ST/ESA/STAT/SER.S/37

Department of Economic and Social Affairs
Statistics Division

Département des affaires économiques et sociales
Division de statistique

Statistical Yearbook 2018 edition

Sixty-first issue

Annuaire statistique 2018 édition

Soixante et unième édition

United Nations | Nations Unies
New York, 2018

Department of Economic and Social Affairs

The Department of Economic and Social Affairs of the United Nations Secretariat is a vital interface between global policies in the economic, social and environmental spheres and national action. The Department works in three main interlinked areas: (i) it compiles, generates and analyses a wide range of economic, social and environmental data and information on which Member States of the United Nations draw to review common problems and to take stock of policy options; (ii) it facilitates the negotiations of Member States in many intergovernmental bodies on joint courses of action to address ongoing or emerging global challenges; and (iii) it advises interested Governments on the ways and means of translating policy frameworks developed in United Nations conferences and summits into programmes at the country level and, through technical assistance, helps build national capacities.

Note

The designations employed and the presentation of material in this publication do not imply the expression of any opinion whatsoever on the part of the Secretariat of the United Nations concerning the legal status of any country, territory, city or area; or of its authorities, or concerning the delimitation of its frontiers or boundaries.

In general, statistics contained in the present publication cover a period up to 2018 and as available to the United Nations Secretariat as of 31 July 2018. They reflect the country nomenclature currently in use.

The term "country" as used in the text of this publication also refers, as appropriate, to territories or areas.

The designations "developed" and "developing" which appear in some tables are intended for statistical convenience and do not necessarily express a judgement about the stage reached by a particular country or area in the development process.

Symbols of the United Nations documents are composed of capital letters combined with figures.

ST/ESA/STAT/SER.S/37

UNITED NATIONS PUBLICATION
Sales No. B.18.XVII.1.H

ISBN 978-92-1-061417-7
e-ISBN 978-92-1-047354-5
ISSN 0082-8459

Département des affaires économiques et sociales

Le Département des affaires économiques et sociales du Secrétariat de l'Organisation des Nations Unies assure le lien essentiel entre les politiques adoptées au plan international dans les domaines économique, social et écologique et les mesures prises au plan national. Il mène ses activités dans trois grands domaines interdépendants : i) il compile, produit et analyse une grand variété de données et d'informations économiques, sociales et écologiques dont les États Membres de l'ONU tirent parti pour examiner les problèmes communs et faire le point sur les possibilités d'action; (ii) il facilite les négociations que les États Membres mènent dans un grand nombre d'organes intergouvernementaux sur les moyens d'action à employer conjointement pour faire face aux problèmes mondiaux existants ou naissants; et (iii) il aide les gouvernements intéressés à traduire les orientations politiques établies lors des conférences et sommets de l'ONU en programmes nationaux et contribue à renforcer les capacités des pays en leur apportant une assistance technique.

Note

Les appellations employées dans la présente publication et la présentation de données qui y figurent n'impliquent, de la part du Secrétariat de l'Organisation des Nations Unies, aucune prise de position quant au statut juridique des pays, territoires, villes ou zones, ou de leurs autorités, ni quant au tracé de leurs frontières ou limites.

En règle générale, les statistiques contenues dans la présente publication couvrent pour la période jusqu'en 2018 et sont celles dont disposait le Secrétariat de l'Organisation des Nations Unies au 31 juillet 2018. Elles reflètent donc la nomenclature de pays en vigueur à l'époque.

Le terme « pays », tel qu'il est utilisé dans la présente publication peut également désigner des territoires ou des zones.

Les appellations « développées » et « en développement » qui figurent dans certains tableaux sont employées à des fins exclusivement statistiques et n'expriment pas nécessairement un jugement quant au niveau de développement atteint par tel pays ou telle région.

Les cotes des documents de l'Organisation des Nations Unies se composent de lettres majuscules et de chiffres.

ST/ESA/STAT/SER.S/37

PUBLICATION DES NATIONS UNIES
Numéro de vente: B.18.XVII.1.H

ISBN 978-92-1-061417-7
e-ISBN 978-92-1-047354-5
ISSN 0082-8459

Preface

The 2018 edition of the United Nations *Statistical Yearbook* is the sixty-first issue of the publication, prepared by the Statistics Division of the Department of Economic and Social Affairs. Ever since the compilation of data for the *Statistical Yearbook* series was initiated in 1948, it has consistently provided a wide range of internationally available statistics on social, economic and environmental conditions and activities at the national, regional and world levels.

The contents of the Yearbook continue to be under review and additional tables are expected to be introduced in future editions. Please send any comments or views to our email address, statistics@un.org. The tables include series covering an appropriate historical period, depending upon data availability and space constraints, for as many countries, territories and statistical areas of the world as available. The tables cover a period up to 2018, with some of the data being estimated.

The *Yearbook* tables are based on data which have been compiled by the Statistics Division mainly from official national and international sources as these are more authoritative and comprehensive, more generally available as time series and more comparable among countries than other sources. These sources include the United Nations Statistics Division in the fields of national accounts, industry, energy and international trade, the United Nations Statistics Division and the Population Division in the field of demographic statistics, and over 20 offices of the United Nations system and international organizations in other specialized fields. In some cases, official sources have been supplemented by other sources and estimates, where these have been subjected to professional scrutiny and debate and are consistent with other independent sources.

The United Nations agencies and other international, national and specialized organizations which furnished data are listed under "Source" at the end of each table. Acknowledgement is gratefully made for their generous and valuable cooperation in continually providing data.

After the first table, which presents key world aggregates and totals, the *Yearbook* is organized in three parts as follows; part one, relating to population and social topics; part two, relating to economic activity; and part three relating to energy, environment and infrastructure. The tables in the three parts are presented mainly by countries or areas, and world and regional aggregates are shown where available.

The four annexes contain information on country and area nomenclature (annex I), summary technical notes on statistical definitions, methods and sources for all tables of the *Yearbook* (annex II), the conversion coefficients and factors used in certain tables (annex III), and a list of those tables which were added, omitted or discontinued since the last issue of the *Yearbook* (annex IV).

The *Statistical Yearbook* is prepared by the Statistical Dissemination Section, Statistical Services Branch of the Statistics Division, Department of Economic and Social Affairs of the United Nations Secretariat. The programme managers are Matthias Reister and Ian Rutherford, the chief editor is Anuradha Chimata; and David Carter, Mohamed Nabassoua, Jaspreet Doung and Zin Lin provide production assistance. Bogdan Dragovic provided IT support.

Comments on the present *Yearbook* and its future evolution are welcome. They may be sent via e-mail to statistics@un.org or to the United Nations Statistics Division, Statistical Dissemination Section, New York, NY 10017, USA.

Préface

L'Annuaire statistique des Nations Unies 2018 est la cinquante-neuvième édition de cette publication, préparée par la Division de statistique du Département des affaires économiques et sociales. Depuis son instauration en 1948 comme outil de compilation des données statistiques internationales, l'*Annuaire statistique* s'efforce de constamment diffuser un large éventail de statistiques disponibles sur les activités et conditions économiques et sociales, aux niveaux national, régional et mondial.

Le contenu de l'Annuaire est actuellement en cours de révision et des tableaux seront inclus dans les prochaines éditions. Pour tout commentaire, veuillez envoyer un courriel à notre adresse électronique : statistics@un.org. Les tableaux présentent des séries qui couvrent une période historique appropriée, en fonction de la disponibilité des données et des contraintes d'espace, pour autant de pays, territoires et zones statistiques du monde comme disponibles. Les tableaux couvrent généralement la période allant jusqu'en 2017.

Les tableaux de l'*Annuaire* sont construits essentiellement à partir des données compilées par la Division de statistique et provenant de sources officielles, nationales et internationales ; c'est en effet la meilleure source si l'on veut des données fiables, complètes et comparables, et si l'on a besoin de séries chronologiques. Ces sources sont: la Division de statistique du Secrétariat de l'Organisation des Nations Unies pour ce qui concerne la comptabilité nationale, l'industrie, l'énergie et le commerce extérieur, la Division de statistique et la Division de la population du Secrétariat de l'Organisation des Nations Unies pour les statistiques démographiques; et plus de 20 bureaux du système des Nations Unies et d'organisations internationales pour les autres domaines spécialisés. Dans quelques cas, les données officielles sont complétées par des informations et des estimations provenant d'autres sources qui ont été examinées par des spécialistes et confirmées par des sources indépendantes.

Les institutions spécialisées des Nations Unies et les autres organisations internationales, nationales et spécialisées qui ont fourni des données sont énumérées dans la "Source" sur chaque tableau. Les auteurs de l'*Annuaire statistique* les remercient de leur précieuse et généreuse collaboration.

Après le premier tableau qui fournit les principaux agrégats et totaux au niveau mondial, l'*Annuaire* est groupés en trois parties. La première partie est consacrée à la population et aux questions sociales, la deuxième est consacrée à l'activité économique, et la dernière est consacrée à l'énergie, environnement et infrastructures. Dans ces trois parties, les tableaux sont généralement présentés par pays ou régions, mais les agrégats mondiaux ou régionaux sont indiqués si disponibles.

Les quatre annexes donnent des renseignements sur la nomenclature des pays et des zones (annexe I), des notes récapitulatives sur les définitions, méthodes statistiques et techniques utilisées dans les sources de chaque tableau de *l'Annuaire* (annexe II), ainsi que sur les coefficients et facteurs de conversion employés dans les différents tableaux (annexe III), enfin une liste de nouveaux tableaux, de tableaux omis ou supprimés depuis la dernière édition est disponible (annexe IV).

L'Annuaire statistique est préparé par la Section de la diffusion statistique, Service des statistiques de services de la Division de statistique, Département des affaires économiques et sociales du Secrétariat de l'Organisation des Nations Unies. Les responsables du programme sont Matthias Reister et Ian Rutherford, le rédacteur en chef est Anuradha Chimata ; et David Carter, Mohamed Nabassoua, Jaspreet Doung et Zin Lin fournissent une assistance à la production. Bogdan Dragovic est responsable du support en informatique.

Les observations sur la présente édition de l'*Annuaire* et les suggestions de modification pour l'avenir seront reçues avec intérêt. Elles peuvent être envoyées par message électronique à statistics@un.org, ou adressées à la Division de statistique des Nations Unies, Section de la diffusion statistique, New York, NY 10017 (États-Unis d'Amérique).

Explanatory notes

Symbols and conventions used in the tables

.	A point is used to indicate decimals.
-	A hyphen between years, for example, 2010-2015, indicates the full period involved, including the beginning and end
/	A slash indicates a financial year, school year or crop year, for example 2014/15.
...	Data are not available or not applicable.
*	Data are provisional, estimated or include a major revision.
#	Marked break in the time series.
~0	Not zero, but less than half of the unit employed.
-~0	Not zero, but negative and less than half of the unit employed.

A space is used as a thousands separator, for example 1 000 is one thousand. Subtotals and percentages in the tables do not necessarily add to totals because of rounding.

Country notes and nomenclature

As a general rule, the data presented in the *Yearbook* relate to a given country or area as described in the complete list of countries and territories, see annex I.

References to statistical sources and methods in tables

For brevity the *Yearbook* omits specific information on the source or methodology for individual data points, and when a data point is estimated no distinction is made between whether the estimation was done by the international or national organization. See the technical notes to the tables in annex II for the primary source which may provide this information.

Units of measurement

The metric system of weights and measures has been employed throughout the *Yearbook*. For conversion coefficients and factors, see annex III.

Notes explicatives

Signes et conventions employés dans les tableaux

.	Les décimales sont précédées d'un point.
-	Un tiret entre des années, par exemple "2013-2014", indique que la période est embrassée dans sa totalité, y compris la première et la dernière année.
/	Une barre oblique renvoie à un exercice financier, à une année scolaire ou à une campagne agricole, par exemple
...	Données non disponibles ou non applicables.
*	Données provisoire, estimatif ou avec une révision majeure.
#	Discontinuité notable dans la série chronologique.
~0	Non nul mais inférieur à la moitié de l'unité employée
-~0	Non nul mais négatif et inférieur à la moitié de l'unité employée

Le séparateur utilisé pour les milliers est l'espace : par exemple, 1 000 correspond à un millier. Les chiffres étant arrondis, les sous-totaux ou pourcentages ne correspondent pas toujours à la somme exacte des éléments figurant dans les tableaux.

Notes sur les pays et nomenclature

En règle générale, les données renvoient au pays ou zone en question que décrite dans la liste complète des pays et territoires figure à l'annexe I.

Références à des sources et des méthodes statistiques dans les tableaux

Par souci de brièveté, l'*Annuaire* omet les informations relatives aux sources et méthodologies employées pour les points de données individuels. De plus, quand un point de données est estimé aucune distinction n'est faite entre une estimation provenant d'une organisation internationale ou d'une organisation nationale. Voir les notes techniques relatives aux tableaux dans l'annexe II ou se trouvent les références aux différentes sources contentant ces informations.

Unités de mesure

Le système métrique de poids et mesures a été utilisé dans tout l'*Annuaire.* On trouvera à l'annexe III les coefficients et facteurs de conversion.

Contents

Preface iii
Explanatory notes v
Introduction 1

I. *World summary*
1. World statistics – selected series 7

Part One: Population and social statistics

II. *Population and migration*
2. Population, surface area and density 13
3. Population and rates of growth in urban areas and capital cities 35
4. International migrants and refugees 55

III. *Gender*
5. Proportion of seats held by women in national parliament 77
6. Ratio of girls to boys in primary, secondary and tertiary education 82

IV. *Education*
7. Education at the primary, secondary and tertiary levels 95
8. Teaching staff at the primary, secondary and tertiary levels 116
9. Public expenditure on education 133

V. *Health*
10. Health personnel 147
11. Expenditure on health 157

VI. *Crime*
12. Intentional homicides and other crimes 167

Part Two: Economic activity

VII. *National accounts*
13. Gross domestic product and gross domestic product per capita 183
14. Gross value added by kind of economic activity 203

VIII. *Finance*
15. Balance of payments summary 217
16. Exchange rates 230

IX. *Labour market*
17. Labour force and unemployment 243
18. Employment by economic activity 260

X. *Price and production indices*
19. Consumer price indices 277
20. Agricultural production indices 288

XI. *International merchandise trade*
21. Total imports, exports and balance of trade 301
22. Major trading partners 318

Part Three: Energy, environment and infrastructure

XII. *Energy*
23. Production, trade and supply of energy 335

XIII. *Environment*
24. Land 357
25. Threatened species 375

XIV. *Science and technology*
26. Population employed in research and development (R&D) 395
27. Gross domestic expenditure on research and development (R&D) 404
28. Patents 413

XV. *Communication*
29. Internet usage 423

XVI. *International tourism and transport*
30. Tourist/visitor arrivals and tourism expenditure 429

XVII. *Development assistance*
31. Net disbursements of official development assistance to recipients 441
32. Net disbursements of official development assistance from donors 457

Annexes

I. Country and area nomenclature, regional and other groupings 461
II. Technical notes 471
III. Conversion coefficients and factors 498
IV. Tables added, omitted and discontinued 500

Note: See **Annex IV** for table names presented in previous issues of the *Statistical Yearbook* which are not contained in the present issue.

Table des matières

Préface iv
Notes explicatives vi
Introduction 4

I. *Aperçu mondial*
1. Statistiques mondiales – séries principales 7

Première partie: Population et statistiques sociales

II. *Population et migration*
2. Population, superficie et densité 13
3. Population et taux de croissance dans les zones urbaines et capitales 35
4. Migrants internationaux et réfugiés 55

III. *La situation de femmes*
5. Proportion de sièges occupés par des femmes au parlement national 77
6. Rapport filles/garçons dans l'enseignement primaire, secondaire et supérieur 82

IV. *Éducation*
7. Enseignement primaire, secondaire et supérieur 95
8. Personnel enseignant au niveau primaire, secondaire et supérieur 116
9. Dépenses publiques afférentes à l'éducation 133

V. *Santé*
10. Le personnel de santé 147
11. Dépenses de santé 157

VI. *Criminalité*
12. Homicides intentionnels et autres crimes 167

Deuxième partie: Activité économique

VII. *Comptes nationaux*
13. Produit intérieur brut et produit intérieur brut par habitant 183
14. Valeur ajoutée par type d'activité économique 203

VIII. *Finances*
15. Résumé de la balance des paiements 217
16. Cours des changes 230

IX. *Marché du travail*
17. Population active et chômage 243
18. Emploi par activité économique 260

X. *Indices des prix et de la production*
19. Indices des prix à la consommation 277
20. Indices de la production agricole 288

XI. *Commerce international des marchandises*
21. Total des importations, des exportations et balance commerciale 301
22. Partenaire commercial principal 318

Troisième partie: Énergie, environnement et infrastructures

XII. *Énergie*
23. Production, commerce et fourniture d'énergie 335

XIII. *Environnement*
24. Terres 357
25. Espèces menacées 375

XIV. *Science et technologie*
26. Population employé dans la recherche et le développement (R–D) 395
27. Dépenses intérieures brutes de recherche et développement (R–D) 404
28. Brevets 413

XV. *Communication*
29. Utilisation d'internet 423

XVI. *Tourisme et transport internationaux*
30. Arrivées de touristes/visiteurs et dépenses touristiques 429

XVII. *Aide au développement*
31. Décaissements nets d'aide publique au développement aux bénéficiaires 441
32. Décaissements nets d'aide publique au développement par des donateurs 457

Annexes

I. Nomenclature des pays et des zones, groupements régionaux et autres groupements 466
II. Notes techniques 484
III. Coefficients et facteurs de conversion 498
IV. Tableaux ajoutés, supprimés et discontinues 501

Voir Annexe IV pour les tableaux publiés dans les éditions précédentes de l'Annuaire statistique mais qui n'ont pas été repris dans la présente édition.

Introduction

The 2018 edition of the United Nations *Statistical Yearbook* is the sixty-first issue of this publication, prepared by the Statistics Division, Department of Economic and Social Affairs, of the United Nations Secretariat. The contents of the *Yearbook* continue to be under review and the number of tables has been reduced as a result. Additional tables are expected to be introduced in future editions. Please send any comments or views to our email address, statistics@un.org. The tables include series covering an appropriate historical period, depending upon data availability (as of 31 July 2018) and space constraints, for as many countries, territories and statistical areas of the world as available. The tables cover a period up to 2018, with some of the data being estimated.

Objective and content of the Statistical Yearbook

The main purpose of the *Statistical Yearbook* is to provide in a single volume a comprehensive compilation of internationally available statistics on social, economic and environmental conditions and activities, at world, regional and national levels, for an appropriate historical period.

Most of the statistics presented in the *Yearbook* are extracted from more detailed, specialized databases prepared by the Statistics Division and by many other international statistical services. Thus, while the specialized databases concentrate on monitoring topics and trends in particular social, economic and environmental fields, the *Statistical Yearbook* tables aim to provide data for a comprehensive, overall description of social, economic and environmental structures, conditions, changes and activities. The objective has been to collect, systematize, coordinate and present in a consistent way the most essential components of comparable statistical information which can give a broad picture of social, economic and environmental processes.

The content of the *Statistical Yearbook* is planned to serve a general readership. The *Yearbook* endeavours to provide information for various bodies of the United Nations system as well as for other international organizations, governments and non-governmental organizations, national statistical, economic and social policy bodies, scientific and educational institutions, libraries and the public. Data published in the *Statistical Yearbook* may also be of interest to companies and enterprises and to agencies engaged in market research. The *Statistical Yearbook* thus provides information on a wide range of social, economic and environmental issues which are of concern in the United Nations system and among the governments and peoples of the world. A particular value of the *Yearbook* is that it facilitates meaningful analysis of issues by systematizing and coordinating the data across many fields and shedding light on such interrelated issues as:

- General economic growth and related economic conditions;
- Gender equality;
- Population by sex and rate of increase, surface area and density;
- Unemployment, inflation and prices;
- Energy production and consumption;
- Expansion of trade;
- The financial situation of countries;
- Education;
- Improvement in general living conditions;
- Pollution and protection of the environment;
- Assistance provided to developing countries for social, economic and environmental development purposes.

Organization of the Yearbook

After the first table which presents key world aggregates and totals, the tables of the *Yearbook* are grouped into three parts as follows:

- Part One: Population and Social Statistics (chapters II-VI: tables 2-12);
- Part Two: Economic Activity (chapters VII-XI: tables 13-22);
- Part Three: Energy, environment and infrastructure (chapters XII-XVII: tables 23-32).

The first table provides a summary picture of development at the global level. More specific and detailed information for analysis concerning regions, individual countries or areas are presented in the three thematic parts.

Part One, Population and Social Statistics, comprises 12 tables which contain more detailed statistical series on population and migration, gender, education, health and crime.

Part Two, Economic Activity, comprises 10 tables on national accounts, finance, labour market, price and production indices and international merchandise trade.

Part Three, Energy, environment and infrastructure, comprises 10 tables on energy, environment, science and technology, international tourism and transport, communication and development assistance.

Annexes and regional groupings of countries or areas

The annexes to the *Statistical Yearbook*, and the section "Explanatory notes" preceding the Introduction, provide additional essential information on the *Yearbook*'s contents and presentation of data.

Annex I provides information on countries or areas covered in the *Yearbook* tables and on their arrangement in geographical regions and economic or other groupings. The geographical groupings shown in the *Yearbook* are generally based on continental regions unless otherwise indicated. However, strict consistency in this regard is impossible. A wide range of classifications is used for different purposes in the various international agencies and other sources of statistics for the *Yearbook*. These classifications vary in response to administrative and analytical requirements.

Annex II provide brief descriptions of major statistical concepts, definitions and classifications required for interpretation and analysis of the data.

Annex III provides detailed information on conversion coefficients and factors used in various tables, and Annex IV provides a list of tables added, omitted and discontinued in the present edition of the *Yearbook*. Some Tables do not feature in this edition of the *Yearbook* due to space limitations or an insufficient amount of new data being available. Their titles nevertheless are still listed in this Annex since it is planned that they will be published in a later issue as new data are compiled by the collecting agency and where space permits.

Data comparability, quality and relevance

The major challenge continuously facing the *Statistical Yearbook* is to present series which are as comparable across countries as the available statistics permit. Considerable efforts have already been made among the international suppliers of data and by the staff of the *Statistical Yearbook* to ensure the compatibility of various series by aligning time periods, base years, prices chosen for valuation, and so on. This is indispensable in relating various bodies of data to each other and in facilitating analysis across different sectors. In general, the data presented reflect the methodological recommendations of the United Nations Statistical Commission issued in various United Nations publications, and of other international bodies concerned with statistics. The use of international recommendations promotes international comparability of the data and ensures a degree of compatibility regarding the underlying concepts, definitions and classifications relating to different series. However, much work remains to be done in this area and, for this reason, some tables serve only as a first source of data and require further adjustment before being used for more in-depth analytical studies. While on the whole, a significant degree of comparability has been achieved in international statistics, there will remain some limitations, for a variety of reasons.

One common cause of non-comparability of economic data is different valuations of statistical aggregates such as national income, wages and salaries, output of industries and so forth. Conversion of these and similar series originally expressed in national prices into a common currency, for example into United States dollars, through the use of exchange rates, is not always satisfactory owing to frequent wide fluctuations in market rates and differences between official rates and rates which would be indicated by unofficial markets or purchasing power parities. The use of different kinds of sources for obtaining data is another cause of incomparability. This is true, for example, in the case of employment and unemployment, where data are obtained from different sources, namely household and labour force sample surveys, establishment censuses or surveys, official estimates, social insurance statistics and employment office statistics, which are not fully comparable in many cases. Non-comparability of data may also result from differences in the institutional patterns of countries. Certain variations in social, economic and environmental organization and institutions may have an impact on the comparability of the data even if the underlying concepts and definitions are identical. These and other causes of non-comparability of the data are briefly explained in the technical note associated with each table (see Annex II).

A further set of challenges relate to timeliness, quality and relevance of the data contained in the *Yearbook*. Users generally demand the most up-to-date statistics. However, due to the different development stages of statistical capacity in different countries, data for the most recent years may only be available for a small number of countries. For a global print publication, therefore, a balance has to be struck between presenting the most updated information and satisfactory country coverage. Of course the United Nations Statistics Division's website offers greater flexibility in presenting continuously updated information and is therefore a useful complement to the annual print publication. Furthermore, as most of the information presented in this *Yearbook* is collected through specialized United Nations agencies and partners, the timeliness is continuously enhanced by improving the communication and data flow between countries and the specialized agencies on the one hand, and between the United Nations Statistics Division and the specialized agencies on the other. The development of new XML-based data transfer protocols will address this issue and is expected to make international data flows more efficient in the future.

Data quality at the international level is a function of the data quality at the national level. The United Nations Statistics Division in close cooperation with its partners among the UN agencies and the international statistical system continues to support countries' efforts to improve both the coverage and the quality of their data. Metadata, as for example reflected in the footnotes and technical notes of this publication, are an important service to the user to allow an informed assessment of the quality of the data. Given the wide variety of sources for the *Yearbook*, there is of course an equally wide variety of data formats and accompanying metadata. An important challenge for the United Nations Statistics Division and its partners for the future is to work further towards the standardization, or at least harmonization, of metadata.

A crucial challenge is to maintain the relevance of the series included in the *Yearbook*. As new policy concerns enter the developmental debate, the United Nations Statistics Division will need to introduce new series that describe concerns that have gained prominence as well as to prune data as they become outdated and continue to update the recurrent *Yearbook* series that still address those issues which are most pertinent. Often choosing the appropriate moment when the statistical information on new topics has matured sufficiently so as to be able to disseminate meaningful global data can be challenging. Furthermore, a balance has to continuously be found between the ever-increasing amount of information available for dissemination and the space limitations of the print version of the *Statistical Yearbook*. International comparability, data availability, data quality and relevance will remain the key criteria to guide the United Nations Statistics Division in its selection.

Needless to say, more can always be done to improve the *Statistical Yearbook*'s scope, coverage, design, metadata and timeliness. The *Yearbook* team continually strives to improve upon each of these aspects and to make its publication as responsive as possible to its users' needs and expectations, while at the same time focusing on a manageable body of data and metadata. Since data disseminated in digital form have clear advantages over those in print, as much of the *Yearbook* information as possible will continue to be included in the Statistics Division's online databases. Please feel welcome to provide feedback and suggestions to statistics@un.org.

Introduction

L'*Annuaire statistique* des Nations Unies 2018 est la cinquante-neuvième édition de cette publication, établi par la Division de statistique du Département des affaires économiques et sociales du Secrétariat de l'Organisation des Nations Unies. Le contenu de l'*Annuaire* est actuellement en cours de révision, de ce fait le nombre de tableaux a été réduit. Des tableaux seront inclus dans les prochaines éditions. Pour tout commentaire, veuillez envoyer un courriel à notre adresse électronique : statistics@un.org. Les tableaux présentent des séries qui couvrent une période historique appropriée, en fonction de la disponibilité des données (à la date du 31 juillet 2018) et des contraintes d'espace, pour autant de pays, territoires et zones statistiques du monde comme disponibles. Les tableaux couvrent généralement pour la période jusqu'à 2018.

Objectif et contenu de l'Annuaire statistique

Le principal objectif de *l'Annuaire statistique* est de fournir en un seul volume un inventaire complet de statistiques internationales concernant la situation et les activités sociales, économiques et environnementales aux niveaux mondial, régional et national, sur une période adéquate.

La plupart des données qui figurent dans l'*Annuaire statistique* proviennent de bases de données spécialisées davantage détaillées, préparées par la Division de statistique et par bien d'autres services statistiques internationaux. Tandis que les bases de données spécialisées se concentrent sur le suivi de domaines socioéconomiques et environnementaux particuliers, les données de l'*Annuaire* sont présentées de telle sorte qu'elles fournissent une description globale et exhaustive des structures, conditions, transformations et activités socioéconomiques et environnementaux. On a cherché à recueillir, systématiser, coordonner et présenter de manière cohérente les principales informations statistiques comparables, de manière à dresser un tableau général des processus socioéconomiques et environnementaux.

Le contenu de l'*Annuaire statistique* a été élaboré en vue d'un lectorat large. Les renseignements fournis devraient ainsi pouvoir être utilisés par les divers organismes du système des Nations Unies, mais aussi par d'autres organisations internationales, les gouvernements et les organisations non gouvernementales, les organismes nationaux de statistique et de politique économique et sociale, les institutions scientifiques et les établissements d'enseignement, les bibliothèques et les particuliers. Les données publiées dans l'*Annuaire* peuvent également intéresser les sociétés et entreprises, et les organismes spécialisés dans les études de marché. L'*Annuaire* présente des informations sur un large éventail de questions socioéconomiques et environnementales liées aux préoccupations actuelles du système des Nations Unies, des gouvernements et des peuples du monde entier. Une qualité particulière de l'*Annuaire* est de faciliter une analyse approfondie de ces questions en systématisant et en articulant les données d'un domaine/secteur à l'autre, et en apportant un éclairage sur des sujets interdépendants, tels que :

- La croissance économique générale, et les conditions économiques qui lui sont liées;
- La situation de femmes;
- La population, taux d'accroissement, superficie et densité;
- Le chômage, l'inflation et les prix;
- La production et la consommation d'énergie;
- L'expansion des échanges;
- La situation financière des pays;
- L'éducation;
- L'amélioration des conditions de vie;
- La pollution et la protection de l'environnement;
- L'assistance aux pays en développement à des fins socioéconomiques et environnementaux.

Présentation de l'Annuaire

Après le premier tableau qui fournit les principaux agrégats et totaux au niveau mondial, l'Annuaire est groupés en trois parties comme suit:

- Première partie: Statistiques démographiques et sociales (chapitres II à VI, tableaux 2 à 12)
- Deuxième partie: Activité économique (chapitres VII à XI, tableaux 13 à 22)
- Troisième partie: Energie, environnement et infrastructures (chapitres XII à XVII, tableaux 23 à 32)

Le premier tableau donne un aperçu du développement à l'échelon mondial, tandis que les trois autres parties contiennent des renseignements plus précis et détaillés qui se prêtent mieux à une analyse par régions, pays ou par zones. Chacune de ces trois parties est subdivisée en unités thématiques.

La première partie, intitulée "Population et statistiques sociales", comporte 12 tableaux où figurent des séries plus détaillées concernant la population et la migration, la situation des femmes, l'éducation, la santé et la criminalité.

La deuxième partie, intitulée "Activité économique", comporte 10 tableaux qui présentent des statistiques concernant les comptes nationaux, le finances, le marché du travail, les indices des prix et de la production, et au commence international des marchandises. Les tableaux traitant de certains produits de base associent autant que possible les données relatives à la consommation aux valeurs concernant la production.

La troisième partie, intitulée "Energie, environnement et infrastructures", comprend 10 tableaux relatifs à l'énergie, l'environnement, la science et technologie, au tourisme et transport internationaux, à la communication et à l'aide au développement.

Annexes et groupements régionaux des pays et zones

Les annexes à l'*Annuaire statistique*, et la section intitulée "Notes explicatives" qui précède l'introduction, offrent d'importantes informations complémentaires quant à la teneur et à la présentation des données figurant dans le présent ouvrage.

L'annexe I donne des renseignements sur les pays ou zones couverts par les tableaux de l'*Annuaire* et sur leur regroupement en régions géographiques et groupements économiques ou autres. Sauf indication contraire, les groupements géographiques figurant dans l'*Annuaire* sont généralement fondés sur les régions continentales, mais une présentation absolument systématique est impossible à cet égard car les diverses institutions internationales et autres sources de statistiques employées pour la confection de l'*Annuaire* emploient, selon l'objet de l'exercice, des classifications fort différentes en réponse à diverses exigences d'ordre administratif ou analytique.

L'annexe II contient les notes techniques de chaque chapitre apportent une brève description des principales notions, définitions et classifications statistiques nécessaires pour interpréter et analyser les données.

L'annexe III fournit des renseignements sur les coefficients et facteurs de conversion employés dans les différents tableaux, et l'annexe IV contient la liste de tableaux qui ont été ajoutés omis ou supprimés dans la présente édition de l'*Annuaire*. Certains tableaux ne figurent pas dans cet *Annuaire* en raison du manque d'espace ou de données nouvelles. Comme ils seront repris dans une prochaine édition à mesure que des données nouvelles seront dépouillées par l'office statistique d'origine, ses titres figurent toujours dans la table des matières.

Comparabilité, qualité et pertinence des statistiques

Le défi majeur auquel l'*Annuaire Statistique* fait continuellement face est de présenter des séries aussi comparables entre les pays que la disponibilité des statistiques le permettent. Les sources internationales de données et les auteurs de l'*Annuaire* ont réalisé des efforts considérables pour faire en sorte que diverses séries soient compatibles, en harmonisant les périodes de référence, les années de base, les prix utilisés pour les évaluations, etc. Cette démarche est indispensable si l'on veut rapprocher divers ensembles de données, et faciliter l'analyse intersectorielle de l'économie. De façon générale, les données sont présentées selon les recommandations méthodologiques formulées par la Commission de statistique des Nations Unies, et par les autres entités internationales impliquées dans les statistiques. Le respect des recommandations internationales tend non seulement à promouvoir la comparabilité internationale des données, mais elle assure également une certaine comparabilité entre les concepts, les définitions et classifications utilisés. Mais comme il reste encore beaucoup à faire dans ce domaine, les données présentées dans certains tableaux n'ont qu'une valeur indicative, et nécessiteront des ajustements plus poussés avant de pouvoir servir à des analyses approfondies. Bien que l'on soit parvenu, dans l'ensemble, à un degré de comparabilité appréciable en matière de statistiques internationales, diverses raisons expliquent que subsistent encore de nombreuses limitations.

Une cause commune de non comparabilité des données économiques réside dans la diversité des méthodes d'évaluation employées pour comptabiliser des agrégats tels que le revenu national, les salaires et traitements, la production des différentes branches d'activité industrielle, etc. Il n'est pas toujours satisfaisant de ramener la valeur des séries de ce type—exprimée à l'origine en prix nationaux—à une monnaie commune (par exemple le dollar des États-Unis) car les taux de change du marché connaissent fréquemment de fortes fluctuations, et parce que les taux officiels ne coïncident pas avec ceux des marchés officieux ni avec les parités réelles de pouvoir d'achat. Le recours à des sources diverses pour la collecte des données est un autre facteur qui limite la comparabilité. C'est le cas, par exemple, des données d'emploi et de chômage, obtenues par des moyens aussi peu comparables que les sondages, le dépouillement des registres d'assurances sociales et les enquêtes auprès des entreprises. Dans certains cas, les données ne sont pas comparables en raison de différences entre les structures institutionnelles des pays. Des changements dans l'organisation et les institutions sociales, économiques et environnementales peuvent affecter la comparabilité des données, même si les concepts et définitions sont fondamentalement identiques. Ces causes, et d'autres, de non comparabilité des données sont brièvement expliquées dans les notes techniques associée à chaque tableau (voir annexe II).

Un autre ensemble de défis à relever concerne la fraîcheur, la qualité et la pertinence des données présentées dans l'*Annuaire*. Les utilisateurs exigent généralement des données les plus récentes possibles. Toutefois, selon le niveau de développement de la capacité statistique des pays, les données pour les dernières années peuvent n'être disponibles que pour un nombre limité de pays. Dans le cadre d'une publication mondiale, un équilibre doit être trouvé entre la présentation de l'information la plus récente et une couverture géographique satisfaisante. Bien entendu, le site Internet de la Division de statistique des Nations Unies offre une plus grande flexibilité, puisqu'il propose une information actualisée au fil de l'eau, et constitue ainsi un complément utile à la publication papier annuelle. Par ailleurs, étant donné que la plupart des informations présentées dans cet *Annuaire* sont collectées parmi les agences spécialisées des Nations Unies et autres partenaires, la fraîcheur des données est continuellement améliorée, grâce à une meilleure communication et un meilleur échange de données entre les pays et les agences spécialisées d'une part, et entre la Division de statistique des Nations Unies et les agences spécialisées d'autre part. Le développement de nouveaux protocoles de transfert de données basés sur le langage XML devrait contribuer à rendre, à l'avenir, les échanges de données internationales encore plus efficaces.

La qualité des données au niveau international est fonction de la qualité des données au niveau national. La Division de statistique des Nations Unies, en étroite collaboration avec ses partenaires dans les agences de l'ONU et dans le système statistique international, continue de soutenir les efforts des pays pour améliorer à la fois la couverture et la qualité de leurs données. Des métadonnées, comme l'illustrent les notes de bas de page et les notes techniques de cette publication, constituent un important service fourni à l'utilisateur pour lui permettre d'évaluer de manière avisée la qualité des données. Etant donné la grande variété des sources de l'*Annuaire*, il y a bien entendu une non moins grande variété de formats de données et de métadonnées associées. Un important défi que la Division de statistique des Nations Unies et ses partenaires doivent relever dans le futur est d'aboutir à la standardisation, ou au moins l'harmonisation, des métadonnées.

Le défi majeur reste la constance de la pertinence des séries présentées dans l'*Annuaire*. Au fur et à mesure que de nouvelles préoccupations politiques pénètrent le débat lié au développement, la Division de statistique des Nations Unies doit introduire dans l'*Annuaire* de nouvelles séries qui leur sont liées, et, ce faisant, effectuer une coupe sombre parmi les données qui lui semblent dépassées, tout en s'assurant de continuer à actualiser les séries récurrentes de qui paraissent encore pertinentes. Souvent, choisir le moment idoine auquel les données statistiques sur de nouveaux thèmes sont suffisamment matures pour qu'elles puissent, au niveau mondial, être diffusées sans hésitation, est un défi en soi. Par ailleurs, un équilibre doit continuellement être trouvé entre le volume toujours croissant d'informations disponibles à la diffusion, et les contraintes d'espace de la version papier de l'*Annuaire* statistique. La comparabilité internationale, la disponibilité, la qualité et la pertinence des données devront rester les principaux critères à considérer par la Division de statistique des Nations Unies dans sa sélection.

Inutile de dire qu'il est toujours possible d'améliorer l'*Annuaire* statistique en ce qui concerne son champ, sa couverture, sa conception générale, ses métadonnées et sa mise à jour. L'équipe en charge de l'*Annuaire* s'évertue en permanence à améliorer chacun de ces aspects, et de faire en sorte que cette publication réponde au plus près aux besoins et aux attentes de ses utilisateurs, sans toutefois oublier de mettre l'accent sur un corpus gérable de données et de métadonnées. Puisqu'il est avéré que les données diffusées de manière digitale ont des avantages comparés à celles diffusées sur papier, autant d'informations de l'*Annuaire* que possible continueront d'être incluses dans les bases de données électroniques de la Division de statistique. L'*Annuaire* statistique garde toujours une place de choix parmi les produits de la Division de statistique comme une ressource utile pour une compréhension général de la situation sociale, économique et environnementale globale. N'hésitez pas à nous faire part de vos commentaires et suggestions à statistics@un.org

1 World statistics: selected series

Population and social statistics, economic activity and energy, environment and infrastructure

Statistiques mondiales : séries principales

Population et statistiques sociales, activité économique et énergie, environnement et infrastructures

Population and Migration • Population et migration

Series Séries	Unit or base Unité ou base	2005	2010	2014	2015	2016	2017	2018
Population [1]	million	6 542.2	6 958.2		7 383.0			7 632.82
Population density [1] Densité de population [1]	per km² pour km²	50.3	53.5		56.8			58.7
Population, male [1] Population, hommes [1]	million	3 296.1	3 508.2		3 724.1			3 850.7
Population, female [1] Population, femmes [1]	million	3 246.0	3 450.0		3 658.9			3 782.1
Sex ratio [1] Rapport des sexes [1]	males per 100 females hom. p. 100 fem.	101.5	101.7		101.8			101.8
Population age distribution, 0-14 [1] Répartition par âge de la population, 0-14 [1]	percentage of pop. pourcentage de la pop.	28.0	26.8		26.1			25.8
Population age distribution, 60+ [1] Répartition par âge de la population, 60+ [1]	percentage of pop. pourcentage de la pop.	10.3	11.1		12.3			13.0

Series Séries	Unit or base Unité ou base	2005	2010	2014	2015	2016	2017	2018
Urban population Population urbaine	percentage of pop. pourcentage de la pop.	49.2	51.7		53.9			55.3
Total annual urban growth rate [2] Taux d'accroissement urbaine annuel [2]	percentage of pop. pourcentage de la pop.	2.3	2.2		2.0			...
Total annual rural growth rate [2] Taux d'accroissement rurale annuel [2]	percentage of pop. pourcentage de la pop.	0.3	0.2		0.2			...

Series Séries	Unit or base Unité ou base	2005	2010	2014	2015	2016	2017	2018
International migrant stock: total Stock de migrants internationaux : total	thousand millier	191 531	220 019		243 700		257 715	...
International migrant stock: total Stock de migrants internationaux : total	percentage of pop. pourcentage de la pop.	2.9	3.2		3.3		3.4	...
International migrant stock: male Stock de migrants internationaux : hommes	percentage of pop. pourcentage de la pop.	3.0	3.2		3.4		3.5	...
International migrant stock : female Stock de migrants internationaux : fémmes	percentage of pop. pourcentage de la pop.	2.9	3.1		3.2		3.3	...
Refugees Réfugiés	thousand millier	...	...		15 098		18 474	...
Asylum seekers Demandeurs d'asile	thousand millier	...	...		2 344		2 955	...
Other of concern to UNHCR Autres personnes relevant de la comp. du HCR	thousand millier	...	...		40 518		45 980	...
Total population of concern to UNHCR Population totale de préoccupation pour le HCR	thousand millier	...	...		57 960		67 408	...

Gender • Le genre

Series Séries	Unit or base Unité ou base	2005	2010	2014	2015	2016	2017	2018
Seats held by women in national parliament Pro. de sièges occupés par les fem. au par. nat.	percentage of seats pourcentage du sièges	15.9	19.0	22.1	22.3	22.7	23.4	23.4
Girls to boys in primary education Filles/garçons dans l'enseigne. primaire	ratio rapport	0.95	0.97	0.99	1.00	...	...	...
Girls to boys in secondary education Filles/garçons dans l'enseigne. secondaire	ratio rapport	0.95	0.97	0.99	0.99	...	...	...
Girls to boys in tertiary education Filles/garçons dans l'enseigne. supérieur	ratio rapport	1.05	1.08	1.11	1.12	...	...	...

Education • Enseignement

Series Séries	Unit or base Unité ou base	2005	2010	2014	2015	2016	2017	2018
Students enrolled in primary education Les étudiants inscrits dans l'enseignement primaire	thousand millier	679 990	697 100		723 319	740 231		
Gross enrollment ratio - primary, male Taux brut de scolarisation - primaire, hommes	percentage pourcentage	104.8	105.9		103.1	104.1		
Gross enrollment ratio - primary, female Taux brut de scolarisation - primaire, fémmes	percentage pourcentage	99.8	103.0		102.8	104.6		
Students enrolled in secondary education Les étudiants inscrits dans l'enseignement second.	thousand millier	509 100	546 263		581 620	585 517		
Gross enrollment ratio - secondary, male Taux brut de scolarisation - secondaire, hommes	percentage pourcentage	65.7	72.4		76.7	76.9		
Gross enrollment ratio - secondary, female Taux brut de scolarisation – secondaire, fémmes	percentage pourcentage	62.1	69.8		75.7	75.9		
Students enrolled in tertiary education Les étudiants inscrits dans l'enseigne. supérieur	thousand millier	139 648	181 506		214 083	215 945		
Gross enrollment ratio - tertiary, male Taux brut de scolarisation - tertiaire, hommes	percentage pourcentage	23.7	28.3		34.2	34.7		
Gross enrollment ratio – tertiary, female Taux brut de scolarisation – tertiaire, féminin	percentage pourcentage	24.8	30.4		38.1	39.0		
Teaching staff at the primary level Personnel enseignant au niveau primaire	thousand millier	26 889	28 658		31 144	31 316		
Teaching staff at the secondary level Personnel enseignant au niveau secondaire	thousand millier	28 398	32 347		33 353	34 117		
Teaching staff at the tertiary level Personnel enseignant au niveau supérieur	thousand millier	9 217	11 143		12 880	13 027		
Pupils to teachers in the primary level Élèves/enseignant dans l'enseigne. primaire	ratio rapport	25.3	24.4		23.2	23.6		
Pupils to teachers ratio in the secondary level Élèves/enseignant dans l'enseigne. secondaire	ratio rapport	17.9	16.9		17.4	17.2		

Crime • La criminalité

Series Séries	Unit or base Unité ou base	2005	2010	2014	2015	2016	2017	2018
Intentional homicide rate [3] Homicides volontaires [3]	per 100,000 population pour 100,000 pop.	...	...	...	5.3	...	...	...

National Accounts • Comptes nationaux

Series Séries	Unit or base Unité ou base	2005	2010	2014	2015	2016	2017	2018
GDP in current prices PIB aux prix courants	billion US $ milliard $ E.-U.	47 602	66 010	78 914	74 696	75 649	...	...
GDP per capita PIB par habitant	US $ $ E.-U.	7 278	9 489	10 815	10 120	10 134	...	...
GDP in constant 2005 prices PIB aux prix constants	billion US $ milliard $ E.-U.	58 203	66 010	73 597	75 639	77 490	...	...
GDP real rates of growth Taux de croissance	percentage pourcentage	3.8	4.3	2.8	2.8	2.4	...	...

Labour market • Marché du travail

Series Séries	Unit or base Unité ou base	2005	2010	2014	2015	2016	2017	2018
Labour force - total Force de travail - total	percentage of pop. pourcentage de la pop.	64.3	62.8		62.1			61.8
Labour force - male Force de travail - hommes	percentage of pop. pourcentage de la pop.	77.4	76.2		75.5			75.0
Labour force - female Force de travail - femmes	percentage of pop. pourcentage de la pop.	51.4	49.4		48.8			48.5
Unemployment rate - total Chômage - total	percent. of active pop. pour. de la pop. active	6.0	5.8		5.5			5.5
Unemployment rate - male Chômage - mâle	percent. of active pop. pour. de la pop. active	5.6	5.5		5.2			5.2
Unemployment rate - female Chômage - femmes	percent. of active pop. pour. de la pop. active	6.5	6.2		5.9			6.0

1 World statistics: selected series *(continued)*

Population and social statistics, economic activity and energy, environment and infrastructure

Statistiques mondiales : séries principales *(suite)*

Population et statistiques sociales, activité économique et énergie, environnement et infrastructures

Series Séries	Unit or base Unité ou base	2005	2010	2014	2015	2016	2017	2018
Employment in agriculture - total L'emploi dans agriculture - total	percent. of employees pourcent. des employ.	35.2	30.8		27.2			26.0
Employment in agriculture - male L'emploi dans agriculture - hommes	percent. of employees pourcent. des employ.	34.1	30.2		26.7			25.4
Employment in agriculture - female L'emploi dans agriculture - femmes	percent. of employees pourcent. des employ.	37.1	31.8		28.0			26.8
Employment in industry - total L'emploi dans industrie - total	percent. of employees pourcent. des employ.	22.6	23.0		22.7			22.4
Employment in industry - male L'emploi dans industrie - hommes	percent. of employees pourcent. des employ.	25.5	26.8		27.2			27.0
Employment in industry - female L'emploi in industrie - femmes	percent. of employees pourcent. des employ.	18.3	17.1		15.7			15.1
Employment in services - total L'emploi dans services - total	percent. of employees pourcent. des employ.	42.1	46.2		50.1			51.7
Employment in services - male L'emploi dans services - hommes	percent. of employees pourcent. des employ.	40.5	43.1		46.1			47.6
Employment in services - female L'emploi dans services - femmes	percent. of employees pourcent. des employ.	44.6	51.1		56.2			58.2

Price and production indices • Indices de la production

Series Séries	Unit or base Unité ou base	2005	2010	2014	2015	2016	2017	2018
Agriculture (gross) Agriculture (brut)	2004-2006 = 100	99.9	112.9	124.6	125.9	127.3	...	...
Food (gross) Ailmentaires (brut)	2004-2006 = 100	99.9	113.4	125.0	126.4	127.8	...	...

International merchandise trade • Commerce international des marchandises

Series Séries	Unit or base Unité ou base	2005	2010	2014	2015	2016	2017	2018
Exports FOB Exportations FOB	billion US $ milliard $ E.-U.	10 373	15 100	18 833	16 407	15 861	17 177	...
Imports CIF Importations CIF	billion US $ milliard $ E.-U.	10 577	15 262	18 763	16 453	15 960	17 507	...
Balance Balance	billion US $ milliard $ E.-U.	-204	-162	70	-46	-100	-330	...

Energy • Ènergie

Series Séries	Unit or base Unité ou base	2005	2010	2014	2015	2016	2017	2018
Primary energy production Production d'énergie primaire	petajoules pétajoules	476 469	530 321	567 004	572 353	...	...	...
Net imports Importations nettes	petajoules pétajoules	-13 751	-13 098	-16 670	-18 196	...	...	...
Changes in stocks Variations des stocks	petajoules pétajoules	-289	12	3 205	2 469	...	...	...
Total supply Approvisionnement total	petajoules pétajoules	463 007	517 211	547 128	551 688	...	...	...
Supply per capita Approvisionnement par habitant	gigajoules gigajoules	71	75	75	75	...	...	...

Environment • Environnement

Series Séries	Unit or base Unité ou base	2005	2010	2014	2015	2016	2017	2018
Land area Terres superficie	1,000 hectares	13 011 699	13 009 625		13 008 983	...	...	...
Arable land Terres arables	000 hectares	1 405 843	1 388 254		1 425 919	...	...	...
Arable land Terres arables	percentage of land pourcent. de la superf.	10.8	10.7		11.0	...	...	...
Forest cover Superficie forestière	1,000 hectares	4 032 743	4 015 673		3 999 134	...	...	...
Forest cover Superficie forestière	percentage of land pourcent. de la superf.	31.0	30.9		30.7	...	...	...

Series Séries	Unit or base Unité ou base	2005	2010	2014	2015	2016	2017	2018
Permanent crops Cultures permanentes	1,000 hectares	148 372	159 210		164 831	...	...	...
Permanent crops Cultures permanentes	percentage of land pourcent. de la superf.	1.1	1.2		1.3	...	...	...
Sites protected for terrestrial biodiversity Sites pour la bio. terre. dans aires protég	percentage of sites pourcentage du sites	40.1	44.4		46.5	46.6	46.7	46.7

Science and technology • Science et technologie

Series Séries	Unit or base Unité ou base	2005	2010	2014	2015	2016	2017	2018
Grant of patents Brevets délivrés	per million population par million d'habitants	634 000	915 500	1 179 900	1 241 100	1 351 600	...	...
Gross domestic expenditure on R & D Dépenses intérieures brutes de R-D	percentage of GDP pourcentage du PIB	1.5	1.6	1.7	...	...	...	...

Communication • Internet users

Series Séries	Unit or base Unité ou base	2005	2010	2014	2015	2016	2017	2018
Internet usage Utilisation d'internet	% of individuals % de personnes	15.6	28.7	39.7	43.0	45.7	...	...

Development assistance • Aide au developpement

Series Séries	Unit or base Unité ou base	2005	2010	2014	2015	2016	2017	2018
Net ODA received: bilateral APD nette reçue : bilatérale	million US $ million $ E.-U.	82 923	94 441	119 778	117 372	116 519	...	...
Net ODA received: multilateral APD nette reçue : multilatérale	million US $ million $ E.-U.	25 620	37 133	41 952	35 368	40 493	...	...
Net ODA received: total APD nette reçue : total	million US $ million $ E.-U.	108 542	131 574	161 730	152 740	157 011	...	...
Net ODA received: total APD nette reçue : total	% of recipients' GNI % du RNB des bénéfic.	1.2	0.7	0.6	0.6	0.6	...	...

Source:
These data are presented in other tables of this Yearbook; please refer to the relevant table for source notes and last access data.

Source:
Ces données sont présentées dans d'autres tableaux du présent Annuaire, veuillez donc vous reporter au tableau correspondant pour les notes de source et la date du dernier accès.

1 Mid-year estimates and projections (medium fertility variant).

2 Data refers to a 5-year period preceding the reference year.

3 Data is for 2015, or latest available data from 2010 onwards.

1 Les estimations et projections approximative (variante moyenne fécondité) au milieu de l'année.

2 Les données se réfèrent a période de 5 ans précédant l'année de référence.

3 Données pour 2015, ou dernières données disponibles à partir de 2010.

Part One

Population and social statistics

Chapter II Population and migration (tables 2 - 4)

Chapter III Gender (tables 5 and 6)

Chapter IV Education (tables 7 - 9)

Chapter V Health (tables 10 and 11)

Chapter VI Crime (table 12)

Première partie

Population et statistiques sociales

Chapitre II Population et migration (tableaux 2 - 4)

Chapitre III La situation des femmes (tableaux 5 et 6)

Chapitre IV Éducation (tableaux 7 - 9)

Chapitre V Santé (tableaux 10 et 11)

Chapitre VI Criminalité (tableau 12)

2 Population, surface area and density

Population, superficie et densité

Country or area Pays ou zone	Year Année	Mid-year population estimates and projections (millions) Estimations et projections de population au milieu de l'année (millions) Total	 Male Hommes	 Females Femmes	Sex Ratio (males per 100 females) Rapport des sexes (hommes pour 100 femmes)	Population age distribution (percentage) Répartition par âge de la population (pourcentage) Aged 0 to 14 years old âgée de 0 à 14 ans	 Aged 60+ years old âgée de 60 ans ou plus	Population density (per km²) Densité de population (pour km²)	Surface area Superficie (000 km²)
Total, all countries or areas	**2005**	**6 542.16**	**3 296.12**	**3 246.04**	**101.5**	**28.0**	**10.3**	**50.3**	**...**
Total, tous pays ou zones	**2010**	**6 958.17**	**3 508.24**	**3 449.93**	**101.7**	**26.8**	**11.1**	**53.5**	**...**
	2015	**7 383.01**	**3 724.13**	**3 658.88**	**101.8**	**26.1**	**12.3**	**56.8**	**136 162**
	2018[1]	**7 632.82**	**3 850.72**	**3 782.10**	**101.8**	**25.8**	**13.0**	**58.7**	**...**
Africa	2005	924.76	460.95	463.80	99.4	41.8	5.2	31.2	...
Afrique	2010	1 049.45	523.31	526.14	99.5	41.4	5.2	35.4	...
	2015	1 194.37	596.26	598.11	99.7	41.0	5.4	40.3	30 311
	2018[1]	1 287.92	643.30	644.62	99.8	40.6	5.5	43.4	...
Northern Africa	2005	187.83	94.37	93.47	101.0	33.3	7.0	24.2	...
Afrique septentrionale	2010	204.31	102.50	101.81	100.7	31.9	7.4	26.3	...
	2015	225.14	113.06	112.07	100.9	32.3	8.0	29.0	7 880
	2018[1]	237.78	119.46	118.32	101.0	32.3	8.5	30.6	...
Sub-Saharan Africa	2005	736.93	366.59	370.34	99.0	44.0	4.7	33.7	...
Afrique subsaharienne	2010	845.14	420.80	424.33	99.2	43.7	4.7	38.6	...
	2015	969.23	483.19	486.04	99.4	43.1	4.8	44.3	22 431[2]
	2018[1]	1 050.14	523.84	526.30	99.5	42.5	4.8	48.0	...
Eastern Africa	2005	300.60	148.83	151.77	98.1	45.5	4.5	45.1	...
Afrique orientale	2010	346.99	171.95	175.04	98.2	44.8	4.5	52.0	...
	2015	399.46	198.12	201.33	98.4	43.4	4.6	59.9	7 005
	2018[1]	433.64	215.20	218.44	98.5	42.4	4.7	65.0	...
Middle Africa	2005	111.95	55.56	56.39	98.5	45.6	4.6	17.2	...
Afrique centrale	2010	131.35	65.31	66.04	98.9	45.7	4.5	20.2	...
	2015	153.74	76.56	77.18	99.2	45.7	4.5	23.7	6 613
	2018[1]	168.54	83.99	84.55	99.3	45.3	4.6	25.9	...
Southern Africa	2005	55.76	27.34	28.42	96.2	32.6	6.6	21.0	...
Afrique australe	2010	59.02	28.95	30.07	96.3	31.2	7.0	22.3	...
	2015	63.42	31.11	32.31	96.3	30.1	7.8	23.9	2 675
	2018[1]	65.97	32.35	33.63	96.2	29.6	8.2	24.9	...
Western Africa	2005[3]	268.61	134.86	133.75	100.8	44.0	4.6	44.3	...
Afrique occidentale	2010[3]	307.78	154.59	153.19	100.9	44.1	4.6	50.8	...
	2015	352.61[3]	177.39[3]	175.22[3]	101.2[3]	43.9[3]	4.5[3]	58.1[3]	6 138
	2018[1,3]	381.98	192.31	189.67	101.4	43.6	4.6	63.0	...
Americas [2]	2005	889.20	439.77	449.43	97.9	26.5	11.8	22.9	...
Amériques [2]	2010	940.50	465.09	475.41	97.8	24.8	13.0	24.2	...
	2015	988.38	488.80	499.58	97.8	23.2	14.6	25.5	42 322
	2018[1]	1 015.86	502.39	513.47	97.8	22.4	15.7	26.2	...
Northern America	2005	327.55	161.70[4]	165.84[4]	97.5[4]	20.6[4]	16.8[4]	17.6	...
Amérique septentrionale	2010	342.94	169.46[4]	173.47[4]	97.7[4]	19.8[4]	18.5[4]	18.4	...
	2015	356.00	176.16[4]	179.84[4]	98.0[4]	18.9[4]	20.7[4]	19.1	21 776
	2018[1,4]	363.84	180.17	183.67	98.1	18.6	22.2	19.5	...
Latin America & the Caribbean	2005	561.66	278.07	283.59	98.1	29.9	8.8	27.9	...
Amérique latine et Caraïbes	2010	597.56	295.63	301.94	97.9	27.6	9.8	29.7	...
	2015	632.38	312.64	319.74	97.8	25.6	11.2	31.4	20 546
	2018[1]	652.01	322.21	329.80	97.7	24.5	12.1	32.4	...
Caribbean	2005	40.12	19.89[5]	20.23[5]	98.3[5]	28.2[5]	11.1[5]	177.5	...
Caraïbes	2010	41.72	20.67[5]	21.06[5]	98.1[5]	26.5[5]	12.0[5]	184.6	...
	2015	43.31	21.44[5]	21.87[5]	98.0[5]	25.0[5]	13.3[5]	191.6	234
	2018[1]	44.16	21.84[5]	22.31[5]	97.9[5]	24.3[5]	14.1[5]	195.4	...
Central America	2005	148.21	73.52	74.69	98.4	33.6	7.5	60.4	...
Amérique centrale	2010	160.56	79.67	80.89	98.5	31.0	8.2	65.5	...
	2015	172.64	85.68	86.95	98.5	28.6	9.3	70.4	2 480
	2018[1]	179.62	89.15	90.46	98.6	27.3	10.0	73.2	...
South America	2005	373.33	184.66[6]	188.66[6]	97.9[6]	28.6[6]	9.1[6]	21.4	...
Amérique du Sud	2010	395.28	195.29[6]	199.99[6]	97.6[6]	26.4[6]	10.2[6]	22.6	...
	2015	416.44	205.52[6]	210.91[6]	97.4[6]	24.4[6]	11.8[6]	23.8	17 832
	2018[1]	428.24	211.22[6]	217.02[6]	97.3[6]	23.4[6]	12.8[6]	24.5	...

Country or area Pays ou zone	Year Année	Mid-year population estimates and projections (millions) Estimations et projections de population au milieu de l'année (millions) Total	Male Hommes	Females Femmes	Sex Ratio (males per 100 females) Rapport des sexes (hommes pour 100 femmes)	Population age distribution (percentage) Répartition par âge de la population (pourcentage) Aged 0 to 14 years old âgée de 0 à 14 ans	Aged 60+ years old âgée de 60 ans ou plus	Population density (per km²) Densité de population (pour km²)	Surface area Superficie (000 km²)
Asia	2005	3 964.34	2 026.43	1 937.91	104.6	27.4	9.3	127.7	...
Asie	2010	4 194.43	2 145.95	2 048.47	104.8	25.6	10.1	135.2	...
	2015	4 419.90	2 261.59	2 158.31	104.8	24.6	11.6	142.4	31 915
	2018[1]	4 545.13	2 325.45	2 219.69	104.8	24.0	12.5	146.5	...
Central Asia	2005	58.74	28.96	29.77	97.3	31.0	7.3	15.0	...
Asie centrale	2010	63.16	31.19	31.97	97.6	28.7	7.0	16.1	...
	2015	68.71	33.97	34.73	97.8	29.1	7.8	17.5	4 103[2]
	2018[1]	71.86	35.54	36.32	97.9	29.6	8.5	18.3	...
Eastern Asia	2005	1 555.01	794.78	760.23	104.5	19.4	12.4	134.5	...
Asie orientale	2010	1 595.83	816.14	779.69	104.7	17.5	14.1	138.0	...
	2015	1 635.15	836.81	798.34	104.8	17.2	16.8	141.4	11 799
	2018[1]	1 653.88	846.48	807.40	104.8	17.1	18.1	143.1	...
South-central Asia	2005	1 641.83	846.20	795.63	106.4	33.3	7.1	159.0	...
Asie centrale et du Sud	2010	1 768.53	910.40	858.13	106.1	31.4	7.5	171.3	...
	2015	1 892.01	973.04	918.98	105.9	29.5	8.4	183.2	10 791
	2018[1]	1 963.31	1 009.20	954.11	105.8	28.4	9.0	190.1	...
South-eastern Asia	2005	561.77	279.94	281.83	99.3	30.0	7.6	129.4	...
Asie du Sud-Est	2010	597.33	298.52	298.81	99.9	28.0	8.1	137.6	...
	2015	634.61	317.03	317.58	99.8	26.7	9.3	146.2	4 495
	2018[1]	655.64	327.31	328.32	99.7	26.0	10.2	151.0	...
Southern Asia	2005	1 583.09	817.24	765.85	106.7	33.4	7.1	247.4	...
Asie méridionale	2010	1 705.37	879.21	826.16	106.4	31.5	7.5	266.5	...
	2015	1 823.31	939.06	884.25	106.2	29.5	8.4	284.9	6 688[2]
	2018[1]	1 891.45	973.66	917.80	106.1	28.3	9.1	295.5	...
Western Asia	2005	205.73	105.50	100.23	105.3	33.4	7.2	42.8	...
Asie occidentale	2010	232.74	120.90	111.84	108.1	31.0	7.3	48.4	...
	2015	258.12	134.71	123.41	109.2	29.9	7.9	53.7	4 831
	2018[1]	272.30	142.45	129.85	109.7	29.1	8.4	56.7	...
Europe	2005	730.29	352.16	378.13	93.1	15.9	20.6	33.0	...
Europe	2010	737.16	355.52	381.64	93.2	15.5	22.0	33.3	...
	2015	740.81	357.69	383.12	93.4	15.8	23.9	33.5	23 049
	2018[1]	742.65	358.94	383.70	93.5	15.9	25.0	33.6	...
Eastern Europe	2005	297.51	140.23	157.28	89.2	15.4	18.2	16.5	...
Europe orientale	2010	294.54	138.45	156.09	88.7	14.8	19.3	16.3	...
	2015	293.24	137.96	155.28	88.8	15.9	21.5	16.2	18 814
	2018[1]	291.95	137.38	154.57	88.9	16.6	22.9	16.2	...
Northern Europe	2005	96.38	47.16[7]	49.22[7]	95.8[7]	18.0[7]	21.1[7]	56.6	...
Europe septentrionale	2010	100.31	49.25[7]	51.07[7]	96.4[7]	17.4[7]	22.6[7]	58.9	...
	2015	103.10	50.78[7]	52.32[7]	97.1[7]	17.5[7]	23.7[7]	60.6	1 810
	2018[1]	104.76	51.69[7]	53.07[7]	97.4[7]	17.7[7]	24.4[7]	61.5	...
Southern Europe	2005	150.39	73.64[8]	76.76[8]	95.9[8]	15.1[8]	22.5[8]	116.1	...
Europe méridionale	2010	153.94	75.33[8]	78.61[8]	95.8[8]	14.8[8]	24.1[8]	118.9	...
	2015	152.44	74.43[8]	78.01[8]	95.4[8]	14.6[8]	26.1[8]	117.7	1 317
	2018[1]	151.86	74.19[8]	77.67[8]	95.5[8]	14.2[8]	27.3[8]	117.3	...
Western Europe	2005	186.01	91.14[9]	94.87[9]	96.1[9]	16.4[9]	22.6[9]	171.5	...
Europe occidentale	2010	188.37	92.49[9]	95.88[9]	96.5[9]	15.9[9]	24.3[9]	173.6	...
	2015	192.03	94.52[9]	97.52[9]	96.9[9]	15.5[9]	25.8[9]	177.0	1 108
	2018[1]	194.07	95.68[9]	98.39[9]	97.2[9]	15.4[9]	26.8[9]	178.9	...
Oceania	2005	33.57	16.80	16.77	100.2	24.9	14.1	4.0	...
Océanie	2010	36.64	18.37	18.27	100.5	24.0	15.3	4.3	...
	2015	39.54	19.79	19.76	100.2	23.6	16.5	4.7	8 564
	2018[1]	41.26	20.64	20.62	100.1	23.5	17.2	4.9	...
Australia and New Zealand	2005	24.37	12.13	12.25	99.0	20.1	17.3	3.1	...
Australie et Nouvelle-Zélande	2010	26.49	13.21	13.28	99.4	19.3	18.8	3.3	...
	2015	28.41	14.13	14.28	98.9	19.0	20.3	3.6	8 012
	2018[1]	29.52	14.68	14.85	98.9	19.2	21.2	3.7	...

Country or area Pays ou zone	Year Année	Mid-year population estimates and projections (millions) Estimations et projections de population au milieu de l'année (millions) Total	 Male Hommes	 Females Femmes	Sex Ratio (males per 100 females) Rapport des sexes (hommes pour 100 femmes)	Population age distribution (percentage) Répartition par âge de la population (pourcentage) Aged 0 to 14 years old âgée de 0 à 14 ans	 Aged 60+ years old âgée de 60 ans ou plus	Population density (per km²) Densité de population (pour km²)	Surface area Superficie (000 km²)
Melanesia Mélanésie	2005	8.05	4.09	3.96	103.5	38.1	5.4	15.2	...
	2010	8.98	4.57	4.41	103.5	37.1	5.8	17.0	...
	2015	9.93	5.05	4.88	103.5	35.7	6.4	18.8	541
	2018[1]	10.52	5.35	5.17	103.4	34.8	6.8	19.9	...
Micronesia Micronésie	2005	0.50	0.25[10]	0.25[10]	101.0[10]	33.3[10]	6.5[10]	158.6	...
	2010	0.50	0.25[10]	0.25[10]	101.7[10]	32.1[10]	7.8[10]	158.7	...
	2015	0.52	0.26[10]	0.26[10]	101.6[10]	30.0[10]	9.6[10]	163.7	3
	2018[1]	0.53	0.27[10]	0.26[10]	101.5[10]	28.8[10]	10.8[10]	167.8	...
Polynesia Polynésie	2005	0.64[11]	0.33[12]	0.31[12]	104.7[12]	33.9[12]	7.7[12]	79.4[11]	...
	2010	0.66[11]	0.34[12]	0.32[12]	104.0[12]	31.9[12]	8.4[12]	81.5[11]	...
	2015	0.68[11]	0.34[12]	0.33[12]	103.6[12]	30.6[12]	9.6[12]	83.7[11]	8
	2018[1]	0.69[11]	0.35[12]	0.34[12]	103.4[12]	29.5[12]	10.6[12]	85.5[11]	...
Afghanistan Afghanistan	2005	25.07	12.97	12.10	107.2	47.6	3.6	38.4	...
	2010	28.80	14.80	14.01	105.7	47.8	3.9	44.1	...
	2015	33.74	17.39	16.35	106.4	44.5	4.0	51.7	653
	2018[1]	36.37	18.74	17.64	106.2	42.6	4.2	55.7	...
Albania Albanie	2005	3.08	1.54	1.54	100.6	26.5	12.3	112.4	...
	2010	2.94	1.48	1.47	100.7	22.5	15.0	107.3	...
	2015	2.92	1.48	1.45	102.0	18.0	17.8	106.7	29
	2018[1]	2.93	1.48	1.45	101.8	17.1	19.7	107.1	...
Algeria Algérie	2005	33.29	16.84	16.45	102.3	29.1	7.0	14.0	...
	2010	36.12	18.23	17.89	101.9	27.2	7.8	15.2	...
	2015	39.87	20.13	19.74	102.0	28.7	8.9	16.7	2 382
	2018[1]	42.01	21.22	20.79	102.0	29.5	9.6	17.6	...
American Samoa Samoa américaines	2000	0.06	...	...	104.4[13,14]	38.8[13,14]	5.4[13,14]	287.6	...
	2005	0.06	...	...	...	...	...	295.6	...
	2010	0.06	...	...	103.0[13,14]	35.0[13,14]	6.7[13,14]	278.2	...
	2015	0.06	...	...	...	...	...	277.7	~0
	2016	0.06[1]	...	...	# 103.6	# 33.3	# 9.0	278.0[1]	...
	2018[1]	0.06	...	...	...	...	...	278.4	...
Andorra Andorre	2005	0.08	...	...	109.0[13,15]	15.1[13,15]	16.1[13,15]	167.8	...
	2010	0.08	...	...	108.5[13,15]	14.0[13,15]	18.6[13,15]	179.7	...
	2015	0.08	...	...	101.7[13,15]	...	...	166.0	~0
	2016	0.08[1]	...	...	102.3[13,15]	14.4[13,15]	19.0[13,15]	164.4[1]	...
	2018[1]	0.08	...	...	...	...	...	163.7	...
Angola Angola	2005	19.55	9.56	10.00	95.6	47.2	3.7	15.7	...
	2010	23.37	11.43	11.94	95.8	47.3	3.6	18.7	...
	2015	27.86	13.65	14.21	96.1	47.1	3.9	22.3	1 247
	2018[1]	30.77	15.09	15.68	96.3	46.6	4.1	24.7	...
Anguilla Anguilla	2001	0.01	...	...	97.3	27.7	10.2	126.4	...
	2005	0.01	...	...	...	...	...	140.4	...
	2010	0.01	...	...	...	...	...	153.0	...
	2011	0.01	...	...	* 97.6	* 23.3	* 7.6[16]	155.0	...
	2015	0.01	...	...	...	...	...	162.3	~0
	2018[1]	0.02	...	...	...	...	...	167.2	...
Antigua and Barbuda Antigua-et-Barbuda	2005	0.09	0.04	0.05	92.1	28.4	9.3	202.8	...
	2010	0.09	0.05	0.05	92.0	26.6	8.9	215.1	...
	2015	0.10	0.05	0.05	92.2	24.6	10.1	227.1	~0
	2018[1]	0.10	0.05	0.05	92.3	23.6	11.3	234.2	...
Argentina Argentine	2005	39.15	19.15	20.00	95.8	26.9	13.8	14.3	...
	2010	41.22	20.16	21.06	95.7	25.9	14.4	15.1	...
	2015	43.42	21.25	22.17	95.8	25.2	15.1	15.9	2 780
	2018[1]	44.69	21.88	22.81	95.9	24.7	15.6	16.3	...
Armenia Arménie	2005	2.98	1.40	1.58	88.8	21.5	14.4	104.7	...
	2010	2.88	1.35	1.53	87.9	19.5	14.8	101.1	...
	2015	2.92	1.37	1.55	88.7	19.8	15.8	102.5	30
	2018[1]	2.93	1.38	1.55	88.8	20.1	17.5	103.1	...

2 Population, surface area and density *(continued)*

Population, superficie et densité *(suite)*

Country or area Pays ou zone	Year Année	Mid-year population estimates and projections (millions) Estimations et projections de population au milieu de l'année (millions) Total	Male Hommes	Females Femmes	Sex Ratio (males per 100 females) Rapport des sexes (hommes pour 100 femmes)	Population age distribution (percentage) Répartition par âge de la population (pourcentage) Aged 0 to 14 years old âgée de 0 à 14 ans	Aged 60+ years old âgée de 60 ans ou plus	Population density (per km²) Densité de population (pour km²)	Surface area Superficie (000 km²)
Aruba Aruba	2005	0.10	0.05	0.05	90.7	21.5	12.6	555.7	...
	2010	0.10	0.05	0.05	91.1	20.9	15.5	564.8	...
	2015	0.10	0.05	0.05	90.6	18.7	18.4	579.7	~0
	2018[1]	0.11	0.05	0.06	90.3	17.7	20.4	587.1	...
Australia Australie	2005[17]	20.24	10.10	10.14	99.6	19.8	17.4	2.6	...
	2010[17]	22.12	11.06	11.06	100.0	19.0	18.9	2.9	...
	2015	23.80[17]	11.86[17]	11.94[17]	99.4[17]	18.8[17]	20.4[17]	3.1[17]	7 692[18]
	2018[1,17]	24.77	12.34	12.43	99.3	19.1	21.2	3.2	...
Austria Autriche	2005	8.25	4.01	4.24	94.6	16.0	22.1	100.2	...
	2010	8.41	4.10	4.31	95.1	14.7	23.3	102.1	...
	2015	8.68	4.25	4.43	95.9	14.1	24.3	105.3	84
	2018[1]	8.75	4.29	4.46	96.3	14.1	25.5	106.2	...
Azerbaijan Azerbaïdjan	2005[19]	8.54	4.21	4.33	97.1	26.2	8.5	103.3	...
	2010[19]	9.03	4.48	4.56	98.2	22.8	8.1	109.3	...
	2015	9.62[19]	4.79[19]	4.83[19]	99.1[19]	22.9[19]	9.3[19]	116.4[19]	87
	2018[1,19]	9.92	4.94	4.98	99.3	23.3	10.6	120.1	...
Bahamas Bahamas	2005	0.33	0.16	0.17	95.4	25.6	9.4	32.9	...
	2010	0.36	0.18	0.18	95.6	22.5	10.5	36.0	...
	2015	0.39	0.19	0.20	95.9	20.7	12.6	38.6	14
	2018[1]	0.40	0.20	0.20	96.0	20.5	14.0	39.9	...
Bahrain Bahreïn	2005	0.89	0.53	0.36	150.5	25.7	3.4	1 170.0	...
	2010	1.24	0.77	0.47	165.8	20.3	3.5	1 632.7	...
	2015	1.37	0.85	0.53	161.3	20.8	4.1	1 805.1	1
	2018[1]	1.57	0.99	0.57	173.0	19.2	4.9	2 061.8	...
Bangladesh Bangladesh	2005	143.43	73.05	70.38	103.8	34.4	6.6	1 101.9	...
	2010	152.15	76.94	75.21	102.3	32.1	6.9	1 168.8	...
	2015	161.20	81.34	79.86	101.9	29.4	7.1	1 238.4	148
	2018[1]	166.37	83.86	82.51	101.6	27.8	7.5	1 278.1	...
Barbados Barbade	2005	0.27	0.13	0.14	92.3	20.7	15.5	637.2	...
	2010	0.28	0.13	0.15	92.2	19.9	17.3	650.2	...
	2015	0.28	0.14	0.15	92.0	19.4	19.8	661.0	~0
	2018[1]	0.29	0.14	0.15	91.8	18.9	21.6	666.0	...
Belarus Bélarus	2005	9.62	4.49	5.13	87.5	15.6	18.6	47.4	...
	2010	9.47	4.40	5.07	86.9	14.8	19.1	46.7	...
	2015	9.49	4.41	5.07	87.0	16.1	20.4	46.7	208
	2018[1]	9.45	4.40	5.05	87.0	17.0	21.8	46.6	...
Belgium Belgique	2005	10.55	5.17	5.37	96.3	17.2	22.1	348.3	...
	2010	10.94	5.37	5.57	96.5	16.9	23.2	361.3	...
	2015	11.29	5.55	5.74	96.7	17.0	24.0	372.8	31
	2018[1]	11.50	5.68	5.82	97.7	17.2	24.9	379.7	...
Belize Belize	2005	0.28	0.14	0.14	101.0	39.0	4.7	12.4	...
	2010	0.32	0.16	0.16	100.1	35.7	5.7	14.1	...
	2015	0.36	0.18	0.18	99.4	32.5	5.9	15.8	23
	2018[1]	0.38	0.19	0.19	99.0	30.9	6.3	16.8	...
Benin Bénin	2005	7.98	3.96	4.03	98.2	44.4	5.0	70.8	...
	2010	9.20	4.57	4.63	98.7	43.8	4.9	81.6	...
	2015	10.58	5.27	5.31	99.3	43.0	5.0	93.8	115
	2018[1]	11.49	5.73	5.75	99.6	42.4	5.0	101.9	...
Bermuda Bermudes	2005	0.07	...	...	91.8[13,20]	18.4[13]	16.4[13]	1 302.6	...
	2010	0.06	...	...	92.4[13,21]	17.4[13]	18.7[13]	1 279.1	...
	2015	0.06	...	...	91.4[13,21]	15.3[13,21]	23.4[13,21]	1 240.1	~0
	2017	0.06[1]	...	...	91.4[13,21]	14.8[13,21]	24.9[13,21]	1 227.0[1]	...
	2018[1]	0.06	...	...	...	...	...	1 221.4	...
Bhutan Bhoutan	2005	0.66	0.34	0.31	110.6	34.9	5.7	17.2	...
	2010	0.73	0.39	0.34	112.7	30.6	6.2	19.1	...
	2015	0.79	0.42	0.37	113.4	27.4	6.9	20.7	38
	2018[1]	0.82	0.43	0.38	112.9	26.2	7.5	21.4	...

Country or area Pays ou zone	Year Année	Mid-year population estimates and projections (millions) / Estimations et projections de population au milieu de l'année (millions): Total	Male Hommes	Females Femmes	Sex Ratio (males per 100 females) Rapport des sexes (hommes pour 100 femmes)	Population age distribution (percentage) / Répartition par âge de la population (pourcentage): Aged 0 to 14 years old âgée de 0 à 14 ans	Aged 60+ years old âgée de 60 ans ou plus	Population density (per km²) Densité de population (pour km²)	Surface area Superficie (000 km²)
Bolivia (Plurin. State of)	2005	9.13	4.57	4.55	100.5	36.6	7.8	8.4	...
Bolivie (État plurin. de)	2010	9.92	4.97	4.95	100.5	34.7	8.3	9.2	...
	2015	10.72	5.37	5.35	100.3	32.4	9.2	9.9	1 099[22]
	2018[1]	11.22	5.61	5.60	100.2	31.3	9.6	10.4	...
Bonaire, St. Eustatius & Saba	2005	0.01	...	...	...	...	...	43.9	...
Bonaire, St-Eustache et	2010	0.02	...	...	...	...	...	63.8	...
Saba	2018[1]	0.03	...	...	...	...	...	78.4	...
Bosnia and Herzegovina	2005	3.78	1.86	1.92	96.6	17.7	17.4	74.1	...
Bosnie-Herzégovine	2010	3.72	1.83	1.89	96.5	15.7	19.2	73.0	...
	2015	3.54	1.74	1.80	96.4	14.5	22.4	69.3	51
	2018[1]	3.50	1.72	1.78	96.5	14.2	23.9	68.7	...
Botswana	2005	1.86	0.92	0.94	97.5	35.1	5.0	3.3	...
Botswana	2010	2.01	1.00	1.02	97.8	33.0	5.3	3.6	...
	2015	2.21	1.09	1.12	97.7	31.8	6.1	3.9	582
	2018[1]	2.33	1.15	1.18	97.8	31.2	6.5	4.1	...
Brazil	2005	186.92	92.22	94.69	97.4	27.4	8.7	22.4	...
Brésil	2010	196.80	96.93	99.86	97.1	24.9	10.0	23.5	...
	2015	205.96	101.28	104.68	96.8	22.5	11.9	24.6	8 516
	2018[1]	210.87	103.60	107.27	96.6	21.4	13.1	25.2	...
British Virgin Islands	2001	0.02	...	...	106.1	26.3	7.4	140.6	...
Îles Vierges britanniques	2005	0.02	...	...	...	...	...	154.5	...
	2010	0.03	...	...	97.1	22.3	9.7	181.5	...
	2015	0.03	...	...	...	...	...	200.8	~0
	2018[1]	0.03	...	...	...	...	...	211.5	...
Brunei Darussalam	2005	0.37	0.19	0.18	104.3	27.8	4.8	69.3	...
Brunéi Darussalam	2010	0.39	0.20	0.19	106.7	26.0	5.4	73.7	...
	2015	0.42	0.22	0.20	106.3	23.7	7.1	79.2	6
	2018[1]	0.43	0.22	0.21	106.0	22.6	8.5	82.4	...
Bulgaria	2005	7.68	3.74	3.94	94.8	13.6	23.1	70.8	...
Bulgarie	2010	7.40	3.61	3.80	94.9	13.3	25.3	68.2	...
	2015	7.18	3.49	3.69	94.7	14.0	27.1	66.1	111
	2018[1]	7.04	3.42	3.62	94.6	14.4	27.9	64.8	...
Burkina Faso	2005	13.42	6.62	6.80	97.4	46.5	4.1	49.1	...
Burkina Faso	2010	15.61	7.74	7.87	98.3	46.2	3.9	57.0	...
	2015	18.11	9.02	9.09	99.2	45.6	3.8	66.2	273
	2018[1]	19.75	9.86	9.89	99.6	44.9	3.9	72.2	...
Burundi	2005	7.42	3.65	3.77	96.8	45.7	4.2	289.1	...
Burundi	2010	8.77	4.31	4.46	96.5	44.1	4.0	341.4	...
	2015	10.20	5.02	5.18	96.7	44.8	4.2	397.2	28
	2018[1]	11.22	5.52	5.69	97.0	45.1	4.4	436.8	...
Cabo Verde	2005	0.47	0.23	0.24	95.8	38.1	7.2	117.8	...
Cabo Verde	2010	0.50	0.25	0.25	98.7	34.0	6.7	124.7	...
	2015	0.53	0.27	0.27	99.2	31.2	6.7	132.2	4
	2018[1]	0.55	0.28	0.28	99.4	29.8	7.0	137.3	...
Cambodia	2005	13.27	6.44	6.83	94.3	37.1	5.3	75.2	...
Cambodge	2010	14.31	6.97	7.34	95.0	33.3	5.9	81.1	...
	2015	15.52	7.57	7.95	95.2	31.6	6.8	87.9	181
	2018[1]	16.25	7.93	8.32	95.3	31.2	7.2	92.0	...
Cameroon	2005	17.42	8.70	8.72	99.7	44.0	5.0	36.9	...
Cameroun	2010	19.97	9.99	9.99	100.0	43.5	4.9	42.2	...
	2015	22.83	11.42	11.41	100.1	43.0	4.8	48.3	476
	2018[1]	24.68	12.35	12.33	100.2	42.5	4.8	52.2	...
Canada	2005	32.29	16.01	16.28	98.3	17.7	17.9	3.6	...
Canada	2010	34.17	16.95	17.22	98.5	16.5	20.0	3.8	...
	2015	35.95	17.83	18.12	98.4	16.0	22.4	4.0	9 985
	2018[1]	36.95	18.34	18.61	98.5	16.1	24.0	4.1	...

Country or area Pays ou zone	Year Année	Mid-year population estimates and projections (millions) Estimations et projections de population au milieu de l'année (millions): Total	Male Hommes	Females Femmes	Sex Ratio (males per 100 females) Rapport des sexes (hommes pour 100 femmes)	Population age distribution (percentage) Répartition par âge de la population (pourcentage): Aged 0 to 14 years old âgée de 0 à 14 ans	Aged 60+ years old âgée de 60 ans ou plus	Population density (per km²) Densité de population (pour km²)	Surface area Superficie (000 km²)
Cayman Islands	2005	0.05	...	...	101.0[13]	...	...	202.6	...
Îles Caïmanes	2010	0.06	...	...	97.8[13,23]	18.1[13,23]	8.6[13,23]	231.3	...
	2015	0.06	...	...	100.4[13]	18.3[13]	6.7[13,16]	249.8	~0
	2018[1]	0.06	...	...	...	...	...	259.8	...
Central African Republic	2005	4.13	2.03	2.09	97.2	42.2	5.7	6.6	...
République centrafricaine	2010	4.45	2.19	2.25	97.4	42.5	5.5	7.1	...
	2015	4.55	2.24	2.30	97.3	43.7	5.5	7.3	623
	2018[1]	4.74	2.34	2.40	97.3	42.8	5.5	7.6	...
Chad	2005	10.07	5.03	5.04	99.7	49.1	4.2	8.0	...
Tchad	2010	11.89	5.95	5.94	100.0	48.6	4.0	9.4	...
	2015	14.01	7.01	7.00	100.2	47.6	4.0	11.1	1 284
	2018[1]	15.35	7.69	7.67	100.2	46.9	4.0	12.2	...
Channel Islands [24]	2005	0.15	0.08	0.08	96.6	16.3	20.4	812.1	...
Îles Anglo-Normandes [24]	2010	0.16	0.08	0.08	98.1	15.3	21.7	839.9	...
	2015	0.16	0.08	0.08	98.3	14.7	23.7	861.9	~0
	2018[1]	0.17	0.08	0.08	98.5	14.5	25.0	874.1	...
Chile	2005	16.15	7.99	8.16	97.9	24.6	11.8	21.7	...
Chili	2010	16.99	8.41	8.58	98.0	22.5	13.2	22.9	...
	2015	17.76	8.80	8.97	98.1	20.8	15.2	23.9	756
	2018[1]	18.20	9.02	9.18	98.2	20.1	16.5	24.5	...
China	2005[25]	1 321.62	679.54	642.08	105.8	19.9	11.0	140.8	...
Chine	2010[25]	1 359.76	699.88	659.87	106.1	17.8	12.6	144.8	...
	2015	1 397.03[25]	719.76[25]	677.27[25]	106.3[25]	17.7[25]	15.4[25]	148.8[25]	9 600
	2018[1,25]	1 415.05	729.20	685.85	106.3	17.6	16.6	150.7	...
China, Hong Kong SAR	2005	6.83	3.28	3.55	92.2	14.4	15.6	6 502.6	...
Chine, RAS de Hong Kong	2010	7.03	3.30	3.73	88.4	11.9	18.4	6 690.7	...
	2015	7.25	3.35	3.90	85.9	11.2	21.8	6 900.7	1
	2018[1]	7.43	3.41	4.02	84.8	11.9	24.3	7 075.1	...
China, Macao SAR	2005	0.48	0.23	0.25	90.5	16.9	9.6	16 139.1	...
Chine, RAS de Macao	2010	0.54	0.26	0.28	92.3	12.7	11.0	17 958.8	...
	2015	0.60	0.29	0.31	92.2	12.4	14.4	20 098.4	~0[26]
	2018[1]	0.63	0.30	0.33	92.4	13.8	17.0	21 151.1	...
Colombia	2005	43.29	21.38	21.91	97.6	28.9	7.6	39.0	...
Colombie	2010	45.92	22.64	23.28	97.3	26.4	9.0	41.4	...
	2015	48.23	23.74	24.49	97.0	24.3	10.8	43.5	1 142
	2018[1]	49.46	24.33	25.14	96.8	23.1	12.1	44.6	...
Comoros	2005	0.61	0.31	0.30	101.4	42.3	4.6	328.7	...
Comores	2010	0.69	0.35	0.34	101.6	41.0	4.5	370.6	...
	2015	0.78	0.39	0.39	101.7	40.1	4.7	417.7	2
	2018[1]	0.83	0.42	0.41	101.8	39.5	5.0	447.3	...
Congo	2005	3.72	1.86	1.86	99.9	41.6	5.2	10.9	...
Congo	2010	4.39	2.19	2.19	100.1	41.7	5.0	12.8	...
	2015	5.00	2.50	2.50	100.1	42.4	5.1	14.6	342
	2018[1]	5.40	2.70	2.70	100.1	42.1	5.2	15.8	...
Cook Islands	2001	0.02	...	...	106.6	30.0	10.6	76.3	...
Îles Cook	2005	0.02	...	...	...	...	...	82.1	...
	2006	0.02	...	...	* 103.1	* 26.1	* 11.9	82.1	...
	2010	0.02	...	...	...	...	...	77.3	...
	2015	0.02	...	...	...	...	...	72.7	~0
	2016	0.02[1]	...	...	# 97.4	# 26.9	# 14.2	72.4[1]	...
	2018[1]	0.02	...	...	...	...	...	72.5	...
Costa Rica	2005	4.25	2.13	2.12	100.6	27.4	9.4	83.2	...
Costa Rica	2010	4.55	2.28	2.27	100.4	24.6	11.1	89.0	...
	2015	4.81	2.41	2.40	100.1	22.3	12.8	94.2	51
	2018[1]	4.95	2.48	2.48	100.0	21.4	14.1	97.0	...
Côte d'Ivoire	2005	18.34	9.40	8.94	105.2	44.1	4.6	57.7	...
Côte d'Ivoire	2010	20.40	10.41	9.99	104.2	43.7	4.7	64.2	...
	2015	23.11	11.73	11.38	103.1	42.7	4.7	72.7	322
	2018[1]	24.91	12.61	12.30	102.5	42.3	4.8	78.3	...

Country or area Pays ou zone	Year Année	Mid-year population estimates and projections (millions) Estimations et projections de population au milieu de l'année (millions) Total	Male Hommes	Females Femmes	Sex Ratio (males per 100 females) Rapport des sexes (hommes pour 100 femmes)	Population age distribution (percentage) Répartition par âge de la population (pourcentage) Aged 0 to 14 years old âgée de 0 à 14 ans	Aged 60+ years old âgée de 60 ans ou plus	Population density (per km²) Densité de population (pour km²)	Surface area Superficie (000 km²)
Croatia Croatie	2005	4.38	2.11	2.27	92.9	15.7	21.9	78.2	...
	2010	4.33	2.08	2.24	92.9	15.4	23.8	77.3	...
	2015	4.24	2.04	2.20	93.0	14.8	25.8	75.7	57
	2018[1]	4.16	2.01	2.16	93.1	14.7	27.2	74.4	...
Cuba Cuba	2005	11.28	5.66	5.62	100.7	19.4	15.2	106.0	...
	2010	11.33	5.68	5.66	100.4	17.4	17.0	106.5	...
	2015	11.46	5.74	5.73	100.2	16.3	19.4	107.7	110
	2018[1]	11.49	5.75	5.74	100.1	15.9	20.5	107.9	...
Curaçao Curaçao	2005	0.13	0.06	0.07	88.2	21.1	17.2	291.4	...
	2010	0.15	0.07	0.08	84.8	19.9	18.8	332.5	...
	2015	0.16	0.07	0.09	84.3	18.9	21.9	355.9	~0
	2018[1]	0.16	0.07	0.09	84.7	18.5	23.4	363.9	...
Cyprus Chypre	2005[27]	1.03	0.52	0.51	102.6	20.0	14.9	111.2	...
	2010[27]	1.11	0.56	0.56	99.7	17.8	16.1	120.4	...
	2015	1.16[27]	0.58[27]	0.58[27]	100.3[27]	16.9[27]	17.7[27]	125.6[27]	9
	2018[1,27]	1.19	0.59	0.59	100.1	16.8	18.9	128.7	...
Czechia Tchéquie	2005	10.26	5.00	5.26	95.0	14.7	19.8	132.8	...
	2010	10.54	5.17	5.36	96.4	14.2	22.4	136.4	...
	2015	10.60	5.21	5.39	96.6	15.1	24.9	137.3	79
	2018[1]	10.63	5.22	5.40	96.7	15.5	25.8	137.6	...
Dem. People's Rep. Korea Rép. pop. dém. de Corée	2005	23.90	11.67	12.23	95.4	24.7	11.9	198.5	...
	2010	24.59	12.02	12.58	95.6	22.8	12.9	204.2	...
	2015	25.24	12.35	12.90	95.7	21.1	12.7	209.6	121
	2018[1]	25.61	12.53	13.08	95.7	20.4	14.1	212.7	...
Dem. Rep. of the Congo Rép. dém. du Congo	2005	54.75	27.20	27.55	98.8	45.8	4.7	24.2	...
	2010	64.52	32.12	32.40	99.1	46.1	4.7	28.5	...
	2015	76.20	38.00	38.20	99.5	46.3	4.7	33.6	2 345
	2018[1]	84.01	41.92	42.08	99.6	46.2	4.7	37.1	...
Denmark Danemark	2005	5.42	2.69	2.74	98.1	18.7	21.2	127.8	...
	2010	5.55	2.76	2.80	98.5	17.9	23.3	130.9	...
	2015	5.69	2.83	2.86	98.9	16.8	24.8	134.1	43
	2018[1]	5.75	2.86	2.89	99.0	16.4	25.6	135.6	...
Djibouti Djibouti	2005	0.78	0.39	0.39	101.0	37.9	5.2	33.8	...
	2010	0.85	0.43	0.42	100.9	34.8	5.8	36.7	...
	2015	0.93	0.47	0.46	100.8	32.0	6.2	40.0	23
	2018[1]	0.97	0.49	0.48	100.7	30.6	6.6	41.9	...
Dominica Dominique	2001	0.07	...	...	101.5[28]	29.0[29]	13.2[29]	92.9	...
	2005	0.07	...	...	101.4	...	...	94.2	...
	2006	0.07	...	...	103.7	29.5	13.3	94.4	...
	2010	0.07	...	...	101.4	...	...	95.3	...
	2014	0.07	...	...	103.0	...	...	97.0	1
	2015	0.07	...	...	...	...	...	97.5	1
	2018[1]	0.07	...	...	...	...	...	99.1	...
Dominican Republic République dominicaine	2005	9.24	4.62	4.62	100.0	33.2	8.0	191.2	...
	2010	9.90	4.94	4.96	99.7	31.4	8.7	204.8	...
	2015	10.53	5.25	5.28	99.3	30.0	9.7	217.9	49
	2018[1]	10.88	5.42	5.47	99.1	29.0	10.5	225.2	...
Ecuador Équateur	2005	13.74	6.88	6.86	100.3	32.7	8.0	55.3	...
	2010	14.93	7.47	7.46	100.1	30.7	8.7	60.1	...
	2015	16.14	8.07	8.07	100.0	29.0	9.9	65.0	257
	2018[1]	16.86	8.43	8.44	99.9	28.2	10.7	67.9	...
Egypt Égypte	2005	76.78	38.71	38.07	101.7	33.3	7.1	77.1	...
	2010	84.11	42.47	41.64	102.0	32.1	7.5	84.5	...
	2015	93.78	47.41	46.37	102.2	33.1	7.7	94.2	1 002
	2018[1]	99.38	50.25	49.13	102.3	33.3	8.0	99.8	...
El Salvador El Salvador	2005	6.03	2.88	3.15	91.4	34.8	9.1	291.0	...
	2010	6.16	2.92	3.25	89.9	31.6	10.0	297.5	...
	2015	6.31	2.97	3.34	88.9	28.3	11.1	304.7	21[30]
	2018[1]	6.41	3.01	3.40	88.4	27.1	11.8	309.4	...

Country or area / Pays ou zone	Year / Année	Mid-year population estimates and projections (millions) / Estimations et projections de population au milieu de l'année (millions): Total	Male / Hommes	Females / Femmes	Sex Ratio (males per 100 females) / Rapport des sexes (hommes pour 100 femmes)	Population age distribution (percentage) / Répartition par âge de la population (pourcentage): Aged 0 to 14 years old / âgée de 0 à 14 ans	Aged 60+ years old / âgée de 60 ans ou plus	Population density (per km²) / Densité de population (pour km²)	Surface area / Superficie (000 km²)
Equatorial Guinea / Guinée équatoriale	2005	0.76	0.40	0.36	112.6	39.5	5.3	27.0	...
	2010	0.95	0.52	0.43	118.8	38.4	4.8	33.9	...
	2015	1.18	0.65	0.53	123.0	37.4	4.6	41.9	28
	2018[1]	1.31	0.73	0.59	124.3	37.0	4.4	46.8	...
Eritrea / Érythrée	2005	3.97	1.99	1.98	100.1	41.0	5.5	39.3	...
	2010	4.39	2.20	2.19	100.2	41.6	5.5	43.5	...
	2015	4.85	2.43	2.42	100.4	42.3	5.3	48.0	118
	2018[1]	5.19	2.60	2.59	100.5	41.5	5.3	51.4	...
Estonia / Estonie	2005	1.36	0.63	0.73	86.8	15.2	21.9	32.0	...
	2010	1.33	0.62	0.71	87.2	15.1	23.2	31.4	...
	2015	1.32	0.62	0.70	87.9	16.1	25.1	31.0	45
	2018[1]	1.31	0.61	0.69	88.3	16.6	26.2	30.8	...
Ethiopia / Éthiopie	2005	76.73	38.28	38.45	99.5	46.2	4.9	76.7	...
	2010	87.70	43.77	43.93	99.6	44.5	5.1	87.7	...
	2015	99.87	49.86	50.01	99.7	41.6	5.2	99.9	1 104
	2018[1]	107.53	53.70	53.84	99.7	40.0	5.3	107.5	...
Falkland Islands (Malvinas) [31] / Îles Falkland (Malvinas) [31]	2001	~0.00	...	...	121.5	15.0	12.0	0.2	...
	2005	~0.00	...	...	...	...	...	0.2	...
	2006	~0.00	...	...	113.2	15.9	14.0	0.2	...
	2010	~0.00	...	...	...	...	...	0.2	...
	2012	~0.00	...	...	110.5[32]	16.4[32]	15.7[32]	0.2	...
	2015	~0.00	...	...	...	...	...	0.2	12
	2018[1]	~0.00	...	...	...	...	...	0.2	...
Faroe Islands / Îles Féroé	2005	0.05	...	...	108.0[13]	...	...	34.6	...
	2008	0.05	...	...	108.1[13]	22.0[13]	19.3[13]	34.7	...
	2010	0.05	...	...	108.0[13]	...	...	34.8	...
	2015	0.05	...	...	107.2[13]	21.0[13]	22.5[13]	35.1	1
	2018[1]	0.05	...	...	...	...	...	35.5	...
Fiji / Fidji	2005	0.82	0.42	0.40	104.0	30.5	6.9	45.0	...
	2010	0.86	0.44	0.42	104.2	29.0	7.9	47.1	...
	2015	0.89	0.45	0.44	103.4	28.7	9.3	48.8	18
	2018[1]	0.91	0.46	0.45	102.9	28.3	10.3	49.9	...
Finland [33] / Finlande [33]	2005	5.26	2.57	2.68	95.9	17.3	21.5	17.3	...
	2010	5.37	2.63	2.73	96.4	16.5	24.8	17.7	...
	2015	5.48	2.70	2.78	96.9	16.4	27.1	18.0	338
	2018[1]	5.54	2.73	2.81	97.3	16.5	28.1	18.2	...
France / France	2005	61.23	30.04	31.19	96.3	18.4	20.9	111.8	...
	2010	63.03	30.93	32.09	96.4	18.4	23.1	115.1	...
	2015	64.46	31.67	32.78	96.6	18.3	25.0	117.7	552
	2018[1]	65.23	32.08	33.15	96.8	18.0	26.1	119.1	...
French Guiana / Guyane française	2005	0.20	0.10	0.10	98.2	36.1	5.7	2.5	...
	2010	0.23	0.12	0.12	99.9	35.3	6.5	2.8	...
	2015	0.27	0.13	0.13	100.0	33.9	7.9	3.3	84
	2018[1]	0.29	0.14	0.14	100.0	32.8	8.7	3.5	...
French Polynesia / Polynésie française	2005	0.25	0.13	0.12	105.3	27.7	8.0	69.6	...
	2010	0.27	0.14	0.13	104.7	25.2	9.3	73.2	...
	2015	0.28	0.14	0.14	104.0	23.9	11.1	75.9	4
	2018[1]	0.29	0.15	0.14	103.6	22.9	12.4	78.1	...
Gabon / Gabon	2005	1.40	0.70	0.70	100.3	39.0	7.7	5.4	...
	2010	1.64	0.84	0.80	104.2	37.0	7.0	6.4	...
	2015	1.93	0.99	0.94	105.7	35.8	6.4	7.5	268
	2018[1]	2.07	1.06	1.01	105.5	35.9	6.3	8.0	...
Gambia / Gambie	2005	1.44	0.72	0.73	98.4	46.3	4.0	142.7	...
	2010	1.69	0.84	0.85	98.1	46.3	3.7	167.2	...
	2015	1.98	0.98	1.00	98.0	45.7	3.8	195.4	11
	2018[1]	2.16	1.07	1.09	98.0	45.1	3.8	213.8	...

Country or area Pays ou zone	Year Année	Mid-year population estimates and projections (millions) Estimations et projections de population au milieu de l'année (millions) Total	 Male Hommes	 Females Femmes	Sex Ratio (males per 100 females) Rapport des sexes (hommes pour 100 femmes)	Population age distribution (percentage) Répartition par âge de la population (pourcentage) Aged 0 to 14 years old âgée de 0 à 14 ans	 Aged 60+ years old âgée de 60 ans ou plus	Population density (per km²) Densité de population (pour km²)	Surface area Superficie (000 km²)
Georgia Géorgie	2005[34]	4.49	2.12	2.37	89.5	19.5	18.2	64.6	...
	2010[34]	4.23	2.01	2.22	90.5	18.0	18.8	60.9	...
	2015	3.95[34]	1.89[34]	2.07[34]	91.3[34]	18.7[34]	20.3[34]	56.9[34]	70
	2018[1,34]	3.91	1.87	2.04	91.3	19.4	21.1	56.2	...
Germany Allemagne	2005	81.67	39.91	41.76	95.6	14.4	24.9	234.3	...
	2010	80.89	39.66	41.24	96.2	13.6	26.1	232.1	...
	2015	81.71	40.19	41.52	96.8	13.1	27.3	234.4	357
	2018[1]	82.29	40.55	41.75	97.1	13.1	28.4	236.1	...
Ghana Ghana	2005	21.54	10.76	10.78	99.9	40.6	5.2	94.7	...
	2010	24.51	12.13	12.38	98.0	39.6	5.4	107.7	...
	2015	27.58	13.72	13.86	99.0	38.8	5.2	121.2	239
	2018[1]	29.46	14.69	14.78	99.4	38.3	5.4	129.5	...
Gibraltar Gibraltar	2001	0.03	...	...	98.5[35]	18.4[35]	20.5[35]	3 137.4	...
	2005	0.03	...	...	97.3[36]	...	...	3 208.5	...
	2010	0.03	...	...	99.2[36]	...	...	3 318.9	...
	2012	0.03	...	...	99.6[13,36]	18.1[13,36]	22.4[13,36]	3 362.3	...
	2015	0.03	...	...	101.8[36]	...	...	3 422.8	~0
	2018[1]	0.03	...	...	...	...	...	3 473.3	...
Greece Grèce	2005	11.30	5.60	5.71	98.1	15.1	22.5	87.7	...
	2010	11.45	5.64	5.80	97.2	14.9	24.0	88.8	...
	2015	11.22	5.52	5.69	97.0	14.5	25.7	87.0	132
	2018[1]	11.14	5.48	5.66	96.9	14.1	26.9	86.4	...
Greenland Groenland	2005	0.06	...	...	113.4[13,15]	25.0[13,15]	9.6[13,15]	0.1	...
	2010	0.06	...	...	112.6[13,15]	22.6[13,15]	10.9[13,15]	0.1	...
	2015	0.06	...	...	111.9[13,15]	21.1[13,15]	12.7[13,15]	0.1	2 166
	2016	0.06[1]	...	...	112.1[13,15]	21.0[13,15]	13.2[13,15]	0.1[1]	...
	2018[1]	0.06	...	...	...	...	...	0.1	...
Grenada Grenade	2005	0.10	0.05	0.05	98.8	30.0	9.9	302.8	...
	2010	0.10	0.05	0.05	99.8	27.5	9.6	307.9	...
	2015	0.11	0.05	0.05	100.6	26.5	10.2	314.2	~0
	2018[1]	0.11	0.05	0.05	101.0	26.3	10.7	318.6	...
Guadeloupe Guadeloupe	2005[37]	0.44	0.21	0.23	94.2	23.8	15.6	260.1	...
	2010[37]	0.45	0.21	0.24	87.4	22.0	19.3	266.7	...
	2015	0.45[37]	0.21[37]	0.24[37]	86.6[37]	19.4[37]	22.4[37]	266.5[37]	2
	2018[1,37]	0.45	0.21	0.24	86.2	18.2	24.3	265.8	...
Guam Guam	2005	0.16	0.08	0.08	104.0	29.5	9.2	293.3	...
	2010	0.16	0.08	0.08	103.3	27.5	11.1	295.3	...
	2015	0.16	0.08	0.08	102.7	25.4	13.2	299.6	1
	2018[1]	0.17	0.08	0.08	102.5	24.4	14.4	306.9	...
Guatemala Guatemala	2005	13.10	6.42	6.67	96.2	42.3	5.9	122.2	...
	2010	14.63	7.19	7.44	96.5	39.4	6.1	136.5	...
	2015	16.25	8.00	8.26	96.8	36.2	6.7	151.7	109
	2018[1]	17.25	8.49	8.76	97.0	34.4	7.0	160.9	...
Guinea Guinée	2005	9.68	4.84	4.84	99.9	44.0	5.1	39.4	...
	2010	10.79	5.40	5.39	100.1	43.5	4.9	43.9	...
	2015	12.09	6.06	6.03	100.5	42.7	5.1	49.2	246
	2018[1]	13.05	6.55	6.51	100.6	42.0	5.2	53.1	...
Guinea-Bissau Guinée-Bissau	2005	1.38	0.67	0.71	95.4	43.6	4.5	49.1	...
	2010	1.56	0.76	0.79	96.2	42.3	4.6	55.3	...
	2015	1.77	0.87	0.90	96.7	41.7	4.9	63.0	36
	2018[1]	1.91	0.94	0.97	96.9	41.3	5.0	67.8	...
Guyana Guyana	2005	0.75	0.38	0.37	100.4	36.2	6.0	3.8	...
	2010	0.75	0.37	0.37	100.1	32.7	7.2	3.8	...
	2015	0.77	0.39	0.38	101.5	29.8	8.1	3.9	215
	2018[1]	0.78	0.40	0.39	102.1	28.6	8.9	4.0	...
Haiti Haïti	2005	9.26	4.58	4.69	97.7	38.0	6.4	336.1	...
	2010	10.00	4.94	5.06	97.8	35.9	6.5	362.8	...
	2015	10.71	5.30	5.41	97.9	33.7	7.1	388.6	28
	2018[1]	11.11	5.49	5.62	97.8	32.6	7.4	403.2	...

Country or area Pays ou zone	Year Année	Mid-year population estimates and projections (millions) Estimations et projections de population au milieu de l'année (millions) Total	Male Hommes	Females Femmes	Sex Ratio (males per 100 females) Rapport des sexes (hommes pour 100 femmes)	Population age distribution (percentage) Répartition par âge de la population (pourcentage) Aged 0 to 14 years old âgée de 0 à 14 ans	Aged 60+ years old âgée de 60 ans ou plus	Population density (per km²) Densité de population (pour km²)	Surface area Superficie (000 km²)
Holy See Saint-Siège	2000	~0.00	...	...	196.7[15,38]	...	...	1 784.1	...
	2005	~0.00	...	...	...	...	...	1 813.6	...
	2009	~0.00	...	...	219.2	...	...	1 806.8	...
	2010	~0.00	...	...	...	...	...	1 804.5	...
	2015	~0.00	...	...	...	...	...	1 825.0	~0[39]
	2018[1]	~0.00	...	...	...	...	...	1 820.5	...
Honduras Honduras	2005	7.37	3.67	3.70	99.1	39.9	5.5	65.9	...
	2010	8.19	4.08	4.11	99.3	36.6	5.8	73.2	...
	2015	8.96	4.47	4.49	99.4	33.0	6.6	80.1	112
	2018[1]	9.42	4.70	4.72	99.5	31.0	7.1	84.2	...
Hungary Hongrie	2005	10.09	4.79	5.30	90.3	15.5	21.4	111.4	...
	2010	9.93	4.71	5.22	90.3	14.9	22.1	109.7	...
	2015	9.78	4.65	5.13	90.6	14.4	25.0	108.1	93
	2018[1]	9.69	4.61	5.08	90.8	14.3	26.3	107.0	...
Iceland Islande	2005	0.30	0.15	0.15	100.6	22.2	15.8	2.9	...
	2010	0.32	0.16	0.16	101.5	20.8	16.9	3.2	...
	2015	0.33	0.17	0.16	100.7	20.3	19.1	3.3	103
	2018[1]	0.34	0.17	0.17	100.8	20.0	20.6	3.4	...
India Inde	2005	1 144.12	593.06	551.06	107.6	32.8	7.3	384.8	...
	2010	1 230.98	638.47	592.51	107.8	30.9	7.8	414.0	...
	2015	1 309.05	678.56	630.49	107.6	28.7	8.9	440.3	3 287
	2018[1]	1 354.05	701.55	652.50	107.5	27.4	9.6	455.4	...
Indonesia Indonésie	2005	226.71	113.82	112.89	100.8	30.0	7.4	125.1	...
	2010	242.52	122.28	120.25	101.7	29.0	7.4	133.9	...
	2015	258.16	130.04	128.12	101.5	27.9	8.1	142.5	1 911
	2018[1]	266.80	134.27	132.52	101.3	27.0	8.9	147.3	...
Iran (Islamic Republic of) Iran (Rép. islamique d')	2005	70.42	35.96	34.46	104.4	26.1	6.8	43.2	...
	2010	74.57	37.72	36.85	102.3	23.5	7.1	45.8	...
	2015	79.36	39.94	39.42	101.3	23.6	8.2	48.7	1 629[40]
	2018[1]	82.01	41.23	40.78	101.1	23.7	9.1	50.4	...
Iraq Iraq	2005	27.01	13.65	13.36	102.2	42.0	5.1	62.2	...
	2010	30.76	15.55	15.21	102.2	41.7	4.8	70.8	...
	2015	36.12	18.28	17.84	102.4	40.7	5.0	83.2	435
	2018[1]	39.34	19.92	19.42	102.6	40.2	5.0	90.6	...
Ireland Irlande	2005	4.21	2.10	2.11	99.8	20.2	14.8	61.2	...
	2010	4.63	2.31	2.32	99.3	20.7	16.1	67.2	...
	2015	4.70	2.33	2.37	98.4	21.7	18.4	68.2	70
	2018[1]	4.80	2.38	2.42	98.5	21.5	19.4	69.7	...
Isle of Man Île de Man	2005	0.08	...	...	96.9[13]	17.3[13]	22.1[13]	133.5	...
	2009	0.08	...	...	98.4[13]	16.4[13]	24.1[13]	139.2	...
	2010	0.08	...	...	98.6[13]	...	...	140.5	...
	2015	0.08	...	...	99.3[13]	16.3[13]	25.7[13]	145.9	1
	2016	0.08[1]	...	...	98.2[13]	16.0[13]	26.9[13]	146.9[1]	...
	2018[1]	0.08	...	...	...	...	...	148.8	...
Israel Israël	2005	6.60	3.26	3.35	97.4	27.9	13.2	305.1	...
	2010	7.43	3.67	3.76	97.6	27.3	14.9	343.2	...
	2015	8.06	4.00	4.07	98.4	27.9	15.8	372.7	22
	2018[1]	8.45	4.20	4.25	98.8	27.8	16.3	390.6	...
Italy Italie	2005	58.81	28.61	30.20	94.8	14.1	25.1	199.9	...
	2010	59.73	29.02	30.71	94.5	14.0	26.9	203.1	...
	2015	59.50	28.96	30.54	94.8	13.7	28.6	202.3	302
	2018[1]	59.29	28.92	30.38	95.2	13.4	29.8	201.6	...
Jamaica Jamaïque	2005	2.74	1.36	1.39	98.0	30.1	10.8	253.4	...
	2010	2.82	1.40	1.42	98.6	27.0	11.6	260.1	...
	2015	2.87	1.43	1.44	99.0	23.5	13.0	265.2	11
	2018[1]	2.90	1.44	1.46	99.0	22.6	13.9	267.7	...

Country or area Pays ou zone	Year Année	Mid-year population estimates and projections (millions) Estimations et projections de population au milieu de l'année (millions) Total	Male Hommes	Females Femmes	Sex Ratio (males per 100 females) Rapport des sexes (hommes pour 100 femmes)	Population age distribution (percentage) Répartition par âge de la population (pourcentage) Aged 0 to 14 years old âgée de 0 à 14 ans	Aged 60+ years old âgée de 60 ans ou plus	Population density (per km²) Densité de population (pour km²)	Surface area Superficie (000 km²)
Japan Japon	2005	128.34	62.89	65.45	96.1	13.8	26.3	352.0	...
	2007	128.51	62.92	65.58	95.9	13.6	27.9	352.5	378[41]
	2010	128.55	62.88	65.67	95.7	13.4	30.3	352.6	...
	2018[1]	127.19	62.09	65.09	95.4	12.8	33.6	348.9	...
Jordan Jordanie	2005	5.71	2.95	2.77	106.6	37.8	5.3	64.4	...
	2010	7.18	3.66	3.52	104.1	37.0	5.4	80.9	...
	2015	9.16	4.64	4.52	102.7	36.0	5.5	103.2	89
	2018[1]	9.90	5.02	4.89	102.6	35.2	5.8	111.6	...
Kazakhstan Kazakhstan	2005	15.54	7.49	8.05	93.0	24.5	10.1	5.8	...
	2010	16.40	7.93	8.47	93.6	24.0	9.9	6.1	...
	2015	17.75	8.60	9.15	93.9	26.8	10.7	6.6	2 725
	2018[1]	18.40	8.91	9.49	93.9	28.3	11.3	6.8	...
Kenya Kenya	2005	36.05	17.91	18.14	98.7	43.8	3.7	63.3	...
	2010	41.35	20.55	20.80	98.8	43.2	3.8	72.7	...
	2015	47.24	23.48	23.76	98.8	41.3	4.1	83.0	592
	2018[1]	50.95	25.32	25.63	98.8	40.1	4.3	89.5	...
Kiribati Kiribati	2005	0.09	0.05	0.05	97.1	36.9	5.4	114.0	...
	2010	0.10	0.05	0.05	97.0	36.1	5.4	126.7	...
	2015	0.11	0.06	0.06	97.2	34.9	6.1	138.8	1[42]
	2018[1]	0.12	0.06	0.06	97.3	35.3	6.5	146.2	...
Kuwait Koweït	2005	2.28	1.34	0.93	144.2	26.0	3.6	127.8	...
	2010	3.00	1.73	1.26	137.1	23.2	3.4	168.2	...
	2015	3.94	2.26	1.67	135.0	20.9	4.1	220.9	18
	2018[1]	4.20	2.41	1.79	134.8	21.2	5.3	235.5	...
Kyrgyzstan Kirghizistan	2005	5.08	2.52	2.56	98.3	31.0	7.1	26.5	...
	2010	5.42	2.68	2.74	97.7	29.9	6.4	28.3	...
	2015	5.87	2.91	2.96	98.3	31.1	7.2	30.6	200
	2018[1]	6.13	3.04	3.09	98.3	32.1	7.8	32.0	...
Lao People's Dem. Rep. Rép. dém. populaire lao	2005	5.75	2.85	2.90	98.4	40.3	5.5	24.9	...
	2010	6.25	3.11	3.14	99.0	36.3	5.6	27.1	...
	2015	6.66	3.32	3.34	99.4	33.7	6.1	28.9	237
	2018[1]	6.96	3.47	3.49	99.6	32.5	6.4	30.2	...
Latvia Lettonie	2005	2.25	1.03	1.22	84.7	14.7	22.5	36.2	...
	2010	2.12	0.97	1.15	84.5	14.1	23.6	34.1	...
	2015	1.99	0.91	1.08	84.8	15.1	25.4	32.0	65
	2018[1]	1.93	0.89	1.04	85.0	15.6	26.6	31.0	...
Lebanon Liban	2005	3.99	2.03	1.96	103.3	27.9	10.7	389.7	...
	2010	4.34	2.21	2.13	104.1	23.7	11.9	424.0	...
	2015	5.85	2.94	2.91	100.9	24.0	11.5	572.0	10
	2018[1]	6.09	3.06	3.04	100.7	22.6	12.3	595.7	...
Lesotho Lesotho	2005	1.95	0.94	1.01	93.5	39.4	6.3	64.2	...
	2010	2.04	0.99	1.05	93.9	37.3	6.6	67.2	...
	2015	2.17	1.05	1.12	94.2	35.7	6.7	71.6	30
	2018[1]	2.26	1.10	1.16	94.5	35.3	6.7	74.5	...
Liberia Libéria	2005	3.26	1.64	1.63	100.6	43.3	4.9	33.9	...
	2010	3.95	1.99	1.96	101.2	43.3	4.8	41.0	...
	2015	4.50	2.27	2.23	101.7	42.4	4.8	46.7	111
	2018[1]	4.85	2.45	2.40	101.9	41.5	4.9	50.4	...
Libya Libye	2005	5.79	2.99	2.81	106.5	30.1	5.9	3.3	...
	2010	6.17	3.15	3.02	104.3	28.4	6.0	3.5	...
	2015	6.24	3.15	3.09	102.0	28.6	6.5	3.5	1 676
	2018[1]	6.47	3.26	3.21	101.6	27.9	6.8	3.7	...
Liechtenstein Liechtenstein	2005	0.03	...	...	97.0[13]	17.5[13]	16.8[13]	217.8	...
	2010	0.04	...	...	97.9	16.0	20.1	225.0	...
	2015	0.04	...	...	98.4[13]	15.0[13]	22.5[13]	233.8	~0
	2016	0.04[1]	...	...	98.4[13]	14.9[13]	22.7[13]	235.4[1]	...
	2018[1]	0.04	...	...	...	...	...	238.5	...

Country or area Pays ou zone	Year Année	Mid-year population estimates and projections (millions) Estimations et projections de population au milieu de l'année (millions) Total	Male Hommes	Females Femmes	Sex Ratio (males per 100 females) Rapport des sexes (hommes pour 100 femmes)	Population age distribution (percentage) Répartition par âge de la population (pourcentage) Aged 0 to 14 years old âgée de 0 à 14 ans	Aged 60+ years old âgée de 60 ans ou plus	Population density (per km²) Densité de population (pour km²)	Surface area Superficie (000 km²)
Lithuania Lituanie	2005	3.34	1.55	1.79	86.8	16.8	21.1	53.4	...
	2010	3.12	1.44	1.69	85.3	14.8	22.4	49.8	...
	2015	2.93	1.35	1.58	85.4	14.6	24.5	46.8	65
	2018[1]	2.88	1.33	1.55	85.5	15.0	25.7	45.9	...
Luxembourg Luxembourg	2005	0.46	0.23	0.23	97.4	18.6	19.0	176.8	...
	2010	0.51	0.25	0.26	98.7	17.6	19.0	196.1	...
	2015	0.57	0.28	0.28	100.8	16.4	19.1	218.8	3
	2018[1]	0.59	0.30	0.29	101.1	16.5	19.9	227.9	...
Madagascar Madagascar	2005	18.34	9.13	9.21	99.2	44.7	4.4	31.5	...
	2010	21.15	10.54	10.62	99.3	43.5	4.3	36.4	...
	2015	24.23	12.08	12.15	99.4	41.6	4.6	41.7	587
	2018[1]	26.26	13.10	13.16	99.5	40.7	4.9	45.1	...
Malawi Malawi	2005	13.04	6.44	6.60	97.5	46.7	4.4	138.3	...
	2010	15.17	7.50	7.67	97.8	46.2	4.5	160.9	...
	2015	17.57	8.70	8.87	98.1	44.7	4.3	186.4	118
	2018[1]	19.16	9.50	9.67	98.2	43.7	4.2	203.3	...
Malaysia Malaisie	2005[43]	25.66	13.15	12.51	105.1	30.5	7.1	78.1	...
	2010[43]	28.11	14.49	13.62	106.3	27.9	7.9	85.6	...
	2015	30.72[43]	15.88[43]	14.85[43]	106.9[43]	25.0[43]	9.1[43]	93.5[43]	330
	2018[1,43]	32.04	16.53	15.52	106.5	24.0	10.0	97.5	...
Maldives Maldives	2005	0.32	0.17	0.15	111.5	31.6	6.3	1 062.8	...
	2010	0.36	0.20	0.16	121.1	25.5	6.0	1 215.0	...
	2015	0.42	0.24	0.18	130.2	23.4	6.0	1 394.7	~0
	2018[1]	0.44	0.25	0.19	132.2	23.4	6.6	1 480.9	...
Mali Mali	2005	12.80	6.37	6.43	99.1	46.9	4.6	10.5	...
	2010	15.08	7.53	7.54	99.8	47.5	4.2	12.4	...
	2015	17.47	8.74	8.73	100.0	47.9	4.0	14.3	1 240
	2018[1]	19.11	9.57	9.54	100.3	47.5	3.9	15.7	...
Malta Malte	2005	0.41	0.20	0.20	99.1	17.7	18.8	1 271.2	...
	2010	0.42	0.21	0.21	99.1	15.2	22.9	1 300.3	...
	2015	0.43	0.21	0.21	100.6	14.4	25.1	1 336.3	~0
	2018[1]	0.43	0.22	0.22	100.9	14.5	26.6	1 350.3	...
Marshall Islands Îles Marshall	2004	0.05	...	...	104.0[44,45]	40.6[44,45]	3.6[44,45]	289.3	...
	2005	0.05	...	...	...	...	...	289.2	...
	2010	0.05	...	...	105.2[44,45]	40.9[44,45]	4.5[44,45]	291.3	...
	2015	0.05	...	...	...	...	...	294.4	~0
	2016	0.05[1]	...	...	# 104.5	# 39.0	# 5.5	294.8[1]	
	2018[1]	0.05	...	...	...	...	...	295.4	...
Martinique Martinique	2005	0.40	0.19	0.21	87.3	21.1	18.0	374.6	...
	2010	0.39	0.18	0.21	85.8	19.6	20.6	372.6	...
	2015	0.39	0.18	0.21	83.9	18.4	24.3	364.0	1
	2018[1]	0.39	0.18	0.21	83.3	17.6	26.4	363.3	...
Mauritania Mauritanie	2005	3.13	1.57	1.56	100.4	42.1	4.8	3.0	...
	2010	3.61	1.81	1.80	100.9	41.2	4.8	3.5	...
	2015	4.18	2.11	2.08	101.4	40.2	4.9	4.1	1 031
	2018[1]	4.54	2.29	2.25	101.7	39.7	5.1	4.4	...
Mauritius Maurice	2005[46]	1.22	0.61	0.62	98.3	24.7	9.6	602.0	...
	2010[46]	1.25	0.62	0.63	98.3	21.9	12.1	614.8	...
	2015	1.26[46]	0.62[46]	0.64[46]	98.1[46]	19.4[46]	15.4[46]	620.4[46]	2[47]
	2018[1,46]	1.27	0.63	0.64	97.7	17.9	17.2	624.8	...
Mayotte Mayotte	2005	0.18	0.09	0.09	97.2	42.4	4.8	474.9	...
	2010	0.21	0.10	0.11	95.6	42.9	5.1	556.6	...
	2018[1]	0.26	0.13	0.13	96.8	40.2	5.9	692.5	...
Mexico Mexique	2005	108.47	53.95	54.53	98.9	32.3	7.7	55.8	...
	2010	117.32	58.39	58.93	99.1	29.8	8.4	60.4	...
	2015	125.89	62.68	63.21	99.2	27.5	9.6	64.8	1 964
	2018[1]	130.76	65.11	65.65	99.2	26.3	10.4	67.3	...

Country or area Pays ou zone	Year Année	Mid-year population estimates and projections (millions) Estimations et projections de population au milieu de l'année (millions) Total	Male Hommes	Females Femmes	Sex Ratio (males per 100 females) Rapport des sexes (hommes pour 100 femmes)	Population age distribution (percentage) Répartition par âge de la population (pourcentage) Aged 0 to 14 years old âgée de 0 à 14 ans	Aged 60+ years old âgée de 60 ans ou plus	Population density (per km²) Densité de population (pour km²)	Surface area Superficie (000 km²)
Micronesia (Fed. States of) Micronésie (États féd. de)	2005	0.11	0.05	0.05	103.3	38.8	5.5	151.7	...
	2010	0.10	0.05	0.05	104.3	36.9	6.2	148.0	...
	2015	0.10	0.05	0.05	105.0	34.1	7.5	149.2	1
	2018[1]	0.11	0.05	0.05	105.2	32.7	8.2	151.8	...
Monaco Monaco	2000	0.03	...	...	94.3[13]	13.2[13]	28.9[13]	21 531.5	...
	2005	0.03	...	...	...	...	...	22 679.9	...
	2008	0.04	...	...	94.7[13]	12.7[13]	31.2[13]	24 062.4	...
	2010	0.04	...	...	...	...	...	24 895.3	...
	2015	0.04	...	...	...	...	...	25 709.4	~0
	2018[1]	0.04	...	...	...	...	...	26 105.4	...
Mongolia Mongolie	2005	2.53	1.26	1.27	99.0	28.9	5.6	1.6	...
	2010	2.71	1.35	1.37	98.5	27.0	5.7	1.7	...
	2015	2.98	1.47	1.50	98.1	28.8	6.2	1.9	1 564
	2018[1]	3.12	1.54	1.58	97.8	29.9	6.8	2.0	...
Montenegro Monténégro	2005	0.62	0.30	0.31	96.6	20.2	17.0	45.8	...
	2010	0.62	0.31	0.32	97.1	19.2	17.9	46.4	...
	2015	0.63	0.31	0.32	97.3	18.5	20.4	46.7	14
	2018[1]	0.63	0.31	0.32	97.4	18.0	21.7	46.8	...
Montserrat Montserrat	2001	~0.00	...	...	116.6	19.3	19.9	45.1	...
	2004	~0.00	...	...	112.7	...	...	46.4	...
	2005	~0.00	...	...	...	...	...	47.8	...
	2006	~0.00	...	...	108.7[48]	19.6[48]	19.0[48]	48.5	...
	2010	~0.00	...	...	...	...	...	49.4	...
	2011	0.01	...	...	107.2[13]	19.7[13]	19.6[13]	49.9	...
	2015	0.01	...	...	...	...	...	51.2	~0
	2016	0.01[1]	...	...	106.0	...	...	51.5[1]	...
	2018[1]	0.01	...	...	...	...	...	52.0	...
Morocco Maroc	2005	30.52	15.08	15.45	97.6	30.8	8.2	68.4	...
	2010	32.41	15.97	16.44	97.2	28.5	8.6	72.6	...
	2015	34.80	17.22	17.58	97.9	27.7	10.0	78.0	447
	2018[1]	36.19	17.93	18.26	98.2	27.2	11.0	81.1	...
Mozambique Mozambique	2005	20.92	10.11	10.82	93.4	45.6	4.8	26.6	...
	2010	24.22	11.76	12.46	94.4	45.7	4.8	30.8	...
	2015	28.01	13.66	14.35	95.2	45.2	4.8	35.6	799
	2018[1]	30.53	14.92	15.61	95.6	44.5	4.8	38.8	...
Myanmar Myanmar	2005	48.48	23.68	24.80	95.5	30.9	7.0	74.2	...
	2010	50.16	24.48	25.68	95.3	30.0	7.5	76.8	...
	2015	52.40	25.59	26.81	95.5	27.9	8.9	80.2	677
	2018[1]	53.86	26.30	27.55	95.5	26.3	9.7	82.4	...
Namibia Namibie	2005	2.03	0.99	1.04	94.5	39.8	5.0	2.5	...
	2010	2.17	1.05	1.12	93.9	38.4	5.2	2.6	...
	2015	2.43	1.18	1.25	94.5	37.0	5.4	2.9	824
	2018[1]	2.59	1.26	1.33	94.8	36.5	5.6	3.1	...
Nauru Nauru	2002	0.01	...	...	104.2	38.1	2.5	504.0	...
	2005	0.01	...	...	...	...	...	505.7	...
	2010	0.01	...	...	...	...	...	501.3	...
	2015	0.01	...	...	...	...	...	563.0	~0
	2016	0.01[1]	...	...	# 101.9	# 39.5	# 4.0	567.4[1]	...
	2018[1]	0.01	...	...	...	...	...	565.6	...
Nepal Népal	2005	25.64	12.72	12.92	98.5	39.7	6.7	178.9	...
	2010	27.02	13.18	13.84	95.2	37.0	7.4	188.5	...
	2015	28.66	13.90	14.75	94.2	32.6	8.5	199.9	147
	2018[1]	29.62	14.39	15.23	94.5	30.2	8.8	206.7	...
Netherlands Pays-Bas	2005	16.37	8.12	8.25	98.4	18.3	19.3	485.4	...
	2010	16.68	8.28	8.40	98.6	17.5	22.0	494.7	...
	2015	16.94	8.42	8.52	98.9	16.8	24.1	502.3	42
	2018[1]	17.08	8.50	8.58	99.1	16.2	25.5	506.7	...

Country or area Pays ou zone	Year Année	Mid-year population estimates and projections (millions) Estimations et projections de population au milieu de l'année (millions) Total	Male Hommes	Females Femmes	Sex Ratio (males per 100 females) Rapport des sexes (hommes pour 100 femmes)	Population age distribution (percentage) Répartition par âge de la population (pourcentage) Aged 0 to 14 years old âgée de 0 à 14 ans	Aged 60+ years old âgée de 60 ans ou plus	Population density (per km²) Densité de population (pour km²)	Surface area Superficie (000 km²)
New Caledonia Nouvelle-Calédonie	2005	0.23	0.12	0.12	101.1	27.5	10.3	12.7	...
	2010	0.25	0.13	0.12	102.9	24.1	13.1	13.7	...
	2015	0.27	0.14	0.13	101.9	22.8	13.8	14.7	19
	2018[1]	0.28	0.14	0.14	101.4	22.3	14.5	15.3	...
New Zealand Nouvelle-Zélande	2005	4.14	2.03	2.11	96.0	21.5	16.4	15.7	...
	2010	4.37	2.15	2.22	96.5	20.5	18.4	16.6	...
	2015	4.61	2.27	2.35	96.7	20.0	20.0	17.5	268
	2018[1]	4.75	2.34	2.41	96.7	19.8	21.3	18.0	...
Nicaragua Nicaragua	2005	5.38	2.66	2.72	97.5	36.0	6.1	44.7	...
	2010	5.74	2.83	2.91	97.1	32.8	6.5	47.7	...
	2015	6.08	3.00	3.08	97.2	30.0	7.8	50.5	130
	2018[1]	6.28	3.10	3.19	97.3	28.6	8.7	52.2	...
Niger Niger	2005	13.62	6.78	6.83	99.3	49.2	4.1	10.8	...
	2010	16.43	8.21	8.22	99.9	50.0	4.1	13.0	...
	2015	19.90	9.97	9.93	100.4	50.2	4.1	15.7	1 267
	2018[1]	22.31	11.19	11.12	100.7	50.1	4.2	17.6	...
Nigeria Nigéria	2005	138.94	70.16	68.78	102.0	43.7	4.6	152.6	...
	2010	158.58	80.20	78.37	102.3	44.0	4.5	174.1	...
	2015	181.18	91.77	89.41	102.6	44.1	4.5	198.9	924
	2018[1]	195.88	99.28	96.60	102.8	43.8	4.5	215.1	...
Niue Nioué	2005	~0.00	...	...	94.8[13]	26.1[13]	15.1[13]	6.5	...
	2010	~0.00	...	...	101.9[13]	25.7[13]	16.8[13]	6.3	...
	2015	~0.00	...	...	...	...	...	6.3	~0
	2016	~0.00[1]	...	...	# 100.0	# 22.8	# 20.1	6.2[1]	...
	2018[1]	~0.00	...	...	...	...	...	6.2	...
Northern Mariana Islands Îles Mariannes du Nord	2005	0.06	...	...	83.3[44]	22.9[44,49]	3.7[44,49]	138.6	...
	2010	0.05	...	...	106.2	26.7	5.8	118.3	...
	2015	0.05	...	...	...	...	...	119.2	~0
	2016	0.06[1]	...	...	# 107.1	# 23.5	# 10.0	119.6[1]	...
	2018[1]	0.06	...	...	...	...	...	120.0	...
Norway [50] Norvège [50]	2005	4.63	2.30	2.33	98.5	19.6	19.8	12.7	...
	2010	4.89	2.44	2.44	100.0	18.8	21.0	13.4	...
	2015	5.20	2.62	2.58	101.4	18.0	21.8	14.2	386
	2018[1]	5.35	2.70	2.65	102.0	17.8	22.6	14.7	...
Oman Oman	2005	2.51	1.42	1.09	130.2	32.5	4.1	8.1	...
	2010	3.04	1.83	1.21	152.0	25.7	3.9	9.8	...
	2015	4.20	2.72	1.48	184.4	22.2	3.8	13.6	310
	2018[1]	4.83	3.20	1.63	195.7	21.6	4.1	15.6	...
Other non-specified areas Autres zones non-spécifiées	2005	22.60	11.48	11.12	103.2	19.2	13.1	638.3	...
	2010	23.10	11.63	11.47	101.4	16.1	14.9	652.4	...
	2018[1]	23.69	11.81	11.88	99.4	13.2	21.0	669.1	...
Pakistan Pakistan	2005	153.91	79.33	74.58	106.4	38.2	6.5	199.7	...
	2010	170.56	87.69	82.87	105.8	36.2	6.6	221.3	...
	2015	189.38	97.29	92.09	105.6	35.0	6.6	245.7	796
	2018[1]	200.81	103.15	97.67	105.6	34.7	6.8	260.5	...
Palau Palaos	2005	0.02	...	...	116.2[13]	24.1[13]	8.2[13]	43.3	...
	2010	0.02	...	...	...	...	...	44.5	...
	2015	0.02	...	...	114.6[13]	20.5[13]	12.1[13]	46.3	~0
	2016	0.02[1]	...	...	# 113.3	# 20.3	# 13.1	46.7[1]	...
	2018[1]	0.02	...	...	...	...	...	47.7	...
Panama Panama	2005	3.33	1.68	1.65	101.3	30.4	8.8	44.8	...
	2010	3.64	1.83	1.81	100.9	29.1	9.7	49.0	...
	2015	3.97	1.99	1.98	100.6	27.9	10.8	53.4	75
	2018[1]	4.16	2.09	2.08	100.4	27.1	11.7	56.0	...
Papua New Guinea Papouasie-Nvl-Guinée	2005	6.31	3.21	3.10	103.4	39.1	5.1	13.9	...
	2010	7.11	3.62	3.49	103.5	38.3	5.4	15.7	...
	2015	7.92	4.03	3.89	103.5	36.6	5.9	17.5	463
	2018[1]	8.42	4.28	4.14	103.5	35.6	6.2	18.6	...

Country or area Pays ou zone	Year Année	Mid-year population estimates and projections (millions) Estimations et projections de population au milieu de l'année (millions) Total	Male Hommes	Females Femmes	Sex Ratio (males per 100 females) Rapport des sexes (hommes pour 100 femmes)	Population age distribution (percentage) Répartition par âge de la population (pourcentage) Aged 0 to 14 years old âgée de 0 à 14 ans	Aged 60+ years old âgée de 60 ans ou plus	Population density (per km²) Densité de population (pour km²)	Surface area Superficie (000 km²)
Paraguay Paraguay	2005	5.80	2.93	2.86	102.6	35.3	7.1	14.6	...
	2010	6.21	3.15	3.06	103.0	32.7	7.9	15.6	...
	2015	6.64	3.37	3.27	103.0	30.1	9.0	16.7	407
	2018[1]	6.90	3.50	3.40	102.9	29.1	9.6	17.4	...
Peru Pérou	2005	27.61	13.80	13.81	99.9	31.7	8.1	21.6	...
	2010	29.37	14.68	14.70	99.8	29.4	8.9	22.9	...
	2015	31.38	15.67	15.70	99.8	27.9	10.0	24.5	1 285
	2018[1]	32.55	16.26	16.29	99.8	27.1	10.7	25.4	...
Philippines Philippines	2005	86.27	43.36	42.91	101.0	37.1	5.4	289.3	...
	2010	93.73	47.31	46.42	101.9	33.9	6.5	314.3	...
	2015	101.72	51.24	50.48	101.5	32.2	7.3	341.1	300
	2018[1]	106.51	53.58	52.93	101.2	31.5	7.8	357.2	...
Poland Pologne	2005	38.36	18.57	19.79	93.9	16.6	17.0	125.3	...
	2010	38.32	18.53	19.79	93.6	15.2	19.4	125.1	...
	2015	38.27	18.48	19.78	93.4	14.9	22.6	125.0	313
	2018[1]	38.10	18.40	19.70	93.4	14.9	24.6	124.4	...
Portugal Portugal	2005	10.57	5.11	5.46	93.7	15.4	22.5	115.4	...
	2010	10.65	5.10	5.55	91.9	15.0	24.7	116.3	...
	2015	10.42	4.94	5.48	90.0	14.1	27.0	113.8	92
	2018[1]	10.29	4.87	5.42	89.9	13.4	28.3	112.4	...
Puerto Rico Porto Rico	2005	3.77	1.81	1.96	92.3	22.3	16.7	424.5	...
	2010	3.72	1.79	1.93	92.5	20.6	18.1	419.0	...
	2015	3.67	1.77	1.91	92.5	18.7	19.7	414.2	9
	2018[1]	3.66	1.76	1.90	92.6	17.6	20.8	412.5	...
Qatar Qatar	2005	0.86	0.58	0.28	208.4	21.7	2.5	74.5	...
	2010	1.78	1.35	0.43	313.7	13.1	1.8	153.3	...
	2015	2.48	1.87	0.61	306.6	13.8	2.3	213.7	12
	2018[1]	2.69	2.02	0.68	298.6	13.9	3.1	232.1	...
Republic of Korea République de Corée	2005	48.71	24.43	24.27	100.7	18.8	12.8	501.0	...
	2010	49.55	24.83	24.72	100.4	16.1	15.3	509.6	...
	2015	50.59	25.32	25.27	100.2	13.9	18.4	520.4	100
	2018[1]	51.16	25.60	25.57	100.1	13.4	21.1	526.2	...
Republic of Moldova République de Moldova	2005[51]	4.16	1.99	2.17	91.9	18.5	13.6	126.6	...
	2010[51]	4.08	1.96	2.12	92.6	16.5	14.1	124.3	...
	2015	4.07[51]	1.95[51]	2.11[51]	92.5[51]	15.7[51]	16.5[51]	123.8[51]	34
	2018[1,51]	4.04	1.94	2.10	92.1	15.8	18.0	123.0	...
Réunion Réunion	2005	0.79	0.39	0.40	96.4	26.9	10.3	316.6	...
	2010	0.83	0.40	0.43	93.9	25.4	12.2	332.2	...
	2015	0.86	0.42	0.45	93.9	24.3	15.3	345.3	3
	2018[1]	0.88	0.43	0.46	93.9	23.2	17.0	353.3	...
Romania Roumanie	2005	21.43	10.45	10.99	95.1	15.9	19.6	93.1	...
	2010	20.44	9.92	10.52	94.4	15.8	21.4	88.8	...
	2015	19.88	9.63	10.24	94.0	15.4	23.9	86.4	238
	2018[1]	19.58	9.49	10.10	94.0	15.2	25.3	85.1	...
Russian Federation Fédération de Russie	2005	143.62	66.83	76.78	87.0	15.2	17.2	8.8	...
	2010	143.15	66.39	76.77	86.5	14.9	18.0	8.7	...
	2015	143.89	66.85	77.04	86.8	16.8	20.1	8.8	17 098
	2018[1]	143.96	66.91	77.06	86.8	17.8	21.5	8.8	...
Rwanda Rwanda	2005	8.99	4.39	4.60	95.6	41.7	4.1	364.5	...
	2010	10.25	5.02	5.23	95.9	41.8	4.1	415.4	...
	2015	11.63	5.70	5.93	96.2	40.8	4.6	471.4	26
	2018[1]	12.50	6.13	6.37	96.2	39.8	5.0	506.7	...
Saint Helena [52] Sainte-Hélène [52]	2005	~0.00	...	...	...	...	...	11.0	...
	2010	~0.00	...	...	...	...	...	10.7	...
	2015	~0.00	...	...	...	...	...	10.3	~0
	2018[1]	~0.00	...	...	...	...	...	10.4	...

Country or area Pays ou zone	Year Année	Mid-year population estimates and projections (millions) Estimations et projections de population au milieu de l'année (millions) Total	 Male Hommes	 Females Femmes	Sex Ratio (males per 100 females) Rapport des sexes (hommes pour 100 femmes)	Population age distribution (percentage) Répartition par âge de la population (pourcentage) Aged 0 to 14 years old âgée de 0 à 14 ans	 Aged 60+ years old âgée de 60 ans ou plus	Population density (per km²) Densité de population (pour km²)	Surface area Superficie (000 km²)
Saint Kitts and Nevis	2000	0.05	...	...	101.9	28.0	9.9	174.5	...
Saint-Kitts-et-Nevis	2005	0.05	...	...	* 95.7	...	...	187.0	...
	2010	0.05	...	...	* 95.7	...	...	197.9	...
	2011	0.05	...	...	* 97.0	...	...	200.0	...
	2015	0.05	...	...	...	...	...	208.8	~0
	2018[1]	0.06	...	...	...	...	...	214.8	...
Saint Lucia	2005	0.16	0.08	0.08	95.8	27.7	9.8	268.4	...
Sainte-Lucie	2010	0.17	0.08	0.09	96.4	23.2	12.1	282.9	...
	2015	0.18	0.09	0.09	96.0	19.7	13.1	290.5	1[53]
	2018[1]	0.18	0.09	0.09	95.8	18.5	14.1	294.5	...
Saint Pierre and Miquelon	2005	0.01	...	...	...	...	...	27.2	...
Saint-Pierre-et-Miquelon	2006	0.01	...	...	98.2	19.1	17.8	27.2	...
	2010	0.01	...	...	...	...	...	27.3	...
	2015	0.01	...	...	...	...	...	27.3	~0
	2018[1]	0.01	...	...	...	...	...	27.6	...
Saint Vincent & Grenadines	2005	0.11	0.05	0.05	102.0	28.5	9.4	278.8	...
Saint-Vincent-Grenadines	2010	0.11	0.06	0.05	102.0	26.5	9.5	280.3	...
	2015	0.11	0.06	0.05	101.8	24.5	10.9	280.7	~0
	2018[1]	0.11	0.06	0.05	101.7	23.5	12.2	282.6	...
Samoa	2005	0.18	0.09	0.09	107.4	39.6	6.9	63.6	...
Samoa	2010	0.19	0.10	0.09	106.5	38.3	7.2	65.8	...
	2015	0.19	0.10	0.09	106.6	37.2	8.0	68.5	3
	2018[1]	0.20	0.10	0.10	106.6	36.4	8.7	69.9	...
San Marino	2004	0.03	...	...	96.2[15]	15.2[15]	21.5[15]	481.1	...
Saint-Marin	2005	0.03	...	...	96.1[15]	...	...	487.3	...
	2010	0.03	...	...	* 93.5	* 20.9[54]	* 21.6[55]	518.5	...
	2015	0.03	...	...	94.9[15]	15.0[15]	24.1[15]	549.3	~0
	2018[1]	0.03	...	...	...	...	...	559.3	...
Sao Tome and Principe	2005	0.16	0.08	0.08	98.8	44.1	5.6	162.1	...
Sao Tomé-et-Principe	2010	0.17	0.09	0.09	99.0	44.1	4.7	182.1	...
	2015	0.20	0.10	0.10	99.2	43.4	4.3	203.7	1
	2018[1]	0.21	0.10	0.10	99.2	42.4	4.4	217.5	...
Saudi Arabia	2005	23.91	13.31	10.60	125.5	33.8	4.4	11.1	...
Arabie saoudite	2010	27.43	15.40	12.03	128.1	29.8	4.5	12.8	...
	2015	31.56	17.89	13.66	130.9	26.0	5.2	14.7	2 207
	2018[1]	33.55	19.21	14.34	134.0	24.9	5.8	15.6	...
Senegal	2005	11.25	5.52	5.73	96.2	43.7	4.9	58.4	...
Sénégal	2010	12.92	6.32	6.59	95.9	43.2	4.7	67.1	...
	2015	14.98	7.35	7.63	96.4	43.1	4.7	77.8	197[56]
	2018[1]	16.29	8.01	8.29	96.7	42.7	4.7	84.6	...
Serbia	2005[57]	9.22	4.50	4.71	95.6	18.6	19.0	105.4	...
Serbie	2010[57]	9.03	4.42	4.61	95.7	17.3	21.0	103.2	...
	2015	8.85[57]	4.33[57]	4.53[57]	95.6[57]	16.7[57]	23.8[57]	101.2[57]	88[58]
	2018[1,57]	8.76	4.28	4.48	95.6	16.3	24.8	100.2	...
Seychelles	2005	0.09	0.04	0.04	99.9	24.9	9.2	192.9	...
Seychelles	2010	0.09	0.05	0.04	106.5	22.8	10.0	198.7	...
	2015	0.09	0.05	0.05	98.2	21.7	12.4	203.8	~0
	2018[1]	0.10	0.05	0.05	97.2	22.4	13.8	207.0	...
Sierra Leone	2005	5.66	2.79	2.87	97.3	44.4	4.1	78.4	...
Sierra Leone	2010	6.46	3.19	3.27	97.6	44.0	4.1	89.5	...
	2015	7.24	3.58	3.66	98.0	42.7	4.1	100.3	72
	2018[1]	7.72	3.82	3.90	98.2	41.7	4.2	107.0	...
Singapore	2005	4.49	2.23	2.26	98.5	19.1	12.6	6 415.8	...
Singapour	2010	5.07	2.50	2.57	97.4	17.3	14.1	7 248.9	...
	2015	5.54	2.73	2.80	97.6	15.5	17.9	7 907.5	1[59]
	2018[1]	5.79	2.86	2.93	97.7	14.7	20.4	8 274.1	...

Country or area Pays ou zone	Year Année	Mid-year population estimates and projections (millions) Estimations et projections de population au milieu de l'année (millions) Total	 Male Hommes	 Females Femmes	Sex Ratio (males per 100 females) Rapport des sexes (hommes pour 100 femmes)	Population age distribution (percentage) Répartition par âge de la population (pourcentage) Aged 0 to 14 years old âgée de 0 à 14 ans	 Aged 60+ years old âgée de 60 ans ou plus	Population density (per km²) Densité de population (pour km²)	Surface area Superficie (000 km²)
Sint Maarten (Dutch part) St-Martin (partie néerland.)	2005	0.03	...	...	93.9[13]	...	...	956.8	...
	2010	0.03	...	...	91.0[13]	...	...	974.2	...
	2013	0.04	...	...	95.8[13]	21.0[13]	10.4[13]	1 071.7	~0
	2014	0.04	...	...	95.7[13]	...	...	1 108.7	~0
	2015	0.04	...	...	...	...	...	1 139.7	~0
	2018[1]	0.04	...	...	...	...	...	1 192.7	...
Slovakia Slovaquie	2005	5.40	2.62	2.78	94.1	16.8	16.1	112.3	...
	2010	5.40	2.62	2.78	94.2	15.3	17.8	112.4	...
	2015	5.44	2.64	2.80	94.6	15.3	20.7	113.1	49[60]
	2018[1]	5.45	2.65	2.80	94.6	15.5	22.3	113.3	...
Slovenia Slovénie	2005	2.00	0.97	1.02	95.4	14.0	20.8	99.1	...
	2010	2.05	1.01	1.03	97.9	14.1	22.2	101.5	...
	2015	2.07	1.03	1.05	98.5	14.7	25.1	103.0	20
	2018[1]	2.08	1.03	1.05	98.7	15.1	26.8	103.3	...
Solomon Islands Îles Salomon	2005	0.47	0.24	0.23	104.5	41.3	4.8	16.8	...
	2010	0.53	0.27	0.26	103.3	40.8	5.1	18.9	...
	2015	0.59	0.30	0.29	103.4	39.6	5.2	21.0	29
	2018[1]	0.62	0.32	0.31	103.4	38.5	5.5	22.3	...
Somalia Somalie	2005	10.41	5.21	5.20	100.2	47.9	4.3	16.6	...
	2010	12.05	6.02	6.04	99.7	47.7	4.3	19.2	...
	2015	13.91	6.93	6.98	99.3	46.7	4.3	22.2	638
	2018[1]	15.18	7.56	7.62	99.3	46.3	4.4	24.2	...
South Africa Afrique du Sud	2005	48.82	23.96	24.86	96.4	31.7	6.7	40.2	...
	2010	51.58	25.33	26.26	96.5	30.4	7.2	42.5	...
	2015	55.29	27.15	28.14	96.5	29.3	8.0	45.6	1 221
	2018[1]	57.40	28.16	29.24	96.3	28.8	8.5	47.3	...
South Sudan Soudan du sud	2005	8.11	4.05	4.06	99.6	44.3	5.1	13.3	...
	2010	10.07	5.03	5.03	99.9	43.3	5.3	16.5	...
	2015	11.88	5.95	5.93	100.3	42.1	5.1	19.4	659
	2018[1]	12.92	6.47	6.44	100.5	41.5	5.1	21.1	...
Spain Espagne	2005[61]	44.04	21.72	22.32	97.3	14.3	21.6	88.3	...
	2010[61]	46.79	23.13	23.66	97.8	14.6	22.4	93.8	...
	2015	46.40[61]	22.77[61]	23.63[61]	96.4[61]	14.9[61]	24.4[61]	93.0[61]	506
	2018[1,61]	46.40	22.76	23.64	96.3	14.6	25.8	93.0	...
Sri Lanka Sri Lanka	2005	19.52	9.63	9.90	97.2	25.6	10.4	311.3	...
	2010	20.20	9.83	10.37	94.8	25.4	11.8	322.1	...
	2015	20.71	9.98	10.74	93.0	24.6	13.9	330.3	66
	2018[1]	20.95	10.06	10.89	92.4	23.7	15.4	334.1	...
State of Palestine État de Palestine	2005[62]	3.58	1.81	1.76	102.9	45.6	4.0	594.0	...
	2010[62]	4.07	2.06	2.00	102.9	42.4	4.3	675.6	...
	2015	4.66[62]	2.36[62]	2.30[62]	102.9[62]	40.1[62]	4.5[62]	774.6[62]	6
	2018[1,62]	5.05	2.56	2.49	102.9	39.3	4.7	839.3	...
Sudan Soudan	2005	30.91	15.50	15.41	100.6	43.5	4.9	17.5	...
	2010	34.39	17.15	17.23	99.5	43.0	5.1	19.5	...
	2018[1]	41.51	20.75	20.76	99.9	40.5	5.6	23.5	...
Suriname Suriname	2005	0.50	0.25	0.25	101.5	30.8	8.5	3.2	...
	2010	0.53	0.26	0.26	101.2	28.7	9.1	3.4	...
	2015	0.55	0.28	0.28	100.9	26.9	9.9	3.5	164
	2018[1]	0.57	0.29	0.28	100.7	26.2	10.6	3.6	...
Eswatini Eswatini	2005	1.11	0.54	0.57	93.8	42.1	4.6	64.3	...
	2010	1.20	0.58	0.62	94.2	39.5	4.7	69.9	...
	2015	1.32	0.64	0.68	94.0	37.6	4.8	76.7	17
	2018[1]	1.39	0.67	0.72	93.9	37.0	4.9	80.9	...
Sweden Suède	2005	9.04	4.48	4.56	98.4	17.4	23.5	22.0	...
	2010	9.39	4.68	4.71	99.2	16.5	24.9	22.9	...
	2015	9.76	4.88	4.88	99.9	17.3	25.2	23.8	439
	2018[1]	9.98	5.00	4.98	100.3	17.7	25.6	24.3	...

Country or area Pays ou zone	Year Année	Mid-year population estimates and projections (millions) Estimations et projections de population au milieu de l'année (millions): Total	Male Hommes	Females Femmes	Sex Ratio (males per 100 females) Rapport des sexes (hommes pour 100 femmes)	Population age distribution (percentage) Répartition par âge de la population (pourcentage): Aged 0 to 14 years old âgée de 0 à 14 ans	Aged 60+ years old âgée de 60 ans ou plus	Population density (per km²) Densité de population (pour km²)	Surface area Superficie (000 km²)
Switzerland Suisse	2005	7.41	3.63	3.78	95.9	16.3	21.3	187.5	...
	2010	7.83	3.86	3.98	97.0	15.1	22.8	198.2	...
	2015	8.32	4.12	4.20	98.0	14.8	23.5	210.5	41
	2018[1]	8.54	4.24	4.31	98.3	14.9	24.5	216.2	...
Syrian Arab Republic République arabe syrienne	2005	18.29	9.33	8.96	104.2	39.1	4.9	99.6	...
	2010	21.02	10.61	10.41	101.9	36.4	5.1	114.5	...
	2015	18.74	9.48	9.26	102.3	38.1	6.4	102.0	185
	2018[1]	18.28	9.23	9.06	101.9	35.7	7.1	99.6	...
Tajikistan Tadjikistan	2005	6.85	3.45	3.40	101.3	38.1	5.1	49.0	...
	2010	7.64	3.85	3.79	101.6	35.7	4.9	54.6	...
	2015	8.55	4.30	4.25	101.1	35.1	5.5	61.1	143
	2018[1]	9.11	4.57	4.54	100.8	35.3	6.0	65.1	...
Thailand Thaïlande	2005	65.43	32.18	33.25	96.8	21.3	11.1	128.1	...
	2010	67.21	32.94	34.27	96.1	19.2	12.9	131.6	...
	2015	68.66	33.53	35.13	95.4	18.0	15.6	134.4	513
	2018[1]	69.18	33.71	35.47	95.0	17.0	17.6	135.4	...
TFYR of Macedonia ex-R.Y. de Macédoine	2005	2.06	1.03	1.03	99.9	20.2	15.3	81.7	...
	2010	2.07	1.03	1.04	99.8	17.9	16.4	82.1	...
	2015	2.08	1.04	1.04	100.0	16.8	18.6	82.4	26
	2018[1]	2.09	1.04	1.04	100.0	16.6	19.9	82.7	...
Timor-Leste Timor-Leste	2005	1.03	0.52	0.51	102.8	49.2	4.3	69.0	...
	2010	1.11	0.56	0.55	103.2	45.6	5.1	74.6	...
	2015	1.24	0.63	0.61	103.2	44.0	5.4	83.5	15
	2018[1]	1.32	0.67	0.65	103.2	43.5	5.5	89.0	...
Togo Togo	2005	5.68	2.82	2.86	98.7	42.6	4.5	104.5	...
	2010	6.50	3.24	3.27	99.1	42.5	4.4	119.6	...
	2015	7.42	3.70	3.72	99.3	42.0	4.5	136.4	57
	2018[1]	7.99	3.98	4.01	99.4	41.3	4.6	146.9	...
Tokelau Tokélaou	2001	~0.00	...	...	98.1	40.7	9.5	150.3	...
	2005	~0.00	...	...	...	...	...	120.8	...
	2006	~0.00	...	...	102.6	36.6	11.3	116.7	...
	2010	~0.00	...	...	...	...	...	114.0	...
	2015	~0.00	...	...	...	...	...	125.2	~0
	2016	~0.00[1]	...	...	# 100.0	# 28.3	# 12.2	128.2[1]	...
	2018[1]	~0.00	...	...	...	...	...	131.9	...
Tonga Tonga	2005	0.10	0.05	0.05	100.6	38.2	8.3	140.3	...
	2010	0.10	0.05	0.05	100.3	37.4	8.0	144.6	...
	2015	0.11	0.05	0.05	100.6	36.7	8.1	147.7	1
	2018[1]	0.11	0.05	0.05	100.7	35.4	8.7	151.4	...
Trinidad and Tobago Trinité-et-Tobago	2005	1.30	0.64	0.65	98.3	21.8	10.8	252.8	...
	2010	1.33	0.66	0.67	98.0	20.7	12.4	258.9	...
	2015	1.36	0.67	0.69	97.4	20.8	14.2	265.1	5
	2018[1]	1.37	0.68	0.70	96.9	20.5	15.5	267.6	...
Tunisia Tunisie	2005	10.10	5.03	5.07	99.2	25.5	10.0	65.0	...
	2010	10.64	5.28	5.36	98.4	23.3	10.4	68.5	...
	2015	11.27	5.57	5.70	97.7	23.7	11.7	72.6	164
	2018[1]	11.66	5.76	5.90	97.7	24.0	12.6	75.0	...
Turkey Turquie	2005	67.90	33.42	34.48	96.9	28.6	9.6	88.2	...
	2010	72.33	35.56	36.76	96.7	26.9	10.4	94.0	...
	2015	78.27	38.50	39.77	96.8	25.6	11.5	101.7	784
	2018[1]	81.92	40.37	41.55	97.2	24.6	12.3	106.4	...
Turkmenistan Turkménistan	2005	4.75	2.34	2.42	96.8	32.6	6.1	10.1	...
	2010	5.09	2.50	2.58	96.8	29.5	6.1	10.8	...
	2015	5.57	2.74	2.83	97.0	30.4	6.8	11.8	488
	2018[1]	5.85	2.88	2.97	97.0	30.8	7.6	12.5	...

Country or area Pays ou zone	Year Année	Mid-year population estimates and projections (millions) Estimations et projections de population au milieu de l'année (millions) Total	Male Hommes	Females Femmes	Sex Ratio (males per 100 females) Rapport des sexes (hommes pour 100 femmes)	Population age distribution (percentage) Répartition par âge de la population (pourcentage) Aged 0 to 14 years old âgée de 0 à 14 ans	Aged 60+ years old âgée de 60 ans ou plus	Population density (per km²) Densité de population (pour km²)	Surface area Superficie (000 km²)
Turks and Caicos Islands	2001	0.02	...	...	99.1	28.6	5.2	21.2	...
Îles Turques-et-Caïques	2005	0.03	...	...	99.1[13,44]	...	...	27.8	...
	2010	0.03	...	...	106.7[13,44]	...	...	32.6	...
	2015	0.03	...	...	103.8[13,44]	19.8[13,44]	6.9[13,44]	36.1	1[63]
	2017	0.04[1]	...	...	104.1[13,44]	19.2[13,44]	7.6[13,44]	37.3[1]	...
	2018[1]	0.04	...	...	...	...	...	37.9	...
Tuvalu	2002	0.01	...	...	97.9	36.2	8.6	321.2	...
Tuvalu	2005	0.01	...	...	...	...	...	334.2	...
	2010	0.01	...	...	...	...	...	351.0	...
	2015	0.01	...	...	...	...	...	366.7	~0
	2016	0.01[1]	...	...	102.0	31.1	9.9	369.9[1]	...
	2018[1]	0.01	...	...	...	...	...	376.2	...
Uganda	2005	28.54	14.13	14.41	98.1	49.8	3.6	142.9	...
Ouganda	2010	33.92	16.84	17.07	98.6	49.3	3.4	169.7	...
	2015	40.14	19.96	20.18	98.9	48.2	3.3	200.9	242
	2018[1]	44.27	22.02	22.25	99.0	47.4	3.3	221.6	...
Ukraine	2005[64]	46.89	21.75	25.14	86.5	14.6	20.4	80.9	...
Ukraine	2010[64]	45.79	21.14	24.66	85.7	14.1	21.0	79.0	...
	2015	44.66[64]	20.64[64]	24.02[64]	85.9[64]	15.1[64]	22.5[64]	77.1[64]	604
	2018[1,64]	44.01	20.35	23.66	86.0	15.8	23.5	76.0	...
United Arab Emirates	2005	4.58	3.22	1.36	236.2	18.4	1.7	54.8	...
Émirats arabes unis	2010	8.27	6.16	2.11	292.1	13.4	1.5	98.9	...
	2015	9.15	6.69	2.46	272.2	13.8	2.0	109.5	84
	2018[1]	9.54	6.88	2.67	257.9	13.9	2.6	114.1	...
United Kingdom	2005	60.29	29.51	30.77	95.9	18.0	21.2	249.2	...
Royaume-Uni	2010	63.31	31.10	32.21	96.6	17.5	22.7	261.7	...
	2015	65.40	32.23	33.17	97.2	17.6	23.5	270.3	242
	2018[1]	66.57	32.87	33.71	97.5	17.8	24.2	275.2	...
United Rep. of Tanzania	2005[65]	39.41	19.44	19.97	97.3	45.3	4.6	44.5	...
Rép.-Unie de Tanzanie	2010[65]	46.10	22.75	23.35	97.4	45.3	4.7	52.0	...
	2015	53.88[65]	26.63[65]	27.25[65]	97.7[65]	45.2[65]	4.6[65]	60.8[65]	947
	2018[1,65]	59.09	29.23	29.86	97.9	44.7	4.7	66.7	...
United States of America	2005	295.13	145.63	149.50	97.4	20.9	16.7	32.3	...
États-Unis d'Amérique	2010	308.64	152.45	156.19	97.6	20.2	18.4	33.7	...
	2015	319.93	158.27	161.66	97.9	19.2	20.6	35.0	9 834
	2018[1]	326.77	161.77	165.00	98.0	18.8	22.0	35.7	...
United States Virgin Islands	2005	0.11	0.05	0.06	93.5	22.4	16.6	308.0	...
Îles Vierges américaines	2010	0.11	0.05	0.06	91.8	20.8	20.4	303.3	...
	2015	0.11	0.05	0.05	91.2	20.4	24.0	299.9	~0
	2018[1]	0.10	0.05	0.05	91.0	20.0	26.0	299.8	...
Uruguay	2005	3.33	1.61	1.72	93.3	23.8	17.9	19.0	...
Uruguay	2010	3.37	1.63	1.75	93.1	22.5	18.4	19.3	...
	2015	3.43	1.66	1.78	93.3	21.4	19.1	19.6	174
	2018[1]	3.47	1.68	1.79	93.5	20.9	19.7	19.8	...
Uzbekistan	2005	26.51	13.17	13.34	98.8	32.6	6.6	62.3	...
Ouzbékistan	2010	28.61	14.23	14.38	99.0	29.1	6.2	67.2	...
	2015	30.98	15.43	15.54	99.3	28.1	7.1	72.8	449
	2018[1]	32.37	16.14	16.23	99.4	28.0	7.9	76.1	...
Vanuatu	2005	0.21	0.11	0.10	104.1	39.7	5.2	17.2	...
Vanuatu	2010	0.24	0.12	0.12	103.1	38.2	5.7	19.4	...
	2015	0.26	0.13	0.13	102.6	36.5	6.5	21.7	12
	2018[1]	0.28	0.14	0.14	102.3	35.8	6.8	23.1	...
Venezuela (Boliv. Rep. of)	2005	26.78	13.41	13.38	100.2	31.7	7.4	30.4	...
Venezuela (Rép. boliv. du)	2010	29.03	14.49	14.54	99.7	29.8	8.3	32.9	...
	2015	31.16	15.51	15.64	99.2	28.2	9.4	35.3	912
	2018[1]	32.38	16.10	16.28	98.9	27.3	10.2	36.7	...

Country or area Pays ou zone	Year Année	Mid-year population estimates and projections (millions) Estimations et projections de population au milieu de l'année (millions) Total	Male Hommes	Females Femmes	Sex Ratio (males per 100 females) Rapport des sexes (hommes pour 100 femmes)	Population age distribution (percentage) Répartition par âge de la population (pourcentage) Aged 0 to 14 years old âgée de 0 à 14 ans	Aged 60+ years old âgée de 60 ans ou plus	Population density (per km²) Densité de population (pour km²)	Surface area Superficie (000 km²)
Viet Nam Viet Nam	2005	84.31	41.52	42.79	97.0	27.2	8.6	271.9	...
	2010	88.47	43.68	44.79	97.5	23.7	8.9	285.3	...
	2015	93.57	46.28	47.29	97.9	23.1	10.3	301.8	331
	2018[1]	96.49	47.76	48.74	98.0	23.0	11.6	311.2	...
Wallis and Futuna Islands Îles Wallis-et-Futuna	2003	0.01	...	...	100.6	...	...	104.7	...
	2005	0.01	...	...	...	...	...	104.1	...
	2008	0.01	...	...	98.4	...	...	99.9	...
	2010	0.01	...	...	...	...	...	95.9	...
	2015	0.01	...	...	...	...	...	86.2	~0
	2016	0.01[1]	...	...	# 93.4	25.5	15.4	85.0[1]	...
	2018[1]	0.01	...	...	...	...	...	83.5	...
Western Sahara Sahara occidental	2005	0.44	0.23	0.21	111.5	31.5	3.6	1.6	...
	2010	0.48	0.25	0.23	111.2	29.4	3.8	1.8	...
	2015	0.53	0.28	0.25	110.5	28.5	4.8	2.0	266[66]
	2018[1]	0.57	0.30	0.27	109.9	27.7	5.7	2.1	...
Yemen Yémen	2005	20.58	10.40	10.18	102.1	45.7	4.2	39.0	...
	2010	23.61	11.93	11.68	102.1	42.5	4.4	44.7	...
	2015	26.92	13.60	13.32	102.1	40.6	4.5	51.0	528
	2018[1]	28.92	14.61	14.31	102.1	39.6	4.6	54.8	...
Zambia Zambie	2005	12.05	5.97	6.09	98.1	47.0	3.9	16.2	...
	2010	13.85	6.86	6.99	98.3	46.8	3.8	18.6	...
	2015	16.10	7.99	8.11	98.5	45.4	3.7	21.7	753
	2018[1]	17.61	8.74	8.87	98.5	44.5	3.7	23.7	...
Zimbabwe Zimbabwe	2005	12.94	6.31	6.63	95.3	41.8	4.5	33.4	...
	2010	14.09	6.86	7.23	94.9	41.5	4.3	36.4	...
	2015	15.78	7.68	8.10	94.8	41.5	4.2	40.8	391
	2018[1]	16.91	8.24	8.67	95.1	41.0	4.2	43.7	...

Source:

United Nations Population Division, New York, World Population Prospects: The 2017 Revision, last accessed June 2017.
United Nations Population Division, New York, World Population Prospects: The 2017 Revision; supplemented by data from the United Nations Statistics Division, New York, Demographic Yearbook 2015 and Secretariat for the Pacific Community (SPC) for small countries or areas, last accessed June 2017.
United Nations Statistics Division, New York, "Demographic Yearbook 2015" and the demographic statistics database, last accessed June 2017.

Source:

Organisation des Nations Unies, Division de la population, New York, « World Population Prospects: The 2017 Revision », denier accès juin 2017.
Organisation des Nations Unies, Division de la population, New York, « World Population Prospects: The 2017 Revision »; complétées par des données de l'Organisation des Nations Unies, Division de statistique, New York, Annuaire démographique 2015 et Secrétariat de la Communauté du Pacifique (SCP) pour petits pays ou zones, denier accès juin 2017.
Organisation des Nations Unies, Division de statistique, New York, Annuaire démographique 2015 et recueil de statistiques démographiques, denier accès juin 2017.

1 Projected estimate (medium fertility variant).
2 Calculated by the United Nations Statistics Division.
3 Including Saint Helena.
4 Including Bermuda, Greenland, and Saint Pierre and Miquelon.
5 Including Anguilla, Bonaire, Sint Eustatius and Saba, British Virgin Islands, Cayman Islands, Dominica, Montserrat, Saint Kitts and Nevis, Sint Maarten (Dutch part) and Turks and Caicos Islands.
6 Including Falkland Islands (Malvinas).
7 Including the Faroe Islands and the Isle of Man.
8 Including Andorra, Gibraltar, Holy See, and San Marino.
9 Including Liechtenstein and Monaco.
10 Including Marshall Islands, Nauru, Northern Mariana Islands and Palau.
11 Including Pitcairn.

1 Projection approximative (variante moyenne fécondité).
2 Calculés par la Division de statistique des Nations Unies.
3 Y compris Sainte-Hélène.
4 Y compris les Bermudes, le Groenland et Saint-Pierre-et-Miquelon.
5 Y compris Anguilla, les îles Bonaire, Saint-Eustache et Saba, les îles Caïmans, la Dominique, Montserrat, Saint-Kitts-et-Nevis, Saint-Martin (partie néerlandaise), les îles Turques-et-Caïques et les îles Vierges britanniques.
6 Y compris les îles Falkland (Malvinas)
7 Y compris les îles Féroé et l'île de Man.
8 Y compris Andorre, Gibraltar, Saint-Siège, et Saint-Marin.
9 Y compris le Liechtenstein et Monaco.
10 Y compris les îles Mariannes du Nord, les îles Marshall, Nauru et Palaos.
11 Y compris Pitcairn.

12 Including American Samoa, Cook Islands, Niue, Pitcairn, Tokelau, Tuvalu, and Wallis and Futuna Islands.
13 De jure population.
14 Including armed forces stationed in the area.
15 Population statistics are compiled from registers.
16 Population aged 65 years and over.
17 Including Christmas Island, Cocos (Keeling) Islands and Norfolk Island.
18 Including Norfolk Island.
19 Including Nagorno-Karabakh.
20 Data refer to projections based on the 2000 population census.
21 Data refer to projections based on the 2010 Population Census.
22 Data updated according to "Superintendencia Agraria". Interior waters correspond to natural or artificial bodies of water or snow.
23 Excluding the institutional population.
24 Refers to Guernsey and Jersey.
25 For statistical purposes, the data for China do not include those for the Hong Kong Special Administrative Region (Hong Kong SAR), Macao Special Administrative Region (Macao SAR) and Taiwan Province of China.
26 Inland waters include the reservoirs.
27 Refers to the whole country.
28 Excluding residents of institutions.
29 Data have not been adjusted for underenumeration, estimated at 1.4 per cent.
30 The total surface is 21 040.79 square kilometres, without taking into account the last ruling of The Hague.
31 A dispute exists between the Governments of Argentina and the United Kingdom of Great Britain and Northern Ireland concerning sovereignty over the Falkland Islands (Malvinas).
32 Excluding military personnel and their families, visitors and transients.
33 Including Åland Islands.
34 Including Abkhazia and South Ossetia.
35 Excluding families of military personnel, visitors and transients.
36 Excluding military personnel, visitors and transients.
37 Including Saint Barthélemy and Saint Martin (French part).
38 Including nationals outside the country.
39 Surface area is 0.44 Km2.
40 Land area only.
41 Data refer to 1 October.
42 Land area only. Excluding 84 square km of uninhabited islands.
43 Including Sabah and Sarawak.
44 Estimates should be viewed with caution as these are derived from scarce data.
45 Projections are prepared by the Secretariat of the Pacific Community based on 1999 census of population and housing.
46 Including Agalega, Rodrigues and Saint Brandon.
47 Excluding the islands of Saint Brandon and Agalega.
48 Intercensus data.
49 Refers to the island of Saipan.
50 Including Svalbard and Jan Mayen Islands.
51 Including the Transnistria region.
52 Including Ascension and Tristan da Cunha.
53 Refers to habitable area. Excludes Saint Lucia's Forest Reserve.
54 Population aged 0 to 20 years.
55 Population aged 61 years and over.
56 Surface area is based on the 2002 population and housing census.

12 Y compris les îles Cook, Nioué, Pitcairn, Samoa américaines, Tokélaou, Tuvalu, et les îles Wallis-et-Futuna.
13 Population de droit.
14 Y compris les militaires en garnison sur le territoire.
15 Les statistiques de la population sont compilées à partir des registres.
16 Population âgée de 65 ans ou plus.
17 Y compris l'île Christmas, les îles des Cocos (Keeling) et l'île Norfolk.
18 Y compris l'île Norfolk.
19 Y compris le Haut-Karabakh.
20 Les données se réfèrent aux projections basées sur le recensement de la population 2000.
21 Les données se réfèrent aux projections basées sur le recensement de la population de 2010.
22 Données actualisées d'après la « Superintendencia Agraria ». Les eaux intérieures correspondent aux étendues d'eau naturelles ou artificielles et aux étendues neigeuses.
23 Non compris la population dans les institutions.
24 Se rapporte à Guernesey et Jersey.
25 Pour la présentation des statistiques, les données pour la Chine ne comprennent pas la région administrative spéciale de Hong Kong (Hong Kong RAS), la région administrative spéciale de Macao (Macao RAS) et la province chinoise de Taïwan.
26 Les eaux intérieures comprennent les réservoirs.
27 Ensemble du pays.
28 À l'exclusion de personnes en établissements de soins.
29 Les données n'ont pas été ajustées pour le sous-dénombrement, estimé à 1,4 pour cent.
30 La superficie totale est égale à 21 040.79 km2, excluant la dernière décision de la Haye.
31 La souveraineté sur les îles Falkland (Malvinas) fait l'objet d'un différend entre le Gouvernement argentin et le Gouvernement du Royaume-Uni de Grande-Bretagne et d'Irlande du Nord.
32 À l'exclusion des personnels militaires et leurs familles, les personnes de passage et les visiteurs.
33 Y compris les Îles d'Åland.
34 Y compris l'Abkhazie et l'Ossétie du Sud.
35 Non compris les familles des militaires, ni les visiteurs et voyageurs en transit.
36 À l'exclusion des personnels militaires, les personnes de passage et les visiteurs.
37 Y compris Saint-Barthélemy et Saint-Martin (partie française).
38 Y compris les ressortissants étrangers.
39 Superficie: 0,44 Km2.
40 La superficie des terres seulement.
41 Les données se réfèrent au 1er octobre.
42 La superficie des terres seulement. Exclut des îles inhabitées d'une superficie de 84 kilomètres carrés.
43 Y compris Sabah et Sarawak.
44 Les montants estimatifs sont à prendre avec prudence, car calculés à partir de données peu nombreuses.
45 Les projections sont préparées par le Secrétariat de la Communauté du Pacifique en fonction du recensement de la population et du logement de 1999.
46 Y compris Agalega, Rodrigues et Saint-Brandon.
47 Non compris les îles Saint-Brandon et Agalega.
48 Données intercensitaires.
49 Fait référence seulement à l'île de Saipan.
50 Y compris les îles Svalbard-et-Jan Mayen.
51 Y compris la région de Transnistrie.
52 Y compris Ascension et Tristan da Cunha.
53 S'applique à la zone habitable. Exclut la réserve forestière de Sainte-Lucie.
54 Population âgée de 0 à 20 ans.
55 Population âgée de 61 ans ou plus.
56 La superficie est fondée sur les données provenant du recensement de la population et du logement de 2002.

57 Including Kosovo.
58 Changes in total area per year are the result of new measuring and correcting of the administrative borders between former Yugoslavian countries.
59 The land area of Singapore comprises the mainland and other islands.
60 Excluding inland water.
61 Including Canary Islands, Ceuta and Melilla.
62 Including East Jerusalem.
63 Including low water level for all islands (area to shoreline).
64 Including Crimea.
65 Including Zanzibar.
66 Comprising the Northern Region (former Saguia el Hamra) and Southern Region (former Rio de Oro).

57 Y compris Kosovo.
58 Les changements des totaux par année résultent de nouvelles mesures et de corrections des frontières administratives entre pays ex-yougoslaves.
59 La superficie terrestre de Singapour comprend l'île principale et les autres îles.
60 Exception faite des eaux intérieures.
61 Y compris les îles Canaries, Ceuta et Melilla.
62 Y compris Jérusalem-Est.
63 Y compris le niveau de basses eaux pour toutes les îles.
64 Y compris Crimea.
65 Y compris Zanzibar.
66 Comprend la région septentrionale (ancien Saguia el Hamra) et la région méridionale (ancien Rio de Oro).

3 Population and rates of growth in urban areas and capital cities

Population et taux de croissance dans les zones urbaines et capitales

Region, country or area Région, pays ou zone	Year Année	Urban % Urbaine %	Annual growth rate (%) Taux d'accroissement annuel (%) Urban pop. urbaine %	 Rural pop. rurale %	Capital Capitale	Population (000s) Population (000s)	% of total % de totale	% of urban % d'urbaine
Total, all countries or areas	**2005**	**49.2**	**2.3[1]**	**0.3[1]**		...	...	...
Total, tous pays ou zones	**2010**	**51.7**	**2.2[1]**	**0.2[1]**		...	...	...
	2015	**53.9**	**2.0[1]**	**0.2[1]**		...	...	...
	2018	**55.3**	**...**	**...**		...	...	...
Africa	2005	36.9	3.5[1]	1.9[1]		...	...	...
Afrique	2010	38.9	3.6[1]	1.9[1]		...	...	...
	2015	41.2	3.7[1]	1.8[1]		...	...	...
	2018	42.5	...	...		...	...	...
Northern Africa	2005	49.3	2.1[1]	1.3[1]		...	...	...
Afrique septentrionale	2010	50.5	2.1[1]	1.2[1]		...	...	...
	2015	51.4	2.3[1]	1.6[1]		...	...	...
	2018	52.0	...	...		...	...	...
Sub-Saharan Africa	2005	33.7	4.1[1]	2.0[1]		...	...	...
Afrique subsaharienne	2010	36.1	4.1[1]	2.0[1]		...	...	...
	2015	38.8	4.1[1]	1.9[1]		...	...	...
	2018	40.4	...	...		...	...	...
Eastern Africa	2005	22.5	4.2[1]	2.4[1]		...	...	...
Afrique orientale	2010	24.4	4.4[1]	2.4[1]		...	...	...
	2015	26.6	4.6[1]	2.2[1]		...	...	...
	2018	28.0	...	...		...	...	...
Middle Africa	2005	42.6	4.4[1]	2.1[1]		...	...	...
Afrique centrale	2010	45.2	4.4[1]	2.3[1]		...	...	...
	2015	47.9	4.3[1]	2.1[1]		...	...	...
	2018	49.5	...	...		...	...	...
Southern Africa	2005	56.5	2.3[1]	0.1[1]		...	...	...
Afrique australe	2010	59.4	2.1[1]	-0.2[1]		...	...	...
	2015	62.1	2.3[1]	0.1[1]		...	...	...
	2018	63.6	...	...		...	...	...
Western Africa	2005	37.8	4.4[1]	1.6[1]		...	...	...
Afrique occidentale	2010	41.1	4.4[1]	1.6[1]		...	...	...
	2015	44.5	4.3[1]	1.6[1]		...	...	...
	2018	46.4	...	...		...	...	...
Northern America	2005	80.0	1.1[1]	0.1[1]		...	...	...
Amérique septentrionale	2010	80.8	1.1[1]	0.1[1]		...	...	...
	2015	81.6	1.0[1]	-0.1[1]		...	...	...
	2018	82.2	...	...		...	...	...
Latin America & the Caribbean	2005	77.1	1.7[1]	-0.1[1]		...	...	...
Amérique latine et Caraïbes	2010	78.6	1.6[1]	-0.1[1]		...	...	...
	2015	79.9	1.5[1]	-0.2[1]		...	...	...
	2018	80.7	...	...		...	...	...
Caribbean	2005	65.4	1.7[1]	-0.6[1]		...	...	...
Caraïbes	2010	67.8	1.5[1]	-0.6[1]		...	...	...
	2015	70.0	1.4[1]	-0.7[1]		...	...	...
	2018	71.3	...	...		...	...	...
Central America	2005	70.3	1.9[1]	0.3[1]		...	...	...
Amérique centrale	2010	72.1	2.1[1]	0.4[1]		...	...	...
	2015	73.7	1.9[1]	0.2[1]		...	...	...
	2018	74.7	...	...		...	...	...
South America	2005	81.1	1.7[1]	-0.2[1]		...	...	...
Amérique du Sud	2010	82.4	1.5[1]	-0.3[1]		...	...	...
	2015	83.5	1.3[1]	-0.3[1]		...	...	...
	2018	84.1	...	...		...	...	...
Asia	2005	41.2	3.1[1]	~0.0[1]		...	...	...
Asie	2010	44.8	2.8[1]	-0.1[1]		...	...	...
	2015	48.0	2.4[1]	-0.2[1]		...	...	...
	2018	49.9	...	...		...	...	...

Region, country or area Région, pays ou zone	Year Année	Urban % Urbaine %	Annual growth rate (%) Taux d'accroissement annuel (%) Urban pop. urbaine %	 Rural pop. rurale %	Capital Capitale	Population (000s) Population (000s)	% of total % de totale	% of urban % d'urbaine
Central Asia Asie centrale	2005	46.8	1.6[1]	0.7[1]		...	...	...
	2010	48.0	1.9[1]	1.0[1]		...	...	...
	2015	48.1	1.7[1]	1.6[1]		...	...	...
	2018	48.2	...	...		...	...	...
Eastern Asia Asie orientale	2005	48.3	3.3[1]	-1.7[1]		...	...	...
	2010	54.4	2.9[1]	-2.0[1]		...	...	...
	2015	59.8	2.4[1]	-2.0[1]		...	...	...
	2018	62.9	...	...		...	...	...
South-eastern Asia Asie du Sud-Est	2005	41.1	3.0[1]	0.3[1]		...	...	...
	2010	44.3	2.7[1]	0.1[1]		...	...	...
	2015	47.2	2.5[1]	0.2[1]		...	...	...
	2018	48.9	...	...		...	...	...
Southern Asia Asie méridionale	2005	30.7	2.8[1]	1.2[1]		...	...	...
	2010	32.5	2.6[1]	1.0[1]		...	...	...
	2015	34.5	2.5[1]	0.8[1]		...	...	...
	2018	35.8	...	...		...	...	...
Western Asia Asie occidentale	2005	65.8	2.7[1]	1.0[1]		...	...	...
	2010	68.2	3.2[1]	1.0[1]		...	...	...
	2015	70.4	2.7[1]	0.7[1]		...	...	...
	2018	71.6	...	...		...	...	...
Europe Europe	2005	71.9	0.3[1]	-0.5[1]		...	...	...
	2010	72.9	0.5[1]	-0.5[1]		...	...	...
	2015	73.9	0.3[1]	-0.6[1]		...	...	...
	2018	74.5	...	...		...	...	...
Eastern Europe Europe orientale	2005	68.5	-0.4[1]	-0.6[1]		...	...	...
	2010	68.9	-0.1[1]	-0.5[1]		...	...	...
	2015	69.3	~0.0[1]	-0.3[1]		...	...	...
	2018	69.6	...	...		...	...	...
Northern Europe Europe septentrionale	2005	78.9	0.6[1]	-0.5[1]		...	...	...
	2010	80.1	1.1[1]	-0.4[1]		...	...	...
	2015	81.4	0.9[1]	-0.9[1]		...	...	...
	2018	82.2	...	...		...	...	...
Southern Europe Europe méridionale	2005	67.8	1.0[1]	-0.2[1]		...	...	...
	2010	69.2	0.9[1]	-0.4[1]		...	...	...
	2015	70.6	0.2[1]	-1.1[1]		...	...	...
	2018	71.5	...	...		...	...	...
Western Europe Europe occidentale	2005	77.3	0.7[1]	-0.8[1]		...	...	...
	2010	78.5	0.6[1]	-0.9[1]		...	...	...
	2015	79.4	0.6[1]	-0.4[1]		...	...	...
	2018	79.9	...	...		...	...	...
Oceania Océanie	2005	68.0	1.3[1]	1.6[1]		...	...	...
	2010	68.1	1.8[1]	1.7[1]		...	...	...
	2015	68.1	1.5[1]	1.5[1]		...	...	...
	2018	68.2	...	...		...	...	...
Australia and New Zealand Australie et Nouvelle-Zélande	2005	84.9	1.3[1]	0.8[1]		...	...	...
	2010	85.3	1.8[1]	1.0[1]		...	...	...
	2015	85.8	1.5[1]	0.8[1]		...	...	...
	2018	86.1	...	...		...	...	...
Melanesia Mélanésie	2005	18.9	2.2[1]	2.3[1]		...	...	...
	2010	19.0	2.3[1]	2.2[1]		...	...	...
	2015	19.2	2.2[1]	2.0[1]		...	...	...
	2018	19.4	...	...		...	...	...
Micronesia Micronésie	2005	65.9	0.3[1]	~0.0[1]		...	...	...
	2010	66.6	0.2[1]	-0.4[1]		...	...	...
	2015	67.9	1.0[1]	-0.2[1]		...	...	...
	2018	68.7	...	...		...	...	...
Polynesia Polynésie	2005	43.5	1.3[1]	0.6[1]		...	...	...
	2010	44.3	0.9[1]	0.2[1]		...	...	...
	2015	44.5	0.6[1]	0.4[1]		...	...	...
	2018	44.4	...	...		...	...	...

Population and rates of growth in urban areas and capital cities *(continued)*

Population et taux de croissance dans les zones urbaines et capitales *(suite)*

Region, country or area Région, pays ou zone	Year Année	Urban % Urbaine %	Annual growth rate (%) Taux d'accroissement annuel (%) Urban pop. urbaine %	 Rural pop. rurale %	Capital Capitale	Population (000s) Population (000s)	% of total % de totale	% of urban % d'urbaine
Afghanistan	2005	22.7	5.0[1]	4.3[1]	Kabul	2 905	11.6	51.0
Afghanistan	2010	23.7	3.7[1]	2.5[1]	Kaboul	3 289	11.4	48.1
	2015	24.8	4.0[1]	2.9[1]		3 724	11.0	44.5
	2018	25.5	...	...		4 012	...	...
Albania	2005	46.7	2.0[1]	-2.1[1]	Tirana	372	12.1	25.8
Albanie	2010	52.2	1.3[1]	-3.1[1]		409	13.9	26.6
	2015	57.4	1.8[1]	-2.5[1]		449	15.4	26.8
	2018	60.3	...	...		476	...	...
Algeria	2005	63.8	2.6[1]	-0.7[1]	Algiers	2 282[2]	6.9[2]	10.7[2]
Algérie	2010	67.5	2.8[1]	-0.5[1]	Alger	2 432[2]	6.7[2]	10.0[2]
	2015	70.8	2.9[1]	-0.2[1]		2 592[2]	6.5[2]	9.2[2]
	2018	72.6	...	...		2 694[2]	...	...
American Samoa	2005	88.1	0.4[1]	1.4[1]	Pago Pago	...	...	...
Samoa américaines	2010	87.6	-1.3[1]	-0.4[1]		...	...	...
	2015	87.2	-0.1[1]	0.5[1]		...	...	...
	2018	87.2	...	...		49	...	...
Andorra	2005	90.3	3.3[1]	8.6[1]	Andorra la Vella	...	...	...
Andorre	2010	88.8	1.0[1]	4.2[1]	Andorre-la-Vieille	...	...	...
	2015	88.3	-1.7[1]	-0.8[1]		...	...	...
	2018	88.1	...	...		23	...	...
Angola	2005	56.0	5.7[1]	0.9[1]	Luanda	3 872[3]	19.8[3]	35.4[3]
Angola	2010	59.8	4.9[1]	1.8[1]		5 300[3]	22.7[3]	37.9[3]
	2015	63.4	4.7[1]	1.6[1]		7 023[3]	25.2[3]	39.7[3]
	2018	65.5	...	...		7 774[3]	...	...
Anguilla	2005	100.0	2.6[1]	0.0[1]	The Valley	...	...	...
Anguilla	2010	100.0	1.7[1]	0.0[1]		...	...	...
	2015	100.0	1.2[1]	0.0[1]		...	...	...
	2018	100.0	...	...		1	...	...
Antigua and Barbuda	2005	29.2	-0.6[1]	2.2[1]	Saint John's	...	...	...
Antigua-et-Barbuda	2010	26.2	-1.0[1]	2.0[1]	Saint-Johns	...	...	...
	2015	25.0	0.1[1]	1.4[1]		...	...	...
	2018	24.6	...	...		21	...	...
Argentina	2005	90.0	1.3[1]	-0.6[1]	Buenos Aires	13 330[4]	34.1[4]	37.8[4]
Argentine	2010	90.8	1.2[1]	-0.7[1]		14 246[4]	34.6[4]	38.0[4]
	2015	91.5	1.2[1]	-0.4[1]		14 706[4]	33.9[4]	37.0[4]
	2018	91.9	...	...		14 967[4]	...	...
Armenia	2005	63.9	-0.8[1]	-0.2[1]	Yerevan	1 087	36.5	57.0
Arménie	2010	63.4	-0.9[1]	-0.4[1]	Erevan	1 066	37.0	58.4
	2015	63.1	0.2[1]	0.5[1]		1 071	36.7	58.2
	2018	63.1	...	...		1 080	...	...
Aruba	2005	44.9	1.1[1]	2.6[1]	Oranjestad	...	...	...
Aruba	2010	43.1	-0.5[1]	1.0[1]		...	...	...
	2015	43.1	0.5[1]	0.5[1]		...	...	...
	2018	43.4	...	...		30	...	...
Australia	2005	84.6[5]	1.3[1,5]	0.7[1,5]	Canberra	366[6]	1.8[6]	2.1[6]
Australie	2010	85.2[5]	1.9[1,5]	1.0[1,5]		398[6]	1.8[6]	2.1[6]
	2015	85.7[5]	1.6[1,5]	0.8[1,5]		429[6]	1.8[6]	2.1[6]
	2018	86.0[5]	...	...		448[6]	...	...
Austria	2005	58.8	-~0.0[1]	1.1[1]	Vienna	1 641	19.9	33.8
Autriche	2010	57.4	-0.1[1]	1.1[1]	Vienne	1 731	20.6	35.9
	2015	57.7	0.7[1]	0.5[1]		1 835	21.1	36.6
	2018	58.3	...	...		1 901	...	...
Azerbaijan	2005	52.4[7]	1.4[1,7]	0.6[1,7]	Baku	1 867[8]	21.9[8]	41.7[8]
Azerbaïdjan	2010	53.4[7]	1.5[1,7]	0.7[1,7]	Bakou	2 062[8]	22.8[8]	42.7[8]
	2015	54.7[7]	1.7[1,7]	0.7[1,7]		2 206[8]	22.9[8]	41.9[8]
	2018	55.7[7]	...	...		2 286[8]	...	...
Bahamas	2005	82.2	2.1[1]	1.8[1]	Nassau	...	...	...
Bahamas	2010	82.4	1.9[1]	1.6[1]		...	...	...
	2015	82.7	1.5[1]	1.0[1]		...	...	...
	2018	83.0	...	...		280	...	...

3 Population and rates of growth in urban areas and capital cities *(continued)*

Population et taux de croissance dans les zones urbaines et capitales *(suite)*

Region, country or area Région, pays ou zone	Year Année	Urban % Urbaine %	Annual growth rate (%) Taux d'accroissement annuel (%) Urban pop. urbaine %	 Rural pop. rurale %	Capital Capitale	Population (000s) Population (000s)	% of total % de totale	% of urban % d'urbaine
Bahrain Bahreïn	2005	88.4	5.8[1]	5.7[1]	Manama	198[9]	22.3[9]	25.2[9]
	2010	88.6	6.7[1]	6.3[1]		292[9]	23.5[9]	26.6[9]
	2015	89.0	2.1[1]	1.4[1]		441[9]	32.1[9]	36.1[9]
	2018	89.3	...	...		565[9]	...	...
Bangladesh Bangladesh	2005	26.8	4.3[1]	0.9[1]	Dhaka Dacca	12 331[10]	8.6[10]	32.1[10]
	2010	30.5	3.7[1]	0.2[1]		14 731[10]	9.7[10]	31.8[10]
	2015	34.3	3.5[1]	~0.0[1]		17 597[10]	10.9[10]	31.8[10]
	2018	36.6	...	...		19 578[10]	...	...
Barbados Barbade	2005	32.8	-0.3[1]	0.6[1]	Bridgetown	...	...	...
	2010	31.9	-0.2[1]	0.7[1]		...	...	...
	2015	31.2	-0.1[1]	0.5[1]		...	...	...
	2018	31.1	...	...		89	...	...
Belarus Bélarus	2005	72.4	~0.0[1]	-2.3[1]	Minsk	1 775[8]	18.4[8]	25.5[8]
	2010	74.7	0.3[1]	-2.1[1]		1 850[8]	19.5[8]	26.2[8]
	2015	77.2	0.7[1]	-2.1[1]		1 945[8]	20.5[8]	26.6[8]
	2018	78.6	...	...		2 005[8]	...	...
Belgium Belgique	2005	97.4	0.6[1]	-1.5[1]	Brussels Bruxelles	1 853[11]	17.6[11]	18.0[11]
	2010	97.7	0.8[1]	-1.3[1]		1 926[11]	17.6[11]	18.0[11]
	2015	97.9	0.7[1]	-1.4[1]		2 002[11]	17.7[11]	18.1[11]
	2018	98.0	...	...		2 050[11]	...	...
Belize Belize	2005	45.3	2.7[1]	2.7[1]	Belmopan	...	...	...
	2010	45.2	2.5[1]	2.6[1]		...	...	...
	2015	45.4	2.3[1]	2.2[1]		...	...	...
	2018	45.7	...	...		23	...	...
Benin Bénin	2005	40.5	4.1[1]	2.3[1]	Porto-Novo [12]	...	...	...
	2010	43.1	4.1[1]	2.0[1]		...	...	...
	2015	45.7	4.0[1]	1.9[1]		...	...	...
	2018	47.3	...	...		285	...	...
Bermuda Bermudes	2005	100.0	0.3[1]	0.0[1]	Hamilton	...	...	...
	2010	100.0	-0.4[1]	0.0[1]		...	...	...
	2015	100.0	-0.6[1]	0.0[1]		...	...	...
	2018	100.0	...	...		10	...	...
Bhutan Bhoutan	2005	31.0	6.7[1]	1.2[1]	Thimphu Thimphou	...	...	...
	2010	34.8	4.4[1]	0.9[1]		...	...	...
	2015	38.7	3.7[1]	0.3[1]		...	...	...
	2018	40.9	...	...		203	...	...
Bolivia (Plurin. State of) Bolivie (État plurin. de)	2005	64.2	2.6[1]	0.5[1]	Sucre [13]	...	...	...
	2010	66.4	2.4[1]	0.4[1]		...	...	...
	2015	68.4	2.1[1]	0.4[1]		...	...	...
	2018	69.4	...	...		278	...	...
Bonaire, St. Eustatius & Saba Bonaire, St-Eustache et Saba	2005	74.8	--0.0[1]	0.2[1]	Kralendijk	...	...	...
	2010	74.7	7.5[1]	7.5[1]		...	...	...
	2015	74.8	3.2[1]	3.2[1]		...	...	...
	2018	74.9	...	...		11[14]	...	...
Bosnia and Herzegovina Bosnie-Herzégovine	2005	44.0	0.8[1]	-0.5[1]	Sarajevo	342[15]	9.0[15]	20.6[15]
	2010	45.6	0.4[1]	-0.9[1]		342[15]	9.2[15]	20.2[15]
	2015	47.2	-0.3[1]	-1.6[1]		342[15]	9.7[15]	20.5[15]
	2018	48.2	...	...		343[15]	...	...
Botswana Botswana	2005	55.9	2.4[1]	0.2[1]	Gaborone	...	...	...
	2010	62.4	3.8[1]	-1.5[1]		...	...	...
	2015	67.2	3.3[1]	-0.9[1]		...	...	...
	2018	69.4	...	...		269	...	...
Brazil Brésil	2005	82.8	1.7[1]	-0.5[1]	Brasilia	3 301[16]	1.8[16]	2.1[16]
	2010	84.3	1.4[1]	-0.8[1]		3 710[16]	1.9[16]	2.2[16]
	2015	85.8	1.2[1]	-1.0[1]		4 168[16]	2.0[16]	2.4[16]
	2018	86.6	...	...		4 470[16]	...	...
British Virgin Islands Îles Vierges britanniques	2005	43.2	3.0[1]	1.8[1]	Road Town	...	...	...
	2010	44.8	4.0[1]	2.7[1]		...	...	...
	2015	46.6	2.8[1]	1.4[1]		...	...	...
	2018	47.7	...	...		15	...	...

3 Population and rates of growth in urban areas and capital cities *(continued)*

Population et taux de croissance dans les zones urbaines et capitales *(suite)*

Region, country or area Région, pays ou zone	Year Année	Urban % Urbaine %	Annual growth rate (%) Taux d'accroissement annuel (%) Urban pop. urbaine %	 Rural pop. rurale %	Capital Capitale	Population (000s) Population (000s)	% of total % de totale	% of urban % d'urbaine
Brunei Darussalam Brunéi Darussalam	2005	73.2	2.4[1]	0.4[1]	Bandar Seri Begawan	...	...	...
	2010	75.0	1.7[1]	-0.1[1]		...	...	...
	2015	76.7	1.9[1]	~0.0[1]		...	...	...
	2018	77.6	...	...		41	...	...
Bulgaria Bulgarie	2005	70.6	-0.3[1]	-1.9[1]	Sofia	1 169	15.2	21.6
	2010	72.3	-0.3[1]	-1.9[1]		1 216	16.4	22.7
	2015	74.0	-0.2[1]	-1.9[1]		1 256	17.5	23.6
	2018	75.0	...	...		1 272	...	...
Burkina Faso Burkina Faso	2005	21.5	6.7[1]	2.0[1]	Ouagadougou	1 328	9.9	45.9
	2010	24.6	5.7[1]	2.2[1]		1 742	11.2	45.3
	2015	27.5	5.2[1]	2.2[1]		2 200	12.2	44.1
	2018	29.4	...	...		2 531	...	...
Burundi Burundi	2005	9.4	5.5[1]	2.7[1]	Bujumbura	412	5.6	59.2
	2010	10.6	5.9[1]	3.0[1]		556	6.3	59.6
	2015	12.1	5.6[1]	2.7[1]		751	7.4	61.0
	2018	13.0	...	...		899	...	...
Cabo Verde Cabo Verde	2005	57.7	3.3[1]	-0.2[1]	Praia Praïa	...	...	...
	2010	61.8	2.5[1]	-0.9[1]		...	...	...
	2015	64.3	2.0[1]	-0.2[1]		...	...	...
	2018	65.7	...	...		168	...	...
Cambodia Cambodge	2005	19.2	2.4[1]	1.6[1]	Phnom Penh	1 317[17]	9.9[17]	51.8[17]
	2010	20.3	2.6[1]	1.2[1]		1 523[17]	10.6[17]	52.4[17]
	2015	22.2	3.4[1]	1.1[1]		1 779[17]	11.5[17]	51.7[17]
	2018	23.4	...	...		1 952[17]	...	...
Cameroon Cameroun	2005	48.5	3.9[1]	1.5[1]	Yaoundé	1 781	10.2	21.1
	2010	51.6	3.9[1]	1.5[1]		2 349	11.8	22.8
	2015	54.6	3.8[1]	1.4[1]		3 097	13.6	24.8
	2018	56.4	...	...		3 656	...	...
Canada Canada	2005	80.1	1.1[1]	0.3[1]	Ottawa	1 122[18]	3.5[18]	4.3[18]
	2010	80.9	1.3[1]	0.3[1]		1 218[18]	3.6[18]	4.4[18]
	2015	81.3	1.1[1]	0.7[1]		1 308[18]	3.6[18]	4.5[18]
	2018	81.4	...	...		1 363[19]	...	...
Cayman Islands Îles Caïmanes	2005	100.0	3.1[1]	0.0[1]	George Town	...	...	...
	2010	100.0	2.6[1]	0.0[1]		...	...	...
	2015	100.0	1.5[1]	0.0[1]		...	...	...
	2018	100.0	...	...		35	...	...
Central African Republic République centrafricaine	2005	38.1	2.1[1]	1.8[1]	Bangui	644	15.6	41.0
	2010	38.9	1.9[1]	1.2[1]		717	16.1	41.4
	2015	40.3	1.1[1]	--0.0[1]		798	17.6	43.6
	2018	41.4	...	...		851	...	...
Chad Tchad	2005	21.8	3.9[1]	3.7[1]	N'Djamena	827	8.2	37.7
	2010	22.0	3.5[1]	3.3[1]		991	8.3	37.9
	2015	22.5	3.8[1]	3.1[1]		1 187	8.5	37.6
	2018	23.1	...	...		1 323	...	...
Channel Islands Îles Anglo-Normandes	2005[20]	30.7	0.9[1]	0.7[1]	Saint Helier [21] Saint-Hélier [21]	...	...	...
	2010[20]	31.1	0.9[1]	0.6[1]		...	...	...
	2015[20]	31.0	0.5[1]	0.5[1]		...	...	...
	2018	30.9[20]	...	...		34	...	...
Chile Chili	2005	86.8	1.3[1]	0.1[1]	Santiago	6 025[22]	37.3[22]	43.0[22]
	2010	87.1	1.1[1]	0.6[1]		6 269[22]	36.9[22]	42.4[22]
	2015	87.4	1.0[1]	0.4[1]		6 523[22]	36.7[22]	42.0[22]
	2018	87.6	...	...		6 680[22]	...	...
China Chine	2005	42.5[23]	4.0[1,23]	-1.6[1,23]	Beijing	12 991[24]	1.0[24]	2.3[24]
	2010	49.2[23]	3.5[1,23]	-1.9[1,23]		16 441[24]	1.2[24]	2.5[24]
	2015	55.5[23]	2.9[1,23]	-2.1[1,23]		18 421[24]	1.3[24]	2.4[24]
	2018	59.2[23]	...	...		19 618[24]	...	...
China, Hong Kong SAR Chine, RAS de Hong Kong	2005	100.0	0.5[1]	0.0[1]	Hong Kong	6 828[25]	100.0[25]	100.0[25]
	2010	100.0	0.6[1]	0.0[1]		7 025[25]	100.0[25]	100.0[25]
	2015	100.0	0.6[1]	0.0[1]		7 246[25]	100.0[25]	100.0[25]
	2018	100.0	...	...		7 429[25]	...	...

3 Population and rates of growth in urban areas and capital cities *(continued)*

Population et taux de croissance dans les zones urbaines et capitales *(suite)*

Region, country or area Région, pays ou zone	Year Année	Urban % Urbaine %	Annual growth rate (%) Taux d'accroissement annuel (%) Urban pop. urbaine %	 Rural pop. rurale %	Capital Capitale	Population (000s) Population (000s)	% of total % de totale	% of urban % d'urbaine
China, Macao SAR Chine, RAS de Macao	2005	100.0	2.4[1]	0.0[1]	Macao	483	100.0	100.0
	2010	100.0	2.1[1]	0.0[1]		537	100.0	100.0
	2015	100.0	2.3[1]	0.0[1]		601	100.0	100.0
	2018	100.0	...	...		632	...	...
Colombia Colombie	2005	76.0	1.9[1]	-0.3[1]	Bogota	7 299[26]	16.9[26]	22.2[26]
	2010	78.0	1.7[1]	-0.5[1]		8 418[26]	18.3[26]	23.5[26]
	2015	79.8	1.4[1]	-0.7[1]		9 708[26]	20.1[26]	25.2[26]
	2018	80.8	...	...		10 574[26]	...	...
Comoros Comores	2005	27.9	2.3[1]	2.5[1]	Moroni	...	...	...
	2010	28.0	2.5[1]	2.4[1]		...	...	...
	2015	28.5	2.7[1]	2.3[1]		...	...	...
	2018	29.0	...	...		62	...	...
Congo Congo	2005	61.0	3.6[1]	1.7[1]	Brazzaville	1 269	34.1	56.0
	2010	63.3	4.0[1]	2.1[1]		1 576	35.9	56.8
	2015	65.5	3.3[1]	1.3[1]		1 958	39.2	59.8
	2018	66.9	...	...		2 230	...	...
Cook Islands Îles Cook	2005	71.0	3.4[1]	-2.0[1]	Avarua	...	...	...
	2010	73.3	-0.6[1]	-2.8[1]		...	...	...
	2015	74.4	-0.9[1]	-2.1[1]		...	...	...
	2018	75.1	...	...		13[27]	...	...
Costa Rica Costa Rica	2005	65.7	3.7[1]	-1.9[1]	San José	1 114[28]	26.2[28]	39.9[28]
	2010	71.7	3.1[1]	-2.5[1]		1 202[28]	26.4[28]	36.9[28]
	2015	76.9	2.5[1]	-2.9[1]		1 297[28]	27.0[28]	35.1[28]
	2018	79.3	...	...		1 358[28]	...	...
Côte d'Ivoire Côte d'Ivoire	2005	45.2	2.8[1]	1.1[1]	Yamoussoukro [29]	...	...	...
	2010	47.3	3.0[1]	1.4[1]		...	...	...
	2015	49.4	3.4[1]	1.7[1]		...	...	...
	2018	50.8	...	...		231	...	...
Croatia Croatie	2005	54.3	0.1[1]	-0.6[1]	Zagreb	690[30]	15.8[30]	29.0[30]
	2010	55.2	0.1[1]	-0.6[1]		688[30]	15.9[30]	28.8[30]
	2015	56.2	-0.1[1]	-0.9[1]		687[30]	16.2[30]	28.9[30]
	2018	56.9	...	...		686[30]	...	...
Cuba Cuba	2005	76.1	0.5[1]	-0.4[1]	Havana La Havane	2 180	19.3	25.4
	2010	76.6	0.2[1]	-0.3[1]		2 143	18.9	24.7
	2015	76.9	0.3[1]	--0.0[1]		2 124	18.5	24.1
	2018	77.0	...	...		2 136	...	...
Curaçao Curaçao	2005	90.5	-0.5[1]	0.1[1]	Willemstad	...	...	...
	2010	89.9	2.5[1]	3.9[1]		...	...	...
	2015	89.4	1.2[1]	2.4[1]		...	...	...
	2018	89.1	...	...		144[31]	...	...
Cyprus Chypre	2005[32]	68.3	1.6[1]	2.0[1]	Nicosia Nicosie	...	...	...
	2010[32]	67.6	1.4[1]	2.0[1]		...	...	...
	2015[32]	66.9	0.7[1]	1.2[1]		...	...	...
	2018	66.8[32]	...	...		269	...	...
Czechia Tchéquie	2005	73.6	-0.2[1]	0.2[1]	Prague	1 199	11.7	15.9
	2010	73.3	0.4[1]	0.8[1]		1 234	11.7	16.0
	2015	73.5	0.2[1]	--0.0[1]		1 269	12.0	16.3
	2018	73.8	...	...		1 292	...	...
Dem. People's Rep. Korea Rép. pop. dém. de Corée	2005	59.8	1.0[1]	0.6[1]	Pyongyang	2 805	11.7	19.6
	2010	60.4	0.8[1]	0.3[1]		2 861	11.6	19.3
	2015	61.3	0.8[1]	0.1[1]		2 970	11.8	19.2
	2018	61.9	...	...		3 038	...	...
Dem. Rep. of the Congo Rép. dém. du Congo	2005	37.5	4.3[1]	2.3[1]	Kinshasa	7 589	13.9	37.0
	2010	40.0	4.6[1]	2.5[1]		9 382	14.5	36.3
	2015	42.7	4.6[1]	2.4[1]		11 598	15.2	35.6
	2018	44.5	...	...		13 171	...	...
Denmark Danemark	2005	85.9	0.5[1]	-0.7[1]	Copenhagen Copenhague	1 127[33]	20.8[33]	24.2[33]
	2010	86.8	0.7[1]	-0.9[1]		1 192[33]	21.5[33]	24.7[33]
	2015	87.5	0.6[1]	-0.7[1]		1 271[33]	22.3[33]	25.5[33]
	2018	87.9	...	...		1 321[33]	...	...

Population and rates of growth in urban areas and capital cities *(continued)*

Population et taux de croissance dans les zones urbaines et capitales *(suite)*

Region, country or area Région, pays ou zone	Year Année	Urban % Urbaine %	Annual growth rate (%) Taux d'accroissement annuel (%) Urban pop. urbaine %	 Rural pop. rurale %	Capital Capitale	Population (000s) Population (000s)	% of total % de totale	% of urban % d'urbaine
Djibouti Djibouti	2005	76.8	1.8[1]	1.6[1]	Djibouti	442[34]	56.5[34]	73.6[34]
	2010	77.0	1.7[1]	1.5[1]		485[34]	57.0[34]	74.0[34]
	2015	77.4	1.8[1]	1.4[1]		531[34]	57.3[34]	74.0[34]
	2018	77.8	...	...		562[34]	...	...
Dominica Dominique	2005	66.6	0.7[1]	-0.5[1]	Roseau	...	...	...
	2010	68.1	0.7[1]	-0.7[1]		...	...	...
	2015	69.6	0.9[1]	-0.5[1]		...	...	...
	2018	70.5	...	...		15	...	...
Dominican Republic République dominicaine	2005	67.4	3.3[1]	-1.7[1]	Santo Domingo Saint-Domingue	2 297[35]	24.9[35]	36.9[35]
	2010	73.8	3.2[1]	-3.0[1]		2 601[35]	26.3[35]	35.6[35]
	2015	78.6	2.5[1]	-2.8[1]		2 945[35]	28.0[35]	35.6[35]
	2018	81.1	...	...		3 172[35]	...	...
Ecuador Équateur	2005	61.7	2.1[1]	1.0[1]	Quito	1 479	10.8	17.5
	2010	62.7	2.0[1]	1.2[1]		1 598	10.7	17.1
	2015	63.4	1.8[1]	1.2[1]		1 734	10.7	16.9
	2018	63.8	...	...		1 822	...	...
Egypt Égypte	2005	43.0	2.0[1]	1.8[1]	Cairo Le Caire	15 174[36]	19.8[36]	45.9[36]
	2010	43.0	1.8[1]	1.8[1]		16 899[36]	20.1[36]	46.7[36]
	2015	42.8	2.1[1]	2.3[1]		18 820[36]	20.1[36]	46.9[36]
	2018	42.7	...	...		20 076[36]	...	...
El Salvador El Salvador	2005	61.6	1.5[1]	-0.8[1]	San Salvador	1 074[37]	17.8[37]	28.9[37]
	2010	65.5	1.6[1]	-1.6[1]		1 086[37]	17.6[37]	26.9[37]
	2015	69.7	1.7[1]	-2.1[1]		1 099[37]	17.4[37]	25.0[37]
	2018	72.0	...	...		1 107[37]	...	...
Equatorial Guinea Guinée équatoriale	2005	57.7	7.4[1]	0.5[1]	Malabo	...	...	...
	2010	65.9	7.2[1]	0.2[1]		...	...	...
	2015	70.6	5.6[1]	1.3[1]		...	...	...
	2018	72.1	...	...		297	...	...
Eritrea Érythrée	2005	31.1	6.3[1]	1.9[1]	Asmara	558	14.1	45.2
	2010	35.2	4.5[1]	0.8[1]		670	15.3	43.4
	2015	38.2	3.6[1]	1.0[1]		803	16.6	43.4
	2018	40.1	...	...		896	...	...
Estonia Estonie	2005	68.7	-0.8[1]	-0.2[1]	Tallinn Tallin	397	29.3	42.6
	2010	68.1	-0.5[1]	0.1[1]		394	29.6	43.5
	2015	68.4	-0.2[1]	-0.5[1]		416	31.6	46.3
	2018	68.9	...	...		437	...	...
Eswatini Eswatini	2005	22.0	0.2[1]	1.0[1]	Mbabane [38]	...	...	...
	2010	22.5	2.1[1]	1.6[1]		...	...	...
	2015	23.3	2.6[1]	1.6[1]		...	...	...
	2018	23.8	...	...		68[38]	...	...
Ethiopia Éthiopie	2005	15.7	4.1[1]	2.6[1]	Addis Ababa Addis-Abeba	2 634	3.4	21.9
	2010	17.3	4.6[1]	2.3[1]		3 126	3.6	20.6
	2015	19.4	4.9[1]	2.1[1]		3 871	3.9	19.9
	2018	20.8	...	...		4 400	...	...
Falkland Islands (Malvinas) [39] Îles Falkland (Malvinas) [39]	2005	70.8	1.3[1]	-1.7[1]	Stanley	...	...	...
	2010	73.7	0.2[1]	-2.6[1]		...	...	...
	2015	76.3	1.0[1]	-1.8[1]		...	...	...
	2018	77.7	...	...		2	...	...
Faroe Islands Îles Féroé	2005	39.8	2.2[1]	-0.7[1]	Tórshavn	...	...	...
	2010	40.9	0.7[1]	-0.3[1]		...	...	...
	2015	41.6	0.5[1]	-0.1[1]		...	...	...
	2018	42.1	...	...		21	...	...
Fiji Fidji	2005	49.9	1.1[1]	-0.5[1]	Suva	...	...	...
	2010	52.2	1.8[1]	--0.0[1]		...	...	...
	2015	54.7	1.7[1]	-0.4[1]		...	...	...
	2018	56.2	...	...		178	...	...
Finland Finlande	2005	82.9[40]	0.4[1,40]	-0.6[1,40]	Helsinki	1 067	20.3	24.5
	2010	83.8[40]	0.6[1,40]	-0.6[1,40]		1 126	21.0	25.1
	2015	85.2[40]	0.8[1,40]	-1.5[1,40]		1 222	22.3	26.2
	2018	85.4[40]	...	...		1 279	...	...

Population and rates of growth in urban areas and capital cities *(continued)*

Population et taux de croissance dans les zones urbaines et capitales *(suite)*

Region, country or area Région, pays ou zone	Year Année	Urban % Urbaine %	Annual growth rate (%) Taux d'accroissement annuel (%) Urban pop. urbaine %	 Rural pop. rurale %	Capital Capitale	Population (000s) Population (000s)	% of total % de totale	% of urban % d'urbaine
France France	2005	77.1	0.9[1]	-0.5[1]	Paris	10 092	16.5	21.4
	2010	78.4	0.9[1]	-0.5[1]		10 460	16.6	21.2
	2015	79.7	0.8[1]	-0.8[1]		10 734	16.7	20.9
	2018	80.4	...	...		10 901	...	...
French Guiana Guyane française	2005	81.1	5.0[1]	2.4[1]	Cayenne	...	...	...
	2010	82.9	3.2[1]	0.8[1]		...	...	...
	2015	84.5	3.1[1]	0.8[1]		...	...	...
	2018	85.3	...	...		58	...	...
French Polynesia Polynésie française	2005	57.4	1.9[1]	0.8[1]	Papeete	...	...	...
	2010	60.3	2.0[1]	-0.4[1]		...	...	...
	2015	61.7	1.2[1]	~0.0[1]		...	...	...
	2018	61.8	...	...		136[41]	...	...
Gabon Gabon	2005	82.5	3.5[1]	-1.1[1]	Libreville	563	40.1	48.7
	2010	85.5	3.9[1]	-0.7[1]		649	39.5	46.2
	2015	88.1	3.9[1]	-0.7[1]		747	38.7	43.9
	2018	89.4	...	...		813	...	...
Gambia Gambie	2005	52.0	4.8[1]	1.5[1]	Banjul	368[42]	25.5[42]	49.0[42]
	2010	55.7	4.5[1]	1.6[1]		393[42]	23.3[42]	41.8[42]
	2015	59.2	4.4[1]	1.4[1]		420[42]	21.3[42]	35.9[42]
	2018	61.3	...	...		437[42]	...	...
Georgia Géorgie	2005	53.6[43]	-0.7[1,43]	-1.4[1,43]	Tbilisi Tbilissi	1 081	24.1	44.9
	2010	55.5[43]	-0.5[1,43]	-2.0[1,43]		1 079	25.5	45.9
	2015	57.4[43]	-0.7[1,43]	-2.2[1,43]		1 078	27.3	47.5
	2018	58.6[43]	...	...		1 077	...	...
Germany Allemagne	2005	76.0	0.3[1]	-0.8[1]	Berlin	3 391	4.2	5.5
	2010	77.0	0.1[1]	-1.0[1]		3 450	4.3	5.5
	2015	77.2	0.3[1]	-~0.0[1]		3 514	4.3	5.6
	2018	77.3	...	...		3 552	...	...
Ghana Ghana	2005	47.3	4.1[1]	1.3[1]	Accra	1 854	8.6	18.2
	2010	50.7	4.0[1]	1.2[1]		2 060	8.4	16.6
	2015	54.1	3.6[1]	0.9[1]		2 290	8.3	15.3
	2018	56.1	...	...		2 439	...	...
Gibraltar Gibraltar	2005	100.0	0.6[1]	0.0[1]	Gibraltar	...	...	...
	2010	100.0	0.7[1]	0.0[1]		...	...	...
	2015	100.0	0.6[1]	0.0[1]		...	...	...
	2018	100.0	...	...		35	...	...
Greece Grèce	2005	74.5	0.8[1]	-1.0[1]	Athens Athènes	3 180[44]	28.1[44]	37.8[44]
	2010	76.3	0.7[1]	-1.2[1]		3 170[44]	27.7[44]	36.3[44]
	2015	78.0	0.1[1]	-1.9[1]		3 161[44]	28.2[44]	36.1[44]
	2018	79.1	...	...		3 156[44]	...	...
Greenland Groenland	2005	82.9	0.6[1]	-1.1[1]	Nuuk	...	...	...
	2010	84.4	0.3[1]	-2.0[1]		...	...	...
	2015	86.1	0.3[1]	-2.4[1]		...	...	...
	2018	86.8	...	...		18	...	...
Grenada Grenade	2005	35.9	0.4[1]	0.2[1]	Saint George's Saint-Georges	...	...	...
	2010	35.9	0.3[1]	0.3[1]		...	...	...
	2015	36.0	0.5[1]	0.4[1]		...	...	...
	2018	36.3	...	...		39[45]	...	...
Guadeloupe Guadeloupe	2005[46]	98.4	0.7[1]	0.7[1]	Basse-Terre	...	...	...
	2010[46]	98.4	0.5[1]	0.4[1]		...	...	...
	2015[46]	98.4	-~0.0[1]	-0.4[1]		...	...	...
	2018	98.5[46]	...	...		58	...	...
Guam Guam	2005	93.6	0.5[1]	-1.1[1]	Hagåtña	...	...	...
	2010	94.1	0.2[1]	-1.4[1]		...	...	...
	2015	94.5	0.4[1]	-1.2[1]		...	...	...
	2018	94.8	...	...		147	...	...
Guatemala Guatemala	2005	46.9	3.0[1]	1.8[1]	Guatemala City Guatemala	2 302	17.6	37.5
	2010	48.4	2.8[1]	1.6[1]		2 560	17.5	36.2
	2015	50.0	2.7[1]	1.5[1]		2 738	16.8	33.7
	2018	51.1	...	...		2 851	...	...

Population and rates of growth in urban areas and capital cities *(continued)*

Population et taux de croissance dans les zones urbaines et capitales *(suite)*

Region, country or area Région, pays ou zone	Year Année	Urban % Urbaine %	Annual growth rate (%) / Taux d'accroissement annuel (%): Urban pop. urbaine %	Rural pop. rurale %	Capital Capitale	Population (000s) Population (000s)	% of total % de totale	% of urban % d'urbaine
Guinea Guinée	2005	32.3	2.8[1]	1.5[1]	Conakry	1 345	13.9	43.1
	2010	33.7	3.0[1]	1.8[1]		1 518	14.1	41.8
	2015	35.1	3.1[1]	1.8[1]		1 714	14.2	40.3
	2018	36.1	...	...		1 843	...	...
Guinea-Bissau Guinée-Bissau	2005	38.2	3.1[1]	1.5[1]	Bissau	336	24.3	63.8
	2010	40.1	3.4[1]	1.7[1]		409	26.3	65.5
	2015	42.1	3.6[1]	1.9[1]		497	28.1	66.6
	2018	43.4	...	...		558	...	...
Guyana Guyana	2005	27.8	-0.7[1]	0.2[1]	Georgetown	...	...	...
	2010	26.6	-1.0[1]	0.2[1]		...	...	...
	2015	26.4	0.4[1]	0.6[1]		...	...	...
	2018	26.6	...	...		110	...	...
Haiti Haïti	2005	42.6	5.2[1]	-0.7[1]	Port-au-Prince	2 171	23.4	55.0
	2010	47.5	3.7[1]	-0.2[1]		2 141	21.4	45.1
	2015	52.4	3.3[1]	-0.6[1]		2 439	22.8	43.4
	2018	55.3	...	...		2 637	...	...
Holy See Saint-Siège	2005	100.0	0.3[1]	0.0[1]	Vatican City Cité du Vatican	...	...	...
	2010	100.0	-0.1[1]	0.0[1]		...	...	...
	2015	100.0	0.2[1]	0.0[1]		...	...	...
	2018	100.0	...	...		1	...	...
Honduras Honduras	2005	48.6	3.8[1]	1.3[1]	Tegucigalpa	882	12.0	24.6
	2010	51.9	3.4[1]	0.8[1]		1 043	12.7	24.5
	2015	55.2	3.0[1]	0.4[1]		1 233	13.8	24.9
	2018	57.1	...	...		1 363	...	...
Hungary Hongrie	2005	66.4	0.3[1]	-1.3[1]	Budapest	1 756	17.4	26.2
	2010	68.9	0.4[1]	-1.9[1]		1 734	17.5	25.4
	2015	70.5	0.2[1]	-1.3[1]		1 746	17.8	25.3
	2018	71.4	...	...		1 759	...	...
Iceland Islande	2005	93.0	1.1[1]	-0.7[1]	Reykjavik	...	...	...
	2010	93.6	1.8[1]	~0.0[1]		...	...	...
	2015	93.7	0.6[1]	0.2[1]		...	...	...
	2018	93.8	...	...		216	...	...
India Inde	2005	29.2	2.8[1]	1.2[1]	New Delhi	18 691[47]	1.6[47]	5.6[47]
	2010	30.9	2.6[1]	1.0[1]		21 988[47]	1.8[47]	5.8[47]
	2015	32.8	2.4[1]	0.7[1]		25 866[47]	2.0[47]	6.0[47]
	2018	34.0	...	...		28 514[47]	...	...
Indonesia Indonésie	2005	45.9	3.2[1]	~-0.0[1]	Jakarta	8 988[48]	4.0[48]	8.6[48]
	2010	49.9	3.0[1]	-0.2[1]		9 626[48]	4.0[48]	8.0[48]
	2015	53.3	2.6[1]	-0.2[1]		10 173[48]	3.9[48]	7.4[48]
	2018	55.3	...	...		10 517[48]	...	...
Iran (Islamic Republic of) Iran (Rép. islamique d')	2005	67.6	2.3[1]	-0.8[1]	Tehran Téhéran	7 652	10.9	16.1
	2010	70.6	2.0[1]	-0.8[1]		8 059	10.8	15.3
	2015	73.4	2.0[1]	-0.7[1]		8 555	10.8	14.7
	2018	74.9	...	...		8 896	...	...
Iraq Iraq	2005	68.8	2.8[1]	2.6[1]	Baghdad Bagdad	5 327	19.7	28.7
	2010	69.1	2.7[1]	2.4[1]		5 652	18.4	26.6
	2015	69.9	3.4[1]	2.7[1]		6 351	17.6	25.2
	2018	70.5	...	...		6 812	...	...
Ireland Irlande	2005	60.5	2.3[1]	1.2[1]	Dublin	1 037	24.6	40.7
	2010	61.5	2.2[1]	1.3[1]		1 100	23.8	38.6
	2015	62.5	0.6[1]	-0.2[1]		1 163	24.7	39.6
	2018	63.2	...	...		1 201	...	...
Isle of Man Île de Man	2005	51.9	1.0[1]	0.9[1]	Douglas	...	...	...
	2010	52.0	1.0[1]	1.0[1]		...	...	...
	2015	52.2	0.9[1]	0.7[1]		...	...	...
	2018	52.6	...	...		27	...	...
Israel Israël	2005	91.5	1.9[1]	1.1[1]	Jerusalem [50] Jérusalem [50]	719[49]	10.9[49]	11.9[49]
	2010	91.8	2.4[1]	1.6[1]		781[49]	10.5[49]	11.5[49]
	2015	92.2	1.7[1]	0.8[1]		858[49]	10.6[49]	11.5[49]
	2018	92.4	...	...		907[49]	...	...

3 Population and rates of growth in urban areas and capital cities *(continued)*

Population et taux de croissance dans les zones urbaines et capitales *(suite)*

Region, country or area Région, pays ou zone	Year Année	Urban % Urbaine %	Annual growth rate (%) Taux d'accroissement annuel (%) Urban pop. urbaine %	 Rural pop. rurale %	Capital Capitale	Population (000s) Population (000s)	% of total % de totale	% of urban % d'urbaine
Italy Italie	2005	67.7	0.7[1]	0.2[1]	Rome	3 807[51]	6.5[51]	9.6[51]
	2010	68.3	0.5[1]	-0.1[1]		3 957[51]	6.6[51]	9.7[51]
	2015	69.6	0.3[1]	-0.9[1]		4 113[51]	6.9[51]	9.9[51]
	2018	70.4	…	…		4 210[51]	…	…
Jamaica Jamaïque	2005	52.8	1.0[1]	0.2[1]	Kingston	581	21.2	40.1
	2010	53.7	0.9[1]	0.1[1]		584	20.7	38.6
	2015	54.8	0.8[1]	-0.1[1]		587	20.4	37.3
	2018	55.7	…	…		589	…	…
Japan Japon	2005	86.0	1.9[1]	-8.3[1]	Tokyo	35 622[52]	27.8[52]	32.3[52]
	2010	90.8	1.1[1]	-8.4[1]		36 860[52]	28.7[52]	31.6[52]
	2015	91.4	~0.0[1]	-1.4[1]		37 256[52]	29.1[52]	31.9[52]
	2018	91.6	…	…		37 468[52]	…	…
Jordan Jordanie	2005	79.5	2.6[1]	1.1[1]	Amman	1 094	19.2	24.1
	2010	86.1	6.2[1]	-3.2[1]		1 397	19.4	22.6
	2015	90.3	5.8[1]	-2.3[1]		1 783	19.5	21.6
	2018	91.0	…	…		2 065	…	…
Kazakhstan Kazakhstan	2005	56.5	0.8[1]	0.5[1]	Astana	538	3.5	6.1
	2010	56.8	1.2[1]	0.9[1]		664	4.0	7.1
	2015	57.2	1.7[1]	1.4[1]		894	5.0	8.8
	2018	57.4	…	…		1 068	…	…
Kenya Kenya	2005	21.7	4.4[1]	2.3[1]	Nairobi	2 677	7.4	34.3
	2010	23.6	4.4[1]	2.3[1]		3 237	7.8	33.2
	2015	25.7	4.4[1]	2.1[1]		3 914	8.3	32.3
	2018	27.0	…	…		4 386	…	…
Kiribati Kiribati	2005	43.6	2.1[1]	1.6[1]	Bairiki	…	…	…
	2010	47.4	3.8[1]	0.7[1]		…	…	…
	2015	51.6	3.5[1]	0.1[1]		3	…	…
	2018	54.1	…	…		…	…	…
Kuwait Koweït	2005	100.0	2.3[1]	0.0[1]	Kuwait City Koweït	1 548[53]	68.0[53]	68.0[53]
	2010	100.0	5.5[1]	0.0[1]		1 994[53]	66.5[53]	66.5[53]
	2015	100.0	5.4[1]	0.0[1]		2 568[53]	65.3[53]	65.3[53]
	2018	100.0	…	…		2 989[53]	…	…
Kyrgyzstan Kirghizistan	2005	35.3	0.6[1]	0.6[1]	Bishkek Bichkek	798	15.7	44.5
	2010	35.3	1.3[1]	1.3[1]		844	15.6	44.1
	2015	35.8	1.8[1]	1.4[1]		936	16.0	44.6
	2018	36.4	…	…		996	…	…
Lao People's Dem. Rep. Rép. dém. populaire lao	2005	27.2	5.8[1]	0.2[1]	Vientiane	572	9.9	36.6
	2010	30.1	3.7[1]	0.8[1]		606	9.7	32.3
	2015	33.1	3.2[1]	0.4[1]		642	9.6	29.1
	2018	35.0	…	…		665	…	…
Latvia Lettonie	2005	68.0	-1.2[1]	-1.1[1]	Riga	712	31.6	46.5
	2010	67.8	-1.3[1]	-1.1[1]		665	31.4	46.2
	2015	68.0	-1.2[1]	-1.3[1]		646	32.4	47.7
	2018	68.1	…	…		637	…	…
Lebanon Liban	2005	86.6	4.3[1]	3.3[1]	Beirut Beyrouth	1 777[54,55]	44.6[54,55]	51.5[54,55]
	2010	87.3	1.8[1]	0.6[1]		1 990[54,55]	45.9[54,55]	52.5[54,55]
	2015	88.1	6.2[1]	4.7[1]		2 229[54,55]	38.1[54,55]	43.2[54,55]
	2018	88.6	…	…		2 385[54,55]	…	…
Lesotho Lesotho	2005	22.2	3.4[1]	0.2[1]	Maseru	…	…	…
	2010	24.8	3.1[1]	0.2[1]		…	…	…
	2015	26.9	2.9[1]	0.7[1]		…	…	…
	2018	28.2	…	…		202	…	…
Liberia Libéria	2005	46.1	3.2[1]	1.8[1]	Monrovia	1 202	36.9	80.0
	2010	47.8	4.6[1]	3.2[1]		1 056	26.7	55.9
	2015	49.8	3.4[1]	1.8[1]		1 270	28.2	56.6
	2018	51.2	…	…		1 418	…	…
Libya Libye	2005	77.1	1.7[1]	1.0[1]	Tripoli	1 058	18.3	23.7
	2010	78.1	1.5[1]	0.4[1]		1 095	17.8	22.7
	2015	79.3	0.5[1]	-0.9[1]		1 134	18.2	22.9
	2018	80.1	…	…		1 158	…	…

3 Population and rates of growth in urban areas and capital cities *(continued)*

Population et taux de croissance dans les zones urbaines et capitales *(suite)*

Region, country or area Région, pays ou zone	Year Année	Urban % Urbaine %	Annual growth rate (%) Taux d'accroissement annuel (%) Urban pop. urbaine %	 Rural pop. rurale %	Capital Capitale	Population (000s) Population (000s)	% of total % de totale	% of urban % d'urbaine
Liechtenstein Liechtenstein	2005	14.7	0.4[1]	1.0[1]	Vaduz	...	...	...
	2010	14.5	0.3[1]	0.7[1]		...	...	...
	2015	14.3	0.5[1]	0.8[1]		...	...	...
	2018	14.3	...	...		5	...	...
Lithuania Lituanie	2005	66.6	-1.0[1]	-0.7[1]	Vilnius	535	16.0	24.0
	2010	66.8	-1.3[1]	-1.4[1]		526	16.8	25.2
	2015	67.2	-1.1[1]	-1.6[1]		531	18.1	27.0
	2018	67.7	...	...		536	...	...
Luxembourg Luxembourg	2005	86.6	1.5[1]	-2.3[1]	Luxembourg	...	...	...
	2010	88.5	2.5[1]	-1.1[1]		...	...	...
	2015	90.2	2.6[1]	-0.9[1]		...	...	...
	2018	91.0	...	...		120	...	...
Madagascar Madagascar	2005	28.8	4.2[1]	2.6[1]	Antananarivo	1 561	8.5	29.5
	2010	31.9	4.9[1]	2.0[1]		2 021	9.6	29.9
	2015	35.2	4.7[1]	1.7[1]		2 618	10.8	30.7
	2018	37.2	...	...		3 058	...	...
Malawi Malawi	2005	15.1	3.3[1]	2.6[1]	Lilongwe	590	4.5	30.1
	2010	15.5	3.7[1]	2.9[1]		731	4.8	31.0
	2015	16.3	3.9[1]	2.8[1]		905	5.2	31.6
	2018	16.9	...	...		1 030	...	...
Malaysia Malaisie	2005	66.6[56]	3.5[1,56]	-0.6[1,56]	Kuala Lumpur [58]	4 927[57]	19.2[57]	28.8[57]
	2010	70.9[56]	3.1[1,56]	-0.9[1,56]		5 810[57]	20.7[57]	29.1[57]
	2015	74.2[56]	2.7[1,56]	-0.6[1,56]		6 851[57]	22.3[57]	30.0[57]
	2018	76.0[56]	...	...		7 564[57]	...	...
Maldives Maldives	2005	33.8	6.5[1]	0.8[1]	Male Malé	...	...	...
	2010	36.4	4.2[1]	1.9[1]		...	...	...
	2015	38.5	3.9[1]	2.1[1]		...	...	...
	2018	39.8	...	...		177	...	...
Mali Mali	2005	32.1	5.5[1]	2.0[1]	Bamako	1 486	11.6	36.2
	2010	36.0	5.6[1]	2.1[1]		1 886	12.5	34.7
	2015	40.0	5.0[1]	1.7[1]		2 219	12.7	31.8
	2018	42.4	...	...		2 447	...	...
Malta Malte	2005	93.6	0.8[1]	-3.2[1]	Valletta La Valette	...	...	...
	2010	94.1	0.5[1]	-0.9[1]		...	...	...
	2015	94.4	0.6[1]	-0.6[1]		...	...	...
	2018	94.6	...	...		213[59]	...	...
Marshall Islands Îles Marshall	2005	71.1	0.7[1]	-1.7[1]	Majuro	...	...	...
	2010	73.6	0.8[1]	-1.6[1]		...	...	...
	2015	75.8	0.8[1]	-1.6[1]		...	...	...
	2018	77.0	...	...		31	...	...
Martinique Martinique	2005	89.3	0.4[1]	1.2[1]	Fort-de-France	...	...	...
	2010	89.1	-0.2[1]	0.4[1]		...	...	...
	2015	89.0	-0.5[1]	-0.3[1]		...	...	...
	2018	89.0	...	...		79	...	...
Mauritania Mauritanie	2005	42.1	4.9[1]	1.5[1]	Nouakchott	684	21.8	51.9
	2010	46.6	4.9[1]	1.2[1]		851	23.6	50.6
	2015	51.1	4.8[1]	1.2[1]		1 058	25.3	49.5
	2018	53.7	...	...		1 205	...	...
Mauritius Maurice	2005[60]	42.1	0.3[1]	0.8[1]	Port Louis Port-Louis	...	...	...
	2010[60]	41.6	0.2[1]	0.6[1]		...	...	...
	2015[60]	41.0	-0.1[1]	0.4[1]		...	...	...
	2018	40.8[60]	...	...		149	...	...
Mayotte Mayotte	2005	50.2	4.4[1]	2.4[1]	Mamoudzou	...	...	...
	2010	49.0	2.7[1]	3.7[1]		...	...	...
	2015	47.0	2.0[1]	3.6[1]		...	...	...
	2018	46.1	...	...		6	...	...
Mexico Mexique	2005	76.3	1.7[1]	--~0.0[1]	Mexico City Mexico	19 276[61]	17.8[61]	23.3[61]
	2010	77.8	2.0[1]	0.3[1]		20 137[61]	17.2[61]	22.1[61]
	2015	79.3	1.8[1]	~0.0[1]		21 340[61]	17.0[61]	21.4[61]
	2018	80.2	...	...		21 581[61]	...	...

Population and rates of growth in urban areas and capital cities *(continued)*

Population et taux de croissance dans les zones urbaines et capitales *(suite)*

Region, country or area Région, pays ou zone	Year Année	Urban % Urbaine %	Annual growth rate (%) Taux d'accroissement annuel (%) Urban pop. urbaine %	Rural pop. rurale %	Capital Capitale	Population (000s) Population (000s)	% of total % de totale	% of urban % d'urbaine
Micronesia (Fed. States of) Micronésie (États féd. de)	2005	22.3	-0.2[1]	-0.2[1]	Palikir	...	...	...
	2010	22.3	-0.5[1]	-0.5[1]		...	...	...
	2015	22.5	0.3[1]	0.1[1]		...	...	...
	2018	22.7	...	...		7	...	...
Monaco Monaco	2005	100.0	1.0[1]	0.0[1]	Monaco	...	...	...
	2010	100.0	1.9[1]	0.0[1]		...	...	...
	2015	100.0	0.6[1]	0.0[1]		...	...	...
	2018	100.0	...	...		39	...	...
Mongolia Mongolie	2005	62.5	2.8[1]	-1.6[1]	Ulaanbaatar Oulan-Bator	933	36.9	59.1
	2010	67.6	3.0[1]	-1.5[1]		1 138	41.9	62.1
	2015	68.2	2.1[1]	1.4[1]		1 365	45.8	67.2
	2018	68.4	...	...		1 520	...	...
Montenegro Monténégro	2005	62.5	1.4[1]	-1.9[1]	Podgorica	...	...	...
	2010	64.1	0.8[1]	-0.7[1]		...	...	...
	2015	65.8	0.6[1]	-0.8[1]		...	...	...
	2018	66.8	...	...		177[62]	...	...
Montserrat Montserrat	2005	9.3	29.3[1]	-2.3[1]	Brades Estate	...	...	...
	2010	9.2	0.3[1]	0.7[1]		...	...	...
	2015	9.0	0.5[1]	0.7[1]		...	...	...
	2018	9.1	...	...		~0	...	...
Morocco Maroc	2005	55.2	1.8[1]	0.3[1]	Rabat	1 635[63]	5.4[63]	9.7[63]
	2010	58.0	2.2[1]	-0.1[1]		1 714[63]	5.3[63]	9.1[63]
	2015	60.8	2.4[1]	~0.0[1]		1 796[63]	5.2[63]	8.5[63]
	2018	62.5	...	...		1 847[63]	...	...
Mozambique Mozambique	2005	30.0	3.5[1]	2.7[1]	Maputo	1 072	5.1	17.1
	2010	31.8	4.1[1]	2.4[1]		1 097	4.5	14.2
	2015	34.4	4.5[1]	2.1[1]		1 100	3.9	11.4
	2018	36.0	...	...		1 102	...	...
Myanmar Myanmar	2005	27.9	1.7[1]	0.8[1]	Nay Pyi Taw	148	0.3	1.1
	2010	28.9	1.3[1]	0.4[1]		234	0.5	1.6
	2015	29.9	1.5[1]	0.6[1]		376	0.7	2.4
	2018	30.6	...	...		500	...	...
Namibia Namibie	2005	36.6	3.8[1]	0.1[1]	Windhoek	268	13.2	36.1
	2010	41.6	3.9[1]	-0.3[1]		314	14.5	34.7
	2015	46.9	4.6[1]	0.3[1]		368	15.2	32.3
	2018	50.0	...	...		404	...	...
Nauru Nauru	2005	100.0	0.2[1]	0.0[1]	Yaren	...	...	...
	2010	100.0	-0.2[1]	0.0[1]		...	...	...
	2015	100.0	2.3[1]	0.0[1]		...	...	...
	2018	100.0	...	...		11[64]	...	...
Nepal Népal	2005	15.1	4.0[1]	1.1[1]	Kathmandu Katmandou	790[65]	3.1[65]	20.3[65]
	2010	16.8	3.1[1]	0.7[1]		965[65]	3.6[65]	21.3[65]
	2015	18.6	3.2[1]	0.7[1]		1 179[65]	4.1[65]	22.2[65]
	2018	19.7	...	...		1 330[65]	...	...
Netherlands Pays-Bas	2005	82.6	2.0[1]	-5.2[1]	Amsterdam [66]	1 025	6.3	7.6
	2010	87.1	1.4[1]	-5.6[1]		1 065	6.4	7.3
	2015	90.2	1.0[1]	-5.1[1]		1 106	6.5	7.2
	2018	91.5	...	...		1 132	...	...
New Caledonia Nouvelle-Calédonie	2005	64.0	2.4[1]	0.7[1]	Nouméa	...	...	...
	2010	67.1	2.5[1]	-0.3[1]		...	...	...
	2015	69.4	2.1[1]	--~0.0[1]		...	...	...
	2018	70.7	...	...		198	...	...
New Zealand Nouvelle-Zélande	2005	86.3	1.5[1]	0.9[1]	Wellington	371	9.0	10.4
	2010	86.2	1.1[1]	1.4[1]		387	8.9	10.3
	2015	86.3	1.1[1]	0.8[1]		402	8.7	10.1
	2018	86.5	...	...		411	...	...
Nicaragua Nicaragua	2005	55.9	1.6[1]	1.0[1]	Managua	910	16.9	30.3
	2010	56.9	1.6[1]	0.8[1]		992	17.3	30.4
	2015	57.9	1.5[1]	0.7[1]		1 027	16.9	29.2
	2018	58.5	...	...		1 048	...	...

3 Population and rates of growth in urban areas and capital cities *(continued)*

Population et taux de croissance dans les zones urbaines et capitales *(suite)*

Region, country or area Région, pays ou zone	Year Année	Urban % Urbaine %	Annual growth rate (%) Taux d'accroissement annuel (%) Urban pop. urbaine %	 Rural pop. rurale %	Capital Capitale	Population (000s) Population (000s)	% of total % de totale	% of urban % d'urbaine
Niger Niger	2005	16.2	3.7[1]	3.6[1]	Niamey	821	6.0	37.1
	2010	16.2	3.7[1]	3.8[1]		954	5.8	35.8
	2015	16.2	3.9[1]	3.8[1]		1 109	5.6	34.3
	2018	16.4	...	...		1 214	...	...
Nigeria Nigéria	2005	39.1	4.8[1]	1.2[1]	Abuja	1 316[67]	0.9[67]	2.4[67]
	2010	43.5	4.8[1]	1.1[1]		1 814[67]	1.1[67]	2.6[67]
	2015	47.8	4.6[1]	1.1[1]		2 442[67]	1.3[67]	2.8[67]
	2018	50.3	...	...		2 919[67]	...	...
Niue Nioué	2005	35.2	-1.1[1]	-3.1[1]	Alofi	...	...	...
	2010	38.7	1.2[1]	-1.7[1]		...	...	...
	2015	42.6	1.9[1]	-1.3[1]		...	...	...
	2018	44.8	...	...		1	...	...
Northern Mariana Islands Îles Mariannes du Nord	2005	90.6	-1.5[1]	-2.5[1]	Garapan	...	...	...
	2010	90.9	-3.1[1]	-4.0[1]		4	...	...
	2015	91.4	0.2[1]	-0.8[1]		...	...	...
	2018	91.6	...	...		...	...	...
Norway Norvège	2005	77.7[68]	1.0[1,68]	-0.8[1,68]	Oslo	818	17.7	22.7
	2010	79.1[68]	1.4[1,68]	-0.3[1,68]		898	18.4	23.2
	2015	81.1[68]	1.7[1,68]	-0.8[1,68]		969	18.6	23.0
	2018	82.2[68]	...	...		1 012	...	...
Oman Oman	2005	72.4	2.3[1]	1.4[1]	Muscat Mascate	622[69]	24.8[69]	34.2[69]
	2010	75.2	4.6[1]	1.7[1]		721[69]	23.7[69]	31.6[69]
	2015	81.4	8.0[1]	0.7[1]		1 180[69]	28.1[69]	34.6[69]
	2018	84.5	...	...		1 447[69]	...	...
Pakistan Pakistan	2005	34.0	2.7[1]	1.8[1]	Islamabad	676	0.4	1.3
	2010	35.0	2.6[1]	1.7[1]		804	0.5	1.3
	2015	36.0	2.7[1]	1.8[1]		957	0.5	1.4
	2018	36.7	...	...		1 061	...	...
Palau Palaos	2005	71.2	1.0[1]	0.2[1]	Melekeok	...	...	...
	2010	74.8	1.6[1]	-2.2[1]		...	...	...
	2015	78.2	1.7[1]	-2.1[1]		...	...	...
	2018	79.9	...	...		11[70]	...	...
Panama Panama	2005	63.7	2.4[1]	1.1[1]	Panama City Panama	1 352[71]	40.6[71]	63.8[71]
	2010	65.1	2.2[1]	1.0[1]		1 504[71]	41.3[71]	63.4[71]
	2015	66.7	2.2[1]	0.8[1]		1 673[71]	42.2[71]	63.2[71]
	2018	67.7	...	...		1 783[71]	...	...
Papua New Guinea Papouasie-Nvl-Guinée	2005	13.1	2.4[1]	2.5[1]	Port Moresby	281	4.5	34.0
	2010	13.0	2.2[1]	2.4[1]		312	4.4	33.7
	2015	13.0	2.2[1]	2.2[1]		345	4.4	33.5
	2018	13.2	...	...		367	...	...
Paraguay Paraguay	2005	57.6	2.6[1]	0.7[1]	Asunción	2 134[72]	36.8[72]	63.9[72]
	2010	59.3	1.9[1]	0.6[1]		2 587[72]	41.7[72]	70.3[72]
	2015	60.8	1.8[1]	0.6[1]		2 967[72]	44.7[72]	73.6[72]
	2018	61.6	...	...		3 222[72]	...	...
Peru Pérou	2005	75.0	1.8[1]	-0.3[1]	Lima	8 081[73]	29.3[73]	39.0[73]
	2010	76.4	1.6[1]	0.1[1]		8 920[73]	30.4[73]	39.7[73]
	2015	77.4	1.6[1]	0.5[1]		9 813[73]	31.3[73]	40.4[73]
	2018	77.9	...	...		10 391[73]	...	...
Philippines Philippines	2005	45.7	1.8[1]	2.2[1]	Manila Manille	10 751[74]	12.5[74]	27.3[74]
	2010	45.3	1.5[1]	1.8[1]		11 887[74]	12.7[74]	28.0[74]
	2015	46.3	2.1[1]	1.3[1]		12 860[74]	12.6[74]	27.3[74]
	2018	46.9	...	...		13 482[74]	...	...
Poland Pologne	2005	61.5	-0.2[1]	~0.0[1]	Warsaw Varsovie	1 684	4.4	7.1
	2010	60.9	-0.2[1]	0.3[1]		1 703	4.4	7.3
	2015	60.3	-0.2[1]	0.3[1]		1 740	4.5	7.5
	2018	60.1	...	...		1 768	...	...
Portugal Portugal	2005	57.5	1.5[1]	-1.0[1]	Lisbon Lisbonne	2 742[75]	25.9[75]	45.1[75]
	2010	60.6	1.2[1]	-1.3[1]		2 812[75]	26.4[75]	43.6[75]
	2015	63.5	0.5[1]	-2.0[1]		2 883[75]	27.7[75]	43.6[75]
	2018	65.2	...	...		2 927[75]	...	...

Region, country or area Région, pays ou zone	Year Année	Urban % Urbaine %	Annual growth rate (%) Taux d'accroissement annuel (%) Urban pop. urbaine %	 Rural pop. rurale %	Capital Capitale	Population (000s) Population (000s)	% of total % de totale	% of urban % d'urbaine
Puerto Rico Porto Rico	2005	94.1	-0.2[1]	0.8[1]	San Juan	2 493[76]	66.2[76]	70.4[76]
	2010	93.8	-0.3[1]	0.7[1]		2 478[76]	66.7[76]	71.1[76]
	2015	93.6	-0.3[1]	0.4[1]		2 463[76]	67.1[76]	71.6[76]
	2018	93.6	...	...		2 454[76]	...	...
Qatar Qatar	2005	97.4	7.8[1]	0.6[1]	Doha	373[77]	43.1[77]	44.3[77]
	2010	98.5	14.7[1]	3.4[1]		524[77]	29.4[77]	29.9[77]
	2015	98.9	6.7[1]	-0.4[1]		590[77]	23.8[77]	24.0[77]
	2018	99.1	...	...		633[77]	...	...
Republic of Korea République de Corée	2005	81.3	1.0[1]	-1.2[1]	Seoul Séoul	9 822[78]	20.2[78]	24.8[78]
	2010	81.9	0.5[1]	-0.3[1]		9 796[78]	19.8[78]	24.1[78]
	2015	81.6	0.3[1]	0.7[1]		9 897[78]	19.6[78]	24.0[78]
	2018	81.5	...	...		9 963[78]	...	...
Republic of Moldova République de Moldova	2005	42.8[79]	-1.0[1,79]	0.4[1,79]	Chisinau	585	14.1	32.9
	2010	42.6[79]	-0.4[1,79]	-0.3[1,79]		555	13.6	31.9
	2015	42.5[79]	-0.2[1,79]	-0.0[1,79]		526	12.9	30.5
	2018	42.6[79]	...	...		510	...	...
Réunion Réunion	2005	96.3	2.5[1]	-16.0[1]	Saint-Denis	...	...	...
	2010	98.5	1.4[1]	-17.1[1]		...	...	...
	2015	99.3	0.9[1]	-15.6[1]		...	...	...
	2018	99.6	...	...		147	...	...
Romania Roumanie	2005	53.2	-0.6[1]	-0.7[1]	Bucharest Bucarest	1 912	8.9	16.8
	2010	53.8	-0.7[1]	-1.2[1]		1 889	9.2	17.2
	2015	53.9	-0.5[1]	-0.6[1]		1 849	9.3	17.3
	2018	54.0	...	...		1 821	...	...
Russian Federation Fédération de Russie	2005	73.5	-0.4[1]	-0.5[1]	Moscow Moscou	10 751	7.5	10.2
	2010	73.7	-0.0[1]	-0.2[1]		11 461	8.0	10.9
	2015	74.1	0.2[1]	-0.2[1]		12 049	8.4	11.3
	2018	74.4	...	...		12 410	...	...
Rwanda Rwanda	2005	16.9	4.8[1]	1.8[1]	Kigali	668	7.4	43.9
	2010	16.9	2.6[1]	2.6[1]		797	7.8	45.9
	2015	17.0	2.6[1]	2.5[1]		951	8.2	48.1
	2018	17.2	...	...		1 058	...	...
Saint Helena Sainte-Hélène	2005[80]	39.9	-3.8[1]	-3.4[1]	Jamestown	...	...	...
	2010[80]	39.5	-0.7[1]	-0.3[1]		...	...	...
	2015[80]	39.5	-0.7[1]	-0.7[1]		...	...	...
	2018	39.8[80]	...	...		1	...	...
Saint Kitts and Nevis Saint-Kitts-et-Nevis	2005	32.0	0.9[1]	1.6[1]	Basseterre	...	...	...
	2010	31.3	0.7[1]	1.3[1]		...	...	...
	2015	30.8	0.8[1]	1.2[1]		...	...	...
	2018	30.8	...	...		14	...	...
Saint Lucia Sainte-Lucie	2005	23.1	-2.9[1]	2.1[1]	Castries	...	...	...
	2010	18.5	-3.4[1]	2.2[1]		...	...	...
	2015	18.5	0.6[1]	0.5[1]		...	...	...
	2018	18.7	...	...		22	...	...
Saint Pierre and Miquelon Saint-Pierre-et-Miquelon	2005	89.9	0.1[1]	-1.3[1]	Saint-Pierre	...	...	...
	2010	89.9	-0.0[1]	0.0[1]		...	...	...
	2015	89.9	0.1[1]	-0.8[1]		...	...	...
	2018	89.9	...	...		6	...	...
Saint Vincent & Grenadines Saint-Vincent-Grenadines	2005	47.0	1.0[1]	-0.5[1]	Kingstown	...	...	...
	2010	49.0	0.9[1]	-0.6[1]		...	...	...
	2015	51.0	0.8[1]	-0.8[1]		...	...	...
	2018	52.2	...	...		27	...	...
Samoa Samoa	2005	21.2	-0.1[1]	0.8[1]	Apia	...	...	...
	2010	20.1	-0.4[1]	1.0[1]		...	...	...
	2015	18.9	-0.4[1]	1.1[1]		...	...	...
	2018	18.2	...	...		36	...	...
San Marino Saint-Marin	2005	94.5	1.5[1]	-2.1[1]	San Marino Saint-Marin	...	...	...
	2010	95.7	1.5[1]	-4.0[1]		...	...	...
	2015	96.7	1.4[1]	-4.2[1]		...	...	...
	2018	97.2	...	...		4	...	...

3 Population and rates of growth in urban areas and capital cities *(continued)*

Population et taux de croissance dans les zones urbaines et capitales *(suite)*

Region, country or area Région, pays ou zone	Year Année	Urban % Urbaine %	Annual growth rate (%) Taux d'accroissement annuel (%) Urban pop. urbaine %	 Rural pop. rurale %	Capital Capitale	Population (000s) Population (000s)	% of total % de totale	% of urban % d'urbaine
Sao Tome and Principe	2005	59.2	4.4[1]	-0.3[1]	Sao Tome	...	...	...
Sao Tomé-et-Principe	2010	65.0	4.2[1]	-0.7[1]	Sao Tomé	...	...	...
	2015	70.2	3.8[1]	-1.0[1]		...	...	...
	2018	72.8	...	...		80	...	...
Saudi Arabia	2005	81.0	3.1[1]	1.7[1]	Riyadh	4 252	17.8	22.0
Arabie saoudite	2010	82.1	3.0[1]	1.6[1]	Riyad	5 220	19.0	23.2
	2015	83.2	3.1[1]	1.5[1]		6 218	19.7	23.7
	2018	83.8	...	...		6 907	...	...
Senegal	2005	41.7	3.3[1]	2.1[1]	Dakar	2 135[81]	19.0[81]	45.5[81]
Sénégal	2010	43.8	3.7[1]	2.0[1]		2 427[81]	18.8[81]	42.9[81]
	2015	45.9	3.9[1]	2.2[1]		2 758[81]	18.4[81]	40.2[81]
	2018	47.2	...	...		2 978[81]	...	...
Serbia	2005	53.9[82]	-0.2[1,82]	-1.1[1,82]	Belgrade	1 303[83]	14.1[83]	26.2[83]
Serbie	2010	55.0[82]	~0.0[1,82]	-0.9[1,82]		1 336[83]	14.8[83]	26.9[83]
	2015	55.7[82]	-0.1[1,82]	-0.7[1,82]		1 369[83]	15.5[83]	27.8[83]
	2018	56.1[82]	...	...		1 389[83]	...	...
Seychelles	2005	51.7	2.3[1]	1.3[1]	Victoria	...	...	...
Seychelles	2010	53.3	1.2[1]	-0.1[1]		...	...	...
	2015	55.4	1.3[1]	-0.4[1]		...	...	...
	2018	56.7	...	...		28	...	...
Sierra Leone	2005	36.9	5.0[1]	3.9[1]	Freetown	786	13.9	37.6
Sierra Leone	2010	38.9	3.7[1]	2.0[1]		905	14.0	36.1
	2015	40.8	3.3[1]	1.6[1]		1 043	14.4	35.3
	2018	42.1	...	...		1 136	...	...
Singapore	2005	100.0	2.8[1]	0.0[1]	Singapore	4 491	100.0	100.0
Singapour	2010	100.0	2.4[1]	0.0[1]	Singapour	5 074	100.0	100.0
	2015	100.0	1.7[1]	0.0[1]		5 535	100.0	100.0
	2018	100.0	...	...		5 792	...	...
Sint Maarten (Dutch part)	2005	100.0	0.4[1]	0.0[1]	Philipsburg	...	...	...
St-Martin (partie néerland.)	2010	100.0	0.4[1]	0.0[1]		...	...	...
	2015	100.0	3.1[1]	0.0[1]		...	...	...
	2018	100.0	...	...		41[84]	...	...
Slovakia	2005	55.6	-0.2[1]	0.3[1]	Bratislava	426	7.9	14.2
Slovaquie	2010	54.7	-0.3[1]	0.4[1]		414	7.7	14.0
	2015	53.9	-0.2[1]	0.5[1]		422	7.8	14.4
	2018	53.7	...	...		430	...	...
Slovenia	2005	51.5	0.4[1]	-0.2[1]	Ljubljana	...	...	...
Slovénie	2010	52.7	0.9[1]	~0.0[1]		...	...	...
	2015	53.8	0.7[1]	-0.2[1]		...	...	...
	2018	54.5	...	...		286	...	...
Solomon Islands	2005	17.8	5.0[1]	2.1[1]	Honiara	...	...	...
Îles Salomon	2010	20.0	4.7[1]	1.8[1]		...	...	...
	2015	22.4	4.3[1]	1.6[1]		...	...	...
	2018	23.7	...	...		82	...	...
Somalia	2005	36.3	4.6[1]	1.9[1]	Mogadishu	1 415[67]	13.6[67]	37.4[67]
Somalie	2010	39.3	4.5[1]	2.0[1]	Mogadiscio	1 353[67]	11.2[67]	28.6[67]
	2015	43.2	4.8[1]	1.5[1]		1 783[67]	12.8[67]	29.6[67]
	2018	45.0	...	...		2 082[67]	...	...
South Africa	2005	59.5	2.2[1]	~0.0[1]	Pretoria [85]	1 334	2.7	4.6
Afrique du Sud	2010	62.2	2.0[1]	-0.3[1]		1 666	3.2	5.2
	2015	64.8	2.2[1]	-~0.0[1]		2 081	3.8	5.8
	2018	66.4	...	...		2 378	...	...
South Sudan	2005	17.2	4.6[1]	3.7[1]	Juba	202	2.5	14.5
Soudan du sud	2010	17.9	5.1[1]	4.2[1]	Djouba	255	2.5	14.2
	2015	18.9	4.4[1]	3.1[1]		321	2.7	14.3
	2018	19.6	...	...		369	...	...
Spain	2005	77.3[86]	1.7[1,86]	0.6[1,86]	Madrid	5 383	12.2	15.8
Espagne	2010	78.4[86]	1.5[1,86]	0.1[1,86]		5 787	12.4	15.8
	2015	79.6[86]	0.1[1,86]	-1.3[1,86]		6 221	13.4	16.8
	2018	80.3[86]	...	...		6 497	...	...

3 Population and rates of growth in urban areas and capital cities *(continued)*

Population et taux de croissance dans les zones urbaines et capitales *(suite)*

Region, country or area Région, pays ou zone	Year Année	Urban % Urbaine %	Annual growth rate (%) / Taux d'accroissement annuel (%): Urban pop. urbaine %	Rural pop. rurale %	Capital Capitale	Population (000s) Population (000s)	% of total % de totale	% of urban % d'urbaine
Sri Lanka	2005	18.3	0.7[1]	0.8[1]	Colombo [87]	614	3.1	17.2
Sri Lanka	2010	18.2	0.6[1]	0.7[1]		574	2.8	15.6
	2015	18.3	0.5[1]	0.5[1]		581	2.8	15.4
	2018	18.5	...	...		600	...	...
State of Palestine	2005[49]	73.1	2.4[1]	1.3[1]	East Jerusalem [88]	...	...	...
État de Palestine	2010[49]	74.1	2.9[1]	1.7[1]	Jérusalem-Est [88]	...	...	...
	2015[49]	75.4	3.1[1]	1.8[1]		...	...	...
	2018	76.2[49]	...	...		275[88]	...	...
Sudan	2005	32.8	2.7[1]	2.4[1]	Khartoum	3 979	12.9	39.3
Soudan	2010	33.1	2.3[1]	2.0[1]		4 517	13.1	39.7
	2015	33.9	2.8[1]	2.1[1]		5 128	13.3	39.2
	2018	34.6	...	...		5 534	...	...
Suriname	2005	66.7	1.2[1]	1.0[1]	Paramaribo	...	...	...
Suriname	2010	66.3	1.0[1]	1.3[1]		...	...	...
	2015	66.1	0.9[1]	1.2[1]		...	...	...
	2018	66.1	...	...		239[89]	...	...
Sweden	2005	84.3	0.4[1]	-0.0[1]	Stockholm	1 248[90]	13.8[90]	16.4[90]
Suède	2010	85.1	0.9[1]	-0.2[1]		1 360[90]	14.5[90]	17.0[90]
	2015	86.6	1.1[1]	-1.3[1]		1 495[90]	15.3[90]	17.7[90]
	2018	87.4	...	...		1 583[90]	...	...
Switzerland	2005	73.5	0.7[1]	0.6[1]	Bern	367	5.0	6.7
Suisse	2010	73.6	1.1[1]	1.0[1]	Berne	387	4.9	6.7
	2015	73.7	1.2[1]	1.1[1]		409	4.9	6.7
	2018	73.8	...	...		422	...	...
Syrian Arab Republic	2005	53.8	2.9[1]	1.4[1]	Damascus	2 200[55]	12.0[55]	22.4[55]
République arabe syrienne	2010	55.6	3.4[1]	2.0[1]	Damas	2 401[55]	11.4[55]	20.5[55]
	2015	52.2	-3.6[1]	-0.8[1]		2 223[55]	11.9[55]	22.7[55]
	2018	54.2	...	...		2 320[55]	...	...
Tajikistan	2005	26.5	2.0[1]	2.0[1]	Dushanbe	640	9.3	35.2
Tadjikistan	2010	26.5	2.2[1]	2.2[1]	Douchanbé	721	9.4	35.6
	2015	26.7	2.4[1]	2.2[1]		812	9.5	35.5
	2018	27.1	...	...		873	...	...
Thailand	2005	37.4	4.3[1]	-1.1[1]	Bangkok	7 272	11.1	29.7
Thaïlande	2010	43.9	3.7[1]	-1.6[1]		8 269	12.3	28.1
	2015	47.7	2.1[1]	-1.0[1]		9 403	13.7	28.7
	2018	49.9	...	...		10 156	...	...
TFYR of Macedonia	2005	57.5	-0.1[1]	0.7[1]	Skopje	485	23.6	40.9
ex-R.Y. de Macédoine	2010	57.1	-0.1[1]	0.3[1]		521	25.2	44.1
	2015	57.4	0.2[1]	-0.1[1]		560	26.9	46.9
	2018	58.0	...	...		584	...	...
Timor-Leste	2005	26.0	4.7[1]	2.8[1]	Dili	...	...	...
Timor-Leste	2010	27.7	2.8[1]	1.1[1]		...	...	...
	2015	29.5	3.5[1]	1.7[1]		...	...	...
	2018	30.6	...	...		281	...	...
Togo	2005	35.2	4.0[1]	2.0[1]	Lomé	1 315	23.1	65.8
Togo	2010	37.5	4.0[1]	2.0[1]		1 466	22.6	60.1
	2015	40.1	4.0[1]	1.8[1]		1 635	22.0	55.0
	2018	41.7	...	...		1 746	...	...
Tokelau	2005	0.0	0.0[1]	-5.0[1]		...	...	...
Tokélaou	2010	0.0	0.0[1]	-1.2[1]		...	...	...
	2015	0.0	0.0[1]	1.9[1]		...	...	...
	2018	0.0	...	...		...	...	...
Tonga	2005	23.2	0.7[1]	0.6[1]	Nuku'alofa	...	...	...
Tonga	2010	23.4	0.8[1]	0.5[1]		...	...	...
	2015	23.3	0.3[1]	0.5[1]		...	...	...
	2018	23.1	...	...		23	...	...
Trinidad and Tobago	2005	55.0	0.1[1]	0.9[1]	Port of Spain	547[67]	42.2[67]	76.8[67]
Trinité-et-Tobago	2010	54.0	0.1[1]	0.9[1]		546[67]	41.1[67]	76.1[67]
	2015	53.3	0.2[1]	0.8[1]		545[67]	40.1[67]	75.2[67]
	2018	53.2	...	...		544[67]	...	...

Population and rates of growth in urban areas and capital cities *(continued)*

Population et taux de croissance dans les zones urbaines et capitales *(suite)*

			Annual growth rate (%) Taux d'accroissement annuel (%)					
Region, country or area Région, pays ou zone	Year Année	Urban % Urbaine %	Urban pop. urbaine %	Rural pop. rurale %	Capital Capitale	Population (000s) Population (000s)	% of total % de totale	% of urban % d'urbaine
Tunisia	2005	65.2	1.4[1]	-0.2[1]	Tunis	1 859[91]	18.4[91]	28.2[91]
Tunisie	2010	66.7	1.5[1]	0.2[1]		2 014[91]	18.9[91]	28.4[91]
	2015	68.1	1.6[1]	0.3[1]		2 183[91]	19.4[91]	28.5[91]
	2018	68.9	...	...		2 291[91]	...	...
Turkey	2005	67.8	2.4[1]	-0.4[1]	Ankara	3 638[92]	5.4[92]	7.9[92]
Turquie	2010	70.8	2.1[1]	-0.7[1]		4 166[92]	5.8[92]	8.1[92]
	2015	73.6	2.4[1]	-0.4[1]		4 633[92]	5.9[92]	8.0[92]
	2018	75.1	...	...		4 919[92]	...	...
Turkmenistan	2005	47.1	1.5[1]	0.6[1]	Ashgabat	592	12.4	26.4
Turkménistan	2010	48.5	2.0[1]	0.8[1]	Achgabat	668	13.1	27.1
	2015	50.3	2.5[1]	1.1[1]		753	13.5	26.9
	2018	51.6	...	...		810	...	...
Turks and Caicos Islands	2001	85.4	...	...	Cockburn Town	~0	...	...
Îles Turques-et-Caïques	2005	87.7	7.5[1]	2.1[1]		...	...	...
	2010	90.2	3.7[1]	-1.4[1]		...	...	...
	2015	92.2	2.5[1]	-2.4[1]		...	...	...
	2018	93.1	...	...		...	...	...
Tuvalu	2005	49.7	2.8[1]	-0.2[1]	Funafuti	...	...	...
Tuvalu	2010	54.8	2.9[1]	-1.2[1]		...	...	...
	2015	59.7	2.6[1]	-1.4[1]		...	...	...
	2018	62.4	...	...		7	...	...
Uganda	2005	17.0	6.2[1]	2.9[1]	Kampala	1 576[93]	5.5[93]	32.6[93]
Ouganda	2010	19.4	6.1[1]	2.9[1]		2 016[93]	5.9[93]	30.7[93]
	2015	22.1	6.0[1]	2.7[1]		2 577[93]	6.4[93]	29.1[93]
	2018	23.8	...	...		2 986[93]	...	...
Ukraine	2005	67.8[94]	-0.6[1,94]	-1.2[1,94]	Kyiv	2 673	5.7	8.4
Ukraine	2010	68.6[94]	-0.2[1,94]	-1.0[1,94]	Kiev	2 795	6.1	8.9
	2015	69.1[94]	-0.4[1,94]	-0.8[1,94]		2 895	6.5	9.4
	2018	69.4[94]	...	...		2 957	...	...
United Arab Emirates	2005	82.3	8.0[1]	5.3[1]	Abu Dhabi	655	14.3	17.4
Émirats arabes unis	2010	84.1	12.3[1]	9.7[1]	Abou Dhabi	912	11.0	13.1
	2015	85.7	2.4[1]	-0.1[1]		1 203	13.1	15.3
	2018	86.5	...	...		1 420	...	...
United Kingdom	2005	79.9	0.8[1]	-0.8[1]	London	7 501[95]	12.4[95]	15.6[95]
Royaume-Uni	2010	81.3	1.3[1]	-0.5[1]	Londres	8 044[95]	12.7[95]	15.6[95]
	2015	82.6	1.0[1]	-0.8[1]		8 661[95]	13.2[95]	16.0[95]
	2018	83.4	...	...		9 046[95]	...	...
United Rep. of Tanzania	2005[96]	24.8	5.0[1]	2.2[1]	Dodoma	...	...	...
Rép.-Unie de Tanzanie	2010[96]	28.1	5.6[1]	2.2[1]		...	...	...
	2015[96]	31.6	5.5[1]	2.1[1]		...	...	...
	2018	33.8[96]	...	...		262	...	...
United States of America	2005	79.9	1.1[1]	0.1[1]	Washington, D.C.	4 264	1.4	1.8
États-Unis d'Amérique	2010	80.8	1.1[1]	~0.0[1]		4 604	1.5	1.8
	2015	81.7	0.9[1]	-0.2[1]		4 972	1.6	1.9
	2018	82.3	...	...		5 207	...	...
United States Virgin Islands	2005	93.7	0.1[1]	-3.3[1]	Charlotte Amalie	...	...	...
Îles Vierges américaines	2010	94.6	-0.1[1]	-3.5[1]		...	...	...
	2015	95.4	-0.1[1]	-3.2[1]		...	...	...
	2018	95.7	...	...		52	...	...
Uruguay	2005	93.3	0.3[1]	-3.5[1]	Montevideo	1 613[97]	48.5[97]	52.0[97]
Uruguay	2010	94.4	0.5[1]	-3.3[1]		1 659[97]	49.2[97]	52.1[97]
	2015	95.0	0.5[1]	-2.1[1]		1 707[97]	49.8[97]	52.4[97]
	2018	95.3	...	...		1 737[97]	...	...
Uzbekistan	2005	48.5	2.3[1]	0.4[1]	Tashkent	2 169	8.2	16.9
Ouzbékistan	2010	51.0	2.5[1]	0.6[1]	Tachkent	2 244	7.8	15.4
	2015	50.8	1.5[1]	1.7[1]		2 379	7.7	15.1
	2018	50.5	...	...		2 464	...	...
Vanuatu	2005	23.1	3.7[1]	2.1[1]	Port Vila	...	...	...
Vanuatu	2010	24.5	3.6[1]	2.1[1]	Port-Vila	...	...	...
	2015	25.0	2.7[1]	2.1[1]		...	...	...
	2018	25.3	...	...		53	...	...

Population and rates of growth in urban areas and capital cities *(continued)*

Population et taux de croissance dans les zones urbaines et capitales *(suite)*

Region, country or area Région, pays ou zone	Year Année	Urban % Urbaine %	Annual growth rate (%) Taux d'accroissement annuel (%) Urban pop. urbaine %	 Rural pop. rurale %	Capital Capitale	Population (000s) Population (000s)	% of total % de totale	% of urban % d'urbaine
Venezuela (Boliv. Rep. of) Venezuela (Rép. boliv. du)	2005	88.0	1.9[1]	1.1[1]	Caracas	2 886[98]	10.8[98]	12.3[98]
	2010	88.1	1.6[1]	1.4[1]		2 899[98]	10.0[98]	11.3[98]
	2015	88.2	1.4[1]	1.3[1]		2 920[98]	9.4[98]	10.6[98]
	2018	88.2	...	...		2 935[98]	...	...
Viet Nam Viet Nam	2005	27.3	3.2[1]	0.2[1]	Hanoi Hanoï	2 160[99]	2.6[99]	9.4[99]
	2010	30.4	3.1[1]	0.1[1]		2 811[99]	3.2[99]	10.4[99]
	2015	33.8	3.2[1]	0.1[1]		3 657[99]	3.9[99]	11.6[99]
	2018	35.9	...	...		4 283[99]	...	...
Wallis and Futuna Islands Îles Wallis-et-Futuna	2005	0.0	0.0[1]	0.1[1]	Matu-Utu	...	...	...
	2010	0.0	0.0[1]	-1.6[1]		...	...	...
	2015	0.0	0.0[1]	-2.1[1]		...	...	...
	2018	0.0	...	...		1	...	...
Western Sahara Sahara occidental	2005	86.0	6.7[1]	6.3[1]	El Aaiún	...	...	...
	2010	86.3	1.9[1]	1.5[1]		...	...	...
	2015	86.5	1.9[1]	1.5[1]		...	...	...
	2018	86.7	...	...		232	...	...
Yemen Yémen	2005	28.9	4.8[1]	2.1[1]	Sana'a Sanaa	1 741[67]	8.5[67]	29.2[67]
	2010	31.8	4.6[1]	1.9[1]		2 084[67]	8.8[67]	27.8[67]
	2015	34.8	4.4[1]	1.7[1]		2 495[67]	9.3[67]	26.7[67]
	2018	36.6	...	...		2 779[67]	...	...
Zambia Zambie	2005	36.9	3.9[1]	2.0[1]	Lusaka	1 357	11.3	30.5
	2010	39.4	4.1[1]	2.0[1]		1 723	12.4	31.6
	2015	41.9	4.3[1]	2.2[1]		2 187	13.6	32.4
	2018	43.5	...	...		2 524	...	...
Zimbabwe Zimbabwe	2005	34.1	1.3[1]	1.0[1]	Harare	1 450	11.2	32.8
	2010	33.2	1.2[1]	2.0[1]		1 475	10.5	31.5
	2015	32.4	1.8[1]	2.5[1]		1 500	9.5	29.4
	2018	32.2	...	...		1 515	...	...

Source:

United Nations Population Division, New York, World Urbanization Prospects: The 2018 Revision, last accessed May 2018.

Source:

Organisation des Nations Unies (ONU), Division de la population, New York, « Perspectives de l'urbanisation mondiale : révision de 2018 », denier accès mai 2018.

1 Data refers to a 5-year period preceding the reference year.
2 Refers to the Governorate of Grand Algiers.
3 Refers to the urban population of the province of Luanda.
4 Refers to Gran Buenos Aires.
5 Including Christmas Island, Cocos (Keeling) Islands and Norfolk Island.
6 Refers to Significant Urban Areas as of 2001.
7 Including Nagorno-Karabakh.
8 Including communities under the authority of the Town Council.
9 Refers to the urban area of the municipality of Al-Manamah.
10 Mega city.
11 Refers to the population of Brussels-Capital Region and "communes" of the agglomeration and suburbs.
12 Porto-Novo is the constitutional capital and Cotonou is the economic capital.
13 La Paz is the seat of government and Sucre is the constitutional capital.
14 Refers to the island of Bonaire.
15 Refers to the municipalities of Stari Grad Sarajevo, Centar Sarajevo, Novo Sarajevo, Novi Grad Sarajevo and Ilidza.
16 Refers to the "Região Integrada de Desenvolvimento do Distrito Federal e Entorno".

1 Les données se réfèrent a période de 5 ans précédant l'année de référence.
2 Fait référence au Gouvernorat du Grand Alger.
3 Fait référence à la population urbaine de la province de Luanda.
4 Fait référence au Gran Buenos Aires.
5 Y compris l'île Christmas, les îles des Cocos (Keeling) et l'île Norfolk.
6 Désigne les zones urbaines importantes en 2001.
7 Y compris le Haut-Karabakh.
8 Y compris les communautés sous l'autorité du conseil municipal.
9 Fait référence à la zone urbaine de la municipalité d'Al-Manama.
10 Mégapole.
11 Concernent la population de Bruxelles-Capitale et les « communes » de l'agglomération et des banlieues.
12 Porto-Novo est la capitale constitutionnelle, Cotonou est la capitale économique.
13 La Paz est le siège du gouvernement, Sucre est la capitale constitutionnelle.
14 Fait référence à l'île de Bonaire.
15 Désigne les municipalités de Stari Grad Sarajevo, de Centar Sarajevo, de Novo Sarajevo, de Novi Grad Sarajevo et d'Ilidza.
16 Fait reference a la région de développement intégré du District fédéral et les régions avoisinantes.

3 Population and rates of growth in urban areas and capital cities *(continued)*

Population et taux de croissance dans les zones urbaines et capitales *(suite)*

17 Refers to the municipality of Phnom Penh including suburban areas.
18 Refers to the Census Metropolitan Area.
19 Refers to Ottawa-Gatineau, the Census Metropolitan Area.
20 Refers to Guernsey and Jersey.
21 The capital of the Bailiwick of Jersey.
22 Refers to the urban population of Santiago Metropolitan Area Region.
23 For statistical purposes, the data for China do not include those for the Hong Kong Special Administrative Region (Hong Kong SAR), Macao Special Administrative Region (Macao SAR) and Taiwan Province of China.
24 Refers to all city districts (excluding Yanqing District) meeting the criteria such as contiguous built-up areas, being the location of the local government, being a Street or Having a Resident Committee.
25 Consists of the population of Hong Kong Island, New Kowloon the new towns in New Territories and the marine areas.
26 Refers to the nuclei of Santa Fe de Bogotá, Soacha, Chia and Funza.
27 Refers to the island of Rarotonga.
28 Refers to the urban population of cantons.
29 Yamoussoukro is the capital and Abidjan is the administrative capital.
30 Refers to the settlement of Zagreb.
31 Total population of Curaçao excluding some neighborhoods (see source).
32 Refers to the whole country.
33 Refers to the Greater Copenhagen Region, consisting of (parts of) 16 municipalities.
34 Refers to the population of the "cercle".
35 Refers to the urban population of the Municipalities of Santo Domingo de Guzmán, Santo Domingo Este, Santo Domingo Oeste, and Santo Domingo Norte.
36 Refers to Greater Cairo as the sum of the Governorate of Al-Qahirah (Cairo) and the surrounding districts of the Governorates of Al-Jizah (Giza) and Al-Qalyūbyah (Qalyubia).
37 Refers to the urban parts of the municipalities San Salvador, Mejicanos, Soyapango, Delgado, Ilopango, Cuscatancingo, Ayutuxtepeque and San Marcos.
38 Mbabane is the administrative capital and Lobamba is the legislative capital.
39 A dispute exists between the Governments of Argentina and the United Kingdom of Great Britain and Northern Ireland concerning sovereignty over the Falkland Islands (Malvinas).
40 Including Åland Islands.
41 Refers to the total population in the communes of Arue, Faaa, Mahina, Papara, Papeete, Pirae and Punaauia.
42 Refers to the local government areas of Banjul and Kanifing.
43 Including Abkhazia and South Ossetia.
44 Refers to the localities of Calithèa, Peristérion and Piraeus, among others.
45 Refers to Saint George Parish.
46 Including Saint Barthélemy and Saint Martin (French part).
47 Refers to the Delhi metropolitan area that is not restricted to state boundaries (National Capital Territory), includes contiguous suburban cities and towns, such as Faridabad, Gurgaon, and Ghaziabad.
48 Refers to the functional urban area.
49 Including East Jerusalem.
50 Designation and data provided by Israel. The position of the UN on Jerusalem is stated in A/RES/181 (II) and subsequent General Assembly and Security Council resolutions.
51 Refers to the official Metropolitan City.
52 Major metropolitan areas.

17 Fait référence à la municipalité de Phnom Penh, y compris les banlieues.
18 Fait référence à la région métropolitaine de recensement.
19 Fait référence à l'Ottawa-Gatineau, la région métropolitaine de recensement.
20 Se rapporte à Guernesey et Jersey.
21 La capitale du bailliage de Jersey.
22 Les données se réfèrent à la population urbaine de la région métropolitaine de Santiago.
23 Pour la présentation des statistiques, les données pour la Chine ne comprennent pas la région administrative spéciale de Hong Kong (Hong Kong RAS), la région administrative spéciale de Macao (Macao RAS) et la province chinoise de Taïwan.
24 Les données réfèrent à tous les districts de la ville (à l'exclusion du district de Yanqing) répondant à des critères tels que les agglomérations contiguës, le fait d'être une Comité de résidents.
25 Composé de la population de l'île de Hong Kong, des villes nouvelles des Nouveaux Territoires de New Kowloon, et des zones marines.
26 Fait référence au principaux foyers de Santa Fe de Bogotá, Soacha, Chia et Funza.
27 Fait référence à l'île de Rarotonga.
28 Fait référence à la population urbaine des cantons.
29 Yamoussoukro est la capitale et Abidjan est la capitale administrative.
30 Fait référence à l'accord de Zagreb.
31 Population totale de Curaçao à l'exception de certains quartiers (voir la source).
32 Ensemble du pays.
33 Fait référence à la région du Grand-Copenhague, composé de (ou des parties de) 16 communes.
34 Fait référence à la population du « cercle ».
35 Les données se réfèrent à la population urbaine des municipalités de Santo Domingo de Guzmán, de Santo Domingo Este, de Santo Domingo Oeste et de Santo Domingo Norte.
36 Les données se réfèrent au Grand Caire comme étant la somme du Gouvernorat d'Al-Qahirah (Le Caire) et des districts environnants des gouvernorats d'Al-Jizah (Giza) et d'Al-Qalyūbyah (Qalyubia).
37 Parties urbaines de San Salvador, Mejicanos, Soyapango, Delgado, Ilopango, Cuscatancingo, Ayutuxtepeque et San Marcos.
38 Mbabane est la capitale administrative, Lobamba est la capitale législative.
39 La souveraineté sur les îles Falkland (Malvinas) fait l'objet d'un différend entre le Gouvernement argentin et le Gouvernement du Royaume-Uni de Grande-Bretagne et d'Irlande du Nord.
40 Y compris les Îles d'Åland.
41 Fait référence à la population totale des communes de Arue, Faaa, Mahina, Papara, Papeete, Pirate et Punaauia.
42 Fait référence aux zones du gouvernement local de Banjul et de Kanifing.
43 Y compris l'Abkhazie et l'Ossétie du Sud.
44 Fait référence, entre autres, aux localités de Calithea, Peristérion et Pirée.
45 Fait référence à la paroisse Saint-George.
46 Y compris Saint-Barthélemy et Saint-Martin (partie française).
47 Les données se rapportent à la région métropolitaine qui n'est pas limitée aux limites des États (Territoire de la capitale nationale). Des villes et banlieues contiguës de banlieue, telles que Faridabad, Gurgaon et Ghaziabad sont incluses dans Delhi.
48 Fait référence aux zones urbaines fonctionnelles.
49 Y compris Jérusalem-Est.
50 Désignation et données fournies par Israël. Voir la résolution A/RES/81 (II) et les résolutions ultérieures de l'Assemblée générale et du Conseil de sécurité pour la position de l'ONU sur Jérusalem.
51 Les données se réfèrent la ville métropolitaine officielle.
52 Principales zones métropolitaines.

53 Data refers to the Governorates of Capital, Hawalli, Al-Farwaniya and Mubarak Al-Kabeer.
54 Excluding Syrian refugees.
55 Estimates should be viewed with caution as these are derived from scarce data.
56 Including Sabah and Sarawak.
57 Refers to the Greater Kuala Lumpur.
58 Kuala Lumpur is the capital and Putrajaya is the administrative capital.
59 Refers to the localities of the Northern Harbour and Southern Harbour.
60 Including Agalega, Rodrigues and Saint Brandon.
61 Refers to the total population in 76 municipalities of the Metropolitan Area of Mexico City.
62 Refers to the urban population of Podgorica municipality.
63 Including Salé and Temara.
64 Refers to Nauru.
65 Refers to the municipality.
66 Amsterdam is the capital and The Hague is the seat of government.
67 Data refers to the urban agglomeration.
68 Including Svalbard and Jan Mayen Islands.
69 Refers to Muscat governorate.
70 Refers to Koror.
71 Refers to the metropolitan area of Panama City.
72 Refers to the district of Asunción and the 19 districts of Central Department.
73 Refers to the Province of Lima and the Constitutional Province of Callao.
74 Refers to the National Capital Region.
75 Refers to Grande Lisboa, the Peninsula of Setúbal, and the municipality Azambuja.
76 Refers to the Metropolitan Statistical Area.
77 Does not include the populations from the industrial area and zone 58.
78 Refers to Seoul Special City.
79 Including the Transnistria region.
80 Including Ascension and Tristan da Cunha.
81 Refers to the sum of the Departments of Dakar, Pikinie and Guédiawaye, in Dakar Region.
82 Including Kosovo.
83 Refers to the urban population of Belgrade area.
84 Refers to the total population of Sint Maarten.
85 Pretoria is the administrative capital, Cape Town is the legislative capital and Bloemfontein is the judiciary capital.
86 Including Canary Islands, Ceuta and Melilla.
87 Colombo is the capital and Sri Jayewardenepura Kotte is the legislative capital.
88 Designation and data provided by the State of Palestine. The position of the UN on Jerusalem is stated in A/RES/181 (II) and subsequent General Assembly and Security Council resolutions.
89 Refers to the total population of the District of Paramaribo.
90 Refers to "tätort" (according to the administrative divisions of 2005).
91 Refers to Grand Tunis.
92 Refers to Altindag, Cankaya, Etimesgut, Golbasi, Keçioren, Mamak, Sincan and Yenimahalle.
93 Data includes Kira, Makindye Ssabagabo and Nansana.
94 Including Crimea.
95 Data refer to "Urban area" (Greater London).
96 Including Zanzibar.
97 Data refer to the department of Montevideo and localities of the departments of Canelones and San José (Cerámicas del Sur and Ciudad del Plata).
98 Refers to multiple municipalities and parishes (see source).
99 Refers to urban population in the city districts.

53 Les données se réfèrent aux gouvernorats de la capitale, Hawalli, Al-Farwaniya et Mubarak Al-Kabeer.
54 À l'exclusion des réfugiés syriens.
55 Les montants estimatifs sont à prendre avec prudence, car calculés à partir de données peu nombreuses.
56 Y compris Sabah et Sarawak.
57 Fait référence au Grand Kuala Lumpur.
58 Kuala Lumpur est la capitale, Putrajaya est la capitale administrative.
59 Désigne les localités du port nord et du port sud.
60 Y compris Agalega, Rodrigues et Saint-Brandon.
61 Fait référence à la population totale de 76 municipalités de la zone métropolitaine de Mexico.
62 Désigne la population urbaine de la municipalité de Podgorica.
63 Y compris Salé and Temara.
64 Fait référence à la Nauru.
65 Fait référence à la commune.
66 Amsterdam est la capitale, La Haye est le siège du gouvernement.
67 Les données se rapportent à l'agglomération urbaine.
68 Y compris les îles Svalbard-et-Jan Mayen.
69 Fait référence au gouvernorat de Mascate.
70 Fait référence au Koror.
71 Fait référence à l'agglomération métropolitaine de la ville de Panama.
72 Désigne le district d'Asunción et les 19 districts du département central.
73 Fait référence à la province de Lima et à la province constitutionnelle de Callao.
74 Fait référence à la région de la capitale nationale.
75 Fait référence à « Grande Lisboa », la Péninsule de Setúbal et la municipalité Azambuja.
76 Fait référence à la zone statistique métropolitaine.
77 Ne comprend pas les populations de la zone industrielle et de la zone 58.
78 Fait référence à Séoul Special City.
79 Y compris la région de Transnistrie.
80 Y compris Ascension et Tristan da Cunha.
81 Désigne la somme des départements de Dakar, Pikinie et Guédiawaye, dans la région de Dakar.
82 Y compris Kosovo.
83 Désigne la population urbaine de la région de Belgrade.
84 Se réfère à la population totale de Sint Maarten.
85 Pretoria est la capitale administrative, Cape Town est la capitale législative et Bloemfontein est la capitale judiciaire.
86 Y compris les îles Canaries, Ceuta et Melilla.
87 Colombo est la capitale, Sri Jayewardenepura Kotte est la capitale législative.
88 Désignation et données fournies par l'État de Palestine. La position de l'Organisation des Nations Unies sur Jérusalem est indiquée dans la résolution A/RES/81 (II), puis dans les résolutions ultérieures de l'Assemblée générale et du Conseil de sécurité.
89 Fait référence à la population totale du district de Paramaribo.
90 Fait référence à « tätort » (selon les divisions administratives de 2005).
91 Fait référence au Grand Tunis.
92 Fait référence à Altindag, Cankaya, Etimesgut, Golbasi, Keçiören, Mamak, Sincan et Yenimahalle.
93 Les données comprennent également Kira, Makindye Ssabagabo et Nansana.
94 Y compris Crimea.
95 Les données se réfèrent à "zone urbaine" (Greater London).
96 Y compris Zanzibar.
97 Les données concernent le département de Montevideo et les localités des départements de Canelones et de San José (Cerámicas del Sur et Ciudad del Plata).
98 Fait référence à plusieurs municipalités et paroisses (voir source).
99 Fait référence à la population dans les districts urbains.

4 International migrants and refugees

International migrant stock (number and percentage) and refugees and others of concern to UNHCR

Migrants internationaux et réfugiés

Stock de migrants internationaux (nombre et pourcentage) et réfugiés et autres personnes relevant de la compétence du HCR

Region, country or area Région, pays ou zone	Year Année	International Migrant Stock (mid-year) Stock de migrants internationaux (milieu de l'année) Total Total	% of total pop. % de la pop. totale MF/HF	M/H	F	Refugees and others of concern to UNHCR (mid-year) Réfugiés et autres personnes relevant de la compétence du HCR (milieu de l'année) Refugees& Réfugiés&	Asylum seekers Demandeurs d'asile	Other&& Autres&&	Total pop. Pop. totale
Total, all countries or areas **Total, tous pays ou zones**	**2005**	**190 531 600**	**2.9**	**3.0**	**2.9**	...	...	...	...
	2010	**220 019 266**	**3.2**	**3.2**	**3.1**	...	...	...	...
	2015	**247 585 744**	**3.4**	**3.4**	**3.3**	**15 097 633**	**2 343 919**	**40 518 150**	**57 959 702**
	2017	**257 715 425**	**3.4**	**3.5**	**3.3**	**18 473 853**	**2 954 666**	**45 979 852**	**67 408 371**
Africa Afrique	2005	15 462 306	1.7	1.8	1.5	...	...	...	...
	2010	17 007 249	1.6	1.7	1.5	...	...	...	...
	2015	23 436 088	2.0	2.1	1.8	4 493 139	1 044 031	11 530 138	17 067 308
	2017	24 650 223	2.0	2.1	1.8	6 134 401	589 255	15 203 541	21 927 197
Northern Africa [1] Afrique septentrionale [1]	2005	1 731 939	0.9	1.1	0.7	...	...	...	...
	2010	1 893 613	0.9	1.1	0.8	...	...	...	...
	2015	2 354 732	1.0	1.2	0.9	...	...	...	...
	2017	2 410 056	1.0	1.2	0.9	...	...	...	...
Sub-Saharan Africa [2] Afrique subsaharienne [2]	2005	14 272 361	1.9	2.0	1.7	...	...	...	...
	2010	15 691 999	1.8	1.9	1.7	...	...	...	...
	2015	21 705 234	2.2	2.3	2.0	...	...	...	...
	2017	22 975 988	2.2	2.3	2.1	...	...	...	...
Eastern Africa Afrique orientale	2005	4 745 792	1.6	1.7	1.5	...	...	...	...
	2010	4 657 063	1.3	1.4	1.3	...	...	...	...
	2015	6 920 965	1.7	1.8	1.7	...	...	...	...
	2017	7 591 799	1.8	1.8	1.8	...	...	...	...
Middle Africa Afrique centrale	2005	1 928 828	1.7	1.8	1.7	...	...	...	...
	2010	2 139 979	1.6	1.7	1.6	...	...	...	...
	2015	3 436 978	2.2	2.3	2.2	...	...	...	...
	2017	3 539 697	2.2	2.2	2.1	...	...	...	...
Southern Africa Afrique australe	2005	1 439 426	2.6	3.1	2.1	...	...	...	...
	2010	2 357 093	4.0	4.7	3.3	...	...	...	...
	2015	4 112 793	6.5	7.3	5.7	...	...	...	...
	2017	4 338 205	6.7	7.5	5.8	...	...	...	...
Western Africa Afrique occidentale	2005	5 616 321	2.1	2.2	1.9	...	...	...	...
	2010	5 959 501	1.9	2.1	1.8	...	...	...	...
	2015	6 610 620	1.9	2.0	1.8	...	...	...	...
	2017	6 770 466	1.8	1.9	1.7	...	...	...	...
Northern America Amérique septentrionale	2005	45 363 387	13.8	13.9	13.8	...	...	...	...
	2010	50 970 996	14.9	14.7	15.0	...	...	...	...
	2015	55 766 224	15.7	15.4	16.0	416 385	238 989	...	655 374
	2017	57 664 154	16.0	15.6	16.3	380 675	725 314	...	1 105 989
Latin America & the Caribbean Amérique latine et Caraïbes	2005	7 237 476	1.3	1.3	1.3	...	...	...	...
	2010	8 246 652	1.4	1.4	1.4	...	...	...	...
	2015	9 272 027	1.5	1.5	1.5	336 552	37 378	6 697 290	7 071 220
	2017	9 508 189	1.5	1.5	1.5	323 973	117 507	7 774 202	8 215 682
Caribbean Caraïbes	2005	1 333 118	3.3	3.5	3.2	...	...	...	...
	2010	1 353 589	3.2	3.4	3.2	...	...	...	...
	2015	1 385 784	3.2	3.3	3.1	...	...	...	...
	2017	1 399 747	3.2	3.3	3.1	...	...	...	...
Central America Amérique centrale	2005	1 385 713	0.9	0.9	0.9	...	...	...	...
	2010	1 749 940	1.1	1.1	1.1	...	...	...	...
	2015	2 043 212	1.2	1.2	1.2	...	...	...	...
	2017	2 092 819	1.2	1.2	1.2	...	...	...	...
South America Amérique du Sud	2005	4 518 645	1.2	1.2	1.2	...	...	...	...
	2010	5 143 123	1.3	1.3	1.3	...	...	...	...
	2015	5 843 031	1.4	1.4	1.4	...	...	...	...
	2017	6 015 623	1.4	1.4	1.4	...	...	...	...
Asia Asie	2005	53 243 730	1.3	1.4	1.2	...	...	...	...
	2010	65 921 788	1.6	1.8	1.4	...	...	...	...
	2015	76 558 152	1.7	1.9	1.5	8 178 380	320 437	19 921 907	28 420 724
	2017	79 586 709	1.8	2.0	1.5	9 067 704	502 166	20 251 046	29 820 916

4

International migrants and refugees *(continued)*
International migrant stock (number and percentage) and refugees and others of concern to UNHCR

Migrants internationaux et réfugiés *(suite)*
Stock de migrants internationaux (nombre et pourcentage) et réfugiés et autres personnes relevant de la compétence du HCR

Region, country or area Région, pays ou zone	Year Année	International Migrant Stock (mid-year) Stock de migrants internationaux (milieu de l'année) Total Total	% of total pop. % de la pop. totale MF/HF	M/H	F	Refugees and others of concern to UNHCR (mid-year) Réfugiés et autres personnes relevant de la compétence du HCR (milieu de l'année) Refugees[&] Réfugiés[&]	Asylum seekers Demandeurs d'asile	Other[&&] Autres[&&]	Total pop. Pop. totale
Central Asia	2005	5 238 699	8.9	8.3	9.5	...	...	...	...
Asie centrale	2010	5 262 414	8.3	8.0	8.7	...	...	...	...
	2015	5 393 504	7.9	7.6	8.1	...	...	...	...
	2017	5 462 972	7.7	7.5	7.9	...	...	...	...
Eastern Asia	2005	6 229 524	0.4	0.4	0.4	...	...	...	...
Asie orientale	2010	7 061 814	0.4	0.4	0.5	...	...	...	...
	2015	7 600 768	0.5	0.4	0.5	...	...	...	...
	2017	7 776 716	0.5	0.4	0.5	...	...	...	...
South-eastern Asia	2005	6 522 343	1.2	1.2	1.1	...	...	...	...
Asie du Sud-Est	2010	8 673 693	1.5	1.5	1.4	...	...	...	...
	2015	9 609 923	1.5	1.6	1.5	...	...	...	...
	2017	9 873 600	1.5	1.6	1.5	...	...	...	...
Southern Asia	2005	13 722 011	0.9	0.9	0.9	...	...	...	...
Asie méridionale	2010	14 307 646	0.8	0.9	0.8	...	...	...	...
	2015	14 173 830	0.8	0.8	0.8	...	...	...	...
	2017	13 582 402	0.7	0.7	0.7	...	...	...	...
Western Asia	2005	21 531 153	10.5	12.6	8.2	...	...	...	...
Asie occidentale	2010	30 616 221	13.2	16.5	9.5	...	...	...	...
	2015	39 780 127	15.4	18.9	11.6	...	...	...	...
	2017	42 891 019	16.0	19.6	12.1	...	...	...	...
Europe	2005	63 201 280	8.7	8.7	8.6	...	...	...	...
Europe	2010	70 747 947	9.6	9.6	9.6	...	...	...	...
	2015	74 501 508	10.1	10.0	10.1	1 626 214	678 737	2 368 815	4 673 766
	2017	77 895 217	10.5	10.4	10.6	2 508 981	983 967	2 751 063	6 244 011
Eastern Europe	2005	19 747 392	6.6	6.7	6.6	...	...	...	...
Europe orientale	2010	19 127 781	6.5	6.5	6.5	...	...	...	...
	2015	19 880 519	6.8	6.8	6.7	...	...	...	...
	2017	20 121 711	6.9	6.9	6.8	...	...	...	...
Northern Europe	2005	9 588 814	9.9	9.7	10.2	...	...	...	...
Europe septentrionale	2010	11 810 676	11.8	11.5	12.0	...	...	...	...
	2015	13 188 813	12.8	12.5	13.1	...	...	...	...
	2017	13 946 390	13.4	13.1	13.7	...	...	...	...
Southern Europe	2005	11 974 334	8.0	7.9	8.0	...	...	...	...
Europe méridionale	2010	16 205 444	10.5	10.5	10.6	...	...	...	...
	2015	15 830 496	10.4	10.0	10.8	...	...	...	...
	2017	15 957 631	10.5	10.1	10.9	...	...	...	...
Western Europe	2005	21 890 740	11.8	11.9	11.7	...	...	...	...
Europe occidentale	2010	23 604 046	12.5	12.4	12.6	...	...	...	...
	2015	25 601 680	13.3	13.2	13.4	...	...	...	...
	2017	27 869 485	14.4	14.4	14.5	...	...	...	...
Oceania	2005	6 023 421	17.9	17.9	18.2	...	...	...	...
Océanie	2010	7 124 634	19.4	19.4	19.8	...	...	...	...
	2015	8 051 745	20.4	20.1	20.8	46 963	24 347	...	71 310
	2017	8 410 933	20.7	20.4	21.2	58 119	36 457	...	94 576
Australia and New Zealand	2005	5 717 982	23.5	23.3	23.6	...	...	...	...
Australie et Nouvelle-Zélande	2010	6 830 423	25.8	25.6	26.0	...	...	...	...
	2015	7 750 276	27.3	26.9	27.7	...	...	...	...
	2017	8 102 983	27.8	27.3	28.3	...	...	...	...
Melanesia	2005	103 878	1.3	1.4	1.1	...	...	...	...
Mélanésie	2010	105 684	1.2	1.3	1.0	...	...	...	...
	2015	114 595	1.2	1.3	1.0	...	...	...	...
	2017	118 078	1.1	1.3	1.0	...	...	...	...
Micronesia	2005	128 390	25.5	35.4	36.6	...	...	...	...
Micronésie	2010	115 948	23.0	31.7	31.8	...	...	...	...
	2015	115 311	22.2	30.6	30.3	...	...	...	...
	2017	117 601	22.3	30.6	30.3	...	...	...	...

International migrants and refugees *(continued)*

International migrant stock (number and percentage) and refugees and others of concern to UNHCR

Migrants internationaux et réfugiés *(suite)*

Stock de migrants internationaux (nombre et pourcentage) et réfugiés et autres personnes relevant de la compétence du HCR

Region, country or area Région, pays ou zone	Year Année	International Migrant Stock (mid-year) Stock de migrants internationaux (milieu de l'année) Total Total	% of total pop. % de la pop. totale MF/HF	M/H	F	Refugees and others of concern to UNHCR (mid-year) Réfugiés et autres personnes relevant de la compétence du HCR (milieu de l'année) Refugees& Réfugiés&	Asylum seekers Demandeurs d'asile	Other&& Autres&&	Total pop. Pop. totale
Polynesia Polynésie	2005	73 171	11.4	14.4	12.8	...	...	...	...
	2010	72 579	11.0	13.7	12.3	...	...	...	...
	2015	71 563	10.6	13.0	11.7	...	...	...	...
	2017	72 271	10.5	12.9	11.6	...	...	...	...
Afghanistan Afghanistan	2005	87 300	0.3	0.4	0.3	32[3]	14[3]	159 551[3]	159 597[3]
	2010	102 246	0.4	0.4	0.3	6 434[3]	30[3]	1 193 523[3]	1 199 987[3]
	2015	489 749	1.5	1.4	1.5	225 714	101	1 195 604	1 421 419
	2017	133 612	0.4	0.4	0.4	87 119	205	2 101 881[4]	2 189 205
Albania Albanie	2005	64 739	2.1	2.1	2.1	56[3]	35[3]	1[3]	92[3]
	2010	52 784	1.8	1.8	1.8	76[3]	23[3]	...	99[3]
	2015	52 031	1.8	1.8	1.8	154	501	7 443	8 098
	2017	52 484	1.8	1.8	1.8	113	2 743	4 860[5]	7 716
Algeria Algérie	2005	197 422[6]	0.6[6]	0.6[6]	0.5[6]	94 101[3]	306[3]	...	94 407[3]
	2010	216 964[6]	0.6[6]	0.6[6]	0.6[6]	94 144[3]	304[3]	...	94 448[3]
	2015	239 473[6]	0.6[6]	0.6[6]	0.6[6]	94 144[7]	5 892	...	100 036
	2017	248 624[6]	0.6[6]	0.6[6]	0.6[6]	94 248[7]	5 986	...	100 234
American Samoa Samoa américaines	2005	24 233	41.0	...	...	...	...	...	...
	2010	23 555	42.3	...	...	...	...	...	...
	2015	23 513	42.3	...	...	...	...	...	...
	2017	23 561	42.3	...	...	...	...	...	...
Andorra [8] Andorre [8]	2005	50 298	63.8	...	...	...	...	...	...
	2010	52 053	61.6	...	...	...	...	...	...
	2015	42 082	53.9	...	...	...	...	...	...
	2017	41 039	53.3	...	...	...	...	...	...
Angola Angola	2005	61 329[6]	0.3[6]	0.3[6]	0.3[6]	13 984[3]	885[3]	45[3]	14 914[3]
	2010	76 549[6]	0.3[6]	0.3[6]	0.3[6]	15 155[3]	4 241[3]	...	19 396[3]
	2015	632 178[6]	2.3[6]	2.2[6]	2.3[6]	15 555[3]	30 143[3]	2 887	45 698[3]
	2017	638 499[6]	2.1[6]	2.1[6]	2.2[6]	48 232	30 192	...	78 424
Anguilla Anguilla	2005	4 684	37.1	...	...	...	...	...	...
	2010	5 103	37.1	...	...	...	...	...	...
	2015	5 470	37.4	...	...	...	...	...	...
	2016	...	...	...	...	1	...	...	1
	2017	5 579	37.4	...	...	...	...	...	...
Antigua and Barbuda Antigua-et-Barbuda	2005	24 741	27.7	25.8	29.5	...	...	...	...
	2010	26 412	27.9	26.0	29.7	...	...	...	...
	2015	28 083	28.1	26.1	29.9	...	10	...	10
	2017	28 646	28.1	26.1	29.9	1	...	...	1
Argentina Argentine	2005	1 673 088	4.3	4.0	4.5	3 074[3]	825[3]	2[3]	3 901[3]
	2010	1 805 957	4.4	4.1	4.6	3 276[3]	947[3]	...	4 223[3]
	2015	2 086 302	4.8	4.5	5.1	3 523	897	...	4 420
	2017	2 164 524	4.9	4.6	5.2	3 322	4 010	396	7 728
Armenia Arménie	2005	469 119[6]	15.7[6]	13.7[6]	17.6[6]	219 550[3]	70[3]	...	219 620[3]
	2010	221 560[6]	7.7[6]	6.7[6]	8.6[6]	3 296[3]	23[3]	82 525[3]	85 844[3]
	2015	191 199[6]	6.6[6]	5.6[6]	7.4[6]	15 690	114	238	16 042
	2017	190 719[6]	6.5[6]	5.6[6]	7.3[6]	17 922	71	613	18 606
Aruba Aruba	2005	32 540	32.5	30.6	34.3	...	...	...	...
	2010	34 327	33.8	31.6	35.7	...	1[3]	...	1[3]
	2015	36 114	34.6	32.5	36.5	...	2	...	2
	2017	36 356	34.5	32.4	36.5	1	5	...	6
Australia Australie	2005	4 878 030[9]	24.1[9]	24.0[9]	24.3[9]	64 964[3]	1 822[3]	8[3]	66 794[3]
	2010	5 882 980[9]	26.6[9]	26.4[9]	26.8[9]	21 805[3]	3 760[3]	15[3]	25 580[3]
	2015	6 710 540[9]	28.2[9]	27.8[9]	28.6[9]	35 582	22 837[10,11]	...	58 419
	2017	7 035 560[9]	28.8[9]	28.3[9]	29.3[9]	46 576	35 825[10]	...	82 401
Austria Autriche	2005	1 136 270	13.8	13.5	14.0	21 230[3]	40 710[3]	830[3]	62 770[3]
	2010	1 275 992	15.2	14.9	15.5	42 630[3]	25 625[3]	470[3]	68 725[3]
	2015	1 492 374	17.2	16.9	17.5	60 747[11]	30 900[11]	570[11]	92 217[11]
	2017	1 660 283	19.0	18.6	19.4	104 375	65 515	980	170 870

International migrants and refugees *(continued)*

International migrant stock (number and percentage) and refugees and others of concern to UNHCR

Migrants internationaux et réfugiés *(suite)*

Stock de migrants internationaux (nombre et pourcentage) et réfugiés et autres personnes relevant de la compétence du HCR

		International Migrant Stock (mid-year) Stock de migrants internationaux (milieu de l'année)	% of total pop. % de la pop. totale			Refugees and others of concern to UNHCR (mid-year) Réfugiés et autres personnes relevant de la compétence du HCR (milieu de l'année)			
Region, country or area Région, pays ou zone	Year Année	Total Total	MF/HF	M/H	F	Refugees& Réfugiés&	Asylum seekers Demandeurs d'asile	Other&& Autres&&	Total pop. Pop. totale
Azerbaijan Azerbaïdjan	2005	302 220[6,12]	3.5[6,12]	3.2[6,12]	3.9[6,12]	3 004[3]	115[3]	581 194[3]	584 313[3]
	2010	276 901[6,12]	3.1[6,12]	2.9[6,12]	3.2[6,12]	1 891[3]	17[3]	594 969[3]	596 877[3]
	2015	264 241[6,12]	2.7[6,12]	2.6[6,12]	2.8[6,12]	1 357	262	626 477	628 096
	2017	259 241[6,12]	2.6[6,12]	2.5[6,12]	2.7[6,12]	1 196	358	616 714	618 268
Bahamas Bahamas	2005	45 595	13.8	14.7	13.0	...	...	...	...
	2010	54 736	15.2	15.8	14.6	28[3]	9[3]	...	37[3]
	2015	59 306	15.3	15.8	14.8	7	19	30	56
	2016	...	...	...	...	11	17	97	125
	2017	61 806	15.6	16.1	15.1	14	23	...	37
Bahrain Bahreïn	2005	404 018[8]	45.4[8]	54.0[8]	32.5[8]	...	15[3]	...	15[3]
	2010	657 856[8]	53.0[8]	61.5[8]	39.0[8]	165[3]	69[3]	...	234[3]
	2015	704 137[8]	51.3[8]	60.1[8]	37.2[8]	277	78	...	355
	2017	722 649[8]	48.4[8]	55.8[8]	36.0[8]	262	109	...	371
Bangladesh Bangladesh	2005	1 166 700[6]	0.8[6]	0.9[6]	0.8[6]	21 098[3]	58[3]	250 094[3]	271 250[3]
	2010	1 345 546[6]	0.9[6]	0.9[6]	0.8[6]	229 253[3]	...	...	229 253[3]
	2015	1 422 805[6]	0.9[6]	0.9[6]	0.8[6]	232 975[13]	11	...	232 986
	2017	1 500 921[6]	0.9[6]	1.0[6]	0.9[6]	307 424[14]	104	2	307 530
Barbados Barbade	2005	30 624	11.2	10.3	12.0	...	...	...	...
	2010	32 825	11.7	11.0	12.4	...	...	...	...
	2015	34 475	12.1	11.4	12.8	1	...	...	1
	2017	34 660	12.1	11.4	12.8	...	5	...	5
Belarus Bélarus	2005	1 106 982	11.5	11.3	11.7	725[3]	56[3]	12 421[3]	13 202[3]
	2010	1 090 378	11.5	11.3	11.7	589[3]	66[3]	7 734[3]	8 389[3]
	2015	1 082 905	11.4	11.2	11.6	1 369	257	6 302	7 928
	2017	1 078 652	11.4	11.2	11.5	1 930	112	5 915	7 957
Belgium Belgique	2005	882 031[8]	8.4[8]	8.7[8]	8.0[8]	15 282[3]	18 913[3]	398[3]	34 593[3]
	2010	1 119 256[8]	10.2[8]	10.6[8]	9.9[8]	17 892[3]	18 288[3]	696[3]	36 876[3]
	2015	1 252 380[8]	11.1[8]	11.5[8]	10.7[8]	31 115	9 396	5 267	45 778
	2016[3]	...	...	...	...	42 168	24 111	2 630	68 909
	2017[8]	1 268 411	11.1	11.4	10.8	...	...	...	...
Belize Belize	2005	41 424[6]	14.6[6]	14.8[6]	14.5[6]	624[3]	14[3]	...	638[3]
	2010	46 360[6]	14.4[6]	14.6[6]	14.2[6]	134[3]	30[3]	2[3]	166[3]
	2015	54 674[6]	15.2[6]	15.4[6]	15.1[6]	...	146	...	146
	2016	...	...	...	...	165	2 761	200	3 126
	2017	59 998[6]	16.0[6]	16.2[6]	15.8[6]	...	2 666	2 442	5 108
Benin Bénin	2005	171 499[6,8]	2.1[6,8]	2.4[6,8]	1.9[6,8]	30 294[3]	1 695[3]	77[3]	32 066[3]
	2010	209 267[6,8]	2.3[6,8]	2.5[6,8]	2.0[6,8]	7 139[3]	101[3]	47[3]	7 287[3]
	2015	245 399[6,8]	2.3[6,8]	2.6[6,8]	2.0[6,8]	488	84	...	572
	2017	253 284[6,8]	2.3[6,8]	2.6[6,8]	2.0[6,8]	968	188	...	1 156
Bermuda Bermudes	2005	18 276	28.1	...	...	...	...	...	...
	2010	18 884	29.5	...	...	...	...	...	...
	2015	19 126	30.8	...	...	...	...	...	...
	2017	18 954	30.9	...	...	...	...	...	...
Bhutan Bhoutan	2005	40 279	6.1	9.5	2.4	...	...	...	...
	2010	48 420	6.7	10.2	2.7	...	...	...	...
	2015	51 106	6.5	9.9	2.6	...	...	...	...
	2017	52 296	6.5	9.9	2.6	...	...	...	...
Bolivia (Plurin. State of) Bolivie (État plurin. de)	2005	107 745	1.2	1.2	1.1	535[3]	3[3]	2[3]	540[3]
	2010	122 846	1.2	1.3	1.2	695[3]	41[3]	3[3]	739[3]
	2015	142 989	1.3	1.4	1.3	767	8	...	775
	2017	148 837	1.3	1.4	1.3	797	6	...	803
Bonaire, St. Eustatius & Saba Bonaire, St-Eustache et Saba	2010	11 445	54.7	...	...	...	1[3,15]	...	1[3,15]
	2015	13 002	52.9	...	...	...	...	...	...
	2017	13 508	53.2	...	...	...	...	...	...
Bosnia and Herzegovina Bosnie-Herzégovine	2005	* 47 272[6]	* 1.3[6]	* 1.2[6]	* 1.3[6]	10 568[3]	215[3]	188 735[3]	199 518[3]
	2010	* 38 792[6]	* 1.0[6]	* 1.0[6]	* 1.1[6]	7 016[3]	153[3]	171 790[3]	178 959[3]
	2015	* 38 574[6]	* 1.1[6]	* 1.1[6]	* 1.1[6]	6 805	11	137 035	143 851
	2017	* 37 100[6]	* 1.1[6]	* 1.0[6]	* 1.1[6]	5 265	92	151 064	156 421

International migrants and refugees *(continued)*

International migrant stock (number and percentage) and refugees and others of concern to UNHCR

Migrants internationaux et réfugiés *(suite)*

Stock de migrants internationaux (nombre et pourcentage) et réfugiés et autres personnes relevant de la compétence du HCR

		International Migrant Stock (mid-year) Stock de migrants internationaux (milieu de l'année)				Refugees and others of concern to UNHCR (mid-year) Réfugiés et autres personnes relevant de la compétence du HCR (milieu de l'année)			
			% of total pop. % de la pop. totale						
Region, country or area Région, pays ou zone	Year Année	Total Total	MF/HF	M/H	F	Refugees& Réfugiés&	Asylum seekers Demandeurs d'asile	Other&& Autres&&	Total pop. Pop. totale
Botswana	2005	88 829[8]	4.8[8]	5.4[8]	4.2[8]	3 109[3]	47[3]	592[3]	3 748[3]
Botswana	2010	120 912[8]	6.0[8]	6.7[8]	5.3[8]	2 986[3]	249[3]	111[3]	3 346[3]
	2015	160 644[8]	7.3[8]	8.0[8]	6.5[8]	2 164	248	...	2 412
	2017	166 430[8]	7.3[8]	8.0[8]	6.5[8]	2 149	86	635	2 870
Brazil	2005	638 582	0.3	0.4	0.3	3 458[3]	195[3]	4 093[3]	7 746[3]
Brésil	2010	592 568	0.3	0.3	0.3	4 357[3]	872[3]	8[3]	5 237[3]
	2015	716 568	0.3	0.4	0.3	7 762	17 902	40 338	66 002
	2017	735 557	0.4	0.4	0.3	10 129	53 949	43 875	107 953
British Virgin Islands	2005	15 016	64.8	...	...	...	...	...	...
Îles Vierges britanniques	2010	17 074	62.7	...	...	2[3]	...	...	2[3]
	2015	19 132	63.5	...	...	...	...	...	...
	2017	19 959	64.0	...	...	...	1	...	1
Brunei Darussalam	2005	98 441	27.0	29.6	24.2	...	...	...	...
Brunéi Darussalam	2010	100 587	25.9	28.3	23.3	...	...	20 992[3]	20 992[3]
	2015	102 733	24.6	27.0	22.0	...	...	20 524	20 524
	2017	108 612	25.3	27.9	22.6	...	...	20 524	20 524
Bulgaria	2005	61 074	0.8	0.7	0.9	4 413[3]	805[3]	...	5 218[3]
Bulgarie	2010	76 287	1.0	0.9	1.1	5 530[3]	1 412[3]	...	6 942[3]
	2015	133 803	1.9	1.7	2.0	11 046[11]	7 840	67	18 953
	2017	153 803	2.2	2.0	2.4	18 678	8 995	67	27 740
Burkina Faso	2005	596 972[6]	4.4[6]	4.3[6]	4.6[6]	511[3]	784[3]	7[3]	1 302[3]
Burkina Faso	2010	673 904[6]	4.3[6]	4.1[6]	4.5[6]	531[3]	534[3]	9[3]	1 074[3]
	2015	704 676[6]	3.9[6]	3.7[6]	4.1[6]	34 027	180	...	34 207
	2017	708 921[6]	3.7[6]	3.5[6]	3.9[6]	34 033	176	...	34 209
Burundi	2005	172 874[6]	2.3[6]	2.3[6]	2.3[6]	20 681[3]	19 900[3]	12 988[3]	53 569[3]
Burundi	2010	235 259[6]	2.7[6]	2.7[6]	2.7[6]	29 365[3]	12 062[3]	159 338[3]	200 765[3]
	2015	289 810[6]	2.8[6]	2.8[6]	2.8[6]	54 126	2 733	80 851	137 710
	2017	299 569[6]	2.8[6]	2.8[6]	2.8[6]	59 424	3 870	123 643[16]	186 937
Cabo Verde	2005	12 700	2.7	2.8	2.5	...	...	1[3]	1[3]
Cabo Verde	2010	14 373	2.9	2.9	2.8	...	...	...	...
	2015	14 924	2.8	2.8	2.8	...	...	115	115
	2017	15 295	2.8	2.8	2.8	...	...	115	115
Cambodia	2005	114 031	0.9	0.9	0.8	127[3]	68[3]	207[3]	402[3]
Cambodge	2010	81 977	0.6	0.6	0.5	129[3]	51[3]	...	180[3]
	2015	73 963	0.5	0.5	0.4	80	33	131	244
	2017	76 329	0.5	0.5	0.4	70	54	10	134
Cameroon	2005	258 737	1.5	1.6	1.3	52 042[3]	6 766[3]	7 444[3]	66 252[3]
Cameroun	2010	289 091	1.4	1.6	1.3	104 275[3]	2 383[3]	66[3]	106 724[3]
	2015	508 357	2.2	2.2	2.3	302 293	7 835	81 693	391 821
	2017	540 266	2.2	2.2	2.3	322 777	4 409	226 260	553 446
Canada	2005	6 078 985	18.8	18.2	19.4	147 171[3]	20 552[3]	12[3]	167 735[3]
Canada	2010	6 761 226	19.8	19.1	20.5	165 549[3]	51 025[3]	7[3]	216 581[3]
	2015	7 561 226	21.0	20.3	21.8	135 888[3]	19 951[3]	...	155 839[3]
	2017	7 861 226	21.5	20.7	22.2	101 256	33 261	...	134 517
Cayman Islands	2005[8]	21 655	44.5	...	...	...	...	...	...
Îles Caïmanes	2010	24 057[8]	43.3[8]	...	...	1[3]	4[3]	...	5[3]
	2015	23 726[8]	39.6[8]	...	...	6	1	100	107
	2017	24 355[8]	39.6[8]	...	...	25	32	...	57
Central African Republic	2005	94 449[8]	2.3[8]	2.5[8]	2.1[8]	24 569[3]	1 960[3]	2 167[3]	28 696[3]
République centrafricaine	2010	93 466[8]	2.1[8]	2.3[8]	1.9[8]	21 574[3]	1 219[3]	192 531[3]	215 324[3]
	2015	81 598[8]	1.8[8]	1.9[8]	1.7[8]	7 906	394	508 904	517 204
	2017	88 774[8]	1.9[8]	2.0[8]	1.8[8]	11 426	511	637 685	649 622
Chad	2005	352 062[6]	3.5[6]	3.2[6]	3.8[6]	275 412[3]	68[3]	...	275 480[3]
Tchad	2010	416 924[6]	3.5[6]	3.1[6]	3.9[6]	347 939[3]	110[3]	185 000[3]	533 049[3]
	2015	516 968[6]	3.7[6]	3.4[6]	4.0[6]	420 774	2 749	50 000	473 523
	2017	489 690[6]	3.3[6]	3.0[6]	3.5[6]	400 705	1 914	161 060	563 679

4 International migrants and refugees *(continued)*

International migrant stock (number and percentage) and refugees and others of concern to UNHCR

Migrants internationaux et réfugiés *(suite)*

Stock de migrants internationaux (nombre et pourcentage) et réfugiés et autres personnes relevant de la compétence du HCR

Region, country or area Région, pays ou zone	Year Année	International Migrant Stock (mid-year) Stock de migrants internationaux (milieu de l'année) Total Total	% of total pop. % de la pop. totale MF/HF	M/H	F	Refugees and others of concern to UNHCR (mid-year) Réfugiés et autres personnes relevant de la compétence du HCR (milieu de l'année) Refugees& Réfugiés&	Asylum seekers Demandeurs d'asile	Other&& Autres&&	Total pop. Pop. totale
Channel Islands [17] Îles Anglo-Normandes [17]	2005	70 941	46.0	44.3	47.6	...	...	...	...
	2010	77 581	48.6	46.8	50.4	...	...	...	...
	2015	82 307	50.3	48.5	52.0	...	...	...	...
	2017	83 082	50.3	48.4	52.1	...	...	...	...
Chile Chili	2005	273 384	1.7	1.6	1.8	806[3]	107[3]	...	913[3]
	2010	369 436	2.2	2.1	2.3	1 621[3]	274[3]	...	1 895[3]
	2015	469 436	2.6	2.5	2.8	1 798	719	...	2 517
	2017	488 571	2.7	2.6	2.8	1 736	5 195	...	6 931
China [18] Chine [18]	2005	678 947[8]	0.1[8]	0.1[8]	~0.0[8]	301 041[3]	84[3]	1[3]	301 126[3]
	2010	849 861[8]	0.1[8]	0.1[8]	0.1[8]	300 986[3]	122[3]	...	301 108[3]
	2015	978 046[8]	0.1[8]	0.1[8]	0.1[8]	301 057[19]	564	...	301 621
	2017	999 527[8]	0.1[8]	0.1[8]	0.1[8]	317 238[19]	732	...	317 970
China, Hong Kong SAR Chine, RAS de Hong Kong	2005	2 721 235	39.9	36.2	43.2	1 934[3]	1 097[3]	...	3 031[3]
	2010	2 779 950	39.6	34.8	43.8	154[3]	486[3]	3[3]	643[3]
	2015	2 838 665	39.2	33.4	44.1	151	9 940	1	10 092
	2016	...	...	...	...	140	2 315	1	2 456
	2017	2 883 051	39.1	33.6	43.9	93	...	1	94
China, Macao SAR Chine, RAS de Macao	2005	279 308	57.9	56.9	58.8	...	...	...	...
	2010	318 506	59.3	56.8	61.6	...	9[3]	1[3]	10[3]
	2015	342 703	57.0	54.0	59.8	...	6	...	6
	2017	353 654	56.8	53.8	59.6	...	5	...	5
Colombia Colombie	2005	107 612	0.2	0.3	0.2	155[3]	41[3]	2 000 009[3]	2 000 205[3]
	2010	124 271	0.3	0.3	0.3	212[3]	167[3]	3 672 065[3]	3 672 444[3]
	2015	139 134	0.3	0.3	0.3	219	56	6 520 304	6 520 579
	2017	142 319	0.3	0.3	0.3	258	542	7 524 010	7 524 810
Comoros Comores	2005	13 209	2.2	2.0	2.3	1[3]	...	...	1[3]
	2010	12 618	1.8	1.7	1.9	...	...	...	...
	2015	12 555	1.6	1.5	1.7	...	...	...	...
	2017	12 555	1.5	1.5	1.6	...	...	...	...
Congo Congo	2005	315 238	8.5	9.2	7.7	66 075[3]	3 486[3]	8 079[3]	77 640[3]
	2010	419 649	9.6	10.4	8.7	133 112[3]	5 524[3]	59[3]	138 695[3]
	2015	392 996	7.9	8.6	7.1	61 492	3 248	1 070	65 810
	2017	398 890	7.6	8.3	6.9	47 436	6 903	84 398	138 737
Cook Islands Îles Cook	2005	3 277	16.6	...	...	...	...	...	...
	2010	3 769	20.3	...	...	...	...	...	...
	2015	4 152	23.8	...	...	...	...	...	...
	2017	4 213	24.2	...	...	...	...	...	...
Costa Rica Costa Rica	2005	358 175[6]	8.4[6]	8.3[6]	8.6[6]	11 253[3]	223[3]	...	11 476[3]
	2010	405 404[6]	8.9[6]	8.6[6]	9.2[6]	19 505[3]	375[3]	40[3]	19 920[3]
	2015	411 697[6]	8.6[6]	8.2[6]	8.9[6]	3 475	1 819	2 613	7 907
	2017	414 214[6]	8.4[6]	8.1[6]	8.8[6]	4 414	5 594	216	10 224
Côte d'Ivoire Côte d'Ivoire	2005	2 010 824[8]	11.0[8]	11.8[8]	10.0[8]	41 627[3]	2 443[3]	71 050[3]	115 120[3]
	2010	2 095 185[8]	10.3[8]	11.1[8]	9.4[8]	26 218[3]	256[3]	538 068[3]	564 542[3]
	2015	2 175 399[8]	9.4[8]	10.3[8]	8.5[8]	1 972	667	724 131	726 770
	2017	2 197 152[8]	9.0[8]	9.9[8]	8.2[8]	1 468	342	698 343	700 153
Croatia Croatie	2005	579 273[6]	13.2[6]	12.9[6]	13.6[6]	2 927[3]	8[3]	7 932[3]	10 867[3]
	2010	573 248[6]	13.2[6]	12.9[6]	13.6[6]	936[3]	81[3]	24 463[3]	25 480[3]
	2015	575 738[6]	13.6[6]	13.1[6]	14.1[6]	710	90	16 684	17 484
	2017	560 483[6]	13.4[6]	12.8[6]	13.9[6]	346	605	12 489	13 440
Cuba Cuba	2005	17 023	0.2	0.1	0.2	706[3]	32[3]	...	738[3]
	2010	14 818	0.1	0.1	0.1	411[3]	11[3]	1[3]	423[3]
	2015	13 336	0.1	0.1	0.1	313	12	...	325
	2017	13 136	0.1	0.1	0.1	325	20	...	345
Curaçao Curaçao	2010	34 627	23.5	21.0	25.6	7[3]	2[3]	...	9[3]
	2015	37 611	23.8	21.4	25.8	44	41	...	85
	2017	38 396	23.9	21.5	26.0	62	107	...	169

4 International migrants and refugees *(continued)*
International migrant stock (number and percentage) and refugees and others of concern to UNHCR

Migrants internationaux et réfugiés *(suite)*
Stock de migrants internationaux (nombre et pourcentage) et réfugiés et autres personnes relevant de la compétence du HCR

Region, country or area Région, pays ou zone	Year Année	International Migrant Stock (mid-year) Stock de migrants internationaux (milieu de l'année) Total Total	% of total pop. % de la pop. totale MF/HF	M/H	F	Refugees and others of concern to UNHCR (mid-year) Réfugiés et autres personnes relevant de la compétence du HCR (milieu de l'année) Refugees& Réfugiés&	Asylum seekers Demandeurs d'asile	Other&& Autres&&	Total pop. Pop. totale
Cyprus Chypre	2005	117 165[20]	11.4[20]	9.7[20]	13.2[20]	701[3]	13 067[3]	1[3]	13 769[3]
	2010	188 472[20]	16.9[20]	14.8[20]	19.0[20]	3 394[3]	5 396[3]	...	8 790[3]
	2015	192 020[20]	16.5[20]	14.5[20]	18.6[20]	5 763	2 339	6 000	14 102
	2017	188 973[20]	16.0[20]	14.0[20]	18.0[20]	9 238	3 812	6 000	19 050
Czechia Tchéquie	2005	322 540[8]	3.1[8]	3.6[8]	2.7[8]	1 802[3]	924[3]	...	2 726[3]
	2010	398 493[8]	3.8[8]	4.6[8]	3.0[8]	2 449[3]	1 065[3]	1[3]	3 515[3]
	2015	416 454[8]	3.9[8]	4.6[8]	3.3[8]	3 137[11]	409	1 502	5 048
	2017	433 290[8]	4.1[8]	4.8[8]	3.4[8]	3 644	827	1 502	5 973
Dem. People's Rep. Korea Rép. pop. dém. de Corée	*2005	40 097	0.2	0.2	0.2	...	...	...	...
	*2010	44 010	0.2	0.2	0.2	...	...	...	...
	*2015	48 458	0.2	0.2	0.2	...	...	...	...
	*2017	48 939	0.2	0.2	0.2	...	...	...	...
Dem. Rep. of the Congo Rép. dém. du Congo	2005	622 869[6]	1.1[6]	1.1[6]	1.2[6]	204 341[3]	140[3]	47 435[3]	251 916[3]
	2010	588 950[6]	0.9[6]	0.9[6]	0.9[6]	166 336[3]	932[3]	2 196 591[3]	2 363 859[3]
	2015	824 492[6]	1.1[6]	1.1[6]	1.1[6]	* 160 271	1 124	1 839 611	2 001 006
	2017	879 223[6]	1.1[6]	1.1[6]	1.1[6]	533 656[21]	1 218	3 998 573	4 533 447
Denmark Danemark	2005	440 383	8.1	7.9	8.3	44 374[3]	510[3]	573[3]	45 457[3]
	2010	509 740	9.2	8.9	9.4	17 922[3]	3 363[3]	3 238[3]	24 523[3]
	2015	595 876	10.5	10.3	10.6	17 785[11]	4 566	4 984	27 335
	2017	656 789	11.5	11.4	11.5	34 977	4 502	7 610	47 089
Djibouti Djibouti	2005	92 091[6]	11.8[6]	13.0[6]	10.5[6]	10 456[3]	19[3]	7 668[3]	18 143[3]
	2010	101 575[6]	11.9[6]	12.5[6]	11.4[6]	15 104[3]	732[3]	7[3]	15 843[3]
	2015	112 351[6]	12.1[6]	12.7[6]	11.5[6]	14 787	2 586	...	17 373
	2017	116 089[6]	12.1[6]	12.7[6]	11.6[6]	18 548	8 579	97	27 224
Dominica Dominique	2005	4 744	6.7	...	...	...	...	...	...
	2010	5 765	8.1	...	...	...	...	...	...
	2015	6 720	9.2	...	...	...	...	...	...
	2017	6 782	9.2	...	...	...	...	...	...
Dominican Republic République dominicaine	2005	376 001	4.1	4.9	3.2	...	...	...	...
	2010	393 720	4.0	4.8	3.1	599[3]	1 759[3]	...	2 358[3]
	2015	415 564	3.9	4.8	3.1	609[22]	752[22]	133 770[22]	135 131[22]
	2017	424 964	3.9	4.8	3.1	592	835	...	1 427
Ecuador Équateur	2005	187 404[6]	1.4[6]	1.4[6]	1.3[6]	10 063[3]	2 489[3]	250 001[3]	262 553[3]
	2010	325 366[6]	2.2[6]	2.2[6]	2.1[6]	121 249[3]	49 887[3]	...	171 136[3]
	2015	387 513[6]	2.4[6]	2.5[6]	2.3[6]	121 535[3]	11 583[3]	...	133 118[3]
	2017	399 068[6]	2.4[6]	2.5[6]	2.3[6]	102 610	19 006	...	121 616
Egypt Égypte	2005	274 001[6]	0.4[6]	0.4[6]	0.3[6]	88 946[3]	11 005[3]	203[3]	100 154[3]
	2010	295 714[6]	0.4[6]	0.4[6]	0.3[6]	95 056[3]	14 303[3]	570[3]	109 929[3]
	2015	565 931[6]	0.6[6]	0.7[6]	0.5[6]	226 344	30 019	21	256 384
	2017	478 310[6]	0.5[6]	0.5[6]	0.5[6]	223 964	54 465	18	278 447
El Salvador El Salvador	2005	36 019[6]	0.6[6]	0.6[6]	0.6[6]	49[3]	1[3]	44[3]	94[3]
	2010	40 324[6]	0.7[6]	0.7[6]	0.7[6]	38[3]	18[3]	...	56[3]
	2015	42 045[6]	0.7[6]	0.7[6]	0.7[6]	48	...	...	48
	2017	42 323[6]	0.7[6]	0.7[6]	0.7[6]	43	3	3 322	3 368
Equatorial Guinea [8] Guinée équatoriale [8]	2005	6 588	0.9	0.9	0.8	...	...	...	...
	2010	8 658	0.9	0.9	0.9	...	...	...	...
	2015	209 611	17.8	24.9	9.1	...	...	...	...
	2017	221 865	17.5	24.4	9.0	...	...	...	...
Eritrea Érythrée	2005	* 14 314	* 0.4	* 0.4	* 0.3	4 418[3]	1 591[3]	31[3]	6 040[3]
	2010	* 15 676	* 0.4	* 0.4	* 0.3	4 809[3]	137[3]	13[3]	4 959[3]
	2015	* 15 941	* 0.3	* 0.4	* 0.3	2 944	1	22	2 967
	2016	...	...	...	...	2 293	5	6	2 304
	2017	* 16 041	* 0.3	* 0.4	* 0.3	2 381	...	19	2 400
Estonia Estonie	2005	233 701	17.2	15.0	19.2	7[3]	8[3]	136 000[3]	136 015[3]
	2010	217 890	16.4	14.1	18.3	39[3]	10[3]	100 983[3]	101 032[3]
	2015	194 664	14.8	13.0	16.4	117	117	86 522[23]	86 756
	2017	192 962	14.7	13.1	16.1	402	43	81 382[23]	81 827

International migrants and refugees *(continued)*

International migrant stock (number and percentage) and refugees and others of concern to UNHCR

Migrants internationaux et réfugiés *(suite)*

Stock de migrants internationaux (nombre et pourcentage) et réfugiés et autres personnes relevant de la compétence du HCR

Region, country or area Région, pays ou zone	Year Année	International Migrant Stock (mid-year) Stock de migrants internationaux (milieu de l'année) Total Total	% of total pop. % de la pop. totale MF/HF	M/H	F	Refugees and others of concern to UNHCR (mid-year) Réfugiés et autres personnes relevant de la compétence du HCR (milieu de l'année) Refugees& Réfugiés&	Asylum seekers Demandeurs d'asile	Other&& Autres&&	Total pop. Pop. totale
Eswatini	2005	27 097[6]	2.5[6]	2.8[6]	2.2[6]	760[3]	256[3]	...	1 016[3]
Eswatini	2010	30 476[6]	2.5[6]	2.7[6]	2.4[6]	759[3]	...	...	759[3]
	2015	31 993[6]	2.4[6]	2.6[6]	2.3[6]	539	321	4	864
	2017	33 263[6]	2.4[6]	2.6[6]	2.3[6]	770	462	10	1 242
Ethiopia	2005	514 242[6]	0.7[6]	0.7[6]	0.6[6]	100 817[3]	209[3]	4 110[3]	105 136[3]
Éthiopie	2010	567 720[6]	0.6[6]	0.7[6]	0.6[6]	154 295[3]	1 028[3]	47[3]	155 370[3]
	2015	1 162 576[6]	1.2[6]	1.2[6]	1.1[6]	702 467	2 871	348	705 686
	2017	1 227 143[6]	1.2[6]	1.2[6]	1.1[6]	841 285	1 929	536	843 750
Falkland Islands (Malvinas)	2005	1 166	39.7	...	...	...	...	...	...
Îles Falkland (Malvinas)	2010	1 436	50.4	...	...	...	...	...	...
	2015	1 571	54.2	...	...	...	...	...	...
	2017	1 579	54.3	...	...	...	...	...	...
Faroe Islands	2005	4 583	9.5	...	...	...	...	...	...
Îles Féroé	2010	5 096	10.5	...	...	...	...	...	...
	2015	5 517	11.3	...	...	...	...	...	...
	2017	5 735	11.6	...	...	...	...	...	...
Fiji	2005	12 435	1.5	1.6	1.5	...	...	...	...
Fidji	2010	13 351	1.6	1.6	1.5	1[3]	6[3]	...	7[3]
	2015	13 751	1.5	1.6	1.4	12	8	...	20
	2017	13 911	1.5	1.6	1.4	11	4	...	15
Finland	2005	192 169[24]	3.7[24]	3.7[24]	3.6[24]	11 809[3]	...	849[3]	12 658[3]
Finlande	2010	248 135[24]	4.6[24]	4.8[24]	4.5[24]	8 724[3]	2 097[3]	3 133[3]	13 954[3]
	2015	314 856[24]	5.7[24]	5.9[24]	5.6[24]	11 798[11]	2 622	1 928	16 348
	2017	343 582[24]	6.2[24]	6.4[24]	6.0[24]	19 939	3 520	2 671	26 130
France	2005	6 737 600	11.0	11.0	11.0	137 316[3]	41 279[3]	946[3]	179 541[3]
France	2010	7 196 481	11.4	11.3	11.5	200 687[3]	48 576[3]	1 171[3]	250 434[3]
	2015	7 918 382	12.3	12.1	12.5	264 972	53 827	1 290	320 089
	2017	7 902 783	12.2	11.9	12.4	321 119	55 606	1 363	378 088
French Guiana	2005	86 468	42.4	42.3	42.5	...	...	...	...
Guyane française	2010	96 288	41.1	39.8	42.4	...	...	...	...
	2015	106 108	39.5	37.5	41.5	...	...	...	...
	2017	111 718	39.5	37.5	41.5	...	...	...	...
French Polynesia	2005	32 286	12.7	14.1	11.2	...	...	...	...
Polynésie française	2010	31 640	11.8	13.2	10.4	...	...	...	...
	2015	30 058	10.8	12.1	9.5	...	...	...	...
	2017	30 687	10.8	12.1	9.5	...	...	...	...
Gabon	2005	214 123[8]	15.3[8]	17.4[8]	13.1[8]	8 545[3]	4 843[3]	291[3]	13 679[3]
Gabon	2010	243 992[8]	14.9[8]	16.7[8]	13.0[8]	9 015[3]	4 132[3]	84[3]	13 231[3]
	2015	268 384[8]	13.9[8]	15.4[8]	12.3[8]	1 008	1 886	...	2 894
	2017	280 197[8]	13.8[8]	15.4[8]	12.2[8]	957	105	3	1 065
Gambia	2005	181 905	12.6	13.4	11.8	7 330[3]	602[3]	42[3]	7 974[3]
Gambie	2010	185 763	11.0	11.7	10.3	8 378[3]	74[3]	31[3]	8 483[3]
	2015	192 540	9.7	10.4	9.1	11 773	2	...	11 775
	2017	205 063	9.8	10.4	9.1	7 973	5	33	8 011
Georgia	2005	72 311[25]	1.6[25]	1.5[25]	1.7[25]	2 497[3]	8[3]	236 097[3]	238 602[3]
Géorgie	2010	73 034[25]	1.7[25]	1.6[25]	1.8[25]	639[3]	44[3]	361 547[3]	362 230[3]
	2015	76 685[25]	1.9[25]	1.8[25]	2.1[25]	1 659	587	266 060	268 306
	2017	78 218[25]	2.0[25]	1.8[25]	2.2[25]	2 167	344	276 271	278 782
Germany	2005	9 402 447	11.5	11.7	11.3	700 016[3]	71 624[3]	12 340[3]	783 980[3]
Allemagne	2010	9 812 263	12.1	12.2	12.0	594 269[3]	51 991[3]	24 378[3]	670 638[3]
	2015	10 220 418	12.5	12.5	12.5	250 299	311 551	11 978	573 828
	2017	12 165 083	14.8	15.0	14.7	864 686	459 503	12 957	1 337 146
Ghana	2005	304 436	1.4	1.5	1.3	53 537[3]	5 496[3]	1 212[3]	60 245[3]
Ghana	2010	337 017	1.4	1.4	1.3	13 828[3]	749[3]	184[3]	14 761[3]
	2015	399 471	1.4	1.5	1.4	18 476	2 855	...	21 331
	2016	...	...	...	...	16 409	2 048	8 871	27 328
	2017	417 642	1.4	1.5	1.4	11 976	1 376	...	13 352

4

International migrants and refugees *(continued)*

International migrant stock (number and percentage) and refugees and others of concern to UNHCR

Migrants internationaux et réfugiés *(suite)*

Stock de migrants internationaux (nombre et pourcentage) et réfugiés et autres personnes relevant de la compétence du HCR

Region, country or area Région, pays ou zone	Year Année	International Migrant Stock (mid-year) Stock de migrants internationaux (milieu de l'année) Total Total	% of total pop. % de la pop. totale MF/HF	M/H	F	Refugees and others of concern to UNHCR (mid-year) Réfugiés et autres personnes relevant de la compétence du HCR (milieu de l'année) Refugees& Réfugiés&	Asylum seekers Demandeurs d'asile	Other&& Autres&&	Total pop. Pop. totale
Gibraltar Gibraltar	2005	9 211	28.7	...	...	...	...	...	...
	2010	10 369	31.2	...	...	...	...	...	...
	2015	11 065	32.3	...	...	...	...	...	...
	2017	11 152	32.3	...	...	...	...	...	...
Greece Grèce	2005	1 190 707	10.5	10.5	10.6	2 390[3]	8 867[3]	3 000[3]	14 257[3]
	2010	1 321 149	11.5	11.4	11.7	1 444[3]	55 724[3]	260[3]	57 428[3]
	2015	1 242 924	11.1	10.3	11.8	8 231	29 157	214	37 602
	2017	1 220 395	10.9	10.1	11.7	41 977	38 277	73	80 327
Greenland Groenland	2005	6 686	11.7	...	...	...	...	...	...
	2010	6 226	11.0	...	...	...	...	...	...
	2015	6 009	10.7	...	...	...	...	...	...
	2017	6 014	10.6	...	...	...	...	...	...
Grenada Grenade	2005	6 902	6.7	6.7	6.7	...	...	...	...
	2010	6 980	6.7	6.6	6.7	...	3[3]	...	3[3]
	2015	7 057	6.6	6.5	6.7	...	...	...	...
	2017	7 124	6.6	6.5	6.7	1	1	...	2
Guadeloupe [26] Guadeloupe [26]	2005	89 065	20.3	19.4	21.1	...	...	...	...
	2010	94 942	21.1	20.3	21.7	...	...	...	...
	2015	98 507	21.9	21.0	22.6	...	...	...	...
	2017	99 350	22.1	21.2	22.9	...	...	...	...
Guam Guam	2005	74 743	47.2	47.8	46.5	...	...	...	...
	2010	75 416	47.3	48.0	46.5	...	...	...	...
	2015	76 089	47.0	47.9	46.2	...	...	...	...
	2017	78 027	47.5	48.4	46.6	...	...	...	...
Guatemala Guatemala	2005	57 252[6]	0.4[6]	0.4[6]	0.5[6]	391[3]	3[3]	...	394[3]
	2010	66 384[6]	0.5[6]	0.4[6]	0.5[6]	138[3]	2[3]	...	140[3]
	2015	78 352[6]	0.5[6]	0.5[6]	0.5[6]	202	73	...	275
	2017	81 528[6]	0.5[6]	0.5[6]	0.5[6]	312	41	21 600	21 953
Guinea Guinée	2005	229 611[6,8]	2.4[6,8]	2.3[6,8]	2.4[6,8]	63 525[3]	3 808[3]	29 645[3]	96 978[3]
	2010	177 998[6,8]	1.6[6,8]	1.7[6,8]	1.6[6,8]	14 113[3]	764[3]	117[3]	14 994[3]
	2015	126 386[6,8]	1.0[6,8]	1.2[6,8]	0.9[6,8]	8 704	293	...	8 997
	2017	122 796[6,8]	1.0[6,8]	1.1[6,8]	0.8[6,8]	5 105	105	1	5 211
Guinea-Bissau Guinée-Bissau	2005	20 736[6]	1.5[6]	1.5[6]	1.5[6]	7 616[3]	166[3]	...	7 782[3]
	2010	21 061[6]	1.4[6]	1.4[6]	1.4[6]	7 679[3]	330[3]	5[3]	8 014[3]
	2015	22 333[6]	1.3[6]	1.2[6]	1.3[6]	8 684	123	...	8 807
	2017	23 405[6]	1.3[6]	1.2[6]	1.3[6]	9 323	27	...	9 350
Guyana Guyana	2005	10 868	1.4	1.5	1.3	...	...	...	...
	2010	13 126	1.8	1.9	1.6	7[3]	...	...	7[3]
	2015	15 384	2.0	2.1	1.9	11	1	...	12
	2017	15 530	2.0	2.1	1.9	11	...	...	11
Haiti Haïti	2005	30 468	0.3	0.4	0.3	...	...	...	...
	2010	35 104	0.4	0.4	0.3	...	4[3]	...	4[3]
	2015	39 529	0.4	0.4	0.3	5	5	...	10
	2017	40 533	0.4	0.4	0.3	5	22	2 710[27]	2 737
Holy See Saint-Siège	*2005	798	100.0	...	...	...	...	...	...
	*2010	794	100.0	...	...	...	...	...	...
	*2015	803	100.0	...	...	...	...	...	...
	*2017	792	100.0	...	...	...	...	...	...
Honduras Honduras	2005	27 875[6]	0.4[6]	0.4[6]	0.4[6]	22[3]	50[3]	...	72[3]
	2010	27 288[6]	0.3[6]	0.4[6]	0.3[6]	14[3]	...	1[3]	15[3]
	2015	38 317[6]	0.4[6]	0.5[6]	0.4[6]	23	19	...	42
	2017	38 700[6]	0.4[6]	0.4[6]	0.4[6]	22	12	175 600	175 634
Hungary Hongrie	2005	366 787[6]	3.6[6]	3.6[6]	3.6[6]	8 046[3]	684[3]	192[3]	8 922[3]
	2010	436 616[6]	4.4[6]	4.5[6]	4.3[6]	5 414[3]	367[3]	62[3]	5 843[3]
	2015	475 508[6]	4.9[6]	5.1[6]	4.7[6]	4 192	24 431	128	28 751
	2017	503 787[6]	5.2[6]	5.4[6]	4.9[6]	5 069	754	137	5 960

International migrants and refugees *(continued)*

International migrant stock (number and percentage) and refugees and others of concern to UNHCR

Migrants internationaux et réfugiés *(suite)*

Stock de migrants internationaux (nombre et pourcentage) et réfugiés et autres personnes relevant de la compétence du HCR

Region, country or area Région, pays ou zone	Year Année	International Migrant Stock (mid-year) Stock de migrants internationaux (milieu de l'année) Total Total	% of total pop. % de la pop. totale MF/HF	M/H	F	Refugees and others of concern to UNHCR (mid-year) Réfugiés et autres personnes relevant de la compétence du HCR (milieu de l'année) Refugees& Réfugiés&	Asylum seekers Demandeurs d'asile	Other&& Autres&&	Total pop. Pop. totale
Iceland Islande	2005	25 492	8.6	8.4	8.9	293[3]	29[3]	53[3]	375[3]
	2010	35 091	11.0	10.9	11.0	83[3]	39[3]	113[3]	235[3]
	2015	39 072	11.8	11.5	12.2	104	225	119	448
	2017	41 853	12.5	12.3	12.7	308	366	85	759
India Inde	2005	5 923 642[6]	0.5[6]	0.5[6]	0.5[6]	139 283[3]	303[3]	2 792[3]	142 378[3]
	2010	5 436 012[6]	0.4[6]	0.4[6]	0.4[6]	184 821[3]	3 746[3]	5 109[3]	193 676[3]
	2015	5 240 960[6]	0.4[6]	0.4[6]	0.4[6]	200 383	5 381	…	205 764
	2017	5 188 550[6]	0.4[6]	0.4[6]	0.4[6]	196 662	9 814	…	206 476
Indonesia Indonésie	2005	289 568[6]	0.1[6]	0.1[6]	0.1[6]	89[3]	58[3]	263[3]	410[3]
	2010	305 416[6]	0.1[6]	0.1[6]	0.1[6]	811[3]	2 071[3]	12[3]	2 894[3]
	2015	338 124[6]	0.1[6]	0.2[6]	0.1[6]	5 277	7 911	…	13 188
	2017	345 930[6]	0.1[6]	0.2[6]	0.1[6]	8 819	5 274	…	14 093
Iran (Islamic Republic of) Iran (Rép. islamique d')	2005	2 568 930[6]	3.6[6]	3.9[6]	3.4[6]	974 302[3]	140[3]	344 914[3]	1 319 356[3]
	2010	2 761 561[6]	3.7[6]	4.2[6]	3.2[6]	1 073 366[3]	1 775[3]	10 168[3]	1 085 309[3]
	2015	2 726 420[6]	3.4[6]	3.6[6]	3.3[6]	979 441	42	8	979 491
	2017	2 699 155[6]	3.3[6]	3.5[6]	3.1[6]	978 698	84	3	978 785
Iraq Iraq	2005	132 915[6,8]	0.5[6,8]	0.6[6,8]	0.4[6,8]	50 177[3]	1 948[3]	1 526 104[3]	1 578 229[3]
	2010	117 389[6,8]	0.4[6,8]	0.5[6,8]	0.3[6,8]	34 655[3]	3 073[3]	1 758 603[3]	1 796 331[3]
	2015	359 381[6,8]	1.0[6,8]	1.1[6,8]	0.8[6,8]	288 035	7 420	4 016 205[28]	4 311 660
	2017	366 568[6,8]	1.0[6,8]	1.1[6,8]	0.8[6,8]	273 516	12 680	4 640 941[29]	4 927 137
Ireland Irlande	2005	589 046	14.0	14.7	13.2	7 113[3]	2 414[3]	4[3]	9 531[3]
	2010	730 542	15.8	15.6	15.9	9 107[3]	5 129[3]	1[3]	14 237[3]
	2015	749 943	16.0	15.4	16.5	6 125[3]	4 267[3]	100[3]	10 492[3]
	2017	806 549	16.9	16.7	17.2	5 731	5 123	100	10 954
Isle of Man Île de Man	2005	41 475	54.5	…	…	…	…	…	…
	2010	43 447	54.3	…	…	…	…	…	…
	2015	45 221	54.4	…	…	…	…	…	…
	2017	45 872	54.4	…	…	…	…	…	…
Israel Israël	2005	1 889 503[6]	28.6[6]	26.6[6]	30.5[6]	609[3]	939[3]	…	1 548[3]
	2010	1 950 615[6]	26.3[6]	24.3[6]	28.2[6]	25 471[3]	5 575[3]	9[3]	31 055[3]
	2015	2 011 727[6]	24.9[6]	22.8[6]	27.0[6]	38 500	6 591	88	45 179
	2017	1 962 123[6]	23.6[6]	21.5[6]	25.6[6]	35 851	27 759	42	63 652
Italy Italie	2005	3 954 785	6.7	6.4	7.1	20 675[3]	…	940[3]	21 615[3]
	2010	5 787 898	9.7	9.2	10.2	56 397[3]	4 076[3]	858[3]	61 331[3]
	2015	5 805 325	9.8	9.1	10.4	93 715[11]	48 307	606	142 628
	2017	5 907 461	10.0	9.3	10.6	157 839	134 327	715	292 881
Jamaica Jamaïque	2005	24 314	0.9	0.9	0.9	…	…	…	…
	2010	23 677	0.8	0.9	0.8	21[3]	…	…	21[3]
	2015	23 167	0.8	0.8	0.8	15	3	…	18
	2017	23 332	0.8	0.8	0.8	15	9	…	24
Japan Japon	2005	2 012 916[8]	1.6[8]	1.5[8]	1.7[8]	1 941[3]	533[3]	1 770[3]	4 244[3]
	2010	2 134 151[8]	1.7[8]	1.5[8]	1.8[8]	2 586[3]	3 047[3]	1 397[3]	7 030[3]
	2015	2 232 189[8]	1.7[8]	1.6[8]	1.9[8]	* 2 419	* 10 705	* 631	* 13 755
	2017	2 321 476[8]	1.8[8]	1.7[8]	2.0[8]	* 2 530	* 24 679	* 626	* 27 835
Jordan Jordanie	2005	2 325 414[6,8]	40.7[6,8]	40.1[6,8]	41.3[6,8]	965[3]	16 570[3]	329[3]	17 864[3]
	2010	2 722 983[6,8]	37.9[6,8]	37.8[6,8]	38.0[6,8]	450 915[3]	2 159[3]	107[3]	453 181[3]
	2015	3 112 026[6,8]	34.0[6,8]	33.8[6,8]	34.2[6,8]	664 102[30]	20 693	…	684 795
	2017	3 233 553[6,8]	33.3[6,8]	33.1[6,8]	33.5[6,8]	692 240[30]	40 876	…	733 116[30]
Kazakhstan Kazakhstan	2005	3 102 962	20.0	19.7	20.2	7 265[3]	65[3]	50 598[3]	57 928[3]
	2010	3 334 623	20.3	20.5	20.2	4 406[3]	314[3]	7 969[3]	12 689[3]
	2015	3 546 778	20.0	20.5	19.5	662	149	7 038	7 849
	2017	3 635 168	20.0	20.4	19.5	622	191	7 209	8 022
Kenya Kenya	2005	756 894[6]	2.1[6]	2.2[6]	2.0[6]	251 271[3]	16 460[3]	481[3]	268 212[3]
	2010	926 959[6]	2.2[6]	2.2[6]	2.2[6]	402 905[3]	27 966[3]	320 083[3]	750 954[3]
	2015	1 084 357[6]	2.3[6]	2.3[6]	2.3[6]	552 272	40 341	21 231	613 844
	2017	1 078 572[6]	2.2[6]	2.2[6]	2.2[6]	433 457	52 554	18 500	504 511

4

International migrants and refugees *(continued)*

International migrant stock (number and percentage) and refugees and others of concern to UNHCR

Migrants internationaux et réfugiés *(suite)*

Stock de migrants internationaux (nombre et pourcentage) et réfugiés et autres personnes relevant de la compétence du HCR

Region, country or area Région, pays ou zone	Year Année	International Migrant Stock (mid-year) Stock de migrants internationaux (milieu de l'année) Total Total	% of total pop. % de la pop. totale MF/HF	M/H	F	Refugees and others of concern to UNHCR (mid-year) Réfugiés et autres personnes relevant de la compétence du HCR (milieu de l'année) Refugees[&] Réfugiés[&]	Asylum seekers Demandeurs d'asile	Other[&&] Autres[&&]	Total pop. Pop. totale
Kiribati	2005	2 487	2.7	2.9	2.5	...	...	...	...
Kiribati	2010	2 868	2.8	3.0	2.6	...	...	...	...
	2015	2 919	2.6	2.8	2.4	...	...	...	...
	2017	3 022	2.6	2.8	2.4	...	...	...	...
Kuwait	2005	1 333 327[6,8]	58.6[6,8]	68.3[6,8]	44.5[6,8]	1 523[3]	203[3]	101 000[3]	102 726[3]
Koweït	2010	1 871 537[6,8]	62.4[6,8]	75.6[6,8]	44.4[6,8]	184[3]	3 275[3]	93 000[3]	96 459[3]
	2015	2 866 136[6,8]	72.8[6,8]	83.5[6,8]	58.4[6,8]	593	1 040	93 000	94 633
	2017	3 123 431[6,8]	75.5[6,8]	89.4[6,8]	56.8[6,8]	844	810	93 000	94 654
Kyrgyzstan	2005	312 897	6.2	5.1	7.2	2 598[3]	498[3]	100 004[3]	103 100[3]
Kirghizistan	2010	231 511	4.3	3.5	5.0	2 458[3]	554[3]	301 164[3]	304 176[3]
	2015	204 382	3.5	2.8	4.1	433	168	13 678	14 279
	2017	200 294	3.3	2.7	3.9	350	102	2 272	2 724
Lao People's Dem. Rep. [6,8]	2005	20 371	0.4	0.4	0.3	...	...	...	...
Rép. dém. populaire lao [6,8]	2010	32 473	0.5	0.6	0.5	...	...	...	...
	2015	44 575	0.7	0.7	0.6	...	...	...	...
	2017	45 466	0.7	0.7	0.6	...	...	...	...
Latvia	2005	376 725	16.7	15.0	18.2	11[3]	9[3]	418 638[3]	418 658[3]
Lettonie	2010	313 786	14.8	12.8	16.5	68[3]	53[3]	326 906[3]	327 027[3]
	2015	265 418	13.3	11.4	15.0	195	171	262 802[31]	263 168
	2017	256 889	13.2	11.3	14.8	546	126	242 736[32]	243 408[32]
Lebanon	2005	756 784[6]	19.0[6]	19.3[6]	18.7[6]	1 078[3]	1 450[3]	451[3]	2 979[3]
Liban	2010	820 655[6]	18.9[6]	19.3[6]	18.5[6]	8 063[3]	1 417[3]	40[3]	9 520[3]
	2015	1 973 204[6]	33.7[6]	32.3[6]	35.2[6]	1 172 388	10 851	5 813	1 189 052
	2017	1 939 212[6]	31.9[6]	30.6[6]	33.2[6]	1 003 076	13 630	4 314	1 021 020
Lesotho	2005[6,8]	6 290	0.3	0.4	0.3	...	...	...	...
Lesotho	2010[6,8]	6 414	0.3	0.4	0.3	...	...	...	...
	2015	6 572[6,8]	0.3[6,8]	0.3[6,8]	0.3[6,8]	44	1	...	45
	2017	6 749[6,8]	0.3[6,8]	0.3[6,8]	0.3[6,8]	59	3	...	62
Liberia	2005	87 188	2.7	3.1	2.2	10 168[3]	29[3]	498 604[3]	508 801[3]
Libéria	2010	99 129	2.5	2.9	2.2	24 743[3]	28[3]	1 855[3]	26 626[3]
	2015	113 779	2.5	2.9	2.2	38 904	18	1 486	40 408
	2017	98 630	2.1	2.4	1.8	13 380	22	374	13 776
Libya	2005	625 212[8]	10.8[8]	14.9[8]	6.4[8]	12 166[3]	200[3]	35[3]	12 401[3]
Libye	2010	683 998[8]	11.1[8]	15.5[8]	6.4[8]	7 923[3]	3 194[3]	37[3]	11 154[3]
	2015	771 146[8]	12.4[8]	17.4[8]	7.2[8]	27 948	8 904	434 869	471 721
	2017	788 419[8]	12.4[8]	17.5[8]	7.2[8]	9 450	32 430	300 019	341 899
Liechtenstein	2005	18 898	54.2	...	...	150[3]	60[3]	...	210[3]
Liechtenstein	2010	22 342	62.1	...	...	92[3]	44[3]	6[3]	142[3]
	2015	23 799	63.6	...	...	107	75	2	184
	2017	24 683	65.1	...	...	177	113	...	290
Lithuania	2005	201 209	6.0	6.1	6.0	531[3]	55[3]	8 709[3]	9 295[3]
Lituanie	2010	160 772	5.1	4.8	5.4	803[3]	71[3]	3 679[3]	4 553[3]
	2015	136 021	4.6	4.3	5.0	1 055	54	3 583	4 692
	2017	124 706	4.3	3.9	4.7	1 283	144	3 251	4 678
Luxembourg	2005	150 618	32.9	33.2	32.6	1 822[3]	...	74[3]	1 896[3]
Luxembourg	2010	248 888	49.0	50.0	48.0	3 254[3]	697[3]	173[3]	4 124[3]
	2015	260 573	46.0	46.6	45.4	1 192	831	81	2 104
	2016[3]	...	...	...	...	2 046	2 213	83	4 342
	2017	264 073	45.3	45.8	44.7	...	...	...	...
Madagascar	2005[8]	26 058	0.1	0.2	0.1	...	...	...	...
Madagascar	2010	28 905[8]	0.1[8]	0.2[8]	0.1[8]	...	...	1[3]	1[3]
	2015	32 075[8]	0.1[8]	0.2[8]	0.1[8]	10	9	...	19
	2017	33 844[8]	0.1[8]	0.2[8]	0.1[8]	43	46	...	89
Malawi	2005	221 661[6]	1.7[6]	1.6[6]	1.8[6]	4 240[3]	5 331[3]	49[3]	9 620[3]
Malawi	2010	217 722[6]	1.4[6]	1.4[6]	1.5[6]	5 740[3]	9 362[3]	131[3]	15 233[3]
	2015	232 803[6]	1.3[6]	1.3[6]	1.4[6]	8 963	13 669	...	22 632
	2017	237 104[6]	1.3[6]	1.2[6]	1.3[6]	8 904	23 066	395	32 365

International migrants and refugees *(continued)*
International migrant stock (number and percentage) and refugees and others of concern to UNHCR

Migrants internationaux et réfugiés *(suite)*
Stock de migrants internationaux (nombre et pourcentage) et réfugiés et autres personnes relevant de la compétence du HCR

Region, country or area Région, pays ou zone	Year Année	International Migrant Stock (mid-year) Stock de migrants internationaux (milieu de l'année) Total Total	% of total pop. % de la pop. totale MF/HF	M/H	F	Refugees and others of concern to UNHCR (mid-year) Réfugiés et autres personnes relevant de la compétence du HCR (milieu de l'année) Refugees& Réfugiés&	Asylum seekers Demandeurs d'asile	Other&& Autres&&	Total pop. Pop. totale
Malaysia Malaisie	2005	1 722 344[6,8,33]	6.7[6,8,33]	7.6[6,8,33]	5.8[6,8,33]	33 693[3]	10 838[3]	61 555[3]	106 086[3]
	2010	2 406 011[6,8,33]	8.6[6,8,33]	9.9[6,8,33]	7.1[6,8,33]	81 516[3]	11 339[3]	120 015[3]	212 870[3]
	2015	2 650 617[6,8,33]	8.6[6,8,33]	10.1[6,8,33]	7.1[6,8,33]	97 573	54 400	120 000	271 973
	2017	2 703 629[6,8,33]	8.5[6,8,33]	10.0[6,8,33]	7.0[6,8,33]	95 903	51 764	90 558[34]	238 225
Maldives [8] Maldives [8]	2005	45 045	14.1	16.1	11.9	…	…	…	…
	2010	54 659	15.0	20.9	7.9	…	…	…	…
	2015	64 273	15.4	23.8	4.4	…	…	…	…
	2017	67 026	15.4	23.7	4.4	…	…	…	…
Mali Mali	2005	256 797[6]	2.0[6]	2.1[6]	1.9[6]	11 233[3]	1 833[3]	…	13 066[3]
	2010	336 607[6]	2.2[6]	2.3[6]	2.2[6]	13 558[3]	1 703[3]	…	15 261[3]
	2015	365 145[6]	2.1[6]	2.1[6]	2.0[6]	14 970	386	132 953	148 309
	2017	383 721[6]	2.1[6]	2.1[6]	2.0[6]	17 586	373	65 895	83 854
Malta Malte	2005	24 560	6.0	5.9	6.2	1 939[3]	149[3]	…	2 088[3]
	2010	33 008	7.9	8.3	7.6	6 136[3]	1 295[3]	…	7 431[3]
	2015	42 430	9.9	10.6	9.3	6 095	425	…	6 520
	2017	45 539	10.6	11.2	9.9	8 314	1 307	…	9 621
Marshall Islands Îles Marshall	2005	2 417	4.6	…	…	…	…	…	…
	2010	3 089	5.9	…	…	…	…	…	…
	2015	3 284	6.2	…	…	…	…	…	…
	2017	3 292	6.2	…	…	…	…	…	…
Martinique Martinique	2005	57 034	14.4	14.0	14.7	…	…	…	…
	2010	59 575	15.1	14.4	15.6	…	…	…	…
	2015	61 731	16.0	15.3	16.6	…	…	…	…
	2017	61 579	16.0	15.4	16.5	…	…	…	…
Mauritania Mauritanie	2005	58 119[6,8]	1.9[6,8]	2.1[6,8]	1.6[6,8]	632[3]	92[3]	29 500[3]	30 224[3]
	2010	84 679[6,8]	2.3[6,8]	2.7[6,8]	2.0[6,8]	26 717[3]	241[3]	9[3]	26 967[3]
	2015	166 552[6,8]	4.0[6,8]	4.5[6,8]	3.5[6,8]	76 851	407	…	77 258
	2017	168 438[6,8]	3.8[6,8]	4.3[6,8]	3.3[6,8]	79 029	706	…	79 735
Mauritius Maurice	2005[8,35]	19 647	1.6	1.5	1.7	…	…	…	…
	2010[8,35]	24 836	2.0	2.1	1.9	…	…	…	…
	2015[8,35]	28 585	2.3	2.5	2.0	…	…	…	…
	2017	28 713[8,35]	2.3[8,35]	2.5[8,35]	2.0[8,35]	3	…	…	3
Mayotte Mayotte	2005	63 176	35.5	35.7	35.2	…	…	…	…
	2010	72 757	34.9	33.8	35.9	…	…	…	…
	2015	73 992	30.8	29.0	32.6	…	…	…	…
	2017	74 399	29.4	27.7	31.1	…	…	…	…
Mexico Mexique	2005	712 487[6]	0.7[6]	0.7[6]	0.6[6]	3 229[3]	161[3]	…	3 390[3]
	2010	969 538[6]	0.8[6]	0.8[6]	0.8[6]	1 395[3]	172[3]	6[3]	1 573[3]
	2015	1 193 155[6]	0.9[6]	1.0[6]	0.9[6]	2 158	…	68	2 226
	2017	1 224 169[6]	0.9[6]	1.0[6]	0.9[6]	7 186	6 653	13	13 852
Micronesia (Fed. States of) Micronésie (États féd. de)	2005	2 905	2.7	2.9	2.6	…	…	…	…
	2010	2 805	2.7	2.8	2.6	…	…	…	…
	2015	2 756	2.6	2.8	2.5	…	34	…	34
	2016	…	…	…	…	3	1	…	4
	2017	2 785	2.6	2.8	2.5	4	…	…	4
Monaco Monaco	2005	21 312	63.1	…	…	…	…	…	…
	2010	21 132	57.0	…	…	…	1[3]	…	1[3]
	2015	21 042	54.9	…	…	33	…	…	33
	2016[3]	…	…	…	…	27	…	…	27
	2017	21 255	54.9	…	…	…	…	…	…
Mongolia Mongolie	2005	11 475[8]	0.5[8]	0.6[8]	0.3[8]	…	2[3]	581[3]	583[3]
	2010	16 061[8]	0.6[8]	0.9[8]	0.3[8]	12[3]	1[3]	260[3]	273[3]
	2015	17 620[8]	0.6[8]	0.9[8]	0.3[8]	11	5	16	32
	2017	18 204[8]	0.6[8]	0.9[8]	0.3[8]	8	3	19	30
Montenegro Monténégro	2010	78 507	12.6	10.3	14.8	16 364[3]	5[3]	1 886[3]	18 255[3]
	2015	82 541	13.1	10.8	15.4	6 203	7	13 602	19 812
	2017	70 984	11.3	9.0	13.5	919	57	12 005	12 981

4 International migrants and refugees *(continued)*

International migrant stock (number and percentage) and refugees and others of concern to UNHCR

Migrants internationaux et réfugiés *(suite)*

Stock de migrants internationaux (nombre et pourcentage) et réfugiés et autres personnes relevant de la compétence du HCR

Region, country or area Région, pays ou zone	Year Année	International Migrant Stock (mid-year) Stock de migrants internationaux (milieu de l'année) Total Total	% of total pop. % de la pop. totale MF/HF	M/H	F	Refugees and others of concern to UNHCR (mid-year) Réfugiés et autres personnes relevant de la compétence du HCR (milieu de l'année) Refugees& Réfugiés&	Asylum seekers Demandeurs d'asile	Other&& Autres&&	Total pop. Pop. totale
Montserrat Montserrat	2005	1 244	26.0	...	...	...	...	...	...
	2010	1 277	25.8	...	...	...	14[3]	...	14[3]
	2015	1 351	26.4	...	...	...	...	...	...
	2017	1 364	26.3	...	...	...	...	...	...
Morocco Maroc	2005	54 379[8]	0.2[8]	0.2[8]	0.2[8]	219[3]	1 843[3]	4[3]	2 066[3]
	2010	70 909[8]	0.2[8]	0.2[8]	0.2[8]	792[3]	280[3]	...	1 072[3]
	2015	92 424[8]	0.3[8]	0.3[8]	0.3[8]	2 144	2 216	...	4 360
	2017	95 835[8]	0.3[8]	0.3[8]	0.3[8]	5 167	1 887	...	7 054
Mozambique Mozambique	2005	204 830[6]	1.0[6]	1.0[6]	0.9[6]	1 954[3]	4 015[3]	40[3]	6 009[3]
	2010	214 612[6]	0.9[6]	0.9[6]	0.9[6]	4 077[3]	5 914[3]	1[3]	9 992[3]
	2015	238 930[6]	0.9[6]	0.9[6]	0.9[6]	4 552	14 257	7	18 816
	2017	246 954[6]	0.8[6]	0.8[6]	0.8[6]	4 787	16 324	21 543	42 654
Myanmar Myanmar	2005	83 025[8]	0.2[8]	0.2[8]	0.2[8]	...	...	236 495[3]	236 495[3]
	2010	76 414[8]	0.2[8]	0.2[8]	0.1[8]	...	...	859 403[3]	859 403[3]
	2015	73 308[8]	0.1[8]	0.2[8]	0.1[8]	...	...	1 466 501[36]	1 466 501
	2016	...	...	...	...	...	1	1 392 096[36]	1 392 097
	2017	74 660[8]	0.1[8]	0.2[8]	0.1[8]	...	...	1 277 777[37]	1 277 777
Namibia Namibie	2005	106 274	5.2	5.8	4.7	5 307[3]	1 073[3]	2 752[3]	9 132[3]
	2010	102 405	4.7	5.2	4.2	7 254[3]	1 421[3]	93[3]	8 768[3]
	2015	96 888	4.0	4.4	3.6	1 659	1 100	1 684	4 443
	2017	95 067	3.8	4.2	3.4	1 972	1 860	77	3 909
Nauru Nauru	2005[8]	2 253	22.3	...	...	...	...	...	...
	2010[8]	2 112	21.1	...	...	...	...	...	...
	2015	3 678[8]	32.7[8]	...	...	506[3]	290	...	796
	2017	3 710[8]	32.7[8]	...	...	506	302	...	808
Nepal Népal	2005	679 457[6]	2.7[6]	1.8[6]	3.4[6]	126 436[3]	1 272[3]	410 929[3]	538 637[3]
	2010	578 657[6]	2.1[6]	1.4[6]	2.8[6]	89 808[3]	938[3]	800 571[3]	891 317[3]
	2015	509 855[6]	1.8[6]	1.1[6]	2.4[6]	36 287	57	409[38]	36 753
	2017	502 670[6]	1.7[6]	1.1[6]	2.3[6]	23 566	115	757[38]	24 438
Netherlands Pays-Bas	2005	1 736 127	10.6	10.4	10.8	118 189[3]	14 664[3]	6 872[3]	139 725[3]
	2010	1 832 510	11.0	10.6	11.3	74 961[3]	13 053[3]	2 095[3]	90 109[3]
	2015	1 996 318	11.8	11.3	12.3	82 494[11]	8 097	1 951	92 542
	2016[3]	...	...	...	...	101 744	10 411	1 951	114 106
	2017	2 056 520	12.1	11.6	12.5	...	...	...	...
New Caledonia Nouvelle-Calédonie	2005	55 405	23.8	25.6	22.0	...	...	...	...
	2010	61 158	24.4	25.8	22.9	...	...	...	...
	2015	64 290	23.9	25.5	22.3	...	...	...	...
	2017	66 001	23.9	25.5	22.2	...	...	...	...
New Zealand Nouvelle-Zélande	2005	839 952	20.3	20.1	20.5	5 307[3]	396[3]	6[3]	5 709[3]
	2010	947 443	21.7	21.4	22.0	2 307[3]	216[3]	1[3]	2 524[3]
	2015	1 039 736	22.5	22.2	22.9	1 349[11]	251	...	1 600
	2017	1 067 423	22.7	22.3	23.0	1 467	324	...	1 791
Nicaragua Nicaragua	2005	34 918[6]	0.6[6]	0.7[6]	0.6[6]	227[3]	1[3]	...	228[3]
	2010	37 333[6]	0.7[6]	0.7[6]	0.6[6]	64[3]	12[3]	...	76[3]
	2015	40 262[6]	0.7[6]	0.7[6]	0.6[6]	361	25	5	391
	2017	41 159[6]	0.7[6]	0.7[6]	0.6[6]	330	405	2	737
Niger Niger	2005	124 461[6]	0.9[6]	0.9[6]	1.0[6]	301[3]	48[3]	37[3]	386[3]
	2010	126 464[6]	0.8[6]	0.7[6]	0.8[6]	314[3]	18[3]	5[3]	337[3]
	2015	252 998[6]	1.3[6]	1.2[6]	1.3[6]	82 064	122	120 000	202 186
	2017	295 610[6]	1.4[6]	1.3[6]	1.5[6]	162 135	98	147 712	309 945
Nigeria Nigéria	2005	969 294[6,8]	0.7[6,8]	0.8[6,8]	0.6[6,8]	9 019[3]	420[3]	3 290[3]	12 729[3]
	2010	988 679[6,8]	0.6[6,8]	0.7[6,8]	0.5[6,8]	8 747[3]	1 815[3]	34[3]	10 596[3]
	2015	1 199 115[6,8]	0.7[6,8]	0.7[6,8]	0.6[6,8]	1 279	909	1 508 017	1 510 205
	2017	1 235 088[6,8]	0.6[6,8]	0.7[6,8]	0.6[6,8]	1 415	614	2 476 290	2 478 319
Niue Nioué	2005	522	31.0	...	...	...	...	...	...
	2010	545	33.4	...	...	...	...	...	...
	2015	557	34.2	...	...	...	...	...	...
	2017	553	34.2	...	...	...	...	...	...

International migrants and refugees *(continued)*
International migrant stock (number and percentage) and refugees and others of concern to UNHCR

Migrants internationaux et réfugiés *(suite)*
Stock de migrants internationaux (nombre et pourcentage) et réfugiés et autres personnes relevant de la compétence du HCR

Region, country or area Région, pays ou zone	Year Année	International Migrant Stock (mid-year) Stock de migrants internationaux (milieu de l'année) Total Total	% of total pop. % de la pop. totale MF/HF	M/H	F	Refugees and others of concern to UNHCR (mid-year) Réfugiés et autres personnes relevant de la compétence du HCR (milieu de l'année) Refugees& Réfugiés&	Asylum seekers Demandeurs d'asile	Other&& Autres&&	Total pop. Pop. totale
Northern Mariana Islands Îles Mariannes du Nord	2005	37 542	58.9	...	...	...	...	...	...
	2010	24 168	44.4	...	...	...	...	...	...
	2015	21 648	39.5	...	...	...	...	...	...
	2017	21 777	39.5	...	...	...	...	...	...
Norway Norvège	2005	361 144[39]	7.8[39]	7.7[39]	7.9[39]	43 034[3]	...	1 143[3]	44 177[3]
	2010	526 799[39]	10.8[39]	11.0[39]	10.6[39]	40 260[3]	12 473[3]	3 150[3]	55 883[3]
	2015	746 375[39]	14.4[39]	14.9[39]	13.8[39]	47 043[11]	5 885	1 997	54 925
	2017	798 944[39]	15.1[39]	15.6[39]	14.5[39]	60 118	4 861	3 251	68 230
Oman Oman	2005	666 160[8]	26.5[8]	37.2[8]	12.7[8]	7[3]	4[3]	...	11[3]
	2010	816 221[8]	26.8[8]	35.9[8]	13.0[8]	78[3]	13[3]	...	91[3]
	2015	1 814 591[8]	43.2[8]	55.1[8]	21.3[8]	122	268	...	390
	2017	2 073 292[8]	44.7[8]	57.0[8]	21.0[8]	315	366	...	681
Pakistan Pakistan	2005	3 171 132[6]	2.1[6]	2.2[6]	2.0[6]	1 084 694[3]	3 426[3]	461 123[3]	1 549 243[3]
	2010	3 941 586[6]	2.3[6]	2.4[6]	2.3[6]	1 900 621[3]	2 095[3]	2 248 308[3]	4 151 024[3]
	2015	3 628 956[6]	1.9[6]	1.9[6]	1.9[6]	1 540 854	6 103	1 893 008	3 439 965
	2017	3 398 154[6]	1.7[6]	1.7[6]	1.7[6]	1 406 794	3 233	452 131	1 862 158
Palau Palaos	2005	6 043	30.4	...	...	...	...	...	...
	2010	5 490	26.8	...	...	...	...	...	...
	2015	4 937	23.2	...	...	1	...	...	1
	2016	...	...	...	...	...	1	...	1
	2017	4 988	23.0	...	...	5	...	...	5
Panama Panama	2005	117 563	3.5	3.6	3.5	1 730[3]	433[3]	10 273[3]	12 436[3]
	2010	157 309	4.3	4.4	4.2	17 073[3]	479[3]	6[3]	17 558[3]
	2015	184 710	4.7	4.8	4.5	17 303	2 038	2	19 343
	2017	190 728	4.7	4.8	4.5	17 373	5 627	2	23 002
Papua New Guinea Papouasie-Nvl-Guinée	2005	29 967[6,8]	0.5[6,8]	0.6[6,8]	0.4[6,8]	9 999[3]	4[3]	135[3]	10 138[3]
	2010	25 424[6,8]	0.4[6,8]	0.5[6,8]	0.3[6,8]	9 698[3]	1[3]	...	9 699[3]
	2015	30 782[6,8]	0.4[6,8]	0.5[6,8]	0.3[6,8]	9 510	400	...	9 910
	2017	32 389[6,8]	0.4[6,8]	0.5[6,8]	0.3[6,8]	9 547	2	...	9 549
Paraguay Paraguay	2005	168 243	2.9	3.0	2.8	50[3]	8[3]	...	58[3]
	2010	160 299	2.6	2.6	2.5	107[3]	8[3]	...	115[3]
	2015	156 462	2.4	2.4	2.3	161	39	...	200
	2017	160 519	2.4	2.4	2.3	214	31	...	245
Peru Pérou	2005	77 541	0.3	0.3	0.3	848[3]	336[3]	1[3]	1 185[3]
	2010	84 066	0.3	0.3	0.3	1 146[3]	264[3]	1[3]	1 411[3]
	2015	91 481	0.3	0.3	0.3	1 407	366	...	1 773
	2017	93 780	0.3	0.3	0.3	1 746	10 436	...	12 182
Philippines Philippines	2005	257 468[6,8]	0.3[6,8]	0.3[6,8]	0.3[6,8]	96[3]	42[3]	775[3]	913[3]
	2010	208 599[6,8]	0.2[6,8]	0.2[6,8]	0.2[6,8]	243[3]	73[3]	139 577[3]	139 893[3]
	2015	211 862[6,8]	0.2[6,8]	0.2[6,8]	0.2[6,8]	254	163	385 746	386 163
	2017	218 530[6,8]	0.2[6,8]	0.2[6,8]	0.2[6,8]	451	227	510 506[40]	511 184
Poland Pologne	2005	722 509	1.9	1.6	2.2	4 604[3]	1 627[3]	75[3]	6 306[3]
	2010	642 417	1.7	1.4	1.9	15 555[3]	2 126[3]	763[3]	18 444[3]
	2015	611 855	1.6	1.4	1.8	15 741[11]	2 470	10 825	29 036
	2017	640 937	1.7	1.5	1.9	12 002	2 902	10 825	25 729
Portugal Portugal	2005	771 184	7.3	7.4	7.2	363[3]	...	...	363[3]
	2010	762 825	7.2	7.3	7.0	384[3]	72[3]	31[3]	487[3]
	2015	864 814	8.3	8.1	8.5	699[11]	641	14	1 354
	2016[3]	...	...	...	...	1 194	858	14	2 066
	2017	880 188	8.5	8.4	8.6	...	...	...	...
Puerto Rico Porto Rico	2005	352 144	9.4	9.2	9.5	...	...	...	...
	2010	304 969	8.2	8.0	8.4	...	...	...	...
	2015	280 494	7.6	7.4	7.8	...	...	...	...
	2017	273 494	7.5	7.2	7.7	...	...	...	...
Qatar Qatar	2005	646 026[8]	74.7[8]	85.3[8]	52.6[8]	46[3]	28[3]	...	74[3]
	2010	1 456 413[8]	81.8[8]	89.4[8]	58.1[8]	51[3]	16[3]	1 200[3]	1 267[3]
	2015	1 687 640[8]	68.0[8]	75.7[8]	44.4[8]	133	100	1 200	1 433
	2017	1 721 392[8]	65.2[8]	72.9[8]	42.1[8]	188	125	1 200	1 513

4

International migrants and refugees *(continued)*

International migrant stock (number and percentage) and refugees and others of concern to UNHCR

Migrants internationaux et réfugiés *(suite)*

Stock de migrants internationaux (nombre et pourcentage) et réfugiés et autres personnes relevant de la compétence du HCR

Region, country or area Région, pays ou zone	Year Année	International Migrant Stock (mid-year) Stock de migrants internationaux (milieu de l'année) Total Total	% of total pop. % de la pop. totale MF/HF	M/H	F	Refugees and others of concern to UNHCR (mid-year) Réfugiés et autres personnes relevant de la compétence du HCR (milieu de l'année) Refugees& Réfugiés&	Asylum seekers Demandeurs d'asile	Other&& Autres&&	Total pop. Pop. totale
Republic of Korea	2005	485 546[8]	1.0[8]	1.2[8]	0.8[8]	69[3]	519[3]	...	588[3]
République de Corée	2010	919 275[8]	1.9[8]	2.1[8]	1.6[8]	358[3]	712[3]	179[3]	1 249[3]
	2015	1 143 087[8]	2.3[8]	2.5[8]	2.0[8]	1 313	5 102	200	6 615
	2017	1 151 865[8]	2.3[8]	2.5[8]	2.0[8]	2 051	7 107	196	9 354
Republic of Moldova	2005	173 957[41]	4.2[41]	3.8[41]	4.5[41]	84[3]	148[3]	1 543[3]	1 775[3]
République de Moldova	2010	157 668[41]	3.9[41]	3.1[41]	4.6[41]	148[3]	81[3]	2 032[3]	2 261[3]
	2015	142 904[41]	3.5[41]	2.6[41]	4.4[41]	389	164	6 233	6 786
	2017	140 045[41]	3.5[41]	2.5[41]	4.3[41]	408	70	4 692	5 170
Réunion	2005	115 076	14.5	15.2	13.9	...	...	...	...
Réunion	2010	123 029	14.8	15.6	14.1	...	...	...	...
	2015	127 209	14.7	15.4	14.1	...	...	...	...
	2017	129 153	14.7	15.4	14.1	...	...	...	...
Romania	2005	145 162	0.7	0.6	0.7	2 056[3]	264[3]	400[3]	2 720[3]
Roumanie	2010	166 126	0.8	0.8	0.8	1 021[3]	388[3]	321[3]	1 730[3]
	2015	281 048	1.4	1.5	1.3	2 426	138	294	2 858
	2017	370 753	1.9	2.1	1.7	3 423	101	240	3 764
Russian Federation	2005	11 667 588	8.1	8.7	7.6	1 523[3]	292[3]	481 282[3]	483 097[3]
Fédération de Russie	2010	11 194 710	7.8	8.3	7.4	4 922[3]	1 463[3]	126 170[3]	132 555[3]
	2015	11 643 276	8.1	8.5	7.7	315 313	2 423	113 474[42]	431 210
	2017	11 651 509	8.1	8.5	7.7	188 374	3 420	90 774[42]	282 568
Rwanda	2005	432 797[6]	4.8[6]	4.9[6]	4.7[6]	45 206[3]	4 301[3]	14 849[3]	64 356[3]
Rwanda	2010	436 787[6]	4.3[6]	4.4[6]	4.2[6]	55 398[3]	290[3]	2[3]	55 690[3]
	2015	441 525[6]	3.8[6]	3.9[6]	3.7[6]	132 743	253	2 557	135 553
	2017	443 088[6]	3.6[6]	3.7[6]	3.6[6]	157 996	445	15 322	173 763
Saint Helena [43]	2005	487	11.4	...	...	...	...	...	...
Sainte-Hélène [43]	2010	569	13.6	...	...	...	...	...	...
	2015	604	15.0	...	...	...	...	...	...
	2017	606	15.0	...	...	...	...	...	...
Saint Kitts and Nevis	2005	6 682	13.7	...	...	...	...	...	...
Saint-Kitts-et-Nevis	2010	7 245	14.1	...	...	...	...	...	...
	2015	7 443	13.7	...	...	1	...	...	1
	2017	7 587	13.7	...	...	...	...	...	...
Saint Lucia	2005	11 468	7.0	7.2	6.8	...	...	...	...
Sainte-Lucie	2010	12 100	7.0	7.2	6.8	...	6[3]	1[3]	7[3]
	2015	12 771	7.2	7.4	7.0	2	2	60	64
	2016	...	...	...	...	2	1	...	3
	2017	12 889	7.2	7.4	7.0	2	...	...	2
Saint Pierre and Miquelon	2005	1 147	18.3	...	...	...	...	...	...
Saint-Pierre-et-Miquelon	2010	1 017	16.2	...	...	...	...	...	...
	2015	986	15.7	...	...	...	...	...	...
	2017	990	15.7	...	...	...	...	...	...
Saint Vincent & Grenadines	2005	4 395	4.0	3.9	4.2	...	...	...	...
Saint-Vincent-Grenadines	2010	4 485	4.1	4.0	4.2	...	...	...	...
	2015	4 577	4.2	4.1	4.3	...	...	...	...
	2017	4 595	4.2	4.1	4.3	...	...	...	...
Samoa	2005	5 746	3.2	3.2	3.2	...	...	...	...
Samoa	2010	5 122	2.8	2.7	2.8	...	...	...	...
	2015	4 929	2.5	2.5	2.6	...	...	...	...
	2016	...	...	...	...	...	3	...	3
	2017	4 879	2.5	2.4	2.6	3	...	...	3
San Marino [8]	2005	4 218	14.4	...	...	...	...	...	...
Saint-Marin [8]	2010	4 399	14.1	...	...	...	...	...	...
	2015	5 174	15.7	...	...	...	...	...	...
	2017	5 243	15.7	...	...	...	...	...	...
Sao Tome and Principe [8]	2005	3 433	2.2	2.2	2.2	...	...	...	...
Sao Tomé-et-Principe [8]	2010	2 700	1.5	1.6	1.5	...	...	...	...
	2015	2 394	1.2	1.2	1.2	...	...	...	...
	2017	2 293	1.1	1.1	1.1	...	...	...	...

International migrants and refugees *(continued)*

International migrant stock (number and percentage) and refugees and others of concern to UNHCR

Migrants internationaux et réfugiés *(suite)*

Stock de migrants internationaux (nombre et pourcentage) et réfugiés et autres personnes relevant de la compétence du HCR

Region, country or area Région, pays ou zone	Year Année	International Migrant Stock (mid-year) Stock de migrants internationaux (milieu de l'année) Total Total	% of total pop. % de la pop. totale MF/HF	M/H	F	Refugees and others of concern to UNHCR (mid-year) Réfugiés et autres personnes relevant de la compétence du HCR (milieu de l'année) Refugees[&] Réfugiés[&]	Asylum seekers Demandeurs d'asile	Other[&&] Autres[&&]	Total pop. Pop. totale
Saudi Arabia Arabie saoudite	2005	6 501 819[6,8]	27.2[6,8]	33.6[6,8]	19.2[6,8]	240 701[3]	212[3]	70 084[3]	310 997[3]
	2010	8 429 956[6,8]	30.7[6,8]	38.5[6,8]	20.8[6,8]	582[3]	87[3]	70 000[3]	70 669[3]
	2015	10 771 366[6,8]	34.1[6,8]	41.7[6,8]	24.2[6,8]	211	93	70 000	70 304
	2017	12 185 284[6,8]	37.0[6,8]	44.4[6,8]	27.2[6,8]	149	45	70 000	70 194
Senegal Sénégal	2005	238 298[6]	2.1[6]	2.3[6]	2.0[6]	20 712[3]	2 629[3]	12[3]	23 353[3]
	2010	256 092[6]	2.0[6]	2.1[6]	1.8[6]	20 672[3]	2 177[3]	1 401[3]	24 250[3]
	2015	263 242[6]	1.8[6]	1.9[6]	1.6[6]	14 304	2 956	...	17 260
	2017	265 601[6]	1.7[6]	1.8[6]	1.5[6]	14 565	3 313	...	17 878
Serbia [44] Serbie [44]	2005	845 120	9.2	8.3	10.0	148 264[3]	33[3]	338 641[3]	486 938[3]
	2010	826 066	9.1	8.3	10.0	73 608[3]	209[3]	238 810[3]	312 627[3]
	2015	807 441	9.1	8.2	10.0	35 309	464	223 949	259 722
	2017	801 903	9.1	8.2	10.0	33 704	205	220 378	254 287
Seychelles Seychelles	2005	8 997	10.1	13.1	7.2	...	...	...	...
	2010	11 420	12.5	16.6	8.2	...	...	...	...
	2015	12 791	13.6	19.3	8.1	...	...	...	...
	2017	12 926	13.6	19.4	8.1	...	1	...	1
Sierra Leone Sierra Leone	2005	149 615[6]	2.6[6]	2.9[6]	2.4[6]	59 965[3]	177[3]	6 202[3]	66 344[3]
	2010	97 452[6]	1.5[6]	1.7[6]	1.4[6]	8 363[3]	210[3]	38[3]	8 611[3]
	2015	91 213[6]	1.3[6]	1.4[6]	1.1[6]	1 371	16	...	1 387
	2017	95 248[6]	1.3[6]	1.4[6]	1.1[6]	693	1	...	694
Singapore Singapour	2005	1 710 594	38.1	34.0	42.1	3[3]	1[3]	...	4[3]
	2010	2 164 794	42.7	38.2	47.0	7[3]	...	...	7[3]
	2015	2 543 638	46.0	41.1	50.7	...	...	1	1
	2017	2 623 404	46.0	41.1	50.7	...	...	1	1
Sint Maarten (Dutch part) St-Martin (partie néerland.)	2005	13 100	40.3	...	...	...	...	...	...
	2010	26 200	79.1	...	...	1[3]	3[3]	...	4[3]
	2015	27 295	70.4	...	...	3	5	...	8
	2017	28 260	70.4	...	...	5	6	...	11
Slovakia Slovaquie	2005	130 491	2.4	2.2	2.6	368[3]	2 707[3]	...	3 075[3]
	2010	146 319	2.7	2.6	2.9	461[3]	267[3]	911[3]	1 639[3]
	2015	177 624	3.3	3.4	3.2	799[11]	61	1 671	2 531
	2017	184 642	3.4	3.5	3.3	984	27	1 528	2 539
Slovenia Slovénie	2005	197 276	9.9	11.0	8.8	251[3]	185[3]	715[3]	1 151[3]
	2010	253 786	12.4	14.0	10.9	314[3]	121[3]	4 119[3]	4 554[3]
	2015	237 616	11.5	13.1	9.9	283	43	4	330
	2017	244 790	11.8	13.4	10.2	551	326	4	881
Solomon Islands Îles Salomon	2005	3 271	0.7	0.8	0.6	...	...	...	...
	2010	2 760	0.5	0.6	0.5	...	...	...	...
	2015	2 585	0.4	0.5	0.4	3	...	...	3
	2016	...	...	...	...	3	...	...	3
	2017	2 532	0.4	0.5	0.4	...	...	...	...
Somalia Somalie	2005	* 20 670[6]	* 0.2[6]	* 0.2[6]	* 0.2[6]	493[3]	98[3]	400 000[3]	400 591[3]
	2010	* 23 995[6]	* 0.2[6]	* 0.2[6]	* 0.2[6]	1 937[3]	24 111[3]	1 463 780[3]	1 489 828[3]
	2015	* 41 578[6]	* 0.3[6]	* 0.3[6]	* 0.3[6]	3 582	9 320	1 152 073	1 164 975
	2017	* 44 868[6]	* 0.3[6]	* 0.3[6]	* 0.3[6]	12 925	13 558	1 594 105	1 620 588
South Africa Afrique du Sud	2005	1 210 936[6]	2.5[6]	3.0[6]	2.0[6]	29 714[3]	140 095[3]	100[3]	169 909[3]
	2010	2 096 886[6]	4.1[6]	4.8[6]	3.4[6]	57 899[3]	171 702[3]	134[3]	229 735[3]
	2015	3 816 696[6]	6.9[6]	7.8[6]	6.0[6]	114 512	798 080	...	912 592
	2017	4 036 696[6]	7.1[6]	8.1[6]	6.2[6]	92 296	215 860[45]	...	308 156
South Sudan Soudan du sud	2010[6]	257 905	2.6	2.6	2.5	...	...	...	...
	2015	844 122[6]	7.1[6]	7.2[6]	7.0[6]	265 887	632	1 792 014[46]	2 058 533
	2017	845 239[6]	6.7[6]	6.8[6]	6.6[6]	274 920	2 400	1 944 735	2 222 055
Spain Espagne	2005	4 107 226[47]	9.3[47]	9.9[47]	8.8[47]	5 374[3]	...	27[3]	5 401[3]
	2010	6 280 065[47]	13.4[47]	14.0[47]	12.9[47]	3 820[3]	2 712[3]	31[3]	6 563[3]
	2015	5 891 208[47]	12.7[47]	12.7[47]	12.7[47]	5 798[11]	11 020	440	17 258
	2017	5 947 106[47]	12.8[47]	12.7[47]	12.9[47]	15 557	20 360	485	36 402

4 International migrants and refugees *(continued)*

International migrant stock (number and percentage) and refugees and others of concern to UNHCR

Migrants internationaux et réfugiés *(suite)*

Stock de migrants internationaux (nombre et pourcentage) et réfugiés et autres personnes relevant de la compétence du HCR

Region, country or area Région, pays ou zone	Year Année	International Migrant Stock (mid-year) Stock de migrants internationaux (milieu de l'année) Total Total	% of total pop. % de la pop. totale MF/HF	M/H	F	Refugees and others of concern to UNHCR (mid-year) Réfugiés et autres personnes relevant de la compétence du HCR (milieu de l'année) Refugees[&] Réfugiés[&]	Asylum seekers Demandeurs d'asile	Other[&&] Autres[&&]	Total pop. Pop. totale
Sri Lanka Sri Lanka	2005	39 526[6]	0.2[6]	0.2[6]	0.2[6]	106[3]	121[3]	351 884[3]	352 111[3]
	2010	38 959[6]	0.2[6]	0.2[6]	0.2[6]	223[3]	138[3]	434 903[3]	435 264[3]
	2015	39 706[6]	0.2[6]	0.2[6]	0.2[6]	848	461	50 499[48]	51 808
	2017	40 018[6]	0.2[6]	0.2[6]	0.2[6]	651	634	40 445	41 730
State of Palestine État de Palestine	2005[49,50]	266 617	7.5	6.6	8.3	...	...	...	...
	2010[49,50]	258 032	6.3	5.6	7.2	...	...	...	...
	2015	255 507[49,50]	5.5[49,50]	4.8[49,50]	6.2[49,50]	...	...	3	3
	2017[49,50]	253 735	5.2	4.5	5.8	...	...	...	...
Sudan Soudan	2005[3]	...	...	...	...	147 256	4 425	878 067	1 029 748
	2010	578 363[6]	1.7[6]	1.7[6]	1.6[6]	178 308[3]	6 046[3]	1 767 167[3]	1 951 521[3]
	2015	623 878[6]	1.6[6]	1.6[6]	1.6[6]	356 191	11 448	2 400 270[51]	2 767 909
	2017	735 821[6]	1.8[6]	1.8[6]	1.8[6]	538 797	17 839	2 311 162	2 867 798
Suriname Suriname	2005[8]	33 664	6.7	7.3	6.2	...	...	...	...
	2010	39 713[8]	7.5[8]	8.2[8]	6.9[8]	1[3]	7[3]	...	8[3]
	2015	46 836[8]	8.5[8]	9.2[8]	7.7[8]	1	...	...	1
	2017	47 699[8]	8.5[8]	9.2[8]	7.7[8]	15	72	1	88
Sweden Suède	2005	1 125 790	12.5	12.0	12.9	74 915[3]	15 702[3]	5 785[3]	96 402[3]
	2010	1 337 214	14.2	13.9	14.6	82 629[3]	18 635[3]	9 545[3]	110 809[3]
	2015	1 602 522	16.4	16.1	16.7	142 207[11]	56 135	27 167	225 509
	2017	1 747 710	17.6	17.4	17.9	235 853	67 140	36 036	339 029
Switzerland Suisse	2005	1 805 437	24.4	25.4	23.3	48 030[3]	14 428[3]	990[3]	63 448[3]
	2010	2 075 182	26.5	24.3	28.6	48 813[3]	12 916[3]	127[3]	61 856[3]
	2015	2 416 394	29.0	28.7	29.3	69 390	17 085	76	86 551
	2017	2 506 394	29.6	29.2	29.9	88 066	26 648	64	114 778
Syrian Arab Republic République arabe syrienne	2005	876 410[6,8]	4.8[6,8]	4.8[6,8]	4.8[6,8]	26 089[3]	1 898[3]	300 001[3]	327 988[3]
	2010	1 785 115[6,8]	8.5[6,8]	8.6[6,8]	8.4[6,8]	1 005 472[3]	2 446[3]	300 194[3]	1 308 112[3]
	2015	993 940[6,8]	5.3[6,8]	5.4[6,8]	5.3[6,8]	149 200[52]	4 839	7 792 500	7 946 539
	2017	1 013 818[6,8]	5.5[6,8]	5.6[6,8]	5.5[6,8]	19 006[52]	16 665	6 508 914[52]	6 544 585
Tajikistan Tadjikistan	2005	280 444	4.1	3.5	4.7	1 018[3]	22[3]	25[3]	1 065[3]
	2010	278 152	3.6	3.1	4.2	3 131[3]	1 656[3]	2 338[3]	7 125[3]
	2015	275 059	3.2	2.8	3.7	1 782	79	10 082[53]	11 943
	2017	273 259	3.1	2.6	3.5	2 612	474	15 047	18 133
Thailand Thaïlande	2005	2 163 447[6]	3.3[6]	3.4[6]	3.2[6]	117 053[3]	32 163[3]	136[3]	149 352[3]
	2010	3 224 131[6]	4.8[6]	4.9[6]	4.7[6]	96 675[3]	10 250[3]	542 505[3]	649 430[3]
	2015	3 486 526[6]	5.1[6]	5.2[6]	4.9[6]	110 372	8 166	506 718[54]	625 256
	2017	3 588 873[6]	5.2[6]	5.4[6]	5.1[6]	104 532	3 360	485 569[55]	593 461
TFYR of Macedonia ex-R.Y. de Macédoine	2005	127 667	6.2	5.2	7.2	1 274[3]	723[3]	2 451[3]	4 448[3]
	2010	129 701	6.3	5.2	7.3	1 398[3]	161[3]	1 731[3]	3 290[3]
	2015	130 730	6.3	5.2	7.3	828	43	717	1 588
	2017	130 972	6.3	5.2	7.3	592	22	598	1 212
Timor-Leste Timor-Leste	2005	11 286	1.1	1.1	1.1	3[3]	10[3]	...	13[3]
	2010	11 535	1.0	1.0	1.0	1[3]	4[3]	...	5[3]
	2015	11 784	0.9	0.9	1.0	...	...	5	5
	2017	12 063	0.9	0.9	0.9	...	...	2	2
Togo Togo	2005	203 379[6,8]	3.6[6,8]	3.6[6,8]	3.5[6,8]	9 287[3]	420[3]	9 012[3]	18 719[3]
	2010	255 262[6,8]	3.9[6,8]	4.0[6,8]	3.9[6,8]	14 051[3]	151[3]	5[3]	14 207[3]
	2015	276 844[6,8]	3.7[6,8]	3.8[6,8]	3.7[6,8]	21 877	687	...	22 564
	2017	283 966[6,8]	3.6[6,8]	3.7[6,8]	3.6[6,8]	12 558	726	1	13 285
Tokelau Tokélaou	2005	258	21.4	...	...	...	...	...	...
	2010	429	37.6	...	...	...	...	...	...
	2015	487	38.9	...	...	...	...	...	...
	2017	504	38.8	...	...	...	...	...	...
Tonga Tonga	2005	4 301	4.3	4.6	3.9	...	...	...	...
	2010	4 589	4.4	4.8	4.0	...	3[3]	...	3[3]
	2015	4 877	4.6	5.0	4.2	...	...	...	...
	2017	4 952	4.6	5.0	4.2	...	...	...	...

International migrants and refugees *(continued)*

International migrant stock (number and percentage) and refugees and others of concern to UNHCR

Migrants internationaux et réfugiés *(suite)*

Stock de migrants internationaux (nombre et pourcentage) et réfugiés et autres personnes relevant de la compétence du HCR

Region, country or area Région, pays ou zone	Year Année	International Migrant Stock (mid-year) Stock de migrants internationaux (milieu de l'année) Total Total	% of total pop. % de la pop. totale MF/HF	M/H	F	Refugees and others of concern to UNHCR (mid-year) Réfugiés et autres personnes relevant de la compétence du HCR (milieu de l'année) Refugees[&] Réfugiés[&]	Asylum seekers Demandeurs d'asile	Other[&&] Autres[&&]	Total pop. Pop. totale
Trinidad and Tobago Trinité-et-Tobago	2005	44 812	3.5	3.2	3.7	...	...	...	...
	2010	48 226	3.6	3.5	3.7	29[3]	102[3]	...	131[3]
	2015	49 883	3.7	3.6	3.7	121	59	...	180
	2017	50 214	3.7	3.6	3.7	206	488	13	707
Tunisia Tunisie	2005	35 040[8]	0.3[8]	0.4[8]	0.3[8]	87[3]	26[3]	...	113[3]
	2010	43 172[8]	0.4[8]	0.4[8]	0.4[8]	89[3]	23[3]	3[3]	115[3]
	2015	56 701[8]	0.5[8]	0.5[8]	0.5[8]	824	156	3	983
	2017	57 663[6]	0.5[6]	0.5[6]	0.5[6]	601	34	3	638
Turkey Turquie	2005	1 319 236[6]	1.9[6]	1.9[6]	2.0[6]	2 399[3]	4 872[3]	1 434[3]	8 705[3]
	2010	1 367 034[6]	1.9[6]	1.8[6]	2.0[6]	10 032[3]	6 715[3]	1 086[3]	17 833[3]
	2015	4 131 302[6]	5.3[6]	5.0[6]	5.5[6]	1 838 848[56]	145 335	1 086	1 985 269
	2017	4 881 966[6]	6.0[6]	5.8[6]	6.3[6]	3 203 785[56]	266 177	117	3 470 079
Turkmenistan Turkménistan	2005	213 051	4.5	4.0	4.9	11 963[3]	2[3]	45[3]	12 010[3]
	2010	197 979	3.9	3.6	4.2	62[3]	...	20 000[3]	20 062[3]
	2015	196 386	3.5	3.3	3.7	27	...	7 144	7 171
	2017	195 061	3.4	3.2	3.6	22	...	3 390	3 412
Turks and Caicos Islands Îles Turques-et-Caïques	2005	13 115	49.6	...	...	...	...	...	...
	2010	17 216	55.5	...	...	...	...	...	...
	2015	22 719	66.2	...	...	4	4	...	8
	2017	24 534	69.2	...	...	5	...	...	5
Tuvalu [8] Tuvalu [8]	2005	183	1.8	...	...	...	...	...	...
	2010	154	1.5	...	...	...	...	...	...
	2015	141	1.3	...	...	...	...	...	...
	2017	143	1.3	...	...	...	...	...	...
Uganda Ouganda	2005	652 968[6]	2.3[6]	2.3[6]	2.3[6]	257 256[3]	1 809[3]	1 636[3]	260 701[3]
	2010	529 160[6]	1.6[6]	1.6[6]	1.6[6]	135 801[3]	20 804[3]	437 775[3]	594 380[3]
	2015	1 197 162[6]	3.0[6]	2.8[6]	3.1[6]	428 397	38 068	180 000	646 465
	2017	1 692 120[6]	3.9[6]	3.7[6]	4.2[6]	1 269 758	39 940	180 000	1 489 698
Ukraine Ukraine	2005	5 050 302[57]	10.8[57]	10.0[57]	11.5[57]	2 346[3]	1 618[3]	72 896[3]	76 860[3]
	2010	4 818 767[57]	10.5[57]	9.8[57]	11.1[57]	3 022[3]	2 981[3]	40 357[3]	46 360[3]
	2015	4 915 142[57]	11.0[57]	10.2[57]	11.7[57]	3 232	6 169	1 417 179	1 426 580
	2017	4 964 293[57]	11.2[57]	10.4[57]	11.9[57]	3 253	6 282	1 835 463[58]	1 844 998
United Arab Emirates Émirats arabes unis	2005	3 281 036[6,8]	71.6[6,8]	74.2[6,8]	65.5[6,8]	104[3]	79[3]	...	183[3]
	2010	7 316 611[6,8]	88.5[6,8]	88.7[6,8]	87.9[6,8]	538[3]	86[3]	...	624[3]
	2015	7 995 126[6,8]	87.3[6,8]	89.2[6,8]	82.3[6,8]	424	378	...	802
	2017	8 312 524[6,8]	88.4[6,8]	91.2[6,8]	81.2[6,8]	807	872	...	1 679
United Kingdom Royaume-Uni	2005	5 926 156	9.8	9.5	10.1	303 181[3]	12 500[3]	909[3]	316 590[3]
	2010	7 604 583	12.0	11.8	12.2	238 150[3]	14 880[3]	229[3]	253 259[3]
	2015	8 411 021	12.9	12.5	13.2	117 234[11]	37 829	16	155 079
	2017	8 841 717	13.4	12.9	13.8	121 280	31 353	85	152 718
United Rep. of Tanzania Rép.-Unie de Tanzanie	2005	770 846[6,59]	2.0[6,59]	2.5[6,59]	1.4[6,59]	548 824[3]	307[3]	81 519[3]	630 650[3]
	2010	308 600[6,59]	0.7[6,59]	0.7[6,59]	0.7[6,59]	109 286[3]	1 247[3]	163 269[3]	273 802[3]
	2015	413 309[6,59]	0.8[6,59]	0.8[6,59]	0.8[6,59]	159 014	1 150	168 019	328 183
	2017	492 574[6,59]	0.9[6,59]	0.9[6,59]	0.9[6,59]	306 025	37 139	168 785	511 949
United States of America États-Unis d'Amérique	2005	39 258 293	13.3	13.5	13.1	379 340[3]	169 743[3]	76[3]	549 159[3]
	2010	44 183 643	14.3	14.2	14.4	264 569[3]	6 285[3]	89[3]	270 943[3]
	2015	48 178 877	15.1	14.8	15.3	* 267 222[11]	224 508	...	491 730
	2017	49 776 970	15.3	15.1	15.6	279 419	692 053[60]	...	971 472[60]
United States Virgin Islands Îles Vierges américaines	2005	56 647	52.6	51.3	53.7	...	...	...	...
	2010	56 684	53.4	52.6	54.1	...	...	...	...
	2015	56 721	54.0	53.4	54.6	...	...	...	...
	2017	56 745	54.1	53.5	54.7	...	...	...	...
Uruguay Uruguay	2005	82 318	2.5	2.3	2.6	121[3]	9[3]	...	130[3]
	2010	76 263	2.3	2.1	2.4	189[3]	40[3]	...	229[3]
	2015	78 799	2.3	2.2	2.4	289	68	...	357
	2017	79 586	2.3	2.2	2.4	318	772	...	1 090

4 International migrants and refugees *(continued)*

International migrant stock (number and percentage) and refugees and others of concern to UNHCR

Migrants internationaux et réfugiés *(suite)*

Stock de migrants internationaux (nombre et pourcentage) et réfugiés et autres personnes relevant de la compétence du HCR

		International Migrant Stock (mid-year) Stock de migrants internationaux (milieu de l'année)				Refugees and others of concern to UNHCR (mid-year) Réfugiés et autres personnes relevant de la compétence du HCR (milieu de l'année)			
			% of total pop. % de la pop. totale						
Region, country or area Région, pays ou zone	Year Année	Total Total	MF/HF	M/H	F	Refugees& Réfugiés&	Asylum seekers Demandeurs d'asile	Other&& Autres&&	Total pop. Pop. totale
Uzbekistan Ouzbékistan	2005	1 329 345	5.0	4.5	5.5	43 950[3]	587[3]	5[3]	44 542[3]
	2010	1 220 149	4.3	3.9	4.6	311[3]	...	2[3]	313[3]
	2015	1 170 899	3.8	3.5	4.0	118	...	86 703[61]	86 821
	2017	1 159 190	3.6	3.4	3.9	22	...	86 425[62]	86 447
Vanuatu Vanuatu	2005	2 800	1.3	1.3	1.4	...	...	...	...
	2010	2 991	1.3	1.2	1.3	4[3]	...	...	4[3]
	2015	3 187	1.2	1.2	1.2	...	1	...	1
	2017	3 245	1.2	1.2	1.2	...	...	...	...
Venezuela (Boliv. Rep. of) Venezuela (Rép. boliv. du)	2005	1 070 562	4.0	4.0	4.0	408[3]	5 912[3]	200 001[3]	206 321[3]
	2010	1 331 488	4.6	4.6	4.6	201 547[3]	15 859[3]	...	217 406[3]
	2015	1 404 448	4.5	4.5	4.5	174 191	704	...	174 895
	2017	1 426 336	4.5	4.5	4.4	171 878	933	...	172 811
Viet Nam Viet Nam	2005	51 768[6,8]	0.1[6,8]	0.1[6,8]	~0.0[6,8]	2 357[3]	...	15 000[3]	17 357[3]
	2010	61 756[6,8]	0.1[6,8]	0.1[6,8]	0.1[6,8]	1 928[3]	...	10 200[3]	12 128[3]
	2015	72 793[6,8]	0.1[6,8]	0.1[6,8]	0.1[6,8]	...	...	11 000	11 000
	2017	76 104[6,8]	0.1[6,8]	0.1[6,8]	0.1[6,8]	...	...	11 000	11 000
Wallis and Futuna Islands Îles Wallis-et-Futuna	2005	2 365	16.2	...	...	...	...	...	...
	2010	2 776	20.7	...	...	...	...	...	...
	2015	2 849	23.6	...	...	...	...	...	...
	2017	2 779	23.6	...	...	...	...	...	...
Western Sahara Sahara occidental	*2005	3 891	0.9	1.0	0.8	...	...	...	...
	*2010	4 493	0.9	1.0	0.8	...	...	...	...
	*2015	5 179	1.0	1.1	0.8	...	...	...	...
	*2017	5 384	1.0	1.1	0.8	...	...	...	...
Yemen Yémen	2005	171 073[6,8]	0.8[6,8]	0.9[6,8]	0.7[6,8]	81 937[3]	798[3]	48[3]	82 783[3]
	2010	285 837[6,8]	1.2[6,8]	1.3[6,8]	1.1[6,8]	190 092[3]	2 557[3]	315 929[3]	508 578[3]
	2015	379 899[6,8]	1.4[6,8]	1.5[6,8]	1.4[6,8]	263 047	9 902	1 267 590	1 540 539
	2017	384 321[6,8]	1.4[6,8]	1.4[6,8]	1.3[6,8]	270 905	9 306	2 926 569	3 206 780
Zambia Zambie	2005	252 749[6]	2.1[6]	2.2[6]	2.0[6]	155 718[3]	146[3]	29 833[3]	185 697[3]
	2010	149 637[6]	1.1[6]	1.1[6]	1.1[6]	47 857[3]	325[3]	9 687[3]	57 869[3]
	2015	155 428[6]	1.0[6]	1.0[6]	0.9[6]	25 737	2 606	23 415	51 758
	2017	156 982[6]	0.9[6]	0.9[6]	0.9[6]	29 509	3 871	25 088	58 468
Zimbabwe Zimbabwe	2005	392 693[6]	3.0[6]	3.5[6]	2.5[6]	13 850[3]	118[3]	7[3]	13 975[3]
	2010	397 891[6]	2.8[6]	3.3[6]	2.4[6]	4 435[3]	416[3]	...	4 851[3]
	2015	403 866[6]	2.6[6]	3.0[6]	2.2[6]	6 085	123	* 301 883	308 091
	2017	403 866[6]	2.4[6]	2.9[6]	2.1[6]	7 567	1 297	2 106[63]	10 970

Source:

United Nations Population Division, New York, International migrant stock: The 2017 Revision, last accessed January 2018.

United Nations High Commissioner for Refugees (UNHCR), Geneva, UNHCR Population Statistics Database, last accessed February 2018.

& Number of refugees or persons in refugee-like situations as reported by the Office of the United Nations High Commissioner for Refugees (UNHCR). && Figure includes sum of returned refugees, internally displaced persons (IDPs) protected/assisted by UNHCR, including people in IDP like situations, returned IDPs, Persons under UNHCR's stateless mandate, and others of concern to UNHCR categories.

1 Excluding Sudan.

Source:

Organisation des Nations Unies, Division de la population, New York, « International migrant stock: The 2017 Revision », derniér accéss janvier 2018.
Haut-Commissariat des Nations Unies pour les réfugiés (HCR), Genève, base de données statistique du HCR, dernier accès février 2018.

&Nombre de réfugiés ou de personnes en situation analogue à celle de réfugiés, tel que donné par le Bureau des Nations Unies. && Les chiffres correspondent au total des réfugiés rapatriés, des personnes déplacées protégées ou assistées par le HCR, notamment celles se trouvant dans une situation analogue à celle des personnes déplacées, des personnes déplacées de retour, des apatrides relevant du mandat du HCR et d'autres catégories de personnes relevant de la compétence du HCR.

1 Exclut le Soudan.

2 Including Sudan.
3 Data as at the end of December.
4 The number of IDPs in Afghanistan is decreased due to the revision of methodology.
5 The statelessness figure refers to a census from 2011 and has been adjusted to reflect the number of persons with undetermined nationality who had their nationality confirmed in 2011-mid 2017.
6 Including refugees.
7 According to the Government of Algeria, there are an estimated 165,000 Sahrawi refugees in the Tindouf camps.
8 Refers to foreign citizens.
9 Including Christmas Island, Cocos (Keeling) Islands and Norfolk Island.
10 Asylum-seekers are based on the number of applications lodged for protection visas.
11 Data relates to the end of 2014.
12 Including Nagorno-Karabakh.
13 The refugee population includes 200,000 persons originating from Myanmar in a refugee-like situation. The Government of Bangladesh estimates the population to be between 300,000 and 500,000.
14 The refugee population includes 274,000 persons originating from Myanmar in a refugee-like situation. The Government of Bangladesh estimates the population to be between 300,000 and 500,000.
15 Bonaire only.
16 Refugee returnees in Burundi are cumulative as of June 2017. These includes both registered and unregistered refugees.
17 Refers to Guernsey and Jersey.
18 For statistical purposes, the data for China do not include those for the Hong Kong Special Administrative Region (Hong Kong SAR), Macao Special Administrative Region (Macao SAR) and Taiwan Province of China.
19 The 300,000 Vietnamese refugees are well integrated and in practice receive protection from the Government of China.
20 Including northern Cyprus.
21 Refugee population includes 60,280 refugee-like from Central African Rep. who are new arrivals from January to June 2017.
22 Revised estimate includes only individuals born in the country where both parents were born abroad. This estimate does not include subsequent generations of individuals of foreign descent as such it does not include all persons without nationality.
23 Almost all people recorded as being stateless have permanent residence and enjoy more rights than foreseen in the 1954 Convention relating to the Status of Stateless Persons.
24 Including Åland Islands.
25 Including Abkhazia and South Ossetia.
26 Including Saint Barthélemy and Saint Martin (French part).
27 Figure refers to individuals without a nationality who were born in the Dominican Republic prior to January 2010 and who were identified by UNHCR in Haiti since June 2015.
28 Including an estimate for stateless persons populations in line with Law 26 of 2006, which allows stateless persons to apply for nationality in certain circumstances.
29 Pending a more accurate study into stateless in Iraq, the estimate of stateless persons in Iraq has been adjusted to reflect the reduction of statelessness in line with Law 26 of 2006, which allows stateless persons to apply for nationality in certain circumstances.
30 Includes Iraqi refugees registered with UNHCR.
31 The figure of stateless persons includes persons covered by two separate Laws; Law on Stateless Persons dated 17 February 2004 and the Law on the Status of Those Former USSR Citizens who are not Citizens of Latvia or of Any Other State.

2 Y compris le Soudan.
3 Données à la fin de décembre.
4 Le nombre de personnes déplacées en Afghanistan est diminué en raison de la révision de la méthodologie.
5 Le chiffre d'apatridie fait référence à un recensement de 2011 et a été ajusté pour refléter le nombre de personnes de nationalité indéterminée dont la nationalité a été confirmée en 2011-mi-2017.
6 Y compris les réfugiés.
7 Selon le Gouvernement algérien, les camps de Tindouf accueillent environ 165 000 réfugiés sahraouis.
8 Se rapportent aux citoyens étrangers.
9 Y compris l'île Christmas, les îles des Cocos (Keeling) et l'île Norfolk.
10 Les chiffres de l'Australie concernant les demandeurs d'asile sont établis sur la base du nombre de demandes de visa de protection présentées.
11 Le nombre se rapporte à fin 2014.
12 Y compris le Haut-Karabakh.
13 Au nombre des réfugiés figurent 200 000 personnes originaires du Myanmar se trouvant dans une situation analogue à celle des réfugiés. Le Gouvernement bangladais estime que le nombre de réfugiés se situe entre 300 000 et 500 000.
14 Au nombre des réfugiés figurent 274,000 personnes originaires du Myanmar se trouvant dans une situation analogue à celle des réfugiés. Le Gouvernement bangladais estime que le nombre de réfugiés se situe entre 300 000 et 500 000.
15 Bonaire seulement.
16 Les réfugiés rapatriés au Burundi sont cumulatifs en juin 2017. Sont inclus les réfugiés enregistrés ou non enregistrés.
17 Se rapporte à Guernesey et Jersey.
18 Pour la présentation des statistiques, les données pour la Chine ne comprennent pas la région administrative spéciale de Hong Kong (Hong Kong RAS), la région administrative spéciale de Macao (Macao RAS) et la province chinoise de Taïwan.
19 Les 300 000 réfugiés vietnamiens sont bien intégrés et, dans la pratique, recoivent la protection du Gouvernement chinois.
20 Y compris la partie nord de Chypre.
21 La population réfugiée comprend 60 280 qui se trouvent dans des situations semblables à celles de réfugiés en provenance de la République centrafricaine, qui sont de nouveaux arrivants de janvier à juin 2017.
22 Cette réestimation concerne uniquement les personnes nées dans le pays dont les deux parents sont nés à l'étranger. Cette estimation ne comprend pas les générations futures de personnes d'origine étrangère tels que les apatrides.
23 La quasi totalité des personnes enregistrées comme apatrides ont une résidence permanente et jouissent de davantage de droits que ceux prévus par la Convention de 1954 relative au statut des apatrides.
24 Y compris les Îles d'Åland.
25 Y compris l'Abkhazie et l'Ossétie du Sud.
26 Y compris Saint-Barthélemy et Saint-Martin (partie française).
27 Chiffre correspond aux individus sans nationalité qui sont nés en République Dominicaine avant Janvier 2010 et qui ont été identifiés par le HCR en Haïti depuis Juin 2015.
28 Y compris une estimation des populations apatrides conforme à la loi 26 de 2006,qui permet aux apatrides de demander la nationalité dans certaines circonstances.
29 En attendant une étude plus précise sur les apatrides en Irak, l'estimation des apatrides en Irak a été ajustée pour refléter la réduction de l'apatridie conformément à la loi 26 de 2006, qui permet aux apatrides de demander la nationalité dans certaines circonstances.
30 Y compris réfugiés iraquiens enregistrés par le HCR.
31 Le nombres d'apatrides comprend les personnes couvertes par deux lois distinctes: La loi sur les apatrides du 17 février 2004 et la loi relative au Statut des citoyens de l'ex-URSS qui ne sont pas citoyens de la Lettonie ou d'un autre État.

32 Non-citizens of Latvia is the only category of residents who are not Latvian citizens, but who enjoy the right to reside in Latvia ex lege (all others require a resident permit) and an immediate right to acquire citizenship through registration and/or naturalisation (depending on age).
33 Including Sabah and Sarawak.
34 The updated statelessness figure is based on a registration and community legal assistance programme undertaken in West Malaysia by a local NGO with technical support from UNHCR, which began in 2014. During 2016, 874 persons of those registered acquired Malaysian nationality.
35 Including Agalega, Rodrigues and Saint Brandon.
36 Stateless persons population refers to persons without citizeship in Rakhine State only.
37 This figure is an estimate of persons without any citizenship in Rakhine state derived from the 2014 census. It does not include an estimated 118,000 stateless IDPs, persons in an IDP-like situation who are also of concern under the statelessness mandate because they are already included within the figures on IDPs.
38 Various studies estimate that a large number of individuals lack citizenship certificates in Nepal. While these individuals are not all necessarily stateless, UNHCR has been working closely with the Government of Nepal and partners to address this situation.
39 Including Svalbard and Jan Mayen Islands.
40 The updated statelessness figure is based on a registration exercise covering 28 municipalities that has taken place between 2014 and 2016. 4,112 of the registered group were confirmed as Filipino, Indonesian or dual nationals during 2016.
41 Including the Transnistria region.
42 Stateless persons refers to census figure from 2010 adjusted to reflect the number of people who acquired nationality since 2011.
43 Including Ascension and Tristan da Cunha.
44 Including Kosovo.
45 An adjustment to 2015 and 2016 end of year figures, in particular for the number of asylum applications pending on appeal and review, has resulted in a substantially lower figure for numbers of asylum seekers reported in South Africa.
46 Internally displaced persons (IDP) figure in South Sudan includes 105,000 people who are in an IDP-like situation.
47 Including Canary Islands, Ceuta and Melilla.
48 The statistics of the remaining IDPs, while provided by the Government authorities at the district level, are being reviewed by the central authorities. Once this review has been concluded, the statistics will be changed accordingly.
49 Including East Jerusalem.
50 Refugees are not part of the foreign-born migrant stock in the State of Palestine.
51 Internally displaced persons (IDP) figure in Sudan includes 77,300 people who are in an IDP-like situation.
52 The figure for Iraqi refugees is a Government estimate.
53 Figure refers to a registration exercise in three regions and 637 persons registered as stateless by the Ministry of Internal Affairs of Tajikistan.
54 Figure of stateless persons in Thailand refers to 2011.
55 The figure on the number of registered stateless persons has been updated by the Royal Thai Government. It includes an increase of 61,070 persons who are expected to form a large proportion of the group which will benefit from positive changes introduced to the nationality framework in December 2016. In addition, it reflects decreases as a result of 8,814 stateless persons acquiring Thai nationality in 2016 and 8,377 cases that were de-registered because of death or duplicate registration.

32 Les non-ressortissants de la Lettonie sont les seuls résidents qui, sans être des citoyens lettons, jouissent du droit de résider en Lettonie ex lege (tous les autres ont besoin d'un permis de séjour) et du droit d'acquérir immédiatement la nationalité par enregistrement ou naturalisation (en fonction de leur âge).
33 Y compris Sabah et Sarawak.
34 Le chiffre actualisé sur l'apatridie est basé sur un programme d'enregistrement et d'assistance juridique communautaire entrepris en Malaisie occidentale par une ONG locale avec le soutien technique du HCR, qui a débuté en 2014. En 2016, 874 personnes enregistrées ont acquis la nationalité malaisienne.
35 Y compris Agalega, Rodrigues et Saint-Brandon.
36 Les apatrides s'entendent des personnes dépourvues de nationalité, dans l'État de Rakhine uniquement.
37 Ce chiffre est une estimation des personnes sans citoyenneté dans l'État de Rakhine dérivées du recensement de 2014. Il n'inclut pas environ 118 000 personnes déplacées apatrides, des personnes dans une situation de type PDI qui sont également préoccupantes dans le cadre du mandat sur l'apatridie parce qu'elles sont déjà incluses dans les chiffres sur les PDI.
38 Selon différentes études, un grand nombre de personnes ne disposeraient pas de certificat de nationalité au Népal. Elles ne sont pas nécessairement toutes apatrides, mais le HCR travaille en coopération étroite avec les autorités népalaises et des partenaires pour régler la situation.
39 Y compris les îles Svalbard-et-Jan Mayen.
40 Le chiffre mis à jour sur l'apatridie est basé sur un exercice d'enregistrement couvrant 28 municipalités qui a eu lieu entre 2014 et 2016. 4 112 du groupe enregistré ont été confirmés en tant que Philippins, Indonésiens ou binationaux en 2016.
41 Y compris la région de Transnistrie.
42 Le nombre d'apatrides se rapporte aux données du recensement effectué en 2010, ajustées pour tenir compte du nombre de personnes ayant acquis la nationalité depuis 2011.
43 Y compris Ascension et Tristan da Cunha.
44 Y compris Kosovo.
45 Un ajustement des chiffres de fin d'année 2015 et 2016, en particulier pour le nombre de demandes d'asile pendantes en appel et en révision, a abouti à un chiffre sensiblement inférieur pour le nombre de demandeurs d'asile signalés en Afrique du Sud.
46 Au nombre des déplacés au Soudan du Sud figurent 105 000 personnes dans une situation analogue à celle des déplacés.
47 Y compris les îles Canaries, Ceuta et Melilla.
48 Les statistiques relatives au reste des déplacés ont été fournies par les autorités locales au niveau des districts, mais examinées par les autorités centrales, et seront ajustées en fonction des résultats de l'examen.
49 Y compris Jérusalem-Est.
50 Les réfugiés ne sont pas comptabilisés parmi les migrants nés à l'étranger qui se trouvent dans l'État de Palestine.
51 Au nombre des déplacés au Soudan figurent 77 300 personnes dans une situation analogue à celles des déplacés.
52 Le nombre de réfugiés iraquiens est une estimation du Gouvernement.
53 Les chiffres se rapportent aux enregistrements effectués dans trois régions; 637 personnes ont été enregistrées comme apatrides par le Ministère de l'intérieur tadjik.
54 Les chiffres relatifs au nombre d'apatrides en Thaïlande remontent à 2011.
55 Le chiffre concernant le nombre d'apatrides enregistrés a été mis à jour par le gouvernement royal thaïlandais. Il comprend une augmentation de 61 070 personnes qui devraient former une grande partie du groupe qui bénéficiera des changements positifs introduits dans le cadre de la nationalité en décembre 2016. En outre, il reflète des diminutions dues au fait que 8 814 apatrides ayant acquis la nationalité thaïlandaise en 2016 et 8 377 cas qui ont été radiés en raison d'un décès ou d'un double enregistrement.

56 Refugee figure for Syrians in Turkey is a Government estimate.
57 Including Crimea.
58 Internally displaced persons (IDP) figure in Ukraine includes 800,000 people who are in an IDP-like situation.
59 Including Zanzibar.
60 Pending asylum applications for U.S. Citizenship and Immigration Services at start-2017 and mid-2017 are multiplied by inflation factor (1.518).
61 Figure of stateless persons refers to those with permanent residence reported in 2010 by the Government. Information on other categories of stateless persons is not available.
62 The statelessness figure refers to stateless persons with permanent residence reported by the Government in 2010. The figure has been adjusted to reflect the acquisition of nationality of 179 formerly stateless persons. Information on other categories of stateless persons is not available.
63 A study is being pursued to provide a revised estimate of statelessness figure.

56 Le nombre de réfugiés syriens en Turquie est une estimation du Gouvernement.
57 Y compris Crimea.
58 Le chiffre sur les personnes déplacées à l'intérieur de leur propre pays (PDI) en Ukraine inclut 800000 personnes qui sont dans une situation similaire aux PDI.
59 Y compris Zanzibar.
60 Les demandes d'asile pendantes pour les services de citoyenneté et d'immigration des États-Unis au début de 2017 et à la mi-2017 sont multipliées par le facteur d'inflation (1,518).
61 Le nombre d'apatrides renvoit au nombre de résidents permanents recensés en 2010 par le Gouvernement. On ne dispose d'aucune information sur d'autres catégories d'apatrides.
62 Le chiffre relatif à l'apatridie fait référence aux personnes apatrides avec résidence permanente déclarées par le gouvernement en 2010. Ce chiffre a été ajusté pour refléter l'acquisition de la nationalité de 179 anciens apatrides. Les informations sur les autres catégories d'apatrides ne sont pas disponibles.
63 Une étude est en cours pour fournir une estimation révisée du chiffre d'apatridie.

5 Proportion of seats held by women in national parliament

Percentage, as of February each year

Proportion de sièges occupés par les femmes au parlement national

Pourcentage, données disponibles en février de chaque année

Region, country or area&	Last Election date Dernière date de l'élection	1990	2000	2005	2010	2014	2015	2016	2017	2018	Région, pays ou zone&
Total, all countries or areas		**...**	**13.3**	**15.9**	**19.0**	**22.1**	**22.3**	**22.7**	**23.4**	**23.4**	**Total, tous pays ou zones**
Africa		...	10.4	13.9	17.4	23.0	23.0	23.3	23.7	23.4	Afrique
Northern Africa		...	4.5	8.7	10.9	24.1	22.0	23.2	23.8	22.6	Afrique septentrionale
Sub-Saharan Africa		...	11.5	14.4	18.4	22.8	22.6	23.3	23.7	23.6	Afrique subsaharienne
Eastern Africa		...	11.9	16.6	21.6	27.3	27.2	28.9	29.7	30.0	Afrique orientale
Middle Africa		...	8.6	11.2	13.5	18.7	18.1	18.1	17.4	16.4	Afrique centrale
Southern Africa		...	22.5	24.6	33.4	33.2	33.4	33.4	33.4	33.7	Afrique australe
Western Africa		...	8.2	10.2	11.6	14.6	14.5	14.0	14.9	14.8	Afrique occidentale
Americas		...	15.4	18.8	22.1	25.2	26.5	27.3	28.3	28.5	Amériques
Northern America		...	16.3	17.5	19.0	21.1	21.8	22.3	22.2	22.8	Amérique septentrionale
Latin America & the Caribbean		...	15.2	19.0	22.7	25.9	27.4	28.2	29.4	29.5	Amérique latine et Caraïbes
Caribbean		...	20.6	26.0	29.4	32.9	33.1	33.0	33.8	33.7	Caraïbes
Central America		...	14.3	17.4	21.6	29.3	30.1	32.5	33.1	32.5	Amérique centrale
South America		...	12.5	15.8	19.2	19.6	22.2	22.7	24.5	24.8	Amérique du Sud
Asia		...	12.1	13.4	16.8	17.5	17.8	17.9	18.4	17.9	Asie
Central Asia		...	7.0	13.4	20.0	23.2	21.8	21.1	21.3	21.3	Asie centrale
Eastern Asia		...	18.2	18.1	18.7	19.9	20.4	20.4	20.5	20.9	Asie orientale
South-eastern Asia		...	12.3	15.5	19.3	18.4	17.8	18.3	19.3	19.1	Asie du Sud-Est
Southern Asia		...	6.8	8.8	18.2	16.0	17.6	17.7	18.0	13.9	Asie méridionale
Western Asia		...	5.2	5.7	9.3	12.8	12.8	13.2	13.8	14.3	Asie occidentale
Europe		...	16.8	20.5	23.2	26.4	26.7	27.2	28.0	28.9	Europe
Eastern Europe		...	9.5	14.1	15.2	16.3	16.9	17.6	19.4	20.0	Europe orientale
Northern Europe		...	27.0	28.0	29.6	30.9	30.4	32.5	33.3	33.8	Europe septentrionale
Southern Europe		...	11.0	17.1	23.0	29.4	30.0	29.0	29.4	29.9	Europe méridionale
Western Europe		...	23.0	25.8	28.4	32.5	32.0	32.2	32.1	34.0	Europe occidentale
Oceania		...	11.3	11.2	13.2	13.4	13.2	13.4	15.0	15.5	Océanie
Australia and New Zealand		...	25.5	26.3	30.1	29.5	28.8	28.8	31.1	33.0	Australie et Nouvelle-Zélande
Melanesia		...	3.9	3.2	1.4	1.9	4.2	4.6	4.6	3.5	Mélanésie
Micronesia		...	2.5	2.4	2.4	4.7	4.7	5.5	7.8	7.8	Micronésie
Polynesia		...	4.4	3.2	5.2	4.3	4.4	4.4	7.7	8.7	Polynésie
Afghanistan	2010-09	3.7	...	...	27.3	27.7	27.7	27.7	27.7	27.7	Afghanistan
Albania	2017-06	28.8	5.2	6.4	16.4	20.0	20.7	20.7	22.9	27.9	Albanie
Algeria	2017-05	2.4	3.2	6.2	7.7	31.6	31.6	31.6	31.6	25.8	Algérie
Andorra	2015-03	...	7.1	14.3	35.7	50.0	50.0	39.3	32.1	32.1	Andorre
Angola	2017-08	14.5	15.5	15.0	38.6	36.8	36.8	36.8	38.2	30.5	Angola
Antigua and Barbuda	2014-06	0.0	...	10.5	10.5	10.5	11.1	11.1	11.1	11.1	Antigua-et-Barbuda
Argentina	2017-10	6.3	28.0	33.7	38.5	36.6	36.2	35.8	38.9	38.9	Argentine
Armenia	2017-04	35.6	3.1	5.3	9.2	10.7	10.7	10.7	9.9	18.1	Arménie
Australia	2016-07	6.1	22.4	24.7	27.3	26.0	26.7	26.7	28.7	28.7	Australie
Austria	2017-10	11.5	26.8	33.9	27.9	32.2	30.6	30.6	30.6	34.4	Autriche
Azerbaijan	2015-11	...	12.0	10.5	11.4	15.6	15.6	16.9	16.8	16.8	Azerbaïdjan
Bahamas	2017-05	4.1	15.0	20.0	12.2	13.2	13.2	13.2	13.2	12.8	Bahamas
Bahrain	2014-11	...	...	0.0	2.5	10.0	7.5	7.5	7.5	7.5	Bahreïn
Bangladesh	2014-01	10.3	9.1	2.0	18.6	6.4	20.0	20.0	20.3	20.3	Bangladesh
Barbados	2013-02	3.7	10.7	13.3	10.0	16.7	16.7	16.7	16.7	16.7	Barbade
Belarus	2016-09	...	4.5	29.4	31.8	26.6	27.3	27.3	34.5	34.5	Bélarus
Belgium	2014-05	8.5	23.3	34.7	38.0	41.3	39.3	39.3	38.0	38.0	Belgique
Belize	2015-11	0.0	6.9	6.7	0.0	3.1	3.1	3.1	9.4	9.4	Belize
Benin	2015-04	2.9	6.0	7.2	10.8	8.4	8.4	7.2	7.2	7.2	Bénin
Bhutan	2013-07	2.0	2.0	9.3	8.5	8.5	8.5	8.5	8.5	8.5	Bhoutan
Bolivia (Plurin. State of)	2014-10	9.2	11.5	19.2	22.3	25.4	53.1	53.1	53.1	53.1	Bolivie (État plurin. de)
Bosnia and Herzegovina	2014-10	...	28.6	16.7	19.0	21.4	21.4	21.4	21.4	21.4	Bosnie-Herzégovine
Botswana	2014-10	5.0	...	11.1	7.9	9.5	9.5	9.5	9.5	9.5	Botswana
Brazil	2014-10	5.3	5.7	8.6	8.8	8.6	9.0	9.9	10.7	10.7	Brésil
Brunei Darussalam	2017-01	...	...	...	...	...	...	...	9.1	9.1	Brunéi Darussalam
Bulgaria	2017-03	21.0	10.8	26.3	20.8	24.6	20.4	20.4	19.2	23.8	Bulgarie
Burkina Faso	2015-11	...	8.1	11.7	15.3	18.9	13.3	9.4	11.0	11.0	Burkina Faso
Burundi	2015-06	...	6.0	18.4	31.4	30.5	30.5	36.4	36.4	36.4	Burundi

5

Proportion of seats held by women in national parliament *(continued)*
Percentage, as of February each year

Proportion de sièges occupés par les femmes au parlement national *(suite)*
Pourcentage, données disponibles en février de chaque année

Region, country or area&	Last Election date Dernière date de l'élection	1990	2000	2005	2010	2014	2015	2016	2017	2018	Région, pays ou zone&
Cabo Verde	2016-03	12.0	11.1	11.1	18.1	20.8	20.8	20.8	23.6	23.6	Cabo Verde
Cambodia	2013-07	...	8.2	9.8	21.1	20.3	20.3	20.3	20.3	20.3	Cambodge
Cameroon	2013-09	14.4	5.6	8.9	13.9	31.1	31.1	31.1	31.1	31.1	Cameroun
Canada	2015-10	13.3	20.6	21.1	22.1	25.1	25.2	26.0	26.3	27.0	Canada
Central African Republic	2016-02	3.8	7.3	...	9.6	...	...	...	8.6	8.6	République centrafricaine
Chad	2011-02	...	2.4	6.5	5.2	14.9	14.9	14.9	12.8	12.8	Tchad
Chile	2013-11	...	10.8	12.5	14.2	15.8	15.8	15.8	15.8	...	Chili
China	2013-03	21.3	21.8	20.2	21.3	23.4	23.6	23.6	23.7	24.2	Chine
Colombia	2014-03	4.5	11.8	12.0	8.4	12.1	19.9	19.9	18.7	18.7	Colombie
Comoros	2015-01	0.0	...	3.0	3.0	3.0	...	3.0	6.1	6.1	Comores
Congo	2017-07	14.3	12.0	8.5	7.3	7.4	7.4	7.4	7.4	11.3	Congo
Costa Rica	2014-02	10.5	19.3	35.1	36.8	38.6	33.3	33.3	35.1	35.1	Costa Rica
Côte d'Ivoire	2016-12	5.7	...	8.5	8.9	9.4	9.2	9.2	11.5	10.6	Côte d'Ivoire
Croatia	2016-09	...	...	21.7	23.5	23.8	25.8	15.2	19.9	18.5	Croatie
Cuba	2013-02	33.9	27.6	36.0	43.2	48.9	48.9	48.9	48.9	48.9	Cuba
Cyprus	2016-05	1.8	5.4	16.1	12.5	12.5	12.5	12.5	17.9	17.9	Chypre
Czechia	2017-10	...	15.0	17.0	15.5	19.5	19.0	20.0	20.0	22.0	Tchéquie
Dem. People's Rep. Korea	2014-03	21.1	20.1	20.1	15.6	15.6	16.3	16.3	16.3	16.3	Rép. pop. dém. de Corée
Dem. Rep. of the Congo	2011-11	5.4	...	12.0	8.4	10.6	8.9	8.9	8.9	8.9	Rép. dém. du Congo
Denmark	2015-06	30.7	37.4	38.0	38.0	39.1	38.0	37.4	37.4	37.4	Danemark
Djibouti	2013-02	0.0	0.0	10.8	13.8	12.7	12.7	12.7	10.8	10.8	Djibouti
Dominica	2014-12	10.0	9.4	19.4	14.3	12.9	21.9	21.9	25.0	25.0	Dominique
Dominican Republic	2016-05	7.5	16.1	17.3	19.7	20.8	20.8	20.8	26.8	26.8	République dominicaine
Ecuador	2017-02	4.5	17.4	16.0	32.3	41.6	41.6	41.6	41.6	38.0	Équateur
Egypt	2015-10	3.9	2.0	2.9	1.8	...	...	14.9	14.9	14.9	Égypte
El Salvador	2015-03	11.7	16.7	10.7	19.0	26.2	27.4	32.1	32.1	32.1	El Salvador
Equatorial Guinea	2017-11	13.3	5.0	18.0	10.0	24.0	24.0	24.0	24.0	20.0	Guinée équatoriale
Eritrea	1994-02	...	14.7	22.0	22.0	22.0	22.0	22.0	22.0	22.0	Érythrée
Estonia	2015-03	...	17.8	18.8	22.8	19.0	19.8	23.8	26.7	26.7	Estonie
Eswatini	2013-09	3.6	3.1	10.8	13.6	6.2	6.2	6.2	6.2	6.2	Eswatini
Ethiopia	2015-05	...	2.0	7.7	21.9	27.8	27.8	38.8	38.8	38.8	Éthiopie
Fiji	2014-09	...	11.3	8.5	...	...	14.0	16.0	16.0	16.0	Fidji
Finland	2015-04	31.5	37.0	37.5	40.0	42.5	42.5	41.5	42.0	42.0	Finlande
France	2017-06	6.9	10.9	12.2	18.9	26.2	26.2	26.2	25.8	39.0	France
Gabon	2011-12	13.3	8.3	9.2	14.7	15.0	14.2	14.2	17.1	17.1	Gabon
Gambia	2017-04	7.8	2.0	13.2	7.5	9.4	9.4	9.4	9.4	10.3	Gambie
Georgia	2016-10	...	7.2	9.4	5.1	12.0	11.3	11.3	16.0	16.0	Géorgie
Germany	2017-09	...	30.9	32.8	32.8	36.5	36.5	36.5	37.0	30.7	Allemagne
Ghana	2016-12	...	9.0	10.9	8.3	10.9	10.9	10.9	12.7	12.7	Ghana
Greece	2015-09	6.7	6.3	14.0	17.3	21.0	23.0	19.7	18.3	18.3	Grèce
Grenada	2013-02	...	...	26.7	13.3	33.3	33.3	33.3	33.3	33.3	Grenade
Guatemala	2015-09	7.0	7.1	8.2	12.0	13.3	13.3	13.9	12.7	12.7	Guatemala
Guinea	2013-09	...	8.8	19.3	...	21.9	21.9	21.9	21.9	21.9	Guinée
Guinea-Bissau	2014-04	20.0	...	14.0	10.0	11.0	13.7	13.7	13.7	13.7	Guinée-Bissau
Guyana	2015-05	36.9	18.5	30.8	30.0	31.3	31.3	30.4	31.9	31.9	Guyana
Haiti	2015-08	...	3.6	3.6	4.1	4.2	4.2	0.0	2.6	2.5	Haïti
Honduras	2017-11	10.2	9.4	5.5	18.0	25.8	25.8	25.8	25.8	21.1	Honduras
Hungary	2014-04	20.7	8.3	9.1	11.1	9.4	10.1	10.1	10.1	10.1	Hongrie
Iceland	2017-10	20.6	34.9	30.2	42.9	39.7	41.3	41.3	47.6	38.1	Islande
India	2014-04	5.0	9.0	8.3	10.8	11.4	12.0	12.0	11.8	11.8	Inde
Indonesia	2014-04	12.4	...	11.3	18.0	18.6	17.1	17.1	19.8	19.8	Indonésie
Iran (Islamic Republic of)	2016-02	1.5	4.9	4.1	2.8	3.1	3.1	3.1	5.9	5.9	Iran (Rép. islamique d')
Iraq	2014-04	10.8	6.4	...	25.5	25.2	26.5	26.5	25.3	25.3	Iraq
Ireland	2016-02	7.8	12.0	13.3	13.9	15.7	16.3	16.3	22.2	22.2	Irlande
Israel	2015-03	6.7	11.7	15.0	19.2	22.5	22.5	26.7	27.5	27.5	Israël
Italy	2013-02	12.9	11.1	11.5	21.3	31.4	31.0	31.0	31.0	31.0	Italie
Jamaica	2016-02	5.0	13.3	11.7	13.3	12.7	12.7	12.7	17.5	17.5	Jamaïque
Japan	2017-10	1.4	4.6	7.1	11.3	8.1	9.5	9.5	9.3	10.1	Japon
Jordan	2016-09	0.0	0.0	5.5	6.4	12.0	12.0	12.0	15.4	15.4	Jordanie

5 Proportion of seats held by women in national parliament *(continued)*

Percentage, as of February each year

Proportion de sièges occupés par les femmes au parlement national *(suite)*

Pourcentage, données disponibles en février de chaque année

Region, country or area&	Last Election date Dernière date de l'élection	1990	2000	2005	2010	2014	2015	2016	2017	2018	Région, pays ou zone&
Kazakhstan	2016-03	...	10.4	10.4	17.8	25.2	26.2	26.2	27.1	27.1	Kazakhstan
Kenya	2017-07	1.1	3.6	7.1	9.8	19.1	19.7	19.7	19.4	21.8	Kenya
Kiribati	2015-12	0.0	4.9	4.8	4.3	8.7	8.7	6.5	6.5	6.5	Kiribati
Kuwait	2016-11	...	0.0	0.0	7.7	4.6	1.5	1.5	3.1	3.1	Koweït
Kyrgyzstan	2015-10	...	1.4	10.0	25.6	23.3	23.3	19.2	19.2	19.2	Kirghizistan
Lao People's Dem. Rep.	2016-03	6.3	21.2	22.9	25.2	25.0	25.0	25.0	27.5	27.5	Rép. dém. populaire lao
Latvia	2014-10	...	17.0	21.0	22.0	25.0	18.0	18.0	16.0	16.0	Lettonie
Lebanon	2009-06	0.0	2.3	2.3	3.1	3.1	3.1	3.1	3.1	3.1	Liban
Lesotho	2017-06	...	3.8	11.7	24.2	26.7	26.7	25.0	25.0	22.1	Lesotho
Liberia	2017-10	...	...	5.3	12.5	11.0	11.0	11.0	12.3	9.9	Libéria
Libya	2014-06	...	...	...	7.7	16.5	16.0	16.0	16.0	16.0	Libye
Liechtenstein	2017-02	4.0	4.0	12.0	24.0	20.0	20.0	20.0	12.0	12.0	Liechtenstein
Lithuania	2016-10	...	17.5	22.0	19.1	24.1	23.4	23.4	21.3	21.3	Lituanie
Luxembourg	2013-10	13.3	16.7	23.3	20.0	28.3	28.3	28.3	28.3	28.3	Luxembourg
Madagascar	2013-12	6.5	8.0	6.9	...	23.1	20.5	20.5	19.2	19.2	Madagascar
Malawi	2014-05	9.8	8.3	14.0	20.8	22.3	16.7	16.7	16.7	16.7	Malawi
Malaysia	2013-05	5.1	...	9.1	9.9	10.4	10.4	10.4	10.4	10.4	Malaisie
Maldives	2014-03	6.3	...	12.0	6.5	6.8	5.9	5.9	5.9	5.9	Maldives
Mali	2013-11	...	12.2	10.2	10.2	9.5	9.5	8.8	8.8	8.8	Mali
Malta	2017-06	2.9	9.2	9.2	8.7	14.3	12.9	12.9	12.5	11.9	Malte
Marshall Islands	2015-11	...	...	3.0	3.0	3.0	3.0	9.1	9.1	9.1	Îles Marshall
Mauritania	2013-11	...	3.8	3.7	22.1	25.2	25.2	25.2	25.2	25.2	Mauritanie
Mauritius	2014-12	7.1	7.6	5.7	17.1	18.8	11.6	11.6	11.6	11.6	Maurice
Mexico	2015-06	12.0	18.2	22.6	27.6	37.4	38.0	42.4	42.6	42.6	Mexique
Micronesia (Fed. States of)	2017-03	...	0.0	0.0	0.0	0.0	0.0	0.0	0.0	0.0	Micronésie (États féd. de)
Monaco	2013-02	11.1	22.2	20.8	26.1	20.8	20.8	20.8	20.8	20.8	Monaco
Mongolia	2016-06	24.9	7.9	6.8	3.9	14.9	14.9	14.5	17.1	17.1	Mongolie
Montenegro	2016-10	...	...	...	11.1	14.8	17.3	17.3	23.5	23.5	Monténégro
Morocco	2016-10	0.0	0.6	10.8	10.5	17.0	17.0	17.0	20.5	20.5	Maroc
Mozambique	2014-10	15.7	...	34.8	39.2	39.2	39.6	39.6	39.6	39.6	Mozambique
Myanmar	2015-11	...	...	...	...	5.6	6.2	9.9	10.2	10.2	Myanmar
Namibia	2014-11	6.9	22.2	25.0	26.9[1]	25.6	41.3	41.3	41.3	46.2	Namibie
Nauru	2016-07	5.6	0.0	0.0	0.0	5.3	5.3	5.3	10.5	10.5	Nauru
Nepal	2017-12	6.1	5.9	...	33.2	29.9	29.5	29.5	29.6	* 3.6	Népal
Netherlands	2017-03	21.3	36.0	36.7	42.0	38.7	37.3	37.3	38.0	36.0	Pays-Bas
New Zealand	2017-09	14.4	29.2	28.3	33.6	33.9	31.4	31.4	34.2	38.3	Nouvelle-Zélande
Nicaragua	2016-11	14.8	9.7	20.7	20.7	40.2	39.1	41.3	45.7	45.7	Nicaragua
Niger	2016-02	5.4	1.2	12.4	9.7	13.3	13.3	13.3	17.0	17.0	Niger
Nigeria	2015-03	...	...	4.7	7.0	6.7	6.7	5.6	5.6	5.6	Nigéria
Norway	2017-09	35.8	36.4	38.2	39.6	39.6	39.6	39.6	39.6	41.4	Norvège
Oman	2015-10	...	...	2.4	0.0	1.2	1.2	1.2	1.2	1.2	Oman
Pakistan	2013-05	10.1	...	21.3	22.2	20.7	20.7	20.6	20.6	20.6	Pakistan
Palau	2016-11	...	0.0	0.0	0.0	0.0	0.0	0.0	12.5	12.5	Palaos
Panama	2014-05	7.5	...	16.7	8.5	8.5	19.3	18.3	18.3	18.3	Panama
Papua New Guinea	2017-06	0.0	1.8	0.9	0.9	2.7	2.7	2.7	2.7	0.0	Papouasie-Nvl-Guinée
Paraguay	2013-04	5.6	2.5	10.0	12.5	15.0	15.0	15.0	13.8	13.8	Paraguay
Peru	2016-04	5.6	10.8	18.3	27.5	22.3	22.3	22.3	27.7	27.7	Pérou
Philippines	2016-05	9.1	12.4	15.3	21.0	27.3	27.2	27.2	29.5	29.5	Philippines
Poland	2015-10	13.5	13.0	20.2	20.0	24.3	24.1	27.4	28.0	28.0	Pologne
Portugal	2015-10	7.6	18.7	19.1	27.4	31.3	31.3	34.8	34.8	34.8	Portugal
Qatar	2013-07	...	...	...	0.0	0.0	0.0	0.0	0.0	9.8	Qatar
Republic of Korea	2016-04	2.0	3.7	13.0	14.7	15.7	16.3	16.3	17.0	17.0	République de Corée
Republic of Moldova	2014-11	...	8.9	15.8	23.8	18.8	20.8	21.8	22.8	22.8	République de Moldova
Romania	2016-12	34.4	7.3	11.4	11.4	13.5	13.7	13.7	20.7	20.7	Roumanie
Russian Federation	2016-09	...	7.7	9.8	14.0	13.6	13.6	13.6	15.8	15.8	Fédération de Russie
Rwanda	2013-09	17.1	17.1	48.8	56.3	63.8	63.8	63.8	61.3	61.3	Rwanda
Saint Kitts and Nevis	2015-02	6.7	13.3	0.0	6.7	6.7	6.7	13.3	13.3	13.3	Saint-Kitts-et-Nevis
Saint Lucia	2016-06	0.0	11.1	11.1	11.1	16.7	16.7	16.7	16.7	16.7	Sainte-Lucie
Saint Vincent & Grenadines	2015-12	9.5	4.8	22.7	21.7	13.0	13.0	13.0	13.0	13.0	Saint-Vincent-Grenadines

5 Proportion of seats held by women in national parliament *(continued)*
Percentage, as of February each year

Proportion de sièges occupés par les femmes au parlement national *(suite)*
Pourcentage, données disponibles en février de chaque année

Region, country or area&	Last Election date Dernière date de l'élection	1990	2000	2005	2010	2014	2015	2016	2017	2018	Région, pays ou zone&
Samoa	2016-03	0.0	8.2	6.1	8.2	4.1	6.1	6.1	10.0	10.0	Samoa
San Marino	2016-11	11.7	13.3	16.7	16.7	18.3	16.7	16.7	26.7	26.7	Saint-Marin
Sao Tome and Principe	2014-10	11.8	9.1	9.1	7.3	18.2	18.2	18.2	18.2	18.2	Sao Tomé-et-Principe
Saudi Arabia	2016-12	...	...	0.0	0.0	19.9	19.9	19.9	19.9	19.9	Arabie saoudite
Senegal	2017-07	12.5	12.1	19.2	22.7	43.3	42.7	42.7	42.7	41.8	Sénégal
Serbia	2016-04	...	...	...	21.6	33.6	34.0	34.0	34.4	34.4	Serbie
Serbia and Monten. [former]		...	5.1	7.9	...	...	...	...	...	...	Serbie-et-Monténégro [anc.]
Seychelles	2016-09	16.0	23.5	29.4	23.5	43.8	43.8	43.8	21.2	21.2	Seychelles
Sierra Leone	2012-11	...	8.8	14.5	13.2	12.1	12.4	12.4	12.4	12.4	Sierra Leone
Singapore	2015-09	4.9	4.3	16.0	23.4	25.3	25.3	23.1	23.8	23.0	Singapour
Slovakia	2016-03	...	12.7	16.7	18.0	18.7	18.7	18.7	20.0	20.0	Slovaquie
Slovenia	2014-07	...	7.8	12.2	14.4	33.3	36.7	36.7	36.7	36.7	Slovénie
Solomon Islands	2014-11	0.0	2.0	0.0	0.0	2.0	2.0	2.0	2.0	2.0	Îles Salomon
Somalia	2016-10	4.0	...	...	6.9	13.8	13.8	13.8	24.2	24.4	Somalie
South Africa	2014-05	2.8	30.0	32.8	44.5	44.8	41.5	42.0	42.2	42.4	Afrique du Sud
South Sudan	2016-08	...	...	...	...	26.5	26.5	26.5	28.5	28.5	Soudan du sud
Spain	2016-06	14.6	21.6	36.0	36.6	39.7	41.1	40.0	39.1	39.1	Espagne
Sri Lanka	2015-08	4.9	4.9	4.9	5.8	5.8	5.8	5.8	5.8	5.8	Sri Lanka
Sudan	2015-04	...	...	...	...	24.3	24.3	30.5	30.5	30.5	Soudan
Sudan [former]		...	...	9.7	18.9	...	...	...	...	...	Soudan [anc.]
Suriname	2015-05	7.8	15.7	19.6	25.5	11.8	11.8	25.5	25.5	25.5	Suriname
Sweden	2014-09	38.4	42.7	45.3	46.4	45.0	43.6	43.6	43.6	43.6	Suède
Switzerland	2015-10	14.0	22.5	25.0	29.0	31.0	30.5	32.0	32.5	32.5	Suisse
Syrian Arab Republic	2016-04	9.2	10.4	12.0	12.4	12.0	12.4	12.4	13.2	13.2	République arabe syrienne
Tajikistan	2015-03	...	2.8	12.7	17.5	15.9	16.9	19.0	19.0	19.0	Tadjikistan
Thailand	2014-08	2.8	5.6	8.8	13.3	15.8	6.1	6.1	4.9	4.8	Thaïlande
TFYR of Macedonia	2016-12	...	7.5	19.2	32.5	34.1	33.3	33.3	31.7	37.5	ex-R.Y. de Macédoine
Timor-Leste	2017-07	...	...	25.3	29.2	38.5	38.5	38.5	38.5	32.3	Timor-Leste
Togo	2013-07	5.2	...	6.2	11.1	16.5	17.6	17.6	17.6	17.6	Togo
Tonga	2017-11	0.0	...	0.0	3.1	3.6	0.0	0.0	3.8	7.4	Tonga
Trinidad and Tobago	2015-09	16.7	11.1	19.4	26.8	28.6	28.6	31.0	31.0	31.0	Trinité-et-Tobago
Tunisia	2014-10	4.3	11.5	22.8	27.6	28.1	31.3	31.3	31.3	31.3	Tunisie
Turkey	2015-11	1.3	4.2	4.4	9.1	14.4	14.4	14.9	14.9	14.6	Turquie
Turkmenistan	2013-12	26.0	26.0	...	16.8	26.4	25.8	25.8	25.8	25.8	Turkménistan
Tuvalu	2015-03	7.7	0.0	0.0	0.0	6.7	6.7	6.7	6.7	6.7	Tuvalu
Uganda	2016-02	12.2	17.9	23.9	31.5	35.0	35.0	35.0	34.3	34.3	Ouganda
Ukraine	2014-10	...	7.8	5.3	8.0	9.7	11.8	12.1	12.3	12.3	Ukraine
United Arab Emirates	2015-10	0.0	0.0	0.0	22.5	17.5	17.5	22.5	20.0	22.5	Émirats arabes unis
United Kingdom	2017-06	6.3	18.4	18.1	19.5	22.6	22.8	29.4	30.0	32.0	Royaume-Uni
United Rep. of Tanzania	2015-10	...	16.4	21.4	30.7	36.0	36.0	36.6	36.4	37.2	Rép.-Unie de Tanzanie
United States of America	2016-11	6.6	13.3	14.9	16.8	18.3	19.4	19.4	19.1	19.5	États-Unis d'Amérique
Uruguay	2014-10	6.1	12.1	12.1	14.1	13.1	13.1	16.2	20.2	20.2	Uruguay
Uzbekistan	2014-12	...	6.8	17.5	22.0	22.0	16.0	16.0	16.0	16.0	Ouzbékistan
Vanuatu	2016-01	4.3	0.0	3.8	3.8	0.0	0.0	0.0	0.0	0.0	Vanuatu
Venezuela (Boliv. Rep. of)	2015-12	10.0	12.1	9.7	17.5	17.0	17.0	14.4	22.2	22.2	Venezuela (Rép. boliv. du)
Viet Nam	2016-05	17.7	26.0	27.3	25.8	24.3	24.3	24.3	26.7	26.7	Viet Nam
Yemen	2003-04	4.1	0.7	0.3	0.3	0.3	0.3	0.0	0.0	0.0	Yémen
Zambia	2016-08	6.6	10.1	12.0	14.0	10.8	12.7	12.7	18.0	18.0	Zambie
Zimbabwe	2013-07	11.0	14.0	10.0	15.0	31.5	31.5	31.5	32.6	33.2	Zimbabwe

Source:

Inter-Parliamentary Union (IPU), Geneva, "Women in National Parliament" dataset and the Millennium Development Goals Indicators database, last accessed February 2018.

Source:

Union interparlementaire, Genève, données des « Les femmes dans les parlements nationaux » et la base de données des Objectifs du Millénaire pour le développement, dernier accès février 2018.

& The data are as at 1 February for 2014 – 2018, as at 31 January for 2005 and 2010, and as at 25 January for 2000.

& Les données sont au 1er février en 2014 – 2018, au 31 janvier en 2005 et 2010, et au 25 janvier en 2000.

5

Proportion of seats held by women in national parliament *(continued)*
Percentage, as of February each year

Proportion de sièges occupés par les femmes au parlement national *(suite)*
Pourcentage, données disponibles en février de chaque année

1 Figure excludes 11 members yet to be sworn in.

1 Ce chiffre ne tient pas compte de 11 membres qui n'avaient pas encore été assermentés.

6

Ratio of girls to boys in primary, secondary and tertiary education

Rapport filles/garçons dans l'enseignement primaire, secondaire et supérieur

Region, country or area	1985	1995	2005	2010	2014	2015	2016	Région, pays ou zone
Total, all countries or areas								**Total, tous pays ou zones**
Primary education	**0.85**	**0.90**	**0.95**	**0.97**	**0.99**	**1.00**	**...**	**Enseignement primaire**
Secondary education	*** 0.81**	**0.88**	**0.95**	**0.97**	**0.99**	**0.99**	**...**	**Enseignement secondaire**
Tertiary education	*** 0.85**	*** 0.95**	**1.05**	**1.08**	**1.11**	**1.12**	**...**	**Enseignement supérieur**
Northern Africa								**Afrique septentrionale**
Primary education	0.78	0.86	0.93	0.95	0.96	* 0.97	0.97	Enseignement primaire
Secondary education	0.71	0.86	* 0.99	0.98	* 0.99	* 0.99	0.99	Enseignement secondaire
Tertiary education	* 0.62	* 0.76	0.96	1.07	1.08	1.11	1.16	Enseignement supérieur
Sub-Saharan Africa								**Afrique subsaharienne**
Primary education	0.81	0.84	0.88	0.93	0.94	* 0.94	0.95	Enseignement primaire
Secondary education	* 0.64	* 0.80	0.78	0.82	* 0.86	* 0.86	0.86	Enseignement secondaire
Tertiary education	* 0.46	* 0.59	0.67	0.67	* 0.69	* 0.71	0.71	Enseignement supérieur
Northern America								**Amérique septentrionale**
Primary education	1.01	0.99	0.99	0.99	1.00	1.00	1.00	Enseignement primaire
Secondary education	1.02	1.01	1.02	1.01	1.01	* 1.01	1.01	Enseignement secondaire
Tertiary education	1.13	1.28	1.40	1.39	1.35	1.34	1.35	Enseignement supérieur
Latin America & the Caribbean								**Amérique latine et Caraïbes**
Primary education	0.98	* 0.97	0.97	0.97	0.98	0.98	0.98	Enseignement primaire
Secondary education	* 1.03	* 1.08	1.08	1.08	1.06	1.06	1.06	Enseignement secondaire
Tertiary education	* 0.88	* 1.09	1.22	1.31	1.31	* 1.32	1.32	Enseignement supérieur
Eastern Asia								**Asie orientale**
Primary education	0.85	0.95	* 1.00	0.99	1.00	1.00	1.01	Enseignement primaire
Secondary education	0.77	0.89	* 0.98	1.00	1.02	1.02	1.02	Enseignement secondaire
Tertiary education	* 0.48	* 0.64	0.86	1.00	1.10	1.13	1.14	Enseignement supérieur
South-eastern Asia								**Asie du Sud-Est**
Primary education	0.95	0.97	0.97	1.01	0.98	0.97	0.97	Enseignement primaire
Secondary education	* 0.87	* 0.92	0.99	1.01	1.01	* 1.00	1.02	Enseignement secondaire
Tertiary education	* 0.87	0.94	* 0.99	1.07	1.19	1.20	1.22	Enseignement supérieur
Southern Asia								**Asie méridionale**
Primary education	0.69	0.81	* 0.95	1.00	1.06	1.06	1.09	Enseignement primaire
Secondary education	* 0.53	0.66	0.85	0.93	0.99	1.00	1.00	Enseignement secondaire
Tertiary education	0.43	0.54	0.74	0.76	0.96	0.95	0.96	Enseignement supérieur
Western Asia								**Asie occidentale**
Primary education	0.85	* 0.88	0.91	0.93	* 0.93	* 0.94	0.94	Enseignement primaire
Secondary education	* 0.69	* 0.75	0.86	0.90	* 0.92	* 0.92	0.92	Enseignement secondaire
Tertiary education	0.63	0.77	0.90	0.93	0.96	0.97	0.97	Enseignement supérieur
Europe								**Europe**
Primary education	* 0.99	0.99	0.99	1.00	1.00	1.00	1.00	Enseignement primaire
Secondary education	* 1.02	1.02	1.00	0.99	1.00	1.00	1.00	Enseignement secondaire
Tertiary education	* 1.08	1.14	1.28	1.29	1.23	1.23	1.22	Enseignement supérieur
Oceania								**Océanie**
Primary education	0.96	0.97	0.98	0.97	0.96	0.97	0.97	Enseignement primaire
Secondary education	* 0.99	0.99	0.97	0.93	0.90	* 0.89	0.89	Enseignement secondaire
Tertiary education	0.92	1.06	1.25	1.35	1.41	* 1.43	1.42	Enseignement supérieur
Afghanistan								**Afghanistan**
Primary education	0.49	0.51	0.59	0.69	0.70	0.69	...	Enseignement primaire
Secondary education	0.46	0.37	0.33	0.50	0.56	0.56	...	Enseignement secondaire
Tertiary education	...	...	...	...	0.28	...	...	Enseignement supérieur
Albania								**Albanie**
Primary education	0.98	0.96	0.99	0.98	0.98	0.97	0.97	Enseignement primaire
Secondary education	0.91	0.98	0.95	0.99	0.93	0.93	0.93	Enseignement secondaire
Tertiary education	0.86	1.08	1.42	1.34	1.52	1.53	1.58	Enseignement supérieur
Algeria								**Algérie**
Primary education	0.79	0.88	0.92	0.94	0.95	0.95	0.95	Enseignement primaire
Secondary education	0.73	0.89	1.10	1.04	...	...	...	Enseignement secondaire
Tertiary education	...	...	1.28	1.44	1.53	1.56	1.67	Enseignement supérieur
Angola								**Angola**
Primary education	...	...	...	0.79	...	...	...	Enseignement primaire
Secondary education	...	...	...	0.67	...	...	...	Enseignement secondaire
Tertiary education	...	...	...	...	...	0.77	...	Enseignement supérieur
Antigua and Barbuda								**Antigua-et-Barbuda**
Primary education	...	...	...	0.92	0.93	0.94	...	Enseignement primaire
Secondary education	...	...	...	1.01	1.01	1.02	...	Enseignement secondaire
Tertiary education	...	...	...	2.53	...	...	...	Enseignement supérieur

6

Ratio of girls to boys in primary, secondary and tertiary education *(continued)*

Rapport filles/garçons dans l'enseignement primaire, secondaire et supérieur *(suite)*

Region, country or area	1985	1995	2005	2010	2014	2015	2016	Région, pays ou zone
Argentina								**Argentine**
Primary education	1.00	...	0.99	0.99	1.00	1.00	...	Enseignement primaire
Secondary education	1.12	...	1.10	1.10	1.07	1.06	...	Enseignement secondaire
Tertiary education	1.11	...	1.46	1.51	1.62	1.64	...	Enseignement supérieur
Armenia								**Arménie**
Primary education	...	1.02	1.02	...	...	1.02	1.01	Enseignement primaire
Secondary education	...	...	...	...	...	1.05	...	Enseignement secondaire
Tertiary education	...	...	1.40	1.22	1.14	1.19	1.27	Enseignement supérieur
Aruba								**Aruba**
Primary education	...	...	0.94	0.99	0.97	...	...	Enseignement primaire
Secondary education	...	...	1.00	1.05	...	...	...	Enseignement secondaire
Tertiary education	...	...	1.44	1.41	2.27	2.26	...	Enseignement supérieur
Australia								**Australie**
Primary education	0.99	1.00	1.02	1.00	1.00	1.00	1.00	Enseignement primaire
Secondary education	...	1.00	...	...	...	0.87	0.87	Enseignement secondaire
Tertiary education	0.95	1.05	...	...	...	1.45	1.43	Enseignement supérieur
Austria								**Autriche**
Primary education	0.99	0.99	1.00	0.99	0.99	0.99	0.99	Enseignement primaire
Secondary education	0.93	0.94	0.95	0.96	0.96	0.96	0.96	Enseignement secondaire
Tertiary education	0.84	0.94	...	...	1.19	1.19	1.19	Enseignement supérieur
Azerbaijan								**Azerbaïdjan**
Primary education	...	1.12	* 0.95	* 0.99	* 0.99	* 0.98	* 0.99	Enseignement primaire
Secondary education	...	1.02	...	...	...	...	...	Enseignement secondaire
Tertiary education	...	0.88	...	* 0.99	* 1.14	* 1.16	* 1.19	Enseignement supérieur
Bahamas								**Bahamas**
Primary education	1.01	1.00	0.99	1.02	...	...	1.05	Enseignement primaire
Secondary education	1.16	1.00	1.00	1.05	...	...	1.06	Enseignement secondaire
Tertiary education	...	2.71	...	...	...	...	...	Enseignement supérieur
Bahrain								**Bahreïn**
Primary education	1.00	1.01	1.04	...	1.02	1.01	1.02	Enseignement primaire
Secondary education	0.92	1.04	1.11	1.01	1.01	1.00	1.01	Enseignement secondaire
Tertiary education	1.39	1.62	3.06	...	1.98	1.92	1.87	Enseignement supérieur
Bangladesh								**Bangladesh**
Primary education	0.69	...	1.05	* 1.06	...	1.08	1.06	Enseignement primaire
Secondary education	0.40	...	1.07	1.12	...	1.13	1.10	Enseignement secondaire
Tertiary education	0.24	...	0.52	...	0.74	...	0.70	Enseignement supérieur
Barbados								**Barbade**
Primary education	0.96	...	1.00	* 1.02	1.01	1.00	1.01	Enseignement primaire
Secondary education	1.02	...	0.99	* 1.01	1.03	1.03	1.05	Enseignement secondaire
Tertiary education	0.98	...	...	2.18	...	...	...	Enseignement supérieur
Belarus								**Bélarus**
Primary education	...	0.96	0.97	1.00	1.00	1.00	1.00	Enseignement primaire
Secondary education	...	...	...	0.97	0.98	0.99	0.98	Enseignement secondaire
Tertiary education	...	...	1.37	* 1.45	1.33	1.33	1.29	Enseignement supérieur
Belgium								**Belgique**
Primary education	1.01	0.99	1.00	1.00	1.00	1.00	...	Enseignement primaire
Secondary education	1.03	1.08	1.12	1.14	1.13	1.14	...	Enseignement secondaire
Tertiary education	0.87	1.02	1.25	1.27	1.30	1.31	...	Enseignement supérieur
Belize								**Belize**
Primary education	...	0.96	0.96	0.96	0.95	0.95	0.95	Enseignement primaire
Secondary education	...	1.03	1.03	1.08	1.05	1.02	1.01	Enseignement secondaire
Tertiary education	...	...	1.58	1.60	...	1.61	1.62	Enseignement supérieur
Benin								**Bénin**
Primary education	0.50	0.57	0.79	0.89	0.92	0.93	...	Enseignement primaire
Secondary education	0.41	...	...	...	0.69	0.71	...	Enseignement secondaire
Tertiary education	* 0.21	0.21	...	0.35	0.37	0.40	0.43	Enseignement supérieur
Bermuda								**Bermudes**
Primary education	1.01	1.00	1.05	...	0.97	0.98	...	Enseignement primaire
Secondary education	...	...	1.13	1.18	1.14	1.12	...	Enseignement secondaire
Tertiary education	...	...	...	2.11	1.89	2.32	...	Enseignement supérieur
Bhutan								**Bhoutan**
Primary education	0.53	0.78	0.98	1.03	1.02	1.01	1.01	Enseignement primaire
Secondary education	...	...	0.89	1.02	1.07	1.06	1.10	Enseignement secondaire
Tertiary education	...	...	0.64	0.61	...	...	...	Enseignement supérieur

Ratio of girls to boys in primary, secondary and tertiary education *(continued)*

Rapport filles/garçons dans l'enseignement primaire, secondaire et supérieur *(suite)*

Region, country or area	1985	1995	2005	2010	2014	2015	2016	Région, pays ou zone
Bolivia (Plurin. State of)								**Bolivie (État plurin. de)**
Primary education	...	0.96	0.99	0.98	0.97	0.97	0.98	Enseignement primaire
Secondary education	...	...	0.94	0.99	0.99	0.98	0.98	Enseignement secondaire
Botswana								**Botswana**
Primary education	1.11	1.01	0.98	...	0.97	...	...	Enseignement primaire
Secondary education	1.13	1.10	1.03	...	...	...	...	Enseignement secondaire
Tertiary education	0.82	0.91	0.89	...	1.25	1.37	1.43	Enseignement supérieur
Brazil								**Brésil**
Primary education	...	...	* 0.94	...	* 0.96	* 0.97	...	Enseignement primaire
Secondary education	...	...	* 1.10	...	* 1.08	* 1.05	...	Enseignement secondaire
Tertiary education	...	...	* 1.29	...	* 1.35	* 1.40	...	Enseignement supérieur
Brunei Darussalam								**Brunéi Darussalam**
Primary education	...	0.95	0.96	1.00	1.00	0.99	0.99	Enseignement primaire
Secondary education	...	...	0.98	1.01	1.00	1.00	1.01	Enseignement secondaire
Tertiary education	...	...	1.99	1.87	1.69	1.65	1.60	Enseignement supérieur
Bulgaria								**Bulgarie**
Primary education	1.00	0.99	0.99	1.00	0.99	0.99	0.99	Enseignement primaire
Secondary education	0.99	1.00	0.96	0.96	0.97	0.97	0.97	Enseignement secondaire
Tertiary education	1.21	1.60	1.16	1.32	1.26	1.28	1.25	Enseignement supérieur
Burkina Faso								**Burkina Faso**
Primary education	0.60	0.66	0.80	0.91	0.97	0.97	0.98	Enseignement primaire
Secondary education	0.55	...	0.71	0.76	0.87	0.92	0.95	Enseignement secondaire
Tertiary education	0.29	0.28	0.45	0.48	0.49	0.52	0.51	Enseignement supérieur
Burundi								**Burundi**
Primary education	0.67	0.79	0.84	0.97	1.01	1.01	1.01	Enseignement primaire
Secondary education	0.50	...	* 0.71	0.68	0.84	0.91	0.97	Enseignement secondaire
Tertiary education	* 0.34	...	* 0.37	0.50	0.31	...	...	Enseignement supérieur
Cabo Verde								**Cabo Verde**
Primary education	0.97	...	0.96	0.93	0.93	0.93	0.93	Enseignement primaire
Secondary education	...	...	1.13	1.19	1.12	1.10	1.10	Enseignement secondaire
Tertiary education	...	...	1.07	1.29	1.43	1.42	1.45	Enseignement supérieur
Cambodia								**Cambodge**
Primary education	...	0.82	0.93	0.94	0.95	0.99	0.97	Enseignement primaire
Tertiary education	...	0.18	0.46	0.59	...	0.82	...	Enseignement supérieur
Cameroon								**Cameroun**
Primary education	0.84	0.90	* 0.84	0.86	0.89	0.90	0.90	Enseignement primaire
Secondary education	0.61	0.69	0.79	...	0.85	0.86	0.86	Enseignement secondaire
Tertiary education	...	...	* 0.66	0.82	0.78	0.81	...	Enseignement supérieur
Canada								**Canada**
Primary education	0.98	0.99	0.99	1.01	1.01	1.01	1.00	Enseignement primaire
Secondary education	1.00	1.00	0.98	0.98	1.01	1.01	1.01	Enseignement secondaire
Tertiary education	...	1.17	...	...	...	...	...	Enseignement supérieur
Central African Republic								**République centrafricaine**
Primary education	0.56	...	0.69	0.71	...	...	0.76	Enseignement primaire
Secondary education	...	...	...	...	...	...	0.64	Enseignement secondaire
Tertiary education	...	...	...	0.32	...	...	...	Enseignement supérieur
Chad								**Tchad**
Primary education	0.38	0.49	0.68	0.74	0.76	0.78	0.78	Enseignement primaire
Secondary education	0.18	0.24	* 0.35	0.42	0.45	0.45	0.46	Enseignement secondaire
Tertiary education	0.09	...	0.06	* 0.17	* 0.20	...	...	Enseignement supérieur
Chile								**Chili**
Primary education	0.97	...	0.95	0.97	0.97	0.97	0.97	Enseignement primaire
Secondary education	1.06	...	1.01	1.03	1.01	1.01	1.01	Enseignement secondaire
Tertiary education	0.78	0.86	0.96	1.08	1.13	1.13	1.14	Enseignement supérieur
China [1]								**Chine** [1]
Primary education	0.83	0.95	...	0.98	1.00	1.00	1.01	Enseignement primaire
Secondary education	0.70	0.85	...	1.00	...	...	...	Enseignement secondaire
Tertiary education	...	...	0.90	1.06	1.16	1.19	1.21	Enseignement supérieur
China, Hong Kong SAR								**Chine, RAS de Hong Kong**
Secondary education	1.08	...	1.01	1.00	0.97	0.97	0.97	Enseignement secondaire
Tertiary education	...	...	1.01	* 0.99	1.11	1.13	1.14	Enseignement supérieur
China, Macao SAR								**Chine, RAS de Macao**
Primary education	...	...	0.94	0.98	0.99	0.98	0.99	Enseignement primaire
Secondary education	...	...	0.93	0.97	0.97	0.99	1.00	Enseignement secondaire
Tertiary education	...	...	0.67	0.96	1.28	1.30	1.33	Enseignement supérieur

6

Ratio of girls to boys in primary, secondary and tertiary education *(continued)*

Rapport filles/garçons dans l'enseignement primaire, secondaire et supérieur *(suite)*

Region, country or area	1985	1995	2005	2010	2014	2015	2016	Région, pays ou zone
Colombia								**Colombie**
Primary education	1.03	0.99	0.98	0.98	0.97	0.97	0.97	Enseignement primaire
Secondary education	1.03	1.16	1.11	1.10	1.08	1.07	1.06	Enseignement secondaire
Tertiary education	0.96	1.05	1.08	1.10	1.15	1.16	1.16	Enseignement supérieur
Comoros								**Comores**
Primary education	0.90	...	...	...	0.93	...	...	Enseignement primaire
Secondary education	...	...	...	...	1.07	...	...	Enseignement secondaire
Tertiary education	...	...	...	0.74	0.81	...	...	Enseignement supérieur
Congo								**Congo**
Primary education	0.96	0.85	0.93	0.94	...	...	...	Enseignement primaire
Secondary education	0.75	...	...	...	...	...	...	Enseignement secondaire
Tertiary education	0.18	...	...	...	...	...	...	Enseignement supérieur
Cook Islands								**Îles Cook**
Primary education	...	...	* 1.03	* 0.99	* 0.96	* 0.91	* 0.94	Enseignement primaire
Secondary education	...	...	* 1.13	* 1.09	* 1.10	* 1.09	* 1.06	Enseignement secondaire
Costa Rica								**Costa Rica**
Primary education	0.97	0.99	0.97	0.98	0.99	0.99	1.01	Enseignement primaire
Secondary education	1.09	1.08	1.04	1.04	1.05	1.04	1.05	Enseignement secondaire
Tertiary education	...	...	...	...	1.24	1.31	1.24	Enseignement supérieur
Côte d'Ivoire								**Côte d'Ivoire**
Primary education	0.70	0.73	...	...	0.87	0.88	0.89	Enseignement primaire
Secondary education	...	...	...	...	0.70	0.71	0.73	Enseignement secondaire
Tertiary education	...	0.33	...	0.52	0.59	0.66	...	Enseignement supérieur
Croatia								**Croatie**
Primary education	...	1.00	1.00	1.00	1.00	1.00	1.01	Enseignement primaire
Secondary education	...	1.04	1.03	1.07	1.04	1.05	1.05	Enseignement secondaire
Tertiary education	...	1.01	1.21	1.34	1.37	1.35	1.38	Enseignement supérieur
Cuba								**Cuba**
Primary education	0.94	0.99	0.97	0.98	0.95	0.94	...	Enseignement primaire
Secondary education	1.06	1.12	1.02	1.01	1.03	1.04	...	Enseignement secondaire
Tertiary education	1.20	1.46	* 1.69	1.65	...	1.41	1.41	Enseignement supérieur
Cyprus								**Chypre**
Primary education	0.99	* 1.00	* 1.00	* 1.00	* 1.01	* 1.00	...	Enseignement primaire
Secondary education	1.05	* 1.01	* 1.02	* 1.01	* 1.00	* 0.99	...	Enseignement secondaire
Tertiary education	0.90	* 1.27	* 1.13	* 0.90	* 1.42	* 1.36	...	Enseignement supérieur
Czechia								**Tchéquie**
Primary education	0.97	1.00	0.99	1.00	1.00	1.00	...	Enseignement primaire
Secondary education	1.07	1.03	1.02	1.01	1.00	1.01	...	Enseignement secondaire
Tertiary education	0.74	0.96	1.16	1.40	1.40	1.41	...	Enseignement supérieur
Dem. People's Rep. Korea								**Rép. pop. dém. de Corée**
Secondary education	...	...	...	...	...	1.01	...	Enseignement secondaire
Tertiary education	...	...	...	...	...	0.55	...	Enseignement supérieur
Dem. Rep. of the Congo								**Rép. dém. du Congo**
Primary education	0.65	0.69	...	0.87	0.91	0.99	...	Enseignement primaire
Secondary education	0.41	0.61	...	0.58	0.62	0.64	...	Enseignement secondaire
Denmark								**Danemark**
Primary education	1.00	1.00	1.00	1.00	0.99	0.99	0.99	Enseignement primaire
Secondary education	0.99	1.03	1.04	1.01	1.04	1.05	1.03	Enseignement secondaire
Tertiary education	1.02	1.12	1.38	1.45	1.41	1.40	1.36	Enseignement supérieur
Djibouti								**Djibouti**
Primary education	0.73	0.78	0.82	...	0.87	0.89	0.89	Enseignement primaire
Secondary education	0.61	0.69	0.67	...	0.81	0.80	0.82	Enseignement secondaire
Tertiary education	...	...	0.73	0.69	...	...	...	Enseignement supérieur
Dominica								**Dominique**
Primary education	...	1.14	1.00	0.98	1.00	0.98	0.97	Enseignement primaire
Secondary education	...	...	1.08	1.09	0.98	0.99	...	Enseignement secondaire
Tertiary education	2.04	...	...	...	...	...	...	Enseignement supérieur
Dominican Republic								**République dominicaine**
Primary education	1.03	...	0.95	0.88	0.91	0.91	0.92	Enseignement primaire
Secondary education	...	...	1.20	1.13	1.11	1.10	1.10	Enseignement secondaire
Tertiary education	...	...	...	...	1.62	1.84	1.79	Enseignement supérieur
Ecuador								**Équateur**
Primary education	0.99	0.99	1.00	1.00	1.00	1.00	1.00	Enseignement primaire
Secondary education	1.02	...	1.01	1.05	1.04	1.04	1.04	Enseignement secondaire
Tertiary education	...	...	...	...	...	1.16	...	Enseignement supérieur

6

Ratio of girls to boys in primary, secondary and tertiary education *(continued)*

Rapport filles/garçons dans l'enseignement primaire, secondaire et supérieur *(suite)*

Region, country or area	1985	1995	2005	2010	2014	2015	2016	Région, pays ou zone
Egypt								**Égypte**
Primary education	0.79	0.89	0.95	0.97	1.00	...	1.00	Enseignement primaire
Secondary education	0.68	0.88	...	0.97	0.99	...	0.98	Enseignement secondaire
Tertiary education	0.51	...	0.84	0.92	0.89	0.96	1.02	Enseignement supérieur
El Salvador								**El Salvador**
Primary education	...	0.98	0.97	0.95	0.96	0.96	0.96	Enseignement primaire
Secondary education	...	...	1.00	0.99	1.01	1.01	1.00	Enseignement secondaire
Tertiary education	0.73	0.97	1.12	1.11	1.10	1.11	1.12	Enseignement supérieur
Equatorial Guinea								**Guinée équatoriale**
Primary education	...	...	0.97	0.99	...	0.99	...	Enseignement primaire
Secondary education	...	...	0.74	...	...	...	...	Enseignement secondaire
Eritrea								**Érythrée**
Primary education	...	0.81	0.81	0.85	0.85	0.86	...	Enseignement primaire
Secondary education	...	0.72	0.60	0.77	0.82	0.85	...	Enseignement secondaire
Tertiary education	...	0.16	...	0.38	0.49	0.65	0.71	Enseignement supérieur
Estonia								**Estonie**
Primary education	0.98	0.97	0.97	0.99	1.00	1.00	...	Enseignement primaire
Secondary education	...	1.12	1.04	1.00	1.00	1.00	...	Enseignement secondaire
Tertiary education	...	1.10	1.68	1.66	1.51	1.52	...	Enseignement supérieur
Eswatini								**Eswatini**
Primary education	0.98	0.97	0.93	0.91	0.91	0.91	...	Enseignement primaire
Secondary education	...	...	1.01	0.99	0.99	0.99	...	Enseignement secondaire
Tertiary education	...	...	1.06	...	...	...	...	Enseignement supérieur
Ethiopia								**Éthiopie**
Primary education	0.65	0.60	0.84	0.92	0.92	0.91	...	Enseignement primaire
Secondary education	...	0.80	0.60	0.83	...	0.96	...	Enseignement secondaire
Tertiary education	...	0.26	0.32	0.43	0.48	...	...	Enseignement supérieur
Fiji								**Fidji**
Primary education	0.99	1.00	...	...	...	0.99	...	Enseignement primaire
Secondary education	1.03	...	...	...	...	...	...	Enseignement secondaire
Tertiary education	0.61	...	* 1.19	...	...	...	...	Enseignement supérieur
Finland								**Finlande**
Primary education	1.00	1.00	0.99	0.99	1.00	0.99	1.00	Enseignement primaire
Secondary education	1.17	1.15	1.05	1.05	1.10	1.10	1.10	Enseignement secondaire
Tertiary education	0.98	1.17	1.21	1.22	1.20	1.20	1.19	Enseignement supérieur
France								**France**
Primary education	0.98	0.98	0.99	0.99	1.00	1.00	...	Enseignement primaire
Secondary education	1.09	0.99	1.00	1.01	1.01	1.01	...	Enseignement secondaire
Tertiary education	1.03	1.26	1.29	1.27	1.25	1.25	...	Enseignement supérieur
Gabon								**Gabon**
Primary education	0.98	1.00	...	...	...	...	...	Enseignement primaire
Secondary education	0.71	0.84	...	...	...	...	...	Enseignement secondaire
Gambia								**Gambie**
Primary education	0.61	0.75	1.03	1.03	1.06	1.07	1.08	Enseignement primaire
Secondary education	0.41	0.54	...	* 0.95	...	...	...	Enseignement secondaire
Tertiary education	...	0.54	...	0.68	...	...	...	Enseignement supérieur
Georgia								**Géorgie**
Primary education	...	0.99	0.98	1.01	0.99	1.00	1.00	Enseignement primaire
Secondary education	...	0.92	0.98	...	1.03	1.03	1.02	Enseignement secondaire
Tertiary education	...	1.31	1.05	1.28	1.26	1.23	1.15	Enseignement supérieur
Germany								**Allemagne**
Primary education	...	0.99	1.00	1.00	0.99	0.99	...	Enseignement primaire
Secondary education	...	0.97	0.98	0.95	0.95	0.95	...	Enseignement secondaire
Tertiary education	...	0.80	...	...	0.95	0.98	...	Enseignement supérieur
Ghana								**Ghana**
Primary education	0.80	0.90	0.96	...	1.00	1.00	1.02	Enseignement primaire
Secondary education	0.63	0.72	* 0.83	...	0.94	0.95	0.97	Enseignement secondaire
Tertiary education	...	...	0.53	...	0.66	0.69	0.72	Enseignement supérieur
Greece								**Grèce**
Primary education	1.00	1.02	0.98	0.98	0.99	0.99	...	Enseignement primaire
Secondary education	0.99	1.01	0.95	0.94	0.94	0.93	...	Enseignement secondaire
Tertiary education	1.04	1.05	1.11	1.04	0.99	...	...	Enseignement supérieur
Grenada								**Grenade**
Primary education	0.94	0.93	0.97	0.97	0.98	0.96	0.97	Enseignement primaire
Secondary education	1.18	...	* 1.02	1.03	0.99	1.00	1.04	Enseignement secondaire
Tertiary education	...	...	...	...	...	1.16	1.28	Enseignement supérieur

Ratio of girls to boys in primary, secondary and tertiary education *(continued)*

Rapport filles/garçons dans l'enseignement primaire, secondaire et supérieur *(suite)*

Region, country or area	1985	1995	2005	2010	2014	2015	2016	Région, pays ou zone
Guatemala								**Guatemala**
Primary education	0.85	0.87	0.94	0.98	0.97	0.97	0.97	Enseignement primaire
Secondary education	...	...	0.92	0.94	0.95	0.94	0.95	Enseignement secondaire
Tertiary education	...	...	...	...	1.12	1.18	...	Enseignement supérieur
Guinea								**Guinée**
Primary education	0.46	0.51	0.80	0.82	0.85	...	...	Enseignement primaire
Secondary education	0.36	...	* 0.50	...	0.66	...	...	Enseignement secondaire
Tertiary education	0.34	...	0.23	0.33	0.45	...	...	Enseignement supérieur
Guinea-Bissau								**Guinée-Bissau**
Primary education	0.51	0.58	...	0.93	...	...	...	Enseignement primaire
Secondary education	0.27	...	...	...	...	...	...	Enseignement secondaire
Guyana								**Guyana**
Primary education	1.02	0.97	1.00	1.00	...	...	...	Enseignement primaire
Secondary education	1.00	...	1.03	1.06	...	...	...	Enseignement secondaire
Tertiary education	0.94	0.89	2.14	2.42	...	...	...	Enseignement supérieur
Haiti								**Haïti**
Primary education	0.87	0.95	...	...	...	...	...	Enseignement primaire
Honduras								**Honduras**
Primary education	1.00	1.01	1.00	1.00	0.98	0.99	0.99	Enseignement primaire
Secondary education	...	...	...	1.23	1.17	1.19	1.16	Enseignement secondaire
Tertiary education	...	...	...	1.15	1.37	1.37	...	Enseignement supérieur
Hungary								**Hongrie**
Primary education	1.00	0.99	0.98	0.99	0.99	1.00	1.00	Enseignement primaire
Secondary education	1.00	1.04	0.99	0.99	1.01	1.01	1.00	Enseignement secondaire
Tertiary education	1.18	1.13	1.46	1.36	1.29	1.26	1.25	Enseignement supérieur
Iceland								**Islande**
Primary education	...	1.00	0.98	1.01	0.99	1.00	...	Enseignement primaire
Secondary education	...	0.97	1.01	1.02	1.04	1.01	...	Enseignement secondaire
Tertiary education	...	1.40	1.92	1.79	1.74	1.79	...	Enseignement supérieur
India								**Inde**
Primary education	0.70	0.81	...	* 1.02	1.11	1.12	1.17	Enseignement primaire
Secondary education	...	0.64	* 0.82	0.93	1.01	1.01	1.02	Enseignement secondaire
Tertiary education	0.45	0.57	0.70	0.73	0.98	0.99	1.00	Enseignement supérieur
Indonesia								**Indonésie**
Primary education	0.95	0.97	* 0.97	1.04	0.98	0.97	0.96	Enseignement primaire
Secondary education	...	0.86	* 0.99	1.01	1.00	1.01	1.04	Enseignement secondaire
Tertiary education	0.49	0.63	...	0.90	1.13	1.13	1.11	Enseignement supérieur
Iran (Islamic Republic of)								**Iran (Rép. islamique d')**
Primary education	0.79	0.93	0.98	0.99	1.05	1.05	...	Enseignement primaire
Secondary education	0.70	0.83	0.96	0.98	0.99	1.00	...	Enseignement secondaire
Tertiary education	...	...	1.06	0.99	0.93	0.89	0.91	Enseignement supérieur
Iraq								**Iraq**
Primary education	0.86	...	...	...	...	...	...	Enseignement primaire
Secondary education	0.57	...	...	...	...	...	...	Enseignement secondaire
Tertiary education	0.41	...	* 0.60	...	...	...	...	Enseignement supérieur
Ireland								**Irlande**
Primary education	1.00	1.00	0.99	1.00	1.00	1.00	1.00	Enseignement primaire
Secondary education	1.10	1.06	1.10	1.05	1.01	1.02	1.02	Enseignement secondaire
Tertiary education	0.79	1.02	1.26	1.12	1.05	1.07	...	Enseignement supérieur
Israel								**Israël**
Primary education	1.03	...	1.01	1.00	1.00	1.01	1.01	Enseignement primaire
Secondary education	1.07	...	0.99	1.02	1.02	1.01	1.02	Enseignement secondaire
Tertiary education	...	...	1.33	...	1.34	1.38	1.40	Enseignement supérieur
Italy								**Italie**
Primary education	1.00	0.99	0.99	0.99	0.99	0.99	...	Enseignement primaire
Secondary education	0.99	1.00	0.99	0.99	0.98	0.98	...	Enseignement secondaire
Tertiary education	0.85	1.14	1.37	1.43	1.38	1.36	...	Enseignement supérieur
Jamaica								**Jamaïque**
Primary education	1.02	...	...	...	...	...	...	Enseignement primaire
Secondary education	1.09	...	1.06	1.08	1.08	1.07	1.05	Enseignement secondaire
Tertiary education	...	...	...	2.31	...	1.73	...	Enseignement supérieur
Japan								**Japon**
Primary education	1.00	1.00	1.01	1.00	1.00	1.00	...	Enseignement primaire
Secondary education	1.02	1.02	1.01	1.01	1.01	1.01	...	Enseignement secondaire
Tertiary education	0.55	0.83	0.89	0.89	0.93	0.94	...	Enseignement supérieur

Ratio of girls to boys in primary, secondary and tertiary education *(continued)*

Rapport filles/garçons dans l'enseignement primaire, secondaire et supérieur *(suite)*

Region, country or area	1985	1995	2005	2010	2014	2015	2016	Région, pays ou zone
Jordan								**Jordanie**
Primary education	1.05	1.01	…	…	…	…	…	Enseignement primaire
Secondary education	1.04	…	1.03	1.04	1.04	…	…	Enseignement secondaire
Tertiary education	0.95	…	1.09	1.14	…	1.09	1.07	Enseignement supérieur
Kazakhstan								**Kazakhstan**
Primary education	…	1.01	1.00	1.01	1.00	1.00	1.00	Enseignement primaire
Secondary education	…	…	…	1.01	1.03	1.04	1.03	Enseignement secondaire
Tertiary education	…	1.29	…	1.27	1.26	1.28	1.24	Enseignement supérieur
Kenya								**Kenya**
Primary education	0.96	0.98	0.96	…	* 1.01	1.00	1.00	Enseignement primaire
Secondary education	0.75	…	* 0.95	…	…	…	…	Enseignement secondaire
Tertiary education	0.35	…	* 0.60	…	…	…	…	Enseignement supérieur
Kiribati								**Kiribati**
Primary education	1.00	1.03	1.01	…	1.04	1.03	1.03	Enseignement primaire
Secondary education	1.01	1.24	1.15	…	…	…	…	Enseignement secondaire
Kuwait								**Koweït**
Primary education	0.94	1.01	1.04	0.99	1.03	1.04	1.04	Enseignement primaire
Secondary education	0.93	1.06	* 1.09	1.02	* 1.07	1.08	…	Enseignement secondaire
Tertiary education	1.16	1.58	…	…	…	…	…	Enseignement supérieur
Kyrgyzstan								**Kirghizistan**
Primary education	…	1.02	0.98	0.99	0.99	0.99	0.99	Enseignement primaire
Secondary education	…	…	1.00	1.00	1.01	1.02	1.00	Enseignement secondaire
Tertiary education	…	1.26	1.26	1.30	1.30	1.30	1.28	Enseignement supérieur
Lao People's Dem. Rep.								**Rép. dém. populaire lao**
Primary education	0.79	0.81	0.87	0.92	0.95	0.96	0.96	Enseignement primaire
Secondary education	…	0.66	0.75	0.83	0.91	0.93	0.93	Enseignement secondaire
Tertiary education	0.54	0.41	0.71	0.77	0.93	0.96	1.00	Enseignement supérieur
Latvia								**Lettonie**
Primary education	…	0.97	0.96	1.00	0.99	0.99	…	Enseignement primaire
Secondary education	…	1.07	1.00	0.98	0.97	0.99	…	Enseignement secondaire
Tertiary education	1.46	…	1.78	1.76	1.42	1.54	…	Enseignement supérieur
Lebanon								**Liban**
Primary education	0.92	0.99	* 0.92	0.91	0.92	0.91	0.91	Enseignement primaire
Secondary education	0.94	1.16	* 1.01	1.02	1.01	0.99	1.00	Enseignement secondaire
Tertiary education	0.60	…	1.05	1.04	1.16	…	…	Enseignement supérieur
Lesotho								**Lesotho**
Primary education	1.26	1.14	1.00	0.97	0.97	0.97	0.97	Enseignement primaire
Secondary education	1.46	…	1.29	1.41	1.36	1.34	1.35	Enseignement secondaire
Tertiary education	1.00	1.34	1.35	…	1.43	1.50	…	Enseignement supérieur
Liberia								**Libéria**
Primary education	…	…	…	…	0.92	0.90	…	Enseignement primaire
Secondary education	…	…	…	…	0.78	0.78	…	Enseignement secondaire
Tertiary education	…	…	…	0.53	…	…	…	Enseignement supérieur
Libya								**Libye**
Primary education	…	…	0.99	…	…	…	…	Enseignement primaire
Secondary education	…	…	* 1.19	…	…	…	…	Enseignement secondaire
Liechtenstein								**Liechtenstein**
Primary education	…	…	…	* 0.94	* 0.99	* 0.98	* 0.96	Enseignement primaire
Secondary education	…	…	…	* 0.85	* 0.81	* 0.78	* 0.78	Enseignement secondaire
Tertiary education	…	…	…	* 0.62	* 0.48	* 0.49	* 0.55	Enseignement supérieur
Lithuania								**Lituanie**
Primary education	…	0.97	1.00	0.99	1.00	1.00	1.00	Enseignement primaire
Secondary education	…	1.05	0.99	0.98	0.96	0.96	0.95	Enseignement secondaire
Tertiary education	…	1.44	1.56	1.50	1.46	1.44	1.40	Enseignement supérieur
Luxembourg								**Luxembourg**
Primary education	…	…	1.00	1.01	1.00	1.00	…	Enseignement primaire
Secondary education	…	1.01	1.05	1.03	1.02	1.04	…	Enseignement secondaire
Tertiary education	0.52	…	…	1.11	…	1.11	…	Enseignement supérieur
Madagascar								**Madagascar**
Primary education	0.93	1.04	0.96	0.98	1.00	1.00	1.00	Enseignement primaire
Secondary education	…	…	* 0.96	…	0.98	* 0.99	0.99	Enseignement secondaire
Tertiary education	…	0.83	0.89	0.91	0.92	0.90	…	Enseignement supérieur
Malawi								**Malawi**
Primary education	0.81	0.91	1.01	1.02	1.02	1.02	1.03	Enseignement primaire
Secondary education	0.49	0.68	0.80	0.90	0.91	* 0.92	0.89	Enseignement secondaire
Tertiary education	0.29	0.42	* 0.54	0.61	…	…	…	Enseignement supérieur

6 Ratio of girls to boys in primary, secondary and tertiary education *(continued)*

Rapport filles/garçons dans l'enseignement primaire, secondaire et supérieur *(suite)*

Region, country or area	1985	1995	2005	2010	2014	2015	2016	Région, pays ou zone
Malaysia								**Malaisie**
Primary education	0.99	1.00	1.00	1.01	1.00	1.00	1.01	Enseignement primaire
Secondary education	1.02	1.09	…	…	1.08	1.09	1.06	Enseignement secondaire
Tertiary education	0.84	…	…	…	1.39	1.34	1.20	Enseignement supérieur
Maldives								**Maldives**
Primary education	…	0.97	0.97	…	…	0.98	1.00	Enseignement primaire
Secondary education	…	1.05	…	…	…	…	…	Enseignement secondaire
Tertiary education	…	…	…	…	2.06	…	…	Enseignement supérieur
Mali								**Mali**
Primary education	0.61	0.69	0.79	0.86	0.89	0.90	0.88	Enseignement primaire
Secondary education	…	0.49	* 0.62	0.69	0.74	0.79	0.74	Enseignement secondaire
Tertiary education	0.15	0.18	…	0.41	0.42	0.42	…	Enseignement supérieur
Malta								**Malte**
Primary education	0.94	0.97	0.98	1.01	1.02	1.02	1.04	Enseignement primaire
Secondary education	0.97	0.93	0.96	0.89	1.05	1.07	1.04	Enseignement secondaire
Tertiary education	0.45	0.99	1.35	1.35	1.31	1.37	1.37	Enseignement supérieur
Marshall Islands								**Îles Marshall**
Primary education	…	…	1.26	…	…	1.00	1.02	Enseignement primaire
Secondary education	…	…	1.00	…	…	1.10	1.10	Enseignement secondaire
Mauritania								**Mauritanie**
Primary education	0.69	0.84	1.03	1.04	1.06	1.05	1.06	Enseignement primaire
Secondary education	…	0.58	0.88	* 0.85	0.91	0.93	0.97	Enseignement secondaire
Tertiary education	…	0.21	0.34	0.41	…	0.50	0.51	Enseignement supérieur
Mauritius								**Maurice**
Primary education	0.99	1.00	1.00	1.01	1.02	1.02	1.02	Enseignement primaire
Secondary education	0.91	…	* 0.98	* 1.05	1.02	1.04	1.06	Enseignement secondaire
Tertiary education	0.60	1.00	* 1.03	1.21	1.23	1.31	…	Enseignement supérieur
Mexico								**Mexique**
Primary education	0.97	0.97	0.98	0.99	1.01	1.01	1.01	Enseignement primaire
Secondary education	0.90	1.01	1.09	1.09	1.06	1.07	1.09	Enseignement secondaire
Tertiary education	…	0.88	1.04	1.04	1.01	1.00	1.02	Enseignement supérieur
Micronesia (Fed. States of)								**Micronésie (États féd. de)**
Primary education	…	…	0.97	…	0.99	1.00	…	Enseignement primaire
Secondary education	…	…	1.08	…	…	…	…	Enseignement secondaire
Mongolia								**Mongolie**
Primary education	0.97	1.03	1.00	0.98	0.98	0.98	0.98	Enseignement primaire
Secondary education	…	1.33	1.11	1.07	…	1.02	1.01	Enseignement secondaire
Tertiary education	…	…	1.65	1.54	1.44	1.38	1.39	Enseignement supérieur
Montenegro								**Monténégro**
Primary education	…	…	1.00	0.99	…	0.99	0.97	Enseignement primaire
Secondary education	…	…	1.03	1.01	…	1.00	1.00	Enseignement secondaire
Tertiary education	…	…	1.58	1.25	…	…	1.25	Enseignement supérieur
Montserrat								**Montserrat**
Primary education	…	…	* 1.04	…	…	…	…	Enseignement primaire
Secondary education	…	…	* 1.10	…	…	…	…	Enseignement secondaire
Morocco								**Maroc**
Primary education	0.64	0.74	0.91	0.94	0.95	0.95	0.95	Enseignement primaire
Secondary education	0.68	0.74	0.85	0.87	…	…	…	Enseignement secondaire
Tertiary education	…	0.71	0.80	0.90	0.97	0.96	0.93	Enseignement supérieur
Mozambique								**Mozambique**
Primary education	0.77	0.71	0.84	0.90	* 0.92	* 0.92	…	Enseignement primaire
Secondary education	0.45	0.61	0.69	0.81	* 0.91	* 0.92	…	Enseignement secondaire
Tertiary education	0.29	0.30	0.48	0.65	0.71	0.73	0.79	Enseignement supérieur
Myanmar								**Myanmar**
Primary education	0.91	0.94	1.00	0.99	0.97	…	…	Enseignement primaire
Secondary education	…	…	0.97	1.05	1.03	…	…	Enseignement secondaire
Tertiary education	…	1.58	…	…	…	…	…	Enseignement supérieur
Namibia								**Namibie**
Primary education	…	0.99	0.99	0.97	…	…	…	Enseignement primaire
Secondary education	…	1.16	1.12	…	…	…	…	Enseignement secondaire
Tertiary education	…	1.53	0.85	…	…	…	…	Enseignement supérieur
Nauru								**Nauru**
Primary education	…	…	* 1.05	…	* 0.92	…	* 1.03	Enseignement primaire
Secondary education	…	…	* 1.13	…	* 1.03	…	* 1.03	Enseignement secondaire

6 Ratio of girls to boys in primary, secondary and tertiary education *(continued)*

Rapport filles/garçons dans l'enseignement primaire, secondaire et supérieur *(suite)*

Region, country or area	1985	1995	2005	2010	2014	2015	2016	Région, pays ou zone
Nepal								**Népal**
Primary education	0.45	0.69	0.92	1.07	1.08	1.08	1.08	Enseignement primaire
Secondary education	0.31	0.59	* 0.81	* 0.95	* 1.06	* 1.07	* 1.07	Enseignement secondaire
Tertiary education	...	...	0.54	0.61	...	1.02	1.07	Enseignement supérieur
Netherlands								**Pays-Bas**
Primary education	1.03	0.98	0.98	1.00	1.00	1.00	1.00	Enseignement primaire
Secondary education	0.97	0.95	0.98	0.99	...	1.02	1.02	Enseignement secondaire
Tertiary education	0.73	0.93	1.08	1.12	...	1.14	1.13	Enseignement supérieur
New Zealand								**Nouvelle-Zélande**
Primary education	0.98	1.00	0.99	1.00	1.00	1.01	1.01	Enseignement primaire
Secondary education	1.02	0.98	1.06	1.05	1.06	1.06	1.06	Enseignement secondaire
Tertiary education	0.88	1.25	...	1.46	1.44	1.41	1.41	Enseignement supérieur
Nicaragua								**Nicaragua**
Primary education	1.11	1.04	0.99	0.99	...	...	...	Enseignement primaire
Secondary education	2.09	...	1.16	1.13	...	...	...	Enseignement secondaire
Tertiary education	1.30	1.05	...	...	...	...	...	Enseignement supérieur
Niger								**Niger**
Primary education	0.58	0.62	0.72	0.81	0.85	0.85	0.86	Enseignement primaire
Secondary education	...	...	0.62	0.66	0.70	0.70	0.73	Enseignement secondaire
Tertiary education	0.17	...	0.34	0.36	...	...	...	Enseignement supérieur
Nigeria								**Nigéria**
Primary education	0.81	0.83	0.84	* 0.91	...	...	...	Enseignement primaire
Secondary education	...	...	0.83	0.87	...	...	...	Enseignement secondaire
Tertiary education	0.35	...	0.71	0.74	...	...	...	Enseignement supérieur
Niue								**Nioué**
Primary education	...	...	* 0.89	...	* 0.98	* 0.82	* 0.95	Enseignement primaire
Secondary education	...	...	* 1.63	...	* 1.25	* 1.10	...	Enseignement secondaire
Norway								**Norvège**
Primary education	1.00	1.00	1.00	1.00	1.00	1.00	1.00	Enseignement primaire
Secondary education	1.06	0.95	1.01	0.98	0.97	0.97	0.97	Enseignement secondaire
Tertiary education	1.05	1.25	1.52	1.62	1.45	1.46	1.48	Enseignement supérieur
Oman								**Oman**
Primary education	0.76	0.99	0.99	...	1.06	1.04	1.03	Enseignement primaire
Secondary education	0.46	0.95	0.96	...	...	0.98	0.94	Enseignement secondaire
Tertiary education	0.73	1.18	1.07	1.44	1.94	1.87	1.82	Enseignement supérieur
Pakistan								**Pakistan**
Primary education	0.52	...	0.77	0.85	0.85	0.85	0.85	Enseignement primaire
Secondary education	0.36	...	...	0.77	0.79	0.79	0.81	Enseignement secondaire
Tertiary education	...	...	0.87	...	1.06	0.87	0.87	Enseignement supérieur
Palau								**Palaos**
Primary education	...	...	...	...	* 0.96	...	...	Enseignement primaire
Secondary education	...	...	...	...	* 1.05	...	...	Enseignement secondaire
Panama								**Panama**
Primary education	0.95	...	0.97	0.96	0.97	0.97	...	Enseignement primaire
Secondary education	1.12	...	1.07	1.06	1.07	1.05	...	Enseignement secondaire
Tertiary education	1.40	...	1.64	1.53	1.59	1.57	...	Enseignement supérieur
Papua New Guinea								**Papouasie-Nvl-Guinée**
Primary education	...	0.87	0.85	...	...	...	...	Enseignement primaire
Secondary education	...	0.68	...	...	...	...	...	Enseignement secondaire
Tertiary education	0.31	0.47	...	...	...	...	...	Enseignement supérieur
Paraguay								**Paraguay**
Primary education	0.94	0.97	0.97	0.96	...	...	...	Enseignement primaire
Secondary education	...	1.07	1.03	1.06	...	...	...	Enseignement secondaire
Tertiary education	...	...	1.13	1.42	...	...	...	Enseignement supérieur
Peru								**Pérou**
Primary education	0.96	0.97	1.01	1.01	1.00	1.00	1.00	Enseignement primaire
Secondary education	0.90	0.93	0.98	1.00	1.00	1.00	1.00	Enseignement secondaire
Tertiary education	...	...	1.03	...	...	...	...	Enseignement supérieur
Philippines								**Philippines**
Primary education	1.00	0.99	0.99	...	...	0.97	...	Enseignement primaire
Secondary education	1.07	...	1.12	...	...	1.09	...	Enseignement secondaire
Tertiary education	...	1.37	1.23	1.25	1.28	...	...	Enseignement supérieur
Poland								**Pologne**
Primary education	...	0.99	0.99	0.99	1.00	1.01	1.01	Enseignement primaire
Secondary education	...	1.01	0.99	0.99	0.97	0.97	0.97	Enseignement secondaire
Tertiary education	1.30	1.41	1.41	1.52	1.54	1.52	1.51	Enseignement supérieur

6 Ratio of girls to boys in primary, secondary and tertiary education *(continued)*

Rapport filles/garçons dans l'enseignement primaire, secondaire et supérieur *(suite)*

Region, country or area	1985	1995	2005	2010	2014	2015	2016	Région, pays ou zone
Portugal								**Portugal**
Primary education	0.95	0.95	0.95	0.97	0.96	0.96	0.97	Enseignement primaire
Secondary education	...	1.08	1.10	1.03	0.98	0.97	0.97	Enseignement secondaire
Tertiary education	1.14	1.34	1.31	1.18	1.16	1.13	1.12	Enseignement supérieur
Puerto Rico								**Porto Rico**
Primary education	...	...	...	1.04	1.01	1.02	...	Enseignement primaire
Secondary education	...	...	...	1.06	1.06	1.07	...	Enseignement secondaire
Tertiary education	...	...	...	1.48	1.41	1.41	...	Enseignement supérieur
Qatar								**Qatar**
Primary education	0.98	1.00	0.97	1.01	1.03	1.01	0.99	Enseignement primaire
Secondary education	0.94	0.97	0.94	1.04	1.38	1.26	1.17	Enseignement secondaire
Tertiary education	3.08	5.60	* 3.52	5.32	6.36	6.95	7.37	Enseignement supérieur
Republic of Korea								**République de Corée**
Primary education	1.01	1.03	0.99	1.00	1.01	1.00	...	Enseignement primaire
Secondary education	0.94	1.00	1.02	0.99	1.00	1.00	...	Enseignement secondaire
Tertiary education	0.47	0.57	0.64	0.74	0.76	0.77	...	Enseignement supérieur
Republic of Moldova								**République de Moldova**
Primary education	...	0.99	* 0.99	* 1.00	* 1.00	* 0.99	...	Enseignement primaire
Secondary education	...	1.04	* 1.04	* 1.02	* 1.01	* 1.01	...	Enseignement secondaire
Tertiary education	...	1.15	* 1.46	* 1.34	* 1.32	* 1.34	...	Enseignement supérieur
Romania								**Roumanie**
Primary education	...	1.00	0.99	0.98	...	0.98	0.99	Enseignement primaire
Secondary education	...	1.03	1.02	0.99	0.99	0.99	0.99	Enseignement secondaire
Tertiary education	0.81	0.94	1.26	1.37	1.24	1.23	1.24	Enseignement supérieur
Russian Federation								**Fédération de Russie**
Primary education	...	0.99	1.00	...	1.01	1.01	1.01	Enseignement primaire
Secondary education	...	...	0.99	...	0.98	0.98	0.99	Enseignement secondaire
Tertiary education	...	...	1.37	...	1.20	1.21	1.20	Enseignement supérieur
Rwanda								**Rwanda**
Primary education	0.95	...	1.01	1.03	1.02	1.01	1.00	Enseignement primaire
Secondary education	0.78	...	0.89	0.99	1.10	1.09	1.10	Enseignement secondaire
Tertiary education	0.16	...	...	0.78	0.83	0.78	0.76	Enseignement supérieur
Saint Lucia								**Sainte-Lucie**
Primary education	1.00	...	0.96	...	...	...	...	Enseignement primaire
Secondary education	1.64	...	1.18	0.99	0.99	0.99	1.01	Enseignement secondaire
Tertiary education	0.83	...	2.72	2.58	2.09	1.90	1.95	Enseignement supérieur
Saint Vincent & Grenadines								**Saint-Vincent-Grenadines**
Primary education	...	...	0.91	0.93	0.97	0.97	0.98	Enseignement primaire
Secondary education	1.49	...	1.25	1.02	0.97	0.97	0.99	Enseignement secondaire
Samoa								**Samoa**
Primary education	...	1.03	1.01	0.99	1.00	1.00	1.01	Enseignement primaire
Secondary education	...	1.12	1.13	1.14	1.13	1.11	1.10	Enseignement secondaire
San Marino								**Saint-Marin**
Primary education	...	...	...	* 1.13	...	...	...	Enseignement primaire
Secondary education	...	...	...	* 1.02	...	...	...	Enseignement secondaire
Tertiary education	...	...	...	* 1.46	...	...	...	Enseignement supérieur
Sao Tome and Principe								**Sao Tomé-et-Principe**
Primary education	...	...	0.96	0.99	0.96	0.96	0.95	Enseignement primaire
Secondary education	...	...	1.06	1.02	* 1.10	1.11	1.13	Enseignement secondaire
Tertiary education	...	...	...	0.97	0.87	1.03	...	Enseignement supérieur
Saudi Arabia								**Arabie saoudite**
Primary education	...	...	* 0.98	0.99	0.97	1.01	0.98	Enseignement primaire
Secondary education	...	...	* 0.94	...	* 0.77	...	...	Enseignement secondaire
Tertiary education	0.66	0.91	1.48	1.15	0.99	1.01	1.00	Enseignement supérieur
Senegal								**Sénégal**
Primary education	0.68	0.77	0.96	1.06	1.12	1.12	1.12	Enseignement primaire
Secondary education	0.50	...	0.75	0.87	1.00	0.98	1.01	Enseignement secondaire
Tertiary education	* 0.26	...	...	* 0.59	0.60	0.60	0.60	Enseignement supérieur
Serbia								**Serbie**
Primary education	...	...	* 1.01	* 1.00	* 1.00	* 1.00	* 1.00	Enseignement primaire
Secondary education	...	...	* 1.03	* 1.02	* 1.02	* 1.01	* 1.01	Enseignement secondaire
Tertiary education	...	...	* 1.30	* 1.30	* 1.31	* 1.33	* 1.31	Enseignement supérieur
Seychelles								**Seychelles**
Primary education	1.04	1.02	0.98	1.03	0.98	0.99	0.99	Enseignement primaire
Secondary education	1.02	1.00	1.07	* 1.06	1.03	1.05	1.07	Enseignement secondaire
Tertiary education	...	...	...	...	2.58	2.16	1.85	Enseignement supérieur

Ratio of girls to boys in primary, secondary and tertiary education *(continued)*

Rapport filles/garçons dans l'enseignement primaire, secondaire et supérieur *(suite)*

Region, country or area	1985	1995	2005	2010	2014	2015	2016	Région, pays ou zone
Sierra Leone								**Sierra Leone**
Primary education	0.67	...	...	...	...	1.01	1.01	Enseignement primaire
Secondary education	0.47	...	...	...	...	0.86	0.91	Enseignement secondaire
Tertiary education	0.30	...	...	...	...	...	...	Enseignement supérieur
Singapore								**Singapour**
Secondary education	...	...	...	...	...	...	* 0.99	Enseignement secondaire
Slovakia								**Slovaquie**
Primary education	...	1.00	0.99	0.99	0.99	0.99	...	Enseignement primaire
Secondary education	...	1.05	1.01	1.01	1.01	1.01	...	Enseignement secondaire
Tertiary education	...	1.00	1.29	1.55	1.55	...	...	Enseignement supérieur
Slovenia								**Slovénie**
Primary education	...	1.00	0.98	0.99	1.00	1.00	...	Enseignement primaire
Secondary education	...	1.03	0.99	0.99	1.00	1.00	...	Enseignement secondaire
Tertiary education	1.06	1.34	1.42	1.49	1.45	1.47	...	Enseignement supérieur
Solomon Islands								**Îles Salomon**
Primary education	...	...	0.95	0.98	0.97	0.99	0.99	Enseignement primaire
Secondary education	...	...	0.83	0.86	...	...	...	Enseignement secondaire
Somalia								**Somalie**
Primary education	0.52	...	...	...	...	...	...	Enseignement primaire
Secondary education	0.55	...	...	...	...	...	...	Enseignement secondaire
South Africa								**Afrique du Sud**
Primary education	...	0.98	0.96	0.96	0.96	0.93	...	Enseignement primaire
Secondary education	...	...	1.07	1.06	1.09	0.99	...	Enseignement secondaire
Tertiary education	...	...	...	...	1.41	...	...	Enseignement supérieur
South Sudan								**Soudan du sud**
Primary education	...	...	...	...	...	0.71	...	Enseignement primaire
Secondary education	...	...	...	...	...	0.54	...	Enseignement secondaire
Spain								**Espagne**
Primary education	0.99	0.98	0.99	1.00	1.01	1.01	1.01	Enseignement primaire
Secondary education	1.05	1.09	1.07	1.02	1.00	1.00	1.01	Enseignement secondaire
Tertiary education	0.96	1.16	1.23	1.24	1.19	1.18	1.19	Enseignement supérieur
Sri Lanka								**Sri Lanka**
Primary education	0.96	0.97	0.99	0.98	0.98	0.98	0.98	Enseignement primaire
Secondary education	1.11	1.08	...	1.01	...	...	1.03	Enseignement secondaire
Tertiary education	0.70	...	...	1.79	1.29	1.54	1.55	Enseignement supérieur
State of Palestine								**État de Palestine**
Primary education	...	0.99	0.99	0.98	0.99	1.00	1.00	Enseignement primaire
Secondary education	...	0.96	1.05	1.08	1.10	1.10	1.10	Enseignement secondaire
Tertiary education	...	...	1.01	1.34	1.55	1.58	1.59	Enseignement supérieur
Sudan								**Soudan**
Primary education	...	...	0.88	0.90	...	0.92	...	Enseignement primaire
Secondary education	...	...	0.93	0.87	...	0.99	...	Enseignement secondaire
Tertiary education	...	...	1.13	1.17	1.06	...	...	Enseignement supérieur
Suriname								**Suriname**
Primary education	0.98	...	0.98	0.99	1.01	1.01	1.00	Enseignement primaire
Secondary education	...	...	1.33	1.28	1.37	1.32	...	Enseignement secondaire
Tertiary education	1.12	...	...	...	...	...	...	Enseignement supérieur
Sweden								**Suède**
Primary education	1.01	1.01	1.00	0.99	1.06	1.04	...	Enseignement primaire
Secondary education	1.13	1.15	1.00	0.99	1.14	1.14	...	Enseignement secondaire
Tertiary education	1.14	1.26	1.54	1.53	1.54	1.53	...	Enseignement supérieur
Switzerland								**Suisse**
Primary education	1.01	1.00	1.00	1.00	1.00	1.00	0.99	Enseignement primaire
Secondary education	0.91	0.94	0.94	0.97	0.97	0.97	0.96	Enseignement secondaire
Tertiary education	0.48	0.60	0.87	0.99	1.02	1.03	1.02	Enseignement supérieur
Syrian Arab Republic								**République arabe syrienne**
Primary education	0.86	0.91	0.97	0.97	...	...	...	Enseignement primaire
Secondary education	0.66	0.83	0.96	1.00	...	...	...	Enseignement secondaire
Tertiary education	0.52	0.72	0.90	0.86	1.05	1.14	1.19	Enseignement supérieur
Tajikistan								**Tadjikistan**
Primary education	...	0.97	0.97	0.98	0.99	0.99	0.99	Enseignement primaire
Secondary education	...	...	0.83	0.87	...	...	...	Enseignement secondaire
Tertiary education	...	...	0.48	0.53	0.61	0.67	0.71	Enseignement supérieur

Ratio of girls to boys in primary, secondary and tertiary education *(continued)*

Rapport filles/garçons dans l'enseignement primaire, secondaire et supérieur *(suite)*

Region, country or area	1985	1995	2005	2010	2014	2015	2016	Région, pays ou zone
Thailand								**Thaïlande**
Primary education	...	...	0.97	0.99	1.01	0.94	...	Enseignement primaire
Secondary education	...	...	* 1.05	1.07	1.05	0.96	...	Enseignement secondaire
Tertiary education	...	...	1.12	1.28	1.35	1.44	...	Enseignement supérieur
TFYR of Macedonia								**ex-R.Y. de Macédoine**
Primary education	...	0.99	0.98	0.99	0.99	1.00	...	Enseignement primaire
Secondary education	...	0.99	0.97	0.97	0.97	0.98	...	Enseignement secondaire
Tertiary education	...	1.23	1.38	1.16	1.26	1.25	...	Enseignement supérieur
Timor-Leste								**Timor-Leste**
Primary education	...	...	0.91	0.96	0.99	0.99	0.98	Enseignement primaire
Secondary education	...	...	0.97	1.00	1.07	1.07	1.07	Enseignement secondaire
Tertiary education	...	...	...	0.72	...	...	...	Enseignement supérieur
Togo								**Togo**
Primary education	0.62	0.68	0.85	0.90	0.94	0.95	0.95	Enseignement primaire
Secondary education	0.31	0.35	0.53	...	...	...	...	Enseignement secondaire
Tertiary education	...	0.15	...	...	0.42	0.43	0.43	Enseignement supérieur
Tokelau								**Tokélaou**
Primary education	...	...	...	...	...	...	* 0.88	Enseignement primaire
Secondary education	...	...	...	...	...	...	* 1.02	Enseignement secondaire
Tonga								**Tonga**
Primary education	0.99	0.99	0.97	0.98	0.99	...	...	Enseignement primaire
Secondary education	1.09	...	...	1.07	1.09	...	...	Enseignement secondaire
Tertiary education	1.42	...	...	...	...	...	...	Enseignement supérieur
Trinidad and Tobago								**Trinité-et-Tobago**
Primary education	1.02	1.00	* 0.97	0.97	...	...	...	Enseignement primaire
Secondary education	1.02	...	...	...	...	...	...	Enseignement secondaire
Tertiary education	0.61	...	...	...	...	...	...	Enseignement supérieur
Tunisia								**Tunisie**
Primary education	0.82	0.92	0.96	0.97	0.97	0.97	0.97	Enseignement primaire
Secondary education	0.68	0.91	1.08	1.07	...	...	1.11	Enseignement secondaire
Tertiary education	0.59	0.78	1.23	1.53	1.63	1.64	1.71	Enseignement supérieur
Turkey								**Turquie**
Primary education	0.90	0.92	0.95	0.99	1.00	0.99	...	Enseignement primaire
Secondary education	...	0.65	0.83	0.92	0.97	0.97	...	Enseignement secondaire
Tertiary education	0.46	0.62	0.73	0.81	0.87	0.87	...	Enseignement supérieur
Turkmenistan								**Turkménistan**
Primary education	...	...	...	...	0.98	...	...	Enseignement primaire
Secondary education	...	...	...	...	0.96	...	...	Enseignement secondaire
Tertiary education	...	...	...	...	0.64	...	...	Enseignement supérieur
Tuvalu								**Tuvalu**
Primary education	...	...	* 0.96	...	* 0.99	* 0.99	...	Enseignement primaire
Secondary education	...	...	...	...	* 1.23	* 1.27	...	Enseignement secondaire
Uganda								**Ouganda**
Primary education	0.79	0.84	0.99	1.02	...	1.02	1.03	Enseignement primaire
Tertiary education	0.30	0.48	...	0.79	0.78	...	...	Enseignement supérieur
Ukraine								**Ukraine**
Primary education	...	...	1.00	1.01	1.02	...	...	Enseignement primaire
Secondary education	...	...	* 0.93	* 0.98	0.98	...	...	Enseignement secondaire
Tertiary education	...	...	1.24	1.26	1.15	...	...	Enseignement supérieur
United Arab Emirates								**Émirats arabes unis**
Primary education	0.95	0.98	...	1.02	1.03	1.01	0.97	Enseignement primaire
Secondary education	0.93	1.05	...	...	...	...	0.94	Enseignement secondaire
Tertiary education	2.11	...	...	2.79	2.25	2.14	1.99	Enseignement supérieur
United Kingdom								**Royaume-Uni**
Primary education	1.00	...	1.00	0.99	1.00	1.00	...	Enseignement primaire
Secondary education	1.03	0.99	1.03	1.00	1.04	1.03	...	Enseignement secondaire
Tertiary education	0.84	1.06	1.39	1.34	1.32	1.34	...	Enseignement supérieur
United Rep. of Tanzania								**Rép.-Unie de Tanzanie**
Primary education	1.00	0.98	0.95	1.01	1.02	1.03	...	Enseignement primaire
Secondary education	0.59	0.80	...	0.79	...	...	...	Enseignement secondaire
Tertiary education	0.17	0.19	* 0.47	0.78	...	0.51	...	Enseignement supérieur
United States of America								**États-Unis d'Amérique**
Primary education	1.02	0.99	0.99	0.99	1.00	1.00	...	Enseignement primaire
Secondary education	1.03	1.01	1.02	1.01	1.01	1.01	...	Enseignement secondaire
Tertiary education	1.16	1.30	...	...	...	...	...	Enseignement supérieur

Ratio of girls to boys in primary, secondary and tertiary education *(continued)*

Rapport filles/garçons dans l'enseignement primaire, secondaire et supérieur *(suite)*

Region, country or area	1985	1995	2005	2010	2014	2015	2016	Région, pays ou zone
Uruguay								**Uruguay**
Primary education	0.99	0.99	0.97	0.97	0.98	0.98	...	Enseignement primaire
Secondary education	...	1.20	1.15	1.14	...	...	...	Enseignement secondaire
Tertiary education	...	...	1.74	...	...	...	...	Enseignement supérieur
Uzbekistan								**Ouzbékistan**
Primary education	...	0.96	1.00	0.98	0.98	0.98	0.99	Enseignement primaire
Secondary education	...	...	0.97	1.00	0.99	0.99	0.99	Enseignement secondaire
Tertiary education	...	...	0.69	0.68	0.62	0.63	0.65	Enseignement supérieur
Vanuatu								**Vanuatu**
Primary education	...	...	0.97	0.99	...	0.98	...	Enseignement primaire
Secondary education	...	...	...	1.00	...	1.06	...	Enseignement secondaire
Venezuela (Boliv. Rep. of)								**Venezuela (Rép. boliv. du)**
Primary education	0.99	...	0.98	0.97	0.98	0.97	0.97	Enseignement primaire
Secondary education	1.26	...	1.13	1.10	1.08	1.08	1.08	Enseignement secondaire
Viet Nam								**Viet Nam**
Primary education	0.95	0.99	0.95	0.95	0.99	0.99	1.00	Enseignement primaire
Tertiary education	...	...	0.71	1.00	1.05	1.00	1.24	Enseignement supérieur
Yemen								**Yémen**
Primary education	...	...	0.74	0.82	...	...	0.87	Enseignement primaire
Secondary education	...	...	0.49	0.62	...	...	0.73	Enseignement secondaire
Tertiary education	...	...	0.36	0.44	...	...	...	Enseignement supérieur
Zambia								**Zambie**
Primary education	0.90	0.92	0.95	1.01	...	...	...	Enseignement primaire
Zimbabwe								**Zimbabwe**
Primary education	0.95	0.97	...	...	...	...	...	Enseignement primaire
Secondary education	0.68	0.84	...	...	...	...	...	Enseignement secondaire
Tertiary education	...	...	...	0.79	...	0.90	...	Enseignement supérieur

Source:

United Nations Educational, Scientific and Cultural Organization (UNESCO), Montreal, the UNESCO Institute for Statistics (UIS) statistics database, last accessed May 2018.

1 For statistical purposes, the data for China do not include those for the Hong Kong Special Administrative Region (Hong Kong SAR) and Macao Special Administrative Region (Macao SAR).

Source:

Organisation des Nations Unies pour l'éducation, la science et la culture (UNESCO), Montréal, base de données statistiques de l'Institut de statistique (ISU) de l'UNESCO, dernier accès mai 2018.

1 Pour la présentation des statistiques, les données pour la Chine ne comprennent pas la Région Administrative Spéciale de Hong Kong (Hong Kong RAS) et la Région Administrative Spéciale de Macao (Macao RAS).

7

Enrollment in primary, secondary and tertiary education levels

Number of students enrolled (thousands) and gross enrollment ratio by sex

Enseignement primaire, secondaire et supérieur

Nombre d'élèves inscrits (milliers) et taux brut de scolarisation par sexe

Region, country or area Région, pays ou zone	Year & Année &	Primary education Enseignement primaire Total ('000)	Gross enrollment ratio Taux brut de scolarisation M/H	F	Secondary education Enseignement secondaire Total ('000)	Gross enrollment ratio Taux brut de scolarisation M /H	F	Tertiary education Enseignement supérieur Total ('000)	Gross enrollment ratio Taux brut de scolarisation M/H	F
Total, all countries or areas Total, tous pays ou zones	**2005**	**678 990**	**104.8**	**99.8**	**509 100**	**65.7**	**62.1**	**139 648**	**23.7**	**24.8**
	2010	**697 101**	**105.9**	**103.0**	**546 263**	**72.4**	**69.8**	**181 506**	**28.3**	**30.4**
	2014	**716 242**	**103.3**	**102.7**	**579 906**	**76.7**	**75.7**	**211 455**	**33.5**	**37.2**
	2015	**723 319**	**103.1**	**102.8**	**581 620**	**76.8**	**75.7**	**214 083**	**34.2**	**38.1**
	2016	**740 231**	**104.1**	**104.6**	**585 517**	**76.9**	**75.9**	**215 945**	**34.7**	**39.0**
Northern Africa Afrique septentrionale	2005	23 023	97.5	90.3	* 16 909	* 68.7	* 67.8	4 586	23.8	23.0
	2010	23 598	101.4	96.0	17 399	72.2	70.4	5 515	25.8	27.7
	2014	25 169	100.3	96.7	* 18 464	* 77.9	* 77.2	5 884	28.0	30.2
	2015	* 25 787	* 100.7	* 97.2	* 18 689	* 78.5	* 77.8	6 332	30.1	33.3
	2016	26 477	101.1	97.7	* 19 049	* 79.3	* 78.4	6 471	30.5	35.2
Sub-Saharan Africa Afrique subsaharienne	2005	113 402	99.9	88.1	32 003	35.6	27.8	4 075	7.0	4.7
	2010	135 891	100.8	93.3	44 900	43.3	35.5	5 820	8.9	5.9
	2014	153 640	101.6	95.4	* 53 961	* 45.2	* 39.0	* 7 277	* 9.9	* 6.9
	2015	156 980	100.9	95.3	* 55 914	* 45.5	* 39.2	* 7 417	* 9.9	* 7.0
	*2016	160 987	100.8	95.5	57 726	45.6	39.4	7 429	9.9	7.0
Northern America Amérique septentrionale	2005	26 780	99.0	98.0	27 039	94.3	95.9	18 573	67.8	95.0
	2010	26 565	99.9	99.1	26 809	93.5	94.3	21 799	75.7	105.4
	2014	26 792	98.9	98.8	26 895	96.6	97.6	21 116	72.0	97.2
	2015	27 094	99.4	99.7	27 063	97.9	98.9	20 950	71.7	96.4
	*2016	27 177	99.3	99.6	26 953	98.0	99.1	20 939	71.7	96.5
Latin America & the Caribbean Amérique latine et Caraïbes	2005	69 066	117.5	114.0	58 887	83.5	90.3	16 088	27.6	33.8
	2010	67 190	115.4	111.9	61 100	85.7	92.8	21 646	34.7	45.3
	2014	65 327	109.3	107.3	64 190	91.5	97.2	24 700	39.7	51.9
	2015	65 407	109.8	108.2	64 041	91.8	96.8	25 312	40.4	53.4
	*2016	65 494	109.6	107.7	63 892	92.1	97.2	26 170	41.9	55.1
Eastern Asia Asie orientale	2005	* 126 355	* 104.7	* 104.6	* 115 443	* 69.9	* 68.7	28 737	25.1	21.6
	2010	113 547	107.4	105.9	113 719	89.3	89.2	39 209	27.6	27.7
	2014	106 629	98.8	98.9	102 449	91.9	93.8	50 191	41.9	46.3
	2015	107 284	98.8	99.0	99 599	91.0	93.1	51 555	45.0	50.8
	2016	109 530	100.0	100.5	97 350	89.8	91.5	52 060	47.4	54.2
South-eastern Asia Asie du Sud-Est	2005	68 305	106.9	103.9	40 675	62.4	62.1	11 062	* 20.7	* 20.4
	2010	68 448	107.2	107.8	45 687	70.0	71.0	14 283	25.3	26.9
	2014	68 898	108.1	106.0	50 158	78.7	79.5	17 381	28.3	33.7
	2015	68 715	108.1	105.1	51 344	81.0	81.4	15 800	25.7	30.8
	2016	68 681	108.2	104.8	* 51 207	* 80.3	* 81.7	16 738	27.1	33.0
Southern Asia Asie méridionale	2005	* 181 476	* 106.1	* 100.6	120 645	55.3	46.8	16 055	11.7	8.7
	2010	191 840	107.5	107.0	143 371	61.9	57.4	28 470	19.5	14.9
	2014	196 559	104.7	111.0	168 938	69.6	69.2	40 029	24.4	23.3
	2015	197 691	104.7	111.5	170 483	70.0	69.6	42 209	25.7	24.4
	2016	206 470	107.8	117.8	175 001	71.5	71.4	42 239	25.5	24.4
Western Asia Asie occidentale	2005	24 169	105.1	95.7	19 612	79.0	68.2	5 184	27.9	25.1
	2010	25 425	105.7	98.3	22 269	79.3	71.7	7 514	36.1	33.7
	2014	* 26 143	* 104.6	* 97.6	* 25 007	* 85.1	* 78.0	10 570	48.8	47.0
	2015	* 26 701	* 104.6	* 98.3	* 25 206	* 85.2	* 78.1	11 219	51.6	50.0
	*2016	26 731	103.0	96.4	25 410	85.2	78.2	11 272	52.2	50.5
Europe Europe	2005	38 461	102.3	101.5	65 270	98.1	98.0	32 142	55.3	70.9
	2010	36 749	102.7	102.1	58 629	101.8	101.0	33 676	60.1	77.3
	2014	38 128	102.1	102.2	57 900	108.5	108.1	30 627	63.2	77.6
	2015	38 485	101.6	101.7	57 455	108.7	108.2	29 627	63.0	77.4
	*2016	39 170	102.3	102.4	57 166	108.7	108.4	28 974	63.4	77.6
Oceania Océanie	2005	3 142	91.7	89.7	* 3 575	* 112.8	* 109.5	* 1 658	* 58.7	* 73.4
	2010	3 596	101.5	98.5	* 3 776	* 115.9	* 108.2	* 2 014	* 62.5	* 84.5
	2014	4 346	109.5	105.6	* 3 844	* 116.4	* 104.6	* 2 172	* 63.4	* 89.6
	2015	4 350	107.4	103.8	3 844	* 116.3	103.7	2 207	64.2	91.6
	2016	4 424	107.0	103.4	3 792	* 113.7	100.9	2 223	65.4	92.6

7

Enrollment in primary, secondary and tertiary education levels *(continued)*

Number of students enrolled (thousands) and gross enrollment ratio by sex

Enseignement primaire, secondaire et supérieur *(suite)*

Nombre d'élèves inscrits (milliers) et taux brut de scolarisation par sexe

Region, country or area Région, pays ou zone	Year & Année &	Primary education Enseignement primaire Total ('000)	Gross enrollment ratio Taux brut de scolarisation M/H	F	Secondary education Enseignement secondaire Total ('000)	Gross enrollment ratio Taux brut de scolarisation M/H	F	Tertiary education Enseignement supérieur Total ('000)	Gross enrollment ratio Taux brut de scolarisation M/H	F
Afghanistan Afghanistan	2004	4 430	149.7	65.0	594	29.4	6.1	28	1.9	0.5
	2005	4 319	126.9	74.5	651	28.6	9.3	...	...	...
	2009	4 946	118.5	78.7	1 716	61.0	29.4	95	6.1	1.4
	2010	5 279	120.6	82.7	2 044	68.6	34.3	...	...	...
	2014	6 218	125.7	88.1	2 603	68.6	38.6	263	13.0	3.6
	2015	6 334	126.2	87.2	2 699	68.4	38.6	...	...	...
	2017	6 401	124.0	84.3	2 924	69.6	39.7	...	...	...
Albania Albanie	2005	238	101.6	100.6	407	80.2	76.4	63	19.1	27.2
	2010	225	94.6	93.0	356	89.1	88.1	122	38.6	51.6
	2014	196	108.6	106.7	333	99.9	92.5	174	56.7	86.3
	2015	188	111.2	108.2	315	99.3	92.0	161	53.3	81.7
	2016	180	111.1	108.3	294	98.3	91.5	147	48.2	76.1
Algeria Algérie	2005	4 362	111.8	103.4	3 654	75.2	82.4	792	18.2	23.3
	2010	3 312	118.9	111.4	4 616	95.3	98.7	1 144	24.4	35.3
	2011	3 363	120.1	112.6	4 573	97.8	101.5	1 189	25.5	37.0
	2014	3 765	121.3	115.3	...	...	...	1 245	27.4	41.9
	2015	3 925	118.5	112.8	...	...	...	1 289	28.8	45.1
	2016	4 118	116.6	110.6	...	...	...	1 440	32.1	53.6
American Samoa Samoa américaines	2007	...	...	...	...	...	...	2	...	...
Andorra Andorre	2005	4	...	...	4	...	...	~0	...	...
	2008	4	...	...	4	...	...	~0	...	...
	2010	4	...	...	4	...	...	...	...	...
	2014	4	...	...	4	...	...	~0	...	...
	2015	4	...	...	4	...	...	1	...	...
	2016	4	...	...	4	...	...	1	...	...
Angola Angola	2002	...	...	...	* 462	* 16.7	* 13.6	13	* 0.9	* 0.6
	2005	...	...	...	...	...	...	48	...	...
	2006	...	...	...	...	...	...	49	...	...
	2010	4 273	117.6	92.8	850	31.9	21.2	...	...	...
	2011	5 027	146.7	91.2	885	32.9	20.7	143	9.3	3.4
	2013	...	...	...	...	...	...	219	10.1	7.9
	2015	...	...	...	...	...	...	221	9.6	7.4
Anguilla Anguilla	2005	1	...	...	1	...	...	~0	...	...
	2008	2	...	...	1	...	...	~0	...	...
	2010	2	...	...	1	...	...	...	...	...
	2011	2	...	...	1	...	...	...	...	...
Antigua and Barbuda Antigua-et-Barbuda	2000	13	...	...	5	* 72.6	* 65.7	...	...	...
	2010	11	98.1	89.9	8	98.8	100.0	1	8.3	20.9
	2012	10	91.7	85.7	8	90.4	104.2	2	14.1	29.2
	2014	10	91.1	84.4	8	93.1	94.0	...	...	...
	2015	10	90.2	85.1	8	92.7	94.6	...	...	...
Argentina Argentine	2005	4 873	117.7	116.6	3 884	89.8	98.4	2 083	52.1	75.8
	2010	4 947	117.5	115.9	4 213	97.1	106.6	2 521	59.1	89.2
	2014	4 780	110.2	109.7	4 451	103.4	110.3	2 869	63.5	102.9
	2015	4 784	110.1	109.7	4 502	104.0	110.2	2 966	65.3	106.8
Armenia Arménie	2000	180	98.0	99.3	409	87.8	96.5	93	31.5	39.3
	2005	125	94.6	96.3	370	...	...	115	32.8	46.0
	2009	115	109.2	112.8	313	101.2	99.0	146	45.7	56.6
	2010	102	...	...	306	...	...	146	47.6	58.0
	2014	143	...	...	245	...	...	113	43.9	50.1
	2015	145	94.1	95.5	240	84.0	88.4	106	42.4	50.5
	2016	148	94.0	94.8	...	...	...	109	45.0	57.1
Aruba Aruba	2005	10	114.9	107.8	7	95.8	96.1	2	25.9	37.3
	2010	10	114.5	113.0	7	93.5	98.3	2	31.1	43.9
	2012	9	102.8	105.4	8	110.2	112.1	3	30.5	45.6
	2014	10	118.9	115.2	...	...	...	1	10.1	23.0
	2015	...	...	...	...	...	...	1	9.4	21.4

Enrollment in primary, secondary and tertiary education levels *(continued)*

Number of students enrolled (thousands) and gross enrollment ratio by sex

Enseignement primaire, secondaire et supérieur *(suite)*

Nombre d'élèves inscrits (milliers) et taux brut de scolarisation par sexe

Region, country or area Région, pays ou zone	Year & Année &	Primary education Enseignement primaire Total ('000)	Gross enrollment ratio Taux brut de scolarisation M/H	F	Secondary education Enseignement secondaire Total ('000)	Gross enrollment ratio Taux brut de scolarisation M /H	F	Tertiary education Enseignement supérieur Total ('000)	Gross enrollment ratio Taux brut de scolarisation M/H	F
Australia Australie	2005	1 935	101.8	103.3	...	...	...	...	...	...
	2010	2 015	106.0	105.8	...	...	...	...	...	...
	2014	2 169	106.2	105.9	...	...	...	...	...	...
	2015	2 141	102.2	102.2	2 709	168.9	146.8	1 903	98.5	142.3
	2016	2 180	101.4	101.3	2 662	164.5	142.7	1 919	100.8	144.1
Austria Autriche	2005	363	100.9	100.8	781	102.8	97.8	...	...	...
	2010	328	100.5	99.1	744	100.8	96.8	385	...	...
	2014	327	101.7	101.1	697	101.2	97.5	421	72.2	86.1
	2015	328	102.2	101.4	691	101.9	98.3	426	73.6	87.9
	2016	329	102.5	102.0	687	102.9	98.9	431	76.4	90.8
Azerbaijan Azerbaïdjan	2005	568	* 98.2	* 92.8	...	...	...	...	...	...
	2010	482	* 94.2	* 93.2	...	...	...	181	* 19.4	* 19.2
	2014	518	* 106.6	* 105.5	...	...	...	195	* 21.7	* 24.8
	2015	551	* 107.4	* 105.6	...	...	...	204	* 23.6	* 27.5
	2016	581	* 106.9	* 105.9	...	...	...	208	* 25.0	* 29.7
Bahamas Bahamas	2005	37	109.9	108.4	32	89.4	89.1	...	...	...
	2010	34	106.9	109.0	34	90.2	95.1	...	...	...
	2016	31	92.9	97.9	28	87.9	93.1	...	...	...
Bahrain Bahreïn	2005	83	94.1	97.5	72	91.5	101.5	19	13.0	39.9
	2006	90	96.1	101.0	74	92.1	101.1	18	12.2	38.3
	2010	...	...	...	80	92.2	93.5	...	...	...
	2014	104	98.9	100.5	90	98.5	99.3	38	29.0	57.6
	2015	108	100.6	101.8	92	102.4	101.9	39	30.9	59.4
	2016	112	100.1	102.2	96	103.4	104.3	41	33.7	63.0
Bangladesh Bangladesh	2005	16 219	96.3	100.8	10 109	44.0	46.9	912	8.1	4.2
	2009	* 16 539	* 97.1	* 101.9	10 907	46.6	50.3	1 582	13.1	7.8
	2010	* 16 987	* 99.2	* 105.5	11 334	47.2	53.0	...	...	...
	2013	19 586	117.7	122.9	13 314	55.9	60.6	...	...	...
	2014	...	...	...	...	...	...	2 068	15.4	11.4
	2015	19 068	115.5	124.7	14 567	59.7	67.3	...	...	...
	2016	18 605	115.2	122.1	15 788	65.6	72.5	2 699	20.3	14.2
Barbados Barbade	2001	24	99.8	98.7	21	103.3	103.7	8	23.0	57.0
	2005	22	96.3	96.0	21	109.1	108.0	...	...	...
	2010	* 23	* 98.9	* 100.6	* 19	* 101.6	* 102.2	13	43.9	95.9
	2011	* 23	* 98.4	* 98.4	20	101.7	105.5	12	40.3	90.6
	2014	21	93.1	94.2	21	107.9	110.7	...	...	...
	2015	21	92.8	93.2	21	106.8	110.4	...	...	...
	2016	21	92.0	93.2	20	104.7	109.6	...	...	...
Belarus Bélarus	2005	380	99.4	96.1	...	...	...	529	56.8	77.8
	2010	358	103.8	103.6	763	109.3	105.8	569	* 65.0	* 94.0
	2014	369	98.1	98.5	649	105.7	103.8	518	77.6	103.6
	2015	387	99.5	99.6	644	105.6	104.1	477	76.2	101.0
	2016	410	101.7	102.1	644	105.2	103.5	444	76.3	98.4
Belgium Belgique	2005	739	100.7	100.2	1 200	151.1	169.1	390	54.5	67.9
	2010	732	102.0	101.8	1 203	146.9	167.3	445	60.0	75.9
	2014	774	103.7	103.6	1 210	152.3	172.7	496	63.5	82.8
	2015	783	103.2	103.1	1 218	153.6	174.7	505	64.8	84.7
Belize Belize	2005	50	115.8	110.8	29	75.3	77.7	5	12.5	19.7
	2010	53	114.8	110.3	33	72.5	78.2	7	16.8	26.9
	2013	53	114.6	109.4	37	78.5	81.8	8	18.3	30.1
	2014	52	114.4	109.0	37	78.1	81.7	...	...	...
	2015	52	115.8	110.4	38	79.8	81.8	9	17.9	28.7
	2016	52	117.5	111.7	41	86.6	87.8	9	18.5	30.0
Benin Bénin	2001	1 055	106.7	74.4	* 257	* 32.1	* 15.2	28	* 7.2	* 1.8
	2004	1 320	117.2	89.9	345	39.2	18.4	41	...	...
	2005	1 318	112.4	89.0	...	...	...	42	...	...
	2010	1 788	126.9	113.2	...	...	...	114	20.3	7.2
	2014	2 133	134.6	124.4	897	66.4	45.8	150	23.3	8.5
	2015	2 238	137.2	127.6	964	68.5	48.9	131	19.3	7.7
	2016	...	...	...	...	...	...	132	18.4	7.9

Enrollment in primary, secondary and tertiary education levels *(continued)*
Number of students enrolled (thousands) and gross enrollment ratio by sex

Enseignement primaire, secondaire et supérieur *(suite)*
Nombre d'élèves inscrits (milliers) et taux brut de scolarisation par sexe

Region, country or area / Région, pays ou zone	Year & / Année &	Primary education / Enseignement primaire: Total ('000)	Primary: Gross enrollment ratio / Taux brut de scolarisation: M/H	Primary: Gross enrollment ratio: F	Secondary education / Enseignement secondaire: Total ('000)	Secondary: Gross enrollment ratio / Taux brut de scolarisation: M/H	Secondary: Gross enrollment ratio: F	Tertiary education / Enseignement supérieur: Total ('000)	Tertiary: Gross enrollment ratio / Taux brut de scolarisation: M/H	Tertiary: Gross enrollment ratio: F
Bermuda / Bermudes	2005	5	96.8	101.5	5	76.0	85.9	...	...	...
	2006	5	93.7	100.7	5	74.4	81.0	1	18.7	41.6
	2010	4	...	...	4	72.3	85.4	1	19.3	40.6
	2014	4	88.8	86.1	4	68.0	77.4	1	19.1	36.1
	2015	4	91.3	89.4	4	67.7	75.5	1	14.7	34.1
	2017	...	...	...	...	...	...	1	12.7	21.3
Bhutan / Bhoutan	2005	99	92.2	90.0	42	46.7	41.7	4	5.7	3.7
	2010	110	105.2	107.9	60	63.0	64.2	5	8.4	5.1
	2013	104	102.0	103.4	69	72.1	77.4	9	12.1	8.9
	2014	102	99.4	101.1	74	78.8	84.5	...	...	...
	2015	99	97.3	98.4	74	80.4	85.6	...	...	...
	2016	97	94.7	95.3	74	80.2	87.8	...	...	...
Bolivia (Plurin. State of) / Bolivie (État plurin. de)	2005	1 513	115.5	114.4	1 038	89.6	84.3	...	...	...
	2010	1 429	105.7	103.6	1 058	83.6	82.6	...	...	...
	2014	1 346	98.8	95.8	1 132	85.8	84.9	...	...	...
	2015	1 344	98.5	95.7	1 153	87.1	85.7	...	...	...
	2016	1 354	98.8	96.5	1 160	87.3	85.6	...	...	...
Bosnia and Herzegovina / Bosnie-Herzégovine	2005	...	...	...	...	...	...	84	...	...
	2010	175	...	...	323	...	...	105	...	...
	2014	161	...	...	297	...	...	112	...	...
	2015	163	...	...	278	...	...	108	...	...
	2016	162	...	...	263	...	...	107	...	...
Botswana / Botswana	2005	329	109.5	107.8	173	80.0	82.4	20	9.7	8.6
	2006	330	110.3	107.9	177	80.6	85.0	22	11.1	9.1
	2008	327	109.7	106.6	168	75.0	81.9	31	...	...
	2009	331	111.4	107.4	...	...	...	48	...	...
	2010	...	...	...	...	...	...	42	...	...
	2014	341	107.2	103.5	...	...	...	55	22.9	28.5
	2015	...	...	...	...	...	...	61	23.9	32.6
	2017	...	...	...	...	...	...	50	19.5	27.3
Brazil / Brésil	2005	18 661	* 137.2	* 129.2	24 863	* 96.5	* 106.2	4 572	* 22.8	* 29.3
	2009	17 452	* 133.9	* 128.2	23 617	* 91.5	* 102.1	6 115	* 31.9	* 42.2
	2010	16 893	...	...	23 539	...	...	6 553	...	...
	2014	16 630	* 113.0	* 109.0	24 225	* 98.3	* 105.8	8 072	* 41.9	* 56.7
	2015	17 036	* 116.8	* 113.8	23 502	* 97.2	* 102.2	8 285	* 42.4	* 59.3
British Virgin Islands / Îles Vierges britanniques	2004	3	...	...	2	...	...	1	...	...
	2005	3	...	...	2	...	...	...	...	...
	2009	3	...	...	2	...	...	1	...	...
	2010	3	...	...	2	...	...	...	...	...
	2014	3	...	...	2	...	...	...	...	...
	2015	3	...	...	2	...	...	1	...	...
Brunei Darussalam / Brunéi Darussalam	2005	46	112.8	108.4	44	97.3	95.8	5	9.7	19.4
	2010	44	106.8	106.3	49	98.9	99.5	6	10.9	20.4
	2014	41	105.4	105.0	49	99.0	98.9	11	23.7	40.1
	2015	40	105.5	104.7	47	95.6	96.0	11	23.5	38.6
	2016	40	107.1	106.2	46	92.8	94.0	11	23.8	38.3
Bulgaria / Bulgarie	2005	290	103.8	102.8	686	91.0	87.3	238	42.1	48.9
	2010	260	108.7	108.3	532	92.1	88.2	287	50.0	66.1
	2014	259	98.9	98.1	519	105.9	102.3	283	60.0	75.6
	2015	262	97.6	96.5	501	104.0	100.6	279	62.0	79.1
	2016	262	95.3	94.3	487	101.4	98.3	267	63.7	79.3
Burkina Faso / Burkina Faso	2005	1 271	64.6	51.8	295	16.7	11.8	28	3.2	1.4
	2010	2 048	81.6	74.3	538	24.8	18.9	51	4.8	2.3
	2014	2 594	88.5	86.2	842	32.4	28.3	81	6.8	3.3
	2015	2 707	89.5	87.2	966	35.1	32.3	84	6.6	3.5
	2016	2 873	92.1	90.1	1 058	36.7	34.9	95	7.3	3.8

7 Enrollment in primary, secondary and tertiary education levels *(continued)*

Number of students enrolled (thousands) and gross enrollment ratio by sex

Enseignement primaire, secondaire et supérieur *(suite)*

Nombre d'élèves inscrits (milliers) et taux brut de scolarisation par sexe

Region, country or area Région, pays ou zone	Year & Année &	Primary education Enseignement primaire			Secondary education Enseignement secondaire			Tertiary education Enseignement supérieur		
			Gross enrollment ratio Taux brut de scolarisation			Gross enrollment ratio Taux brut de scolarisation			Gross enrollment ratio Taux brut de scolarisation	
		Total ('000)	M/H	F	Total ('000)	M/H	F	Total ('000)	M/H	F
Burundi Burundi	2005	1 037	89.7	75.4	* 171	* 15.8	* 11.2	17	* 3.7	* 1.4
	2010	1 850	141.8	137.0	338	28.7	19.5	29	4.6	2.3
	2014	2 047	137.1	138.6	583	43.5	36.8	51	8.3	2.5
	2015	2 072	133.5	134.8	664	47.3	43.0	...	...	...
	2016	2 110	130.5	131.3	723	49.2	47.6	...	...	...
Cabo Verde Cabo Verde	2005	83	114.7	110.1	53	66.7	75.3	4	7.3	7.8
	2010	71	106.1	99.0	62	79.1	94.0	10	15.7	20.2
	2014	67	103.9	96.4	60	81.3	91.5	13	19.2	27.5
	2015	66	101.6	95.0	59	81.1	89.5	13	18.0	25.6
	2016	64	99.9	93.4	58	80.7	88.4	13	17.9	26.0
Cambodia Cambodge	2004	2 763	137.3	126.4	* 630	* 36.7	* 25.7	45	3.9	1.8
	2005	2 695	135.6	126.0	...	...	...	57	4.7	2.1
	2008	2 341	127.7	119.7	* 930	* 48.7	* 41.6	137	12.1	6.2
	2010	2 273	127.4	120.2	...	...	...	195	17.7	10.5
	2011	2 224	126.4	117.9	...	...	...	223	19.7	12.1
	2014	2 129	120.0	113.6	...	...	...	...	...	...
	2015	2 179	117.5	116.7	...	...	...	217	14.4	11.8
	2016	2 106	111.6	108.8	...	...	...	...	...	...
Cameroon Cameroun	2005	2 978	* 115.1	* 96.6	784	31.0	24.5	* 100	* 7.2	* 4.7
	2009	3 351	116.7	101.1	1 269	45.2	37.9	174	10.3	8.2
	2010	3 510	118.9	102.8	...	...	...	220	12.6	10.3
	2014	4 143	122.9	109.5	2 000	63.8	54.4	350	18.7	14.7
	2015	4 370	125.5	112.8	2 108	65.3	56.0	372	19.3	15.5
	2016	4 481	125.3	112.9	2 207	66.4	57.1	...	...	...
Canada Canada	2005	2 321	97.4	96.6	2 602	102.1	99.8	...	...	...
	2010	2 168	98.4	98.9	2 612	103.5	101.1	...	...	...
	2014	2 249	101.2	102.4	2 661	109.5	110.1	...	...	...
	2015	2 304	102.4	103.2	2 642	110.4	111.4	...	...	...
	2016	2 319	101.4	101.5	2 641	112.2	113.9	...	...	...
Cayman Islands Îles Caïmanes	2003	...	...	...	...	...	...	1	...	...
	2005	3	...	...	3	...	...	...	...	...
	2008	4	...	...	3	...	...	1	...	...
	2013	4	...	...	3	...	...	...	...	...
Central African Republic République centrafricaine	2000	...	...	...	...	...	...	6	3.1	0.6
	*2001	459	91.8	62.7	70	15.5	8.1	...	...	...
	*2002	411	81.4	54.4	72	...	...	...	...	...
	2004	363	69.3	46.0	...	...	...	6	...	...
	2005	412	76.0	52.3	...	...	...	...	...	...
	2009	608	101.4	71.9	93	17.5	9.7	10	3.5	1.5
	2010	637	104.3	74.2	...	...	...	11	4.0	1.3
	2012	662	103.6	77.0	126	23.2	11.9	13	4.3	1.6
	2016	814	120.0	91.5	119	18.8	12.0	...	...	...
Chad Tchad	2005	1 262	85.5	58.0	* 245	* 23.2	* 8.1	12	2.7	0.2
	2010	1 727	94.9	69.8	430	31.7	13.4	* 22	* 3.6	* 0.6
	2014	2 443	116.4	88.9	509	31.8	14.4	* 42	* 5.7	* 1.1
	2015	2 270	104.4	81.0	513	31.0	14.0	...	...	...
	2016	2 213	99.0	77.0	535	31.0	14.3	...	...	...
Chile Chili	2005	1 721	109.2	104.3	1 630	94.8	96.0	664	49.7	47.7
	2010	1 547	102.8	99.9	1 518	91.4	94.3	988	66.2	71.5
	2014	1 469	99.5	96.6	1 556	98.8	100.1	1 205	81.2	91.5
	2015	1 478	100.1	97.2	1 546	99.4	100.4	1 222	83.2	93.7
	2016	1 494	101.2	98.4	1 530	99.1	100.2	1 237	84.5	96.4
China [1] Chine [1]	2003	121 662	119.2	118.6	95 625	63.6	60.0	15 186	16.6	13.8
	2005	...	...	...	...	...	...	20 601	19.8	17.9
	2010	101 019	108.2	106.6	99 218	88.1	88.0	31 047	23.3	24.8
	2013	98 871	103.9	103.8	94 324	94.2	95.9	34 091	29.6	33.6
	2014	95 107	99.1	99.3	88 692	...	...	41 924	38.3	44.6
	2015	95 958	99.2	99.5	86 127	...	...	43 367	41.7	49.5
	2016	98 189	100.6	101.2	83 956	...	...	43 886	44.2	53.3

Enrollment in primary, secondary and tertiary education levels *(continued)*
Number of students enrolled (thousands) and gross enrollment ratio by sex

Enseignement primaire, secondaire et supérieur *(suite)*
Nombre d'élèves inscrits (milliers) et taux brut de scolarisation par sexe

Region, country or area Région, pays ou zone	Year & Année &	Primary education Enseignement primaire Total ('000)	Gross enrollment ratio Taux brut de scolarisation M/H	F	Secondary education Enseignement secondaire Total ('000)	Gross enrollment ratio Taux brut de scolarisation M /H	F	Tertiary education Enseignement supérieur Total ('000)	Gross enrollment ratio Taux brut de scolarisation M/H	F
China, Hong Kong SAR Chine, RAS de Hong Kong	2005	451	...	...	498	81.3	81.9	152	33.0	33.3
	2010	349	...	...	508	87.5	87.1	265	* 59.2	* 58.9
	2014	324	109.4	107.1	416	102.1	99.0	305	65.0	72.5
	2015	333	110.5	107.9	394	102.9	99.9	299	64.9	73.1
	2016	341	108.3	106.0	372	104.4	100.9	300	67.2	76.6
China, Macao SAR Chine, RAS de Macao	2005	37	102.8	96.6	47	89.3	83.2	23	65.7	44.2
	2010	25	96.6	94.8	38	89.0	86.2	29	56.0	54.0
	2014	23	101.3	100.5	32	94.5	92.0	30	57.0	72.9
	2015	24	104.1	102.6	30	95.6	94.1	31	62.0	80.7
	2016	26	106.5	105.1	29	99.5	99.1	32	67.3	89.4
Colombia Colombie	2005	5 298	128.7	126.2	4 297	79.3	87.7	1 224	28.0	30.4
	2010	5 085	125.4	123.1	5 080	97.3	106.9	1 674	37.6	41.3
	2014	4 543	115.7	111.7	4 828	95.1	102.6	2 221	49.5	57.1
	2015	4 479	115.4	111.6	4 794	94.8	101.5	2 294	51.5	59.9
	2016	4 448	115.7	112.2	4 785	95.2	101.2	2 394	54.4	63.1
Comoros Comores	2003	104	120.8	99.5	38	43.5	36.5	2	3.5	2.7
	2004	104	114.5	101.6	43	49.8	38.0	...	...	...
	2008	111	113.0	104.1	...	...	...	...	...	...
	2010	...	...	...	...	...	...	4	6.6	4.9
	2014	120	108.6	101.2	70	59.1	63.1	6	9.9	8.0
Congo Congo	2003	510	100.4	94.3	204	46.5	32.0	* 12	* 5.3	* 2.1
	2004	584	112.0	105.0	* 235	* 48.2	* 40.7	...	...	...
	2005	597	111.4	103.5	...	...	...	...	...	...
	2009	672	109.0	101.5	...	...	...	23	10.3	2.2
	2010	705	110.0	103.8	...	...	...	...	...	...
	2012	734	100.6	107.8	339	55.8	48.4	39	12.2	7.7
	2013	...	...	...	...	...	...	37	10.6	8.0
Cook Islands Îles Cook	2005	2	* 110.2	* 113.0	2	* 75.1	* 84.9	...	...	...
	2010	2	* 104.6	* 103.6	2	* 80.7	* 88.1	...	...	...
	2012	2	* 111.5	* 105.8	2	* 94.6	* 101.2	1	* 41.2	* 50.1
	2014	2	* 109.8	* 105.0	2	* 85.0	* 93.6	...	...	...
	2015	2	* 109.1	* 99.8	2	* 85.8	* 93.3	...	...	...
	2016	2	* 111.7	* 105.2	2	* 84.9	* 90.1	...	...	...
Costa Rica Costa Rica	2004	558	116.7	114.0	340	80.8	84.3	109	24.5	30.2
	2005	542	114.4	111.5	347	82.6	86.2	...	...	...
	2010	521	118.1	115.8	414	100.1	104.3	...	...	...
	2014	476	111.3	110.3	460	117.2	123.6	217	47.5	58.8
	2015	473	110.1	109.5	460	120.7	125.6	218	46.6	60.9
	2016	476	109.7	110.3	463	122.8	129.5	218	48.4	59.8
Côte d'Ivoire Côte d'Ivoire	*2003	2 046	79.3	63.5	...	...	...	...	...	...
	2009	2 383	79.4	64.8	...	...	...	* 153	* 11.3	* 6.0
	2010	...	...	...	...	...	...	144	10.4	5.4
	2014	3 177	94.2	82.0	1 418	46.4	32.7	177	10.8	6.3
	2015	3 371	97.6	85.9	1 587	50.4	36.1	193	10.8	7.2
	2016	3 617	102.1	91.3	1 727	53.3	38.8	...	...	...
Croatia Croatie	2005	196	103.3	103.4	400	91.7	94.8	135	40.5	49.2
	2010	167	91.9	92.0	389	96.5	103.4	150	46.3	62.1
	2014	161	99.1	98.8	370	97.0	100.6	166	57.2	78.4
	2015	162	97.9	98.2	360	96.0	100.6	162	57.1	77.3
	2016	163	95.0	95.8	349	95.6	100.0	162	57.0	78.5
Cuba Cuba	2005	895	99.7	96.8	937	91.6	93.1	472	* 46.6	* 78.8
	2010	853	104.0	102.2	809	90.8	91.4	801	72.4	119.2
	2013	772	101.4	100.0	787	91.8	92.8	373	36.9	61.5
	2014	763	104.1	99.0	830	97.8	100.3	302	...	...
	2015	746	103.8	97.9	825	98.6	102.2	261	29.9	42.2
	2016	...	...	...	...	...	...	245	28.4	40.1
Curaçao Curaçao	2013	21	176.3	169.2	11	84.1	91.1	2	13.0	29.6

Enrollment in primary, secondary and tertiary education levels *(continued)*
Number of students enrolled (thousands) and gross enrollment ratio by sex

Enseignement primaire, secondaire et supérieur *(suite)*
Nombre d'élèves inscrits (milliers) et taux brut de scolarisation par sexe

Region, country or area / Région, pays ou zone	Year & / Année &	Primary education / Enseignement primaire: Total ('000)	Primary: Gross enrollment ratio Taux brut de scolarisation: M/H	Primary: Gross enrollment ratio Taux brut de scolarisation: F	Secondary education / Enseignement secondaire: Total ('000)	Secondary: Gross enrollment ratio Taux brut de scolarisation: M /H	Secondary: Gross enrollment ratio Taux brut de scolarisation: F	Tertiary education / Enseignement supérieur: Total ('000)	Tertiary: Gross enrollment ratio Taux brut de scolarisation: M/H	Tertiary: Gross enrollment ratio Taux brut de scolarisation: F
Cyprus / Chypre	2005	61	* 100.9	* 100.8	64	* 95.7	* 97.5	20	* 31.2	* 35.3
	2010	55	* 101.6	* 101.6	64	* 90.9	* 92.0	32	* 50.9	* 45.6
	2014	53	* 98.7	* 99.6	59	* 99.4	* 99.5	34	* 44.1	* 62.6
	2015	54	* 99.3	* 99.3	57	* 100.1	* 99.4	37	* 51.1	* 69.4
Czechia / Tchéquie	2005	503	99.9	98.5	975	94.8	96.6	336	44.8	52.0
	2010	463	104.0	103.6	837	94.4	94.9	437	53.6	74.9
	2014	511	98.6	98.6	781	104.4	104.9	419	54.9	76.9
	2015	535	99.3	99.7	770	104.6	105.6	396	53.8	75.7
Dem. People's Rep. Korea / Rép. pop. dém. de Corée	2009	1 547	99.4	99.4	2 474	102.1	102.1	593	40.8	20.6
	2011	...	...	...	...	...	...	600	...	...
	2015	1 358	...	...	2 148	92.5	93.5	565	36.0	19.9
Dem. Rep. of the Congo / Rép. dém. du Congo	2002	5 455	74.9	59.1	...	...	...	...	...	...
	2009	10 244	108.2	92.8	3 399	53.1	29.9	378	10.3	3.2
	2010	10 572	107.0	93.1	3 484	52.2	30.1	...	...	...
	2013	12 601	111.8	101.3	3 996	52.9	32.8	443	9.5	4.3
	2014	13 535	115.5	105.0	4 388	56.1	34.9	...	...	...
	2015	13 763	108.4	107.6	4 619	56.3	36.0	...	...	...
Denmark / Danemark	2005	414	98.8	98.7	465	121.9	126.5	232	67.7	93.4
	2010	403	99.5	99.7	504	119.0	120.0	241	60.4	87.4
	2014	467	101.9	100.7	554	126.7	132.1	301	67.4	95.3
	2015	469	102.1	100.8	553	127.3	133.4	314	68.7	96.3
	2016	472	102.4	101.2	541	127.3	131.0	315	68.8	94.0
Djibouti / Djibouti	2005	51	47.8	39.4	30	27.4	18.3	2	2.7	1.9
	2009	56	58.9	53.0	44	38.5	28.4	3	4.0	2.8
	2010	...	...	...	...	...	...	3	4.1	2.8
	2011	61	64.2	58.4	51	42.1	33.8	5	6.0	4.0
	2014	64	69.5	60.6	59	47.3	38.2	...	...	...
	2015	63	68.0	60.4	59	48.0	38.5	...	...	...
	2017	62	67.5	60.2	61	48.1	40.1	...	...	...
Dominica / Dominique	2005	9	99.4	99.4	7	103.3	111.7	...	...	...
	2010	8	110.0	107.6	7	92.8	101.4	...	...	...
	2014	8	117.9	118.0	6	98.0	96.2	...	...	...
	2015	8	117.2	114.8	6	101.2	99.8	...	...	...
	2016	7	114.1	110.5	...	...	...	...	...	...
Dominican Republic / République dominicaine	2003	1 375	* 112.4	* 113.4	...	...	...	287	25.9	40.7
	2005	1 290	108.6	103.3	808	63.6	76.0	...	...	...
	2010	1 318	114.1	100.5	905	71.5	80.6	...	...	...
	2014	1 268	105.4	95.7	931	74.4	82.4	456	36.3	58.8
	2015	1 307	108.1	98.7	929	74.1	81.7	480	35.4	65.0
	2016	1 287	105.7	97.7	929	73.7	80.7	506	38.0	68.2
Ecuador / Équateur	2005	1 998	112.0	111.5	1 053	61.5	62.2	...	...	...
	2008	...	...	...	...	...	...	535	36.0	41.5
	2010	2 099	115.7	116.0	1 571	86.6	91.0	...	...	...
	2012	2 128	117.5	117.6	1 750	95.7	99.8	573	34.6	45.3
	2013	2 089	114.8	115.4	1 823	99.1	103.7	586	...	...
	2014	2 068	113.1	113.5	1 883	102.4	106.6	...	...	...
	2015	2 094	113.7	114.0	1 942	105.7	109.8	669	42.2	49.0
	2017	1 951	103.7	104.7	1 930	105.6	108.6	...	...	...
Egypt / Égypte	2004	* 7 928	* 97.8	* 94.7	* 8 330	* 81.0	* 76.8	2 261	31.1	25.2
	2005	9 564	99.4	94.2	...	...	...	2 352	31.8	26.8
	2010	10 542	105.1	102.0	6 846	70.1	68.2	2 646	31.5	28.9
	2014	11 128	101.3	101.0	8 208	83.4	83.0	2 544	32.4	29.0
	2015	...	...	...	...	...	...	2 869	35.8	34.4
	2016	11 764	103.6	103.7	8 745	86.7	85.2	2 789	34.0	34.8
El Salvador / El Salvador	2005	1 045	120.7	116.6	524	68.0	68.0	122	21.8	24.3
	2010	940	118.1	112.8	577	69.6	69.2	150	24.9	27.5
	2014	777	109.0	104.4	625	77.0	77.5	176	26.7	29.2
	2015	741	105.2	100.9	600	75.4	76.0	179	26.6	29.5
	2016	711	102.2	98.2	572	74.3	74.2	181	26.4	29.6

7 Enrollment in primary, secondary and tertiary education levels *(continued)*

Number of students enrolled (thousands) and gross enrollment ratio by sex

Enseignement primaire, secondaire et supérieur *(suite)*

Nombre d'élèves inscrits (milliers) et taux brut de scolarisation par sexe

Region, country or area Région, pays ou zone	Year & Année &	Primary education Enseignement primaire Total ('000)	Primary: Gross enrollment ratio Taux brut de scolarisation M/H	Primary: Gross enrollment ratio Taux brut de scolarisation F	Secondary education Enseignement secondaire Total ('000)	Secondary: Gross enrollment ratio Taux brut de scolarisation M /H	Secondary: Gross enrollment ratio Taux brut de scolarisation F	Tertiary education Enseignement supérieur Total ('000)	Tertiary: Gross enrollment ratio Taux brut de scolarisation M/H	Tertiary: Gross enrollment ratio Taux brut de scolarisation F
Equatorial Guinea Guinée équatoriale	2000	73	111.9	92.3	21	32.2	14.4	1	2.4	1.2
	2005	76	90.8	87.7	26	29.8	22.0	...	...	...
	2010	85	69.4	68.4	...	...	...	...	...	...
	2012	92	69.0	68.6	...	...	...	...	...	...
	2015	93	61.8	61.3	...	...	...	...	...	...
Eritrea Érythrée	2004	375	84.0	67.4	194	35.3	20.1	5	1.9	0.3
	2005	378	84.1	68.2	217	38.4	23.0	...	...	...
	2010	286	57.1	48.7	248	41.8	32.0	12	3.7	1.4
	2014	362	60.1	51.2	270	41.4	33.8	13	3.7	1.8
	2015	362	58.0	50.0	246	35.8	30.4	11	3.0	1.9
	2016	...	...	...	...	...	...	10	2.7	1.9
Estonia Estonie	2005	86	100.2	97.6	124	101.0	104.7	68	50.9	85.8
	2010	73	103.8	102.3	95	105.3	105.3	69	51.6	85.9
	2014	77	98.0	97.6	78	108.4	107.9	60	58.6	88.6
	2015	80	96.9	97.0	78	111.1	110.7	55	57.6	87.4
Eswatini Eswatini	2005	222	106.2	99.1	71	46.9	47.5	6	4.6	4.9
	2006	230	111.2	103.3	77	50.5	51.3	6	4.5	4.4
	2010	241	118.2	107.9	89	58.2	57.7	...	...	...
	2013	239	115.0	104.8	93	62.9	61.3	8	5.3	5.5
	2014	240	114.0	104.1	97	65.2	64.3	...	...	...
	2015	241	112.8	102.9	100	67.3	66.8	...	...	...
Ethiopia Éthiopie	2005	10 020	86.0	71.9	2 488	30.8	18.5	191	4.2	1.3
	2010	13 635	95.4	88.1	4 207	38.0	31.5	578	10.2	4.4
	2012	14 532	98.0	91.0	4 929	39.6	35.7	693	11.1	5.2
	2014	15 733	104.1	95.6	...	...	...	757	10.9	5.3
	2015	16 198	106.8	97.0	5 029	35.8	34.4	...	...	...
Fiji Fidji	2004	113	113.4	111.8	102	88.0	93.9	13	14.6	17.4
	*2005	...	...	...	...	...	...	13	14.7	17.6
	2009	101	105.9	104.3	98	83.1	90.9	...	...	...
	2012	103	104.5	105.5	97	84.3	93.4	...	...	...
	2013	105	105.1	106.2	...	...	...	...	...	...
	2015	109	106.0	105.1	...	...	...	...	...	...
Finland Finlande	2005	382	98.8	98.0	431	109.3	114.3	306	83.3	100.5
	2010	347	99.8	99.2	427	105.2	110.1	304	84.3	103.1
	2014	352	100.8	100.4	537	139.7	153.5	306	80.8	97.3
	2015	355	100.8	100.2	540	142.9	157.4	302	79.9	95.8
	2016	360	100.6	100.2	540	145.0	159.7	297	79.8	94.5
France France	2005	4 015	109.6	108.2	6 036	113.7	114.1	2 187	48.5	62.4
	2010	4 159	109.0	107.8	5 873	112.0	112.8	2 245	51.0	65.0
	2014	4 189	106.3	106.0	5 947	110.6	111.9	2 389	57.0	71.5
	2015	4 256	107.5	107.2	5 983	110.6	111.6	2 424	58.1	72.8
Gabon Gabon	2002	282	142.9	142.0	* 105	...	...	...	...	...
	2003	280	139.5	138.5	...	...	...	10	10.5	6.1
	2011	318	140.8	136.6	...	...	...	...	...	...
Gambia Gambie	2004	205	92.7	93.5	...	...	...	2	1.9	0.4
	2005	205	88.7	91.5	...	...	...	...	...	...
	2010	229	82.6	84.9	* 124	* 58.5	* 55.7	3	2.6	1.8
	2012	244	81.6	85.4	...	...	...	5	3.7	2.5
	2014	275	85.9	90.7	...	...	...	...	...	...
	2015	294	88.5	94.5	...	...	...	...	...	...
	2017	330	93.3	101.0	...	...	...	...	...	...
Georgia Géorgie	2005	338	90.8	88.6	316	80.8	79.1	174	44.9	47.0
	2008	311	101.5	100.1	305	89.9	86.4	130	* 30.9	* 37.6
	2009	299	101.9	101.4	342	...	...	95	22.8	28.8
	2010	289	101.4	102.2	...	...	...	106	25.7	32.8
	2014	285	105.4	104.7	282	97.3	99.8	121	36.0	45.3
	2015	289	104.1	104.5	278	100.6	103.3	128	41.1	50.3
	2016	291	102.4	102.8	275	103.2	105.5	137	48.3	55.7

Enrollment in primary, secondary and tertiary education levels *(continued)*

Number of students enrolled (thousands) and gross enrollment ratio by sex

Enseignement primaire, secondaire et supérieur *(suite)*

Nombre d'élèves inscrits (milliers) et taux brut de scolarisation par sexe

Region, country or area Région, pays ou zone	Year [&] Année [&]	Primary education Enseignement primaire Total ('000)	Gross enrollment ratio Taux brut de scolarisation M/H	F	Secondary education Enseignement secondaire Total ('000)	Gross enrollment ratio Taux brut de scolarisation M /H	F	Tertiary education Enseignement supérieur Total ('000)	Gross enrollment ratio Taux brut de scolarisation M/H	F
Germany Allemagne	2005	3 306	103.1	102.9	8 268	103.3	100.8	...	...	...
	2010	3 068	103.1	102.8	7 664	106.4	101.2	...	...	...
	2014	2 863	101.8	101.1	7 201	103.3	98.7	2 912	65.7	62.6
	2015	2 879	102.7	102.1	7 113	103.4	98.6	2 978	66.9	65.6
Ghana Ghana	2005	2 930	90.4	86.9	* 1 370	* 44.9	* 37.2	120	7.7	4.1
	2009	3 659	102.7	100.8	1 812	52.8	46.3	203	11.4	6.7
	2014	4 117	105.4	105.3	2 266	57.8	54.2	402	19.1	12.7
	2015	4 342	108.6	108.7	2 440	61.0	57.8	418	19.1	13.2
	2016	4 358	105.7	107.3	2 512	61.3	59.3	422	18.7	13.4
	2017	4 393	104.1	105.5	2 551	61.2	59.6	...	...	...
Gibraltar Gibraltar	2001	2	...	...	2	...	...	...	...	...
	2009	3	...	...	2	...	...	...	...	...
	2016	3	...	...	2	...	...	...	...	...
Greece Grèce	2005	650	96.4	94.3	716	100.4	95.8	647	80.8	90.0
	2010	643	96.4	94.7	717	105.4	99.0	642	100.0	103.7
	2014	629	94.5	93.4	668	101.9	96.2	677	118.0	116.9
	2015	644	95.5	94.6	663	102.6	95.9	...	...	...
Grenada Grenade	2005	14	98.4	95.5	* 13	* 96.9	* 98.7	...	...	...
	2009	14	107.6	101.5	11	100.7	100.8	7	44.9	60.9
	2010	14	105.1	101.5	12	106.2	109.4	...	...	...
	2014	13	103.9	102.2	10	101.2	100.5	...	...	...
	2015	13	106.7	102.9	9	99.3	99.0	9	84.6	97.9
	2016	13	103.1	99.6	9	98.8	102.5	9	80.3	102.7
Guatemala Guatemala	2002	2 076	107.3	98.8	608	44.8	40.3	112	10.2	7.5
	2005	2 345	113.3	106.3	754	51.0	47.1	...	...	...
	2007	2 449	114.0	108.7	864	54.7	51.5	234	16.6	17.1
	2010	2 653	116.6	114.3	1 082	63.9	60.2	233	...	...
	2014	2 417	104.1	101.0	1 166	64.2	60.9	299	16.7	18.7
	2015	2 382	103.1	99.9	1 221	66.3	62.5	367	19.5	23.1
	2016	2 351	102.4	99.1	1 220	65.2	61.8	...	...	...
Guinea Guinée	2005	1 207	87.6	70.2	* 420	* 38.8	* 19.3	24	4.7	1.1
	2008	1 364	91.6	76.7	531	43.4	25.1	80	13.5	4.4
	2010	1 453	94.1	77.5	...	...	...	99	15.6	5.2
	2014	1 730	101.7	86.1	716	48.6	31.9	118	15.5	6.9
Guinea-Bissau Guinée-Bissau	2000	150	87.8	58.9	26	22.8	12.4	...	...	...
	2005	252	...	...	51	...	...	3	...	...
	2006	269	...	...	55	...	...	4	...	...
	2010	279	122.1	114.1	...	...	...	...	...	...
Guyana Guyana	2005	117	99.9	100.2	71	83.9	86.6	7	7.4	15.9
	2010	99	96.7	96.7	81	87.2	92.8	8	6.9	16.6
	2012	94	95.1	97.1	86	96.6	100.9	9	7.6	15.6
Honduras Honduras	2004	1 257	109.1	108.5	...	...	...	* 123	* 13.2	* 19.0
	2005	1 232	105.5	105.4	...	...	...	...	...	...
	2010	1 275	105.2	104.9	655	61.3	75.3	170	18.0	20.8
	2014	1 150	96.0	94.2	620	57.3	67.1	186	16.7	22.8
	2015	1 154	96.7	95.8	638	58.0	69.2	195	17.4	23.7
	2016	1 145	96.6	95.8	652	59.8	69.6	...	...	...
Hungary Hongrie	2005	431	99.1	97.1	960	96.7	95.8	436	53.0	77.5
	2010	388	101.2	100.5	905	97.7	96.4	389	54.1	73.8
	2014	393	102.2	101.5	858	103.9	104.5	329	45.5	58.9
	2015	396	102.5	102.1	827	102.7	103.3	308	43.5	54.7
	2016	394	102.0	101.7	805	102.3	102.3	295	42.8	53.5
Iceland Islande	2005	31	98.0	95.7	33	110.5	112.1	15	48.1	92.5
	2010	30	99.0	99.6	36	106.5	108.2	18	56.8	101.5
	2014	30	98.7	97.7	38	116.6	120.7	20	59.8	104.1
	2015	30	98.7	98.6	37	118.6	119.6	19	54.7	98.0

7 Enrollment in primary, secondary and tertiary education levels *(continued)*

Number of students enrolled (thousands) and gross enrollment ratio by sex

Enseignement primaire, secondaire et supérieur *(suite)*

Nombre d'élèves inscrits (milliers) et taux brut de scolarisation par sexe

Region, country or area / Région, pays ou zone	Year & / Année &	Primary education / Enseignement primaire: Total ('000)	Primary: Gross enrollment ratio Taux brut de scolarisation M/H	Primary: Gross enrollment ratio Taux brut de scolarisation F	Secondary education / Enseignement secondaire: Total ('000)	Secondary: Gross enrollment ratio Taux brut de scolarisation M/H	Secondary: Gross enrollment ratio Taux brut de scolarisation F	Tertiary education / Enseignement supérieur: Total ('000)	Tertiary: Gross enrollment ratio Taux brut de scolarisation M/H	Tertiary: Gross enrollment ratio Taux brut de scolarisation F
India	2003	125 569	104.3	101.5	81 050	55.0	44.2	11 295	12.7	8.5
Inde	2005	...	...	...	89 462	* 59.2	* 48.7	11 777	12.5	8.8
	2010	138 414	* 108.1	* 110.4	107 687	65.5	60.9	20 741	20.6	15.0
	2014	137 809	102.3	114.0	129 439	73.8	74.8	30 306	25.7	25.3
	2015	138 518	102.7	115.0	129 542	73.5	74.5	32 107	27.0	26.7
	2016	145 803	106.1	123.9	132 161	74.6	75.8	32 392	26.9	27.0
Indonesia	2004	29 142	109.6	108.0	16 354	62.1	61.6	3 551	18.5	14.7
Indonésie	2005	29 150	* 109.5	* 106.1	15 993	* 60.4	* 59.8	* 3 662	...	...
	2010	30 342	108.0	112.2	19 976	74.1	75.0	5 001	24.2	21.8
	2014	29 838	106.0	103.4	22 587	83.6	83.5	6 463	27.8	31.4
	2015	29 700	105.8	102.4	23 756	86.9	87.8	5 108	21.9	24.8
	2016	29 450	105.4	101.4	23 633	84.5	87.7	6 141	26.5	29.5
Iran (Islamic Republic of)	2005	6 207	100.7	98.2	9 066	76.9	74.1	2 126	22.2	23.5
Iran (Rép. islamique d')	2010	5 630	105.7	104.8	7 347	82.2	80.6	3 791	42.7	42.2
	2014	7 441	106.3	111.5	5 795	88.4	87.8	4 685	68.0	63.2
	2015	7 670	105.8	111.6	5 712	88.8	89.1	4 803	75.7	67.2
	2016	...	...	...	...	...	...	4 348	72.0	65.5
Iraq	2004	4 335	113.1	95.2	1 706	56.7	38.2	413	19.8	11.8
Iraq	*2005	...	...	...	...	...	...	425	20.0	11.9
	2007	4 864	117.0	98.7	2 038	61.0	45.6	...	...	...
Ireland	2005	454	106.8	106.2	317	104.5	114.5	187	47.9	60.6
Irlande	2010	506	106.4	106.9	336	120.6	126.1	194	59.5	66.5
	2014	536	101.8	102.1	348	126.0	127.9	204	75.6	79.3
	2015	545	101.2	101.3	355	125.9	128.6	215	80.8	86.3
	2016	554	100.8	100.8	360	124.7	127.7	218	...	...
Israel	2005	722	103.3	103.8	673	105.0	104.4	311	50.1	66.4
Israël	2009	786	102.6	103.2	694	100.9	103.1	343	54.5	70.7
	2010	807	104.0	104.5	708	100.9	103.3	360	...	...
	2014	862	103.8	104.2	768	101.1	102.6	377	56.7	76.2
	2015	884	104.2	104.8	785	102.0	103.0	374	54.6	75.5
	2016	897	103.2	104.1	809	103.2	105.0	378	53.7	75.2
Italy	2005	2 771	101.8	100.7	4 507	98.5	97.8	2 015	54.2	74.2
Italie	2010	2 822	102.4	101.4	4 626	102.7	101.3	1 980	54.7	78.0
	2014	2 863	102.0	101.1	4 597	103.9	101.6	1 854	53.5	73.8
	2015	2 856	101.6	100.8	4 606	104.3	102.0	1 826	53.6	72.7
Jamaica	2002	330	96.3	96.1	228	83.1	86.1	45	11.7	25.5
Jamaïque	2004	331	96.1	96.4	246	88.0	91.9	52	...	...
	2005	326	...	...	246	87.1	92.4	48	...	...
	2010	294	...	...	260	88.2	95.5	71	16.4	37.8
	2013	278	...	...	229	79.1	85.2	74	16.6	38.0
	2014	266	...	...	224	78.6	84.9	...	...	...
	2015	259	...	...	215	77.8	83.5	75	19.8	34.2
	2016	253	...	...	217	82.0	86.3	...	...	...
Japan	2005	7 232	100.1	100.6	7 710	97.9	98.5	4 038	57.3	51.1
Japon	2010	7 099	101.4	101.8	7 296	100.1	100.8	3 836	61.2	54.8
	2014	6 715	99.4	99.7	7 227	101.0	101.8	3 862	65.1	60.6
	2015	6 638	98.6	99.0	7 221	101.8	102.5	3 845	65.1	61.3
Jordan	2004	800	99.0	100.0	616	83.8	86.2	214	35.2	39.8
Jordanie	2005	805	...	...	626	83.8	86.3	218	35.9	39.0
	2010	820	...	...	710	79.4	82.5	247	34.9	39.7
	2012	849	...	...	724	73.7	75.7	307	39.4	45.5
	2014	980	...	...	749	68.9	71.3	...	...	...
	2015	...	...	...	...	...	...	313	35.8	39.0
	2016	1 050	...	...	...	...	...	316	35.0	37.5
Kazakhstan	2000	1 208	95.6	95.9	1 994	90.3	95.2	418	28.9	34.4
Kazakhstan	2005	1 024	101.5	101.4	...	...	...	...	...	...
	2010	958	107.7	108.3	1 818	97.2	97.7	757	40.3	51.1
	2014	1 122	111.5	111.6	1 662	104.4	107.1	727	42.6	53.9
	2015	1 196	110.6	110.8	1 679	107.6	111.4	658	40.3	51.5
	2017	1 357	107.1	108.8	1 768	112.6	113.6	627	43.9	55.5

7

Enrollment in primary, secondary and tertiary education levels *(continued)*
Number of students enrolled (thousands) and gross enrollment ratio by sex

Enseignement primaire, secondaire et supérieur *(suite)*
Nombre d'élèves inscrits (milliers) et taux brut de scolarisation par sexe

Region, country or area Région, pays ou zone	Year & Année &	Primary education Enseignement primaire Total ('000)	Gross enrollment ratio Taux brut de scolarisation M/H	 F	Secondary education Enseignement secondaire Total ('000)	Gross enrollment ratio Taux brut de scolarisation M /H	 F	Tertiary education Enseignement supérieur Total ('000)	Gross enrollment ratio Taux brut de scolarisation M/H	 F
Kenya Kenya	2005	6 076	103.5	99.4	* 2 468	* 48.8	* 46.6	* 114	* 3.7	* 2.2
	2009	7 150	107.4	105.2	3 204	60.7	54.9	168	4.7	3.3
	*2014	8 158	107.8	108.5	...	...	...	...	...	...
	2015	8 169	106.0	105.9	...	...	...	...	...	...
	2016	8 290	105.1	105.5	...	...	...	...	...	...
Kiribati Kiribati	2005	16	111.2	112.8	12	83.1	95.3	...	...	...
	2008	16	108.3	113.1	12	82.9	91.5	...	...	...
	2009	16	108.0	113.7	...	...	...	...	...	...
	2014	16	111.2	115.2	...	...	...	...	...	...
	2015	16	102.8	106.2	...	...	...	...	...	...
	2016	17	103.7	106.4	...	...	...	...	...	...
Kuwait Koweït	2004	158	97.9	106.9	267	99.1	104.9	* 37	* 12.2	* 28.1
	2005	203	102.7	106.4	* 244	* 104.4	* 114.2	...	...	...
	2010	214	103.0	101.5	264	96.8	99.0	...	...	...
	2013	239	102.0	105.5	279	92.2	96.9	72	23.0	42.7
	2014	253	101.8	105.1	* 283	* 90.5	* 96.5	...	...	...
	2015	264	100.4	104.4	302	94.0	101.4	...	...	...
	2016	271	98.8	102.7	...	...	...	...	...	...
Kyrgyzstan Kirghizistan	2005	434	99.6	98.1	721	86.4	86.8	220	37.8	47.5
	2010	391	99.8	99.0	694	87.7	87.3	261	36.6	47.7
	2014	435	109.0	108.0	651	91.7	92.5	268	40.3	52.4
	2015	451	108.3	107.5	643	92.6	94.1	265	41.2	53.7
	2016	470	106.9	105.8	660	97.5	97.6	250	40.4	51.6
Lao People's Dem. Rep. Rép. dém. populaire lao	2005	891	119.6	104.6	394	49.5	37.4	47	9.1	6.4
	2010	916	128.6	118.7	435	51.1	42.4	118	18.8	14.4
	2014	871	121.7	116.0	601	61.7	56.3	132	18.9	17.7
	2015	850	117.1	112.5	640	66.0	61.1	130	18.5	17.7
	2016	828	112.6	108.3	665	68.9	64.0	123	17.2	17.2
Latvia Lettonie	2005	84	96.0	91.8	272	99.5	99.5	131	54.9	97.8
	2010	114	108.7	108.7	147	97.0	94.6	113	48.8	85.9
	2014	115	98.8	98.1	122	112.5	109.7	90	55.2	78.1
	2015	117	98.8	98.0	118	112.8	111.7	86	53.9	83.2
Lebanon Liban	2005	* 476	* 107.8	* 99.0	* 378	* 80.2	* 80.8	166	43.0	45.2
	2010	462	109.5	100.0	383	74.5	76.0	202	47.4	49.3
	2014	481	98.5	90.2	370	61.6	62.0	229	39.6	45.8
	2015	491	96.7	88.5	382	61.6	61.1	216	...	...
	2016	487	93.2	85.1	384	59.9	60.1	221	...	...
Lesotho Lesotho	2005	422	117.2	117.0	94	34.5	44.4	8	3.1	4.2
	2006	425	117.7	117.4	96	34.8	45.0	9	3.4	4.3
	2010	389	111.8	109.0	126	42.3	59.7	...	...	...
	2014	366	107.8	104.8	131	44.3	60.0	24	8.3	11.8
	2015	362	106.5	103.0	133	45.7	61.4	22	7.3	10.9
	2016	361	105.7	102.1	129	44.5	60.2	...	...	...
Liberia Libéria	2000	496	129.9	95.7	136	40.8	29.7	52	25.0	13.8
	2009	605	105.3	94.4	...	...	...	...	...	...
	2010	...	...	...	...	...	...	33	12.1	6.5
	2012	...	...	...	...	...	...	44	14.3	9.0
	2014	684	99.8	91.8	223	42.6	33.2	...	...	...
	2015	684	98.7	89.3	227	42.0	32.6	...	...	...
Libya Libye	2003	739	104.9	101.7	* 798	* 100.7	* 107.2	* 375	* 57.5	* 63.6
	2005	714	102.8	101.7	702	* 84.5	* 100.8	...	...	...
	2006	755	111.5	107.0	733	90.2	106.0	...	...	...
Liechtenstein Liechtenstein	2004	2	* 109.9	* 108.5	3	* 117.2	* 103.9	1	* 35.7	* 13.3
	2005	2	...	...	3	...	...	1	...	...
	2010	2	* 108.6	* 102.3	3	* 117.6	* 100.0	1	* 44.3	* 27.4
	2014	2	* 103.1	* 102.3	3	* 127.8	* 103.3	1	* 50.8	* 24.1
	2015	2	* 106.5	* 104.8	3	* 130.7	* 101.7	1	* 44.8	* 21.9
	2016	2	* 107.5	* 103.4	3	* 130.3	* 101.9	1	* 45.3	* 24.8

7

Enrollment in primary, secondary and tertiary education levels *(continued)*
Number of students enrolled (thousands) and gross enrollment ratio by sex

Enseignement primaire, secondaire et supérieur *(suite)*
Nombre d'élèves inscrits (milliers) et taux brut de scolarisation par sexe

Region, country or area / Région, pays ou zone	Year & / Année &	Primary education / Enseignement primaire: Total ('000)	Primary: Gross enrollment ratio Taux brut de scolarisation: M/H	Primary: F	Secondary education / Enseignement secondaire: Total ('000)	Secondary: Gross enrollment ratio Taux brut de scolarisation: M /H	Secondary: F	Tertiary education / Enseignement supérieur: Total ('000)	Tertiary: Gross enrollment ratio / Taux brut de scolarisation: M/H	Tertiary: F
Lithuania / Lituanie	2005	158	94.6	94.2	424	103.7	102.7	195	62.9	98.0
	2010	122	100.9	99.7	343	102.2	100.3	201	68.7	103.2
	2014	108	100.2	100.3	277	105.7	101.3	148	56.0	81.7
	2015	108	100.1	100.4	263	105.8	101.3	141	55.2	79.4
	2016	110	101.4	101.3	251	105.6	100.7	134	55.2	77.5
Luxembourg / Luxembourg	2003	34	99.5	99.3	35	93.6	98.7	3	11.1	13.3
	2005	35	100.7	100.9	36	92.9	97.9	...	...	...
	2010	35	97.1	98.1	43	99.9	102.9	5	17.3	19.2
	2012	35	96.9	97.2	44	98.5	102.0	6	18.2	20.7
	2014	35	96.9	97.3	47	101.1	103.5	...	...	...
	2015	36	98.6	98.6	47	100.1	103.9	7	18.7	20.8
Madagascar / Madagascar	2005	3 598	142.0	135.8	* 621	* 21.9	* 21.0	45	2.8	2.5
	2009	4 324	151.0	147.6	* 1 022	* 31.6	29.7	68	3.7	3.3
	2010	4 242	145.0	142.4	...	...	...	74	3.8	3.5
	2014	4 611	145.4	145.0	1 494	38.7	38.0	113	5.0	4.6
	2015	4 764	147.3	147.3	* 1 536	* 38.7	* 38.3	117	5.0	4.6
	2016	4 734	143.7	144.0	1 561	38.4	38.2	...	...	...
Malawi / Malawi	2005	2 868	123.5	125.1	516	29.6	23.8	6	* 0.6	* 0.3
	2010	3 417	131.5	134.6	692	33.8	30.3	10	0.8	0.5
	2011	3 564	133.4	136.9	736	* 34.8	31.4	12	0.9	0.6
	2014	4 097	140.8	143.7	920	40.0	36.2	...	...	...
	2015	4 205	139.6	142.8	* 962	* 40.4	* 37.1	...	...	...
	2016	4 281	137.2	141.3	952	39.5	35.3	...	...	...
Malaysia / Malaisie	2005	3 202	100.0	100.0	...	...	...	...	...	...
	2010	3 234	99.8	100.7	...	...	...	...	...	...
	2014	3 178	104.5	104.7	2 846	81.4	88.2	1 128	31.1	43.1
	2015	3 108	103.4	103.2	2 801	81.5	88.6	1 302	36.4	48.8
	2016	3 101	103.1	103.8	2 760	82.6	87.9	1 337	40.3	48.3
Maldives / Maldives	2003	66	128.2	124.1	29	64.0	73.2	~0	0.1	0.3
	2004	63	127.7	122.7	* 29	* 64.0	* 74.6	...	...	...
	2005	58	121.1	117.0	...	...	...	...	...	...
	2008	47	111.7	107.2	...	...	...	...	...	...
	2009	45	109.3	105.4	...	...	...	5	9.5	13.4
	2010	42	...	...	...	...	...	...	...	...
	2014	40	...	...	...	...	...	...	...	...
	2015	42	102.3	99.8	...	...	...	6	9.9	20.5
	2016	44	101.4	101.7	...	...	...	...	...	...
Mali / Mali	2002	1 227	75.2	56.6	...	...	...	23	2.8	1.4
	2005	1 506	82.5	64.8	430	* 31.8	* 19.6	...	...	...
	2010	2 019	89.6	76.8	758	46.4	31.9	81	8.6	3.6
	2014	2 182	81.5	72.3	961	50.4	37.3	88	8.4	3.5
	2015	2 227	79.6	71.5	945	46.4	36.8	83	7.7	3.2
	2016	2 356	81.8	72.2	1 014	49.1	36.6	...	...	...
Malta / Malte	2005	30	98.0	95.7	40	104.5	100.3	9	27.5	37.3
	2010	25	98.7	99.3	37	109.7	98.0	11	31.6	42.7
	2014	24	101.1	102.8	30	92.2	96.5	13	38.9	50.9
	2015	25	102.2	104.7	29	91.7	98.1	13	40.3	55.2
	2016	25	102.6	106.6	29	93.8	97.8	13	41.5	56.8
Marshall Islands / Îles Marshall	2002	9	124.6	116.1	6	71.7	74.4	1	14.2	18.3
	2005	8	103.0	129.9	5	75.6	75.7	...	...	...
	2009	8	107.4	107.9	5	101.4	104.4	...	...	...
	2011	9	105.7	105.0	...	...	...	...	...	...
	2012	...	...	...	...	...	...	1	44.6	41.2
	2015	8	93.5	93.3	5	73.1	80.4	...	...	...
	2016	8	88.6	90.0	6	69.8	76.5	...	...	...

7 Enrollment in primary, secondary and tertiary education levels *(continued)*

Number of students enrolled (thousands) and gross enrollment ratio by sex

Enseignement primaire, secondaire et supérieur *(suite)*

Nombre d'élèves inscrits (milliers) et taux brut de scolarisation par sexe

Region, country or area Région, pays ou zone	Year & Année &	Primary education Enseignement primaire Total ('000)	Gross enrollment ratio Taux brut de scolarisation M/H	F	Secondary education Enseignement secondaire Total ('000)	Gross enrollment ratio Taux brut de scolarisation M /H	F	Tertiary education Enseignement supérieur Total ('000)	Gross enrollment ratio Taux brut de scolarisation M/H	F
Mauritania Mauritanie	2005	444	89.4	91.9	93	23.6	20.7	9	4.3	1.5
	2010	531	94.2	98.3	* 110	* 21.8	* 18.6	15	6.2	2.5
	2013	569	93.5	98.0	171	30.1	28.1	19	7.3	3.3
	2014	592	94.5	99.8	179	31.0	28.3	...	...	...
	2015	633	98.8	103.7	188	31.4	29.2	21	7.2	3.6
	2016	601	91.0	96.8	200	32.0	31.1	20	6.9	3.5
Mauritius Maurice	2005	124	103.3	103.1	* 129	* 89.7	* 87.6	* 21	* 21.0	* 21.7
	2010	117	102.5	103.1	* 127	* 87.2	* 91.3	33	30.5	36.9
	2014	105	101.4	103.5	133	99.0	100.8	40	35.1	43.2
	2015	102	102.0	103.8	129	95.3	99.5	38	32.4	42.5
	2016	97	101.6	103.4	123	90.8	96.0	...	...	...
	2017	...	...	...	...	...	...	38	34.0	43.8
Mexico Mexique	2005	14 700	105.6	103.7	10 564	76.5	83.3	2 385	23.0	23.8
	2010	14 906	105.6	104.6	11 682	80.9	87.9	2 847	25.8	26.8
	2014	14 627	104.8	105.5	12 993	89.1	94.7	3 419	30.1	30.3
	2015	14 398	103.8	104.5	13 473	91.9	98.7	3 515	30.8	30.8
	2016	14 297	103.7	104.2	13 725	93.3	101.4	4 244	36.5	37.3
Micronesia (Fed. States of) Micronésie (États féd. de)	*2000	...	...	...	...	...	...	2	...	...
	2005	19	112.7	109.8	14	80.1	86.7	...	...	...
	2007	19	111.0	112.4	...	...	...	...	...	...
	2014	14	98.0	97.2	...	...	...	...	...	...
	2015	14	95.4	95.7	...	...	...	...	...	...
Monaco Monaco	2004	2	...	...	3	...	...	...	...	...
	2010	2	...	...	3	...	...	...	...	...
	2014	2	...	...	3	...	...	...	...	...
	2015	2	...	...	3	...	...	...	...	...
	2016	2	...	...	3	...	...	1	...	...
Mongolia Mongolie	2005	251	98.0	98.0	339	85.6	95.0	124	33.8	55.9
	2010	274	127.1	124.2	276	88.4	94.8	166	42.5	65.3
	2014	239	102.9	100.8	...	...	...	175	52.9	75.9
	2015	251	102.2	100.3	282	90.4	92.4	180	57.7	79.7
	2016	274	105.4	103.0	306	100.0	100.6	163	54.1	75.3
Montenegro Monténégro	2005	38	112.8	112.6	68	93.3	95.8	11	17.2	27.2
	2010	35	111.2	109.6	70	99.7	101.0	24	46.5	58.3
	2012	38	96.9	97.8	63	92.8	93.6	...	...	...
	2015	38	96.1	94.8	61	92.7	92.7	...	...	...
	2016	38	97.4	94.6	59	90.6	90.5	25	50.8	63.4
Montserrat Montserrat	2005	1	* 114.6	* 118.7	~0	* 111.0	* 122.5	...	...	...
	2007	~0	* 101.2	* 112.9	~0	* 101.1	* 103.2	...	...	...
	2009	~0	...	...	~0	...	...	~0	...	...
	2010	...	...	...	...	...	...	~0	...	...
	2014	~0	...	...	~0	...	...	...	...	...
Morocco Maroc	2005	4 023	110.8	100.5	1 948	54.0	46.0	368	13.0	10.5
	2010	3 945	112.8	106.2	2 393	67.5	58.8	447	15.2	13.7
	2012	4 017	113.0	107.7	2 554	75.0	64.1	606	20.1	18.6
	2014	4 030	112.2	107.1	...	...	...	789	25.7	24.8
	2015	4 039	112.2	106.2	...	...	...	877	28.9	27.7
	2016	4 102	113.0	107.3	...	...	...	974	33.2	30.7
Mozambique Mozambique	2005	3 943	105.7	88.9	306	15.6	10.8	28	1.9	0.9
	2010	5 278	116.0	104.2	672	27.0	22.0	104	5.6	3.6
	2014	* 5 705	* 110.0	* 101.0	* 1 026	* 34.2	* 31.0	157	7.1	5.0
	2015	* 5 902	* 110.9	* 101.7	* 1 073	* 34.3	* 31.5	175	7.5	5.5
	2016	...	...	...	...	...	...	197	7.9	6.2
Myanmar Myanmar	2001	4 782	101.0	98.9	2 302	39.6	37.2	553	...	...
	2005	4 948	101.0	101.2	2 589	46.1	44.7	...	...	...
	2007	5 014	...	...	2 686	47.5	47.5	508	9.1	12.5
	2010	5 126	99.1	98.3	2 852	48.3	50.7	...	...	...
	2012	...	...	...	...	...	...	634	12.5	15.3
	2014	5 177	103.3	100.5	3 191	51.8	53.2	...	...	...
	2017	5 322	113.3	109.9	3 748	57.7	63.4	771	13.0	19.0

7 Enrollment in primary, secondary and tertiary education levels *(continued)*

Number of students enrolled (thousands) and gross enrollment ratio by sex

Enseignement primaire, secondaire et supérieur *(suite)*

Nombre d'élèves inscrits (milliers) et taux brut de scolarisation par sexe

Region, country or area Région, pays ou zone	Year & Année &	Primary education Enseignement primaire Total ('000)	Gross enrollment ratio Taux brut de scolarisation M/H	F	Secondary education Enseignement secondaire Total ('000)	Gross enrollment ratio Taux brut de scolarisation M /H	F	Tertiary education Enseignement supérieur Total ('000)	Gross enrollment ratio Taux brut de scolarisation M/H	F
Namibia Namibie	2005	404	109.5	108.2	148	59.9	66.9	14	7.4	6.3
	2007	410	110.6	108.2	158	60.1	69.0	...	...	...
	2008	407	110.0	107.2	...	...	...	20	8.2	10.4
	2010	407	109.2	105.8	...	...	...	...	...	...
	2013	425	113.5	109.1	...	...	...	...	...	...
Nauru Nauru	2005	2	*122.3	*128.5	1	*44.4	*50.3	...	...	...
	2008	1	*90.1	*96.0	1	*57.6	*68.9	...	...	...
	2014	2	*110.4	*101.1	1	*81.7	*83.9	...	...	...
	2016	2	*105.7	*108.5	1	*76.5	*79.0	...	...	...
Nepal Népal	2005	4 030	120.4	110.2	2 054	*53.5	*43.5	187	10.3	5.6
	2010	4 901	137.6	146.9	*2 694	*60.3	*57.4	377	17.9	11.0
	2013	4 577	133.0	143.4	*3 111	*64.5	*67.5	477	18.6	15.3
	2014	4 402	129.6	140.1	*3 164	*64.9	*68.9	459	...	...
	2015	4 335	129.8	140.4	*3 176	*64.8	*69.6	445	14.8	15.1
	2016	4 265	130.3	140.7	*3 277	*67.1	*72.1	361	11.4	12.2
	2017	4 135	130.1	138.4	*3 337	*67.6	*75.0	...	...	...
Netherlands Pays-Bas	2005	1 278	107.9	105.5	1 411	119.5	117.2	565	56.4	61.1
	2010	1 294	108.5	108.1	1 475	122.9	121.2	651	60.3	67.3
	2012	1 277	105.8	105.8	1 550	130.1	127.9	794	73.0	80.4
	2014	1 223	102.4	102.4	*1 574	...	...	...	...	...
	2015	1 208	102.7	102.7	1 613	132.6	134.6	843	75.2	86.1
	2016	1 192	103.3	103.3	1 611	131.6	133.8	837	75.6	85.3
Netherlands Antilles [former] Antilles néerlandaises [anc.]	2002	23	...	...	15	...	...	2	...	...
New Zealand Nouvelle-Zélande	2005	353	100.1	99.3	526	117.1	123.6	240	...	...
	2010	348	101.0	101.3	512	116.4	121.8	266	67.4	98.7
	2014	360	97.5	97.8	492	111.9	119.1	261	64.4	92.6
	2015	368	97.7	98.2	487	111.5	118.1	270	67.3	94.9
	2016	377	98.5	99.2	484	111.0	117.8	271	68.2	96.4
Nicaragua Nicaragua	2002	923	116.4	116.6	383	55.3	65.8	100	16.8	18.7
	2005	945	121.9	120.2	438	63.7	74.1	...	...	...
	2010	924	123.8	122.7	465	69.8	78.8	...	...	...
Niger Niger	2005	1 064	56.2	40.2	182	12.0	7.4	11	1.7	0.6
	2010	1 726	69.1	56.0	307	16.1	10.7	17	2.2	0.8
	2012	2 051	74.5	62.3	389	18.6	12.3	22	2.6	0.9
	2014	2 277	75.3	64.1	515	22.0	15.3	...	...	...
	2015	2 445	77.4	66.0	595	24.1	17.0	...	...	...
	2016	2 611	79.1	68.1	718	27.3	19.9	...	...	...
Nigeria Nigéria	2005	22 115	109.8	92.6	6 398	38.1	31.7	1 392	12.3	8.7
	2010	*21 558	*89.1	*80.9	9 057	47.1	41.2	1 395	11.0	8.1
	2011	23 669	93.7	87.4	9 591	49.1	41.9	1 513	12.0	8.3
	2013	26 168	95.2	92.8	12 533	58.8	53.5	...	...	...
Niue Nioué	2005	~0	*118.9	*105.9	~0	*71.3	*116.5	...	...	...
	2014	~0	*127.4	*125.3	~0	*100.0	*124.7	...	...	...
	2015	~0	*147.2	*120.2	~0	*104.1	*114.1	...	...	...
	2016	~0	*132.5	*125.3	...	...	...	...	...	...
Norway Norvège	2005	430	98.4	98.7	403	113.2	114.3	214	62.4	95.1
	2010	424	98.9	99.2	435	113.5	111.7	225	56.5	91.2
	2014	426	99.9	99.8	439	114.6	110.8	264	63.7	92.2
	2015	431	100.0	99.8	437	114.7	111.2	268	63.8	92.9
	2016	438	100.3	100.1	437	115.9	112.5	277	65.4	96.6
Oman Oman	2005	312	93.2	92.1	302	89.3	86.0	48	17.9	19.1
	2009	302	104.9	100.7	322	101.8	97.1	76	19.7	27.4
	2010	...	...	...	...	...	...	78	19.7	28.5
	2013	320	106.5	112.5	293	99.1	100.5	105	23.1	41.2
	2014	337	107.4	113.5	...	...	...	118	25.4	49.3
	2015	351	106.9	111.3	287	104.3	102.3	127	29.2	54.5
	2016	368	107.2	110.1	294	110.4	103.9	132	32.8	59.7

7

Enrollment in primary, secondary and tertiary education levels *(continued)*

Number of students enrolled (thousands) and gross enrollment ratio by sex

Enseignement primaire, secondaire et supérieur *(suite)*

Nombre d'élèves inscrits (milliers) et taux brut de scolarisation par sexe

Region, country or area / Région, pays ou zone	Year & / Année &	Primary education / Enseignement primaire: Total ('000)	Primary: Gross enrollment ratio Taux brut de scolarisation: M/H	Primary: F	Secondary education / Enseignement secondaire: Total ('000)	Secondary: Gross enrollment ratio Taux brut de scolarisation: M/H	Secondary: F	Tertiary education / Enseignement supérieur: Total ('000)	Tertiary: Gross enrollment ratio Taux brut de scolarisation: M/H	Tertiary: F
Pakistan	2005	17 258	98.9	76.1	6 852	...	...	783	5.3	4.6
Pakistan	2009	18 468	100.7	86.0	9 433	39.1	31.0	* 1 226	* 7.5	* 6.3
	2010	18 756	102.7	87.5	9 655	40.2	31.0	...	...	...
	2014	19 432	100.4	85.5	11 287	46.2	36.5	1 932	10.0	10.7
	2015	19 847	99.4	84.9	12 078	49.3	39.1	1 872	10.6	9.2
	2016	21 551	105.2	89.7	12 597	50.7	41.1	1 856	10.4	9.0
Palau	*2002	...	...	...	...	...	...	~0	25.6	52.3
Palaos	2004	2	* 104.6	* 101.1	2	* 97.7	* 99.9	...	...	...
	2005	2	...	...	2	...	...	...	...	...
	2007	2	...	...	2	...	...	...	...	...
	2013	2	* 115.9	* 113.5	2	* 115.4	* 118.3	1	* 50.6	* 78.1
	2014	2	* 117.0	* 112.5	2	* 112.3	* 118.3	...	...	...
Panama	2005	430	109.1	105.3	256	65.7	70.3	126	32.1	52.5
Panama	2010	440	107.0	103.0	284	69.2	73.5	139	35.1	53.7
	2014	427	100.3	97.7	312	72.4	77.8	145	34.5	54.8
	2015	418	97.3	94.7	317	73.9	77.8	157	36.8	58.0
Papua New Guinea	2005	532	61.9	52.4	...	...	...	...	...	...
Papouasie-Nvl-Guinée	2008	601	63.2	55.9	...	...	...	...	...	...
	2012	1 427	117.9	106.6	378	45.2	34.0	...	...	...
Paraguay	2005	934	113.5	110.3	529	66.0	67.8	156	24.3	27.5
Paraguay	2010	839	105.9	101.8	561	66.5	70.2	225	29.1	41.2
	2012	838	107.6	104.3	631	74.2	79.1	...	...	...
Peru	2005	4 077	117.0	118.0	2 470	86.3	84.6	908	32.8	33.6
Pérou	2006	4 026	116.3	117.3	2 540	88.4	87.7	951	33.3	35.4
	2010	3 763	109.8	111.0	2 675	94.5	94.9	...	...	...
	2014	3 496	101.4	101.4	2 671	95.7	95.5	...	...	...
	2015	3 513	101.7	101.7	2 682	95.7	95.8	...	...	...
	2016	3 577	103.0	103.3	2 753	98.2	97.9	...	...	...
Philippines	2005	13 084	106.5	105.4	6 352	78.3	87.6	2 403	24.7	30.4
Philippines	2009	13 687	108.6	107.5	6 767	80.9	87.5	2 625	25.6	31.6
	2010	...	...	...	...	...	...	2 774	26.4	33.0
	2013	14 460	115.4	113.7	7 220	84.0	91.5	3 317	29.7	37.5
	2014	...	...	...	...	...	...	3 563	31.3	40.1
	2015	14 453	114.6	111.3	7 319	84.8	92.1	...	...	...
	2017	...	...	...	...	...	...	3 589	30.5	40.3
Poland	2005	2 724	94.8	94.3	3 445	99.9	99.3	2 118	52.9	74.7
Pologne	2010	2 235	97.0	96.2	2 842	96.2	95.8	2 149	59.6	90.8
	2014	2 153	99.2	99.4	2 641	107.9	104.3	1 763	54.2	83.2
	2015	2 306	104.6	105.4	2 548	108.3	104.8	1 665	53.3	80.7
	2016	2 481	109.6	110.6	2 463	108.5	105.5	1 600	53.2	80.6
Portugal	2005	753	120.3	114.6	670	92.8	102.1	381	47.9	62.6
Portugal	2010	734	112.7	109.4	721	104.8	107.7	384	59.9	70.7
	2014	674	109.8	105.3	769	116.9	114.1	362	60.4	69.9
	2015	657	108.5	104.4	779	120.0	116.4	338	57.6	65.3
	2016	639	107.1	103.3	766	119.1	115.9	343	59.5	66.4
Puerto Rico	2010	300	92.5	95.8	291	80.8	85.4	249	69.9	103.2
Porto Rico	2014	259	87.4	88.7	266	78.7	83.8	241	70.1	98.8
	2015	251	86.0	87.5	279	83.9	89.3	241	70.7	99.4
Qatar	2005	70	107.1	103.7	56	102.3	96.0	* 10	* 8.8	* 31.1
Qatar	2010	89	104.7	105.9	69	99.2	103.3	14	4.8	25.6
	2014	117	98.0	100.8	88	72.6	100.5	25	6.2	39.2
	2015	130	102.4	103.6	96	82.0	103.6	28	6.3	43.9
	2016	139	104.0	103.4	98	85.8	100.7	28	6.4	47.1
Republic of Korea	2005	4 032	101.4	100.7	3 796	96.0	98.2	3 210	110.8	70.9
République de Corée	2010	3 306	101.7	101.7	3 959	96.6	96.1	3 270	116.7	86.8
	2014	2 736	96.8	97.3	3 579	100.5	100.5	3 318	105.2	80.2
	2015	2 722	97.4	97.8	3 397	100.1	100.3	3 268	104.6	80.6

7

Enrollment in primary, secondary and tertiary education levels ***(continued)***
Number of students enrolled (thousands) and gross enrollment ratio by sex

Enseignement primaire, secondaire et supérieur ***(suite)***
Nombre d'élèves inscrits (milliers) et taux brut de scolarisation par sexe

Region, country or area Région, pays ou zone	Year & Année &	Primary education Enseignement primaire Total ('000)	Gross enrollment ratio Taux brut de scolarisation M/H	F	Secondary education Enseignement secondaire Total ('000)	Gross enrollment ratio Taux brut de scolarisation M /H	F	Tertiary education Enseignement supérieur Total ('000)	Gross enrollment ratio Taux brut de scolarisation M/H	F
Republic of Moldova République de Moldova	2005	184	* 98.6	* 97.2	394	* 86.2	* 90.0	130	* 29.5	* 42.9
	2010	141	* 93.7	* 93.3	308	* 87.0	* 89.0	130	* 32.7	* 43.7
	2014	138	* 93.3	* 92.9	246	* 86.8	* 87.9	116	* 35.9	* 47.3
	2015	139	* 92.9	* 91.9	233	* 85.8	* 86.5	109	* 35.3	* 47.4
	2016	138	...	...	227	...	...	103	...	...
Romania Roumanie	2005	970	109.2	107.7	2 090	82.9	84.5	739	40.2	50.8
	2010	842	98.3	96.8	1 822	97.6	96.8	1 000	55.3	75.9
	2012	807	97.0	95.1	1 714	96.8	95.6	705	45.0	56.9
	2014	...	...	...	1 609	93.2	92.2	579	42.7	52.7
	2015	947	91.1	89.7	1 563	91.2	90.6	542	42.2	51.8
	2016	939	90.0	88.9	1 515	89.3	88.6	535	43.0	53.3
Russian Federation Fédération de Russie	2005	5 309	95.2	95.4	12 433	83.4	82.5	9 003	61.3	84.3
	2009	5 015	99.0	99.5	9 614	85.7	84.3	9 330	64.3	86.9
	2014	5 726	98.3	99.0	9 061	101.5	99.5	6 996	71.6	86.3
	2015	5 983	100.3	101.1	9 385	105.5	103.3	6 592	73.0	88.4
	2016	6 199	101.8	102.3	9 567	105.6	104.0	6 182	74.7	89.3
Rwanda Rwanda	2004	1 753	135.4	134.4	204	15.6	14.1	25	3.5	2.0
	2005	1 858	137.2	138.1	219	17.3	15.4	28	...	...
	2010	2 299	143.3	146.9	426	33.1	32.8	63	6.4	5.0
	2014	2 399	134.9	138.0	587	38.0	41.6	78	8.4	6.9
	2015	2 451	134.7	136.3	568	35.8	38.9	80	9.0	7.0
	2016	2 546	137.3	136.8	572	34.9	38.4	82	9.1	6.9
Saint Kitts and Nevis Saint-Kitts-et-Nevis	2005	6	...	...	* 4	...	...	...	...	...
	2008	6	...	...	4	...	...	1	...	...
	2010	6	...	...	* 4	...	...	...	...	...
	2014	6	...	...	4	...	...	3	...	...
	2015	5	...	...	4	...	...	4	...	...
	2016	5	...	...	4	...	...	...	...	...
Saint Lucia Sainte-Lucie	2005	24	105.1	100.5	14	71.5	84.0	2	7.0	19.0
	2007	22	103.3	98.1	15	83.5	92.8	1	5.2	12.0
	2010	19	...	...	16	95.2	94.1	2	7.0	18.0
	2014	17	...	...	14	88.0	87.4	3	10.9	22.8
	2015	17	...	...	13	88.6	87.8	3	11.5	21.9
	2016	16	...	...	13	87.4	88.3	3	13.0	25.4
Saint Vincent & Grenadines Saint-Vincent-Grenadines	2005	18	123.9	112.3	10	79.5	99.5	...	...	...
	2010	14	108.8	101.2	11	106.3	108.8	...	...	...
	2014	13	106.4	103.0	10	106.2	103.2	...	...	...
	2015	13	105.9	103.2	10	107.8	105.0	...	...	...
	2016	13	104.6	102.1	10	107.6	106.2	...	...	...
Samoa Samoa	2000	28	95.9	97.3	22	73.7	83.9	1	7.8	7.2
	2005	31	109.0	109.8	24	78.2	88.2	...	...	...
	2010	31	111.5	109.9	26	82.3	93.6	...	...	...
	2014	31	105.9	106.2	26	81.9	92.2	...	...	...
	2015	32	106.5	106.6	26	80.7	89.5	...	...	...
	2016	33	107.0	108.3	26	80.3	88.6	...	...	...
San Marino Saint-Marin	2000	1	...	...	1	...	...	1	...	...
	2004	1	...	...	...	...	...	...	...	...
	2010	2	* 88.8	* 100.6	2	* 96.3	* 98.2	1	* 53.0	* 77.3
	2012	2	* 93.9	* 92.6	2	* 93.5	* 95.9	1	* 50.5	* 69.9
Sao Tome and Principe Sao Tomé-et-Principe	2005	30	129.0	124.0	8	41.3	43.8	...	...	...
	2010	34	118.3	117.1	10	51.1	52.0	1	4.3	4.2
	2014	34	109.1	104.7	19	* 71.0	* 77.8	2	10.2	8.8
	2015	36	110.9	106.0	22	77.9	86.2	2	12.8	13.3
	2017	37	112.4	108.1	26	83.5	96.0	...	...	...
Saudi Arabia Arabie saoudite	2005	* 3 098	* 96.2	* 94.7	* 2 610	* 89.7	* 84.4	604	23.8	35.2
	2009	3 255	105.5	102.8	* 2 997	* 100.0	* 88.6	758	27.8	35.3
	2010	3 321	106.5	105.6	...	...	...	904	34.0	39.1
	2014	3 737	120.0	116.4	* 3 419	* 131.3	* 101.5	1 497	58.2	57.7
	2015	3 845	120.2	121.1	...	...	...	1 528	60.3	60.9
	2016	3 735	117.3	115.2	...	...	...	1 622	66.5	66.7

7

Enrollment in primary, secondary and tertiary education levels *(continued)*

Number of students enrolled (thousands) and gross enrollment ratio by sex

Enseignement primaire, secondaire et supérieur *(suite)*

Nombre d'élèves inscrits (milliers) et taux brut de scolarisation par sexe

Region, country or area Région, pays ou zone	Year & Année &	Primary education Enseignement primaire			Secondary education Enseignement secondaire			Tertiary education Enseignement supérieur		
			Gross enrollment ratio Taux brut de scolarisation			Gross enrollment ratio Taux brut de scolarisation			Gross enrollment ratio Taux brut de scolarisation	
		Total ('000)	M/H	F	Total ('000)	M /H	F	Total ('000)	M/H	F
Senegal Sénégal	2005	1 444	80.6	77.5	406	25.2	18.9	* 59	...	...
	2010	1 695	80.9	85.4	725	38.2	33.3	* 92	* 9.3	* 5.5
	2014	1 927	79.4	89.0	1 095	49.6	49.5	141	13.0	7.7
	2015	1 977	78.8	88.3	1 136	50.7	49.7	145	13.0	7.8
	2016	2 034	78.4	87.9	* 1 117	* 47.8	* 48.4	150	13.2	7.9
Serbia Serbie	2005	325	* 102.5	* 103.0	632	* 87.3	* 90.0	225	* 38.6	* 50.1
	2010	283	* 96.1	* 95.6	591	* 90.5	* 92.4	227	* 42.8	* 55.6
	2014	285	* 100.9	* 101.4	548	* 93.3	* 95.4	243	* 50.5	* 66.0
	2015	279	* 101.5	* 101.2	553	* 96.0	* 97.4	241	* 50.2	* 66.9
	2016	273	* 100.7	* 100.5	545	* 95.6	* 96.9	251	* 53.9	* 70.9
Seychelles Seychelles	2005	9	110.1	108.0	9	79.0	84.8	...	...	...
	2010	9	108.8	112.1	8	* 72.5	* 77.0	...	...	...
	2014	9	116.5	114.3	7	86.1	88.9	~0	4.0	10.5
	2015	9	116.5	115.7	7	90.2	94.3	1	10.4	22.5
	2016	9	113.2	112.4	7	89.9	96.1	1	14.7	27.2
Sierra Leone Sierra Leone	2001	554	87.1	60.9	156	* 28.3	* 20.0	9	2.8	1.1
	*2002	...	...	...	...	...	...	9	2.7	1.1
	2013	1 300	115.1	114.6	417	41.6	35.5	...	...	...
	2015	1 360	112.2	113.3	449	41.1	35.4	...	...	...
	2016	1 413	114.4	115.2	488	42.4	38.6	...	...	...
Singapore Singapour	2009	295	...	...	232	...	...	199	...	...
	2010	...	...	...	...	...	...	213	...	...
	2013	...	...	...	...	...	...	255	...	...
	2016	237	* 100.9	* 100.7	180	* 108.6	* 107.7	...	...	...
Sint Maarten (Dutch part) St-Martin (partie néerland.)	2014	4	...	...	3	...	...	~0	...	...
	2015	...	...	...	...	...	...	~0	...	...
Slovakia Slovaquie	2005	242	98.8	97.6	663	92.8	93.7	181	35.4	45.6
	2010	212	101.9	101.0	550	91.8	92.8	235	45.0	69.6
	2014	214	100.2	99.3	465	90.1	91.2	198	41.6	64.3
	2015	216	98.9	98.1	454	90.5	91.5	...	...	...
Slovenia Slovénie	2005	93	101.0	99.3	181	97.4	96.8	112	65.6	93.4
	2010	107	99.4	98.5	138	99.2	98.1	115	72.3	107.3
	2014	112	99.1	99.2	145	110.1	109.8	91	67.4	97.6
	2015	116	99.2	99.6	143	109.6	109.9	86	65.3	95.6
Solomon Islands Îles Salomon	2005	75	103.2	97.8	22	33.2	27.4	...	...	...
	2010	95	116.0	113.1	40	51.9	44.9	...	...	...
	2012	98	114.0	111.6	42	49.5	47.0	...	...	...
	2014	102	114.8	111.6	...	...	...	...	...	...
	2015	104	114.1	112.9	...	...	...	...	...	...
	2016	107	115.4	114.0	...	...	...	...	...	...
Somalia Somalie	2007	457	30.3	16.8	87	8.2	3.8	...	...	...
South Africa Afrique du Sud	2005	7 314	104.5	100.7	4 658	87.2	93.1	...	...	...
	2010	7 024	99.9	95.8	4 690	89.4	94.7	...	...	...
	2014	7 195	100.6	96.3	5 221	97.2	106.4	1 019	16.4	23.2
	2015	7 556	106.6	99.0	5 279	103.5	102.0	1 051	...	...
South Sudan Soudan du sud	2011	1 451	101.8	67.4	134	12.0	6.1	...	...	...
	2015	1 274	77.8	55.1	164	12.8	6.9	...	...	...
Spain Espagne	2005	2 485	103.6	102.2	3 108	113.6	121.1	1 809	60.4	74.2
	2010	2 721	105.7	105.2	3 185	122.8	125.5	1 879	70.3	87.1
	2014	2 961	103.6	104.8	3 288	129.6	130.1	1 982	81.3	96.8
	2015	3 010	103.8	105.0	3 313	129.6	129.3	1 964	82.2	97.0
	2016	3 028	103.3	104.5	3 329	127.5	128.4	1 969	83.5	99.2
Sri Lanka Sri Lanka	2005	1 611	99.9	99.3	...	...	...	...	...	...
	2010	1 721	101.0	98.4	2 525	96.3	97.5	262	11.7	20.9
	2013	1 767	101.8	99.4	2 606	97.5	101.9	298	14.8	22.9
	2014	1 778	102.4	100.1	...	...	...	302	16.8	21.7
	2015	1 778	102.7	100.6	...	...	...	308	15.6	24.0
	2016	1 771	103.0	100.8	2 619	96.0	99.3	290	14.8	22.9

Enrollment in primary, secondary and tertiary education levels *(continued)*
Number of students enrolled (thousands) and gross enrollment ratio by sex

Enseignement primaire, secondaire et supérieur *(suite)*
Nombre d'élèves inscrits (milliers) et taux brut de scolarisation par sexe

Region, country or area Région, pays ou zone	Year & Année &	Primary education Enseignement primaire Total ('000)	Gross enrollment ratio Taux brut de scolarisation M/H	F	Secondary education Enseignement secondaire Total ('000)	Gross enrollment ratio Taux brut de scolarisation M /H	F	Tertiary education Enseignement supérieur Total ('000)	Gross enrollment ratio Taux brut de scolarisation M/H	F
State of Palestine État de Palestine	2005	387	88.5	87.9	657	87.7	91.7	138	40.6	41.2
	2010	403	91.9	90.1	711	82.4	89.0	197	41.1	54.9
	2014	442	95.5	94.9	709	78.6	86.4	214	34.6	53.8
	2015	450	94.4	94.4	721	79.4	87.2	221	34.5	54.4
	2016	459	93.9	94.0	733	79.9	88.0	218	33.1	52.8
Sudan Soudan	2005	3 177	67.5	59.2	1 344	40.2	37.3	364	11.5	13.0
	2010	4 024	75.8	68.1	1 687	45.6	39.6	523	14.7	17.3
	2013	4 292	76.1	68.5	1 871	45.0	42.5	640	16.8	18.7
	2014	...	...	...	...	...	...	632	16.5	17.5
	2015	4 518	76.7	70.3	2 060	46.1	45.5	...	...	...
Sudan [former] Soudan [anc.]	2000	2 567	...	...	980	...	...	* 204	...	...
	2005	3 278	...	...	* 1 370	...	...	...	...	...
	2009	4 744	...	...	1 837	...	...	...	...	...
Suriname Suriname	2002	64	105.7	104.3	42	63.4	88.7	5	9.6	15.8
	2005	66	106.7	104.6	46	59.6	79.3	...	...	...
	2010	71	116.7	115.9	50	63.2	81.1	...	...	...
	2014	70	117.5	119.2	52	62.8	86.1	...	...	...
	2015	72	120.7	121.6	55	68.1	89.7	...	...	...
	2016	72	120.9	121.0	...	...	...	...	...	...
Sweden Suède	2005	658	95.9	95.7	735	104.3	103.8	427	64.8	99.9
	2010	576	101.7	101.2	731	98.6	97.6	455	58.5	89.6
	2014	757	117.7	124.2	827	124.8	141.6	429	49.3	75.7
	2015	792	120.5	125.5	844	131.5	150.0	429	49.6	75.6
Switzerland Suisse	2005	524	102.1	101.8	575	97.9	92.1	200	48.9	42.4
	2010	493	102.8	102.3	605	97.2	94.3	249	53.0	52.5
	2014	484	103.2	103.3	616	101.2	98.2	290	56.5	57.5
	2015	490	104.1	103.8	614	102.9	99.4	294	56.7	58.3
	2016	498	104.8	104.0	610	104.2	100.3	295	57.3	58.4
Syrian Arab Republic République arabe syrienne	2005	2 252	121.9	118.4	2 389	71.2	68.1	361	19.1	17.1
	2010	2 429	120.8	116.5	2 732	72.3	72.4	574	27.8	24.0
	2013	1 547	77.3	74.7	1 857	49.3	49.3	660	34.0	34.5
	2014	...	...	...	...	...	...	792	42.4	44.6
	2015	...	...	...	...	...	...	773	41.0	46.7
	2016	...	...	...	...	...	...	697	36.0	42.7
Tajikistan Tadjikistan	2005	693	100.2	96.9	984	88.5	73.6	149	28.0	13.4
	2010	682	100.4	98.0	1 032	89.7	78.3	196	29.9	15.8
	2013	665	99.5	97.5	1 063	92.0	82.7	195	29.1	16.3
	2014	662	96.5	95.3	...	...	...	209	30.4	18.4
	2015	683	95.8	94.5	...	...	...	225	31.5	21.0
	2017	771	99.5	98.1	...	...	...	265	35.2	26.4
Thailand Thaïlande	2005	5 975	103.3	100.4	4 533	* 71.9	* 75.4	2 359	42.0	47.2
	2010	5 147	97.4	96.2	4 807	79.6	85.3	2 427	44.3	56.5
	2014	5 182	101.3	102.8	6 792	117.2	123.5	2 433	42.7	57.8
	2015	5 081	103.5	97.5	6 757	123.0	118.1	2 235	37.8	54.2
TFYR of Macedonia ex-R.Y. de Macédoine	2005	110	94.5	92.5	214	* 82.8	80.2	49	24.6	34.1
	2010	111	88.0	86.7	197	83.4	81.0	62	34.7	40.4
	2014	108	92.0	90.8	171	81.8	79.3	61	34.0	42.8
	2015	109	94.1	93.7	169	82.6	81.2	64	36.7	45.9
Timor-Leste Timor-Leste	2002	184	...	...	53	...	...	* 6	* 8.1	* 9.3
	2005	178	93.2	85.2	75	53.2	51.8	...	...	...
	2010	230	121.4	116.3	102	60.6	60.8	19	21.9	15.8
	2014	246	122.5	120.7	119	60.3	64.8	...	...	...
	2015	244	117.3	115.5	129	65.7	70.3	...	...	...
	2016	236	110.6	108.3	140	71.7	77.1	...	...	...

7

Enrollment in primary, secondary and tertiary education levels *(continued)*

Number of students enrolled (thousands) and gross enrollment ratio by sex

Enseignement primaire, secondaire et supérieur *(suite)*

Nombre d'élèves inscrits (milliers) et taux brut de scolarisation par sexe

Region, country or area Région, pays ou zone	Year & Année &	Primary education Enseignement primaire Total ('000)	Gross enrollment ratio Taux brut de scolarisation M/H	F	Secondary education Enseignement secondaire Total ('000)	Gross enrollment ratio Taux brut de scolarisation M/H	F	Tertiary education Enseignement supérieur Total ('000)	Gross enrollment ratio Taux brut de scolarisation M/H	F
Togo Togo	2005	997	122.5	104.1	404	58.8	31.3	...	...	...
	2007	1 022	118.7	102.8	409	* 57.9	* 30.7	33	...	...
	2010	1 287	133.7	120.6	...	...	...	56	...	...
	2011	1 300	130.2	118.5	546	...	...	63	...	...
	2014	1 413	126.6	119.4	...	...	...	67	14.4	6.0
	2015	1 414	123.0	116.5	...	...	...	71	15.0	6.4
	2016	1 498	127.0	120.8	...	...	...	83	17.1	7.4
Tokelau Tokélaou	2003	~0	* 101.8	* 132.6	~0	* 83.3	* 75.8	...	...	...
	2016	~0	* 107.7	* 95.2	~0	* 69.6	* 70.7	...	...	...
Tonga Tonga	2002	17	111.7	106.7	15	105.5	116.3	1	* 4.2	* 7.1
	2003	18	118.2	111.9	16	...	...	1	4.8	8.0
	2004	17	114.2	108.5	14	...	...	...	...	...
	2005	17	113.4	110.1	...	...	...	...	...	...
	2010	17	109.4	107.3	15	100.4	107.2	...	...	...
	2014	17	108.6	107.4	15	86.4	94.2	...	...	...
Trinidad and Tobago Trinité-et-Tobago	2004	* 137	* 103.4	* 100.0	* 105	* 82.6	* 88.5	17	10.6	13.4
	*2005	130	100.7	97.8	...	...	...	...	...	...
	2010	131	108.0	104.3	...	...	...	...	...	...
Tunisia Tunisie	2005	1 184	114.0	109.3	1 239	81.4	88.3	327	28.6	35.1
	2010	1 030	109.0	105.3	1 164	87.5	93.4	370	27.8	42.6
	2011	1 028	109.4	106.0	1 152	90.0	94.2	362	26.7	43.1
	2014	1 089	114.8	111.5	1 020	...	...	332	26.4	43.1
	2015	1 115	116.0	112.7	1 008	...	...	323	26.4	43.3
	2016	1 139	116.2	113.2	1 047	88.1	97.9	294	24.1	41.2
Turkey Turquie	2005	6 678	105.8	100.5	6 345	91.6	76.1	2 106	38.2	27.9
	2010	6 635	102.0	100.6	7 531	87.9	80.5	3 529	62.1	50.5
	2014	5 575	106.8	106.3	10 899	104.4	101.6	5 473	93.1	80.8
	2015	5 434	103.6	102.9	10 969	104.4	101.7	6 063	101.8	88.9
Turkmenistan Turkménistan	2014	359	89.2	87.5	651	87.6	84.0	44	9.7	6.2
Turks and Caicos Islands Îles Turques-et-Caïques	2005	2	...	...	2	...	...	...	...	...
	2009	3	...	...	2	...	...	...	...	...
	2010	...	...	...	...	...	...	~0	...	...
	2014	3	...	...	2	...	...	...	...	...
	2015	3	...	...	2	...	...	~0	...	...
Tuvalu Tuvalu	2001	1	* 94.9	* 106.9	1	* 67.4	* 74.1	...	...	...
	2005	1	* 101.4	* 97.6	...	...	...	...	...	...
	2006	1	* 102.4	* 97.6	...	...	...	...	...	...
	2014	1	* 114.2	* 112.9	1	* 78.4	* 96.5	...	...	...
	2015	1	* 119.6	* 118.8	1	* 85.0	* 108.2	...	...	...
Uganda Ouganda	2004	7 377	127.3	125.4	733	21.1	17.0	88	4.4	2.7
	2005	7 224	120.2	119.2	...	...	...	...	...	...
	2007	7 538	116.5	117.0	1 032	26.3	21.6	...	...	...
	2010	8 375	115.9	117.7	...	...	...	121	4.4	3.5
	2013	8 459	105.6	107.6	...	...	...	...	...	...
	2014	...	...	...	...	...	...	165	5.2	4.0
	2015	8 264	97.2	99.0	...	...	...	...	...	...
	2016	8 656	98.3	101.3	...	...	...	...	...	...
Ukraine Ukraine	2005	1 946	106.6	106.2	4 043	* 99.2	* 91.8	2 605	63.1	78.0
	2010	1 540	98.5	99.1	3 133	* 96.7	* 94.3	2 635	71.2	89.5
	2014	1 685	98.9	100.9	2 714	97.8	95.7	2 146	77.6	89.5
	2015	1 537	...	...	2 370	...	...	1 776	...	...
	2016	1 599	...	...	2 326	...	...	1 690	...	...
United Arab Emirates Émirats arabes unis	2005	263	...	...	...	...	...	...	...	...
	2010	327	96.9	98.9	...	...	...	102	10.7	29.9
	2014	410	103.6	106.3	...	...	...	143	19.7	44.3
	2015	461	112.8	114.3	...	...	...	157	23.7	50.6
	2016	468	112.8	108.9	442	98.6	93.0	160	26.7	53.2

7

Enrollment in primary, secondary and tertiary education levels *(continued)*
Number of students enrolled (thousands) and gross enrollment ratio by sex

Enseignement primaire, secondaire et supérieur *(suite)*
Nombre d'élèves inscrits (milliers) et taux brut de scolarisation par sexe

Region, country or area Région, pays ou zone	Year & Année &	Primary education Enseignement primaire Total ('000)	Gross enrollment ratio Taux brut de scolarisation M/H	F	Secondary education Enseignement secondaire Total ('000)	Gross enrollment ratio Taux brut de scolarisation M /H	F	Tertiary education Enseignement supérieur Total ('000)	Gross enrollment ratio Taux brut de scolarisation M/H	F
United Kingdom Royaume-Uni	2005	4 635	106.3	106.2	5 761	103.9	107.0	2 288	49.5	68.9
	2010	4 422	105.0	104.5	5 538	102.9	103.2	2 479	50.7	67.9
	2014	4 737	107.7	107.5	6 557	124.9	129.9	2 353	49.4	65.4
	2015	4 617	102.0	101.8	6 375	123.6	127.5	2 330	49.2	65.8
United Rep. of Tanzania Rép.-Unie de Tanzanie	2005	7 541	104.9	99.7	...	...	...	* 52	* 2.0	* 0.9
	2010	8 419	97.1	97.7	1 826	34.3	27.1	85	2.4	1.9
	2013	8 232	84.9	86.2	2 052	33.1	30.3	158	4.8	2.5
	2014	8 223	81.7	83.6	...	...	...	...	...	...
	2015	8 298	79.5	82.0	...	...	...	182	5.2	2.7
	2016	...	...	...	...	...	...	179	...	...
United States of America États-Unis d'Amérique	2005	24 455	99.2	98.1	24 432	93.6	95.5	17 272	...	...
	2010	24 393	100.1	99.2	24 193	92.5	93.6	20 428	...	...
	2014	24 538	98.6	98.5	24 230	95.4	96.4	19 700	...	...
	2015	24 786	99.2	99.4	24 417	96.7	97.7	19 532	...	...
United States Virgin Islands Îles Vierges américaines	2007	...	...	...	...	...	...	2	...	...
Uruguay Uruguay	2005	366	115.3	112.4	323	94.2	108.5	111	33.2	57.9
	2006	365	116.9	113.6	323	93.5	108.5	113	34.5	58.0
	2010	342	113.9	110.2	287	84.6	96.2	132	...	...
	2014	322	109.8	107.3	339	...	...	160	...	...
	2015	317	108.6	106.2	340	...	...	146	...	...
Uzbekistan Ouzbékistan	2005	2 383	96.8	96.7	4 516	89.9	87.3	266	11.9	8.2
	2010	1 971	94.5	92.8	4 449	89.6	89.6	289	11.1	7.6
	2014	2 034	98.9	97.3	4 083	92.2	91.2	260	9.9	6.2
	2015	2 135	100.1	98.6	3 964	92.1	91.0	262	10.0	6.3
	2017	2 391	103.9	102.3	3 893	93.6	92.4	281	11.3	6.9
Vanuatu Vanuatu	2004	39	122.4	120.0	14	45.8	39.5	* 1	* 5.9	* 3.5
	2005	39	119.2	116.1	...	...	...	...	...	...
	2010	42	123.0	121.9	20	59.6	59.5	...	...	...
	2013	44	125.2	122.2	...	...	...	...	...	...
	2015	46	120.7	118.7	21	53.4	56.4	...	...	...
	2017	...	...	...	0	...	...	...	...	...
Venezuela (Boliv. Rep. of) Venezuela (Rép. boliv. du)	2003	3 450	104.0	101.9	1 866	63.4	72.9	* 983	* 38.4	* 41.2
	2004	3 453	104.0	101.8	1 954	66.1	75.3	* 1 050	...	...
	2005	3 449	103.7	101.6	2 028	68.6	77.5	...	...	...
	2008	3 439	103.0	100.3	2 224	76.1	83.8	2 109	* 57.8	* 97.7
	2009	3 462	103.3	100.5	2 252	77.3	84.5	2 123	...	...
	2010	3 458	102.9	99.9	2 255	77.2	84.7	...	...	...
	2014	3 493	101.6	99.3	2 567	88.1	94.8	...	...	...
	2015	3 476	100.9	98.2	2 523	86.2	92.8	...	...	...
	2016	3 383	97.8	95.2	2 428	82.5	88.9	...	...	...
Viet Nam Viet Nam	2005	7 773	99.5	94.5	...	...	...	1 355	18.7	13.3
	2010	6 923	107.6	102.2	...	...	...	2 020	22.6	22.7
	2014	7 435	109.9	108.5	...	...	...	2 692	29.7	31.2
	2015	7 544	109.1	108.3	...	...	...	2 467	28.8	28.8
	2016	7 790	109.8	110.1	...	...	...	2 307	25.3	31.3
Yemen Yémen	2005	3 220	100.6	74.4	1 455	60.7	29.7	200	13.9	5.1
	2010	3 427	99.5	81.2	1 561	53.4	33.2	272	14.6	6.4
	2011	3 641	104.0	84.8	1 643	55.5	35.2	267	13.7	6.1
	2013	3 875	105.4	88.5	1 768	57.4	39.5	...	...	...
	2016	3 900	98.6	86.1	1 916	58.9	42.8	...	...	...
Zambia Zambie	2005	2 573	112.5	107.4	...	...	...	...	...	...
	2010	2 899	104.5	105.9	...	...	...	...	...	...
	2012	3 135	106.8	107.7	...	...	...	57	4.6	3.5
	2013	3 075	102.0	102.7	...	...	...	...	...	...
Zimbabwe Zimbabwe	2003	2 362	98.5	97.2	758	40.8	36.8	...	...	...
	2010	...	...	...	...	...	...	95	6.8	5.4
	2013	2 663	99.5	97.9	957	47.6	46.7	94	6.5	5.5
	2015	...	...	...	...	...	...	136	8.9	8.0

Enrollment in primary, secondary and tertiary education levels *(continued)*

Number of students enrolled (thousands) and gross enrollment ratio by sex

Enseignement primaire, secondaire et supérieur *(suite)*

Nombre d'élèves inscrits (milliers) et taux brut de scolarisation par sexe

Source:

United Nations Educational, Scientific and Cultural Organization (UNESCO), Montreal, the UNESCO Institute for Statistics (UIS) statistics database, last accessed May 2018.

& Data relate to the calendar year in which the academic year ends.

1 For statistical purposes, the data for China do not include those for the Hong Kong Special Administrative Region (Hong Kong SAR), Macao Special Administrative Region (Macao SAR) and Taiwan Province of China.

Source:

Organisation des Nations Unies pour l'éducation, la science et la culture (UNESCO), Montréal, base de données statistiques de l'Institut de statistique (ISU) de l'UNESCO, dernier accès mai 2018.

& Les données se réfèrent à l'année civile durant laquelle l'année scolaire se termine.

1 Pour la présentation des statistiques, les données pour la Chine ne comprennent pas la région administrative spéciale de Hong Kong (Hong Kong RAS), la région administrative spéciale de Macao (Macao RAS) et la province chinoise de Taïwan.

8 Teaching staff at the primary, secondary and tertiary levels

Number of teachers and Pupil teacher ratio

Personnel enseignant au niveau primaire, secondaire et supérieur

Nombre d'enseignants et ratio élèves/enseignant par niveau d'enseignement

Region, country or area / Région, pays ou zone	Year & / Année &	Primary education / Enseignant primaire: Total / Totale ('000)	Primary education / Enseignant primaire: Pupil-teacher ratio / Ratio élèves/ enseignant	Secondary education / Enseignant secondaire: Total / Totale ('000)	Secondary education / Enseignant secondaire: Pupil-teacher ratio / Ratio élèves/ enseignant	Tertiary education / Enseignant supérieur: Total / Totale ('000)	Tertiary education / Enseignant supérieur: Pupil-teacher ratio / Ratio élèves/ enseignant
Total, all countries or areas	**2005**	*** 26 888**	*** 25.3**	*** 28 398**	*** 17.9**	**9 217**	**...**
Total, tous pays ou zones	**2010**	**28 658**	**24.3**	**32 248**	**16.9**	**11 143**	**...**
	2015	**31 145**	**23.2**	**33 353**	**17.4**	**12 880**	**...**
	2016	**31 316**	**23.6**	**34 117**	**17.2**	*** 13 027**	**...**
Northern Africa	2005	944	24.4	* 994	* 17.0	* 173	...
Afrique septentrionale	2010	969	24.3	* 1 165	* 14.9	* 209	...
	*2015	1 171	22.0	1 198	15.6	259	...
	2016	1 175	22.5	* 1 209	* 15.8	* 260	...
Sub-Saharan Africa	2005	2 577	44.0	1 165	27.5	* 179	...
Afrique subsaharienne	2010	3 168	42.9	* 1 858	* 24.2	* 262	...
	*2015	4 085	38.4	2 594	21.6	340	...
	*2016	4 187	38.4	2 601	22.2	...	...
Northern America	2005	1 865	14.4	1 774	15.2	1 367	...
Amérique septentrionale	2010	1 920	13.8	1 898	14.1	1 638	...
	2015	1 847	14.7	1 803	15.0	1 767	...
	*2016	1 853	14.7	1 795	15.0	1 734	...
Latin America & the Caribbean	2005	2 935	23.5	3 469	17.0	* 1 227	...
Amérique latine et Caraïbes	2010	2 908	23.1	3 542	17.3	* 1 658	...
	2015	2 991	21.9	3 912	16.4	1 779	...
	*2016	2 987	21.9	3 900	16.4	1 865	...
Eastern Asia	2005	* 6 683	* 18.9	* 6 495	* 17.8	2 179	...
Asie orientale	2010	6 656	17.1	7 431	15.3	2 405	...
	2012	6 574	16.9	7 592	14.4	* 2 534	...
	2015	6 565	16.3	7 281	13.7	...	...
	2016	6 609	16.6	7 258	13.4	...	...
South-eastern Asia	2005	2 941	23.2	2 229	18.3	565	...
Asie du Sud-Est	2010	3 251	21.1	* 2 696	* 16.9	* 679	...
	*2015	3 701	18.6	2 752	18.7	691	...
	2016	3 883	17.7	* 2 834	* 18.1	* 766	...
Southern Asia	*2005	4 583	39.6	4 151	29.1	760	...
Asie méridionale	2010	* 5 275	* 36.4	5 699	25.2	* 1 292	...
	2015	6 055	32.6	5 747	29.7	1 866	...
	2016	5 855	35.3	6 342	27.6	1 905	...
Western Asia	2005	* 1 288	* 18.8	* 1 271	* 15.4	307	...
Asie occidentale	2010	* 1 440	* 17.7	* 1 528	* 14.6	372	...
	2015	* 1 600	* 16.7	* 1 731	* 14.6	480	...
	*2016	1 570	17.0	1 815	14.0	489	...
Europe	2005	2 673	14.4	5 836	11.2	2 272	...
Europe	2010	2 673	13.7	* 5 469	* 10.7	* 2 412	...
	2015	2 685	14.3	5 331	10.8	2 376	...
	*2016	2 752	14.2	5 325	10.7	2 330	...
Oceania	*2005	157	20.0	...	...	85	...
Océanie	*2010	172	20.9	...	...	103	...
	2013	* 190	* 22.5	...	...	68	...
	*2014	...	...	...	...	110	...
Afghanistan	2004	...	...	...	...	2	15.5
Afghanistan	2007	110	42.8	33	31.6	...	...
	2009	115	42.8	...	...	3	28.5
	2010	119	44.4	...	...	...	...
	2014	...	...	...	...	11	23.9
	2015	143	44.3	72	37.7	...	...
	2017	144	44.3	75	38.9	...	...
Albania	2001	13	21.8	22	17.0	3	13.5
Albanie	2003	12	21.5	22	17.7	...	...
	2010	11	19.7	24	14.8	...	...
	2014	10	18.9	23	14.3	7	23.6
	2015	10	18.6	23	13.5	...	...
	2016	10	18.2	24	12.2	9	16.4

8

Teaching staff at the primary, secondary and tertiary levels *(continued)*
Number of teachers and Pupil teacher ratio

Personnel enseignant au niveau primaire, secondaire et supérieur *(suite)*
Nombre d'enseignants et ratio élèves/enseignant par niveau d'enseignement

Region, country or area Région, pays ou zone	Year & Année &	Primary education / Enseignant primaire Total Totale ('000)	Primary education / Enseignant primaire Pupil-teacher ratio Ratio élèves/ enseignant	Secondary education / Enseignant secondaire Total Totale ('000)	Secondary education / Enseignant secondaire Pupil-teacher ratio Ratio élèves/ enseignant	Tertiary education / Enseignant supérieur Total Totale ('000)	Tertiary education / Enseignant supérieur Pupil-teacher ratio Ratio élèves/ enseignant
Algeria Algérie	2005	171	25.4	...	...	28	27.9
	2010	142	23.3	...	...	40	28.8
	2015	165	23.8	...	...	54	24.0
	2016	170	24.2	...	...	56	25.7
American Samoa Samoa américaines	2007	...	...	...	...	~0	...
Andorra Andorre	2004	~0	12.7	~0	7.1	~0	3.9
	2005	~0	11.5	~0	7.8	...	...
	2008	~0	10.0	...	...	~0	5.3
	2009	~0	10.3	...	...	~0	...
	2010	~0	9.6	...	...	...	...
	2015	~0	9.9	1	8.1	~0	4.6
	2016	~0	10.1	1	7.9	~0	3.9
Angola Angola	*2001	...	...	22	19.0	...	...
	*2002	...	...	...	...	1	9.8
	2006	...	...	...	...	1	37.9
	2010	94	45.6	...	...	...	...
	2011	118	42.5	32	27.4	8	18.2
	2015	...	...	...	...	9	25.5
Anguilla Anguilla	2005	~0	15.4	* ~0	* 12.5	~0	1.4
	2007	~0	16.1	~0	10.4	~0	3.9
	2008	~0	14.1	...	...	~0	3.9
	2010	~0	14.5	...	...	...	...
	2011	~0	14.8	~0	8.5	...	...
Antigua and Barbuda Antigua-et-Barbuda	2000	1	18.7	~0	13.4	...	...
	2010	1	15.1	1	12.2	~0	6.8
	2012	1	13.8	1	11.6	~0	8.2
	2015	1	14.3	1	11.5	...	...
Argentina Argentine	2004	274	18.0	254	15.4	142	14.9
	2005	279	17.4	257	15.1	...	...
	2008	289	17.2	324	12.2	...	...
	2009	...	...	...	...	142	16.8
Armenia Arménie	2005	6	21.2	...	...	17	6.8
	2007	7	19.3	...	...	16	8.3
	2010	...	...	...	...	16	9.2
	2015	...	...	...	...	16	6.8
	2016	...	...	...	...	15	7.2
Aruba Aruba	2005	1	18.1	1	14.2	~0	9.2
	2010	1	16.8	1	13.8	~0	10.4
	2012	1	14.8	1	15.1	~0	9.9
	2015	...	...	...	...	~0	13.6
Australia Australie	2013	...	...	...	...	51	...
Austria Autriche	2005	29	12.4	71	11.0	...	...
	2010	30	11.0	75	10.0	47	8.3
	2015	31	10.6	72	9.6	61	7.0
	2016	32	10.3	73	9.4	58	7.4
Azerbaijan Azerbaïdjan	2005	42	13.4	...	...	...	...
	2010	44	11.0	...	...	26	7.0
	2015	41	13.5	...	...	21	9.7
	2016	38	15.5	130	...	21	10.1
Bahamas Bahamas	*2004	2	16.8	2	14.2	...	...
	2005	...	...	2	13.6	...	...
	2010	2	14.1	3	12.1	...	...
	2016	2	19.0	2	11.8	...	...
Bahrain Bahreïn	2003	...	...	...	...	1	22.3
	*2004	...	...	...	...	1	...
	2015	9	11.7	9	9.9	3	15.4
	2016	9	12.1	10	9.8	2	19.0

8 Teaching staff at the primary, secondary and tertiary levels *(continued)*

Number of teachers and Pupil teacher ratio

Personnel enseignant au niveau primaire, secondaire et supérieur *(suite)*

Nombre d'enseignants et ratio élèves/enseignant par niveau d'enseignement

Region, country or area Région, pays ou zone	Year & Année &	Primary education / Enseignant primaire: Total Totale ('000)	Primary education / Enseignant primaire: Pupil-teacher ratio Ratio élèves/enseignant	Secondary education / Enseignant secondaire: Total Totale ('000)	Secondary education / Enseignant secondaire: Pupil-teacher ratio Ratio élèves/enseignant	Tertiary education / Enseignant supérieur: Total Totale ('000)	Tertiary education / Enseignant supérieur: Pupil-teacher ratio Ratio élèves/enseignant
Bangladesh Bangladesh	2005	345	47.0	423	23.9	52	17.4
	2009	361	* 45.8	387	28.2	59	26.9
	2010	395	* 43.0	400	28.3	...	...
	2013	...	...	378	35.2	...	...
	2014	...	...	...	...	90	22.9
	2015	528	36.1	...	...	...	...
	2016	548	33.9	436	36.2	93	29.0
Barbados Barbade	*2001	1	17.0	1	17.2	1	13.5
	2005	1	15.1	* 1	* 15.9	...	...
	2006	...	...	1	14.6	...	...
	2007	2	14.5	...	...	1	14.5
	*2010	2	13.0	...	...	...	...
	2015	2	13.4	1	17.5	...	...
	2016	2	13.3	1	18.6	...	...
Belarus Bélarus	2005	24	16.0	...	...	42	12.7
	2010	24	15.0	...	...	41	14.0
	2015	22	17.6	77	8.4	33	14.6
	2016	22	18.3	78	8.3	29	15.1
Belgium Belgique	2002	64	11.9	109	10.6	23	15.7
	2005	64	11.5	...	...	26	15.1
	2010	66	11.0	...	...	29	15.4
	2015	70	11.2	129	9.4	29	17.6
Belize Belize	2005	2	23.6	* 2	* 18.7	...	...
	2010	2	22.2	2	16.8	...	...
	2015	3	20.4	2	16.3	1	14.2
	2016	3	20.5	2	18.4	1	14.7
Benin Bénin	2001	20	53.5	* 12	* 21.6	* 1	* 29.4
	2004	26	51.6	* 14	* 23.9	...	...
	2005	28	46.8	...	...	...	...
	2010	39	46.4	...	...	6	17.8
	2011	42	44.2	...	...	6	17.3
	2015	50	45.0	93	10.3	...	...
Bermuda Bermudes	2005	1	8.3	1	7.0	~0	...
	2010	1	7.4	1	5.4	~0	15.3
	2015	~0	10.4	1	6.3	~0	18.7
	2016	~0	...	1	...	...	...
	2017	...	...	...	...	~0	11.8
Bhutan Bhoutan	2005	3	31.1	1	28.1	...	...
	2010	4	25.9	3	21.4	1	6.7
	2012	5	24.0	3	19.9	1	7.7
	2015	2	40.0	6	12.1	...	...
	2016	3	38.0	7	11.4	...	...
Bolivia (Plurin. State of) Bolivie (État plurin. de)	2015	74	18.1	55	20.8	...	...
	2016	74	18.4	58	20.0	...	...
Bosnia and Herzegovina Bosnie-Herzégovine	2010	...	...	...	...	8	12.4
	2015	9	17.2	27	10.1	10	11.3
	2016	9	17.3	27	9.7	10	11.2
Botswana Botswana	2005	13	25.6	13	13.8	...	...
	2007	13	25.2	13	13.8	...	...
	2009	13	25.5	...	...	...	...
	2012	14	23.4	...	...	2	21.8
	2013	15	22.6	...	...	...	...
	2016	...	...	...	...	3	20.1
Brazil Brésil	2005	887	21.0	1 612	15.4	293	15.6
	2010	762	22.2	1 413	16.7	345	19.0
	2015	792	21.5	1 429	16.5	429	19.3
British Virgin Islands Îles Vierges britanniques	2004	~0	13.9	~0	9.3	~0	10.9
	2005	~0	14.9	~0	9.3	...	...
	2009	~0	13.5	~0	8.7	~0	11.5
	2010	~0	13.2	~0	8.7	...	...
	2015	~0	11.7	~0	8.1	~0	9.5

8

Teaching staff at the primary, secondary and tertiary levels *(continued)*
Number of teachers and Pupil teacher ratio

Personnel enseignant au niveau primaire, secondaire et supérieur *(suite)*
Nombre d'enseignants et ratio élèves/enseignant par niveau d'enseignement

Region, country or area Région, pays ou zone	Year & Année &	Primary education Enseignant primaire Total Totale ('000)	 Pupil-teacher ratio Ratio élèves/ enseignant	Secondary education Enseignant secondaire Total Totale ('000)	 Pupil-teacher ratio Ratio élèves/ enseignant	Tertiary education Enseignant supérieur Total Totale ('000)	 Pupil-teacher ratio Ratio élèves/ enseignant
Brunei Darussalam	2005	5	10.1	4	10.1	1	8.5
Brunéi Darussalam	2009	4	12.0	5	10.5	1	9.6
	2010	4	11.3	...	...	1	8.3
	2015	4	10.0	5	8.8	1	11.9
	2016	4	10.2	5	8.6	1	11.6
Bulgaria	2005	18	16.2	57	12.0	21	11.3
Bulgarie	2010	15	17.5	44	12.1	21	13.8
	2014	15	17.7	39	13.2	23	12.3
	2016	15	17.6	39	12.6	23	11.8
Burkina Faso	2003	23	44.7	8	31.3	...	...
Burkina Faso	2005	27	47.2	...	...	2	14.1
	2010	39	52.4	18	30.3	3	17.7
	2015	64	42.2	38	25.2	5	18.3
	2016	69	41.5	45	23.4	5	19.2
Burundi	2005	21	48.7	*7	*22.8	1	16.1
Burundi	2010	37	50.6	11	29.9	2	16.4
	2014	47	43.7	16	37.2	2	25.2
	2015	48	43.2	19	35.8	...	...
	2016	42	49.7	23	32.1	...	...
Cabo Verde	2005	3	26.0	2	23.5	~0	8.1
Cabo Verde	2010	3	23.6	4	17.5	1	11.0
	2015	3	21.9	4	16.4	1	9.2
	2016	3	21.5	4	16.0	1	9.6
Cambodia	2003	49	56.2	24	23.6	2	17.4
Cambodge	2005	51	53.2	...	...	2	22.7
	2006	51	50.4	27	30.0	3	29.0
	2007	49	50.9	30	28.9	...	...
	2010	47	48.4	...	...	...	...
	2015	48	45.5	...	...	12	17.7
	2016	50	42.5	...	...	...	...
Cameroon	2005	*62	*47.8	*48	*16.2	3	*31.5
Cameroun	2008	70	46.0	43	26.3	4	38.5
	2010	77	45.8	...	...	*4	*52.0
	2014	94	44.2	98	20.4	*7	*52.3
	2015	105	41.5	106	19.9	...	...
	2016	105	42.7	115	19.3	...	...
Canada							
Canada	2000	141	17.4	...	...	133	...
Cayman Islands	2001	~0	15.2	*~0	*9.8	*~0	*18.8
Îles Caïmanes	2005	~0	12.8	*~0	*10.3	...	...
	2008	~0	12.1	~0	8.9	~0	26.8
	2012	~0	13.3	1	5.3	...	...
	2013	~0	13.0	...	...	...	...
Central African Republic	2000	...	...	...	...	~0	19.5
République centrafricaine	2005	5	88.6	...	...	...	...
	2009	6	94.6	1	80.1	~0	30.7
	2010	8	84.3	2	...	...	...
	2011	8	81.3	2	66.8	~0	34.6
	2012	8	80.1	2	68.1	...	...
	2016	10	83.4	3	34.6	...	...
Chad	2005	20	63.2	*7	*33.5	1	9.5
Tchad	2009	27	61.0	13	32.3	2	8.6
	2010	28	62.2	13	32.5	...	...
	2011	31	62.6	14	32.0	2	10.9
	2015	41	55.5	19	27.5	...	...
	2016	39	56.9	20	27.1	...	...
Chile	2005	66	26.1	66	24.8	...	...
Chili	2010	66	23.4	69	21.9	70	14.1
	2013	75	19.5	75	21.0	78	15.0
	2015	80	18.4	80	19.4	...	...

8 Teaching staff at the primary, secondary and tertiary levels *(continued)*
Number of teachers and Pupil teacher ratio

Personnel enseignant au niveau primaire, secondaire et supérieur *(suite)*
Nombre d'enseignants et ratio élèves/enseignant par niveau d'enseignement

Region, country or area Région, pays ou zone	Year & Année &	Primary education / Enseignant primaire: Total Totale ('000)	Primary education / Enseignant primaire: Pupil-teacher ratio Ratio élèves/ enseignant	Secondary education / Enseignant secondaire: Total Totale ('000)	Secondary education / Enseignant secondaire: Pupil-teacher ratio Ratio élèves/ enseignant	Tertiary education / Enseignant supérieur: Total Totale ('000)	Tertiary education / Enseignant supérieur: Pupil-teacher ratio Ratio élèves/ enseignant
China [1] Chine [1]	2003	5 779	21.1	5 138	18.6	* 742	* 20.5
	2005	...	...	...	...	1 404	14.7
	2010	5 997	16.8	6 417	15.5	1 557	19.9
	2011	5 939	16.8	6 431	15.2	1 607	19.5
	2015	5 889	16.3	6 234	13.8	...	...
	2016	5 933	16.5	6 220	13.5	...	...
China, Hong Kong SAR Chine, RAS de Hong Kong	2005	25	18.3	* 28	* 18.1	...	...
	2010	23	15.2	* 30	* 16.7	...	...
	2015	24	13.7	* 30	* 13.0	...	...
	2016	25	13.7	* 30	* 12.4	...	...
China, Macao SAR Chine, RAS de Macao	2005	2	23.2	2	22.4	2	15.4
	2010	2	16.1	2	16.2	2	14.4
	2015	2	14.1	3	11.4	2	15.4
	2016	2	13.9	3	10.7	2	15.9
Colombia Colombie	2005	187	28.3	164	26.2	94	13.1
	2009	181	29.3	187	26.7	* 110	* 14.2
	2010	181	28.1	187	27.1	...	...
	2015	188	23.8	187	25.6	149	15.4
	2016	184	24.2	184	26.0	153	15.7
Comoros Comores	2003	3	35.9	3	11.3	~0	13.7
	2004	3	35.0	3	13.8	...	...
	2008	4	30.2	...	...	...	...
	2010	...	...	...	...	~0	17.1
	2013	4	27.8	8	8.7	~0	25.7
	2014	...	...	8	8.6	~0	26.3
Congo Congo	2003	8	65.2	* 7	* 28.1	* 1	* 13.8
	2004	7	82.8	* 7	* 34.3	...	...
	2009	10	64.4	...	...	1	20.0
	2010	14	49.1	...	...	...	...
	2012	17	44.4	18	18.7	3	11.8
	2013	...	...	...	...	3	12.3
Cook Islands Îles Cook	2005	~0	16.1	~0	15.6	...	...
	2010	~0	15.0	~0	16.2	...	...
	2015	~0	17.2	~0	13.9	~0	...
	2016	~0	17.4	~0	15.7	~0	...
Costa Rica Costa Rica	2002	24	22.6	15	18.8	...	...
	2005	25	21.3	...	...	...	...
	2010	29	17.9	27	15.5	...	...
	2015	37	12.7	33	14.0	...	...
	2016	40	12.0	36	12.7	...	...
Côte d'Ivoire Côte d'Ivoire	*2003	48	42.4	...	...	...	...
	2009	57	42.1	...	...	...	...
	2010	...	...	...	...	10	14.2
	2014	75	42.5	64	22.3	19	9.1
	2015	80	42.1	...	...	19	10.3
	2016	85	42.5	67	25.8	...	...
Croatia Croatie	2005	11	17.5	39	10.1	...	...
	2010	12	14.3	48	8.1	16	9.5
	2015	12	13.7	51	7.0	16	10.1
Cuba Cuba	2005	87	10.3	85	11.1	91	5.2
	2010	93	9.1	85	9.5	153	5.2
	2015	84	8.9	91	9.0	57	4.6
	2016	...	...	...	...	61	4.0
Cyprus Chypre	2005	3	17.7	6	11.3	1	13.8
	2010	4	13.8	7	9.8	3	12.6
	2015	5	11.9	6	10.4	3	12.7
	2016	5	...	7	...	3	...
Czechia Tchéquie	2005	31	16.2	93	10.4	24	13.8
	2006	30	15.7	92	10.5	23	15.0
	2010	25	18.7	76	11.0	...	...
	2013	26	18.9	69	11.5	16	26.0

8 Teaching staff at the primary, secondary and tertiary levels *(continued)*
Number of teachers and Pupil teacher ratio

Personnel enseignant au niveau primaire, secondaire et supérieur *(suite)*
Nombre d'enseignants et ratio élèves/enseignant par niveau d'enseignement

Region, country or area Région, pays ou zone	Year & Année &	Primary education Enseignant primaire Total Totale ('000)	Primary education Pupil-teacher ratio Ratio élèves/ enseignant	Secondary education Enseignant secondaire Total Totale ('000)	Secondary education Pupil-teacher ratio Ratio élèves/ enseignant	Tertiary education Enseignant supérieur Total Totale ('000)	Tertiary education Pupil-teacher ratio Ratio élèves/ enseignant
Dem. People's Rep. Korea Rép. pop. dém. de Corée	2009	70	22.0	124	20.0	69	8.6
	2015	66	20.5	123	17.5	63	9.0
Dem. Rep. of the Congo Rép. dém. du Congo	2002	159	34.3	...	...	...	...
	2009	274	37.3	212	16.0	23	16.4
	2010	286	37.0	218	16.0	...	...
	2013	340	37.1	281	14.2	29	15.3
	2015	415	33.2	324	14.2	...	...
Denmark Danemark	2001	40	9.9	44	10.1	...	...
	2014	44	10.7	49	11.3	28	10.7
	2015	...	...	...	...	37	8.5
Djibouti Djibouti	2002	...	...	1	31.9	* ~0	* 15.2
	2004	1	34.5	...	...	~0	12.3
	2005	...	...	...	...	~0	17.7
	2009	2	34.1	1	29.7	~0	20.1
	2010	...	...	...	...	~0	20.5
	2011	2	35.2	2	27.9	~0	19.2
	2015	2	33.0	3	22.8	...	...
	2017	2	30.4	3	22.7	...	...
Dominica Dominique	2005	1	18.2	~0	15.1	...	...
	2010	1	16.0	1	13.2	...	...
	2015	1	14.0	1	10.7	...	...
	2016	1	13.1	1	...	...	...
Dominican Republic République dominicaine	2003	...	...	...	...	11	25.8
	2005	53	24.3	31	26.4	...	...
	2010	52	25.5	32	28.2	...	...
	2015	71	18.3	42	22.1	19	25.5
	2016	69	18.5	...	...	20	25.9
Ecuador Équateur	2001	85	23.1	* 69	* 13.6	15	...
	2005	87	22.9	* 76	* 13.9	...	...
	2008	...	...	...	...	27	19.9
	2010	91	23.1	77	20.4	...	...
	2015	85	24.7	84	23.0	40	16.6
	2017	78	25.1	88	21.9	...	...
Egypt Égypte	*2004	363	21.9	488	17.1	81	28.0
	*2005	373	25.6	...	...	...	...
	2009	382	27.2	549	12.1	...	...
	2010	380	27.7	...	...	...	...
	2014	...	...	...	...	107	23.9
	2016	510	23.1	591	14.8	...	...
El Salvador El Salvador	2005	24	43.2	* 18	* 28.9	8	15.2
	2009	31	31.0	23	24.4	9	16.2
	2010	...	...	...	...	9	16.5
	2015	25	29.7	19	30.8	10	18.1
	2016	25	28.3	20	29.3	10	18.1
Equatorial Guinea Guinée équatoriale	2000	2	43.4	* 1	* 23.2	~0	4.9
	2003	2	32.0	...	...	...	...
	2005	...	...	1	19.2	...	...
	2010	3	27.2	...	...	...	...
	2015	4	23.2	...	...	...	...
Eritrea Érythrée	2004	8	46.7	4	47.8	~0	10.8
	2005	8	47.5	4	51.3	...	...
	2010	8	38.0	6	38.7	1	19.2
	2015	8	43.3	6	38.9	1	19.5
	2016	9	...	6	...	1	14.1
Estonia Estonie	2001	8	14.1	12	10.1	7	8.8
	2005	...	...	...	...	6	10.7
	2006	8	10.6	...	...	* 6	* 10.7
	2010	6	11.7	11	8.8	...	...
	2013	7	11.5	10	8.1	...	...

8

Teaching staff at the primary, secondary and tertiary levels *(continued)*
Number of teachers and Pupil teacher ratio

Personnel enseignant au niveau primaire, secondaire et supérieur *(suite)*
Nombre d'enseignants et ratio élèves/enseignant par niveau d'enseignement

Region, country or area Région, pays ou zone	Year & Année &	Primary education Enseignant primaire Total Totale ('000)	Primary education Enseignant primaire Pupil-teacher ratio Ratio élèves/enseignant	Secondary education Enseignant secondaire Total Totale ('000)	Secondary education Enseignant secondaire Pupil-teacher ratio Ratio élèves/enseignant	Tertiary education Enseignant supérieur Total Totale ('000)	Tertiary education Enseignant supérieur Pupil-teacher ratio Ratio élèves/enseignant
Eswatini Eswatini	2005	7	32.9	4	16.7	~0	13.7
	2006	7	33.3	4	19.3	~0	12.3
	2010	7	32.3	5	18.1	...	...
	2013	9	28.1	6	16.0	~0	17.6
	2015	9	27.6	6	15.8	1	...
Ethiopia Éthiopie	2000	87	67.3	...	...	2	27.1
	2005	...	...	...	...	5	39.4
	2009	234	57.9	82	47.4	12	34.1
	2010	252	54.1	98	43.1	...	...
	2011	260	55.1	113	40.3	...	...
	*2012	...	...	122	40.4	...	...
	2014	...	...	...	...	24	31.2
Fiji Fidji	2004	4	28.2	*5	*22.4	...	...
	2008	4	26.0	5	18.7	...	...
	2012	4	28.0	5	19.3	...	...
Finland Finlande	2005	25	15.5	42	10.3	19	16.4
	2010	25	14.0	43	9.9	15	19.7
	2014	26	13.3	42	12.8	16	19.3
	2016	27	13.3	41	13.2	15	19.9
France France	2004	203	18.6	511	11.4	136	15.9
	2005	216	18.6	528	11.4	...	...
	2010	234	17.8	463	12.7	...	...
	2013	229	18.2	457	12.9	110	21.3
Gabon Gabon	2003	8	36.0	...	...	...	...
	2011	13	24.5	...	...	...	...
Gambia Gambie	2004	5	38.5	...	...	~0	11.4
	2005	6	36.6	...	...	...	...
	*2010	6	37.5	...	...	...	...
	2012	7	33.9	...	...	~0	23.2
	2015	8	37.1	6	...	...	...
	2017	9	38.7	7	...	...	...
Georgia Géorgie	2003	17	14.5	49	9.2	29	5.5
	2005	...	...	...	...	29	5.9
	2009	*34	*8.9	*45	*7.6	12	7.7
	2010	...	...	...	...	13	7.9
	2015	32	9.0	38	7.2	18	7.1
	2016	33	8.8	37	7.4	19	7.3
Germany Allemagne	2002	236	14.3	590	14.3	277	...
	2005	234	14.1	596	13.9	...	...
	2010	242	12.7	594	12.9	...	...
	2015	236	12.2	586	12.1	396	7.5
	2016	238	...	589	...	402	...
Ghana Ghana	2005	89	32.8	*73	*18.8	...	...
	2009	111	33.1	99	18.3	...	...
	*2010	121	...	112	...	...	...
	2015	139	31.3	147	16.6	14	28.9
	2016	143	30.6	148	17.0	15	27.3
	2017	161	27.3	163	15.6	...	...
Gibraltar Gibraltar	2001	~0	20.7	~0	11.7	...	...
	2009	~0	16.0	~0	5.9	...	...
	2016	~0	13.7	~0	16.8	...	...
Greece Grèce	2005	59	11.1	86	8.3	27	23.8
	2007	62	10.3	87	7.9	29	20.8
	2014	67	9.4	80	8.3	15	44.5
	2015	67	9.6	76	8.7	...	...
Grenada Grenade	2004	1	17.7	*1	*20.1	...	...
	2005	1	18.2	...	...	...	...
	2010	1	16.1	1	15.5	...	...
	2015	1	17.0	1	11.9	2	4.3
	2016	1	15.5	1	11.9	2	4.3

Teaching staff at the primary, secondary and tertiary levels *(continued)*
Number of teachers and Pupil teacher ratio

Personnel enseignant au niveau primaire, secondaire et supérieur *(suite)*
Nombre d'enseignants et ratio élèves/enseignant par niveau d'enseignement

Region, country or area Région, pays ou zone	Year & Année &	Primary education Enseignant primaire Total Totale ('000)	Primary education Pupil-teacher ratio Ratio élèves/ enseignant	Secondary education Enseignant secondaire Total Totale ('000)	Secondary education Pupil-teacher ratio Ratio élèves/ enseignant	Tertiary education Enseignant supérieur Total Totale ('000)	Tertiary education Pupil-teacher ratio Ratio élèves/ enseignant
Guatemala Guatemala	2002	69	30.1	44	13.7	4	27.7
	*2003	...	...	...	...	4	...
	2005	76	31.1	48	15.8	...	...
	2010	99	26.9	77	14.0	...	...
	2014	105	23.0	92	12.7	...	...
	2015	117	20.4	...	...	...	...
	2016	108	21.7	98	12.4	...	...
Guinea Guinée	2005	27	44.9	12	* 34.4	...	...
	2008	31	44.1	16	33.3	...	...
	2010	34	42.2	...	...	5	19.1
	2011	35	44.1	19	33.1	6	17.9
	2014	38	45.6	...	...	6	18.7
Guinea-Bissau Guinée-Bissau	2000	3	44.1	* 2	* 15.0	...	...
	2006	4	62.2	1	37.3	~0	147.6
	2010	5	51.9	...	...	...	...
Guyana Guyana	2005	4	28.0	* 4	* 18.0	1	12.6
	2010	4	24.6	4	21.4	1	10.6
	2012	4	23.2	4	20.3	1	13.1
Honduras Honduras	2004	38	32.9	17	...	* 7	* 17.1
	*2005	42	29.1	...	...	...	...
	2009	37	33.9	...	...	...	...
	2010	...	...	...	...	9	19.8
	2015	40	29.1	40	16.1	10	20.0
	2016	40	28.4	45	14.5	...	...
Hungary Hongrie	2005	41	10.4	97	9.9	25	17.2
	2010	37	10.6	89	10.2	25	15.8
	2015	36	11.0	80	10.3	21	14.6
	2016	37	10.8	81	10.0	22	13.6
Iceland Islande	2005	...	...	...	...	2	8.5
	2010	...	...	...	...	2	8.6
	2012	3	9.9	...	...	2	8.7
	2015	3	10.1	...	...	...	...
India Inde	2003	3 038	41.3	2 507	32.3	428	26.4
	2004	...	...	2 586	32.7	539	22.0
	2010	...	...	4 252	25.3	...	...
	2015	4 399	31.5	4 093	31.7	1 322	24.3
	2016	4 140	35.2	4 639	28.5	1 364	23.7
Indonesia Indonésie	2005	1 428	20.4	1 282	12.5	272	* 13.5
	2010	1 596	19.0	1 641	12.2	271	18.4
	2014	1 802	16.6	1 460	15.5	258	25.0
	2016	2 107	14.0	1 674	14.1	277	22.2
Iran (Islamic Republic of) Iran (Rép. islamique d')	2005	285	21.7	...	...	115	18.4
	2009	278	20.5	...	...	164	20.5
	2010	...	...	...	...	174	21.8
	2015	286	26.8	336	17.0	315	15.3
	2016	...	...	...	...	311	14.0
Iraq Iraq	2004	211	20.5	91	18.8	19	22.1
	*2005	...	...	...	...	19	22.1
	2007	287	17.0	148	13.7	...	...
Ireland Irlande	2005	25	17.9	...	...	12	16.0
	2010	32	15.8	...	...	13	15.4
	2012	32	16.1	...	...	...	...
Israel Israël	*2005	55	13.0	68	9.9	...	...
	*2009	60	13.1	71	9.8	...	...
	2010	62	13.1	...	...	...	...
	2015	73	12.1	...	...	...	...
Italy Italie	2005	264	10.5	428	10.5	94	21.4
	2007	273	10.3	451	10.1	104	19.5
	2010	...	...	...	...	106	18.7
	2015	237	12.0	408	11.3	90	20.3

8

Teaching staff at the primary, secondary and tertiary levels *(continued)*
Number of teachers and Pupil teacher ratio

Personnel enseignant au niveau primaire, secondaire et supérieur *(suite)*
Nombre d'enseignants et ratio élèves/enseignant par niveau d'enseignement

Region, country or area Région, pays ou zone	Year & Année &	Primary education / Enseignant primaire: Total Totale ('000)	Primary: Pupil-teacher ratio Ratio élèves/ enseignant	Secondary education / Enseignant secondaire: Total Totale ('000)	Secondary: Pupil-teacher ratio Ratio élèves/ enseignant	Tertiary education / Enseignant supérieur: Total Totale ('000)	Tertiary: Pupil-teacher ratio Ratio élèves/ enseignant
Jamaica Jamaïque	2002	...	...	* 12	* 19.3	2	22.8
	2004	12	27.5	13	19.1	...	...
	2010	...	...	18	14.3	...	...
	2015	12	22.0	13	16.4	...	...
	2016	10	25.6	12	18.1	...	...
Japan Japon	2005	383	18.9	610	12.6	497	8.1
	2010	399	17.8	614	11.9	528	7.3
	2015	410	16.2	634	11.4	550	7.0
Jordan Jordanie	2003	* 39	* 19.9	* 34	* 17.9	7	26.8
	2005	...	...	...	...	8	26.4
	2010	...	...	...	...	10	24.6
	2014	58	16.9	51	14.6	...	...
	2015	...	...	...	...	14	22.5
	2016	57	18.4	...	...	20	15.8
Kazakhstan Kazakhstan	2000	...	...	...	...	31	13.4
	2005	59	17.3	...	...	...	...
	2010	59	16.2	...	...	49	15.5
	2015	74	16.2	224	7.5	51	13.0
	2017	65	20.8	268	6.6	47	13.4
Kenya Kenya	*2005	145	42.0	91	27.2	...	...
	*2009	165	43.3	96	33.4	...	...
	*2015	267	30.7	199	...	...	...
Kiribati Kiribati	2005	1	24.7	1	17.0	...	...
	2008	1	25.0	1	17.4	...	...
	2014	1	26.4	...	...	...	...
	2016	1	25.7	...	...	...	...
Kuwait Koweït	2004	12	12.8	25	10.6	* 2	* 17.0
	2005	17	12.1	...	...	...	...
	2009	25	8.6	* 31	* 8.2	...	...
	2010	26	8.4	...	...	...	...
	2015	30	8.9	40	7.6	...	...
	2016	31	8.9	42	...	...	...
Kyrgyzstan Kirghizistan	2005	18	24.5	54	13.4	13	16.5
	2010	16	24.3	48	14.3	17	14.9
	2015	17	26.2	60	10.8	21	12.8
	2016	19	25.0	60	11.0	21	11.9
Lao People's Dem. Rep. Rép. dém. populaire lao	2005	28	31.5	16	24.8	2	20.7
	2010	32	28.8	21	20.2	5	22.5
	2015	35	24.2	* 34	* 18.7	12	10.6
	2016	36	23.0	* 36	* 18.3	11	10.7
Latvia Lettonie	2005	7	12.2	25	10.8	6	20.9
	2010	10	11.9	16	9.0	7	16.3
	2015	11	11.1	15	8.0	7	12.6
Lebanon Liban	2005	* 33	* 14.6	* 42	* 9.0	21	8.0
	2010	33	14.1	43	8.9	25	8.0
	2014	39	12.3	48	7.7	46	5.0
	2016	40	12.2	50	7.7	...	...
Lesotho Lesotho	2005	10	41.6	3	27.0	1	14.2
	2006	10	40.8	4	25.8	1	13.3
	2010	12	33.8	* 5	* 24.5	...	...
	2014	11	32.8	* 6	* 23.5	1	29.3
	2015	11	33.1	6	24.0	...	...
	2016	11	33.8	6	23.2	...	...
Liberia Libéria	2000	13	38.3	...	...	1	72.3
	*2001	...	...	...	...	1	...
	2009	22	27.4	...	...	...	...
	2010	...	...	...	...	1	24.4
	2012	...	...	...	...	2	21.6
	2015	22	30.4	12	18.4	...	...
Libya Libye	*2003	...	...	...	...	16	23.9

8

Teaching staff at the primary, secondary and tertiary levels *(continued)*
Number of teachers and Pupil teacher ratio

Personnel enseignant au niveau primaire, secondaire et supérieur *(suite)*
Nombre d'enseignants et ratio élèves/enseignant par niveau d'enseignement

Region, country or area Région, pays ou zone	Year & Année &	Primary education / Enseignant primaire: Total Totale ('000)	Primary education / Enseignant primaire: Pupil-teacher ratio Ratio élèves/ enseignant	Secondary education / Enseignant secondaire: Total Totale ('000)	Secondary education / Enseignant secondaire: Pupil-teacher ratio Ratio élèves/ enseignant	Tertiary education / Enseignant supérieur: Total Totale ('000)	Tertiary education / Enseignant supérieur: Pupil-teacher ratio Ratio élèves/ enseignant
Liechtenstein Liechtenstein	2005	~0	8.6	~0	9.6	...	...
	2009	~0	6.5	~0	9.3	...	...
	2010	~0	6.1	...	...	...	...
	2015	~0	7.8	~0	9.9	~0	6.3
	2016	~0	7.7	~0	9.7	~0	6.5
Lithuania Lituanie	2005	11	14.1	43	9.9	13	14.9
	2010	10	12.8	39	8.8	14	14.3
	2015	8	12.9	33	7.9	13	10.8
	2016	8	13.2	33	7.7	13	10.5
Luxembourg Luxembourg	2005	3	11.3	3	10.3	...	...
	2010	4	9.3	5	8.5	1	5.4
	2015	4	8.5	5	9.4	1	8.9
Madagascar Madagascar	2005	67	53.6	* 29	* 21.6	2	25.5
	2009	90	47.9	44	* 23.5	4	16.3
	2010	106	40.1	...	...	4	16.6
	2014	111	41.7	65	23.1	6	18.8
	2015	116	41.2	...	...	6	18.7
	2016	117	40.6	...	...	...	...
Malawi Malawi	2005	...	...	...	...	1	7.5
	2010	* 43	* 79.3	* 16	* 43.2	1	11.6
	2011	* 47	* 76.1	* 17	* 42.1	1	13.6
	*2015	60	69.5	25	37.9	...	...
Malaysia Malaisie	2005	190	16.9	...	...	...	...
	2010	257	12.6	...	...	...	...
	2015	270	11.5	...	...	82	15.9
	2016	267	11.6	209	13.2	96	13.9
Maldives Maldives	2003	4	18.2	2	13.7	~0	1.9
	2005	3	20.1	...	...	...	...
	2010	4	11.7	...	...	...	...
	2015	4	10.3	...	...	...	...
	2016	4	10.3	...	...	...	...
Mali Mali	2000	16	65.3	* 9	* 29.0	* 1	* 20.5
	2005	28	54.4	...	...	...	...
	2009	38	50.1	* 29	* 23.4	...	...
	2010	40	50.4	...	...	...	...
	2015	52	42.7	49	19.2	...	...
	2016	60	39.1	52	19.5	...	...
Malta Malte	2005	2	18.4	3	11.5	1	11.4
	2008	2	17.5	4	10.6	1	9.8
	2010	2	14.3	...	...	1	9.0
	2015	2	13.5	4	7.8	2	8.1
	2016	2	13.0	4	7.2	2	7.9
Marshall Islands Îles Marshall	2002	1	16.9	~0	16.7	~0	18.8
	*2003	...	...	~0	14.9	...	...
	2012	...	...	...	...	~0	19.6
Mauritania Mauritanie	2005	11	40.3	3	31.0	~0	24.6
	2006	11	41.4	* 4	* 26.2	~0	28.8
	2010	14	37.2	...	...	~0	38.4
	2013	16	35.4	...	...	~0	43.0
	2015	18	35.8	6	33.5	...	...
	2016	17	36.4	8	26.4	...	...
Mauritius Maurice	2005	6	22.3	7	* 17.4	...	...
	2010	5	21.5	8	* 15.3	1	30.4
	2015	5	18.8	10	12.9	...	...
	2016	5	17.8	10	12.6	...	...
Mexico Mexique	2005	519	28.3	593	17.8	251	9.5
	2010	530	28.1	652	17.9	310	9.2
	2015	535	26.9	838	16.1	364	9.7
	2016	535	26.7	842	16.3	...	...
Micronesia (Fed. States of) Micronésie (États féd. de)	*2000	...	...	...	...	~0	17.1
	*2015	1	19.7	...	...	...	...

8 Teaching staff at the primary, secondary and tertiary levels *(continued)*
Number of teachers and Pupil teacher ratio

Personnel enseignant au niveau primaire, secondaire et supérieur *(suite)*
Nombre d'enseignants et ratio élèves/enseignant par niveau d'enseignement

Region, country or area Région, pays ou zone	Year & Année &	Primary education Enseignant primaire Total Totale ('000)	Primary education Enseignant primaire Pupil-teacher ratio Ratio élèves/ enseignant	Secondary education Enseignant secondaire Total Totale ('000)	Secondary education Enseignant secondaire Pupil-teacher ratio Ratio élèves/ enseignant	Tertiary education Enseignant supérieur Total Totale ('000)	Tertiary education Enseignant supérieur Pupil-teacher ratio Ratio élèves/ enseignant
Monaco Monaco	2001	~0	22.3	~0	10.8	...	...
	2004	...	...	~0	11.1	...	...
	2008	...	...	1	5.8	...	...
	2015	~0	12.6	~0	8.1	...	...
	2016	~0	13.7	...	...	~0	6.9
Mongolia Mongolie	2005	7	34.2	15	22.4	8	15.4
	2010	9	30.2	19	14.5	9	18.9
	2015	9	28.2	21	13.5	9	20.3
	2016	9	29.7	22	14.1	13	12.5
Montenegro Monténégro	2016	...	...	...	...	2	15.2
Montserrat Montserrat	2005	~0	20.4	~0	11.5	...	...
	2009	~0	13.1	~0	13.3	...	...
	2014	~0	11.0	~0	12.7	...	...
Morocco Maroc	2004	148	27.6	* 100	* 18.7	19	18.5
	2005	148	27.1	...	...	19	19.0
	2009	145	26.6	...	...	20	21.4
	2010	150	26.2	...	...	...	...
	2015	156	25.9	...	...	33	26.9
	2016	154	26.6	...	...	34	28.5
Mozambique Mozambique	2005	59	66.3	* 10	* 32.2	3	9.4
	2010	90	58.5	* 20	* 34.1	6	16.2
	2014	104	* 54.8	* 26	* 40.0	10	15.2
	2015	108	* 54.7	* 27	* 39.7	...	...
Myanmar Myanmar	2001	148	32.3	75	30.8	11	52.6
	2005	160	30.9	78	33.1	...	...
	2007	172	29.1	82	32.8	11	47.6
	2010	182	28.2	84	34.1	...	...
	2012	...	...	...	...	25	25.3
	2014	188	27.6	100	31.8	...	...
	2017	241	22.0	156	24.0	13	57.2
Namibia Namibie	2003	13	31.6	6	25.2	1	13.1
	2005	13	30.8	6	25.1	...	...
	2007	14	29.9	6	24.6	...	...
	2008	14	29.4	...	...	1	16.4
	2010	14	29.8	...	...	...	...
	2014	...	...	...	...	3	...
Nauru Nauru	2005	~0	27.9	~0	15.4	...	...
	2007	~0	19.9	~0	20.9	...	...
	2008	~0	22.4	...	...	...	...
	2014	~0	39.5	~0	22.8	...	...
	2016	~0	40.2	~0	24.8	...	...
Nepal Népal	2003	110	35.7	53	34.7	...	...
	2005	101	39.7	...	...	7	27.2
	2007	113	40.0	...	...	10	25.7
	2010	154	31.9	* 84	* 32.0	...	...
	2013	179	25.6	* 107	* 29.2	8	60.0
	2015	188	23.1	* 111	* 28.6	...	...
	2017	198	20.9	* 116	* 28.8	...	...
Netherlands Pays-Bas	2005	...	...	107	13.1	45	12.7
	2010	...	...	107	13.7	52	12.6
	2015	104	11.6	112	14.5	63	13.5
	2016	102	11.7	112	14.4	65	12.9
Netherlands Antilles [former] Antilles néerlandaises [anc.]	2002	1	...	1	...	* ~0	...
New Zealand Nouvelle-Zélande	2005	22	16.3	36	14.7	15	15.9
	2010	24	14.5	35	14.5	17	16.0
	2015	25	14.5	35	13.8	16	16.7
Nicaragua Nicaragua	2002	26	35.2	* 11	* 33.9	7	15.3
	2005	28	33.6	13	33.7	...	...
	2010	31	30.2	15	30.8	...	...

8

Teaching staff at the primary, secondary and tertiary levels *(continued)*
Number of teachers and Pupil teacher ratio

Personnel enseignant au niveau primaire, secondaire et supérieur *(suite)*
Nombre d'enseignants et ratio élèves/enseignant par niveau d'enseignement

Region, country or area Région, pays ou zone	Year & Année &	Primary education / Enseignant primaire: Total Totale ('000)	Primary education / Enseignant primaire: Pupil-teacher ratio Ratio élèves/ enseignant	Secondary education / Enseignant secondaire: Total Totale ('000)	Secondary education / Enseignant secondaire: Pupil-teacher ratio Ratio élèves/ enseignant	Tertiary education / Enseignant supérieur: Total Totale ('000)	Tertiary education / Enseignant supérieur: Pupil-teacher ratio Ratio élèves/ enseignant
Niger	2005	24	43.7	7	27.4	1	14.9
Niger	2010	45	38.6	10	30.8	2	11.3
	2012	53	38.8	...	...	2	12.3
	2014	64	35.8	21	25.1	...	...
	2015	...	36.6	21	28.0	...	...
	2016	72	36.3	27	26.7	...	...
Nigeria	2004	598	35.8	155	40.6	37	34.8
Nigéria	2005	599	36.9	159	40.2	...	...
	2010	574	* 37.6	390	23.2	57	24.6
	2011	...	...	...	...	67	22.6
Niue	2004	~0	11.5	~0	8.4	...	...
Nioué	2005	...	...	~0	8.2	...	...
	2015	~0	17.3	~0	7.9	...	...
	2016	~0	15.5	...	...	...	...
Norway	2001	...	...	...	...	15	12.3
Norvège	2015	49	8.9	51	8.5	27	9.9
Oman	*2003	16	19.9	16	17.4	...	...
Oman	2005	...	...	...	...	3	16.2
	2010	...	...	...	...	5	16.8
	2015	...	...	...	...	8	16.2
	2016	...	...	...	...	8	16.2
Pakistan	2005	450	38.3	* 295	* 23.3	...	...
Pakistan	2009	465	39.7	...	...	* 63	* 19.3
	2010	464	40.5	...	...	...	...
	2015	428	46.3	* 572	* 21.1	107	17.6
	2016	452	47.6	* 590	* 21.4	...	...
Palau	2000	~0	15.7	~0	15.1	* ~0	* 10.9
Palaos	*2002	...	...	...	...	~0	10.5
	2013	...	...	...	...	~0	8.2
Panama	2005	18	24.2	16	15.6	11	11.0
Panama	2010	19	23.5	19	15.3	15	9.2
	2015	19	21.9	24	13.3	15	10.6
Papua New Guinea	*2001	14	36.2	...	...	...	...
Papouasie-Nvl-Guinée	2012	32	45.2	14	27.4	...	...
Paraguay	*2004	33	27.8	44	11.8	...	...
Paraguay	2012	35	24.2	34	18.4	...	...
Peru	2002	171	25.1	134	18.9	56	14.8
Pérou	2005	177	23.0	148	16.7	...	...
	2010	191	19.7	167	16.0	...	...
	2015	195	18.0	190	14.1	...	...
	2016	195	18.3	192	14.3	...	...
Philippines	2005	373	35.1	168	37.9	* 113	* 21.3
Philippines	2009	435	31.4	194	34.8	...	...
	2015	478	30.3	279	26.2	...	...
	2017	...	...	...	...	151	23.7
Poland	2005	236	11.5	296	11.6	95	22.3
Pologne	2010	240	9.3	273	10.4	103	20.9
	2015	220	10.5	273	9.3	97	17.1
Portugal	2005	72	10.5	94	7.1	37	10.4
Portugal	2010	68	10.8	98	7.3	36	10.6
	2015	49	13.3	78	9.9	32	10.4
Puerto Rico	2010	26	11.7	26	11.1	16	15.4
Porto Rico	2015	18	13.9	15	18.9	16	14.8
Qatar	2005	6	11.1	5	11.6	1	* 14.6
Qatar	2010	7	12.0	7	9.9	2	8.6
	2015	11	11.6	9	10.7	2	12.9
	2016	12	11.6	10	10.2	2	12.6
Republic of Korea	2005	144	27.9	210	18.1	191	16.8
République de Corée	2010	158	20.9	225	17.6	223	14.7
	2015	164	16.6	236	14.4	225	14.5
	2016	164	...	233	...	220	...

8 Teaching staff at the primary, secondary and tertiary levels *(continued)*

Number of teachers and Pupil teacher ratio

Personnel enseignant au niveau primaire, secondaire et supérieur *(suite)*

Nombre d'enseignants et ratio élèves/enseignant par niveau d'enseignement

Region, country or area Région, pays ou zone	Year & Année &	Primary education / Enseignant primaire: Total Totale ('000)	Primary education / Enseignant primaire: Pupil-teacher ratio Ratio élèves/ enseignant	Secondary education / Enseignant secondaire: Total Totale ('000)	Secondary education / Enseignant secondaire: Pupil-teacher ratio Ratio élèves/ enseignant	Tertiary education / Enseignant supérieur: Total Totale ('000)	Tertiary education / Enseignant supérieur: Pupil-teacher ratio Ratio élèves/ enseignant
Republic of Moldova République de Moldova	2005	10	18.0	31	12.8	8	16.7
	2010	9	15.4	29	10.5	8	16.8
	2015	8	17.5	25	9.3	7	16.5
	2016	8	17.4	25	9.2	7	15.8
Romania Roumanie	2005	57	17.0	162	12.9	31	23.9
	2010	52	16.1	146	12.5	31	32.1
	2015	50	18.9	129	12.1	28	19.5
	2016	49	19.3	125	12.1	27	19.9
Russian Federation Fédération de Russie	2005	* 317	* 16.7	* 1 306	* 9.5	625	14.4
	2009	278	18.1	1 136	8.5	670	13.9
	2012	282	19.6	1 046	8.8	554	14.4
	2015	297	20.1	...	...	627	10.5
Rwanda Rwanda	2005	27	69.0	8	28.7	* 2	* 15.3
	2009	33	68.3	15	22.6	3	18.7
	2010	36	64.6	...	...	3	22.2
	2015	42	58.3	30	19.2	3	23.9
	2016	44	58.5	31	18.6	3	32.5
Saint Kitts and Nevis Saint-Kitts-et-Nevis	2005	~0	17.6	* ~0	* 9.9	...	...
	2010	~0	14.1	~0	* 9.3	...	...
	2015	~0	15.1	1	8.3	~0	7.6
	2016	~0	13.9	1	7.9	...	...
Saint Lucia Sainte-Lucie	2005	1	22.0	1	16.9	~0	12.6
	2010	1	18.5	* 1	* 15.7	~0	9.3
	2015	1	15.5	1	11.7	~0	10.2
	2016	1	15.1	1	11.8	~0	10.1
Saint Vincent & Grenadines Saint-Vincent-Grenadines	*2004	1	17.2	1	18.1	...	...
	2010	1	16.3	1	16.8	...	...
	2015	1	14.9	1	15.0	...	...
	2016	1	14.5	1	14.3	...	...
Samoa Samoa	2000	1	24.0	1	21.2	~0	7.8
	2002	1	27.2	1	21.0	...	...
	2010	1	30.2	1	21.5	...	...
	2016	...	...	1	27.7	...	...
San Marino Saint-Marin	2004	~0	6.3	...	...	...	...
	2010	~0	6.5	~0	14.5	...	...
	2012	~0	6.3	...	...	...	...
Sao Tome and Principe Sao Tomé-et-Principe	2005	1	30.8	* ~0	* 21.7	...	...
	2009	1	26.2	...	...	...	...
	2010	...	...	...	...	~0	8.1
	2015	1	38.8	1	20.8	~0	8.0
	2016	1	32.2	1	24.8	...	...
	2017	1	31.2	...	...	...	...
Saudi Arabia Arabie saoudite	2005	* 273	* 11.3	* 234	* 11.1	27	22.5
	2009	* 285	* 11.4	* 264	* 11.3	39	19.2
	2010	298	11.2	...	...	50	18.2
	2014	347	10.8	312	* 11.0	74	20.3
	2015	353	10.9	...	...	77	19.8
	2016	320	11.7	...	...	80	20.3
Senegal Sénégal	2005	35	41.7	* 15	* 26.4	...	...
	2010	50	33.7	...	...	...	...
	2015	62	32.1	56	20.4	6	25.8
	2016	64	31.7	57	* 19.7	5	33.4
Serbia Serbie	2010	17	16.4	62	9.6	15	15.3
	2015	18	15.2	65	8.5	11	22.5
	2016	19	14.5	66	8.2	11	22.6
Seychelles Seychelles	2005	1	13.7	1	14.4	...	...
	2010	1	12.5	1	12.8	...	...
	2015	1	13.7	1	12.0	~0	14.4
	2016	1	14.0	1	11.6	~0	19.4

8 Teaching staff at the primary, secondary and tertiary levels *(continued)*
Number of teachers and Pupil teacher ratio

Personnel enseignant au niveau primaire, secondaire et supérieur *(suite)*
Nombre d'enseignants et ratio élèves/enseignant par niveau d'enseignement

Region, country or area Région, pays ou zone	Year & Année &	Primary education / Enseignant primaire: Total Totale ('000)	Primary education / Enseignant primaire: Pupil-teacher ratio Ratio élèves/ enseignant	Secondary education / Enseignant secondaire: Total Totale ('000)	Secondary education / Enseignant secondaire: Pupil-teacher ratio Ratio élèves/ enseignant	Tertiary education / Enseignant supérieur: Total Totale ('000)	Tertiary education / Enseignant supérieur: Pupil-teacher ratio Ratio élèves/ enseignant
Sierra Leone Sierra Leone	2001	15	37.3	6	26.6	1	7.7
	*2002	...	...	...	...	1	7.5
	2015	40	33.8	22	20.5	...	...
	2016	38	37.3	22	22.0	...	...
Singapore Singapour	2009	17	17.4	16	14.9	15	13.1
	2010	...	...	...	...	15	13.8
	2013	...	...	...	...	19	13.5
Sint Maarten (Dutch part) St-Martin (partie néerland.)	2012	~0	11.3	~0	11.8	~0	3.3
	2014	...	...	~0	7.6	~0	3.6
	2015	...	...	...	...	~0	3.6
Slovakia Slovaquie	2005	14	17.5	51	13.1	13	14.3
	2010	14	15.2	46	12.0	13	17.6
	2014	14	15.2	42	11.1	13	15.5
	2015	14	15.2	41	11.2	13	...
Slovenia Slovénie	2005	6	15.1	16	11.2	4	25.1
	2010	6	17.0	15	9.1	7	16.5
	2015	7	16.9	14	10.2	7	12.0
Solomon Islands Îles Salomon	*2000	...	...	1	10.1	...	...
	2010	5	19.9	1	28.1	...	...
	2012	5	19.1	2	25.9	...	...
	2015	4	25.7	2	...	...	...
	2016	4	25.2	...	...	...	...
Somalia Somalie	2007	13	35.5	5	19.3	...	...
South Africa Afrique du Sud	2005	* 233	* 31.4	142	32.9	...	...
	2009	* 212	* 33.6	187	25.0	...	...
	2010	238	29.5	...	...	...	...
	2015	249	30.3	190	27.8	...	...
South Sudan Soudan du sud	*2015	27	46.8	6	27.5	...	...
Spain Espagne	2005	181	13.8	280	11.1	145	12.5
	2010	219	12.4	295	10.8	155	12.1
	2015	228	13.2	276	12.0	157	12.5
Sri Lanka Sri Lanka	2005	73	21.9	...	...	...	...
	2010	72	23.9	...	...	...	...
	2012	72	24.4	150	17.3	...	...
	2015	77	23.2	...	...	...	...
	2016	76	23.2	150	17.4	...	...
State of Palestine État de Palestine	2005	16	24.5	25	26.6	* 5	* 30.5
	2010	14	27.8	32	22.5	7	27.2
	2015	19	24.0	36	19.9	8	26.1
	2016	19	23.8	37	19.6	8	28.9
Sudan Soudan	2014	...	...	...	...	14	46.0
Sudan [former] Soudan [anc.]	*2000	...	...	...	...	4	45.5
	2005	113	29.0	64	* 21.5	...	...
	*2009	124	38.4	83	22.2	...	...
Suriname Suriname	2005	4	18.6	3	13.9	...	...
	2010	5	14.9	4	13.8	...	...
	2015	5	14.3	4	13.2	...	...
	2016	5	14.2	...	...	...	...
Sweden Suède	2005	66	10.1	76	9.7	38	11.3
	2010	60	9.5	75	9.7	29	15.6
	2015	65	12.1	66	12.9	34	12.6
Switzerland Suisse	2005	...	...	...	...	34	5.9
	2010	...	...	...	...	40	6.2
	2012	45	10.8	65	9.3	46	5.8
	2014	48	10.1	...	...	33	8.9
Syrian Arab Republic République arabe syrienne	2002	115	25.3	65	18.1	...	...
	2015	...	...	...	...	12	64.4

8 Teaching staff at the primary, secondary and tertiary levels *(continued)*
Number of teachers and Pupil teacher ratio

Personnel enseignant au niveau primaire, secondaire et supérieur *(suite)*
Nombre d'enseignants et ratio élèves/enseignant par niveau d'enseignement

Region, country or area Région, pays ou zone	Year & Année &	Primary education / Enseignant primaire: Total Totale ('000)	Primary education / Enseignant primaire: Pupil-teacher ratio Ratio élèves/ enseignant	Secondary education / Enseignant secondaire: Total Totale ('000)	Secondary education / Enseignant secondaire: Pupil-teacher ratio Ratio élèves/ enseignant	Tertiary education / Enseignant supérieur: Total Totale ('000)	Tertiary education / Enseignant supérieur: Pupil-teacher ratio Ratio élèves/ enseignant
Tajikistan Tadjikistan	2005	32	21.3	60	16.4	10	14.9
	2010	27	25.2	60	17.1	13	14.8
	2011	29	23.3	68	15.4	13	14.5
	2015	31	22.3	...	...	13	17.6
	2017	35	22.3	...	...	16	16.7
Thailand Thaïlande	2002	326	18.6	* 173	* 24.0	64	33.6
	*2003	...	...	...	...	66	33.6
	2008	348	16.0	223	21.2	* 76	* 32.1
	2010	317	16.3	...	...	...	...
	2015	301	16.9	240	28.2	104	21.5
TFYR of Macedonia ex-R.Y. de Macédoine	2005	6	19.4	15	14.7	3	16.9
	2010	7	15.9	17	11.9	3	17.8
	2015	8	14.4	18	9.4	* 4	* 17.7
Timor-Leste Timor-Leste	2002	4	47.2	2	29.5	* ~0	* 51.6
	2004	4	50.7	3	27.6	...	...
	2005	...	...	3	23.7	...	...
	2009	7	29.8	...	...	1	14.0
	2010	8	30.2	4	23.0	...	...
	2011	8	31.4	4	24.3	...	...
Togo Togo	2005	30	33.6	13	30.5	~0	...
	2007	26	39.1	* 12	* 35.5	~0	69.2
	2010	32	40.6	...	...	...	...
	2011	32	40.9	21	26.2	...	...
	2015	34	41.7	...	...	3	26.2
	2016	36	41.4	...	...	3	30.7
Tokelau Tokélaou	2003	~0	5.8	~0	7.1	...	...
	2016	~0	11.9	...	...	...	...
Tonga Tonga	2000	1	22.1	1	14.6	* ~0	* 5.1
	2002	1	22.1	1	14.4	...	...
	2005	1	20.3	...	...	...	...
	2010	1	24.9	1	14.9	...	...
	2014	1	21.9	1	13.4	...	...
Trinidad and Tobago Trinité-et-Tobago	2004	* 8	* 17.5	...	...	2	9.7
	*2005	8	16.5	...	...	...	...
	*2009	7	17.6	...	...	...	...
Tunisia Tunisie	2005	59	20.0	72	17.2	17	19.6
	2010	60	17.1	88	13.3	21	17.4
	2011	59	17.4	85	13.6	22	16.8
	2012	61	17.1	...	...	22	15.9
	2015	71	15.8	...	...	...	...
	2016	70	16.2	...	...	...	...
Turkey Turquie	2005	...	...	...	...	82	25.7
	2010	...	...	...	...	105	33.5
	2015	295	18.4	594	18.5	149	40.7
Turkmenistan Turkménistan	2014	...	...	...	...	8	5.4
Turks and Caicos Islands Îles Turques-et-Caïques	2003	~0	15.2	~0	8.7	...	...
	2014	~0	9.3	~0	8.8	...	...
	2015	...	...	~0	9.6	...	...
Tuvalu Tuvalu	2004	~0	19.2	...	...	...	...
	2015	~0	12.7	~0	6.2	...	...
Uganda Ouganda	2004	147	50.1	40	18.5	4	21.2
	2005	140	51.7	* 40	...	...	...
	2007	152	49.6	56	18.5	...	...
	2010	172	48.6	66	...	5	22.6
	2011	170	47.8	...	...	6	24.5
	2014	191	...	64	...	...	...
	2015	193	42.9	...	...	...	...
	2016	203	42.7	...	...	...	...

8 Teaching staff at the primary, secondary and tertiary levels *(continued)*

Number of teachers and Pupil teacher ratio

Personnel enseignant au niveau primaire, secondaire et supérieur *(suite)*

Nombre d'enseignants et ratio élèves/enseignant par niveau d'enseignement

Region, country or area Région, pays ou zone	Year & Année &	Primary education Enseignant primaire Total Totale ('000)	Primary education Enseignant primaire Pupil-teacher ratio Ratio élèves/ enseignant	Secondary education Enseignant secondaire Total Totale ('000)	Secondary education Enseignant secondaire Pupil-teacher ratio Ratio élèves/ enseignant	Tertiary education Enseignant supérieur Total Totale ('000)	Tertiary education Enseignant supérieur Pupil-teacher ratio Ratio élèves/ enseignant
Ukraine	2000	105	19.9	389	13.4	* 146	* 12.4
Ukraine	2005	104	18.7	...	...	187	13.9
	2010	98	15.7	...	...	201	13.1
	2014	100	16.9	...	...	195	11.0
	2015	...	...	340	7.0	169	10.5
	2016	125	12.8	331	7.0	163	10.4
United Arab Emirates	2005	17	15.2	...	...	...	...
Émirats arabes unis	2009	20	15.6	...	...	5	18.6
	2010	19	16.8	...	...	...	...
	2015	20	23.6	...	...	9	17.8
	2016	19	24.5	46	9.5	9	17.0
United Kingdom	2005	265	17.5	388	14.9	122	18.7
Royaume-Uni	2008	244	18.3	* 375	* 14.3	134	17.4
	2010	252	17.5	...	...	140	17.7
	2014	272	17.4	414	15.8	152	15.5
	2015	...	...	412	15.5	149	15.7
United Rep. of Tanzania	2005	135	55.9	...	...	3	* 18.8
Rép.-Unie de Tanzanie	2010	166	50.8	...	...	4	18.9
	2012	181	45.6	80	26.4	5	34.4
	2014	191	43.1	...	...	...	...
United States of America	2005	1 731	14.1	1 635	14.9	1 208	14.3
États-Unis d'Amérique	2010	1 795	13.6	1 758	13.8	1 439	14.2
	2015	1 714	14.5	1 661	14.7	1 581	12.4
United States Virgin Islands Îles Vierges américaines	2007	...	...	...	...	~0	...
Uruguay	2005	18	20.2	22	14.6	12	9.3
Uruguay	2010	25	13.8	25	11.3	17	8.0
	2015	27	11.8	...	...	21	7.1
Uzbekistan	2005	119	19.9	339	13.3	20	13.3
Ouzbékistan	2010	111	17.8	342	13.0	23	12.5
	2015	112	19.0	371	10.7	24	10.7
	2017	113	21.2	377	10.3	24	11.7
Vanuatu	2001	2	23.7	1	15.1	~0	25.0
Vanuatu	2002	2	23.2	...	...	* ~0	* 24.9
	2004	2	20.0	...	...	...	...
	2010	2	21.7	...	...	...	...
	2015	2	26.6	1	20.6	...	...
Venezuela (Boliv. Rep. of)	*2004	...	...	...	...	82	12.8
Venezuela (Rép. boliv. du)	*2009	...	...	...	...	165	12.9
Viet Nam	2005	361	21.6	...	...	48	28.4
Viet Nam	2010	348	19.9	...	...	70	29.0
	2015	392	19.2	...	...	91	27.1
	2016	397	19.6	...	...	94	24.6
Yemen	*2005	...	...	...	...	7	29.2
Yémen	2007	...	...	...	...	7	32.2
	2010	111	30.8	...	...	...	...
	*2012	122	30.3	...	...	...	...
	2016	145	26.9	...	...	...	...
Zambia	*2005	46	56.5	...	...	...	...
Zambie	*2010	55	53.0	...	...	...	...
	*2013	64	47.9	...	...	...	...
Zimbabwe	2003	61	38.6	34	22.3	...	...
Zimbabwe	2010	...	...	...	...	4	23.2
	2013	73	36.4	43	22.5	6	17.0
	2015	...	...	...	...	8	17.9

Source:

United Nations Educational, Scientific and Cultural Organization (UNESCO), Montreal, the UNESCO Institute for Statistics (UIS) statistics database, last accessed May 2018.

& Data relate to the calendar year in which the academic year ends.

1 For statistical purposes, the data for China do not include those for the Hong Kong Special Administrative Region (Hong Kong SAR) and Macao Special Administrative Region (Macao SAR).

Source:

Organisation des Nations Unies pour l'éducation, la science et la culture (UNESCO), Montréal, base de données statistiques de l'Institut de statistique (ISU) de l'UNESCO, dernier accès mai 2018.

& Les données se réfèrent à l'année civile durant laquelle l'année scolaire se termine.

1 Pour la présentation des statistiques, les données pour la Chine ne comprennent pas la Région Administrative Spéciale de Hong Kong (Hong Kong RAS) et la Région Administrative Spéciale de Macao (Macao RAS).

9 Public expenditure on education

By expenditure type, level of education, total government expenditure and GDP

Dépenses publiques afférentes à l'éducation

Par type de dépenses, niveau de scolarité, dépenses publiques totales et PIB

Country or area Pays ou zone	Year Année	Percentage of total expenditure in public institutions / Pourcentage des dépenses publiques totales en faveur de l'éducation: Current expenditure Dépenses courantes	Staff Compensation Rémunération du personnel	Capital expenditure Dépenses en Capital	Percentage of government expenditure on education by level / Pourcentage des dépenses publiques selon le niveau d'enseignement: Pre-primary Préprimaire	Primary Primaire	Secondary Secondaire	Tertiary Tertiaire	As % of Govt. Expenditure En % des dépenses du gouvt.	As % of GDP En % du PIB
Afghanistan	2010	9.3	72.4	18.3	...	62.1	26.7	9.0	17.1	3.5
Afghanistan	2015	9.0	71.4	19.6	...	56.7	24.4	16.0	12.5	3.2
Albania	2005	...	...	...	...	...	...	...	11.4	3.2
Albanie	2007	...	...	...	...	...	...	...	11.2	3.3
	2015	12.5	79.5	8.1	...	56.8	21.6	21.2	11.3	3.5
	2017	...	...	...	...	60.2	18.6	19.5	...	...
Algeria Algérie	2008	...	...	...	...	...	...	27.0	11.4	4.3
Andorra	2005	...	...	...	16.9	24.1	20.6	3.9	...	1.6
Andorre	2010	30.9	36.7	1.7	14.6	28.9	20.9	3.9	...	3.1
	2016	64.1	35.1	0.8	12.7	21.5	24.0	5.9	9.7	3.3
Angola	2005	...	...	...	...	36.5	55.2	8.3	8.0	2.8
Angola	2006	...	...	24.3	13.5	31.4	42.4	8.7	7.5	2.9
	2010	...	...	...	...	...	...	...	8.7	3.5
Anguilla	2005	6.7	80.9	...	1.9	28.5	51.3	18.3	...	...
Anguilla	2008	* 9.8	* 69.4	* 20.8	1.6	39.4	56.1	2.8	...	2.8
Antigua and Barbuda	2002	25.7	...	3.9	2.1	28.6	35.2	6.7	11.7	3.4
Antigua-et-Barbuda	2009	21.6	73.2	5.2	0.3	41.6	48.4	7.4	6.9	2.5
Argentina	2004	11.6	87.6	0.8	8.3	36.7	37.8	17.2	15.2	3.5
Argentine	2005	...	...	...	7.9	34.2	41.7	16.2	15.8	3.9
	2010	9.9	85.9	4.2	7.4	33.1	39.7	19.9	15.0	5.0
	2015	7.2	82.0	10.8	8.1	30.0	41.3	20.5	14.1	5.9
Armenia	2005	...	...	...	...	...	...	...	13.6	2.7
Arménie	2009	...	...	...	11.3	...	...	9.4	13.5	3.8
	2010	...	...	...	...	...	...	11.7	12.4	3.2
	2016	8.2	82.5	9.3	11.9	20.7	51.1	13.2	10.2	2.8
Aruba	2005	6.1	90.7	3.2	6.8	26.7	26.8	11.5	18.9	4.7
Aruba	2009	5.7	87.0	...	...	...	...	...	21.5	5.9
	2010	...	...	...	...	...	...	...	22.1	6.7
	2015	6.9	93.1	...	5.2	23.8	30.7	25.1	22.9	6.5
Australia	2000	24.7	68.3	7.0	1.2	34.1	38.6	23.4	13.4	4.9
Australie	2005	...	...	...	1.0	34.6	39.7	22.2	13.6	4.9
	2010	...	...	...	1.2	36.8	36.8	22.3	14.3	5.6
	2014	27.0	64.6	8.4	2.9	32.6	32.4	26.5	13.9	5.2
Austria	2005	23.2	72.1	4.7	7.4	19.0	45.9	27.3	10.3	5.2
Autriche	2010	24.9	70.2	4.9	10.3	17.1	44.4	27.7	10.8	5.7
	2014	26.2	68.9	5.0	8.8	16.3	40.4	32.5	10.4	5.4
Azerbaijan	2005	31.6	66.8	1.6	6.9	...	...	6.9	13.2	3.0
Azerbaïdjan	2010	32.6	64.8	2.5	7.1	...	...	14.0	8.7	2.8
	2015	45.9	52.0	2.2	9.5	...	55.7	12.8	7.6	3.0
Bahamas Bahamas	*2000	...	...	...	...	...	...	...	18.9	2.9
Bahrain	2008	...	...	...	...	...	...	...	10.6	2.5
Bahreïn	2012	13.8	82.3	3.8	...	...	...	...	8.3	2.6
	2013	...	...	...	...	32.1	43.4	24.4	7.2	2.5
	2015	...	...	...	...	33.0	44.2	...	7.3	2.7
	2016	...	...	...	...	...	...	...	7.6	2.7
Bangladesh	2004	...	...	...	...	40.0	48.5	11.5	16.0	1.9
Bangladesh	2009	21.2	59.8	19.0	...	44.7	40.2	13.5	14.0	1.9
	2012	4.3	95.2	0.5	...	44.6	39.1	14.7	15.6	2.2
	*2016	...	...	...	...	43.0	38.2	16.9	18.1	2.5

9

Public expenditure on education *(continued)*
By expenditure type, level of education, total government expenditure and GDP

Dépenses publiques afférentes à l'éducation *(suite)*
Par type de dépenses, niveau de scolarité, dépenses publiques totales et PIB

Country or area Pays ou zone	Year Année	Percentage of total expenditure in public institutions / Pourcentage des dépenses publiques totales en faveur de l'éducation: Current expenditure Dépenses courantes	Staff Compensation Rémunération du personnel	Capital expenditure Dépenses en Capital	Percentage of government expenditure on education by level / Pourcentage des dépenses publiques selon le niveau d'enseignement: Pre-primary Préprimaire	Primary Primaire	Secondary Secondaire	Tertiary Tertiaire	As % of Govt. Expenditure En % des dépenses du gouvt.	As % of GDP En % du PIB
Barbados Barbade	2005	16.2	79.9	4.0	* 6.3	* 27.9	31.7	31.6	19.1	5.6
	2008	14.5	78.6	6.9	0.4	36.9	29.4	30.1	15.6	5.1
	2010	10.5	83.4	6.2	…	…	29.6	32.5	18.1	6.1
	2016	50.5	45.3	4.2	…	29.6	39.3	31.1	14.4	5.1
Belarus Bélarus	2005	30.1	65.2	4.8	17.4	…	…	25.5	12.6	5.9
	2010	26.5	62.6	10.9	19.0	…	…	17.1	11.8	5.2
	2011	26.8	65.4	7.8	21.0	…	…	17.3	11.6	4.7
	2016	28.6	67.5	4.0	…	…	…	16.1	10.8	5.0
	2017	…	…	…	…	…	50.2	17.0	…	…
Belgium Belgique	2005	11.7	85.5	2.8	9.6	23.6	43.1	21.7	11.2	5.8
	2010	11.9	84.3	3.8	9.5	23.5	42.5	22.2	12.0	6.4
	2014	13.7	81.5	4.8	10.7	23.2	42.0	22.0	12.0	6.6
Belize Belize	2003	* 18.4	* 62.3	* 19.3	…	…	…	…	16.2	5.2
	2004	…	…	…	0.6	42.6	39.2	10.8	16.8	5.3
	2010	…	…	…	1.5	46.1	41.1	8.7	23.1	6.6
	2015	…	…	…	4.9	32.9	41.2	11.8	21.2	6.7
	2017	…	…	…	4.6	31.8	41.0	10.9	…	7.4
Benin Bénin	2001	15.2	56.8	28.0	* 1.2	* 55.4	* 25.1	18.3	15.3	3.2
	2005	13.3	73.0	13.7	…	* 46.0	* 32.8	21.2	18.8	3.6
	2010	6.2	85.7	8.2	2.6	52.8	28.0	15.6	26.1	5.0
	2015	22.2	69.5	8.3	4.3	49.8	23.7	22.1	17.5	4.4
Bermuda Bermudes	2005	…	…	…	* 7.0	* 40.7	* 52.3	…	12.1	2.0
	2010	…	…	…	8.9	30.8	45.4	13.5	12.9	2.6
	2015	18.6	79.9	1.5	7.0	30.7	44.3	…	9.0	1.7
	2017	…	…	…	6.5	32.2	44.4	17.0	…	1.5
Bhutan Bhoutan	2005	…	…	…	…	22.3	50.9	14.1	22.8	7.1
	2010	…	…	…	…	29.9	53.9	15.1	11.8	4.0
	2014	…	…	…	…	32.0	55.7	10.3	17.0	5.9
	2015	50.1	35.9	14.0	…	…	41.5	…	25.5	7.4
Bolivia (Plurin. State of) Bolivie (État plurin. de)	2000	…	…	14.5	6.3	* 40.5	* 18.5	28.9	18.7	5.5
	2003	…	…	…	3.3	44.1	24.3	21.6	19.9	6.4
	2009	31.8	68.2	…	2.6	40.5	26.0	29.7	22.6	8.1
	2010	…	…	…	2.8	39.4	26.3	29.9	24.1	7.6
	2014	19.9	63.3	16.8	5.0	41.6	27.1	26.2	16.8	7.3
Botswana Botswana	2005	…	…	…	…	30.0	39.6	27.9	25.8	10.7
	2009	…	…	9.8	…	17.8	32.7	41.5	20.5	9.6
Brazil Brésil	2005	23.6	70.3	6.1	8.2	34.0	38.8	19.0	11.3	4.5
	2010	24.3	68.5	7.2	7.6	31.3	44.7	16.4	14.6	5.6
	2011	20.7	73.2	6.1	8.8	29.3	45.1	16.8	15.3	5.7
	2014	24.1	69.4	6.6	…	26.8	43.1	19.3	15.7	5.9
British Virgin Islands Îles Vierges britanniques	*2004	2.4	90.3	7.4	…	…	…	…	…	…
	2005	0.7	99.3	…	0.1	33.7	31.2	34.2	…	…
	2007	15.1	77.8	7.1	0.1	28.4	37.7	33.1	…	3.7
	2010	…	…	…	0.1	34.1	34.0	…	…	4.4
	2015	…	…	…	~0.0	16.6	19.0	22.1	…	6.3
Brunei Darussalam Brunéi Darussalam	2000	…	…	…	…	…	…	…	8.9	3.7
	2010	…	…	…	…	28.5	46.8	24.4	5.3	2.0
	2016	30.6	66.2	3.2	0.7	19.5	60.8	18.9	11.4	4.4
Bulgaria Bulgarie	2005	26.7	63.2	10.1	16.9	20.3	45.9	16.9	12.1	4.1
	2010	28.4	66.6	5.1	22.5	19.6	43.0	14.8	11.2	3.9
	2013	20.9	71.8	7.3	25.3	19.7	38.9	15.9	11.4	4.1
Burkina Faso Burkina Faso	2005	…	…	…	0.2	71.2	10.3	9.6	19.5	4.4
	2007	8.0	56.7	35.3	0.6	67.0	15.7	15.2	17.9	4.6
	2010	…	…	…	…	60.3	18.0	18.8	17.3	3.9
	2015	…	…	…	0.1	57.9	22.1	13.7	18.0	4.2

9

Public expenditure on education *(continued)*
By expenditure type, level of education, total government expenditure and GDP

Dépenses publiques afférentes à l'éducation *(suite)*
Par type de dépenses, niveau de scolarité, dépenses publiques totales et PIB

		Percentage of total expenditure in public institutions Pourcentage des dépenses publiques totales en faveur de l'éducation			Percentage of government expenditure on education by level Pourcentage des dépenses publiques selon le niveau d'enseignement					
Country or area Pays ou zone	**Year Année**	**Current expenditure Dépenses courantes**	**Staff Compensation Rémunération du personnel**	**Capital expenditure Dépenses en Capital**	**Pre-primary Préprimaire**	**Primary Primaire**	**Secondary Secondaire**	**Tertiary Tertiaire**	**As % of Govt. Expenditure En % des dépenses du gouvt.**	**As % of GDP En % du PIB**
Burundi Burundi	2004	15.7	57.8	26.6	~0.0	50.7	29.5	18.3	9.2	3.7
	2005	...	...	...	...	51.6	33.1	15.3	11.0	3.6
	2010	23.7	68.5	7.9	~0.0	45.4	27.9	18.0	16.6	6.8
	2012	20.5	77.6	1.9	~0.0	44.0	24.2	20.6	16.4	5.8
	2013	...	...	...	~0.0	45.4	26.8	24.2	17.2	5.4
Cabo Verde Cabo Verde	2002	...	...	...	...	43.8	29.8	17.5	19.8	7.9
	2004	3.3	80.0	16.7	...	...	...	...	20.8	7.5
	*2005	2.1	82.4	16.7	...	...	...	...	...	...
	2008	...	...	15.9	0.3	36.3	36.6	11.3	18.2	5.5
	2009	...	...	...	...	44.1	33.0	14.0	15.9	5.3
	2010	15.6	77.1	7.3	...	...	...	...	14.2	5.6
	2016	12.2	82.8	4.9	1.1	39.1	40.8	17.6	17.9	5.4
	2017	...	...	...	1.0	38.1	39.9	17.2	...	...
Cambodia Cambodge	2001	...	...	...	1.1	74.4	11.2	...	11.4	1.7
	2002	...	...	...	1.0	64.6	...	...	10.1	1.7
	2004	...	...	...	...	...	...	...	12.4	1.7
	2010	...	...	...	1.7	50.0	42.5	5.8	7.7	1.5
	2012	57.3	42.7	...	2.0	49.2	44.1	...	7.5	1.6
	2013	...	...	...	2.7	49.7	41.5	6.1	9.9	2.0
	2014	...	...	0.5	2.6	48.5	44.1	...	9.1	1.9
Cameroon Cameroun	2005	...	...	...	...	35.1	52.0	12.6	21.4	2.9
	2010	6.5	80.2	13.4	3.9	34.2	52.7	9.0	18.8	3.0
	2012	...	...	...	3.5	36.2	52.6	7.8	15.2	2.7
	2013	10.7	75.7	13.6	4.0	33.9	...	10.2	13.8	2.8
Canada Canada	2000	26.0	70.5	3.6	3.9	...	...	...	13.0	5.4
	2005	25.4	70.0	4.6	...	...	...	...	12.2	4.8
	2010	24.5	65.8	9.7	...	...	...	35.4	12.3	5.4
	2011	24.1	65.5	10.4	...	...	26.4	35.6	12.2	5.3
	2013	23.4	68.8	7.8	...	...	...	...	...	...
Cayman Islands Îles Caïmanes	2005	...	...	...	1.2	49.3	49.5	...	...	...
	2006	2.4	97.6	...	...	46.0	54.0	...	...	...
Central African Republic République centrafricaine	2005	...	79.2	2.2	...	...	...	...	9.7	1.6
	2008	13.5	84.2	2.3	...	...	25.9	17.5	7.9	1.3
	2010	...	...	1.1	2.3	53.3	24.0	20.5	6.5	1.2
	2011	...	...	...	...	...	...	27.3	7.8	1.2
Chad Tchad	2005	...	...	...	...	45.8	35.5	18.7	14.7	1.7
	2010	...	...	31.3	0.4	51.6	27.4	19.8	8.1	2.0
	2011	...	...	20.8	0.3	40.7	34.9	16.3	10.1	2.3
	2012	2.6	75.5	21.9	...	46.7	20.7	30.3	9.2	2.2
	2013	...	...	...	...	...	24.7	31.7	12.5	2.9
Chile Chili	2005	17.5	78.1	4.4	9.6	37.4	39.0	14.0	16.2	3.3
	2009	18.1	78.9	3.0	12.8	36.4	35.2	15.6	17.0	4.2
	2010	...	...	...	13.4	31.7	32.5	22.3	17.8	4.2
	2015	...	...	...	13.2	25.6	29.4	25.7	19.6	4.9
China, Hong Kong SAR Chine, RAS de Hong Kong	2005	...	...	...	2.3	23.1	33.8	28.4	22.5	4.1
	2010	...	...	12.7	3.8	20.9	35.5	27.8	19.9	3.5
	2012	...	...	18.2	3.9	18.7	33.6	32.8	18.6	3.5
	2016	...	...	...	4.8	21.3	33.0	30.4	18.1	3.3
	2017	...	...	...	5.3	21.7	32.6	28.6	...	3.3
China, Macao SAR Chine, RAS de Macao	2000	...	...	...	* 7.6	* 24.8	* 25.0	28.4	...	3.3
	2003	...	...	...	...	* 24.8	...	41.1	11.7	2.8
	2005	...	...	...	...	...	...	45.6	10.5	2.3
	2010	19.5	39.0	41.5	...	...	...	48.4	15.4	2.6
	2015	31.7	59.1	9.2	...	...	57.8	42.2	13.4	3.0

9 Public expenditure on education *(continued)*

By expenditure type, level of education, total government expenditure and GDP

Dépenses publiques afférentes à l'éducation *(suite)*

Par type de dépenses, niveau de scolarité, dépenses publiques totales et PIB

Country or area Pays ou zone	Year Année	Percentage of total expenditure in public institutions / Pourcentage des dépenses publiques totales en faveur de l'éducation: Current expenditure Dépenses courantes	Staff Compensation Rémunération du personnel	Capital expenditure Dépenses en Capital	Percentage of government expenditure on education by level / Pourcentage des dépenses publiques selon le niveau d'enseignement: Pre-primary Préprimaire	Primary Primaire	Secondary Secondaire	Tertiary Tertiaire	As % of Govt. Expenditure En % des dépenses du gouvt.	As % of GDP En % du PIB
Colombia	2004	23.4	71.0	5.7	* 2.7	* 48.3	* 35.7	13.3	15.4	4.1
Colombie	2005	...	...	...	2.6	47.4	36.1	13.8	15.5	4.0
	2010	6.8	71.0	22.3	5.8	35.9	34.8	22.1	16.4	4.8
	2016	5.4	72.1	22.5	5.8	36.0	34.7	23.0	16.0	4.5
	2017	...	...	...	5.8	36.0	34.7	23.0	...	...
Comoros	2002	...	...	...	* 0.4	* 45.2	* 40.1	* 7.7	15.8	3.9
Comores	2008	...	...	...	...	61.7	23.7	14.6	29.2	7.7
	2015	4.8	95.2	...	7.1	54.6	27.7	10.4	15.3	4.3
Congo	2005	...	...	...	* 2.9	* 27.3	* 41.2	* 25.9	7.6	1.8
Congo	2010	...	...	...	4.6	31.0	53.3	10.9	29.0	6.2
Cook Islands	2000	...	...	...	7.1	50.6	36.5	...	6.7	...
Îles Cook	2013	...	...	...	11.4	40.4	40.6	7.6	8.8	3.0
	2014	15.7	84.3	...	...	...	...	9.2	11.6	3.9
	2016	34.1	63.3	2.6	...	...	...	11.5	...	4.7
Costa Rica	2004	...	...	...	7.9	45.5	27.8	18.8	20.4	4.9
Costa Rica	2010	...	...	...	5.4	41.9	31.5	18.4	22.9	6.6
	2016	14.8	81.2	4.0	5.8	34.0	32.0	23.0	23.4	7.1
	2017	...	...	...	5.7	33.0	31.1	23.9	...	...
Côte d'Ivoire	2000	...	...	...	* ~0.0	* 41.6	* 32.7	22.0	20.8	3.7
Côte d'Ivoire	2001	...	...	...	...	* 42.2	...	19.4	23.2	3.7
	2005	...	...	...	...	...	...	20.0	21.8	4.1
	2010	21.8	71.2	7.0	2.0	42.7	33.1	22.2	22.8	4.6
	*2015	21.4	72.7	5.9	3.0	41.4	34.2	21.4	21.2	4.8
Croatia	2004	30.0	65.6	4.4	9.2	...	...	18.1	8.1	3.8
Croatie	2010	23.0	70.6	6.4	13.8	...	...	18.3	9.0	4.3
	2011	21.4	74.4	4.3	14.1	...	...	22.2	8.5	4.2
	2013	27.3	69.4	3.2	...	...	...	21.9	9.5	4.6
	2014	28.3	72.8	3.8	...	...	...	...	...	...
Cuba	2005	34.3	52.6	13.2	8.3	30.3	37.7	22.1	...	10.6
Cuba	2007	46.7	50.2	3.1	8.1	30.1	36.0	25.1	...	11.9
	2010	40.5	58.6	0.9	6.8	29.0	29.1	...	...	12.8
Curaçao										
Curaçao	2013	13.9	86.1	...	9.2	27.5	33.9	5.3	...	4.9
Cyprus	2005	9.8	76.9	13.4	4.9	27.3	44.9	22.9	15.8	6.2
Chypre	2010	11.5	77.5	11.0	5.5	31.0	43.0	20.5	15.7	6.6
	2014	12.2	85.0	2.8	5.8	32.8	43.8	17.6	15.5	6.1
Czechia	2005	34.4	56.0	9.7	9.8	14.5	51.3	21.0	9.3	3.9
Tchéquie	2010	38.4	51.5	10.1	11.4	16.2	45.7	22.5	9.5	4.1
	2014	37.3	51.5	11.1	13.6	18.6	43.5	20.0	9.5	4.0
Dem. Rep. of the	2010	2.6	87.8	9.6	0.6	33.3	33.7	24.0	9.6	1.6
Congo	2013	1.7	81.4	16.9	1.0	61.6	14.4	22.0	17.8	2.2
Rép. dém. du										
Congo	2015	...	...	...	...	...	...	23.8	12.5	2.3
Denmark	2005	20.7	74.1	5.3	8.6	23.3	36.3	28.7	15.8	8.1
Danemark	2010	18.0	74.9	7.1	11.5	23.7	34.5	27.3	15.1	8.6
	2013	20.1	73.5	6.3	13.9	24.9	32.4	26.9	15.2	8.5
	2014	19.9	73.7	6.4	...	27.2	40.0	30.7	13.8	7.6
Djibouti	2005	...	42.2	2.7	...	...	...	...	22.7	8.4
Djibouti	2007	...	38.8	4.6	...	19.0	...	...	22.5	8.4
	2010	...	...	...	...	34.1	37.3	16.5	12.3	4.5
Dominica	2012	...	100.0	...	...	...	...	...	...	...
Dominique	2015	...	...	...	1.9	45.8	43.4	8.9	10.5	3.4
Dominican	2002	16.6	76.7	6.7	2.1	62.8	...	...	12.1	2.0
Republic	*2003	...	...	...	...	...	...	...	9.7	1.9
République	2004	24.1	72.6	3.4	...	...	...	...	...	...
dominicaine	2007	15.5	66.9	17.6	4.2	58.7	18.0	14.5	12.6	2.0

9

Public expenditure on education *(continued)*
By expenditure type, level of education, total government expenditure and GDP

Dépenses publiques afférentes à l'éducation *(suite)*
Par type de dépenses, niveau de scolarité, dépenses publiques totales et PIB

Country or area Pays ou zone	Year Année	Percentage of total expenditure in public institutions / Pourcentage des dépenses publiques totales en faveur de l'éducation: Current expenditure Dépenses courantes	Staff Compensation Rémunération du personnel	Capital expenditure Dépenses en Capital	Percentage of government expenditure on education by level / Pourcentage des dépenses publiques selon le niveau d'enseignement: Pre-primary Préprimaire	Primary Primaire	Secondary Secondaire	Tertiary Tertiaire	As % of Govt. Expenditure En % des dépenses du gouvt.	As % of GDP En % du PIB
Ecuador	2000	16.7	78.1	5.2	...	38.3	34.6	5.2	5.0	1.2
Équateur	2010	...	...	...	21.4	32.4	10.4	35.8	13.0	4.5
	2015	...	...	...	21.1	23.3	12.1	43.5	12.8	5.0
Egypt	2005	...	...	...	...	...	...	...	14.4	4.8
Égypte	2008	...	...	...	...	...	...	...	10.5	3.8
El Salvador	2005	27.3	66.9	5.8	* 8.5	* 51.0	* 29.1	* 11.1	* 14.7	* 2.7
El Salvador	2008	37.8	51.7	10.5	9.1	38.0	22.0	...	19.4	3.7
	2010	...	...	...	7.9	42.7	30.1	12.2	16.2	3.5
	2016	25.0	68.0	7.0	9.2	47.2	35.3	8.0	16.1	3.5
Eritrea	2002	8.6	31.0	60.4	...	26.0	35.4	14.9	5.6	3.5
Érythrée	2004	...	...	41.7	...	23.1	21.1	31.9	5.7	3.1
	2006	22.7	57.7	19.6	...	...	...	...	5.2	2.1
Estonia	2002	28.8	56.3	15.0	5.2	28.0	40.9	19.7	15.3	5.5
Estonie	2004	...	...	9.5	6.4	25.8	46.3	17.4	14.5	4.9
	2005	...	...	...	7.4	25.3	43.7	18.9	14.5	4.8
	2010	...	...	...	7.8	24.6	40.1	21.7	13.6	5.5
	2013	28.9	57.7	13.4	7.3	30.7	29.4	28.2	12.6	4.8
	2014	26.7	64.0	9.3	...	24.6	26.1	26.2	14.3	5.5
Eswatini	2005	...	...	...	~0.0	39.9	34.9	23.9	20.9	6.5
Eswatini	2010	...	...	...	0.2	47.2	35.5	16.6	18.3	6.1
	2014	36.2	59.3	4.5	1.1	50.8	34.1	13.3	24.9	7.1
Ethiopia	*2002	...	...	...	...	...	...	...	16.2	3.6
Éthiopie	2010	21.0	44.8	34.1	~0.0	28.4	25.0	43.9	26.3	4.5
	2013	19.7	44.2	36.1	0.4	24.0	29.3	42.7	27.0	4.5
Fiji	2004	...	...	...	0.2	39.1	32.6	15.9	22.0	6.2
Fidji	2005	...	...	...	...	...	...	...	18.8	5.1
	2009	...	...	...	...	...	...	...	15.4	4.5
	2011	...	...	...	0.4	44.4	15.9	13.0	14.9	4.2
	2013	1.2	98.7	0.1	...	38.6	...	22.6	14.0	3.9
Finland	2005	32.1	60.9	7.0	5.5	20.8	41.9	31.8	12.2	6.0
Finlande	2010	33.6	60.3	6.1	5.8	19.9	42.4	31.8	11.9	6.5
	2014	34.0	59.7	6.3	10.7	19.1	37.5	27.9	12.3	7.2
France	2005	15.6	74.5	9.9	11.4	20.2	47.1	21.1	10.4	5.5
France	2010	17.4	73.2	9.4	11.6	20.4	45.0	22.6	10.1	5.7
	2014	17.0	74.8	8.2	12.7	20.6	43.7	22.6	9.7	5.5
Gabon	*2000	...	...	...	...	...	...	...	17.7	3.8
Gabon	2010	...	...	...	3.6	29.6	28.3	37.8	13.3	3.1
	2014	...	45.5	...	3.8	29.2	28.9	37.8	11.2	2.7
Gambia	2005	...	...	...	...	61.4	23.1	14.3	5.3	1.1
Gambie	2010	10.8	46.4	42.8	...	65.3	23.4	9.9	17.6	4.2
	2012	7.4	50.4	42.2	...	60.0	31.4	7.4	13.8	4.1
	2013	...	...	...	...	51.8	35.5	10.7	10.3	2.8
Georgia	2005	...	...	...	...	...	...	...	11.2	2.5
Géorgie	2008	...	...	...	10.7	36.0	37.0	11.6	8.9	2.9
	*2009	...	...	...	12.3	...	...	...	9.0	3.2
	2012	...	...	...	14.4	34.3	32.1	19.2	6.7	2.0
	2016	...	...	...	...	...	...	11.1	12.7	3.8
Germany	2010	19.8	70.6	9.6	9.1	13.5	45.5	27.2	10.4	4.9
Allemagne	2014	20.0	72.9	7.1	8.9	12.8	42.0	26.6	11.1	4.9
Ghana	2005	22.3	63.0	14.7	5.9	39.5	32.5	22.1	23.4	7.4
Ghana	2010	14.3	68.8	16.9	6.1	30.9	37.1	25.9	20.7	5.5
	2014	18.2	73.3	8.6	7.3	21.7	37.0	18.3	21.0	6.2
Gibraltar Gibraltar	2016	12.2	69.5	18.3	...	...	...	...	...	...
Greece Grèce	2005	11.0	67.3	21.7	...	...	33.9	36.1	8.7	4.0

Public expenditure on education *(continued)*
By expenditure type, level of education, total government expenditure and GDP

Dépenses publiques afférentes à l'éducation *(suite)*
Par type de dépenses, niveau de scolarité, dépenses publiques totales et PIB

Country or area Pays ou zone	Year Année	Percentage of total expenditure in public institutions / Pourcentage des dépenses publiques totales en faveur de l'éducation: Current expenditure Dépenses courantes	Staff Compensation Rémunération du personnel	Capital expenditure Dépenses en Capital	Percentage of government expenditure on education by level / Pourcentage des dépenses publiques selon le niveau d'enseignement: Pre-primary Préprimaire	Primary Primaire	Secondary Secondaire	Tertiary Tertiaire	As % of Govt. Expenditure En % des dépenses du gouvt.	As % of GDP En % du PIB
Grenada	2003	8.3	82.2	9.5	5.7	36.4	35.8	9.8	10.8	3.9
Grenade	2016	...	...	...	1.9	56.8	23.4	9.6	42.8	10.3
Guatemala	2008	9.9	65.2	11.5	10.0	59.8	12.8	10.8	23.3	3.2
Guatemala	2010	...	...	0.1	11.2	55.6	14.8	11.3	19.3	2.8
	2016	25.0	72.4	2.6	12.1	55.5	13.3	14.6	23.4	2.8
Guinea	2005	...	...	...	...	...	...	30.6	10.9	1.8
Guinée	2010	...	...	7.7	...	38.9	24.9	36.2	12.4	2.5
	2014	12.6	75.0	12.4	^ 0.1	38.9	21.9	39.1	12.0	2.4
Guinea-Bissau	2010	12.5	61.5	26.0	0.7	46.7	46.7	5.0	9.1	1.9
Guinée-Bissau	2013	0.9	48.3	50.8	0.8	64.4	30.4	3.9	16.2	2.1
Guyana	2004	37.6	51.8	10.6	11.6	32.1	26.5	6.2	11.1	5.5
Guyana	2005	23.1	62.3	14.6	...	...	...	...	13.8	8.1
	2010	22.8	68.4	8.7	11.5	29.1	33.4	5.3	12.0	3.6
	2012	22.5	62.9	14.6	11.6	30.6	33.3	5.1	10.3	3.2
Honduras										
Honduras	2013	15.6	79.7	4.7	7.3	48.9	25.3	18.5	19.9	5.9
Hungary	2005	21.0	71.6	7.4	14.2	20.1	40.4	18.9	10.8	5.3
Hongrie	2010	27.1	62.5	10.4	14.4	17.8	40.3	20.1	9.7	4.8
	2013	31.6	63.7	4.7	15.5	20.5	34.5	21.3	8.6	4.2
	2014	25.1	66.3	8.7	...	12.5	42.8	16.4	9.5	4.6
Iceland	2005	23.6	67.9	8.5	6.7	35.0	33.6	19.1	17.8	7.4
Islande	2010	20.8	72.6	6.6	9.6	32.4	31.2	21.5	14.6	7.2
	2013	32.1	62.7	5.3	11.5	28.6	27.9	19.4	17.7	7.8
India	2005	9.0	86.2	4.8	1.3	35.6	42.9	19.6	11.2	3.2
Inde	2010	...	...	...	1.1	25.2	37.0	36.1	11.8	3.4
	2013	...	...	...	1.6	28.4	41.4	28.5	14.1	3.8
Indonesia	*2005	...	...	...	...	...	...	...	15.1	2.7
Indonésie	2010	33.6	54.5	11.9	0.7	44.4	24.3	16.1	16.7	2.8
	2014	25.0	63.3	11.7	1.8	43.7	26.8	15.1	17.7	3.3
	2015	24.1	64.1	11.9	...	42.6	27.0	15.8	20.6	3.6
Iran (Islamic Republic of)	2002	...	...	8.2	0.9	25.9	36.3	18.5	26.3	4.5
	2005	...	...	...	1.0	22.4	34.6	15.4	22.3	4.1
Iran (Rép. islamique d')	2010	...	...	...	1.0	24.7	49.2	21.4	18.8	3.7
	2016	20.8	75.1	4.1	0.3	28.9	36.5	29.8	19.3	3.4
Ireland	2005	17.4	74.2	8.4	0.1	33.6	34.8	23.3	13.6	4.5
Irlande	2010	19.7	71.6	8.7	1.6	35.3	33.8	22.2	9.3	6.0
	2014	20.9	72.9	6.2	2.0	36.4	33.3	20.8	13.0	4.9
Israel	2005	25.1	68.8	6.1	10.7	37.5	28.9	16.6	12.8	5.8
Israël	2010	18.7	72.9	8.4	11.0	41.2	25.7	16.9	13.7	5.5
	2014	15.8	75.1	9.1	12.3	38.1	29.1	15.3	14.3	5.7
Italy	2005	20.9	71.9	7.2	10.3	24.6	46.5	17.2	9.0	4.2
Italie	2010	20.5	74.7	4.8	10.0	25.0	42.9	18.8	8.7	4.4
	2014	22.8	72.4	4.8	11.2	24.5	42.4	19.6	8.0	4.1
Jamaica	2004	7.5	88.1	4.5	5.6	32.6	41.9	18.8	11.7	3.9
Jamaïque	2005	...	...	...	4.9	* 34.2	* 38.0	22.1	14.3	4.6
	2008	4.9	85.6	9.4	5.5	30.2	42.6	15.7	19.1	6.2
	2009	7.0	93.0	...	8.2	33.2	37.1	20.3	17.6	6.2
	2010	...	...	...	4.0	36.3	36.6	21.8	16.1	6.4
	2016	18.2	79.1	2.7	3.8	35.9	38.9	18.2	19.1	5.3
	2017	...	...	...	3.8	35.9	38.9	18.2	...	5.4
Japan	2005	20.2	70.8	9.1	2.7	35.7	38.4	17.3	10.3	3.4
Japon	2010	20.3	66.4	13.3	2.7	34.9	36.8	20.1	9.4	3.6
	2014	21.3	64.8	13.9	2.8	33.1	37.8	20.8	9.2	3.6
Jordan										
Jordanie	2016	14.0	77.9	8.1	0.5	42.5	37.0	19.9	13.5	3.9

Country or area Pays ou zone	Year Année	Percentage of total expenditure in public institutions / Pourcentage des dépenses publiques totales en faveur de l'éducation: Current expenditure Dépenses courantes	Staff Compensation Rémunération du personnel	Capital expenditure Dépenses en Capital	Percentage of government expenditure on education by level / Pourcentage des dépenses publiques selon le niveau d'enseignement: Pre-primary Préprimaire	Primary Primaire	Secondary Secondaire	Tertiary Tertiaire	As % of Govt. Expenditure En % des dépenses du gouvt.	As % of GDP En % du PIB
Kazakhstan	2005	40.6	53.2	6.2	3.8	…	…	12.3	10.2	2.3
Kazakhstan	2009	34.2	56.8	9.0	6.8	…	…	13.1	13.0	3.1
	2010	32.8	57.8	9.4	…	…	…	…	…	…
	2016	33.6	62.3	4.1	11.8	0.7	68.6	11.6	13.9	3.0
Kenya	2004	…	…	…	1.6	62.1	23.4	12.9	26.7	6.8
Kenya	2005	…	…	…	…	…	…	…	27.5	7.3
	2006	…	…	…	0.1	54.1	21.7	15.4	25.1	7.0
	2010	…	…	…	…	…	…	…	20.6	5.5
	2015	31.6	60.9	7.5	1.8	36.3	41.8	13.1	16.7	5.3
Kiribati										
Kiribati	2001	…	…	…	…	34.3	…	…	11.5	12.0
Kuwait	2005	17.4	74.9	7.7	9.8	19.8	36.2	32.6	13.9	4.7
Koweït	*2006	…	…	…	9.6	20.4	36.2	32.6	13.4	3.8
Kyrgyzstan	2005	28.4	66.2	5.4	6.2	…	…	19.2	16.5	4.9
Kirghizistan	2010	29.1	64.5	6.5	8.1	…	…	15.5	15.7	5.8
	2014	17.6	69.1	13.3	10.7	…	…	4.6	16.1	5.5
	2015	16.2	68.1	15.7	…	…	…	…	16.3	6.0
Lao People's Dem.	2002	…	…	…	1.9	45.0	19.0	12.6	16.2	2.8
Rep.	2005	…	…	…	1.6	62.5	…	…	13.7	2.4
Rép. dém.	2010	16.7	65.0	18.3	6.8	46.5	29.9	16.2	7.3	1.7
populaire lao	2014	12.4	72.6	15.0	6.6	40.6	38.6	13.8	12.2	2.9
Latvia	2004	22.0	69.7	8.4	13.0	16.3	56.4	13.4	14.5	4.9
Lettonie	2010	21.6	65.7	12.7	16.8	28.5	38.4	15.9	11.8	5.1
	2014	24.1	58.0	17.9	16.2	30.0	31.2	21.3	14.0	5.3
Lebanon	2005	1.6	94.7	3.7	…	…	…	28.8	8.4	2.7
Liban	2010	0.1	88.0	11.9	…	…	…	27.2	5.5	1.6
	2011	0.1	86.8	13.1	…	…	…	26.5	5.7	1.6
	2013	2.4	97.6	…	…	…	17.1	28.7	8.6	2.5
Lesotho	2001	…	…	8.7	…	53.2	23.8	18.6	23.8	9.4
Lesotho	2005	…	…	…	…	* 43.0	* 18.3	* 36.4	32.4	12.1
	2008	…	…	* 1.7	0.1	36.0	20.5	36.4	24.7	11.4
Liberia	2008	47.4	41.4	11.2	…	…	…	…	7.3	3.2
Libéria	2012	…	…	…	…	30.7	34.5	* 31.6	8.1	2.8
Liechtenstein	2004	…	…	…	6.5	29.0	42.6	13.9	…	2.4
Liechtenstein	2007	19.3	80.7	…	6.9	30.6	47.2	9.1	…	1.9
	2008	30.2	69.8	…	7.3	31.1	52.4	…	…	2.0
	2010	18.9	68.4	12.6	…	…	…	…	…	…
	2011	20.7	73.9	5.4	7.1	38.6	47.4	…	…	2.6
Lithuania	2005	20.1	73.0	6.8	12.1	14.9	50.6	21.0	14.6	4.9
Lituanie	2010	19.5	72.9	7.6	12.9	16.7	44.9	23.6	12.9	5.3
	2014	20.7	65.3	14.0	11.2	15.2	37.7	29.6	13.2	4.5
Luxembourg	2001	11.2	71.3	17.5	…	…	…	…	9.3	3.6
Luxembourg	2014	13.9	74.3	11.8	14.3	30.8	42.2	12.6	9.6	4.0
Madagascar	2005	* 24.4	* 43.8	31.8	…	57.3	18.9	10.1	18.0	3.8
Madagascar	2008	31.3	58.7	10.0	0.4	53.6	22.1	15.4	16.3	2.9
	2009	…	…	…	0.3	52.3	18.2	15.4	22.6	3.2
	2012	…	…	* 4.6	0.2	47.4	19.3	15.2	20.3	2.7
	2013	29.6	67.4	3.1	…	…	…	…	14.0	2.1
Malawi	2001	…	…	…	…	45.2	22.5	15.3	…	4.5
Malawi	2003	…	…	…	…	54.9	21.1	…	16.6	3.2
	2010	…	…	4.9	~0.0	34.8	24.1	29.8	12.5	3.5
	2013	14.5	71.7	13.8	~0.0	36.7	24.4	28.4	20.4	5.4
	2016	…	…	3.1	…	43.9	28.8	23.1	17.2	4.7
Malaysia	2004	30.2	56.8	13.1	1.1	29.6	35.1	33.4	21.0	5.9
Malaisie	2009	15.7	68.8	15.5	1.2	27.7	32.8	35.9	18.5	6.0
	2010	…	…	…	1.2	28.6	33.7	34.5	18.4	5.0
	2016	24.4	67.6	8.1	3.4	33.8	39.4	23.4	20.6	4.8

9 Public expenditure on education *(continued)*
By expenditure type, level of education, total government expenditure and GDP

Dépenses publiques afférentes à l'éducation *(suite)*
Par type de dépenses, niveau de scolarité, dépenses publiques totales et PIB

		Percentage of total expenditure in public institutions Pourcentage des dépenses publiques totales en faveur de l'éducation			Percentage of government expenditure on education by level Pourcentage des dépenses publiques selon le niveau d'enseignement					
Country or area Pays ou zone	Year Année	Current expenditure Dépenses courantes	Staff Compensation Rémunération du personnel	Capital expenditure Dépenses en Capital	Pre-primary Préprimaire	Primary Primaire	Secondary Secondaire	Tertiary Tertiaire	As % of Govt. Expenditure En % des dépenses du gouvt.	As % of GDP En % du PIB
Maldives Maldives	2005	...	...	...	...	54.1	...	...	13.0	5.0
	2010	20.5	78.3	1.2	12.7	42.5	25.0	7.3	12.5	4.1
	2016	38.4	60.8	0.7	10.8	36.4	21.6	20.6	11.1	4.3
Mali Mali	2005	...	...	...	...	...	...	...	16.3	3.5
	2010	40.9	54.1	5.0	0.2	25.3	53.8	20.7	16.5	3.3
	2015	34.4	61.8	3.8	0.3	45.1	33.0	20.8	18.2	3.8
Malta Malte	2004	14.5	79.9	5.6	5.2	21.1	39.8	11.0	10.6	4.5
	2010	17.5	72.4	10.1	7.4	21.6	45.7	22.8	15.7	6.5
	2014	13.2	79.1	7.8	7.2	21.0	33.0	19.3	17.5	7.2
Marshall Islands Îles Marshall	2002	* 22.6	* 75.0	* 2.4	...	45.5	38.9	14.7	14.8	8.7
	2003	...	...	...	...	...	...	...	22.5	12.2
	2006	42.8	35.8	21.4	...	...	...	...	...	...
Mauritania Mauritanie	*2004	...	...	...	...	...	...	...	8.2	2.5
	2010	...	...	...	0.5	47.5	23.2	18.8	16.0	3.6
	*2016	...	...	...	0.5	55.9	25.9	17.7	9.3	2.6
Mauritius Maurice	2005	...	...	...	1.5	27.2	44.2	11.3	17.1	4.2
	2010	...	...	13.5	1.4	27.0	52.6	9.4	14.6	3.6
	2016	...	...	...	1.2	21.6	63.7	6.4	20.0	5.0
	2017	...	...	...	1.2	23.8	61.6	6.2	...	5.1
Mexico Mexique	2005	11.2	85.7	3.1	10.4	39.1	30.3	17.5	22.2	4.9
	2010	10.3	85.7	3.9	10.2	36.0	30.3	19.7	19.4	5.2
	2011	10.6	85.5	3.9	10.4	35.5	30.7	18.1	19.0	5.1
	2014	12.9	82.8	4.3	...	32.8	32.0	21.3	19.1	5.3
Micronesia (Fed. States of) Micronésie (États féd. de)	*2000	...	...	...	...	...	...	...	10.0	6.7
	2015	...	...	...	...	...	...	...	22.4	12.5
Monaco Monaco	2004	2.1	90.9	7.0	4.3	15.4	45.8	4.4	5.9	1.2
	2010	8.4	90.7	0.9	3.2	15.3	37.7	...	6.4	1.3
	2016	8.5	80.8	10.7	3.0	12.7	31.5	...	6.6	1.4
Mongolia Mongolie	2000	55.8	43.4	0.8	...	...	...	...	16.1	5.6
	2002	...	...	4.9	14.1	...	...	15.5	20.3	7.2
	2004	...	...	...	18.5	25.1	32.8	18.4	13.6	4.3
	2010	...	...	...	22.0	26.9	33.7	6.7	14.7	4.6
	2016	26.8	59.2	14.0	25.1	28.7	28.3	11.0	12.8	5.2
Montserrat Montserrat	2001	* 27.5	* 41.4	* 31.2	13.6	20.6	29.5	5.5	...	...
	2004	...	...	...	...	20.5	...	...	...	...
	2009	...	...	...	...	...	...	...	...	5.1
Morocco Maroc	2008	...	...	...	~0.0	35.5	43.1	...	17.5	5.3
	2009	...	...	...	...	37.7	41.9	20.2	17.3	5.3
Mozambique Mozambique	2005	...	...	22.6	...	...	...	...	22.7	4.4
	2006	...	...	26.8	...	57.7	29.3	12.1	18.6	4.3
	2013	22.2	58.5	19.3	...	49.2	30.6	13.7	19.0	6.5
Myanmar Myanmar	2011	9.4	77.2	13.4	...	50.5	23.5	19.1	5.4	0.8
	2017	22.4	57.2	20.3	0.5	36.0	39.4	11.3	...	2.2
Namibia Namibie	2000	19.3	73.6	7.2	0.2	58.8	27.2	12.0	21.9	7.0
	2003	...	...	...	0.5	63.1	25.8	9.1	20.3	6.1
	2008	...	* 79.9	...	0.4	47.6	18.7	9.9	25.1	6.5
	2010	22.1	77.0	0.8	...	40.0	23.5	23.1	26.2	8.3
Nauru Nauru	2002	...	...	...	...	67.5	...	...	...	...
	*2007	20.8	56.9	...	...	...	...	...	...	...
Nepal Népal	2003	...	...	...	...	* 56.5	22.1	10.3	21.3	3.1
	2005	...	...	...	...	...	...	...	22.3	3.4
	2010	18.0	69.2	12.8	1.0	55.7	30.5	12.7	16.0	3.6
	2015	24.9	64.1	11.0	2.1	53.8	33.3	10.8	17.0	3.7

9

Public expenditure on education *(continued)*
By expenditure type, level of education, total government expenditure and GDP

Dépenses publiques afférentes à l'éducation *(suite)*
Par type de dépenses, niveau de scolarité, dépenses publiques totales et PIB

Country or area Pays ou zone	Year Année	Percentage of total expenditure in public institutions / Pourcentage des dépenses publiques totales en faveur de l'éducation: Current expenditure Dépenses courantes	Staff Compensation Rémunération du personnel	Capital expenditure Dépenses en Capital	Percentage of government expenditure on education by level / Pourcentage des dépenses publiques selon le niveau d'enseignement: Pre-primary Préprimaire	Primary Primaire	Secondary Secondaire	Tertiary Tertiaire	As % of Govt. Expenditure En % des dépenses du gouvt.	As % of GDP En % du PIB
Netherlands Pays-Bas	2005	17.5	69.8	12.7	7.7	25.9	39.4	26.8	12.2	5.2
	2010	18.5	69.6	11.9	6.9	24.3	40.7	28.0	11.5	5.6
	2014	20.3	67.7	12.1	6.7	22.5	40.3	30.6	12.0	5.5
New Zealand Nouvelle-Zélande	2005	...	...	...	3.3	25.7	42.6	23.1	18.0	6.3
	2010	...	...	...	6.7	24.4	38.7	26.8	16.9	7.0
	2015	...	...	...	7.6	23.2	37.0	25.6	18.1	6.3
Nicaragua Nicaragua	2002	10.7	80.1	9.2	...	...	...	...	15.7	2.4
	*2003	...	...	...	...	...	...	...	14.9	2.4
	2004	...	...	11.7	...	...	...	...	...	...
	2010	10.7	46.2	11.4	3.6	39.8	13.2	26.0	22.8	4.5
Niger Niger	2003	...	...	...	...	72.6	...	...	13.8	2.4
	2010	14.2	77.9	7.9	2.4	61.0	21.3	12.6	18.1	3.7
	2015	31.8	56.3	11.9	7.6	45.8	32.2	13.5	18.5	6.0
Niue Nioué	2002	...	...	...	...	28.8	50.7	...	...	...
	2016	10.3	89.7	...	5.2	37.0	56.9	...	...	...
	2017	...	...	...	5.7	33.4	60.1	...	...	...
Norway Norvège	2005	22.4	66.9	10.7	4.1	25.0	35.7	32.4	16.8	6.9
	2010	21.3	67.4	11.3	4.9	26.7	35.3	29.6	15.3	6.7
	2014	18.6	70.6	10.7	9.8	21.6	27.0	28.6	17.0	7.7
Oman Oman	2002	...	...	14.4	...	46.8	43.2	10.0	11.1	4.3
	2005	...	...	...	...	50.5	41.8	7.6	10.1	3.5
	2009	...	...	...	...	33.0	40.2	26.9	10.9	4.2
	2016	14.6	66.5	18.8	...	42.2	37.1	20.7	12.0	6.2
	2017	...	...	...	...	42.6	37.5	19.9	...	...
Pakistan Pakistan	2005	12.3	49.2	38.5	...	...	...	...	13.8	2.3
	2007	14.8	59.1	26.1	...	...	...	...	15.4	2.6
	2010	...	...	...	...	...	...	...	11.9	2.3
	2016	...	...	13.7	16.6	43.7	29.0	10.7	12.6	2.5
	2017	...	...	...	...	...	...	10.2	...	2.8
Palau Palaos	2001	...	...	...	* 14.6	* 44.9	9.6	20.7	15.3	7.6
	*2002	...	...	...	...	...	...	...	15.5	7.6
Panama Panama	2002	11.1	67.9	21.0	2.2	32.1	29.2	28.1	17.0	4.2
	*2004	...	...	...	4.0	34.5	25.9	28.4	14.6	3.6
	2008	...	...	14.1	...	...	...	...	14.9	3.6
	2011	...	...	...	3.0	23.5	22.4	22.2	13.0	3.2
Paraguay Paraguay	2004	6.2	89.4	4.4	7.6	46.6	29.8	15.9	18.2	3.4
	2010	9.5	65.5	6.5	6.7	38.5	36.1	18.5	18.8	3.8
	2012	11.7	79.9	8.4	6.1	38.3	33.0	22.4	19.6	5.0
Peru Pérou	2005	9.3	81.3	9.4	8.1	35.6	31.4	10.7	14.3	2.8
	2010	14.5	64.6	20.9	12.0	39.9	34.2	13.8	13.6	2.9
	2016	30.2	51.6	18.2	15.6	34.8	32.5	17.0	17.8	3.8
Philippines Philippines	2005	11.1	85.5	3.4	0.1	52.0	26.8	13.3	12.4	2.4
	2009	18.4	73.4	8.2	1.7	55.0	29.7	12.0	13.2	2.7
Poland Pologne	2005	32.6	60.5	6.9	9.9	31.0	36.6	21.8	12.3	5.4
	2010	29.3	61.4	9.3	10.0	31.0	35.5	22.8	11.1	5.1
	2014	24.7	68.0	7.3	12.4	31.4	31.4	24.1	11.6	4.9
Portugal Portugal	2005	10.2	86.2	3.6	7.4	30.6	40.8	18.1	10.9	5.1
	2010	12.1	84.1	3.8	7.2	27.0	44.0	20.2	10.4	5.4
	2014	12.8	84.3	2.8	8.3	29.9	42.3	17.8	9.9	5.1
Puerto Rico Porto Rico	2014	37.4	58.0	4.6	7.4	22.0	24.6	36.8	20.0	6.0
Qatar Qatar	2005	...	...	...	...	...	...	...	13.7	4.0
	2009	...	...	...	4.4	17.6	14.7	...	14.8	3.4
	2010	...	...	...	...	...	...	...	13.8	4.5
	2014	45.5	22.7	31.9	...	...	...	...	12.7	3.6
	2016	16.1	60.0	23.9	...	...	...	...	...	...

Public expenditure on education *(continued)*

By expenditure type, level of education, total government expenditure and GDP

Dépenses publiques afférentes à l'éducation *(suite)*

Par type de dépenses, niveau de scolarité, dépenses publiques totales et PIB

		Percentage of total expenditure in public institutions Pourcentage des dépenses publiques totales en faveur de l'éducation			Percentage of government expenditure on education by level Pourcentage des dépenses publiques selon le niveau d'enseignement					
Country or area Pays ou zone	Year Année	Current expenditure Dépenses courantes	Staff Compensation Rémunération du personnel	Capital expenditure Dépenses en Capital	Pre-primary Préprimaire	Primary Primaire	Secondary Secondaire	Tertiary Tertiaire	As % of Govt. Expenditure En % des dépenses du gouvt.	As % of GDP En % du PIB
Republic of Korea République de Corée	2005	24.0	58.7	17.4	1.6	35.4	41.5	14.0	...	3.9
	2009	27.2	55.8	17.0	2.2	32.6	38.2	17.1	...	4.7
	2015	25.2	62.7	12.1	8.3	31.5	39.4	20.8	...	5.1
Republic of Moldova République de Moldova	2005	...	...	...	...	...	...	...	19.3	7.2
	2010	29.1	62.6	8.2	19.5	18.0	37.3	18.0	22.3	9.1
	2016	32.7	58.6	8.7	22.3	22.5	34.8	16.2	18.5	6.7
Romania Roumanie	2005	34.4	59.1	6.5	9.1	* 13.8	* 44.3	23.2	10.8	3.5
	2010	27.1	62.2	10.8	10.0	16.4	35.8	28.5	9.1	3.5
	2014	27.7	67.3	5.0	10.8	13.7	40.9	21.6	9.2	3.1
Russian Federation Fédération de Russie	2005	...	...	...	13.9	...	...	21.1	12.0	3.8
	2008	...	...	...	15.0	...	...	23.1	12.0	4.1
	2012	24.5	66.4	9.1	...	...	...	21.2	11.1	3.8
	2014	20.6	69.8	9.6	...	...	...	...	...	...
Rwanda Rwanda	2000	...	47.3	20.3	* 0.5	* 48.2	* 16.7	* 34.7	18.8	4.1
	2001	24.4	33.8	41.8	...	...	...	...	25.3	5.7
	2010	25.1	58.7	16.1	0.2	36.7	30.7	22.7	17.5	4.9
	*2016	44.8	42.2	13.0	7.7	34.6	52.8	1.7	12.3	3.5
Saint Kitts and Nevis Saint-Kitts-et-Nevis	2005	...	...	...	...	...	...	...	11.1	3.9
	2007	...	...	...	...	...	...	...	13.1	4.3
	2015	...	...	...	15.6	21.4	40.2	15.4	8.6	2.8
	2016	18.6	61.7	19.8	...	...	...	...	...	...
Saint Lucia Sainte-Lucie	2004	26.1	73.2	0.7	0.4	47.2	33.4	...	15.0	4.1
	2005	...	...	...	...	...	...	...	16.3	5.1
	2006	28.4	45.3	26.3	...	...	...	...	19.0	5.3
	*2010	...	...	...	1.8	42.3	45.6	4.6	14.2	3.9
	2011	...	...	...	1.5	42.3	45.1	* 5.0	13.8	3.9
	2015	...	...	11.7	1.4	34.2	43.8	...	16.5	4.4
	2016	...	...	...	...	26.4	30.8	...	22.4	5.7
Saint Vincent & Grenadines Saint-Vincent-Grenadines	2005	14.6	51.9	33.6	0.3	41.0	31.7	3.7	22.6	6.4
	2010	5.6	94.4	...	2.0	41.4	36.3	7.0	15.5	5.1
	2016	...	...	...	...	37.5	32.7	...	20.1	5.8
	2017	...	...	...	...	37.2	32.3	...	...	...
Samoa Samoa	2001	...	...	...	* 0.7	* 36.2	* 29.8	33.2	12.8	3.8
	*2002	...	...	...	...	45.8	...	...	12.8	3.8
	2008	...	...	...	...	...	...	...	16.1	5.1
	2016	...	...	...	0.9	37.0	42.8	9.2	10.5	4.1
San Marino Saint-Marin	2010	4.2	95.8	...	19.0	31.7	39.5	9.8	10.8	2.3
	2011	5.0	95.0	...	20.2	33.3	35.8	10.8	10.6	2.4
Sao Tome and Principe Sao Tomé-et-Principe	2005	...	...	...	...	...	...	...	12.1	5.3
	2010	...	...	...	...	...	...	...	19.3	9.7
	2014	...	...	...	12.0	55.8	22.6	9.6	12.3	3.7
Saudi Arabia Arabie saoudite	2005	...	...	...	...	...	...	...	19.3	5.4
	2008	...	...	...	...	...	...	...	19.3	5.1
Senegal Sénégal	2005	...	...	...	0.9	41.8	22.4	22.0	21.8	5.1
	2010	18.3	72.6	9.1	1.1	43.2	27.9	26.8	24.0	6.5
	2015	23.6	61.7	14.7	4.0	34.2	29.3	32.1	23.8	7.1
Serbia Serbie	2010	22.4	75.1	2.5	0.5	45.9	23.3	29.1	10.5	4.6
	2015	19.4	78.7	1.9	0.7	45.3	22.9	30.1	9.2	4.0
Seychelles Seychelles	2002	23.9	66.4	9.7	* 10.5	* 32.0	* 26.1	17.4	9.2	5.2
	2003	31.8	59.3	8.9	* 8.6	* 32.8	* 28.9	...	12.0	5.4
	2006	29.8	56.7	13.5	4.1	...	...	17.9	11.0	4.8
	2011	18.7	71.3	10.0	...	24.0	16.2	32.5	10.4	3.6

Public expenditure on education *(continued)*
By expenditure type, level of education, total government expenditure and GDP

Dépenses publiques afférentes à l'éducation *(suite)*
Par type de dépenses, niveau de scolarité, dépenses publiques totales et PIB

Country or area Pays ou zone	Year Année	Percentage of total expenditure in public institutions / Pourcentage des dépenses publiques totales en faveur de l'éducation: Current expenditure Dépenses courantes	Staff Compensation Rémunération du personnel	Capital expenditure Dépenses en Capital	Percentage of government expenditure on education by level / Pourcentage des dépenses publiques selon le niveau d'enseignement: Pre-primary Préprimaire	Primary Primaire	Secondary Secondaire	Tertiary Tertiaire	As % of Govt. Expenditure En % des dépenses du gouvt.	As % of GDP En % du PIB
Sierra Leone Sierra Leone	*2005	...	...	...	...	...	...	...	15.5	2.8
	2010	28.3	69.1	2.5	...	50.7	26.4	19.6	12.8	2.6
	2011	24.5	74.3	1.2	...	52.6	26.3	17.9	12.4	2.7
	2014	...	...	0.5	...	43.1	23.4	30.7	15.1	2.7
	2016	...	...	...	...	35.7	12.0	52.1	12.5	2.9
Singapore Singapour	2005	...	...	...	...	...	...	...	19.8	3.2
	2010	...	...	9.2	...	20.8	25.0	35.1	17.2	3.1
	2013	...	...	8.2	...	22.0	23.0	35.3	20.0	2.9
Slovakia Slovaquie	2005	34.1	60.2	5.6	10.1	17.1	48.9	21.0	9.5	3.8
	2010	30.8	57.0	12.2	9.4	20.7	46.9	19.6	9.8	4.1
	2015	32.0	53.0	15.0	10.5	19.1	37.9	29.9	10.2	4.6
Slovenia Slovénie	2003	21.0	69.4	9.6	9.2	* 21.8	* 46.6	22.3	13.7	5.7
	2005	20.6	69.4	10.0	10.4	...	...	22.0	13.3	5.6
	2010	21.4	70.0	8.7	10.3	28.5	37.1	24.0	12.1	5.6
	2014	20.8	66.6	12.6	12.2	28.2	33.2	19.8	11.3	5.3
Solomon Islands Îles Salomon	2010	...	...	...	...	...	...	...	17.5	10.0
South Africa Afrique du Sud	2005	20.9	66.3	2.9	0.6	42.9	32.6	15.1	19.9	5.1
	2006	...	69.8	* 3.5	0.5	45.1	31.1	12.8	18.0	5.1
	2009	...	...	* 3.8	0.9	41.1	30.9	12.5	18.3	5.2
	2010	...	...	...	1.1	42.5	31.4	11.9	18.0	5.7
	2014	29.5	67.2	3.3	1.5	38.8	30.7	12.2	19.1	6.0
	2016	27.2	67.5	...	...	...	...	...	18.1	5.9
South Sudan Soudan du sud	2014	34.7	48.8	16.5	0.6	57.5	16.6	24.7	4.1	1.7
	2016	6.5	93.5	...	0.3	36.4	12.2	50.4	0.8	1.8
	2017	...	...	...	0.1	48.6	18.5	31.5	...	...
Spain Espagne	2005	16.7	73.5	9.8	12.4	25.8	39.5	22.4	10.8	4.1
	2010	17.7	71.6	10.8	14.1	25.5	37.0	23.4	10.6	4.8
	2014	18.5	76.3	5.3	11.3	26.3	36.7	22.5	9.5	4.3
Sri Lanka Sri Lanka	2010	9.9	75.5	14.6	...	25.0	53.2	16.4	8.6	1.7
	2015	18.3	62.4	19.3	...	28.3	47.1	19.4	11.0	2.2
	2016	...	...	29.0	...	34.9	50.4	12.1	17.7	3.5
State of Palestine État de Palestine	2010	...	...	...	...	...	...	...	...	6.7
	2016	10.4	84.7	4.9	...	...	...	...	...	5.7
Sudan Soudan	2005	...	...	...	...	...	...	...	6.0	1.6
	2009	...	...	...	...	...	...	...	10.8	2.2
Sweden Suède	2005	28.4	65.0	6.6	7.8	26.2	38.2	27.5	12.7	6.6
	2010	31.3	63.1	5.6	10.2	24.3	35.6	29.0	13.2	6.6
	2014	29.7	65.2	5.1	16.9	22.8	27.5	25.3	15.2	7.7
Switzerland Suisse	2005	15.5	75.3	9.1	3.6	29.7	37.7	26.0	15.8	5.2
	2010	16.2	75.2	8.6	3.7	28.0	41.3	25.3	15.4	4.9
	2014	15.6	74.4	10.0	4.7	29.6	37.6	26.4	15.5	5.1
Syrian Arab Republic République arabe syrienne	2002	...	...	...	...	44.4	33.4	21.0	16.8	5.0
	2004	...	...	...	...	...	...	24.8	17.1	5.4
	2009	...	...	...	...	38.9	36.9	24.2	19.2	5.1
Tajikistan Tadjikistan	2005	...	...	...	3.8	...	...	7.4	15.3	3.5
	2010	...	...	...	5.0	...	...	10.1	15.3	4.0
	2015	...	...	14.0	5.3	...	...	9.9	16.4	5.2
Thailand Thaïlande	2004	...	...	...	10.4	31.0	24.0	20.6	21.5	4.0
	2005	...	...	...	13.6	...	...	21.7	20.5	3.9
	2010	45.8	50.9	3.3	5.7	40.1	28.6	16.5	16.2	3.5
	2013	45.8	49.2	5.0	5.4	41.1	29.8	15.6	19.1	4.1
	2014	31.8	62.5	5.7	...	...	...	...	...	...
TFYR of Macedonia ex-R.Y. de Macédoine	2002	10.8	87.1	2.1	...	...	...	15.0	8.6	3.3

9 Public expenditure on education *(continued)*

By expenditure type, level of education, total government expenditure and GDP

Dépenses publiques afférentes à l'éducation *(suite)*

Par type de dépenses, niveau de scolarité, dépenses publiques totales et PIB

Country or area Pays ou zone	Year Année	Percentage of total expenditure in public institutions / Pourcentage des dépenses publiques totales en faveur de l'éducation: Current expenditure Dépenses courantes	Staff Compensation Rémunération du personnel	Capital expenditure Dépenses en Capital	Percentage of government expenditure on education by level / Pourcentage des dépenses publiques selon le niveau d'enseignement: Pre-primary Préprimaire	Primary Primaire	Secondary Secondaire	Tertiary Tertiaire	As % of Govt. Expenditure En % des dépenses du gouvt.	As % of GDP En % du PIB
Timor-Leste	2010	52.5	37.8	9.7	...	...	...	10.4	9.2	11.0
Timor-Leste	2014	46.4	49.5	4.0	1.2	64.9	29.8	4.1	6.7	7.5
Togo	2000	20.9	69.1	10.0	...	48.6	29.3	17.4	24.4	4.5
Togo	2005	...	...	...	...	41.8	...	...	17.7	3.4
	2010	14.7	74.7	10.6	2.6	51.7	25.6	16.7	19.6	4.4
	2016	7.1	90.5	2.4	1.6	64.1	16.0	17.9	16.0	5.1
	2017	...	...	...	1.2	46.9	32.4	19.1	...	...
Tonga Tonga	2004	...	...	...	...	44.4	30.1	21.7	18.1	3.9
Trinidad and Tobago Trinité-et-Tobago	2003	...	...	...	0.6	39.2	36.8	...	13.9	3.1
Tunisia	2000	8.2	77.3	14.5	...	* 33.3	* 45.0	* 21.7	* 24.6	* 6.2
Tunisie	2002	...	...	11.6	...	* 32.9	* 44.4	22.8	22.9	5.8
	2005	...	...	...	...	* 34.3	* 41.6	24.1	26.7	6.5
	2008	...	...	10.0	...	27.7	47.3	25.0	25.3	6.3
	2010	...	...	10.4	...	...	...	28.2	24.8	6.3
	2015	...	...	...	...	...	71.6	23.9	22.9	6.6
Turkey	2004	12.6	66.3	21.1	...	...	...	27.9	8.6	3.0
Turquie	2006	14.9	74.6	10.6	...	...	...	31.9	8.0	2.8
	2014	16.2	70.4	13.5	...	23.8	36.4	35.5	13.1	4.4
Turkmenistan Turkménistan	2012	...	...	33.7	28.1	...	...	9.2	20.8	3.0
Turks and Caicos	2002	9.8	61.1	29.2	* 5.0	* 21.1	31.7	22.9	...	...
Islands	2003	...	...	...	...	* 21.6	28.0	37.2	...	...
Îles Turques-et-	2005	13.7	69.5	16.8	...	* 30.0	47.7	...	...	...
Caïques	2015	...	...	17.6	...	36.1	41.5	22.4	14.3	3.3
Uganda	2004	12.1	62.7	25.2	...	61.2	17.3	11.9	20.3	5.0
Ouganda	2010	51.1	35.5	13.4	...	47.3	39.4	13.3	10.1	2.4
	2014	48.3	39.1	12.6	...	59.2	24.6	16.3	10.9	2.3
Ukraine	2000	...	...	8.3	11.1	...	...	32.3	11.4	4.2
Ukraine	2005	...	...	...	11.0	...	...	29.5	13.7	6.1
	2009	...	...	...	12.5	...	...	32.4	15.1	7.3
	2014	...	...	2.2	16.3	18.0	27.8	31.5	13.1	5.9
United Kingdom	2005	18.5	73.5	8.0	5.9	26.5	45.4	22.3	13.2	5.0
Royaume-Uni	2010	29.8	58.8	11.4	5.2	30.1	48.3	16.4	13.1	5.8
	2015	23.5	73.9	2.6	3.5	32.2	41.0	22.8	13.8	5.6
United Rep. of	2005	...	...	...	5.8	56.0	12.9	21.7	18.1	4.6
Tanzania	2009	...	...	...	4.4	41.9	16.7	33.8	17.4	4.0
Rép.-Unie de	2010	...	...	...	...	...	11.3	28.3	19.6	4.6
Tanzanie	2014	...	...	...	6.0	49.2	18.3	21.4	17.3	3.5
United States of America	2010	20.5	69.4	10.1	6.5	32.4	35.4	25.7	13.1	5.4
États-Unis d'Amérique	2014	21.6	69.7	8.7	6.6	31.0	34.6	27.5	13.5	5.0
Uruguay	2005	14.5	80.8	4.7	8.9	33.8	35.5	21.8	9.4	2.7
Uruguay	2006	14.1	80.2	5.7	8.7	33.3	36.0	22.0	9.9	2.9
	2011	14.9	80.5	4.6	10.2	27.9	33.2	26.8	14.9	4.4
	2015	13.4	82.6	4.0	...	...	...	...	...	...
Vanuatu	2001	1.1	51.7	47.2	0.1	27.9	57.4	10.5	40.1	9.0
Vanuatu	2003	...	...	...	...	...	...	...	44.8	8.4
	2008	11.4	87.4	1.2	0.5	49.7	32.9	5.9	21.4	5.8
	2009	8.8	89.5	1.7	0.1	54.3	29.7	...	18.7	5.0
	2015	...	...	...	0.1	41.3	28.7	...	22.3	5.5
Venezuela (Boliv. Rep. of) Venezuela (Rép. boliv. du)	2009	20.2	76.9	2.9	11.6	31.5	19.0	22.6	20.7	6.9

9 Public expenditure on education *(continued)*
By expenditure type, level of education, total government expenditure and GDP

Dépenses publiques afférentes à l'éducation *(suite)*
Par type de dépenses, niveau de scolarité, dépenses publiques totales et PIB

Country or area Pays ou zone	Year Année	Percentage of total expenditure in public institutions / Pourcentage des dépenses publiques totales en faveur de l'éducation: Current expenditure Dépenses courantes	Staff Compensation Rémunération du personnel	Capital expenditure Dépenses en Capital	Percentage of government expenditure on education by level / Pourcentage des dépenses publiques selon le niveau d'enseignement: Pre-primary Préprimaire	Primary Primaire	Secondary Secondaire	Tertiary Tertiaire	As % of Govt. Expenditure En % des dépenses du gouvt.	As % of GDP En % du PIB
Viet Nam	2010	32.3	42.4	25.3	13.3	30.0	42.2	14.5	17.1	5.1
Viet Nam	2013	31.3	46.9	21.9	15.7	29.7	39.6	15.0	18.5	5.7
Yemen	*2001	...	...	...	...	...	...	...	30.3	9.2
Yémen	2008	...	...	25.7	...	...	...	...	12.5	5.2
Zambia	2004	25.2	73.0	1.8	...	63.9	13.3	18.0	10.6	2.5
Zambie	2005	...	...	...	...	59.8	14.5	25.8	7.7	1.7
	2008	...	...	...	...	...	...	...	5.7	1.1
Zimbabwe	2010	...	...	...	...	51.6	25.6	22.8	8.7	1.8
Zimbabwe	2014	...	...	...	2.0	47.8	26.9	16.8	30.0	7.5

Source:

United Nations Educational, Scientific and Cultural Organization (UNESCO), Montreal, the UNESCO Institute for Statistics (UIS) statistics database, last accessed May 2018.

Source:

Organisation des Nations Unies pour l'éducation, la science et la culture (UNESCO), Montréal, base de données statistiques de l'Institut de statistique (ISU) de l'UNESCO, dernier accès mai 2018.

10 Health Personnel

Number of health workers and workforce density (per 1 000 population)

Le personnel de santé

Personnel de santé et densité (pour 1 000 habitants)

Country or area Pays ou zone	Year Année	Physicians Médecins Number Nombre	Per 1 000 Pour 1 000	Dentists Dentistes Number Nombre	Per 1 000 Pour 1 000	Pharmacists Pharmaciens Number Nombre	Per 1 000 Pour 1 000	Nurses and midwives Infirmières et Sages-femmes Number Nombre	Per 1 000 Pour 1 000
Afghanistan	2001	4 104	0.2	…	…	525	~0.0	…	…
Afghanistan	2005	…	…	…	…	900	~0.0	14 930	0.6
	2008	4 834	0.2	382	~0.0	829	~0.0	13 780	0.5
	2009	6 037	0.2	…	…	847	~0.0	17 257	0.6
	2010	6 901	0.2	…	…	814	~0.0	…	…
	2014	9 954	0.3	111	~0.0	1 711	0.1	11 399	0.4
	2016	9 842	0.3	120	~0.0	1 675	0.1	…	…
Albania	2006	…	…	1 035	0.3	…	…	…	…
Albanie	2010	3 640	1.3	…	…	1 324	0.5	…	…
	2013	3 709	1.3	…	…	2 441	0.8	…	…
Algeria	2002	35 368	1.1	9 553	0.3	6 333	0.2	69 749	2.2
Algérie	2005	33 952	1.0	9 022	0.3	6 104	0.2	…	…
	2007	40 857	1.2	11 010	0.3	8 232	0.2	65 919	1.9
Andorra	2003	244	3.3	44	0.6	68	0.9	…	…
Andorre	2015	260	3.7	64	0.9	82	1.2	313	4.4
Angola	2004	1 165	0.1	222	~0.0	919	0.1	18 485	1.1
Angola	2009	2 956	0.1	…	…	…	…	29 592	1.4
Argentina	2004	122 623	3.2	35 592	0.9	19 510	0.5	18 685	0.5
Argentine	2013	166 187	3.9	…	…	…	…	179 175	4.2
Armenia	2010	8 177	2.8	1 257	0.4	123	~0.0	16 386	5.5
Arménie	2014	8 425	2.8	1 138	0.4	150	0.1	16 302	5.4
Australia	2001	47 875	2.5	21 296	1.1	13 956	0.7	187 837	9.7
Australie	2009	62 800	2.9	14 500	0.7	21 800	1.0	201 300	9.2
	2010	…	…	…	…	19 237	0.9	…	…
	2015	83 804	3.5	13 849	0.6	20 297	0.8	296 701	12.4
	2016	…	…	…	…	…	…	305 462	12.6
Austria	2010	40 105	4.8	4 685	0.6	5 579	0.7	65 698	7.8
Autriche	2015	44 002	5.2	4 906	0.6	6 104	0.7	70 955	8.3
	2016	44 816	5.2	4 954	0.6	…	…	…	…
Azerbaijan	2010	33 085	3.6	2 467	0.3	1 831	0.2	72 717	8.0
Azerbaïdjan	2014	32 756	3.4	2 601	0.3	1 897	0.2	66 166	6.9
Bahamas	2008	947	2.7	115	0.3	160	0.5	1 391	4.0
Bahamas	2011	830	2.3	130	0.4	292	0.8	1 458	4.0
Bahrain	2005	928	1.1	243	0.3	164	0.2	2 389	2.8
Bahreïn	2010	1 178	0.9	294	0.2	196	0.2	3 052	2.4
	2015	1 270	0.9	216	0.2	222	0.2	3 422	2.5
Bangladesh	2002	…	…	1 886	~0.0	7 622	0.1	…	…
Bangladesh	2005	42 881	0.3	2 344	~0.0	…	…	39 471	0.3
	2010	53 643	0.4	6 252	~0.0	58 388	0.4	28 228	0.2
	2015	75 915	0.5	6 520	~0.0	89 631	0.6	42 965	0.3
Barbados									
Barbade	2005	489	1.8	94	0.3	251	0.9	1 311	4.8
Belarus	2010	33 325	3.5	5 087	0.5	2 731	0.3	104 872	11.0
Bélarus	2014	38 671	4.1	5 414	0.6	3 240	0.3	108 490	11.4
Belgium	2005	21 599	2.0	7 731	0.7	…	…	…	…
Belgique	2010	31 815	2.9	7 675	0.7	12 629	1.2	108 935	10.0
	2015	34 020	3.0	8 291	0.7	13 643	1.2	122 127	10.8
	2016	…	…	…	…	…	…	126 091	11.1
Belize	2000	251	1.0	32	0.1	…	…	303	1.2
Belize	2009	241	0.8	12	~0.0	112	0.4	570	1.8
Benin	2004	311	~0.0	12	~0.0	11	~0.0	5 789	0.7
Bénin	2008	542	0.1	37	~0.0	20	~0.0	7 129	0.8
	2016	1 709	0.2	9	~0.0	13	~0.0	6 681	0.6
Bhutan	2004	118	0.2	58	0.1	78	0.1	515	0.8
Bhoutan	2007	144	0.2	65	0.1	87	0.1	545	0.8
	2008	171	0.2	…	…	89	0.1	666	1.0
	2016	299	0.4	…	…	23	~0.0	1 185	1.5

10 Health Personnel *(continued)*

Number of health workers and workforce density (per 1 000 population)

Le personnel de santé *(suite)*

Personnel de santé et densité (pour 1 000 habitants)

Country or area Pays ou zone	Year Année	Physicians / Médecins: Number Nombre	Physicians / Médecins: Per 1 000 Pour 1 000	Dentists / Dentistes: Number Nombre	Dentists / Dentistes: Per 1 000 Pour 1 000	Pharmacists / Pharmaciens: Number Nombre	Pharmacists / Pharmaciens: Per 1 000 Pour 1 000	Nurses and midwives / Infirmières et Sages-femmes: Number Nombre	Nurses and midwives / Infirmières et Sages-femmes: Per 1 000 Pour 1 000
Bolivia (Plurin. State of)	2001	10 329	1.2	5 997	0.7	4 670	0.6	18 091	2.1
Bolivie (État plurin. de)	2010	4 406	0.4	976	0.1	567	0.1	8 366	0.8
	2011	4 771	0.5	1 130	0.1	660	0.1	10 139	1.0
Bosnia and Herzegovina	2010	6 665	1.7	797	0.2	371	0.1	21 560	5.6
Bosnie-Herzégovine	2013	7 211	1.9	809	0.2	429	0.1	22 052	5.8
	2014	...	...	825	0.2	441	0.1	22 465	5.9
Botswana	2004	715	0.4	38	~0.0	333	0.2	4 753	2.6
Botswana	2005	466	0.3	...	...	...	...	4 468	2.4
	2009	693	0.3	145	0.1	365	0.2	5 816	2.9
	2012	819	0.4	...	...	...	...	5 816	2.7
Brazil	2005	310 138	1.6	207 904	1.1	99 696	0.5	703 813	3.7
Brésil	2010	355 006	1.8	242 266	1.2	142 841	0.7	1 446 403	7.3
	2013	378 354	1.9	...	...	...	...	1 520 533	7.4
Brunei Darussalam	2005	390	1.1	73	0.2	41	0.1	2 006	5.5
Brunéi Darussalam	2010	563	1.4	86	0.2	43	0.1	2 907	7.4
	2015	739	1.7	183	0.4	71	0.2	2 756	6.5
Bulgaria	2001	...	...	...	...	1 020	0.1	...	...
Bulgarie	2010	27 963	3.8	6 389	0.9	...	...	38 280	5.2
	2014	28 801	4.0	7 054	1.0	...	...	38 298	5.3
Burkina Faso	2004	708	0.1	58	~0.0	343	~0.0	6 557	0.5
Burkina Faso	2010	713	~0.0	32	~0.0	339	~0.0	8 645	0.6
	2012	787	~0.0	38	~0.0	351	~0.0	10 459	0.6
Burundi	2004	200	~0.0	14	~0.0	76	~0.0	1 348	0.2
Burundi	2011	...	...	...	...	172	~0.0	...	...
Cabo Verde	2010	292	0.6	4	~0.0	4	~0.0	543	1.1
Cabo Verde	2011	292	0.6	3	~0.0	5	~0.0	543	1.1
	2015	410	0.8	...	...	...	...	654	1.3
Cambodia	2000	2 047	0.2	209	~0.0	564	~0.0	11 125	0.9
Cambodge	2010	3 294	0.2	242	~0.0	548	~0.0	12 251	0.9
	2014	2 192	0.1	377	~0.0	615	~0.0	14 579	1.0
Cameroon	2005	1 049	0.1	26	~0.0	27	~0.0	6 705	0.4
Cameroun	2010	1 712	0.1	58	~0.0	42	~0.0	10 714	0.5
Canada	2004	60 612	1.9	35 834	1.1	28 537	0.9	316 512	9.9
Canada	2005	...	...	...	...	...	...	321 159	10.0
	2008	65 440	2.0	41 798	1.3	29 010	0.9	343 699	10.3
	2009	...	...	...	...	30 553	0.9	350 547	10.4
	2010	69 648	2.0	...	...	...	...	318 565	9.3
	2015	91 268	2.5	...	...	35 238	1.0	353 738	9.8
Central African Republic	2004	331	0.1	13	~0.0	17	~0.0	1 613	0.4
République centrafricaine	2009	205	~0.0	12	~0.0	12	~0.0	1 097	0.3
Chad	2004	345	~0.0	15	~0.0	37	~0.0	2 499	0.3
Tchad	2006	368	~0.0	...	...	...	...	1 891	0.2
	2013	573	~0.0	...	...	72	~0.0	4 057	0.3
Chile	2005	15 865	1.0	12	~0.0	36	~0.0	2 103	0.1
Chili	2009	17 382	1.0	15	~0.0	39	~0.0	2 443	0.1
China	2002	1 463 573	1.1	...	...	357 659	0.3	1 246 545	1.0
Chine	2005	...	...	51 012	~0.0	349 533	0.3	1 349 589	1.0
	2010	1 972 840	1.5	...	...	353 916	0.3	2 048 071	1.5
	2015	5 016 816	3.6	...	...	423 294	0.3	3 241 469	2.3
Colombia	2005	62 807	1.5	37 371	0.9	...	...	25 845	0.6
Colombie	2010	71 980	1.6	44 858	1.0	...	...	30 119	0.1
	2014	87 050	1.8	...	...	...	...	51 593	1.1
Comoros									
Comores	2004	115	0.2	29	~0.0	41	0.1	588	1.0
Congo	2004	756	0.2	12	~0.0	99	~0.0	3 672	1.1
Congo	2007	401	0.1	...	...	63	~0.0	3 492	0.9
Cook Islands	2004	20	1.0	10	0.5	2	0.1	80	4.2
Îles Cook	2009	24	1.2	19	0.9	8	0.4	116	5.8
Costa Rica	2000	5 204	1.3	1 905	0.5	2 101	0.5	3 653	0.9
Costa Rica	2013	5 411	1.2	599	0.1	891	0.2	3 745	0.8

Health Personnel *(continued)*
Number of health workers and workforce density (per 1 000 population)

Le personnel de santé *(suite)*
Personnel de santé et densité (pour 1 000 habitants)

Country or area Pays ou zone	Year Année	Physicians / Médecins: Number Nombre	Physicians / Médecins: Per 1 000 Pour 1 000	Dentists / Dentistes: Number Nombre	Dentists / Dentistes: Per 1 000 Pour 1 000	Pharmacists / Pharmaciens: Number Nombre	Pharmacists / Pharmaciens: Per 1 000 Pour 1 000	Nurses and midwives / Infirmières et Sages-femmes: Number Nombre	Nurses and midwives / Infirmières et Sages-femmes: Per 1 000 Pour 1 000
Côte d'Ivoire	2005	1 698	0.1	204	~0.0	128	~0.0	8 988	0.5
Côte d'Ivoire	2008	2 746	0.1	274	~0.0	413	~0.0	9 231	0.5
Croatia	2010	12 304	2.9	3 158	0.7	2 851	0.7	26 553	6.2
Croatie	2014	13 302	3.1	3 327	0.8	3 024	0.7	27 714	6.5
	2015	...	...	3 614	0.9	2 797	0.7	...	...
Cuba	2002	67 079	6.0	9 955	0.9	...	...	83 880	7.5
Cuba	2005	70 594	6.3	10 554	0.9	...	...	...	...
	2010	76 506	6.8	12 144	1.1	4 656	0.4	103 014	9.1
	2014	85 563	7.5	21 032	1.8	3 058	0.3	90 765	8.0
Cyprus	2002	...	...	...	...	144	0.1	2 994	3.1
Chypre	2009	2 313	2.1	757	0.7	...	...	3 806	3.5
	2010	2 399	2.2	772	0.7	181	0.2	...	...
	2014	2 880	2.5	839	0.7	188	0.2	4 750	4.1
Czechia	2010	37 661	3.6	7 263	0.7	6 061	0.6	89 233	8.5
Tchéquie	2013	38 776	3.7	7 426	0.7	6 383	0.6	88 425	8.4
	2015	...	...	8 461	0.8	6 965	0.7	88 744	8.4
Dem. People's Rep. Korea	2003	74 597	3.2	8 315	0.4	13 497	0.6	93 414	4.0
Rép. pop. dém. de Corée	2008	79 931	3.3	4 314	0.2	8 622	0.4	100 768	4.2
	2014	87 780	3.5	4 740	0.2	9 463	0.4	...	...
Dem. Rep. of the Congo Rép. dém. du Congo	2009	5 832	0.1	79	~0.0	495	~0.0	61 368	1.0
Denmark	2005	17 350	3.2	4 634	0.9	...	...	81 219	15.0
Danemark	2010	19 881	3.6	4 485	0.8	2 623	0.5	89 431	16.1
	2014	20 639	3.7	4 244	0.8	2 862	0.5	96 078	17.0
Djibouti	2004	129	0.2	10	~0.0	18	~0.0	296	0.4
Djibouti	2005	140	0.2	...	...	41	0.1	450	0.6
	2006	185	0.2	...	...	16	~0.0	...	...
	2008	...	...	...	...	266	0.3	...	...
	2014	201	0.2	19	~0.0	210	0.2	488	0.6
Dominica Dominique	2001	124	1.8	21	0.3	18	0.3	438	6.3
Dominican Republic	2000	15 670	1.8	7 000	0.8	3 330	0.4	15 352	1.8
République dominicaine	2008	10 385	1.1	1 205	0.1	...	...	...	...
	2009	...	...	1 785	0.2	...	...	12 686	1.3
	2011	14 983	1.5	1 910	0.2	...	...	13 374	1.3
Ecuador	2003	20 020	1.5	2 213	0.2	497	~0.0	20 372	1.5
Équateur	2009	23 614	1.6	3 363	0.2	664	~0.0	27 764	1.9
	2011	25 277	1.7	4 183	0.3	810	0.1	31 635	2.1
Egypt	2004	...	...	9 917	0.1	...	...	146 761	2.0
Égypte	2005	179 900	2.4	...	...	...	...	...	...
	2009	225 565	2.8	...	...	...	...	...	...
	2014	72 901	0.8	14 753	0.2	29 507	0.3	128 445	1.4
El Salvador	2005	10 355	1.7	4 255	0.7	2 280	0.4	2 084	0.4
El Salvador	2008	11 542	1.9	4 669	0.8	2 316	0.4	2 929	0.5
Equatorial Guinea Guinée équatoriale	2004	153	0.3	15	~0.0	121	0.2	271	0.4
Eritrea Érythrée	2004	215	0.1	16	~0.0	107	~0.0	2 505	0.6
Estonia	2000	6 118	4.4	1 747	1.2	580	0.4	12 087	8.6
Estonie	2010	4 319	3.2	1 198	0.9	842	0.6	8 524	6.4
	2015	4 502	3.4	1 239	0.9	948	0.7	8 357	6.4
Eswatini	2004	171	0.2	32	~0.0	70	0.1	6 828	6.2
Eswatini	2009	173	0.1	59	0.1	51	~0.0	1 626	1.4
Ethiopia	2003	1 936	~0.0	93	~0.0	805	~0.0	15 544	0.2
Éthiopie	2005	2 453	~0.0	...	...	1 619	~0.0	18 809	0.2
	2009	2 152	~0.0	...	...	2 661	~0.0	21 488	0.3
Fiji	2003	380	0.5	60	0.1	90	0.1	1 660	2.0
Fidji	2009	372	0.4	171	0.2	76	0.1	1 957	2.3
	2015	747	0.8	241	0.3	95	0.1	2 621	2.9

Health Personnel *(continued)*

Number of health workers and workforce density (per 1 000 population)

Le personnel de santé *(suite)*

Personnel de santé et densité (pour 1 000 habitants)

Country or area Pays ou zone	Year Année	Physicians / Médecins: Number Nombre	Physicians / Médecins: Per 1 000 Pour 1 000	Dentists / Dentistes: Number Nombre	Dentists / Dentistes: Per 1 000 Pour 1 000	Pharmacists / Pharmaciens: Number Nombre	Pharmacists / Pharmaciens: Per 1 000 Pour 1 000	Nurses and midwives / Infirmières et Sages-femmes: Number Nombre	Nurses and midwives / Infirmières et Sages-femmes: Per 1 000 Pour 1 000
Finland Finlande	2002	16 446	3.2	6 674	1.3	5 829	1.1	78 402	15.1
	2010	16 030	3.0	4 234	0.8	5 944	1.1	76 500	14.3
	2014	17 511	3.2	3 925	0.7	5 988	1.1	82 368	15.0
France France	2003	…	…	40 648	0.7	63 909	1.1	439 115	7.3
	2005	…	…	…	…	…	…	469 036	7.7
	2007	227 683	3.7	41 444	0.7	70 498	1.1	500 863	8.1
	2008	…	…	41 422	0.7	72 160	1.2	494 895	7.9
	2015	207 789	3.2	42 602	0.7	70 247	1.1	682 896	10.6
	2016	209 367	3.2	43 026	0.7	70 025	1.1	…	…
Gabon Gabon	2004	395	0.3	66	~0.0	63	~0.0	6 778	5.0
	2016	715	0.4	42	~0.0	118	0.1	5 109	2.9
Gambia Gambie	2005	166	0.1	10	~0.0	11	~0.0	732	0.5
	2008	175	0.1	47	~0.0	75	~0.0	1 411	0.9
	2015	213	0.1	20	~0.0	104	0.1	3 222	1.6
Georgia Géorgie	2010	18 227	4.3	1 257	0.3	353	0.1	17 104	4.0
	2014	19 270	4.8	2 152	0.5	308	0.1	16 023	4.0
Germany Allemagne	2010	303 645	3.8	66 427	0.8	50 604	0.6	1 014 000	12.6
	2015	338 129	4.2	69 863	0.9	52 568	0.7	1 113 000	13.8
Ghana Ghana	2004	3 240	0.2	393	~0.0	1 388	0.1	19 707	0.9
	2008	2 587	0.1	148	~0.0	1 673	0.1	22 834	1.0
	2010	2 325	0.1	…	…	…	…	22 507	0.9
Greece Grèce	2010	69 265	6.2	14 661	1.3	11 160	1.0	40 978	3.7
	2014	68 807	6.3	13 746	1.3	11 579	1.1	37 842	3.4
	2015	…	…	…	…	…	…	37 320	3.4
Grenada Grenade	2003	58	0.6	13	0.1	22	0.2	366	3.6
	2006	69	0.7	19	0.2	21	0.2	398	3.9
	2011	…	…	…	…	89	0.8	…	…
Guatemala Guatemala	2007	…	…	2 376	0.2	…	…	…	…
	2009	12 940	0.9	…	…	…	…	12 452	0.9
Guinea Guinée	2004	987	0.1	60	~0.0	…	…	4 408	0.5
	2005	940	0.1	33	~0.0	199	~0.0	…	…
	2016	977	0.1	…	…	142	~0.0	4 765	0.4
Guinea-Bissau Guinée-Bissau	2004	188	0.1	22	~0.0	27	~0.0	1 072	0.7
	2009	124	0.1	13	~0.0	21	~0.0	1 042	0.7
Guyana Guyana	2000	366	0.5	30	~0.0	…	…	1 738	2.3
	2009	161	0.2	46	0.1	87	0.1	989	1.3
	2010	161	0.2	…	…	…	…	399	0.5
Honduras Honduras	2000	3 676	0.6	1 371	0.2	926	0.1	8 528	1.4
	2005	2 680	0.4	…	…	…	…	7 796	1.1
Hungary Hongrie	2005	32 563	3.2	…	…	…	…	…	…
	2010	28 686	2.9	5 257	0.5	5 821	0.6	63 838	6.4
	2015	30 486	3.1	5 936	0.6	7 039	0.7	65 367	6.6
Iceland Islande	2005	1 070	3.6	314	1.1	299	1.0	4 378	14.8
	2010	1 142	3.6	299	0.9	365	1.1	4 875	15.3
	2015	1 249	3.8	278	0.8	370	1.1	5 387	16.4
	2016	…	…	278	0.8	365	1.1	5 035	15.2
India Inde	2003	625 400	0.6	47 318	~0.0	559 408	0.5	1 382 901	1.2
	2005	660 801	0.6	55 344	~0.0	…	…	1 481 270	1.3
	2009	757 377	0.6	104 603	0.1	655 801	0.5	1 702 555	1.4
	2010	816 629	0.7	…	…	656 101	0.5	1 894 968	1.5
	2016	1 005 281	0.8	197 734	0.1	741 548	0.6	2 778 248	2.1
Indonesia Indonésie	2003	29 499	0.1	7 093	~0.0	7 580	~0.0	179 959	0.8
	2010	33 736	0.1	18 454	0.1	11 758	~0.0	256 625	1.1
	2012	49 853	0.2	24 147	0.1	…	…	338 501	1.4
	2015	…	…	12 740	~0.0	30 329	0.1	335 646	1.3
Iran (Islamic Republic of) Iran (Rép. islamique d')	2005	61 870	0.9	13 210	0.2	13 900	0.2	98 020	1.4
	2014	116 536	1.5	27 783	0.4	17 750	0.2	121 166	1.6
Iraq Iraq	2010	19 738	0.6	4 799	0.2	5 675	0.2	…	…
	2014	30 131	0.9	7 891	0.2	8 609	0.2	63 850	1.8

Health Personnel *(continued)*

Number of health workers and workforce density (per 1 000 population)

Le personnel de santé *(suite)*

Personnel de santé et densité (pour 1 000 habitants)

Country or area / Pays ou zone	Year / Année	Physicians / Médecins: Number / Nombre	Physicians / Médecins: Per 1 000 / Pour 1 000	Dentists / Dentistes: Number / Nombre	Dentists / Dentistes: Per 1 000 / Pour 1 000	Pharmacists / Pharmaciens: Number / Nombre	Pharmacists / Pharmaciens: Per 1 000 / Pour 1 000	Nurses and midwives / Infirmières et Sages-femmes: Number / Nombre	Nurses and midwives / Infirmières et Sages-femmes: Per 1 000 / Pour 1 000
Ireland / Irlande	2010	...	...	2 721	0.6	4 567	1.0	...	...
	2011	12 215	2.6	2 667	0.6	4 791	1.0	57 685	12.4
	2015	13 446	2.9	2 828	0.6	5 191	1.1	...	...
	2016	13 959	3.0	...	...	...	...	...	...
Israel / Israël	2010	25 333	3.4	6 367	0.9	5 733	0.8	35 900	4.8
	2015	28 833	3.6	6 633	0.8	6 233	0.8	40 900	5.1
Italy / Italie	2016	240 481	4.0	47 098	0.8	66 454	1.1	341 949	5.7
Jamaica / Jamaïque	2003	2 253	0.9	212	0.1	...	...	4 374	1.7
	2008	1 103	0.4	244	0.1	172	0.1	2 930	1.1
	2016	1 322	0.5	186	0.1	157	0.1	4 669	1.7
Japan / Japon	2004	270 371	2.1	95 197	0.8	241 369	1.9	1 210 633	9.6
	2010	283 548	2.2	98 739	0.8	197 616	1.6	1 320 623	10.4
	2014	300 075	2.4	100 994	0.8	216 077	1.7	1 425 322	11.2
Jordan / Jordanie	2005	12 909	2.4	4 194	0.8	7 100	1.3	17 428	3.3
	2010	16 212	2.5	5 691	0.9	9 151	1.4	25 661	3.9
	2015	26 019	3.4	6 806	0.9	12 076	1.6	23 651	3.1
Kazakhstan / Kazakhstan	2010	57 179	3.5	6 657	0.4	11 265	0.7	135 125	8.3
	2013	59 872	3.5	6 406	0.4	13 828	0.8	146 072	8.5
	2014	56 873	3.3	6 430	0.4	14 163	0.8	...	...
Kenya / Kenya	2002	4 506	0.1	1 340	~0.0	...	...	...	...
	2004	...	...	...	...	3 094	0.1	16 146	0.5
	2010	7 129	0.2	898	~0.0	3 097	0.1	29 678	0.7
	2014	9 149	0.2	1 090	~0.0	2 355	0.1	70 975	1.6
Kiribati / Kiribati	2004	...	...	3	~0.0	2	~0.0	260	2.9
	2008	25	0.3	18	0.2	22	0.2	361	3.7
	2013	22	0.2	27	0.2	15	0.1	501	4.6
Kuwait / Koweït	2001	...	...	673	0.3	722	0.4	9 197	4.6
	2009	5 340	1.9	1 054	0.4	888	0.3	13 554	4.7
	2010	7 269	2.4	1 634	0.5	...	...	19 535	6.4
	2014	9 789	2.6	2 427	0.6	1 814	0.5	23 710	6.3
	2015	10 150	2.6	2 587	0.7	...	...	27 430	7.0
Kyrgyzstan / Kirghizistan	2010	10 277	1.9	1 022	0.2	169	~0.0	32 658	6.0
	2013	10 838	1.9	981	0.2	317	0.1	36 546	6.4
	2014	10 833	1.9	965	0.2	242	~0.0	...	...
Lao People's Dem. Rep. / Rép. dém. populaire lao	2005	1 614	0.3	...	...	...	...	5 724	1.0
	2009	1 211	0.2	324	0.1	...	...	5 322	0.9
	2014	3 286	0.5	341	0.1	1 276	0.2	6 416	1.0
Latvia / Lettonie	2005	8 207	3.7	1 450	0.7	...	...	10 350	4.6
	2010	6 517	3.1	1 488	0.7	1 433	0.7	10 922	5.2
	2015	6 324	3.2	1 419	0.7	1 574	0.8	9 661	4.9
Lebanon / Liban	2001	11 505	3.4	4 283	1.3	3 359	1.0	4 157	1.2
	2005	...	...	...	...	4 105	1.0	4 720	1.2
	2010	11 583	2.7	5 395	1.2	5 508	1.3	8 791	2.0
	2014	13 358	2.4	5 627	1.0	7 609	1.4	14 377	2.6
Lesotho / Lesotho	2003	89	~0.0	16	~0.0	62	~0.0	1 123	0.6
Liberia / Libéria	2004	103	~0.0	13	~0.0	35	~0.0	1 035	0.3
	2010	90	~0.0	23	~0.0	46	~0.0	1 805	0.5
Libya / Libye	2004	7 070	1.2	850	0.1	1 130	0.2	27 160	4.8
	2009	12 009	1.9	3 792	0.6	2 275	0.4	42 982	6.9
	2014	13 095	2.1	4 583	0.7	3 928	0.6	43 216	6.9
Lithuania / Lituanie	2003	...	...	...	...	2 270	0.7	...	...
	2010	12 226	3.9	2 456	0.8	...	...	23 722	7.6
	2015	12 605	4.4	2 644	0.9	...	...	23 172	8.1
Luxembourg / Luxembourg	2010	1 404	2.8	422	0.8	374	0.7	5 786	11.4
	2015	1 656	2.9	506	0.9	396	0.7	6 990	12.3
	2016	1 683	2.9	550	1.0	...	...	...	...

Country or area Pays ou zone	Year Année	Physicians / Médecins Number Nombre	Physicians / Médecins Per 1 000 Pour 1 000	Dentists / Dentistes Number Nombre	Dentists / Dentistes Per 1 000 Pour 1 000	Pharmacists / Pharmaciens Number Nombre	Pharmacists / Pharmaciens Per 1 000 Pour 1 000	Nurses and midwives / Infirmières et Sages-femmes Number Nombre	Nurses and midwives / Infirmières et Sages-femmes Per 1 000 Pour 1 000
Madagascar	2005	3 303	0.2	197	~0.0	8	0.0	6 418	0.4
Madagascar	2010	4 130	0.2	195	~0.0	7	0.0	4 724	0.2
	2012	3 188	0.1	181	~0.0	6	0.0	4 858	0.2
Malawi	2004	266	~0.0	...	...	...	...	7 264	0.6
Malawi	2009	265	~0.0	180	~0.0	221	~0.0	4 812	0.3
Malaysia	2002	17 020	0.7	2 160	0.1	2 880	0.1	43 380	1.8
Malaisie	2010	32 979	1.2	9 995	0.4	11 077	0.4	90 199	3.2
	2015	46 491	1.5	15 294	0.5	15 819	0.5	125 100	4.1
Maldives	2004	302	1.0	14	~0.0	241	0.8	886	3.0
Maldives	2010	525	1.6	32	0.1	247	0.7	1 868	5.6
	2015	1 313	3.6	62	0.2	391	1.1	2 990	8.2
Mali	2004	1 053	0.1	84	~0.0	351	~0.0	8 338	0.7
Mali	2010	1 291	0.1	103	~0.0	135	~0.0	6 715	0.4
Malta	2010	1 279	3.1	184	0.4	301	0.7	2 990	7.3
Malte	2015	1 636	3.9	206	0.5	558	1.3	3 827	9.1
Marshall Islands	2007	31	0.6	13	0.2	6	0.1	188	3.6
Îles Marshall	2012	24	0.5	26	0.5	7	0.1	187	3.6
Mauritania	2004	313	0.1	64	~0.0	81	~0.0	1 893	0.6
Mauritanie	2009	445	0.1	93	~0.0	123	~0.0	2 303	0.7
Mauritius	2004	1 303	1.1	233	0.2	1 428	1.2	4 604	3.8
Maurice	2010	1 500	1.2	260	0.2	400	0.3	3 600	2.9
	2015	2 550	2.0	380	0.3	497	0.4	4 261	3.3
Mexico	2000	195 897	1.9	78 281	0.8	3 189	~0.0	88 678	0.9
Mexique	2010	228 028	1.9	13 225	0.1	...	...	275 171	2.3
	2015	283 414	2.2	15 915	0.1	...	...	335 959	2.6
Micronesia (Fed. States of)	2005	62	0.6	13	0.1	16	0.2	249	2.3
Micronésie (États féd. de)	2008	64	0.6	40	0.4	16	0.2	280	2.7
	2009	20	0.2	...	...	...	...	375	3.6
Monaco Monaco	2014	250	6.6	38	1.0	98	2.6	772	20.5
Mongolia	2002	6 732	2.8	337	0.1	1 093	0.4	8 826	3.6
Mongolie	2010	7 497	2.8	533	0.2	1 176	0.4	9 876	3.6
	2011	7 943	2.9	652	0.2	1 284	0.5	10 143	3.7
	2014	9 300	3.2	...	...	3 451	1.2	11 836	4.1
	2015	9 653	3.3	...	...	1 504	0.5	...	...
Montenegro	2010	1 268	2.0	26	~0.0	91	0.1	3 542	5.7
Monténégro	2015	1 466	2.3	25	~0.0	109	0.2	3 592	5.7
Morocco	2004	15 991	0.5	3 091	0.1	7 366	0.2	24 328	0.8
Maroc	2009	20 682	0.7	2 668	0.1	9 006	0.3	29 689	0.9
	2014	20 947	0.6	4 655	0.1	...	...	29 592	0.9
Mozambique	2004	514	~0.0	159	~0.0	618	~0.0	6 183	0.3
Mozambique	2010	1 145	~0.0	448	~0.0	1 221	0.1	9 507	0.4
	2013	1 452	0.1	418	~0.0	1 491	0.1	10 620	0.4
Myanmar	2004	17 791	0.4	1 396	~0.0	127	~0.0	...	...
Myanmar	2005	18 584	0.4	1 756	~0.0	...	...	36 521	0.7
	2010	26 435	0.5	2 849	0.1	...	...	45 200	0.9
	2012	29 832	0.6	3 355	0.1	...	...	48 871	0.9
Namibia	2004	598	0.3	113	0.1	288	0.1	6 145	3.1
Namibie	2007	774	0.4	90	~0.0	376	0.2	5 750	2.8
Nauru	2004	10	1.0	1	0.1	10	1.0	63	6.2
Nauru	2008	10	1.0	1	0.1	...	...	69	6.9
	2009	10	1.0	3	0.3	7	0.7	...	...
	2010	10	1.0	...	...	...	...	...	...
	2011	14	1.4	6	0.6	10	1.0	70	7.0
Nepal	2004	5 384	0.2	359	~0.0	358	~0.0	11 825	0.5
Népal	2012	13 925	0.5	...	...	4 200	0.2	43 130	1.6
	2014	16 854	0.6	...	...	...	...	57 495	2.0
Netherlands	2010	...	...	...	...	3 308	0.2	...	...
Pays-Bas	2014	57 762	3.4	8 596	0.5	3 635	0.2	177 818	10.5
	2015	58 858	3.5	8 561	0.5	3 597	0.2	...	...

10

Health Personnel *(continued)*

Number of health workers and workforce density (per 1 000 population)

Le personnel de santé *(suite)*

Personnel de santé et densité (pour 1 000 habitants)

Country or area Pays ou zone	Year Année	Physicians Médecins Number Nombre	Per 1 000 Pour 1 000	Dentists Dentistes Number Nombre	Per 1 000 Pour 1 000	Pharmacists Pharmaciens Number Nombre	Per 1 000 Pour 1 000	Nurses and midwives Infirmières et Sages-femmes Number Nombre	Per 1 000 Pour 1 000
New Zealand Nouvelle-Zélande	2001	9 027	2.3	2 586	0.7	1 179	0.3	33 249	8.5
	2002	8 190	2.1	1 620	0.4	...	...	...	...
	2007	9 757	2.3	1 877	0.4	2 889	0.7	44 491	10.5
	2010	11 412	2.6	...	...	2 749	0.6	46 218	10.6
	2015	13 862	3.1	...	...	3 074	0.7	49 799	11.0
	2016	...	...	...	...	3 147	0.7	50 895	11.1
Nicaragua Nicaragua	2005	2 717	0.5	246	~0.0	...	...	6 294	1.2
	2010	4 239	0.7	258	~0.0	...	...	7 366	1.3
	2014	5 495	0.9	260	~0.0	...	...	8 323	1.4
Niger Niger	2004	296	~0.0	15	~0.0	20	~0.0	2 818	0.2
	2008	288	~0.0	16	~0.0	21	~0.0	2 115	0.1
Nigeria Nigéria	2005	39 210	0.3	2 113	~0.0	12 072	0.1	213 425	1.5
	2008	56 526	0.4	3 781	~0.0	18 682	0.1	224 943	1.5
	2009	58 363	0.4	2 464	~0.0	...	...	...	...
	2011	...	...	...	...	17 022	0.1	...	...
Niue Nioué	2004	4	2.3	2	1.2	1	0.6	22	12.8
	2008	3	1.8	4	2.5	1	0.6	16	9.8
Norway Norvège	2010	20 114	4.1	4 293	0.9	3 120	0.6	81 428	16.6
	2015	22 848	4.4	4 434	0.9	3 863	0.7	92 880	17.8
Oman Oman	2005	4 182	1.7	448	0.2	1 665	0.7	9 277	3.7
	2010	5 862	2.0	654	0.2	2 784	0.9	12 865	4.4
	2016	8 914	1.9	1 149	0.2	4 104	0.9	19 331	4.2
Pakistan Pakistan	2004	116 298	0.8	7 862	0.1	8 102	0.1	71 764	0.5
	2005	126 350	0.8	...	...	...	...	...	...
	2010	144 901	0.9	10 508	0.1	...	...	100 397	0.6
	2015	184 711	1.0	16 652	0.1	...	...	94 766	0.5
Palau Palaos	2004	...	...	...	...	...	...	120	6.1
	2007	...	...	5	0.2	1	0.1	...	...
	2010	29	1.4	...	...	...	...	120	5.9
	2014	25	1.2	...	...	...	...	111	5.3
Panama Panama	2005	4 488	1.4	938	0.3	...	...	6 675	2.0
	2010	5 121	1.4	1 091	0.3	...	...	9 021	2.5
	2011	5 551	1.5	1 114	0.3	...	...	8 579	2.3
	2013	6 068	1.6	1 037	0.3	...	...	...	...
Papua New Guinea Papouasie-Nvl-Guinée	2000	275	0.1	90	~0.0	...	...	2 841	0.5
	2009	...	...	121	~0.0	...	...	...	...
	2010	376	0.1	...	...	...	...	3 643	0.5
	2012	...	...	...	...	354	~0.0	...	...
Paraguay Paraguay	2002	6 355	1.2	3 182	0.6	1 868	0.3	10 261	1.9
	2012	8 203	1.3	1 054	0.2	...	...	6 689	1.0
Peru Pérou	2009	27 272	0.9	3 570	0.1	1 822	0.1	37 672	1.3
	2012	33 669	1.1	4 471	0.1	1 528	0.1	45 024	1.5
Philippines Philippines	2004	93 862	1.1	45 903	0.5	49 667	0.6	488 434	5.8
	2011	...	...	...	...	84 000	0.9	...	...
	2015	...	...	1 922	~0.0	...	...	24 169	0.2
Poland Pologne	2010	83 201	2.2	12 549	0.3	25 203	0.7	223 385	5.8
	2015	88 437	2.3	12 603	0.3	28 121	0.7	219 845	5.7
Portugal Portugal	2005	36 138	3.4	5 056	0.5	9 494	0.9	48 155	4.6
	2009	40 095	3.8	6 605	0.6	11 347	1.1	59 601	5.6
	2010	40 672	3.8	8 105	0.8	7 674	0.7	...	...
	2014	46 036	4.4	9 125	0.9	8 379	0.8	66 340	6.4
	2016	...	...	...	...	8 785	0.9	...	...
Qatar Qatar	2005	2 150	2.6	690	0.8	1 100	1.3	4 880	5.8
	2006	2 313	2.3	486	0.5	1 056	1.1	6 185	6.3
	2010	6 919	3.9	...	...	...	...	10 615	6.0
	2014	4 267	2.0	1 242	0.6	2 023	0.9	12 381	5.7
Republic of Korea République de Corée	2005	85 369	1.8	21 581	0.5	54 829	1.2	222 301	4.7
	2010	98 293	2.0	20 936	0.4	32 152	0.7	229 819	4.7
	2016	117 450	2.3	24 150	0.5	33 946	0.7	348 401	6.9

10 Health Personnel *(continued)*

Number of health workers and workforce density (per 1 000 population)

Le personnel de santé *(suite)*

Personnel de santé et densité (pour 1 000 habitants)

Country or area Pays ou zone	Year Année	Physicians / Médecins Number Nombre	Per 1 000 Pour 1 000	Dentists / Dentistes Number Nombre	Per 1 000 Pour 1 000	Pharmacists / Pharmaciens Number Nombre	Per 1 000 Pour 1 000	Nurses and midwives / Infirmières et Sages-femmes Number Nombre	Per 1 000 Pour 1 000
Republic of Moldova République de Moldova	2010	9 962	2.4	1 641	0.4	1 779	0.4	23 869	5.8
	2013	10 432	2.6	1 751	0.4	1 901	0.5	23 103	5.7
	2015	13 012	3.2	1 778	0.4	...	...	18 343	4.5
Romania Roumanie	2002	43 093	2.0	13 205	0.6	15 121	0.7	...	...
	2010	50 778	2.5	12 959	0.6	13 534	0.7	121 084	6.0
	2013	52 828	2.7	14 248	0.7	16 231	0.8	126 978	6.4
Russian Federation Fédération de Russie	2010	715 800	5.0	...	...	...	...	1 038 459	7.3
	2015	570 260	4.0	...	...	...	...	1 245 594	8.7
Rwanda Rwanda	2004	432	~0.0	...	...	278	~0.0	3 647	0.4
	2010	568	0.1	122	~0.0	56	~0.0	6 975	0.7
	2015	742	0.1	127	~0.0	114	~0.0	9 661	0.8
Saint Kitts and Nevis Saint-Kitts-et-Nevis	2001	49	1.1	15	0.3	...	...	294	6.4
Saint Lucia Sainte-Lucie	2001	130	0.8	27	0.2	23	0.1	371	2.3
	2004	68	0.4	7	~0.0	...	...	375	2.3
	2005	83	0.5	...	...	...	...	326	2.0
	2009	18	0.1	5	~0.0	...	...	...	...
	2010	...	...	28	0.2	...	...	...	...
Saint Vincent & Grenadines Saint-Vincent-Grenadines	2001	62	0.6	21	0.2	23	0.2	476	4.4
Samoa Samoa	2003	50	0.3	10	0.1	20	0.1	310	1.7
	2005	50	0.3	...	...	3	~0.0	...	...
	2008	85	0.5	63	0.3	59	0.3	348	1.9
	2010	64	0.3	45	0.2	...	...	286	1.5
San Marino Saint-Marin	2014	201	6.4	22	0.7	22	0.7	287	9.1
Sao Tome and Principe Sao Tomé-et-Principe	2004	81	0.5	11	0.1	24	0.2	308	2.1
Saudi Arabia Arabie saoudite	2000	14 950	0.7	...	...	...	...	36 495	1.7
	2001	14 464	0.7	1 581	0.1	...	...	...	...
	2010	66 014	2.4	...	...	14 928	0.5	129 792	4.6
	2014	79 313	2.6	12 301	0.4	21 639	0.7	160 811	5.2
Senegal Sénégal	2004	594	0.1	97	~0.0	85	~0.0	3 287	0.3
	2008	741	0.1	105	~0.0	127	~0.0	5 254	0.4
	2016	1 066	0.1	178	~0.0	170	~0.0	4 822	0.3
Serbia Serbie	2010	22 316	2.5	2 530	0.3	2 247	0.2	48 060	5.3
	2014	21 900	2.5	2 310	0.3	2 344	0.3	47 424	5.3
	2015	...	...	2 704	0.3	4 398	0.5	41 771	4.7
Seychelles Seychelles	2005	104	1.2	10	0.1	7	0.1	390	4.4
	2010	100	1.1	19	0.2	4	~0.0	412	4.4
	2012	93	1.0	14	0.1	4	~0.0	419	4.4
Sierra Leone Sierra Leone	2004	168	~0.0	5	~0.0	340	0.1	2 510	0.5
	2010	136	~0.0	6	~0.0	113	~0.0	1 842	0.3
Singapore Singapour	2005	6 748	1.5	1 277	0.3	1 330	0.3	20 167	4.5
	2010	8 819	1.7	1 506	0.3	1 814	0.4	29 340	5.8
	2016	12 967	2.3	2 198	0.4	2 875	0.5	40 561	7.1
Slovakia Slovaquie	2009	17 798	3.3	2 633	0.5	2 917	0.5	34 477	6.4
	2010	...	...	...	...	...	...	36 493	6.7
	2015	18 719	3.5	2 647	0.5	6 008	1.1	32 664	6.0
Slovenia Slovénie	2010	4 979	2.4	1 259	0.6	1 102	0.5	16 871	8.2
	2015	5 830	2.8	1 392	0.7	1 295	0.6	18 277	8.8
Solomon Islands Îles Salomon	2005	89	0.2	52	0.1	53	0.1	694	1.5
	2008	89	0.2	...	...	...	...	...	...
	2009	...	...	...	...	...	...	1 080	2.1
	2013	107	0.2	58	0.1	75	0.1	998	1.8
Somalia Somalie	2006	300	~0.0	...	...	...	...	965	0.1
	2014	309	~0.0	...	...	...	...	825	0.1

10 Health Personnel *(continued)*

Number of health workers and workforce density (per 1 000 population)

Le personnel de santé *(suite)*

Personnel de santé et densité (pour 1 000 habitants)

Country or area Pays ou zone	Year Année	Physicians / Médecins: Number Nombre	Physicians / Médecins: Per 1 000 Pour 1 000	Dentists / Dentistes: Number Nombre	Dentists / Dentistes: Per 1 000 Pour 1 000	Pharmacists / Pharmaciens: Number Nombre	Pharmacists / Pharmaciens: Per 1 000 Pour 1 000	Nurses and midwives / Infirmières et Sages-femmes: Number Nombre	Nurses and midwives / Infirmières et Sages-femmes: Per 1 000 Pour 1 000
South Africa Afrique du Sud	2004	34 829	0.7	5 994	0.1	12 521	0.3	184 459	3.9
	2005	...	...	...	...	...	...	191 269	4.0
	2010	37 599	0.7	8 812	0.2	...	...	283 052	5.5
	2016	44 949	0.8	11 817	0.2	36 980	0.7	287 458	5.2
Spain Espagne	2005	199 123	4.5	22 150	0.5	59 498	1.4	231 001	5.3
	2010	175 033	3.8	27 826	0.6	43 000	0.9	239 867	5.1
	2014	176 665	3.8	33 286	0.7	54 567	1.2	239 333	5.2
	2015	178 600	3.9	...	...	55 400	1.2	245 533	5.3
Sri Lanka Sri Lanka	2004	10 479	0.5	1 245	0.1	907	~0.0	33 233	1.7
	2005	10 198	0.5	954	~0.0	...	...	27 514	1.4
	2007	11 023	0.6	1 743	0.1	886	~0.0	40 678	2.1
	2010	14 668	0.7	1 046	0.1	...	...	35 367	1.8
	2015	18 243	0.9	1 390	0.1	1 504	0.1	57 887	2.8
Sudan Soudan	2004	7 552	0.2	1 082	~0.0	3 558	0.1	31 496	1.0
	2008	10 813	0.3	772	~0.0	386	~0.0	32 439	0.9
	2014	...	...	...	...	...	...	45 541	1.2
Suriname Suriname	2004	400	0.8	42	0.1	...	...	2 580	5.3
Sweden Suède	2010	36 524	3.9	7 509	0.8	7 135	0.8	111 000	11.8
	2014	40 637	4.2	7 777	0.8	7 367	0.8	115 237	11.9
Switzerland Suisse	2010	29 803	3.8	4 109	0.5	4 230	0.5	127 659	16.3
	2015	34 762	4.2	4 200	0.5	4 498	0.5	151 288	18.2
	2016	35 592	4.2	...	...	...	...	...	...
Syrian Arab Republic République arabe syrienne	2005	28 247	1.6	15 725	0.9	13 218	0.7	34 604	1.9
	2010	31 194	1.5	15 984	0.8	16 554	0.8	40 053	1.9
	2014	29 025	1.5	16 585	0.9	27 715	1.5	43 210	2.3
Tajikistan Tadjikistan	2003	12 688	1.9	...	...	680	0.1	...	...
	2005	13 272	2.0	...	...	...	...	...	...
	2010	12 778	1.7	1 234	0.2	...	...	33 764	4.5
	2014	14 219	1.7	1 289	0.2	...	...	43 762	5.3
Thailand Thaïlande	2004	18 918	0.3	4 129	0.1	7 413	0.1	96 704	1.5
	2010	26 244	0.4	17 222	0.3	8 700	0.1	138 710	2.1
	2015	31 959	0.5	...	...	12 231	0.2	155 876	2.3
TFYR of Macedonia ex-R.Y. de Macédoine	2010	5 541	2.7	1 599	0.8	692	0.3	9 899	4.8
	2015	5 975	2.9	1 824	0.9	1 029	0.5	7 884	3.8
Timor-Leste Timor-Leste	2004	79	0.1	45	~0.0	14	~0.0	1 795	1.9
	2010	84	0.1	44	~0.0	130	0.1	1 255	1.2
	2011	84	0.1	46	~0.0	131	0.1	1 283	1.2
	2015	...	...	18	~0.0	170	0.1	1 545	1.3
Togo Togo	2004	244	~0.0	19	~0.0	134	~0.0	1 937	0.4
	2008	349	0.1	19	~0.0	11	~0.0	1 816	0.3
Tonga Tonga	2001	35	0.4	33	0.3	17	0.2	341	3.5
	2002	30	0.3	...	...	...	...	350	3.5
	2003	...	...	23	0.2	...	...	...	...
	2009	62	0.6	37	0.4	15	0.1	378	3.7
	2010	58	0.6	...	...	...	...	400	3.8
	2013	...	...	39	0.4	27	0.3	408	3.9
Trinidad and Tobago Trinité-et-Tobago	2003	1 038	0.8	249	0.2	525	0.4	3 980	3.1
	2010	2 402	1.8	343	0.3	641	0.5	3 905	2.9
	2011	2 431	1.8	343	0.3	650	0.5	4 379	3.3
Tunisia Tunisie	2004	13 330	1.3	2 452	0.2	2 909	0.3	28 537	2.8
	2005	9 422	0.9	1 850	0.2	2 114	0.2	...	...
	2010	12 996	1.2	3 130	0.3	3 236	0.3	23 836	2.2
	2015	14 507	1.3	...	...	...	...	29 851	2.7
	2016	...	...	...	...	...	...	30 049	2.6
Turkey Turquie	2005	100 853	1.5	18 149	0.3	22 756	0.3	121 723	1.8
	2010	123 447	1.7	21 432	0.3	26 506	0.4	215 458	3.0
	2014	135 616	1.7	22 996	0.3	27 199	0.4	248 108	3.2
	2015	...	...	24 834	0.3	27 530	0.4	205 889	2.6

10 Health Personnel *(continued)*
Number of health workers and workforce density (per 1 000 population)

Le personnel de santé *(suite)*
Personnel de santé et densité (pour 1 000 habitants)

Country or area / Pays ou zone	Year / Année	Physicians / Médecins: Number / Nombre	Physicians / Médecins: Per 1 000 / Pour 1 000	Dentists / Dentistes: Number / Nombre	Dentists / Dentistes: Per 1 000 / Pour 1 000	Pharmacists / Pharmaciens: Number / Nombre	Pharmacists / Pharmaciens: Per 1 000 / Pour 1 000	Nurses and midwives / Infirmières et Sages-femmes: Number / Nombre	Nurses and midwives / Infirmières et Sages-femmes: Per 1 000 / Pour 1 000
Turkmenistan / Turkménistan	2002	20 032	4.4	876	0.2	1 626	0.4	43 359	9.4
	2010	11 570	2.3	586	0.1	928	0.2	23 994	4.8
	2014	12 161	2.3	631	0.1	926	0.2	25 312	4.8
Tuvalu / Tuvalu	2003	10	1.0	2	0.2	2	0.2	50	5.2
	2008	10	1.0	4	0.4	2	0.2	64	6.5
	2009	12	1.2	…	…	…	…	…	…
Uganda / Ouganda	2005	3 361	0.1	440	~0.0	762	~0.0	37 625	1.3
	2015	3 645	0.1	276	~0.0	45	~0.0	25 305	0.6
Ukraine / Ukraine	2010	159 495	3.5	30 147	0.7	1 818	~0.0	362 236	7.9
	2014	134 986	3.0	26 954	0.6	1 521	~0.0	316 771	7.0
United Arab Emirates / Émirats arabes unis	2004	…	…	1 368	0.3	2 006	0.5	14 362	3.6
	2005	6 946	1.6	…	…	…	…	14 844	3.3
	2007	9 215	1.5	2 053	0.3	2 817	0.5	17 336	2.9
	2010	12 752	1.5	…	…	…	…	24 362	2.9
	2014	14 154	1.6	2 814	0.3	3 344	0.4	27 812	3.1
United Kingdom / Royaume-Uni	2010	169 163	2.7	32 423	0.5	40 641	0.6	630 394	10.1
	2016	183 938	2.8	34 867	0.5	56 542	0.9	548 291	8.4
United Rep. of Tanzania / Rép.-Unie de Tanzanie	2002	822	~0.0	267	~0.0	365	~0.0	13 292	0.4
	2006	…	…	230	~0.0	…	…	9 440	0.2
	2014	1 157	~0.0	1 037	~0.0	1 839	~0.0	21 552	0.4
United States of America / États-Unis d'Amérique	2000	730 801	2.6	463 663	1.6	249 642	0.9	2 669 603	9.4
	2004	793 648	2.7	…	…	…	…	…	…
	2005	…	…	…	…	…	…	2 927 000	9.9
	2010	752 572	2.4	…	…	275 000	0.9	…	…
	2014	820 251	2.6	…	…	…	…	…	…
Uruguay / Uruguay	2002	12 384	3.7	3 936	1.2	…	…	2 880	0.9
	2008	13 197	3.9	2 476	0.7	1 035	0.3	19 595	5.8
Uzbekistan / Ouzbékistan	2010	72 522	2.6	4 693	0.2	1 074	~0.0	349 800	12.6
	2014	72 237	2.5	4 520	0.2	1 243	~0.0	368 250	12.5
Vanuatu / Vanuatu	2004	30	0.1	…	…	…	…	360	1.8
	2008	26	0.1	3	~0.0	2	~0.0	380	1.7
	2012	46	0.2	17	0.1	29	0.1	549	2.2
Venezuela (Boliv. Rep. of) / Venezuela (Rép. boliv. du)	2001	48 000	1.9	13 680	0.5	…	…	28 000	1.1
Viet Nam / Viet Nam	2005	51 466	0.6	…	…	23 218	0.3	69 665	0.8
	2010	61 398	0.7	…	…	30 687	0.3	109 094	1.2
	2016	77 539	0.8	…	…	32 997	0.3	135 432	1.4
Yemen / Yémen	2004	6 739	0.3	850	~0.0	2 638	0.1	13 746	0.7
	2009	7 127	0.3	…	…	…	…	…	…
	2010	…	…	897	~0.0	2 295	0.1	16 590	0.7
	2014	8 148	0.3	543	~0.0	2 716	0.1	19 828	0.8
Zambia / Zambie	2004	1 499	0.1	491	~0.0	…	…	…	…
	2005	646	0.1	…	…	…	…	8 369	0.7
	2010	836	0.1	246	~0.0	317	~0.0	9 932	0.7
	2016	1 514	0.1	312	~0.0	1 159	0.1	14 807	0.9
Zimbabwe / Zimbabwe	2004	2 086	0.2	…	…	883	0.1	…	…
	2009	827	0.1	182	~0.0	2 528	0.2	16 668	1.2
	2010	916	0.1	239	~0.0	…	…	17 029	1.2
	2014	1 176	0.1	250	~0.0	392	~0.0	17 795	1.2

Source:

World Health Organisation (WHO), Geneva, WHO Global Health Workforce statistics database, last accessed April 2018.

Source:

Organisation mondiale de la santé (OMS), Genève, base de données de l'OMS sur les statistiques relatives aux personnels de santé, dernier accès avril 2018.

11 Expenditure on health

Percentage of GDP and of government expenditure

Dépenses de santé

Pourcentage du PIB et des dépenses du gouvernement

Region, country or area[&]	2000	2005	2010	2013	2014	2015	Région, pays ou zone[&]
Afghanistan							**Afghanistan**
Current expenditure (% GDP)	...	9.9	8.6	8.8	9.7	10.3	Dépenses courantes (% du PIB)
Domestic General govt.(% expend. total)	...	3.4	2.3	1.8	1.9	2.0	Dépenses intérieures (en % du totale)
Albania							**Albanie**
Current expenditure (% GDP)	6.8	6.3	5.0	6.3	7.0	6.8	Dépenses courantes (% du PIB)
Domestic General govt.(% expend. total)	7.1	9.7	8.5	9.5	9.6	9.5	Dépenses intérieures (en % du totale)
Algeria							**Algérie**
Current expenditure (% GDP)	3.5	3.2	5.1	6.0	6.5	7.1	Dépenses courantes (% du PIB)
Domestic General govt.(% expend. total)	8.6	8.1	9.5	11.9	11.6	10.7	Dépenses intérieures (en % du totale)
Andorra							**Andorre**
Current expenditure (% GDP)	9.3	9.8	11.6	14.2	12.0	12.0	Dépenses courantes (% du PIB)
Domestic General govt.(% expend. total)	13.0	15.1	16.4	15.8	18.5	18.5	Dépenses intérieures (en % du totale)
Angola							**Angola**
Current expenditure (% GDP)	2.5	4.0	2.7	3.0	2.8	2.9	Dépenses courantes (% du PIB)
Domestic General govt.(% expend. total)	2.3	5.1	4.3	4.6	3.7	3.7	Dépenses intérieures (en % du totale)
Antigua and Barbuda							**Antigua-et-Barbuda**
Current expenditure (% GDP)	4.1	4.4	5.5	5.4	5.7	4.8	Dépenses courantes (% du PIB)
Domestic General govt.(% expend. total)	11.2	12.0	16.3	15.5	17.8	14.9	Dépenses intérieures (en % du totale)
Argentina							**Argentine**
Current expenditure (% GDP)	5.0	6.4	6.8	6.4	6.4	6.8	Dépenses courantes (% du PIB)
Domestic General govt.(% expend. total)	4.6	10.9	11.7	11.9	12.4	12.3	Dépenses intérieures (en % du totale)
Armenia							**Arménie**
Current expenditure (% GDP)	6.5	7.0	5.3	8.3	7.0	10.1	Dépenses courantes (% du PIB)
Domestic General govt.(% expend. total)	4.2	7.4	6.4	6.2	6.3	6.1	Dépenses intérieures (en % du totale)
Australia							**Australie**
Current expenditure (% GDP)	7.6	8.0	8.5	8.8	9.1	9.4	Dépenses courantes (% du PIB)
Domestic General govt.(% expend. total)	15.2	16.3	16.3	16.5	16.6	...	Dépenses intérieures (en % du totale)
Austria							**Autriche**
Current expenditure (% GDP)	9.2	9.6	10.1	10.2	10.3	10.3	Dépenses courantes (% du PIB)
Domestic General govt.(% expend. total)	...	14.0	14.5	15.0	14.7	15.1	Dépenses intérieures (en % du totale)
Azerbaijan							**Azerbaïdjan**
Current expenditure (% GDP)	3.8	7.4	4.9	5.4	5.7	6.7	Dépenses courantes (% du PIB)
Domestic General govt.(% expend. total)	5.4	5.2	4.1	4.2	4.1	4.1	Dépenses intérieures (en % du totale)
Bahamas							**Bahamas**
Current expenditure (% GDP)	5.1	5.9	7.4	7.4	7.3	7.4	Dépenses courantes (% du PIB)
Domestic General govt.(% expend. total)	18.6	16.2	15.2	15.0	12.8	14.2	Dépenses intérieures (en % du totale)
Bahrain							**Bahreïn**
Current expenditure (% GDP)	3.4	3.0	3.3	4.3	4.6	5.2	Dépenses courantes (% du PIB)
Domestic General govt.(% expend. total)	10.2	8.6	8.5	8.2	10.6	9.5	Dépenses intérieures (en % du totale)
Bangladesh [1]							**Bangladesh** [1]
Current expenditure (% GDP)	* 2.4	* 2.8	* 2.7	* 2.7	* 2.7	* 2.6	Dépenses courantes (% du PIB)
Domestic General govt.(% expend. total)	* 5.2	* 4.1	* 4.1	* 2.8	* 2.6	* 2.8	Dépenses intérieures (en % du totale)
Barbados							**Barbade**
Current expenditure (% GDP)	5.2	6.3	6.9	8.2	7.7	7.5	Dépenses courantes (% du PIB)
Domestic General govt.(% expend. total)	7.8	9.2	9.0	8.8	8.0	7.4	Dépenses intérieures (en % du totale)
Belarus							**Bélarus**
Current expenditure (% GDP)	5.5	6.3	5.3	5.8	5.4	6.1	Dépenses courantes (% du PIB)
Domestic General govt.(% expend. total)	12.1	9.8	9.5	8.7	8.7	8.5	Dépenses intérieures (en % du totale)
Belgium							**Belgique**
Current expenditure (% GDP)	7.9	9.0	9.9	10.4	10.4	10.5	Dépenses courantes (% du PIB)
Domestic General govt.(% expend. total)	...	14.3	15.2	15.2	15.4	16.0	Dépenses intérieures (en % du totale)
Belize							**Belize**
Current expenditure (% GDP)	3.9	4.4	5.8	5.8	5.8	6.2	Dépenses courantes (% du PIB)
Domestic General govt.(% expend. total)	5.8	8.0	...	11.9	9.8	11.1	Dépenses intérieures (en % du totale)
Benin							**Bénin**
Current expenditure (% GDP)	4.3	4.0	4.1	3.9	3.6	4.0	Dépenses courantes (% du PIB)
Domestic General govt.(% expend. total)	6.2	4.8	4.9	5.0	4.1	3.4	Dépenses intérieures (en % du totale)
Bhutan [1]							**Bhoutan** [1]
Current expenditure (% GDP)	* 4.2	* 3.5	* 3.2	* 3.3	* 3.2	* 3.5	Dépenses courantes (% du PIB)
Domestic General govt.(% expend. total)	...	* 6.8	* 6.5	* 6.9	* 7.8	* 9.1	Dépenses intérieures (en % du totale)
Bolivia (Plurin. State of)							**Bolivie (État plurin. de)**
Current expenditure (% GDP)	4.3	5.0	5.1	5.5	5.8	6.4	Dépenses courantes (% du PIB)
Domestic General govt.(% expend. total)	8.3	8.6	9.9	8.6	8.7	9.8	Dépenses intérieures (en % du totale)

11 Expenditure on health *(continued)*
Percentage of GDP and of government expenditure

Dépenses de santé *(suite)*
Pourcentage du PIB et des dépenses du gouvernement

Region, country or area[&]	2000	2005	2010	2013	2014	2015	Région, pays ou zone[&]
Bosnia and Herzegovina							**Bosnie-Herzégovine**
Current expenditure (% GDP)	7.1	9.1	9.0	9.5	9.6	9.4	Dépenses courantes (% du PIB)
Domestic General govt.(% expend. total)	7.3	10.8	12.5	14.6	14.4	14.9	Dépenses intérieures (en % du totale)
Botswana							**Botswana**
Current expenditure (% GDP)	5.8	5.3	5.6	5.4	5.3	6.0	Dépenses courantes (% du PIB)
Domestic General govt.(% expend. total)	10.9	10.5	7.9	8.6	8.3	8.8	Dépenses intérieures (en % du totale)
Brazil							**Brésil**
Current expenditure (% GDP)	8.4	8.0	8.0	8.0	8.4	8.9	Dépenses courantes (% du PIB)
Domestic General govt.(% expend. total)	10.1	8.4	8.4	8.3	8.3	7.7	Dépenses intérieures (en % du totale)
Brunei Darussalam [2]							**Brunéi Darussalam [2]**
Current expenditure (% GDP)	2.5	2.2	2.3	2.1	2.2	2.6	Dépenses courantes (% du PIB)
Domestic General govt.(% expend. total)	5.7	6.4	5.8	5.8	5.9	6.4	Dépenses intérieures (en % du totale)
Bulgaria [3]							**Bulgarie [3]**
Current expenditure (% GDP)	5.9	6.9	7.1	7.8	8.5	8.2	Dépenses courantes (% du PIB)
Domestic General govt.(% expend. total)	8.5	11.2	10.9	10.8	10.7	10.3	Dépenses intérieures (en % du totale)
Burkina Faso							**Burkina Faso**
Current expenditure (% GDP)	3.3	4.4	5.9	6.1	5.6	5.4	Dépenses courantes (% du PIB)
Domestic General govt.(% expend. total)	4.7	6.3	5.8	6.5	7.8	7.2	Dépenses intérieures (en % du totale)
Burundi							**Burundi**
Current expenditure (% GDP)	* 6.8	* 9.4	* 11.3	* 8.2	* 6.8	* 8.2	Dépenses courantes (% du PIB)
Domestic General govt.(% expend. total)	* 5.9	* 5.5	* 4.9	* 4.4	* 4.4	* 11.8	Dépenses intérieures (en % du totale)
Cabo Verde							**Cabo Verde**
Current expenditure (% GDP)	4.8	4.8	4.5	4.4	5.0	4.8	Dépenses courantes (% du PIB)
Domestic General govt.(% expend. total)	7.5	8.8	7.3	8.8	10.9	10.8	Dépenses intérieures (en % du totale)
Cambodia [1,4]							**Cambodge [1,4]**
Current expenditure (% GDP)	6.4	7.1	6.9	6.9	6.2	6.0	Dépenses courantes (% du PIB)
Domestic General govt.(% expend. total)	8.6	11.5	6.8	6.8	5.9	6.1	Dépenses intérieures (en % du totale)
Cameroon							**Cameroun**
Current expenditure (% GDP)	* 4.3	* 4.5	* 5.0	* 4.9	* 4.9	* 5.1	Dépenses courantes (% du PIB)
Domestic General govt.(% expend. total)	* 4.8	* 5.2	* 5.1	* 3.2	* 2.6	* 3.1	Dépenses intérieures (en % du totale)
Canada							**Canada**
Current expenditure (% GDP)	8.3	9.1	10.6	10.1	10.0	10.4	Dépenses courantes (% du PIB)
Domestic General govt.(% expend. total)	14.8	17.1	17.8	18.6	19.0	19.1	Dépenses intérieures (en % du totale)
Central African Republic							**République centrafricaine**
Current expenditure (% GDP)	* 3.5	* 4.5	* 3.8	* 4.4	* 4.7	* 4.8	Dépenses courantes (% du PIB)
Domestic General govt.(% expend. total)	* 8.5	* 7.6	* 4.4	* 3.4	* 4.9	* 4.1	Dépenses intérieures (en % du totale)
Chad							**Tchad**
Current expenditure (% GDP)	* 6.2	* 4.9	* 4.1	* 4.8	* 4.6	* 4.6	Dépenses courantes (% du PIB)
Domestic General govt.(% expend. total)	* 12.4	* 12.4	* 3.5	* 8.2	* 5.7	* 6.3	Dépenses intérieures (en % du totale)
Chile							**Chili**
Current expenditure (% GDP)	7.0	6.6	6.8	7.4	7.6	8.1	Dépenses courantes (% du PIB)
Domestic General govt.(% expend. total)	16.3	17.3	17.1	19.1	19.3	19.6	Dépenses intérieures (en % du totale)
China							**Chine**
Current expenditure (% GDP)	* 4.5	* 4.3	* 4.5	* 4.9	* 5.0	* 5.3	Dépenses courantes (% du PIB)
Domestic General govt.(% expend. total)	* 6.2	* 7.9	* 9.4	* 9.6	* 9.9	* 10.1	Dépenses intérieures (en % du totale)
Colombia							**Colombie**
Current expenditure (% GDP)	5.5	5.5	6.1	6.0	6.4	6.2	Dépenses courantes (% du PIB)
Domestic General govt.(% expend. total)	13.6	13.6	14.1	12.9	12.7	12.2	Dépenses intérieures (en % du totale)
Comoros							**Comores**
Current expenditure (% GDP)	* 12.1	* 10.1	* 8.7	* 8.3	* 8.0	* 8.0	Dépenses courantes (% du PIB)
Domestic General govt.(% expend. total)	* 9.7	* 6.6	* 3.4	* 3.8	* 3.8	* 3.8	Dépenses intérieures (en % du totale)
Congo							**Congo**
Current expenditure (% GDP)	* 1.7	1.9	2.0	2.4	2.4	3.4	Dépenses courantes (% du PIB)
Domestic General govt.(% expend. total)	2.3	2.0	4.2	2.5	2.6	3.1	Dépenses intérieures (en % du totale)
Cook Islands [1]							**Îles Cook [1]**
Current expenditure (% GDP)	3.2	4.2	3.5	3.3	3.3	2.7	Dépenses courantes (% du PIB)
Domestic General govt.(% expend. total)	9.6	9.6	9.3	6.7	5.7	5.1	Dépenses intérieures (en % du totale)
Costa Rica							**Costa Rica**
Current expenditure (% GDP)	6.5	6.7	8.1	8.3	8.2	8.1	Dépenses courantes (% du PIB)
Domestic General govt.(% expend. total)	17.6	17.7	21.0	21.3	20.2	18.8	Dépenses intérieures (en % du totale)
Côte d'Ivoire							**Côte d'Ivoire**
Current expenditure (% GDP)	5.7	5.4	6.1	5.1	5.2	5.4	Dépenses courantes (% du PIB)
Domestic General govt.(% expend. total)	4.5	4.0	4.0	5.0	4.1	5.0	Dépenses intérieures (en % du totale)
Croatia							**Croatie**
Current expenditure (% GDP)	7.7	6.9	8.1	7.3	7.5	7.4	Dépenses courantes (% du PIB)
Domestic General govt.(% expend. total)	14.8	13.0	14.6	12.2	12.0	11.7	Dépenses intérieures (en % du totale)

Region, country or area&	2000	2005	2010	2013	2014	2015	Région, pays ou zone&
Cyprus							**Chypre**
Current expenditure (% GDP)	5.3	5.3	6.3	6.9	6.8	6.8	Dépenses courantes (% du PIB)
Domestic General govt.(% expend. total)	6.5	5.4	7.2	7.7	6.2	7.1	Dépenses intérieures (en % du totale)
Czechia							**Tchéquie**
Current expenditure (% GDP)	5.7	6.4	6.9	7.8	7.7	7.3	Dépenses courantes (% du PIB)
Domestic General govt.(% expend. total)	...	13.3	13.5	15.3	15.0	14.3	Dépenses intérieures (en % du totale)
Dem. Rep. of the Congo							**Rép. dém. du Congo**
Current expenditure (% GDP)	1.4	3.0	4.0	3.9	4.4	4.3	Dépenses courantes (% du PIB)
Domestic General govt.(% expend. total)	1.5	2.3	3.1	4.0	4.1	5.0	Dépenses intérieures (en % du totale)
Denmark							**Danemark**
Current expenditure (% GDP)	8.1	9.1	10.4	10.2	10.3	10.3	Dépenses courantes (% du PIB)
Domestic General govt.(% expend. total)	12.8	14.9	15.5	15.4	15.6	15.8	Dépenses intérieures (en % du totale)
Djibouti [5]							**Djibouti** [5]
Current expenditure (% GDP)	4.1	4.5	4.3	4.1	4.1	4.4	Dépenses courantes (% du PIB)
Domestic General govt.(% expend. total)	6.1	5.3	7.0	6.7	6.1	4.1	Dépenses intérieures (en % du totale)
Dominica							**Dominique**
Current expenditure (% GDP)	4.7	4.6	5.1	5.0	5.2	5.4	Dépenses courantes (% du PIB)
Domestic General govt.(% expend. total)	8.4	9.5	8.5	9.7	10.7	10.6	Dépenses intérieures (en % du totale)
Dominican Republic							**République dominicaine**
Current expenditure (% GDP)	4.2	4.6	5.6	6.0	6.1	6.2	Dépenses courantes (% du PIB)
Domestic General govt.(% expend. total)	6.6	7.8	13.6	14.0	11.9	9.5	Dépenses intérieures (en % du totale)
Ecuador							**Équateur**
Current expenditure (% GDP)	3.3	5.6	7.5	8.5	8.6	8.5	Dépenses courantes (% du PIB)
Domestic General govt.(% expend. total)	5.5	7.2	9.2	10.0	10.4	11.0	Dépenses intérieures (en % du totale)
Egypt							**Égypte**
Current expenditure (% GDP)	5.2	5.2	4.4	4.6	4.1	4.2	Dépenses courantes (% du PIB)
Domestic General govt.(% expend. total)	6.1	5.0	4.3	4.1	4.1	4.2	Dépenses intérieures (en % du totale)
El Salvador							**El Salvador**
Current expenditure (% GDP)	8.0	7.2	6.9	6.9	6.8	6.9	Dépenses courantes (% du PIB)
Domestic General govt.(% expend. total)	18.1	19.0	16.8	17.8	18.3	19.1	Dépenses intérieures (en % du totale)
Equatorial Guinea							**Guinée équatoriale**
Current expenditure (% GDP)	* 2.5	* 0.8	* 1.5	* 1.7	* 1.8	* 2.7	Dépenses courantes (% du PIB)
Domestic General govt.(% expend. total)	* 2.5	* 2.1	* 1.0	* 1.5	* 1.3	* 1.3	Dépenses intérieures (en % du totale)
Eritrea							**Érythrée**
Current expenditure (% GDP)	* 5.6	* 5.3	* 3.7	* 3.2	* 3.4	* 3.3	Dépenses courantes (% du PIB)
Domestic General govt.(% expend. total)	* 2.6	* 1.1	* 1.9	* 1.3	* 1.7	* 1.8	Dépenses intérieures (en % du totale)
Estonia							**Estonie**
Current expenditure (% GDP)	5.2	5.0	6.3	6.0	6.2	6.5	Dépenses courantes (% du PIB)
Domestic General govt.(% expend. total)	...	11.2	11.6	11.8	12.2	12.2	Dépenses intérieures (en % du totale)
Eswatini							**Eswatini**
Current expenditure (% GDP)	4.6	5.9	8.2	7.3	7.2	7.0	Dépenses courantes (% du PIB)
Domestic General govt.(% expend. total)	10.5	12.6	18.8	16.6	13.7	14.9	Dépenses intérieures (en % du totale)
Ethiopia							**Éthiopie**
Current expenditure (% GDP)	4.4	4.1	5.5	4.1	4.0	4.0	Dépenses courantes (% du PIB)
Domestic General govt.(% expend. total)	7.0	7.2	5.2	6.2	4.1	6.0	Dépenses intérieures (en % du totale)
Fiji							**Fidji**
Current expenditure (% GDP)	* 3.7	* 3.5	* 3.6	* 3.5	* 3.7	* 3.6	Dépenses courantes (% du PIB)
Domestic General govt.(% expend. total)	* 10.0	* 9.6	* 8.5	* 7.3	* 7.0	* 7.2	Dépenses intérieures (en % du totale)
Finland							**Finlande**
Current expenditure (% GDP)	6.8	8.0	8.9	9.5	9.5	9.4	Dépenses courantes (% du PIB)
Domestic General govt.(% expend. total)	10.5	12.7	12.5	12.9	12.7	12.8	Dépenses intérieures (en % du totale)
France							**France**
Current expenditure (% GDP)	9.5	10.2	10.7	10.9	11.1	11.1	Dépenses courantes (% du PIB)
Domestic General govt.(% expend. total)	...	15.1	14.9	15.1	15.3	15.3	Dépenses intérieures (en % du totale)
Gabon							**Gabon**
Current expenditure (% GDP)	2.9	2.8	2.5	2.8	2.5	2.7	Dépenses courantes (% du PIB)
Domestic General govt.(% expend. total)	5.2	5.1	6.8	5.3	6.4	7.0	Dépenses intérieures (en % du totale)
Gambia							**Gambie**
Current expenditure (% GDP)	3.6	4.9	5.7	6.1	7.0	6.7	Dépenses courantes (% du PIB)
Domestic General govt.(% expend. total)	7.1	10.0	7.8	6.0	7.6	10.6	Dépenses intérieures (en % du totale)
Georgia [6]							**Géorgie** [6]
Current expenditure (% GDP)	7.4	8.3	9.5	8.4	8.4	7.9	Dépenses courantes (% du PIB)
Domestic General govt.(% expend. total)	6.4	5.6	6.1	6.7	7.8	10.5	Dépenses intérieures (en % du totale)
Germany							**Allemagne**
Current expenditure (% GDP)	9.8	10.3	11.0	11.0	11.1	11.2	Dépenses courantes (% du PIB)
Domestic General govt.(% expend. total)	17.5	17.0	19.5	20.6	21.0	21.4	Dépenses intérieures (en % du totale)

Region, country or area&	2000	2005	2010	2013	2014	2015	Région, pays ou zone&
Ghana							**Ghana**
Current expenditure (% GDP)	5.1	6.3	6.5	5.8	5.5	5.9	Dépenses courantes (% du PIB)
Domestic General govt.(% expend. total)	6.1	10.0	10.1	10.1	5.8	7.1	Dépenses intérieures (en % du totale)
Greece							**Grèce**
Current expenditure (% GDP)	7.2	9.0	9.6	8.3	7.9	8.4	Dépenses courantes (% du PIB)
Domestic General govt.(% expend. total)	...	...	12.6	8.3	9.1	9.1	Dépenses intérieures (en % du totale)
Grenada							**Grenade**
Current expenditure (% GDP)	5.1	5.3	6.1	5.6	5.3	5.0	Dépenses courantes (% du PIB)
Domestic General govt.(% expend. total)	6.8	9.9	9.8	7.9	7.1	7.4	Dépenses intérieures (en % du totale)
Guatemala							**Guatemala**
Current expenditure (% GDP)	5.2	6.6	6.4	6.2	6.2	5.7	Dépenses courantes (% du PIB)
Domestic General govt.(% expend. total)	13.2	13.8	13.9	15.6	16.2	14.9	Dépenses intérieures (en % du totale)
Guinea							**Guinée**
Current expenditure (% GDP)	5.0	4.5	4.4	4.7	4.3	4.5	Dépenses courantes (% du PIB)
Domestic General govt.(% expend. total)	2.9	3.0	1.9	2.6	2.7	2.7	Dépenses intérieures (en % du totale)
Guinea-Bissau							**Guinée-Bissau**
Current expenditure (% GDP)	* 6.3	* 6.3	* 6.2	* 4.7	* 6.3	* 6.9	Dépenses courantes (% du PIB)
Domestic General govt.(% expend. total)	* 14.3	* 14.1	* 5.5	* 14.7	* 9.0	* 9.5	Dépenses intérieures (en % du totale)
Guyana							**Guyana**
Current expenditure (% GDP)	4.4	5.4	4.6	5.0	5.1	4.5	Dépenses courantes (% du PIB)
Domestic General govt.(% expend. total)	7.1	6.3	5.7	8.1	8.6	7.8	Dépenses intérieures (en % du totale)
Haiti							**Haïti**
Current expenditure (% GDP)	6.9	5.5	10.2	7.2	7.2	6.9	Dépenses courantes (% du PIB)
Domestic General govt.(% expend. total)	10.9	4.0	2.5	3.0	2.9	3.3	Dépenses intérieures (en % du totale)
Honduras							**Honduras**
Current expenditure (% GDP)	6.3	7.2	8.2	8.2	7.7	7.6	Dépenses courantes (% du PIB)
Domestic General govt.(% expend. total)	13.9	12.2	13.0	11.0	10.5	11.3	Dépenses intérieures (en % du totale)
Hungary							**Hongrie**
Current expenditure (% GDP)	6.8	8.0	7.6	7.3	7.1	7.2	Dépenses courantes (% du PIB)
Domestic General govt.(% expend. total)	...	11.5	10.2	9.8	9.8	9.7	Dépenses intérieures (en % du totale)
Iceland							**Islande**
Current expenditure (% GDP)	9.0	9.2	8.8	8.7	8.8	8.6	Dépenses courantes (% du PIB)
Domestic General govt.(% expend. total)	...	18.0	14.4	16.0	15.7	16.4	Dépenses intérieures (en % du totale)
India [2]							**Inde** [2]
Current expenditure (% GDP)	* 4.2	* 3.8	* 3.3	# * 3.7	* 3.6	* 3.9	Dépenses courantes (% du PIB)
Domestic General govt.(% expend. total)	* 3.3	* 3.0	* 3.2	# * 3.1	* 3.0	* 3.4	Dépenses intérieures (en % du totale)
Indonesia							**Indonésie**
Current expenditure (% GDP)	2.0	2.8	3.5	3.4	3.4	3.3	Dépenses courantes (% du PIB)
Domestic General govt.(% expend. total)	3.8	4.2	6.2	6.6	7.1	7.4	Dépenses intérieures (en % du totale)
Iran (Islamic Republic of)							**Iran (Rép. islamique d')**
Current expenditure (% GDP)	* 5.2	* 6.0	* 7.8	* 6.3	* 7.1	* 7.6	Dépenses courantes (% du PIB)
Domestic General govt.(% expend. total)	* 11.0	* 9.4	* 11.9	* 16.0	* 22.6	* 22.6	Dépenses intérieures (en % du totale)
Iraq							**Iraq**
Current expenditure (% GDP)	...	2.9	3.3	3.2	3.4	3.4	Dépenses courantes (% du PIB)
Domestic General govt.(% expend. total)	...	3.2	4.8	2.4	2.4	1.7	Dépenses intérieures (en % du totale)
Ireland							**Irlande**
Current expenditure (% GDP)	5.9	7.6	10.5	10.4	9.9	7.8	Dépenses courantes (% du PIB)
Domestic General govt.(% expend. total)	...	...	...	18.3	18.2	18.4	Dépenses intérieures (en % du totale)
Israel							**Israël**
Current expenditure (% GDP)	6.8	7.1	7.1	7.1	7.4	7.4	Dépenses courantes (% du PIB)
Domestic General govt.(% expend. total)	...	...	10.8	11.0	...	...	Dépenses intérieures (en % du totale)
Italy							**Italie**
Current expenditure (% GDP)	7.6	8.4	9.0	9.0	9.0	9.0	Dépenses courantes (% du PIB)
Domestic General govt.(% expend. total)	12.1	13.7	14.1	13.3	13.4	13.4	Dépenses intérieures (en % du totale)
Jamaica							**Jamaïque**
Current expenditure (% GDP)	5.8	4.1	5.4	5.8	5.5	5.9	Dépenses courantes (% du PIB)
Domestic General govt.(% expend. total)	11.8	6.7	8.8	11.7	10.7	12.6	Dépenses intérieures (en % du totale)
Japan							**Japon**
Current expenditure (% GDP)	7.2	7.8	9.2	10.8	10.8	10.9	Dépenses courantes (% du PIB)
Domestic General govt.(% expend. total)	14.8	17.8	18.9	22.3	22.6	...	Dépenses intérieures (en % du totale)
Jordan							**Jordanie**
Current expenditure (% GDP)	9.6	8.9	8.1	7.3	7.4	6.3	Dépenses courantes (% du PIB)
Domestic General govt.(% expend. total)	12.8	11.6	18.4	12.7	12.6	12.4	Dépenses intérieures (en % du totale)
Kazakhstan							**Kazakhstan**
Current expenditure (% GDP)	4.2	4.0	4.2	3.8	3.6	3.9	Dépenses courantes (% du PIB)
Domestic General govt.(% expend. total)	9.2	9.2	13.0	12.0	11.4	10.9	Dépenses intérieures (en % du totale)

Region, country or area&	2000	2005	2010	2013	2014	2015	Région, pays ou zone&
Kenya							**Kenya**
Current expenditure (% GDP)	5.2	5.1	6.4	5.7	5.5	5.2	Dépenses courantes (% du PIB)
Domestic General govt.(% expend. total)	9.4	7.5	7.3	7.3	6.6	6.3	Dépenses intérieures (en % du totale)
Kiribati [1,7]							**Kiribati** [1,7]
Current expenditure (% GDP)	8.6	11.5	9.4	9.4	9.6	7.6	Dépenses courantes (% du PIB)
Domestic General govt.(% expend. total)	11.4	11.4	10.6	9.0	7.0	6.3	Dépenses intérieures (en % du totale)
Kuwait							**Koweït**
Current expenditure (% GDP)	2.5	2.4	2.8	2.6	3.2	4.0	Dépenses courantes (% du PIB)
Domestic General govt.(% expend. total)	5.2	6.8	5.2	5.7	6.2	6.2	Dépenses intérieures (en % du totale)
Kyrgyzstan							**Kirghizistan**
Current expenditure (% GDP)	4.4	7.5	7.1	8.2	8.3	8.2	Dépenses courantes (% du PIB)
Domestic General govt.(% expend. total)	7.1	12.8	9.2	10.3	10.7	9.9	Dépenses intérieures (en % du totale)
Lao People's Dem. Rep. [8]							**Rép. dém. populaire lao** [8]
Current expenditure (% GDP)	4.7	4.8	3.2	2.7	2.6	2.8	Dépenses courantes (% du PIB)
Domestic General govt.(% expend. total)	6.7	5.8	3.0	2.8	2.8	3.8	Dépenses intérieures (en % du totale)
Latvia							**Lettonie**
Current expenditure (% GDP)	7.9	8.9	8.6	7.5	7.8	5.8	Dépenses courantes (% du PIB)
Domestic General govt.(% expend. total)	7.4	9.5	8.2	8.8	8.8	8.9	Dépenses intérieures (en % du totale)
Lebanon							**Liban**
Current expenditure (% GDP)	10.7	7.6	7.5	7.5	7.4	7.4	Dépenses courantes (% du PIB)
Domestic General govt.(% expend. total)	7.5	9.2	10.3	13.0	13.7	14.3	Dépenses intérieures (en % du totale)
Lesotho							**Lesotho**
Current expenditure (% GDP)	5.8	5.3	6.2	7.9	8.6	8.4	Dépenses courantes (% du PIB)
Domestic General govt.(% expend. total)	7.7	5.9	6.0	6.0	8.8	9.3	Dépenses intérieures (en % du totale)
Liberia							**Libéria**
Current expenditure (% GDP)	3.8	8.5	10.0	9.2	14.1	15.2	Dépenses courantes (% du PIB)
Domestic General govt.(% expend. total)	7.7	7.1	3.7	5.3	3.6	2.7	Dépenses intérieures (en % du totale)
Libya							**Libye**
Current expenditure (% GDP)	* 3.4	* 2.6	* 3.4	...	...	...	Dépenses courantes (% du PIB)
Domestic General govt.(% expend. total)	* 6.0	* 5.8	* 4.3	...	...	...	Dépenses intérieures (en % du totale)
Lithuania							**Lituanie**
Current expenditure (% GDP)	5.8	5.6	6.8	6.1	6.2	6.5	Dépenses courantes (% du PIB)
Domestic General govt.(% expend. total)	10.2	11.1	11.6	11.4	11.9	12.2	Dépenses intérieures (en % du totale)
Luxembourg							**Luxembourg**
Current expenditure (% GDP)	5.9	7.2	7.0	6.5	6.3	6.0	Dépenses courantes (% du PIB)
Domestic General govt.(% expend. total)	12.8	13.7	13.6	12.6	12.5	12.1	Dépenses intérieures (en % du totale)
Madagascar							**Madagascar**
Current expenditure (% GDP)	* 5.3	* 5.5	* 5.4	* 4.0	* 4.9	* 5.2	Dépenses courantes (% du PIB)
Domestic General govt.(% expend. total)	* 12.4	* 8.1	* 15.5	* 10.3	* 13.9	* 15.6	Dépenses intérieures (en % du totale)
Malawi							**Malawi**
Current expenditure (% GDP)	4.4	6.1	7.2	11.6	9.7	9.3	Dépenses courantes (% du PIB)
Domestic General govt.(% expend. total)	7.4	6.5	6.5	8.6	8.8	10.8	Dépenses intérieures (en % du totale)
Malaysia							**Malaisie**
Current expenditure (% GDP)	2.4	2.9	3.3	3.7	3.9	4.0	Dépenses courantes (% du PIB)
Domestic General govt.(% expend. total)	4.7	5.7	6.4	6.9	7.9	8.3	Dépenses intérieures (en % du totale)
Maldives							**Maldives**
Current expenditure (% GDP)	7.4	8.8	# * 9.3	11.0	13.0	11.5	Dépenses courantes (% du PIB)
Domestic General govt.(% expend. total)	8.8	7.7	# * 13.6	22.2	24.9	22.8	Dépenses intérieures (en % du totale)
Mali							**Mali**
Current expenditure (% GDP)	5.1	5.0	4.4	5.4	5.8	5.8	Dépenses courantes (% du PIB)
Domestic General govt.(% expend. total)	5.0	8.4	3.2	3.6	4.5	4.5	Dépenses intérieures (en % du totale)
Malta							**Malte**
Current expenditure (% GDP)	6.5	8.7	8.2	8.9	9.5	9.6	Dépenses courantes (% du PIB)
Domestic General govt.(% expend. total)	11.8	14.2	12.9	14.2	14.0	14.2	Dépenses intérieures (en % du totale)
Marshall Islands [8,9]							**Îles Marshall** [8,9]
Current expenditure (% GDP)	25.2	26.3	19.3	19.5	18.8	22.1	Dépenses courantes (% du PIB)
Domestic General govt.(% expend. total)	26.1	11.7	14.2	20.4	19.0	21.2	Dépenses intérieures (en % du totale)
Mauritania							**Mauritanie**
Current expenditure (% GDP)	4.5	4.5	3.3	3.6	4.2	4.6	Dépenses courantes (% du PIB)
Domestic General govt.(% expend. total)	2.5	3.9	4.2	5.3	5.2	5.5	Dépenses intérieures (en % du totale)
Mauritius							**Maurice**
Current expenditure (% GDP)	3.0	3.7	4.7	4.7	5.4	5.5	Dépenses courantes (% du PIB)
Domestic General govt.(% expend. total)	6.9	7.4	8.1	8.0	10.5	9.9	Dépenses intérieures (en % du totale)
Mexico							**Mexique**
Current expenditure (% GDP)	4.9	5.9	6.0	6.0	5.7	5.9	Dépenses courantes (% du PIB)
Domestic General govt.(% expend. total)	...	11.3	10.9	11.3	10.5	11.3	Dépenses intérieures (en % du totale)

Region, country or area&	2000	2005	2010	2013	2014	2015	Région, pays ou zone&
Micronesia (Fed. States of) [8]							**Micronésie (États féd. de)** [8]
Current expenditure (% GDP)	7.7	11.5	12.9	11.9	12.4	13.1	Dépenses courantes (% du PIB)
Domestic General govt.(% expend. total)	2.6	4.5	3.4	4.6	5.8	6.1	Dépenses intérieures (en % du totale)
Monaco							**Monaco**
Current expenditure (% GDP)	* 1.7	* 2.1	* 2.3	* 2.1	* 2.1	* 2.0	Dépenses courantes (% du PIB)
Domestic General govt.(% expend. total)	* 6.9	* 7.9	* 9.2	* 9.2	* 8.3	* 8.1	Dépenses intérieures (en % du totale)
Mongolia							**Mongolie**
Current expenditure (% GDP)	5.5	4.2	4.2	4.0	3.8	3.9	Dépenses courantes (% du PIB)
Domestic General govt.(% expend. total)	12.3	9.0	6.5	4.9	4.9	6.0	Dépenses intérieures (en % du totale)
Montenegro							**Monténégro**
Current expenditure (% GDP)	6.7	7.7	5.9	6.0	5.9	6.0	Dépenses courantes (% du PIB)
Domestic General govt.(% expend. total)	15.0	14.7	8.2	8.7	8.7	8.8	Dépenses intérieures (en % du totale)
Morocco							**Maroc**
Current expenditure (% GDP)	4.0	4.8	5.9	5.6	5.7	5.5	Dépenses courantes (% du PIB)
Domestic General govt.(% expend. total)	4.0	4.0	7.5	7.6	7.7	7.7	Dépenses intérieures (en % du totale)
Mozambique							**Mozambique**
Current expenditure (% GDP)	* 3.7	* 6.4	* 5.1	* 4.7	* 5.5	* 5.4	Dépenses courantes (% du PIB)
Domestic General govt.(% expend. total)	* 14.5	* 15.4	* 1.4	* 3.0	* 4.4	* 1.2	Dépenses intérieures (en % du totale)
Myanmar [2,10]							**Myanmar** [2,10]
Current expenditure (% GDP)	* 1.8	* 1.8	* 1.9	* 2.0	* 4.9	* 4.9	Dépenses courantes (% du PIB)
Domestic General govt.(% expend. total)	* 1.2	* 1.1	* 1.2	* 2.7	* 4.3	* 4.9	Dépenses intérieures (en % du totale)
Namibia							**Namibie**
Current expenditure (% GDP)	11.5	12.4	9.5	8.6	8.2	8.9	Dépenses courantes (% du PIB)
Domestic General govt.(% expend. total)	20.5	20.9	15.4	14.0	12.9	12.9	Dépenses intérieures (en % du totale)
Nauru [1,7,11]							**Nauru** [1,7,11]
Current expenditure (% GDP)	13.5	12.6	10.7	4.9	5.5	4.8	Dépenses courantes (% du PIB)
Domestic General govt.(% expend. total)	9.7	18.0	7.3	6.5	6.6	5.2	Dépenses intérieures (en % du totale)
Nepal [12]							**Népal** [12]
Current expenditure (% GDP)	3.6	4.5	5.0	5.7	5.8	6.1	Dépenses courantes (% du PIB)
Domestic General govt.(% expend. total)	4.2	6.2	4.8	5.2	5.6	5.5	Dépenses intérieures (en % du totale)
Netherlands							**Pays-Bas**
Current expenditure (% GDP)	7.1	9.3	10.4	10.9	10.9	10.7	Dépenses courantes (% du PIB)
Domestic General govt.(% expend. total)	...	14.7	17.8	19.1	19.0	19.0	Dépenses intérieures (en % du totale)
New Zealand							**Nouvelle-Zélande**
Current expenditure (% GDP)	7.5	8.3	9.7	9.4	9.4	9.3	Dépenses courantes (% du PIB)
Domestic General govt.(% expend. total)	17.1	20.0	19.7	22.0	...	...	Dépenses intérieures (en % du totale)
Nicaragua							**Nicaragua**
Current expenditure (% GDP)	5.2	5.5	6.5	7.4	7.6	7.8	Dépenses courantes (% du PIB)
Domestic General govt.(% expend. total)	10.8	12.3	13.5	16.8	17.6	17.4	Dépenses intérieures (en % du totale)
Niger							**Niger**
Current expenditure (% GDP)	5.7	7.2	6.2	6.1	5.9	7.2	Dépenses courantes (% du PIB)
Domestic General govt.(% expend. total)	8.4	12.3	8.1	6.6	5.2	4.6	Dépenses intérieures (en % du totale)
Nigeria							**Nigéria**
Current expenditure (% GDP)	2.6	3.8	3.3	3.4	3.3	3.6	Dépenses courantes (% du PIB)
Domestic General govt.(% expend. total)	2.1	3.6	2.7	3.6	3.5	5.3	Dépenses intérieures (en % du totale)
Niue [1,7,11]							**Nioué** [1,7,11]
Current expenditure (% GDP)	7.9	10.1	9.8	7.3	7.7	6.3	Dépenses courantes (% du PIB)
Domestic General govt.(% expend. total)	6.3	2.7	2.1	2.1	2.1	2.2	Dépenses intérieures (en % du totale)
Norway							**Norvège**
Current expenditure (% GDP)	7.7	8.3	8.9	8.9	9.3	10.0	Dépenses courantes (% du PIB)
Domestic General govt.(% expend. total)	...	16.5	16.8	17.2	17.4	17.5	Dépenses intérieures (en % du totale)
Oman							**Oman**
Current expenditure (% GDP)	3.1	2.6	2.7	2.8	3.5	3.8	Dépenses courantes (% du PIB)
Domestic General govt.(% expend. total)	7.0	6.1	6.7	5.4	6.7	6.7	Dépenses intérieures (en % du totale)
Pakistan							**Pakistan**
Current expenditure (% GDP)	3.1	2.9	2.6	2.6	2.7	2.7	Dépenses courantes (% du PIB)
Domestic General govt.(% expend. total)	5.9	3.7	2.8	3.2	3.5	3.7	Dépenses intérieures (en % du totale)
Palau [8]							**Palaos** [8]
Current expenditure (% GDP)	* 9.5	* 9.0	* 11.5	* 11.8	* 11.9	* 10.6	Dépenses courantes (% du PIB)
Domestic General govt.(% expend. total)	* 8.2	* 8.5	* 8.4	* 13.4	* 13.1	* 13.1	Dépenses intérieures (en % du totale)
Panama							**Panama**
Current expenditure (% GDP)	7.5	6.6	6.6	6.6	6.8	7.0	Dépenses courantes (% du PIB)
Domestic General govt.(% expend. total)	20.3	10.0	11.3	11.0	11.4	11.3	Dépenses intérieures (en % du totale)
Papua New Guinea							**Papouasie-Nvl-Guinée**
Current expenditure (% GDP)	3.0	3.7	3.1	4.9	4.5	3.8	Dépenses courantes (% du PIB)
Domestic General govt.(% expend. total)	8.3	7.8	7.1	9.5	9.0	8.7	Dépenses intérieures (en % du totale)

Region, country or area&	2000	2005	2010	2013	2014	2015	Région, pays ou zone&
Paraguay							**Paraguay**
Current expenditure (% GDP)	5.8	5.0	6.2	7.0	7.6	7.8	Dépenses courantes (% du PIB)
Domestic General govt.(% expend. total)	6.7	5.7	9.0	9.9	11.2	10.8	Dépenses intérieures (en % du totale)
Peru							**Pérou**
Current expenditure (% GDP)	4.4	4.6	4.7	4.8	5.1	5.3	Dépenses courantes (% du PIB)
Domestic General govt.(% expend. total)	11.2	12.5	11.6	12.8	13.6	14.4	Dépenses intérieures (en % du totale)
Philippines							**Philippines**
Current expenditure (% GDP)	* 3.2	* 3.9	* 4.3	* 4.5	* 4.2	* 4.4	Dépenses courantes (% du PIB)
Domestic General govt.(% expend. total)	* 6.5	* 6.6	* 7.2	* 6.3	* 6.4	* 7.4	Dépenses intérieures (en % du totale)
Poland							**Pologne**
Current expenditure (% GDP)	5.3	5.8	6.4	6.4	6.2	6.3	Dépenses courantes (% du PIB)
Domestic General govt.(% expend. total)	...	...	...	10.6	10.4	10.7	Dépenses intérieures (en % du totale)
Portugal							**Portugal**
Current expenditure (% GDP)	8.4	9.4	9.8	9.1	9.0	9.0	Dépenses courantes (% du PIB)
Domestic General govt.(% expend. total)	13.8	14.4	13.2	12.2	11.5	12.3	Dépenses intérieures (en % du totale)
Qatar							**Qatar**
Current expenditure (% GDP)	2.0	2.6	1.8	2.1	2.4	3.1	Dépenses courantes (% du PIB)
Domestic General govt.(% expend. total)	3.9	6.6	4.1	6.2	6.3	6.3	Dépenses intérieures (en % du totale)
Republic of Korea							**République de Corée**
Current expenditure (% GDP)	4.0	5.1	6.5	6.9	7.1	7.4	Dépenses courantes (% du PIB)
Domestic General govt.(% expend. total)	8.7	9.7	12.2	12.2	12.5	12.9	Dépenses intérieures (en % du totale)
Republic of Moldova [13]							**République de Moldova** [13]
Current expenditure (% GDP)	5.8	9.6	12.2	10.3	10.3	10.2	Dépenses courantes (% du PIB)
Domestic General govt.(% expend. total)	8.5	13.6	13.6	12.5	12.8	12.2	Dépenses intérieures (en % du totale)
Romania							**Roumanie**
Current expenditure (% GDP)	4.2	5.5	5.7	5.2	5.0	5.0	Dépenses courantes (% du PIB)
Domestic General govt.(% expend. total)	8.8	13.3	11.5	11.6	11.4	10.8	Dépenses intérieures (en % du totale)
Russian Federation							**Fédération de Russie**
Current expenditure (% GDP)	5.4	5.1	5.3	5.5	5.7	5.6[14]	Dépenses courantes (% du PIB)
Domestic General govt.(% expend. total)	9.7	9.9	8.6	9.1	9.2	9.6[14]	Dépenses intérieures (en % du totale)
Rwanda							**Rwanda**
Current expenditure (% GDP)	* 4.6	* 7.5	* 9.3	* 7.9	* 8.2	* 7.9	Dépenses courantes (% du PIB)
Domestic General govt.(% expend. total)	* 5.3	* 9.6	* 7.0	* 6.8	* 9.2	* 6.2	Dépenses intérieures (en % du totale)
Saint Kitts and Nevis							**Saint-Kitts-et-Nevis**
Current expenditure (% GDP)	4.8	5.1	5.7	5.6	5.7	5.6	Dépenses courantes (% du PIB)
Domestic General govt.(% expend. total)	5.8	6.4	6.0	5.8	6.5	6.5	Dépenses intérieures (en % du totale)
Saint Lucia							**Sainte-Lucie**
Current expenditure (% GDP)	4.9	5.6	6.6	7.3	5.8	6.0	Dépenses courantes (% du PIB)
Domestic General govt.(% expend. total)	8.5	6.4	6.6	5.7	7.0	8.5	Dépenses intérieures (en % du totale)
Saint Vincent & Grenadines							**Saint-Vincent-Grenadines**
Current expenditure (% GDP)	3.8	3.7	4.4	4.4	4.2	4.2	Dépenses courantes (% du PIB)
Domestic General govt.(% expend. total)	11.9	10.5	9.8	10.6	9.8	10.0	Dépenses intérieures (en % du totale)
Samoa [1]							**Samoa** [1]
Current expenditure (% GDP)	5.5	5.2	5.3	6.1	6.0	5.6	Dépenses courantes (% du PIB)
Domestic General govt.(% expend. total)	11.8	10.4	10.4	10.6	10.1	11.5	Dépenses intérieures (en % du totale)
San Marino							**Saint-Marin**
Current expenditure (% GDP)	5.1	4.1	5.8	7.0	6.9	6.8	Dépenses courantes (% du PIB)
Domestic General govt.(% expend. total)	11.8	11.8	12.6	14.3	14.3	14.3	Dépenses intérieures (en % du totale)
Sao Tome and Principe							**Sao Tomé-et-Principe**
Current expenditure (% GDP)	9.7	12.1	5.3	9.1	8.9	9.8	Dépenses courantes (% du PIB)
Domestic General govt.(% expend. total)	9.0	12.4	4.6	8.4	10.6	10.7	Dépenses intérieures (en % du totale)
Saudi Arabia							**Arabie saoudite**
Current expenditure (% GDP)	4.2	3.4	3.5	4.4	5.1	5.8	Dépenses courantes (% du PIB)
Domestic General govt.(% expend. total)	9.2	8.8	6.7	8.7	9.3	10.1	Dépenses intérieures (en % du totale)
Senegal							**Sénégal**
Current expenditure (% GDP)	4.6	4.6	4.0	3.8	3.9	4.0	Dépenses courantes (% du PIB)
Domestic General govt.(% expend. total)	9.1	8.0	4.8	3.7	4.4	4.2	Dépenses intérieures (en % du totale)
Serbia [15]							**Serbie** [15]
Current expenditure (% GDP)	6.5	8.7	10.1	9.9	9.8	9.4	Dépenses courantes (% du PIB)
Domestic General govt.(% expend. total)	13.6	14.2	14.1	13.7	12.5	12.3	Dépenses intérieures (en % du totale)
Seychelles							**Seychelles**
Current expenditure (% GDP)	4.6	3.9	3.6	3.5	3.4	3.4	Dépenses courantes (% du PIB)
Domestic General govt.(% expend. total)	6.8	9.3	9.0	8.5	9.7	10.0	Dépenses intérieures (en % du totale)
Sierra Leone							**Sierra Leone**
Current expenditure (% GDP)	9.9	9.8	9.2	11.6	19.7	18.3	Dépenses courantes (% du PIB)
Domestic General govt.(% expend. total)	12.7	8.5	6.1	5.2	7.6	7.9	Dépenses intérieures (en % du totale)

Expenditure on health *(continued)*
Percentage of GDP and of government expenditure

Dépenses de santé *(suite)*
Pourcentage du PIB et des dépenses du gouvernement

Region, country or area&	2000	2005	2010	2013	2014	2015	Région, pays ou zone&
Singapore [2,16]							**Singapour [2,16]**
Current expenditure (% GDP)	3.4	3.0	3.2	3.7	3.9	4.3	Dépenses courantes (% du PIB)
Domestic General govt.(% expend. total)	6.7	6.9	8.9	11.8	12.3	12.0	Dépenses intérieures (en % du totale)
Slovakia							**Slovaquie**
Current expenditure (% GDP)	5.3	6.6	7.8	7.5	6.9	6.9	Dépenses courantes (% du PIB)
Domestic General govt.(% expend. total)	...	12.5	13.3	13.5	13.2	12.0	Dépenses intérieures (en % du totale)
Slovenia							**Slovénie**
Current expenditure (% GDP)	7.8	8.0	8.6	8.8	8.5	8.5	Dépenses courantes (% du PIB)
Domestic General govt.(% expend. total)	...	13.0	12.8	10.3	12.0	12.7	Dépenses intérieures (en % du totale)
Solomon Islands							**Îles Salomon**
Current expenditure (% GDP)	5.8	10.1	7.4	6.8	8.4	8.0	Dépenses courantes (% du PIB)
Domestic General govt.(% expend. total)	23.1	20.0	7.5	10.4	11.2	10.6	Dépenses intérieures (en % du totale)
South Africa [17]							**Afrique du Sud [17]**
Current expenditure (% GDP)	7.4	6.7	7.4	7.7	7.9	8.2	Dépenses courantes (% du PIB)
Domestic General govt.(% expend. total)	10.9	10.5	13.5	14.0	14.1	14.1	Dépenses intérieures (en % du totale)
South Sudan							**Soudan du sud**
Current expenditure (% GDP)	...	...	...	* 2.1	* 2.1	* 2.5	Dépenses courantes (% du PIB)
Domestic General govt.(% expend. total)	...	...	...	* 1.4	* 1.9	* 1.6	Dépenses intérieures (en % du totale)
Spain							**Espagne**
Current expenditure (% GDP)	6.8	7.7	9.0	9.0	9.1	9.2	Dépenses courantes (% du PIB)
Domestic General govt.(% expend. total)	...	14.4	14.8	14.1	14.2	14.9	Dépenses intérieures (en % du totale)
Sri Lanka							**Sri Lanka**
Current expenditure (% GDP)	# 4.1	# 3.8	# 3.0	# 2.8	# 2.8	# 3.0	Dépenses courantes (% du PIB)
Domestic General govt.(% expend. total)	# 10.1	# 10.1	# 7.8	# 9.2	# 9.1	# 7.9	Dépenses intérieures (en % du totale)
Sudan							**Soudan**
Current expenditure (% GDP)	* 3.6[18]	* 4.1[18]	* 5.3[18]	* 6.3	* 5.3	* 6.3	Dépenses courantes (% du PIB)
Domestic General govt.(% expend. total)	* 11.8[18]	* 8.1[18]	* 9.5[18]	* 8.7	* 11.5	* 18.1	Dépenses intérieures (en % du totale)
Suriname							**Suriname**
Current expenditure (% GDP)	8.4	7.7	5.4	5.7	5.8	6.5	Dépenses courantes (% du PIB)
Domestic General govt.(% expend. total)	11.6	8.3	9.6	8.3	8.8	10.5	Dépenses intérieures (en % du totale)
Sweden							**Suède**
Current expenditure (% GDP)	7.4	8.3	8.5	11.1	11.1	11.0	Dépenses courantes (% du PIB)
Domestic General govt.(% expend. total)	...	12.8	13.6	17.7	18.0	18.4	Dépenses intérieures (en % du totale)
Switzerland							**Suisse**
Current expenditure (% GDP)	9.3	10.3	10.7	11.4	11.6	12.1	Dépenses courantes (% du PIB)
Domestic General govt.(% expend. total)	...	...	22.7	23.9	24.3	25.2	Dépenses intérieures (en % du totale)
Syrian Arab Republic							**République arabe syrienne**
Current expenditure (% GDP)	4.6	4.1	3.4	...	...	...	Dépenses courantes (% du PIB)
Domestic General govt.(% expend. total)	5.6	7.3	5.1	...	...	...	Dépenses intérieures (en % du totale)
Tajikistan							**Tadjikistan**
Current expenditure (% GDP)	4.3	5.2	5.8	6.3	6.7	6.9	Dépenses courantes (% du PIB)
Domestic General govt.(% expend. total)	4.6	4.3	4.9	6.4	7.0	6.1	Dépenses intérieures (en % du totale)
Thailand [8]							**Thaïlande [8]**
Current expenditure (% GDP)	* 3.2	* 3.4	* 3.6	* 3.5	* 3.7	* 3.8	Dépenses courantes (% du PIB)
Domestic General govt.(% expend. total)	* 13.2	* 15.3	* 16.4	* 16.5	* 16.8	* 16.6	Dépenses intérieures (en % du totale)
TFYR of Macedonia							**ex-R.Y. de Macédoine**
Current expenditure (% GDP)	3.9	8.4	7.0	6.5	6.2	6.1	Dépenses courantes (% du PIB)
Domestic General govt.(% expend. total)	0.4	14.5	13.4	12.3	12.1	12.1	Dépenses intérieures (en % du totale)
Timor-Leste							**Timor-Leste**
Current expenditure (% GDP)	...	* 1.3	* 1.3	* 1.7	* 2.3	* 3.1	Dépenses courantes (% du PIB)
Domestic General govt.(% expend. total)	...	* 10.4	* 3.8	* 4.9	* 4.8	* 4.2	Dépenses intérieures (en % du totale)
Togo							**Togo**
Current expenditure (% GDP)	3.8	4.2	6.3	6.6	6.5	6.6	Dépenses courantes (% du PIB)
Domestic General govt.(% expend. total)	2.4	3.8	7.4	4.7	5.1	5.7	Dépenses intérieures (en % du totale)
Tonga [1]							**Tonga [1]**
Current expenditure (% GDP)	4.1	4.6	4.9	5.0	5.2	5.9	Dépenses courantes (% du PIB)
Domestic General govt.(% expend. total)	11.4	10.6	9.0	10.3	8.8	8.4	Dépenses intérieures (en % du totale)
Trinidad and Tobago							**Trinité-et-Tobago**
Current expenditure (% GDP)	4.0	4.9	5.2	5.1	5.2	6.0	Dépenses courantes (% du PIB)
Domestic General govt.(% expend. total)	6.5	9.1	7.7	8.3	7.9	8.5	Dépenses intérieures (en % du totale)
Tunisia							**Tunisie**
Current expenditure (% GDP)	5.0	5.4	5.9	6.9	6.8	6.7	Dépenses courantes (% du PIB)
Domestic General govt.(% expend. total)	10.7	11.4	12.8	12.5	13.6	13.6	Dépenses intérieures (en % du totale)
Turkey							**Turquie**
Current expenditure (% GDP)	4.6	4.9	5.1	4.4	4.3	4.1	Dépenses courantes (% du PIB)
Domestic General govt.(% expend. total)	...	10.5	...	10.4	10.5	10.1	Dépenses intérieures (en % du totale)

Expenditure on health *(continued)*
Percentage of GDP and of government expenditure

Dépenses de santé *(suite)*
Pourcentage du PIB et des dépenses du gouvernement

Region, country or area&	2000	2005	2010	2013	2014	2015	Région, pays ou zone&
Turkmenistan							**Turkménistan**
Current expenditure (% GDP)	6.9	9.6	5.0	5.2	5.5	6.3	Dépenses courantes (% du PIB)
Domestic General govt.(% expend. total)	13.3	10.3	8.7	8.7	8.7	8.7	Dépenses intérieures (en % du totale)
Tuvalu							**Tuvalu**
Current expenditure (% GDP)	* 24.2	* 11.1	* 14.4	* 13.8	* 14.7	* 15.0	Dépenses courantes (% du PIB)
Domestic General govt.(% expend. total) [7]	11.9	11.6	14.8	16.5	16.1	12.1	Dépenses intérieures (en % du totale) [7]
Uganda [19]							**Ouganda** [19]
Current expenditure (% GDP)	8.0	11.3	10.7	7.2	7.3	7.3	Dépenses courantes (% du PIB)
Domestic General govt.(% expend. total)	9.4	10.7	7.5	7.7	7.0	5.6	Dépenses intérieures (en % du totale)
Ukraine [20]							**Ukraine** [20]
Current expenditure (% GDP)	5.3	6.1	6.4	6.9	6.1	6.1	Dépenses courantes (% du PIB)
Domestic General govt.(% expend. total)	9.2	11.6	10.5	10.9	8.8	8.3	Dépenses intérieures (en % du totale)
United Arab Emirates							**Émirats arabes unis**
Current expenditure (% GDP)	3.5	2.3	3.9	3.6	3.7	3.5	Dépenses courantes (% du PIB)
Domestic General govt.(% expend. total)	7.6	8.4	8.5	8.5	8.0	8.0	Dépenses intérieures (en % du totale)
United Kingdom							**Royaume-Uni**
Current expenditure (% GDP)	6.0	7.2	8.5	9.9	9.8	9.9	Dépenses courantes (% du PIB)
Domestic General govt.(% expend. total)	13.8	14.5	15.0	17.7	18.0	18.5	Dépenses intérieures (en % du totale)
United Rep. of Tanzania [21]							**Rép.-Unie de Tanzanie** [21]
Current expenditure (% GDP)	...	...	...	* 6.6	* 6.4	* 6.1	Dépenses courantes (% du PIB)
Domestic General govt.(% expend. total)	* 6.1	* 12.6	* 7.3	* 6.3	* 7.0	* 7.4	Dépenses intérieures (en % du totale)
United States of America							**États-Unis d'Amérique**
Current expenditure (% GDP)	12.5	14.5	16.4	16.3	16.5	16.8	Dépenses courantes (% du PIB)
Domestic General govt.(% expend. total)	16.4	18.1	18.5	20.6	21.7	22.6	Dépenses intérieures (en % du totale)
Uruguay							**Uruguay**
Current expenditure (% GDP)	9.1	8.6	8.4	9.1	9.1	9.2	Dépenses courantes (% du PIB)
Domestic General govt.(% expend. total)	13.9	18.4	18.7	20.1	20.0	20.0	Dépenses intérieures (en % du totale)
Uzbekistan							**Ouzbékistan**
Current expenditure (% GDP)	5.3	5.3	5.5	5.9	5.9	6.2	Dépenses courantes (% du PIB)
Domestic General govt.(% expend. total)	6.4	7.7	8.2	9.2	9.3	9.3	Dépenses intérieures (en % du totale)
Vanuatu [22]							**Vanuatu** [22]
Current expenditure (% GDP)	1.4	1.9	2.8	5.4	3.6	3.5	Dépenses courantes (% du PIB)
Domestic General govt.(% expend. total)	3.4	4.0	4.6	17.2	10.6	11.8	Dépenses intérieures (en % du totale)
Venezuela (Boliv. Rep. of)							**Venezuela (Rép. boliv. du)**
Current expenditure (% GDP)	4.4	4.0	4.5	3.5	3.6	3.2	Dépenses courantes (% du PIB)
Domestic General govt.(% expend. total)	6.5	5.2	5.7	4.1	3.8	3.1	Dépenses intérieures (en % du totale)
Viet Nam							**Viet Nam**
Current expenditure (% GDP)	* 4.4	* 5.0	* 5.9	* 6.4	* 5.8	* 5.7	Dépenses courantes (% du PIB)
Domestic General govt.(% expend. total)	* 9.5	* 8.7	* 8.6	* 9.8	* 8.5	* 7.9	Dépenses intérieures (en % du totale)
Yemen							**Yémen**
Current expenditure (% GDP)	* 4.1	* 4.6	* 5.2	* 5.8	* 5.6	* 6.0	Dépenses courantes (% du PIB)
Domestic General govt.(% expend. total)	* 7.5	* 4.5	* 3.8	* 3.2	* 2.8	* 2.2	Dépenses intérieures (en % du totale)
Zambia							**Zambie**
Current expenditure (% GDP)	7.9	7.4	4.6	5.1	5.1	5.4	Dépenses courantes (% du PIB)
Domestic General govt.(% expend. total)	9.2	6.9	3.3	6.0	6.4	6.8	Dépenses intérieures (en % du totale)
Zimbabwe							**Zimbabwe**
Current expenditure (% GDP)	...	...	11.6	7.7	8.9	10.3	Dépenses courantes (% du PIB)
Domestic General govt.(% expend. total)	...	...	5.2	7.8	6.5	8.2	Dépenses intérieures (en % du totale)

Source:

World Health Organization (WHO), Geneva, WHO Global Health Expenditure database, last accessed March 2018.

Source:

Organisation mondiale de la santé (OMS), Genève, base de données de l'OMS sur les dépenses de santé mondiales, dernier accès mars 2018.

& These estimates are in line with the 2011 System of Health Accounts (SHA).

& Ces estimations sont conformes au Système de comptes de la santé (SCS) de 2011.

11 Expenditure on health *(continued)*
Percentage of GDP and of government expenditure

Dépenses de santé *(suite)*
Pourcentage du PIB et des dépenses du gouvernement

1	Data refer to fiscal years beginning 1 July.	1	Les données se réfèrent aux exercices budgétaires commençant le 1er juillet.
2	Data refer to fiscal years beginning 1 April.	2	Les données se réfèrent aux exercices budgétaires commençant le 1er avril.
3	Health expenditure data do not include funds from foreign origin flowing in the health financing system.	3	Les données sur les dépenses de santé n'incluent pas les fonds d'origine étrangère qui entrent dans le système de financement de la santé.
4	2012 data are based on a health accounts study based on SHA2011. Numbers were converted to SHA 1.0 format for comparability.	4	Les données de 2012 sont basées sur une étude sur les comptes de santé basée sur SHA2011. Les nombres ont été convertis au format SHA 1.0 pour la comparabilité.
5	Care should be taken interpreting the 2011-2014 out of pocket estimates and related total current health spending (SHA 2011) because of limitations in available household expenditure data.	5	Des précautions doivent être prises pour interpréter les estimations des dépenses personnelles de 2011-2014 et les dépenses de santé actuelles totales connexes (SHA 2011) en raison des limites dans les données disponibles sur les dépenses des ménages.
6	As a result of recent health-care reforms, public compulsory insurance has since 2008 been implemented by private insurance companies. The voucher cost of this insurance is treated as general government health expenditure.	6	L'assurance publique obligatoire est réalisée depuis 2008 par des sociétés privées dont le coût des coupons est traité comme dépense publique de santé du fait des réformes des soins de santé.
7	General government expenditure (GGE) can be larger than the Gross domestic product (GDP) because government accounts for a very large part of domestic consumption and because a large part of domestic consumption in the country is accounted for by imports.	7	Les dépenses publiques peuvent être supérieure au produit intérieur brut (PIB) parce que le gouvernement contribue très largement à la consommation intérieure et aussi une grande partie de la consommation intérieure du pays et représentée par les importations.
8	Data refer to fiscal years ending 30 September.	8	Les données se réfèrent aux exercices budgétaires finissant le 30 septembre.
9	Health expenditure indicators are high as they spend a lot on health using direct funding from the United States and also from their domestic funds. Current health expenditure is mostly government.	9	Les indicateurs de dépenses de santé sont élevés car ils dépensent beaucoup pour la santé en utilisant le financement direct de - États-Unis et aussi de leurs fonds nationaux. Dépenses de santé est principalement le gouvernement.
10	Country is still reporting data based on SHA1.0.	10	Le pays rapporte toujours des données basées sur SHA1.0.
11	Indicators are sensitive to external funds flowing in to the country.	11	Les indicateurs sont sensibles aux fonds externes vers le pays.
12	Data refer to fiscal years ending 15 July.	12	Les données se réfèrent aux exercices budgétaires finissant le 15 juillet.
13	Excluding the Transnistria region.	13	Non compris la région de Transnistrie.
14	From 2015 the data is adjusted by WHO in accordance with United Nations General Assembly Resolution A/RES/68/262.	14	À partir de 2015 les données sont ajustées conformes à la résolution A/RES/68/262.
15	Excluding Kosovo and Metohija.	15	Non compris Kosovo et Metohija.
16	Medisave is classified as Social insurance scheme, considering that it is a compulsory payment.	16	Medisave est classé comme régime d'assurance sociale, considérant qu'il s'agit d'un paiement obligatoire.
17	Data refer to fiscal years ending 31 March.	17	Les données se réfèrent aux exercices budgétaires finissant le 31 mars.
18	Including South Sudan.	18	Y compris le Sud Soudan.
19	Unlike other countries, in Uganda Fiscal Years starting on July 1 and ending in June 30 are converted to the previous year and that is a special request from the country.	19	Contrairement aux autres pays, en Ouganda, les années fiscales commençant le 1er juillet et se terminant le 30 juin sont converties en années précédentes et il s'agit d'une demande spéciale du pays.
20	Excludes the temporarily occupied territory of the Autonomous Republic of Crimea and Sevastopol.	20	Excluent le territoire temporairement occupé de la République autonome de Crimée et de Sébastopol.
21	Tanzania mainland only, excluding Zanzibar.	21	Tanzanie continentale seulement, Zanzibar non compris.
22	Government expenditures show fluctuations due to variations in capital investment.	22	Les dépenses publiques manifestent des fluctuations du fait de variations des investissements.

12 Intentional homicides and other crimes

By type of crime per 100 000 population and homicide victims by sex

Homicides intentionnels et autres crimes

Par type de crime pour 100 000 habitants et victimes d'homicides par sexe

		Intentional homicides Homicides volontaires			Other crimes (per 100 000 pop.) Autres infractions (pour 100 000 hab.)				
		Per 100 000 Pour 100 000	Victims (%) Victimes (%)						
Country or area Pays ou zone	Year Année		Male Hommes	Female Femmes	Assault Agression	Kidnapping Enlèvement	Theft Vol simple	Robbery Vol qualifié	Sexual Violence Violences Sexuelles
Total, all countries or areas [1] Total, tous pays ou zones [1]	**2015**	**5.3**	...	...	...	...	...	...	...
Sub-Saharan Africa [1] Afrique subsaharienne [1]	2015	9.6	...	...	...	...	...	...	...
Latin America & the Caribbean [1] Amérique latine et Caraïbes [1]	2015	22.3	...	...	...	...	...	...	...
South-central Asia [1] Asie centrale et du Sud [1]	2015	3.7	...	...	...	...	...	...	...
Australia and New Zealand [1] Australie et Nouvelle-Zélande [1]	2015	1.0	...	...	...	...	...	...	...
Oceania [1,2] Océanie [1,2]	2015	8.8	...	...	...	...	...	...	...
Afghanistan	2010	3.4	...	...	...	...	...	...	...
Afghanistan	2012	6.3	11.8	0.6	...	...	...	...	...
Albania	2005	5.0	8.6	1.4	5.4	...	96.9	6.5	2.9
Albanie	2010	4.3	7.3	1.3	6.1	0.3	137.1	8.1	2.7
	2015	2.3	3.5	1.0	5.8	0.3	248.1	8.1	5.1
Algeria	2005	0.6	...	...	# 99.0	0.3	...	# 75.6	...
Algérie	2010	0.7	...	...	# 114.8	0.5	# 141.7	# 51.3	# 10.5
	2015	1.4	2.3	0.4	# 123.8	1.3	# 125.0	# 65.6	# 8.5
American Samoa	2005	10.1	...	...	...	...	...	...	...
Samoa américaines	2010	9.0	...	...	...	...	...	...	...
	2015	7.2	...	...	...	...	...	...	...
Andorra	2004	1.3	...	...	...	...	...	...	...
Andorre	2008	1.2	0.0	2.4	122.6	...	1 141.1	4.7	17.5
	2010	...	0.0	0.0	116.1	...	1 323.2	9.5	11.9
	2011	1.2	2.3	0.0	174.9	...	1 291.2	6.1	20.7
	2014	...	0.0	0.0	169.0	1.4	1 286.0	9.6	22.0
	2015	...	0.0	0.0	188.7	...	1 484.3	11.4	15.6
Angola Angola	2012	4.8	7.8	2.1	...	...	...	...	...
Anguilla	2004	8.1	...	...	...	...	...	...	...
Anguilla	2009	7.4	...	...	...	...	...	...	...
	2014	27.7	...	...	...	...	...	...	...
Antigua and Barbuda	2002	5.8	9.2	2.8	...	...	...	...	...
Antigua-et-Barbuda	2005	3.4	...	...	...	...	...	...	...
	2008	17.3	24.8	10.4	...	...	...	...	...
	2010	6.3	...	...	...	...	...	...	...
	2012	10.3	...	...	...	...	...	...	...
Argentina	2005	...	...	...	363.0	...	775.7	907.7	...
Argentine	2008	...	...	...	359.7	...	703.8	957.9	26.3
	2015	6.5	11.5	1.7	417.6	...	626.3	1 020.4	37.1
Armenia	2005	1.9	3.4	0.7	6.0	0.7	81.7	8.9	1.7
Arménie	2010	1.9	3.4	0.7	5.2	1.3	123.6	12.0	2.8
	2012	2.3	3.4	1.2	5.3	1.3	134.9	10.4	3.5
	2015	2.6	3.9	1.4	5.4	1.9	177.8	...	4.0
Aruba	2005	6.0	10.5	1.9	...	...	...	...	...
Aruba	2010	3.9	8.3	0.0	...	...	...	...	...
	2014	1.9	4.1	0.0	...	...	...	...	...
Australia	2005	1.3	1.6	1.0	...	...	# 2 556.6	...	...
Australie	2010	1.0	1.2	0.8	309.8	# 2.8	# 2 153.4	# 66.0	# 85.1
	2015	1.0	1.3	0.7	279.9	# 2.2	# 2 122.5	# 37.4	# 89.2
Austria	2005	0.7	0.7	0.6	43.9	0.1	2 149.7	57.9	20.3
Autriche	2010	0.7	0.7	0.7	43.0	0.1	1 857.2	51.4	39.3
	2015	0.5	0.7	0.4	40.5	~0.0	1 630.9	40.0	39.0

Intentional homicides and other crimes *(continued)*

By type of crime per 100 000 population and homicide victims by sex

Homicides intentionnels et autres crimes *(suite)*

Par type de crime pour 100 000 habitants et victimes d'homicides par sexe

		Intentional homicides Homicides volontaires			Other crimes (per 100 000 pop.) Autres infractions (pour 100 000 hab.)				
		Per 100 000 Pour 100 000	Victims (%) Victimes (%)						
Country or area Pays ou zone	Year Année		Male Hommes	Female Femmes	Assault Agression	Kidnapping Enlèvement	Theft Vol simple	Robbery Vol qualifié	Sexual Violence Violences Sexuelles
Azerbaijan Azerbaïdjan	2005	2.2	...	...	1.9	0.3	25.1	2.3	...
	2010	2.3	3.2	1.4	1.9	~0.0	42.5	3.2	2.2
	2014	2.5	3.2	1.8	1.7	~0.0	60.9	2.5	2.2
Bahamas Bahamas	2005	15.8	27.4	4.7	...	7.3	440.4	...	133.3
	2010	26.1	45.4	7.6	848.9	5.0	545.7	93.1	85.6
	2012	29.8	55.5	5.3	841.1	7.5	533.1	98.6	80.3
	2015	37.7	...	...	...	...	...	...	...
Bahrain Bahreïn	2005	0.4	...	...	406.9	1.4	1 114.1	48.4	...
	2006	0.7	...	...	367.2	2.2	888.6	24.8	...
	2008	0.5	...	...	327.5	...	681.0	27.4	15.7
	2010	0.9	...	...	...	...	...	...	...
	2011	0.5	0.7	0.3	...	...	...	...	...
	2014	0.5	...	...	...	...	...	...	...
Bangladesh Bangladesh	2005	2.5	...	...	0.4	0.9	8.8	0.6	...
	2006	2.9	...	...	0.4	0.8	9.0	0.6	...
	2010	2.6	...	...	...	...	...	...	...
	2015	2.5	3.9	1.0	...	...	...	...	...
Barbados Barbade	2005	10.6	15.1	6.4	631.7	8.4	412.4	120.4	70.1
	2010	11.1	17.1	5.5	540.5	4.3	739.4	174.2	60.5
	2015	10.9	20.6	2.0	518.6	4.9	596.0	105.6	68.3
Belarus Bélarus	2005	8.6	...	...	19.9	0.4	# 1 070.4	119.9	8.5
	2010	4.2	6.0	2.7	12.2	0.2	# 775.3	49.9	3.9
	2014	3.6	5.1	2.3	8.7	0.3	# 426.6	25.9	4.8
Belgium Belgique	2005	2.1[3]	2.5	1.7	638.3	8.7	2 058.2	# 1 814.0	57.3
	2010	1.7[3]	2.2	1.2	711.4	10.3	2 089.3	# 218.3	64.9
	2014	1.9[3]	2.3	1.4	625.7	10.2	1 856.7	# 195.1	60.3
	2015	1.9[3]	...	...	600.0	10.1	1 651.3	# 195.6	55.1
Belize Belize	2004	28.6	46.8	10.2	...	...	...	...	...
	2005	28.6	...	...	...	3.2	592.4	235.5	...
	2009	30.9	56.0	5.7	165.3	0.6	375.6	173.6	64.4
	2010	40.1	70.2	10.0	...	...	259.9	148.3	40.4
	2014	35.0	63.3	6.8	296.3	1.1	234.9	86.4	42.4
	2015	33.1	61.4	5.0	...	...	...	...	...
Benin Bénin	2005	7.2	...	...	...	...	...	...	...
	2010	6.6	...	...	...	...	...	...	...
	2015	6.2	10.0	2.4	...	...	...	...	...
Bermuda Bermudes	2004	1.5	0.0	2.9	668.6	# 3.1	1 541.7	118.4	...
	2005	3.1	6.5	0.0	...	...	...	...	...
	2010	10.9	23.0	0.0	964.8	# 1.6	950.7	154.8	143.9
	2015	6.5	13.6	0.0	922.5	# 1.6	1 029.0	74.2	137.1
Bhutan Bhoutan	2005	1.7	...	...	...	...	...	...	...
	2010	2.2	...	...	9.3	0.1	67.9	6.5	9.9
	2013	3.1	...	...	1.7	0.1	76.5	5.4	8.5
	2014	...	...	...	...	0.8	69.5	...	10.6
	2015	1.5	2.4	0.5	...	...	...	...	...
Bolivia (Plurin. State of) Bolivie (État plurin. de)	2005	5.2	...	...	66.0	1.1	41.6	93.9	18.9
	2008	8.6	14.4	2.9	72.8	1.3	50.3	137.4	26.8
	2010	12.8	...	...	85.2	0.9	50.9	125.7	39.8
	2012	11.9	...	...	72.5	1.0	50.8	140.8	47.1
	2015	6.3	8.0	4.5	...	...	...	...	...
Bosnia and Herzegovina Bosnie-Herzégovine	2002	2.4	3.5	1.3	...	...	...	...	...
	2005	1.9	...	...	# 35.7	0.2	# 480.4	19.7	...
	2008	1.8	...	...	# 38.4	0.2	# 168.1	19.4	4.4
	2010	1.5	2.5	0.5	# 13.2	~0.0	# 296.3	...	3.8
	2014	1.4	2.2	0.6	# 15.5	0.1	# 155.4	26.9	3.5
	2015	1.6	2.2	1.0	# 26.0	...	# 127.9	...	4.3

12

Intentional homicides and other crimes *(continued)*
By type of crime per 100 000 population and homicide victims by sex

Homicides intentionnels et autres crimes *(suite)*
Par type de crime pour 100 000 habitants et victimes d'homicides par sexe

Country or area Pays ou zone	Year Année	Intentional homicides / Homicides volontaires: Per 100 000 Pour 100 000	Victims (%) / Victimes (%): Male Hommes	Victims (%) / Victimes (%): Female Femmes	Other crimes (per 100 000 pop.) / Autres infractions (pour 100 000 hab.): Assault Agression	Kidnapping Enlèvement	Theft Vol simple	Robbery Vol qualifié	Sexual Violence Violences Sexuelles
Botswana	2005	15.7	...	...	...	...	...	...	...
Botswana	2010	15.0	27.9	2.5	852.5	0.2	1 451.1	117.3	...
	2014	...	...	...	758.9	0.1	1 335.9	76.5	123.9
Brazil	2005	23.3	43.5	3.8	...	...	...	...	...
Brésil	2010	22.0	40.8	3.7	360.4	0.2	696.2	544.3	23.4
	2013	26.8	49.8	4.4	323.9	0.2	873.8	495.7	27.5
	2015	28.4	53.1	4.4	...	...	...	...	...
British Virgin Islands	2004	17.7	...	...	...	...	...	...	...
Îles Vierges britanniques	2006	8.4	...	...	...	...	...	...	...
Brunei Darussalam	2000	1.2	1.2	1.2	...	...	...	...	...
Brunéi Darussalam	2004	0.6	...	...	151.0	0.3	295.8	3.1	...
	2005	0.5	...	...	146.5	...	332.2	2.5	...
	2006	0.8	...	...	122.5	...	308.6	0.5	...
	2010	0.3	...	...	...	...	...	...	...
	2013	0.5	...	...	...	...	...	...	...
Bulgaria	2005	2.6	3.9	1.3	47.6	2.5	561.3	48.9	13.5
Bulgarie	2010	2.0	3.4	0.7	41.0	1.6	681.5	50.5	9.4
	2015	1.8	2.9	0.8	35.3	1.0	535.9	27.2	8.4
Burkina Faso	2005	0.5	...	...	...	...	...	...	...
Burkina Faso	2010	0.6	...	...	...	...	...	...	...
	2015	0.4	0.6	0.2	...	...	...	...	...
Burundi	2010	4.0	...	...	3.2	0.3	...	32.1	7.4
Burundi	2014	5.7	9.5	2.0	5.1	0.7	7.5	41.6	11.7
	2015	4.5	7.6	1.5	...	...	...	...	...
Cabo Verde	2005	9.3	...	...	...	...	...	...	...
Cabo Verde	2010	7.8	...	...	834.1	1.2	764.9	626.9	41.4
	2015	8.6	14.7	2.6	807.9	1.0	799.4	1 051.3	42.3
Cambodia	2005	3.4	...	...	...	...	...	...	...
Cambodge	2010	2.3	...	...	...	...	...	...	...
	2011	1.8	3.2	0.6	...	...	...	...	...
Cameroon	2003	6.1	...	...	# 17.4	...	# 68.8	...	...
Cameroun	#2005	...	...	...	17.3	...	66.3	...	...
	2010	5.0	...	...	# 23.9	2.2	# 79.7	# 79.7	# 10.0
	2012	4.2	6.8	1.5	# 26.6	2.5	# 72.7	# 72.7	# 9.2
	2014	...	...	...	# 31.5	3.3	# 111.0	# 111.0	# 3.1
	2015	...	...	...	# 20.6	4.2	# 69.8	# 69.8	...
Canada	2005	2.1	3.0	1.1	165.7	12.1	2 033.4	100.6	81.7
Canada	2010	1.6	2.4	0.9	162.4	12.6	1 594.8	89.3	78.8
	2015	1.7	2.4	1.0	140.3	9.9	1 402.7	61.4	76.0
Cayman Islands	2005	6.2	...	...	...	...	...	...	...
Îles Caïmanes	2010	16.2	...	...	...	...	...	...	...
	2014	8.4	...	...	...	...	...	...	...
Chad	2005	10.7	...	...	...	...	...	...	...
Tchad	2010	9.7	...	...	...	...	...	...	...
	2015	9.0	14.4	3.6	...	...	...	...	...
Channel Islands	2005	0.6	...	...	...	...	...	...	...
Îles Anglo-Normandes	2010	0.0	...	...	...	...	...	...	...
Chile	2005	3.6	6.2	1.0	...	# 0.9	964.6	403.0	...
Chili	2010	3.2	5.3	1.1	130.8	# 1.5	1 098.9	480.0	76.5
	2015	3.0	5.3	0.7	89.0	# 1.5	1 025.6	593.2	65.6
China [4]	2005	1.6	...	...	...	...	...	...	...
Chine [4]	2010	1.0	...	...	...	...	...	...	...
	2014	0.7	0.9	0.5	...	...	...	...	...
	2015	0.7	...	...	...	...	...	...	...
China, Hong Kong SAR	2004	0.7	0.8	0.6	114.2	~0.0	548.1	32.7	20.4
Chine, RAS de Hong Kong	2005	0.5	0.6	0.4	118.3	...	514.6	24.5	21.3
	2010	0.5	0.5	0.5	108.7	~0.0	491.1	11.1	26.3
	2013	0.9	0.8	1.0	92.5	~0.0	441.1	7.0	24.9
	2015	0.3	...	...	...	...	...	...	...

Intentional homicides and other crimes *(continued)*

By type of crime per 100 000 population and homicide victims by sex

Homicides intentionnels et autres crimes *(suite)*

Par type de crime pour 100 000 habitants et victimes d'homicides par sexe

Country or area Pays ou zone	Year Année	Intentional homicides / Homicides volontaires: Per 100 000 Pour 100 000	Victims (%) / Victimes (%): Male Hommes	Female Femmes	Other crimes (per 100 000 pop.) / Autres infractions (pour 100 000 hab.): Assault Agression	Kidnapping Enlèvement	Theft Vol simple	Robbery Vol qualifié	Sexual Violence Violences Sexuelles
China, Macao SAR Chine, RAS de Macao	2005	0.8	...	...	...	...	...	...	...
	2010	0.4	0.8	0.0	# 343.4	# 0.4	# 526.0	# 33.3	# 8.4
	2013	0.2	0.0	0.3	# 299.3	# 0.2	# 529.2	# 26.4	# 9.3
	2015	0.2	0.0	0.3	# 275.7	...	# 450.5	# 19.2	# 9.7
Colombia Colombie	2005	41.8	77.7	6.8	70.3	1.9	158.8	93.9	# 10.6
	2010	33.7	62.9	5.3	115.7	0.6	200.0	133.8	# 14.8
	2015	26.5	49.3	4.4	180.2	0.4	300.5	210.1	# 45.1
Comoros Comores	2005	9.5	...	...	...	...	...	...	...
	2010	8.5	...	...	...	...	...	...	...
	2015	7.7	11.6	3.7	...	...	...	...	...
Congo Congo	2005	10.6	...	...	...	...	...	...	...
	2010	9.9	...	...	...	...	...	...	...
	2015	9.3	14.1	4.5	...	...	...	...	...
Cook Islands Îles Cook	2012	3.5	...	...	...	...	...	...	...
Costa Rica Costa Rica	2005	7.9	12.9	2.9	...	0.3	196.8	# 501.1	...
	2010	11.6	20.5	2.7	175.0	0.2	445.5	# 950.1	143.3
	2013	8.7	15.9	1.5	174.7	0.1	696.6	# 1 018.9	154.7
	2014	10.0	17.9	2.1	...	0.1	...	# 1 095.6	...
	2015	11.6	...	...	...	...	...	...	...
Côte d'Ivoire Côte d'Ivoire	2005	14.7	...	...	...	...	...	...	...
	2008	...	...	...	52.6	...	...	3.1	3.7
	2010	12.6	...	...	...	...	...	...	...
	2015	11.6	15.6	7.5	...	...	...	...	...
Croatia Croatie	2005	1.6	1.9	1.2	26.3	0.5	# 694.3	35.6	14.2
	2010	1.4	1.4	1.4	22.8	0.3	# 314.5	28.8	9.2
	2014	0.8	0.9	0.8	18.0	~0.0	# 283.0	29.8	14.2
	2015	0.9	1.1	0.7	19.0	...	# 319.5	30.9	14.3
Cuba Cuba	2005	6.1	9.1	3.0	...	...	...	...	...
	2010	4.5	6.7	2.2	...	...	...	...	...
	2015	5.4	8.4	2.4	...	...	...	...	...
Curaçao Curaçao	2005	20.1	33.0	8.7	...	...	...	...	...
	2007	19.2	36.5	4.1	...	...	...	...	...
Cyprus Chypre	2005	1.9	3.5	0.4	12.8	1.6	116.3	8.1	10.9
	2010	0.7	1.3	0.2	15.7	2.5	151.3	14.1	7.2
	2015	1.3	2.2	0.3	12.1	2.1	78.8	8.0	8.6
Czechia Tchéquie	2005	1.1	1.3	0.9	212.0	0.1	1 506.5	54.3	18.1
	2010	1.0	1.0	1.0	172.0	0.1	1 202.2	38.3	12.7
	2015	0.8	0.7	0.9	148.6	~0.0	1 319.3	19.2	13.5
Dem. People's Rep. Korea Rép. pop. dém. de Corée	*2005	5.0	...	...	...	...	...	...	...
	*2010	4.8	...	...	...	...	...	...	...
	*2015	4.4	...	...	...	...	...	...	...
Dem. Rep. of the Congo Rép. dém. du Congo	2005	14.6	...	...	...	...	...	...	...
	2010	14.3	...	...	...	...	...	...	...
	2015	13.5	22.0	5.1	...	...	...	...	...
Denmark Danemark	2005	1.0	1.4	0.6	205.2	...	3 103.2	53.9	...
	2010	0.8	0.7	0.8	31.6	...	4 354.3	60.8	36.2
	2015	1.0	1.2	0.8	25.8	...	3 430.5	35.9	38.4
Djibouti Djibouti	2005	8.1	...	...	...	...	...	...	...
	2010	7.4	...	...	...	...	...	...	...
	2015	6.5	10.6	2.3	...	...	...	...	...
Dominica Dominique	2005	11.3	...	...	...	...	...	...	...
	2010	21.0	...	...	...	...	...	...	...
	2011	8.4	...	...	...	...	...	...	...

12 Intentional homicides and other crimes *(continued)*

By type of crime per 100 000 population and homicide victims by sex

Homicides intentionnels et autres crimes *(suite)*

Par type de crime pour 100 000 habitants et victimes d'homicides par sexe

Country or area Pays ou zone	Year Année	Intentional homicides / Homicides volontaires: Per 100 000 Pour 100 000	Victims (%) / Victimes (%): Male Hommes	Female Femmes	Other crimes (per 100 000 pop.) / Autres infractions (pour 100 000 hab.): Assault Agression	Kidnapping Enlèvement	Theft Vol simple	Robbery Vol qualifié	Sexual Violence Violences Sexuelles
Dominican Republic République dominicaine	2005	25.9	47.2	4.6	...	0.2	...	...	...
	2006	22.9	41.9	3.8	...	0.2	...	...	...
	2010	25.0	45.8	4.2	...	...	...	...	...
	2014	17.4	31.3	3.6	48.3	0.2	235.3	144.2	2.8
Ecuador Équateur	2005	15.4	28.4	2.4	56.5	0.3	# 43.4	346.7	...
	2010	17.6	31.9	3.2	30.2	0.2	# 33.6	362.3	24.5
	2014	8.2	14.1	2.4	46.7	0.2	# 152.8	570.6	19.0
	2015	6.5	10.9	2.2	...	...	...	...	...
Egypt Égypte	2005	0.7	1.2	0.2	...	~0.0	46.7	0.6	...
	2010	2.2	3.9	0.5	0.2	0.1	94.1	0.9	0.2
	2011	3.1	5.5	0.8	0.4	0.3	104.0	3.2	0.1
	2012	2.5	4.4	0.6	...	...	...	...	...
El Salvador El Salvador	2005	64.4	121.0	12.6	# 77.8	0.1	# 180.3	# 81.7	...
	2010	64.7	117.4	17.3	# 64.4	0.5	# 160.2	# 89.7	# 37.0
	2015	105.4	204.8	17.2	# 96.1	0.3	# 139.4	# 84.2	# 72.5
Equatorial Guinea Guinée équatoriale	2005	2.9	...	...	...	...	...	...	...
	2010	2.6	...	...	...	...	...	...	...
	2015	2.3	3.4	0.9	...	...	...	...	...
Eritrea Érythrée	2005	9.6	...	...	...	...	...	...	...
	2010	8.9	...	...	...	...	...	...	...
	2015	8.0	12.6	3.4	...	...	...	...	...
Estonia Estonie	2005	8.3	13.4	3.9	9.7	# 0.2	2 246.3	97.8	29.7
	2008	6.4	10.8	2.6	10.5	# 0.2	1 677.0	67.8	27.5
	2010	5.3	8.6	2.3	7.7	...	1 895.7	45.0	20.6
	2013	3.9	5.5	2.6	7.5	# 0.1	1 247.3	36.1	28.9
	2015	3.2	5.2	1.4	7.5	...	865.0	25.7	42.9
Eswatini Eswatini	2004	13.3	...	...	1 332.4	8.8	1 904.6	309.8	...
	2005	13.7	...	...	...	...	...	...	...
	2010	17.3	30.9	4.5	...	...	...	...	...
Ethiopia Éthiopie	2005	9.4	...	...	...	...	...	...	...
	2010	8.5	...	...	...	...	...	...	...
	2015	7.6	11.3	3.9	...	...	...	...	...
Fiji Fidji	2005	2.8	3.3	2.2	...	...	...	...	...
	2010	2.3	3.2	1.4	...	...	...	...	...
	2014	2.3	1.8	2.8	...	...	...	...	...
Finland Finlande	2005	2.3	3.3	1.3	# 580.7	~0.0	2 384.1	34.6	# 36.6
	2010	2.2	3.5	1.0	# 37.2	~0.0	1 852.5	28.1	# 45.0
	2015	1.5	2.4	0.6	# 28.4	~0.0	1 771.0	28.2	# 54.0
France France	2005	1.6	...	...	# 242.7	3.3	# 1 363.5	# 203.5	# 39.0
	2010	1.3	...	...	# 368.3	3.3	# 1 862.3	# 192.2	# 36.5
	2015	1.6	2.0	1.2	# 379.1	6.2	# 1 906.9	# 162.9	# 52.1
French Guiana Guyane française	2005	22.1	...	...	...	...	...	...	...
	2009	13.2	21.6	4.8	...	...	...	...	...
French Polynesia Polynésie française	2009	0.4	...	...	...	...	...	...	...
Gabon Gabon	2005	11.0	...	...	...	...	...	...	...
	2010	8.7	...	...	...	...	...	...	...
	2015	8.0	12.6	3.2	...	...	...	...	...
Gambia Gambie	2005	9.8	...	...	...	...	...	...	...
	2010	9.8	...	...	...	...	...	...	...
	2015	9.1	16.6	1.8	...	...	...	...	...
Georgia Géorgie	2005	9.0	15.6	3.0	8.2	2.0	363.2	46.6	3.7
	2010	4.4	7.9	1.3	3.0	0.1	267.5	15.0	3.9
	2014	2.7	3.9	1.6	5.7	...	236.9	11.7	3.3
Germany Allemagne	2005	1.1	1.2	0.9	# 608.4	# 2.1	# 2 750.2	67.5	67.9
	2010	1.0	1.0	1.0	# 177.7	# 6.1	# 1 516.7	59.9	45.5
	2015	0.8	0.9	0.8	# 157.9	# 5.9	# 1 657.2	55.4	42.5

12

Intentional homicides and other crimes *(continued)*
By type of crime per 100 000 population and homicide victims by sex

Homicides intentionnels et autres crimes *(suite)*
Par type de crime pour 100 000 habitants et victimes d'homicides par sexe

Country or area Pays ou zone	Year Année	Intentional homicides / Homicides volontaires: Per 100 000 Pour 100 000	Victims (%) / Victimes (%): Male Hommes	Victims (%) / Victimes (%): Female Femmes	Other crimes (per 100 000 pop.) / Autres infractions (pour 100 000 hab.): Assault Agression	Kidnapping Enlèvement	Theft Vol simple	Robbery Vol qualifié	Sexual Violence Violences Sexuelles
Ghana Ghana	2005	1.8	...	...	...	...	...	...	...
	2010	1.7	...	...	...	...	...	...	...
	2011	1.7	2.4	1.0	...	...	...	...	...
Gibraltar Gibraltar	2010	3.0	...	...	...	...	...	...	...
Greece Grèce	2005	1.2	1.6	0.8	# 70.3	0.2	557.0	18.8	5.7
	2010	1.5	2.5	0.6	# 9.9	1.6	1 060.3	54.4	4.6
	2015	0.8	1.1	0.5	# 14.8	0.8	915.6	39.4	5.1
Greenland Groenland	2005	17.6	...	...	...	...	...	...	...
	2010	19.4	...	...	...	...	...	...	...
	2015	7.1	...	...	...	...	...	...	...
Grenada Grenade	2005	10.7	15.6	5.8	1 839.7	...	1 761.0	43.7	146.7
	2010	9.6	15.3	3.8	1 100.5	...	918.1	24.8	106.0
	2015	5.6	7.5	3.8	462.4	...	1 948.1	71.1	196.6
Guadeloupe Guadeloupe	2005	5.2	10.1	0.7	...	...	...	...	...
	2009	8.0	14.5	2.3	...	...	...	...	...
Guam Guam	2005	4.4	...	...	...	...	...	...	...
	2010	1.9	...	...	...	...	...	...	...
	2011	2.5	3.6	1.4	...	...	...	...	...
Guatemala Guatemala	2005	40.8	75.0	7.8	46.2	0.4	32.6	# 83.3	2.4
	2010	40.7	73.3	9.3	50.6	0.9	44.2	# 22.0	3.4
	2012	33.8	61.0	7.4	39.6	0.5	59.3	# 24.9	4.3
	2014	31.4	55.8	7.8	37.3	0.3	...	# 19.4	...
	2015	29.4	...	...	...	...	...	...	...
Guinea Guinée	2005	10.1	...	...	3.0	0.2	...	...	...
	2007	...	...	...	2.9	0.2	13.3	1.5	0.3
	2008	...	...	...	...	0.2	...	...	...
	2010	9.4	...	...	...	...	...	...	...
	2015	8.8	13.8	3.8	...	...	...	...	...
Guinea-Bissau Guinée-Bissau	2005	11.7	...	...	...	...	...	...	...
	2010	10.5	...	...	...	...	...	...	...
	2015	9.5	10.6	8.6	...	...	...	...	...
Guyana Guyana	2005	18.9	30.3	7.5	...	...	...	...	32.2
	2010	18.8	29.2	8.3	# 1 484.3	0.3	518.5	145.4	19.5
	2011	17.4	25.6	9.1	...	0.1	252.6	157.6	39.3
	2015	19.4	31.3	7.3	# 1 208.3	...	674.1	190.7	49.5
Haiti Haïti	2010	6.8	...	...	...	...	...	...	...
	2012	10.0	15.7	4.5	...	...	...	...	...
Holy See Saint-Siège	2010	0.0	...	...	...	...	...	...	...
	2015	0.0	...	...	...	...	...	...	...
Honduras Honduras	2005	43.6	...	...	...	...	...	...	...
	2010	76.1	143.3	9.4	...	...	59.7	...	...
	2015	57.5	104.5	10.6	16.4	0.5	36.1	127.2	18.4
Hungary Hongrie	2005	1.6	1.8	1.4	122.2	0.1	1 250.5	29.5	# 8.5
	2010	1.4	1.6	1.2	145.5	0.2	1 340.0	33.9	# 12.9
	2014	1.5	1.7	1.3	136.3	~0.0	1 081.3	19.8	# 7.8
	2015	2.3	2.6	2.0	...	...	...	...	...
Iceland Islande	2005	1.0	2.0	0.0	...	...	1 072.0	16.5	97.1
	2010	0.6	1.2	0.0	17.9	...	1 547.0	13.2	68.2
	2015	0.9	1.8	0.0	25.8	...	1 224.0	16.1	108.7
India Inde	2005	3.9	5.0	2.8	23.7	2.0	23.9	1.5	5.5
	2010	3.8	4.5	3.0	23.5	3.1	26.8	1.9	5.9
	2013	3.6	4.2	2.9	26.2	5.1	29.1	2.9	9.2
	2015	3.4	4.0	2.7	...	...	...	...	...
Indonesia Indonésie	2004	0.6	...	...	...	...	...	...	...
	2010	0.4	...	...	# 13.2	0.2	10.1	4.1	...
	2014	0.5	0.7	0.3	# 14.5	0.1	9.6	4.6	2.2
	2015	0.6	...	...	# 5.7	0.2	10.2	4.6	2.0

12

Intentional homicides and other crimes *(continued)*
By type of crime per 100 000 population and homicide victims by sex

Homicides intentionnels et autres crimes *(suite)*
Par type de crime pour 100 000 habitants et victimes d'homicides par sexe

Country or area Pays ou zone	Year Année	Intentional homicides / Homicides volontaires: Per 100 000 Pour 100 000	Victims (%) / Victimes (%): Male Hommes	Female Femmes	Other crimes (per 100 000 pop.) / Autres infractions (pour 100 000 hab.): Assault Agression	Kidnapping Enlèvement	Theft Vol simple	Robbery Vol qualifié	Sexual Violence Violences Sexuelles
Iran (Islamic Republic of)	2004	2.9	...	...	...	...	158.5	...	...
Iran (Rép. islamique d')	2009	3.0	...	...	...	...	...	...	...
	2014	2.5	4.3	0.6	...	...	...	...	...
Iraq	2010	8.7[5]	14.2	3.2	98.3[6]	5.3[6]	31.1[6]	...	...
Iraq	2013	9.9[5]	16.3	3.2	96.2[6]	2.7[6]	36.7[6]	...	...
	2014[6]	...	...	...	83.2	3.7	34.8	...	...
Ireland	2005	1.2	2.1	0.4	296.9	1.8	1 400.7	57.7	42.8
Irlande	2010	1.1	2.0	0.3	325.7	2.9	1 416.8	69.2	51.2
	2013	1.1	1.9	0.3	270.7	2.7	1 527.8	60.1	43.0
	2015	0.6	...	...	317.4	3.3	1 481.6	54.9	50.2
Isle of Man Île de Man	2015	1.2	...	...	...	...	...	...	...
Israel	2005	2.5	3.5	1.5	774.0	6.3	1 897.3	65.6	69.6
Israël	2010	2.0	3.1	0.9	620.0	3.6	974.9	39.2	66.8
	2011	2.0	3.1	0.9	569.4	3.5	936.2	36.3	60.5
	2014	1.5	2.4	0.6	...	...	...	...	...
	2015	1.4	...	...	...	...	...	...	...
Italy	2005	1.0	1.7	0.5	96.5	0.6	# 1 870.8	112.1	6.9
Italie	2010	0.9	1.3	0.5	108.9	0.6	# 1 584.3	80.6	8.1
	2015	0.8	1.2	0.4	107.1	0.5	# 1 748.2	58.6	6.7
Jamaica	2005	61.0	109.5	13.4	...	1.2	...	...	40.8
Jamaïque	2008	58.0	105.1	11.7	...	1.6	...	97.9	54.2
	2010	51.4	93.1	10.2	# 51.3	...	...	104.2	54.2
	2013	42.1	75.5	9.1	# 178.0	0.8	75.4	96.4	95.8
	2015	42.1	76.4	8.0	...	0.5	...	68.3	79.2
Japan	2005	0.5	0.5	0.5	47.5	0.2	727.1	4.7	8.5
Japon	2010	0.4	0.4	0.4	20.9	0.2	485.5	3.2	6.6
	2014	0.3	0.3	0.3	21.0	0.2	356.2	2.4	6.8
	2015	0.3	0.2	0.3	...	...	...	...	...
Jordan	2005	1.2	...	...	275.2	0.5	132.5	11.6	...
Jordanie	2006	1.7	...	...	283.8	0.6	161.8	14.5	...
	2010	1.6	2.1	1.1	...	...	187.2	...	...
	2012	2.0	3.3	0.6	...	...	193.1	...	...
	2015	1.7	...	...	...	...	...	...	...
Kazakhstan	#2004	13.6	...	...	...	...	...	...	...
Kazakhstan	2005	...	...	...	...	0.6	408.6	84.6	...
	2010	# 8.5	13.2	4.1	9.8	0.8	367.8	65.8	2.2
	2015	# 4.8	7.0	2.7	5.1	0.5	1 185.3	69.2	2.7
Kenya	2005	3.0	...	...	36.0	0.4	34.5	19.6	7.3
Kenya	2010	4.7	...	...	34.9	0.2	29.7	7.1	11.9
	2015	4.8	7.0	2.6	32.4	0.2	20.7	6.2	13.4
Kiribati	2001	4.7	...	...	...	...	...	...	...
Kiribati	2010	3.9	...	...	...	...	...	...	...
	2012	7.5	12.2	2.9	...	...	...	...	...
Kosovo	2010	6.0	9.6	2.3	205.9	2.4	834.3	31.0	8.2
Kosovo	2014	2.3	3.8	0.7	48.7	1.2	834.2	22.9	2.9
	2015	1.7	2.8	0.6	...	...	...	...	...
Kuwait	2005	1.8	1.9	1.7	26.3	12.4	432.5	19.0	16.4
Koweït	2009	1.7	2.3	1.0	23.8	12.4	282.1	22.8	17.7
	2010	2.0	2.7	1.0	...	...	...	...	...
	2012	1.8	2.6	0.7	...	...	...	...	...
Kyrgyzstan	2005	8.3	13.1	3.5	5.2	# 0.5	# 241.1	53.1	# 0.3
Kirghizistan	2009	7.8	10.9	4.9	6.7	# 0.1	# 203.3	43.6	# 0.6
	2010	19.8	...	...	9.8	# 1.5	# 180.9	51.2	...
	2013	3.6	...	...	5.3	# 0.7	# 173.6	28.1	# 1.3
	2015	5.2	...	...	6.0	# 0.9	# 166.6	...	# 1.3
Lao People's Dem. Rep.	2005	9.6	...	...	...	...	...	...	...
Rép. dém. populaire lao	2010	8.0	...	...	...	...	...	...	...
	2015	7.0	10.8	3.2	...	...	...	...	...

Intentional homicides and other crimes *(continued)*

By type of crime per 100 000 population and homicide victims by sex

Homicides intentionnels et autres crimes *(suite)*

Par type de crime pour 100 000 habitants et victimes d'homicides par sexe

Country or area Pays ou zone	Year Année	Intentional homicides / Homicides volontaires: Per 100 000 Pour 100 000	Victims (%) / Victimes (%): Male Hommes	Victims (%) / Victimes (%): Female Femmes	Other crimes (per 100 000 pop.) / Autres infractions (pour 100 000 hab.): Assault Agression	Kidnapping Enlèvement	Theft Vol simple	Robbery Vol qualifié	Sexual Violence Violences Sexuelles
Latvia Lettonie	2005	5.6	...	...	# 49.4	0.3	# 1 090.3	97.1	# 32.4
	2010	3.3	...	...	# 58.7	0.4	# 1 227.4	51.3	# 11.1
	2015	3.4	4.1	2.7	# 27.1	0.9	# 983.9	39.5	# 23.7
Lebanon Liban	2010	3.8	...	...	219.0	12.9	662.1	# 0.5	4.8
	2015	3.9	6.6	1.2	132.8	16.9	427.8	# 39.8	3.5
Lesotho Lesotho	2009	35.8	...	...	368.4	3.1	225.9	63.8	...
	2010	37.4	...	...	...	...	...	...	...
	2015	41.2	75.6	8.9	...	...	...	...	...
Liberia Libéria	2010	3.3	...	...	...	...	...	...	...
	2012	3.2	5.1	1.4	...	...	...	...	...
Libya Libye	2005	3.7	...	...	...	...	...	...	...
	2010	3.1	...	...	...	...	...	...	...
	2015	2.5	4.0	1.0	...	...	...	...	...
Liechtenstein Liechtenstein	2005	0.0	...	...	203.7	...	502.1	2.9	51.7
	2010	2.8	...	...	212.3	...	479.7	5.5	16.5
	2015	0.0	...	...	327.7	...	514.2	8.0	24.0
Lithuania Lituanie	2005	11.1	17.5	5.6	12.2	2.1	826.1	155.7	16.7
	2010	7.0	10.0	4.4	7.9	2.2	849.6	87.3	16.5
	2015	5.9	9.1	3.1	7.4	1.7	699.0	55.2	13.0
Luxembourg Luxembourg	2004	0.4	0.4	0.4	...	...	...	...	...
	2005	0.9	...	...	...	...	...	...	...
	2010	2.0	2.0	2.0	487.3	5.3	1 421.2	74.2	# 41.5
	2014	0.7	0.7	0.7	572.6	9.3	1 843.2	110.5	# 51.4
Madagascar Madagascar	2005	10.0	...	...	...	...	...	...	...
	2010	9.2	...	...	16.4	...	0.3	14.9	3.3
	2015	7.7	12.1	3.3	9.0	0.1	0.9	7.2	4.6
Malawi Malawi	2005	1.5	...	...	...	...	...	...	...
	2010	3.4	...	...	...	...	...	...	...
	2012	1.7	2.7	0.8	...	...	...	...	...
Malaysia Malaisie	2005	2.4	...	...	16.5	...	133.0	59.7	...
	2006	2.2	...	...	21.8	...	141.4	81.6	...
	2010	1.9	3.0	0.7	...	...	...	...	...
	2013	2.1	...	...	...	...	...	...	...
Maldives Maldives	2003	1.3	...	...	...	...	...	90.9	...
	2004	...	...	...	...	0.3	...	155.7	...
	2010	1.6	...	...	444.4	7.8	1 203.0	164.5	157.3
	2013	0.8	1.1	0.3	367.1	2.3	1 903.4	207.6	163.2
Mali Mali	2005	12.7	...	...	...	...	...	...	...
	2010	12.2	...	...	...	...	...	...	...
	2015	10.9	16.7	5.1	...	...	...	...	...
Malta Malte	2005	1.0	1.0	1.0	...	...	2 420.6	# 64.5	...
	2010	1.0	1.4	0.5	# 43.7	...	1 885.4	# 47.6	# 22.1
	2015	0.9	0.9	0.9	# 43.7	...	2 066.8	# 57.8	# 24.8
Martinique Martinique	2005	4.8	...	...	...	...	...	...	...
	2009	2.8	4.4	1.4	...	...	...	...	...
Mauritania Mauritanie	2005	12.4	...	...	...	...	...	...	...
	2010	10.9	...	...	...	...	...	...	...
	2015	9.9	14.6	5.2	...	...	...	...	...
Mauritius Maurice	2005	3.0	3.9	2.1	10.0	...	# 1 172.3	110.5	25.7
	2010	2.6	4.0	1.3	19.1	2.8	# 864.0	86.9	34.6
	2011	2.7	4.2	1.3	18.4	4.0	# 729.9	65.0	37.2
	2015	1.7	2.4	0.9	...	...	...	...	...
Mayotte Mayotte	2009	5.9	...	...	...	...	...	...	...
Mexico Mexique	2005	9.1	16.0	2.4	# 217.9	# 0.3	# 77.3	# 470.1	# 26.1
	2010	22.0	40.0	4.1	# 194.5	# 1.1	# 111.3	# 622.3	# 28.8
	2015	16.5	29.3	3.8	# 35.8	# 0.9	# 114.2	# 129.2	# 31.8

12 Intentional homicides and other crimes *(continued)*

By type of crime per 100 000 population and homicide victims by sex

Homicides intentionnels et autres crimes *(suite)*

Par type de crime pour 100 000 habitants et victimes d'homicides par sexe

Country or area Pays ou zone	Year Année	Intentional homicides / Homicides volontaires: Per 100 000 Pour 100 000	Victims (%) / Victimes (%): Male Hommes	Female Femmes	Other crimes (per 100 000 pop.) / Autres infractions (pour 100 000 hab.): Assault Agression	Kidnapping Enlèvement	Theft Vol simple	Robbery Vol qualifié	Sexual Violence Violences Sexuelles
Micronesia (Fed. States of) Micronésie (États féd. de)	2005	4.6	...	...	...	...	...	...	...
	2010	4.5	...	...	...	...	...	...	...
	2015	4.7	6.9	2.4	...	...	...	...	...
Monaco Monaco	2005	3.0	...	...	458.5	...	958.4	20.7	...
	2006	2.9	...	...	407.2	5.8	1 006.3	11.6	...
	2010	0.0	...	...	...	...	...	...	...
	2015	0.0	...	...	...	...	...	...	...
Mongolia Mongolie	2005	15.8	...	...	118.4	~0.0	264.5	23.1	13.4
	2009	8.2	12.1	4.4	216.1	~0.0	238.8	28.2	13.0
	2010	8.8	12.8	4.9	214.6	...	213.0	19.2	13.3
	2013	7.1	10.5	3.9	264.6	0.1	275.7	21.7	14.2
	2015	6.2	9.6	2.9	272.5	...	309.9	18.2	12.1
Montenegro Monténégro	2005	3.6	...	...	# 25.2	...	249.8	# 14.0	5.7
	2010	2.4	2.6	2.2	# 31.0	0.3	85.2	# 0.5	5.8
	2013	1.6	2.9	0.3	# 27.7	0.2	118.3	# 25.8	4.0
	2015	2.7	4.5	0.9	# 22.4	...	132.2	# 24.9	4.2
Montserrat Montserrat	2005	20.9	...	...	...	...	...	...	...
	2008	20.4	...	...	...	...	...	...	...
	2012	19.9	...	...	...	...	...	...	...
Morocco Maroc	2005	1.5	...	...	107.4	1.0	204.4	49.4	3.1
	2009	1.4	2.4	0.3	98.1	1.0	247.2	81.8	10.3
	2010	1.4	...	...	...	...	...	...	...
	2013	1.3	2.2	0.4	202.6	2.9	322.3	44.4	12.9
	2015	1.2	1.9	0.6	...	...	...	...	...
Mozambique Mozambique	2005	5.2	...	...	6.0	...	26.3	32.3	3.7
	2009	3.5	...	...	2.2	...	20.1	22.3	2.6
	2010	3.6	...	...	...	...	...	...	...
	2011	3.4	5.8	1.1	...	...	...	...	...
Myanmar Myanmar	2005	1.4	...	...	...	...	...	...	...
	2010	1.6	2.7	0.6	5.2	...	3.3	~0.0	0.5
	2013	2.4	4.1	0.8	4.7	~0.0	4.8	~0.0	0.7
	2014	2.4	4.0	0.8	10.3	0.0	5.6	0.2	...
	2015	2.2	3.7	0.7	9.0	...	5.4	0.3	...
Namibia Namibie	2004	17.5	...	...	...	...	...	...	...
	2010	14.4	...	...	...	...	...	...	...
	2012	17.1	31.7	3.5	...	...	...	...	...
Nauru Nauru	2012	0.0	...	...	...	...	...	...	...
Nepal Népal	2005	3.4	...	...	4.1	0.5	2.0	0.9	...
	2006	2.4	...	...	4.1	1.0	2.1	0.6	...
	2010	3.0	...	...	...	...	...	...	...
	2014	2.0	3.1	0.9	...	...	...	...	...
Netherlands Pays-Bas	2005	1.1	1.4	0.7	# 410.6	# 5.6	# 4 641.6	# 100.7	# 44.6
	2010	0.9	1.1	0.6	# 362.4	# 3.9	# 3 981.0	# 97.0	# 57.8
	2015	0.6	0.7	0.5	# 281.8	# 2.5	# 3 214.8	# 56.8	# 43.5
New Caledonia Nouvelle-Calédonie	2009	3.2	...	...	...	...	...	...	...
New Zealand Nouvelle-Zélande	2005	1.5[3]	1.7	1.3	234.2	# 7.0	3 088.4	56.2	59.6
	2010	1.0	1.0	1.0	257.7	# 5.2	2 676.6	57.0	66.7
	2013	1.0	1.5	0.5	200.5	# 4.4	2 280.1	45.5	83.7
	2014	1.0	1.4	0.6	220.2	# 5.2	...	44.9	83.2
Nicaragua Nicaragua	2005	13.6	...	...	359.4	0.2	269.8	# 397.4	...
	2010	13.7	25.0	2.7	319.7	0.1	182.2	# 495.5	# 63.2
	2015	8.6	15.3	2.1	...	...	...	...	...
Niger Niger	2012	4.4	6.9	2.0	...	...	...	...	...

Intentional homicides and other crimes *(continued)*
By type of crime per 100 000 population and homicide victims by sex

Homicides intentionnels et autres crimes *(suite)*
Par type de crime pour 100 000 habitants et victimes d'homicides par sexe

Country or area Pays ou zone	Year Année	Intentional homicides / Homicides volontaires: Per 100 000 Pour 100 000	Victims (%) / Victimes (%): Male Hommes	Victims (%) / Victimes (%): Female Femmes	Other crimes (per 100 000 pop.) / Autres infractions (pour 100 000 hab.): Assault Agression	Kidnapping Enlèvement	Theft Vol simple	Robbery Vol qualifié	Sexual Violence Violences Sexuelles
Nigeria Nigéria	2005	11.8	...	...	...	...	...	...	...
	2010	10.7	...	...	11.4	0.5	12.9	1.4	1.1
	2013	...	...	...	9.5	0.3	13.9	1.1	1.0
	2015	9.8	14.6	5.0	...	...	...	...	...
Niue Nioué	2012	0.0	...	...	...	...	...	...	...
Norway Norvège	2005	0.7	0.8	0.6	# 64.0	...	2 996.7	# 31.3	42.4
	2010	0.6	0.6	0.6	# 59.8	...	2 590.0	# 34.5	50.1
	2014	0.6	0.6	0.5	# 46.2	...	2 193.7	# 20.7	51.6
	2015	0.5	0.4	0.5	...	...	...	...	...
Oman Oman	2005	2.1	...	...	...	...	...	...	...
	2008	1.7	...	...	78.5	0.3	207.9	9.6	6.9
	2010	1.6	...	...	...	...	...	...	...
	2014	0.7	0.8	0.4	...	...	...	...	...
Other non-specified areas Autres zones non-spécifiées	2001	1.4	...	...	...	...	...	...	...
	2010	0.8	...	...	...	...	...	...	...
	2015	0.8	138.7	53.3	...	...	...	...	...
Pakistan Pakistan	2005	6.4	...	...	...	...	...	...	...
	2010	7.7	...	...	...	...	...	...	...
	2015	5.0	7.5	2.3	...	...	...	...	...
Palau Palaos	2012	3.1	...	...	...	...	...	...	...
Panama Panama	2005	10.9	19.6	2.2	...	# 0.5	# 421.1	# 158.1	# 23.6
	2010	12.6	23.4	1.7	167.4	# 1.1	# 504.4	# 262.6	# 27.8
	2015	11.3	20.0	2.5	72.4	# 0.4	# 480.4	# 207.9	# 80.2
Papua New Guinea Papouasie-Nvl-Guinée	2000	8.3	...	...	...	...	...	...	...
	2007	7.8	11.9	3.6	...	...	...	...	...
Paraguay Paraguay	2005	15.3	...	...	38.6	~0.0	...	...	...
	2010	11.9	21.2	2.4	31.4	0.1	502.1	220.3	54.7
	2015	9.3	16.6	1.7	10.3	~0.0	572.7	317.2	74.8
Peru Pérou	2005	...	...	...	53.2	# 1.8	189.9	165.1	...
	2010	...	...	...	64.9	# 1.6	190.1	193.4	18.0
	2015	7.2	11.7	2.6	79.0	# 0.7	301.1	264.4	18.2
Philippines Philippines	2005	# 7.5	...	...	...	0.1	# 13.0	# 9.0	...
	2010	# 9.5	16.2	2.7	...	~0.0	# 78.4	# 38.8	2.3
	2012	# 8.8	15.1	2.3	...	~0.0	# 45.4	# 28.1	1.9
	#2014	9.7	...	...	...	...	113.8	44.1	...
	#2015	9.5	...	...	...	...	...	...	...
Poland Pologne	2005	1.4[3]	2.2	0.7	...	0.1	725.0	109.6	...
	2010	1.1[3]	1.6	0.7	28.5	0.1	528.6	50.2	8.0
	2014	0.7[3]	1.1	0.4	18.5	0.8	433.4	24.5	11.6
	2015	0.8[3]	...	...	14.3	0.6	357.8	21.1	7.8
Portugal Portugal	2005	1.3	2.0	0.6	374.2	4.2	876.1	192.9	15.5
	2010	1.2	1.6	0.8	8.2	4.7	898.1	193.1	20.2
	2014	0.9	0.9	0.9	5.2	3.6	875.2	149.9	22.4
	2015	1.0	...	...	4.5	3.6	835.0	149.5	23.6
Puerto Rico Porto Rico	2005	20.5	39.5	2.9	...	...	...	...	...
	2010	27.4	53.5	3.2	73.2	...	721.7	175.7	...
	2015	16.8	33.1	1.8	76.3	...	665.0	110.5	...
Qatar Qatar	2004	0.7	0.8	0.4	40.7	0.8	100.3	2.9	...
	2005	0.7	0.3	1.4	...	...	107.2	...	...
	2006	0.5	0.6	0.3	...	...	105.5	...	...
	2010	0.2	0.3	0.0	...	...	...	...	...
	2014	0.4	0.4	0.3	...	...	...	...	...
Republic of Korea République de Corée	2005	...	...	...	...	...	396.6	10.9	...
	2010	...	...	...	# 595.5	0.5	548.8	9.0	37.1
	2014	0.7	0.7	0.8	# 100.4	0.4	531.7	3.2	42.1
	2015	0.7	0.7	0.8	...	...	...	...	...

12

Intentional homicides and other crimes *(continued)*

By type of crime per 100 000 population and homicide victims by sex

Homicides intentionnels et autres crimes *(suite)*

Par type de crime pour 100 000 habitants et victimes d'homicides par sexe

		Intentional homicides Homicides volontaires			Other crimes (per 100 000 pop.) Autres infractions (pour 100 000 hab.)				
		Per 100 000 Pour 100 000	Victims (%) Victimes (%)						
Country or area Pays ou zone	Year Année		Male Hommes	Female Femmes	Assault Agression	Kidnapping Enlèvement	Theft Vol simple	Robbery Vol qualifié	Sexual Violence Violences Sexuelles
Republic of Moldova République de Moldova	2005	7.1	9.8	4.6	# 9.5	0.4	276.7	4.5	9.5
	2010	6.5	10.8	2.5	# 10.2	0.9	334.1	4.5	13.6
	2014	3.2	4.2	2.3	# 7.9	2.2	410.8	3.1	15.9
Réunion Réunion	2005	3.2	4.5	1.8	...	...	...	...	...
	2009	1.8	2.3	1.4	...	...	...	...	...
Romania Roumanie	2005	2.1[3]	3.0	1.2	# 41.6	# 1.3	# 201.8	# 15.5	...
	2010	2.0[3]	2.7	1.3	# 60.6	# 1.6	# 240.6	# 12.2	# 7.3
	2015	1.5[3]	2.0	1.0	# 1.5	# 1.5	# 555.8	# 17.2	# 8.9
Russian Federation Fédération de Russie	2005	24.8 #	40.1	11.5	40.3	0.8	1 095.2	239.8	12.9
	2009	14.9	24.1	7.0	30.1	0.4	830.4	143.5	12.5
	2010	...	...	...	21.2	0.4	774.2	114.9	10.6
	2015	11.5[7]	...	...	16.6	0.2	709.9	50.7	11.3
Rwanda Rwanda	2010	2.8	...	...	19.5	0.1	...	20.1	...
	2013	3.2	...	...	29.8	0.2	...	25.0	15.7
	2015	2.5	4.0	1.1	...	...	...	...	...
Saint Helena Sainte-Hélène	2005	0.0	...	...	...	...	...	...	...
	2009	0.0	...	...	...	...	...	...	...
Saint Kitts and Nevis Saint-Kitts-et-Nevis	2005	16.5	...	...	...	...	...	...	...
	2010	40.8	...	...	296.1	3.8	1 018.1	166.2	118.4
	2011	65.4	...	...	258.5	5.7	926.5	124.5	120.8
	2012	34.2	...	...	...	...	...	...	...
Saint Lucia Sainte-Lucie	2004	22.8	41.7	4.7	...	...	...	...	...
	2005	25.0	...	...	...	...	...	...	...
	2010	25.5	45.5	6.3	...	...	...	...	...
	2014	19.3	39.3	0.0	...	...	...	...	...
Saint Pierre and Miquelon Saint-Pierre-et-Miquelon	2009	15.9	...	...	...	...	...	...	...
Saint Vincent & Grenadines Saint-Vincent-Grenadines	2005	23.9	34.6	13.0	1 151.3	1.8	1 777.5	67.1	104.8
	2010	22.9	39.9	5.5	1 197.5	1.8	1 739.0	107.0	153.7
	2012	25.6	...	...	1 017.1	3.7	1 923.5	146.3	160.1
	2013	...	...	...	...	...	...	136.3	209.5
Samoa Samoa	2010	8.6	...	...	...	...	...	...	...
	2013	3.1	4.8	1.4	...	...	...	...	...
San Marino Saint-Marin	2005	0.0	...	...	...	...	...	...	...
	2010	0.0	...	...	...	...	...	...	...
	2011	0.0	...	...	...	...	...	...	...
Sao Tome and Principe Sao Tomé-et-Principe	2004	...	...	...	0.7	...	...	...	...
	2009	2.9	...	...	3.0	...	3.0	...	...
	2010	3.4	...	...	...	...	9.4	0.6	...
	2011	3.4	5.2	1.5	2.3	...	11.5	0.6	...
Saudi Arabia Arabie saoudite	2005	1.2	...	...	...	...	...	...	...
	2007	1.0	...	...	...	...	...	...	...
	2015	1.5	1.8	1.1	1.4	...	...	0.3	0.1
Senegal Sénégal	2005	9.3	...	...	2.5	...	...	24.4	...
	2010	8.5	...	...	2.4	...	19.3	19.3	...
	2015	7.4	12.3	2.7	...	~0.0	16.5	16.5	1.7
Serbia Serbie	2005	1.6	2.3	1.0	17.6	0.3	# 182.5	32.5	5.8
	2010	1.4	2.0	0.9	15.4	0.2	# 175.7	40.0	5.4
	2015	1.2	1.7	0.7	12.9	0.2	# 255.4	34.2	3.8
Seychelles Seychelles	2004	11.4	18.8	4.1	...	...	...	...	...
	2010	9.8	16.4	2.9	...	...	...	...	...
	2014	17.2	29.1	5.3	...	...	...	...	...
	2015	7.5	...	...	...	...	...	...	...
Sierra Leone Sierra Leone	2005	1.7	...	...	...	...	...	...	...
	2008	3.0	...	...	359.9	...	190.2	3.3	11.3
	2010	2.5	...	...	...	...	...	...	...
	2015	1.7	2.7	0.8	...	...	...	...	...

12 Intentional homicides and other crimes *(continued)*

By type of crime per 100 000 population and homicide victims by sex

Homicides intentionnels et autres crimes *(suite)*

Par type de crime pour 100 000 habitants et victimes d'homicides par sexe

Country or area Pays ou zone	Year Année	Intentional homicides / Homicides volontaires: Per 100 000 Pour 100 000	Victims (%) / Victimes (%): Male Hommes	Female Femmes	Other crimes (per 100 000 pop.) / Autres infractions (pour 100 000 hab.): Assault Agression	Kidnapping Enlèvement	Theft Vol simple	Robbery Vol qualifié	Sexual Violence Violences Sexuelles
Singapore Singapour	2003	0.6	...	...	13.9	0.1	354.6	22.9	...
	2005	0.5	...	...	13.5	...	470.9	24.3	...
	2006	0.4	0.5	0.2	13.8	~0.0	413.3	20.5	30.3
	2010	0.4	0.6	0.1	8.5	...	359.8	10.2	31.1
	2015	0.3	0.4	0.1	8.4	...	266.0	2.2	26.0
Slovakia Slovaquie	2005	1.7	2.3	1.2	72.4	0.3	350.9	35.6	...
	2010	1.5	1.9	1.1	44.9	0.1	452.5	22.0	10.4
	2015	0.8	1.1	0.5	35.0	~0.0	444.0	9.9	3.0
Slovenia Slovénie	2005	1.0	1.0	1.0	115.4	0.2	1 477.0	21.5	15.6
	2010	0.7	0.7	0.8	106.3	0.2	1 408.6	22.6	18.3
	2015	1.0	0.9	1.1	74.5	0.2	1 102.7	11.2	7.4
Solomon Islands Îles Salomon	2005	5.5	...	...	258.5	...	219.3	5.1	43.5
	2008	3.8	5.7	1.8	217.9	...	174.4	10.3	24.2
Somalia Somalie	2005	5.0	...	...	...	...	...	...	...
	2010	5.3	...	...	...	...	...	...	...
	2015	4.3	6.5	2.2	...	...	...	...	...
South Africa Afrique du Sud	2005	38.0	...	...	...	...	...	...	...
	2010	30.8	51.9	10.4	...	...	...	...	...
	2011	29.8	51.3	9.0	...	...	...	...	...
	2015	33.8	...	...	...	...	...	...	...
South Sudan Soudan du sud	2012	13.9	21.6	6.2	...	...	...	...	...
Spain Espagne	2005	1.2	1.8	0.6	# 394.1	0.5	...	...	...
	2010	0.9	1.1	0.7	# 53.8	0.3	# 310.3	181.1	21.4
	2015	0.7	0.8	0.5	# 63.0	0.2	# 446.1	140.0	21.4
Sri Lanka Sri Lanka	2004	# 7.1	...	...	109.3	4.5	135.8	41.0	...
	#2005	6.2	...	...	...	...	...	...	...
	2010	# 3.8	6.1	1.6	319.9	1.0	62.8	31.9	4.4
	2013	# 3.0	4.8	1.4	316.4	1.0	55.8	23.1	4.8
	2015	# 2.4	3.8	1.0	...	...	...	...	...
State of Palestine État de Palestine	2005	2.4	...	...	# 183.6	# 5.6	# 122.3	# 5.7	...
	2010	0.8	1.1	0.5	# 7.0	# 0.5	# 67.4	# 69.9	4.4
	2012	0.6	1.0	0.2	# 8.1	# 0.3	# 45.3	# 46.4	2.8
	2013	0.5	...	...	...	...	...	# 84.5	3.0
	2015	1.0	...	...	...	...	...	...	...
Sudan Soudan	2008	5.2	8.0	2.4	...	1.8	220.6	8.9	...
Suriname Suriname	2004	9.3	...	...	...	...	2 778.8	...	...
	2005	13.8	...	...	...	...	...	...	...
	2008	8.3	12.7	3.9	...	...	...	...	...
Sweden Suède	2005	0.9	1.2	0.7	804.5	...	4 926.0	104.1	129.7
	2010	1.0	1.4	0.6	59.6	...	3 921.9	98.3	150.6
	2015	1.1	1.7	0.6	47.4	...	3 815.5	86.5	155.8
Switzerland Suisse	2005	1.0	1.0	1.0	# 109.3	# 3.3	# 1 922.4	# 53.7	...
	2009	0.7	0.6	0.7	# 6.8	# 4.6	# 1 616.4	# 65.0	# 85.9
	2010	0.7	0.7	0.7	# 6.2	...	# 2 059.6	# 56.3	# 31.8
	2015	0.7	0.7	0.7	# 7.4	# 0.1	# 1 759.6	# 39.5	# 32.7
Syrian Arab Republic République arabe syrienne	2004	2.4	...	...	36.0	0.8	65.3	3.1	...
	2005	2.4	...	...	34.0	0.2	...	4.2	...
	2008	2.6	...	...	2.8	0.1	32.4	4.3	0.4
	2010	2.2	3.4	1.0	...	...	...	...	...
Tajikistan Tadjikistan	2005	2.3	...	...	...	...	52.3	...	...
	2010	2.4	4.1	0.6	72.4	1.9	46.9	3.2	2.6
	2011	1.6	2.8	0.4	48.2	2.2	47.3	3.7	2.6
Thailand Thaïlande	2005	7.3	13.0	1.9	# 42.9	~0.0	92.4	...	...
	2010	5.4	9.7	1.3	# 13.7	~0.0	81.5	# 2.8	2.9
	2014	3.9	6.7	1.2	# 18.7	~0.0	58.9	# 2.1	1.8
	2015	3.5	...	...	# 20.1	0.5	57.9	# 2.2	6.0

12 Intentional homicides and other crimes *(continued)*

By type of crime per 100 000 population and homicide victims by sex

Homicides intentionnels et autres crimes *(suite)*

Par type de crime pour 100 000 habitants et victimes d'homicides par sexe

		Intentional homicides Homicides volontaires			Other crimes (per 100 000 pop.) Autres infractions (pour 100 000 hab.)				
			Victims (%) Victimes (%)						
Country or area Pays ou zone	Year Année	Per 100 000 Pour 100 000	Male Hommes	Female Femmes	Assault Agression	Kidnapping Enlèvement	Theft Vol simple	Robbery Vol qualifié	Sexual Violence Violences Sexuelles
TFYR of Macedonia ex-R.Y. de Macédoine	2005	2.1	3.4	0.9	...	1.2	...	34.7	...
	2010	2.1	2.7	1.4	12.0	0.8	237.4	29.3	6.0
	2014	1.6	2.2	1.0	10.4	0.4	240.1	14.7	6.5
Timor-Leste Timor-Leste	2005	4.5	...	...	...	...	...	...	...
	2010	3.5	...	...	...	...	...	...	...
	2015	3.9	6.2	1.6	...	...	...	...	...
Togo Togo	2005	10.7	...	...	...	...	...	...	...
	2010	9.6	...	...	...	...	...	...	...
	2015	9.0	14.9	3.2	...	...	...	...	...
Tonga Tonga	2005	4.0	7.9	0.0	...	...	...	...	...
	2010	1.0	1.9	0.0	...	...	...	...	...
	2012	1.0	0.0	1.9	...	...	...	...	...
Trinidad and Tobago Trinité-et-Tobago	2005	29.8	54.0	6.0	61.8	4.5	212.2	375.4	61.9
	2010	35.6	63.9	7.9	46.4	0.5	307.9	385.7	57.8
	2015	30.9	58.3	4.2	44.1	0.3	137.5	181.5	51.1
Tunisia Tunisie	2005	2.6	...	...	...	...	...	...	...
	2010	2.7	...	...	...	...	...	...	...
	2012	3.0	5.1	1.0	...	...	...	...	...
Turkey Turquie	2005	4.9	8.1	1.8	155.8	12.9	152.9	21.2	4.5
	2010	4.2	6.8	1.7	305.5	18.8	248.4	11.9	5.8
	2012	4.3	7.1	1.6	350.5	17.9	279.1	13.8	7.4
Turkmenistan Turkménistan	2004	4.4	...	...	...	2.7	...	3.8	...
	2005	4.3	...	...	1.9	...	35.0	3.4	...
	2006	4.2	6.8	1.7	1.7	...	29.8	2.9	...
Turks and Caicos Islands Îles Turques-et-Caïques	2005	0.0	...	...	...	...	...	...	...
	2009	6.6	...	...	...	...	...	...	...
	2014	5.9	...	...	...	...	...	...	...
Tuvalu Tuvalu	2005	0.0	...	...	...	...	...	...	...
	2010	9.5	...	...	...	...	...	...	...
	2012	18.6	...	...	...	...	...	...	...
Uganda Ouganda	2005	8.7	...	...	125.1	...	196.3	26.1	50.3
	2010	9.3	15.2	3.5	69.3	# 0.5	70.7	18.2	26.1
	2014	11.5	18.8	4.3	38.4	# 0.6	45.2	9.6	36.2
Ukraine Ukraine	2005	6.5	9.5	3.8	14.3	0.4	398.9	100.5	4.1
	2010	4.3	6.6	2.4	8.8	0.6	558.1	51.0	3.0
	2014	6.3	...	...	...	...	...	...	...
United Arab Emirates Émirats arabes unis	2004	0.7	...	...	...	12.7	# 277.6	11.0	...
	2005	1.2	...	...	16.0	19.2	...	9.6	...
	2006	0.7	...	...	14.7	18.8	...	10.8	...
	2010	0.8	0.8	0.9	...	...	...	...	...
	2015	0.7	0.7	0.4	3.5	0.9	# 67.8	9.0	4.1
United Kingdom Royaume-Uni	2005	1.4	1.8	1.0	1 010.6[8]	5.2[8]	3 368.8[8]	183.3[8]	88.0[8]
	2010	1.2	1.5	0.9	658.8[8]	3.1[8]	2 654.9[8]	136.8[8]	81.5[8]
	2014	0.9	1.1	0.7	649.3[8]	3.8[8]	2 208.6[8]	87.5[8]	137.0[8]
	2015	1.0	1.2	0.8	...	...	...	...	...
United Rep. of Tanzania Rép.-Unie de Tanzanie	2004	7.6	...	...	...	...	...	...	...
	2010	8.4	14.7	2.4	...	...	...	26.1	~0.0
	2015	7.0	11.5	2.5	4.4	...	0.3	17.6	0.1
United States of America États-Unis d'Amérique	2005	5.7	9.1	2.4	291.2	...	2 290.6	141.0	...
	2010	4.8	7.5	2.1	252.3	...	2 002.3	119.1	...
	2015	5.0	7.9	2.1	237.6	...	1 773.4	101.7	...
United States Virgin Islands Îles Vierges américaines	2005	34.3	65.3	5.4	...	...	...	...	...
	2010	52.8	96.5	12.6	...	...	...	...	...
	2012	49.3	99.2	3.6	...	...	...	...	...
Uruguay Uruguay	2003	5.9	...	...	...	0.1	2 904.9	291.7	...
	2004	6.0	...	...	...	...	3 179.5	277.5	...
	2005	5.7	...	...	...	...	...	291.7	...
	2010	6.1	10.1	2.3	15.4	...	2 823.3	409.8	...
	2015	8.5	14.7	2.8	13.6	0.3	3 043.6	566.0	46.1

12 Intentional homicides and other crimes *(continued)*
By type of crime per 100 000 population and homicide victims by sex

Homicides intentionnels et autres crimes *(suite)*
Par type de crime pour 100 000 habitants et victimes d'homicides par sexe

Country or area Pays ou zone	Year Année	Intentional homicides / Homicides volontaires: Per 100 000 Pour 100 000	Victims (%) / Victimes (%): Male Hommes	Female Femmes	Other crimes (per 100 000 pop.) / Autres infractions (pour 100 000 hab.): Assault Agression	Kidnapping Enlèvement	Theft Vol simple	Robbery Vol qualifié	Sexual Violence Violences Sexuelles
Uzbekistan	2005	3.4	...	...	...	...	...	...	...
Ouzbékistan	2008	3.0	4.9	1.2	...	...	...	...	...
Vanuatu	2005	2.5	...	...	...	...	...	...	...
Vanuatu	2010	2.3	...	...	...	...	...	...	...
	2015	2.1	3.2	1.1	...	...	...	...	...
Venezuela (Boliv. Rep. of)	2005	37.2	70.2	4.2	...	...	...	...	...
Venezuela (Rép. boliv. du)	2010	45.1	84.8	5.4	...	...	...	...	...
	2012	53.8	101.5	6.3	...	...	...	...	...
	2014	61.9	...	...	...	...	...	...	...
Viet Nam	2005	1.2	...	...	...	...	...	...	...
Viet Nam	2010	1.5	...	...	...	...	...	...	...
	2011	1.5	2.6	0.4	...	...	...	...	...
Yemen	2005	4.6	...	...	...	0.5	...	...	...
Yémen	2009	4.3	...	...	0.1	0.2	...	1.9	0.3
	2010	4.7	...	...	...	...	...	...	...
	2013	6.7	10.3	3.0	...	...	...	...	...
Zambia	2000	7.6	...	...	...	...	...	...	...
Zambie	2010	5.9	...	...	...	...	...	...	...
	2015	5.3	8.6	2.1	...	...	...	...	...
Zimbabwe	2005	10.4	...	...	712.5	0.3	851.1	85.8	...
Zimbabwe	2008	...	...	...	379.7	1.6	677.7	65.2	...
	2010	5.0	...	...	...	...	...	...	...
	2012	6.7	11.5	2.0	...	...	...	...	...

Source:

United Nations Office on Drugs and Crime (UNODC), Vienna, UNODC Statistics database, last accessed May 2018.

1 Data is for 2015, or latest available data from 2010 onwards.
2 Excludes Australia and New Zealand.
3 Data refer to offences, not victims, of intentional homicide.
4 For statistical purposes, the data for China do not include those for the Hong Kong Special Administrative Region (Hong Kong SAR), Macao Special Administrative Region (Macao SAR) and Taiwan Province of China.
5 Excluding victims of terrorist attacks.
6 Data refer to Central Iraq.
7 Include victims of attempted homicide.
8 England and Wales only.

Source:

Office des Nations Unies contre la drogue et le crime (ONUDC), Vienne, base de données statistiques de l'ONUDC, dernier accès mai 2018.

1 Données pour 2015, ou dernières données disponibles à partir de 2010.
2 Exclut l'Australie et la Nouvelle-Zélande.
3 Les données concernent les infractions, et non les victimes, d'homicides volontaires.
4 Pour la présentation des statistiques, les données pour la Chine ne comprennent pas la région administrative spéciale de Hong Kong (Hong Kong RAS), la région administrative spéciale de Macao (Macao RAS) et la province chinoise de Taïwan.
5 À l'exclusion des victimes d'attaques terroristes.
6 Les données se réfèrent l'Iraq central.
7 Inclure les victimes de tentative d'homicide.
8 Se rapporte seulement a l'Angleterre et au pays de Galles.

Part Two

Economic activity

Chapter VII	National accounts (tables 13 and 14)
Chapter VIII	Finance (tables 15 and 16)
Chapter IX	Labour market (tables 17 and 18)
Chapter X	Price and production indices (tables 19 and 20)
Chapter XI	International merchandise trade (tables 21 and 22)

Deuxième partie

Activité économique

Chapitre VII	Compatibilités nationales (tableaux 13 et 14)
Chapitre VIII	Finances (tableaux 15 et 16)
Chapitre IX	Marché du travail (tableaux 17 et 18)
Chapitre X	Indices des prix et de la production (tableaux 19 et 20)
Chapitre XI	Commerce international des marchandises (tableaux 21 et 22)

13 Gross domestic product and gross domestic product per capita

In millions of US dollars at current and constant 2010 prices; per capita US dollars; real rates of growth

Produit intérieur brut et produit intérieur brut par habitant

En millions de dollars É.-U. aux prix courants et constants de 2010; par habitant en dollars É.U.; taux de croissance réels

Country or area	1985	1995	2005	2010	2014	2015	2016	Pays ou zone
Total, all countries or areas								**Total, tous pays ou zones**
GDP at current prices	**13 517 692**	**31 101 565**	**47 601 561**	**66 010 167**	**78 913 668**	**74 696 419**	**75 648 868**	**PIB aux prix courants**
GDP per capita	**2 775**	**5 409**	**7 278**	**9 489**	**10 815**	**10 120**	**10 134**	**PIB par habitant**
GDP at constant prices	**31 823 976**	**42 267 728**	**58 202 560**	**66 010 167**	**73 597 005**	**75 638 559**	**77 489 958**	**PIB aux prix constants**
Growth rates	**3.7**	**3.1**	**3.8**	**4.3**	**2.8**	**2.8**	**2.4**	**Taux de croissance**
Africa								**Afrique**
GDP at current prices	511 495	577 167	1 120 031	1 948 202	2 494 180	2 288 021	2 143 440	PIB aux prix courants
GDP per capita	927	800	1 213	1 859	2 145	1 918	1 752	PIB par habitant
GDP at constant prices	792 383	966 766	1 513 474	1 948 202	2 213 660	2 289 017	2 330 450	PIB aux prix constants
Growth rates	3.6	3.1	6.0	5.3	3.8	3.4	1.8	Taux de croissance
Northern Africa								**Afrique septentrionale**
GDP at current prices	142 523	207 392	373 106	648 507	768 597	744 739	700 350	PIB aux prix courants
GDP per capita	1 103	1 270	1 908	3 182	3 488	3 316	3 060	PIB par habitant
GDP at constant prices	264 050	333 874	519 909	648 507	656 139	684 819	708 381	PIB aux prix constants
Growth rates	5.8	1.7	5.7	4.6	1.5	4.4	3.4	Taux de croissance
Sub-Saharan Africa								**Afrique subsaharienne**
GDP at current prices	368 972	369 775	746 926	1 299 694	1 725 583	1 543 282	1 443 090	PIB aux prix courants
GDP per capita	873	662	1 026	1 540	1 831	1 594	1 451	PIB par habitant
GDP at constant prices	528 333	632 892	993 565	1 299 694	1 557 521	1 604 199	1 622 068	PIB aux prix constants
Growth rates	2.6	3.9	6.1	5.6	4.8	3.0	1.1	Taux de croissance
Eastern Africa								**Afrique orientale**
GDP at current prices	61 768	67 945	111 507	215 107	319 868	315 310	320 971	PIB aux prix courants
GDP per capita	374	309	382	622	826	792	784	PIB par habitant
GDP at constant prices	71 294	95 247	143 890	215 107	267 933	283 464	297 105	PIB aux prix constants
Growth rates	2.2	4.6	6.4	7.3	6.7	5.8	4.8	Taux de croissance
Middle Africa								**Afrique centrale**
GDP at current prices	35 105	35 990	99 285	184 993	286 578	232 370	225 212	PIB aux prix courants
GDP per capita	569	427	887	1 408	1 923	1 511	1 420	PIB par habitant
GDP at constant prices	91 717	82 183	137 442	184 993	225 650	230 401	230 401	PIB aux prix constants
Growth rates	1.6	6.7	8.8	4.2	4.9	2.1	0.0	Taux de croissance
Southern Africa								**Afrique australe**
GDP at current prices	62 927	168 964	279 559	406 247	386 872	349 875	328 201	PIB aux prix courants
GDP per capita	1 645	3 518	5 013	6 884	6 188	5 517	5 105	PIB par habitant
GDP at constant prices	214 759	249 548	347 130	406 247	451 513	457 815	459 923	PIB aux prix constants
Growth rates	-1.0	3.3	5.1	3.3	2.0	1.4	0.5	Taux de croissance
Western Africa								**Afrique occidentale**
GDP at current prices	209 172	96 876	256 575	493 347	732 265	645 727	568 706	PIB aux prix courants
GDP per capita	1 325	469	955	1 603	2 133	1 831	1 570	PIB par habitant
GDP at constant prices	150 563	205 914	365 101	493 347	612 425	632 519	634 640	PIB aux prix constants
Growth rates	9.1	3.3	6.0	7.3	6.1	3.3	0.3	Taux de croissance
Americas								**Amériques**
GDP at current prices	5 494 937	10 237 896	17 129 485	21 925 902	25 550 116	25 151 882	25 404 270	PIB aux prix courants
GDP per capita	8 190	13 110	19 289	23 343	26 130	25 480	25 496	PIB par habitant
GDP at constant prices	11 214 675	14 811 586	20 394 849	21 925 902	23 942 406	24 395 461	24 573 633	PIB aux prix constants
Growth rates	4.1	2.5	3.5	3.4	2.2	1.9	0.7	Taux de croissance
Northern America								**Amérique septentrionale**
GDP at current prices	4 713 297	8 271 824	14 269 644	16 585 997	19 228 743	19 681 665	20 162 646	PIB aux prix courants
GDP per capita	17 665	28 030	43 566	48 365	54 404	55 286	56 228	PIB par habitant
GDP at constant prices	8 574 418	11 407 612	15 940 446	16 585 997	17 996 008	18 476 667	18 750 666	PIB aux prix constants
Growth rates	4.3	2.8	3.3	2.6	2.6	2.7	1.5	Taux de croissance
Latin America & the Caribbean								**Amérique latine et Caraïbes**
GDP at current prices	781 641	1 966 072	2 859 841	5 339 905	6 321 373	5 470 217	5 241 624	PIB aux prix courants
GDP per capita	1 934	4 047	5 102	8 954	10 125	8 667	8 218	PIB par habitant
GDP at constant prices	2 640 257	3 403 974	4 454 403	5 339 905	5 946 398	5 918 794	5 822 967	PIB aux prix constants
Growth rates	3.6	1.5	4.3	5.8	1.0	-0.5	-1.6	Taux de croissance
Caribbean								**Caraïbes**
GDP at current prices	69 215	119 701	221 428	288 787	331 709	341 434	347 035	PIB aux prix courants
GDP per capita	2 223	3 369	5 655	7 086	7 891	8 063	8 139	PIB par habitant
GDP at constant prices	151 340	183 383	263 027	288 787	306 611	313 418	314 896	PIB aux prix constants
Growth rates	0.8	4.0	3.4	1.8	1.4	2.2	0.5	Taux de croissance
Central America								**Amérique centrale**
GDP at current prices	254 231	412 617	974 370	1 212 738	1 531 332	1 401 752	1 321 586	PIB aux prix courants
GDP per capita	2 453	3 253	6 574	7 553	8 994	8 120	7 552	PIB par habitant
GDP at constant prices	662 931	795 163	1 109 318	1 212 738	1 369 308	1 416 145	1 459 096	PIB aux prix constants
Growth rates	2.6	-5.2	2.5	5.0	3.0	3.4	3.0	Taux de croissance

13 Gross domestic product and gross domestic product per capita *(continued)*

In millions of US dollars at current and constant 2010 prices; per capita US dollars; real rates of growth

Produit intérieur brut et produit intérieur brut par habitant *(suite)*

En millions de dollars É.-U. aux prix courants et constants de 2010; par habitant en dollars É.U.; taux de croissance réels

Country or area	1985	1995	2005	2010	2014	2015	2016	Pays ou zone
South America								**Amérique du Sud**
GDP at current prices	458 194	1 433 755	1 664 043	3 838 379	4 458 331	3 727 031	3 573 003	PIB aux prix courants
GDP per capita	1 701	4 433	4 460	9 716	10 820	8 956	8 504	PIB par habitant
GDP at constant prices	1 825 986	2 425 428	3 082 058	3 838 379	4 270 480	4 189 231	4 048 975	PIB aux prix constants
Growth rates	4.2	3.7	5.0	6.4	0.3	-1.9	-3.3	Taux de croissance
Asia								**Asie**
GDP at current prices	2 881 897	9 192 930	12 349 162	20 837 705	26 984 909	26 734 466	27 538 651	PIB aux prix courants
GDP per capita	1 010	2 635	3 115	4 968	6 167	6 049	6 172	PIB par habitant
GDP at constant prices	6 739 396	10 989 470	16 268 085	20 837 705	25 171 939	26 275 445	27 507 325	PIB aux prix constants
Growth rates	5.2	5.1	5.7	7.4	4.4	4.4	4.7	Taux de croissance
Central Asia								**Asie centrale**
GDP at current prices	...	38 937	90 474	220 593	345 100	302 381	252 467	PIB aux prix courants
GDP per capita	...	729	1 540	3 493	5 106	4 401	3 618	PIB par habitant
GDP at constant prices	...	89 432	157 611	220 593	288 433	297 761	306 136	PIB aux prix constants
Growth rates	...	-6.9	9.2	7.5	5.7	3.2	2.8	Taux de croissance
Eastern Asia								**Asie orientale**
GDP at current prices	1 927 587	7 179 561	8 547 753	13 584 987	17 701 539	17 896 854	18 489 486	PIB aux prix courants
GDP per capita	1 510	4 906	5 497	8 513	10 875	10 946	11 262	PIB par habitant
GDP at constant prices	4 650 215	7 464 418	10 704 134	13 584 987	16 266 627	16 939 873	17 692 682	PIB aux prix constants
Growth rates	7.1	4.9	5.1	7.4	4.2	4.1	4.4	Taux de croissance
South-eastern Asia								**Asie du Sud-Est**
GDP at current prices	243 732	703 207	958 929	1 980 866	2 531 839	2 450 641	2 558 569	PIB aux prix courants
GDP per capita	609	1 449	1 707	3 316	4 036	3 862	3 987	PIB par habitant
GDP at constant prices	524 011	1 052 280	1 525 960	1 980 866	2 414 862	2 524 245	2 643 640	PIB aux prix constants
Growth rates	0.7	7.9	5.7	7.8	4.5	4.5	4.7	Taux de croissance
Southern Asia								**Asie méridionale**
GDP at current prices	367 121	611 440	1 258 642	2 524 007	3 031 267	3 116 265	3 317 296	PIB aux prix courants
GDP per capita	346	463	795	1 480	1 684	1 709	1 797	PIB par habitant
GDP at constant prices	692 236	1 052 360	1 811 397	2 524 007	3 077 766	3 264 505	3 519 669	PIB aux prix constants
Growth rates	4.2	6.0	7.4	8.4	6.7	6.1	7.8	Taux de croissance
Western Asia								**Asie occidentale**
GDP at current prices	343 457	659 785	1 493 364	2 527 253	3 375 164	2 968 325	2 920 834	PIB aux prix courants
GDP per capita	2 967	3 959	7 269	10 872	13 344	11 514	11 122	PIB par habitant
GDP at constant prices	872 934	1 330 979	2 068 984	2 527 253	3 124 250	3 249 061	3 345 197	PIB aux prix constants
Growth rates	-0.7	4.2	6.9	5.8	3.5	4.0	3.0	Taux de croissance
Europe								**Europe**
GDP at current prices	4 415 131	10 618 830	16 100 999	19 821 579	22 178 005	19 056 682	19 026 676	PIB aux prix courants
GDP per capita	5 732	14 556	21 996	26 824	29 887	25 659	25 596	PIB par habitant
GDP at constant prices	12 399 880	14 586 638	18 727 946	19 821 579	20 620 642	20 982 785	21 347 160	PIB aux prix constants
Growth rates	2.5	2.1	2.5	2.3	1.6	1.8	1.7	Taux de croissance
Eastern Europe								**Europe orientale**
GDP at current prices	1 124 250	786 133	1 621 006	2 849 342	3 474 507	2 582 612	2 515 689	PIB aux prix courants
GDP per capita	3 023	2 540	5 449	9 674	11 837	8 807	8 589	PIB par habitant
GDP at constant prices	2 220 893	1 683 128	2 415 627	2 849 342	3 105 432	3 091 860	3 129 300	PIB aux prix constants
Growth rates	1.6	-1.0	5.6	3.5	1.4	-0.4	1.2	Taux de croissance
Northern Europe								**Europe septentrionale**
GDP at current prices	810 063	2 163 509	3 972 776	4 244 137	5 103 178	4 702 513	4 497 618	PIB aux prix courants
GDP per capita	9 782	23 258	41 341	42 431	49 894	45 744	43 520	PIB par habitant
GDP at constant prices	2 332 082	2 995 237	4 123 877	4 244 137	4 564 372	4 731 268	4 833 765	PIB aux prix constants
Growth rates	4.0	3.2	3.2	2.1	2.8	3.7	2.2	Taux de croissance
Southern Europe								**Europe méridionale**
GDP at current prices	783 494	2 120 827	3 606 121	4 304 357	4 218 585	3 617 495	3 693 991	PIB aux prix courants
GDP per capita	5 514	14 667	23 983	27 967	27 611	23 736	24 281	PIB par habitant
GDP at constant prices	2 694 172	3 319 249	4 243 142	4 304 357	4 096 850	4 172 807	4 248 438	PIB aux prix constants
Growth rates	2.5	3.0	1.9	0.6	0.7	1.9	1.8	Taux de croissance
Western Europe								**Europe occidentale**
GDP at current prices	1 697 323	5 548 361	6 901 095	8 423 742	9 381 736	8 154 061	8 319 377	PIB aux prix courants
GDP per capita	9 786	30 432	36 704	44 223	48 491	41 979	42 669	PIB par habitant
GDP at constant prices	5 152 734	6 589 025	7 945 301	8 423 742	8 853 988	8 986 851	9 135 657	PIB aux prix constants
Growth rates	2.2	2.0	1.5	2.9	1.5	1.5	1.7	Taux de croissance
Oceania								**Océanie**
GDP at current prices	214 231	474 741	901 884	1 476 780	1 706 457	1 465 368	1 535 831	PIB aux prix courants
GDP per capita	8 664	16 420	27 109	40 627	44 112	37 329	38 561	PIB par habitant
GDP at constant prices	677 642	913 269	1 298 207	1 476 780	1 648 358	1 695 850	1 731 391	PIB aux prix constants
Growth rates	3.8	3.9	3.0	2.3	2.5	2.9	2.1	Taux de croissance

13 Gross domestic product and gross domestic product per capita *(continued)*

In millions of US dollars at current and constant 2010 prices; per capita US dollars; real rates of growth

Produit intérieur brut et produit intérieur brut par habitant *(suite)*

En millions de dollars É.-U. aux prix courants et constants de 2010; par habitant en dollars É.U.; taux de croissance réels

Country or area	1985	1995	2005	2010	2014	2015	2016	Pays ou zone
Australia and New Zealand								**Australie et Nouvelle-Zélande**
GDP at current prices	206 097	455 727	877 210	1 440 378	1 658 562	1 420 860	1 491 980	PIB aux prix courants
GDP per capita	10 848	20 951	35 989	54 374	59 147	50 005	51 829	PIB par habitant
GDP at constant prices	660 883	887 608	1 267 022	1 440 378	1 607 365	1 652 991	1 687 466	PIB aux prix constants
Growth rates	3.8	4.0	3.0	2.2	2.5	2.8	2.1	Taux de croissance
Melanesia								**Mélanésie**
GDP at current prices	5 971	13 533	17 353	28 121	39 070	36 679	35 782	PIB aux prix courants
GDP per capita	1 179	2 118	2 156	3 130	4 011	3 693	3 534	PIB par habitant
GDP at constant prices	11 529	18 957	22 689	28 121	32 651	34 324	35 180	PIB aux prix constants
Growth rates	2.5	0.8	3.6	8.5	5.6	5.1	2.5	Taux de croissance
Micronesia								**Micronésie**
GDP at current prices	256	544	718	860	1 040	1 049	1 100	PIB aux prix courants
GDP per capita	1 222	2 065	2 560	2 975	3 471	3 469	3 605	PIB par habitant
GDP at constant prices	714	844	862	860	993	1 049	1 083	PIB aux prix constants
Growth rates	2.4	3.9	1.5	3.5	4.8	5.6	3.2	Taux de croissance
Polynesia								**Polynésie**
GDP at current prices	1 906	4 937	6 603	7 421	7 785	6 780	6 969	PIB aux prix courants
GDP per capita	4 184	9 689	11 674	12 636	12 931	11 183	11 406	PIB par habitant
GDP at constant prices	4 516	5 859	7 634	7 421	7 348	7 486	7 661	PIB aux prix constants
Growth rates	5.4	0.8	1.6	-1.6	1.5	1.9	2.3	Taux de croissance
Afghanistan								**Afghanistan**
GDP at current prices	3 322	3 236	6 622	16 078	21 331	20 608	20 235	PIB aux prix courants
GDP per capita	282	189	264	558	651	611	584	PIB par habitant
GDP at constant prices	11 604	7 011	10 244	16 078	21 271	20 890	21 634	PIB aux prix constants
Growth rates	0.3	49.9	9.9	3.2	3.1	-1.8	3.6	Taux de croissance
Albania								**Albanie**
GDP at current prices	2 324	2 393	8 052	11 927	13 228	11 335	11 864	PIB aux prix courants
GDP per capita	783	770	2 615	4 056	4 529	3 877	4 054	PIB par habitant
GDP at constant prices	5 911	5 424	9 222	11 927	12 750	13 035	13 474	PIB aux prix constants
Growth rates	1.8	13.3	5.5	3.7	1.8	2.2	3.4	Taux de croissance
Algeria								**Algérie**
GDP at current prices	57 866	41 971	103 198	161 207	213 810	165 874	159 049	PIB aux prix courants
GDP per capita	2 564	1 452	3 100	4 463	5 466	4 160	3 917	PIB par habitant
GDP at constant prices	88 592	93 203	142 230	161 207	183 025	189 797	196 061	PIB aux prix constants
Growth rates	3.7	3.8	5.9	3.6	3.8	3.7	3.3	Taux de croissance
Andorra								**Andorre**
GDP at current prices	439	1 491	3 256	3 355	3 351	2 812	2 858	PIB aux prix courants
GDP per capita	9 837	23 359	41 281	39 734	42 293	36 040	36 987	PIB par habitant
GDP at constant prices	1 602	2 151	3 851	3 355	3 231	3 258	3 298	PIB aux prix constants
Growth rates	2.3	2.8	7.4	-5.4	2.3	0.8	1.2	Taux de croissance
Angola								**Angola**
GDP at current prices	9 125	6 642	36 971	83 799	145 712	115 143	106 918	PIB aux prix courants
GDP per capita	860	466	1 891	3 586	5 413	4 133	3 711	PIB par habitant
GDP at constant prices	27 523	27 009	56 312	83 799	102 821	103 777	103 087	PIB aux prix constants
Growth rates	3.5	15.0	15.0	4.7	4.1	0.9	-0.7	Taux de croissance
Anguilla								**Anguilla**
GDP at current prices	27	104	229	268	311	330	338	PIB aux prix courants
GDP per capita	4 072	10 583	18 129	19 459	21 533	22 597	22 861	PIB par habitant
GDP at constant prices	62	145	256	268	273	281	284	PIB aux prix constants
Growth rates	12.9	-2.3	13.1	-4.5	5.0	3.2	1.1	Taux de croissance
Antigua and Barbuda								**Antigua-et-Barbuda**
GDP at current prices	245	577	1 015	1 148	1 280	1 365	1 460	PIB aux prix courants
GDP per capita	3 508	7 841	11 372	12 127	12 947	13 659	14 462	PIB par habitant
GDP at constant prices	502	766	1 143	1 148	1 222	1 271	1 339	PIB aux prix constants
Growth rates	7.7	-4.4	6.4	-7.2	5.1	4.1	5.3	Taux de croissance
Argentina								**Argentine**
GDP at current prices	95 530	279 701	200 622	426 487	567 050	634 019	545 866	PIB aux prix courants
GDP per capita	3 144	7 993	5 125	10 346	13 193	14 603	12 449	PIB par habitant
GDP at constant prices	204 283	268 814	335 871	426 487	446 703	458 528	447 990	PIB aux prix constants
Growth rates	-7.0	-2.8	8.9	10.1	-2.5	2.6	-2.3	Taux de croissance
Armenia								**Arménie**
GDP at current prices	...	1 372	5 226	9 875	11 610	10 553	10 572	PIB aux prix courants
GDP per capita	...	426	1 753	3 432	3 995	3 618	3 615	PIB par habitant
GDP at constant prices	...	3 520	8 172	9 875	11 852	12 236	12 259	PIB aux prix constants
Growth rates	...	6.9	13.9	2.2	3.6	3.2	0.2	Taux de croissance

13 Gross domestic product and gross domestic product per capita *(continued)*

In millions of US dollars at current and constant 2010 prices; per capita US dollars; real rates of growth

Produit intérieur brut et produit intérieur brut par habitant *(suite)*

En millions de dollars É.-U. aux prix courants et constants de 2010; par habitant en dollars É.U.; taux de croissance réels

Country or area	1985	1995	2005	2010	2014	2015	2016	Pays ou zone
Aruba								**Aruba**
GDP at current prices	385	1 321	2 331	2 391	2 650	2 693	2 667	PIB aux prix courants
GDP per capita	6 108	16 442	23 303	23 513	25 528	25 807	25 444	PIB par habitant
GDP at constant prices	881	2 099	2 702	2 391	2 565	2 554	2 548	PIB aux prix constants
Growth rates	9.1	2.5	1.2	-3.4	0.8	-0.5	-0.2	Taux de croissance
Australia								**Australie**
GDP at current prices	181 990	392 576	762 488	1 293 794	1 457 607	1 243 240	1 304 463	PIB aux prix courants
GDP per capita	11 570	21 717	37 674	58 490	62 093	52 238	54 069	PIB par habitant
GDP at constant prices	579 362	791 027	1 131 094	1 293 794	1 445 331	1 485 305	1 514 685	PIB aux prix constants
Growth rates	4.1	3.9	3.0	2.4	2.4	2.8	2.0	Taux de croissance
Austria								**Autriche**
GDP at current prices	69 388	241 054	315 967	391 893	441 885	382 066	390 800	PIB aux prix courants
GDP per capita	9 112	30 169	38 282	46 599	51 184	44 024	44 857	PIB par habitant
GDP at constant prices	224 388	290 786	367 502	391 893	409 027	412 966	419 081	PIB aux prix constants
Growth rates	2.5	2.7	2.1	1.9	0.6	1.0	1.5	Taux de croissance
Azerbaijan								**Azerbaïdjan**
GDP at current prices	...	3 081	13 245	52 906	75 240	53 076	37 847	PIB aux prix courants
GDP per capita	...	396	1 551	5 857	7 917	5 519	3 892	PIB par habitant
GDP at constant prices	...	9 514	24 782	52 906	57 758	58 132	56 685	PIB aux prix constants
Growth rates	...	-11.8	28.0	4.6	2.7	0.6	-2.5	Taux de croissance
Bahamas								**Bahamas**
GDP at current prices	2 880	5 117	9 836	10 096	10 844	11 240	11 262	PIB aux prix courants
GDP per capita	12 271	18 264	29 875	27 979	28 374	29 056	28 785	PIB par habitant
GDP at constant prices	6 551	7 344	10 214	10 096	10 282	9 967	9 983	PIB aux prix constants
Growth rates	4.8	4.4	3.4	1.5	-1.2	-3.1	0.2	Taux de croissance
Bahrain								**Bahreïn**
GDP at current prices	4 475	6 787	15 969	25 713	33 388	31 126	32 179	PIB aux prix courants
GDP per capita	10 669	12 040	17 959	20 722	24 983	22 689	22 579	PIB par habitant
GDP at constant prices	7 940	12 142	19 620	25 713	29 922	30 779	31 779	PIB aux prix constants
Growth rates	-16.1	1.9	6.8	4.3	4.4	2.9	3.3	Taux de croissance
Bangladesh								**Bangladesh**
GDP at current prices	19 169	37 866	57 628	114 508	173 062	194 466	220 837	PIB aux prix courants
GDP per capita	206	319	402	753	1 086	1 206	1 355	PIB par habitant
GDP at constant prices	33 762	50 806	85 320	114 508	146 014	155 582	166 649	PIB aux prix constants
Growth rates	3.0	4.9	6.0	5.6	6.1	6.6	7.1	Taux de croissance
Barbados								**Barbade**
GDP at current prices	1 425	2 275	3 897	4 365	4 413	4 463	4 553	PIB aux prix courants
GDP per capita	5 569	8 585	14 223	15 613	15 574	15 704	15 975	PIB par habitant
GDP at constant prices	3 203	3 429	4 196	4 365	4 413	4 453	4 528	PIB aux prix constants
Growth rates	1.1	2.0	4.0	0.3	0.1	0.9	1.7	Taux de croissance
Belarus								**Bélarus**
GDP at current prices	...	14 360	31 310	57 232	78 813	56 455	47 408	PIB aux prix courants
GDP per capita	...	1 416	3 254	6 042	8 309	5 952	5 001	PIB par habitant
GDP at constant prices	...	20 657	40 282	57 232	63 129	60 712	59 109	PIB aux prix constants
Growth rates	...	-10.4	9.4	7.7	1.7	-3.8	-2.6	Taux de croissance
Belgium								**Belgique**
GDP at current prices	86 728	289 571	387 356	483 549	531 076	455 200	467 955	PIB aux prix courants
GDP per capita	8 746	28 428	36 727	44 205	47 336	40 326	41 199	PIB par habitant
GDP at constant prices	283 439	357 104	450 522	483 549	501 072	508 109	515 558	PIB aux prix constants
Growth rates	1.7	2.4	2.1	2.7	1.4	1.4	1.5	Taux de croissance
Belize								**Belize**
GDP at current prices	209	587	1 114	1 397	1 706	1 743	1 741	PIB aux prix courants
GDP per capita	1 268	2 834	3 933	4 344	4 852	4 850	4 745	PIB par habitant
GDP at constant prices	358	708	1 235	1 397	1 553	1 598	1 588	PIB aux prix constants
Growth rates	1.0	4.2	3.0	3.3	4.1	2.9	-0.6	Taux de croissance
Benin								**Bénin**
GDP at current prices	1 130	2 345	4 804	6 970	9 575	8 457	8 894	PIB aux prix courants
GDP per capita	264	397	602	758	931	800	818	PIB par habitant
GDP at constant prices	2 604	3 727	5 773	6 970	8 552	8 979	9 428	PIB aux prix constants
Growth rates	7.5	10.1	1.7	2.1	6.5	5.0	5.0	Taux de croissance
Bermuda								**Bermudes**
GDP at current prices	1 428	2 557	4 868	5 855	5 700	5 923	6 127	PIB aux prix courants
GDP per capita	24 241	40 780	74 745	91 552	91 372	95 528	99 363	PIB par habitant
GDP at constant prices	3 726	4 273	5 840	5 855	5 250	5 281	5 275	PIB aux prix constants
Growth rates	4.2	5.4	1.7	-2.5	-0.3	0.6	-0.1	Taux de croissance

13 Gross domestic product and gross domestic product per capita *(continued)*

In millions of US dollars at current and constant 2010 prices; per capita US dollars; real rates of growth

Produit intérieur brut et produit intérieur brut par habitant *(suite)*

En millions de dollars É.-U. aux prix courants et constants de 2010; par habitant en dollars É.U.; taux de croissance réels

Country or area	1985	1995	2005	2010	2014	2015	2016	Pays ou zone
Bhutan								**Bhoutan**
GDP at current prices	172	289	819	1 585	1 959	2 058	2 213	PIB aux prix courants
GDP per capita	369	562	1 247	2 179	2 523	2 614	2 774	PIB par habitant
GDP at constant prices	214	491	1 008	1 585	1 941	2 069	2 235	PIB aux prix constants
Growth rates	5.7	6.8	7.1	11.7	5.7	6.6	8.0	Taux de croissance
Bolivia (Plurin. State of)								**Bolivie (État plurin. de)**
GDP at current prices	4 122	6 715	9 549	19 650	32 996	33 000	33 806	PIB aux prix courants
GDP per capita	664	887	1 046	1 981	3 124	3 077	3 105	PIB par habitant
GDP at constant prices	8 325	11 383	15 697	19 650	24 475	25 664	26 759	PIB aux prix constants
Growth rates	-1.0	4.7	4.4	4.1	5.5	4.9	4.3	Taux de croissance
Bosnia and Herzegovina								**Bosnie-Herzégovine**
GDP at current prices	...	2 034	11 223	17 176	18 559	16 210	16 910	PIB aux prix courants
GDP per capita	...	529	2 968	4 615	5 204	4 584	4 808	PIB par habitant
GDP at constant prices	...	4 249	14 922	17 176	17 804	18 351	18 941	PIB aux prix constants
Growth rates	...	20.8	3.9	0.9	1.1	3.1	3.2	Taux de croissance
Botswana								**Botswana**
GDP at current prices	838	4 731	9 931	12 787	16 251	14 406	15 566	PIB aux prix courants
GDP per capita	704	3 015	5 351	6 346	7 494	6 521	6 917	PIB par habitant
GDP at constant prices	2 856	6 649	10 231	12 787	16 425	16 146	16 839	PIB aux prix constants
Growth rates	9.2	7.0	4.6	8.6	4.1	-1.7	4.3	Taux de croissance
Brazil								**Brésil**
GDP at current prices	187 426	778 053	891 634	2 208 838	2 456 044	1 803 650	1 795 926	PIB aux prix courants
GDP per capita	1 381	4 794	4 770	11 224	12 027	8 757	8 649	PIB par habitant
GDP at constant prices	1 102 866	1 400 990	1 774 773	2 208 838	2 423 235	2 331 897	2 248 072	PIB aux prix constants
Growth rates	7.8	4.2	3.2	7.5	0.5	-3.8	-3.6	Taux de croissance
British Virgin Islands								**Îles Vierges britanniques**
GDP at current prices	45	389	853	876	938	955	971	PIB aux prix courants
GDP per capita	3 396	21 114	36 802	32 183	31 689	31 698	31 677	PIB par habitant
GDP at constant prices	100	563	921	876	887	889	892	PIB aux prix constants
Growth rates	1.4	24.1	15.5	-0.1	1.3	0.3	0.3	Taux de croissance
Brunei Darussalam								**Brunéi Darussalam**
GDP at current prices	4 425	5 245	10 561	13 707	17 098	12 930	11 400	PIB aux prix courants
GDP per capita	19 712	17 650	28 923	35 267	41 529	30 968	26 939	PIB par habitant
GDP at constant prices	10 494	11 205	13 264	13 707	13 693	13 638	13 301	PIB aux prix constants
Growth rates	-1.5	4.5	0.4	2.6	-2.5	-0.4	-2.5	Taux de croissance
Bulgaria								**Bulgarie**
GDP at current prices	16 486	14 433	29 636	50 610	56 733	50 199	53 240	PIB aux prix courants
GDP per capita	1 837	1 723	3 857	6 835	7 855	6 994	7 465	PIB par habitant
GDP at constant prices	37 424	35 336	42 593	50 610	52 732	54 639	56 793	PIB aux prix constants
Growth rates	2.7	2.9	7.1	1.3	1.3	3.6	3.9	Taux de croissance
Burkina Faso								**Burkina Faso**
GDP at current prices	1 569	2 404	5 463	8 980	12 377	10 419	11 695	PIB aux prix courants
GDP per capita	203	238	407	575	704	575	627	PIB par habitant
GDP at constant prices	2 627	3 681	6 872	8 980	11 250	11 688	12 379	PIB aux prix constants
Growth rates	8.5	5.7	8.7	8.4	4.3	3.9	5.9	Taux de croissance
Burundi								**Burundi**
GDP at current prices	1 171[1]	1 000	1 117	2 032	2 706	2 814	2 874	PIB aux prix courants
GDP per capita	249[1]	168	150	232	274	276	273	PIB par habitant
GDP at constant prices	1 461	1 563	1 630	2 032	2 414	2 407	2 448	PIB aux prix constants
Growth rates	11.7	-7.0	0.9	5.1	4.2	-0.3	1.7	Taux de croissance
Cabo Verde								**Cabo Verde**
GDP at current prices	157	558	1 105	1 664	1 858	1 596	1 639	PIB aux prix courants
GDP per capita	497	1 434	2 329	3 313	3 530	2 995	3 038	PIB par habitant
GDP at constant prices	430	671	1 302	1 664	1 774	1 792	1 860	PIB aux prix constants
Growth rates	8.6	7.5	6.5	1.5	0.6	1.0	3.8	Taux de croissance
Cambodia								**Cambodge**
GDP at current prices	1 059	3 309	6 293	11 242	16 778	18 050	20 017	PIB aux prix courants
GDP per capita	137	311	474	786	1 099	1 163	1 270	PIB par habitant
GDP at constant prices	1 824	3 688	8 138	11 242	14 858	15 904	16 998	PIB aux prix constants
Growth rates	4.7	5.9	13.2	6.0	7.1	7.0	6.9	Taux de croissance
Cameroon								**Cameroun**
GDP at current prices	9 597	9 641	17 944	26 144	34 943	30 916	32 217	PIB aux prix courants
GDP per capita	955	716	1 030	1 309	1 571	1 354	1 374	PIB par habitant
GDP at constant prices	19 199	14 338	22 023	26 144	31 763	33 558	35 052	PIB aux prix constants
Growth rates	2.4	3.5	2.0	3.4	5.9	5.7	4.5	Taux de croissance

13 Gross domestic product and gross domestic product per capita *(continued)*

In millions of US dollars at current and constant 2010 prices; per capita US dollars; real rates of growth

Produit intérieur brut et produit intérieur brut par habitant *(suite)*

En millions de dollars É.-U. aux prix courants et constants de 2010; par habitant en dollars É.U.; taux de croissance réels

Country or area	1985	1995	2005	2010	2014	2015	2016	Pays ou zone
Canada								**Canada**
GDP at current prices	364 761	604 014	1 169 393	1 613 463	1 792 883	1 552 808	1 529 760	PIB aux prix courants
GDP per capita	14 098	20 594	36 218	47 221	50 355	43 194	42 154	PIB par habitant
GDP at constant prices	890 993	1 102 814	1 524 530	1 613 463	1 779 610	1 796 368	1 822 734	PIB aux prix constants
Growth rates	4.7	2.7	3.2	3.1	2.6	0.9	1.5	Taux de croissance
Cayman Islands								**Îles Caïmanes**
GDP at current prices	416	1 296	3 042	3 267	3 629	3 734	3 844	PIB aux prix courants
GDP per capita	21 544	40 930	62 559	58 859	61 332	62 264	63 261	PIB par habitant
GDP at constant prices	995	1 993	3 366	3 267	3 477	3 570	3 633	PIB aux prix constants
Growth rates	3.5	4.8	6.5	-2.7	2.6	2.7	1.8	Taux de croissance
Central African Republic								**République centrafricaine**
GDP at current prices	905	1 167	1 413	2 034	1 756	1 633	1 810	PIB aux prix courants
GDP per capita	344	348	342	457	389	359	394	PIB par habitant
GDP at constant prices	1 426	1 591	1 723	2 034	1 366	1 431	1 496	PIB aux prix constants
Growth rates	3.3	5.2	2.4	3.6	1.0	4.8	4.5	Taux de croissance
Chad								**Tchad**
GDP at current prices	987	1 643	6 681	9 791	14 683	11 695	11 267	PIB aux prix courants
GDP per capita	194	235	664	824	1 082	835	780	PIB par habitant
GDP at constant prices	2 130	2 959	6 743	9 791	11 393	11 894	11 490	PIB aux prix constants
Growth rates	7.9	1.4	7.9	13.4	3.4	4.4	-3.4	Taux de croissance
Chile								**Chili**
GDP at current prices	18 985	75 099	122 965	218 538	260 990	242 518	247 046	PIB aux prix courants
GDP per capita	1 559	5 253	7 615	12 860	14 817	13 653	13 794	PIB par habitant
GDP at constant prices	56 647	118 979	181 652	218 538	258 957	264 790	268 998	PIB aux prix constants
Growth rates	2.0	10.6	6.2	5.8	1.9	2.3	1.6	Taux de croissance
China [2]								**Chine** [2]
GDP at current prices	312 617	736 870	2 308 800	6 066 351	10 534 527	11 226 185	11 218 281	PIB aux prix courants
GDP per capita	292	594	1 747	4 461	7 578	8 036	7 993	PIB par habitant
GDP at constant prices	564 254	1 473 518	3 551 064	6 066 351	8 290 517	8 862 562	9 505 298	PIB aux prix constants
Growth rates	13.4	11.0	11.4	10.6	7.3	6.9	7.3	Taux de croissance
China, Hong Kong SAR								**Chine, RAS de Hong Kong**
GDP at current prices	35 700	144 652	181 569	228 639	291 460	309 406	320 912	PIB aux prix courants
GDP per capita	6 688	23 559	26 593	32 545	40 511	42 702	43 943	PIB par habitant
GDP at constant prices	71 742	134 780	188 650	228 639	258 222	264 404	269 813	PIB aux prix constants
Growth rates	0.8	2.4	7.4	6.8	2.8	2.4	2.0	Taux de croissance
China, Macao SAR								**Chine, RAS de Macao**
GDP at current prices	1 349	6 996	12 092	28 124	55 348	45 362	45 311	PIB aux prix courants
GDP per capita	4 756	18 139	25 059	52 375	94 004	75 485	74 018	PIB par habitant
GDP at constant prices	4 967	9 852	16 526	28 124	41 067	32 199	31 921	PIB aux prix constants
Growth rates	0.7	3.3	8.1	25.3	-1.2	-21.6	-0.9	Taux de croissance
Colombia								**Colombie**
GDP at current prices	49 322	110 292	146 566	287 018	378 196	291 520	282 463	PIB aux prix courants
GDP per capita	1 590	2 946	3 386	6 251	7 913	6 045	5 806	PIB par habitant
GDP at constant prices	118 422	183 904	229 937	287 018	348 484	359 120	366 159	PIB aux prix constants
Growth rates	3.1	5.2	4.7	4.0	4.4	3.1	2.0	Taux de croissance
Comoros								**Comores**
GDP at current prices	240	483	787	1 068	1 313	1 104	1 150	PIB aux prix courants
GDP per capita	675	1 016	1 287	1 549	1 728	1 421	1 445	PIB par habitant
GDP at constant prices	643	759	922	1 068	1 309	1 307	1 336	PIB aux prix constants
Growth rates	2.0	3.6	2.8	3.8	3.4	-0.2	2.2	Taux de croissance
Congo								**Congo**
GDP at current prices	2 161	2 116	6 087	12 281	14 077	8 493	7 778	PIB aux prix courants
GDP per capita	1 016	756	1 637	2 800	2 890	1 700	1 517	PIB par habitant
GDP at constant prices	6 917	6 902	9 489	12 281	14 547	14 932	14 653	PIB aux prix constants
Growth rates	-1.2	4.0	7.6	8.7	6.8	2.6	-1.9	Taux de croissance
Cook Islands								**Îles Cook**
GDP at current prices	28	106	183	255	318	285	290	PIB aux prix courants
GDP per capita	1 591	5 588	9 262	13 758	18 056	16 350	16 698	PIB par habitant
GDP at constant prices	140	201	257	255	282	293	304	PIB aux prix constants
Growth rates	8.8	-4.4	-1.1	-3.0	6.2	3.8	3.7	Taux de croissance
Costa Rica								**Costa Rica**
GDP at current prices	4 989	11 507	19 952	37 269	50 656	54 840	57 436	PIB aux prix courants
GDP per capita	1 827	3 278	4 697	8 199	10 647	11 406	11 825	PIB par habitant
GDP at constant prices	12 177	19 824	29 540	37 269	43 186	45 226	47 184	PIB aux prix constants
Growth rates	0.7	4.1	3.9	5.0	3.7	4.7	4.3	Taux de croissance

13 Gross domestic product and gross domestic product per capita *(continued)*

In millions of US dollars at current and constant 2010 prices; per capita US dollars; real rates of growth

Produit intérieur brut et produit intérieur brut par habitant *(suite)*

En millions de dollars É.-U. aux prix courants et constants de 2010; par habitant en dollars É.U.; taux de croissance réels

Country or area	1985	1995	2005	2010	2014	2015	2016	Pays ou zone
Côte d'Ivoire								**Côte d'Ivoire**
GDP at current prices	6 978[1]	11 105[1]	17 085	24 885	35 316	32 835	36 768	PIB aux prix courants
GDP per capita	683[1]	764[1]	932	1 220	1 567	1 421	1 552	PIB par habitant
GDP at constant prices	15 125	18 833	22 299	24 885	31 201	34 060	37 041	PIB aux prix constants
Growth rates	4.5	7.1	1.7	2.0	8.8	9.2	8.8	Taux de croissance
Croatia								**Croatie**
GDP at current prices	...	22 388	45 416	59 829	57 630	49 425	51 231	PIB aux prix courants
GDP per capita	...	4 849	10 374	13 823	13 536	11 668	12 159	PIB par habitant
GDP at constant prices	...	39 566	58 278	59 829	57 862	59 221	60 977	PIB aux prix constants
Growth rates	...	6.8	4.2	-1.4	-0.1	2.3	3.0	Taux de croissance
Cuba								**Cuba**
GDP at current prices	22 921	30 428	42 644	64 328	80 656	87 206	89 689	PIB aux prix courants
GDP per capita	2 273	2 790	3 779	5 676	7 050	7 609	7 815	PIB par habitant
GDP at constant prices	45 176	31 019	49 481	64 328	70 729	73 869	73 232	PIB aux prix constants
Growth rates	1.6	2.5	11.2	2.4	1.0	4.4	-0.9	Taux de croissance
Curaçao								**Curaçao**
GDP at current prices	...	...	2 345	2 951	3 158	3 152	3 121	PIB aux prix courants
GDP per capita	...	...	18 120	19 994	20 180	19 948	19 586	PIB par habitant
GDP at constant prices	...	...	2 786	2 951	2 908	2 916	2 888	PIB aux prix constants
Growth rates	...	...	...	0.1	-1.1	0.3	-1.0	Taux de croissance
Cyprus [3]								**Chypre** [3]
GDP at current prices	2 711	9 933	18 694	25 561	23 358	19 677	20 046	PIB aux prix courants
GDP per capita	5 011	15 265	25 311	30 817	27 400	23 231	23 631	PIB par habitant
GDP at constant prices	8 652	15 640	22 573	25 561	23 055	23 512	24 225	PIB aux prix constants
Growth rates	4.7	9.9	3.7	1.3	-1.4	2.0	3.0	Taux de croissance
Czechia								**Tchéquie**
GDP at current prices	...	59 536	135 990	207 016	207 818	186 830	195 305	PIB aux prix courants
GDP per capita	...	5 748	13 257	19 648	19 608	17 619	18 406	PIB par habitant
GDP at constant prices	...	138 634	183 583	207 016	214 124	225 493	231 340	PIB aux prix constants
Growth rates	...	6.2	6.4	2.3	2.7	5.3	2.6	Taux de croissance
Dem. People's Rep. Korea								**Rép. pop. dém. de Corée**
GDP at current prices	12 075	4 849	13 031	13 945	17 396	16 283	16 789	PIB aux prix courants
GDP per capita	722	222	548	570	696	648	665	PIB par habitant
GDP at constant prices	16 158	12 982	14 023	13 945	14 543	14 377	14 933	PIB aux prix constants
Growth rates	3.7	-4.4	3.8	-0.5	1.0	-1.1	3.9	Taux de croissance
Dem. Rep. of the Congo								**Rép. dém. du Congo**
GDP at current prices	7 524	8 947	11 965	21 566	35 909	37 918	40 337	PIB aux prix courants
GDP per capita	252	215	219	334	487	498	512	PIB par habitant
GDP at constant prices	24 387	16 680	16 467	21 566	29 311	31 338	32 090	PIB aux prix constants
Growth rates	0.5	0.7	6.1	7.1	9.5	6.9	2.4	Taux de croissance
Denmark								**Danemark**
GDP at current prices	62 659	185 008	264 467	321 995	352 994	301 298	306 900	PIB aux prix courants
GDP per capita	12 252	35 356	48 779	57 967	62 323	52 964	53 730	PIB par habitant
GDP at constant prices	213 347	257 078	318 623	321 995	335 436	340 826	347 520	PIB aux prix constants
Growth rates	4.0	3.0	2.3	1.9	1.6	1.6	2.0	Taux de croissance
Djibouti								**Djibouti**
GDP at current prices	369	510	709	1 067	1 589	1 737	1 892	PIB aux prix courants
GDP per capita	868	808	905	1 254	1 742	1 873	2 007	PIB par habitant
GDP at constant prices	577	669	787	1 067	1 301	1 385	1 472	PIB aux prix constants
Growth rates	-0.2	5.6	3.2	3.5	6.0	6.5	6.3	Taux de croissance
Dominica								**Dominique**
GDP at current prices	117	260	370	494	524	535	581	PIB aux prix courants
GDP per capita	1 586	3 639	5 245	6 912	7 195	7 314	7 907	PIB par habitant
GDP at constant prices	243	344	413	494	508	495	508	PIB aux prix constants
Growth rates	1.3	2.0	-0.3	1.2	4.4	-2.5	2.6	Taux de croissance
Dominican Republic								**République dominicaine**
GDP at current prices	5 618	15 747	35 510	53 132	65 231	68 103	71 584	PIB aux prix courants
GDP per capita	866	1 995	3 844	5 368	6 269	6 468	6 722	PIB par habitant
GDP at constant prices	15 871	23 622	39 218	53 132	63 468	67 937	72 452	PIB aux prix constants
Growth rates	-2.1	5.5	9.3	8.3	7.6	7.0	6.6	Taux de croissance
Ecuador								**Équateur**
GDP at current prices	17 141	24 421	41 507	69 555	102 292	100 177	98 010	PIB aux prix courants
GDP per capita	1 895	2 135	3 022	4 657	6 432	6 205	5 982	PIB par habitant
GDP at constant prices	33 225	44 018	58 876	69 555	86 503	86 639	84 761	PIB aux prix constants
Growth rates	3.9	2.3	5.3	3.5	4.0	0.2	-2.2	Taux de croissance

13 Gross domestic product and gross domestic product per capita *(continued)*

In millions of US dollars at current and constant 2010 prices; per capita US dollars; real rates of growth

Produit intérieur brut et produit intérieur brut par habitant *(suite)*

En millions de dollars É.-U. aux prix courants et constants de 2010; par habitant en dollars É.U.; taux de croissance réels

Country or area	1985	1995	2005	2010	2014	2015	2016	Pays ou zone
Egypt								**Égypte**
GDP at current prices	23 801	65 758	94 456	214 630	296 979	317 750	270 144	PIB aux prix courants
GDP per capita	474	1 032	1 230	2 552	3 235	3 388	2 823	PIB par habitant
GDP at constant prices	63 151	102 915	159 056	214 630	233 070	247 761	258 409	PIB aux prix constants
Growth rates	6.8	4.6	4.5	5.1	2.2	6.3	4.3	Taux de croissance
El Salvador								**El Salvador**
GDP at current prices	5 732	9 501	17 094	21 418	25 054	26 052	26 797	PIB aux prix courants
GDP per capita	1 164	1 693	2 835	3 474	3 989	4 127	4 224	PIB par habitant
GDP at constant prices	10 326	15 289	19 962	21 418	23 041	23 570	24 128	PIB aux prix constants
Growth rates	2.0	6.4	3.6	1.4	1.4	2.3	2.4	Taux de croissance
Equatorial Guinea								**Guinée équatoriale**
GDP at current prices	88	215	8 520	16 299	21 737	12 597	10 678	PIB aux prix courants
GDP per capita	246	427	11 250	17 136	19 246	10 717	8 742	PIB par habitant
GDP at constant prices	574	926	12 349	16 299	18 103	16 468	14 998	PIB aux prix constants
Growth rates	12.9	11.7	8.9	-8.9	0.4	-9.0	-8.9	Taux de croissance
Eritrea								**Érythrée**
GDP at current prices	...	640	1 098	2 117	4 052	4 783	5 414	PIB aux prix courants
GDP per capita	...	207	277	482	854	987	1 093	PIB par habitant
GDP at constant prices	...	1 844	2 201	2 117	2 664	2 791	2 893	PIB aux prix constants
Growth rates	...	20.9	1.5	2.2	5.0	4.8	3.7	Taux de croissance
Estonia								**Estonie**
GDP at current prices	...	4 423	14 003	19 503	26 225	22 567	23 338	PIB aux prix courants
GDP per capita	...	3 086	10 330	14 640	19 892	17 157	17 782	PIB par habitant
GDP at constant prices	...	10 494	19 902	19 503	22 957	23 341	23 823	PIB aux prix constants
Growth rates	...	4.3	9.6	2.3	2.9	1.7	2.1	Taux de croissance
Eswatini								**Eswatini**
GDP at current prices	539	1 902	3 176	4 436	4 462	4 156	4 007	PIB aux prix courants
GDP per capita	764	1 979	2 872	3 688	3 446	3 151	2 983	PIB par habitant
GDP at constant prices	1 427	2 799	3 625	4 436	5 249	5 470	5 469	PIB aux prix constants
Growth rates	1.9	4.8	1.8	3.8	3.8	4.2	-~0.0	Taux de croissance
Ethiopia								**Éthiopie**
GDP at current prices	...	7 587	12 164	26 311	54 163	63 079	70 315	PIB aux prix courants
GDP per capita	...	132	159	300	556	632	687	PIB par habitant
GDP at constant prices	...	9 196	15 699	26 311	39 442	43 538	46 831	PIB aux prix constants
Growth rates	...	6.1	11.8	12.6	10.3	10.4	7.6	Taux de croissance
Fiji								**Fidji**
GDP at current prices	1 143	1 993	2 980	3 140	4 484	4 362	4 671	PIB aux prix courants
GDP per capita	1 605	2 570	3 627	3 652	5 062	4 890	5 197	PIB par habitant
GDP at constant prices	1 753	2 423	3 033	3 140	3 617	3 756	3 771	PIB aux prix constants
Growth rates	-3.9	2.5	0.7	3.0	5.6	3.8	0.4	Taux de croissance
Finland								**Finlande**
GDP at current prices	55 914	134 196	204 431	247 800	272 609	232 439	238 503	PIB aux prix courants
GDP per capita	11 385	26 215	38 873	46 181	49 931	42 401	43 339	PIB par habitant
GDP at constant prices	141 128	163 434	237 928	247 800	247 075	247 054	251 815	PIB aux prix constants
Growth rates	3.5	4.2	2.8	3.0	-0.6	-~0.0	1.9	Taux de croissance
France [4]								**France** [4]
GDP at current prices	555 201	1 609 794	2 203 624	2 646 837	2 849 305	2 433 562	2 465 454	PIB aux prix courants
GDP per capita	9 773	26 853	34 843	40 629	42 924	36 504	36 826	PIB par habitant
GDP at constant prices	1 615 113	2 033 100	2 547 190	2 646 837	2 748 202	2 777 538	2 810 525	PIB aux prix constants
Growth rates	1.6	2.1	1.6	2.0	0.9	1.1	1.2	Taux de croissance
French Polynesia								**Polynésie française**
GDP at current prices	1 716	4 421	5 703	6 081	6 170	5 283	5 418	PIB aux prix courants
GDP per capita	9 795	20 542	22 374	22 704	22 399	19 026	19 335	PIB par habitant
GDP at constant prices	3 751	4 934	6 344	6 081	5 943	6 032	6 140	PIB aux prix constants
Growth rates	5.4	0.5	1.4	-2.5	1.3	1.5	1.8	Taux de croissance
Gabon								**Gabon**
GDP at current prices	4 639	5 519	9 579	12 882	17 412	13 660	13 863	PIB aux prix courants
GDP per capita	5 589	5 081	6 827	7 854	9 283	7 077	7 002	PIB par habitant
GDP at constant prices	9 452	11 669	12 189	12 882	16 108	16 755	17 288	PIB aux prix constants
Growth rates	-2.3	5.0	1.1	6.8	5.0	4.0	3.2	Taux de croissance
Gambia								**Gambie**
GDP at current prices	654	786	624	952	849	939	986	PIB aux prix courants
GDP per capita	894	737	432	563	443	475	484	PIB par habitant
GDP at constant prices	398	524	758	952	1 020	1 064	1 087	PIB aux prix constants
Growth rates	3.4	0.9	-0.9	6.5	0.9	4.3	2.2	Taux de croissance

13

Gross domestic product and gross domestic product per capita *(continued)*
In millions of US dollars at current and constant 2010 prices; per capita US dollars; real rates of growth

Produit intérieur brut et produit intérieur brut par habitant *(suite)*
En millions de dollars É.-U. aux prix courants et constants de 2010; par habitant en dollars É.U.; taux de croissance réels

Country or area	1985	1995	2005	2010	2014	2015	2016	Pays ou zone
Georgia								**Géorgie**
GDP at current prices	...	2 703	6 411	11 638	16 510	13 993	14 333	PIB aux prix courants
GDP per capita	...	539	1 429	2 750	4 135	3 541	3 651	PIB par habitant
GDP at constant prices	...	4 766	9 011	11 638	14 355	14 768	15 174	PIB aux prix constants
Growth rates	...	2.6	9.6	6.2	4.6	2.9	2.7	Taux de croissance
Germany								**Allemagne**
GDP at current prices	729 751	2 591 447	2 861 339	3 417 095	3 890 607	3 375 611	3 477 796	PIB aux prix courants
GDP per capita	9 390	31 898	35 035	42 241	47 744	41 313	42 456	PIB par habitant
GDP at constant prices	2 183 636	2 840 972	3 213 777	3 417 095	3 646 040	3 709 598	3 781 699	PIB aux prix constants
Growth rates	2.3	1.7	0.7	4.1	1.9	1.7	1.9	Taux de croissance
Ghana								**Ghana**
GDP at current prices	6 605	10 361	17 199	32 174	39 087	37 338	42 794	PIB aux prix courants
GDP per capita	519	618	798	1 313	1 450	1 354	1 517	PIB par habitant
GDP at constant prices	9 574	14 915	23 884	32 174	44 751	46 468	48 080	PIB aux prix constants
Growth rates	5.1	4.0	6.2	7.9	4.0	3.8	3.5	Taux de croissance
Greece								**Grèce**
GDP at current prices	47 816	136 886	247 777	299 362	237 030	195 542	192 691	PIB aux prix courants
GDP per capita	4 794	12 687	21 925	26 154	21 042	17 431	17 230	PIB par habitant
GDP at constant prices	185 846	210 286	304 331	299 362	245 795	245 080	244 481	PIB aux prix constants
Growth rates	2.5	2.1	0.6	-5.5	0.7	-0.3	-0.2	Taux de croissance
Greenland								**Groenland**
GDP at current prices	407	1 193	1 656	2 307	2 551	2 220	2 283	PIB aux prix courants
GDP per capita	7 661	21 379	29 081	40 724	45 247	39 384	40 469	PIB par habitant
GDP at constant prices	1 351	1 501	1 982	2 307	2 287	2 325	2 329	PIB aux prix constants
Growth rates	3.7	3.7	2.7	2.7	-0.8	1.7	0.2	Taux de croissance
Grenada								**Grenade**
GDP at current prices	136	278	695	771	912	984	1 016	PIB aux prix courants
GDP per capita	1 359	2 775	6 755	7 366	8 571	9 212	9 469	PIB par habitant
GDP at constant prices	325	470	807	771	844	896	913	PIB aux prix constants
Growth rates	8.1	2.1	13.3	-0.5	7.4	6.2	1.9	Taux de croissance
Guatemala								**Guatemala**
GDP at current prices	9 967	13 066	27 211	41 338	58 722	63 767	68 763	PIB aux prix courants
GDP per capita	1 210	1 255	2 078	2 825	3 688	3 924	4 147	PIB par habitant
GDP at constant prices	17 225	24 523	34 551	41 338	47 896	49 879	51 409	PIB aux prix constants
Growth rates	-0.6	5.0	3.3	2.9	4.2	4.1	3.1	Taux de croissance
Guinea								**Guinée**
GDP at current prices	2 848	5 260	4 063	6 853	8 778	8 767	8 476	PIB aux prix courants
GDP per capita	560	668	420	635	744	725	684	PIB par habitant
GDP at constant prices	2 771	4 122	5 964	6 853	8 263	8 632	9 204	PIB aux prix constants
Growth rates	5.0	4.7	3.0	4.2	3.7	4.5	6.6	Taux de croissance
Guinea-Bissau								**Guinée-Bissau**
GDP at current prices	415	800	587	849	1 027	1 014	1 123	PIB aux prix courants
GDP per capita	462	703	425	546	595	573	618	PIB par habitant
GDP at constant prices	459	644	720	849	933	981	1 031	PIB aux prix constants
Growth rates	4.3	4.0	4.3	4.6	0.2	5.1	5.1	Taux de croissance
Guyana								**Guyana**
GDP at current prices	737	991	1 315	2 259	3 077	3 179	3 437	PIB aux prix courants
GDP per capita	956	1 302	1 752	3 026	4 031	4 137	4 444	PIB par habitant
GDP at constant prices	1 232	1 541	1 826	2 259	2 730	2 813	2 908	PIB aux prix constants
Growth rates	2.4	5.0	-2.0	4.1	3.9	3.1	3.4	Taux de croissance
Haiti								**Haïti**
GDP at current prices	2 665	2 696	4 154	6 708	8 661	8 355	7 647	PIB aux prix courants
GDP per capita	417	345	448	671	819	780	705	PIB par habitant
GDP at constant prices	6 649	5 865	6 462	6 708	7 804	7 899	8 012	PIB aux prix constants
Growth rates	0.6	9.9	1.8	-5.5	2.8	1.2	1.4	Taux de croissance
Honduras								**Honduras**
GDP at current prices	4 342	4 724	9 757	15 839	19 757	20 844	21 517	PIB aux prix courants
GDP per capita	1 014	828	1 323	1 933	2 243	2 326	2 361	PIB par habitant
GDP at constant prices	6 557	9 104	13 268	15 839	18 142	18 803	19 482	PIB aux prix constants
Growth rates	4.2	4.1	6.1	3.7	3.1	3.6	3.6	Taux de croissance
Hungary								**Hongrie**
GDP at current prices	23 643	46 432	113 035	130 923	140 118	122 879	125 817	PIB aux prix courants
GDP per capita	2 237	4 486	11 207	13 187	14 278	12 559	12 900	PIB par habitant
GDP at constant prices	101 303	92 465	132 349	130 923	139 305	143 996	147 183	PIB aux prix constants
Growth rates	-0.3	1.5	4.4	0.7	4.2	3.4	2.2	Taux de croissance

13 Gross domestic product and gross domestic product per capita *(continued)*

In millions of US dollars at current and constant 2010 prices; per capita US dollars; real rates of growth

Produit intérieur brut et produit intérieur brut par habitant *(suite)*

En millions de dollars É.-U. aux prix courants et constants de 2010; par habitant en dollars É.U.; taux de croissance réels

Country or area	1985	1995	2005	2010	2014	2015	2016	Pays ou zone
Iceland								**Islande**
GDP at current prices	3 008	7 182	16 691	13 311	17 291	16 922	20 270	PIB aux prix courants
GDP per capita	12 453	26 835	56 585	41 553	52 643	51 242	60 966	PIB par habitant
GDP at constant prices	6 844	8 106	12 725	13 311	14 623	15 222	16 318	PIB aux prix constants
Growth rates	3.3	0.1	6.7	-3.6	1.9	4.1	7.2	Taux de croissance
India								**Inde**
GDP at current prices	219 581	358 024	812 059	1 650 635	2 039 198	2 132 755	2 259 642	PIB aux prix courants
GDP per capita	281	373	710	1 341	1 576	1 629	1 706	PIB par habitant
GDP at constant prices	341 279	596 573	1 107 189	1 650 635	2 123 009	2 293 063	2 456 031	PIB aux prix constants
Growth rates	5.5	7.6	9.3	10.3	7.5	8.0	7.1	Taux de croissance
Indonesia								**Indonésie**
GDP at current prices	102 171	236 456	304 372	755 094	890 815	861 256	932 259	PIB aux prix courants
GDP per capita	617	1 195	1 343	3 113	3 492	3 336	3 570	PIB par habitant
GDP at constant prices	214 637	437 210	571 205	755 094	942 185	988 128	1 037 688	PIB aux prix constants
Growth rates	2.5	8.2	5.7	6.2	5.0	4.9	5.0	Taux de croissance
Iran (Islamic Republic of)								**Iran (Rép. islamique d')**
GDP at current prices	76 257	114 364	226 452	491 099	443 976	393 436	425 403	PIB aux prix courants
GDP per capita	1 611	1 888	3 216	6 586	5 662	4 958	5 299	PIB par habitant
GDP at constant prices	222 796	262 362	403 657	491 099	487 095	480 662	545 053	PIB aux prix constants
Growth rates	1.9	2.4	3.2	5.8	4.6	-1.3	13.4	Taux de croissance
Iraq								**Iraq**
GDP at current prices	12 074	3 477	36 268	117 138	199 221	167 658	160 021	PIB aux prix courants
GDP per capita	775	172	1 343	3 808	5 691	4 642	4 301	PIB par habitant
GDP at constant prices	49 034	29 296	88 107	117 138	183 567	190 891	211 878	PIB aux prix constants
Growth rates	-~0.0	-18.3	4.4	5.5	0.2	4.0	11.0	Taux de croissance
Ireland								**Irlande**
GDP at current prices	21 296	69 225	211 645	221 951	258 099	290 617	304 819	PIB aux prix courants
GDP per capita	5 974	18 958	50 237	47 969	55 075	61 832	64 497	PIB par habitant
GDP at constant prices	66 216	104 518	214 349	221 951	251 765	316 109	332 361	PIB aux prix constants
Growth rates	3.1	9.6	6.0	1.8	8.3	25.6	5.1	Taux de croissance
Israel								**Israël**
GDP at current prices	27 425	100 344	142 463	233 611	308 415	299 094	317 748	PIB aux prix courants
GDP per capita	6 717	18 813	21 576	31 459	38 837	37 088	38 788	PIB par habitant
GDP at constant prices	75 491	132 135	188 880	233 611	270 858	277 976	288 988	PIB aux prix constants
Growth rates	4.0	8.7	4.1	5.5	3.5	2.6	4.0	Taux de croissance
Italy								**Italie**
GDP at current prices	450 706	1 170 824	1 852 616	2 125 058	2 151 733	1 832 347	1 858 913	PIB aux prix courants
GDP per capita	7 905	20 449	31 503	35 578	36 112	30 794	31 279	PIB par habitant
GDP at constant prices	1 499 984	1 866 192	2 158 722	2 125 058	2 043 486	2 063 873	2 083 323	PIB aux prix constants
Growth rates	2.8	2.9	0.9	1.7	0.1	1.0	0.9	Taux de croissance
Jamaica								**Jamaïque**
GDP at current prices	2 605	6 578	11 244	13 219	13 898	14 187	14 057	PIB aux prix courants
GDP per capita	1 114	2 592	4 097	4 692	4 856	4 940	4 879	PIB par habitant
GDP at constant prices	8 555	12 565	13 545	13 219	13 523	13 643	13 831	PIB aux prix constants
Growth rates	-4.6	1.0	0.9	-1.5	0.7	0.9	1.4	Taux de croissance
Japan								**Japon**
GDP at current prices	1 400 715	5 449 118	4 755 410	5 700 098	4 848 733	4 379 869	4 936 212	PIB aux prix courants
GDP per capita	11 491	43 118	37 054	44 341	37 833	34 224	38 640	PIB par habitant
GDP at constant prices	3 669 898	5 063 810	5 672 311	5 700 098	5 914 022	5 979 746	6 040 651	PIB aux prix constants
Growth rates	6.3	2.7	1.7	4.2	0.3	1.1	1.0	Taux de croissance
Jordan								**Jordanie**
GDP at current prices	5 119	6 732	12 589	26 425	35 827	37 517	38 655	PIB aux prix courants
GDP per capita	1 768	1 472	2 203	3 679	4 067	4 096	4 088	PIB par habitant
GDP at constant prices	9 280	12 246	19 529	26 425	29 501	30 206	30 812	PIB aux prix constants
Growth rates	-2.7	6.2	8.1	2.3	3.1	2.4	2.0	Taux de croissance
Kazakhstan								**Kazakhstan**
GDP at current prices	...	20 563	57 124	148 047	221 416	184 388	135 005	PIB aux prix courants
GDP per capita	...	1 282	3 676	9 028	12 661	10 388	7 505	PIB par habitant
GDP at constant prices	...	59 128	109 540	148 047	186 500	188 652	190 469	PIB aux prix constants
Growth rates	...	-8.2	9.7	7.3	4.2	1.2	1.0	Taux de croissance
Kenya								**Kenya**
GDP at current prices	9 110	13 428	21 506	40 000	61 445	63 768	70 526	PIB aux prix courants
GDP per capita	464	491	597	967	1 335	1 350	1 455	PIB par habitant
GDP at constant prices	16 538	23 533	31 367	40 000	49 505	52 334	55 395	PIB aux prix constants
Growth rates	4.3	4.4	5.9	8.4	5.5	5.7	5.8	Taux de croissance

13

Gross domestic product and gross domestic product per capita *(continued)*

In millions of US dollars at current and constant 2010 prices; per capita US dollars; real rates of growth

Produit intérieur brut et produit intérieur brut par habitant *(suite)*

En millions de dollars É.-U. aux prix courants et constants de 2010; par habitant en dollars É.U.; taux de croissance réels

Country or area	1985	1995	2005	2010	2014	2015	2016	Pays ou zone
Kiribati								**Kiribati**
GDP at current prices	30	56	112	153	178	167	174	PIB aux prix courants
GDP per capita	468	720	1 215	1 493	1 611	1 487	1 518	PIB par habitant
GDP at constant prices	105	123	155	153	171	184	191	PIB aux prix constants
Growth rates	-4.6	-0.6	5.0	-1.6	0.4	7.5	4.2	Taux de croissance
Kosovo								**Kosovo**
GDP at current prices	...	5 304	3 680	5 830	7 387	6 440	6 714	PIB aux prix courants
GDP per capita	...	2 351	2 074	3 354	4 214	3 668	3 811	PIB par habitant
GDP at constant prices	...	4 213	4 536	5 830	6 551	6 819	7 096	PIB aux prix constants
Growth rates	...	8.1	3.9	3.3	1.2	4.1	4.1	Taux de croissance
Kuwait								**Koweït**
GDP at current prices	21 446	26 554	80 798	115 416	162 656	114 059	110 346	PIB aux prix courants
GDP per capita	12 333	16 487	35 490	38 497	43 003	28 980	27 229	PIB par habitant
GDP at constant prices	42 081	65 562	108 938	115 416	137 146	139 679	143 113	PIB aux prix constants
Growth rates	-4.3	1.4	10.6	-2.4	0.5	1.8	2.5	Taux de croissance
Kyrgyzstan								**Kirghizistan**
GDP at current prices	...	1 492	2 460	4 794	7 468	6 678	6 551	PIB aux prix courants
GDP per capita	...	327	485	884	1 293	1 139	1 100	PIB par habitant
GDP at constant prices	...	2 440	3 859	4 794	5 836	6 062	6 294	PIB aux prix constants
Growth rates	...	-5.4	-0.2	-0.5	4.0	3.9	3.8	Taux de croissance
Lao People's Dem. Rep.								**Rép. dém. populaire lao**
GDP at current prices	626	1 852	2 946	7 313	13 268	14 390	15 806	PIB aux prix courants
GDP per capita	170	382	512	1 171	2 018	2 159	2 339	PIB par habitant
GDP at constant prices	1 616	2 692	4 982	7 313	9 911	10 631	11 378	PIB aux prix constants
Growth rates	5.1	7.5	6.8	8.1	7.6	7.3	7.0	Taux de croissance
Latvia								**Lettonie**
GDP at current prices	...	5 407	16 922	23 765	31 419	27 009	27 573	PIB aux prix courants
GDP per capita	...	2 155	7 514	11 216	15 584	13 554	13 993	PIB par habitant
GDP at constant prices	...	12 779	24 351	23 765	27 496	28 276	28 863	PIB aux prix constants
Growth rates	...	-0.8	10.7	-3.9	1.9	2.8	2.1	Taux de croissance
Lebanon								**Liban**
GDP at current prices	2 275	11 506	21 490	38 420	47 833	49 459	50 458	PIB aux prix courants
GDP per capita	850	3 793	5 390	8 858	8 537	8 452	8 400	PIB par habitant
GDP at constant prices	20 297	20 531	26 598	38 420	41 730	42 070	42 491	PIB aux prix constants
Growth rates	24.3	6.5	2.7	8.0	2.0	0.8	1.0	Taux de croissance
Lesotho								**Lesotho**
GDP at current prices	297	955	1 559	2 394	2 521	2 335	2 241	PIB aux prix courants
GDP per capita	202	542	800	1 173	1 175	1 074	1 017	PIB par habitant
GDP at constant prices	807	1 339	1 888	2 394	2 825	2 983	3 069	PIB aux prix constants
Growth rates	9.4	4.6	2.7	6.5	2.3	5.6	2.9	Taux de croissance
Liberia								**Libéria**
GDP at current prices	1 076	209	706	1 292	2 053	2 669	2 757	PIB aux prix courants
GDP per capita	491	101	217	327	468	593	598	PIB par habitant
GDP at constant prices	1 197	174	662	1 292	1 712	1 871	1 862	PIB aux prix constants
Growth rates	-2.0	-4.3	5.3	7.3	5.2	9.3	-0.5	Taux de croissance
Libya								**Libye**
GDP at current prices	29 887	28 292	45 451	80 942	30 774	37 367	42 960	PIB aux prix courants
GDP per capita	7 715	5 717	7 846	13 121	4 960	5 993	6 826	PIB par habitant
GDP at constant prices	45 138	44 062	60 808	80 942	25 620	24 059	24 534	PIB aux prix constants
Growth rates	8.3	-2.2	10.3	4.3	-24.0	-6.1	2.0	Taux de croissance
Liechtenstein								**Liechtenstein**
GDP at current prices	681	2 695	4 046	5 621	6 658	6 290	6 194	PIB aux prix courants
GDP per capita	24 995	87 414	116 095	156 127	179 318	168 177	164 437	PIB par habitant
GDP at constant prices	2 441	3 456	5 047	5 621	5 889	5 912	5 986	PIB aux prix constants
Growth rates	7.0	1.9	4.8	7.4	3.0	0.4	1.2	Taux de croissance
Lithuania								**Lituanie**
GDP at current prices	...	6 702	26 141	37 130	48 557	41 509	42 773	PIB aux prix courants
GDP per capita	...	1 848	7 817	11 886	16 394	14 157	14 707	PIB par habitant
GDP at constant prices	...	19 321	35 022	37 130	43 808	44 699	45 747	PIB aux prix constants
Growth rates	...	3.3	7.7	1.6	3.5	2.0	2.3	Taux de croissance
Luxembourg								**Luxembourg**
GDP at current prices	4 738	21 588	37 346	53 212	66 327	57 784	58 631	PIB aux prix courants
GDP per capita	12 915	52 894	81 571	104 772	119 226	101 959	101 835	PIB par habitant
GDP at constant prices	16 821	30 556	47 158	53 212	59 611	61 317	63 207	PIB aux prix constants
Growth rates	2.8	5.9	3.2	4.9	5.8	2.9	3.1	Taux de croissance

Gross domestic product and gross domestic product per capita *(continued)*
In millions of US dollars at current and constant 2010 prices; per capita US dollars; real rates of growth

Produit intérieur brut et produit intérieur brut par habitant *(suite)*
En millions de dollars É.-U. aux prix courants et constants de 2010; par habitant en dollars É.U.; taux de croissance réels

Country or area	1985	1995	2005	2010	2014	2015	2016	Pays ou zone
Madagascar								**Madagascar**
GDP at current prices	2 789	3 723	5 936	10 401	11 867	11 406	11 222	PIB aux prix courants
GDP per capita	277	276	324	492	503	471	451	PIB par habitant
GDP at constant prices	6 015	6 775	9 151	10 401	11 304	11 650	12 139	PIB aux prix constants
Growth rates	1.2	1.7	4.6	0.6	2.7	3.1	4.2	Taux de croissance
Malawi								**Malawi**
GDP at current prices	2 028	2 474	3 656	6 960	5 965	6 430	5 318	PIB aux prix courants
GDP per capita	281	250	280	459	349	366	294	PIB par habitant
GDP at constant prices	3 029	3 653	4 867	6 960	8 214	8 444	8 695	PIB aux prix constants
Growth rates	4.7	9.0	3.3	6.9	6.6	2.8	3.0	Taux de croissance
Malaysia								**Malaisie**
GDP at current prices	31 200	88 833	143 534	255 018	338 073	296 284	296 531	PIB aux prix courants
GDP per capita	2 000	4 334	5 594	9 071	11 184	9 644	9 508	PIB par habitant
GDP at constant prices	59 287	128 614	204 864	255 018	314 337	329 952	344 045	PIB aux prix constants
Growth rates	-1.1	9.8	5.3	7.4	6.0	5.0	4.3	Taux de croissance
Maldives								**Maldives**
GDP at current prices	166	566	1 163	2 588	3 697	4 007	4 224	PIB aux prix courants
GDP per capita	875	2 229	3 649	7 100	9 057	9 576	9 875	PIB par habitant
GDP at constant prices	513	1 169	1 749	2 588	3 317	3 391	3 600	PIB aux prix constants
Growth rates	13.0	7.1	-13.1	7.3	7.3	2.2	6.2	Taux de croissance
Mali								**Mali**
GDP at current prices	1 260	2 837	6 245	10 679	14 388	13 038	14 002	PIB aux prix courants
GDP per capita	161	295	488	708	848	746	778	PIB par habitant
GDP at constant prices	1 276	2 762	6 457	10 679	14 761	15 885	17 135	PIB aux prix constants
Growth rates	8.5	37.2	10.4	10.9	7.8	7.6	7.9	Taux de croissance
Malta								**Malte**
GDP at current prices	1 156	3 697	6 393	8 741	11 217	10 286	10 999	PIB aux prix courants
GDP per capita	3 311	9 722	15 716	21 005	26 358	24 054	25 616	PIB par habitant
GDP at constant prices	3 159	5 562	7 909	8 741	10 290	11 017	11 625	PIB aux prix constants
Growth rates	2.6	6.3	3.8	3.5	8.2	7.1	5.5	Taux de croissance
Marshall Islands								**Îles Marshall**
GDP at current prices	44	121	138	165	183	179	183	PIB aux prix courants
GDP per capita	1 155	2 379	2 651	3 143	3 462	3 386	3 449	PIB par habitant
GDP at constant prices	83	160	152	165	176	177	182	PIB aux prix constants
Growth rates	-6.3	8.2	2.9	6.4	-0.9	0.6	2.9	Taux de croissance
Mauritania								**Mauritanie**
GDP at current prices	1 085	1 681	2 184	4 338	5 362	4 783	4 667	PIB aux prix courants
GDP per capita	613	722	698	1 202	1 319	1 144	1 085	PIB par habitant
GDP at constant prices	1 775	2 332	3 387	4 338	5 382	5 549	5 643	PIB aux prix constants
Growth rates	3.4	-2.4	9.0	4.8	5.6	3.1	1.7	Taux de croissance
Mauritius								**Maurice**
GDP at current prices	1 152	4 273	6 775	10 004	12 803	11 682	12 216	PIB aux prix courants
GDP per capita	1 134	3 786	5 544	8 016	10 184	9 275	9 679	PIB par habitant
GDP at constant prices	2 806	5 131	7 939	10 004	11 555	11 956	12 403	PIB aux prix constants
Growth rates	6.9	4.4	1.8	4.4	3.7	3.5	3.7	Taux de croissance
Mexico								**Mexique**
GDP at current prices	219 661	360 073	877 477	1 057 801	1 314 390	1 169 625	1 076 914	PIB aux prix courants
GDP per capita	2 839	3 829	8 089	9 016	10 581	9 291	8 444	PIB par habitant
GDP at constant prices	601 246	707 431	982 737	1 057 801	1 184 651	1 223 395	1 259 036	PIB aux prix constants
Growth rates	2.8	-6.3	2.3	5.1	2.8	3.3	2.9	Taux de croissance
Micronesia (Fed. States of)								**Micronésie (États féd. de)**
GDP at current prices	108	222	251	297	318	315	330	PIB aux prix courants
GDP per capita	1 262	2 063	2 360	2 862	3 057	3 018	3 144	PIB par habitant
GDP at constant prices	192	293	301	297	283	296	296	PIB aux prix constants
Growth rates	16.6	4.2	2.1	2.0	-2.2	4.9	-0.1	Taux de croissance
Monaco								**Monaco**
GDP at current prices	1 059	3 070	4 203	5 362	7 060	6 259	6 468	PIB aux prix courants
GDP per capita	36 724	100 041	124 374	144 561	185 145	163 394	168 004	PIB par habitant
GDP at constant prices	3 101	3 903	4 890	5 362	6 809	7 146	7 375	PIB aux prix constants
Growth rates	1.6	2.1	1.6	2.2	7.2	4.9	3.2	Taux de croissance
Mongolia								**Mongolie**
GDP at current prices	1 218	1 678	2 926	7 189	12 227	11 750	11 160	PIB aux prix courants
GDP per capita	634	730	1 158	2 650	4 182	3 947	3 686	PIB par habitant
GDP at constant prices	3 185	3 338	5 253	7 189	11 409	11 680	11 792	PIB aux prix constants
Growth rates	5.7	6.3	7.3	6.4	7.9	2.4	1.0	Taux de croissance

13 Gross domestic product and gross domestic product per capita *(continued)*
In millions of US dollars at current and constant 2010 prices; per capita US dollars; real rates of growth

Produit intérieur brut et produit intérieur brut par habitant *(suite)*
En millions de dollars É.-U. aux prix courants et constants de 2010; par habitant en dollars É.U.; taux de croissance réels

Country or area	1985	1995	2005	2010	2014	2015	2016	Pays ou zone
Montenegro								**Monténégro**
GDP at current prices	...	1 215	2 279	4 138	4 588	4 020	4 374	PIB aux prix courants
GDP per capita	...	1 958	3 697	6 628	7 309	6 400	6 958	PIB par habitant
GDP at constant prices	...	2 004	3 439	4 138	4 379	4 528	4 661	PIB aux prix constants
Growth rates	...	14.3	4.2	2.7	1.8	3.4	2.9	Taux de croissance
Montserrat								**Montserrat**
GDP at current prices	44	69	49	56	59	59	62	PIB aux prix courants
GDP per capita	3 850	6 728	10 229	11 228	11 570	11 556	12 044	PIB par habitant
GDP at constant prices	101	113	54	56	65	65	67	PIB aux prix constants
Growth rates	5.9	-8.8	3.1	-2.8	2.0	0.4	2.0	Taux de croissance
Morocco [5]								**Maroc** [5]
GDP at current prices	15 111	38 728	62 545	93 217	110 081	101 187	103 607	PIB aux prix courants
GDP per capita	670	1 430	2 049	2 876	3 208	2 907	2 937	PIB par habitant
GDP at constant prices	35 111	45 626	70 187	93 217	110 594	116 062	119 976	PIB aux prix constants
Growth rates	6.3	-6.6	3.0	4.0	4.0	4.9	3.4	Taux de croissance
Mozambique								**Mozambique**
GDP at current prices	5 752	2 572	7 724	10 154	16 961	14 798	10 930	PIB aux prix courants
GDP per capita	443	163	369	419	623	528	379	PIB par habitant
GDP at constant prices	1 914	2 688	7 096	10 154	13 423	14 308	14 858	PIB aux prix constants
Growth rates	-8.8	2.2	8.7	6.7	7.4	6.6	3.8	Taux de croissance
Myanmar								**Myanmar**
GDP at current prices	6 607	7 764	11 931	41 445	66 300	62 543	65 698	PIB aux prix courants
GDP per capita	177	180	246	826	1 277	1 193	1 242	PIB par habitant
GDP at constant prices	7 496	8 935	24 375	41 445	54 999	58 845	62 182	PIB aux prix constants
Growth rates	2.9	6.9	13.6	10.2	8.0	7.0	5.7	Taux de croissance
Namibia								**Namibie**
GDP at current prices	1 606	3 942	7 121	11 282	12 786	11 571	10 947	PIB aux prix courants
GDP per capita	1 399	2 382	3 504	5 192	5 393	4 770	4 415	PIB par habitant
GDP at constant prices	4 418	6 059	9 159	11 282	13 992	14 830	14 990	PIB aux prix constants
Growth rates	0.5	3.9	2.5	6.0	6.4	6.0	1.1	Taux de croissance
Nauru								**Nauru**
GDP at current prices	33	35	26	62	114	90	103	PIB aux prix courants
GDP per capita	4 043	3 496	2 600	6 234	10 307	7 955	9 119	PIB par habitant
GDP at constant prices	212	93	40	62	157	162	178	PIB aux prix constants
Growth rates	-2.8	-7.9	-12.1	20.1	36.5	2.8	10.4	Taux de croissance
Nepal								**Népal**
GDP at current prices	2 741	4 534	8 259	16 281	19 738	20 801	20 914	PIB aux prix courants
GDP per capita	164	212	322	602	697	726	722	PIB par habitant
GDP at constant prices	5 401	8 694	13 056	16 281	19 472	20 119	20 202	PIB aux prix constants
Growth rates	6.1	3.5	3.1	4.8	6.0	3.3	0.4	Taux de croissance
Netherlands								**Pays-Bas**
GDP at current prices	142 011	446 514	678 517	836 390	879 635	757 999	777 228	PIB aux prix courants
GDP per capita	9 784	28 867	41 456	50 135	52 082	44 750	45 753	PIB par habitant
GDP at constant prices	449 975	594 222	785 109	836 390	851 636	870 890	890 136	PIB aux prix constants
Growth rates	2.6	3.1	2.2	1.4	1.4	2.3	2.2	Taux de croissance
Netherlands Antilles [former]								**Antilles néerlandaises [anc.]**
GDP at current prices	1 190	2 571	3 053	3 848	...	...	...	PIB aux prix courants
GDP per capita	7 024	14 734	18 852	21 290	...	...	...	PIB par habitant
GDP at constant prices	2 818	3 522	3 569	3 848	...	...	...	PIB aux prix constants
Growth rates	-2.1	1.6	1.1	-0.3	...	...	...	Taux de croissance
New Caledonia								**Nouvelle-Calédonie**
GDP at current prices	855	3 628	6 236	9 355	10 463	9 174	9 446	PIB aux prix courants
GDP per capita	5 480	19 024	26 801	37 266	39 411	34 094	34 641	PIB par habitant
GDP at constant prices	3 302	6 162	7 713	9 355	10 453	10 834	11 157	PIB aux prix constants
Growth rates	4.5	5.9	3.6	6.9	3.4	3.6	3.0	Taux de croissance
New Zealand								**Nouvelle-Zélande**
GDP at current prices	24 108	63 151	114 722	146 584	200 955	177 621	187 517	PIB aux prix courants
GDP per capita	7 376	17 184	27 742	33 543	44 004	38 492	40 233	PIB par habitant
GDP at constant prices	81 521	96 581	135 929	146 584	162 034	167 686	172 781	PIB aux prix constants
Growth rates	1.6	4.6	3.3	1.0	3.1	3.5	3.0	Taux de croissance
Nicaragua								**Nicaragua**
GDP at current prices	3 606	4 118	6 300	8 759	11 880	12 748	13 230	PIB aux prix courants
GDP per capita	972	893	1 171	1 526	1 975	2 096	2 151	PIB par habitant
GDP at constant prices	5 563	5 135	7 663	8 759	10 903	11 432	11 970	PIB aux prix constants
Growth rates	-4.1	5.9	4.3	4.4	4.8	4.9	4.7	Taux de croissance

13

Gross domestic product and gross domestic product per capita *(continued)*
In millions of US dollars at current and constant 2010 prices; per capita US dollars; real rates of growth

Produit intérieur brut et produit intérieur brut par habitant *(suite)*
En millions de dollars É.-U. aux prix courants et constants de 2010; par habitant en dollars É.U.; taux de croissance réels

Country or area	1985	1995	2005	2010	2014	2015	2016	Pays ou zone
Niger								**Niger**
GDP at current prices	1 531	1 786	3 369	5 719	8 230	7 218	7 528	PIB aux prix courants
GDP per capita	221	188	247	348	430	363	364	PIB par habitant
GDP at constant prices	2 795	3 044	4 445	5 719	7 405	7 698	8 086	PIB aux prix constants
Growth rates	7.7	3.3	7.4	8.4	7.5	4.0	5.0	Taux de croissance
Nigeria								**Nigéria**
GDP at current prices	178 821	49 030	180 502	369 062	568 499	494 583	404 649	PIB aux prix courants
GDP per capita	2 139	454	1 299	2 327	3 222	2 730	2 176	PIB par habitant
GDP at constant prices	99 925	139 274	266 817	369 062	452 284	464 282	456 775	PIB aux prix constants
Growth rates	11.3	2.1	6.5	7.8	6.3	2.7	-1.6	Taux de croissance
Norway								**Norvège**
GDP at current prices	65 417	152 028	308 722	429 131	499 339	386 663	371 069	PIB aux prix courants
GDP per capita	15 751	34 813	66 645	87 831	97 142	74 361	70 617	PIB par habitant
GDP at constant prices	235 051	307 138	409 135	429 131	458 626	467 662	472 766	PIB aux prix constants
Growth rates	5.6	4.2	2.6	0.7	2.0	2.0	1.1	Taux de croissance
Oman								**Oman**
GDP at current prices	10 281	13 650	31 082	58 641	81 034	69 832	63 171	PIB aux prix courants
GDP per capita	6 861	6 193	12 377	19 281	20 458	16 627	14 277	PIB par habitant
GDP at constant prices	23 487	35 967	44 279	58 641	67 859	71 695	73 886	PIB aux prix constants
Growth rates	14.5	4.8	2.5	4.8	2.5	5.7	3.1	Taux de croissance
Pakistan								**Pakistan**
GDP at current prices	38 840	77 266	117 708	174 508	248 949	267 523	282 506	PIB aux prix courants
GDP per capita	421	629	765	1 023	1 342	1 413	1 462	PIB par habitant
GDP at constant prices	59 288	98 511	147 540	174 508	202 809	212 366	224 558	PIB aux prix constants
Growth rates	7.6	5.0	7.7	1.6	4.7	4.7	5.7	Taux de croissance
Palau								**Palaos**
GDP at current prices	41	110	191	183	246	298	310	PIB aux prix courants
GDP per capita	2 997	6 378	9 611	8 956	11 683	13 982	14 428	PIB par habitant
GDP at constant prices	122	176	214	183	207	230	235	PIB aux prix constants
Growth rates	5.4	10.0	0.2	3.0	5.4	11.4	1.9	Taux de croissance
Panama								**Panama**
GDP at current prices	5 725	9 042	15 465	28 917	49 166	52 132	55 188	PIB aux prix courants
GDP per capita	2 580	3 300	4 643	7 937	12 594	13 134	13 680	PIB par habitant
GDP at constant prices	9 478	13 149	20 363	28 917	39 935	42 242	44 299	PIB aux prix constants
Growth rates	5.1	1.8	7.2	5.8	6.1	5.8	4.9	Taux de croissance
Papua New Guinea								**Papouasie-Nvl-Guinée**
GDP at current prices	3 682	7 274	7 312	14 205	22 207	21 315	19 694	PIB aux prix courants
GDP per capita	970	1 486	1 158	1 998	2 863	2 691	2 436	PIB par habitant
GDP at constant prices	5 838	9 416	10 877	14 205	17 002	18 128	18 588	PIB aux prix constants
Growth rates	3.6	-3.3	3.9	11.2	7.4	6.6	2.5	Taux de croissance
Paraguay								**Paraguay**
GDP at current prices	4 017[6]	8 066[6]	8 735	20 048	30 881	27 283	27 165	PIB aux prix courants
GDP per capita	1 094	1 694	1 507	3 228	4 713	4 109	4 039	PIB par habitant
GDP at constant prices	8 524[6]	12 183[6]	15 707	20 048	24 671	25 402	26 405	PIB aux prix constants
Growth rates	4.0[6]	5.4[6]	2.1	13.1	4.7	3.0	4.0	Taux de croissance
Peru								**Pérou**
GDP at current prices	14 529	53 371	76 080	147 528	201 047	189 210	192 210	PIB aux prix courants
GDP per capita	743[6]	2 220[6]	2 755	5 022	6 491	6 030	6 049	PIB par habitant
GDP at constant prices	64 566	75 500	105 785	147 528	180 386	186 251	193 482	PIB aux prix constants
Growth rates	2.1	7.4	6.3	8.3	2.4	3.3	3.9	Taux de croissance
Philippines								**Philippines**
GDP at current prices	34 052	82 121	103 072	199 591	284 585	292 774	304 906	PIB aux prix courants
GDP per capita	627	1 176	1 195	2 130	2 843	2 878	2 951	PIB par habitant
GDP at constant prices	75 004	105 213	156 874	199 591	250 838	266 056	284 477	PIB aux prix constants
Growth rates	-7.3	4.7	4.8	7.6	6.1	6.1	6.9	Taux de croissance
Poland								**Pologne**
GDP at current prices	73 333	142 138	306 127	479 321	545 172	477 356	471 402	PIB aux prix courants
GDP per capita	1 975	3 696	7 980	12 507	14 237	12 475	12 332	PIB par habitant
GDP at constant prices	231 201	252 408	379 768	479 321	535 609	556 201	572 132	PIB aux prix constants
Growth rates	3.6	7.0	3.5	3.6	3.3	3.8	2.9	Taux de croissance
Portugal								**Portugal**
GDP at current prices	27 118	118 132	197 300	238 303	229 630	199 420	204 837	PIB aux prix courants
GDP per capita	2 716	11 639	18 674	22 371	21 930	19 141	19 750	PIB par habitant
GDP at constant prices	126 436	181 279	231 124	238 303	223 971	228 052	231 562	PIB aux prix constants
Growth rates	2.8	4.3	0.8	1.9	0.9	1.8	1.5	Taux de croissance

13

Gross domestic product and gross domestic product per capita *(continued)*
In millions of US dollars at current and constant 2010 prices; per capita US dollars; real rates of growth

Produit intérieur brut et produit intérieur brut par habitant *(suite)*
En millions de dollars É.-U. aux prix courants et constants de 2010; par habitant en dollars É.U.; taux de croissance réels

Country or area	1985	1995	2005	2010	2014	2015	2016	Pays ou zone
Puerto Rico								**Porto Rico**
GDP at current prices	20 574	43 246	83 915	98 381	102 446	103 144	105 035	PIB aux prix courants
GDP per capita	6 106	11 721	22 286	26 470	27 833	28 076	28 636	PIB par habitant
GDP at constant prices	49 122	78 847	105 342	98 381	96 593	95 518	93 029	PIB aux prix constants
Growth rates	2.1	4.5	-2.0	-0.4	-1.2	-1.1	-2.6	Taux de croissance
Qatar								**Qatar**
GDP at current prices	6 153[1]	8 041	43 998	123 627	206 225	164 641	152 452	PIB aux prix courants
GDP per capita	16 582[1]	15 660	50 873	69 466	86 853	66 347	59 324	PIB par habitant
GDP at constant prices	15 602	21 460	54 006	123 627	158 802	164 441	168 097	PIB aux prix constants
Growth rates	-2.1	2.4	7.5	16.7	4.0	3.6	2.2	Taux de croissance
Republic of Korea								**République de Corée**
GDP at current prices	100 273	556 129	898 137	1 094 499	1 411 334	1 382 764	1 411 246	PIB aux prix courants
GDP per capita	2 457	12 277	18 439	22 088	28 011	27 331	27 785	PIB par habitant
GDP at constant prices	220 570	543 606	894 708	1 094 499	1 234 340	1 268 781	1 304 659	PIB aux prix constants
Growth rates	7.7	9.6	3.9	6.5	3.3	2.8	2.8	Taux de croissance
Republic of Moldova								**République de Moldova**
GDP at current prices	...	1 767	2 988	5 812	7 983	6 513	6 773	PIB aux prix courants
GDP per capita	...	407	719	1 423	1 962	1 602	1 668	PIB par habitant
GDP at constant prices	...	3 992	4 960	5 812	7 065	7 034	7 335	PIB aux prix constants
Growth rates	...	-1.4	7.5	7.1	4.8	-0.4	4.3	Taux de croissance
Romania								**Roumanie**
GDP at current prices	50 742	37 657	99 699	167 998	199 495	177 524	186 691	PIB aux prix courants
GDP per capita	2 196	1 640	4 652	8 219	9 988	8 931	9 439	PIB par habitant
GDP at constant prices	135 872	111 404	145 503	167 998	182 337	189 517	198 648	PIB aux prix constants
Growth rates	-0.1	7.1	4.2	-0.8	3.1	3.9	4.8	Taux de croissance
Russian Federation								**Fédération de Russie**
GDP at current prices	...	399 472	764 016	1 524 917	2 003 922	1 326 324	1 246 015	PIB aux prix courants
GDP per capita	...	2 694	5 320	10 652	13 939	9 218	8 655	PIB par habitant
GDP at constant prices	...	878 983	1 281 320	1 524 917	1 679 246	1 631 754	1 628 082	PIB aux prix constants
Growth rates	...	-4.1	6.4	4.5	0.7	-2.8	-0.2	Taux de croissance
Rwanda								**Rwanda**
GDP at current prices	1 813	1 230	2 581	5 774	8 016	8 279	8 474	PIB aux prix courants
GDP per capita	296	208	287	563	707	712	711	PIB par habitant
GDP at constant prices	2 265	1 587	3 875	5 774	7 633	8 311	8 806	PIB aux prix constants
Growth rates	4.4	33.5	9.4	7.3	7.6	8.9	5.9	Taux de croissance
Saint Kitts and Nevis								**Saint-Kitts-et-Nevis**
GDP at current prices	106	300	543	705	848	878	910	PIB aux prix courants
GDP per capita	2 524	6 987	11 178	13 708	15 776	16 178	16 597	PIB par habitant
GDP at constant prices	262	455	689	705	808	840	859	PIB aux prix constants
Growth rates	8.6	5.8	8.8	-2.2	6.0	4.0	2.2	Taux de croissance
Saint Lucia								**Sainte-Lucie**
GDP at current prices	249	617	935	1 244	1 405	1 450	1 397	PIB aux prix courants
GDP per capita	1 970	4 199	5 714	7 210	7 962	8 184	7 848	PIB par habitant
GDP at constant prices	536	904	1 121	1 244	1 239	1 263	1 272	PIB aux prix constants
Growth rates	7.5	1.1	-1.7	-1.0	0.4	1.9	0.7	Taux de croissance
Saint Vincent & Grenadines								**Saint-Vincent-Grenadines**
GDP at current prices	133	312	551	681	725	757	765	PIB aux prix courants
GDP per capita	1 277	2 887	5 065	6 232	6 633	6 912	6 980	PIB par habitant
GDP at constant prices	295	436	637	681	707	720	729	PIB aux prix constants
Growth rates	6.2	7.5	2.5	-3.3	1.0	1.8	1.3	Taux de croissance
Samoa								**Samoa**
GDP at current prices	85	196	434	679	824	774	822	PIB aux prix courants
GDP per capita	532	1 151	2 414	3 648	4 286	3 995	4 214	PIB par habitant
GDP at constant prices	373	405	644	679	704	725	767	PIB aux prix constants
Growth rates	3.9	6.0	5.1	4.3	1.9	2.9	5.8	Taux de croissance
San Marino								**Saint-Marin**
GDP at current prices	318	1 020	2 027	2 139	1 845	1 570	1 591	PIB aux prix courants
GDP per capita	14 017	39 407	69 338	68 767	56 492	47 627	47 910	PIB par habitant
GDP at constant prices	998	1 515	2 355	2 139	1 721	1 729	1 747	PIB aux prix constants
Growth rates	2.8	9.3	2.3	-4.6	-0.9	0.5	1.0	Taux de croissance
Sao Tome and Principe								**Sao Tomé-et-Principe**
GDP at current prices	79	99	126	197	349	316	343	PIB aux prix courants
GDP per capita	759	780	811	1 130	1 824	1 615	1 715	PIB par habitant
GDP at constant prices	108	110	148	197	237	246	247	PIB aux prix constants
Growth rates	9.3	2.0	7.1	6.7	6.5	3.8	0.1	Taux de croissance

13 Gross domestic product and gross domestic product per capita *(continued)*

In millions of US dollars at current and constant 2010 prices; per capita US dollars; real rates of growth

Produit intérieur brut et produit intérieur brut par habitant *(suite)*

En millions de dollars É.-U. aux prix courants et constants de 2010; par habitant en dollars É.U.; taux de croissance réels

Country or area	1985	1995	2005	2010	2014	2015	2016	Pays ou zone
Saudi Arabia								**Arabie saoudite**
GDP at current prices	103 894	143 152	328 461	528 207	756 350	651 757	639 617	PIB aux prix courants
GDP per capita	7 877	7 641	13 740	19 260	24 575	20 653	19 817	PIB par habitant
GDP at constant prices	207 527	349 402	461 602	528 207	651 958	678 730	688 219	PIB aux prix constants
Growth rates	-9.8	0.2	5.6	5.0	3.7	4.1	1.4	Taux de croissance
Senegal								**Sénégal**
GDP at current prices	2 807	4 873	8 708	12 926	15 280	13 676	14 605	PIB aux prix courants
GDP per capita	433	557	774	1 001	1 050	913	948	PIB par habitant
GDP at constant prices	5 467	6 861	10 866	12 926	14 787	15 790	16 823	PIB aux prix constants
Growth rates	3.8	4.7	5.6	4.2	4.1	6.8	6.5	Taux de croissance
Serbia								**Serbie**
GDP at current prices	...	21 823[7]	26 252[8]	39 460[8]	44 211[8]	37 160[8]	38 300[8]	PIB aux prix courants
GDP per capita	...	2 208[7]	3 528[8]	5 412[8]	6 199[8]	5 237[8]	5 426[8]	PIB par habitant
GDP at constant prices	...	24 046[7]	34 596[8]	39 460[8]	39 882[8]	40 184[8]	41 308[8]	PIB aux prix constants
Growth rates	...	5.7[7]	5.5[8]	0.6[8]	-1.8[8]	0.8[8]	2.8[8]	Taux de croissance
Seychelles								**Seychelles**
GDP at current prices	204	614	919	970	1 343	1 377	1 434	PIB aux prix courants
GDP per capita	2 922	8 005	10 357	10 612	14 401	14 691	15 217	PIB par habitant
GDP at constant prices	392	596	783	970	1 174	1 233	1 251	PIB aux prix constants
Growth rates	10.3	-0.6	9.0	5.9	4.5	5.0	1.5	Taux de croissance
Sierra Leone								**Sierra Leone**
GDP at current prices	1 376	1 179	1 650	2 578	5 015	4 215	3 675	PIB aux prix courants
GDP per capita	362	276	292	399	708	582	497	PIB par habitant
GDP at constant prices	2 087	1 874	1 998	2 578	3 985	3 164	3 357	PIB aux prix constants
Growth rates	2.3	-10.0	4.5	5.3	4.6	-20.6	6.1	Taux de croissance
Singapore								**Singapour**
GDP at current prices	18 555	87 892	127 418	236 420	308 155	296 835	296 946	PIB aux prix courants
GDP per capita	6 858	25 265	28 372	46 592	56 559	53 626	52 814	PIB par habitant
GDP at constant prices	44 696	102 240	170 716	236 420	283 689	289 172	294 945	PIB aux prix constants
Growth rates	-0.7	7.0	7.5	15.2	3.6	1.9	2.0	Taux de croissance
Sint Maarten (Dutch part)								**St-Martin (partie néerland.)**
GDP at current prices	...	...	708	896	1 058	1 066	1 072	PIB aux prix courants
GDP per capita	...	...	21 762	27 065	28 064	27 521	27 116	PIB par habitant
GDP at constant prices	...	...	805	896	938	942	947	PIB aux prix constants
Growth rates	...	...	...	1.1	1.6	0.5	0.4	Taux de croissance
Slovakia								**Slovaquie**
GDP at current prices	...	19 959	48 965	89 501	100 948	87 501	89 769	PIB aux prix courants
GDP per capita	...	3 713	9 069	16 561	18 581	16 087	16 489	PIB par habitant
GDP at constant prices	...	46 643	70 976	89 501	97 555	101 311	104 679	PIB aux prix constants
Growth rates	...	5.8	6.8	5.0	2.8	3.9	3.3	Taux de croissance
Slovenia								**Slovénie**
GDP at current prices	...	21 274	36 345	48 014	49 905	43 072	44 709	PIB aux prix courants
GDP per capita	...	10 683	18 206	23 477	24 099	20 760	21 517	PIB par habitant
GDP at constant prices	...	29 973	44 069	48 014	47 888	48 970	50 512	PIB aux prix constants
Growth rates	...	4.1	4.0	1.2	3.0	2.3	3.1	Taux de croissance
Solomon Islands								**Îles Salomon**
GDP at current prices	160	365	429	720	1 101	1 060	1 134	PIB aux prix courants
GDP per capita	591	1 015	914	1 363	1 913	1 804	1 892	PIB par habitant
GDP at constant prices	303	510	516	720	826	841	868	PIB aux prix constants
Growth rates	2.8	10.0	12.8	10.6	2.0	1.8	3.2	Taux de croissance
Somalia								**Somalie**
GDP at current prices	810	1 122	2 316	1 071	1 375	1 332	1 318	PIB aux prix courants
GDP per capita	119	146	222	89	102	96	92	PIB par habitant
GDP at constant prices	1 011	732	944	1 071	1 187	1 218	1 250	PIB aux prix constants
Growth rates	9.5	0.0	3.0	2.6	2.6	2.6	2.6	Taux de croissance
South Africa								**Afrique du Sud**
GDP at current prices	59 648	157 434	257 772	375 348	350 852	317 406	295 440	PIB aux prix courants
GDP per capita	1 768	3 741	5 280	7 276	6 433	5 741	5 274	PIB par habitant
GDP at constant prices	205 250	232 702	322 227	375 348	413 022	418 387	419 556	PIB aux prix constants
Growth rates	-1.2	3.1	5.3	3.0	1.7	1.3	0.3	Taux de croissance
South Sudan								**Soudan du sud**
GDP at current prices	...	...	...	15 206	15 848	13 408	6 534	PIB aux prix courants
GDP per capita	...	...	...	1 510	1 374	1 128	534	PIB par habitant
GDP at constant prices	...	...	...	15 206	11 952	12 556	12 596	PIB aux prix constants
Growth rates	...	...	...	-1.8	22.2	5.1	0.3	Taux de croissance

13 Gross domestic product and gross domestic product per capita *(continued)*
In millions of US dollars at current and constant 2010 prices; per capita US dollars; real rates of growth

Produit intérieur brut et produit intérieur brut par habitant *(suite)*
En millions de dollars É.-U. aux prix courants et constants de 2010; par habitant en dollars É.U.; taux de croissance réels

Country or area	1985	1995	2005	2010	2014	2015	2016	Pays ou zone
Spain								**Espagne**
GDP at current prices	180 305	612 943	1 157 248	1 431 617	1 376 911	1 197 790	1 237 255	PIB aux prix courants
GDP per capita	4 643	15 366	26 276	30 598	29 597	25 816	26 695	PIB par habitant
GDP at constant prices	700 751	940 939	1 358 052	1 431 617	1 371 018	1 418 075	1 464 509	PIB aux prix constants
Growth rates	2.3	2.8	3.7	~0.0	1.4	3.4	3.3	Taux de croissance
Sri Lanka								**Sri Lanka**
GDP at current prices	6 873	15 293	27 932	56 726	79 356	80 612	81 322	PIB aux prix courants
GDP per capita	425	838	1 431	2 808	3 848	3 892	3 910	PIB par habitant
GDP at constant prices	17 380	26 744	41 633	56 726	72 838	76 363	79 707	PIB aux prix constants
Growth rates	5.0	5.5	6.2	8.0	5.0	4.8	4.4	Taux de croissance
State of Palestine								**État de Palestine**
GDP at current prices	1 005	3 283	4 832	8 913	12 716	12 673	13 397	PIB aux prix courants
GDP per capita	571	1 254	1 351	2 192	2 802	2 718	2 796	PIB par habitant
GDP at constant prices	2 115	4 804	6 983	8 913	10 866	11 238	11 701	PIB aux prix constants
Growth rates	-0.6	7.1	10.8	8.1	-0.2	3.4	4.1	Taux de croissance
Sudan								**Soudan**
GDP at current prices	...	...	...	54 459	69 350	79 546	82 887	PIB aux prix courants
GDP per capita	...	...	...	1 584	1 838	2 058	2 094	PIB par habitant
GDP at constant prices	...	...	...	54 459	56 810	59 594	61 381	PIB aux prix constants
Growth rates	...	...	...	8.8	1.6	4.9	3.0	Taux de croissance
Sudan [former]								**Soudan [anc.]**
GDP at current prices	6 624	12 847	35 183	69 665	...	...	...	PIB aux prix courants
GDP per capita	292	435	902	1 567	...	...	...	PIB par habitant
GDP at constant prices	16 497	26 296	52 248	69 665	...	...	...	PIB aux prix constants
Growth rates	5.4	6.0	9.0	6.6	...	...	...	Taux de croissance
Suriname								**Suriname**
GDP at current prices	1 196	844	2 193	4 368	5 241	4 826	3 278	PIB aux prix courants
GDP per capita	3 221	1 903	4 395	8 303	9 565	8 725	5 871	PIB par habitant
GDP at constant prices	2 507	2 478	3 483	4 368	4 900	4 773	4 527	PIB aux prix constants
Growth rates	14.0	~0.0	3.9	5.2	0.3	-2.6	-5.1	Taux de croissance
Sweden								**Suède**
GDP at current prices	112 514	264 053	389 043	488 378	573 818	497 918	514 476	PIB aux prix courants
GDP per capita	13 462	29 882	43 042	52 009	59 221	50 998	52 297	PIB par habitant
GDP at constant prices	285 180	332 659	451 444	488 378	519 342	542 826	560 758	PIB aux prix constants
Growth rates	2.2	4.0	2.8	6.0	2.6	4.5	3.3	Taux de croissance
Switzerland								**Suisse**
GDP at current prices	107 765	342 626	408 697	583 783	709 183	679 289	668 851	PIB aux prix courants
GDP per capita	16 692	48 817	55 153	74 538	86 174	81 648	79 609	PIB par habitant
GDP at constant prices	373 821	434 925	524 104	583 783	625 702	633 375	642 090	PIB aux prix constants
Growth rates	3.7	0.5	3.1	3.0	2.4	1.2	1.4	Taux de croissance
Syrian Arab Republic								**République arabe syrienne**
GDP at current prices	10 050	13 547	28 397	60 465	34 077	28 378	22 163	PIB aux prix courants
GDP per capita	944	944	1 552	2 877	1 775	1 515	1 203	PIB par habitant
GDP at constant prices	22 117	31 119	47 588	60 465	33 194	31 435	30 366	PIB aux prix constants
Growth rates	6.1	7.0	6.2	3.4	0.4	-5.3	-3.4	Taux de croissance
Tajikistan								**Tadjikistan**
GDP at current prices	...	1 218	2 312	5 642	9 237	7 855	6 952	PIB aux prix courants
GDP per capita	...	211	337	738	1 105	919	796	PIB par habitant
GDP at constant prices	...	2 597	4 126	5 642	7 122	7 547	8 068	PIB aux prix constants
Growth rates	...	-12.4	6.7	6.5	6.7	6.0	6.9	Taux de croissance
Thailand								**Thaïlande**
GDP at current prices	40 240	168 998	189 318	341 105	406 521	399 234	407 026	PIB aux prix courants
GDP per capita	773	2 841	2 894	5 075	5 942	5 815	5 911	PIB par habitant
GDP at constant prices	85 347	209 559	283 767	341 105	382 430	393 678	410 601	PIB aux prix constants
Growth rates	4.6	8.1	4.2	7.5	0.9	2.9	4.3	Taux de croissance
TFYR of Macedonia								**ex-R.Y. de Macédoine**
GDP at current prices	...	4 707	6 259	9 407	11 362	10 065	10 746	PIB aux prix courants
GDP per capita	...	2 373	3 038	4 543	5 469	4 840	5 163	PIB par habitant
GDP at constant prices	...	6 063	7 736	9 407	10 222	10 616	10 925	PIB aux prix constants
Growth rates	...	-1.1	4.7	3.4	3.6	3.9	2.9	Taux de croissance
Timor-Leste								**Timor-Leste**
GDP at current prices	...	451	1 850	3 999	4 042	3 102	2 703	PIB aux prix courants
GDP per capita	...	518	1 802	3 604	3 333	2 500	2 131	PIB par habitant
GDP at constant prices	...	817	2 423	3 999	3 088	3 733	3 920	PIB aux prix constants
Growth rates	...	9.5	52.7	-1.3	-26.0	20.9	5.0	Taux de croissance

13 Gross domestic product and gross domestic product per capita *(continued)*

In millions of US dollars at current and constant 2010 prices; per capita US dollars; real rates of growth

Produit intérieur brut et produit intérieur brut par habitant *(suite)*

En millions de dollars É.-U. aux prix courants et constants de 2010; par habitant en dollars É.U.; taux de croissance réels

Country or area	1985	1995	2005	2010	2014	2015	2016	Pays ou zone
Togo								**Togo**
GDP at current prices	860	1 663	2 281	3 426	4 569	4 179	4 449	PIB aux prix courants
GDP per capita	264	389	401	527	632	563	585	PIB par habitant
GDP at constant prices	2 053	2 476	2 898	3 426	4 365	4 616	4 847	PIB aux prix constants
Growth rates	3.7	6.8	-4.7	6.1	5.9	5.7	5.0	Taux de croissance
Tonga								**Tonga**
GDP at current prices	73	203	262	374	436	402	401	PIB aux prix courants
GDP per capita	779	2 115	2 589	3 590	4 118	3 778	3 748	PIB par habitant
GDP at constant prices	242	297	360	374	383	398	411	PIB aux prix constants
Growth rates	6.6	4.0	1.6	3.6	2.1	3.7	3.4	Taux de croissance
Trinidad and Tobago								**Trinité-et-Tobago**
GDP at current prices	7 376	5 329	15 982	22 123	27 267	25 917	24 086	PIB aux prix courants
GDP per capita	6 299	4 246	12 323	16 658	20 131	19 056	17 646	PIB par habitant
GDP at constant prices	8 992	8 603	18 265	22 123	22 616	22 657	22 143	PIB aux prix constants
Growth rates	-4.1	4.0	6.2	3.3	-1.0	0.2	-2.3	Taux de croissance
Tunisia								**Tunisie**
GDP at current prices	9 234	19 795	32 272	44 051	47 604	43 015	41 704	PIB aux prix courants
GDP per capita	1 261	2 172	3 194	4 140	4 272	3 815	3 657	PIB par habitant
GDP at constant prices	15 561	21 771	35 380	44 051	47 020	47 545	48 021	PIB aux prix constants
Growth rates	5.7	2.3	4.0	3.0	2.4	1.1	1.0	Taux de croissance
Turkey								**Turquie**
GDP at current prices	92 554	233 085	501 423	771 877	934 168	859 794	863 712	PIB aux prix courants
GDP per capita	1 884	3 985	7 384	10 672	12 127	10 985	10 863	PIB par habitant
GDP at constant prices	277 716	426 265	658 107	771 877	1 025 434	1 087 840	1 122 475	PIB aux prix constants
Growth rates	4.2	7.2	9.0	8.5	5.2	6.1	3.2	Taux de croissance
Turkmenistan								**Turkménistan**
GDP at current prices	...	2 190	14 182	22 583	43 524	36 052	36 180	PIB aux prix courants
GDP per capita	...	520	2 983	4 439	7 962	6 478	6 389	PIB par habitant
GDP at constant prices	...	8 644	13 789	22 583	34 980	37 254	39 563	PIB aux prix constants
Growth rates	...	-7.2	13.0	9.2	10.3	6.5	6.2	Taux de croissance
Turks and Caicos Islands								**Îles Turques-et-Caïques**
GDP at current prices	58	191	579	687	797	863	918	PIB aux prix courants
GDP per capita	6 142	12 425	21 879	22 159	23 615	25 122	26 291	PIB par habitant
GDP at constant prices	102	279	627	687	742	773	807	PIB aux prix constants
Growth rates	10.7	7.3	14.4	1.0	4.6	4.1	4.4	Taux de croissance
Tuvalu								**Tuvalu**
GDP at current prices	4	12	22	32	37	35	37	PIB aux prix courants
GDP per capita	406	1 274	2 162	3 005	3 419	3 226	3 307	PIB par habitant
GDP at constant prices	10	22	29	32	35	38	39	PIB aux prix constants
Growth rates	-1.8	-5.0	-4.1	-3.1	1.3	9.1	3.0	Taux de croissance
Uganda								**Ouganda**
GDP at current prices	4 742	7 146	11 154	19 803	27 949	25 207	25 308	PIB aux prix courants
GDP per capita	324	348	391	584	720	628	610	PIB par habitant
GDP at constant prices	3 599	6 815	13 403	19 803	23 697	25 041	25 623	PIB aux prix constants
Growth rates	-0.3	9.4	10.0	8.2	4.6	5.7	2.3	Taux de croissance
Ukraine								**Ukraine**
GDP at current prices	...	50 379	89 239	136 012[9]	133 504[9]	91 031[9]	93 270[9]	PIB aux prix courants
GDP per capita	...	990	1 903	2 970[9]	2 974[9]	2 038[9]	2 099[9]	PIB par habitant
GDP at constant prices	...	102 606	134 293	136 012[9]	134 331[9]	121 203[9]	124 000[9]	PIB aux prix constants
Growth rates	...	-12.2	3.1	0.3[9]	-6.6[9]	-9.8[9]	2.3[9]	Taux de croissance
United Arab Emirates								**Émirats arabes unis**
GDP at current prices	41 134	66 603	182 978	289 787	403 137	358 135	348 744	PIB aux prix courants
GDP per capita	29 571	27 198	39 955	35 038	44 443	39 122	37 622	PIB par habitant
GDP at constant prices	103 869	144 762	257 284	289 787	354 076	367 633	378 796	PIB aux prix constants
Growth rates	-2.4	8.2	4.9	1.6	3.3	3.8	3.0	Taux de croissance
United Kingdom								**Royaume-Uni**
GDP at current prices	489 256	1 335 286	2 520 709	2 441 173	3 022 828	2 885 570	2 647 899	PIB aux prix courants
GDP per capita	8 665	23 031	41 812	38 561	46 494	44 124	40 249	PIB par habitant
GDP at constant prices	1 384 318	1 779 711	2 400 398	2 441 173	2 643 243	2 705 252	2 753 793	PIB aux prix constants
Growth rates	4.2	2.5	3.1	1.7	3.1	2.3	1.8	Taux de croissance
United Rep. of Tanzania [10]								**Rép.-Unie de Tanzanie** [10]
GDP at current prices	11 654	7 575	18 072	31 105	48 197	45 628	47 653	PIB aux prix courants
GDP per capita	534	260	471	694	948	870	881	PIB par habitant
GDP at constant prices	9 123	13 412	23 158	31 105	40 489	43 307	46 326	PIB aux prix constants
Growth rates	4.6	3.6	7.4	6.4	7.0	7.0	7.0	Taux de croissance

13 Gross domestic product and gross domestic product per capita *(continued)*

In millions of US dollars at current and constant 2010 prices; per capita US dollars; real rates of growth

Produit intérieur brut et produit intérieur brut par habitant *(suite)*

En millions de dollars É.-U. aux prix courants et constants de 2010; par habitant en dollars É.U.; taux de croissance réels

Country or area	1985	1995	2005	2010	2014	2015	2016	Pays ou zone
Zanzibar								**Zanzibar**
GDP at current prices	...	186	438	746	1 291	1 160	1 207	PIB aux prix courants
GDP per capita	...	235	408	587	936	795	823	PIB par habitant
GDP at constant prices	...	294	572	746	980	1 044	1 115	PIB aux prix constants
Growth rates	...	3.5	4.9	4.3	7.0	6.5	6.8	Taux de croissance
United States of America								**États-Unis d'Amérique**
GDP at current prices	4 346 700	7 664 060	13 093 726	14 964 372	17 427 609	18 120 714	18 624 475	PIB aux prix courants
GDP per capita	18 049	28 849	44 366	48 485	54 852	56 640	57 808	PIB par habitant
GDP at constant prices	7 678 348	10 299 025	14 408 094	14 964 372	16 208 861	16 672 692	16 920 328	PIB aux prix constants
Growth rates	4.2	2.8	3.3	2.5	2.6	2.9	1.5	Taux de croissance
Uruguay								**Uruguay**
GDP at current prices	5 226	21 312	17 363	40 285	57 236	53 274	52 420	PIB aux prix courants
GDP per capita	1 735	6 609	5 221	11 938	16 738	15 525	15 221	PIB par habitant
GDP at constant prices	18 302	26 841	30 157	40 285	47 384	47 559	48 251	PIB aux prix constants
Growth rates	1.5	-1.5	7.5	7.8	3.2	0.4	1.5	Taux de croissance
Uzbekistan								**Ouzbékistan**
GDP at current prices	...	13 474	14 396	39 526	63 455	67 408	67 779	PIB aux prix courants
GDP per capita	...	589	543	1 382	2 081	2 176	2 155	PIB par habitant
GDP at constant prices	...	16 623	26 297	39 526	53 996	58 246	61 741	PIB aux prix constants
Growth rates	...	-0.9	7.0	8.5	8.0	7.9	6.0	Taux de croissance
Vanuatu								**Vanuatu**
GDP at current prices	133	273	395	701	815	767	838	PIB aux prix courants
GDP per capita	1 020	1 621	1 886	2 966	3 148	2 899	3 097	PIB par habitant
GDP at constant prices	334	447	550	701	753	765	796	PIB aux prix constants
Growth rates	1.1	4.7	5.3	1.6	2.3	1.6	4.0	Taux de croissance
Venezuela (Boliv. Rep. of)								**Venezuela (Rép. boliv. du)**
GDP at current prices	59 963	74 889	145 514	393 806	363 282	344 375	291 376	PIB aux prix courants
GDP per capita	3 425	3 375	5 433	13 566	11 819	11 054	9 230	PIB par habitant
GDP at constant prices	207 087	278 797	328 294	393 806	422 051	395 794	330 663	PIB aux prix constants
Growth rates	0.2	4.0	10.3	-1.5	-3.9	-6.2	-16.5	Taux de croissance
Viet Nam								**Viet Nam**
GDP at current prices	4 797	20 736	57 633	115 932	186 205	193 241	205 276	PIB aux prix courants
GDP per capita	79	276	684	1 310	2 012	2 065	2 171	PIB par habitant
GDP at constant prices	23 610	42 924	85 352	115 932	144 835	154 509	164 105	PIB aux prix constants
Growth rates	5.6	9.5	7.5	6.4	6.0	6.7	6.2	Taux de croissance
Yemen								**Yémen**
GDP at current prices	...	5 936	19 041	29 031	33 399	26 899	25 374	PIB aux prix courants
GDP per capita	...	387	925	1 230	1 273	999	920	PIB par habitant
GDP at constant prices	...	11 850	22 923	29 031	22 318	15 799	14 254	PIB aux prix constants
Growth rates	...	16.7	5.1	7.8	-10.6	-29.2	-9.8	Taux de croissance
Zambia								**Zambie**
GDP at current prices	2 772	3 807	8 332	20 265	27 151	21 243	21 063	PIB aux prix courants
GDP per capita	399	417	691	1 463	1 738	1 319	1 270	PIB par habitant
GDP at constant prices	7 820	8 274	13 350	20 265	25 318	26 058	26 999	PIB aux prix constants
Growth rates	-~0.0	2.9	7.2	10.3	4.7	2.9	3.6	Taux de croissance
Zimbabwe								**Zimbabwe**
GDP at current prices	7 548	9 576	6 223	10 052	15 834	16 072	16 124	PIB aux prix courants
GDP per capita	872	846	481	714	1 027	1 019	998	PIB par habitant
GDP at constant prices	5 824	7 729	6 146	10 052	14 372	14 577	14 672	PIB aux prix constants
Growth rates	6.9	0.2	-4.1	15.4	2.8	1.4	0.7	Taux de croissance

Source:

United Nations Statistics Division, New York, National Accounts Statistics: Analysis of Main Aggregates (AMA) database, last accessed February 2018.

Source:

Organisation des Nations Unies, Division de statistique, New York, base de données des statistiques des comptes nationaux : Analyse des principaux agrégats, denier accès février 2018.

1 Data compiled in accordance with the System of National Accounts 1968 (1968 SNA).

2 For statistical purposes, the data for China do not include those for the Hong Kong Special Administrative Region (Hong Kong SAR), Macao Special Administrative Region (Macao SAR) and Taiwan Province of China.

1 Données compilées selon le Système de comptabilité nationale de 1968 (SCN 1968).

2 Pour la présentation des statistiques, les données pour la Chine ne comprennent pas la région administrative spéciale de Hong Kong (Hong Kong RAS), la région administrative spéciale de Macao (Macao RAS) et la province chinoise de Taïwan.

13 Gross domestic product and gross domestic product per capita *(continued)*

In millions of US dollars at current and constant 2010 prices; per capita US dollars; real rates of growth

Produit intérieur brut et produit intérieur brut par habitant *(suite)*

En millions de dollars É.-U. aux prix courants et constants de 2010; par habitant en dollars É.U.; taux de croissance réels

3 Excluding northern Cyprus.
4 Including French Guiana, Guadeloupe, Martinique and Réunion.
5 Including Western Sahara.
6 Does not incorporate value added generated by binational hydroelectric plants.
7 Including Kosovo and Metohija.
8 Excluding Kosovo and Metohija.
9 Excludes the temporarily occupied territory of the Autonomous Republic of Crimea and Sevastopol.
10 Tanzania mainland only, excluding Zanzibar.

3 Chypre du nord non compris.
4 Y compris Guadeloupe, Guyane française, Martinique et Réunion.
5 Y compris les données de Sahara occidental.
6 Ne comprend pas la valeur ajoutée produite par les centrales hydroélectriques binationales.
7 Y compris Kosovo et Metohija.
8 Non compris Kosovo et Metohija.
9 Excluent le territoire temporairement occupé de la République autonome de Crimée et de Sébastopol.
10 Tanzanie continentale seulement, Zanzibar non compris.

14 Gross value added by kind of economic activity

Percentage distribution, current prices

Valeur ajoutée brute par type d'activité économique

Répartition en pourcentage, aux prix courants

Country or area &	1985	1995	2005	2010	2014	2015	2016	Pays ou zone &
Afghanistan								**Afghanistan**
Agriculture	51.2	65.7	35.2	28.8	24.9	22.7	24.1	Agriculture
Industry	24.9	10.5	26.0	21.3	21.4	22.7	22.0	Industrie
Services	23.9	23.8	38.8	49.8	53.6	54.7	53.9	Services
Albania [1]								**Albanie** [1]
Agriculture	38.7	54.3	21.5	20.7	22.9	22.9	22.7	Agriculture
Industry	43.1	26.5	28.7	28.7	24.6	24.2	23.7	Industrie
Services	18.3	19.2	49.8	50.7	52.5	53.0	53.6	Services
Algeria								**Algérie**
Agriculture	8.4	10.4	8.0	8.6	10.7	12.1	12.7	Agriculture
Industry	49.8	47.9	59.7	51.4	43.9	37.2	36.1	Industrie
Services	41.9	41.7	32.3	40.0	45.4	50.7	51.1	Services
Andorra [1]								**Andorre** [1]
Agriculture	0.5	0.5	0.4	0.5	0.6	0.5	0.6	Agriculture
Industry	18.3	18.8	17.3	14.6	11.0	10.8	11.1	Industrie
Services	81.2	80.7	82.3	84.8	88.4	88.6	88.4	Services
Angola								**Angola**
Agriculture	13.8	7.4	5.0	6.1	8.0	9.8	8.0	Agriculture
Industry	43.5	67.4	59.7	51.2	45.4	41.3	46.0	Industrie
Services	42.8	25.2	35.3	42.7	46.6	48.9	46.0	Services
Anguilla								**Anguilla**
Agriculture	5.6	3.3	2.7	2.0	2.2	2.3	2.8	Agriculture
Industry	16.6	14.5	19.3	15.8	15.0	15.4	14.3	Industrie
Services	77.8	82.2	78.0	82.2	82.7	82.4	82.9	Services
Antigua and Barbuda								**Antigua-et-Barbuda**
Agriculture	2.2	1.9	2.0	1.8	1.8	1.9	1.9	Agriculture
Industry	11.4	14.4	16.3	18.2	17.8	18.3	19.8	Industrie
Services	86.4	83.7	81.7	80.0	80.4	79.9	78.3	Services
Argentina								**Argentine**
Agriculture	7.4	5.3	9.3	8.5	8.0	6.0	7.6	Agriculture
Industry	37.7	26.0	33.7	30.1	28.9	28.1	26.7	Industrie
Services	54.9	68.7	57.0	61.4	63.1	65.9	65.8	Services
Armenia [1]								**Arménie** [1]
Agriculture	...	40.3	19.9	17.8	19.9	18.9	17.4	Agriculture
Industry	...	28.4	43.8	34.7	27.8	28.2	26.9	Industrie
Services	...	31.3	36.3	47.4	52.2	52.9	55.7	Services
Aruba								**Aruba**
Agriculture [2]	0.5	0.5	0.4	0.5	0.5	0.5	0.5	Agriculture [2]
Industry [3]	15.9	15.6	19.6	15.4	15.4	15.4	15.4	Industrie [3]
Services	83.5	83.9	80.0	84.2	84.2	84.1	84.2	Services
Australia [1]								**Australie** [1]
Agriculture	4.5	3.7	3.0	2.5	2.6	2.6	2.5	Agriculture
Industry	35.5	28.4	27.9	28.5	25.4	24.3	25.7	Industrie
Services	60.0	67.8	69.1	69.0	72.0	73.1	71.8	Services
Austria [1]								**Autriche** [1]
Agriculture	3.6	2.4	1.4	1.4	1.3	1.2	1.2	Agriculture
Industry	34.5	32.1	30.5	28.7	28.4	28.1	27.7	Industrie
Services	61.9	65.5	68.1	69.9	70.2	70.7	71.0	Services
Azerbaijan [1]								**Azerbaïdjan** [1]
Agriculture	...	26.9	9.8	5.9	5.7	6.7	6.0	Agriculture
Industry	...	32.9	63.2	64.0	57.6	48.9	51.3	Industrie
Services	...	40.3	27.0	30.1	36.7	44.3	42.7	Services
Bahamas [1,4]								**Bahamas** [1,4]
Agriculture	2.2	2.0	1.1	1.2	0.9	0.9	1.0	Agriculture
Industry	13.9	10.4	11.7	12.4	15.3	11.2	12.8	Industrie
Services	84.0	87.6	87.1	86.4	83.8	87.8	86.2	Services
Bahrain [4]								**Bahreïn** [4]
Agriculture	0.8	0.7	0.3	0.3	0.3	0.3	0.3	Agriculture
Industry	38.9	36.1	42.8	45.5	46.9	40.7	39.8	Industrie
Services	60.2	63.2	56.9	54.2	52.8	59.0	59.8	Services
Bangladesh								**Bangladesh**
Agriculture	35.7	26.4	20.1	17.8	16.1	15.3	14.8	Agriculture
Industry	21.5	24.6	27.2	26.1	27.6	27.8	28.8	Industrie
Services	42.8	49.1	52.6	56.0	56.3	57.0	56.5	Services

14 Gross value added by kind of economic activity *(continued)*
Percentage distribution, current prices

Valeur ajoutée brute par type d'activité économique *(suite)*
Répartition en pourcentage, aux prix courants

Country or area [&]	1985	1995	2005	2010	2014	2015	2016	Pays ou zone [&]
Barbados								**Barbade**
Agriculture	4.5	3.5	1.8	1.5	1.6	1.5	1.6	Agriculture
Industry	23.0	16.6	16.9	15.5	15.6	15.2	15.5	Industrie
Services	72.5	79.9	81.3	83.0	82.8	83.3	83.0	Services
Belarus [1]								**Bélarus** [1]
Agriculture	...	16.7	9.7	10.1	8.3	7.2	7.9	Agriculture
Industry	...	37.0	43.1	40.3	40.1	37.7	36.1	Industrie
Services	...	46.3	47.2	49.5	51.7	55.1	56.0	Services
Belgium [1]								**Belgique** [1]
Agriculture	2.6	1.4	0.9	0.9	0.7	0.8	0.7	Agriculture
Industry	31.4	29.0	25.1	23.2	22.0	22.2	22.2	Industrie
Services	66.0	69.6	74.0	76.0	77.3	77.1	77.2	Services
Belize								**Belize**
Agriculture	19.8	19.8	14.7	12.6	15.0	14.3	10.9	Agriculture
Industry	24.3	23.5	16.5	20.7	18.0	16.2	18.0	Industrie
Services	55.9	56.8	68.8	66.7	67.0	69.5	71.1	Services
Benin								**Bénin**
Agriculture	32.4	23.7	27.1	25.4	23.0	22.7	23.0	Agriculture
Industry	15.5	32.5	30.3	24.7	22.7	24.5	24.1	Industrie
Services	52.0	43.8	42.5	49.9	54.3	52.9	52.9	Services
Bermuda								**Bermudes**
Agriculture	0.8	0.8	0.8	0.7	0.6	0.7	0.8	Agriculture
Industry	10.4	10.4	9.7	7.1	5.2	5.4	5.6	Industrie
Services	88.9	88.8	89.5	92.2	94.2	93.9	93.6	Services
Bhutan								**Bhoutan**
Agriculture	42.3	33.2	23.2	17.5	17.7	17.4	17.3	Agriculture
Industry	21.4	33.5	37.3	44.6	42.9	43.2	43.5	Industrie
Services	36.4	33.3	39.5	37.9	39.4	39.4	39.2	Services
Bolivia (Plurin. State of)								**Bolivie (État plurin. de)**
Agriculture	28.7	16.4	13.9	12.4	12.4	12.6	12.9	Agriculture
Industry	28.5	32.1	30.9	35.8	35.0	31.0	29.3	Industrie
Services	42.8	51.5	55.2	51.8	52.6	56.5	57.7	Services
Bosnia and Herzegovina								**Bosnie-Herzégovine**
Agriculture	...	22.0	9.8[1]	8.0[1]	7.0[1]	7.3[1]	7.5[1]	Agriculture
Industry	...	31.8	25.3[1]	26.4[1]	26.0[1]	26.5[1]	27.2[1]	Industrie
Services	...	46.2	64.9[1]	65.6[1]	67.0[1]	66.2[1]	65.3[1]	Services
Botswana								**Botswana**
Agriculture	7.4	4.9	2.0	2.8	2.3	2.4	2.2	Agriculture
Industry	54.3	46.5	47.6	35.7	36.4	33.1	34.7	Industrie
Services	38.3	48.6	50.3	61.6	61.3	64.4	63.1	Services
Brazil								**Brésil**
Agriculture	11.1	5.5[1]	5.5[1]	4.8[1]	5.0[1]	5.0[1]	5.1[1]	Agriculture
Industry	42.3	26.0[1]	28.5[1]	27.4[1]	23.8[1]	22.3[1]	24.8[1]	Industrie
Services	46.6	68.5[1]	66.0[1]	67.8[1]	71.2[1]	72.7[1]	70.1[1]	Services
British Virgin Islands [1]								**Îles Vierges britanniques** [1]
Agriculture	0.7	0.3	0.2	0.2	0.2	0.2	0.2	Agriculture
Industry	4.9	7.0	6.1	5.3	6.7	6.4	6.5	Industrie
Services	94.5	92.7	93.7	94.5	93.1	93.5	93.3	Services
Brunei Darussalam [1]								**Brunéi Darussalam** [1]
Agriculture	0.4	1.1	0.9	0.7	0.8	1.1	1.2	Agriculture
Industry	78.5	53.4	72.0	67.4	66.8	60.2	56.5	Industrie
Services	21.1	45.5	27.1	31.9	32.3	38.7	42.4	Services
Bulgaria [1]								**Bulgarie** [1]
Agriculture	13.0	13.4	8.6	4.8	5.3	4.8	4.7	Agriculture
Industry	53.9	25.6	28.4	27.4	27.1	27.9	28.3	Industrie
Services	33.0	61.0	63.0	67.8	67.6	67.3	67.0	Services
Burkina Faso								**Burkina Faso**
Agriculture	34.9	34.3	38.5	35.1	34.3	33.2	30.3	Agriculture
Industry	19.8	24.8	17.7	20.2	21.6	20.8	25.7	Industrie
Services	45.4	40.9	43.8	44.7	44.1	46.0	44.0	Services
Burundi								**Burundi**
Agriculture	55.8[5]	48.2	43.0	40.7	37.7	39.0	37.7	Agriculture
Industry	16.9[5]	19.2	17.8	16.3	16.7	14.4	15.2	Industrie
Services	27.2[5]	32.6	39.1	43.0	45.7	46.5	47.1	Services

14 Gross value added by kind of economic activity *(continued)*
Percentage distribution, current prices

Valeur ajoutée brute par type d'activité économique *(suite)*
Répartition en pourcentage, aux prix courants

Country or area [&]	1985	1995	2005	2010	2014	2015	2016	Pays ou zone [&]
Cabo Verde								**Cabo Verde**
Agriculture	17.3	15.6	11.7	9.2	9.1	9.7	9.4	Agriculture
Industry	25.4	30.0	22.8	20.8	21.3	20.5	19.9	Industrie
Services	57.3	54.4	65.5	70.1	69.6	69.9	70.6	Services
Cambodia								**Cambodge**
Agriculture	47.0	51.4	32.4	36.0	30.7	28.2	26.3	Agriculture
Industry	13.6	12.9	26.4	23.3	27.2	29.4	31.3	Industrie
Services	39.4	35.7	41.2	40.7	42.2	42.3	42.4	Services
Cameroon [1]								**Cameroun [1]**
Agriculture	15.8	17.5	15.2	15.1	15.3	16.1	16.7	Agriculture
Industry	26.6	28.6	30.3	29.1	29.1	27.4	26.6	Industrie
Services	57.6	53.8	54.6	55.8	55.6	56.6	56.7	Services
Canada								**Canada**
Agriculture	3.5	2.9	1.8	1.4[1]	1.5[1]	1.7[1]	1.7[1]	Agriculture
Industry	35.1	30.7	32.4	28.6[1]	28.7[1]	28.6[1]	28.5[1]	Industrie
Services	61.4	66.4	65.8	70.0[1]	69.7[1]	69.7[1]	69.8[1]	Services
Cayman Islands [1]								**Îles Caïmanes [1]**
Agriculture	0.3	0.2	0.2	0.3	0.3	0.4	0.3	Agriculture
Industry	9.8	9.2	9.1	7.7	7.4	7.5	7.5	Industrie
Services	89.9	90.5	90.6	92.0	92.3	92.2	92.2	Services
Central African Republic								**République centrafricaine**
Agriculture	35.7	36.1	45.0	41.2	30.8	31.4	31.9	Agriculture
Industry	22.2	26.9	18.6	24.0	27.4	26.0	25.5	Industrie
Services	42.1	37.0	36.5	34.8	41.9	42.6	42.6	Services
Chad								**Tchad**
Agriculture	31.7	27.7	26.0	35.9	28.5	29.5	27.5	Agriculture
Industry	14.9	15.0	35.1	36.7	32.4	31.7	32.6	Industrie
Services	53.4	57.3	38.9	27.4	39.1	38.8	39.9	Services
Chile [1]								**Chili [1]**
Agriculture	6.0	6.0	4.6	3.9	4.3	4.3	4.3	Agriculture
Industry	36.1	40.1	39.1	38.8	33.7	32.4	31.3	Industrie
Services	57.8	53.9	56.3	57.3	62.0	63.3	64.4	Services
China [4,6]								**Chine [4,6]**
Agriculture	28.2	19.8	12.0	9.8	9.3	9.1	8.9	Agriculture
Industry	42.8	46.9	47.2	46.6	43.3	41.1	40.0	Industrie
Services	29.0	33.3	40.9	43.6	47.4	49.8	51.2	Services
China, Hong Kong SAR								**Chine, RAS de Hong Kong**
Agriculture [2,7]	0.6	0.2	0.1	0.1	0.1	0.1	0.1	Agriculture [2,7]
Industry [3,8]	26.8	14.1	8.7	7.0	7.2	7.3	7.2	Industrie [3,8]
Services [9]	72.6	85.7	91.3	93.0	92.7	92.7	92.7	Services [9]
China, Macao SAR								**Chine, RAS de Macao**
Industry	24.7	14.5	14.9	7.4	7.5	10.5	8.0	Industrie
Services	75.3	85.5	85.1	92.6	92.5	89.5	92.0	Services
Colombia								**Colombie**
Agriculture	12.3	9.3	8.4	7.1	6.2	6.6	7.1	Agriculture
Industry	31.2	30.0	32.8	35.0	35.7	33.4	32.6	Industrie
Services	56.5	60.7	58.8	57.9	58.1	59.9	60.3	Services
Comoros								**Comores**
Agriculture	26.5	31.9	37.3	41.4	44.5	42.4	42.0	Agriculture
Industry	17.5	11.7	10.9	8.3	10.1	11.6	11.8	Industrie
Services	56.0	56.3	51.8	50.3	45.4	45.9	46.2	Services
Congo								**Congo**
Agriculture	7.6	10.9	4.6	3.7	5.1	7.7	9.3	Agriculture
Industry	54.9	46.9	73.4	78.1	70.9	56.4	51.9	Industrie
Services	37.5	42.2	22.0	18.2	24.0	35.9	38.8	Services
Cook Islands [4]								**Îles Cook [4]**
Agriculture	6.8	7.4	6.9	4.9	9.0	8.3	7.9	Agriculture
Industry	8.8	7.8	9.6	8.5	7.5	9.0	8.1	Industrie
Services	84.5	84.8	83.5	86.6	83.5	82.7	84.0	Services
Costa Rica [1]								**Costa Rica [1]**
Agriculture	14.4	14.0	9.6	7.2	5.6	5.4	5.5	Agriculture
Industry	33.5	29.2	26.9	25.4	22.1	22.1	21.5	Industrie
Services	52.1	56.8	63.6	67.4	72.3	72.5	73.0	Services
Côte d'Ivoire								**Côte d'Ivoire**
Agriculture	28.1[5]	26.6[5]	24.3	26.0	22.9	22.5	20.8	Agriculture
Industry	20.5[5]	22.3[5]	24.5	23.8	29.8	31.8	32.8	Industrie
Services	51.4[5]	51.1[5]	51.3	50.2	47.3	45.7	46.3	Services

14 Gross value added by kind of economic activity *(continued)*
Percentage distribution, current prices

Valeur ajoutée brute par type d'activité économique *(suite)*
Répartition en pourcentage, aux prix courants

Country or area &	1985	1995	2005	2010	2014	2015	2016	Pays ou zone &
Croatia [1]								**Croatie [1]**
Agriculture	...	7.2	5.0	4.8	4.1	4.2	4.1	Agriculture
Industry	...	32.3	29.0	26.9	26.5	26.4	26.4	Industrie
Services	...	60.5	66.0	68.2	69.3	69.4	69.6	Services
Cuba								**Cuba**
Agriculture	9.5	6.4	4.4	3.7	4.0	3.9	3.9	Agriculture
Industry	20.7	25.9	21.8	23.1	22.4	22.6	22.9	Industrie
Services	69.9	67.7	73.8	73.2	73.6	73.5	73.2	Services
Curaçao								**Curaçao**
Agriculture [2]	...	...	0.6	0.5	0.4	0.5	0.4	Agriculture [2]
Industry	...	...	16.4	16.0	19.9	19.8	19.8	Industrie
Services	...	...	83.0	83.5	79.7	79.7	79.8	Services
Cyprus [1,10]								**Chypre [1,10]**
Agriculture	7.6	5.2	3.1	2.4	2.1	2.1	2.1	Agriculture
Industry	27.0	22.0	20.5	16.7	10.7	11.1	11.4	Industrie
Services	65.4	72.8	76.4	80.9	87.2	86.8	86.5	Services
Czechia [1]								**Tchéquie [1]**
Agriculture	...	4.4	2.4	1.7	2.7	2.5	2.5	Agriculture
Industry	...	38.9	37.7	36.8	37.9	37.8	37.6	Industrie
Services	...	56.7	59.8	61.5	59.4	59.7	59.9	Services
Dem. People's Rep. Korea								**Rép. pop. dém. de Corée**
Agriculture	28.3	27.6	25.0	20.8	21.8	21.6	21.7	Agriculture
Industry	48.5	42.0	42.8	48.2	46.9	46.2	47.2	Industrie
Services	23.2	30.3	32.2	31.0	31.3	32.2	31.1	Services
Dem. Rep. of the Congo								**Rép. dém. du Congo**
Agriculture	31.8	57.0	22.3	22.4	19.9	19.7	20.6	Agriculture
Industry	31.0	17.0	32.9	40.5	46.1	44.8	43.1	Industrie
Services	37.1	26.0	44.9	37.0	34.0	35.5	36.2	Services
Denmark [1]								**Danemark [1]**
Agriculture	4.9	3.3	1.3	1.4	1.6	0.9	0.9	Agriculture
Industry	26.5	25.5	26.2	22.8	22.8	22.7	23.5	Industrie
Services	68.6	71.2	72.5	75.8	75.6	76.4	75.6	Services
Djibouti								**Djibouti**
Agriculture	3.1[11]	3.2[11]	3.6	3.6	3.2	3.3	3.3	Agriculture
Industry	21.2[12]	15.4[12]	16.2	19.0	22.7	21.4	21.8	Industrie
Services	75.7	81.3	80.2	77.4	74.0	75.3	74.9	Services
Dominica								**Dominique**
Agriculture	22.7	13.7	13.2	13.8	14.9	15.9	18.0	Agriculture
Industry	13.7	16.0	15.0	14.4	14.7	13.4	13.6	Industrie
Services	63.6	70.3	71.9	71.8	70.4	70.7	68.4	Services
Dominican Republic [1]								**République dominicaine [1]**
Agriculture	13.4	10.7	7.7	6.4	5.4	5.8	6.1	Agriculture
Industry	41.9	35.1	32.5	30.0	31.0	29.8	28.5	Industrie
Services	44.7	54.3	59.8	63.6	63.5	64.4	65.5	Services
Ecuador [1]								**Équateur [1]**
Agriculture	19.6	22.6	10.0	10.2	9.5	10.1	9.6	Agriculture
Industry	30.7	28.0	33.4	36.3	38.6	34.1	37.3	Industrie
Services	49.7	49.4	56.6	53.5	51.9	55.8	53.1	Services
Egypt [13]								**Égypte [13]**
Agriculture	18.4	16.8	14.4	14.0	11.1	11.3	11.9	Agriculture
Industry	31.8	32.7	36.9	37.5	39.0	36.2	32.9	Industrie
Services	49.9	50.9	48.8	48.5	49.9	52.5	55.2	Services
El Salvador								**El Salvador**
Agriculture	18.2	14.0[4]	10.2[4]	12.1[4]	10.8[4]	10.7[4]	10.6[4]	Agriculture
Industry	21.9	28.7[4]	28.7[4]	25.9[4]	25.7[4]	25.6[4]	25.5[4]	Industrie
Services	59.9	57.3[4]	61.1[4]	62.1[4]	63.4[4]	63.7[4]	63.9[4]	Services
Equatorial Guinea								**Guinée équatoriale**
Agriculture	14.5	12.5	1.5	1.1	1.3	2.0	2.5	Agriculture
Industry	20.6	35.8	81.3	74.3	69.8	57.1	50.0	Industrie
Services	64.9	51.6	17.2	24.6	28.9	40.9	47.5	Services
Eritrea								**Érythrée**
Agriculture	...	20.9	24.2	19.1	17.2	17.2	17.3	Agriculture
Industry	...	16.8	21.9	23.1	23.6	23.5	23.5	Industrie
Services	...	62.3	53.9	57.8	59.2	59.3	59.1	Services

14 Gross value added by kind of economic activity *(continued)*
Percentage distribution, current prices

Valeur ajoutée brute par type d'activité économique *(suite)*
Répartition en pourcentage, aux prix courants

Country or area &	1985	1995	2005	2010	2014	2015	2016	Pays ou zone &
Estonia [1]								**Estonie** [1]
Agriculture	...	5.7	3.5	3.2	3.5	3.1	2.6	Agriculture
Industry	...	31.9	29.8	28.0	28.6	27.8	26.9	Industrie
Services	...	62.4	66.7	68.8	67.9	69.1	70.5	Services
Eswatini [1]								**Eswatini** [1]
Agriculture	14.5	7.9	11.3	10.4	9.7	10.2	10.0	Agriculture
Industry	24.8	41.2	40.8	38.7	36.7	36.3	36.9	Industrie
Services	60.7	51.0	47.9	50.9	53.6	53.5	53.1	Services
Ethiopia								**Éthiopie**
Agriculture	...	55.0	45.2	45.3	41.5	38.8	36.8	Agriculture
Industry	...	9.8	13.1	10.4	14.5	17.5	21.0	Industrie
Services	...	35.1	41.7	44.3	44.0	43.7	42.2	Services
Fiji [1]								**Fidji** [1]
Agriculture	16.4	16.4	12.8	10.2	11.8	11.3	13.6	Agriculture
Industry	16.1	17.8	17.9	19.9	18.1	17.9	17.5	Industrie
Services	67.5	65.8	69.2	69.9	70.1	70.7	68.9	Services
Finland [1]								**Finlande** [1]
Agriculture	7.8	4.3	2.6	2.7	2.8	2.5	2.7	Agriculture
Industry	35.1	33.7	33.5	30.0	26.8	27.0	27.1	Industrie
Services	57.1	62.0	63.8	67.3	70.4	70.4	70.2	Services
France [1,14]								**France** [1,14]
Agriculture	3.8	2.7	1.9	1.8	1.7	1.8	1.6	Agriculture
Industry	28.4	24.5	21.5	19.6	19.6	19.6	19.6	Industrie
Services	67.9	72.7	76.6	78.6	78.6	78.6	78.8	Services
French Polynesia								**Polynésie française**
Agriculture	4.7	5.2	3.4	2.5	3.0	3.1	3.1	Agriculture
Industry	21.0	12.5	12.7	12.3	11.8	11.8	11.8	Industrie
Services	74.3	82.3	83.9	85.2	85.2	85.1	85.1	Services
Gabon								**Gabon**
Agriculture	5.0	7.3	5.2	4.6	3.9	4.6	4.1	Agriculture
Industry	58.5	54.5	62.6	55.6	50.9	46.3	50.8	Industrie
Services	36.5	38.2	32.2	39.8	45.2	49.1	45.2	Services
Gambia								**Gambie**
Agriculture	23.3	21.6	28.6	30.7	20.3	20.5	20.6	Agriculture
Industry	10.7	15.1	14.9	13.1	14.5	14.8	13.8	Industrie
Services	66.0	68.4	56.5	56.2	65.2	64.7	65.6	Services
Georgia								**Géorgie**
Agriculture	...	44.4	16.5	8.3	9.1	9.0	9.1	Agriculture
Industry	...	14.3	26.5	22.0	23.6	24.2	24.9	Industrie
Services	...	41.3	57.0	69.8	67.3	66.8	66.0	Services
Germany [1]								**Allemagne** [1]
Agriculture	1.6	1.2	0.9	0.9	0.9	0.7	0.7	Agriculture
Industry	39.4	38.7	34.8	35.8	35.8	35.9	35.9	Industrie
Services	59.0	60.0	64.3	63.4	63.3	63.4	63.4	Services
Ghana								**Ghana**
Agriculture	37.8	34.0	31.8	29.8[1]	21.5[1]	20.3[1]	18.9[1]	Agriculture
Industry	15.8	20.9	20.3	19.1[1]	26.6[1]	25.1[1]	24.2[1]	Industrie
Services	46.4	45.1	47.9	51.1[1]	51.9[1]	54.6[1]	56.9[1]	Services
Greece [1]								**Grèce** [1]
Agriculture	10.2	8.1	4.8	3.3	3.8	4.2	4.0	Agriculture
Industry	27.0	21.6	19.8	15.7	16.0	15.6	16.3	Industrie
Services	62.7	70.3	75.4	81.1	80.1	80.1	79.7	Services
Greenland								**Groenland**
Agriculture	10.5	10.5	10.6	8.3	13.7	12.9	12.8	Agriculture
Industry	14.7	14.7	15.2	17.5	14.2	15.7	15.2	Industrie
Services	74.8	74.7	74.2	74.3	72.1	71.4	72.0	Services
Grenada								**Grenade**
Agriculture	16.1	9.5	3.4	5.2	7.0	8.8	7.3	Agriculture
Industry	16.3	18.6	26.1	16.8	14.7	14.6	15.1	Industrie
Services	67.7	71.9	70.5	78.1	78.3	76.6	77.6	Services
Guatemala								**Guatemala**
Agriculture	27.2	25.4	13.1	11.4	11.0	10.8	10.7	Agriculture
Industry	20.7	20.7	28.6	28.0	28.1	27.2	26.7	Industrie
Services	52.2	53.9	58.3	60.6	60.9	62.0	62.6	Services

Gross value added by kind of economic activity *(continued)*
Percentage distribution, current prices

Valeur ajoutée brute par type d'activité économique *(suite)*
Répartition en pourcentage, aux prix courants

Country or area &	1985	1995	2005	2010	2014	2015	2016	Pays ou zone &
Guinea								**Guinée**
Agriculture	18.3	25.7	14.9	18.6	19.0	20.4	20.2	Agriculture
Industry	31.9	27.2	34.9	34.3	32.3	28.3	36.9	Industrie
Services	49.9	47.1	50.3	47.1	48.7	51.2	42.9	Services
Guinea-Bissau								**Guinée-Bissau**
Agriculture	46.5	55.1	45.4	46.2	42.7	45.0	44.2	Agriculture
Industry	15.6	12.2	14.7	13.5	15.1	14.5	14.7	Industrie
Services	37.9	32.7	39.9	40.3	42.1	40.5	41.1	Services
Guyana								**Guyana**
Agriculture	20.0	37.1	25.7	17.6	17.9	18.9	14.6	Agriculture
Industry	31.6	33.3	28.7	34.5	32.9	32.9	40.3	Industrie
Services	48.4	29.6	45.6	47.9	49.2	48.2	45.1	Services
Haiti								**Haïti**
Agriculture	33.3	24.3	22.4	21.0	17.6	16.4	16.7	Agriculture
Industry	24.7	31.4	32.9	33.7	37.7	38.2	38.0	Industrie
Services	42.0	44.3	44.8	45.4	44.7	45.4	45.3	Services
Honduras								**Honduras**
Agriculture	20.4	20.4	13.1	11.9	12.9	12.8	12.7	Agriculture
Industry	23.8	29.9	27.6	26.2	25.2	26.3	26.6	Industrie
Services	55.8	49.7	59.3	62.0	61.9	60.9	60.7	Services
Hungary [1]								**Hongrie** [1]
Agriculture	16.0	8.4	4.3	3.5	4.7	4.4	4.4	Agriculture
Industry	42.8	30.4	31.3	29.9	30.6	31.7	30.5	Industrie
Services	41.3	61.3	64.5	66.6	64.7	63.9	65.1	Services
Iceland [1]								**Islande** [1]
Agriculture	11.3	11.0	5.7	7.4	6.1	6.2	5.7	Agriculture
Industry	34.2	28.4	24.7	24.7	23.1	22.6	22.4	Industrie
Services	54.5	60.6	69.6	68.0	70.9	71.2	72.0	Services
India [1]								**Inde** [1]
Agriculture	32.7	27.6	19.5	18.9	18.0	17.5	17.4	Agriculture
Industry	31.0	32.8	33.6	32.5	30.2	29.6	28.8	Industrie
Services	36.3	39.6	46.9	48.7	51.8	52.9	53.8	Services
Indonesia [1]								**Indonésie** [1]
Agriculture	19.8	14.2	12.1	14.3	13.7	13.9	14.0	Agriculture
Industry	33.1	38.3	43.1	43.9	43.0	41.3	40.8	Industrie
Services	47.1	47.6	44.8	41.8	43.3	44.7	45.3	Services
Iran (Islamic Republic of)								**Iran (Rép. islamique d')**
Agriculture	13.1	12.4	6.2	6.4	9.9	10.6	9.8	Agriculture
Industry	31.4	38.7	47.7	43.4	39.9	33.2	34.3	Industrie
Services	55.4	48.9	46.1	50.2	50.3	56.3	55.9	Services
Iraq								**Iraq**
Agriculture	13.9[15]	12.3	6.9	5.1	4.9	3.9	4.1	Agriculture
Industry	42.2[15,16]	66.0	63.3	55.4	55.1	43.3	39.8	Industrie
Services	43.9[16]	21.7	29.9	39.4	40.0	52.8	56.1	Services
Ireland [1]								**Irlande** [1]
Agriculture	9.4	6.4	1.2	1.1	1.4	1.0	1.0	Agriculture
Industry	30.6	32.1	34.4	26.1	27.5	41.4	39.3	Industrie
Services	60.0	61.5	64.5	72.9	71.0	57.7	59.7	Services
Israel [1]								**Israël** [1]
Agriculture	4.2	2.0	1.8	1.7	1.3	1.3	1.3	Agriculture
Industry	26.9	26.2	23.0	22.9	22.0	21.0	20.8	Industrie
Services	68.8	71.9	75.2	75.4	76.7	77.7	77.9	Services
Italy [1]								**Italie** [1]
Agriculture	4.6	3.3	2.2	2.0	2.2	2.2	2.1	Agriculture
Industry	33.0	29.1	25.8	24.4	23.4	23.5	23.9	Industrie
Services	62.4	67.6	71.9	73.7	74.5	74.2	74.0	Services
Jamaica								**Jamaïque**
Agriculture	5.4	9.2	5.7	5.9	6.8	7.2	7.6	Agriculture
Industry	28.4	29.4	23.9	20.0	20.8	21.9	21.9	Industrie
Services	66.2	61.4	70.4	74.1	72.4	70.9	70.5	Services
Japan [1]								**Japon** [1]
Agriculture	2.9	1.7[4]	1.1[4]	1.1[4]	1.1[4]	1.1[4]	1.1[4]	Agriculture
Industry	39.5	34.7[4]	30.1[4]	28.5[4]	27.9[4]	28.9[4]	28.0[4]	Industrie
Services	57.5	63.6[4]	68.8[4]	70.4[4]	71.0[4]	70.0[4]	71.0[4]	Services

14 Gross value added by kind of economic activity *(continued)*
Percentage distribution, current prices

Valeur ajoutée brute par type d'activité économique *(suite)*
Répartition en pourcentage, aux prix courants

Country or area &	1985	1995	2005	2010	2014	2015	2016	Pays ou zone &
Jordan								**Jordanie**
Agriculture	5.0	4.3	3.0	3.2	3.6	4.0	4.1	Agriculture
Industry	26.5	27.5	26.9	28.7	27.8	28.1	27.4	Industrie
Services	68.5	68.3	70.1	68.1	68.6	68.0	68.6	Services
Kazakhstan [1]								**Kazakhstan** [1]
Agriculture	...	12.9	6.6	4.7	4.7	5.0	4.9	Agriculture
Industry	...	30.2	39.2	41.9	35.9	32.5	33.6	Industrie
Services	...	56.9	54.2	53.4	59.4	62.5	61.5	Services
Kenya [1]								**Kenya** [1]
Agriculture	28.7	27.6	23.2	27.1	29.6	32.4	34.5	Agriculture
Industry	25.2	20.9	22.3	20.3	18.8	18.6	18.5	Industrie
Services	46.1	51.5	54.5	52.6	51.7	49.1	47.0	Services
Kiribati [13]								**Kiribati** [13]
Agriculture	44.0	26.9	21.8	24.6	24.0	22.6	23.5	Agriculture
Industry	9.4	9.1	9.3	10.3	14.5	14.4	14.2	Industrie
Services	46.6	64.0	68.9	65.1	61.5	63.0	62.4	Services
Kosovo [1]								**Kosovo** [1]
Agriculture	...	7.2	17.1	16.2	14.3	12.6	13.0	Agriculture
Industry	...	32.6	26.6	28.4	26.7	29.1	29.6	Industrie
Services	...	60.2	56.3	55.4	59.0	58.2	57.4	Services
Kuwait								**Koweït**
Agriculture	0.6	0.4	0.3	0.4	0.4	0.6	0.4	Agriculture
Industry	56.4	52.8	60.2	58.2	62.3	48.7	58.8	Industrie
Services	43.0	46.7	39.5	41.4	37.3	50.7	40.8	Services
Kyrgyzstan [1]								**Kirghizistan** [1]
Agriculture	...	43.1	31.3	18.8	16.5	15.4	14.4	Agriculture
Industry	...	21.8	22.1	28.2	26.8	27.5	28.3	Industrie
Services	...	35.1	46.6	53.0	56.7	57.1	57.3	Services
Lao People's Dem. Rep. [1]								**Rép. dém. populaire lao** [1]
Agriculture	39.1	42.8	29.1	23.6	19.7	19.7	19.5	Agriculture
Industry	16.2	15.7	26.2	30.9	31.7	31.0	32.5	Industrie
Services	44.7	41.5	44.7	45.5	48.6	49.4	48.0	Services
Latvia [1]								**Lettonie** [1]
Agriculture	...	8.9	4.3	4.4	3.8	4.1	4.0	Agriculture
Industry	...	30.3	22.9	23.4	22.4	22.3	21.5	Industrie
Services	...	60.8	72.8	72.2	73.8	73.6	74.5	Services
Lebanon [1]								**Liban** [1]
Agriculture	3.7	5.7	4.0	4.3	4.3	3.8	2.9	Agriculture
Industry	23.5	32.3	16.7	15.7	18.6	16.7	11.2	Industrie
Services	72.8	62.0	79.3	80.1	77.1	79.5	85.9	Services
Lesotho [1]								**Lesotho** [1]
Agriculture	16.7	9.2	6.2	5.6	5.8	5.3	5.8	Agriculture
Industry	15.7	32.4	37.7	32.8	33.3	32.9	32.3	Industrie
Services	67.6	58.4	56.1	61.7	60.9	61.7	61.8	Services
Liberia								**Libéria**
Agriculture	35.9	80.5	68.8	70.7	70.7[17]	70.8[17]	72.9[17]	Agriculture
Industry	24.7	5.2	9.8	11.4	11.4[17]	11.4[17]	8.7[17]	Industrie
Services	39.4	14.3	21.5	18.0	17.9[17]	17.9[17]	18.4[17]	Services
Libya								**Libye**
Agriculture	3.5	6.7	2.2	2.5	0.9	0.9	0.9	Agriculture
Industry	58.8	40.3	75.7	74.0	67.1	67.1	67.1	Industrie
Services	37.7	53.0	22.2	23.5	32.0	32.0	32.0	Services
Liechtenstein [1]								**Liechtenstein** [1]
Agriculture	2.5	1.6	5.2	5.2	4.8	4.9	4.8	Agriculture
Industry	32.5	30.1	38.6	39.0	41.0	38.9	40.2	Industrie
Services	65.0	68.4	56.1	55.9	54.2	56.3	55.0	Services
Lithuania [1]								**Lituanie** [1]
Agriculture	...	11.1	4.8	3.3	3.8	3.8	3.3	Agriculture
Industry	...	31.5	32.7	29.1	30.4	29.7	28.7	Industrie
Services	...	57.4	62.5	67.6	65.8	66.5	68.0	Services
Luxembourg [1]								**Luxembourg** [1]
Agriculture	2.0	1.0	0.4	0.3	0.3	0.3	0.3	Agriculture
Industry	28.1	21.2	16.5	12.7	12.7	12.5	12.9	Industrie
Services	70.0	77.8	83.1	87.0	87.0	87.2	86.8	Services

14 Gross value added by kind of economic activity *(continued)*
Percentage distribution, current prices

Valeur ajoutée brute par type d'activité économique *(suite)*
Répartition en pourcentage, aux prix courants

Country or area &	1985	1995	2005	2010	2014	2015	2016	Pays ou zone &
Madagascar								**Madagascar**
Agriculture	39.0	37.6	32.4	28.4	33.6	33.3	34.6	Agriculture
Industry	10.6	11.3	14.1	18.8	11.0	11.1	7.9	Industrie
Services	50.4	51.1	53.5	52.8	55.4	55.6	57.5	Services
Malawi [1]								**Malawi** [1]
Agriculture	50.0	31.9	37.1	31.9	27.5	26.5	25.1	Agriculture
Industry	28.1	21.9	16.8	16.4	16.2	16.5	16.4	Industrie
Services	21.8	46.1	46.1	51.7	56.3	57.1	58.5	Services
Malaysia								**Malaisie**
Agriculture	20.3	12.7[1,4]	8.4[1,4]	10.2[1,4]	9.0[1,4]	8.6[1,4]	8.9[1,4]	Agriculture
Industry	39.2	40.5[1,4]	46.9[1,4]	40.9[1,4]	40.4[1,4]	39.6[1,4]	40.2[1,4]	Industrie
Services	40.5	46.8[1,4]	44.7[1,4]	48.9[1,4]	50.6[1,4]	51.8[1,4]	50.9[1,4]	Services
Maldives [1]								**Maldives** [1]
Agriculture	10.7	7.5	8.7	6.1	6.0	6.5	6.8	Agriculture
Industry	8.2	9.8	13.2	10.2	9.4	10.3	11.2	Industrie
Services	81.1	82.7	78.1	83.8	84.6	83.3	82.0	Services
Mali								**Mali**
Agriculture	36.1	38.8	34.4	34.9	39.3	39.9	39.8	Agriculture
Industry	14.7	18.0	25.9	25.3	20.8	19.6	19.2	Industrie
Services	49.3	43.2	39.6	39.7	39.9	40.5	41.0	Services
Malta [1]								**Malte** [1]
Agriculture	4.4	2.8	2.2	1.7	1.3	1.3	1.4	Agriculture
Industry	33.3	28.5	23.0	19.0	15.1	14.4	13.8	Industrie
Services	62.4	68.7	74.7	79.4	83.6	84.3	84.9	Services
Marshall Islands								**Îles Marshall**
Agriculture	9.7	10.5	9.2	15.6	15.9	14.3	17.0	Agriculture
Industry	12.5	14.0	9.2	11.6	10.7	10.6	10.7	Industrie
Services	77.7	75.6	81.6	72.9	73.4	75.1	72.3	Services
Mauritania								**Mauritanie**
Agriculture	36.1	43.6	29.8	21.3	23.8	27.2	23.4	Agriculture
Industry	27.0	24.7	32.4	40.9	35.7	28.0	36.1	Industrie
Services	36.9	31.6	37.9	37.8	40.5	44.8	40.4	Services
Mauritius								**Maurice**
Agriculture	14.8	9.8	5.7	4.1[1]	3.7[1]	3.5[1]	3.5[1]	Agriculture
Industry	32.2	31.3	26.6	25.3[1]	22.3[1]	21.7[1]	20.9[1]	Industrie
Services	53.1	58.9	67.8	70.7[1]	74.0[1]	74.8[1]	75.6[1]	Services
Mexico								**Mexique**
Agriculture	8.4	4.6[1]	3.2[1]	3.4[1]	3.3[1]	3.4[1]	3.6[1]	Agriculture
Industry	42.6	34.1[1]	34.2[1]	33.7[1]	33.2[1]	31.8[1]	31.3[1]	Industrie
Services	49.0	61.3[1]	62.6[1]	62.9[1]	63.5[1]	64.8[1]	65.1[1]	Services
Micronesia (Fed. States of)								**Micronésie (États féd. de)**
Agriculture	24.5	24.9	24.2	26.7	26.1	27.7	27.3	Agriculture
Industry	7.4	7.2	5.7	7.8	6.4	6.5	6.9	Industrie
Services	68.1	68.0	70.2	65.5	67.5	65.8	65.8	Services
Monaco [1,4]								**Monaco** [1,4]
Industry	12.8	12.8	12.2	12.9	12.6	17.6	18.3	Industrie
Services	87.2	87.2	87.8	87.1	87.4	82.4	81.7	Services
Mongolia [1]								**Mongolie** [1]
Agriculture	9.9[4]	28.5[4]	17.8	13.1	14.7	14.5	13.3	Agriculture
Industry	32.5[4]	33.8[4]	37.4	37.0	34.7	33.8	35.3	Industrie
Services	57.6[4]	37.7[4]	44.8	50.0	50.5	51.7	51.4	Services
Montenegro [1]								**Monténégro** [1]
Agriculture	...	12.1	10.3	9.2	10.0	9.8	9.0	Agriculture
Industry	...	25.3	22.1	20.5	17.7	17.5	19.1	Industrie
Services	...	62.6	67.6	70.3	72.3	72.6	71.8	Services
Montserrat								**Montserrat**
Agriculture	4.0	4.9	0.9	1.1	1.6	1.4	1.7	Agriculture
Industry	17.7	12.3	16.7	13.3	16.0	12.7	12.9	Industrie
Services	78.3	82.8	82.5	85.7	82.5	85.9	85.4	Services
Morocco [18]								**Maroc** [18]
Agriculture	17.4	15.1	13.1	14.4	13.0	14.3	13.6	Agriculture
Industry	32.8	29.6	28.9	28.6	29.5	29.5	29.5	Industrie
Services	49.8	55.3	58.0	56.9	57.5	56.2	56.8	Services
Mozambique								**Mozambique**
Agriculture	47.5	33.5[1]	25.4[1]	28.9[1]	24.5[1]	24.6[1]	24.1[1]	Agriculture
Industry	13.2	14.4[1]	20.7[1]	18.6[1]	20.2[1]	21.0[1]	21.1[1]	Industrie
Services	39.3	52.1[1]	53.8[1]	52.5[1]	55.3[1]	54.4[1]	54.8[1]	Services

14

Gross value added by kind of economic activity *(continued)*
Percentage distribution, current prices

Valeur ajoutée brute par type d'activité économique *(suite)*
Répartition en pourcentage, aux prix courants

Country or area [&]	1985	1995	2005	2010	2014	2015	2016	Pays ou zone [&]
Myanmar [4]								**Myanmar [4]**
Agriculture	48.2	60.0	46.7	36.9	27.8	26.8	25.3	Agriculture
Industry	13.1	9.9	17.5	26.5	34.5	34.5	34.9	Industrie
Services	38.7	30.1	35.8	36.7	37.7	38.8	39.8	Services
Namibia								**Namibie**
Agriculture	7.9	10.5	11.4	9.2	7.1	6.4	6.8	Agriculture
Industry	39.7	24.2	27.3	29.8	31.1	30.6	30.9	Industrie
Services	52.4	65.2	61.3	61.1	61.7	63.0	62.3	Services
Nauru [4]								**Nauru [4]**
Agriculture	6.0	6.4	7.8	4.3	3.2	3.1	3.2	Agriculture
Industry	32.9	27.7	-6.5	48.0	58.8	60.5	58.5	Industrie
Services	61.1	65.8	98.7	47.7	38.0	36.5	38.3	Services
Nepal								**Népal**
Agriculture	49.0	38.9	35.2	35.4	32.6	31.7	31.6	Agriculture
Industry	11.5	17.7	17.1	15.1	14.9	14.8	14.2	Industrie
Services	39.5	43.4	47.7	49.5	52.5	53.4	54.2	Services
Netherlands [1]								**Pays-Bas [1]**
Agriculture	4.1	3.4	2.0	1.9	1.8	1.8	1.8	Agriculture
Industry	33.1	27.0	24.0	22.1	20.5	20.3	20.0	Industrie
Services	62.9	69.6	74.0	76.0	77.7	77.9	78.2	Services
Netherlands Antilles [former]								**Antilles néerlandaises [anc.]**
Agriculture [2]	1.1	0.9	0.8	0.6	...	...	...	Agriculture [2]
Industry	20.5	18.4	15.6	15.7	...	...	...	Industrie
Services	78.4	80.7	83.7	83.7	...	...	...	Services
New Caledonia								**Nouvelle-Calédonie**
Agriculture	1.8	1.8	1.7	1.4	1.4	1.4	1.4	Agriculture
Industry	25.9	22.0	26.6	25.5	26.4	26.0	26.2	Industrie
Services	72.2	76.2	71.7	73.1	72.2	72.6	72.4	Services
New Zealand [1]								**Nouvelle-Zélande [1]**
Agriculture	7.4	7.0	4.9	7.1	5.2	5.0	6.0	Agriculture
Industry	34.1	27.8	25.8	23.0	23.4	23.4	23.0	Industrie
Services	58.5	65.3	69.3	69.9	71.4	71.7	71.1	Services
Nicaragua								**Nicaragua**
Agriculture	14.9	22.4	17.8	18.7	18.5	18.2	17.3	Agriculture
Industry	33.7	22.0	22.9	24.2	27.8	27.2	26.8	Industrie
Services	51.4	55.6	59.3	57.0	53.7	54.6	55.9	Services
Niger								**Niger**
Agriculture	37.0	35.9	45.5	43.8	39.2	39.1	41.1	Agriculture
Industry	20.2	14.3	11.8	16.7	20.7	19.1	18.0	Industrie
Services	42.8	49.7	42.7	39.4	40.2	41.8	40.8	Services
Nigeria [1]								**Nigéria [1]**
Agriculture	23.2	27.0	25.6	23.9	20.2	20.9	21.2	Agriculture
Industry	18.2	25.1	23.7	25.3	24.9	20.4	18.4	Industrie
Services	58.6	47.9	50.7	50.8	54.8	58.8	60.4	Services
Norway [1]								**Norvège [1]**
Agriculture	3.3	3.0	1.6	1.8	1.6	1.9	2.6	Agriculture
Industry	38.3	33.1	42.5	39.1	38.1	37.7	34.6	Industrie
Services	58.3	63.9	55.9	59.2	60.3	60.5	62.8	Services
Oman								**Oman**
Agriculture	2.3	2.9	1.6	1.4	1.2	1.5	1.3	Agriculture
Industry	63.3	49.7	62.1	62.8	60.2	51.1	58.3	Industrie
Services	34.4	47.4	36.3	35.9	38.6	47.3	40.4	Services
Pakistan [1]								**Pakistan [1]**
Agriculture	30.5	28.1	24.5	24.3	24.9	25.1	25.2	Agriculture
Industry	16.7	17.9	21.2	20.6	21.0	20.0	19.2	Industrie
Services	52.8	54.0	54.3	55.1	54.2	54.9	55.6	Services
Palau [1]								**Palaos [1]**
Agriculture	16.7	8.1	4.4	4.5	4.0	3.3	3.4	Agriculture
Industry	25.4	11.1	16.6	10.7	8.3	7.8	8.4	Industrie
Services	57.9	80.8	79.1	84.8	87.7	88.8	88.3	Services
Panama								**Panama**
Agriculture	7.3	7.4	6.8	3.9	3.1	2.8	2.6	Agriculture
Industry	22.1	19.8	16.3	20.3	26.6	27.1	27.9	Industrie
Services	70.6	72.8	76.9	75.8	70.3	70.0	69.6	Services

14 Gross value added by kind of economic activity *(continued)*
Percentage distribution, current prices

Valeur ajoutée brute par type d'activité économique *(suite)*
Répartition en pourcentage, aux prix courants

Country or area &	1985	1995	2005	2010	2014	2015	2016	Pays ou zone &
Papua New Guinea								**Papouasie-Nvl-Guinée**
Agriculture	18.6	22.0	22.7	20.3	20.0	20.1	20.1	Agriculture
Industry	14.4	23.0	34.0	33.6	29.0	28.2	28.1	Industrie
Services	67.0	55.0	43.3	46.0	51.0	51.8	51.8	Services
Paraguay								**Paraguay**
Agriculture	26.5	22.8	19.6	22.5	20.5	19.2	19.0	Agriculture
Industry	24.2[19]	25.7[19]	34.8	30.1	28.8	29.6	31.6	Industrie
Services	49.3	51.5	45.7	47.4	50.6	51.2	49.4	Services
Peru [1]								**Pérou** [1]
Agriculture	10.7	8.9	7.5	7.5	7.5	7.8	7.6	Agriculture
Industry	33.3	32.3	37.7	39.1	34.8	32.8	32.5	Industrie
Services	56.0	58.8	54.7	53.5	57.7	59.4	59.9	Services
Philippines [1,17]								**Philippines** [1,17]
Agriculture	21.2	18.8	12.7	12.3	11.3	10.3	9.7	Agriculture
Industry	38.0	35.0	33.9	32.6	31.4	30.9	30.9	Industrie
Services	40.8	46.1	53.5	55.1	57.3	58.8	59.5	Services
Poland [1]								**Pologne** [1]
Agriculture	14.6	5.6	3.3	2.9	2.9	2.5	2.7	Agriculture
Industry	51.4	37.4	32.8	33.2	33.2	34.1	33.7	Industrie
Services	34.0	57.0	63.9	63.9	63.9	63.4	63.6	Services
Portugal [1]								**Portugal** [1]
Agriculture	13.3	5.4	2.6	2.2	2.3	2.4	2.2	Agriculture
Industry	26.8	28.2	24.6	22.6	21.6	22.4	22.2	Industrie
Services	59.9	66.4	72.7	75.2	76.0	75.3	75.6	Services
Puerto Rico [4]								**Porto Rico** [4]
Agriculture	2.5	1.0	0.6	0.8	0.8	0.8	0.8	Agriculture
Industry	45.3	47.6	47.3	50.7	50.0	50.5	50.4	Industrie
Services	52.2	51.4	52.1	48.4	49.1	48.7	48.8	Services
Qatar [1]								**Qatar** [1]
Agriculture	1.0	1.0	0.1	0.1	0.1	0.2	0.2	Agriculture
Industry	57.8	53.0	74.6	67.5	67.9	56.4	49.7	Industrie
Services	41.3	46.0	25.3	32.4	32.0	43.5	50.1	Services
Republic of Korea [1]								**République de Corée** [1]
Agriculture	13.0	5.9	3.1	2.5	2.3	2.3	2.2	Agriculture
Industry	37.2	39.5	37.5	38.3	38.1	38.3	38.6	Industrie
Services	49.7	54.6	59.4	59.3	59.6	59.4	59.2	Services
Republic of Moldova								**République de Moldova**
Agriculture	...	32.2	19.1	14.1	15.1	13.9	14.0	Agriculture
Industry	...	31.3	22.3	20.0	21.6	21.4	20.3	Industrie
Services	...	36.5	58.6	65.9	63.2	64.7	65.7	Services
Romania [1]								**Roumanie** [1]
Agriculture	15.5	19.2	9.5	6.3	5.3	4.7	4.3	Agriculture
Industry	54.0	38.4	36.0	41.3	35.6	33.7	32.4	Industrie
Services	30.4	42.5	54.5	52.4	59.0	61.6	63.3	Services
Russian Federation								**Fédération de Russie**
Agriculture	...	7.2	5.0	3.9	4.1	4.6	4.7	Agriculture
Industry	...	39.3	38.1	34.7	32.1	32.8	32.4	Industrie
Services	...	53.5	57.0	61.4	63.9	62.7	62.8	Services
Rwanda [1]								**Rwanda** [1]
Agriculture	53.8	44.5	39.3	30.2	30.9	30.2	31.5	Agriculture
Industry	15.7	12.4	13.8	15.8	18.5	18.3	17.6	Industrie
Services	30.5	43.1	46.9	53.9	50.6	51.6	50.8	Services
Saint Kitts and Nevis								**Saint-Kitts-et-Nevis**
Agriculture	5.7	3.3	1.9	1.6	1.4	1.2	1.1	Agriculture
Industry	19.1	24.0	25.4	28.1	27.2	28.1	28.0	Industrie
Services	75.2	72.6	72.6	70.3	71.4	70.7	70.9	Services
Saint Lucia								**Sainte-Lucie**
Agriculture	12.0	7.5	3.5	2.9	2.6	2.7	3.0	Agriculture
Industry	16.0	16.2	18.7	15.5	12.6	12.9	13.5	Industrie
Services	72.1	76.3	77.8	81.6	84.7	84.4	83.5	Services
Saint Vincent & Grenadines								**Saint-Vincent-Grenadines**
Agriculture	15.1	11.2	6.2	7.1	7.7	7.3	8.2	Agriculture
Industry	19.6	20.9	18.6	19.2	17.2	18.0	17.4	Industrie
Services	65.3	67.9	75.1	73.7	75.1	74.7	74.4	Services

14 Gross value added by kind of economic activity *(continued)*
Percentage distribution, current prices

Valeur ajoutée brute par type d'activité économique *(suite)*
Répartition en pourcentage, aux prix courants

Country or area &	1985	1995	2005	2010	2014	2015	2016	Pays ou zone &
Samoa [4]								**Samoa** [4]
Agriculture	22.4	20.1	12.3	9.1	9.2	9.3	10.4	Agriculture
Industry	27.3	27.1	30.6	25.8	25.0	24.2	22.7	Industrie
Services	50.3	52.7	57.2	65.1	65.8	66.6	66.9	Services
San Marino [1]								**Saint-Marin** [1]
Agriculture	~0.0	~0.0	~0.0	~0.0	~0.0	~0.0	~0.0	Agriculture
Industry	40.9	40.9	38.2	35.4	32.8	34.4	34.8	Industrie
Services	59.0	59.1	61.8	64.6	67.2	65.6	65.1	Services
Sao Tome and Principe								**Sao Tomé-et-Principe**
Agriculture	27.6	26.4	18.3	11.8	11.6	12.2	11.5	Agriculture
Industry	17.9	19.6	14.9	18.2	17.3	14.6	16.7	Industrie
Services	54.5	53.9	66.8	70.1	71.1	73.2	71.9	Services
Saudi Arabia [1]								**Arabie saoudite** [1]
Agriculture	3.6	5.9	3.2	2.6	2.2	2.6	2.7	Agriculture
Industry	41.2	48.9	61.8	58.2	57.2	45.1	43.1	Industrie
Services	55.2	45.3	35.0	39.1	40.6	52.2	54.2	Services
Senegal								**Sénégal**
Agriculture	18.1	19.4	16.8	17.5	15.4	16.9	17.1	Agriculture
Industry	22.2	24.7	23.6	23.4	23.9	23.7	23.4	Industrie
Services	59.6	55.9	59.6	59.2	60.7	59.4	59.6	Services
Serbia [1]								**Serbie** [1]
Agriculture	...	20.9	12.0[20]	10.2[20]	9.3[20]	8.2[20]	7.9[20]	Agriculture
Industry	...	35.5	29.3[20]	28.4[20]	30.2[20]	31.4[20]	31.3[20]	Industrie
Services	...	43.6	58.7[20]	61.4[20]	60.5[20]	60.5[20]	60.8[20]	Services
Seychelles								**Seychelles**
Agriculture	6.7	5.9	3.8[1]	2.7[1]	2.8[1]	2.4[1]	2.0[1]	Agriculture
Industry	9.2	13.5	19.4[1]	16.5[1]	14.5[1]	14.0[1]	12.6[1]	Industrie
Services	84.1	80.6	76.8[1]	80.8[1]	82.6[1]	83.6[1]	85.4[1]	Services
Sierra Leone								**Sierra Leone**
Agriculture	41.0	48.1	51.0	55.2	53.3	60.4	59.9	Agriculture
Industry	20.4	9.1	11.6	8.1	16.1	4.7	5.8	Industrie
Services	38.7	42.8	37.4	36.7	30.7	34.9	34.3	Services
Singapore [1]								**Singapour** [1]
Agriculture [2]	1.0	0.2	0.1	~0.0	~0.0	~0.0	~0.0	Agriculture [2]
Industry [3]	33.4	33.8	32.4	27.6	25.6	26.1	26.1	Industrie [3]
Services	65.6	66.1	67.6	72.3	74.4	73.8	73.8	Services
Sint Maarten (Dutch part)								**St-Martin (partie néerland.)**
Agriculture	...	...	0.3	0.1	0.1	0.1	0.1	Agriculture
Industry	...	...	16.4	13.4	11.6	9.8	9.2	Industrie
Services	...	...	83.3	86.5	88.3	90.1	90.7	Services
Slovakia [1]								**Slovaquie** [1]
Agriculture	...	5.6	3.6	2.8	4.5	3.8	3.7	Agriculture
Industry	...	36.8	36.1	35.2	34.6	34.5	34.8	Industrie
Services	...	57.5	60.3	62.0	61.0	61.7	61.5	Services
Slovenia [1]								**Slovénie** [1]
Agriculture	...	4.3	2.6	2.0	2.3	2.3	2.2	Agriculture
Industry	...	34.7	34.1	30.6	32.8	32.6	32.3	Industrie
Services	...	61.0	63.3	67.4	64.8	65.1	65.5	Services
Solomon Islands								**Îles Salomon**
Agriculture	50.4	44.7	30.4	28.7	26.6	27.1	26.9	Agriculture
Industry	8.3	14.4	7.5	13.3	15.2	15.3	15.2	Industrie
Services	41.3	41.0	62.1	57.9	58.2	57.6	57.9	Services
Somalia								**Somalie**
Agriculture	66.1	60.1	60.1	60.2	60.2	60.2	60.2	Agriculture
Industry	7.6	7.3	7.4	7.4	7.4	7.4	7.4	Industrie
Services	26.3	32.6	32.6	32.5	32.5	32.5	32.5	Services
South Africa								**Afrique du Sud**
Agriculture	5.1	3.8	2.7	2.6	2.4	2.3	2.4	Agriculture
Industry	42.8	33.9	30.3	30.2	29.6	29.2	28.9	Industrie
Services	52.1	62.4	67.1	67.2	68.0	68.5	68.6	Services
South Sudan								**Soudan du sud**
Agriculture	...	...	...	5.1	4.9	3.9	4.1	Agriculture
Industry	...	...	...	55.4	55.1	43.3	39.8	Industrie
Services	...	...	...	39.4	40.0	52.8	56.1	Services

14 Gross value added by kind of economic activity *(continued)*
Percentage distribution, current prices

Valeur ajoutée brute par type d'activité économique *(suite)*
Répartition en pourcentage, aux prix courants

Country or area &	1985	1995	2005	2010	2014	2015	2016	Pays ou zone &
Spain [1]								**Espagne** [1]
Agriculture	5.7	4.2	3.0	2.6	2.7	2.8	2.8	Agriculture
Industry	34.9	30.7	30.4	26.0	23.2	23.6	23.5	Industrie
Services	59.4	65.1	66.5	71.4	74.1	73.6	73.8	Services
Sri Lanka [1]								**Sri Lanka** [1]
Agriculture	22.3	16.6	8.8	9.5	8.6	8.8	8.2	Agriculture
Industry	31.9	32.8	31.0	29.7	30.4	29.5	29.6	Industrie
Services	45.8	50.6	60.1	60.9	61.1	61.7	62.2	Services
State of Palestine [1]								**État de Palestine** [1]
Agriculture	13.2	12.6	5.8	6.4	4.4	4.1	4.4	Agriculture
Industry	30.7	31.6	25.8	23.3	22.7	21.8	22.5	Industrie
Services	56.1	55.8	68.3	70.2	72.9	74.0	73.1	Services
Sudan								**Soudan**
Agriculture	...	...	...	42.8	32.1	32.4	31.7	Agriculture
Industry	...	...	...	13.9	21.3	20.1	20.8	Industrie
Services	...	...	...	43.4	46.6	47.6	47.6	Services
Sudan [former]								**Soudan [anc.]**
Agriculture	36.7	37.1	34.5	34.6	...	...	...	Agriculture
Industry	13.2	9.9	21.7	22.9	...	...	...	Industrie
Services	50.1	53.0	43.7	42.5	...	...	...	Services
Suriname								**Suriname**
Agriculture	8.6[13]	29.9	11.3	10.2	10.0	9.9	9.7	Agriculture
Industry	28.5[13]	27.5	37.4	37.9	32.7	27.9	31.8	Industrie
Services	62.9[13]	42.6	51.3	51.9	57.3	62.2	58.4	Services
Sweden [1]								**Suède** [1]
Agriculture	4.5	2.8	1.1	1.6	1.3	1.4	1.3	Agriculture
Industry	33.7	31.3	29.7	28.9	25.7	24.5	24.5	Industrie
Services	61.9	65.9	69.2	69.4	72.9	74.2	74.2	Services
Switzerland [1]								**Suisse** [1]
Agriculture	2.5	1.6	0.9	0.7	0.7	0.7	0.7	Agriculture
Industry	32.5	30.1	27.0	26.6	26.0	25.9	25.8	Industrie
Services	65.0	68.4	72.1	72.7	73.2	73.4	73.5	Services
Syrian Arab Republic [17]								**République arabe syrienne** [17]
Agriculture	21.0	28.2	20.3	19.7	20.6	20.7	20.5	Agriculture
Industry	21.9	18.1	31.2	30.7	30.2	30.0	30.2	Industrie
Services	57.1	53.7	48.5	49.6	49.2	49.3	49.3	Services
Tajikistan								**Tadjikistan**
Agriculture	...	31.6	23.8	21.8	26.8	24.7	23.3	Agriculture
Industry	...	48.4	30.7	27.9	25.5	27.5	29.6	Industrie
Services	...	20.0	45.6	50.3	47.6	47.8	47.1	Services
Thailand [4]								**Thaïlande** [4]
Agriculture	15.8	9.1	9.2	10.5	10.1	8.7	8.3	Agriculture
Industry	31.8	37.6	38.6	40.0	36.9	36.4	35.8	Industrie
Services	52.3	53.3	52.2	49.5	53.0	54.9	55.8	Services
TFYR of Macedonia [1]								**ex-R.Y. de Macédoine** [1]
Agriculture	...	12.5	11.3	11.7	11.7	11.1	10.5	Agriculture
Industry	...	24.7	23.7	24.4	26.3	27.4	28.4	Industrie
Services	...	62.8	64.9	63.9	62.0	61.5	61.1	Services
Timor-Leste								**Timor-Leste**
Agriculture	...	20.0	7.3[1]	4.8[1]	7.0[1]	9.2[1]	7.0[1]	Agriculture
Industry	...	49.3	76.7[1]	79.9[1]	69.8[1]	57.8[1]	69.2[1]	Industrie
Services	...	30.7	16.0[1]	15.3[1]	23.2[1]	33.1[1]	23.8[1]	Services
Togo								**Togo**
Agriculture	29.2	32.7	32.9	33.8	29.1	28.2	28.7	Agriculture
Industry	18.1	20.0	15.9	16.0	18.3	18.0	17.3	Industrie
Services	52.7	47.2	51.2	50.3	52.6	53.8	54.0	Services
Tonga								**Tonga**
Agriculture	37.8	22.1	20.2	18.2	19.4	19.9	19.3	Agriculture
Industry	14.9	22.0	19.1	19.9	18.3	19.1	19.4	Industrie
Services	47.3	55.9	60.6	61.8	62.3	60.9	61.3	Services
Trinidad and Tobago								**Trinité-et-Tobago**
Agriculture	2.9	1.9	0.5	0.4	0.3	0.4	0.4	Agriculture
Industry	42.5	41.7	56.7	51.3	46.9	42.6	37.8	Industrie
Services	54.6	56.3	42.8	48.3	52.8	57.0	61.8	Services

14 Gross value added by kind of economic activity *(continued)*
Percentage distribution, current prices

Valeur ajoutée brute par type d'activité économique *(suite)*
Répartition en pourcentage, aux prix courants

Country or area &	1985	1995	2005	2010	2014	2015	2016	Pays ou zone &
Tunisia [13]								**Tunisie** [13]
Agriculture	14.4	10.5	10.0	8.1	9.5	10.3	9.8	Agriculture
Industry	34.7	29.6	28.8	31.1	28.8	27.8	26.0	Industrie
Services	50.8	59.9	61.3	60.8	61.6	62.0	64.2	Services
Turkey [1]								**Turquie** [1]
Agriculture	16.2	12.4	10.6	10.3	7.5	7.8	7.0	Agriculture
Industry	34.1	38.3	29.0	28.0	31.9	31.7	32.0	Industrie
Services	49.7	49.3	60.4	61.8	60.7	60.5	61.0	Services
Turkmenistan								**Turkménistan**
Agriculture	...	16.9	18.8	14.5	13.3	13.4	13.4	Agriculture
Industry	...	65.3	37.6	48.4	51.3	51.0	51.0	Industrie
Services	...	17.9	43.6	37.0	35.4	35.6	35.6	Services
Turks and Caicos Islands								**Îles Turques-et-Caïques**
Agriculture	1.3	1.3	1.2	0.6	0.6	0.6	0.6	Agriculture
Industry	16.3	16.4	19.7	12.4	11.0	10.4	10.5	Industrie
Services	82.4	82.3	79.1	86.9	88.4	89.0	88.9	Services
Tuvalu								**Tuvalu**
Agriculture	10.8	24.0	22.2	27.6	23.1	21.1	24.3	Agriculture
Industry	13.5	14.0	8.3	4.7	7.8	13.4	8.2	Industrie
Services	75.6	62.0	69.4	67.7	69.1	65.5	67.5	Services
Uganda [1]								**Ouganda** [1]
Agriculture	50.2	40.2	28.6	26.1	26.9	25.7	25.5	Agriculture
Industry	9.5	17.0	22.2	20.4	21.7	22.2	22.7	Industrie
Services	40.3	42.8	49.1	53.5	51.4	52.1	51.8	Services
Ukraine [1]								**Ukraine** [1]
Agriculture	...	14.5	10.0	8.4[21]	11.7[21]	14.2[21]	13.7[21]	Agriculture
Industry	...	41.8	34.1	29.3[21]	26.2[21]	25.6[21]	27.1[21]	Industrie
Services	...	43.7	55.8	62.3[21]	62.2[21]	60.2[21]	59.2[21]	Services
United Arab Emirates [4]								**Émirats arabes unis** [4]
Agriculture	0.9	1.6	1.3	0.8	0.6	0.7	0.8	Agriculture
Industry	60.8	47.5	54.0	52.5	52.8	43.9	40.2	Industrie
Services	38.4	50.9	44.7	46.7	46.6	55.3	59.0	Services
United Kingdom [1]								**Royaume-Uni** [1]
Agriculture	1.3	1.4	0.6	0.7	0.7	0.7	0.6	Agriculture
Industry	33.4	27.5	21.9	20.0	20.0	20.0	20.2	Industrie
Services	65.3	71.1	77.5	79.3	79.3	79.3	79.2	Services
United Rep. of Tanzania [22]								**Rép.-Unie de Tanzanie** [22]
Agriculture	27.6	34.2[1]	30.1[1]	31.7[1]	31.0[1]	31.1[1]	31.2[1]	Agriculture
Industry	13.0	16.7[1]	20.8[1]	21.5[1]	25.0[1]	26.1[1]	27.0[1]	Industrie
Services	59.4	49.2[1]	49.1[1]	46.8[1]	44.0[1]	42.9[1]	41.9[1]	Services
Zanzibar [1]								**Zanzibar** [1]
Agriculture	...	21.3	23.0	32.5	30.7	28.3	28.4	Agriculture
Industry	...	22.5	17.5	19.2	18.6	19.8	20.5	Industrie
Services	...	56.2	59.5	48.3	50.7	51.9	51.1	Services
United States of America [1,17]								**États-Unis d'Amérique** [1,17]
Agriculture	1.6	1.2	1.0	1.1	1.2	1.0	1.0	Agriculture
Industry	28.4	24.3	21.5	20.2	20.6	19.8	19.2	Industrie
Services	70.0	74.5	77.5	78.8	78.2	79.2	79.9	Services
Uruguay								**Uruguay**
Agriculture	12.5	8.1	9.8	8.0	7.4	6.7	6.6	Agriculture
Industry	30.8	25.9	26.6	27.3	27.3	28.0	27.8	Industrie
Services	56.7	66.0	63.6	64.7	65.3	65.3	65.6	Services
Uzbekistan								**Ouzbékistan**
Agriculture	...	31.4	29.5	19.8	18.9	18.3	17.6	Agriculture
Industry	...	30.9	29.1	33.3	32.6	33.0	32.9	Industrie
Services	...	37.7	41.4	46.9	48.5	48.8	49.5	Services
Vanuatu [1]								**Vanuatu** [1]
Agriculture	32.6	30.5	24.1	21.9	26.8	27.3	27.0	Agriculture
Industry	5.9	9.1	8.5	13.0	8.7	11.7	9.6	Industrie
Services	61.5	60.4	67.4	65.0	64.5	61.0	63.5	Services
Venezuela (Boliv. Rep. of)								**Venezuela (Rép. boliv. du)**
Agriculture	6.4	5.9	4.0	5.7	5.4	6.3	5.6	Agriculture
Industry	51.9	47.1	56.9	51.0	39.6	30.5	39.2	Industrie
Services	41.7	47.0	39.2	43.4	55.0	63.2	55.3	Services

14 Gross value added by kind of economic activity *(continued)*

Percentage distribution, current prices

Valeur ajoutée brute par type d'activité économique *(suite)*

Répartition en pourcentage, aux prix courants

Country or area &	1985	1995	2005	2010	2014	2015	2016	Pays ou zone &
Viet Nam [1]								**Viet Nam** [1]
Agriculture	39.0[4]	24.5[4]	19.3[4]	21.0	19.7	18.9	18.1	Agriculture
Industry	21.4[4]	26.1[4]	38.1[4]	36.7	36.9	37.0	36.4	Industrie
Services	39.6[4]	49.4[4]	42.6[4]	42.2	43.4	44.2	45.5	Services
Yemen								**Yémen**
Agriculture	...	17.3	9.6	12.1	13.9	17.4	15.4	Agriculture
Industry	...	27.4	43.8	34.4	36.1	20.6	31.0	Industrie
Services	...	55.3	46.5	53.4	50.0	62.0	53.6	Services
Zambia								**Zambie**
Agriculture	13.3	15.1	15.5	10.0[1]	7.3[1]	5.3[1]	5.1[1]	Agriculture
Industry	50.8	36.8	28.6	34.1[1]	35.3[1]	35.3[1]	35.8[1]	Industrie
Services	35.9	48.1	55.9	55.9[1]	57.4[1]	59.4[1]	59.2[1]	Services
Zimbabwe								**Zimbabwe**
Agriculture	20.8	14.0	12.3	13.4	12.3	11.8	11.2	Agriculture
Industry	27.8	28.8	41.9	28.4	25.8	24.5	24.3	Industrie
Services	51.4	57.2	45.9	58.1	62.0	63.7	64.5	Services

Source:

United Nations Statistics Division, New York, National Accounts Statistics: Analysis of Main Aggregates (AMA) database, last accessed February 2018.

& Table is in ISIC Rev. 3 unless otherwise indicated.

1 Data classified according to ISIC Rev. 4.
2 Including mining and quarrying.
3 Excluding mining and quarrying.
4 At producers' prices.
5 Data compiled in accordance with the System of National Accounts 1968 (1968 SNA).
6 For statistical purposes, the data for China do not include those for the Hong Kong Special Administrative Region (Hong Kong SAR), Macao Special Administrative Region (Macao SAR) and Taiwan Province of China.
7 Excluding hunting and forestry.
8 Includes waste management.
9 Excluding waste management.
10 Excluding northern Cyprus.
11 Excludes hunting.
12 Excludes gas.
13 At factor cost.
14 Including French Guiana, Guadeloupe, Martinique and Réunion.
15 Agricultural services and related activities such as cotton ginning and pressing are included in Industry.
16 Distribution of petroleum products is included in Services.
17 Including taxes less subsidies on production and imports.
18 Including Western Sahara.
19 Does not incorporate value added generated by binational hydroelectric plants.
20 Excluding Kosovo and Metohija.
21 Excludes the temporarily occupied territory of the Autonomous Republic of Crimea and Sevastopol.
22 Tanzania mainland only, excluding Zanzibar.

Source:

Organisation des Nations Unies, Division de statistique, New York, base de données des statistiques des comptes nationaux : Analyse des principaux agrégats, denier accès février 2018.

& Sauf indication contraire la classification utilisée dans ce tableau est la CITI Rev. 3.

1 Classifiées selon la CITI, Rév. 4.
2 Y compris les industries extractives.
3 Non compris les industries extractives.
4 Aux prix à la production.
5 Données compilées selon le Système de comptabilité nationale de 1968 (SCN 1968).
6 Pour la présentation des statistiques, les données pour la Chine ne comprennent pas la région administrative spéciale de Hong Kong (Hong Kong RAS), la région administrative spéciale de Macao (Macao RAS) et la province chinoise de Taïwan.
7 Non compris la chasse et la sylviculture.
8 Y compris la gestion des déchets.
9 Gestion des déchets non-compris.
10 Chypre du nord non compris.
11 Non compris la chasse.
12 Non compris le gaz.
13 Au coût des facteurs.
14 Y compris Guadeloupe, Guyane française, Martinique et Réunion.
15 Les services agricoles et les activités connexes (par exemple l'égrenage du coton, tressage) figurent sous « Industrie».
16 La distribution du gaz est inclue dans la catégorie Services.
17 Y compris les impôts moins les subventions sur la production et les importations.
18 Y compris les données de Sahara occidental.
19 Ne comprend pas la valeur ajoutée produite par les centrales hydroélectriques binationales.
20 Non compris Kosovo et Metohija.
21 Excluent le territoire temporairement occupé de la République autonome de Crimée et de Sébastopol.
22 Tanzanie continentale seulement, Zanzibar non compris.

15 Balance of payments summary

Millions of US dollars

Résumé de la balance des paiements

Millions de dollars É.-U.

Country or area&	1985	1995	2005	2010	2015	2016	2017	Pays ou zone&
Afghanistan								**Afghanistan**
Current account	-243	...	...	-1 505	-4 689	-3 648	-4 683	Compte des transac. courantes
Capital account	0	...	...	2 996	1 630	1 654	1 479	Compte de capital
Financial account	-75	...	...	1 061	-317	524	442	Compte financier
Albania								**Albanie**
Current account	-36	-12	-571	-1 356	-980	-900	-909	Compte des transac. courantes
Capital account	0	389	123	113	139	72	139	Compte de capital
Financial account	-30	432	-245	-797	-681	-686	-1 055	Compte financier
Algeria								**Algérie**
Current account	1 015	...	21 180	# 12 220	-27 229	-26 179	...	Compte des transac. courantes
Capital account	0	...	-3	# 4	~0	1	...	Compte de capital
Financial account	1 141	...	20 988	# 10 921	-27 672	-26 320	...	Compte financier
Angola								**Angola**
Current account	195	-295	5 138	7 506	-10 273	-3 071	...	Compte des transac. courantes
Capital account	0	0	8	1	6	1	...	Compte de capital
Financial account	-460	-314	4 571	7 219	-9 954	-5 628	...	Compte financier
Anguilla								**Anguilla**
Current account	...	-10	-52	-51	-60	-99	...	Compte des transac. courantes
Capital account	...	1	2	4	1	~0	...	Compte de capital
Financial account	...	4	-42	-35	-39	-80	...	Compte financier
Antigua and Barbuda								**Antigua-et-Barbuda**
Current account	-23	-1	-171	-167	93	2	...	Compte des transac. courantes
Capital account	0	4	211	17	38	23	...	Compte de capital
Financial account	-23	24	32	-158	114	6	...	Compte financier
Argentina								**Argentine**
Current account	-952	-5 118	5 274	-1 623	-17 622	-14 693	-30 792	Compte des transac. courantes
Capital account	0	14	89	78	52	371	139	Compte de capital
Financial account	-1 484	-7 777	5 699	-3 803	-18 497	-14 483	-30 394	Compte financier
Armenia								**Arménie**
Current account	...	-221	-124	-1 261	-272	-238	-400	Compte des transac. courantes
Capital account	...	8	84	99	65	35	46	Compte de capital
Financial account	...	-198	-203	-1 318	-357	-432	-467	Compte financier
Aruba								**Aruba**
Current account	...	-~0	105	-460	111	141	...	Compte des transac. courantes
Capital account	...	0	16	4	0	8	...	Compte de capital
Financial account	...	1	148	-446	112	133	...	Compte financier
Australia								**Australie**
Current account	...	# -18 669	-43 343	-44 714	-58 065	-37 026	-32 653	Compte des transac. courantes
Capital account	...	# -300	-121	-287	-457	-605	-395	Compte de capital
Financial account	...	# -18 866	-42 174	-44 105	-54 941	-36 780	-33 652	Compte financier
Austria								**Autriche**
Current account	...	...	6 245	11 478	7 388	8 291	7 709	Compte des transac. courantes
Capital account	...	...	-84	268	-1 914	-659	-311	Compte de capital
Financial account	...	...	168	4 758	4 806	11 059	10 183	Compte financier
Azerbaijan								**Azerbaïdjan**
Current account	...	-401	167	15 040	-222	-1 363	1 685	Compte des transac. courantes
Capital account	...	-2	-~0	0	-44	-40	100	Compte de capital
Financial account	...	-342	83	14 065	-2 352	2 222	2 173	Compte financier
Bahamas								**Bahamas**
Current account	-3	-146	-701	-814	-1 203	-1 106	...	Compte des transac. courantes
Financial account	30	-107	-910	-1 097	-347	58	...	Compte financier
Bahrain								**Bahreïn**
Current account	39	237	1 474	770	# -752	-1 493	-1 600	Compte des transac. courantes
Capital account	0	157	50	50	# 253	874	604	Compte de capital
Financial account	834	1 896	1 674	927	# -1 118	1 693	77	Compte financier
Bangladesh								**Bangladesh**
Current account	-455	-824	# 508	2 109	2 580	928	-6 365	Compte des transac. courantes
Capital account	0	0	# 263	603	442	427	298	Compte de capital
Financial account	-523	-691	# 103	-1 745	2 272	131	-7 519	Compte financier
Barbados								**Barbade**
Current account	60	10	-466	-218	...	...	...	Compte des transac. courantes
Financial account	23	69	-395	-284	...	...	...	Compte financier

Country or area&	1985	1995	2005	2010	2015	2016	2017	Pays ou zone&
Belarus								**Bélarus**
Current account	...	-458	459	-8 280	-1 831	-1 669	-931	Compte des transac. courantes
Capital account	...	7	...	...	5	7	2	Compte de capital
Financial account	...	-282	585	-7 578	-1 322	-746	-396	Compte financier
Belgium								**Belgique**
Current account	...	...	7 703	7 977	-690	487	-790	Compte des transac. courantes
Capital account	...	...	-922	-1 142	122	506	420	Compte de capital
Financial account	...	...	9 221	6 567	1 944	-225	-40	Compte financier
Belize								**Belize**
Current account	9	-17	-151	-46	-175	-163	-131	Compte des transac. courantes
Capital account	0	0	3	5	9	33	16	Compte de capital
Financial account	-7	5	-156	-22	-148	-107	-119	Compte financier
Benin								**Bénin**
Current account	-39	-167	-226	-530	-744	-809	...	Compte des transac. courantes
Capital account	0	88	102	122	125	138	...	Compte de capital
Financial account	-23	-79	-95	-375	-612	-670	...	Compte financier
Bermuda								**Bermudes**
Current account	...	...	...	696	886	766	...	Compte des transac. courantes
Financial account	...	...	...	714	782	694	...	Compte financier
Bhutan								**Bhoutan**
Current account	...	...	...	-323	-572	-618	-546	Compte des transac. courantes
Capital account	...	...	...	150	226	192	186	Compte de capital
Financial account	...	...	...	-105	-367	-446	-364	Compte financier
Bolivia (Plurin. State of)								**Bolivie (État plurin. de)**
Current account	-285	-303	622	874	-1 936	-1 932	-2 377	Compte des transac. courantes
Capital account	0	0	0	0	5	5	5	Compte de capital
Financial account	-92	-413	257	64	-2 822	-2 257	-2 758	Compte financier
Bosnia and Herzegovina								**Bosnie-Herzégovine**
Current account	...	...	-1 844	-1 031	-882	-821	-875	Compte des transac. courantes
Capital account	...	...	276	264	204	168	173	Compte de capital
Financial account	...	...	-1 336	-647	-664	-518	-593	Compte financier
Botswana								**Botswana**
Current account	82	300	1 598	# -533	813	2 145	2 149	Compte des transac. courantes
Capital account	0	12	0	# 0	0	0	0	Compte de capital
Financial account	131	240	2 795	# -821	873	-131	672	Compte financier
Brazil								**Brésil**
Current account	-280	-18 136	13 985	# -75 760	-59 434	-23 546	-9 762	Compte des transac. courantes
Capital account	0	0	52	# 242	461	274	379	Compte de capital
Financial account	-803	-16 337	14 423	# -76 903	-55 145	-16 424	-6 136	Compte financier
Brunei Darussalam								**Brunéi Darussalam**
Current account	...	...	4 033	# 5 016	2 157	1 766	...	Compte des transac. courantes
Capital account	...	...	-8	...	0	0	...	Compte de capital
Financial account	...	...	19	# 4 918	4 508	6 551	...	Compte financier
Bulgaria								**Bulgarie**
Current account	-136	-26	-3 347	# -965	-21	1 243	2 628	Compte des transac. courantes
Capital account	0	0	290	# 398	1 557	1 187	599	Compte de capital
Financial account	463	118	-4 277	# 861	3 279	4 524	2 617	Compte financier
Burkina Faso								**Burkina Faso**
Current account	...	...	-634	-181	-895	-780	...	Compte des transac. courantes
Capital account	...	...	209	180	260	253	...	Compte de capital
Financial account	...	...	-431	16	-626	-534	...	Compte financier
Burundi								**Burundi**
Current account	-41	10	# -6	-301	-373	-355	...	Compte des transac. courantes
Capital account	0	0	# 32	78	56	70	...	Compte de capital
Financial account	-50	16	# -58	-226	-329	-257	...	Compte financier
Cabo Verde								**Cabo Verde**
Current account	-9	-62	-41	-223	-51	-44	-125	Compte des transac. courantes
Capital account	0	21	21	38	19	13	16	Compte de capital
Financial account	-4	-76	-18	-270	-81	-42	-76	Compte financier
Cambodia								**Cambodge**
Current account	...	-186	-307	# -538	-1 692	-1 775	...	Compte des transac. courantes
Capital account	...	92	102	# 331	172	160	...	Compte de capital
Financial account	...	-82	-238	# -373	-1 562	-1 482	...	Compte financier

Balance of payments summary *(continued)*
Millions of US dollars

Résumé de la balance des paiements *(suite)*
Millions de dollars É.-U.

Country or area&	1985	1995	2005	2010	2015	2016	2017	Pays ou zone&
Cameroon								**Cameroun**
Current account	-562	90	-495	-856	-1 173	# -1 037	...	Compte des transac. courantes
Capital account	0	20	204	147	22	# 99	...	Compte de capital
Financial account	-453	-16	-319	-521	-1 125	# -922	...	Compte financier
Canada								**Canada**
Current account	-5 839	-5 061	21 931	-58 160	-56 188	-49 423	-48 800	Compte des transac. courantes
Capital account	-1	-433	-191	-121	-85	-68	-58	Compte de capital
Financial account	-9 987	-1 621	20 405	-58 299	-58 322	-51 482	-40 065	Compte financier
Central African Republic								**République centrafricaine**
Current account	-49	...	...	...	...	...	...	Compte des transac. courantes
Financial account	-56	...	...	...	...	...	...	Compte financier
Chad								**Tchad**
Current account	-87	...	...	...	...	...	...	Compte des transac. courantes
Financial account	-93	...	...	...	...	...	...	Compte financier
Chile								**Chili**
Current account	-1 413	-1 350	1 825	3 069	-5 511	-3 499	-4 146	Compte des transac. courantes
Capital account	0	0	41	6 240	675	7	67	Compte de capital
Financial account	-1 483	-1 218	919	8 480	-5 103	-2 639	-3 110	Compte financier
China								**Chine**
Current account	-11 417	1 618	# 132 378	237 810	304 164	202 203	164 887	Compte des transac. courantes
Capital account	0	0	# 4 102	4 630	316	-344	-94	Compte de capital
Financial account	-11 411	-16 205	# 159 727	185 631	91 521	-27 555	-57 086	Compte financier
China, Hong Kong SAR								**Chine, RAS de Hong Kong**
Current account	...	...	21 575	16 012	10 264	12 711	14 736	Compte des transac. courantes
Capital account	...	...	-74	-571	-28	-48	-83	Compte de capital
Financial account	...	...	19 369	10 867	16 568	12 972	19 769	Compte financier
China, Macao SAR								**Chine, RAS de Macao**
Current account	...	...	2 902	11 089	11 458	12 215	...	Compte des transac. courantes
Capital account	...	...	515	20	-3	-2	...	Compte de capital
Financial account	...	...	1 446	6 787	5 117	12 883	...	Compte financier
Colombia								**Colombie**
Current account	-1 809	-4 516	-1 891	-8 732	-18 586	-12 129	-10 359	Compte des transac. courantes
Financial account	-2 082	-4 564	-1 508	-9 344	-18 260	-12 670	-9 695	Compte financier
Comoros								**Comores**
Current account	-14	-19	-27	-39	...	...	...	Compte des transac. courantes
Capital account	0	0	15	71	...	...	...	Compte de capital
Financial account	-12	-21	-5	35	...	...	...	Compte financier
Congo								**Congo**
Current account	-161	-625	696	900	-4 627	...	...	Compte des transac. courantes
Capital account	0	45	11	2 667	70	...	...	Compte de capital
Financial account	-120	-635	737	3 314	-4 145	...	...	Compte financier
Costa Rica								**Costa Rica**
Current account	-126	-358	-860	-1 214	-1 921	-1 474	-1 717	Compte des transac. courantes
Capital account	0	0	15	54	31	87	41	Compte de capital
Financial account	17	-301	-1 158	-1 642	-2 611	-1 987	-2 131	Compte financier
Côte d'Ivoire								**Côte d'Ivoire**
Current account	...	...	40	465	-201	-414	...	Compte des transac. courantes
Capital account	...	...	185	1 178	264	187	...	Compte de capital
Financial account	...	...	167	1 590	11	-318	...	Compte financier
Croatia								**Croatie**
Current account	...	-1 442	-2 479	-894	2 492	1 390	2 363	Compte des transac. courantes
Capital account	...	0	64	77	345	574	266	Compte de capital
Financial account	...	-1 102	-3 749	-1 867	2 123	1 287	2 037	Compte financier
Curaçao								**Curaçao**
Current account	...	...	...	...	-519	-581	-690	Compte des transac. courantes
Capital account	...	...	...	...	~0	1	~0	Compte de capital
Financial account	...	...	...	...	-483	-529	-685	Compte financier
Cyprus								**Chypre**
Current account	-180	-205	-971	-2 906	-280	-965	-1 452	Compte des transac. courantes
Capital account	0	0	35	78	55	41	120	Compte de capital
Financial account	-142	-150	-719	-2 265	-308	-1 474	-440	Compte financier
Czechia								**Tchéquie**
Current account	...	-1 374	-2 810	-7 351	461	3 016	1 918	Compte des transac. courantes
Capital account	...	6	1 028	1 953	4 130	2 208	2 084	Compte de capital
Financial account	...	-771	-2 113	-6 445	7 080	4 739	4 612	Compte financier

15 Balance of payments summary *(continued)*
Millions of US dollars

Résumé de la balance des paiements *(suite)*
Millions de dollars É.-U.

Country or area&	1985	1995	2005	2010	2015	2016	2017	Pays ou zone&
Dem. Rep. of the Congo								**Rép. dém. du Congo**
Current account	...	...	-389	-2 174	-1 484	-1 334	...	Compte des transac. courantes
Capital account	...	...	-93	10 084	252	-47	...	Compte de capital
Financial account	...	...	-377	9 059	-1 543	-1 473	...	Compte financier
Denmark								**Danemark**
Current account	-2 767	1 855	# 11 007	21 051	26 441	22 458	25 798	Compte des transac. courantes
Capital account	0	...	# 404	84	-1 063	20	162	Compte de capital
Financial account	-3 071	2 929	# 9 060	-1 005	17 814	14 704	23 879	Compte financier
Djibouti								**Djibouti**
Current account	...	78	20	50	-302	-170	...	Compte des transac. courantes
Capital account	...	5	27	55	48	34	...	Compte de capital
Financial account	...	-5	1	-17	-319	-290	...	Compte financier
Dominica								**Dominique**
Current account	-6	-40	-76	-80	-10	5	...	Compte des transac. courantes
Capital account	0	22	15	30	55	136	...	Compte de capital
Financial account	-7	-34	-46	-54	31	131	...	Compte financier
Dominican Republic								**République dominicaine**
Current account	-108	-183	-473	# -4 024	-1 280	-815	-165	Compte des transac. courantes
Capital account	0	1	0	# 4	2 089	2	2	Compte de capital
Financial account	48	-107	-893	# -4 983	-737	-1 558	-1 098	Compte financier
Ecuador								**Équateur**
Current account	76	-1 000	474	-1 583	-2 111	1 442	-255	Compte des transac. courantes
Capital account	0	2 078	73	105	-49	-794	87	Compte de capital
Financial account	244	645	1 168	-1 581	-2 122	548	-186	Compte financier
Egypt								**Égypte**
Current account	-1 816	-254	2 103	-4 504	-17 243	-19 894	-9 336	Compte des transac. courantes
Capital account	0	0	-40	-39	-148	-103	-156	Compte de capital
Financial account	-1 231	18	-364	-6 688	-22 162	-28 943	-13 007	Compte financier
El Salvador								**El Salvador**
Current account	-29	-262	-622	-533	-748	-500	-501	Compte des transac. courantes
Capital account	...	...	94	232	65	70	85	Compte de capital
Financial account	-6	-290	-977	-264	-759	-779	-363	Compte financier
Equatorial Guinea								**Guinée équatoriale**
Current account	...	-123	...	...	...	...	...	Compte des transac. courantes
Capital account	...	53	...	...	...	...	...	Compte de capital
Financial account	...	-60	...	...	...	...	...	Compte financier
Eritrea								**Érythrée**
Current account	...	-31	...	...	...	...	...	Compte des transac. courantes
Financial account	...	-72	...	...	...	...	...	Compte financier
Estonia								**Estonie**
Current account	...	-158	-1 386	344	438	447	825	Compte des transac. courantes
Capital account	...	-1	103	681	470	249	247	Compte de capital
Financial account	...	-150	-1 135	1 098	1 049	427	1 152	Compte financier
Eswatini								**Eswatini**
Current account	-38	-30	-103	-388	1 056	640	...	Compte des transac. courantes
Capital account	0	-~0	-3	14	-2	~0	...	Compte de capital
Financial account	-27	49	-147	-318	775	588	...	Compte financier
Ethiopia								**Éthiopie**
Current account	106	39	-1 568	-425	-7 511	-8 269	...	Compte des transac. courantes
Capital account	0	11	0	0	...	...	...	Compte de capital
Financial account	-63	-72	-1 081	-3 355	-4 708	-4 933	...	Compte financier
Faroe Islands								**Îles Féroé**
Current account	...	...	31	144	...	...	...	Compte des transac. courantes
Fiji								**Fidji**
Current account	19	-113	# -206	-149	-154	-237	-315	Compte des transac. courantes
Capital account	0	116	# 3	3	3	4	4	Compte de capital
Financial account	-2	5	# -338	-157	-174	-209	-323	Compte financier
Finland								**Finlande**
Current account	-806	5 231	# 7 788	2 792	-1 715	-843	1 917	Compte des transac. courantes
Capital account	0	66	# 324	234	90	92	200	Compte de capital
Financial account	-849	3 913	# 3 787	4 364	-7 781	-25 206	-6 626	Compte financier
France								**France**
Current account	-35	10 840	-137	-22 034	-10 774	-21 124	-18 514	Compte des transac. courantes
Capital account	0	442	1 161	1 637	2 017	-29	1 296	Compte de capital
Financial account	256	8 230	-11 143	782	-14 147	-32 739	-58 677	Compte financier

Balance of payments summary *(continued)*
Millions of US dollars

Résumé de la balance des paiements *(suite)*
Millions de dollars É.-U.

Country or area&	1985	1995	2005	2010	2015	2016	2017	Pays ou zone&
French Polynesia								**Polynésie française**
Current account	…	…	9	-18	291	412	…	Compte des transac. courantes
Capital account	…	…	-1	-1	~0	-3	…	Compte de capital
Financial account	…	…	32	-119	315	374	…	Compte financier
Gabon								**Gabon**
Current account	-162	515	1 983	2 453	…	…	…	Compte des transac. courantes
Capital account	0	5	0	1	…	…	…	Compte de capital
Financial account	-225	287	1 568	1 121	…	…	…	Compte financier
Gambia								**Gambie**
Current account	8	-8	-43	17	-99	-96	…	Compte des transac. courantes
Capital account	0	0	1	38	19	7	…	Compte de capital
Financial account	-4	-22	-77	36	-16	~0	…	Compte financier
Georgia								**Géorgie**
Current account	…	…	-696	-1 199	-1 699	-1 848	-1 311	Compte des transac. courantes
Capital account	…	…	56	198	58	56	108	Compte de capital
Financial account	…	…	-613	-1 064	-1 766	-1 770	-1 268	Compte financier
Germany								**Allemagne**
Current account	17 994	-32 186	131 661	193 034	300 804	297 319	297 118	Compte des transac. courantes
Capital account	-741	-3 119	-2 998	1 617	623	3 798	-314	Compte de capital
Financial account	20 714	-37 207	120 502	123 738	264 946	284 328	311 294	Compte financier
Ghana								**Ghana**
Current account	-134	-144	-1 105	-2 747	-2 824	-2 832	-2 003	Compte des transac. courantes
Capital account	0	0	331	338	474	274	241	Compte de capital
Financial account	-71	-276	-710	-3 586	-2 732	-2 022	-1 777	Compte financier
Greece								**Grèce**
Current account	-3 276	-2 864	-18 233	-30 275	-459	-1 964	-1 331	Compte des transac. courantes
Capital account	…	…	2 563	2 776	2 192	1 130	1 042	Compte de capital
Financial account	-3 320	-3 185	-15 737	-28 117	2 999	-939	-947	Compte financier
Grenada								**Grenade**
Current account	3	-42	-193	-204	-38	-34	…	Compte des transac. courantes
Capital account	0	9	24	36	89	37	…	Compte de capital
Financial account	1	-1	-171	-141	59	9	…	Compte financier
Guatemala								**Guatemala**
Current account	-246	-572	-1 241	-563	-96	1 023	1 134	Compte des transac. courantes
Capital account	0	62	0	3	…	…	…	Compte de capital
Financial account	-203	-647	-443	-907	-567	332	720	Compte financier
Guinea								**Guinée**
Current account	…	-216	-160	-327	-1 020	-2 745	…	Compte des transac. courantes
Capital account	…	45	21	47	231	164	…	Compte de capital
Financial account	…	-137	-20	-241	544	-660	…	Compte financier
Guinea-Bissau								**Guinée-Bissau**
Current account	-76	-35	-10	-71	21	10	…	Compte des transac. courantes
Capital account	31	49	45	980	60	30	…	Compte de capital
Financial account	-55	3	30	907	68	27	…	Compte financier
Guyana								**Guyana**
Current account	-97	-135	-96	-246	# -39	128	…	Compte des transac. courantes
Capital account	0	11	52	65	# 70	70	…	Compte de capital
Financial account	-101	-113	-112	-317	# -127	167	…	Compte financier
Haiti								**Haïti**
Current account	-95	-87	7	-102	-271	-72	…	Compte des transac. courantes
Capital account	0	50	0	1 474	22	62	…	Compte de capital
Financial account	-48	88	18	1 738	-399	172	…	Compte financier
Honduras								**Honduras**
Current account	-220	-201	-304	-682	-978	-587	-380	Compte des transac. courantes
Capital account	0	17	848	48	34	11	45	Compte de capital
Financial account	-259	-139	367	-896	-1 075	-595	-677	Compte financier
Hungary								**Hongrie**
Current account	-455	# -1 577	-7 883	346	4 184	7 594	3 743	Compte des transac. courantes
Capital account	0	# 60	740	2 365	5 648	-48	1 686	Compte de capital
Financial account	-530	# 403	-10 073	1 380	7 260	4 242	2 505	Compte financier
Iceland								**Islande**
Current account	-115	# 13	-2 653	-881	895	1 595	879	Compte des transac. courantes
Capital account	0	# -4	-6	-11	-11	-12	-13	Compte de capital
Financial account	-168	# -33	-2 336	-680	895	1 824	698	Compte financier

15 Balance of payments summary *(continued)*
Millions of US dollars

Résumé de la balance des paiements *(suite)*
Millions de dollars É.-U.

Country or area&	1985	1995	2005	2010	2015	2016	2017	Pays ou zone&
India								**Inde**
Current account	-4 141	-5 563	-10 284	-54 516	-22 457	-12 114	-39 073	Compte des transac. courantes
Capital account	0	...	...	50	37	137	37	Compte de capital
Financial account	-3 641	-4 594	-10 730	-56 483	-23 593	-13 601	-37 491	Compte financier
Indonesia								**Indonésie**
Current account	-1 923	-6 431	278	# 5 144	-17 519	-16 952	-17 293	Compte des transac. courantes
Capital account	0	0	334	# 50	17	41	46	Compte de capital
Financial account	-1 272	-8 686	475	# 3 866	-17 941	-17 217	-18 249	Compte financier
Iran (Islamic Republic of)								**Iran (Rép. islamique d')**
Current account	-476	3 358	...	...	...	...	...	Compte des transac. courantes
Financial account	11	3 641	...	...	...	...	...	Compte financier
Iraq								**Iraq**
Current account	...	...	-3 335	6 488	4 121	3 843	...	Compte des transac. courantes
Capital account	...	...	20 489	25	-2	-1	...	Compte de capital
Financial account	...	...	17 604	-2 637	-19 162	-12 461	...	Compte financier
Ireland								**Irlande**
Current account	...	...	-7 150	2 319	31 670	14 349	42 719	Compte des transac. courantes
Capital account	...	...	418	-827	-1 449	-6 129	-29 429	Compte de capital
Financial account	...	...	724	-8 419	36 259	6 238	6 371	Compte financier
Israel								**Israël**
Current account	988	-4 790	4 540	8 372	# 15 359	11 879	10 392	Compte des transac. courantes
Capital account	151	285	253	1 175	# 2 120	2 174	324	Compte de capital
Financial account	22	-3 831	11 351	8 475	# 15 130	7 821	5 941	Compte financier
Italy								**Italie**
Current account	-4 088	25 096	-17 023	-73 018	27 519	47 656	54 333	Compte des transac. courantes
Capital account	222	1 721	1 301	69	4 260	-3 434	-933	Compte de capital
Financial account	-7 735	5 625	-39 697	-106 243	38 603	72 565	54 283	Compte financier
Jamaica								**Jamaïque**
Current account	-271	-99	-1 071	-934	-430	-103	...	Compte des transac. courantes
Capital account	0	21	~0	4	1 467	26	...	Compte de capital
Financial account	-285	-81	-1 080	-785	86	513	...	Compte financier
Japan								**Japon**
Current account	...	...	170 123	220 888	136 472	193 996	195 801	Compte des transac. courantes
Capital account	...	...	-4 878	-4 964	-2 253	-6 580	-2 563	Compte de capital
Financial account	...	...	148 988	244 200	180 933	261 706	157 397	Compte financier
Jordan								**Jordanie**
Current account	-260	-259	-2 271	# -1 882	-3 406	-3 688	-4 251	Compte des transac. courantes
Capital account	0	0	8	# ~0	113	75	42	Compte de capital
Financial account	-290	-401	-1 588	# -1 117	-2 617	-3 269	-2 827	Compte financier
Kazakhstan								**Kazakhstan**
Current account	...	-213	-1 036	1 386	-5 135	-8 874	-5 353	Compte des transac. courantes
Capital account	...	0	5	7 898	132	270	288	Compte de capital
Financial account	...	-864	350	15 338	-9 962	-8 706	-7 321	Compte financier
Kenya								**Kenya**
Current account	-115	-1 578	-252	-2 369	-3 928	-3 376	-4 755	Compte des transac. courantes
Capital account	0	124	103	240	262	206	184	Compte de capital
Financial account	-82	252	-394	-1 987	-4 199	-4 017	-4 743	Compte financier
Kiribati								**Kiribati**
Current account	-2	...	...	~0	79	36	...	Compte des transac. courantes
Capital account	7	...	...	13	16	12	...	Compte de capital
Financial account	~0	...	...	2	106	64	...	Compte financier
Kosovo								**Kosovo**
Current account	...	...	-308	-678	-547	-530	-449	Compte des transac. courantes
Capital account	...	...	20	28	28	15	-13	Compte de capital
Financial account	...	...	-67	-419	-342	-221	-349	Compte financier
Kuwait								**Koweït**
Current account	4 798	5 016	30 071	36 989	8 584	642	7 591	Compte des transac. courantes
Capital account	0	-194	710	2 096	-288	-646	-447	Compte de capital
Financial account	2 879	-298	33 381	46 187	11 542	-3 566	25 580	Compte financier
Kyrgyzstan								**Kirghizistan**
Current account	...	-235	-37	# -475	-1 052	-792	-347	Compte des transac. courantes
Capital account	...	2	43	# -11	79	113	132	Compte de capital
Financial account	...	-341	8	# -394	-769	-265	136	Compte financier
Lao People's Dem. Rep.								**Rép. dém. populaire lao**
Current account	-114	-237	-174	29	-2 277	-1 234	...	Compte des transac. courantes
Financial account	-75	-131	-168	-374	-2 969	-2 701	...	Compte financier

Balance of payments summary *(continued)*
Millions of US dollars

Résumé de la balance des paiements *(suite)*
Millions de dollars É.-U.

Country or area&	1985	1995	2005	2010	2015	2016	2017	Pays ou zone&
Latvia								**Lettonie**
Current account	...	-16	-1 988	494	-130	377	-246	Compte des transac. courantes
Capital account	...	...	211	471	748	275	240	Compte de capital
Financial account	...	-669	-2 073	1 428	-161	489	202	Compte financier
Lebanon								**Liban**
Current account	...	...	-2 748	-7 552	-8 646	-10 555	...	Compte des transac. courantes
Capital account	...	...	27	39	1 801	1 588	...	Compte de capital
Financial account	...	...	-3 329	-457	-9 218	-12 426	...	Compte financier
Lesotho								**Lesotho**
Current account	142	-165	# 166	-158	-78	-198	-166	Compte des transac. courantes
Capital account	8	296	# 26	108	37	49	44	Compte de capital
Financial account	170	254	# 178	-9	-126	-285	-53	Compte financier
Liberia								**Libéria**
Current account	1	...	-184	-415	-860	...	...	Compte des transac. courantes
Capital account	0	...	...	1 594	105	...	...	Compte de capital
Financial account	6	...	-223	1 877	-1 045	...	...	Compte financier
Libya								**Libye**
Current account	1 906	1 672	14 945	16 801	-9 346	-4 705	...	Compte des transac. courantes
Financial account	1 578	1 908	13 448	14 509	-8 999	-5 911	...	Compte financier
Lithuania								**Lituanie**
Current account	...	-614	-1 888	-488	-1 171	-490	418	Compte des transac. courantes
Capital account	...	-39	250	1 412	1 236	628	573	Compte de capital
Financial account	...	-366	-1 239	1 130	802	94	1 562	Compte financier
Luxembourg								**Luxembourg**
Current account	...	...	4 107	3 585	2 882	2 894	3 325	Compte des transac. courantes
Capital account	...	...	1 278	-263	-264	-235	-277	Compte de capital
Financial account	...	...	5 384	3 298	3 092	3 427	3 046	Compte financier
Madagascar								**Madagascar**
Current account	-184	-276	# -772	-964	-316	-38	...	Compte des transac. courantes
Capital account	0	40	# 287	178	130	265	...	Compte de capital
Financial account	-173	-132	# -233	-803	-299	362	...	Compte financier
Malawi								**Malawi**
Current account	-126	-78	-507	-969	-930	-912	-1 021	Compte des transac. courantes
Capital account	0	...	363	710	228	238	229	Compte de capital
Financial account	-21	-162	-109	-6	-838	-696	-664	Compte financier
Malaysia								**Malaisie**
Current account	-600	-8 644	19 980	# 25 644	9 068	7 133	9 450	Compte des transac. courantes
Capital account	0	0	0	# -34	-309	27	-6	Compte de capital
Financial account	-781	-9 405	13 425	# 5 925	70	1 329	2 959	Compte financier
Maldives								**Maldives**
Current account	-6	-18	-273	-196	-302	-1 032	-876	Compte des transac. courantes
Capital account	0	0	0	9	10	...	...	Compte de capital
Financial account	6	-50	-246	-71	-530	-769	-759	Compte financier
Mali								**Mali**
Current account	-210	-284	# -438	-1 190	...	...	...	Compte des transac. courantes
Capital account	81	130	# 206	252	...	...	...	Compte de capital
Financial account	-147	-167	# -261	-907	...	...	...	Compte financier
Malta								**Malte**
Current account	-26	-380	-418	-420	472	786	1 721	Compte des transac. courantes
Capital account	0	13	197	171	187	49	73	Compte de capital
Financial account	-42	-346	-137	-64	439	1 496	1 443	Compte financier
Marshall Islands								**Îles Marshall**
Current account	...	...	# -3	-14	-7	-16	...	Compte des transac. courantes
Capital account	...	...	# 6	19	8	11	...	Compte de capital
Financial account	...	...	# -4	19	29	32	...	Compte financier
Mauritania								**Mauritanie**
Current account	-116	22	...	...	-956	-707	# -709	Compte des transac. courantes
Capital account	0	0	...	...	31	8	# 11	Compte de capital
Financial account	-122	4	...	...	-1 058	-531	# -753	Compte financier
Mauritius								**Maurice**
Current account	-30	-22	-324	-1 006	-587	-515	-878	Compte des transac. courantes
Financial account	22	84	-307	-856	-514	-675	-828	Compte financier
Mexico								**Mexique**
Current account	800	-1 576	-9 053	-5 241	-29 775	-23 321	-19 354	Compte des transac. courantes
Capital account	0	...	0	-167	-87	39	150	Compte de capital
Financial account	-2 117	-5 824	-5 267	-26 478	-42 906	-31 714	-26 599	Compte financier

Balance of payments summary *(continued)*
Millions of US dollars

Résumé de la balance des paiements *(suite)*
Millions de dollars É.-U.

Country or area&	1985	1995	2005	2010	2015	2016	2017	Pays ou zone&
Micronesia (Fed. States of)								**Micronésie (États féd. de)**
Current account	...	...	...	-25	...	...	...	Compte des transac. courantes
Capital account	...	...	...	64	...	...	...	Compte de capital
Financial account	...	...	...	29	...	...	...	Compte financier
Mongolia								**Mongolie**
Current account	-814	39	88	-885	-948	-700	-1 155	Compte des transac. courantes
Capital account	0	...	...	152	116	91	78	Compte de capital
Financial account	-730	49	-107	-794	-1 056	-823	-1 133	Compte financier
Montenegro								**Monténégro**
Current account	...	...	...	# -952	-533	-788	-881	Compte des transac. courantes
Capital account	...	...	...	# -1	-~0	1	~0	Compte de capital
Financial account	...	...	...	# -857	-374	-571	-730	Compte financier
Montserrat								**Montserrat**
Current account	...	-2	-16	-19	-6	-9	...	Compte des transac. courantes
Capital account	...	7	7	13	14	9	...	Compte de capital
Financial account	...	-1	-10	-6	4	6	...	Compte financier
Morocco								**Maroc**
Current account	-891	-1 186	1 041	-3 925	-2 161	-4 531	-3 850	Compte des transac. courantes
Capital account	0	0	0	0	1	...	0	Compte de capital
Financial account	-847	-801	629	-4 092	-1 484	-3 591	-2 676	Compte financier
Mozambique								**Mozambique**
Current account	...	...	-761	-1 679	-5 968	-3 846	-2 558	Compte des transac. courantes
Capital account	...	...	193	357	288	206	196	Compte de capital
Financial account	...	...	-543	-1 267	-5 655	-3 634	-2 354	Compte financier
Myanmar								**Myanmar**
Current account	-205	-258	582	1 574	-2 838	-1 761	-3 945	Compte des transac. courantes
Capital account	0	0	...	...	0	~0	1	Compte de capital
Financial account	-164	-275	-22	-559	-4 290	-3 851	-5 262	Compte financier
Namibia								**Namibie**
Current account	...	176	333	-534	-1 635	-1 595	-296	Compte des transac. courantes
Capital account	...	40	80	187	107	115	155	Compte de capital
Financial account	...	229	541	-724	-1 633	-1 300	-334	Compte financier
Nepal								**Népal**
Current account	-122	-356	153	-128	2 447	-168	-815	Compte des transac. courantes
Capital account	0	0	40	185	162	165	149	Compte de capital
Financial account	-119	-354	332	-123	2 512	553	-250	Compte financier
Netherlands								**Pays-Bas**
Current account	4 248	25 773	41 600	61 820	65 828	65 573	84 830	Compte des transac. courantes
Capital account	-39	-497	82	-4 123	-38 131	-1 748	4 263	Compte de capital
Financial account	3 144	16 928	32 359	51 355	36 974	63 793	58 697	Compte financier
Netherlands Antilles [former]								**Antilles néerlandaises [anc.]**
Current account	403	128	-106	...	...	...	...	Compte des transac. courantes
Capital account	0	63	96	...	...	...	...	Compte de capital
Financial account	396	203	22	...	...	...	...	Compte financier
New Caledonia								**Nouvelle-Calédonie**
Current account	...	...	-112	-1 360	-1 119	-654	...	Compte des transac. courantes
Capital account	...	...	9	2	3	-12	...	Compte de capital
Financial account	...	...	-19	-1 279	-1 121	-860	...	Compte financier
New Zealand								**Nouvelle-Zélande**
Current account	...	...	-8 025	-3 429	-5 214	-4 377	-5 540	Compte des transac. courantes
Capital account	...	...	-1	4 645	227	786	46	Compte de capital
Financial account	...	...	-8 950	1 040	1 023	-5 583	-2 445	Compte financier
Nicaragua								**Nicaragua**
Current account	-771	-722	# -784	-780	-1 145	-989	-694	Compte des transac. courantes
Capital account	45	1 707	# 479	264	375	202	166	Compte de capital
Financial account	-913	1 127	# -369	-351	-1 269	-1 018	-879	Compte financier
Niger								**Niger**
Current account	-64	-152	-312	-1 136	-1 486	-1 181	...	Compte des transac. courantes
Capital account	0	65	49	196	294	387	...	Compte de capital
Financial account	-37	28	-141	-925	-1 207	-803	...	Compte financier
Nigeria								**Nigéria**
Current account	2 604	-802	36 529	13 111	-16 019	2 714	10 381	Compte des transac. courantes
Capital account	0	-14	7 336	0	...	...	...	Compte de capital
Financial account	2 469	-848	26 520	-1 802	4 622	-2 931	4 320	Compte financier

15

Balance of payments summary *(continued)*
Millions of US dollars

Résumé de la balance des paiements *(suite)*
Millions de dollars É.-U.

Country or area&	1985	1995	2005	2010	2015	2016	2017	Pays ou zone&
Norway								**Norvège**
Current account	3 030	5 233	49 967	50 258	31 106	14 301	20 169	Compte des transac. courantes
Capital account	0	-170	-279	-164	-118	-111	-104	Compte de capital
Financial account	1 954	1 116	49 596	42 948	8 138	39 166	18 517	Compte financier
Oman								**Oman**
Current account	-10	-801	5 178	4 634	-10 969	-12 319	...	Compte des transac. courantes
Capital account	0	0	-16	-65	543	515	...	Compte de capital
Financial account	-336	-413	4 310	5 926	-10 860	-13 076	...	Compte financier
Pakistan								**Pakistan**
Current account	-1 067	-3 349	# -3 606	-1 354	-2 776	-7 094	-15 818	Compte des transac. courantes
Capital account	9	0	# 202	109	274	232	408	Compte de capital
Financial account	-1 027	-3 653	# -3 551	-2 433	-2 829	-6 112	-15 837	Compte financier
Palau								**Palaos**
Current account	...	...	# -40	-19	-24	-46	...	Compte des transac. courantes
Capital account	...	...	# 51	30	21	23	...	Compte de capital
Financial account	...	...	# 7	6	29	-7	...	Compte financier
Panama								**Panama**
Current account	75	-471	-1 064	-3 113	-4 274	-3 160	-3 036	Compte des transac. courantes
Capital account	...	9	16	43	27	24	25	Compte de capital
Financial account	-46	-447	-1 288	-2 803	-3 877	-5 336	-6 412	Compte financier
Papua New Guinea								**Papouasie-Nvl-Guinée**
Current account	-122	674	539	-633	4 534	5 181	...	Compte des transac. courantes
Capital account	0	0	33	37	8	2	...	Compte de capital
Financial account	-125	587	575	-672	4 905	5 163	...	Compte financier
Paraguay								**Paraguay**
Current account	-252	-217	-68	49	-301	415	-369	Compte des transac. courantes
Capital account	0	11	20	40	154	163	166	Compte de capital
Financial account	-178	-964	-402	-82	201	1 185	449	Compte financier
Peru								**Pérou**
Current account	102	-4 625	1 148	-3 782	-9 169	-5 304	-2 720	Compte des transac. courantes
Capital account	32	93	106	26	6	14	18	Compte de capital
Financial account	-1 394	-4 280	1 488	-2 402	-9 335	-6 219	-2 367	Compte financier
Philippines								**Philippines**
Current account	-36	-1 980	# 1 990	7 179	7 266	-1 199	-2 518	Compte des transac. courantes
Capital account	0	0	# 79	88	84	62	57	Compte de capital
Financial account	510	-4 074	# 4 244	3 753	4 916	-861	-3 070	Compte financier
Poland								**Pologne**
Current account	-982	854	-7 981	-25 875	-2 659	-1 369	1 584	Compte des transac. courantes
Capital account	...	285	996	8 612	11 331	4 884	6 805	Compte de capital
Financial account	-864	575	-7 028	-31 020	720	-545	1 475	Compte financier
Portugal								**Portugal**
Current account	380	-132	-19 538	-24 202	235	1 201	1 167	Compte des transac. courantes
Capital account	0	0	2 782	3 318	2 321	2 073	2 070	Compte de capital
Financial account	127	-3 325	-17 307	-20 336	2 304	3 359	3 743	Compte financier
Qatar								**Qatar**
Current account	...	...	...	...	13 751	-8 270	6 426	Compte des transac. courantes
Capital account	...	...	...	...	-737	-823	-468	Compte de capital
Financial account	...	...	...	...	13 433	-10 260	7 109	Compte financier
Republic of Korea								**République de Corée**
Current account	-2 079	-9 752	12 655	28 850	105 940	99 243	78 460	Compte des transac. courantes
Capital account	...	...	-1	-63	-60	-46	-31	Compte de capital
Financial account	-3 660	-11 523	18 829	23 190	106 299	102 567	87 100	Compte financier
Republic of Moldova								**République de Moldova**
Current account	...	-85	-226	-481	-468	-286	-617	Compte des transac. courantes
Capital account	...	0	13	5	55	-21	-30	Compte de capital
Financial account	...	-103	-51	-402	-458	-214	-570	Compte financier
Romania								**Roumanie**
Current account	1 381	-1 774	# -8 541	-8 478	-2 156	-3 961	-7 111	Compte des transac. courantes
Capital account	0	242	# 714	259	4 336	4 729	2 563	Compte de capital
Financial account	1 263	-1 076	# -7 358	-7 548	2 503	1 737	-3 838	Compte financier
Russian Federation								**Fédération de Russie**
Current account	...	7 438	84 389	67 452	67 661	24 401	35 173	Compte des transac. courantes
Capital account	...	786	-12 387	-41	-309	-764	-233	Compte de capital
Financial account	...	-7 560	67 015	58 278	70 636	19 115	38 745	Compte financier

15 Balance of payments summary *(continued)*
Millions of US dollars

Résumé de la balance des paiements *(suite)*
Millions de dollars É.-U.

Country or area&	1985	1995	2005	2010	2015	2016	2017	Pays ou zone&
Rwanda								**Rwanda**
Current account	...	...	...	# -427	-1 201	-1 336	-628	Compte des transac. courantes
Capital account	...	...	...	# 286	300	190	190	Compte de capital
Financial account	...	...	...	# -207	-718	-1 078	-537	Compte financier
Saint Kitts and Nevis								**Saint-Kitts-et-Nevis**
Current account	-7	-45	-65	-139	-85	-102	...	Compte des transac. courantes
Capital account	0	6	12	56	49	42	...	Compte de capital
Financial account	-7	-23	-36	-109	-109	-122	...	Compte financier
Saint Lucia								**Sainte-Lucie**
Current account	-13	-36	-129	-203	112	-31	...	Compte des transac. courantes
Capital account	0	12	4	42	14	9	...	Compte de capital
Financial account	-11	-25	-139	-136	112	-48	...	Compte financier
Saint Vincent & Grenadines								**Saint-Vincent-Grenadines**
Current account	4	-40	-102	-208	-113	-122	...	Compte des transac. courantes
Capital account	0	5	12	52	12	8	...	Compte de capital
Financial account	6	-35	-111	-148	-76	-50	...	Compte financier
Samoa								**Samoa**
Current account	2	9	# -48	-44	-25	-32	...	Compte des transac. courantes
Capital account	0	0	# 35	31	44	31	...	Compte de capital
Financial account	6	8	# -9	-21	26	-40	...	Compte financier
Sao Tome and Principe								**Sao Tomé-et-Principe**
Current account	-16	...	-36	-88	-69	-61	-73	Compte des transac. courantes
Capital account	0	...	66	42	32	30	30	Compte de capital
Financial account	-10	...	35	-61	-23	-66	-48	Compte financier
Saudi Arabia								**Arabie saoudite**
Current account	-12 932	-5 318	# 90 060	66 751	-56 724	-23 843	...	Compte des transac. courantes
Capital account	0	0	...	...	-1 062	-897	...	Compte de capital
Financial account	-12 931	-5 318	# 55 607	32 598	-72 516	-91 083	...	Compte financier
Senegal								**Sénégal**
Current account	-360	-244	# -676	-589	...	...	...	Compte des transac. courantes
Capital account	88	209	# 200	302	...	...	...	Compte de capital
Financial account	-269	-55	# -479	-305	...	...	...	Compte financier
Serbia								**Serbie**
Current account	...	...	...	-2 692	-1 751	-1 190	-2 355	Compte des transac. courantes
Capital account	...	...	...	-1	-19	-11	6	Compte de capital
Financial account	...	...	...	-2 078	-1 339	-593	-1 903	Compte financier
Seychelles								**Seychelles**
Current account	-19	1	-174	-214	-257	-286	-296	Compte des transac. courantes
Capital account	0	1	30	275	37	54	52	Compte de capital
Financial account	-17	-26	-144	138	-223	-259	-247	Compte financier
Sierra Leone								**Sierra Leone**
Current account	3	-118	-105	-585	-1 003	-162	...	Compte des transac. courantes
Capital account	0	0	68	118	127	165	...	Compte de capital
Financial account	-6	-97	-96	-445	-421	-47	...	Compte financier
Singapore								**Singapour**
Current account	-4	# 14 445	28 105	55 421	56 493	58 845	60 989	Compte des transac. courantes
Capital account	0	...	...	...	...	...	...	Compte de capital
Financial account	639	# 14 175	29 123	59 958	54 871	58 821	61 116	Compte financier
Sint Maarten (Dutch part)								**St-Martin (partie néerland.)**
Current account	...	...	...	...	18	-25	47	Compte des transac. courantes
Capital account	...	...	...	...	-~0	~0	0	Compte de capital
Financial account	...	...	...	...	40	-22	65	Compte financier
Slovakia								**Slovaquie**
Current account	...	390	-5 125	-4 211	-1 509	-1 291	-2 044	Compte des transac. courantes
Capital account	...	46	-13	1 392	3 078	1 801	900	Compte de capital
Financial account	...	580	-4 741	-3 140	-434	-399	-4 369	Compte financier
Slovenia								**Slovénie**
Current account	...	-75	-681	-55	1 884	2 337	3 132	Compte des transac. courantes
Capital account	...	-6	-137	72	455	-333	-258	Compte de capital
Financial account	...	-276	-637	-1 911	1 846	1 252	1 871	Compte financier
Solomon Islands								**Îles Salomon**
Current account	-28	8	-90	-144	-36	-49	-46	Compte des transac. courantes
Capital account	0	1	28	50	55	53	60	Compte de capital
Financial account	-29	8	-9	-116	20	-34	10	Compte financier
South Africa								**Afrique du Sud**

Country or area&	1985	1995	2005	2010	2015	2016	2017	Pays ou zone&
Current account	2 261	-2 493	-8 015	-5 492	-14 498	-8 083	-8 607	Compte des transac. courantes
Capital account	0	0	30	31	19	16	18	Compte de capital
Financial account	1 350	-3 385	-6 846	-7 508	-16 253	-8 760	-7 522	Compte financier
South Sudan								**Soudan du sud**
Current account	...	...	...	...	-3 087	-2 485	-965	Compte des transac. courantes
Capital account	...	...	...	...	75	81	117	Compte de capital
Financial account	...	...	...	...	-321	-296	-491	Compte financier
Spain								**Espagne**
Current account	2 785	-1 967	-87 005	-56 363	13 380	23 769	25 622	Compte des transac. courantes
Capital account	0	5 861	9 047	6 500	7 801	2 957	3 027	Compte de capital
Financial account	942	261	-75 438	-57 066	26 136	29 441	26 277	Compte financier
Sri Lanka								**Sri Lanka**
Current account	-418	-770	-650	-1 075	-1 883	-1 742	-2 309	Compte des transac. courantes
Capital account	0	116	242	150	46	25	11	Compte de capital
Financial account	-461	-491	-473	-1 778	-2 312	-2 182	-2 184	Compte financier
State of Palestine								**État de Palestine**
Current account	...	-984	-1 365	-1 307	-2 066	-1 941	-1 564	Compte des transac. courantes
Capital account	...	262	386	828	491	682	397	Compte de capital
Financial account	...	-557	-885	-201	-1 960	-1 019	-998	Compte financier
Sudan								**Soudan**
Current account	154	-500	-2 473	# -1 725	-5 461	-4 213	-5 033	Compte des transac. courantes
Capital account	0	...	165	# 378	250	148	227	Compte de capital
Financial account	5	-481	-1 448	# -1 633	-5 117	-3 440	-3 494	Compte financier
Suriname								**Suriname**
Current account	...	...	-144	651	-786	-170	-2	Compte des transac. courantes
Capital account	...	...	15	54	1	19	...	Compte de capital
Financial account	...	...	40	537	-1 036	-412	-146	Compte financier
Sweden								**Suède**
Current account	-1 010	4 940	23 583	29 196	22 557	21 675	17 097	Compte des transac. courantes
Capital account	0	0	290	-681	-981	-395	-596	Compte de capital
Financial account	-1 758	3 388	27 988	34 610	10 192	-17 430	6 855	Compte financier
Switzerland								**Suisse**
Current account	6 039	20 703	55 573	86 701	73 802	63 205	66 558	Compte des transac. courantes
Capital account	...	-462	-2 289	-4 437	-29 501	2 621	841	Compte de capital
Financial account	8 500	11 260	79 876	109 086	40 162	75 266	37 188	Compte financier
Syrian Arab Republic								**République arabe syrienne**
Current account	-958	263	299	-367	...	...	...	Compte des transac. courantes
Capital account	0	20	18	50	...	...	...	Compte de capital
Financial account	-974	318	180	824	...	...	...	Compte financier
Tajikistan								**Tadjikistan**
Current account	...	...	-19	# -540	-472	-362	-35	Compte des transac. courantes
Capital account	...	...	0	# 59	144	144	135	Compte de capital
Financial account	...	...	-95	# -410	-474	-306	-24	Compte financier
Thailand								**Thaïlande**
Current account	-1 537	-13 582	# -7 642	11 486	32 113	48 237	48 126	Compte des transac. courantes
Capital account	0	0	...	245	~0	13	-141	Compte de capital
Financial account	-1 434	-14 778	# -2 435	7 751	22 658	33 867	44 185	Compte financier
TFYR of Macedonia								**ex-R.Y. de Macédoine**
Current account	...	...	-159	-198	-193	-299	-129	Compte des transac. courantes
Capital account	...	...	~0	4	8	12	8	Compte de capital
Financial account	...	...	-165	-193	-187	-298	-146	Compte financier
Timor-Leste								**Timor-Leste**
Current account	...	...	...	1 671	# 225	-533	-339	Compte des transac. courantes
Capital account	...	...	...	31	# 29	30	34	Compte de capital
Financial account	...	...	...	1 703	# 191	-656	-212	Compte financier
Togo								**Togo**
Current account	-27	-122	-204	-200	-461	...	...	Compte des transac. courantes
Capital account	0	3	51	1 388	269	...	...	Compte de capital
Financial account	-28	-139	-141	1 191	-182	...	...	Compte financier
Tonga								**Tonga**
Current account	2	...	-21	-80	-56	...	...	Compte des transac. courantes
Capital account	0	...	13	34	31	...	...	Compte de capital
Financial account	3	...	-20	-57	15	...	...	Compte financier

15 Balance of payments summary *(continued)*
Millions of US dollars

Résumé de la balance des paiements *(suite)*
Millions de dollars É.-U.

Country or area&	1985	1995	2005	2010	2015	2016	2017	Pays ou zone&
Trinidad and Tobago								**Trinité-et-Tobago**
Current account	-48	294	3 881	4 172	1 853	-653	2 325	Compte des transac. courantes
Capital account	0	0	...	...	0	~0	1	Compte de capital
Financial account	-322	298	2 897	4 199	-1 082	-1 899	-232	Compte financier
Tunisia								**Tunisie**
Current account	-581	-774	-299	-2 104	-3 850	-3 694	...	Compte des transac. courantes
Capital account	0	47	127	82	225	95	...	Compte de capital
Financial account	-607	-861	-200	-1 927	-3 619	-3 453	...	Compte financier
Turkey								**Turquie**
Current account	-1 013	-2 338	# -20 980	-44 616	-32 109	-33 137	-47 378	Compte des transac. courantes
Capital account	0	0	# 0	-51	-21	23	16	Compte de capital
Financial account	-1 849	17	# -19 509	-45 128	-22 374	-22 145	-46 512	Compte financier
Turks and Caicos Islands								**Îles Turques-et-Caïques**
Current account	...	...	...	...	151	253	...	Compte des transac. courantes
Financial account	...	...	...	...	454	279	...	Compte financier
Tuvalu								**Tuvalu**
Current account	...	...	-4	-14	...	...	...	Compte des transac. courantes
Capital account	...	...	2	9	...	...	...	Compte de capital
Financial account	...	...	~0	-~0	...	...	...	Compte financier
Uganda								**Ouganda**
Current account	5	-281	51	-1 609	-1 675	-711	-1 128	Compte des transac. courantes
Capital account	0	48	64	49	164	189	175	Compte de capital
Financial account	-48	-204	-400	-1 065	-1 268	-677	-811	Compte financier
Ukraine								**Ukraine**
Current account	...	-1 152	2 534	-3 016	1 616	-1 340	-2 088	Compte des transac. courantes
Capital account	...	6	-43	188	456	92	-4	Compte de capital
Financial account	...	-1 098	2 599	-1 463	1 677	-1 801	-1 567	Compte financier
United Kingdom								**Royaume-Uni**
Current account	3 314	-13 436	-52 165	-92 499	-149 805	-154 873	-106 505	Compte des transac. courantes
Capital account	...	486	-1 439	-1 130	-3 022	-2 171	-1 747	Compte de capital
Financial account	4 358	-4 522	-71 565	-113 190	-138 447	-146 338	-88 854	Compte financier
United Rep. of Tanzania								**Rép.-Unie de Tanzanie**
Current account	-375	-590	-1 093	# -2 211	-4 120	-2 009	...	Compte des transac. courantes
Capital account	0	191	393	# 538	354	328	...	Compte de capital
Financial account	-415	-369	-1 539	# -2 712	-3 303	-1 720	...	Compte financier
United States of America								**États-Unis d'Amérique**
Current account	-124 455	-113 561	-745 246	-430 702	-434 603	-451 692	-466 248	Compte des transac. courantes
Capital account	0	-222	13 115	-158	-43	-59	24 847	Compte de capital
Financial account	-104 677	-82 815	-714 071	-446 426	-333 171	-377 670	-349 192	Compte financier
Uruguay								**Uruguay**
Current account	-98	-213	42	-731	-446	417	926	Compte des transac. courantes
Capital account	0	0	4	0	175	17	5	Compte de capital
Financial account	141	-194	-127	-1 418	-700	-276	644	Compte financier
Vanuatu								**Vanuatu**
Current account	-10	-18	-34	# -42	-82	...	...	Compte des transac. courantes
Capital account	10	31	22	# 21	84	...	...	Compte de capital
Financial account	-5	-20	-29	# -149	52	...	...	Compte financier
Venezuela (Boliv. Rep. of)								**Venezuela (Rép. boliv. du)**
Current account	3 327	2 014	# 25 447	5 585	-16 051	-3 870	...	Compte des transac. courantes
Capital account	0	0	# 0	-211	-3 980	...	...	Compte de capital
Financial account	2 328	1 520	# 21 855	1 644	-22 296	-6 665	...	Compte financier
Viet Nam								**Viet Nam**
Current account	...	...	-560	-4 276	906	8 235	6 124	Compte des transac. courantes
Financial account	...	...	-957	-7 966	-7 607	-2 568	-7 658	Compte financier
Yemen								**Yémen**
Current account	...	...	624	-1 054	-3 026	...	...	Compte des transac. courantes
Capital account	...	...	202	88	0	...	...	Compte de capital
Financial account	...	...	1 040	-900	-2 365	...	...	Compte financier
Zambia								**Zambie**
Current account	-395	...	# -232	1 525	-768	-954	-1 006	Compte des transac. courantes
Capital account	0	...	# 2 560	150	81	55	58	Compte de capital
Financial account	-544	...	# 2 206	1 646	-724	-1 032	-1 001	Compte financier
Zimbabwe								**Zimbabwe**
Current account	-64	...	...	-1 444	-1 521	-591	...	Compte des transac. courantes
Capital account	0	...	...	231	398	242	...	Compte de capital
Financial account	-38	...	...	-411	-1 094	-368	...	Compte financier

15 Balance of payments summary *(continued)*
Millions of US dollars

Résumé de la balance des paiements *(suite)*
Millions de dollars É.-U.

Country or area&	1985	1995	2005	2010	2015	2016	2017	Pays ou zone&
Euro Area								**Zone euro**
Current account	...	...	19 191	-7 825	375 964	428 782	443 905	Compte des transac. courantes
Capital account	...	...	14 237	16 526	-12 783	1 103	-21 649	Compte de capital
Financial account	...	...	48 521	-18 162	294 934	383 501	493 763	Compte financier

Source:

International Monetary Fund (IMF), Washington, D.C., Balance of Payment (BOP) Statistics database, last accessed May 2018.

& Financial account includes reserves and related items.

Source:

Fonds monétaire international (FMI), Washington, D.C., base de données des Statistiques Balance des Paiements, dernier accès mai 2018.

& Compte financier inclut les réserves et les éléments connexes.

16 Exchange rates

National currency per US dollar

Cours des changes

Valeur du dollar E.-U. en monnaie nationale

Country or area	National currency Monnaie nationale	1985	1995	2005	2010	2014	2015	2016	2017	Pays ou zone
Afghanistan										**Afghanistan**
End of period	Afghani (AFN)	42.8	47.5	50.4	45.3	57.8	68.1	66.8	69.5	Fin de période
Period average	afghani (AFN)	39.3	36.6	49.5	46.5	57.3	61.1	67.9	68.0	Moy. sur période
Åland Islands										**Îles d'Åland**
End of period	Euro (EUR)	...	...	0.8	0.7	0.8	0.9	0.9	0.8	Fin de période
Period average [1]	euro (EUR)	...	...	0.8	0.8	0.8	0.9	0.9	0.9	Moy. sur période [1]
Albania										**Albanie**
End of period	Lek (ALL)	...	94.2	103.6	104.0	115.2	125.8	128.2	111.1	Fin de période
Period average	lek (ALL)	...	92.7	99.9	103.9	105.5	126.0	124.1	119.1	Moy. sur période
Algeria										**Algérie**
End of period	Algerian Dinar (DZD)	4.8	52.2	73.4	74.9	87.9	107.1	110.5	114.9	Fin de période
Period average	dinar algérien (DZD)	5.0	47.7	73.3	74.4	80.6	100.7	109.4	111.0	Moy. sur période
Andorra										**Andorre**
End of period	Euro (EUR)	...	...	0.8	0.7	0.8	0.9	0.9	0.8	Fin de période
Period average [1]	euro (EUR)	...	...	0.8	0.8	0.8	0.9	0.9	0.9	Moy. sur période [1]
Angola										**Angola**
End of period	Kwanza (AOA)	0.0	~0.0	80.8	92.6	102.9	135.3	165.9	165.9	Fin de période
Period average	kwanza (AOA)	0.0	0.0	87.2	91.9	98.3	120.1	163.7	165.9	Moy. sur période
Anguilla										**Anguilla**
End of period	E. Caribbean Dollar (XCD) [2]	2.7	2.7	2.7	2.7	2.7	2.7	2.7	2.7	Fin de période
Period average	dollar des Caraïb. (XCD) [2]	2.7	2.7	2.7	2.7	2.7	2.7	2.7	2.7	Moy. sur période
Antigua and Barbuda										**Antigua-et-Barbuda**
End of period	E. Caribbean Dollar (XCD) [2]	2.7	2.7	2.7	2.7	2.7	2.7	2.7	2.7	Fin de période
Period average	dollar des Caraïb. (XCD) [2]	2.7	2.7	2.7	2.7	2.7	2.7	2.7	2.7	Moy. sur période
Argentina										**Argentine**
End of period	Argentine Peso (ARS)	~0.0	1.0	3.0	4.0	8.5	13.1	15.9	18.6	Fin de période
Period average	peso argentin (ARS)	~0.0	1.0	2.9	3.9	8.1	9.2	14.8	16.6	Moy. sur période
Armenia										**Arménie**
End of period	Armenian Dram (AMD)	...	402.0	450.2	363.4	475.0	483.8	483.9	484.1	Fin de période
Period average	dram arménien (AMD)	...	405.9	457.7	373.7	415.9	477.9	480.5	482.7	Moy. sur période
Aruba										**Aruba**
End of period	Aruban Florin (AWG)	...	1.8	1.8	1.8	1.8	1.8	1.8	1.8	Fin de période
Period average	florin de Aruba (AWG)	...	1.8	1.8	1.8	1.8	1.8	1.8	1.8	Moy. sur période
Australia										**Australie**
End of period	Australian Dollar (AUD)	1.5	1.3	1.4	1.0	1.2	1.4	1.4	1.3	Fin de période
Period average	dollar australien (AUD)	1.4	1.3	1.3	1.1	1.1	1.3	1.3	1.3	Moy. sur période
Austria										**Autriche**
End of period	Euro (EUR)	...	...	0.8	0.7	0.8	0.9	0.9	0.8	Fin de période
Period average	euro (EUR)	...	...	0.8	0.8	0.8	0.9	0.9	0.9	Moy. sur période
Azerbaijan										**Azerbaïdjan**
End of period	Azerbaijan manat (AZN)	...	0.9	0.9	0.8	0.8	1.6	1.8	1.7	Fin de période
Period average	manat azerbaïdjan. (AZN)	...	0.9	1.0	0.8	0.8	1.0	1.6	1.7	Moy. sur période
Bahamas										**Bahamas**
End of period	Bahamian Dollar (BSD)	1.0	1.0	1.0	1.0	1.0	1.0	1.0	1.0	Fin de période
Period average	dollar des Bahamas (BSD)	1.0	1.0	1.0	1.0	1.0	1.0	1.0	1.0	Moy. sur période
Bahrain										**Bahreïn**
End of period	Bahraini Dinar (BHD)	0.4	0.4	0.4	0.4	0.4	0.4	0.4	0.4	Fin de période
Period average	dinar de Bahreïn (BHD)	0.4	0.4	0.4	0.4	0.4	0.4	0.4	0.4	Moy. sur période
Bangladesh										**Bangladesh**
End of period	Taka (BDT)	31.0	40.8	66.2	70.7	77.9	78.5	78.7	82.7	Fin de période
Period average	taka (BDT)	28.0	40.3	64.3	69.7	77.6	78.0	78.7	80.4	Moy. sur période
Barbados										**Barbade**
End of period	Barbados Dollar (BBD)	2.0	2.0	2.0	2.0	2.0	2.0	2.0	2.0	Fin de période
Period average	dollar de la Barbade (BBD)	2.0	2.0	2.0	2.0	2.0	2.0	2.0	2.0	Moy. sur période
Belarus										**Bélarus**
End of period	Belarusian Ruble (BYN)	...	0.0	0.2	0.3	1.2	1.9	2.0	2.0	Fin de période
Period average	rouble bélarussien (BYN)	...	~0.0	0.2	0.3	1.0	1.6	2.0	1.9	Moy. sur période
Belgium										**Belgique**
End of period	Euro (EUR)	...	...	0.8	0.7	0.8	0.9	0.9	0.8	Fin de période
Period average	euro (EUR)	...	...	0.8	0.8	0.8	0.9	0.9	0.9	Moy. sur période
Belize										**Belize**
End of period	Belize Dollar (BZD)	2.0	2.0	2.0	2.0	2.0	2.0	2.0	2.0	Fin de période
Period average	dollar du Belize (BZD)	2.0	2.0	2.0	2.0	2.0	2.0	2.0	2.0	Moy. sur période

Country or area	National currency Monnaie nationale	1985	1995	2005	2010	2014	2015	2016	2017	Pays ou zone
Benin										**Bénin**
End of period	CFA Franc BCEAO (XOF) [3]	378.1	490.0	556.0	490.9	540.3	602.5	622.3	546.9	Fin de période
Period average	franc CFA, BCEAO (XOF) [3]	449.3	499.2	527.5	495.3	494.4	591.5	593.0	582.1	Moy. sur période
Bermuda										**Bermudes**
End of period	Bermudian Dollar (BMD)	1.0	1.0	1.0	1.0	1.0	1.0	1.0	1.0	Fin de période
Period average	dollar des Bermudes (BMD)	1.0	1.0	1.0	1.0	1.0	1.0	1.0	1.0	Moy. sur période
Bhutan										**Bhoutan**
End of period	Ngultrum (BTN)	12.2	35.2	45.1	44.8	63.3	66.3	68.0	63.9	Fin de période
Period average	ngultrum (BTN)	12.4	32.4	44.1	45.7	61.0	64.2	67.2	65.1	Moy. sur période
Bolivia (Plurin. State of)										**Bolivie (État plurin. de)**
End of period	Boliviano (BOB)	1.7	4.9	8.0	7.0	6.9	6.9	6.9	6.9	Fin de période
Period average	boliviano (BOB)	0.4	4.8	8.1	7.0	6.9	6.9	6.9	6.9	Moy. sur période
Bosnia and Herzegovina										**Bosnie-Herzégovine**
End of period	Convertible Mark (BAM)	...	...	1.7	1.5	1.6	1.8	1.9	1.6	Fin de période
Period average	marka convertible (BAM)	...	...	1.6	1.5	1.5	1.8	1.8	1.7	Moy. sur période
Botswana										**Botswana**
End of period	Pula (BWP)	2.1	2.8	5.5	6.4	9.5	11.2	10.6	9.9	Fin de période
Period average	pula (BWP)	1.9	2.8	5.1	6.8	9.0	10.1	10.9	10.4	Moy. sur période
Bouvet Island										**Île Bouvet**
End of period	Norwegian Krone (NOK)	7.6	6.3	6.8	5.9	7.4	8.8	8.6	8.2	Fin de période
Period average	couronne norvé. (NOK)	8.6	6.3	6.4	6.0	6.3	8.1	8.4	8.3	Moy. sur période
Brazil										**Brésil**
End of period	Brazilian Real (BRL)	0.0	1.0	2.3	1.7	2.7	3.9	3.3	3.3	Fin de période
Period average	real brésilien (BRL)	0.0	0.9	2.4	1.8	2.4	3.3	3.5	3.2	Moy. sur période
British Indian Ocean Terr.										**Terr. brit. de l'océan Indien**
End of period	Pound Sterling (GBP)	0.7	0.6	0.6	0.6	0.6	0.7	0.8	0.7	Fin de période
Period average	livre sterling (GBP)	0.8	0.6	0.6	0.6	0.6	0.7	0.7	0.8	Moy. sur période
Brunei Darussalam										**Brunéi Darussalam**
End of period	Brunei Dollar (BND)	2.1	1.4	1.7	1.3	1.3	1.4	1.4	1.3	Fin de période
Period average	dollar du Brunéi (BND)	2.2	1.4	1.7	1.4	1.3	1.4	1.4	1.4	Moy. sur période
Bulgaria										**Bulgarie**
End of period	Bulgarian Lev (BGN)	...	0.1	1.7	1.5	1.6	1.8	1.9	1.6	Fin de période
Period average	lev bulgare (BGN)	...	0.1	1.6	1.5	1.5	1.8	1.8	1.7	Moy. sur période
Burkina Faso										**Burkina Faso**
End of period	CFA Franc BCEAO (XOF) [3]	378.1	490.0	556.0	490.9	540.3	602.5	622.3	546.9	Fin de période
Period average	franc CFA, BCEAO (XOF) [3]	449.3	499.2	527.5	495.3	494.4	591.5	593.0	582.1	Moy. sur période
Burundi										**Burundi**
End of period	Burundi Franc (BIF)	112.0	277.9	997.8	1 232.5	1 553.1	1 617.1	1 688.6	1 766.7	Fin de période
Period average	franc burundais (BIF)	120.7	249.8	1 081.6	1 230.8	1 546.7	1 571.9	1 654.6	1 729.1	Moy. sur période
Cabo Verde										**Cabo Verde**
End of period	Cabo Verde Escudo (CVE)	85.4	77.5	93.2	83.0	90.7	100.9	105.5	92.4	Fin de période
Period average	Esc. du Cabo Verde (CVE)	91.6	76.9	88.7	83.3	83.0	99.4	99.7	97.8	Moy. sur période
Cambodia										**Cambodge**
End of period	Riel (KHR)	...	2 526.0	4 112.0	4 051.0	4 075.0	4 051.5	4 044.5	4 041.5	Fin de période
Period average	riel (KHR)	...	2 450.8	4 092.5	4 184.9	4 037.5	4 067.8	4 058.7	4 050.6	Moy. sur période
Cameroon										**Cameroun**
End of period	CFA Franc, BEAC (XAF) [4]	378.1	490.0	556.0	490.9	540.3	602.5	622.3	546.9	Fin de période
Period average	franc CFA, BEAC (XAF) [4]	449.3	499.2	527.5	495.3	494.4	591.5	593.0	582.1	Moy. sur période
Canada										**Canada**
End of period	Canadian Dollar (CAD)	1.4	1.4	1.2	1.0	1.2	1.4	1.3	1.3	Fin de période
Period average	dollar canadien (CAD)	1.4	1.4	1.2	1.0	1.1	1.3	1.3	1.3	Moy. sur période
Cayman Islands [1]										**Îles Caïmanes [1]**
End of period	Cayman Isl. Dollar (KYD)	...	...	...	...	...	0.8	0.8	0.8	Fin de période
Central African Republic										**République centrafricaine**
End of period	CFA Franc, BEAC (XAF) [4]	378.1	490.0	556.0	490.9	540.3	602.5	622.3	546.9	Fin de période
Period average	franc CFA, BEAC (XAF) [4]	449.3	499.2	527.5	495.3	494.4	591.5	593.0	582.1	Moy. sur période
Chad										**Tchad**
End of period	CFA Franc, BEAC (XAF) [4]	378.1	490.0	556.0	490.9	540.3	602.5	622.3	546.9	Fin de période
Period average	franc CFA, BEAC (XAF) [4]	449.3	499.2	527.5	495.3	494.4	591.5	593.0	582.1	Moy. sur période
Channel Islands										**Îles Anglo-Normandes**
End of period	Pound Sterling (GBP)	0.7	0.6	0.6	0.6	0.6	0.7	0.8	0.7	Fin de période
Period average	livre sterling (GBP)	0.8	0.6	0.6	0.6	0.6	0.7	0.7	0.8	Moy. sur période
Chile										**Chili**
End of period	Chilean Peso (CLP)	183.7	407.1	514.2	468.4	607.4	707.3	667.3	615.2	Fin de période
Period average	peso chilien (CLP)	160.9	396.8	559.8	510.3	570.4	654.1	677.0	648.8	Moy. sur période

Country or area	National currency Monnaie nationale	1985	1995	2005	2010	2014	2015	2016	2017	Pays ou zone
China [5]										**Chine** [5]
End of period	Yuan Renminbi (CNY)	3.2	8.3	8.1	6.6	6.1	6.5	6.9	6.5	Fin de période
Period average	yuan (CNY)	2.9	8.4	8.2	6.8	6.1	6.2	6.6	6.8	Moy. sur période
China, Hong Kong SAR										**Chine, RAS de Hong Kong**
End of period	Hong Kong Dollar (HKD)	7.8	7.7	7.8	7.8	7.8	7.8	7.8	7.8	Fin de période
Period average	dollar de Hong Kong (HKD)	7.8	7.7	7.8	7.8	7.8	7.8	7.8	7.8	Moy. sur période
China, Macao SAR										**Chine, RAS de Macao**
End of period	Pataca (MOP)	8.0	8.0	8.0	8.0	8.0	8.0	8.0	8.1	Fin de période
Period average	pataca (MOP)	8.0	8.0	8.0	8.0	8.0	8.0	8.0	8.0	Moy. sur période
Christmas Island										**Île Christmas**
End of period	Australian dollar (AUD)	1.5	1.3	1.4	1.0	1.2	1.4	1.4	1.3	Fin de période
Period average	dollar australien (AUD)	1.4	1.3	1.3	1.1	1.1	1.3	1.3	1.3	Moy. sur période
Cocos (Keeling) Islands										**Îles des Cocos (Keeling)**
End of period	Australian dollar (AUD)	1.5	1.3	1.4	1.0	1.2	1.4	1.4	1.3	Fin de période
Period average	dollar australien (AUD)	1.4	1.3	1.3	1.1	1.1	1.3	1.3	1.3	Moy. sur période
Colombia										**Colombie**
End of period	Colombian Peso (COP)	172.2	987.7	2 284.2	1 989.9	2 392.5	3 149.5	3 000.7	2 971.6	Fin de période
Period average	peso colombien (COP)	142.3	912.8	2 320.8	1 898.6	2 001.8	2 741.9	3 054.1	2 951.3	Moy. sur période
Comoros										**Comores**
End of period	Comorian Franc (KMF)	378.0	367.5	417.0	368.2	405.2	451.9	466.7	410.2	Fin de période
Period average	franc comorien (KMF)	449.3	374.4	395.6	371.5	370.8	443.6	444.8	436.6	Moy. sur période
Congo										**Congo**
End of period	CFA Franc, BEAC (XAF) [4]	378.1	490.0	556.0	490.9	540.3	602.5	622.3	546.9	Fin de période
Period average	franc CFA, BEAC (XAF) [4]	449.3	499.2	527.5	495.3	494.4	591.5	593.0	582.1	Moy. sur période
Cook Islands										**Îles Cook**
End of period	New Zealand Dollar (NZD)	2.0	1.5	1.5	1.3	1.3	1.5	1.4	1.4	Fin de période
Period average	dollar néo-zélandais (NZD)	2.0	1.5	1.4	1.4	1.2	1.4	1.4	1.4	Moy. sur période
Costa Rica										**Costa Rica**
End of period	Costa Rican Colon (CRC)	53.7	194.9	496.7	513.0	539.4	538.4	554.6	569.5	Fin de période
Period average	colon costaricien (CRC)	50.5	179.7	477.8	525.8	538.3	534.6	544.7	567.5	Moy. sur période
Côte d'Ivoire										**Côte d'Ivoire**
End of period	CFA Franc BCEAO (XOF) [3]	378.1	490.0	556.0	490.9	540.3	602.5	622.3	546.9	Fin de période
Period average	franc CFA, BCEAO (XOF) [3]	449.3	499.2	527.5	495.3	494.4	591.5	593.0	582.1	Moy. sur période
Croatia										**Croatie**
End of period	Kuna (HRK)	...	5.3	6.2	5.6	6.3	7.0	7.2	6.3	Fin de période
Period average	kuna (HRK)	...	5.2	6.0	5.5	5.8	6.9	6.8	6.6	Moy. sur période
Cuba [1]										**Cuba** [1]
End of period	Cuban Peso (CUP) [6]	...	...	...	...	...	1.0	1.0	1.0	Fin de période
Curaçao										**Curaçao**
End of period	Neth. Ant. Guilder (ANG) [7]	...	...	...	1.8	1.8	1.8	1.8	1.8	Fin de période
Period average	florin des Ant. néer. (ANG) [7]	...	...	...	...	1.8	1.8	1.8	1.8	Moy. sur période
Cyprus										**Chypre**
End of period	Euro (EUR)	...	...	...	0.7	0.8	0.9	0.9	0.8	Fin de période
Period average	euro (EUR)	...	...	...	0.8	0.8	0.9	0.9	0.9	Moy. sur période
Czechia										**Tchéquie**
End of period	Czech Koruna (CZK)	...	26.6	24.6	18.8	22.8	24.8	25.6	21.3	Fin de période
Period average	couronne tchèque (CZK)	...	26.5	24.0	19.1	20.8	24.6	24.4	23.4	Moy. sur période
Dem. People's Rep. Korea [1]										**Rép. pop. dém. de Corée** [1]
End of period	North Korean Won (KPW)	...	...	...	...	103.0	109.0	110.9	105.0	Fin de période
Dem. Rep. of the Congo										**Rép. dém. du Congo**
End of period	Congolese Franc (CDF)	0.0	0.1	431.3	915.1	924.5	926.8	1 215.6	1 592.2	Fin de période
Period average	franc congolais (CDF)	0.0	0.1	473.9	905.9	925.2	926.0	1 010.3	1 464.4	Moy. sur période
Denmark										**Danemark**
End of period	Danish Krone (DKK)	9.0	5.5	6.3	5.6	6.1	6.8	7.1	6.2	Fin de période
Period average	couronne danoise (DKK)	10.6	5.6	6.0	5.6	5.6	6.7	6.7	6.6	Moy. sur période
Djibouti										**Djibouti**
End of period	Djibouti Franc (DJF)	177.7	177.7	177.7	177.7	177.7	177.7	177.7	177.7	Fin de période
Period average	franc Djibouti (DJF)	177.7	177.7	177.7	177.7	177.7	177.7	177.7	177.7	Moy. sur période
Dominica										**Dominique**
End of period	E. Caribbean Dollar (XCD) [2]	2.7	2.7	2.7	2.7	2.7	2.7	2.7	2.7	Fin de période
Period average	dollar des Caraïb. (XCD) [2]	2.7	2.7	2.7	2.7	2.7	2.7	2.7	2.7	Moy. sur période
Dominican Republic										**République dominicaine**
End of period	Dominican Peso (DOP)	2.9	13.5	34.9	37.9	44.4	45.7	46.7	48.5	Fin de période
Period average	peso dominicain (DOP)	3.1	13.6	30.5	37.3	43.6	45.1	46.1	47.6	Moy. sur période

Exchange rates *(continued)*
National currency per US dollar

Cours des changes *(suite)*
Valeur du dollar E.-U. en monnaie nationale

Country or area	National currency Monnaie nationale	1985	1995	2005	2010	2014	2015	2016	2017	Pays ou zone
Egypt										**Égypte**
End of period	Egyptian Pound (EGP)	0.7	3.4	5.7	5.8	7.1	7.8	18.1	17.7	Fin de période
Period average	livre égyptienne (EGP)	0.7	3.4	5.8	5.6	7.1	7.7	10.0	17.8	Moy. sur période
Equatorial Guinea										**Guinée équatoriale**
End of period	CFA Franc, BEAC (XAF) [4]	378.1	490.0	556.0	490.9	540.3	602.5	622.3	546.9	Fin de période
Period average	franc CFA, BEAC (XAF) [4]	449.3	499.2	527.5	495.3	494.4	591.5	593.0	582.1	Moy. sur période
Eritrea										**Érythrée**
End of period	Nakfa (ERN)	2.1	6.3	15.4	15.4	15.4	15.4	15.4	15.4	Fin de période
Period average	nakfa (ERN)	2.1	6.2	15.4	15.4	15.4	15.4	15.4	15.4	Moy. sur période
Estonia										**Estonie**
End of period	Euro (EUR)	...	...	...	...	0.8	0.9	0.9	0.8	Fin de période
Period average	euro (EUR)	...	...	...	...	0.8	0.9	0.9	0.9	Moy. sur période
Eswatini										**Eswatini**
End of period	Lilangeni (SZL)	2.6	3.6	6.3	6.6	11.6	15.5	13.7	12.3	Fin de période
Period average	lilangeni (SZL)	2.2	3.6	6.4	7.3	10.9	12.8	14.7	13.3	Moy. sur période
Ethiopia										**Éthiopie**
End of period	Ethiopian Birr (ETB)	2.1	6.3	8.7	16.6	20.1	21.1	22.4	27.6	Fin de période
Period average	birr éthiopien (ETB)	2.1	6.2	8.7	14.4	19.6	20.6	21.7	...	Moy. sur période
Falkland Islands (Malvinas)										**Îles Falkland (Malvinas)**
End of period	Falkland Isl. Pound (FKP)	0.7	0.6	0.6	0.6	0.6	0.7	0.8	0.7	Fin de période
Period average	livre de Îles Falkland (FKP)	0.8	0.6	0.6	0.6	0.6	0.7	0.7	0.8	Moy. sur période
Faroe Islands										**Îles Féroé**
End of period	Danish Krone (DKK)	9.0	5.5	6.3	5.6	6.1	6.8	7.1	6.2	Fin de période
Period average	couronne danoise (DKK)	10.6	5.6	6.0	5.6	5.6	6.7	6.7	6.6	Moy. sur période
Fiji										**Fidji**
End of period	Fiji Dollar (FJD)	1.1	1.4	1.7	1.8	2.0	2.1	2.1	2.1	Fin de période
Period average	dollar des Fidji (FJD)	1.2	1.4	1.7	1.9	1.9	2.1	2.1	2.1	Moy. sur période
Finland										**Finlande**
End of period	Euro (EUR)	...	...	0.8	0.7	0.8	0.9	0.9	0.8	Fin de période
Period average	euro (EUR)	...	...	0.8	0.8	0.8	0.9	0.9	0.9	Moy. sur période
France										**France**
End of period	Euro (EUR)	...	...	0.8	0.7	0.8	0.9	0.9	0.8	Fin de période
Period average	euro (EUR)	...	...	0.8	0.8	0.8	0.9	0.9	0.9	Moy. sur période
French Guiana										**Guyane française**
End of period	Euro (EUR)	...	...	0.8	0.7	0.8	0.9	0.9	0.8	Fin de période
Period average [1]	euro (EUR)	...	...	0.8	0.8	0.8	0.9	0.9	0.9	Moy. sur période [1]
French Polynesia										**Polynésie française**
End of period	CFP Franc (XPF) [8]	137.5	89.1	101.2	89.3	98.3	109.6	113.2	99.5	Fin de période
Period average	franc CFP (XPF) [8]	163.4	90.8	96.0	90.1	89.9	107.6	107.9	105.9	Moy. sur période
French Southern Territories										**Terres australes françaises**
End of period	Euro (EUR)	...	...	0.8	0.7	0.8	0.9	0.9	0.8	Fin de période
Period average [1]	euro (EUR)	...	...	0.8	0.8	0.8	0.9	0.9	0.9	Moy. sur période [1]
Gabon										**Gabon**
End of period	CFA Franc, BEAC (XAF) [4]	378.1	490.0	556.0	490.9	540.3	602.5	622.3	546.9	Fin de période
Period average	franc CFA, BEAC (XAF) [4]	449.3	499.2	527.5	495.3	494.4	591.5	593.0	582.1	Moy. sur période
Gambia										**Gambie**
End of period	Dalasi (GMD)	3.5	9.6	28.1	28.4	45.3	39.8	43.9	...	Fin de période
Period average	dalasi (GMD)	3.9	9.5	28.6	28.0	41.7	42.5	43.9	...	Moy. sur période
Georgia										**Géorgie**
End of period	Lari (GEL)	...	1.2	1.8	1.8	1.9	2.4	2.6	2.6	Fin de période
Period average	lari (GEL)	...	...	1.8	1.8	1.8	2.3	2.4	2.5	Moy. sur période
Germany										**Allemagne**
End of period	Euro (EUR)	...	...	0.8	0.7	0.8	0.9	0.9	0.8	Fin de période
Period average	euro (EUR)	...	...	0.8	0.8	0.8	0.9	0.9	0.9	Moy. sur période
Ghana										**Ghana**
End of period	Ghana Cedi (GHS)	~0.0	0.1	0.9	1.5	3.2	3.8	4.2	4.4	Fin de période
Period average	cedi ghanéen (GHS)	~0.0	0.1	0.9	1.4	2.9	3.7	3.9	4.4	Moy. sur période
Gibraltar										**Gibraltar**
End of period	Gibraltar Pound (GIP)	0.7	0.6	0.6	0.6	0.6	0.7	0.8	0.7	Fin de période
Period average	livre de Gibraltar (GIP)	0.8	0.6	0.6	0.6	0.6	0.7	0.7	0.8	Moy. sur période
Greece										**Grèce**
End of period	Euro (EUR)	...	...	0.8	0.7	0.8	0.9	0.9	0.8	Fin de période
Period average	euro (EUR)	...	...	0.8	0.8	0.8	0.9	0.9	0.9	Moy. sur période

Exchange rates *(continued)*
National currency per US dollar

Cours des changes *(suite)*
Valeur du dollar E.-U. en monnaie nationale

Country or area	National currency Monnaie nationale	1985	1995	2005	2010	2014	2015	2016	2017	Pays ou zone
Greenland										**Groenland**
End of period	Danish Krone (DKK)	9.0	5.5	6.3	5.6	6.1	6.8	7.1	6.2	Fin de période
Period average	couronne danoise (DKK)	10.6	5.6	6.0	5.6	5.6	6.7	6.7	6.6	Moy. sur période
Grenada										**Grenade**
End of period	E. Caribbean Dollar (XCD) [2]	2.7	2.7	2.7	2.7	2.7	2.7	2.7	2.7	Fin de période
Period average	dollar des Caraïb. (XCD) [2]	2.7	2.7	2.7	2.7	2.7	2.7	2.7	2.7	Moy. sur période
Guadeloupe										**Guadeloupe**
End of period	Euro (EUR)	...	...	0.8	0.7	0.8	0.9	0.9	0.8	Fin de période
Period average [1]	euro (EUR)	...	...	0.8	0.8	0.8	0.9	0.9	0.9	Moy. sur période [1]
Guatemala										**Guatemala**
End of period	Quetzal (GTQ)	1.0	6.0	7.6	8.0	7.6	7.7	7.5	7.3	Fin de période
Period average	quetzal (GTQ)	1.0	5.8	7.6	8.1	7.7	7.7	7.6	7.4	Moy. sur période
Guernsey										**Guernesey**
End of period	Pound Sterling (GBP)	0.7	0.6	0.6	0.6	0.6	0.7	0.8	0.7	Fin de période
Period average	livre sterling (GBP)	0.8	0.6	0.6	0.6	0.6	0.7	0.7	0.8	Moy. sur période
Guinea										**Guinée**
End of period	Guinean Franc (GNF)	22.5	998.0	4 500.0	6 083.9	7 227.7	8 003.7	9 225.3	...	Fin de période
Period average	franc guinéen (GNF)	24.3	991.4	3 644.3	5 726.1	7 014.1	7 485.5	8 959.7	...	Moy. sur période
Guinea-Bissau										**Guinée-Bissau**
End of period	CFA Franc BCEAO (XOF) [3]	378.1	490.0	556.0	490.9	540.3	602.5	622.3	546.9	Fin de période
Period average	franc CFA, BCEAO (XOF) [3]	449.3	499.2	527.5	495.3	494.4	591.5	593.0	582.1	Moy. sur période
Guyana										**Guyana**
End of period	Guyana Dollar (GYD)	4.2	140.5	200.3	203.5	206.5	206.5	206.5	206.5	Fin de période
Period average	dollar guyanien (GYD)	4.3	142.0	199.9	203.6	206.5	206.5	206.5	206.5	Moy. sur période
Haiti										**Haïti**
End of period	Gourde (HTG)	5.0	16.2	43.0	39.9	46.7	56.7	67.4	...	Fin de période
Period average	gourde (HTG)	5.0	15.1	40.5	39.8	45.2	50.7	63.3	...	Moy. sur période
Heard Is. and McDonald Is.										**Île Heard-et-Îles MacDonald**
End of period	Australian Dollar (AUD)	1.5	1.3	1.4	1.0	1.2	1.4	1.4	1.3	Fin de période
Period average	dollar australien (AUD)	1.4	1.3	1.3	1.1	1.1	1.3	1.3	1.3	Moy. sur période
Holy See										**Saint-Siège**
End of period	Euro (EUR)	...	...	0.8	0.7	0.8	0.9	0.9	0.8	Fin de période
Period average [1]	euro (EUR)	...	...	0.8	0.8	0.8	0.9	0.9	0.9	Moy. sur période [1]
Honduras										**Honduras**
End of period	Lempira (HNL)	2.0	10.3	18.9	18.9	21.5	22.4	23.5	23.6	Fin de période
Period average	lempira (HNL)	2.0	9.5	18.8	18.9	21.0	22.0	22.8	23.5	Moy. sur période
Hungary										**Hongrie**
End of period	Forint (HUF)	47.3	139.5	213.6	208.7	259.1	286.6	293.7	258.8	Fin de période
Period average	forint (HUF)	50.1	125.7	199.6	207.9	232.6	279.3	281.5	274.4	Moy. sur période
Iceland										**Islande**
End of period	Iceland Krona (ISK)	42.1	65.2	63.0	115.1	126.9	129.6	112.8	104.4	Fin de période
Period average	couronne islandaise (ISK)	41.5	64.7	63.0	122.2	116.8	131.9	120.8	106.8	Moy. sur période
India										**Inde**
End of period	Indian Rupee (INR)	12.2	35.2	45.1	44.8	63.3	66.3	68.0	63.9	Fin de période
Period average	roupie indienne (INR)	12.4	32.4	44.1	45.7	61.0	64.2	67.2	65.1	Moy. sur période
Indonesia										**Indonésie**
End of period	Rupiah (IDR)	1 125.0	2 308.0	9 830.0	8 991.0	12 440.0	13 795.0	13 436.0	13 548.0	Fin de période
Period average	rupiah (IDR)	1 110.6	2 248.6	9 704.7	9 090.4	11 865.2	13 389.4	13 308.3	13 380.9	Moy. sur période
Iran (Islamic Republic of)										**Iran (Rép. islamique d')**
End of period	Iranian Rial (IRR)	84.2	1 747.5	9 091.0	10 353.0	27 138.0	30 130.0	32 376.0	36 074.0	Fin de période
Period average	rial iranien (IRR)	91.1	1 748.4	8 964.0	10 254.2	25 941.7	29 011.5	30 914.9	33 226.3	Moy. sur période
Iraq										**Iraq**
End of period	Iraqi Dinar (IQD)	1 938.7	1 938.7	1 487.0	1 170.0	1 166.0	1 182.0	1 182.0	1 184.0	Fin de période
Period average	dinar iraquien (IQD)	2 002.4	2 002.4	1 472.0	1 170.0	1 166.0	1 167.3	1 182.0	1 184.0	Moy. sur période
Ireland										**Irlande**
End of period	Euro (EUR)	...	...	0.8	0.7	0.8	0.9	0.9	0.8	Fin de période
Period average	euro (EUR)	...	...	0.8	0.8	0.8	0.9	0.9	0.9	Moy. sur période
Isle of Man										**Île de Man**
End of period	Pound Sterling (GBP)	0.7	0.6	0.6	0.6	0.6	0.7	0.8	0.7	Fin de période
Period average	livre sterling (GBP)	0.8	0.6	0.6	0.6	0.6	0.7	0.7	0.8	Moy. sur période
Israel										**Israël**
End of period	New Israeli Sheqel (ILS)	1.5	3.1	4.6	3.5	3.9	3.9	3.8	3.5	Fin de période
Period average	nouv. shekel israélien (ILS)	1.2	3.0	4.5	3.7	3.6	3.9	3.8	3.6	Moy. sur période

16 Exchange rates *(continued)*
National currency per US dollar

Cours des changes *(suite)*
Valeur du dollar E.-U. en monnaie nationale

Country or area	National currency Monnaie nationale	1985	1995	2005	2010	2014	2015	2016	2017	Pays ou zone
Italy										**Italie**
End of period	Euro (EUR)	...	...	0.8	0.7	0.8	0.9	0.9	0.8	Fin de période
Period average	euro (EUR)	...	...	0.8	0.8	0.8	0.9	0.9	0.9	Moy. sur période
Jamaica										**Jamaïque**
End of period	Jamaican Dollar (JMD)	5.5	39.6	64.4	85.6	114.4	120.0	128.0	124.3	Fin de période
Period average	dollar jamaïcain (JMD)	5.6	35.1	62.3	87.2	110.9	116.9	125.1	128.0	Moy. sur période
Japan										**Japon**
End of period	Yen (JPY)	200.5	102.8	118.0	81.5	120.6	120.5	116.8	112.9	Fin de période
Period average	yen (JPY)	238.5	94.1	110.2	87.8	105.9	121.0	108.8	112.2	Moy. sur période
Jersey										**Jersey**
End of period	Pound Sterling (GBP)	0.7	0.6	0.6	0.6	0.6	0.7	0.8	0.7	Fin de période
Period average	livre sterling (GBP)	0.8	0.6	0.6	0.6	0.6	0.7	0.7	0.8	Moy. sur période
Jordan										**Jordanie**
End of period	Jordanian Dinar (JOD)	0.4	0.7	0.7	0.7	0.7	0.7	0.7	0.7	Fin de période
Period average	dinar jordanien (JOD)	0.4	0.7	0.7	0.7	0.7	0.7	0.7	0.7	Moy. sur période
Kazakhstan										**Kazakhstan**
End of period	Tenge (KZT)	...	64.0	134.0	147.5	182.4	340.0	333.3	332.3	Fin de période
Period average	tenge (KZT)	...	61.0	132.9	147.4	179.2	221.7	342.2	326.0	Moy. sur période
Kenya										**Kenya**
End of period	Kenyan Shilling (KES)	16.3	55.9	72.4	80.8	90.5	102.3	102.5	103.2	Fin de période
Period average	shilling kényan (KES)	16.4	51.4	75.6	79.2	87.9	98.2	101.5	103.4	Moy. sur période
Kiribati										**Kiribati**
End of period	Australian Dollar (AUD)	1.5	1.3	1.4	1.0	1.2	1.4	1.4	1.3	Fin de période
Period average	dollar australien (AUD)	1.4	1.3	1.3	1.1	1.1	1.3	1.3	1.3	Moy. sur période
Kosovo										**Kosovo**
End of period	Euro (EUR)	...	...	...	0.7	0.8	0.9	0.9	0.8	Fin de période
Period average	euro (EUR)	...	...	...	0.8	0.8	0.9	0.9	0.9	Moy. sur période
Kuwait										**Koweït**
End of period	Kuwaiti Dinar (KWD)	0.3	0.3	0.3	0.3	0.3	0.3	0.3	0.3	Fin de période
Period average	dinar koweïtien (KWD)	0.3	0.3	0.3	0.3	0.3	0.3	0.3	0.3	Moy. sur période
Kyrgyzstan										**Kirghizistan**
End of period	Som (KGS)	...	11.2	41.3	47.1	58.9	75.9	69.2	68.8	Fin de période
Period average	som (KGS)	...	10.8	41.0	46.0	53.7	64.5	69.9	68.9	Moy. sur période
Lao People's Dem. Rep.										**Rép. dém. populaire lao**
End of period	Lao Kip (LAK)	95.0	923.0	10 743.0	8 058.8	8 097.8	8 172.6	8 337.8	8 307.3	Fin de période
Period average	Lao kip (LAK)	55.0	804.7	10 655.2	8 258.8	8 049.0	8 147.9	8 179.3	8 351.5	Moy. sur période
Latvia										**Lettonie**
End of period	Euro (EUR)	...	...	...	...	0.8	0.9	0.9	0.8	Fin de période
Period average	euro (EUR)	...	...	...	...	0.8	0.9	0.9	0.9	Moy. sur période
Lebanon										**Liban**
End of period	Lebanese Pound (LBP)	18.1	1 596.0	1 507.5	1 507.5	1 507.5	1 507.5	1 507.5	1 507.5	Fin de période
Period average	livre libanaise (LBP)	16.4	1 621.4	1 507.5	1 507.5	1 507.5	1 507.5	1 507.5	1 507.5	Moy. sur période
Lesotho										**Lesotho**
End of period	Loti (LSL)	2.6	3.6	6.3	6.6	11.6	15.5	13.7	12.3	Fin de période
Period average	loti (LSL)	2.2	3.6	6.4	7.3	10.9	12.8	14.7	13.3	Moy. sur période
Liberia										**Libéria**
End of period	Liberian Dollar (LRD)	43.3	43.8	56.5	71.5	82.5	88.5	102.5	125.5	Fin de période
Period average	dollar libérien (LRD)	46.4	49.8	57.1	71.4	83.9	86.2	94.4	112.7	Moy. sur période
Libya										**Libye**
End of period	Libyan Dinar (LYD)	0.3	0.4	1.4	1.3	1.3	1.4	1.4	1.4	Fin de période
Period average	dinar libyen (LYD)	0.3	0.4	1.3	1.3	1.3	1.4	1.4	1.4	Moy. sur période
Liechtenstein										**Liechtenstein**
End of period	Swiss Franc (CHF)	2.1	1.2	1.3	0.9	1.0	1.0	1.0	1.0	Fin de période
Period average	franc suisse (CHF)	2.5	1.2	1.2	1.0	0.9	1.0	1.0	1.0	Moy. sur période
Lithuania										**Lituanie**
End of period	Euro (EUR)	...	...	...	...	...	0.9	0.9	0.8	Fin de période
Period average	euro (EUR)	...	...	...	...	...	0.9	0.9	0.9	Moy. sur période
Luxembourg										**Luxembourg**
End of period	Euro (EUR)	...	...	0.8	0.7	0.8	0.9	0.9	0.8	Fin de période
Period average	euro (EUR)	...	...	0.8	0.8	0.8	0.9	0.9	0.9	Moy. sur période
Madagascar										**Madagascar**
End of period	Malagasy Ariary (MGA)	127.2	684.6	2 159.8	2 146.1	2 596.7	3 199.2	3 347.9	3 230.2	Fin de période
Period average	ariary malgache (MGA)	132.5	853.1	2 003.0	2 090.0	2 414.8	2 933.5	3 176.5	3 116.1	Moy. sur période

Exchange rates *(continued)*

National currency per US dollar

Cours des changes *(suite)*

Valeur du dollar E.-U. en monnaie nationale

Country or area	National currency Monnaie nationale	1985	1995	2005	2010	2014	2015	2016	2017	Pays ou zone
Malawi										**Malawi**
End of period	Malawi Kwacha (MWK)	1.7	15.3	123.8	150.8	470.8	672.7	728.6	732.0	Fin de période
Period average	kwacha malawien (MWK)	1.7	15.3	118.4	150.5	424.9	499.6	718.0	730.3	Moy. sur période
Malaysia										**Malaisie**
End of period	Malaysian Ringgit (MYR)	2.4	2.5	3.8	3.1	3.5	4.3	4.5	4.1	Fin de période
Period average	ringgit malaisien (MYR)	2.5	2.5	3.8	3.2	3.3	3.9	4.2	4.3	Moy. sur période
Maldives										**Maldives**
End of period	Rufiyaa (MVR)	7.1	11.8	12.8	12.8	15.4	15.4	15.4	15.4	Fin de période
Period average	rufiyaa (MVR)	7.1	11.8	12.8	12.8	15.4	15.4	15.4	15.4	Moy. sur période
Mali										**Mali**
End of period	CFA Franc BCEAO (XOF) [3]	378.1	490.0	556.0	490.9	540.3	602.5	622.3	546.9	Fin de période
Period average	franc CFA, BCEAO (XOF) [3]	449.3	499.2	527.5	495.3	494.4	591.5	593.0	582.1	Moy. sur période
Malta										**Malte**
End of period	Euro (EUR)	...	...	...	0.7	0.8	0.9	0.9	0.8	Fin de période
Period average	euro (EUR)	...	...	...	0.8	0.8	0.9	0.9	0.9	Moy. sur période
Martinique										**Martinique**
End of period	Euro (EUR)	...	...	0.8	0.7	0.8	0.9	0.9	0.8	Fin de période
Period average [1]	euro (EUR)	...	...	0.8	0.8	0.8	0.9	0.9	0.9	Moy. sur période [1]
Mauritania										**Mauritanie**
End of period	Ouguiya (MRU)	7.7	13.7	27.1	28.2	31.3	33.9	35.6	35.3	Fin de période
Period average	ouguiya (MRU)	7.7	13.0	26.6	27.6	30.3	32.5	35.2	35.8	Moy. sur période
Mauritius										**Maurice**
End of period	Mauritius Rupee (MUR)	14.3	17.7	30.7	30.4	31.7	35.9	36.0	33.5	Fin de période
Period average	roupie mauricienne (MUR)	15.4	17.4	29.5	30.8	30.6	35.1	35.5	34.5	Moy. sur période
Mayotte										**Mayotte**
End of period	Euro (EUR)	...	...	0.8	0.7	0.8	0.9	0.9	0.8	Fin de période
Period average [1]	euro (EUR)	...	...	0.8	0.8	0.8	0.9	0.9	0.9	Moy. sur période [1]
Mexico										**Mexique**
End of period	Mexican Peso (MXN)	0.4	7.6	10.8	12.4	14.7	17.2	20.7	19.8	Fin de période
Period average	peso mexicain (MXN)	0.3	6.4	10.9	12.6	13.3	15.9	18.7	18.9	Moy. sur période
Monaco										**Monaco**
End of period	Euro (EUR)	...	...	0.8	0.7	0.8	0.9	0.9	0.8	Fin de période
Period average [1]	euro (EUR)	...	...	0.8	0.8	0.8	0.9	0.9	0.9	Moy. sur période [1]
Mongolia										**Mongolie**
End of period	Tugrik (MNT)	...	473.6	1 221.0	1 256.5	1 885.6	1 996.0	2 489.5	2 427.1	Fin de période
Period average	tugrik (MNT)	...	448.6	1 205.3	1 357.1	1 817.9	1 970.3	2 140.3	2 439.8	Moy. sur période
Montenegro										**Monténégro**
End of period	Euro (EUR)	...	...	0.8	0.7	0.8	0.9	0.9	0.8	Fin de période
Period average	euro (EUR)	...	...	0.8	0.8	0.8	0.9	0.9	0.9	Moy. sur période
Montserrat										**Montserrat**
End of period	E. Caribbean Dollar (XCD) [2]	2.7	2.7	2.7	2.7	2.7	2.7	2.7	2.7	Fin de période
Period average	dollar des Caraïb. (XCD) [2]	2.7	2.7	2.7	2.7	2.7	2.7	2.7	2.7	Moy. sur période
Morocco										**Maroc**
End of period	Moroccan Dirham (MAD)	9.6	8.5	9.2	8.4	9.0	9.9	10.1	9.3	Fin de période
Period average	dirham marocain (MAD)	10.1	8.5	8.9	8.4	8.4	9.8	9.8	9.7	Moy. sur période
Mozambique										**Mozambique**
End of period	Mozambique Metical (MZN)	~0.0	10.9	24.2	32.6	33.6	45.9	71.4	59.0	Fin de période
Period average	metical de Mozamb. (MZN)	~0.0	9.0	23.1	34.0	31.4	40.0	63.1	63.6	Moy. sur période
Myanmar										**Myanmar**
End of period	Kyat (MMK)	7.8	5.8	6.0	5.6	1 031.5	1 304.0	1 357.5	1 362.0	Fin de période
Period average	kyat (MMK)	8.5	5.7	5.8	5.6	984.4	1 162.6	1 234.9	1 360.4	Moy. sur période
Namibia										**Namibie**
End of period	Namibia Dollar (NAD)	2.6	3.6	6.3	6.6	11.6	15.5	13.6	12.4	Fin de période
Period average	dollar namibien (NAD)	2.2	3.6	6.4	7.3	10.9	12.9	14.7	13.3	Moy. sur période
Nauru										**Nauru**
End of period	Australian Dollar (AUD)	1.5	1.3	1.4	1.0	1.2	1.4	1.4	1.3	Fin de période
Period average	dollar australien (AUD)	1.4	1.3	1.3	1.1	1.1	1.3	1.3	1.3	Moy. sur période
Nepal										**Népal**
End of period	Nepalese Rupee (NPR)	20.7	56.0	74.1	71.7	99.4	107.3	108.0	103.0	Fin de période
Period average	roupie népalaise (NPR)	18.3	51.9	71.4	73.3	97.6	102.4	107.4	104.5	Moy. sur période
Netherlands										**Pays-Bas**
End of period	Euro (EUR)	...	...	0.8	0.7	0.8	0.9	0.9	0.8	Fin de période
Period average	euro (EUR)	...	...	0.8	0.8	0.8	0.9	0.9	0.9	Moy. sur période

Exchange rates *(continued)*
National currency per US dollar

Cours des changes *(suite)*
Valeur du dollar E.-U. en monnaie nationale

Country or area	National currency Monnaie nationale	1985	1995	2005	2010	2014	2015	2016	2017	Pays ou zone
New Caledonia										**Nouvelle-Calédonie**
End of period	CFP Franc (XPF) [8]	137.5	89.1	101.2	89.3	98.3	109.6	113.2	99.5	Fin de période
Period average	franc CFP (XPF) [8]	163.4	90.8	96.0	90.1	89.9	107.6	107.9	105.9	Moy. sur période
New Zealand										**Nouvelle-Zélande**
End of period	New Zealand Dollar (NZD)	2.0	1.5	1.5	1.3	1.3	1.5	1.4	1.4	Fin de période
Period average	dollar néo-zélandais (NZD)	2.0	1.5	1.4	1.4	1.2	1.4	1.4	1.4	Moy. sur période
Nicaragua										**Nicaragua**
End of period	Cordoba Oro (NIO)	0.0	8.0	17.1	21.9	26.6	27.9	29.3	30.8	Fin de période
Period average	cordoba oro (NIO)	0.0	7.6	16.7	21.4	26.0	27.3	28.6	30.1	Moy. sur période
Niger										**Niger**
End of period	CFA Franc BCEAO (XOF) [3]	378.1	490.0	556.0	490.9	540.3	602.5	622.3	546.9	Fin de période
Period average	franc CFA, BCEAO (XOF) [3]	449.3	499.2	527.5	495.3	494.4	591.5	593.0	582.1	Moy. sur période
Nigeria										**Nigéria**
End of period	Naira (NGN)	1.0	21.9	129.0	150.7	169.7	197.0	305.0	306.0	Fin de période
Period average	naira (NGN)	0.9	21.9	131.3	150.3	158.6	192.4	253.5	305.8	Moy. sur période
Niue										**Nioué**
End of period	New Zealand Dollar (NZD)	2.0	1.5	1.5	1.3	1.3	1.5	1.4	1.4	Fin de période
Period average	dollar néo-zélandais (NZD)	2.0	1.5	1.4	1.4	1.2	1.4	1.4	1.4	Moy. sur période
Norfolk Island										**Île Norfolk**
End of period	Australian dollar (AUD)	1.5	1.3	1.4	1.0	1.2	1.4	1.4	1.3	Fin de période
Period average	dollar australien (AUD)	1.4	1.3	1.3	1.1	1.1	1.3	1.3	1.3	Moy. sur période
Norway										**Norvège**
End of period	Norwegian Krone (NOK)	7.6	6.3	6.8	5.9	7.4	8.8	8.6	8.2	Fin de période
Period average	cour. norvégienne (NOK)	8.6	6.3	6.4	6.0	6.3	8.1	8.4	8.3	Moy. sur période
Oman										**Oman**
End of period	Rial Omani (OMR)	0.3	0.4	0.4	0.4	0.4	0.4	0.4	0.4	Fin de période
Period average	rial omanais (OMR)	0.4	0.4	0.4	0.4	0.4	0.4	0.4	0.4	Moy. sur période
Other non-specified areas										**Autres zones non-spécifiées**
End of period	New Taiwan Dollar (TWD)	39.9	27.3	32.9	30.4	31.7	33.1	32.3	29.8	Fin de période
Period average	no. dollar de Taïwan (TWD)	39.9	26.5	32.2	31.7	30.4	31.9	32.3	30.4	Moy. sur période
Pakistan										**Pakistan**
End of period	Pakistan Rupee (PKR)	16.0	34.3	59.8	85.7	100.5	104.9	104.8	110.4	Fin de période
Period average	roupie pakistanaise (PKR)	15.9	31.6	59.5	85.2	101.1	102.8	104.8	105.5	Moy. sur période
Panama										**Panama**
End of period	Balboa (PAB)	1.0	1.0	1.0	1.0	1.0	1.0	1.0	1.0	Fin de période
Period average	balboa (PAB)	1.0	1.0	1.0	1.0	1.0	1.0	1.0	1.0	Moy. sur période
Papua New Guinea										**Papouasie-Nvl-Guinée**
End of period	Kina (PGK)	1.0	1.3	3.1	2.6	2.6	3.0	3.2	3.2	Fin de période
Period average	kina (PGK)	1.0	1.3	3.1	2.7	2.5	2.8	3.1	3.2	Moy. sur période
Paraguay										**Paraguay**
End of period	Guarani (PYG)	320.0	1 979.7	6 120.0	4 573.8	4 626.3	5 806.9	5 766.9	5 590.5	Fin de période
Period average	guaraní (PYG)	306.7	1 963.0	6 178.0	4 735.5	4 462.2	5 204.9	5 670.5	5 618.9	Moy. sur période
Peru										**Pérou**
End of period	Sol (PEN)	0.0	2.3	3.4	2.8	3.0	3.4	3.4	3.2	Fin de période
Period average	sol (PEN)	0.0	2.3	3.3	2.8	2.8	3.2	3.4	3.3	Moy. sur période
Philippines										**Philippines**
End of period	Philippine Piso (PHP)	19.0	26.2	53.1	43.9	44.6	47.2	49.8	49.9	Fin de période
Period average	piso philippin (PHP)	18.6	25.7	55.1	45.1	44.4	45.5	47.5	50.4	Moy. sur période
Pitcairn										**Pitcairn**
End of period	New Zealand dollar (NZD)	2.0	1.5	1.5	1.3	1.3	1.5	1.4	1.4	Fin de période
Period average	dollar néo-zélandais (NZD)	2.0	1.5	1.4	1.4	1.2	1.4	1.4	1.4	Moy. sur période
Poland										**Pologne**
End of period	Zloty (PLN)	~0.0	2.5	3.3	3.0	3.5	3.9	4.2	3.5	Fin de période
Period average	zloty (PLN)	~0.0	2.4	3.2	3.0	3.2	3.8	3.9	3.8	Moy. sur période
Portugal										**Portugal**
End of period	Euro (EUR)	...	...	0.8	0.7	0.8	0.9	0.9	0.8	Fin de période
Period average	euro (EUR)	...	...	0.8	0.8	0.8	0.9	0.9	0.9	Moy. sur période
Qatar										**Qatar**
End of period	Qatari Rial (QAR)	3.6	3.6	3.6	3.6	3.6	3.6	3.6	3.6	Fin de période
Period average	riyal qatari (QAR)	3.6	3.6	3.6	3.6	3.6	3.6	3.6	3.6	Moy. sur période
Republic of Korea										**République de Corée**
End of period	South Korean Won (KRW)	890.2	774.7	1 011.6	1 134.8	1 099.3	1 172.5	1 207.7	1 070.5	Fin de période
Period average	won sud-coréen (KRW)	870.0	771.3	1 024.1	1 156.1	1 053.0	1 131.2	1 160.4	1 130.4	Moy. sur période

Country or area	National currency Monnaie nationale	1985	1995	2005	2010	2014	2015	2016	2017	Pays ou zone
Republic of Moldova										**République de Moldova**
End of period	Moldovan Leu (MDL)	...	4.5	12.8	12.2	15.6	19.7	20.0	17.1	Fin de période
Period average	leu moldove (MDL)	...	4.5	12.6	12.4	14.0	18.8	19.9	18.5	Moy. sur période
Réunion										**Réunion**
End of period	Euro (EUR)	...	...	0.8	0.7	0.8	0.9	0.9	0.8	Fin de période
Period average [1]	euro (EUR)	...	...	0.8	0.8	0.8	0.9	0.9	0.9	Moy. sur période [1]
Romania										**Roumanie**
End of period	Romanian Leu (RON)	~0.0	0.3	3.1	3.2	3.7	4.1	4.3	3.9	Fin de période
Period average	leu roumain (RON)	~0.0	0.2	2.9	3.2	3.4	4.0	4.1	4.1	Moy. sur période
Russian Federation										**Fédération de Russie**
End of period	Russian Ruble (RUB)	...	4.6	28.8	30.5	56.3	72.9	60.7	57.6	Fin de période
Period average	ruble russe (RUB)	...	...	28.3	30.4	38.4	60.9	67.1	58.3	Moy. sur période
Rwanda										**Rwanda**
End of period	Rwanda Franc (RWF)	93.5	299.8	553.7	594.5	694.4	747.4	819.8	843.3	Fin de période
Period average	franc rwandais (RWF)	101.2	262.2	557.8	583.1	681.9	721.0	787.3	831.5	Moy. sur période
Saint Barthélemy										**Saint-Barthélemy**
End of period	Euro (EUR)	...	...	0.8	0.7	0.8	0.9	0.9	0.8	Fin de période
Period average [1]	euro (EUR)	...	...	0.8	0.8	0.8	0.9	0.9	0.9	Moy. sur période [1]
Saint Helena										**Sainte-Hélène**
End of period	Saint Helena Pound (SHP)	0.7	0.6	0.6	0.6	0.6	0.7	0.8	0.7	Fin de période
Period average	livre de Ste.-Hélène (SHP)	0.8	0.6	0.6	0.6	0.6	0.7	0.7	0.8	Moy. sur période
Saint Kitts and Nevis										**Saint-Kitts-et-Nevis**
End of period	E. Caribbean Dollar (XCD) [2]	2.7	2.7	2.7	2.7	2.7	2.7	2.7	2.7	Fin de période
Period average	dollar des Caraïb. (XCD) [2]	2.7	2.7	2.7	2.7	2.7	2.7	2.7	2.7	Moy. sur période
Saint Lucia										**Sainte-Lucie**
End of period	E. Caribbean Dollar (XCD) [2]	2.7	2.7	2.7	2.7	2.7	2.7	2.7	2.7	Fin de période
Period average	dollar des Caraïb. (XCD) [2]	2.7	2.7	2.7	2.7	2.7	2.7	2.7	2.7	Moy. sur période
Saint Martin (French part)										**St-Martin (partie française)**
End of period	Euro (EUR)	...	...	0.8	0.7	0.8	0.9	0.9	0.8	Fin de période
Period average [1]	euro (EUR)	...	...	0.8	0.8	0.8	0.9	0.9	0.9	Moy. sur période [1]
Saint Pierre and Miquelon										**Saint-Pierre-et-Miquelon**
End of period	Euro (EUR)	...	...	0.8	0.7	0.8	0.9	0.9	0.8	Fin de période
Period average [1]	euro (EUR)	...	...	0.8	0.8	0.8	0.9	0.9	0.9	Moy. sur période [1]
Saint Vincent & Grenadines										**Saint-Vincent-Grenadines**
End of period	E. Caribbean Dollar (XCD) [2]	2.7	2.7	2.7	2.7	2.7	2.7	2.7	2.7	Fin de période
Period average	dollar des Caraïb. (XCD) [2]	2.7	2.7	2.7	2.7	2.7	2.7	2.7	2.7	Moy. sur période
Samoa										**Samoa**
End of period	Tala (WST)	2.3	2.5	2.8	2.3	2.4	2.6	2.6	2.5	Fin de période
Period average	tala (WST)	2.3	2.5	2.7	2.5	2.3	2.6	2.6	2.5	Moy. sur période
San Marino										**Saint-Marin**
End of period	Euro (EUR)	...	...	0.8	0.7	0.8	0.9	0.9	0.8	Fin de période
Period average	euro (EUR)	...	...	0.8	0.8	0.8	0.9	0.9	0.9	Moy. sur période
Sao Tome and Principe										**Sao Tomé-et-Principe**
End of period	Dobra (STN)	~0.0	1.8	11.9	18.3	20.1	22.4	23.4	20.5	Fin de période
Period average	dobra (STN)	~0.0	1.4	10.6	18.5	18.5	22.1	22.2	21.7	Moy. sur période
Saudi Arabia										**Arabie saoudite**
End of period	Saudi Riyal (SAR)	3.6	3.8	3.8	3.8	3.8	3.8	3.8	3.8	Fin de période
Period average	rial saoudien (SAR)	3.6	3.8	3.8	3.8	3.8	3.8	3.8	3.8	Moy. sur période
Senegal										**Sénégal**
End of period	CFA Franc BCEAO (XOF) [3]	378.1	490.0	556.0	490.9	540.3	602.5	622.3	546.9	Fin de période
Period average	franc CFA, BCEAO (XOF) [3]	449.3	499.2	527.5	495.3	494.4	591.5	593.0	582.1	Moy. sur période
Serbia										**Serbie**
End of period	Serbian Dinar (RSD)	...	...	72.2	79.3	99.5	111.2	117.1	99.1	Fin de période
Period average	dinar de Serbie (RSD)	...	...	66.7	77.7	88.4	108.8	111.3	107.8	Moy. sur période
Seychelles										**Seychelles**
End of period	Seychelles Rupee (SCR)	6.6	4.9	5.5	12.1	14.0	13.2	13.5	13.8	Fin de période
Period average	roupie seychelloise (SCR)	7.1	4.8	5.5	12.1	12.8	13.3	13.3	13.7	Moy. sur période
Sierra Leone										**Sierra Leone**
End of period	Leone (SLL)	5.2	943.4	2 932.5	4 198.0	4 953.3	5 639.1	7 195.4	7 537.0	Fin de période
Period average	leone (SLL)	5.1	755.2	2 889.6	3 978.1	4 524.2	5 080.8	6 289.9	7 384.4	Moy. sur période
Singapore										**Singapour**
End of period	Singapore Dollar (SGD)	2.1	1.4	1.7	1.3	1.3	1.4	1.4	1.3	Fin de période
Period average	dollar singapourien (SGD)	2.2	1.4	1.7	1.4	1.3	1.4	1.4	1.4	Moy. sur période

Country or area	National currency / Monnaie nationale	1985	1995	2005	2010	2014	2015	2016	2017	Pays ou zone
Sint Maarten (Dutch part)										**St-Martin (partie néerland.)**
End of period	Neth. Ant. Guilder (ANG) [7]	...	...	...	1.8	1.8	1.8	1.8	1.8	Fin de période
Period average	florin des Ant. néer. (ANG) [7]	...	...	...	...	1.8	1.8	1.8	1.8	Moy. sur période
Slovakia										**Slovaquie**
End of period	Euro (EUR)	...	...	...	0.7	0.8	0.9	0.9	0.8	Fin de période
Period average	euro (EUR)	...	...	...	0.8	0.8	0.9	0.9	0.9	Moy. sur période
Slovenia										**Slovénie**
End of period	Euro (EUR)	...	...	...	0.7	0.8	0.9	0.9	0.8	Fin de période
Period average	euro (EUR)	...	...	...	0.8	0.8	0.9	0.9	0.9	Moy. sur période
Solomon Islands										**Îles Salomon**
End of period	Solomon Is. Dollar (SBD) [9]	1.6	3.5	7.6	8.1	7.4	8.1	8.2	7.9	Fin de période
Period average	dol. des Îl. Salomon (SBD) [9]	1.5	3.4	7.5	8.1	7.4	7.9	8.0	7.9	Moy. sur période
Somalia [1]										**Somalie [1]**
End of period	Somali Shilling (SOS)	...	...	...	...	...	24 300.0	24 300.0	24 300.0	Fin de période
South Africa										**Afrique du Sud**
End of period	Rand (ZAR)	2.6	3.6	6.3	6.6	11.6	15.5	13.7	12.3	Fin de période
Period average	rand (ZAR)	2.2	3.6	6.4	7.3	10.9	12.8	14.7	13.3	Moy. sur période
South Georgia & Sandwich Is.										**Géorgie du S.-Îles Sandwich**
End of period	Pound Sterling (GBP)	0.7	0.6	0.6	0.6	0.6	0.7	0.8	0.7	Fin de période
Period average	livre sterling (GBP)	0.8	0.6	0.6	0.6	0.6	0.7	0.7	0.8	Moy. sur période
South Sudan										**Soudan du sud**
End of period	S. Sudan Pound (SSP) [10]	...	...	...	...	3.0	16.6	83.9	127.9	Fin de période
Period average	livre s.-soudanaise (SSP) [10]	...	...	...	...	3.0	4.1	49.4	115.4	Moy. sur période
Spain										**Espagne**
End of period	Euro (EUR)	...	...	0.8	0.7	0.8	0.9	0.9	0.8	Fin de période
Period average	euro (EUR)	...	...	0.8	0.8	0.8	0.9	0.9	0.9	Moy. sur période
Sri Lanka										**Sri Lanka**
End of period	Sri Lanka Rupee (LKR)	27.4	54.0	102.1	111.0	131.0	144.1	149.8	152.9	Fin de période
Period average	roupie sri-lankaise (LKR)	27.2	51.3	100.5	113.1	130.6	135.9	145.6	152.5	Moy. sur période
Sudan										**Soudan**
End of period	Sudanese Pound (SDG)	~0.0	0.5	2.3	2.5	6.0	6.1	6.6	6.7	Fin de période
Period average	livre soudanaise (SDG)	~0.0	0.6	2.4	2.3	5.7	6.0	6.2	6.7	Moy. sur période
Suriname										**Suriname**
End of period	Surinam Dollar (SRD)	~0.0	0.4	2.7	2.7	3.3	4.0	7.4	7.5	Fin de période
Period average	dollar surinamais (SRD)	~0.0	0.4	2.7	2.8	3.3	3.4	6.2	7.5	Moy. sur période
Svalbard and Jan Mayen Is.										**Îles Svalbard-et-Jan Mayen**
End of period	Norwegian Krone (NOK)	7.6	6.3	6.8	5.9	7.4	8.8	8.6	8.2	Fin de période
Period average	cour. norvégienne (NOK)	8.6	6.3	6.4	6.0	6.3	8.1	8.4	8.3	Moy. sur période
Sweden										**Suède**
End of period	Swedish Krona (SEK)	7.6	6.7	8.0	6.7	7.7	8.4	9.1	8.2	Fin de période
Period average	couronne suédoise (SEK)	8.6	7.1	7.5	7.2	6.9	8.4	8.6	8.6	Moy. sur période
Switzerland										**Suisse**
End of period	Swiss Franc (CHF)	2.1	1.2	1.3	0.9	1.0	1.0	1.0	1.0	Fin de période
Period average	franc suisse (CHF)	2.5	1.2	1.2	1.0	0.9	1.0	1.0	1.0	Moy. sur période
Syrian Arab Republic										**République arabe syrienne**
End of period	Syrian Pound (SYP)	3.9	11.2	11.2	11.2	180.9	313.1	498.6	436.5	Fin de période
Period average	livre syrienne (SYP)	3.9	11.2	11.2	11.2	154.1	237.0	460.3	492.6	Moy. sur période
Tajikistan										**Tadjikistan**
End of period	Somoni (TJS)	...	0.3	3.2	4.4	5.3	7.0	7.9	8.8	Fin de période
Period average	somoni (TJS)	...	0.1	3.1	4.4	4.9	6.2	7.8	8.6	Moy. sur période
Thailand										**Thaïlande**
End of period	Baht (THB)	26.7	25.2	41.0	30.2	33.0	36.1	35.8	32.7	Fin de période
Period average	baht (THB)	27.2	24.9	40.2	31.7	32.5	34.3	35.3	33.9	Moy. sur période
TFYR of Macedonia										**ex-R.Y. de Macédoine**
End of period	Denar (MKD)	...	38.0	51.9	46.3	50.6	56.4	58.3	51.3	Fin de période
Period average	denar (MKD)	...	37.9	49.3	46.5	46.4	55.5	55.7	54.7	Moy. sur période
Togo										**Togo**
End of period	CFA Franc BCEAO (XOF) [3]	378.1	490.0	556.0	490.9	540.3	602.5	622.3	546.9	Fin de période
Period average	franc CFA, BCEAO (XOF) [3]	449.3	499.2	527.5	495.3	494.4	591.5	593.0	582.1	Moy. sur période
Tokelau										**Tokélaou**
End of period	New Zealand Dollar (NZD)	2.0	1.5	1.5	1.3	1.3	1.5	1.4	1.4	Fin de période
Period average	dollar néo-zélandais (NZD)	2.0	1.5	1.4	1.4	1.2	1.4	1.4	1.4	Moy. sur période
Tonga										**Tonga**
End of period	Pa'anga (TOP)	1.5	1.3	2.1	1.8	2.0	2.2	2.2	2.2	Fin de période
Period average	pa'anga (TOP)	1.4	1.3	1.9	1.9	1.9	2.1	2.2	2.2	Moy. sur période

Exchange rates *(continued)*
National currency per US dollar

Cours des changes *(suite)*
Valeur du dollar E.-U. en monnaie nationale

Country or area	National currency Monnaie nationale	1985	1995	2005	2010	2014	2015	2016	2017	Pays ou zone
Trinidad and Tobago										**Trinité-et-Tobago**
End of period	TT Dollar (TTD) [11]	3.6	6.0	6.3	6.4	6.4	6.4	6.8	6.8	Fin de période
Period average	dollar de la T-et-T (TTD) [11]	2.5	6.0	6.3	6.4	6.4	6.4	6.7	6.8	Moy. sur période
Tunisia										**Tunisie**
End of period	Tunisian Dinar (TND)	0.8	1.0	1.4	1.4	1.9	2.0	2.3	...	Fin de période
Period average	dinar tunisien (TND)	0.8	1.0	1.3	1.4	1.7	2.0	2.2	2.4	Moy. sur période
Turkey										**Turquie**
End of period	Turkish Lira (TRY)	~0.0	0.1	1.3	1.5	2.3	2.9	3.5	3.8	Fin de période
Period average	livre turque (TRY)	~0.0	0.1	1.3	1.5	2.2	2.7	3.0	3.7	Moy. sur période
Turkmenistan [1]										**Turkménistan** [1]
End of period	Turkmen. Manat (TMT) [12]	...	...	...	...	...	3.5	3.5	3.5	Fin de période
Tuvalu										**Tuvalu**
End of period	Australian Dollar (AUD)	1.5	1.3	1.4	1.0	1.2	1.4	1.4	1.3	Fin de période
Period average	dollar australien (AUD)	1.4	1.3	1.3	1.1	1.1	1.3	1.3	1.3	Moy. sur période
Uganda										**Ouganda**
End of period	Uganda Shilling (UGX)	14.0	1 009.5	1 816.9	2 308.3	2 773.1	3 377.0	3 610.5	3 635.1	Fin de période
Period average	shilling ougandais (UGX)	6.7	968.9	1 780.7	2 177.6	2 599.8	3 240.7	3 420.1	3 611.2	Moy. sur période
Ukraine										**Ukraine**
End of period	Hryvnia (UAH)	...	1.8	5.1	8.0	15.8	24.0	27.2	28.1	Fin de période
Period average	hryvnia (UAH)	...	1.5	5.1	7.9	11.9	21.8	25.6	26.6	Moy. sur période
United Arab Emirates										**Émirats arabes unis**
End of period	UAE Dirham (AED) [13]	3.7	3.7	3.7	3.7	3.7	3.7	3.7	3.7	Fin de période
Period average	dirham des É.A.U. (AED) [13]	3.7	3.7	3.7	3.7	3.7	3.7	3.7	3.7	Moy. sur période
United Kingdom										**Royaume-Uni**
End of period	Pound Sterling (GBP)	0.7	0.6	0.6	0.6	0.6	0.7	0.8	0.7	Fin de période
Period average	livre sterling (GBP)	0.8	0.6	0.6	0.6	0.6	0.7	0.7	0.8	Moy. sur période
United Rep. of Tanzania										**Rép.-Unie de Tanzanie**
End of period	Tanzanian Shilling (TZS)	16.5	550.4	1 165.5	1 453.5	1 725.8	2 148.5	2 172.6	2 230.1	Fin de période
Period average	shilling tanzanien (TZS)	17.5	574.8	1 128.9	1 395.6	1 653.2	1 991.4	2 177.1	2 228.9	Moy. sur période
Uruguay										**Uruguay**
End of period	Peso Uruguayo (UYU)	0.1	7.1	24.1	20.1	24.3	29.9	29.3	28.8	Fin de période
Period average	peso uruguayen (UYU)	0.1	6.4	24.5	20.1	23.3	27.3	30.2	28.7	Moy. sur période
Uzbekistan [1]										**Ouzbékistan** [1]
End of period	Uzbekistan Sum (UZS)	...	...	...	1 640.0	2 418.0	2 780.1	3 218.0	8 125.0	Fin de période
Vanuatu										**Vanuatu**
End of period	Vatu (VUV)	100.3	113.7	112.3	93.2	102.7	110.5	112.3	107.5	Fin de période
Period average	vatu (VUV)	106.0	112.1	109.3	96.9	97.1	109.0	108.5	106.2	Moy. sur période
Venezuela (Boliv. Rep. of)										**Venezuela (Rép. boliv. du)**
End of period	Bolívar (VEF)	~0.0	0.3	2.1	2.6	6.3	6.3	10.0	10.0	Fin de période
Period average	bolívar (VEF)	~0.0	0.2	2.1	2.6	6.3	6.3	9.3	10.0	Moy. sur période
Viet Nam										**Viet Nam**
End of period	Dong (VND)	22.4	11 015.0	15 916.0	18 932.0	21 246.0	21 890.0	22 159.0	22 425.0	Fin de période
Period average	dong (VND)	...	11 038.3	15 858.9	18 612.9	21 148.0	21 697.6	21 935.0	22 370.1	Moy. sur période
Wallis and Futuna Islands										**Îles Wallis-et-Futuna**
End of period	CFP Franc (XPF) [8]	137.5	89.1	101.2	89.3	98.3	109.6	113.2	99.5	Fin de période
Period average	franc CFP (XPF) [8]	163.4	90.8	96.0	90.1	89.9	107.6	107.9	105.9	Moy. sur période
Western Sahara										**Sahara occidental**
End of period	Moroccan Dirham (MAD)	9.6	8.5	9.2	8.4	9.0	9.9	10.1	9.3	Fin de période
Period average	dirham marocain (MAD)	10.1	8.5	8.9	8.4	8.4	9.8	9.8	9.7	Moy. sur période
Yemen										**Yémen**
End of period	Yemeni Rial (YER)	...	57.6	195.1	213.8	214.9	214.9	214.9	214.9	Fin de période
Period average	rial yéménite (YER)	...	40.8	191.5	219.6	214.9	214.9	214.9	214.9	Moy. sur période
Zambia										**Zambie**
End of period	Zambian Kwacha (ZMW)	~0.0	1.0	3.5	4.8	6.4	11.0	9.9	9.9	Fin de période
Period average	kwacha zambien (ZMW)	~0.0	0.9	4.5	4.8	6.2	8.6	10.3	9.5	Moy. sur période
Zimbabwe										**Zimbabwe**
End of period	Zimbabwe Dollar (ZWL)	~0.0	~0.0	80.8	...	...	...	...	...	Fin de période
Period average	dollar du Zimbabwe (ZWL)	~0.0	~0.0	22.4	...	...	...	...	...	Moy. sur période

Source:

International Monetary Fund (IMF), Washington, D.C., the database on International Financial Statistics supplemented by operational rates of exchange for United Nations programmes, last accessed June 2018.

Source:

Fonds monétaire international (FMI), Washington, D.C., base de données des Statistiques Financières Internationales, complétée par les taux de change opérationnels de la Trésorerie de l'ONU, dernier accès juin 2018.

16 Exchange rates *(continued)*
National currency per US dollar

Cours des changes *(suite)*
Valeur du dollar E.-U. en monnaie nationale

1 UN operational exchange rate.
2 East Caribbean Dollar.
3 African Financial Community (CFA) Franc, Central Bank of West African States (BCEAO).
4 African Financial Community (CFA) Franc, Bank of Central African States (BEAC).
5 For statistical purposes, the data for China do not include those for the Hong Kong Special Administrative Region (Hong Kong SAR), Macao Special Administrative Region (Macao SAR) and Taiwan Province of China.
6 The national currency of Cuba is the Cuban Peso (CUP). The convertible peso (CUC) is used by foreigners and tourists in Cuba.
7 Netherlands Antillean Guilder.
8 Communauté financière du Pacifique (CFP) Franc.
9 Solomon Islands Dollar.
10 South Sudanese Pound.
11 Trinidad and Tobago Dollar.
12 Turkmenistan New Manat.
13 United Arab Emirates Dirham.

1 Taux de change opérationnel des Nations Unies.
2 dollar des Caraïbes orientales.
3 franc Communauté financière africaine (CFA), Banque centrale des États de l'Afrique de l'Ouest (BCEAO).
4 franc Communauté financière africaine (CFA), Banque des États de l'Afrique centrale (BEAC).
5 Pour la présentation des statistiques, les données pour la Chine ne comprennent pas la région administrative spéciale de Hong Kong (Hong Kong RAS), la région administrative spéciale de Macao (Macao RAS) et la province chinoise de Taïwan.
6 La monnaie nationale du Cuba est le Peso Cubain (CUP). Le Peso Cubain Convertible (CUC) est utilisé par les touristes et les étrangers à Cuba.
7 florin des Antilles néerlandaises.
8 franc Communauté financière du Pacifique (CFP).
9 dollar des Îles Salomon.
10 livre sud-soudanaise.
11 dollar de la Trinité-et-Tobago.
12 nouveau manat turkmène.
13 dirham des Émirats arabes unis.

17 Labour force participation rate and unemployment rate

Labour force (LF) participation rate and unemployment rate by sex (percent)

Taux d'activité et taux de chômage

Taux d'activité et taux de chômage par sexe (pourcentage)

Region, country or area & / Région, pays ou zone &	Year / Année	Male and Female / Hommes et femmes: LF particip. rate / Taux d'activité	Male and Female / Hommes et femmes: Unemployment rate / Taux de Chômage	Male / Hommes: LF particip. rate / Taux d'activité	Male / Hommes: Unemployment rate / Taux de Chômage	Female / Femmes: LF particip. rate / Taux d'activité	Female / Femmes: Unemployment rate / Taux de Chômage
Total, all countries or areas	***2005**	**64.3**	**6.0**	**77.4**	**5.6**	**51.1**	**6.5**
Total, tous pays ou zones	***2010**	**62.8**	**5.8**	**76.2**	**5.5**	**49.4**	**6.2**
	***2015**	**62.1**	**5.5**	**75.5**	**5.2**	**48.8**	**5.9**
	***2018**	**61.8**	**5.5**	**75.0**	**5.2**	**48.5**	**6.0**
Africa	*2005	63.8	8.4	74.5	7.2	53.4	10.0
Afrique	*2010	64.2	7.8	74.4	6.7	54.4	9.3
	*2015	64.3	7.5	73.6	6.7	55.2	8.6
	*2018	64.5	7.9	73.6	7.0	55.7	9.1
Northern Africa	*2005	47.0	12.5	73.3	10.0	21.0	21.3
Afrique septentrionale	*2010	47.8	11.5	73.9	8.8	22.0	20.3
	*2015	46.9	12.4	72.1	10.0	21.9	20.4
	*2018	46.8	11.5	72.0	9.1	21.9	19.5
Sub-Saharan Africa	*2005	68.9	7.5	74.9	6.4	63.1	8.8
Afrique subsaharienne	*2010	69.0	7.1	74.5	6.1	63.8	8.2
	*2015	69.1	6.6	74.0	5.8	64.4	7.5
	*2018	69.2	7.2	74.0	6.4	64.6	8.2
Eastern Africa	*2005	78.2	6.8	83.1	5.1	73.6	8.6
Afrique orientale	*2010	78.0	7.1	82.6	5.5	73.6	8.8
	*2015	77.2	6.4	81.7	5.0	72.9	7.9
	*2018	77.2	6.5	81.5	5.0	73.0	8.0
Middle Africa	*2005	73.1	7.9	76.2	7.0	70.1	8.9
Afrique centrale	*2010	73.2	5.7	76.2	5.0	70.3	6.5
	*2015	73.3	5.1	76.1	4.5	70.6	5.8
	*2018	73.2	5.4	76.0	4.7	70.6	6.1
Southern Africa	*2005	54.5	24.2	62.7	20.6	46.9	28.6
Afrique australe	*2010	53.3	24.4	61.4	22.5	45.8	26.9
	*2015	55.8	24.7	63.0	22.8	49.0	27.1
	*2018	56.0	27.8	63.2	25.5	49.2	30.6
Western Africa	*2005	60.7	4.5	68.7	4.5	52.7	4.6
Afrique occidentale	*2010	61.1	4.3	67.9	4.1	54.3	4.5
	*2015	61.1	4.0	66.9	4.0	55.4	4.0
	*2018	61.2	5.3	66.8	5.4	55.6	5.1
Americas	*2005	64.9	6.9	76.7	6.1	53.6	8.0
Amériques	*2010	64.4	8.1	75.4	7.6	53.9	8.8
	*2015	63.5	6.2	74.2	5.6	53.3	6.9
	*2018	63.3	6.6	73.8	6.0	53.2	7.5
Northern America	*2005	65.2	5.3	72.2	5.3	58.5	5.2
Amérique septentrionale	*2010	63.9	9.5	70.1	10.3	58.0	8.5
	*2015	62.4	5.5	68.6	5.6	56.3	5.3
	*2018	62.0	4.5	68.1	4.6	56.0	4.4
Latin America & the Caribbean	*2005	64.6	8.0	79.6	6.6	50.3	10.2
Amérique latine et Caraïbes	*2010	64.7	7.3	78.8	6.1	51.3	9.0
	*2015	64.2	6.6	77.7	5.6	51.4	7.9
	*2018	64.1	7.9	77.2	6.8	51.5	9.5
Caribbean	*2005	59.2	8.1	71.5	6.5	47.3	10.3
Caraïbes	*2010	60.1	8.6	71.4	7.4	49.2	10.3
	*2015	60.8	8.2	71.1	6.6	50.7	10.2
	*2018	60.9	8.1	71.2	6.6	51.1	10.0
Central America	*2005	61.5	4.0	81.9	3.7	41.9	4.6
Amérique centrale	*2010	61.8	5.4	80.8	5.3	43.6	5.5
	*2015	62.0	4.4	80.2	4.1	44.5	4.9
	*2018	62.0	3.8	79.8	3.6	44.9	4.2
South America	*2005	66.4	9.4	79.6	7.7	53.7	11.8
Amérique du Sud	*2010	66.3	7.8	78.7	6.2	54.5	10.0
	*2015	65.4	7.2	77.3	6.2	54.1	8.7
	*2018	65.2	9.4	76.8	8.1	54.2	11.1
Central Asia	*2005	64.7	8.1	74.4	7.7	55.5	8.7
Asie centrale	*2010	65.3	7.5	75.4	7.4	55.7	7.7
	*2015	65.9	7.0	76.7	6.7	55.7	7.2
	*2018	66.0	6.5	77.1	6.2	55.4	6.8

17 Labour force participation rate and unemployment rate *(continued)*
Labour force (LF) participation rate and unemployment rate by sex (percent)

Taux d'activité et taux de chômage *(suite)*
Taux d'activité et taux de chômage par sexe (pourcentage)

Region, country or area & Région, pays ou zone &	Year Année	Male and Female Hommes et femmes: LF particip. rate Taux d'activité	Male and Female Hommes et femmes: Unemployment rate Taux de Chômage	Male Hommes: LF particip. rate Taux d'activité	Male Hommes: Unemployment rate Taux de Chômage	Female Femmes: LF particip. rate Taux d'activité	Female Femmes: Unemployment rate Taux de Chômage
Eastern Asia	*2005	71.7	4.2	78.9	4.5	64.3	3.7
Asie orientale	*2010	69.6	4.3	77.1	4.7	61.9	3.7
	*2015	68.6	4.5	76.1	4.9	61.0	3.9
	*2018	67.5	4.5	75.1	4.8	59.7	4.2
South-eastern Asia	*2005	69.2	4.9	82.4	4.6	56.4	5.4
Asie du Sud-Est	*2010	69.1	3.5	81.5	3.3	57.0	3.6
	*2015	68.1	2.9	80.8	2.9	55.7	2.7
	*2018	68.0	3.3	80.0	3.5	56.3	3.1
Southern Asia	*2005	59.2	5.0	83.1	4.6	34.0	6.0
Asie méridionale	*2010	54.9	3.7	80.4	3.4	28.2	4.5
	*2015	54.0	4.0	79.2	3.6	27.7	5.1
	*2018	54.0	4.1	79.1	3.7	27.8	5.2
Western Asia [1]	*2005	48.4	11.1	74.5	9.2	17.4	20.7
Asie occidentale [1]	*2010	50.4	9.0	76.2	6.9	18.2	20.2
	*2015	51.5	8.1	77.3	6.3	18.9	17.7
	*2018	51.4	8.3	77.2	6.8	18.9	16.3
Caucasus [2]	*2005	50.3	10.3	69.7	10.2	32.2	10.6
Caucase [2]	*2010	51.8	10.4	69.7	10.3	35.2	10.7
	*2015	54.5	9.6	71.4	8.9	38.6	10.9
	*2018	54.7	10.1	71.5	9.2	39.0	11.6
Eastern Europe	*2005	58.1	8.5	65.3	8.7	51.9	8.2
Europe orientale	*2010	59.1	7.8	66.9	8.3	52.3	7.3
	*2015	59.7	6.4	67.9	6.7	52.6	6.1
	*2018	59.2	5.3	67.4	5.6	52.1	4.9
Northern Europe	*2005	62.0	5.5	68.9	5.7	55.5	5.2
Europe septentrionale	*2010	61.9	8.6	68.1	9.5	56.1	7.5
	*2015	62.2	6.1	67.6	6.3	56.9	5.8
	*2018	62.2	5.1	67.5	5.3	57.2	4.9
Southern Europe	*2005	53.4	10.4	64.4	8.5	43.0	13.1
Europe méridionale	*2010	53.5	14.3	62.9	13.5	44.6	15.4
	*2015	53.1	17.3	61.4	16.3	45.4	18.5
	*2018	52.8	13.4	60.6	12.3	45.4	14.8
Western Europe	*2005	58.2	9.0	65.8	8.8	51.1	9.3
Europe occidentale	*2010	58.9	7.2	65.4	7.3	52.7	7.1
	*2015	59.0	6.9	64.7	7.2	53.6	6.6
	*2018	58.8	5.9	64.1	6.1	53.7	5.7
Oceania	*2005	65.8	4.5	72.8	4.5	59.0	4.5
Océanie	*2010	66.4	5.0	72.7	5.0	60.2	4.9
	*2015	66.0	5.5	71.6	5.5	60.6	5.3
	*2018	65.9	5.1	71.1	5.1	60.8	5.0
Afghanistan	2005	*53.0	8.5	*87.1	7.6	*16.1	13.6
Afghanistan	*2010	51.7	7.8	86.5	7.1	14.7	12.4
	*2015	53.9	8.9	86.7	7.9	18.7	13.4
	*2018	54.2	8.8	86.7	8.0	19.5	12.4
Albania	*2005	57.9	17.5	67.9	15.9	48.1	19.6
Albanie	2010	*54.3	14.2	*63.0	14.6	*45.7	13.7
	2015	*56.5	17.1	*65.2	17.0	*47.7	17.1
	*2018	55.9	15.1	64.7	15.4	47.0	14.8
Algeria	2005	*42.5	15.3	*71.8	13.0	*12.8	28.1
Algérie	2010	*42.4	10.0	*70.0	8.1	*14.4	19.3
	2015	*41.5	11.2	*67.4	10.0	*15.2	16.7
	*2018	41.4	9.9	67.2	8.2	15.3	17.2
American Samoa [3]	2000	52.9	5.1	58.8	4.9	41.2	6.0
Samoa américaines [3]	#2005	59.9	...	...	...	...	...
	2010	52.8	#9.2	...	...	...	...
Angola	*2005	77.6	21.4	80.6	19.6	74.9	23.2
Angola	*2010	77.8	9.9	80.5	9.3	75.3	10.4
	*2015	77.8	7.3	80.3	6.9	75.4	7.6
	*2018	77.6	8.5	80.0	8.0	75.3	9.1
Anguilla							
Anguilla	2002	72.3	7.8	77.2	6.3	67.2	9.5

17 Labour force participation rate and unemployment rate *(continued)*

Labour force (LF) participation rate and unemployment rate by sex (percent)

Taux d'activité et taux de chômage *(suite)*

Taux d'activité et taux de chômage par sexe (pourcentage)

		Male and Female Hommes et femmes		Male Hommes		Female Femmes	
Region, country or area & Région, pays ou zone &	Year Année	LF particip. rate Taux d'activité	Unemployment rate Taux de Chômage	LF particip. rate Taux d'activité	Unemployment rate Taux de Chômage	LF particip. rate Taux d'activité	Unemployment rate Taux de Chômage
Antigua and Barbuda Antigua-et-Barbuda	2001	71.7	8.4	78.4	8.0	65.9	8.8
Argentina Argentine	2005	* 62.1	11.5	* 75.6	10.0	* 49.4	13.7
	2010	* 59.7	7.4	* 74.0	6.6	* 46.4	8.6
	2015	* 60.0	6.9	* 73.4	5.9	* 47.5	8.4
	*2018	59.7	8.4	73.1	7.0	47.2	10.4
Armenia Arménie	2005	* 55.9	8.2	* 65.9	7.5	* 47.5	9.1
	2010	* 59.6	19.0	* 71.6	17.1	* 49.6	21.3
	2015	* 59.8	18.3	* 70.2	17.4	* 51.2	19.3
	*2018	60.3	18.0	70.8	16.3	51.6	20.1
Aruba Aruba	2001	...	6.9	...	6.5	...	7.4
	#2010[4]	63.9[5]	10.6	68.9[5]	10.8	59.5[5]	10.4
	#2011	63.8	...	69.6	...	58.8	...
Australia Australie	2005	* 64.5	5.0	* 72.2	4.9	* 57.1	5.2
	2010	* 65.5	5.2	* 72.5	5.1	* 58.7	5.4
	2015	* 65.0	6.1	* 71.2	6.1	* 59.1	6.1
	*2018	64.7	5.6	70.4	5.5	59.2	5.6
Austria Autriche	2005	* 58.1	5.6	* 66.1	5.5	* 50.7	5.8
	2010	* 60.0	4.8	* 66.9	5.0	* 53.5	4.6
	2015	* 60.1	5.7	* 66.0	6.1	* 54.5	5.3
	*2018	60.2	5.3	65.8	5.7	54.9	4.9
Azerbaijan Azerbaïdjan	2005	* 63.4	7.3	* 66.0	6.1	* 61.1	8.5
	2010	* 64.0	5.6	* 66.8	4.8	* 61.4	6.5
	2015	* 65.5	5.0	* 68.7	4.1	* 62.5	5.9
	*2018	65.9	5.1	69.2	4.3	62.8	5.9
Bahamas Bahamas	2005	* 75.5	10.2	* 81.6	9.4	* 69.9	11.1
	*2010	75.8	14.3	82.0	14.5	70.1	14.2
	2015	* 75.7	12.0	* 82.0	11.4	* 69.9	12.7
	*2018	75.9	12.3	82.0	11.1	70.1	13.6
Bahrain Bahreïn	*2005	68.6	7.8	86.2	3.4	38.9	24.5
	2010	* 72.2	1.1	* 87.4	0.5	* 43.8	3.7
	*2015	71.6	1.2	87.0	0.5	43.8	3.8
	*2018	72.6	1.4	87.0	0.5	44.2	4.6
Bangladesh Bangladesh	2005	* 57.6	4.3	* 86.2	3.4	* 28.0	7.0
	2010	* 57.0	3.4	* 83.6	3.1	* 30.0	4.2
	*2015	56.5	4.4	80.5	3.3	32.4	7.2
	*2018	56.6	4.4	79.8	3.3	33.2	6.9
Barbados Barbade	2005	* 69.5	9.1	* 75.4	7.9	* 64.2	10.3
	2010	* 68.0	10.7	* 73.1	11.0	* 63.5	10.4
	2015	* 65.7	11.4	* 69.9	12.1	* 61.9	10.6
	*2018	65.5	9.5	69.5	9.0	61.9	10.0
Belarus Bélarus	*2005	60.8	0.9	67.3	0.9	55.4	0.9
	2010	* 63.0	1.2	* 69.5	1.2	* 57.5	1.2
	*2015	64.3	0.5	71.0	0.5	58.6	0.5
	*2018	63.7	0.5	70.3	0.4	58.2	0.5
Belgium Belgique	2005	* 53.2	8.4	* 61.3	7.6	* 45.5	9.5
	2010	* 54.0	8.3	* 60.8	8.1	* 47.5	8.5
	2015	* 53.4	8.5	* 59.1	9.1	* 48.0	7.8
	*2018	53.1	7.2	58.5	7.4	47.8	7.0
Belize Belize	2005	* 63.9	11.0	* 81.9	7.8	* 45.9	16.8
	*2010	67.2	11.3	82.1	7.1	52.4	17.8
	2015	* 66.4	10.0	* 80.9	6.7	* 52.2	15.0
	*2018	67.4	7.6	81.4	4.0	53.7	13.0
Benin Bénin	*2005	71.9	0.9	76.6	1.0	67.3	0.8
	2010	* 71.0	1.0	* 73.0	0.9	* 69.2	1.2
	*2015	70.8	2.6	73.2	2.4	68.4	2.8
	*2018	71.0	2.4	73.1	2.2	68.9	2.6
Bermuda Bermudes	2000	73.8	2.7[3]	79.2	3.1[3]	67.4	2.3[3]
	#2009[3]	82.0	4.5	86.0	6.0	79.0	3.0
	2010[3]	84.0	...	87.0	...	81.0	...
	2012[3,6]	76.1	8.4	80.0	8.7	72.6	8.2
	2013[3,6]	...	6.7	...	...	...	...

17 Labour force participation rate and unemployment rate *(continued)*

Labour force (LF) participation rate and unemployment rate by sex (percent)

Taux d'activité et taux de chômage *(suite)*

Taux d'activité et taux de chômage par sexe (pourcentage)

Region, country or area & Région, pays ou zone &	Year Année	Male and Female Hommes et femmes		Male Hommes		Female Femmes	
		LF particip. rate Taux d'activité	Unemployment rate Taux de Chômage	LF particip. rate Taux d'activité	Unemployment rate Taux de Chômage	LF particip. rate Taux d'activité	Unemployment rate Taux de Chômage
Bhutan Bhoutan	2005	*70.7	3.1	*75.4	2.6	*65.4	3.7
	2010	*69.8	3.3	*74.3	2.7	*64.6	4.2
	2015	*66.6	2.5	*74.1	1.8	*57.8	3.4
	*2018	67.0	2.4	74.3	1.9	58.5	3.3
Bolivia (Plurin. State of) Bolivie (État plurin. de)	2005	*72.5	5.1	*82.6	4.4	*62.5	5.9
	*2010	72.0	2.5	82.0	2.1	62.0	3.1
	2015	*67.0	3.1	*79.7	2.6	*54.5	3.8
	*2018	67.5	3.1	79.9	2.7	55.3	3.8
Bosnia and Herzegovina Bosnie-Herzégovine	*2005	48.9	29.8	60.5	27.7	37.9	33.0
	2010	*48.2	27.2	*59.9	24.9	*37.1	30.8
	2015	*46.7	26.3	*58.4	27.8	*35.7	23.8
	*2018	46.5	26.0	58.5	19.0	35.1	37.1
Botswana Botswana	*2005	62.8	20.7	71.5	17.8	54.4	24.4
	2010	*60.3	17.9	*67.3	14.7	*53.5	21.7
	*2015	71.5	17.5	78.2	14.3	65.0	21.2
	*2018	72.1	18.3	78.6	15.0	66.0	22.0
Brazil Brésil	*2005	67.0	9.3	79.2	7.3	55.4	12.0
	*2010	65.8	8.4	77.7	6.3	54.6	11.2
	2015	*64.1	8.4	*75.4	7.2	*53.4	10.1
	*2018	63.5	11.9	74.5	10.4	53.1	13.9
Brunei Darussalam Brunéi Darussalam	*2005	67.6	5.9	78.0	5.1	56.6	7.0
	*2010	67.5	6.2	76.4	5.5	58.0	7.1
	*2015	67.6	6.8	75.3	6.0	59.4	7.9
	*2018	67.0	7.1	74.5	6.3	59.0	8.2
Bulgaria Bulgarie	2005	*50.4	10.1	*56.4	10.3	*44.7	9.8
	2010	*53.4	10.3	*59.5	10.9	*47.7	9.6
	2015	*54.2	9.1	*60.1	9.8	*48.6	8.4
	*2018	53.4	5.9	59.5	6.3	47.8	5.4
Burkina Faso Burkina Faso	2005	*74.2	4.0	*86.8	3.7	*62.4	4.3
	*2010	70.4	4.7	81.7	3.5	59.7	6.2
	*2015	66.7	6.5	75.4	4.0	58.3	9.5
	*2018	66.3	6.2	75.0	4.1	57.9	8.9
Burundi Burundi	*2005	81.1	1.7	80.2	2.2	82.1	1.2
	*2010	79.3	1.6	78.2	2.1	80.4	1.1
	*2015	78.5	1.6	77.1	2.1	79.9	1.1
	*2018	78.9	1.5	77.5	2.0	80.3	1.1
Cabo Verde Cabo Verde	*2005	59.3	11.2	75.7	10.6	44.2	12.3
	2010	*59.2	10.7	*72.8	*10.1	*46.0	*11.6
	*2015	60.0	10.3	71.6	9.7	48.6	11.1
	*2018	60.7	10.4	71.6	9.7	50.0	11.2
Cambodia Cambodge	*2005	81.5	2.0	86.7	2.2	76.9	1.8
	2010	*85.4	0.4	*89.3	0.4	*81.8	0.3
	*2015	84.5	0.2	88.5	0.2	80.8	0.2
	*2018	84.9	0.2	88.9	0.3	81.2	0.2
Cameroon Cameroun	2005	*75.9	4.4	*81.4	3.6	*70.4	5.3
	2010	*75.9	4.1	*81.4	3.5	*70.6	4.9
	*2015	76.2	4.3	81.3	3.5	71.1	5.2
	*2018	76.2	4.2	81.2	3.4	71.3	5.1
Canada Canada	2005	*66.7	6.8	*72.6	7.0	*60.9	6.5
	2010	*66.6	8.1	*71.4	8.8	*61.9	7.2
	2015	*65.5	6.9	*70.5	7.5	*60.8	6.3
	*2018	65.0	6.3	69.6	6.9	60.6	5.6
Cayman Islands Îles Caïmanes	2005	...	3.5	...	...	...	...
	#2009	84.2[5]	6.0	88.0[5]	7.0	80.6[5]	5.0
	2010	81.8	6.7	...	...	...	...
	2013	83.1	6.3	85.6	6.7	80.6	5.8
Central African Republic République centrafricaine	*2005	71.3	6.2	78.8	5.7	64.1	6.8
	*2010	71.4	6.3	79.0	5.8	64.1	6.9
	*2015	71.7	6.4	80.3	5.9	63.4	7.0
	*2018	71.5	5.8	80.0	5.2	63.3	6.5

17 Labour force participation rate and unemployment rate *(continued)*

Labour force (LF) participation rate and unemployment rate by sex (percent)

Taux d'activité et taux de chômage *(suite)*

Taux d'activité et taux de chômage par sexe (pourcentage)

		Male and Female Hommes et femmes		Male Hommes		Female Femmes	
Region, country or area [&] Région, pays ou zone [&]	Year Année	LF particip. rate Taux d'activité	Unemployment rate Taux de Chômage	LF particip. rate Taux d'activité	Unemployment rate Taux de Chômage	LF particip. rate Taux d'activité	Unemployment rate Taux de Chômage
Chad Tchad	*2005	72.3	5.7	79.9	4.8	64.9	6.8
	*2010	71.9	5.7	79.1	4.8	64.8	6.9
	*2015	71.2	5.7	77.7	4.8	64.8	6.7
	*2018	71.1	5.9	77.5	5.0	64.8	7.0
Channel Islands Îles Anglo-Normandes	*2005	59.2	9.3	68.9	10.5	50.0	7.8
	*2010	58.6	9.7	67.4	11.1	50.2	7.8
	*2015	57.8	9.6	66.1	10.9	49.6	7.8
	*2018	57.1	9.3	65.2	10.0	49.2	8.4
Chile Chili	2005	*55.3	8.0	*73.0	7.0	*38.3	9.8
	2010	*60.8	8.4	*75.0	7.4	*47.1	10.0
	2015	*62.3	6.5	*74.8	6.0	*50.1	7.2
	*2018	62.5	7.1	74.5	6.7	50.8	7.8
China [7] Chine [7]	*2005	73.4	4.1	79.7	4.5	66.8	3.7
	*2010	71.0	4.2	77.9	4.6	63.8	3.7
	*2015	69.7	4.6	76.7	5.1	62.4	4.0
	*2018	68.4	4.7	75.7	5.0	60.9	4.3
China, Hong Kong SAR Chine, RAS de Hong Kong	2005	*60.9	5.6	*71.1	6.5	*51.7	4.4
	2010	*59.1	4.3	*68.1	5.0	*51.4	3.5
	2015	*60.8	3.3	*68.4	3.4	*54.5	3.2
	*2018	60.1	3.2	67.8	3.5	53.8	2.9
China, Macao SAR Chine, RAS de Macao	2005	*64.4	4.2	*72.5	4.5	*57.3	3.8
	2010	*70.8	2.8	*76.9	3.5	*65.3	2.1
	2015	*71.6	1.8	*77.2	2.0	*66.6	1.6
	*2018	70.8	1.9	76.1	2.4	66.0	1.5
Colombia Colombie	2005	*65.1	11.9	*81.7	9.3	*49.3	15.9
	2010	*69.0	10.9	*82.5	8.5	*56.2	14.1
	2015	*70.6	8.2	*82.8	6.3	*59.0	10.9
	*2018	70.5	9.1	82.6	7.3	59.0	11.6
Comoros Comores	*2005	41.8	4.5	50.2	4.4	33.3	4.8
	*2010	42.1	4.4	49.8	4.3	34.4	4.7
	*2015	42.8	4.3	50.1	4.1	35.6	4.6
	*2018	43.2	4.3	50.3	4.1	36.1	4.7
Congo Congo	2005	*68.7	19.8	*70.6	18.5	*66.7	21.2
	*2010	69.5	14.6	71.5	13.6	67.5	15.6
	*2015	69.8	10.0	72.0	9.4	67.5	10.7
	*2018	69.6	11.3	71.9	10.5	67.3	12.1
Cook Islands Îles Cook	2001	74.5[8]	13.1	75.5[8]	11.7	63.0[8]	14.8
	#2006[5]	70.2	6.9	76.1	6.7	64.2	7.3
	2011[5]	71.0	8.2	76.6	8.2	65.4	8.1
Costa Rica Costa Rica	2005	*62.5	6.6	*80.5	5.0	*44.7	9.4
	2010	*60.5	8.9	*77.1	7.6	*44.1	11.3
	2015	*62.2	9.3	*75.7	7.5	*48.8	11.9
	*2018	59.6	8.4	73.9	6.8	45.6	10.9
Côte d'Ivoire Côte d'Ivoire	*2005	63.2	3.5	76.9	2.8	48.3	4.6
	*2010	60.6	3.1	72.3	2.5	48.2	4.0
	*2015	57.9	2.7	67.3	2.1	48.0	3.4
	*2018	57.3	2.6	66.1	2.1	48.2	3.3
Croatia Croatie	2005	*53.3	12.6	*61.1	11.5	*46.2	13.9
	2010	*52.7	11.6	*59.8	11.0	*46.2	12.3
	2015	*52.9	16.2	*59.4	15.5	*47.0	16.9
	*2018	51.1	9.2	57.4	8.7	45.4	9.6
Cuba Cuba	2005	*52.8	1.9	*67.4	1.7	*38.3	2.2
	2010	*55.5	2.5	*68.7	2.4	*42.3	2.7
	2015	*54.7	2.4	*67.6	2.1	*41.9	2.8
	*2018	54.2	2.7	67.3	2.4	41.3	3.1
Curaçao Curaçao	2005	59.4	18.2	65.4	17.1	54.8	19.2
	2008	59.0	10.3	66.5	8.0	53.2	12.5
	#2009[6]	...	9.6	...	7.8	...	11.2
	2013[6]	...	13.0	...	10.5	...	15.4

17 Labour force participation rate and unemployment rate *(continued)*

Labour force (LF) participation rate and unemployment rate by sex (percent)

Taux d'activité et taux de chômage *(suite)*

Taux d'activité et taux de chômage par sexe (pourcentage)

Region, country or area & Région, pays ou zone &	Year Année	Male and Female Hommes et femmes: LF particip. rate Taux d'activité	Male and Female Hommes et femmes: Unemployment rate Taux de Chômage	Male Hommes: LF particip. rate Taux d'activité	Male Hommes: Unemployment rate Taux de Chômage	Female Femmes: LF particip. rate Taux d'activité	Female Femmes: Unemployment rate Taux de Chômage
Cyprus	2005	*63.0	5.3	*72.7	4.6	*53.2	6.4
Chypre	2010	*64.0	6.3	*70.6	6.2	*57.6	6.4
	2015	*62.6	14.9	*67.4	15.2	*57.9	14.6
	*2018	62.7	10.5	67.3	10.0	58.1	11.0
Czechia	2005	*59.5	7.9	*68.9	6.5	*50.8	9.8
Tchéquie	2010	*58.3	7.3	*68.0	6.4	*49.2	8.5
	2015	*59.6	5.1	*68.2	4.2	*51.4	6.1
	*2018	59.7	3.5	68.0	3.0	51.8	4.2
Dem. People's Rep. Korea	*2005	81.4	4.5	87.9	5.3	75.5	3.6
Rép. pop. dém. de Corée	*2010	80.8	4.6	87.2	5.4	74.9	3.7
	*2015	80.5	4.5	87.0	5.3	74.5	3.7
	*2018	80.4	4.7	86.9	5.4	74.4	4.0
Dem. Rep. of the Congo	2005	*72.3	3.7	*73.4	*3.0	*71.2	*4.3
Rép. dém. du Congo	*2010	72.4	3.7	73.6	3.0	71.2	4.4
	*2015	72.4	3.7	73.5	3.0	71.4	4.4
	*2018	72.4	3.7	73.5	3.1	71.4	4.3
Denmark	2005	*65.9	4.8	*71.4	4.4	*60.5	5.3
Danemark	2010	*64.4	7.5	*69.1	8.4	*59.8	6.5
	2015	*62.0	6.2	*66.4	5.9	*57.7	6.4
	*2018	63.0	5.9	67.0	5.5	59.1	6.3
Djibouti	*2005	60.3	6.4	73.8	5.8	46.7	7.4
Djibouti	*2010	59.3	6.2	71.1	5.6	47.6	7.1
	*2015	59.0	5.9	68.8	5.3	49.1	6.7
	*2018	59.1	5.8	68.6	5.2	49.5	6.7
Dominica							
Dominique	2001	57.7	11.0	70.2	12.0	45.0	9.5
Dominican Republic	2005	*64.9	6.5	*81.3	4.7	*48.8	9.5
République dominicaine	2010	*63.9	5.0	*78.7	3.8	*49.3	7.0
	2015	*66.7	5.9	*79.8	3.8	*53.9	9.0
	*2018	66.7	5.5	79.3	3.7	54.4	8.0
Ecuador	2005	*69.1	7.7	*83.2	5.6	*55.3	10.9
Équateur	2010	*65.1	4.1	*80.5	3.5	*49.9	5.0
	2015	*66.6	3.6	*81.2	3.0	*52.2	4.5
	*2018	68.0	5.1	81.2	4.1	55.0	6.5
Egypt	2005	*46.6	11.2	*73.0	7.1	*20.2	26.1
Égypte	2010	*49.3	11.9	*75.8	7.7	*22.8	25.7
	2015	*48.0	13.1	*73.6	9.1	*22.2	26.1
	*2018	48.1	11.8	73.8	8.1	22.3	24.3
El Salvador	2005	*60.9	7.2	*79.0	8.1	*45.5	5.9
El Salvador	2010	*61.3	4.9	*79.1	5.4	*46.4	4.2
	2015	*61.4	4.0	*78.5	4.4	*47.1	3.5
	*2018	61.7	4.6	79.1	5.1	47.3	3.9
Equatorial Guinea	*2005	58.0	5.7	61.5	5.3	53.8	6.3
Guinée équatoriale	*2010	58.8	5.6	61.5	5.3	55.4	6.0
	*2015	59.6	5.5	62.1	5.1	56.1	6.0
	*2018	59.2	7.6	61.7	7.4	55.7	7.8
Eritrea	*2005	79.3	7.0	84.9	6.5	73.8	7.5
Érythrée	*2010	80.6	6.8	86.6	6.3	74.7	7.3
	*2015	81.4	6.6	87.6	6.1	75.4	7.1
	*2018	81.3	6.3	87.3	5.9	75.4	6.8
Estonia	2005	*58.6	8.0	*64.7	9.1	*53.5	6.9
Estonie	2010	*60.5	16.7	*67.1	19.3	*55.0	14.1
	2015	*62.2	6.2	*69.5	6.3	*56.0	6.1
	*2018	62.5	6.7	69.9	7.6	56.2	5.8
Eswatini	*2005	52.6	22.1	68.0	21.5	38.8	23.0
Eswatini	*2010	52.6	27.8	66.3	27.3	40.3	28.5
	*2015	53.8	26.3	66.7	25.9	42.1	27.0
	*2018	54.5	26.4	67.4	26.0	42.9	27.0
Ethiopia	*2005	84.5	5.4	90.8	2.8	78.4	8.3
Éthiopie	*2010	83.6	5.2	90.0	3.0	77.5	7.7
	*2015	83.0	5.0	89.1	3.0	77.0	7.2
	2018	*82.6	*5.3	*87.9	*3.2	*77.4	7.7

17 Labour force participation rate and unemployment rate *(continued)*

Labour force (LF) participation rate and unemployment rate by sex (percent)

Taux d'activité et taux de chômage *(suite)*

Taux d'activité et taux de chômage par sexe (pourcentage)

Region, country or area [&] Région, pays ou zone [&]	Year Année	Male and Female Hommes et femmes: LF particip. rate Taux d'activité	Male and Female Hommes et femmes: Unemployment rate Taux de Chômage	Male Hommes: LF particip. rate Taux d'activité	Male Hommes: Unemployment rate Taux de Chômage	Female Femmes: LF particip. rate Taux d'activité	Female Femmes: Unemployment rate Taux de Chômage
Falkland Islands (Malvinas) [9] Îles Falkland (Malvinas) [9]	2013	# 81.9	1.2	# 86.0	1.1	# 77.2	1.4
Faroe Islands Îles Féroé	2005[3]	...	3.2	...	2.6	...	3.9
	2010[6,10]	81.7	# 6.4	85.3	# 5.1	77.5	# 8.0
	2013[6,10]	82.9	4.0	86.0	3.4	79.4	4.9
Fiji Fidji	2005	* 56.2	4.6	* 73.8	3.7	* 38.1	6.4
	2010	* 56.7	8.9	* 73.9	7.2	* 39.0	12.3
	*2015	58.5	6.1	75.7	4.9	40.9	8.4
	*2018	58.1	6.2	75.2	5.0	40.7	8.6
Finland Finlande	2005	* 60.6	8.4	* 64.8	8.2	* 56.6	8.6
	2010	* 59.8	8.4	* 63.9	9.1	* 56.0	7.6
	2015	* 58.8	9.4	* 62.3	9.9	* 55.5	8.8
	*2018	58.1	8.6	61.7	8.8	54.7	8.3
France France	2005	* 56.2	8.5	* 62.6	7.8	* 50.1	9.3
	2010	* 56.3	8.9	* 62.0	8.7	* 50.9	9.1
	2015	* 55.6	10.4	* 60.7	10.8	* 50.7	9.9
	*2018	55.0	9.7	59.8	9.8	50.5	9.5
French Guiana [6] Guyane française [6]	2005	42.1	24.8	48.2	22.8	36.3	27.0
	2010	48.9	21.0	54.9	17.8	43.2	25.1
	#2013	53.4	21.3	58.8	16.7	48.4	26.3
French Polynesia Polynésie française	*2005	56.7	11.8	65.7	10.9	47.2	13.2
	*2010	56.2	18.0	63.8	17.3	48.2	18.9
	*2015	55.4	21.4	62.3	20.8	48.2	22.2
	*2018	54.6	20.5	61.2	19.8	47.7	21.4
Gabon Gabon	2005	* 47.5	16.9	* 57.3	15.5	* 37.8	19.1
	2010	* 49.2	20.4	* 58.1	14.7	* 39.9	29.1
	*2015	50.9	20.2	58.8	14.4	42.3	28.8
	*2018	51.6	19.5	59.5	14.4	43.2	27.0
Gambia Gambie	*2005	58.5	9.4	68.8	6.9	48.5	12.8
	*2010	59.3	9.4	68.7	6.8	50.3	12.8
	*2015	59.3	9.4	67.9	6.8	51.0	12.7
	*2018	59.3	9.5	67.7	6.9	51.4	12.7
Georgia Géorgie	2005	* 63.4	13.8	* 72.9	14.8	* 55.2	12.7
	2010	* 64.8	16.3	* 75.1	17.9	* 56.0	14.4
	2015	* 68.1	12.0	* 78.7	13.4	* 58.9	10.3
	*2018	67.7	11.5	78.9	13.6	58.0	9.0
Germany Allemagne	2005	* 58.5	11.2	* 66.7	11.4	* 50.7	10.9
	2010	* 59.4	7.0	* 66.5	7.4	* 52.8	6.5
	2015	* 60.3	4.6	* 66.2	5.0	* 54.6	4.2
	*2018	60.4	3.6	66.1	3.9	55.1	3.3
Ghana Ghana	*2005	75.4	4.7	77.7	4.4	73.1	5.0
	2010	* 76.1	5.3	* 78.7	4.9	* 73.8	5.7
	*2015	76.7	2.2	79.0	2.0	74.5	2.3
	*2018	77.1	2.4	79.4	2.2	74.9	2.6
Gibraltar Gibraltar	2001	68.4	...	78.8	...	57.5	...
Greece Grèce	2005	* 53.6	10.0	* 64.9	6.3	* 42.7	15.5
	2010	* 54.4	12.7	* 64.5	10.1	* 44.8	16.3
	2015	* 53.1	24.9	* 61.1	21.8	* 45.5	28.9
	*2018	52.6	19.5	60.2	16.3	45.3	23.5
Greenland Groenland	2005	...	9.3	...	10.4	...	8.0
	2006	...	8.4	...	10.0	...	6.7
	#2013[11,12]	...	9.7	...	9.6	...	9.8
Grenada Grenade	2001	...	10.2	...	9.6	...	10.9
Guadeloupe [6] Guadeloupe [6]	2005	41.8	25.9	46.8	22.4	37.7	29.5
	2010	41.6	23.8	44.2	21.4	39.5	26.0
	#2013	52.7	26.1	56.5	23.8	49.6	28.3
Guam Guam	2005	* 68.2	7.0	* 79.9	7.6	* 56.1	6.1
	2010	* 66.8	8.2	* 78.6	9.0	* 54.8	7.1
	2015	* 65.4	6.9	* 77.2	7.6	* 53.5	5.9
	*2018	64.8	5.9	76.6	6.5	52.8	5.0

17 Labour force participation rate and unemployment rate *(continued)*

Labour force (LF) participation rate and unemployment rate by sex (percent)

Taux d'activité et taux de chômage *(suite)*

Taux d'activité et taux de chômage par sexe (pourcentage)

Region, country or area & Région, pays ou zone &	Year Année	Male and Female Hommes et femmes LF particip. rate Taux d'activité	Male and Female Hommes et femmes Unemployment rate Taux de Chômage	Male Hommes LF particip. rate Taux d'activité	Male Hommes Unemployment rate Taux de Chômage	Female Femmes LF particip. rate Taux d'activité	Female Femmes Unemployment rate Taux de Chômage
Guatemala	*2005	64.9	2.5	87.3	1.9	44.4	3.4
Guatemala	2010	* 62.7	3.7	* 85.6	3.4	* 41.7	4.3
	2015	* 61.5	2.7	* 85.6	2.1	* 39.1	4.0
	*2018	62.1	2.7	85.0	2.1	40.6	3.7
Guinea	*2005	65.1	4.6	67.4	5.6	62.8	3.5
Guinée	*2010	64.7	4.5	66.6	5.6	62.8	3.5
	*2015	64.4	4.5	65.8	5.5	63.0	3.5
	*2018	64.2	4.5	65.4	5.5	63.0	3.4
Guinea-Bissau	*2005	71.5	6.5	79.2	5.9	64.4	7.1
Guinée-Bissau	*2010	71.2	6.3	78.1	5.8	64.7	6.9
	*2015	71.5	6.2	78.0	5.7	65.3	6.8
	*2018	71.7	6.1	78.1	5.5	65.7	6.6
Guyana	*2005	55.8	11.8	78.0	9.8	34.1	16.2
Guyana	*2010	56.3	10.9	76.0	8.5	37.0	15.6
	*2015	57.5	11.9	74.7	9.3	40.2	16.8
	*2018	57.8	11.7	74.5	9.2	40.9	16.4
Haiti	*2005	64.5	15.0	70.1	13.0	59.2	17.3
Haïti	*2010	65.9	15.9	71.4	14.0	60.6	18.1
	*2015	67.6	14.0	72.2	12.3	63.2	16.0
	*2018	68.4	13.9	72.9	12.1	64.1	15.8
Honduras	2005	* 59.5	4.0	* 83.4	3.3	* 36.5	5.4
Honduras	2010	* 64.3	4.1	* 84.8	3.4	* 44.5	5.5
	2015	* 67.9	4.6	* 85.9	3.4	* 50.3	6.5
	*2018	68.1	4.3	85.6	3.7	50.9	5.3
Hungary	2005	* 50.1	7.2	* 58.4	7.0	* 42.9	7.4
Hongrie	2010	* 50.5	11.2	* 58.2	11.6	* 43.8	10.7
	2015	* 54.8	6.8	* 63.4	6.6	* 47.3	7.0
	*2018	55.4	4.0	63.9	4.0	47.9	4.0
Iceland	2005	* 75.8	2.6	* 80.7	2.6	* 70.9	2.5
Islande	2010	* 74.9	7.6	* 79.1	8.3	* 70.6	6.8
	2015	* 77.0	4.0	* 80.9	4.0	* 73.1	4.0
	*2018	76.9	2.8	81.2	2.7	72.5	2.9
India	2005	* 60.6	4.4	* 83.1	4.1	* 36.8	5.0
Inde	2010	* 55.3	3.5	* 80.5	3.3	* 28.6	4.4
	2015	* 53.9	3.5	* 79.1	3.3	* 27.3	4.2
	*2018	53.6	3.5	78.8	3.3	27.0	4.2
Indonesia	2005	* 67.5	7.7	* 85.2	6.7	* 49.9	9.4
Indonésie	2010	* 67.9	5.6	* 83.9	5.1	* 51.9	6.4
	2015	* 65.8	4.5	* 82.7	4.5	* 48.9	4.5
	*2018	66.2	4.4	81.6	4.6	50.7	4.1
Iran (Islamic Republic of)	2005	* 47.4	12.1	* 74.3	10.5	* 19.4	18.4
Iran (Rép. islamique d')	2010	* 43.2	13.5	* 70.0	11.9	* 15.9	20.8
	2015	* 42.8	11.1	* 70.3	9.3	* 15.2	19.3
	*2018	43.9	11.9	71.1	10.1	16.6	19.7
Iraq	2005	* 42.6	18.0	* 70.9	15.6	* 14.5	29.6
Iraq	*2010	46.8	11.2	75.8	9.3	18.1	19.4
	*2015	46.6	7.7	74.7	6.4	18.4	13.2
	*2018	46.7	8.5	74.3	7.2	19.0	13.6
Ireland	2005	* 62.5	4.3	* 72.8	4.6	* 52.4	4.0
Irlande	2010	* 61.2	13.9	* 69.2	17.0	* 53.3	9.8
	2015	* 60.2	9.4	* 68.1	10.8	* 52.6	7.7
	*2018	59.6	6.0	66.7	6.8	52.7	5.0
Isle of Man	2001	63.3	1.6	71.4	1.7	55.7	1.5
Île de Man	2006	62.8	2.4	69.9	2.8	56.3	2.0
	#2011[3]	63.3	3.3[11]	69.3	3.8[11]	57.5	2.8[11]
	#2013[13]	...	2.6	...	3.4	...	1.7
Israel	2005	* 61.7	11.3	* 68.8	11.1	* 55.0	11.6
Israël	2010	* 63.0	8.5	* 69.4	8.9	* 57.0	8.0
	2015	* 64.1	5.3	* 69.5	5.1	* 59.0	5.4
	*2018	64.1	4.3	69.0	4.2	59.3	4.4

17

Labour force participation rate and unemployment rate *(continued)*

Labour force (LF) participation rate and unemployment rate by sex (percent)

Taux d'activité et taux de chômage *(suite)*

Taux d'activité et taux de chômage par sexe (pourcentage)

Region, country or area & / Région, pays ou zone &	Year / Année	Male and Female / Hommes et femmes: LF particip. rate / Taux d'activité	Male and Female / Hommes et femmes: Unemployment rate / Taux de Chômage	Male / Hommes: LF particip. rate / Taux d'activité	Male / Hommes: Unemployment rate / Taux de Chômage	Female / Femmes: LF particip. rate / Taux d'activité	Female / Femmes: Unemployment rate / Taux de Chômage
Italy / Italie	2005	* 49.0	7.7	* 61.0	6.2	* 37.9	10.0
	2010	* 48.0	8.4	* 58.9	7.5	* 37.8	9.6
	2015	* 48.4	11.9	* 58.4	11.3	* 39.0	12.7
	*2018	48.4	11.0	58.0	10.2	39.4	12.1
Jamaica / Jamaïque	2005	* 65.9	10.9	* 76.8	8.3	* 55.6	14.3
	2010	* 66.4	12.4	* 77.1	9.6	* 56.1	16.1
	2015	* 66.8	13.5	* 77.2	10.1	* 56.7	18.0
	*2018	67.4	12.3	77.6	9.5	57.6	16.0
Japan / Japon	2005	* 60.6	4.4	* 73.5	4.6	* 48.4	4.2
	2010	* 60.1	5.1	* 72.1	5.4	* 48.7	4.6
	2015	* 60.0	3.3	* 70.8	3.6	* 49.9	3.0
	*2018	60.0	2.6	70.2	2.8	50.4	2.4
Jordan / Jordanie	2005	* 40.9	14.8	* 67.6	13.0	* 12.2	25.8
	2010	* 41.9	12.5	* 67.3	10.5	* 15.3	21.9
	2015	* 39.1	13.1	* 63.8	11.0	* 13.9	22.7
	*2018	39.0	14.7	63.5	12.4	14.0	25.1
Kazakhstan / Kazakhstan	2005	* 69.5	8.1	* 75.2	6.7	* 64.4	9.6
	2010	* 70.3	5.8	* 75.8	4.9	* 65.4	6.6
	2015	* 70.9	4.9	* 77.0	4.2	* 65.4	5.7
	*2018	70.9	5.1	77.2	4.3	65.2	5.9
Kenya / Kenya	*2005	64.8	10.5	69.7	7.5	60.1	13.9
	*2010	65.9	12.1	70.5	8.6	61.5	16.0
	*2015	65.6	11.6	68.9	8.1	62.4	15.4
	*2018	65.4	11.4	68.5	7.8	62.4	15.3
Kiribati / Kiribati	2005	# 26.4[14]	14.7[15]	# 32.8[14]	12.3[15]	# 20.4[14]	18.2[15]
	2010	# 59.3[14]	30.6[15]	66.8[14]	27.6[15]	52.3[14]	34.1[15]
Kosovo [13] / Kosovo [13]	2005	48.7	41.4	68.3	32.9	29.7	60.5
	2009	47.7	# 45.4	66.9	# 56.4	28.7	# 40.7
	#2012	37.1	30.9	55.5	28.1	17.9	40.0
	#2013	40.6	...	60.2	...	21.1	...
Kuwait / Koweït	2005	* 68.5	2.0	* 82.3	1.9	* 46.3	2.0
	2010	* 70.0	1.8	* 84.6	1.7	* 48.2	2.2
	2015	* 70.5	2.2	* 85.5	1.8	* 48.9	3.1
	*2018	68.6	2.1	83.7	1.8	46.9	2.8
Kyrgyzstan / Kirghizistan	2005	* 64.8	8.1	* 76.1	7.4	* 54.1	9.0
	2010	* 64.1	8.6	* 76.6	7.7	* 52.2	9.9
	2015	* 62.4	7.6	* 75.6	6.5	* 49.8	9.0
	*2018	61.6	7.4	75.9	6.3	48.0	8.9
Lao People's Dem. Rep. / Rép. dém. populaire lao	2005	* 78.8	1.4	* 79.8	1.4	* 77.9	1.3
	2010	* 78.1	0.7	* 79.3	0.8	* 76.8	0.7
	*2015	78.2	0.7	79.6	0.7	76.8	0.6
	*2018	78.4	0.7	79.8	0.7	77.0	0.6
Latvia / Lettonie	2005	* 57.3	10.0	* 65.6	10.1	* 50.4	10.0
	2010	* 59.0	19.5	* 65.3	22.7	* 53.9	16.3
	2015	* 60.2	9.9	* 67.6	11.1	* 54.3	8.6
	*2018	60.4	9.4	67.0	9.8	55.0	8.9
Lebanon / Liban	*2005	46.2	8.1	70.7	7.5	20.4	10.4
	*2010	45.7	6.3	67.8	5.8	22.3	7.8
	*2015	46.9	6.1	70.6	5.8	22.9	7.4
	*2018	47.2	6.3	71.1	6.0	23.3	7.5
Lesotho / Lesotho	*2005	70.4	37.2	77.4	34.9	64.1	39.7
	*2010	67.7	25.9	75.4	22.4	60.7	29.8
	*2015	66.2	27.0	74.0	24.7	59.1	29.5
	*2018	66.6	28.5	74.6	26.2	59.3	31.1
Liberia / Libéria	*2005	56.1	5.6	59.2	6.9	53.0	4.2
	2010	* 56.4	2.3	* 59.3	2.2	* 53.6	2.3
	*2015	55.8	2.3	57.7	2.3	54.0	2.3
	*2018	55.6	2.4	57.3	2.5	53.9	2.4
Libya / Libye	*2005	52.3	20.0	75.5	17.4	27.4	27.7
	*2010	53.8	18.6	77.3	16.3	29.3	25.0
	*2015	52.4	18.4	78.8	15.6	25.8	26.9
	*2018	52.5	15.7	79.1	12.6	25.8	25.0

17

Labour force participation rate and unemployment rate *(continued)*
Labour force (LF) participation rate and unemployment rate by sex (percent)

Taux d'activité et taux de chômage *(suite)*
Taux d'activité et taux de chômage par sexe (pourcentage)

Region, country or area & Région, pays ou zone &	Year Année	Male and Female Hommes et femmes: LF particip. rate Taux d'activité	Male and Female Hommes et femmes: Unemployment rate Taux de Chômage	Male Hommes: LF particip. rate Taux d'activité	Male Hommes: Unemployment rate Taux de Chômage	Female Femmes: LF particip. rate Taux d'activité	Female Femmes: Unemployment rate Taux de Chômage
Liechtenstein	2005	63.0	...	73.7	...	52.8	...
Liechtenstein	2010	61.6	2.6[13]	70.9	2.3[13]	52.6	3.1[13]
	2013	61.9	2.6[13]	70.6	2.3[13]	53.5	3.1[13]
Lithuania	2005	* 56.2	8.3	* 62.9	8.1	* 50.6	8.5
Lituanie	2010	* 57.0	17.8	* 62.3	21.2	* 52.5	14.5
	2015	* 59.3	9.1	* 65.0	10.1	* 54.5	8.2
	*2018	60.5	7.4	66.1	8.5	55.9	6.2
Luxembourg	2005	* 54.8	4.5	* 64.7	3.5	* 45.4	5.8
Luxembourg	2010	* 57.0	4.4	* 65.4	3.8	* 48.8	5.1
	2015	* 59.4	6.7	* 65.2	6.1	* 53.6	7.3
	*2018	57.8	5.6	63.3	5.4	52.3	5.9
Madagascar	2005	* 86.6	2.3	* 89.1	2.2	* 84.2	2.4
Madagascar	2010	* 89.1	3.8	* 91.0	3.7	* 87.1	4.0
	2015	* 86.5	1.8	* 89.6	1.7	* 83.5	1.9
	*2018	86.6	1.8	89.5	1.7	83.8	1.9
Malawi	2005	* 77.1	7.8	* 80.1	6.5	* 74.2	9.1
Malawi	*2010	77.3	6.7	81.8	5.7	73.1	7.8
	*2015	77.1	5.9	82.0	5.0	72.4	6.9
	*2018	77.1	6.1	82.1	5.1	72.4	7.1
Malaysia	2005	* 61.1	3.5	* 77.5	3.3	* 44.0	4.0
Malaisie	2010	* 60.3	3.3	* 76.1	3.1	* 43.5	3.5
	2015	* 64.3	3.1	* 77.4	2.9	* 50.3	3.4
	*2018	64.7	3.4	77.5	3.0	51.0	3.9
Maldives	*2005	63.9	3.8	75.6	3.6	50.4	4.2
Maldives	*2010	66.1	4.6	78.6	4.2	50.1	5.3
	*2015	66.2	5.1	81.8	4.7	44.5	6.0
	*2018	66.3	5.0	82.5	4.6	43.3	6.0
Mali	*2005	53.7	9.5	69.9	8.5	38.2	11.4
Mali	2010	* 65.0	8.1	* 80.5	6.2	* 49.9	11.1
	2015	* 71.3	7.7	* 82.5	7.2	* 60.4	8.4
	*2018	71.8	8.0	82.8	7.4	61.1	8.8
Malta	2005	* 48.4	6.9	* 67.5	6.3	* 29.6	8.4
Malte	2010	* 50.1	6.9	* 66.4	6.7	* 34.1	7.1
	2015	* 54.2	5.4	* 66.8	5.5	* 41.6	5.2
	*2018	54.3	4.2	66.4	3.9	42.3	4.6
Marshall Islands	2006[3]	44.6	...	...	...	...	...
Îles Marshall	2011	41.3	# 4.7	53.3	# 4.9	29.0	# 4.5
Martinique [6]	2005	43.6	18.7	48.5	16.9	39.6	20.4
Martinique [6]	2010	45.9	21.0	49.1	19.7	43.3	22.2
	#2013	53.1	22.8	53.8	22.8	52.6	22.8
Mauritania	*2005	50.6	10.4	71.4	9.7	30.2	12.1
Mauritanie	*2010	49.7	10.2	69.2	9.6	30.4	11.6
	*2015	49.4	10.0	67.8	9.4	30.9	11.3
	*2018	49.4	10.2	67.7	9.5	31.1	11.8
Mauritius	2005	* 58.7	9.6	* 76.8	5.8	* 41.1	16.5
Maurice	2010	* 58.2	7.7	* 74.1	4.6	* 42.8	12.9
	2015	* 59.7	7.9	* 73.6	5.5	* 46.2	11.6
	*2018	58.4	7.0	72.2	4.6	45.1	10.8
Mexico	2005	* 61.0	3.6	* 81.5	3.4	* 41.3	3.9
Mexique	2010	* 61.4	5.3	* 80.1	5.4	* 43.2	5.2
	2015	* 61.4	4.3	* 79.3	4.2	* 43.9	4.5
	*2018	61.3	3.6	78.9	3.6	44.3	3.7
Monaco [16]							
Monaco [16]	2000	45.7	3.6	57.3	2.5	35.1	5.2
Mongolia	2005	* 59.3	3.3	* 64.9	3.5	* 53.7	3.1
Mongolie	2010	* 59.0	6.6	* 65.1	7.1	* 53.1	5.9
	2015	* 60.3	4.9	* 67.2	5.3	* 53.7	4.3
	*2018	59.3	6.7	66.2	7.5	52.7	5.7
Montenegro	2005	* 50.6	30.3	* 59.1	31.1	* 42.7	29.2
Monténégro	2010	* 49.4	19.7	* 56.6	20.0	* 42.6	19.3
	2015	* 48.9	17.5	* 55.6	18.4	* 42.4	16.5
	*2018	48.2	16.4	54.7	17.0	42.0	15.7

17 Labour force participation rate and unemployment rate *(continued)*

Labour force (LF) participation rate and unemployment rate by sex (percent)

Taux d'activité et taux de chômage *(suite)*

Taux d'activité et taux de chômage par sexe (pourcentage)

Region, country or area & Région, pays ou zone &	Year Année	Male and Female Hommes et femmes: LF particip. rate Taux d'activité	Male and Female Hommes et femmes: Unemployment rate Taux de Chômage	Male Hommes: LF particip. rate Taux d'activité	Male Hommes: Unemployment rate Taux de Chômage	Female Femmes: LF particip. rate Taux d'activité	Female Femmes: Unemployment rate Taux de Chômage
Montserrat	#2001	85.2	9.5	89.2	...	80.6	...
Montserrat	2011	...	5.6	...	7.7	...	3.3
Morocco	2005	* 50.8	11.0	* 76.3	10.8	* 26.7	11.6
Maroc	2010	* 49.9	9.1	* 75.6	8.8	* 25.6	9.8
	2015	* 49.1	9.7	* 74.3	9.4	* 25.0	10.4
	*2018	48.9	9.3	73.9	9.0	24.9	10.0
Mozambique	*2005	85.1	21.7	82.9	19.1	87.1	23.9
Mozambique	*2010	81.8	22.2	78.8	20.0	84.4	24.0
	*2015	79.0	25.3	74.8	23.1	82.8	27.1
	*2018	78.6	24.9	74.6	22.7	82.3	26.7
Myanmar	*2005	69.5	0.9	83.9	0.7	56.1	1.0
Myanmar	*2010	67.4	0.8	82.3	0.7	53.5	0.9
	2015	* 65.6	0.8	* 80.5	0.7	* 51.8	0.9
	*2018	64.8	0.8	79.6	0.7	51.1	0.9
Namibia	*2005	57.9	22.2	64.4	19.9	52.0	24.9
Namibie	2010	* 58.9	22.1	* 63.8	19.9	* 54.6	24.4
	*2015	61.0	19.6	64.6	17.9	57.7	21.3
	*2018	62.1	23.3	65.6	21.7	59.0	24.9
Nauru	2002[3]	78.0	22.7	86.8	17.1	69.6	29.6
Nauru	2011	64.0	# 23.0	78.9	# 21.4	49.3	# 25.5
Nepal	*2005	84.2	1.5	88.7	1.7	79.9	1.2
Népal	*2010	83.2	2.1	87.1	2.5	79.6	1.8
	*2015	84.1	3.1	86.2	3.6	82.3	2.6
	*2018	84.1	2.7	85.8	3.2	82.7	2.2
Netherlands	2005	* 64.4	4.7	* 72.3	4.4	* 56.6	5.1
Pays-Bas	2010	* 64.7	4.5	* 71.3	4.4	* 58.2	4.5
	2015	* 64.1	6.9	* 70.1	6.5	* 58.2	7.3
	*2018	63.3	4.3	68.9	3.9	57.9	4.6
Netherlands Antilles [former] 6,14,17	#2009	56.3	...	61.1	...	52.6	...
Antilles néerlandaises [anc.] 6,14,17	2011	57.9	...	62.2	...	54.5	...
New Caledonia	*2005	65.6	15.8	70.6	14.8	60.5	17.0
Nouvelle-Calédonie	*2010	63.2	14.2	68.2	13.3	58.1	15.3
	*2015	62.9	14.6	68.1	13.7	57.7	15.6
	*2018	62.6	14.8	67.9	13.9	57.3	15.9
New Zealand	2005	* 67.2	3.8	* 74.7	3.5	* 60.1	4.1
Nouvelle-Zélande	2010	* 67.2	6.1	* 73.8	5.9	* 61.0	6.4
	2015	* 68.3	5.4	* 74.1	4.9	* 62.8	5.9
	*2018	69.1	5.0	74.7	4.7	63.8	5.4
Nicaragua	2005	* 62.5	5.6	* 82.1	5.3	* 44.1	6.0
Nicaragua	2010	* 64.4	7.8	* 82.9	7.5	* 47.1	8.3
	*2015	66.2	4.5	84.1	3.9	49.5	5.5
	*2018	66.7	4.4	83.9	4.0	50.6	5.1
Niger	2005	* 79.0	3.1	* 90.9	3.9	* 67.8	2.1
Niger	*2010	79.2	0.9	91.1	1.1	67.7	0.6
	*2015	79.0	0.3	90.8	0.4	67.5	0.2
	*2018	78.9	0.4	90.6	0.4	67.5	0.2
Nigeria	*2005	54.8	4.3	61.7	4.3	47.8	4.4
Nigéria	*2010	55.0	3.9	60.7	4.0	49.2	3.8
	2015	* 55.1	4.3	* 59.8	4.7	* 50.4	3.9
	*2018	55.1	7.0	59.7	7.6	50.5	6.3
Niue	2001	75.5	2.2	76.7	2.3	74.8	2.1
Nioué	#2002	...	9.7	...	...	...	...
Northern Mariana Islands 3	2003	81.8	4.6	82.5	5.0	81.3	4.3
Îles Mariannes du Nord 3	2005	...	6.5	...	7.3	...	5.8
	#2010	72.3	11.2	77.6	9.7	66.6	13.0
Norway	2005	* 65.4	4.4	* 70.3	4.6	* 60.7	4.2
Norvège	2010	* 65.7	3.5	* 69.7	4.0	* 61.8	2.9
	2015	* 64.9	4.3	* 68.4	4.6	* 61.3	4.0
	*2018	64.1	4.0	67.4	4.6	60.8	3.4

Labour force participation rate and unemployment rate *(continued)*
Labour force (LF) participation rate and unemployment rate by sex (percent)

Taux d'activité et taux de chômage *(suite)*
Taux d'activité et taux de chômage par sexe (pourcentage)

Region, country or area & / Région, pays ou zone &	Year / Année	Male and Female / Hommes et femmes: LF particip. rate / Taux d'activité	Male and Female / Hommes et femmes: Unemployment rate / Taux de Chômage	Male / Hommes: LF particip. rate / Taux d'activité	Male / Hommes: Unemployment rate / Taux de Chômage	Female / Femmes: LF particip. rate / Taux d'activité	Female / Femmes: Unemployment rate / Taux de Chômage
Oman	*2005	56.1	19.1	77.4	14.6	25.2	39.2
Oman	*2010	61.9	18.2	80.9	14.9	28.7	34.7
	*2015	69.6	15.8	87.4	13.3	30.4	32.0
	*2018	70.6	16.2	87.7	14.0	30.1	31.6
Pakistan	2005	* 52.6	7.7	* 84.1	6.5	* 19.3	13.0
Pakistan	2010	* 51.6	0.7	* 80.1	0.7	* 21.7	0.7
	2015	* 53.2	3.6	* 81.2	2.8	* 23.9	6.2
	*2018	54.5	4.2	82.6	3.3	25.1	7.3
Palau 3							
Palaos 3	2005	67.5	4.2	75.4	3.7	58.1	4.9
Panama	*2005	64.5	9.8	81.1	7.7	47.9	13.3
Panama	*2010	65.4	6.5	82.0	5.3	49.0	8.6
	*2015	65.4	5.3	80.5	4.3	50.5	6.9
	*2017	65.4	6.2	80.4	4.9	50.5	8.1
Papua New Guinea	*2005	72.4	2.5	73.9	3.3	70.9	1.6
Papouasie-Nvl-Guinée	2010	* 71.6	2.0	* 73.0	2.7	* 70.2	1.3
	*2015	70.0	2.6	71.0	3.6	69.1	1.7
	*2018	69.9	2.7	70.8	3.6	68.9	1.7
Paraguay	2005	* 70.3	5.8	* 85.3	4.9	* 55.0	7.3
Paraguay	2010	* 69.0	4.6	* 83.7	3.6	* 53.9	6.1
	2015	* 69.6	4.6	* 82.9	4.2	* 55.9	5.0
	*2018	70.5	5.2	83.8	4.2	56.9	6.6
Peru	2005	* 75.6	4.9	* 84.6	4.8	* 66.7	4.9
Pérou	2010	* 79.1	3.5	* 86.3	3.2	* 72.0	3.8
	2015	* 76.1	3.0	* 84.2	3.0	* 68.1	3.0
	*2018	77.0	3.8	84.7	3.7	69.4	3.8
Philippines	2005	* 62.1	7.8	* 76.6	7.4	* 47.7	8.5
Philippines	2010	* 62.4	3.6	* 76.1	3.5	* 48.6	3.8
	2015	* 62.4	3.0	* 75.4	2.9	* 49.4	3.2
	*2018	62.4	5.9	75.1	5.7	49.8	6.3
Poland	2005	* 55.1	17.8	* 63.0	16.6	* 47.8	19.1
Pologne	2010	* 55.9	9.6	* 64.3	9.3	* 48.3	10.0
	2015	* 56.7	7.5	* 65.1	7.3	* 49.0	7.7
	*2018	56.3	4.2	64.8	4.2	48.5	4.3
Portugal	2005	* 62.0	7.6	* 69.3	6.7	* 55.3	8.6
Portugal	2010	* 61.0	10.8	* 66.9	9.8	* 55.8	11.9
	2015	* 58.6	12.4	* 64.2	12.1	* 53.8	12.8
	*2018	57.8	7.8	63.3	7.7	53.0	7.9
Puerto Rico	2005	* 47.4	11.4	* 59.1	12.2	* 36.9	10.1
Porto Rico	2010	* 44.7	16.4	* 55.0	18.4	* 35.6	13.5
	2015	* 41.7	12.0	* 51.2	13.5	* 33.2	9.9
	*2018	41.5	11.5	50.9	13.0	33.1	9.5
Qatar	*2005	80.2	1.6	94.0	0.9	45.1	5.0
Qatar	2010	* 86.7	0.4	* 95.8	0.1	* 51.1	2.6
	2015	* 87.6	0.2	* 95.0	0.1	* 58.9	0.8
	*2018	86.8	0.2	94.7	0.1	57.8	0.8
Republic of Korea	2005	* 62.1	3.7	* 74.0	4.0	* 50.4	3.3
République de Corée	2010	* 60.8	3.7	* 72.2	4.0	* 49.5	3.3
	2015	* 62.5	3.6	* 73.1	3.7	* 51.9	3.5
	*2018	62.6	3.7	73.2	3.8	52.2	3.5
Republic of Moldova	2005	* 48.5	7.3	* 50.9	8.6	* 46.4	6.0
République de Moldova	2010	* 42.0	7.5	* 45.4	9.0	* 38.9	5.8
	2015	* 44.1	3.7	* 47.3	4.4	* 41.3	2.9
	*2018	42.1	4.4	45.6	5.7	38.9	3.0
Réunion 6	2005	50.1	30.1	60.3	27.6	41.1	33.3
Réunion 6	2010	52.1	28.9	59.9	28.0	45.3	30.0
	#2013	54.9	28.9	61.3	28.3	49.1	29.7
Romania	2005	* 53.5	7.2	* 61.2	7.8	* 46.3	6.4
Roumanie	2010	* 55.0	7.0	* 64.3	7.6	* 46.3	6.2
	2015	* 54.3	6.8	* 64.2	7.5	* 45.2	5.9
	*2018	52.9	5.1	62.8	5.8	43.7	4.3

17 Labour force participation rate and unemployment rate *(continued)*

Labour force (LF) participation rate and unemployment rate by sex (percent)

Taux d'activité et taux de chômage *(suite)*

Taux d'activité et taux de chômage par sexe (pourcentage)

Region, country or area & Région, pays ou zone &	Year Année	Male and Female Hommes et femmes: LF particip. rate Taux d'activité	Male and Female Hommes et femmes: Unemployment rate Taux de Chômage	Male Hommes: LF particip. rate Taux d'activité	Male Hommes: Unemployment rate Taux de Chômage	Female Femmes: LF particip. rate Taux d'activité	Female Femmes: Unemployment rate Taux de Chômage
Russian Federation	2005	* 61.6	7.2	* 68.3	7.7	* 55.9	6.6
Fédération de Russie	2010	* 63.0	7.4	* 70.8	7.9	* 56.5	6.8
	2015	* 63.7	5.6	* 71.9	5.8	* 56.8	5.3
	*2018	63.2	5.0	71.4	5.3	56.3	4.8
Rwanda	*2005	86.0	1.7	86.8	1.4	85.2	1.9
Rwanda	*2010	86.8	3.0	87.6	2.5	86.1	3.5
	*2015	86.4	1.2	86.7	1.1	86.1	1.3
	*2018	86.1	1.4	86.2	1.3	86.0	1.4
Saint Helena	2005	...	5.2	...	...	...	...
Sainte-Hélène	2010	...	2.0	...	...	...	...
Saint Kitts and Nevis Saint-Kitts-et-Nevis	2001	# 68.8	5.1	# 62.8	4.3	# 74.9	5.9
Saint Lucia	2005	* 66.2	18.7	* 75.6	16.4	* 57.3	21.5
Sainte-Lucie	2010	* 66.9	20.6	* 75.3	18.3	* 58.9	23.5
	2015	* 68.0	24.1	* 75.8	21.5	* 60.6	27.1
	*2018	68.5	20.4	75.9	18.8	61.4	22.3
Saint Vincent & Grenadines	*2005	67.9	18.9	80.8	17.6	54.7	20.8
Saint-Vincent-Grenadines	*2010	69.2	18.8	81.0	17.6	57.3	20.6
	*2015	69.5	18.0	80.5	16.9	58.3	19.5
	*2018	69.5	18.3	80.1	17.2	58.7	19.6
Samoa	*2005	33.0	2.1	40.8	1.8	24.6	2.5
Samoa	*2010	32.6	4.8	40.4	4.4	24.3	5.5
	*2015	32.0	8.8	39.6	7.8	23.9	10.5
	*2018	31.4	8.1	38.7	7.2	23.7	9.6
San Marino	2003	66.2	...	79.2	...	53.8	...
Saint-Marin	2010	...	4.4	...	2.1	...	7.3
	#2014[4]	...	6.6	...	4.3	...	9.5
Sao Tome and Principe	2005	* 55.8	16.5	* 73.5	15.1	* 38.8	19.0
Sao Tomé-et-Principe	*2010	57.5	14.6	75.5	13.4	40.1	16.8
	*2015	58.2	13.3	75.7	12.1	41.2	15.4
	*2018	58.0	13.4	75.3	12.3	41.2	15.4
Saudi Arabia	2005	* 50.5	6.1	* 74.0	4.2	* 17.7	17.1
Arabie saoudite	2010	* 51.1	5.6	* 74.4	3.5	* 18.2	17.4
	2015	* 55.6	5.6	* 79.2	2.4	* 22.1	21.7
	*2018	56.4	5.6	79.7	3.3	22.3	17.6
Senegal	*2005	51.2	8.9	69.8	7.2	34.2	12.1
Sénégal	*2010	55.4	10.2	69.6	8.0	42.4	13.6
	2015	* 56.9	4.9	* 69.9	4.8	* 45.0	4.9
	*2018	57.4	4.8	69.9	4.7	45.9	5.1
Serbia	2005	* 54.6	20.9	* 64.5	17.1	* 45.4	25.9
Serbie	2010	* 50.9	19.2	* 59.4	18.5	* 42.9	20.2
	2015	* 52.0	17.9	* 60.5	17.1	* 44.1	19.0
	*2018	53.1	13.1	61.2	12.3	45.6	14.0
Seychelles	2005	72.1	5.5	...	6.1	...	4.9
Seychelles	#2011[6,18]	65.0	4.1	68.3	3.8	61.9	4.5
Sierra Leone	*2005	65.0	3.6	65.7	4.7	64.4	2.4
Sierra Leone	*2010	61.2	4.3	61.9	5.3	60.5	3.2
	*2015	58.2	4.7	59.2	5.6	57.2	3.8
	*2018	57.8	4.4	58.6	5.1	57.0	3.6
Singapore	2005	* 64.2	5.6	* 76.3	5.3	* 52.4	6.1
Singapour	2010	* 66.9	3.2	* 77.2	3.1	* 57.1	3.3
	2015	* 68.9	1.7	* 77.3	1.6	* 60.8	1.7
	*2018	68.3	1.8	76.5	1.8	60.3	1.9
Slovakia	2005	* 59.6	16.3	* 68.6	15.5	* 51.3	17.2
Slovaquie	2010	* 58.8	14.4	* 67.6	14.2	* 50.6	14.6
	2015	* 59.6	11.5	* 67.8	10.3	* 52.0	12.9
	*2018	59.5	6.9	67.4	6.2	52.2	7.6
Slovenia	2005	* 59.2	6.5	* 66.0	6.1	* 52.9	7.0
Slovénie	2010	* 59.2	7.2	* 65.5	7.4	* 53.2	7.1
	2015	* 57.4	9.0	* 62.9	8.1	* 52.0	10.0
	*2018	55.8	6.7	60.4	6.2	51.4	7.2

17 Labour force participation rate and unemployment rate *(continued)*
Labour force (LF) participation rate and unemployment rate by sex (percent)

Taux d'activité et taux de chômage *(suite)*
Taux d'activité et taux de chômage par sexe (pourcentage)

Region, country or area & Région, pays ou zone &	Year Année	Male and Female Hommes et femmes: LF particip. rate Taux d'activité	Male and Female Hommes et femmes: Unemployment rate Taux de Chômage	Male Hommes: LF particip. rate Taux d'activité	Male Hommes: Unemployment rate Taux de Chômage	Female Femmes: LF particip. rate Taux d'activité	Female Femmes: Unemployment rate Taux de Chômage
Solomon Islands Îles Salomon	*2005	72.9	2.2	81.7	2.1	63.9	2.3
	*2010	72.4	2.1	81.4	2.0	63.4	2.2
	*2015	71.6	2.0	80.4	2.0	62.6	2.1
	*2018	71.4	2.1	80.3	2.0	62.4	2.2
Somalia Somalie	*2005	46.7	5.9	76.0	5.7	17.5	6.7
	*2010	46.0	6.0	75.0	5.8	17.5	6.8
	*2015	46.0	6.1	74.3	5.9	18.5	6.8
	*2018	46.2	5.9	74.3	5.7	18.7	6.7
South Africa Afrique du Sud	2005	*53.6	23.8	*61.8	20.1	*45.9	28.5
	2010	*52.4	24.7	*60.5	22.8	*44.7	27.1
	2015	*54.6	25.2	*61.9	23.2	*47.8	27.5
	*2018	54.7	28.5	62.0	26.1	47.9	31.4
South Sudan Soudan du sud	*2005	73.9	12.2	77.2	11.2	70.6	13.2
	*2010	73.2	12.1	75.9	11.2	70.6	13.2
	*2015	72.4	12.0	74.2	11.0	70.7	13.0
	*2018	72.4	11.5	73.8	10.2	70.9	12.9
Spain Espagne	2005	*56.8	9.2	*68.0	7.1	*46.1	12.0
	2010	*59.3	19.9	*67.3	19.6	*51.5	20.2
	2015	*58.3	22.1	*64.7	20.8	*52.3	23.6
	*2018	57.5	15.4	63.3	14.2	52.0	16.8
Sri Lanka Sri Lanka	2005	*56.3	7.7	*76.7	5.6	*36.9	11.8
	2010	*54.7	4.9	*76.3	3.6	*34.8	7.7
	2015	*53.9	4.7	*74.9	3.1	*34.9	7.6
	*2018	53.3	4.1	73.9	2.8	34.9	6.6
State of Palestine État de Palestine	2005	*40.8	23.5	*67.0	24.4	*14.1	19.0
	2010	*40.9	23.7	*66.4	23.1	*14.8	26.6
	2015	*45.4	25.9	*71.3	22.5	*19.0	39.0
	*2018	46.2	28.6	72.1	27.7	19.8	32.0
Sudan Soudan	*2005	49.1	13.0	74.0	10.8	24.5	19.3
	*2010	47.5	12.9	72.7	10.8	23.0	19.2
	*2015	46.7	12.9	70.4	10.8	23.6	18.9
	*2018	46.4	12.8	69.8	10.9	23.5	18.3
Suriname Suriname	*2005	52.2	9.8	65.5	6.0	38.9	16.3
	2010	*53.1	7.6	*65.4	4.5	*41.1	12.4
	2015	*53.6	7.2	*65.1	4.4	*42.2	11.5
	*2018	53.4	8.1	65.1	5.2	41.9	12.5
Sweden Suède	2005	*63.7	7.7	*68.0	7.8	*59.6	7.6
	2010	*63.1	8.6	*67.4	8.7	*58.9	8.5
	2015	*63.9	7.4	*67.3	7.5	*60.6	7.3
	*2018	64.1	6.7	67.3	7.1	60.8	6.3
Switzerland Suisse	2005	*67.0	4.4	*75.0	3.9	*59.5	5.1
	2010	*66.9	4.8	*74.3	4.5	*59.9	5.2
	2015	*68.2	4.8	*74.2	4.7	*62.4	4.9
	*2018	68.3	4.9	73.9	4.8	62.8	4.9
Syrian Arab Republic République arabe syrienne	*2005	46.6	9.9	76.2	6.4	16.2	26.4
	2010	*43.1	8.6	*72.8	6.2	*13.2	21.8
	*2015	41.6	14.6	70.9	10.4	12.1	39.3
	*2018	40.7	12.1	69.7	8.1	11.6	35.7
Tajikistan Tadjikistan	*2005	58.4	11.2	69.5	10.9	47.3	11.6
	*2010	59.1	11.7	71.4	11.7	46.9	11.7
	*2015	59.2	10.4	72.8	9.9	45.7	11.1
	*2018	59.3	10.3	73.5	9.9	45.4	11.0
Thailand Thaïlande	2005	*73.4	1.4	*81.5	1.5	*65.7	1.2
	2010	*72.4	0.6	*80.8	0.6	*64.5	0.6
	2015	*69.1	0.6	*77.8	0.6	*61.0	0.6
	*2018	68.4	1.3	77.0	1.2	60.3	1.3
TFYR of Macedonia ex-R.Y. de Macédoine	2005	*52.8	37.3	*63.8	37.0	*42.0	37.6
	2010	*55.6	32.0	*68.6	31.9	*42.8	32.2
	2015	*55.5	26.1	*67.6	26.7	*43.5	25.1
	*2018	54.9	22.8	67.4	23.4	42.5	21.9

17 Labour force participation rate and unemployment rate *(continued)*
Labour force (LF) participation rate and unemployment rate by sex (percent)

Taux d'activité et taux de chômage *(suite)*
Taux d'activité et taux de chômage par sexe (pourcentage)

Region, country or area & Région, pays ou zone &	Year Année	Male and Female Hommes et femmes: LF particip. rate Taux d'activité	Male and Female Hommes et femmes: Unemployment rate Taux de Chômage	Male Hommes: LF particip. rate Taux d'activité	Male Hommes: Unemployment rate Taux de Chômage	Female Femmes: LF particip. rate Taux d'activité	Female Femmes: Unemployment rate Taux de Chômage
Timor-Leste	*2005	49.2	7.2	66.4	6.5	31.6	8.7
Timor-Leste	2010	* 41.5	3.3	* 56.2	2.8	* 26.5	4.4
	*2015	39.2	3.3	52.9	2.8	25.2	4.4
	*2018	38.6	3.5	52.1	3.0	24.7	4.5
Togo	*2005	80.6	1.9	80.7	2.2	80.5	1.6
Togo	*2010	78.6	1.9	80.3	2.1	77.0	1.6
	*2015	77.8	1.8	79.6	2.1	76.1	1.6
	*2018	77.4	1.8	79.3	2.1	75.6	1.5
Tonga	*2005	60.1	3.0	75.2	3.0	45.5	2.8
Tonga	*2010	59.9	1.1	75.0	1.1	45.4	1.1
	*2015	59.5	1.1	74.3	1.1	45.2	1.1
	*2018	59.5	1.2	74.1	1.2	45.1	1.2
Trinidad and Tobago	2005	* 64.7	8.0	* 76.2	5.8	* 53.5	11.0
Trinité-et-Tobago	2010	* 63.8	5.9	* 75.4	5.1	* 52.5	7.0
	2015	* 62.7	3.4	* 74.3	2.9	* 51.7	4.1
	*2018	61.8	5.1	73.2	4.1	51.0	6.4
Tunisia	2005	* 45.9	12.9	* 68.6	12.1	* 23.9	15.2
Tunisie	2010	* 46.7	13.1	* 69.7	10.9	* 24.5	19.0
	2015	* 47.2	15.2	* 70.8	13.0	* 24.7	21.3
	*2018	46.7	15.1	70.3	12.9	24.1	21.3
Turkey	2005	* 46.0	10.6	* 70.1	10.5	* 23.3	11.0
Turquie	2010	* 47.7	10.7	* 69.6	10.4	* 27.0	11.2
	2015	* 51.0	10.2	* 71.7	9.2	* 31.5	12.5
	*2018	51.5	11.1	71.7	9.8	32.2	14.0
Turkmenistan	*2005	63.5	3.8	75.2	3.7	52.5	3.9
Turkménistan	2010	* 64.2	4.0	* 76.2	4.0	* 52.9	4.0
	*2015	65.4	3.6	78.1	3.4	53.5	3.8
	*2018	65.4	3.3	78.2	3.2	53.2	3.6
Turks and Caicos Islands	2005	# 62.0	8.0	...	...	...	...
Îles Turques-et-Caïques	#2008	64.0	8.3	...	...	...	...
Tuvalu Tuvalu	2005	58.2	6.5	69.6	4.9	47.9	8.6
Uganda	2005	* 70.4	1.9	* 76.1	1.6	* 65.0	2.3
Ouganda	*2010	70.8	4.0	76.0	3.3	65.9	4.8
	*2015	70.7	1.9	75.2	1.4	66.4	2.5
	*2018	70.8	2.2	74.9	1.5	66.7	3.0
Ukraine	2005	* 55.1	7.2	* 62.9	7.5	* 48.5	6.8
Ukraine	2010	* 55.0	8.1	* 63.0	9.3	* 48.4	6.8
	2015	* 54.6	9.1	* 63.3	10.1	* 47.3	8.1
	*2018	53.9	9.0	62.7	10.3	46.6	7.6
United Arab Emirates	2005	* 78.4	3.1	* 92.5	2.6	* 37.2	7.1
Émirats arabes unis	*2010	82.2	3.8	93.3	3.0	42.9	10.1
	*2015	81.3	2.1	93.3	1.6	41.8	5.5
	*2018	79.1	1.8	91.7	1.4	40.6	4.5
United Kingdom	2005	* 61.7	4.8	* 69.2	5.2	* 54.7	4.3
Royaume-Uni	2010	* 61.8	7.8	* 68.6	8.6	* 55.5	6.9
	2015	* 62.2	5.3	* 68.2	5.5	* 56.6	5.1
	*2018	62.3	4.2	68.1	4.3	56.9	4.1
United Rep. of Tanzania	*2005	83.1	4.4	84.4	3.0	81.8	5.9
Rép.-Unie de Tanzanie	*2010	83.1	3.0	84.4	2.1	81.9	3.8
	*2015	83.4	2.1	87.4	1.6	79.5	2.7
	*2018	83.3	2.3	87.5	1.7	79.4	2.9
United States of America	2005	* 65.1	5.1	* 72.2	5.1	* 58.2	5.1
États-Unis d'Amérique	2010	* 63.6	9.6	* 69.9	10.5	* 57.5	8.6
	2015	* 62.0	5.3	* 68.4	5.4	* 55.8	5.2
	*2018	61.6	4.3	68.0	4.3	55.5	4.2
United States Virgin Islands	*2005	64.8	7.7	70.0	6.7	60.1	8.7
Îles Vierges américaines	*2010	63.6	7.3	68.4	6.5	59.4	8.1
	*2015	61.2	7.3	65.3	6.7	57.5	7.9
	*2018	60.4	7.0	64.2	6.5	57.0	7.6

17 Labour force participation rate and unemployment rate *(continued)*

Labour force (LF) participation rate and unemployment rate by sex (percent)

Taux d'activité et taux de chômage *(suite)*

Taux d'activité et taux de chômage par sexe (pourcentage)

Region, country or area & / Région, pays ou zone &	Year / Année	Male and Female / Hommes et femmes: LF particip. rate / Taux d'activité	Male and Female / Hommes et femmes: Unemployment rate / Taux de Chômage	Male / Hommes: LF particip. rate / Taux d'activité	Male / Hommes: Unemployment rate / Taux de Chômage	Female / Femmes: LF particip. rate / Taux d'activité	Female / Femmes: Unemployment rate / Taux de Chômage
Uruguay / Uruguay	2005	* 62.9	12.2	* 74.4	9.5	* 52.5	15.7
	2010	* 65.5	7.2	* 76.7	5.3	* 55.3	9.5
	2015	* 64.9	7.5	* 75.1	6.3	* 55.7	8.9
	*2018	65.0	8.3	74.6	6.7	56.3	10.3
Uzbekistan / Ouzbékistan	*2005	63.2	8.3	74.6	8.4	52.3	8.1
	*2010	64.1	8.2	75.7	8.3	53.0	8.0
	*2015	65.4	7.9	77.5	8.1	53.7	7.8
	*2018	65.7	6.9	78.0	6.9	53.8	6.9
Vanuatu / Vanuatu	*2005	70.4	5.6	79.1	5.1	61.5	6.4
	*2010	70.4	5.4	79.5	4.8	61.2	6.2
	*2015	70.6	5.3	79.7	4.7	61.6	6.0
	*2018	70.6	5.2	79.7	4.6	61.5	5.9
Venezuela (Boliv. Rep. of) / Venezuela (Rép. boliv. du)	2005	* 65.0	11.4	* 80.6	10.4	* 49.7	12.9
	2010	* 64.8	8.5	* 79.3	7.8	* 50.6	9.4
	2015	* 64.3	6.8	* 77.9	6.3	* 51.0	7.6
	*2018	63.6	7.7	77.3	7.1	50.4	8.7
Viet Nam / Viet Nam	*2005	76.8	2.3	81.4	2.1	72.5	2.5
	2010	* 76.9	2.6	* 81.6	2.6	* 72.5	2.6
	2015	* 78.5	2.1	* 83.9	2.2	* 73.4	2.0
	*2018	78.2	2.1	83.4	2.2	73.2	1.9
Western Sahara / Sahara occidental	*2005	55.0	8.1	79.0	6.6	26.9	13.3
	*2010	55.6	7.9	79.5	6.4	28.1	13.0
	*2015	55.8	7.6	79.8	6.1	28.5	12.4
	*2018	55.8	7.3	79.6	6.0	28.9	11.4
Yemen / Yémen	*2005	47.5	16.1	71.3	14.2	23.6	21.9
	*2010	48.2	17.8	71.4	9.7	24.8	41.3
	*2015	49.6	18.1	73.1	13.4	25.8	31.6
	*2017	50.0	16.1	73.7	12.5	26.2	26.4
Zambia / Zambie	*2005	79.5	10.4	85.7	10.8	73.7	9.9
	2010	* 76.5	13.2	* 82.2	12.6	* 71.1	13.8
	*2015	74.9	7.8	80.0	7.2	70.1	8.4
	*2018	74.8	7.8	79.6	7.3	70.1	8.3
Zimbabwe / Zimbabwe	*2005	82.4	4.5	88.2	4.4	77.1	4.7
	*2010	82.6	5.3	88.4	4.7	77.4	5.8
	*2015	83.2	5.2	88.9	6.5	78.1	3.8
	*2018	83.8	5.1	89.3	6.3	78.9	4.0
European Union (EU) / Union européenne (UE)	*2005	56.7	9.0	65.3	8.3	48.7	9.7
	*2010	57.2	9.6	64.8	9.6	50.1	9.5
	*2015	57.4	9.4	64.2	9.3	51.0	9.5
	*2016	57.3	8.6	64.0	8.4	51.0	8.8
	*2017	57.2	8.3	63.9	...	50.9	...

Source:

International Labour Organization (ILO), Geneva, Key Indicators of the Labour Market (KILM 9th edition) and the ILOSTAT database, last accessed February 2018.

Source:

Organisation internationale du Travail (OIT), Genève, Indicateurs Clés du Marché du Travail (ICMT 9e édition) et ILOSTAT base de données, dernier accès février 2018.

& Population aged 15 years and over, unless otherwise footnoted.

& Sauf indication contraire, population âgée de 15 ans et plus.

1 Data excludes Armenia, Azerbaijan, Cyprus, Georgia, Israel and Turkey.
2 Caucasus refers to Armenia, Azerbaijan, Cyprus, Georgia, Israel and Turkey.
3 Population aged 16 years and over.
4 Population aged 14 years and over.
5 Resident population (de jure).

1 Les données excluent l'Arménie, l'Azerbaïdjan, Chypre, la Géorgie, l'Israël et la Turquie.
2 Le Caucase se rapportent à l'Arménie, l'Azerbaïdjan, Chypre, la Géorgie, l'Israël et la Turquie.
3 Population âgée de 16 ans et plus.
4 Population âgée de 14 ans et plus.
5 Population résidente (de droit).

17 Labour force participation rate and unemployment rate *(continued)*
Labour force (LF) participation rate and unemployment rate by sex (percent)

Taux d'activité et taux de chômage *(suite)*
Taux d'activité et taux de chômage par sexe (pourcentage)

6 Excluding the institutional population.
7 For statistical purposes, the data for China do not include those for the Hong Kong Special Administrative Region (Hong Kong SAR), Macao Special Administrative Region (Macao SAR) and Taiwan Province of China.
8 Population aged 15 to 69 years.
9 Population aged 16 to 65 years.
10 Population aged 15 to 74 years.
11 Nationals, residents.
12 Population aged 18 to 64 years.
13 Population aged 15 to 64 years.
14 Persons present (de facto).
15 De facto population.
16 Population aged 17 years and over.
17 Main city or metropolitan area.
18 Excluding some areas.

6 Non compris la population dans les institutions.
7 Pour la présentation des statistiques, les données pour la Chine ne comprennent pas la région administrative spéciale de Hong Kong (Hong Kong RAS), la région administrative spéciale de Macao (Macao RAS) et la province chinoise de Taïwan.
8 Population âgée de 15 à 69 ans.
9 Population âgée de 16 à 65 ans.
10 Population âgée de 15 à 74 ans.
11 Ressortissants, résidents.
12 Population âgée de 18 à 64 ans.
13 Population âgée de 15 à 64 ans.
14 Personnes présentes (de facto).
15 Population de fait.
16 Population âgée de 17 ans et plus.
17 Ville principale ou zone métropolitaine.
18 Certaines régions sont exclues.

18 Employment by economic activity

Percentage of persons employed by sex and ISIC 4 categories; agriculture (agr.), industry (ind.) and services (ser.)

Emploi par activité économique

Personnes employées par sexe et branches de la CITI rév. 4; agriculture (agr.), industrie (ind.) et services (ser.), pourcentage

Region, country or area [+] Région, pays ou zone [+]	Year Année	Male and Female Hommes et femmes			Male Hommes			Female Femmes		
		Agr.	Ind.	Ser.	Agr.	Ind.	Ser.	Agr.	Ind.	Ser.
Total, all countries or areas	***2005**	**35.2**	**22.6**	**42.1**	**34.1**	**25.5**	**40.5**	**37.1**	**18.3**	**44.6**
Total, tous pays ou zones	***2010**	**30.8**	**23.0**	**46.2**	**30.2**	**26.8**	**43.1**	**31.8**	**17.1**	**51.1**
	***2015**	**27.2**	**22.7**	**50.1**	**26.7**	**27.2**	**46.1**	**28.0**	**15.7**	**56.2**
	***2018**	**26.0**	**22.4**	**51.7**	**25.4**	**27.0**	**47.6**	**26.8**	**15.1**	**58.2**
Africa	*2005	58.7	12.0	29.3	55.5	14.7	29.9	63.3	8.3	28.5
Afrique	*2010	54.1	13.3	32.6	51.6	16.3	32.2	57.5	9.3	33.2
	*2015	53.3	13.6	33.1	51.3	16.8	31.9	56.0	9.4	34.6
	*2018	52.9	13.5	33.6	51.0	16.8	32.3	55.4	9.3	35.3
Northern Africa	*2005	34.0	24.0	42.1	31.5	25.2	43.3	43.6	19.2	37.3
Afrique septentrionale	*2010	30.4	27.5	42.1	27.9	29.5	42.7	39.9	20.0	40.1
	*2015	29.0	28.1	42.9	26.5	30.0	43.6	38.3	21.2	40.5
	*2018	28.1	28.0	44.0	25.8	29.9	44.4	36.6	20.9	42.5
Sub-Saharan Africa	*2005	63.6	9.7	26.8	62.4	11.6	26.0	65.0	7.3	27.7
Afrique subsaharienne	*2010	58.7	10.6	30.8	58.3	12.6	29.2	59.1	8.3	32.6
	*2015	57.6	11.1	31.4	57.8	13.3	28.9	57.4	8.5	34.1
	*2018	57.1	11.1	31.8	57.4	13.4	29.2	56.9	8.4	34.8
Eastern Africa	*2005	74.5	7.2	18.3	71.8	8.8	19.4	77.5	5.4	17.1
Afrique orientale	*2010	71.2	7.6	21.2	69.1	9.5	21.4	73.5	5.5	21.0
	*2015	67.4	8.7	23.9	66.2	10.9	22.9	68.8	6.3	24.9
	*2018	66.2	9.0	24.8	65.0	11.4	23.6	67.4	6.3	26.2
Middle Africa	*2005	70.8	11.1	18.1	66.2	13.4	20.4	75.6	8.7	15.7
Afrique centrale	*2010	70.5	10.5	19.0	65.3	13.0	21.8	76.2	7.9	16.0
	*2015	70.9	10.7	18.4	66.2	13.5	20.3	76.0	7.7	16.3
	*2018	71.6	10.1	18.3	66.7	12.9	20.4	76.7	7.2	16.1
Southern Africa	*2005	10.6	24.9	64.5	12.1	32.8	55.0	8.5	13.7	77.8
Afrique australe	*2010	8.1	23.9	67.9	9.1	32.2	58.7	6.9	12.9	80.2
	*2015	8.7	23.5	67.9	9.8	32.7	57.4	7.2	11.6	81.2
	*2018	8.5	23.2	68.4	9.9	31.9	58.3	6.7	11.9	81.5
Western Africa	*2005	54.8	9.6	35.6	58.0	10.6	31.4	50.7	8.4	41.0
Afrique occidentale	*2010	43.9	12.5	43.6	49.2	13.1	37.7	37.2	11.9	51.0
	*2015	45.0	12.6	42.5	50.3	13.4	36.4	38.6	11.6	49.8
	*2018	44.1	12.7	43.3	49.6	13.6	36.9	37.5	11.6	50.9
Americas	*2005	12.2	21.3	66.4	15.7	28.0	56.3	7.3	12.0	80.7
Amériques	*2010	11.1	20.4	68.5	14.8	27.5	57.7	6.2	10.8	83.0
	*2015	9.5	20.7	69.8	13.0	28.0	59.0	4.7	10.7	84.5
	*2018	9.4	20.4	70.2	12.9	27.7	59.4	4.7	10.6	84.8
Northern America	*2005	1.7	21.2	77.2	2.4	30.8	66.8	0.9	9.8	89.3
Amérique septentrionale	*2010	1.7	18.6	79.7	2.4	28.0	69.6	0.9	8.0	91.1
	*2015	1.7	18.9	79.4	2.4	27.9	69.7	0.9	8.4	90.7
	*2018	1.7	18.9	79.5	2.3	27.9	69.8	0.9	8.3	90.8
Latin America & the Caribbean	*2005	19.5	21.5	59.1	23.9	26.3	49.8	12.5	13.8	73.6
Amérique latine et Caraïbes	*2010	16.9	21.5	61.6	21.5	27.2	51.3	10.0	12.8	77.2
	*2015	14.2	21.8	64.0	18.8	28.1	53.1	7.4	12.4	80.2
	*2018	14.1	21.3	64.5	18.7	27.6	53.7	7.3	12.1	80.6
Caribbean	*2005	22.4	18.7	58.9	29.0	23.5	47.5	12.5	11.3	76.1
Caraïbes	*2010	21.8	16.1	62.1	28.6	20.9	50.5	11.9	9.2	78.9
	*2015	20.9	16.3	62.9	27.9	21.3	50.9	11.0	9.3	79.7
	*2018	20.2	16.1	63.7	27.2	21.2	51.6	10.5	8.9	80.6
Central America	*2005	18.4	24.4	57.2	24.9	27.5	47.7	6.0	18.7	75.3
Amérique centrale	*2010	18.0	22.8	59.2	25.0	26.7	48.4	5.6	16.0	78.4
	*2015	16.7	23.7	59.6	23.6	27.8	48.6	4.6	16.4	79.0
	*2018	16.0	24.3	59.7	22.6	28.7	48.7	4.6	16.7	78.7
South America	*2005	19.6	20.7	59.8	23.0	26.1	50.9	14.5	12.6	72.9
Amérique du Sud	*2010	16.1	21.5	62.4	19.5	28.0	52.5	11.3	12.1	76.6
	*2015	12.7	21.5	65.8	16.0	28.8	55.1	8.0	11.3	80.7
	*2018	12.8	20.6	66.6	16.2	27.7	56.1	8.0	10.8	81.2
Central Asia	*2005	35.1	25.4	39.5	32.4	32.9	34.7	38.5	15.8	45.7
Asie centrale	*2010	29.0	29.0	42.0	26.6	37.3	36.1	32.1	18.2	49.7
	*2015	23.6	29.9	46.5	21.3	39.2	39.5	26.8	17.7	55.6
	*2018	22.6	30.2	47.2	20.3	39.7	39.9	25.6	17.5	57.0

18 Employment by economic activity *(continued)*

Percentage of persons employed by sex and ISIC 4 categories; agriculture (agr.), industry (ind.) and services (ser.)

Emploi par activité économique *(suite)*

Personnes employées par sexe et branches de la CITI rév. 4; agriculture (agr.), industrie (ind.) et services (ser.), pourcentage

Region, country or area + / Région, pays ou zone +	Year / Année	Male and Female / Hommes et femmes			Male / Hommes			Female / Femmes		
		Agr.	Ind.	Ser.	Agr.	Ind.	Ser.	Agr.	Ind.	Ser.
Eastern Asia	*2005	32.8	29.2	38.1	29.9	29.9	40.3	36.4	28.4	35.3
Asie orientale	*2010	24.4	29.5	46.1	21.7	32.0	46.3	27.8	26.2	46.0
	*2015	18.5	26.8	54.7	16.2	30.9	52.9	21.5	21.6	56.9
	*2018	15.8	26.1	58.1	13.9	30.6	55.5	18.4	20.2	61.4
South-eastern Asia	*2005	46.4	18.1	35.5	46.7	20.1	33.2	46.0	15.2	38.8
Asie du Sud-Est	*2010	41.1	18.9	40.0	41.9	21.5	36.6	40.0	15.3	44.7
	*2015	34.8	21.4	43.8	35.8	24.8	39.5	33.4	16.7	49.9
	*2018	31.8	21.7	46.5	33.2	25.4	41.5	29.9	16.7	53.4
Southern Asia	*2005	53.5	18.6	27.9	47.3	20.4	32.3	69.5	14.0	16.5
Asie méridionale	*2010	49.7	21.3	29.0	44.1	23.4	32.5	66.7	15.0	18.4
	*2015	43.7	23.3	33.0	38.4	25.3	36.3	59.7	17.1	23.3
	*2018	41.2	23.4	35.5	35.8	25.5	38.7	57.5	16.9	25.6
Western Asia [1]	*2005	13.7	22.8	63.4	12.6	25.8	61.6	20.2	5.7	74.1
Asie occidentale [1]	*2010	10.7	25.6	63.7	9.7	28.8	61.4	16.5	6.1	77.4
	*2015	11.8	25.9	62.3	11.1	29.3	59.6	16.0	6.0	78.1
	*2018	13.3	26.2	60.5	12.8	29.7	57.5	16.2	6.0	77.9
Caucasus [2]	*2005	27.6	22.7	49.7	21.2	28.0	50.8	40.6	12.0	47.4
Caucase [2]	*2010	25.0	22.8	52.2	19.3	28.7	52.0	35.7	11.9	52.4
	*2015	21.8	23.5	54.6	17.4	29.9	52.8	29.8	12.3	58.0
	*2018	20.5	23.4	56.1	16.6	29.6	53.8	27.5	12.2	60.3
Eastern Europe	*2005	13.8	29.9	56.3	15.2	38.4	46.5	12.3	20.8	66.9
Europe orientale	*2010	11.7	28.7	59.7	13.1	38.5	48.4	10.1	18.0	72.0
	*2015	9.8	28.2	62.1	11.3	38.4	50.2	8.1	16.8	75.1
	*2018	9.2	28.1	62.8	10.7	38.4	50.8	7.4	16.7	75.9
Northern Europe	*2005	2.8	23.1	74.1	3.8	34.0	62.2	1.6	10.5	87.9
Europe septentrionale	*2010	2.2	19.9	77.9	3.1	30.3	66.6	1.2	8.3	90.6
	*2015	2.1	19.3	78.6	3.0	29.1	67.9	1.1	8.3	90.6
	*2018	2.0	18.9	79.1	2.8	28.6	68.6	1.0	8.0	91.0
Southern Europe	*2005	8.7	29.3	62.0	8.8	38.6	52.6	8.4	15.5	76.1
Europe méridionale	*2010	7.7	25.6	66.8	8.3	35.1	56.6	6.9	12.6	80.5
	*2015	7.0	23.6	69.4	8.2	32.2	59.6	5.5	12.3	82.2
	*2018	6.7	23.0	70.2	8.0	31.8	60.2	5.2	11.7	83.2
Western Europe	*2005	3.1	26.3	70.7	3.8	36.8	59.4	2.2	13.4	84.5
Europe occidentale	*2010	2.4	24.7	72.9	3.1	35.7	61.3	1.7	11.7	86.7
	*2015	2.1	23.6	74.2	2.7	34.5	62.8	1.5	11.2	87.4
	*2018	2.1	23.3	74.7	2.7	34.1	63.3	1.4	10.9	87.7
Oceania	*2005	14.6	18.3	67.1	15.9	26.6	57.5	13.2	8.1	78.7
Océanie	*2010	9.7	18.3	72.0	11.4	27.1	61.5	7.7	7.7	84.6
	*2015	8.5	17.3	74.2	10.1	26.2	63.7	6.5	7.1	86.4
	*2018	8.5	16.7	74.8	10.3	25.3	64.4	6.5	6.8	86.7
Afghanistan	*2005	71.8	6.6	21.7	70.2	6.5	23.3	81.4	6.8	11.8
Afghanistan	*2010	64.5	6.1	29.4	62.8	6.2	31.0	75.6	5.5	18.8
	*2015	61.1	6.7	32.2	59.0	6.9	34.1	72.4	5.7	21.9
	*2018	62.0	6.8	31.3	59.7	7.0	33.3	73.6	5.5	20.9
Albania	*2005	54.0	19.9	26.2	44.7	25.1	30.2	67.5	12.2	20.4
Albanie	*2010	43.9	19.4	36.7	36.3	25.7	38.0	54.1	10.9	35.0
	*2015	41.4	18.6	40.0	36.7	22.1	41.3	47.8	13.9	38.3
	*2018	38.9	18.7	42.4	34.0	22.3	43.8	45.7	13.8	40.6
Algeria	*2005	20.0	29.8	50.2	20.8	28.9	50.3	14.2	36.0	49.8
Algérie	*2010	16.5	39.4	44.0	17.9	37.5	44.6	8.7	50.3	41.0
	*2015	13.1	47.6	39.3	13.8	45.9	40.4	9.8	55.8	34.4
	*2018	12.8	46.5	40.7	13.6	44.7	41.8	8.9	55.7	35.4
American Samoa [3,4]	2000	3.1	41.7	51.9	...	...	...	...	...	...
Samoa américaines [3,4]	#2010	3.0	23.2	73.8	...	...	...	...	...	...
Angola	*2005	37.5	8.8	53.7	30.0	15.6	54.4	45.5	1.6	53.0
Angola	*2010	47.2	8.8	44.0	40.2	16.2	43.7	54.4	1.2	44.4
	*2015	48.9	8.9	42.2	41.8	16.6	41.6	56.0	1.3	42.8
	*2018	50.4	8.7	40.9	43.5	16.0	40.6	57.4	1.3	41.3
Anguilla [4] / Anguilla [4]	#2001	2.9	18.9	76.7	4.8	32.1	61.7	0.7	3.7	93.9
Antigua and Barbuda [4]	2005	2.8	15.6	81.6	4.4	26.1	69.5	1.2	5.0	93.8
Antigua-et-Barbuda [4]	2008	2.8	15.6	81.6	4.4	26.1	69.5	1.2	5.0	93.8

18 Employment by economic activity *(continued)*

Percentage of persons employed by sex and ISIC 4 categories; agriculture (agr.), industry (ind.) and services (ser.)

Emploi par activité économique *(suite)*

Personnes employées par sexe et branches de la CITI rév. 4; agriculture (agr.), industrie (ind.) et services (ser.), pourcentage

Region, country or area + / Région, pays ou zone +	Year / Année	Male and Female / Hommes et femmes			Male / Hommes			Female / Femmes		
		Agr.	Ind.	Ser.	Agr.	Ind.	Ser.	Agr.	Ind.	Ser.
Argentina	*2005	1.3	23.3	75.5	1.7	31.8	66.6	0.7	10.6	88.7
Argentine	*2010	1.3	23.3	75.4	1.9	32.6	65.6	0.4	9.3	90.3
	*2015	0.5	23.8	75.7	0.8	34.3	64.9	0.2	8.1	91.8
	*2018	0.5	23.2	76.3	0.8	33.6	65.7	0.1	7.7	92.2
Armenia	*2005	40.6	17.7	41.7	35.2	25.3	39.6	47.1	8.7	44.2
Arménie	*2010	38.6	17.4	44.0	31.7	26.7	41.7	47.3	5.8	46.9
	*2015	35.3	15.9	48.8	31.3	23.1	45.7	40.1	7.5	52.4
	*2018	33.2	16.3	50.4	29.5	23.3	47.2	37.7	8.0	54.3
Aruba [4]	#2000	0.5	16.4	82.3	0.8	26.7	71.6	0.2	4.5	94.7
Aruba [4]	#2010[5]	0.6	14.5	84.4	1.0	24.4	74.1	0.3	4.5	94.8
	#2011	0.6	14.0	85.1	0.8	24.4	74.4	0.4	3.3	96.1
Australia	*2005	3.6	21.1	75.3	4.5	30.7	64.9	2.5	9.3	88.2
Australie	*2010	3.2	21.0	75.8	4.0	31.1	64.9	2.3	8.6	89.1
	*2015	2.6	19.5	77.9	3.3	29.4	67.3	1.9	7.7	90.5
	*2018	2.6	19.0	78.5	3.4	28.7	68.0	1.6	7.6	90.8
Austria	2005	5.3	* 27.6	* 67.2	5.3	* 39.7	* 55.1	5.3	* 12.9	* 81.8
Autriche	*2010	5.2	24.9	69.9	5.4	36.5	58.1	5.0	11.5	83.5
	*2015	4.5	25.8	69.7	4.8	37.8	57.4	4.2	12.1	83.7
	*2018	4.2	25.5	70.3	4.6	37.6	57.8	3.8	11.8	84.4
Azerbaijan	*2005	40.5	12.6	46.9	36.5	20.2	43.3	44.6	4.8	50.6
Azerbaïdjan	*2010	38.2	13.7	48.1	32.3	21.0	46.8	44.4	6.2	49.4
	*2015	36.4	14.1	49.6	31.0	21.8	47.2	42.1	5.9	52.1
	*2018	37.5	13.9	48.7	31.7	21.4	47.0	43.6	5.9	50.5
Bahamas	*2005	3.5	17.8	78.7	6.3	29.4	64.3	0.3	5.1	94.6
Bahamas	*2010	3.3	14.7	82.0	5.5	24.7	69.9	1.0	3.8	95.2
	*2015	3.9	12.1	84.0	5.7	19.5	74.8	1.9	3.9	94.3
	*2018	4.0	11.7	84.3	5.9	18.8	75.3	1.9	3.8	94.4
Bahrain	*2005	1.3	30.7	68.0	1.5	35.2	63.3	0.1	9.4	90.6
Bahreïn	*2010	1.1	35.7	63.2	1.4	42.6	56.0	0.1	9.1	90.9
	*2015	0.9	35.4	63.7	1.2	42.4	56.4	~0.0	9.2	90.8
	*2018	1.1	35.6	63.4	1.3	42.1	56.6	0.1	9.2	90.7
Bangladesh	*2005	48.1	14.5	37.4	42.0	15.1	42.9	68.2	12.5	19.3
Bangladesh	2010	47.3	* 17.6	* 35.1	40.9	* 19.2	* 39.8	65.5	* 13.1	* 21.4
	*2015	42.7	20.5	36.9	34.7	22.2	43.1	63.5	15.9	20.7
	*2018	37.6	21.4	41.0	29.1	23.3	47.7	59.2	16.6	24.2
Barbados	*2005	2.4	20.6	77.0	4.3	32.3	63.4	0.4	7.9	91.7
Barbade	*2010	2.8	28.0	69.2	3.7	44.4	51.9	2.0	11.1	86.9
	*2015	2.9	19.3	77.8	4.2	28.6	67.1	1.6	10.0	88.4
	*2018	2.9	19.2	78.0	3.9	29.0	67.1	1.8	9.2	89.0
Belarus	*2005	13.9	35.6	50.5	17.4	44.5	38.0	10.2	26.5	63.3
Bélarus	*2010	10.8	34.6	54.6	13.5	45.4	41.1	8.1	23.7	68.2
	*2015	9.5	32.4	58.1	12.5	44.0	43.6	6.5	20.7	72.8
	*2018	9.7	31.0	59.3	12.7	42.7	44.6	6.6	19.2	74.3
Belgium	2005	2.0	* 24.7	* 73.3	2.5	* 35.0	* 62.6	1.5	* 11.3	* 87.2
Belgique	*2010	1.4	23.4	75.3	1.7	34.3	64.0	0.9	10.1	89.0
	*2015	1.2	21.4	77.4	1.6	32.8	65.7	0.7	8.4	90.9
	*2018	1.3	21.3	77.5	1.7	32.5	65.9	0.8	8.2	91.0
Belize	*2005	19.6	17.9	62.6	27.8	21.7	50.5	3.3	10.3	86.5
Belize	*2010	17.2	18.0	64.8	25.0	22.3	52.7	3.6	10.5	85.9
	*2015	15.9	16.2	67.9	22.7	21.0	56.4	4.8	8.2	87.1
	*2018	15.5	15.4	69.1	23.0	19.5	57.6	3.2	8.8	88.0
Benin	*2005	47.5	11.9	40.6	54.9	14.8	30.3	39.5	8.8	51.7
Bénin	*2010	45.3	10.5	44.2	53.3	13.8	32.9	37.2	7.1	55.6
	*2015	41.8	18.2	40.0	49.2	19.8	31.0	34.2	16.4	49.4
	*2018	42.4	18.6	39.0	49.9	20.0	30.1	34.6	17.2	48.3
Bermuda	2004[6]	1.7	12.1	86.2	3.0	20.5	76.6	0.3	3.1	96.6
Bermudes	#2010[3,4]	1.4	12.9	85.7	2.4	22.6	75.0	0.4	3.2	96.4
	#2012[4,7]	1.7	9.6	88.7	3.0	16.5	80.5	0.3	2.6	97.1
	#2013[3,4,8]	1.6	10.3	87.6	...	...	...	...	...	...
Bhutan	*2005	70.3	4.8	24.9	62.8	6.1	31.1	80.3	3.1	16.6
Bhoutan	*2010	59.6	6.6	33.8	55.0	6.6	38.5	65.9	6.7	27.3
	*2015	58.0	9.7	32.4	52.5	9.9	37.6	66.4	9.3	24.3
	*2018	55.6	9.7	34.7	49.9	10.2	39.9	64.1	9.1	26.8

Employment by economic activity *(continued)*

Percentage of persons employed by sex and ISIC 4 categories; agriculture (agr.), industry (ind.) and services (ser.)

Emploi par activité économique *(suite)*

Personnes employées par sexe et branches de la CITI rév. 4; agriculture (agr.), industrie (ind.) et services (ser.), pourcentage

Region, country or area + Région, pays ou zone +	Year Année	Male and Female Hommes et femmes			Male Hommes			Female Femmes		
		Agr.	Ind.	Ser.	Agr.	Ind.	Ser.	Agr.	Ind.	Ser.
Bolivia (Plurin. State of) Bolivie (État plurin. de)	2005	35.2	* 20.4	* 44.4	34.6	* 27.3	* 38.1	36.0	* 11.2	* 52.8
	*2010	30.1	20.6	49.3	29.7	28.3	42.1	30.6	10.5	58.9
	*2015	27.9	22.5	49.6	27.5	30.4	42.1	28.3	11.0	60.7
	*2018	26.4	22.5	51.1	26.5	30.5	43.0	26.2	11.0	62.8
Bosnia and Herzegovina Bosnie-Herzégovine	*2005	24.6	28.4	47.1	21.9	36.3	41.8	28.9	15.4	55.8
	*2010	19.7	29.1	51.2	18.5	37.3	44.3	21.6	15.6	62.7
	*2015	17.9	37.5	44.6	18.7	42.7	38.6	16.7	29.9	53.4
	*2018	18.6	32.1	49.3	18.8	38.5	42.7	18.0	19.1	62.8
Botswana Botswana	*2005	27.0	17.2	55.9	32.5	20.7	46.8	19.4	12.3	68.3
	*2010	26.4	13.8	59.8	30.6	20.6	48.8	21.0	4.7	74.3
	*2015	26.9	13.8	59.3	31.1	21.0	48.0	21.7	4.8	73.5
	*2018	25.8	13.6	60.6	30.0	20.7	49.3	20.5	4.8	74.8
Brazil Brésil	*2005	20.5	21.5	58.1	23.7	27.2	49.1	15.9	13.2	70.9
	*2010	16.0	22.3	61.7	19.3	29.1	51.6	11.2	12.6	76.1
	*2015	10.2	22.2	67.6	14.0	29.8	56.2	5.1	11.7	83.3
	*2018	10.2	20.9	69.0	14.0	28.2	57.8	4.8	10.8	84.4
British Virgin Islands 4 Îles Vierges britanniques 4	2010	0.5	11.1	87.4	…	…	…	…	…	…
Brunei Darussalam Brunéi Darussalam	*2005	1.0	19.2	79.8	1.5	26.2	72.4	0.3	9.0	90.7
	*2010	0.7	19.3	80.0	1.0	25.7	73.4	0.4	10.0	89.6
	*2015	0.6	18.6	80.9	0.7	24.1	75.3	0.5	11.0	88.5
	*2018	0.5	17.6	81.9	0.6	23.1	76.3	0.4	10.0	89.6
Bulgaria Bulgarie	2005	8.9	* 34.2	* 56.8	10.7	* 38.9	* 50.4	6.8	* 28.8	* 64.3
	2010	6.8	* 33.0	* 60.2	8.2	* 40.7	* 51.0	5.2	* 24.1	* 70.7
	*2015	6.9	29.9	63.3	9.1	36.2	54.7	4.3	22.7	72.9
	*2018	6.1	29.1	64.9	8.2	36.0	55.9	3.7	21.1	75.2
Burkina Faso Burkina Faso	*2005	82.0	5.1	12.9	80.3	6.1	13.7	84.2	3.9	11.9
	*2010	60.9	11.4	27.7	62.5	12.2	25.3	58.7	10.3	30.9
	*2015	29.4	32.0	38.5	36.0	31.2	32.8	20.9	33.1	46.0
	*2018	27.6	32.0	40.4	34.0	31.8	34.2	19.2	32.2	48.6
Burundi Burundi	*2005	91.8	2.6	5.6	86.7	4.4	8.9	96.6	0.9	2.6
	*2010	91.4	2.6	6.1	85.9	4.5	9.6	96.3	0.8	2.9
	*2015	91.6	2.4	6.1	86.1	4.2	9.7	96.5	0.7	2.8
	*2018	91.5	2.5	6.1	85.9	4.3	9.8	96.5	0.8	2.7
Cabo Verde Cabo Verde	*2005	73.2	6.8	20.0	68.2	8.8	23.0	81.3	3.6	15.1
	*2010	69.7	7.3	23.0	64.6	9.5	25.9	77.8	3.8	18.5
	*2015	68.7	7.0	24.4	63.1	9.3	27.6	76.8	3.6	19.7
	*2018	67.2	6.9	25.9	61.6	9.3	29.2	75.3	3.5	21.2
Cambodia Cambodge	*2005	70.8	9.8	19.4	69.4	8.8	21.8	72.2	10.8	17.0
	*2010	54.2	16.3	29.6	53.0	17.0	30.1	55.4	15.5	29.1
	*2015	28.8	26.8	44.4	29.3	27.4	43.4	28.3	26.3	45.4
	*2018	25.7	26.9	47.4	26.3	28.3	45.5	25.2	25.5	49.3
Cameroon Cameroun	*2005	64.9	9.6	25.5	62.0	11.4	26.5	68.3	7.5	24.2
	*2010	64.9	9.3	25.8	62.0	11.1	26.9	68.3	7.2	24.6
	*2015	62.4	9.2	28.5	59.5	11.1	29.4	65.7	6.9	27.4
	*2018	61.6	9.3	29.1	58.8	11.3	29.9	64.9	7.0	28.1
Canada Canada	*2005	2.7	22.1	75.2	3.7	32.1	64.2	1.6	10.6	87.9
	*2010	2.3	19.8	77.9	3.2	30.0	66.8	1.3	8.5	90.2
	*2015	2.0	19.4	78.6	2.8	29.3	67.9	1.2	8.4	90.4
	*2018	1.9	19.5	78.6	2.7	29.3	68.1	1.1	8.7	90.2
Cayman Islands Îles Caïmanes	2005[4]	1.7	22.2	75.5	2.6	39.3	57.3	0.6	3.3	95.7
	#2010	0.6	14.9	84.2	1.1	26.2	72.5	0.1	3.2	96.4
	#2013	0.8	15.5	83.6	1.5	29.0	69.5	0.2	2.0	97.7
Central African Republic République centrafricaine	*2005	86.4	7.0	6.6	82.1	8.6	9.3	91.5	5.1	3.4
	*2010	86.2	7.1	6.8	81.9	8.7	9.4	91.3	5.1	3.6
	*2015	85.6	8.0	6.4	81.7	9.4	8.9	90.5	6.3	3.2
	*2018	85.6	7.9	6.5	81.6	9.4	9.0	90.5	6.2	3.4
Chad Tchad	*2005	87.3	5.3	7.5	83.1	6.8	10.1	92.4	3.4	4.2
	*2010	86.8	6.1	7.1	82.7	7.7	9.6	91.8	4.1	4.1
	*2015	85.9	6.4	7.7	81.5	8.2	10.3	91.3	4.2	4.5
	*2018	87.1	4.9	8.0	82.8	6.5	10.8	92.3	3.1	4.6

18 Employment by economic activity *(continued)*

Percentage of persons employed by sex and ISIC 4 categories; agriculture (agr.), industry (ind.) and services (ser.)

Emploi par activité économique *(suite)*

Personnes employées par sexe et branches de la CITI rév. 4; agriculture (agr.), industrie (ind.) et services (ser.), pourcentage

Region, country or area + / Région, pays ou zone +	Year / Année	Male and Female / Hommes et femmes Agr.	Ind.	Ser.	Male / Hommes Agr.	Ind.	Ser.	Female / Femmes Agr.	Ind.	Ser.
Channel Islands	*2005	20.9	30.2	48.9	26.7	35.4	37.9	13.6	23.6	62.8
Îles Anglo-Normandes	*2010	21.0	30.0	49.0	26.9	35.1	38.0	13.6	23.5	62.9
	*2015	20.2	29.9	49.9	26.0	35.4	38.6	12.8	23.1	64.1
	*2018	19.9	29.7	50.4	25.8	35.2	39.1	12.4	22.8	64.8
Chile	*2005	13.2	23.0	63.9	17.1	29.0	53.9	5.8	11.5	82.8
Chili	*2010	10.6	23.0	66.4	14.1	31.0	54.9	5.1	10.2	84.7
	*2015	9.4	23.3	67.3	12.7	31.6	55.7	4.5	11.2	84.3
	*2018	9.4	22.7	67.9	12.5	31.0	56.5	4.8	10.8	84.4
China 9	*2005	35.8	29.6	34.6	32.8	29.4	37.8	39.5	30.0	30.5
Chine 9	*2010	26.2	30.2	43.6	23.3	32.0	44.6	29.9	27.8	42.3
	*2015	19.6	27.1	53.4	17.0	30.7	52.4	22.8	22.6	54.6
	*2018	16.5	26.3	57.2	14.3	30.4	55.4	19.3	21.1	59.7
China, Hong Kong SAR	*2005	0.3	15.1	84.7	0.3	22.1	77.5	0.2	6.5	93.3
Chine, RAS de Hong Kong	*2010	0.2	13.3	86.5	0.3	20.6	79.1	0.2	5.1	94.7
	*2015	0.2	13.3	86.5	0.3	21.2	78.6	0.2	5.0	94.8
	*2018	0.2	13.0	86.8	0.3	20.8	78.9	0.2	4.8	95.0
China, Macao SAR	*2005	0.1	25.0	74.8	0.1	26.8	73.1	0.1	23.2	76.7
Chine, RAS de Macao	*2010	0.2	13.7	86.1	0.2	20.3	79.5	0.2	6.9	92.9
	*2015	0.3	16.8	83.0	0.2	26.5	73.3	0.3	6.6	93.2
	*2018	0.5	20.0	79.5	0.4	30.5	69.1	0.7	9.2	90.2
Colombia	*2005	20.7	20.0	59.3	28.8	22.0	49.2	7.0	16.8	76.3
Colombie	2010	18.3	* 19.6	* 62.1	26.3	* 22.3	* 51.4	6.5	* 15.5	* 78.0
	*2015	16.0	19.6	64.4	22.8	23.8	53.4	6.5	13.7	79.8
	*2018	16.0	19.2	64.8	22.6	23.6	53.9	6.9	13.1	80.0
Comoros	*2005	55.8	14.3	29.9	50.9	15.7	33.4	63.3	12.2	24.6
Comores	*2010	55.9	14.7	29.5	51.0	16.0	33.0	63.0	12.7	24.3
	*2015	55.4	15.1	29.5	50.5	16.5	33.0	62.2	13.2	24.6
	*2018	54.7	15.5	29.9	49.9	17.0	33.2	61.5	13.3	25.2
Congo	*2005	40.0	23.4	36.6	38.6	23.7	37.7	41.5	23.1	35.4
Congo	*2010	39.1	23.3	37.6	37.6	23.9	38.5	40.8	22.7	36.6
	*2015	36.9	25.2	37.9	35.8	25.6	38.6	38.2	24.8	37.1
	*2018	37.9	25.4	36.7	36.7	25.3	38.0	39.3	25.5	35.3
Cook Islands 10										
Îles Cook 10	2011	4.3	11.7	84.0	6.4	17.7	75.9	1.8	5.0	93.3
Costa Rica	*2005	15.3	21.6	63.1	20.9	26.5	52.7	4.8	12.6	82.7
Costa Rica	*2010	15.1	19.6	65.3	20.9	24.2	55.0	4.7	11.5	83.8
	*2015	12.3	19.2	68.5	17.4	25.1	57.6	4.2	9.6	86.2
	*2018	11.6	18.6	69.9	16.2	24.3	59.5	3.9	9.0	87.2
Côte d'Ivoire	*2005	50.6	6.1	43.3	53.0	8.0	39.0	46.2	2.9	51.0
Côte d'Ivoire	*2010	49.5	5.9	44.6	52.4	7.9	39.8	45.0	2.6	52.4
	*2015	50.0	5.6	44.4	55.2	7.1	37.6	42.3	3.4	54.4
	*2018	47.5	6.3	46.2	52.8	8.2	39.0	39.7	3.7	56.7
Croatia	2005	17.3	* 28.6	* 54.1	16.0	* 37.2	* 46.8	18.9	* 18.1	* 63.0
Croatie	*2010	14.3	27.5	58.3	13.2	38.0	48.8	15.5	14.9	69.6
	*2015	9.2	26.7	64.1	10.8	36.7	52.5	7.4	15.0	77.5
	*2018	7.3	26.9	65.8	9.1	37.6	53.4	5.3	14.4	80.3
Cuba	*2005	20.3	19.1	60.6	26.4	22.5	51.1	9.4	13.1	77.5
Cuba	*2010	18.6	17.1	64.3	24.9	20.5	54.6	8.5	11.5	80.0
	*2015	18.3	16.8	64.9	24.8	20.7	54.6	7.9	10.7	81.4
	*2018	18.5	16.5	65.0	25.0	20.2	54.7	7.8	10.5	81.8
Curaçao 4	2000	1.1	18.0	80.9	2.0	28.6	69.4	0.2	5.6	94.2
Curaçao 4	2005	0.9	15.3	83.8	...	...	...	...	...	...
	2008	1.1	17.6	81.3	...	...	...	...	...	...
Cyprus	2005	4.7	* 24.1	* 71.2	5.7	* 33.7	* 60.6	3.5	* 10.4	* 86.2
Chypre	*2010	3.8	20.4	75.8	4.9	29.7	65.5	2.5	9.2	88.3
	*2015	4.0	16.2	79.8	5.7	24.9	69.5	2.1	6.3	91.6
	*2018	3.5	16.9	79.6	5.1	26.1	68.8	1.5	6.3	92.2
Czechia	2005	4.0	* 39.5	* 56.5	4.9	* 49.4	* 45.7	2.8	* 26.5	* 70.7
Tchéquie	*2010	3.1	38.0	58.9	4.0	49.0	47.0	1.9	23.2	74.9
	*2015	2.9	38.0	59.1	3.9	49.1	47.0	1.6	23.8	74.6
	*2018	2.8	37.5	59.8	3.7	48.6	47.7	1.6	23.4	75.0

Employment by economic activity *(continued)*

Percentage of persons employed by sex and ISIC 4 categories; agriculture (agr.), industry (ind.) and services (ser.)

Emploi par activité économique *(suite)*

Personnes employées par sexe et branches de la CITI rév. 4; agriculture (agr.), industrie (ind.) et services (ser.), pourcentage

Region, country or area [+]	Year	Male and Female			Male			Female		
Région, pays ou zone [+]	Année	Hommes et femmes			Hommes			Femmes		
		Agr.	Ind.	Ser.	Agr.	Ind.	Ser.	Agr.	Ind.	Ser.
Dem. People's Rep. Korea	*2005	67.6	16.3	16.1	63.9	16.4	19.7	71.4	16.2	12.3
Rép. pop. dém. de Corée	*2010	66.8	17.4	15.8	63.6	17.0	19.4	70.3	17.8	11.9
	*2015	67.2	17.1	15.8	63.8	16.9	19.3	70.8	17.3	11.9
	*2018	67.0	17.5	15.5	63.9	17.2	18.9	70.3	17.8	11.9
Dem. Rep. of the Congo	*2005	81.4	13.0	5.7	77.2	14.4	8.4	85.5	11.6	2.9
Rép. dém. du Congo	*2010	79.6	11.7	8.7	73.7	13.0	13.3	85.6	10.5	4.0
	*2015	81.5	11.8	6.7	76.9	13.5	9.6	86.3	10.1	3.7
	*2018	82.0	11.0	7.0	77.1	12.8	10.0	87.0	9.2	3.8
Denmark	2005	3.2	* 23.9	* 72.9	4.6	* 33.9	* 61.6	1.6	* 12.4	* 86.0
Danemark	*2010	2.4	19.6	78.0	3.9	29.1	67.1	0.9	9.2	89.9
	*2015	2.5	19.3	78.2	3.8	27.8	68.4	1.1	9.7	89.3
	*2018	2.5	18.7	78.8	3.9	27.0	69.2	1.0	9.4	89.6
Djibouti	*2005	36.1	24.4	39.6	38.3	18.1	43.7	32.5	34.4	33.0
Djibouti	*2010	33.2	27.4	39.4	35.9	21.1	43.0	29.1	36.9	33.9
	*2015	30.7	30.1	39.2	32.1	25.2	42.8	28.8	37.2	34.0
	*2018	29.1	29.8	41.1	31.2	24.7	44.2	26.0	37.1	36.8
Dominica [6]										
Dominique [6]	#2001	21.0	20.0	58.8	29.4	26.8	43.9	8.3	9.7	81.5
Dominican Republic	*2005	15.3	23.4	61.3	22.3	27.6	50.1	3.1	16.1	80.8
République dominicaine	2010	14.5	* 18.2	* 67.4	21.7	* 23.3	* 55.1	2.8	* 10.0	* 87.3
	*2015	13.3	18.1	68.6	20.6	23.3	56.1	2.2	10.1	87.8
	*2018	11.9	17.6	70.6	18.6	23.3	58.1	1.9	9.1	89.1
Ecuador	*2005	29.1	18.5	52.4	34.0	22.7	43.3	21.5	12.0	66.6
Équateur	2010	27.9	* 18.5	* 53.6	32.2	* 23.1	* 44.7	20.9	* 11.1	* 68.0
	*2015	26.2	19.7	54.2	28.5	25.1	46.4	22.6	11.2	66.3
	*2018	26.8	18.6	54.6	29.6	23.8	46.6	22.6	10.9	66.5
Egypt	*2005	30.9	21.5	47.6	27.5	25.2	47.4	46.7	4.9	48.4
Égypte	*2010	29.1	24.0	46.9	25.5	28.6	46.0	43.9	5.2	50.9
	*2015	25.8	25.1	49.1	22.3	29.9	47.9	40.2	5.6	54.2
	*2018	24.5	25.6	49.9	21.3	30.5	48.1	37.2	5.9	56.9
El Salvador	*2005	20.0	22.2	57.8	30.5	23.7	45.8	4.7	20.1	75.2
El Salvador	*2010	20.8	21.4	57.9	31.8	23.4	44.8	5.3	18.4	76.3
	*2015	18.1	22.2	59.7	28.5	24.1	47.4	3.9	19.5	76.6
	*2018	18.6	21.1	60.3	29.2	24.1	46.7	4.0	17.0	79.0
Equatorial Guinea	*2005	57.2	6.8	36.1	51.5	10.1	38.4	65.0	2.1	32.9
Guinée équatoriale	*2010	54.9	8.0	37.1	49.2	11.8	39.0	63.3	2.5	34.2
	*2015	56.9	7.7	35.4	51.0	11.0	38.0	66.0	2.6	31.4
	*2018	60.4	6.4	33.2	54.4	9.0	36.6	69.7	2.2	28.0
Eritrea	*2005	83.7	7.6	8.7	78.5	9.4	12.1	89.6	5.6	4.7
Érythrée	*2010	84.3	7.3	8.4	79.3	9.0	11.7	90.2	5.3	4.5
	*2015	84.0	7.1	8.9	78.8	8.9	12.3	90.0	5.0	5.0
	*2018	83.8	7.0	9.1	78.5	8.9	12.6	89.9	4.9	5.2
Estonia	2005	5.2	* 34.1	* 60.7	7.2	* 44.1	* 48.8	3.2	* 24.2	* 72.6
Estonie	*2010	4.2	30.3	65.5	5.7	43.1	51.2	2.8	18.0	79.2
	*2015	3.9	30.7	65.4	5.2	43.2	51.6	2.5	17.5	80.0
	*2018	3.8	29.7	66.5	5.6	41.7	52.7	1.9	17.2	80.8
Eswatini	*2005	69.1	14.5	16.4	63.0	18.0	19.0	78.8	8.8	12.4
Eswatini	*2010	68.3	13.7	18.0	61.9	17.4	20.7	78.0	8.1	14.0
	*2015	68.1	13.2	18.7	61.5	17.1	21.4	77.6	7.6	14.9
	*2018	69.4	12.3	18.4	63.0	15.9	21.1	78.6	7.0	14.4
Ethiopia	*2005	80.2	6.7	13.1	84.3	5.2	10.6	75.4	8.4	16.2
Éthiopie	*2010	77.2	6.3	16.6	81.9	5.6	12.5	71.5	7.1	21.4
	*2015	69.9	8.6	21.5	77.3	8.5	14.3	61.3	8.8	29.9
	*2018	67.3	9.6	23.1	75.0	10.0	15.0	58.2	9.2	32.6
Faroe Islands [3,6]										
Îles Féroé [3,6]	2005	11.1	22.2	66.7	20.0	33.3	53.3	8.3	8.3	83.3
Fiji	*2005	44.2	13.4	42.4	44.2	15.5	40.3	44.1	9.2	46.7
Fidji	*2010	42.9	13.7	43.4	43.0	15.8	41.2	42.6	9.4	48.0
	*2015	39.4	13.1	47.5	39.7	15.5	44.7	38.7	8.4	52.9
	*2018	38.6	13.3	48.1	39.0	15.7	45.3	37.8	8.4	53.8
Finland	2005	4.8	* 25.8	* 69.4	6.6	* 38.3	* 55.1	2.9	* 12.3	* 84.8
Finlande	*2010	4.4	23.3	72.3	6.0	35.9	58.1	2.8	9.9	87.3
	*2015	4.2	21.7	74.1	6.1	34.0	59.9	2.2	8.7	89.1
	*2018	3.8	22.1	74.1	5.5	34.4	60.1	2.0	8.8	89.2

18 Employment by economic activity *(continued)*

Percentage of persons employed by sex and ISIC 4 categories; agriculture (agr.), industry (ind.) and services (ser.)

Emploi par activité économique *(suite)*

Personnes employées par sexe et branches de la CITI rév. 4; agriculture (agr.), industrie (ind.) et services (ser.), pourcentage

Region, country or area [+] Région, pays ou zone [+]	Year Année	Male and Female Hommes et femmes			Male Hommes			Female Femmes		
		Agr.	Ind.	Ser.	Agr.	Ind.	Ser.	Agr.	Ind.	Ser.
France	2005	3.6	* 23.8	* 72.6	4.8	* 33.7	* 61.6	2.3	* 12.0	* 85.8
France	*2010	2.9	22.3	74.8	3.9	32.8	63.3	1.8	10.1	88.2
	*2015	2.8	20.4	76.9	3.7	30.3	66.0	1.6	9.3	89.1
	*2018	2.8	20.3	76.9	3.9	30.2	65.9	1.6	9.2	89.3
French Guiana [8,11]	2010	...	14.1	51.5	...	...	...	...	...	...
Guyane française [8,11]	2012	...	14.9	58.3	...	...	...	...	...	...
French Polynesia	*2005	9.2	17.5	73.3	11.7	24.3	64.0	5.4	7.2	87.3
Polynésie française	*2010	9.2	18.2	72.6	11.6	25.9	62.6	5.8	7.4	86.9
	*2015	8.7	17.2	74.1	11.1	25.1	63.8	5.4	6.5	88.1
	*2018	8.6	17.4	74.0	11.0	25.5	63.5	5.3	6.5	88.2
Gabon	*2005	43.3	12.2	44.5	31.1	18.0	50.9	62.6	3.0	34.4
Gabon	*2010	43.1	12.6	44.3	32.1	17.8	50.1	63.3	3.1	33.5
	*2015	41.2	12.7	46.1	30.3	17.9	51.8	60.9	3.3	35.8
	*2018	41.8	12.6	45.5	30.6	18.0	51.5	61.4	3.4	35.3
Gambia	*2005	34.2	16.2	49.6	28.5	24.3	47.3	42.6	4.4	53.0
Gambie	*2010	32.8	14.7	52.5	27.0	22.6	50.3	40.9	3.7	55.5
	*2015	28.4	15.5	56.1	23.5	24.0	52.5	35.1	4.1	60.9
	*2018	26.8	15.4	57.8	22.2	23.8	54.1	33.0	4.1	62.9
Georgia	*2005	54.3	9.3	36.4	51.8	13.7	34.5	57.2	4.4	38.4
Géorgie	*2010	48.2	10.4	41.5	47.4	16.3	36.3	49.1	3.7	47.2
	*2015	41.8	12.2	46.0	41.1	19.5	39.4	42.6	4.0	53.4
	*2018	39.8	12.7	47.5	39.1	20.3	40.6	40.6	4.1	55.4
Germany	2005	2.4	* 29.8	* 67.8	2.9	* 41.1	* 56.0	1.7	* 16.0	* 82.3
Allemagne	2010	1.7	* 28.3	* 70.0	2.0	* 40.2	* 57.8	1.2	* 14.3	* 84.5
	*2015	1.4	27.7	70.9	1.8	39.7	58.5	1.0	13.9	85.2
	*2018	1.3	27.0	71.7	1.6	38.9	59.5	0.9	13.4	85.7
Ghana	*2005	49.0	15.8	35.2	52.2	16.6	31.2	45.8	14.9	39.3
Ghana	*2010	42.0	15.2	42.8	45.9	17.1	37.1	38.1	13.4	48.5
	*2015	42.5	14.0	43.5	46.3	17.5	36.3	38.7	10.4	50.9
	*2018	39.7	14.4	46.0	43.6	18.2	38.2	35.6	10.4	53.9
Greece	2005	12.2	* 22.4	* 65.5	11.3	* 30.0	* 58.7	13.5	* 9.9	* 76.6
Grèce	*2010	12.4	19.6	68.0	12.3	27.5	60.2	12.6	7.8	79.6
	*2015	12.9	14.9	72.2	13.3	19.9	66.8	12.4	8.0	79.7
	*2018	11.9	15.3	72.8	12.3	20.5	67.1	11.2	8.1	80.6
Greenland [11,12] Groenland [11,12]	2011	4.6	12.6	82.5	8.1	20.3	71.3	0.3	3.3	96.2
Guadeloupe [8,11]	2010	...	13.8	64.4	...	...	...	...	...	...
Guadeloupe [8,11]	2012	3.3	13.5	65.5	...	...	...	...	...	...
Guam	*2005	10.1	15.4	74.5	13.3	23.7	63.0	5.6	3.4	91.0
Guam	*2010	9.6	16.6	73.9	12.6	25.5	62.0	5.4	3.8	90.9
	*2015	8.9	15.9	75.2	11.8	24.6	63.6	4.7	3.4	91.9
	*2018	8.8	16.1	75.2	11.6	24.8	63.6	4.6	3.4	92.0
Guatemala	*2005	36.0	20.9	43.1	47.3	21.2	31.6	15.5	20.4	64.1
Guatemala	*2010	37.0	19.8	43.2	48.1	19.8	32.2	16.0	19.8	64.2
	*2015	31.9	18.9	49.2	42.6	19.5	38.0	9.8	17.7	72.5
	*2018	29.0	21.1	49.9	39.0	22.4	38.5	9.2	18.4	72.5
Guernsey Guernesey	2013	1.5	13.6	84.8	1.0	12.2	40.9	0.5	1.4	44.3
Guinea	*2005	70.1	5.8	24.0	66.4	9.6	24.0	74.0	1.9	24.1
Guinée	*2010	70.3	6.0	23.8	66.1	9.9	24.0	74.6	1.9	23.6
	*2015	68.0	5.8	26.3	64.0	9.6	26.4	72.0	1.9	26.1
	*2018	68.0	6.0	26.1	64.2	10.0	25.9	71.8	1.9	26.3
Guinea-Bissau	*2005	84.6	6.9	8.5	79.5	8.9	11.6	90.5	4.6	4.8
Guinée-Bissau	*2010	84.5	6.6	9.0	79.2	8.6	12.2	90.5	4.3	5.2
	*2015	83.7	7.1	9.3	78.4	9.2	12.4	89.7	4.6	5.6
	*2018	83.3	6.9	9.7	78.0	9.1	13.0	89.5	4.5	6.1
Guyana	*2005	23.5	23.9	52.6	30.0	29.1	41.0	7.8	11.5	80.7
Guyana	*2010	17.0	25.1	58.0	22.5	31.5	46.1	5.1	11.1	83.8
	*2015	15.2	24.8	60.0	20.5	32.0	47.5	4.5	10.2	85.3
	*2018	13.2	26.4	60.5	17.9	34.6	47.5	3.7	10.0	86.3
Haiti	*2005	49.8	10.4	39.9	62.9	13.6	23.5	34.3	6.7	59.0
Haïti	*2010	47.2	10.3	42.5	60.1	13.9	26.0	32.1	6.0	61.9
	*2015	42.6	12.1	45.4	55.2	16.8	28.0	28.2	6.7	65.1
	*2018	40.6	12.6	46.8	53.3	17.7	29.1	26.2	6.9	66.9

18 Employment by economic activity *(continued)*

Percentage of persons employed by sex and ISIC 4 categories; agriculture (agr.), industry (ind.) and services (ser.)

Emploi par activité économique *(suite)*

Personnes employées par sexe et branches de la CITI rév. 4; agriculture (agr.), industrie (ind.) et services (ser.), pourcentage

Region, country or area [+] Région, pays ou zone [+]	Year Année	Male and Female Hommes et femmes			Male Hommes			Female Femmes		
		Agr.	Ind.	Ser.	Agr.	Ind.	Ser.	Agr.	Ind.	Ser.
Honduras Honduras	*2005	39.3	20.9	39.8	51.0	19.8	29.2	12.9	23.4	63.7
	*2010	37.8	18.6	43.6	51.4	18.4	30.3	12.3	19.1	68.6
	*2015	28.7	21.8	49.5	41.0	22.3	36.7	7.7	20.9	71.4
	*2018	28.3	21.4	50.4	40.4	22.1	37.5	8.2	20.1	71.7
Hungary Hongrie	2005	4.9	* 32.5	* 62.7	6.7	* 41.9	* 51.4	2.6	* 21.2	* 76.2
	*2010	4.5	30.7	64.8	6.5	40.2	53.4	2.3	19.8	77.9
	*2015	4.9	30.3	64.8	6.8	39.9	53.3	2.7	18.9	78.4
	*2018	4.8	29.9	65.4	6.6	39.6	53.9	2.6	18.5	78.9
Iceland Islande	2005	6.5	* 21.7	* 71.8	9.6	* 31.5	* 58.9	3.1	* 10.6	* 86.3
	*2010	5.6	18.4	76.0	8.6	28.1	63.4	2.2	7.8	90.0
	*2015	4.2	17.8	77.9	6.5	27.7	65.8	1.8	6.9	91.3
	*2018	3.1	15.5	81.4	4.5	24.3	71.3	1.7	5.7	92.7
India Inde	*2005	56.0	18.8	25.2	49.9	20.9	29.2	70.7	13.8	15.5
	*2010	51.5	21.8	26.7	46.5	23.8	29.7	66.8	15.7	17.6
	*2015	44.4	23.9	31.7	40.1	25.8	34.2	57.7	18.0	24.3
	*2018	41.6	23.9	34.5	37.2	25.9	36.9	55.4	17.7	27.0
Indonesia Indonésie	*2005	44.0	18.8	37.2	43.8	20.4	35.8	44.5	15.9	39.7
	*2010	39.2	18.7	42.2	39.6	20.9	39.5	38.4	15.0	46.6
	*2015	33.0	22.0	44.9	33.3	25.8	40.9	32.6	15.8	51.7
	*2018	30.2	21.6	48.2	31.4	25.4	43.2	28.3	15.5	56.1
Iran (Islamic Republic of) Iran (Rép. islamique d')	*2005	24.8	30.4	44.9	22.7	30.8	46.5	33.6	28.4	38.0
	*2010	19.2	32.2	48.6	17.5	33.8	48.8	28.0	24.4	47.6
	*2015	18.0	32.5	49.4	17.1	34.2	48.7	22.8	23.8	53.3
	*2018	16.6	32.4	51.0	15.8	33.9	50.3	20.6	25.3	54.1
Iraq Iraq	*2005	23.0	18.3	58.7	18.8	20.5	60.8	47.8	5.2	46.9
	*2010	23.1	18.7	58.3	17.1	21.9	61.1	51.3	3.6	45.1
	*2015	20.3	19.6	60.1	14.2	23.2	62.6	46.9	3.9	49.3
	*2018	19.2	19.5	61.3	13.2	23.2	63.6	44.6	3.8	51.6
Ireland Irlande	*2005	6.0	27.7	66.3	9.4	39.4	51.2	1.4	11.9	86.7
	*2010	4.6	19.6	75.9	7.5	28.8	63.7	1.1	8.8	90.2
	*2015	5.6	19.1	75.3	9.1	27.8	63.1	1.4	8.5	90.1
	*2018	5.3	19.0	75.8	8.6	27.9	63.5	1.3	8.3	90.5
Isle of Man [4] Île de Man [4]	2001	1.4	16.1	82.5	2.2	25.0	72.9	0.5	5.5	94.0
	2006	1.9	14.8	83.3	2.9	24.0	73.0	0.7	3.9	95.4
Israel Israël	*2005	2.0	21.6	76.4	3.0	31.0	66.0	0.8	10.4	88.8
	*2010	1.6	20.2	78.2	2.3	29.7	68.0	0.8	9.5	89.8
	*2015	1.0	17.7	81.2	1.4	26.3	72.3	0.6	8.1	91.3
	*2018	1.1	17.2	81.8	1.5	25.6	72.9	0.6	7.7	91.7
Italy Italie	2005	4.2	* 30.7	* 65.1	4.8	* 39.2	* 56.0	3.3	* 17.4	* 79.4
	*2010	3.8	28.6	67.6	4.5	38.4	57.1	2.7	14.1	83.2
	*2015	3.8	26.6	69.7	4.7	36.0	59.3	2.4	13.2	84.3
	*2018	3.9	26.1	70.0	4.8	35.5	59.6	2.5	12.9	84.6
Jamaica Jamaïque	*2005	18.1	17.8	64.1	25.0	26.7	48.3	8.4	5.2	86.4
	*2010	20.3	15.9	63.8	28.0	22.3	49.7	9.1	6.8	84.1
	*2015	18.5	15.5	66.0	25.5	22.2	52.3	8.2	5.8	86.0
	*2018	18.4	15.4	66.2	25.6	22.2	52.2	8.2	5.7	86.1
Japan Japon	*2005	4.5	27.8	67.7	4.4	35.1	60.5	4.6	17.4	78.0
	*2010	4.1	25.7	70.2	4.2	33.5	62.3	3.9	14.9	81.1
	*2015	3.6	25.9	70.5	3.9	34.3	61.8	3.2	14.8	82.0
	*2018	3.4	25.3	71.3	3.8	33.8	62.5	2.9	14.2	82.8
Jersey Jersey	2013	4.1	11.7	70.2	…	…	…	…	…	…
Jordan Jordanie	*2005	3.9	26.6	69.5	4.3	27.8	67.9	1.2	17.7	81.1
	*2010	3.7	26.4	69.9	4.2	28.2	67.7	1.3	17.0	81.8
	*2015	3.7	26.8	69.5	4.1	28.5	67.4	1.2	17.8	81.0
	*2018	3.7	26.8	69.5	4.1	28.5	67.4	1.2	17.6	81.2
Kazakhstan Kazakhstan	*2005	32.4	18.0	49.6	33.4	24.6	42.0	31.3	10.9	57.8
	*2010	28.3	18.7	53.0	29.1	25.6	45.3	27.4	11.4	61.2
	*2015	18.0	20.6	61.4	18.9	29.0	52.1	17.1	11.5	71.4
	*2018	17.7	20.8	61.5	18.6	29.2	52.2	16.9	11.6	71.6
Kenya Kenya	*2005	41.5	14.6	44.0	33.7	19.4	46.9	50.8	8.8	40.4
	*2010	39.1	15.3	45.6	31.4	20.6	48.1	48.4	9.0	42.6
	*2015	37.8	14.6	47.7	29.8	20.3	49.9	47.0	7.9	45.1
	*2018	37.2	14.3	48.5	29.3	20.2	50.5	46.4	7.4	46.2

18 Employment by economic activity *(continued)*

Percentage of persons employed by sex and ISIC 4 categories; agriculture (agr.), industry (ind.) and services (ser.)

Emploi par activité économique *(suite)*

Personnes employées par sexe et branches de la CITI rév. 4; agriculture (agr.), industrie (ind.) et services (ser.), pourcentage

Region, country or area + Région, pays ou zone +	Year Année	Male and Female Hommes et femmes Agr.	Ind.	Ser.	Male Hommes Agr.	Ind.	Ser.	Female Femmes Agr.	Ind.	Ser.
Kiribati Kiribati	2005[6]	7.1	8.4	81.1	8.7	10.9	77.3	4.7	4.5	87.8
	2010	22.1	16.1	61.8	32.1	9.1	58.8	9.0	25.3	65.7
Kosovo [11,13] Kosovo [11,13]	2012	4.6	28.4	67.1	4.3	33.3	62.3	5.4	10.1	84.7
Kuwait Koweït	*2005	2.7	20.7	76.6	3.6	27.1	69.3	0.1	2.3	97.7
	*2010	3.1	25.7	71.2	4.3	33.9	61.8	0.1	4.2	95.8
	*2015	3.4	26.6	70.1	4.6	35.2	60.2	0.1	4.5	95.4
	*2018	3.6	26.6	69.9	4.9	35.1	60.0	0.1	4.6	95.3
Kyrgyzstan Kirghizistan	*2005	38.5	17.6	43.9	39.3	22.9	37.8	37.3	10.3	52.4
	*2010	29.9	22.8	47.3	31.3	29.3	39.4	27.9	13.3	58.7
	*2015	29.3	20.9	49.8	27.5	27.7	44.8	31.9	10.8	57.3
	*2018	26.1	22.4	51.5	25.4	29.4	45.2	27.1	11.6	61.3
Lao People's Dem. Rep. Rép. dém. populaire lao	*2005	78.5	5.3	16.2	75.6	6.4	18.0	81.4	4.2	14.4
	2010	71.5	* 8.3	* 20.2	69.3	* 10.0	* 20.7	73.6	* 6.7	* 19.7
	*2015	63.1	9.5	27.4	61.1	11.8	27.1	65.1	7.2	27.7
	*2018	59.9	9.8	30.4	58.1	12.5	29.4	61.7	7.1	31.3
Latvia Lettonie	2005	12.1	* 26.5	* 61.5	15.9	* 35.2	* 48.9	8.0	* 17.2	* 74.8
	*2010	8.6	23.1	68.3	11.8	33.5	54.8	5.7	13.6	80.7
	*2015	7.9	23.7	68.4	10.9	34.7	54.5	5.0	12.7	82.2
	*2018	7.3	23.9	68.8	10.0	35.1	55.0	4.7	12.8	82.5
Lebanon Liban	*2005	3.4	18.8	77.8	4.3	21.8	73.9	~0.0	7.4	92.5
	*2010	2.5	19.2	78.3	3.2	22.9	73.9	~0.0	7.0	93.0
	*2015	3.2	21.9	74.9	4.2	25.8	70.0	0.1	9.2	90.7
	*2018	3.2	20.2	76.6	4.2	24.1	71.7	~0.0	8.0	91.9
Lesotho Lesotho	*2005	25.8	27.3	46.9	36.4	28.5	35.1	13.5	26.0	60.6
	*2010	12.9	39.3	47.8	18.6	48.1	33.4	5.8	28.5	65.7
	*2015	11.1	39.8	49.1	16.1	51.3	32.6	4.9	25.9	69.1
	*2018	10.2	40.5	49.4	14.9	52.1	33.0	4.3	26.2	69.5
Liberia Libéria	*2005	53.0	9.3	37.7	51.4	13.7	35.0	54.8	4.6	40.6
	2010	47.3	* 10.8	* 41.9	47.1	* 15.6	* 37.2	47.5	* 5.5	* 47.1
	*2015	43.4	11.9	44.7	43.8	17.6	38.7	42.9	6.0	51.2
	*2018	42.3	12.0	45.7	42.9	17.7	39.5	41.8	5.9	52.3
Libya Libye	*2005	8.7	28.3	63.1	9.2	30.6	60.3	7.1	20.6	72.4
	*2010	7.3	31.6	61.0	7.7	34.8	57.6	6.3	22.1	71.6
	*2015	16.6	28.8	54.6	17.2	27.9	54.9	14.6	32.1	53.3
	*2018	11.2	25.4	63.4	12.1	25.2	62.7	8.2	25.8	66.0
Lithuania Lituanie	2005	14.3	* 29.1	* 56.7	16.9	* 37.0	* 46.0	11.5	* 20.8	* 67.7
	*2010	8.8	24.6	66.6	11.4	33.4	55.2	6.5	16.6	76.9
	*2015	9.1	25.1	65.9	11.6	34.0	54.4	6.6	16.5	76.9
	*2018	7.6	24.7	67.7	10.1	34.9	55.0	5.2	15.1	79.8
Luxembourg Luxembourg	2005	1.7	* 17.3	* 81.0	2.2	* 25.5	* 72.3	1.1	* 5.8	* 93.1
	*2010	1.1	13.4	85.6	1.4	19.8	78.8	0.7	4.8	94.5
	2015	1.1	* 12.5	* 86.4	1.3	* 19.1	* 79.6	0.8	* 4.4	* 94.9
	*2018	1.0	11.7	87.3	1.3	17.6	81.1	0.6	4.5	95.0
Madagascar Madagascar	*2005	82.0	3.4	14.6	81.5	5.1	13.4	82.5	1.6	15.9
	*2010	74.0	5.5	20.5	75.8	6.0	18.2	72.1	5.0	22.9
	*2015	74.5	9.1	16.4	76.7	8.6	14.7	72.2	9.7	18.2
	*2018	74.2	9.3	16.5	76.6	8.8	14.6	71.8	9.7	18.6
Malawi Malawi	*2005	85.0	9.1	5.9	80.9	10.4	8.7	89.4	7.7	3.0
	*2010	84.8	8.8	6.5	80.6	10.2	9.3	89.3	7.2	3.4
	*2015	84.9	8.3	6.9	80.4	9.8	9.8	89.8	6.6	3.6
	*2018	84.7	8.4	6.9	80.2	10.0	9.8	89.6	6.7	3.7
Malaysia Malaisie	*2005	14.6	29.7	55.6	17.1	32.6	50.3	10.1	24.4	65.5
	*2010	14.2	27.7	58.1	17.1	31.6	51.3	8.9	20.5	70.7
	*2015	12.5	27.5	60.0	15.2	32.5	52.3	7.9	19.2	72.9
	*2018	10.7	27.2	62.1	13.4	32.0	54.7	6.3	19.4	74.3
Maldives Maldives	*2005	14.4	26.1	59.5	17.8	20.7	61.5	8.5	35.4	56.1
	*2010	15.0	16.1	68.8	19.4	15.3	65.3	6.3	17.8	76.0
	*2015	8.0	24.8	67.2	10.0	25.1	65.0	2.7	24.3	73.0
	*2018	7.2	24.7	68.1	9.0	25.1	65.9	2.3	23.5	74.2
Mali Mali	*2005	44.8	15.1	40.1	51.2	16.2	32.6	33.2	13.0	53.8
	*2010	57.5	11.1	31.5	60.8	11.9	27.3	51.9	9.7	38.4
	*2015	62.3	8.3	29.5	62.5	10.0	27.5	61.9	6.0	32.1
	*2018	56.8	8.5	34.7	57.5	10.7	31.9	55.9	5.6	38.5

18 Employment by economic activity *(continued)*

Percentage of persons employed by sex and ISIC 4 categories; agriculture (agr.), industry (ind.) and services (ser.)

Emploi par activité économique *(suite)*

Personnes employées par sexe et branches de la CITI rév. 4; agriculture (agr.), industrie (ind.) et services (ser.), pourcentage

Region, country or area + / Région, pays ou zone +	Year / Année	Male and Female / Hommes et femmes Agr.	Ind.	Ser.	Male / Hommes Agr.	Ind.	Ser.	Female / Femmes Agr.	Ind.	Ser.
Malta / Malte	2005	2.1	* 29.9	* 68.1	2.8	* 35.6	* 61.7	0.6	* 16.8	* 82.6
	*2010	1.3	25.5	73.2	1.9	31.9	66.2	0.3	13.2	86.5
	*2015	1.6	19.8	78.6	2.4	26.7	71.0	0.4	8.9	90.7
	*2018	1.2	19.1	79.6	1.9	25.7	72.4	0.2	8.7	91.1
Marshall Islands [4] / Îles Marshall [4]	#2010	11.0	9.4	79.6	...	...	...	...	...	...
Martinique [8,11] / Martinique [8,11]	2010	4.1	11.9	65.3	...	...	...	...	...	...
	2012	3.9	11.8	69.0	...	...	...	...	...	...
Mauritania / Mauritanie	*2005	77.9	8.9	13.3	74.7	10.5	14.9	85.5	5.1	9.4
	*2010	77.3	7.6	15.1	73.8	9.2	17.0	85.4	3.9	10.7
	*2015	75.9	7.6	16.5	72.2	9.3	18.5	84.2	3.9	12.0
	*2018	75.5	7.2	17.3	71.8	8.8	19.3	83.9	3.5	12.6
Mauritius / Maurice	*2005	10.0	32.4	57.6	10.6	34.2	55.2	8.9	28.8	62.4
	*2010	8.5	28.8	62.7	9.1	32.8	58.2	7.4	21.6	71.0
	*2015	7.5	25.4	67.1	8.7	30.4	60.9	5.7	17.0	77.3
	*2018	7.1	25.7	67.3	7.8	31.5	60.7	5.9	16.0	78.1
Mexico / Mexique	*2005	14.8	25.7	59.5	20.1	29.4	50.6	4.7	18.8	76.6
	*2010	13.9	24.1	62.0	19.4	28.8	51.7	3.8	15.7	80.5
	*2015	13.5	25.1	61.4	19.2	29.9	50.8	3.5	16.5	80.0
	*2018	13.0	25.9	61.2	18.4	31.0	50.7	3.6	17.0	79.4
Mongolia / Mongolie	*2005	45.7	11.9	42.5	46.8	13.9	39.3	44.3	9.5	46.2
	*2010	33.5	16.2	50.2	34.7	20.2	45.1	32.2	11.6	56.2
	*2015	28.5	20.3	51.3	29.7	26.5	43.8	26.9	12.9	60.2
	*2018	29.8	19.2	51.0	31.8	25.0	43.2	27.4	12.5	60.1
Montenegro / Monténégro	*2005	8.6	19.2	72.1	8.5	26.9	64.6	8.9	9.5	81.7
	*2010	6.2	19.0	74.8	7.1	26.7	66.2	5.1	9.4	85.5
	*2015	7.8	17.6	74.7	7.3	26.0	66.7	8.3	7.4	84.3
	*2018	7.4	18.1	74.6	6.9	26.7	66.4	8.0	7.5	84.5
Morocco / Maroc	*2005	45.5	19.5	35.0	39.6	20.8	39.5	61.5	15.9	22.7
	*2010	40.2	22.0	37.8	33.0	25.1	42.0	60.7	13.2	26.1
	*2015	38.6	19.2	42.3	31.8	21.6	46.6	58.1	12.1	29.9
	*2018	37.0	19.5	43.5	30.2	22.0	47.8	56.7	12.3	31.1
Mozambique / Mozambique	*2005	79.3	3.3	17.4	67.9	6.6	25.5	89.4	0.3	10.3
	*2010	77.3	3.4	19.3	65.0	7.0	28.0	88.0	0.3	11.7
	*2015	73.6	4.3	22.2	60.4	8.8	30.8	85.0	0.4	14.7
	*2018	73.1	4.4	22.5	60.1	9.0	30.9	84.5	0.4	15.2
Myanmar / Myanmar	*2005	69.5	11.7	18.8	69.7	12.2	18.1	69.2	11.1	19.7
	*2010	60.6	15.0	24.4	61.4	15.7	22.9	59.5	13.9	26.6
	2015	51.8	* 16.8	* 31.5	52.8	* 18.3	* 28.9	50.2	* 14.6	* 35.2
	*2018	48.3	16.9	34.8	49.5	18.7	31.8	46.6	14.2	39.3
Namibia / Namibie	*2005	26.8	15.3	57.9	31.9	20.3	47.9	20.7	9.4	70.0
	*2010	31.7	12.7	55.6	32.9	19.1	48.0	30.4	5.5	64.2
	*2015	24.3	17.1	58.5	24.9	27.6	47.4	23.7	6.0	70.3
	*2018	20.1	19.7	60.3	22.0	31.3	46.8	18.1	7.4	74.6
Nepal / Népal	*2005	76.0	4.7	19.3	68.0	4.7	27.3	84.4	4.8	10.8
	*2010	74.8	7.5	17.7	64.2	9.2	26.7	85.2	5.8	9.0
	*2015	72.3	7.9	19.8	60.5	9.7	29.9	83.3	6.3	10.4
	*2018	71.3	8.2	20.5	59.2	10.0	30.9	82.5	6.6	10.9
Netherlands / Pays-Bas	2005	3.3	* 20.5	* 76.1	4.3	* 30.2	* 65.5	2.2	* 8.5	* 89.3
	2010	3.1	* 17.6	* 79.3	4.1	* 26.9	* 69.0	1.8	* 6.6	* 91.5
	*2015	2.3	16.4	81.3	3.0	25.2	71.8	1.5	6.1	92.5
	*2018	2.2	16.4	81.5	2.9	25.2	72.0	1.3	6.1	92.6
Netherlands Antilles [former] / Antilles néerlandaises [anc.]	2009	0.8	16.0	83.2	1.6	28.2	70.1	0.2	4.4	95.4
	2011	0.7	15.3	84.0	1.4	27.7	71.0	0.2	4.1	95.7
	2013	0.2	15.9	83.2	...	...	...	...	...	...
New Caledonia / Nouvelle-Calédonie	*2005	4.6	31.8	63.7	6.0	44.8	49.1	2.8	16.1	81.1
	*2010	4.0	33.1	63.0	5.3	45.7	49.0	2.4	17.5	80.1
	*2015	3.5	31.7	64.8	4.8	45.0	50.3	2.1	15.4	82.5
	*2018	3.4	31.7	65.0	4.5	45.2	50.3	1.9	15.2	82.8
New Zealand / Nouvelle-Zélande	*2005	7.2	22.2	70.7	9.0	32.2	58.9	5.0	10.5	84.5
	*2010	6.9	21.0	72.2	9.0	30.8	60.2	4.4	9.7	85.9
	*2015	6.1	22.0	71.9	8.0	32.5	59.5	4.0	10.1	85.9
	*2018	6.5	20.1	73.4	8.5	30.1	61.4	4.4	8.9	86.7

18 Employment by economic activity *(continued)*

Percentage of persons employed by sex and ISIC 4 categories; agriculture (agr.), industry (ind.) and services (ser.)

Emploi par activité économique *(suite)*

Personnes employées par sexe et branches de la CITI rév. 4; agriculture (agr.), industrie (ind.) et services (ser.), pourcentage

Region, country or area + / Région, pays ou zone +	Year / Année	Male and Female / Hommes et femmes			Male / Hommes			Female / Femmes		
		Agr.	Ind.	Ser.	Agr.	Ind.	Ser.	Agr.	Ind.	Ser.
Nicaragua / Nicaragua	*2005	28.9	19.7	51.4	40.7	20.1	39.2	8.1	19.0	72.9
	*2010	32.2	16.5	51.3	46.2	17.3	36.6	9.0	15.2	75.9
	*2015	30.7	18.0	51.3	44.0	20.4	35.6	9.0	14.1	76.9
	*2018	28.8	17.7	53.5	42.0	20.6	37.4	8.1	13.1	78.8
Niger / Niger	*2005	77.6	6.9	15.5	79.9	4.2	15.9	74.7	10.4	14.9
	*2010	77.8	7.2	15.1	80.6	4.3	15.1	74.0	10.9	15.0
	*2015	76.1	7.5	16.5	79.1	4.5	16.5	72.3	11.3	16.5
	*2018	75.3	7.7	17.1	78.4	4.6	17.0	71.2	11.6	17.2
Nigeria / Nigéria	*2005	51.2	8.5	40.4	56.3	8.9	34.8	44.5	7.9	47.6
	*2010	30.6	14.2	55.3	39.5	13.5	46.9	19.5	14.9	65.6
	*2015	36.4	11.8	51.8	44.8	11.5	43.7	26.3	12.2	61.5
	*2018	36.4	11.7	51.9	45.2	11.3	43.6	26.0	12.1	61.8
Niue [4] / Nioué [4]	2001	9.0	20.4	70.1	11.4	28.7	59.4	5.8	8.7	85.1
	#2002	4.8	9.3	85.9	...	...	...	...	...	...
Northern Mariana Islands [3,6] / Îles Mariannes du Nord [3,6]	#2000	1.5	47.2	45.8	...	...	...	...	...	...
Norway / Norvège	2005	3.3	* 20.9	* 75.9	4.8	* 32.3	* 62.9	1.6	* 8.1	* 90.4
	*2010	2.6	19.7	77.8	3.9	31.2	64.9	1.0	7.0	92.0
	*2015	2.0	20.1	77.9	3.0	31.7	65.3	0.9	7.2	91.9
	*2018	2.0	19.5	78.5	3.0	30.8	66.2	1.0	6.9	92.1
Oman / Oman	*2005	6.8	17.8	75.5	7.7	19.2	73.2	1.2	9.2	89.6
	*2010	5.2	36.9	58.0	5.9	41.8	52.4	0.5	5.9	93.7
	*2015	6.0	38.9	55.1	6.6	42.9	50.4	0.6	6.4	93.0
	*2018	6.5	38.2	55.3	7.2	41.9	51.0	0.6	6.5	92.9
Pakistan / Pakistan	*2005	43.1	20.3	36.6	38.2	21.4	40.5	67.4	15.0	17.6
	2010	43.4	* 21.4	* 35.2	35.4	* 24.0	* 40.6	74.1	* 11.5	* 14.4
	*2015	41.0	24.0	35.0	32.6	26.6	40.8	72.1	14.5	13.4
	*2018	41.3	23.9	34.8	32.6	26.5	40.9	72.4	14.4	13.2
Palau [3] / Palaos [3]	2000[6]	7.1	13.8	79.1	9.6	20.7	69.7	3.1	2.6	94.4
	2008[4]	2.4	11.8	85.9	...	...	...	...	...	...
Panama / Panama	*2005	15.7	17.2	67.1	22.1	21.7	56.2	4.3	9.1	86.6
	*2010	17.4	18.7	63.9	23.1	23.9	53.0	7.5	9.7	82.8
	*2015	15.7	19.0	65.3	20.0	24.7	55.3	8.9	9.8	81.3
	*2018	14.5	18.0	67.5	18.6	23.5	57.9	8.2	9.3	82.5
Papua New Guinea / Papouasie-Nvl-Guinée	*2005	52.6	5.8	41.7	56.9	9.5	33.6	48.0	1.9	50.1
	2010	25.8	* 7.5	* 66.7	31.2	* 12.1	* 56.7	20.1	* 2.7	* 77.2
	*2015	20.7	7.5	71.8	25.8	12.4	61.8	15.5	2.5	82.0
	*2018	20.4	7.6	72.0	25.5	12.5	61.9	15.2	2.5	82.3
Paraguay / Paraguay	*2005	32.4	15.7	51.9	38.7	19.9	41.4	22.1	9.0	68.9
	*2010	25.6	19.2	55.2	30.2	25.6	44.2	18.1	8.7	73.2
	*2015	19.7	19.7	60.6	23.4	26.3	50.2	14.0	9.7	76.4
	*2018	20.9	19.5	59.6	25.2	26.7	48.1	14.2	8.4	77.5
Peru / Pérou	*2005	34.8	14.1	51.1	36.6	18.2	45.2	32.6	8.9	58.5
	*2010	27.7	16.9	55.4	28.7	22.6	48.7	26.6	10.1	63.3
	*2015	28.3	16.6	55.2	29.3	22.8	47.9	27.0	9.0	64.0
	*2018	28.0	15.9	56.1	29.7	21.8	48.5	26.0	8.9	65.1
Philippines / Philippines	*2005	36.0	15.6	48.5	43.6	17.8	38.6	23.7	12.0	64.3
	*2010	33.2	15.0	51.8	40.5	18.2	41.3	21.7	9.9	68.4
	*2015	29.2	16.2	54.7	35.8	20.3	43.9	19.0	10.0	71.0
	*2018	25.3	17.8	56.8	31.5	23.2	45.4	16.0	9.8	74.2
Poland / Pologne	2005	17.4	* 29.3	* 53.4	18.0	* 39.0	* 43.1	16.6	* 17.1	* 66.3
	*2010	13.1	30.3	56.6	13.4	41.8	44.8	12.7	16.1	71.2
	*2015	11.5	30.5	57.9	12.5	42.1	45.5	10.4	16.5	73.1
	*2018	10.3	31.1	58.6	11.3	43.1	45.6	9.0	16.5	74.5
Portugal / Portugal	2005	12.1	* 30.4	* 57.6	11.2	* 40.6	* 48.3	13.1	* 18.4	* 68.5
	*2010	11.2	27.3	61.6	11.5	37.5	51.0	10.9	16.0	73.1
	*2015	7.5	24.4	68.1	9.6	33.0	57.5	5.4	15.2	79.4
	*2018	6.7	24.6	68.8	8.6	33.6	57.8	4.6	15.1	80.3
Puerto Rico / Porto Rico	*2005	2.1	19.0	78.9	3.3	24.9	71.8	0.4	10.9	88.8
	*2010	1.6	13.8	84.7	2.6	18.0	79.4	0.2	8.3	91.5
	*2015	3.0	16.7	80.3	5.0	19.3	75.7	0.4	13.3	86.3
	*2018	3.2	16.8	80.1	5.3	19.2	75.6	0.4	13.6	86.0

18 Employment by economic activity *(continued)*

Percentage of persons employed by sex and ISIC 4 categories; agriculture (agr.), industry (ind.) and services (ser.)

Emploi par activité économique *(suite)*

Personnes employées par sexe et branches de la CITI rév. 4; agriculture (agr.), industrie (ind.) et services (ser.), pourcentage

Region, country or area + / Région, pays ou zone +	Year / Année	Male and Female / Hommes et femmes			Male / Hommes			Female / Femmes		
		Agr.	Ind.	Ser.	Agr.	Ind.	Ser.	Agr.	Ind.	Ser.
Qatar / Qatar	*2005	3.1	40.4	56.5	3.6	47.1	49.3	0.1	3.5	96.4
	*2010	1.5	57.2	41.3	1.7	64.1	34.2	~0.0	5.2	94.7
	*2015	1.2	54.1	44.6	1.4	61.9	36.7	~0.0	6.0	94.0
	*2018	1.2	54.6	44.2	1.4	62.4	36.1	~0.0	6.7	93.3
Republic of Korea / République de Corée	*2005	7.9	26.9	65.2	7.3	34.0	58.7	8.9	16.6	74.5
	*2010	6.6	25.0	68.5	6.4	32.4	61.3	6.9	14.3	78.8
	*2015	5.2	25.1	69.7	5.2	33.3	61.6	5.2	13.7	81.1
	*2018	4.8	24.6	70.6	4.9	33.0	62.1	4.7	12.9	82.4
Republic of Moldova / République de Moldova	*2005	40.7	16.0	43.3	41.1	20.8	38.1	40.2	11.5	48.4
	2010	27.5	* 18.7	* 53.8	30.5	* 24.9	* 44.6	24.5	* 12.3	* 63.2
	*2015	34.2	17.9	48.0	38.5	23.9	37.7	29.7	11.8	58.5
	*2018	32.6	17.2	50.3	35.9	22.4	41.7	29.1	11.9	59.0
Réunion [8] / Réunion [8]	2010[11]	4.2	14.1	67.1	...	...	...	...	...	...
	#2012	4.3	12.7	81.7	6.3	20.0	72.0	2.1	4.1	93.0
Romania / Roumanie	2005	32.3	* 30.5	* 37.3	31.7	* 35.1	* 33.2	33.1	* 24.8	* 42.2
	2010	31.0	* 28.3	* 40.7	30.0	* 35.0	* 35.1	32.4	* 19.9	* 47.8
	*2015	25.6	28.5	46.0	25.6	35.0	39.4	25.6	20.0	54.4
	*2018	22.3	28.5	49.2	22.9	35.3	41.8	21.5	19.7	58.8
Russian Federation / Fédération de Russie	*2005	10.2	29.8	60.0	12.3	38.2	49.6	8.0	21.3	70.7
	2010	7.8	* 27.7	* 64.5	9.9	* 37.3	* 52.8	5.6	* 17.8	* 76.6
	*2015	6.7	27.2	66.1	8.2	37.7	54.1	5.1	16.2	78.7
	*2018	6.6	26.8	66.6	8.2	37.1	54.7	4.9	16.0	79.1
Rwanda / Rwanda	*2005	85.6	3.4	11.0	79.1	6.1	14.9	91.9	0.9	7.2
	*2010	79.6	5.5	14.8	70.8	9.5	19.7	88.1	1.7	10.2
	*2015	67.3	8.1	24.6	56.6	13.8	29.5	77.4	2.7	19.9
	*2018	65.7	8.3	26.0	54.8	14.3	31.0	75.9	2.7	21.4
Saint Helena [4,14] / Sainte-Hélène [4,14]	2008	7.3	20.0	72.7	11.8	33.9	54.3	1.7	2.9	95.4
Saint Kitts and Nevis [6] / Saint-Kitts-et-Nevis [6]	#2001	0.2	48.8	42.1	0.4	51.6	34.7	0.1	45.5	50.6
Saint Lucia / Sainte-Lucie	*2005	13.8	20.3	65.9	17.8	27.5	54.7	8.5	10.8	80.6
	*2010	14.6	18.4	67.0	18.7	25.9	55.5	9.4	8.7	82.0
	*2015	14.7	17.0	68.3	18.8	24.2	57.0	9.5	8.0	82.6
	*2018	15.3	17.5	67.3	19.6	25.0	55.5	10.1	8.3	81.6
Saint Vincent & Grenadines / Saint-Vincent-Grenadines	*2005	7.2	12.6	80.3	10.8	16.4	72.9	1.5	6.7	91.9
	*2010	6.9	13.1	80.0	10.4	17.3	72.3	1.5	6.9	91.7
	*2015	6.3	12.4	81.2	9.8	16.7	73.6	1.4	6.3	92.3
	*2018	6.0	12.7	81.3	9.3	17.1	73.6	1.3	6.3	92.4
Samoa / Samoa	*2005	7.1	14.8	78.1	8.4	18.8	72.8	4.8	7.7	87.5
	*2010	5.9	15.3	78.8	7.0	19.4	73.6	3.8	8.2	88.0
	*2015	5.4	14.7	80.0	6.4	18.8	74.8	3.4	7.3	89.3
	*2018	5.8	15.0	79.2	7.0	19.0	74.0	3.8	7.9	88.3
San Marino / Saint-Marin	2005[4]	0.5	39.3	60.2	0.6	50.4	49.1	0.3	23.4	76.3
	#2010	0.3	34.3	65.4	0.4	45.6	54.0	0.2	18.7	81.1
Sao Tome and Principe / Sao Tomé-et-Principe	*2005	27.9	17.2	54.9	34.1	24.1	41.8	16.0	3.9	80.1
	*2010	23.9	16.1	60.0	28.6	20.8	50.7	15.0	7.1	77.9
	*2015	18.8	14.0	67.2	22.9	18.7	58.4	11.0	5.4	83.7
	*2018	16.0	13.9	70.2	19.9	18.8	61.3	8.7	4.8	86.5
Saudi Arabia / Arabie saoudite	*2005	4.0	20.0	75.9	4.6	22.9	72.6	0.4	1.0	98.6
	*2010	4.3	21.4	74.4	4.9	24.3	70.8	0.2	1.6	98.3
	*2015	6.1	22.7	71.2	7.0	26.1	67.0	0.6	1.6	97.9
	*2018	6.4	22.6	71.1	7.3	26.0	66.8	0.6	1.6	97.8
Senegal / Sénégal	*2005	40.6	17.4	42.0	39.9	23.1	37.0	42.1	6.2	51.8
	*2010	53.3	19.7	27.0	49.0	25.1	25.8	60.2	10.9	28.9
	*2015	54.0	20.0	26.0	49.7	25.7	24.6	60.1	11.8	28.1
	*2018	52.8	20.2	27.0	48.5	26.2	25.3	58.8	11.8	29.4
Serbia / Serbie	*2005	23.3	27.6	49.1	23.3	34.4	42.3	23.3	17.5	59.2
	2010	22.7	* 22.3	* 55.0	23.8	* 27.9	* 48.3	21.1	* 14.9	* 64.0
	*2015	19.5	24.5	56.1	21.9	30.2	47.9	16.3	16.9	66.8
	*2018	18.7	24.5	56.9	20.5	30.9	48.6	16.3	16.3	67.4
Seychelles [8,15] / Seychelles [8,15]	2011	3.6	17.9	78.2	6.4	25.3	68.1	0.7	10.4	88.5

18 Employment by economic activity *(continued)*

Percentage of persons employed by sex and ISIC 4 categories; agriculture (agr.), industry (ind.) and services (ser.)

Emploi par activité économique *(suite)*

Personnes employées par sexe et branches de la CITI rév. 4; agriculture (agr.), industrie (ind.) et services (ser.), pourcentage

Region, country or area + / Région, pays ou zone +	Year / Année	Male and Female / Hommes et femmes			Male / Hommes			Female / Femmes		
		Agr.	Ind.	Ser.	Agr.	Ind.	Ser.	Agr.	Ind.	Ser.
Sierra Leone / Sierra Leone	*2005	65.9	6.1	28.0	66.2	11.4	22.4	65.6	1.0	33.4
	*2010	63.7	6.4	29.8	64.7	12.1	23.2	62.8	1.0	36.2
	*2015	60.9	6.2	33.0	61.7	11.6	26.8	60.1	0.9	39.1
	*2018	59.8	6.2	34.0	61.0	11.7	27.3	58.6	0.9	40.6
Singapore / Singapour	*2005	0.9	21.8	77.3	1.2	25.4	73.5	0.6	16.8	82.6
	*2010	0.1	30.4	69.5	0.2	37.2	62.6	0.1	21.5	78.5
	*2015	0.9	16.4	82.7	1.2	20.1	78.7	0.6	11.8	87.6
	*2018	0.1	16.2	83.7	0.2	20.0	79.9	0.1	11.6	88.4
Slovakia / Slovaquie	2005	4.8	*38.8	*56.4	6.4	*49.6	*43.9	2.6	*25.2	*72.1
	*2010	3.2	37.1	59.7	4.4	50.1	45.5	1.8	21.1	77.1
	*2015	3.2	36.1	60.7	4.7	48.4	46.9	1.3	20.8	77.9
	*2018	2.9	36.1	61.1	4.1	48.7	47.3	1.4	20.8	77.9
Slovenia / Slovénie	2005	9.1	*37.1	*53.8	9.1	*46.9	*44.0	9.1	*25.4	*65.5
	*2010	8.8	32.6	58.6	9.1	42.7	48.2	8.5	20.5	70.9
	*2015	7.1	32.0	60.9	7.1	43.5	49.5	7.1	18.2	74.7
	*2018	4.8	31.8	63.4	5.6	43.9	50.5	3.9	17.7	78.4
Solomon Islands / Îles Salomon	*2005	71.2	8.4	20.5	69.5	10.0	20.5	73.3	6.2	20.5
	*2010	69.5	9.1	21.4	67.7	11.2	21.1	71.8	6.3	21.8
	*2015	69.0	9.4	21.6	67.6	11.6	20.8	70.8	6.6	22.6
	*2018	69.7	9.8	20.6	68.4	11.8	19.9	71.4	7.2	21.5
Somalia / Somalie	*2005	86.7	7.2	6.1	85.4	7.7	6.9	92.4	5.0	2.7
	*2010	86.4	7.4	6.2	85.1	8.0	7.0	92.1	5.2	2.7
	*2015	86.1	7.7	6.2	84.7	8.2	7.1	91.8	5.4	2.8
	*2018	86.2	7.6	6.2	84.7	8.2	7.1	91.8	5.3	2.9
South Africa / Afrique du Sud	*2005	7.5	25.7	66.8	8.6	34.3	57.1	6.0	13.5	80.5
	*2010	4.9	24.4	70.7	5.7	32.8	61.5	3.8	13.0	83.2
	*2015	5.6	23.8	70.6	6.7	33.2	60.2	4.2	11.8	84.0
	*2018	5.5	23.4	71.2	6.8	32.0	61.2	3.8	12.0	84.2
South Sudan / Soudan du sud	*2005	56.5	18.9	24.6	57.2	16.0	26.9	55.8	22.0	22.2
	*2010	54.1	19.8	26.1	54.6	17.6	27.8	53.5	22.2	24.3
	*2015	62.4	19.4	18.2	64.6	14.1	21.3	60.1	25.0	14.9
	*2018	65.4	19.5	15.2	68.2	13.1	18.8	62.4	26.3	11.4
Spain / Espagne	2005	5.3	*29.6	*65.1	6.5	*41.1	*52.5	3.5	*12.4	*84.1
	*2010	4.2	23.0	72.8	5.6	33.6	60.9	2.4	9.5	88.0
	*2015	4.1	19.9	76.0	5.8	29.2	65.1	2.1	8.7	89.2
	*2018	4.1	19.3	76.7	5.8	28.7	65.6	2.0	8.2	89.8
Sri Lanka / Sri Lanka	*2005	33.8	27.3	38.9	32.0	26.5	41.6	37.8	29.0	33.3
	*2010	33.6	24.9	41.5	31.4	24.7	43.8	38.2	25.2	36.6
	*2015	28.1	25.5	46.4	26.5	25.7	47.9	31.4	25.3	43.3
	*2018	26.0	25.7	48.3	24.5	26.1	49.4	28.9	24.9	46.2
State of Palestine / État de Palestine	*2005	14.6	26.3	59.2	10.7	30.2	59.1	32.0	8.6	59.4
	*2010	12.8	25.7	61.5	9.6	29.1	61.3	27.9	9.5	62.6
	*2015	8.7	29.2	62.2	7.7	32.8	59.5	13.1	11.7	75.2
	*2018	9.7	29.4	61.0	8.5	33.7	57.9	14.4	12.4	73.1
Sudan / Soudan	*2005	54.8	21.4	23.8	57.4	17.1	25.5	46.1	35.6	18.2
	*2010	49.2	22.6	28.2	51.4	19.2	29.5	42.0	34.3	23.7
	*2015	52.8	18.9	28.3	54.9	15.1	30.0	46.3	31.0	22.7
	*2018	53.2	19.2	27.7	55.4	15.2	29.4	46.2	31.8	22.0
Suriname / Suriname	*2005	7.0	24.2	68.8	8.7	32.6	58.8	3.8	8.4	87.8
	*2010	4.2	23.0	72.8	5.4	32.6	62.0	2.2	6.4	91.3
	*2015	2.4	23.8	73.7	3.4	34.1	62.6	0.9	7.1	92.0
	*2018	2.6	24.4	73.0	3.6	34.4	62.0	1.0	7.7	91.3
Sweden / Suède	*2005	2.0	22.1	75.9	3.0	33.7	63.3	0.9	9.2	89.8
	*2010	2.1	19.9	78.0	3.1	30.9	66.0	1.0	7.6	91.4
	*2015	2.0	18.3	79.7	3.0	28.7	68.3	1.0	6.9	92.1
	*2018	1.8	18.0	80.2	2.6	28.3	69.1	1.0	6.8	92.3
Switzerland / Suisse	2005	3.9	*22.5	*73.6	4.8	*32.0	*63.2	2.8	*11.0	*86.2
	2010	3.5	*22.5	*74.1	4.1	*32.3	*63.6	2.7	*10.7	*86.6
	*2015	3.4	20.8	75.8	3.9	30.0	66.1	2.9	10.1	87.0
	*2018	3.4	20.6	76.0	3.9	29.8	66.3	2.9	10.0	87.1
Syrian Arab Republic / République arabe syrienne	*2005	21.2	26.5	52.2	19.3	29.7	51.0	33.2	7.2	59.6
	*2010	15.2	34.3	50.6	14.2	38.0	47.8	21.4	10.0	68.6
	*2015	20.8	32.4	46.8	20.9	34.6	44.5	19.8	13.4	66.8
	*2018	23.0	33.0	44.0	23.1	35.2	41.8	22.1	14.5	63.5

Employment by economic activity *(continued)*

Percentage of persons employed by sex and ISIC 4 categories; agriculture (agr.), industry (ind.) and services (ser.)

Emploi par activité économique *(suite)*

Personnes employées par sexe et branches de la CITI rév. 4; agriculture (agr.), industrie (ind.) et services (ser.), pourcentage

Region, country or area + Région, pays ou zone +	Year Année	Male and Female Hommes et femmes Agr.	Ind.	Ser.	Male Hommes Agr.	Ind.	Ser.	Female Femmes Agr.	Ind.	Ser.
Tajikistan	*2005	56.7	16.2	27.1	44.1	24.1	31.8	75.1	4.6	20.3
Tadjikistan	*2010	53.1	15.5	31.4	42.4	22.3	35.3	69.4	5.1	25.6
	*2015	51.8	16.1	32.1	40.6	23.5	35.9	69.7	4.4	26.0
	*2018	51.2	16.5	32.3	40.2	24.1	35.8	69.0	4.4	26.6
Thailand	*2005	42.6	20.3	37.1	44.2	21.6	34.2	40.7	18.7	40.6
Thaïlande	2010	38.2	* 20.6	* 41.1	40.1	* 22.7	* 37.2	36.1	* 18.2	* 45.7
	*2015	32.3	23.7	44.0	34.4	26.1	39.6	29.8	20.8	49.4
	*2018	32.0	22.5	45.5	34.2	25.3	40.5	29.4	19.3	51.4
TFYR of Macedonia	*2005	19.5	32.4	48.1	19.4	34.6	46.0	19.6	29.2	51.2
ex-R.Y. de Macédoine	*2010	19.3	29.6	51.1	19.4	32.3	48.3	19.2	25.3	55.5
	*2015	17.9	30.5	51.6	18.1	34.5	47.4	17.5	24.5	58.1
	*2018	16.0	29.7	54.3	16.5	33.4	50.1	15.3	23.8	60.9
Timor-Leste	*2005	60.4	7.9	31.8	60.7	7.9	31.4	59.8	7.7	32.5
Timor-Leste	*2010	50.8	9.3	39.9	51.1	10.2	38.7	50.2	7.4	42.5
	*2015	39.1	13.1	47.8	36.5	15.9	47.6	44.7	7.1	48.2
	*2018	24.9	15.4	59.7	23.5	19.5	57.1	28.1	6.4	65.6
Togo	*2005	42.5	17.9	39.6	47.1	16.0	37.0	38.1	19.8	42.1
Togo	*2010	38.4	18.3	43.4	43.6	16.4	40.0	33.0	20.2	46.8
	*2015	39.4	17.3	43.3	43.9	16.6	39.5	34.9	17.9	47.2
	*2018	36.9	17.3	45.8	41.2	17.1	41.7	32.5	17.5	50.0
Tonga	*2005	31.9	30.3	37.7	49.3	13.5	37.1	4.2	57.2	38.7
Tonga	*2010	31.6	30.7	37.8	48.8	14.3	36.8	4.3	56.5	39.2
	*2015	31.0	30.8	38.2	47.9	14.2	37.9	4.0	57.3	38.7
	*2018	31.6	31.7	36.7	48.7	14.7	36.5	4.1	59.1	36.9
Trinidad and Tobago	*2005	4.3	31.1	64.5	6.1	41.5	52.4	1.7	16.0	82.3
Trinité-et-Tobago	*2010	3.7	30.2	66.1	5.1	41.1	53.8	1.7	14.8	83.5
	*2015	3.7	27.7	68.6	5.1	37.7	57.3	1.8	13.8	84.4
	*2018	3.6	26.8	69.6	5.0	36.4	58.6	1.7	13.3	85.1
Tunisia	*2005	20.8	42.2	37.0	20.1	43.3	36.6	23.0	38.8	38.2
Tunisie	*2010	17.7	44.9	37.3	17.1	46.6	36.3	19.7	39.8	40.4
	*2015	13.2	44.7	42.1	13.8	45.6	40.6	11.4	42.1	46.5
	*2018	13.5	42.7	43.8	14.0	43.9	42.1	12.0	39.0	49.1
Turkey	*2005	25.7	26.3	48.0	18.5	29.7	51.8	46.2	16.7	37.1
Turquie	*2010	23.7	26.2	50.1	17.4	30.4	52.2	39.2	16.0	44.9
	*2015	20.4	27.2	52.4	15.7	32.1	52.2	31.0	16.3	52.8
	*2018	18.8	26.9	54.3	14.8	31.8	53.4	27.6	16.0	56.4
Turkmenistan	*2005	19.1	36.6	44.2	15.7	47.3	37.0	23.8	22.2	54.0
Turkménistan	*2010	12.6	45.1	42.3	9.9	56.9	33.2	16.4	29.0	54.7
	*2015	8.9	45.1	46.1	6.8	57.9	35.3	11.8	27.2	61.1
	*2018	7.9	44.9	47.2	6.0	58.1	35.9	10.5	26.4	63.0
Turks and Caicos Islands [4]	2005	1.4	16.8	70.9	...	...	...	...	...	...
Îles Turques-et-Caïques [4]	#2008	1.2	23.1	74.0	...	...	...	...	...	...
Uganda	*2005	75.3	5.7	19.0	69.3	8.3	22.4	82.1	2.7	15.2
Ouganda	*2010	71.1	7.1	21.8	67.3	9.2	23.5	75.4	4.7	20.0
	*2015	71.0	6.8	22.2	66.2	10.0	23.8	76.4	3.3	20.3
	*2018	68.4	7.0	24.6	63.5	10.5	26.0	73.7	3.3	23.1
Ukraine	*2005	19.4	26.0	54.6	18.8	34.9	46.3	20.0	16.5	63.5
Ukraine	*2010	20.3	25.7	54.0	21.0	35.5	43.5	19.6	15.4	65.0
	*2015	15.3	24.7	60.1	17.2	34.7	48.1	13.1	13.9	73.0
	*2018	14.5	25.7	59.9	16.0	36.0	47.9	12.7	14.5	72.7
United Arab Emirates	*2005	4.9	40.1	55.0	5.6	44.6	49.8	0.1	6.1	93.8
Émirats arabes unis	*2010	0.8	29.3	69.9	0.9	32.0	67.1	~0.0	6.4	93.6
	*2015	0.2	33.6	66.2	0.2	37.4	62.4	~0.0	4.5	95.5
	*2018	0.3	38.7	61.0	0.4	43.2	56.5	~0.0	6.7	93.3
United Kingdom	2005	1.4	* 22.2	* 76.4	1.9	* 33.1	* 65.0	0.7	* 9.4	* 89.9
Royaume-Uni	*2010	1.2	19.2	79.6	1.8	29.5	68.8	0.6	7.4	92.0
	*2015	1.1	18.7	80.2	1.6	28.2	70.2	0.7	7.7	91.7
	*2018	1.1	18.2	80.7	1.5	27.6	70.8	0.6	7.4	92.0
United Rep. of Tanzania	*2005	74.7	4.9	20.5	71.3	7.0	21.7	78.1	2.7	19.2
Rép.-Unie de Tanzanie	*2010	72.2	5.4	22.4	69.1	7.8	23.1	75.4	2.9	21.7
	*2015	67.7	6.2	26.2	64.9	9.3	25.8	70.6	2.9	26.5
	*2018	66.0	6.1	28.0	63.1	9.3	27.6	69.0	2.6	28.4

18 Employment by economic activity *(continued)*

Percentage of persons employed by sex and ISIC 4 categories; agriculture (agr.), industry (ind.) and services (ser.)

Emploi par activité économique *(suite)*

Personnes employées par sexe et branches de la CITI rév. 4; agriculture (agr.), industrie (ind.) et services (ser.), pourcentage

Region, country or area + Région, pays ou zone +	Year Année	Male and Female Hommes et femmes			Male Hommes			Female Femmes		
		Agr.	Ind.	Ser.	Agr.	Ind.	Ser.	Agr.	Ind.	Ser.
United States of America États-Unis d'Amérique	*2005	1.6	21.1	77.4	2.2	30.7	67.1	0.8	9.7	89.5
	*2010	1.6	18.5	79.9	2.3	27.7	70.0	0.8	7.9	91.3
	*2015	1.7	18.9	79.5	2.3	27.7	69.9	0.9	8.4	90.8
	*2018	1.6	18.8	79.6	2.3	27.8	70.0	0.9	8.3	90.9
United States Virgin Islands Îles Vierges américaines	*2005	2.3	11.0	86.7	3.7	17.7	78.6	0.7	3.9	95.5
	*2010	2.2	11.1	86.7	3.6	18.0	78.4	0.7	3.9	95.4
	*2015	2.9	12.0	85.2	4.8	18.9	76.3	1.0	4.9	94.1
	*2018	2.7	11.7	85.6	4.5	18.6	76.9	0.9	4.7	94.4
Uruguay Uruguay	*2005	5.7	22.9	71.5	8.4	30.3	61.3	1.9	12.8	85.4
	2010	11.6	*21.4	*67.0	16.5	*28.8	*54.7	5.1	*11.8	*83.1
	*2015	8.8	20.5	70.7	12.3	29.0	58.7	4.5	9.7	85.8
	*2018	8.0	19.8	72.2	11.5	28.5	60.1	3.7	9.0	87.3
Uzbekistan Ouzbékistan	*2005	34.7	32.2	33.1	30.9	39.6	29.5	39.9	22.0	38.1
	*2010	27.2	37.1	35.7	23.7	45.8	30.5	32.0	25.2	42.8
	*2015	22.9	37.8	39.3	19.7	47.5	32.9	27.3	24.4	48.3
	*2018	21.4	37.7	40.9	18.4	47.7	33.9	25.5	23.6	50.8
Vanuatu Vanuatu	*2005	64.2	5.5	30.3	63.0	8.0	29.0	65.7	2.2	32.1
	*2010	61.4	6.9	31.7	60.1	10.1	29.8	63.2	2.6	34.3
	*2015	63.2	6.0	30.8	62.0	8.9	29.0	64.8	2.2	33.0
	*2018	64.7	6.0	29.4	63.4	8.7	27.8	66.3	2.3	31.4
Venezuela (Boliv. Rep. of) Venezuela (Rép. boliv. du)	*2005	9.8	21.0	69.3	14.5	26.9	58.6	2.0	11.2	86.8
	*2010	9.1	23.9	67.0	13.8	31.2	55.0	1.9	12.6	85.5
	*2015	9.1	23.7	67.3	13.4	31.0	55.6	2.5	12.6	84.9
	*2018	10.0	23.6	66.5	14.5	30.1	55.5	3.2	13.7	83.1
Viet Nam Viet Nam	*2005	54.6	18.9	26.5	52.7	22.6	24.8	56.7	14.9	28.4
	*2010	48.9	21.4	29.7	46.7	25.7	27.6	51.1	16.9	32.0
	*2015	43.9	23.3	32.8	42.4	26.9	30.7	45.6	19.3	35.1
	*2018	39.6	25.3	35.1	38.3	29.2	32.5	41.0	21.2	37.9
Western Sahara Sahara occidental	*2005	38.0	29.2	32.9	40.2	24.8	35.0	30.0	45.1	24.9
	*2010	34.6	30.2	35.2	36.5	26.2	37.3	27.7	44.4	27.9
	*2015	31.8	31.0	37.2	33.6	27.2	39.2	25.6	43.8	30.6
	*2018	30.6	30.9	38.4	32.6	27.1	40.3	24.1	43.5	32.4
Yemen Yémen	*2005	30.1	15.7	54.2	28.2	17.1	54.8	40.0	8.6	51.3
	*2010	24.1	19.0	56.9	23.8	19.4	56.8	28.0	14.6	57.4
	*2015	34.7	14.4	50.9	33.0	14.4	52.6	56.7	14.6	28.8
	*2018	47.7	12.2	40.1	46.3	12.2	41.5	68.6	11.3	20.1
Zambia Zambie	*2005	72.8	6.8	20.4	65.7	10.7	23.6	80.6	2.5	17.0
	*2010	63.4	8.8	27.9	55.4	13.9	30.7	72.4	3.0	24.6
	*2015	53.7	11.5	34.8	45.1	18.3	36.6	63.2	4.0	32.9
	*2018	53.0	12.0	35.0	44.3	19.2	36.5	62.5	4.1	33.4
Zimbabwe Zimbabwe	*2005	72.6	10.4	17.0	65.3	15.8	18.9	80.2	4.8	15.0
	*2010	69.0	9.4	21.6	62.9	15.1	22.0	75.4	3.5	21.2
	*2015	67.2	7.3	25.5	62.9	12.3	24.8	71.6	2.2	26.2
	*2018	68.6	7.4	24.0	64.2	12.4	23.4	73.1	2.4	24.6

Source:

International Labour Organization (ILO), Geneva, Key Indicators of the Labour Market (KILM 9th edition) and the ILOSTAT database, last accessed February 2018.

Source:

Organisation internationale du Travail (OIT), Genève, Indicateurs Clés du Marché du Travail (ICMT 9e édition) et ILOSTAT base de données, dernier accès février 2018.

+ Ages 15 years and over unless indicated otherwise. Table is in ISIC Rev. 4 unless otherwise indicated.

+ Sauf indication contraire, Age 15 ans et plus. Sauf indication contraire, la classification utilisée dans ce tableau est la CITI Rév. 4.

1 Data excludes Armenia, Azerbaijan, Cyprus, Georgia, Israel and Turkey.

2 Caucasus refers to Armenia, Azerbaijan, Cyprus, Georgia, Israel and Turkey.

3 Population aged 16 years and over.

1 Les données excluent l'Arménie, l'Azerbaïdjan, Chypre, la Géorgie, l'Israël et la Turquie.

2 Le Caucase se rapportent à l'Arménie, l'Azerbaïdjan, Chypre, la Géorgie, l'Israël et la Turquie.

3 Population âgée de 16 ans et plus.

4 Data classified according to ISIC Rev. 3.
5 Population aged 14 years and over.
6 Data classified according to ISIC Rev. 2.
7 Population aged 13 years and over.
8 Excluding the institutional population.
9 For statistical purposes, the data for China do not include those for the Hong Kong Special Administrative Region (Hong Kong SAR), Macao Special Administrative Region (Macao SAR) and Taiwan Province of China.
10 Resident population (de jure).
11 Population aged 15 to 64 years.
12 Nationals, residents.
13 Civilians only.
14 Population aged 15 to 69 years.
15 Excluding some areas.

4 Données classifiées selon la CITI, Rév. 3.
5 Population âgée de 14 ans et plus.
6 Données classifiées selon la CITI, Rév. 2.
7 Population âgée de 13 ans et plus.
8 Non compris la population dans les institutions.
9 Pour la présentation des statistiques, les données pour la Chine ne comprennent pas la région administrative spéciale de Hong Kong (Hong Kong RAS), la région administrative spéciale de Macao (Macao RAS) et la province chinoise de Taïwan.
10 Population résidente (de droit).
11 Population âgée de 15 à 64 ans.
12 Ressortissants, résidents.
13 Civils uniquement.
14 Population âgée de 15 à 69 ans.
15 Certaines régions sont exclues.

19 Consumer price indices

General and food (Index base: 2010 = 100)

Indices des prix à la consommation

Généraux et alimentation (Indices base: 2010 = 100)

Country or area	1995	2005	2010	2014	2015	2016	2017	Pays ou zone
Afghanistan								**Afghanistan**
General	...	71.1	100.0	133.1	132.1	137.9	144.8	Généraux
Food	...	...	...	* 101.7	* 100.8	* 106.5	* 113.9	Alimentation
Åland Islands								**Îles d'Åland**
General	# 80.0[1]	# 90.8[1]	# 100.0	108.5	108.6	109.2	111.1	Généraux
Food	...	# 90.3[1]	100.0	114.1	114.3	113.1	113.7	Alimentation
Albania [1]								**Albanie** [1]
General	40.7	86.7	100.0	109.3	111.4	112.8	115.1	Généraux
Food	...	82.8	100.0	113.8	118.8	122.6	127.3	Alimentation
Algeria [2]								**Algérie** [2]
General	51.9	81.8	100.0	120.9	126.7	134.8	142.4	Généraux
Food [1]	...	...	100.0	125.4	131.3	135.7	142.5	Alimentation [1]
Andorra [1]								**Andorre** [1]
General	...	89.6	100.0	104.4	103.3	102.8	105.5	Généraux
Food	...	92.0	100.0	106.4	108.2	109.1	112.3	Alimentation
Angola [3]								**Angola** [3]
General	* # ~0.0	* 53.7	* 100.0	* # 146.0	* 161.1	* 213.2	* 280.8	Généraux
Food	...	* 45.5	* 100.0	* # 153.0	* 167.3	* 222.6	* 286.6	Alimentation
Anguilla								**Anguilla**
General	61.0	81.9	100.0	106.1	105.1	104.5	...	Généraux
Food [1]	...	...	100.0	112.1	111.4	111.0	112.3	Alimentation [1]
Antigua and Barbuda								**Antigua-et-Barbuda**
General	...	89.5	100.0	109.3	110.3	109.8	112.5	Généraux
Argentina [4]								**Argentine** [4]
General	...	...	...	...	...	...	112.9	Généraux
Food	...	...	...	...	...	...	111.7	Alimentation
Armenia								**Arménie**
General	* 44.3	* 76.4	* # 100.0	* # 120.3	* 124.8	* 123.0	* 124.2	Généraux
Food [1]	...	...	* 100.0	* 123.3	* 127.1	* 122.9	* 127.9	Alimentation [1]
Aruba [1]								**Aruba** [1]
General	62.5	84.1	100.0	102.9	103.4	102.5	102.0	Généraux
Food	...	73.6	100.0	109.6	111.9	111.8	112.5	Alimentation
Australia [1,5]								**Australie** [1,5]
General	67.6	86.3	# 100.0	110.4	112.0	113.5	115.7	Généraux
Food	...	...	100.0	106.6	107.6	108.4	109.2	Alimentation
Austria								**Autriche**
General	77.1	91.4	100.0	109.7	110.7	111.7	114.0	Généraux
Food	76.4	88.1	100.0	113.5	114.4	115.2	118.0	Alimentation
Azerbaijan								**Azerbaïdjan**
General	42.7	61.1	100.0	113.2	117.7	132.4	149.5	Généraux
Food [6]	...	...	100.0	113.7	119.6	136.2	159.8	Alimentation [6]
Bahamas [7]								**Bahamas** [7]
General	* # 75.3	* 88.2	* 100.0	* 107.6	* 109.6	* 109.2	* 110.9	Généraux
Food [8]	...	...	...	100.7	106.5	...	...	Alimentation [8]
Bahrain [1]								**Bahreïn** [1]
General	83.8	87.5	100.0	108.6	110.6	113.7	115.2	Généraux
Food	...	...	100.0	111.7	114.5	115.9	117.1	Alimentation
Bangladesh								**Bangladesh**
General	42.5	69.2	100.0	136.1	144.5	152.3	161.1	Généraux
Food [9]	...	...	...	...	...	* 239.1	* 257.9	Alimentation [9]
Barbados [10]								**Barbade** [10]
General [1]	...	...	100.0	# 169.4[11]	167.6[11]	169.7[11]	177.6[11]	Généraux [1]
Food [11]	...	...	...	195.4	200.7	217.5	230.9	Alimentation [11]
Belarus								**Bélarus**
General	* 0.4	* 61.7	* 100.0	340.9	387.0	433.1	459.0	Généraux
Food	...	...	100.0	367.1	389.9	424.1	...	Alimentation
Belgium								**Belgique**
General [1]	75.0	90.4	100.0	108.0	108.6	110.8	112.8	Généraux [1]
Food	71.9	86.3	100.0	109.1	110.4	112.9	114.3	Alimentation
Belize [1]								**Belize** [1]
General	73.5	88.3	100.0	104.7	103.8	104.5	105.7	Généraux
Food [6]	74.0	82.7	100.0	105.2	104.8	104.8	103.6	Alimentation [6]
Benin								**Bénin**
General [12]	* 61.1	* 84.3	* 100.0	* 109.5	* 109.8	* 108.9	* 109.0	Généraux [12]
Food [1]	...	...	* 100.0	* 112.6	* 113.0	* 112.5	* 112.5	Alimentation [1]

Consumer price indices *(continued)*
General and food (Index base: 2010 = 100)

Indices des prix à la consommation *(suite)*
Généraux et alimentation (Indices base: 2010 = 100)

Country or area	1995	2005	2010	2014	2015	2016	2017	Pays ou zone
Bermuda [13]								**Bermudes** [13]
General	...	...	...	148.0	...	...	...	Généraux
Food	...	...	...	151.4	...	...	...	Alimentation
Bhutan								**Bhoutan**
General	56.7	74.8	100.0	139.9	146.2	152.5	158.4	Généraux
Food [14]	...	...	...	* 117.7	* 121.5	* 138.7	* 135.8	Alimentation [14]
Bolivia (Plurin. State of) [1]								**Bolivie (État plurin. de)** [1]
General	46.2	73.0	100.0	128.4	133.7	138.5	142.4	Généraux
Food	...	...	100.0	139.3	145.8	153.8	159.0	Alimentation
Bosnia and Herzegovina								**Bosnie-Herzégovine**
General	...	84.9	100.0	104.8	103.7	102.6	103.8	Généraux
Food	...	* 81.4	* 100.0	* 105.0	* 104.1	* 102.9	...	Alimentation
Botswana [1]								**Botswana** [1]
General	29.5	64.3	100.0	128.9	132.9	136.6	141.1	Généraux
Food	...	56.1	100.0	125.3	126.9	130.3	134.8	Alimentation
Brazil [1]								**Brésil** [1]
General	36.6	79.5	100.0	126.9	138.4	150.4	155.7	Généraux
Food [15]	...	...	100.0	140.7	154.4	173.6	175.3	Alimentation [15]
Brunei Darussalam								**Brunéi Darussalam**
General	90.9	# 95.5	100.0	100.4	100.0	99.3	99.1	Généraux
Food	...	...	* 100.0	* 99.9	* 100.7	* 99.8	* 100.0	Alimentation
Bulgaria [1]								**Bulgarie** [1]
General	1.6	72.7	100.0	106.7	106.6	105.8	107.9	Généraux
Food	2.1	72.4	100.0	112.1	112.5	112.2	116.7	Alimentation
Burkina Faso [16]								**Burkina Faso** [16]
General	66.6	86.9	100.0	107.0	108.0	107.7	108.1	Généraux
Food [17]	...	...	...	...	...	...	* 117.6	Alimentation [17]
Burundi								**Burundi**
General [18]	17.5	61.3	100.0	145.9	154.0	162.6	188.7	Généraux [18]
Food	...	* 57.7	* 100.0	* 139.0	* 147.1	* 157.6	* 195.4	Alimentation
Cabo Verde [1]								**Cabo Verde** [1]
General	64.4	82.6	100.0	108.5	108.6	107.1	107.9	Généraux
Food	...	...	100.0	107.4	109.0	108.3	108.1	Alimentation
Cambodia [19]								**Cambodge** [19]
General	43.1	67.8	100.0	116.1	117.5	121.1	124.6	Généraux
Food [20]	...	...	...	...	...	* 200.0	* 206.7	Alimentation [20]
Cameroon								**Cameroun**
General	* 67.0	* 85.7	* 100.0	* 109.9	* 112.9	* 113.9	* 114.6	Généraux
Food [21]	...	...	...	* 107.6	* 109.8	* 110.9	* 111.0	Alimentation [21]
Canada [1]								**Canada** [1]
General	75.2	91.9	100.0	107.5	108.7	110.2	112.0	Généraux
Food	70.6	86.5	100.0	110.1	114.2	115.9	115.9	Alimentation
Cayman Islands [1]								**Îles Caïmanes** [1]
General	...	...	100.0	106.1	103.6	102.9	...	Généraux
Food	...	...	100.0	114.0	115.8	115.9	...	Alimentation
Central African Republic [22]								**République centrafricaine** [22]
General	* 69.0	* 80.9	* 100.0	* 136.3	* 186.9	...	...	Généraux
Chad [23]								**Tchad** [23]
General	* 61.7	* 85.6	* 100.0	* 111.8	* 115.9	...	...	Généraux
Chile								**Chili**
General	...	...	101.4[24]	104.4[25]	108.9[25]	113.1[25]	115.5[25]	Généraux
Food	...	...	102.2[24]	107.0[25]	114.6[25]	119.0[25]	121.4[25]	Alimentation
China [26]								**Chine** [26]
General	...	...	100.0	113.2	114.9	# 102.0[27]	103.6[27]	Généraux
Food	...	...	100.0	126.5	129.4	# 104.6[6,27]	103.0[6,27]	Alimentation
China, Hong Kong SAR								**Chine, RAS de Hong Kong**
General	89.6	89.5	100.0	119.4	123.0	125.9	127.8	Généraux
Food	...	...	100.0	123.1	127.9	132.2	135.1	Alimentation
China, Macao SAR								**Chine, RAS de Macao**
General	* 77.8	79.7	100.0	125.6[1]	131.3[1]	134.4[1]	136.1[1]	Généraux
Food [1]	...	...	100.0	132.8	139.2	143.3	145.5	Alimentation [1]
Colombia [1]								**Colombie** [1]
General	28.3	79.7	100.0	112.0	117.6	126.4	132.0	Généraux
Food	...	...	100.0	113.9	122.3	136.5	140.1	Alimentation

Consumer price indices *(continued)*
General and food (Index base: 2010 = 100)

Indices des prix à la consommation *(suite)*
Généraux et alimentation (Indices base: 2010 = 100)

Country or area	1995	2005	2010	2014	2015	2016	2017	Pays ou zone
Comoros								**Comores**
General	...	84.4	100.0	...	...	...	...	Généraux
Food [1]	...	...	* 100.0	...	...	...	...	Alimentation [1]
Congo [28]								**Congo** [28]
General	* 55.5	* 78.9	* 100.0	* 113.4	* 118.5	...	...	Généraux
Cook Islands [1,29,30]								**Îles Cook** [1,29,30]
General	...	...	100.0	109.5	111.6	111.3	111.2	Généraux
Food	...	...	100.0	111.9	111.7	113.2	113.5	Alimentation
Costa Rica [1,31]								**Costa Rica** [1,31]
General	20.6	# 63.5	100.0	# 120.5	121.5	121.5	123.5	Généraux
Food	...	...	100.0	118.4	122.1	121.1	123.2	Alimentation
Côte d'Ivoire [32]								**Côte d'Ivoire** [32]
General	* 65.3	* 88.1	* 100.0	* 109.5	* 110.9	* 111.7	* 112.5	Généraux
Food [1,33]	...	* 75.5	* 100.0	* 109.7	* 111.9	* 115.3	* 115.7	Alimentation [1,33]
Croatia								**Croatie**
General	60.3	85.8	100.0	107.9	107.4	106.2	107.4	Généraux
Food	...	...	116.6[9]	108.9	109.3	108.8	112.0	Alimentation
Curaçao [1]								**Curaçao** [1]
General	66.9	84.3	100.0	108.6	108.1	108.1	109.8	Généraux
Food [34]	...	...	100.0	120.0	124.8	126.8	128.9	Alimentation [34]
Cyprus [1,35]								**Chypre** [1,35]
General	...	88.6	100.0	103.9	101.7	100.3	100.8	Généraux
Food	...	...	100.0	103.6	103.6	103.2	102.8	Alimentation
Czechia								**Tchéquie**
General	56.1	87.0	100.0	107.2	107.5	108.2	110.9	Généraux
Food [1]	77.0	89.9	100.0	119.7	118.4	117.3	123.4	Alimentation [1]
Dem. Rep. of the Congo								**Rép. dém. du Congo**
General	~0.0	58.6	100.0	129.1	130.1	133.9	...	Généraux
Food	...	...	...	* 121.0	* 122.0	* 125.7	...	Alimentation
Denmark [1]								**Danemark** [1]
General	72.8	90.0	100.0	106.7	107.1	107.4	108.6	Généraux
Food	...	86.4	100.0	107.9	109.1	109.2	112.2	Alimentation
Djibouti								**Djibouti**
General	...	77.8	100.0	113.4	112.5	115.6	116.2	Généraux
Dominica								**Dominique**
General	74.7	86.0	100.0	103.3	102.5	102.7	103.1	Généraux
Food [36]	...	...	...	* 110.1	* 110.9	* 110.9	* 111.1	Alimentation [36]
Dominican Republic [1]								**République dominicaine** [1]
General	23.2	73.4	100.0	121.4	122.5	124.4	128.5	Généraux
Food	...	74.6	100.0	124.6	133.0	135.9	139.0	Alimentation
Ecuador								**Équateur**
General	6.9	80.4	100.0	# 116.8	121.5	123.6	124.1	Généraux
Food [1]	...	70.7	100.0	120.1	125.2	128.4	129.0	Alimentation [1]
Egypt								**Égypte**
General [37]	36.6	57.8	100.0	142.1	156.8	178.5	231.1	Généraux [37]
Food [38]	...	...	...	...	* 194.1	* 226.4	* 313.9	Alimentation [38]
El Salvador								**El Salvador**
General [37]	59.2	84.5	100.0	109.0	108.2	108.8	109.9	Généraux [37]
Food [39]	...	...	...	...	...	* 119.3	* 119.4	Alimentation [39]
Equatorial Guinea								**Guinée équatoriale**
General	45.8	77.5	# 100.0	116.7	118.6	120.3	121.2	Généraux
Food [1]	...	...	* 100.0	* 121.6	* 123.4	* 118.4	* 120.3	Alimentation [1]
Estonia								**Estonie**
General	42.0	79.1	100.0	112.0	111.5	111.6	115.5	Généraux
Food [1]	...	77.1	100.0	118.6	118.0	117.7	124.8	Alimentation [1]
Eswatini								**Eswatini**
General	34.3	69.5	100.0	129.0	135.4	146.0	155.1	Généraux
Food [14]	...	...	...	* 109.0	* 113.6	* 130.7	* 140.0	Alimentation [14]
Ethiopia								**Éthiopie**
General	* 36.6	* # 44.8	* 100.0	* 192.0	* 211.4	* 226.8	* 249.3	Généraux
Food [1]	...	43.0	100.0	198.8	222.9	237.5	267.1	Alimentation [1]
Fiji [1]								**Fidji** [1]
General	60.4	# 80.8	100.0	114.8	116.4	120.9	124.9	Généraux
Food	...	...	100.0	121.7	127.5	135.2	132.3	Alimentation

Country or area	1995	2005	2010	2014	2015	2016	2017	Pays ou zone
Finland [1]								**Finlande** [1]
General	80.0	91.2	100.0	109.0	108.8	109.2	110.0	Généraux
Food	80.9	90.3	100.0	117.9	115.7	114.4	113.3	Alimentation
France [1,40,41]								**France** [1,40,41]
General	79.5	92.8	100.0	105.5	105.6	105.8	106.8	Généraux
Food	76.3	91.5	100.0	105.3	105.7	106.3	107.3	Alimentation
French Guiana [13]								**Guyane française** [13]
General	...	...	...	125.7	...	...	...	Généraux
Food	...	...	...	135.6	...	...	...	Alimentation
French Polynesia								**Polynésie française**
General [13]	...	...	...	121.7	...	...	...	Généraux [13]
Food [17]	...	...	...	115.5	...	...	...	Alimentation [17]
Gabon								**Gabon**
General [33,42]	* 77.9	* 88.7	* 100.0	* 109.4	* 109.0	* 111.3	...	Généraux [33,42]
Food [1]	...	...	* 100.0	* 112.8	* 115.9	* 115.8	...	Alimentation [1]
Gambia								**Gambie**
General [43]	46.3	81.1	100.0	122.4	130.7	140.1	...	Généraux [43]
Food [44]	...	...	...	...	* 186.0	* 201.3	...	Alimentation [44]
Georgia [45]								**Géorgie** [45]
General	28.6	70.0	100.0	110.3	114.7	117.1	124.2	Généraux
Food	...	...	100.0	115.7	120.5	122.5	130.8	Alimentation
Germany								**Allemagne**
General	80.5	92.5	100.0	106.6	106.9	107.4	109.3	Généraux
Food	84.1	89.1	100.0	111.5	112.3	113.2	116.4	Alimentation
Ghana								**Ghana**
General	7.0	52.9	100.0	150.2	176.0	206.7	232.3	Généraux
Food [46]	...	...	...	* 114.6	* 123.2	* 133.8	* 143.6	Alimentation [46]
Gibraltar [13]								**Gibraltar** [13]
General	...	...	...	142.2	...	...	...	Généraux
Food	...	...	...	169.8	...	...	...	Alimentation
Greece [1]								**Grèce** [1]
General	57.0	85.3	100.0	102.6	100.8	99.9	101.1	Généraux
Food	60.9	86.9	100.0	102.9	104.8	104.5	104.9	Alimentation
Grenada								**Grenade**
General	68.3	82.9	100.0	104.4	103.9	105.6	106.6	Généraux
Food [1]	...	* 74.0	* 100.0	* 109.4	* 110.5	* 108.0	* 108.6	Alimentation [1]
Guadeloupe [1]								**Guadeloupe** [1]
General	...	...	100.0	105.8	106.1	106.0	...	Généraux
Food	...	...	* 100.0	* 107.3	* 109.3	* 110.5	...	Alimentation
Guam [1]								**Guam** [1]
General	...	...	100.0	107.3	106.3	112.7	115.5	Généraux
Food [15,47]	...	...	100.0	120.5	125.2	123.2	121.4	Alimentation [15,47]
Guatemala								**Guatemala**
General	36.0	74.6	# 100.0	119.0	121.8	127.2	132.8	Généraux
Food [48]	...	...	...	134.5	147.0	161.6	176.0	Alimentation [48]
Guinea								**Guinée**
General [49]	...	42.2	100.0	171.6	185.6	200.8	218.7	Généraux [49]
Food [1]	...	...	* 100.0	* 183.4	* 204.5	* 228.0	* 256.4	Alimentation [1]
Guinea-Bissau [50]								**Guinée-Bissau** [50]
General	30.4	84.2	100.0	106.9	108.4	110.2	111.7	Généraux
Food [17,51]	...	...	...	109.4	...	115.5	117.6	Alimentation [17,51]
Guyana [52]								**Guyana** [52]
General	* 43.3	* 73.6	* 100.0	* 110.5	* 109.4	* 110.3	...	Généraux
Haiti								**Haïti**
General	13.5	66.8	100.0	127.5	139.0	158.3	181.5	Généraux
Food [53]	...	...	100.0	130.0	142.2	163.1	186.3	Alimentation [53]
Honduras								**Honduras**
General	* 22.9	* 72.0	* 100.0	* 125.3	* 129.3	* 132.8	* 138.1	Généraux
Food [1]	...	* 70.8	* 100.0	* 122.6	* 126.6	* 127.8	* 129.8	Alimentation [1]
Hungary								**Hongrie**
General	28.7	76.9	100.0	111.5	111.4	111.8	114.5	Généraux
Food	...	...	100.0	115.6	116.6	117.4	120.6	Alimentation
Iceland								**Islande**
General	47.6	67.1	100.0	116.0	117.8	119.8	122.0	Généraux
Food	52.4	65.9	100.0	116.3	119.6	121.2	118.3	Alimentation

19

Consumer price indices *(continued)*
General and food (Index base: 2010 = 100)

Indices des prix à la consommation *(suite)*
Généraux et alimentation (Indices base: 2010 = 100)

Country or area	1995	2005	2010	2014	2015	2016	2017	Pays ou zone
India								**Inde**
General [54]	37.6	65.8	100.0	140.8	147.7	155.0	160.1	Généraux [54]
Food [46]	...	...	...	* 121.2	* 127.2	* 133.9	* 135.7	Alimentation [46]
Indonesia								**Indonésie**
General	19.4	68.7	100.0	124.4	132.3	137.0	142.2	Généraux
Food [34,46]	...	...	...	# 119.5	128.0	137.3	139.9	Alimentation [34,46]
Iran (Islamic Republic of) [55]								**Iran (Rép. islamique d')** [55]
General	...	...	...	81.5	91.6	98.3	106.2	Généraux
Food	...	...	...	82.8	91.5	97.5	109.7	Alimentation
Iraq								**Iraq**
General	13.0	58.6	100.0	116.9	118.5	119.2	119.4	Généraux
Food [1]	...	...	100.0	113.2	112.8	...	...	Alimentation [1]
Ireland [1]								**Irlande** [1]
General	69.0	93.1	100.0	105.0	104.7	104.7	105.1	Généraux
Food	77.3	97.7	100.0	100.5	98.3	97.0	95.0	Alimentation
Isle of Man [13]								**Île de Man** [13]
General	...	...	...	160.8	...	...	...	Généraux
Food	...	...	...	228.4	...	...	...	Alimentation
Israel								**Israël**
General	59.5	87.8	100.0	107.3	106.7	106.1	106.4	Généraux
Food	52.1	79.3	100.0	108.7	108.8	107.8	108.0	Alimentation
Italy								**Italie**
General	71.6[1]	91.0[1]	100.0	107.4	107.5	107.4[1]	108.7[1]	Généraux
Food	72.8[1]	88.9[1]	100.0	107.6	108.8	109.0[1]	111.1[1]	Alimentation
Jamaica [1]								**Jamaïque** [1]
General	19.6	56.0	100.0	136.1	141.1	144.4	150.8	Généraux
Food	...	51.7	100.0	145.8	157.2	163.6	170.7	Alimentation
Japan [1]								**Japon** [1]
General	101.1	100.4	100.0	102.8	103.6	103.5	104.0	Généraux
Food [15]	97.8	96.8	100.0	103.4	106.6	108.4	110.6	Alimentation [15]
Jersey [56]								**Jersey** [56]
General	...	...	...	158.5	...	...	...	Généraux
Food	...	...	...	167.1	...	...	...	Alimentation
Jordan								**Jordanie**
General	57.7	74.5	100.0	117.4	116.4	115.5	119.3	Généraux
Food	...	...	100.0	114.0	115.2	111.2	110.8	Alimentation
Kazakhstan								**Kazakhstan**
General	20.4	61.5	100.0	129.1	137.8	157.6	169.3	Généraux
Food [1]	...	* 58.6	* 100.0	* 129.3	* 136.8	* 154.4	* 167.7	Alimentation [1]
Kenya								**Kenya**
General	25.3	55.5	100.0	140.9	150.2	159.6	172.4	Généraux
Food [1]	...	...	* 100.0	* 154.5	* 172.1	* 189.5	* 214.8	Alimentation [1]
Kiribati								**Kiribati**
General	...	...	* 100.0	* 99.0	* 99.5	...	...	Généraux
Food [1]	...	...	* 100.0	* 94.6	* 94.1	...	...	Alimentation [1]
Kuwait								**Koweït**
General	63.9	76.1	100.0	114.4	118.1	121.9	124.6	Généraux
Food	...	...	* 100.0	* 120.6	* 124.7	* 127.1	* 126.7	Alimentation
Kyrgyzstan								**Kirghizistan**
General	16.7	59.8	100.0	137.4	146.4	146.9	151.6	Généraux
Food	...	55.9	100.0	136.7	141.7	132.5	135.8	Alimentation
Lao People's Dem. Rep.								**Rép. dém. populaire lao**
General	* 6.2	* # 78.5	* # 100.0	* 124.2	* 125.8	* 127.8	* 128.9	Généraux
Food [1]	...	...	* 100.0	* 140.2	* 146.6	* 152.9	* 152.7	Alimentation [1]
Latvia								**Lettonie**
General	42.2	72.1	100.0	107.4	107.6	107.7	110.9	Généraux
Food	45.6	69.1	100.0	112.1	110.7	111.9	118.1	Alimentation
Lebanon								**Liban**
General	...	...	* 100.0	* # 119.4	* 115.0	* 114.1	* 119.1	Généraux
Food [1]	...	...	* 100.0	* 119.8	* 118.5	* 117.1	* 121.3	Alimentation [1]
Lesotho								**Lesotho**
General	69.7	70.9	100.0	123.2	127.1	135.5	142.7	Généraux
Food [1]	...	* 61.9	* 100.0	* 130.4	* 138.4	* 154.8	* 165.5	Alimentation [1]
Liberia								**Libéria**
General	...	61.8	100.0	137.0	147.6	160.6	180.6	Généraux
Food	...	...	* 100.0	* 147.6	* 162.5	* 175.3	* 186.5	Alimentation

Consumer price indices *(continued)*
General and food (Index base: 2010 = 100)

Indices des prix à la consommation *(suite)*
Généraux et alimentation (Indices base: 2010 = 100)

Country or area	1995	2005	2010	2014	2015	2016	2017	Pays ou zone
Libya								**Libye**
General	88.7	79.8	100.0	...	...	...	...	Généraux
Lithuania [1]								**Lituanie** [1]
General	51.3	77.7	100.0	108.6	107.6	108.6	112.6	Généraux
Food	54.2	72.2	100.0	114.3	113.3	114.7	118.8	Alimentation
Luxembourg [1]								**Luxembourg** [1]
General	74.2	89.7	100.0	108.7	109.2	109.5	111.5	Généraux
Food	70.6	87.7	100.0	109.6	110.5	112.2	115.3	Alimentation
Madagascar								**Madagascar**
General	23.2	62.9	100.0	129.9	139.5	148.8	161.2	Généraux
Food [1,53,57]	...	...	...	131.8	140.4	149.4	161.8	Alimentation [1,53,57]
Malawi								**Malawi**
General	* 8.9	* 64.2	* 100.0	* 205.6	* 250.6	* 305.0	* 342.2	Généraux
Food [46]	...	...	...	* 149.4	* 185.1	* 230.9	* 262.4	Alimentation [46]
Malaysia								**Malaisie**
General	69.0	87.7	100.0	110.5	112.8	115.2	119.6	Généraux
Food	...	...	100.0	115.2	119.4	124.0	129.2	Alimentation
Maldives								**Maldives**
General	...	* # 73.3	* 100.0	* 130.8	* 132.0	* 132.7	* 136.4	Généraux
Food [1]	...	...	* 100.0	* 152.3	* 153.0	* 153.9	* 163.3	Alimentation [1]
Mali [58]								**Mali** [58]
General	70.3	85.9	100.0	108.7	110.3	108.3	110.2	Généraux
Food [1,51]	...	...	* 100.0	* 109.6	* 112.9	* 109.2	* 112.0	Alimentation [1,51]
Malta								**Malte**
General	70.0	88.9	100.0	107.0	108.2	# 108.9	110.3	Généraux
Food	...	...	...	158.4[13]	...	* # 96.5[4]	* 99.8[4]	Alimentation
Martinique [1]								**Martinique** [1]
General	...	...	100.0	106.2	106.3	106.1	...	Généraux
Food	...	...	* 100.0	* 108.4	* 110.3	* 111.7	...	Alimentation
Mauritania								**Mauritanie**
General	41.8	75.2	100.0	119.5	# 123.4	125.2	128.1	Généraux
Food [1]	...	...	* 100.0	* 121.7	* 128.6	* 131.5	* 135.6	Alimentation [1]
Mauritius [1]								**Maurice** [1]
General	42.0	72.9	100.0	118.2	119.8	120.9	125.4	Généraux
Food	...	...	100.0	117.0	120.7	122.0	126.6	Alimentation
Mexico [1]								**Mexique** [1]
General	26.4	80.5	100.0	116.2	119.4	122.8	130.2	Généraux
Food [53]	23.8	74.4	100.0	125.0	129.9	135.2	144.4	Alimentation [53]
Micronesia (Fed. States of)								**Micronésie (États féd. de)**
General	...	77.8	100.0	113.1	112.5	...	...	Généraux
Mongolia [1]								**Mongolie** [1]
General	15.8	57.3	100.0	153.7	163.8	165.6	172.0	Généraux
Food	...	...	100.0	158.4	161.4	157.9	164.3	Alimentation
Montenegro								**Monténégro**
General	...	82.2	100.0	109.3	111.0	110.7[1]	113.4[1]	Généraux
Food	...	...	100.0	111.1	114.3	113.4[1]	115.4[1]	Alimentation
Montserrat								**Montserrat**
General	...	* 86.8	* 100.0	* # 109.1	* 107.9	* 107.6	* 108.9	Généraux
Food [59]	...	...	...	* 99.3	* 99.1	* 99.0	* 98.6	Alimentation [59]
Morocco [1]								**Maroc** [1]
General	76.3	89.7	100.0	104.6	106.2	108.0	108.8	Généraux
Food	...	...	100.0	104.8	107.4	110.5	110.5	Alimentation
Mozambique [1]								**Mozambique** [1]
General	...	...	100.0	122.0	126.3	148.3	170.7	Généraux
Food	...	...	100.0	127.7	134.4	170.9	199.0	Alimentation
Myanmar								**Myanmar**
General	5.5	44.5	100.0	# 118.1	129.3	138.3	144.6	Généraux
Food [46]	...	...	...	* 113.1	* 127.9	* 139.7	* 145.9	Alimentation [46]
Namibia [1]								**Namibie** [1]
General	...	71.4	100.0	124.7	128.9	137.6	145.9	Généraux
Food	...	63.0	100.0	131.9	139.4	154.4	162.9	Alimentation
Nepal [60]								**Népal** [60]
General	...	...	...	...	...	...	116.9	Généraux
Food	...	...	...	...	...	...	114.8	Alimentation

19 Consumer price indices *(continued)*
General and food (Index base: 2010 = 100)

Indices des prix à la consommation *(suite)*
Généraux et alimentation (Indices base: 2010 = 100)

Country or area	1995	2005	2010	2014	2015	2016	2017	Pays ou zone
Netherlands								**Pays-Bas**
General	73.7	92.7	100.0	108.5	109.3	109.5	111.0	Généraux
Food [1]	81.4	91.3	100.0	106.7	107.4	108.4	111.3	Alimentation [1]
New Caledonia [1]								**Nouvelle-Calédonie [1]**
General	...	...	100.0	105.7	106.3	107.0	...	Généraux
Food	...	...	* 100.0	* 108.6	* 110.6	* 112.5	...	Alimentation
New Zealand [1]								**Nouvelle-Zélande [1]**
General	71.7	87.0	100.0	107.6	107.9	108.6	110.7	Généraux
Food	...	...	100.0	105.8	106.0	105.3	107.7	Alimentation
Nicaragua								**Nicaragua**
General	...	62.9	100.0	131.6	136.9	141.7	147.2	Généraux
Food [1]	...	57.0	100.0	139.8	146.5	148.7	149.5	Alimentation [1]
Niger [61]								**Niger [61]**
General [33]	68.5	88.5	100.0	104.8	105.8	106.0	108.6	Généraux [33]
Food [17,51]	...	...	...	* 121.8	* 122.4	* 120.9	* 121.8	Alimentation [17,51]
Nigeria [62]								**Nigéria [62]**
General	17.0	61.9	100.0	145.8	158.9	183.9	214.2	Généraux
Food [1]	...	...	100.0	146.8	161.3	185.2	221.3	Alimentation [1]
Norway								**Norvège**
General	73.1	89.3	100.0	106.3	108.6	112.5	114.6	Généraux
Food	74.3	88.3	100.0	105.3	108.4	111.2	111.2	Alimentation
Oman								**Oman**
General	...	76.1	100.0	109.3	109.4	110.6	112.4	Généraux
Food [1]	...	...	* 100.0	* 111.7	* 110.8	* 109.5	* 110.1	Alimentation [1]
Pakistan								**Pakistan**
General	30.3	55.3	# 100.0	141.7	145.3	150.8	156.9	Généraux
Food [63]	...	...	...	* 216.2	* 217.4	* 222.7	* 230.0	Alimentation [63]
Palau								**Palaos**
General	...	80.5	100.0	116.8	117.9	116.7	118.2	Généraux
Food [1]	...	* 73.6	* 100.0	* 114.6	* 116.4	* 112.9	* 115.1	Alimentation [1]
Panama								**Panama**
General [37]	72.9	81.3	100.0	119.5	119.6	120.5	121.6	Généraux [37]
Food [1]	...	* 74.0	* 100.0	* 124.7	* 122.6	* 124.2	* 123.6	Alimentation [1]
Papua New Guinea								**Papouasie-Nvl-Guinée**
General	30.2	77.1	# 100.0	120.6	127.8	136.3	...	Généraux
Food [1]	...	...	* 100.0	* 101.4	* 106.4	* 111.8	...	Alimentation [1]
Paraguay [1,64]								**Paraguay [1,64]**
General	31.0	71.4	100.0	121.0	124.8	129.9	134.6	Généraux
Food	...	58.2	100.0	122.2	125.8	133.1	140.8	Alimentation
Peru [65]								**Pérou [65]**
General	56.8	87.1	100.0	113.7	117.8	122.0	125.4	Généraux
Food [9,15,47]	...	...	...	...	...	...	163.1	Alimentation [9,15,47]
Philippines [46]								**Philippines [46]**
General	...	...	...	106.3	107.0	108.4	111.5	Généraux
Food	...	...	...	108.5	110.5	112.3	115.7	Alimentation
Poland [1]								**Pologne [1]**
General	...	...	100.0	109.0	108.1	107.6	109.6	Généraux
Food	...	...	100.0	110.6	109.1	110.3	114.9	Alimentation
Portugal [1]								**Portugal [1]**
General [66]	69.0	91.8	100.0	106.5	107.0	107.7	109.2	Généraux [66]
Food	77.4	95.1	100.0	106.0	107.0	107.6	109.2	Alimentation
Puerto Rico [1]								**Porto Rico [1]**
General	...	...	100.0	106.0	105.2	104.8	106.7	Généraux
Food [15]	...	...	100.0	108.2	111.1	112.0	112.4	Alimentation [15]
Qatar [25]								**Qatar [25]**
General	...	...	...	103.4	105.2	108.0	108.5	Généraux
Food	...	...	...	100.2	101.1	99.2	101.1	Alimentation
Republic of Korea [1]								**République de Corée [1]**
General	60.2	86.2	100.0	109.1	109.8	110.9	113.1	Généraux
Food	50.6	80.8	100.0	113.7	115.6	118.3	122.3	Alimentation
Republic of Moldova [67,68]								**République de Moldova [67,68]**
General	...	...	100.0	123.8	135.8	144.5	153.9	Généraux
Food [15]	...	...	100.0	124.5	137.1	147.1	159.1	Alimentation [15]
Réunion [13]								**Réunion [13]**
General	...	...	...	126.7	...	...	...	Généraux
Food	...	...	...	137.6	...	...	...	Alimentation

19 Consumer price indices *(continued)*
General and food (Index base: 2010 = 100)

Indices des prix à la consommation *(suite)*
Généraux et alimentation (Indices base: 2010 = 100)

Country or area	1995	2005	2010	2014	2015	2016	2017	Pays ou zone
Romania								**Roumanie**
General	2.7	74.1	# 100.0	114.9	# 114.2	112.4	113.9	Généraux
Food	...	...	...	136.2[9,15]	131.0[9,15]	# 97.4[27]	99.8[27]	Alimentation
Russian Federation								**Fédération de Russie**
General	6.3	61.4	100.0	131.2	151.5	162.2	168.2	Généraux
Food	...	58.4	100.0	133.6	161.7	171.0	175.6	Alimentation
Rwanda [1,37]								**Rwanda** [1,37]
General	...	...	100.0	119.1	122.1	129.1	135.4	Généraux
Food	...	...	100.0	127.3	132.2	146.5	160.4	Alimentation
Saint Kitts and Nevis								**Saint-Kitts-et-Nevis**
General	* 59.6	* 81.7	* 100.0	* 108.1	* 105.7	* 104.9	* 105.5	Généraux
Food [1]	...	...	* 100.0	* 114.4	* 102.2	* 95.9	* 95.6	Alimentation [1]
Saint Lucia								**Sainte-Lucie**
General	* 69.8	* 87.3	* 100.0	* 112.5	* 111.4	* 107.9	* 108.0	Généraux
Food [1]	...	...	* 100.0	* 117.4	* 117.6	* 113.8	* 112.2	Alimentation [1]
Saint Vincent & Grenadines								**Saint-Vincent-Grenadines**
General	* 67.9	* 80.9	* # 100.0	* 106.9	* 105.1	* 104.9	* 107.2	Généraux
Food [1]	...	...	* 100.0	* 110.8	* 109.5	* 108.8	* 111.5	Alimentation [1]
Samoa [66]								**Samoa** [66]
General	* 49.3	* 76.4	* 100.0	* # 107.6	* 108.4	* 109.8	* 111.6	Généraux
San Marino [48]								**Saint-Marin** [48]
General	...	...	...	107.6	107.7	108.4	109.5	Généraux
Food	...	...	...	117.5	121.3	123.7	126.7	Alimentation
Sao Tome and Principe								**Sao Tomé-et-Principe**
General	...	39.2	100.0	146.3	154.0	162.3	171.6	Généraux
Food [59]	...	...	...	...	...	* 105.0	* 111.9	Alimentation [59]
Saudi Arabia [1]								**Arabie saoudite** [1]
General	...	81.4	100.0	112.9	114.4	116.7	115.7	Généraux
Food	...	73.0	100.0	117.9	118.6	117.1	116.2	Alimentation
Senegal [1,69]								**Sénégal** [1,69]
General	...	...	100.0	104.7	105.3	106.9	108.9	Généraux
Food	...	...	100.0	109.1	110.9	113.6	117.2	Alimentation
Serbia								**Serbie**
General	2.6	65.2	100.0	131.1	133.0	134.5	138.7	Généraux
Food	...	...	100.0	130.6	133.2	132.8	137.2	Alimentation
Seychelles [1]								**Seychelles** [1]
General	40.8	54.1	100.0	116.2	120.9	119.6	123.1	Généraux
Food [70]	...	...	100.0	114.6	116.7	116.7	117.7	Alimentation [70]
Sierra Leone [1]								**Sierra Leone** [1]
General	...	...	100.0	125.7	134.1	148.7	175.8	Généraux
Food	...	...	100.0	127.2	137.8	155.1	185.3	Alimentation
Singapore								**Singapour**
General	81.5	88.0	100.0	113.8	113.2	112.6	113.3	Généraux
Food [1]	77.4	85.6	100.0	110.8	112.9	115.3	116.9	Alimentation [1]
Slovakia								**Slovaquie**
General	44.1	86.8	100.0	109.1	108.7	108.2	109.6	Généraux
Food	61.9	89.6	100.0	113.5	113.2	110.0	114.4	Alimentation
Slovenia								**Slovénie**
General	# 44.8	86.8	100.0	# 106.5	105.9	105.9	107.4	Généraux
Food	...	81.3	100.0	112.2	113.2	114.2	116.8	Alimentation
Solomon Islands								**Îles Salomon**
General	28.2	65.8	100.0	126.0	125.3	125.9	126.5	Généraux
Food	...	...	...	* 568.9	* 552.5	* 555.4	* 551.6	Alimentation
South Africa [1,37]								**Afrique du Sud** [1,37]
General	43.4	74.3	100.0	124.6	130.3	# 138.9	146.1	Généraux
Food	34.9	67.1	100.0	131.0	137.5	153.5	164.5	Alimentation
South Sudan								**Soudan du sud**
General	...	...	100.0	217.2	331.9	1 592.4	4 583.7	Généraux
Food [1]	...	...	* 100.0	* 217.9	* 349.4	* 1 660.9	* 4 574.0	Alimentation [1]
Spain [1]								**Espagne** [1]
General	66.7	# 89.0	100.0	107.0	106.5	106.3	108.4	Généraux
Food	67.0	89.2	100.0	107.0	108.2	109.7	111.1	Alimentation
Sri Lanka								**Sri Lanka**
General	23.6[1,71]	# 58.3[1,71]	100.0[1,71]	# 105.5[25]	109.5[25]	113.8[25]	122.6[25]	Généraux
Food	...	...	100.0[1,71]	# 105.2[25]	110.7[25]	114.1[25]	127.0[25]	Alimentation

19 Consumer price indices *(continued)*
General and food (Index base: 2010 = 100)

Indices des prix à la consommation *(suite)*
Généraux et alimentation (Indices base: 2010 = 100)

Country or area	1995	2005	2010	2014	2015	2016	2017	Pays ou zone
State of Palestine								**État de Palestine**
General	...	80.7	100.0	109.4	111.0	110.7	111.0	Généraux
Food	...	71.8	100.0	105.8	107.8	106.2	105.2	Alimentation
Sudan								**Soudan**
General	8.3	60.0	100.0	299.2	349.8	...	...	Généraux
Food [63]	...	...	...	...	* 501.5	...	...	Alimentation [63]
Suriname								**Suriname**
General	7.2	69.0	100.0	130.2	139.2	216.4	264.1	Généraux
Food [1]	...	...	100.0	130.0	141.8	...	...	Alimentation [1]
Sweden								**Suède**
General	84.3	92.7	100.0	103.6	103.6	104.6	106.5	Généraux
Food [1]	86.3	87.2	100.0	105.4	107.9	109.0	111.4	Alimentation [1]
Switzerland [1]								**Suisse [1]**
General	88.4	95.7	100.0	99.3	98.2	97.7	98.3	Généraux
Food	90.4	97.8	100.0	97.9	97.1	97.5	97.9	Alimentation
Syrian Arab Republic								**République arabe syrienne**
General	...	...	100.0	324.2	448.8	662.9	...	Généraux
Food	...	...	100.0	378.0	512.1	807.3	...	Alimentation
Tajikistan [1]								**Tadjikistan [1]**
General	...	...	100.0	132.6	140.2	148.7	159.5	Généraux
Food [15]	...	...	100.0	137.3	146.8	154.4	168.6	Alimentation [15]
Thailand [1]								**Thaïlande [1]**
General	62.9	86.6	100.0	111.3	110.3	110.6	111.3	Généraux
Food	...	...	100.0	121.6	123.0	124.9	124.9	Alimentation
TFYR of Macedonia								**ex-R.Y. de Macédoine**
General	72.8	86.8	100.0	110.0	109.7	109.4	110.9	Généraux
Food [1]	...	83.1	100.0	111.2	111.6	109.9	110.1	Alimentation [1]
Timor-Leste								**Timor-Leste**
General	...	* 74.4	* 100.0	* 142.0	* 142.8	* 140.9	* 141.6	Généraux
Food [14]	...	...	...	* 105.2	* 105.7	* 103.5	* 104.4	Alimentation [14]
Togo [51]								**Togo [51]**
General	65.2	77.6	100.0	108.4	110.3	111.3	110.4	Généraux
Food [1]	...	* 81.5	* 100.0	* 101.1	* 106.6	* 109.9	* 105.4	Alimentation [1]
Tonga								**Tonga**
General	* 39.5	* 76.7	* 100.0	* 111.0	* 109.9	* 112.7	...	Généraux
Food [1]	...	* 75.7	* 100.0	* 114.2	* 116.3	* 117.8	...	Alimentation [1]
Trinidad and Tobago [10]								**Trinité-et-Tobago [10]**
General	42.1	64.6	100.0	# 127.7	133.6	137.7	140.3	Généraux
Food [1]	...	* 39.9	* 100.0	* 157.4	* 170.9	* 183.6	* 189.0	Alimentation [1]
Tunisia								**Tunisie**
General	* 61.2	* 81.6	* # 100.0	* 120.9	* 126.7	* 131.4	* 138.4	Généraux
Food	...	...	100.0	128.3	135.0	138.5	146.2	Alimentation
Turkey [1]								**Turquie [1]**
General	* 1.3	* # 65.9	* 100.0	* 135.7	* 146.1	* 157.4	* 175.0	Généraux
Food	1.5	60.2	100.0	141.5	157.3	166.4	187.5	Alimentation
Uganda [72]								**Ouganda [72]**
General	...	...	...	...	150.8	159.0	167.9	Généraux
Food	...	...	...	...	160.7	169.7	186.8	Alimentation
Ukraine								**Ukraine**
General	9.6	51.2	100.0	121.4	180.5	205.6	235.3	Généraux
Food	...	...	100.0	114.3	166.6	181.6	204.9	Alimentation
United Arab Emirates								**Émirats arabes unis**
General	...	...	# 100.0	105.1	109.3	111.1	113.3	Généraux
Food [1]	...	...	* 100.0	* 116.9	* 118.3	* 119.5	* 121.0	Alimentation [1]
United Kingdom [1]								**Royaume-Uni [1]**
General	...	87.4	100.0	111.8	111.9	112.6	115.6	Généraux
Food	...	78.5	100.0	112.7	109.8	107.2	109.5	Alimentation
United Rep. of Tanzania [73]								**Rép.-Unie de Tanzanie [73]**
General	28.6	66.3	100.0	149.7	# 158.0	166.2	175.0	Généraux
Food	...	...	...	163.0	* 96.6[74]	* 103.8[74]	* 113.3[74]	Alimentation
United States of America [37]								**États-Unis d'Amérique [37]**
General	69.9	89.6	100.0	108.6	108.7	110.1	112.4	Généraux
Food [1]	68.9	87.9	100.0	110.9	112.2	110.8	110.5	Alimentation [1]
Uruguay [1]								**Uruguay [1]**
General	23.0	70.5	100.0	138.1	150.1	164.6	174.8	Généraux
Food	...	64.3	100.0	145.1	158.8	174.1	179.0	Alimentation

19 Consumer price indices *(continued)*
General and food (Index base: 2010 = 100)

Indices des prix à la consommation *(suite)*
Généraux et alimentation (Indices base: 2010 = 100)

Country or area	1995	2005	2010	2014	2015	2016	2017	Pays ou zone
Vanuatu								**Vanuatu**
General	# 67.0	83.9	100.0	104.5	107.1	108.0	...	Généraux
Food [1]	...	...	* 100.0	* 105.4	* 109.2	* 111.6	...	Alimentation [1]
Venezuela (Boliv. Rep. of) [1]								**Venezuela (Rép. boliv. du)** [1]
General	...	...	100.0	348.2	772.0	...	...	Généraux
Food	...	...	100.0	466.7	1 487.2	...	...	Alimentation
Viet Nam								**Viet Nam**
General	40.2	59.9	100.0	# 144.5	145.8	150.5	155.8	Généraux
Food [59]	...	...	...	...	...	* 104.1	* 103.0	Alimentation [59]
Yemen								**Yémen**
General	* 21.3	* # 60.0	* 100.0	* 157.6	...	...	...	Généraux
Zambia								**Zambie**
General	6.7	59.9	# 100.0	130.8	144.0	169.8	180.9	Généraux
Food [24]	...	...	...	* 136.1	* 151.2	* 183.3	* 193.9	Alimentation [24]
Zimbabwe								**Zimbabwe**
General	...	...	100.0	108.8	106.2	104.6	105.5	Généraux
Food [1]	...	...	* 100.0	* 107.2	* 103.6	* 100.2	* 102.7	Alimentation [1]

Source:

United Nations Statistics Division (UNSD), New York, Monthly Bulletin of Statistics (MBS), last accessed May 2018

Source:

Organisation des Nations Unies (ONU), Division de statistique, New York, Bulletin mensuel de statistique (BMS), dernier accès mai 2018.

1 Calculated by the UN Statistics Division from national indices.
2 Algiers
3 Luanda
4 Index base: December 2016=100.
5 Weighted average of index values computed for the 8 capital cities.
6 Including tobacco.
7 New Providence
8 Index base: November 2014=100.
9 Index base: 2005=100.
10 Data refer to the Retail Price Index.
11 Index base: July 2001=100.
12 Cotonou
13 Index base: 2000=100.
14 Index base: December 2012=100.
15 Including alcoholic beverages.
16 Ouagadougou
17 Index base: 2008=100.
18 Bujumbura
19 Phnom Penh
20 Index Base: October to December 2006=100.
21 Base: 2011=100.
22 Bangui
23 N'Djamena
24 Index base: 2009=100.
25 Index base: 2013=100.
26 For statistical purposes, the data for China do not include those for the Hong Kong Special Administrative Region (Hong Kong SAR), Macao Special Administrative Region (Macao SAR) and Taiwan Province of China.
27 Index base: 2015=100.
28 Brazzaville
29 Rarotonga
30 Index base: 2006=100.
31 Central area.
32 Abidjan
33 African population.
34 Food only.
35 Excluding northern Cyprus.
36 Index base: June 2010=100.

1 Les indices ont été calculés par la Division de statistique de l'ONU à partir des indices nationaux.
2 Alger
3 Luanda
4 Indices base: 2016 décembre=100.
5 Moyenne pondérée des données d'index calculées pour les 8 capitales.
6 Y compris le tabac.
7 Nouvelle Providence
8 Indices base: 2014 novembre=100.
9 Indices base: 2005=100.
10 Les données se rapporte à l'index des prix en détail.
11 Indices base: 2001 juillet=100.
12 Cotonou
13 Indices base: 2000=100.
14 Indices base: 2012 décembre=100.
15 Y compris les boissons alcoolisées.
16 Ouagadougou
17 Indices base: 2008=100.
18 Bujumbura
19 Phnom Penh
20 Indices base: octobre au décembre 2006=100.
21 Base : 2011=100.
22 Bangui
23 N'Djamena
24 Indices base: 2009=100.
25 Indices base: 2013=100.
26 Pour la présentation des statistiques, les données pour la Chine ne comprennent pas la région administrative spéciale de Hong Kong (Hong Kong RAS), la région administrative spéciale de Macao (Macao RAS) et la province chinoise de Taïwan.
27 Indices base: 2015=100.
28 Brazzaville
29 Rarotonga
30 Indices base: 2006=100.
31 Région centrale.
32 Abidjan
33 Population Africaine.
34 Alimentation seulement.
35 Chypre du nord non compris.
36 Indices base: 2010 juin=100.

19 Consumer price indices *(continued)*

General and food (Index base: 2010 = 100)

Indices des prix à la consommation *(suite)*

Généraux et alimentation (Indices base: 2010 = 100)

37 Urban areas.
38 Index base: January 2010=100.
39 Index base: December 2009=100.
40 Including French Guiana, Guadeloupe, Martinique and Réunion.
41 All households.
42 Libreville and Owendo.
43 Banjul, Kombo St. Mary
44 Index base: August 2004=100.
45 Five cities.
46 Index base: 2012=100.
47 Including food and beverages consumed away from home.
48 Index base: December 2010=100.
49 Conakry
50 Bissau
51 WAEMU harmonized consumer price index.
52 Georgetown
53 Including alcoholic beverages and tobacco.
54 Industrial workers.
55 Index base: fiscal (solar) year 2016 (21 March 2016 - 20 March 2017)=100.
56 Index base: June 2000=100.
57 Data refer to 7 cities only.
58 Bamako
59 Index base: 2014=100.
60 Index base: 2014/2015=100.
61 Niamey
62 Rural and urban areas.
63 Index base: 2007=100.
64 Refers to the metropolitan area of Asunción.
65 Metropolitan Lima.
66 Excluding rent.
67 Excluding the left side of the river Nistru and the municipality of Bender.
68 Data refer to 8 cities only.
69 Data refer to the national index.
70 Excluding fresh fish.
71 Colombo
72 Index base: 1 July 2009 - 30 June 2010=100.
73 Tanzania mainland only, excluding Zanzibar.
74 Index base: December 2015=100.

37 Zones urbaines.
38 Indices base: 2010 janvier=100.
39 Indices base: 2009 décembre=100.
40 Y compris Guadeloupe, Guyane française, Martinique et Réunion.
41 Tous ménages.
42 Libreville et Owendo.
43 Banjul, Kombo St. Mary
44 Indices base: 2004 août=100.
45 Cinq villes.
46 Indices base: 2012=100.
47 Y compris les aliments et de boissons loin de la maison.
48 Indices base: 2000 décembre=100.
49 Conakry
50 Bissau
51 UEMOA harmonisé l'indice des prix à la consommation.
52 Georgetown
53 Y compris les boissons alcoolisées et le tabac.
54 Ouvriers industriels.
55 Indices base: année fiscale (solaire) 2016 (21 mars 2016 - 20 mars 2017) = 100.
56 Indices base: 2000 juin=100.
57 Les données se réfère à 7 villes seulement.
58 Bamako
59 Indices base: 2014=100.
60 Indices base: 2014/2015=100.
61 Niamey
62 Régions rurales et urbaines.
63 Indices base: 2007=100.
64 Fait référence à la zone métropolitaine d'Asunción.
65 Lima métropolitaine.
66 Sans le loyer.
67 La rive gauche de la rivière Nistru et la municipalité de Bender sont exclues.
68 Les données se réfère à 8 villes seulement.
69 Les données se rapporte à l'indice national.
70 Non compris le poisson frais.
71 Colombo
72 Indices base: 1 juillet 2009 - 30 juin 2010=100.
73 Tanzanie continentale seulement, Zanzibar non compris.
74 Indices base: 2015 décembre=100.

20 Agricultural production indices

Index base: 2004 - 2006 = 100

Indices de la production agricole

Indices base: 2004 - 2006 = 100

Région, pays ou zone	1975	1985	1995	2005	2010	2014	2015	2016	Région, pays ou zone
Total, all countries or areas									**Total, tous pays ou zones**
Agriculture (gross)	**51.3**	**65.5**	**78.3**	**99.9**	**112.9**	**124.6**	**125.9**	**127.3**	**Agriculture (brut)**
Food (gross)	**51.0**	**65.0**	**78.2**	**99.9**	**113.4**	**125.0**	**126.4**	**127.8**	**Produits ailmentaires (brut)**
Africa									**Afrique**
Agriculture (gross)	42.6	50.4	68.8	100.0	117.0	129.0	130.8	129.9	Agriculture (brut)
Food (gross)	41.4	49.3	68.3	99.9	117.8	129.7	131.5	130.5	Produits ailmentaires (brut)
Northern Africa									**Afrique septentrionale**
Agriculture (gross)	36.1	46.2	63.7	98.7	112.2	116.5	119.5	118.4	Agriculture (brut)
Food (gross)	34.4	44.4	63.2	98.6	112.9	117.2	120.2	119.1	Produits ailmentaires (brut)
Eastern Africa									**Afrique orientale**
Agriculture (gross)	51.9	59.9	70.7	99.6	123.9	143.4	144.8	140.0	Agriculture (brut)
Food (gross)	51.2	59.3	69.8	99.6	124.4	144.0	145.6	140.2	Produits ailmentaires (brut)
Middle Africa									**Afrique centrale**
Agriculture (gross)	56.7	64.6	78.1	102.0	132.1	140.5	143.3	149.6	Agriculture (brut)
Food (gross)	53.1	63.1	76.7	101.8	134.0	142.2	145.2	151.7	Produits ailmentaires (brut)
Southern Africa									**Afrique australe**
Agriculture (gross)	65.1	74.7	76.0	103.1	115.5	124.2	119.9	115.4	Agriculture (brut)
Food (gross)	63.3	72.9	75.2	103.0	116.2	124.9	120.5	116.0	Produits ailmentaires (brut)
Western Africa									**Afrique occidentale**
Agriculture (gross)	33.8	39.3	68.1	100.3	113.1	127.6	129.8	130.8	Agriculture (brut)
Food (gross)	33.6	38.9	68.0	100.1	114.3	128.5	130.8	131.9	Produits ailmentaires (brut)
Americas									**Amériques**
Agriculture (gross)	52.1	66.7	77.8	100.0	111.1	120.6	122.1	123.7	Agriculture (brut)
Food (gross)	51.5	66.1	77.8	100.0	111.8	121.6	123.1	124.8	Produits ailmentaires (brut)
Northern America									**Amérique septentrionale**
Agriculture (gross)	63.2	77.3	83.6	100.1	105.5	111.7	111.6	116.1	Agriculture (brut)
Food (gross)	63.4	77.5	83.5	100.0	106.4	112.9	112.8	117.6	Produits ailmentaires (brut)
Caribbean									**Caraïbes**
Agriculture (gross)	87.1	106.0	84.6	97.9	105.3	116.8	119.4	120.6	Agriculture (brut)
Food (gross)	85.5	104.5	84.0	97.8	105.8	117.9	120.4	121.7	Produits ailmentaires (brut)
Central America									**Amérique centrale**
Agriculture (gross)	45.7	61.9	76.8	98.5	110.0	122.0	122.7	128.0	Agriculture (brut)
Food (gross)	43.2	60.4	76.0	98.5	109.8	121.8	122.5	128.0	Produits ailmentaires (brut)
South America									**Amérique du Sud**
Agriculture (gross)	38.2	53.0	70.6	100.3	118.5	131.6	135.1	132.2	Agriculture (brut)
Food (gross)	36.9	51.4	70.7	100.4	119.4	132.6	136.3	133.3	Produits ailmentaires (brut)
Asia									**Asie**
Agriculture (gross)	33.8	48.9	73.3	100.1	118.3	131.9	133.6	135.5	Agriculture (brut)
Food (gross)	33.5	48.3	73.0	100.2	118.8	132.4	134.2	136.2	Produits ailmentaires (brut)
Central Asia									**Asie centrale**
Agriculture (gross)	...	...	78.7	100.3	114.8	137.2	142.6	145.0	Agriculture (brut)
Food (gross)	...	...	75.1	99.6	118.6	144.1	150.4	153.0	Produits ailmentaires (brut)
Eastern Asia									**Asie orientale**
Agriculture (gross)	29.9	45.1	70.1	100.2	118.2	130.4	133.6	136.0	Agriculture (brut)
Food (gross)	29.5	44.0	69.8	100.3	118.7	131.1	134.5	136.9	Produits ailmentaires (brut)
South-eastern Asia									**Asie du Sud-Est**
Agriculture (gross)	32.9	49.6	70.1	99.0	120.1	133.3	133.9	133.2	Agriculture (brut)
Food (gross)	32.6	49.6	70.6	99.1	121.0	133.3	134.0	133.3	Produits ailmentaires (brut)
Southern Asia									**Asie méridionale**
Agriculture (gross)	41.8	56.9	78.7	100.5	120.5	137.8	136.7	139.1	Agriculture (brut)
Food (gross)	41.8	56.6	78.7	100.5	120.2	137.6	136.5	139.0	Produits ailmentaires (brut)
Western Asia									**Asie occidentale**
Agriculture (gross)	43.1	60.1	80.2	101.3	105.8	112.0	115.4	116.8	Agriculture (brut)
Food (gross)	42.4	59.6	79.5	101.4	107.2	113.7	117.2	118.8	Produits ailmentaires (brut)
Europe									**Europe**
Agriculture (gross)	102.5	117.1	97.2	99.1	100.3	109.3	109.0	110.3	Agriculture (brut)
Food (gross)	100.9	115.5	97.2	99.1	100.5	109.5	109.1	110.5	Produits ailmentaires (brut)
Eastern Europe									**Europe orientale**
Agriculture (gross)	142.4	159.0	103.9	98.6	99.3	121.3	118.7	126.6	Agriculture (brut)
Food (gross)	137.5	154.1	103.7	98.6	99.3	121.3	118.7	126.7	Produits ailmentaires (brut)
Northern Europe									**Europe septentrionale**
Agriculture (gross)	76.8	92.4	101.8	100.6	101.0	107.3	109.5	105.6	Agriculture (brut)
Food (gross)	76.8	92.4	101.7	100.6	100.9	107.3	109.5	105.5	Produits ailmentaires (brut)

20

Agricultural production indices *(continued)*
Index base: 2004 - 2006 = 100

Indices de la production agricole *(suite)*
Indices base: 2004 - 2006 = 100

Région, pays ou zone	1975	1985	1995	2005	2010	2014	2015	2016	Région, pays ou zone
Southern Europe									**Europe méridionale**
Agriculture (gross)	77.5	87.8	86.5	98.5	99.7	95.1	98.4	98.6	Agriculture (brut)
Food (gross)	77.6	87.7	86.2	98.3	100.4	95.5	98.8	99.0	Produits ailmentaires (brut)
Western Europe									**Europe occidentale**
Agriculture (gross)	86.4	102.0	96.9	99.8	101.8	108.1	106.3	102.8	Agriculture (brut)
Food (gross)	86.5	102.2	97.0	99.8	101.9	108.1	106.4	102.8	Produits ailmentaires (brut)
Oceania									**Océanie**
Agriculture (gross)	57.9	68.5	82.2	99.2	98.3	110.4	111.3	108.7	Agriculture (brut)
Food (gross)	55.2	65.0	80.0	98.7	99.6	110.5	111.4	108.7	Produits ailmentaires (brut)
Australia and New Zealand									**Australie et Nouvelle-Zélande**
Agriculture (gross)	58.0	68.3	82.3	99.2	97.4	109.9	110.8	108.0	Agriculture (brut)
Food (gross)	55.2	64.6	79.9	98.7	98.8	109.9	110.9	107.9	Produits ailmentaires (brut)
Melanesia									**Mélanésie**
Agriculture (gross)	52.8	68.4	81.1	99.5	109.6	117.3	117.8	118.7	Agriculture (brut)
Food (gross)	52.4	67.7	80.7	98.9	110.2	118.0	118.3	119.2	Produits ailmentaires (brut)
Micronesia									**Micronésie**
Agriculture (gross)	81.2	108.4	84.8	97.2	78.8	81.0	81.9	75.8	Agriculture (brut)
Food (gross)	81.2	108.4	84.8	97.2	78.8	81.0	81.9	75.8	Produits ailmentaires (brut)
Polynesia									**Polynésie**
Agriculture (gross)	114.6	107.6	88.7	100.8	111.1	115.6	117.8	117.2	Agriculture (brut)
Food (gross)	114.5	107.5	88.6	100.8	111.0	115.5	117.8	117.1	Produits ailmentaires (brut)
Afghanistan									**Afghanistan**
Agriculture (gross)	80.7	69.1	85.6	106.6	116.2	124.1	119.7	125.4	Agriculture (brut)
Food (gross)	77.4	67.9	84.5	106.6	116.2	124.1	119.6	125.4	Produits ailmentaires (brut)
Albania									**Albanie**
Agriculture (gross)	50.8	65.4	85.7	98.1	118.9	135.4	138.9	143.4	Agriculture (brut)
Food (gross)	47.8	61.3	84.9	98.0	119.1	135.7	139.3	143.9	Produits ailmentaires (brut)
Algeria									**Algérie**
Agriculture (gross)	35.2	44.3	61.5	98.8	130.1	142.6	150.8	151.5	Agriculture (brut)
Food (gross)	34.9	43.8	61.3	98.7	130.3	142.8	151.1	151.7	Produits ailmentaires (brut)
American Samoa									**Samoa américaines**
Agriculture (gross)	66.0	51.1	62.7	100.3	110.1	112.0	115.1	115.8	Agriculture (brut)
Food (gross)	65.8	51.1	62.7	100.4	110.1	112.0	115.1	115.8	Produits ailmentaires (brut)
Angola									**Angola**
Agriculture (gross)	47.6	36.8	46.0	102.1	166.8	176.8	180.9	191.9	Agriculture (brut)
Food (gross)	36.2	35.4	45.0	102.1	167.5	177.4	181.6	192.9	Produits ailmentaires (brut)
Antigua and Barbuda									**Antigua-et-Barbuda**
Agriculture (gross)	56.6	92.3	92.3	95.1	72.6	79.3	70.8	70.2	Agriculture (brut)
Food (gross)	55.4	91.6	92.4	95.1	72.5	79.2	70.7	70.0	Produits ailmentaires (brut)
Argentina									**Argentine**
Agriculture (gross)	51.7	62.8	75.3	104.6	112.3	123.5	130.8	130.9	Agriculture (brut)
Food (gross)	50.2	61.7	74.2	104.6	112.2	123.4	130.9	131.0	Produits ailmentaires (brut)
Armenia									**Arménie**
Agriculture (gross)	...	...	65.1	108.0	96.0	132.6	140.0	127.2	Agriculture (brut)
Food (gross)	...	...	65.0	108.0	95.8	132.6	140.0	127.1	Produits ailmentaires (brut)
Australia									**Australie**
Agriculture (gross)	58.2	66.0	83.0	99.2	94.9	107.4	107.9	104.4	Agriculture (brut)
Food (gross)	55.6	62.5	80.7	98.5	96.3	106.7	107.2	103.4	Produits ailmentaires (brut)
Austria									**Autriche**
Agriculture (gross)	86.8	95.3	93.4	100.0	98.5	102.9	97.7	100.4	Agriculture (brut)
Food (gross)	86.8	95.3	93.4	100.0	98.5	102.9	97.7	100.4	Produits ailmentaires (brut)
Azerbaijan									**Azerbaïdjan**
Agriculture (gross)	...	...	57.5	104.1	117.2	131.2	139.1	141.4	Agriculture (brut)
Food (gross)	...	...	52.7	103.1	121.5	136.2	144.5	146.9	Produits ailmentaires (brut)
Bahamas									**Bahamas**
Agriculture (gross)	70.6	66.7	79.7	98.8	123.1	129.1	129.7	130.6	Agriculture (brut)
Food (gross)	70.6	66.7	79.7	98.8	123.1	129.1	129.7	130.6	Produits ailmentaires (brut)
Bahrain									**Bahreïn**
Agriculture (gross)	96.8	115.8	119.8	91.1	118.1	200.8	199.2	198.4	Agriculture (brut)
Food (gross)	96.8	115.8	119.8	91.1	118.1	200.8	199.2	198.4	Produits ailmentaires (brut)
Bangladesh									**Bangladesh**
Agriculture (gross)	49.9	59.3	67.5	102.8	128.1	140.3	141.2	144.4	Agriculture (brut)
Food (gross)	49.1	57.5	66.9	102.8	128.5	139.8	140.6	144.0	Produits ailmentaires (brut)
Barbados									**Barbade**
Agriculture (gross)	99.0	106.1	97.3	105.8	91.2	87.1	84.7	84.8	Agriculture (brut)
Food (gross)	99.0	106.1	97.3	105.8	91.2	87.1	84.7	84.8	Produits ailmentaires (brut)

Agricultural production indices *(continued)*
Index base: 2004 - 2006 = 100

Indices de la production agricole *(suite)*
Indices base: 2004 - 2006 = 100

Région, pays ou zone	1975	1985	1995	2005	2010	2014	2015	2016	Région, pays ou zone
Belarus									**Bélarus**
Agriculture (gross)	...	...	90.8	98.0	117.0	124.3	120.6	120.0	Agriculture (brut)
Food (gross)	...	...	90.6	97.9	117.1	124.4	120.7	120.2	Produits ailmentaires (brut)
Belgium									**Belgique**
Agriculture (gross)	...	...	...	99.6	99.7	106.8	106.1	101.1	Agriculture (brut)
Food (gross)	...	...	...	99.6	99.4	106.5	105.7	100.6	Produits ailmentaires (brut)
Belize									**Belize**
Agriculture (gross)	29.2	40.9	67.8	101.3	97.5	103.4	101.8	96.5	Agriculture (brut)
Food (gross)	29.2	40.9	67.8	101.3	97.5	103.5	101.8	96.5	Produits ailmentaires (brut)
Benin									**Bénin**
Agriculture (gross)	25.1	40.3	68.0	104.2	118.1	155.6	147.0	152.6	Agriculture (brut)
Food (gross)	26.8	41.3	63.5	104.1	125.9	162.4	153.0	159.2	Produits ailmentaires (brut)
Bermuda									**Bermudes**
Agriculture (gross)	85.8	92.7	97.2	98.2	108.5	112.4	113.1	112.5	Agriculture (brut)
Food (gross)	85.8	92.7	97.2	98.2	108.5	112.4	113.1	112.5	Produits ailmentaires (brut)
Bhutan									**Bhoutan**
Agriculture (gross)	33.5	45.0	81.7	105.6	94.8	98.4	98.5	101.8	Agriculture (brut)
Food (gross)	33.5	45.0	81.7	105.6	94.7	98.4	98.5	101.8	Produits ailmentaires (brut)
Bolivia (Plurin. State of)									**Bolivie (État plurin. de)**
Agriculture (gross)	40.7	49.4	70.9	99.8	119.8	141.6	147.7	146.6	Agriculture (brut)
Food (gross)	39.6	49.2	70.7	99.8	120.2	142.8	149.1	147.9	Produits ailmentaires (brut)
Bosnia and Herzegovina									**Bosnie-Herzégovine**
Agriculture (gross)	...	...	63.1	97.9	107.1	93.6	105.4	118.1	Agriculture (brut)
Food (gross)	...	...	63.2	97.8	107.5	94.0	105.8	118.6	Produits ailmentaires (brut)
Botswana									**Botswana**
Agriculture (gross)	59.3	66.7	108.9	101.4	124.5	128.2	115.7	119.8	Agriculture (brut)
Food (gross)	59.1	66.5	109.1	101.4	124.7	128.5	116.0	120.1	Produits ailmentaires (brut)
Brazil									**Brésil**
Agriculture (gross)	31.2	49.1	66.8	99.2	122.2	136.4	139.4	135.8	Agriculture (brut)
Food (gross)	30.0	47.6	68.0	99.4	123.3	137.7	141.1	137.1	Produits ailmentaires (brut)
British Virgin Islands									**Îles Vierges britanniques**
Agriculture (gross)	76.3	94.5	93.8	100.1	102.0	103.2	103.0	103.3	Agriculture (brut)
Food (gross)	76.3	94.5	93.8	100.1	102.0	103.2	103.0	103.3	Produits ailmentaires (brut)
Brunei Darussalam									**Brunéi Darussalam**
Agriculture (gross)	32.4	53.5	46.4	75.1	139.1	166.2	169.6	169.1	Agriculture (brut)
Food (gross)	31.2	53.3	46.2	74.9	139.5	166.8	170.2	169.6	Produits ailmentaires (brut)
Bulgaria									**Bulgarie**
Agriculture (gross)	165.7	168.8	129.7	90.0	106.1	112.9	111.3	114.4	Agriculture (brut)
Food (gross)	160.0	165.5	132.5	89.6	107.1	114.8	113.4	117.0	Produits ailmentaires (brut)
Burkina Faso									**Burkina Faso**
Agriculture (gross)	27.3	40.1	59.6	104.0	118.4	124.9	120.8	125.1	Agriculture (brut)
Food (gross)	31.0	44.1	65.8	103.8	125.7	127.4	122.5	127.7	Produits ailmentaires (brut)
Burundi									**Burundi**
Agriculture (gross)	70.7	80.8	83.5	91.7	108.1	108.5	101.0	107.8	Agriculture (brut)
Food (gross)	81.6	90.9	95.3	100.3	113.9	121.5	111.5	120.3	Produits ailmentaires (brut)
Cabo Verde									**Cabo Verde**
Agriculture (gross)	23.1	37.1	72.2	99.4	105.5	94.4	95.5	96.7	Agriculture (brut)
Food (gross)	22.8	37.0	72.2	99.4	105.6	94.2	95.4	96.5	Produits ailmentaires (brut)
Cambodia									**Cambodge**
Agriculture (gross)	25.2	35.9	63.1	104.7	147.9	174.8	177.1	185.5	Agriculture (brut)
Food (gross)	24.7	35.1	61.8	104.6	147.6	176.1	178.5	187.2	Produits ailmentaires (brut)
Cameroon									**Cameroun**
Agriculture (gross)	45.8	53.1	69.2	102.8	139.9	157.0	164.2	175.2	Agriculture (brut)
Food (gross)	44.8	51.4	66.9	102.2	143.7	162.2	169.9	181.8	Produits ailmentaires (brut)
Canada									**Canada**
Agriculture (gross)	54.1	68.7	81.7	102.1	102.7	108.4	110.4	113.1	Agriculture (brut)
Food (gross)	53.7	67.9	80.9	101.9	103.3	108.6	110.6	113.8	Produits ailmentaires (brut)
Cayman Islands									**Îles Caïmanes**
Agriculture (gross)	229.8	231.6	104.7	100.6	100.0	104.9	103.1	103.1	Agriculture (brut)
Food (gross)	229.8	231.6	104.7	100.6	100.0	104.9	103.1	103.1	Produits ailmentaires (brut)
Central African Republic									**République centrafricaine**
Agriculture (gross)	50.6	56.6	77.8	101.3	114.8	117.5	120.3	121.9	Agriculture (brut)
Food (gross)	46.2	52.6	74.3	101.4	114.1	115.3	118.3	119.9	Produits ailmentaires (brut)
Chad									**Tchad**
Agriculture (gross)	40.4	44.8	72.8	105.9	146.7	142.1	140.8	149.7	Agriculture (brut)
Food (gross)	36.8	43.9	71.6	105.6	154.4	146.5	145.0	154.5	Produits ailmentaires (brut)

20 Agricultural production indices *(continued)*
Index base: 2004 - 2006 = 100

Indices de la production agricole *(suite)*
Indices base: 2004 - 2006 = 100

Région, pays ou zone	1975	1985	1995	2005	2010	2014	2015	2016	Région, pays ou zone
Chile									**Chili**
Agriculture (gross)	35.6	43.5	76.6	99.7	107.8	110.6	111.4	113.5	Agriculture (brut)
Food (gross)	35.0	43.0	76.2	99.7	108.0	110.8	111.6	113.7	Produits ailmentaires (brut)
China [1]									**Chine** [1]
Agriculture (gross)	25.5	40.4	67.4	100.2	119.9	132.9	136.5	139.2	Agriculture (brut)
Food (gross)	25.2	39.2	66.9	100.3	120.5	133.8	137.5	140.3	Produits ailmentaires (brut)
China, Hong Kong SAR									**Chine, RAS de Hong Kong**
Agriculture (gross)	162.1	220.8	83.5	98.9	54.8	58.8	59.0	59.2	Agriculture (brut)
Food (gross)	162.1	220.8	83.5	98.9	54.8	58.8	59.0	59.2	Produits ailmentaires (brut)
China, Macao SAR									**Chine, RAS de Macao**
Agriculture (gross)	59.2	65.7	69.6	99.7	95.3	89.6	89.4	90.0	Agriculture (brut)
Food (gross)	59.2	65.7	69.6	99.7	95.3	89.6	89.4	90.0	Produits ailmentaires (brut)
Colombia									**Colombie**
Agriculture (gross)	48.8	58.1	81.5	98.8	100.4	116.0	119.5	115.2	Agriculture (brut)
Food (gross)	45.2	54.7	79.0	98.8	102.2	117.0	119.8	116.2	Produits ailmentaires (brut)
Comoros									**Comores**
Agriculture (gross)	55.2	61.4	89.5	96.3	106.5	106.1	108.7	109.4	Agriculture (brut)
Food (gross)	55.2	61.4	89.5	96.3	106.5	106.1	108.7	109.4	Produits ailmentaires (brut)
Congo									**Congo**
Agriculture (gross)	48.5	61.4	72.4	100.5	121.7	133.3	135.0	137.8	Agriculture (brut)
Food (gross)	48.2	60.6	72.5	100.4	121.9	133.6	135.2	138.1	Produits ailmentaires (brut)
Cook Islands									**Îles Cook**
Agriculture (gross)	326.0	290.2	155.4	99.7	93.9	92.8	92.5	90.9	Agriculture (brut)
Food (gross)	325.6	290.1	154.7	99.7	93.9	92.8	92.5	90.9	Produits ailmentaires (brut)
Costa Rica									**Costa Rica**
Agriculture (gross)	39.0	46.7	77.7	98.2	112.7	128.1	124.9	129.4	Agriculture (brut)
Food (gross)	37.2	43.4	75.0	97.8	114.6	130.6	127.4	132.3	Produits ailmentaires (brut)
Côte d'Ivoire									**Côte d'Ivoire**
Agriculture (gross)	40.9	56.5	77.5	99.8	106.8	128.3	129.0	127.5	Agriculture (brut)
Food (gross)	38.7	53.5	77.6	98.0	108.8	129.5	130.3	128.5	Produits ailmentaires (brut)
Croatia									**Croatie**
Agriculture (gross)	...	...	87.7	100.2	110.8	105.7	110.3	120.7	Agriculture (brut)
Food (gross)	...	...	87.7	100.3	111.1	105.8	110.4	121.0	Produits ailmentaires (brut)
Cuba									**Cuba**
Agriculture (gross)	95.5	130.4	80.4	96.6	87.9	98.1	100.4	102.6	Agriculture (brut)
Food (gross)	94.0	129.5	79.8	96.7	88.2	98.6	100.8	103.3	Produits ailmentaires (brut)
Cyprus									**Chypre**
Agriculture (gross)	65.3	90.7	111.3	98.3	83.8	78.5	80.8	78.6	Agriculture (brut)
Food (gross)	65.3	90.5	111.3	98.3	83.9	78.6	80.9	78.7	Produits ailmentaires (brut)
Czechia									**Tchéquie**
Agriculture (gross)	...	...	110.7	100.2	91.4	100.3	96.1	100.1	Agriculture (brut)
Food (gross)	...	...	110.6	100.2	91.5	100.5	96.3	100.3	Produits ailmentaires (brut)
Dem. People's Rep. Korea									**Rép. pop. dém. de Corée**
Agriculture (gross)	66.5	87.9	75.7	101.0	97.7	102.3	105.2	102.2	Agriculture (brut)
Food (gross)	66.1	87.5	74.9	101.0	97.4	101.7	104.6	101.5	Produits ailmentaires (brut)
Dem. Rep. of the Congo									**Rép. dém. du Congo**
Agriculture (gross)	82.2	102.7	108.1	100.1	104.4	109.6	109.6	108.9	Agriculture (brut)
Food (gross)	79.1	100.2	106.7	100.0	104.4	109.6	109.6	108.9	Produits ailmentaires (brut)
Denmark									**Danemark**
Agriculture (gross)	68.2	85.3	94.2	100.8	101.3	102.8	104.5	101.4	Agriculture (brut)
Food (gross)	68.2	85.3	94.2	100.8	101.3	102.8	104.5	101.4	Produits ailmentaires (brut)
Djibouti									**Djibouti**
Agriculture (gross)	24.0	68.2	75.9	94.9	115.7	132.9	132.8	133.1	Agriculture (brut)
Food (gross)	23.9	68.2	75.9	94.9	115.7	132.9	132.8	133.1	Produits ailmentaires (brut)
Dominica									**Dominique**
Agriculture (gross)	97.7	113.9	110.5	98.8	107.9	110.3	112.5	113.3	Agriculture (brut)
Food (gross)	99.1	114.8	110.8	98.7	108.3	111.0	112.9	113.8	Produits ailmentaires (brut)
Dominican Republic									**République dominicaine**
Agriculture (gross)	64.4	76.6	77.8	98.3	123.5	137.8	142.4	144.8	Agriculture (brut)
Food (gross)	61.0	72.7	76.3	98.2	125.1	140.2	144.8	147.2	Produits ailmentaires (brut)
Ecuador									**Équateur**
Agriculture (gross)	45.2	55.4	78.8	98.4	122.8	119.1	122.1	114.8	Agriculture (brut)
Food (gross)	43.9	53.3	76.5	98.2	123.1	119.8	122.8	115.4	Produits ailmentaires (brut)
Egypt									**Égypte**
Agriculture (gross)	31.1	41.2	67.1	98.8	108.9	120.0	120.9	124.4	Agriculture (brut)
Food (gross)	28.8	38.6	66.5	99.0	109.7	121.3	122.1	125.7	Produits ailmentaires (brut)

20 Agricultural production indices *(continued)*
Index base: 2004 - 2006 = 100

Indices de la production agricole *(suite)*
Indices base: 2004 - 2006 = 100

Région, pays ou zone	1975	1985	1995	2005	2010	2014	2015	2016	Région, pays ou zone
El Salvador									**El Salvador**
Agriculture (gross)	81.8	78.4	87.8	99.3	107.4	108.3	103.7	111.5	Agriculture (brut)
Food (gross)	60.0	64.6	80.3	98.9	105.3	114.3	109.9	118.2	Produits ailmentaires (brut)
Equatorial Guinea									**Guinée équatoriale**
Agriculture (gross)	67.3	70.6	86.5	100.7	108.6	114.4	114.6	115.2	Agriculture (brut)
Food (gross)	59.3	58.2	83.6	101.2	109.6	115.9	116.6	117.3	Produits ailmentaires (brut)
Eritrea									**Érythrée**
Agriculture (gross)	...	...	76.9	107.8	101.9	103.2	102.7	104.4	Agriculture (brut)
Food (gross)	...	...	76.9	107.9	101.8	103.1	102.6	104.3	Produits ailmentaires (brut)
Estonia									**Estonie**
Agriculture (gross)	...	...	110.1	103.1	110.3	136.0	149.8	127.7	Agriculture (brut)
Food (gross)	...	...	110.0	103.1	110.3	136.0	149.8	127.7	Produits ailmentaires (brut)
Eswatini									**Eswatini**
Agriculture (gross)	63.3	88.8	83.4	103.0	106.0	113.6	113.8	113.4	Agriculture (brut)
Food (gross)	60.0	86.6	82.8	102.8	106.4	113.9	114.1	113.7	Produits ailmentaires (brut)
Ethiopia									**Éthiopie**
Agriculture (gross)	...	...	59.8	102.1	138.1	159.0	170.1	163.5	Agriculture (brut)
Food (gross)	...	...	57.9	102.5	137.6	158.3	169.3	162.3	Produits ailmentaires (brut)
Falkland Islands (Malvinas)									**Îles Falkland (Malvinas)**
Agriculture (gross)	99.8	104.2	112.8	102.9	96.4	96.6	96.5	96.4	Agriculture (brut)
Food (gross)	118.6	122.6	134.4	100.0	105.9	106.2	106.0	105.8	Produits ailmentaires (brut)
Faroe Islands									**Îles Féroé**
Agriculture (gross)	93.8	94.2	100.7	100.0	100.0	101.8	100.7	100.7	Agriculture (brut)
Food (gross)	93.8	94.2	100.7	100.0	100.0	101.8	100.7	100.7	Produits ailmentaires (brut)
Fiji									**Fidji**
Agriculture (gross)	63.0	87.6	106.4	98.7	81.5	88.3	85.4	83.6	Agriculture (brut)
Food (gross)	62.8	87.5	106.6	98.7	81.3	88.1	85.3	83.4	Produits ailmentaires (brut)
Finland									**Finlande**
Agriculture (gross)	99.1	106.2	94.9	102.1	93.9	100.8	98.2	97.3	Agriculture (brut)
Food (gross)	99.1	106.2	94.9	102.1	93.9	100.8	98.2	97.3	Produits ailmentaires (brut)
France									**France**
Agriculture (gross)	84.5	99.9	97.8	99.8	98.8	104.0	103.5	95.8	Agriculture (brut)
Food (gross)	84.8	100.3	98.0	99.8	99.0	104.1	103.6	95.8	Produits ailmentaires (brut)
French Guiana									**Guyane française**
Agriculture (gross)	21.1	51.1	104.5	98.2	103.0	134.7	133.0	126.6	Agriculture (brut)
Food (gross)	21.1	51.1	104.5	98.2	103.0	134.7	133.0	126.6	Produits ailmentaires (brut)
French Polynesia									**Polynésie française**
Agriculture (gross)	106.1	90.8	90.7	103.7	99.4	104.0	100.0	101.5	Agriculture (brut)
Food (gross)	105.5	90.7	90.7	103.7	99.4	104.0	100.0	101.5	Produits ailmentaires (brut)
Gabon									**Gabon**
Agriculture (gross)	49.7	67.8	83.8	100.0	111.8	120.7	121.8	123.1	Agriculture (brut)
Food (gross)	52.5	71.2	86.5	100.1	109.1	117.1	117.8	118.9	Produits ailmentaires (brut)
Gambia									**Gambie**
Agriculture (gross)	68.8	56.1	66.1	94.3	133.1	89.3	100.8	106.0	Agriculture (brut)
Food (gross)	68.8	55.6	65.5	94.3	133.2	89.3	100.8	106.0	Produits ailmentaires (brut)
Georgia									**Géorgie**
Agriculture (gross)	...	...	121.2	121.0	67.6	76.7	75.3	73.8	Agriculture (brut)
Food (gross)	...	...	119.1	120.8	68.4	77.9	76.4	74.9	Produits ailmentaires (brut)
Germany									**Allemagne**
Agriculture (gross)	95.4	110.7	91.9	99.9	102.7	111.7	107.8	106.8	Agriculture (brut)
Food (gross)	95.4	110.6	91.8	99.9	102.8	111.7	107.8	106.8	Produits ailmentaires (brut)
Ghana									**Ghana**
Agriculture (gross)	37.7	35.8	63.8	99.8	127.2	150.1	150.6	152.6	Agriculture (brut)
Food (gross)	37.4	35.9	63.5	99.8	127.3	150.1	150.6	152.7	Produits ailmentaires (brut)
Greece									**Grèce**
Agriculture (gross)	79.7	94.7	102.7	104.0	93.9	89.0	87.7	92.7	Agriculture (brut)
Food (gross)	82.2	97.1	101.0	103.3	98.4	90.5	89.3	94.8	Produits ailmentaires (brut)
Greenland									**Groenland**
Agriculture (gross)	61.0	103.4	99.0	99.4	98.0	97.9	97.8	97.8	Agriculture (brut)
Food (gross)	59.1	103.5	99.6	99.2	97.9	97.8	97.8	97.7	Produits ailmentaires (brut)
Grenada									**Grenade**
Agriculture (gross)	139.6	138.2	138.6	78.3	96.5	136.6	136.1	128.0	Agriculture (brut)
Food (gross)	139.7	138.2	138.7	78.3	96.5	136.7	136.2	128.0	Produits ailmentaires (brut)
Guadeloupe									**Guadeloupe**
Agriculture (gross)	135.3	115.1	79.6	102.8	89.2	100.3	95.8	92.2	Agriculture (brut)
Food (gross)	135.0	115.0	79.6	102.8	89.2	100.2	95.8	92.2	Produits ailmentaires (brut)

Agricultural production indices *(continued)*
Index base: 2004 - 2006 = 100

Indices de la production agricole *(suite)*
Indices base: 2004 - 2006 = 100

Région, pays ou zone	1975	1985	1995	2005	2010	2014	2015	2016	Région, pays ou zone
Guam									**Guam**
Agriculture (gross)	67.6	72.5	87.6	99.3	95.5	88.2	79.3	78.0	Agriculture (brut)
Food (gross)	67.6	72.5	87.6	99.3	95.5	88.2	79.3	78.0	Produits ailmentaires (brut)
Guatemala									**Guatemala**
Agriculture (gross)	36.7	43.3	65.1	99.6	124.1	151.6	156.6	157.6	Agriculture (brut)
Food (gross)	32.1	40.1	65.9	99.8	121.9	152.3	158.4	160.1	Produits ailmentaires (brut)
Guinea									**Guinée**
Agriculture (gross)	41.7	49.6	71.5	100.4	120.0	129.2	132.0	134.6	Agriculture (brut)
Food (gross)	42.2	50.2	71.3	100.5	120.0	130.0	132.7	135.4	Produits ailmentaires (brut)
Guinea-Bissau									**Guinée-Bissau**
Agriculture (gross)	33.6	46.5	71.8	100.3	127.8	136.2	139.6	142.6	Agriculture (brut)
Food (gross)	33.6	45.9	71.7	100.2	128.1	136.6	140.1	143.2	Produits ailmentaires (brut)
Guyana									**Guyana**
Agriculture (gross)	79.1	68.8	99.4	94.1	107.6	125.0	145.4	130.0	Agriculture (brut)
Food (gross)	78.9	68.7	99.5	94.1	107.7	125.1	145.6	130.1	Produits ailmentaires (brut)
Haiti									**Haïti**
Agriculture (gross)	90.0	103.0	83.7	101.5	131.7	154.9	158.9	154.6	Agriculture (brut)
Food (gross)	88.6	102.1	83.4	101.4	132.2	156.8	160.4	155.8	Produits ailmentaires (brut)
Honduras									**Honduras**
Agriculture (gross)	39.5	55.4	72.1	102.9	111.2	118.5	121.8	124.3	Agriculture (brut)
Food (gross)	40.8	57.0	72.4	103.7	109.5	115.3	115.6	116.4	Produits ailmentaires (brut)
Hungary									**Hongrie**
Agriculture (gross)	107.7	126.5	91.5	96.5	80.0	98.1	92.1	88.1	Agriculture (brut)
Food (gross)	107.3	126.1	91.5	96.5	80.0	98.1	92.1	88.1	Produits ailmentaires (brut)
Iceland									**Islande**
Agriculture (gross)	105.1	106.5	85.5	98.7	110.1	118.2	122.4	125.9	Agriculture (brut)
Food (gross)	103.7	105.2	85.0	98.7	110.3	118.5	122.8	126.4	Produits ailmentaires (brut)
India									**Inde**
Agriculture (gross)	43.8	59.4	80.8	99.9	124.3	143.5	141.8	144.9	Agriculture (brut)
Food (gross)	43.9	59.5	81.1	99.9	123.2	142.7	140.9	144.2	Produits ailmentaires (brut)
Indonesia									**Indonésie**
Agriculture (gross)	31.2	49.6	75.5	98.1	123.0	139.4	142.4	143.1	Agriculture (brut)
Food (gross)	30.9	49.4	75.9	98.1	123.9	140.5	143.8	144.5	Produits ailmentaires (brut)
Iran (Islamic Republic of)									**Iran (Rép. islamique d')**
Agriculture (gross)	26.3	42.8	69.7	102.6	101.7	111.0	109.6	110.1	Agriculture (brut)
Food (gross)	25.6	42.4	68.6	102.4	102.2	112.0	110.4	111.0	Produits ailmentaires (brut)
Iraq									**Iraq**
Agriculture (gross)	60.5	101.5	95.3	102.5	102.9	120.8	73.0	74.9	Agriculture (brut)
Food (gross)	59.4	101.1	95.8	102.5	102.6	121.0	72.3	74.3	Produits ailmentaires (brut)
Ireland									**Irlande**
Agriculture (gross)	76.8	93.0	98.8	98.2	101.5	103.0	108.9	109.8	Agriculture (brut)
Food (gross)	76.8	93.0	98.7	98.2	101.4	102.9	108.8	109.7	Produits ailmentaires (brut)
Israel									**Israël**
Agriculture (gross)	54.4	69.5	79.7	100.1	104.1	110.0	106.0	108.8	Agriculture (brut)
Food (gross)	52.4	64.9	78.3	100.3	105.0	110.6	106.5	109.4	Produits ailmentaires (brut)
Italy									**Italie**
Agriculture (gross)	88.0	95.3	94.9	100.5	97.0	88.2	92.4	91.6	Agriculture (brut)
Food (gross)	87.9	95.0	94.8	100.5	97.1	88.4	92.6	91.8	Produits ailmentaires (brut)
Jamaica									**Jamaïque**
Agriculture (gross)	73.0	75.0	102.3	96.6	98.1	102.2	101.3	105.1	Agriculture (brut)
Food (gross)	74.0	75.8	103.4	96.3	97.9	102.9	101.8	105.7	Produits ailmentaires (brut)
Japan									**Japon**
Agriculture (gross)	102.8	116.7	109.8	101.0	97.1	96.7	95.6	92.1	Agriculture (brut)
Food (gross)	100.2	115.4	109.7	101.0	97.3	97.0	95.9	92.4	Produits ailmentaires (brut)
Jordan									**Jordanie**
Agriculture (gross)	19.5	44.0	72.0	101.0	127.0	134.8	149.9	145.3	Agriculture (brut)
Food (gross)	19.1	43.3	70.6	101.0	127.1	134.9	150.1	145.4	Produits ailmentaires (brut)
Kazakhstan									**Kazakhstan**
Agriculture (gross)	...	...	87.1	100.3	106.5	125.8	130.9	139.2	Agriculture (brut)
Food (gross)	...	...	87.7	100.1	107.5	126.3	131.3	139.7	Produits ailmentaires (brut)
Kenya									**Kenya**
Agriculture (gross)	36.4	53.2	70.8	103.2	122.6	125.0	126.9	125.8	Agriculture (brut)
Food (gross)	36.1	51.7	69.0	103.3	123.6	125.3	128.4	125.7	Produits ailmentaires (brut)
Kiribati									**Kiribati**
Agriculture (gross)	41.3	72.4	65.0	95.4	60.4	60.7	60.8	60.6	Agriculture (brut)
Food (gross)	41.3	72.4	65.0	95.4	60.4	60.7	60.8	60.6	Produits ailmentaires (brut)

Agricultural production indices *(continued)*
Index base: 2004 - 2006 = 100

Indices de la production agricole *(suite)*
Indices base: 2004 - 2006 = 100

Région, pays ou zone	1975	1985	1995	2005	2010	2014	2015	2016	Région, pays ou zone
Kuwait									**Koweït**
Agriculture (gross)	16.3	51.4	52.4	96.7	130.7	191.2	189.0	190.6	Agriculture (brut)
Food (gross)	16.2	50.8	52.4	96.7	130.8	191.7	189.4	191.1	Produits ailmentaires (brut)
Kyrgyzstan									**Kirghizistan**
Agriculture (gross)	...	...	65.7	97.8	104.7	108.3	114.2	116.9	Agriculture (brut)
Food (gross)	...	...	64.6	97.7	106.5	110.8	117.4	120.3	Produits ailmentaires (brut)
Lao People's Dem. Rep.									**Rép. dém. populaire lao**
Agriculture (gross)	27.9	42.0	53.7	100.3	131.9	192.6	211.5	219.3	Agriculture (brut)
Food (gross)	26.2	42.4	51.8	100.4	130.0	186.0	204.4	211.9	Produits ailmentaires (brut)
Latvia									**Lettonie**
Agriculture (gross)	...	...	113.0	105.0	108.1	127.8	152.3	139.2	Agriculture (brut)
Food (gross)	...	...	113.0	105.0	108.1	127.9	152.4	139.3	Produits ailmentaires (brut)
Lebanon									**Liban**
Agriculture (gross)	41.0	59.6	110.8	96.8	93.3	91.9	91.0	89.1	Agriculture (brut)
Food (gross)	40.9	59.9	111.2	96.8	93.1	91.8	90.9	88.9	Produits ailmentaires (brut)
Lesotho									**Lesotho**
Agriculture (gross)	62.8	68.8	86.6	105.4	106.9	111.8	97.8	95.6	Agriculture (brut)
Food (gross)	62.7	67.9	84.3	105.4	107.0	111.8	97.2	94.9	Produits ailmentaires (brut)
Liberia									**Libéria**
Agriculture (gross)	75.5	94.0	48.9	102.2	104.2	107.7	111.9	113.3	Agriculture (brut)
Food (gross)	74.1	93.1	65.7	101.1	127.2	126.7	132.5	135.7	Produits ailmentaires (brut)
Libya									**Libye**
Agriculture (gross)	49.8	66.7	90.7	100.9	111.6	114.3	116.6	116.7	Agriculture (brut)
Food (gross)	49.1	66.3	90.8	100.8	111.8	114.5	116.9	117.1	Produits ailmentaires (brut)
Liechtenstein									**Liechtenstein**
Agriculture (gross)	44.7	89.6	90.3	99.8	100.6	101.9	99.6	97.0	Agriculture (brut)
Food (gross)	44.7	89.6	90.3	99.8	100.6	101.9	99.6	97.0	Produits ailmentaires (brut)
Lithuania									**Lituanie**
Agriculture (gross)	...	...	97.4	106.1	99.8	126.8	138.5	131.1	Agriculture (brut)
Food (gross)	...	...	97.2	106.1	99.9	126.9	138.6	131.3	Produits ailmentaires (brut)
Luxembourg									**Luxembourg**
Agriculture (gross)	...	...	...	99.3	93.5	97.8	101.9	102.8	Agriculture (brut)
Food (gross)	...	...	...	99.3	93.6	97.8	101.9	102.9	Produits ailmentaires (brut)
Madagascar									**Madagascar**
Agriculture (gross)	70.6	78.2	87.3	103.1	122.6	120.6	117.1	118.3	Agriculture (brut)
Food (gross)	67.8	76.1	86.3	103.5	123.5	121.7	118.2	119.4	Produits ailmentaires (brut)
Malawi									**Malawi**
Agriculture (gross)	37.5	47.9	59.6	85.8	155.7	162.7	151.7	146.3	Agriculture (brut)
Food (gross)	37.4	44.1	52.1	85.6	157.3	166.0	153.9	150.9	Produits ailmentaires (brut)
Malaysia									**Malaisie**
Agriculture (gross)	31.6	46.9	69.8	99.7	110.6	120.8	121.9	122.7	Agriculture (brut)
Food (gross)	20.4	37.6	67.3	100.3	114.6	129.1	129.9	131.2	Produits ailmentaires (brut)
Maldives									**Maldives**
Agriculture (gross)	87.7	110.2	97.3	89.3	75.9	65.7	67.3	67.4	Agriculture (brut)
Food (gross)	87.7	110.2	97.3	89.3	75.9	65.7	67.3	67.4	Produits ailmentaires (brut)
Mali									**Mali**
Agriculture (gross)	31.8	39.6	70.5	102.2	125.7	150.1	157.0	171.3	Agriculture (brut)
Food (gross)	32.8	39.9	68.5	102.4	133.7	152.5	160.1	175.8	Produits ailmentaires (brut)
Malta									**Malte**
Agriculture (gross)	64.5	75.4	95.5	97.1	97.9	95.2	92.9	90.4	Agriculture (brut)
Food (gross)	64.5	75.4	95.5	97.1	97.9	95.3	92.9	90.4	Produits ailmentaires (brut)
Marshall Islands									**Îles Marshall**
Agriculture (gross)	...	...	172.8	96.7	111.9	115.2	110.3	104.1	Agriculture (brut)
Food (gross)	...	...	172.8	96.7	111.9	115.2	110.3	104.1	Produits ailmentaires (brut)
Martinique									**Martinique**
Agriculture (gross)	100.5	98.7	94.5	98.8	82.2	78.1	80.1	78.9	Agriculture (brut)
Food (gross)	100.5	98.7	94.5	98.8	82.2	78.1	80.1	78.9	Produits ailmentaires (brut)
Mauritania									**Mauritanie**
Agriculture (gross)	41.3	54.7	80.8	100.3	108.5	119.7	125.4	120.2	Agriculture (brut)
Food (gross)	41.3	54.7	80.8	100.3	108.5	119.7	125.4	120.2	Produits ailmentaires (brut)
Mauritius									**Maurice**
Agriculture (gross)	67.4	88.6	93.5	98.4	98.7	96.1	94.5	92.1	Agriculture (brut)
Food (gross)	66.1	85.5	92.1	98.5	98.7	96.2	94.6	92.3	Produits ailmentaires (brut)
Mexico									**Mexique**
Agriculture (gross)	44.6	64.6	78.2	98.0	108.0	118.9	119.6	125.7	Agriculture (brut)
Food (gross)	42.9	63.5	77.3	98.0	108.3	118.6	119.5	125.9	Produits ailmentaires (brut)

Agricultural production indices *(continued)*
Index base: 2004 - 2006 = 100

Indices de la production agricole *(suite)*
Indices base: 2004 - 2006 = 100

Région, pays ou zone	1975	1985	1995	2005	2010	2014	2015	2016	Région, pays ou zone
Micronesia (Fed. States of)									**Micronésie (États féd. de)**
Agriculture (gross)	...	...	105.8	99.9	96.4	112.6	127.2	100.8	Agriculture (brut)
Food (gross)	...	...	105.8	99.9	96.4	112.6	127.2	100.8	Produits ailmentaires (brut)
Mongolia									**Mongolie**
Agriculture (gross)	131.8	135.6	115.3	97.0	114.3	156.4	153.3	161.4	Agriculture (brut)
Food (gross)	131.5	136.2	112.5	97.0	115.1	158.7	155.5	163.9	Produits ailmentaires (brut)
Montenegro									**Monténégro**
Agriculture (gross)	...	...	...	...	62.6	65.4	70.9	66.2	Agriculture (brut)
Food (gross)	...	...	...	...	62.6	65.4	70.9	66.3	Produits ailmentaires (brut)
Montserrat									**Montserrat**
Agriculture (gross)	55.4	69.1	97.1	99.7	98.3	103.8	103.9	104.1	Agriculture (brut)
Food (gross)	55.3	69.1	97.2	99.7	98.4	103.8	103.9	104.2	Produits ailmentaires (brut)
Morocco									**Maroc**
Agriculture (gross)	37.7	50.4	56.7	93.1	126.0	134.8	141.7	121.6	Agriculture (brut)
Food (gross)	37.5	50.0	56.3	92.9	126.3	135.2	142.2	121.8	Produits ailmentaires (brut)
Mozambique									**Mozambique**
Agriculture (gross)	58.6	48.5	69.4	96.2	146.0	143.3	140.5	148.9	Agriculture (brut)
Food (gross)	60.0	52.4	74.2	95.8	150.7	144.2	142.1	150.3	Produits ailmentaires (brut)
Myanmar									**Myanmar**
Agriculture (gross)	27.6	45.1	53.3	99.5	135.5	134.3	136.5	137.0	Agriculture (brut)
Food (gross)	27.3	44.6	53.1	99.5	134.7	133.0	135.1	135.5	Produits ailmentaires (brut)
Namibia									**Namibie**
Agriculture (gross)	72.8	69.9	90.6	103.9	89.7	91.7	92.3	93.1	Agriculture (brut)
Food (gross)	72.0	70.0	91.0	104.2	90.2	92.3	92.9	93.7	Produits ailmentaires (brut)
Nauru									**Nauru**
Agriculture (gross)	60.9	67.0	88.8	100.0	106.4	111.7	112.8	113.6	Agriculture (brut)
Food (gross)	60.9	67.0	88.8	100.0	106.4	111.7	112.8	113.6	Produits ailmentaires (brut)
Nepal									**Népal**
Agriculture (gross)	38.4	50.8	75.9	100.3	113.9	138.6	138.3	140.1	Agriculture (brut)
Food (gross)	38.1	50.5	75.9	100.3	113.9	138.6	138.3	140.1	Produits ailmentaires (brut)
Netherlands									**Pays-Bas**
Agriculture (gross)	72.2	97.4	105.7	99.6	111.6	114.8	116.1	117.8	Agriculture (brut)
Food (gross)	72.3	97.4	105.7	99.6	111.6	114.8	116.1	117.9	Produits ailmentaires (brut)
Netherlands Antilles [former]									**Antilles néerlandaises [anc.]**
Agriculture (gross)	125.1	101.6	85.7	97.8	113.6	...	...	...	Agriculture (brut)
Food (gross)	125.1	101.6	85.7	97.8	113.6	...	...	...	Produits ailmentaires (brut)
New Caledonia									**Nouvelle-Calédonie**
Agriculture (gross)	86.0	98.6	98.8	100.1	97.9	106.8	103.6	105.3	Agriculture (brut)
Food (gross)	79.1	96.2	98.8	100.2	98.1	107.0	103.8	105.5	Produits ailmentaires (brut)
New Zealand									**Nouvelle-Zélande**
Agriculture (gross)	57.5	74.2	80.3	99.0	103.9	116.1	118.2	117.3	Agriculture (brut)
Food (gross)	54.1	69.9	78.0	99.1	105.0	117.9	120.1	119.2	Produits ailmentaires (brut)
Nicaragua									**Nicaragua**
Agriculture (gross)	74.0	56.2	60.0	103.7	118.1	129.3	126.9	132.4	Agriculture (brut)
Food (gross)	59.7	48.3	58.4	102.1	119.1	130.0	125.2	130.8	Produits ailmentaires (brut)
Niger									**Niger**
Agriculture (gross)	27.8	34.2	54.1	102.1	146.3	151.7	160.8	172.7	Agriculture (brut)
Food (gross)	27.5	34.1	53.9	102.1	146.6	151.9	161.0	172.9	Produits ailmentaires (brut)
Nigeria									**Nigéria**
Agriculture (gross)	29.8	34.0	67.6	99.6	105.3	118.3	119.9	118.9	Agriculture (brut)
Food (gross)	29.6	34.1	67.7	99.6	105.3	118.9	120.6	119.5	Produits ailmentaires (brut)
Niue									**Nioué**
Agriculture (gross)	101.5	108.8	92.6	99.9	97.2	99.9	100.8	101.3	Agriculture (brut)
Food (gross)	101.5	108.8	92.6	99.9	97.2	99.9	100.8	101.3	Produits ailmentaires (brut)
Norway									**Norvège**
Agriculture (gross)	88.5	103.4	99.5	99.1	102.0	105.9	107.3	107.1	Agriculture (brut)
Food (gross)	88.5	103.4	99.4	99.1	102.1	106.0	107.5	107.2	Produits ailmentaires (brut)
Oman									**Oman**
Agriculture (gross)	19.7	44.9	70.4	111.7	118.5	130.7	142.6	143.7	Agriculture (brut)
Food (gross)	19.7	44.3	70.2	111.7	118.6	130.9	142.9	144.0	Produits ailmentaires (brut)
Pakistan									**Pakistan**
Agriculture (gross)	32.9	48.9	78.1	100.4	110.6	126.7	128.2	127.6	Agriculture (brut)
Food (gross)	33.6	48.0	77.7	100.6	113.4	128.9	130.7	130.0	Produits ailmentaires (brut)
Panama									**Panama**
Agriculture (gross)	77.3	88.4	94.0	98.8	106.5	114.8	114.3	112.2	Agriculture (brut)
Food (gross)	78.1	88.8	94.3	98.8	106.7	115.8	115.2	113.1	Produits ailmentaires (brut)

Région, pays ou zone	1975	1985	1995	2005	2010	2014	2015	2016	Région, pays ou zone
Papua New Guinea									**Papouasie-Nvl-Guinée**
Agriculture (gross)	51.3	65.3	78.1	99.3	111.9	120.1	121.0	122.3	Agriculture (brut)
Food (gross)	50.8	64.3	77.5	98.6	112.7	121.0	121.7	123.1	Produits ailmentaires (brut)
Paraguay									**Paraguay**
Agriculture (gross)	30.6	56.3	70.5	98.1	137.6	162.0	161.6	163.9	Agriculture (brut)
Food (gross)	28.5	50.0	66.7	98.4	142.7	168.1	167.7	170.0	Produits ailmentaires (brut)
Peru									**Pérou**
Agriculture (gross)	43.9	48.1	63.2	99.2	128.9	147.1	148.1	150.1	Agriculture (brut)
Food (gross)	42.8	46.8	63.1	99.8	131.0	150.8	151.3	153.0	Produits ailmentaires (brut)
Philippines									**Philippines**
Agriculture (gross)	44.4	55.2	76.6	99.3	111.9	117.2	115.8	113.4	Agriculture (brut)
Food (gross)	44.2	55.0	76.4	99.4	112.0	117.0	116.0	113.8	Produits ailmentaires (brut)
Poland									**Pologne**
Agriculture (gross)	121.5	118.5	103.4	98.4	101.1	113.2	106.7	113.1	Agriculture (brut)
Food (gross)	120.7	117.7	103.3	98.4	101.1	113.2	106.8	113.1	Produits ailmentaires (brut)
Portugal									**Portugal**
Agriculture (gross)	81.7	83.1	98.4	97.0	105.2	104.1	116.5	107.9	Agriculture (brut)
Food (gross)	81.3	83.0	98.2	97.0	105.4	104.4	116.8	108.2	Produits ailmentaires (brut)
Puerto Rico									**Porto Rico**
Agriculture (gross)	140.0	124.8	117.5	96.4	104.5	102.6	102.3	102.2	Agriculture (brut)
Food (gross)	139.4	123.6	116.7	96.6	105.4	104.1	104.2	104.0	Produits ailmentaires (brut)
Qatar									**Qatar**
Agriculture (gross)	11.4	44.0	105.8	95.5	132.1	160.4	167.5	165.9	Agriculture (brut)
Food (gross)	11.4	44.0	105.8	95.5	132.1	160.4	167.5	165.9	Produits ailmentaires (brut)
Republic of Korea									**République de Corée**
Agriculture (gross)	49.4	70.7	92.5	99.9	101.3	106.1	104.3	102.8	Agriculture (brut)
Food (gross)	47.0	69.8	91.8	99.9	101.3	106.2	104.4	103.0	Produits ailmentaires (brut)
Republic of Moldova									**République de Moldova**
Agriculture (gross)	…	…	131.8	99.8	92.8	108.5	94.9	111.5	Agriculture (brut)
Food (gross)	…	…	130.1	99.8	92.6	109.1	95.4	112.1	Produits ailmentaires (brut)
Réunion									**Réunion**
Agriculture (gross)	55.6	66.5	87.0	99.0	105.2	104.5	101.5	102.4	Agriculture (brut)
Food (gross)	55.6	66.4	87.1	99.0	105.1	104.3	101.3	102.3	Produits ailmentaires (brut)
Romania									**Roumanie**
Agriculture (gross)	89.7	117.1	97.2	95.3	90.2	98.0	91.2	94.5	Agriculture (brut)
Food (gross)	88.5	116.1	97.0	95.3	90.1	98.1	91.2	94.5	Produits ailmentaires (brut)
Russian Federation									**Fédération de Russie**
Agriculture (gross)	…	…	105.3	99.5	98.6	127.8	131.0	138.8	Agriculture (brut)
Food (gross)	…	…	105.1	99.5	98.5	127.7	130.7	138.5	Produits ailmentaires (brut)
Rwanda									**Rwanda**
Agriculture (gross)	44.3	67.9	54.8	100.6	139.5	153.6	149.4	140.1	Agriculture (brut)
Food (gross)	43.8	66.0	54.1	100.7	140.1	154.6	150.0	140.4	Produits ailmentaires (brut)
Saint Kitts and Nevis									**Saint-Kitts-et-Nevis**
Agriculture (gross)	156.4	184.1	138.3	90.8	34.5	39.3	38.0	39.3	Agriculture (brut)
Food (gross)	155.4	183.9	138.3	90.8	34.5	39.3	38.0	39.3	Produits ailmentaires (brut)
Saint Lucia									**Sainte-Lucie**
Agriculture (gross)	186.4	251.9	298.3	90.5	87.3	68.7	65.9	64.9	Agriculture (brut)
Food (gross)	186.3	251.9	298.3	90.5	87.3	68.7	65.9	64.9	Produits ailmentaires (brut)
Saint Pierre and Miquelon									**Saint-Pierre-et-Miquelon**
Agriculture (gross)	2.2	33.1	68.2	93.7	109.7	112.8	114.0	114.9	Agriculture (brut)
Food (gross)	2.2	33.1	68.2	93.7	109.7	112.8	114.0	114.9	Produits ailmentaires (brut)
Saint Vincent & Grenadines									**Saint-Vincent-Grenadines**
Agriculture (gross)	63.2	123.0	101.7	103.8	118.9	113.8	110.9	110.0	Agriculture (brut)
Food (gross)	63.5	123.6	102.0	103.9	119.1	114.0	111.0	110.1	Produits ailmentaires (brut)
Samoa									**Samoa**
Agriculture (gross)	97.1	112.9	82.8	101.1	106.9	114.3	118.8	117.6	Agriculture (brut)
Food (gross)	96.9	112.8	82.5	101.1	106.8	114.2	118.8	117.5	Produits ailmentaires (brut)
Sao Tome and Principe									**Sao Tomé-et-Principe**
Agriculture (gross)	63.8	53.1	66.8	100.8	103.7	123.8	111.1	109.3	Agriculture (brut)
Food (gross)	63.8	53.1	66.8	100.9	103.7	123.9	111.2	109.4	Produits ailmentaires (brut)
Saudi Arabia									**Arabie saoudite**
Agriculture (gross)	21.5	52.1	74.6	100.4	103.3	95.7	101.7	106.5	Agriculture (brut)
Food (gross)	21.5	52.0	74.6	100.4	103.4	95.7	101.7	106.6	Produits ailmentaires (brut)
Senegal									**Sénégal**
Agriculture (gross)	94.2	74.4	91.2	109.7	151.4	124.7	159.3	144.8	Agriculture (brut)
Food (gross)	94.7	74.6	91.4	110.2	153.0	125.6	160.9	146.2	Produits ailmentaires (brut)

Agricultural production indices *(continued)*
Index base: 2004 - 2006 = 100

Indices de la production agricole *(suite)*
Indices base: 2004 - 2006 = 100

Région, pays ou zone	1975	1985	1995	2005	2010	2014	2015	2016	Région, pays ou zone
Serbia									**Serbie**
Agriculture (gross)	...	...	...	...	103.0	101.8	94.6	105.0	Agriculture (brut)
Food (gross)	...	...	...	...	103.1	101.9	94.6	105.2	Produits ailmentaires (brut)
Serbia and Monten. [former]									**Serbie-et-Monténégro [anc.]**
Agriculture (gross)	...	...	98.3	96.5	...	...	...	...	Agriculture (brut)
Food (gross)	...	...	98.2	96.5	...	...	...	...	Produits ailmentaires (brut)
Seychelles									**Seychelles**
Agriculture (gross)	126.2	137.7	154.5	98.8	92.3	107.5	100.2	99.0	Agriculture (brut)
Food (gross)	131.1	141.5	156.6	98.5	95.5	112.0	104.5	103.2	Produits ailmentaires (brut)
Sierra Leone									**Sierra Leone**
Agriculture (gross)	47.6	51.9	56.7	93.5	147.4	171.9	168.9	194.8	Agriculture (brut)
Food (gross)	47.9	49.5	54.4	93.2	148.1	172.0	169.9	197.0	Produits ailmentaires (brut)
Singapore									**Singapour**
Agriculture (gross)	973.7	857.4	163.3	90.1	92.3	111.6	109.4	114.8	Agriculture (brut)
Food (gross)	968.2	857.3	163.3	90.1	92.3	111.6	109.4	114.8	Produits ailmentaires (brut)
Slovakia									**Slovaquie**
Agriculture (gross)	...	...	113.0	101.6	81.8	96.1	85.6	98.1	Agriculture (brut)
Food (gross)	...	...	112.3	101.6	81.9	96.2	85.7	98.2	Produits ailmentaires (brut)
Slovenia									**Slovénie**
Agriculture (gross)	...	...	95.9	99.4	91.1	87.4	91.1	87.9	Agriculture (brut)
Food (gross)	...	...	95.9	99.4	91.1	87.4	91.1	87.9	Produits ailmentaires (brut)
Solomon Islands									**Îles Salomon**
Agriculture (gross)	41.8	72.6	77.7	103.2	110.8	117.1	116.2	112.5	Agriculture (brut)
Food (gross)	41.7	72.6	77.7	103.2	110.8	117.1	116.2	112.5	Produits ailmentaires (brut)
Somalia									**Somalie**
Agriculture (gross)	69.5	90.5	88.1	103.1	104.6	110.1	109.2	107.9	Agriculture (brut)
Food (gross)	69.6	90.6	88.0	103.1	104.6	110.1	109.2	107.9	Produits ailmentaires (brut)
South Africa									**Afrique du Sud**
Agriculture (gross)	65.1	74.8	74.1	103.1	116.7	125.9	121.6	116.6	Agriculture (brut)
Food (gross)	63.2	72.9	73.3	103.0	117.3	126.6	122.3	117.2	Produits ailmentaires (brut)
Spain									**Espagne**
Agriculture (gross)	60.7	73.8	69.7	94.6	103.3	101.6	105.0	103.6	Agriculture (brut)
Food (gross)	60.8	73.7	69.6	94.5	103.6	101.8	105.2	103.9	Produits ailmentaires (brut)
Sri Lanka									**Sri Lanka**
Agriculture (gross)	69.0	89.6	95.7	102.2	123.2	122.0	127.4	128.1	Agriculture (brut)
Food (gross)	64.0	89.4	97.2	102.4	124.8	125.3	130.5	131.2	Produits ailmentaires (brut)
State of Palestine									**État de Palestine**
Agriculture (gross)	...	...	82.2	96.4	75.3	88.2	87.5	87.5	Agriculture (brut)
Food (gross)	...	...	82.3	96.4	75.3	88.2	87.5	87.5	Produits ailmentaires (brut)
Sudan [former]									**Soudan [anc.]**
Agriculture (gross)	38.5	47.5	61.6	101.3	98.5	...	...	...	Agriculture (brut)
Food (gross)	35.3	45.0	61.0	100.9	99.7	...	...	...	Produits ailmentaires (brut)
Suriname									**Suriname**
Agriculture (gross)	90.6	138.8	115.2	98.5	137.3	149.0	144.2	146.5	Agriculture (brut)
Food (gross)	90.5	138.7	115.1	98.5	137.3	149.0	144.2	146.5	Produits ailmentaires (brut)
Sweden									**Suède**
Agriculture (gross)	98.8	112.8	100.4	100.4	94.6	102.2	103.9	100.0	Agriculture (brut)
Food (gross)	98.9	112.9	100.4	100.4	94.5	102.2	103.9	99.9	Produits ailmentaires (brut)
Switzerland									**Suisse**
Agriculture (gross)	97.7	108.5	102.3	99.4	103.2	106.5	103.2	101.5	Agriculture (brut)
Food (gross)	97.6	108.5	102.2	99.4	103.2	106.5	103.2	101.5	Produits ailmentaires (brut)
Syrian Arab Republic									**République arabe syrienne**
Agriculture (gross)	30.9	48.8	65.0	99.6	88.7	63.6	73.4	79.2	Agriculture (brut)
Food (gross)	29.8	48.2	64.5	98.8	91.6	66.9	77.5	83.9	Produits ailmentaires (brut)
Tajikistan									**Tadjikistan**
Agriculture (gross)	...	...	70.4	99.1	123.5	156.3	162.3	159.3	Agriculture (brut)
Food (gross)	...	...	66.5	99.3	137.4	173.6	181.0	177.4	Produits ailmentaires (brut)
Thailand									**Thaïlande**
Agriculture (gross)	41.2	61.6	77.5	98.4	113.6	128.2	121.6	118.3	Agriculture (brut)
Food (gross)	44.7	66.0	80.2	98.3	115.6	125.3	118.2	114.4	Produits ailmentaires (brut)
TFYR of Macedonia									**ex-R.Y. de Macédoine**
Agriculture (gross)	...	...	87.7	99.5	115.3	110.9	121.8	123.2	Agriculture (brut)
Food (gross)	...	...	88.8	99.0	115.3	111.3	123.6	124.8	Produits ailmentaires (brut)
Timor-Leste									**Timor-Leste**
Agriculture (gross)	90.7	83.2	97.8	100.9	123.7	112.5	112.7	111.2	Agriculture (brut)
Food (gross)	99.5	87.3	101.9	100.8	129.0	118.2	118.3	116.8	Produits ailmentaires (brut)

20 Agricultural production indices *(continued)*
Index base: 2004 - 2006 = 100

Indices de la production agricole *(suite)*
Indices base: 2004 - 2006 = 100

Région, pays ou zone	1975	1985	1995	2005	2010	2014	2015	2016	Région, pays ou zone
Togo									**Togo**
Agriculture (gross)	45.0	54.2	75.9	96.8	123.2	141.5	142.5	142.0	Agriculture (brut)
Food (gross)	46.3	52.3	71.8	99.5	129.1	144.1	145.8	145.4	Produits ailmentaires (brut)
Tokelau									**Tokélaou**
Agriculture (gross)	82.2	65.8	90.2	99.9	107.7	112.0	112.9	115.3	Agriculture (brut)
Food (gross)	82.2	65.8	90.2	99.9	107.7	112.0	112.9	115.3	Produits ailmentaires (brut)
Tonga									**Tonga**
Agriculture (gross)	155.2	110.5	96.3	97.5	134.8	134.0	138.6	136.6	Agriçulture (brut)
Food (gross)	155.3	110.5	96.4	97.5	134.8	134.0	138.6	136.6	Produits ailmentaires (brut)
Trinidad and Tobago									**Trinité-et-Tobago**
Agriculture (gross)	109.2	83.6	92.2	98.8	96.2	96.3	96.5	96.0	Agriculture (brut)
Food (gross)	106.6	82.4	92.0	98.8	96.4	96.6	96.8	96.2	Produits ailmentaires (brut)
Tunisia									**Tunisie**
Agriculture (gross)	53.4	60.2	59.1	101.7	106.3	109.4	142.1	117.1	Agriculture (brut)
Food (gross)	53.3	59.8	58.8	101.7	106.4	109.5	142.5	117.2	Produits ailmentaires (brut)
Turkey									**Turquie**
Agriculture (gross)	53.4	69.3	83.1	101.2	109.8	122.1	128.4	129.0	Agriculture (brut)
Food (gross)	52.8	69.2	82.3	101.4	111.3	123.9	130.5	131.2	Produits ailmentaires (brut)
Turkmenistan									**Turkménistan**
Agriculture (gross)	…	…	64.4	103.8	98.3	103.8	99.7	102.0	Agriculture (brut)
Food (gross)	…	…	53.0	102.5	102.0	110.5	105.5	108.4	Produits ailmentaires (brut)
Tuvalu									**Tuvalu**
Agriculture (gross)	48.5	82.6	82.2	100.3	104.1	108.6	109.6	110.7	Agriculture (brut)
Food (gross)	48.5	82.6	82.2	100.3	104.1	108.6	109.6	110.7	Produits ailmentaires (brut)
Uganda									**Ouganda**
Agriculture (gross)	68.2	55.1	76.2	100.4	89.3	94.4	93.8	91.8	Agriculture (brut)
Food (gross)	66.5	54.5	75.7	100.3	88.2	92.0	91.7	89.6	Produits ailmentaires (brut)
Ukraine									**Ukraine**
Agriculture (gross)	…	…	104.3	99.9	106.8	140.6	134.7	153.0	Agriculture (brut)
Food (gross)	…	…	104.1	99.9	106.8	140.6	134.7	153.0	Produits ailmentaires (brut)
United Arab Emirates									**Émirats arabes unis**
Agriculture (gross)	7.4	22.5	67.5	105.5	108.2	83.3	97.7	101.0	Agriculture (brut)
Food (gross)	7.0	22.3	67.5	105.5	108.2	83.3	97.7	101.1	Produits ailmentaires (brut)
United Kingdom									**Royaume-Uni**
Agriculture (gross)	85.7	104.8	106.6	100.3	102.1	108.1	108.2	103.1	Agriculture (brut)
Food (gross)	85.8	105.0	106.6	100.3	102.0	108.1	108.2	103.1	Produits ailmentaires (brut)
United Rep. of Tanzania									**Rép.-Unie de Tanzanie**
Agriculture (gross)	42.7	57.0	68.8	98.1	128.2	181.6	188.2	165.5	Agriculture (brut)
Food (gross)	40.8	57.4	68.3	96.6	129.9	186.0	192.6	168.2	Produits ailmentaires (brut)
United States of America									**États-Unis d'Amérique**
Agriculture (gross)	64.3	78.4	83.8	99.9	105.9	112.1	111.7	116.5	Agriculture (brut)
Food (gross)	64.6	78.7	83.8	99.7	106.8	113.4	113.0	118.0	Produits ailmentaires (brut)
United States Virgin Islands									**Îles Vierges américaines**
Agriculture (gross)	114.7	126.3	92.7	99.2	106.9	109.1	107.2	107.2	Agriculture (brut)
Food (gross)	114.7	126.3	92.7	99.2	106.9	109.1	107.2	107.2	Produits ailmentaires (brut)
Uruguay									**Uruguay**
Agriculture (gross)	56.9	58.7	74.4	101.4	118.6	128.2	128.0	118.3	Agriculture (brut)
Food (gross)	54.6	56.0	71.5	101.5	119.5	129.3	129.1	119.2	Produits ailmentaires (brut)
Uzbekistan									**Ouzbékistan**
Agriculture (gross)	…	…	80.1	99.8	127.4	159.9	168.4	166.5	Agriculture (brut)
Food (gross)	…	…	73.7	98.7	135.0	175.9	186.8	184.5	Produits ailmentaires (brut)
Vanuatu									**Vanuatu**
Agriculture (gross)	80.0	100.5	101.6	100.4	128.4	122.6	122.8	124.0	Agriculture (brut)
Food (gross)	79.9	100.4	101.6	100.4	128.4	122.6	122.8	124.0	Produits ailmentaires (brut)
Venezuela (Boliv. Rep. of)									**Venezuela (Rép. boliv. du)**
Agriculture (gross)	47.5	64.9	79.2	101.3	111.4	121.8	119.7	108.5	Agriculture (brut)
Food (gross)	45.8	63.6	78.4	101.3	111.6	122.7	120.6	109.5	Produits ailmentaires (brut)
Viet Nam									**Viet Nam**
Agriculture (gross)	21.6	36.7	58.2	99.7	119.6	137.3	140.4	138.4	Agriculture (brut)
Food (gross)	22.8	38.7	60.5	100.1	118.5	134.9	137.9	135.5	Produits ailmentaires (brut)
Wallis and Futuna Islands									**Îles Wallis-et-Futuna**
Agriculture (gross)	77.5	83.4	85.7	101.6	104.6	112.0	111.8	111.6	Agriculture (brut)
Food (gross)	77.6	83.4	85.6	101.6	104.6	112.0	111.9	111.7	Produits ailmentaires (brut)
Western Sahara									**Sahara occidental**
Agriculture (gross)	65.5	83.2	96.3	100.4	102.3	98.6	106.6	106.7	Agriculture (brut)
Food (gross)	65.5	83.2	96.3	100.4	102.3	98.6	106.6	106.7	Produits ailmentaires (brut)

20 Agricultural production indices *(continued)*
Index base: 2004 - 2006 = 100

Indices de la production agricole *(suite)*
Indices base: 2004 - 2006 = 100

Région, pays ou zone	1975	1985	1995	2005	2010	2014	2015	2016	Région, pays ou zone
Yemen									**Yémen**
Agriculture (gross)	41.0	45.2	65.3	97.7	135.9	136.7	133.4	140.9	Agriculture (brut)
Food (gross)	40.5	45.6	65.8	97.8	136.3	137.3	133.9	141.4	Produits ailmentaires (brut)
Zambia									**Zambie**
Agriculture (gross)	48.6	50.5	65.6	100.4	164.4	187.4	182.7	182.9	Agriculture (brut)
Food (gross)	53.8	55.2	72.8	98.1	167.0	189.3	183.0	182.4	Produits ailmentaires (brut)
Zimbabwe									**Zimbabwe**
Agriculture (gross)	76.7	99.5	80.0	92.0	97.9	103.5	95.9	100.4	Agriculture (brut)
Food (gross)	74.0	92.8	68.6	89.5	92.0	91.5	83.9	89.1	Produits ailmentaires (brut)
European Union (EU)									**Union européenne (UE)**
Agriculture (gross)	83.1	95.7	95.3	99.0	99.7	103.5	103.2	101.8	Agriculture (brut)
Food (gross)	83.0	95.6	95.2	99.0	99.9	103.6	103.4	102.0	Produits ailmentaires (brut)

Source:

Food and Agriculture Organization of the United Nations (FAO), Rome, FAOSTAT database, last accessed May 2018.

Source:

Organisation des Nations Unies pour l'alimentation et l'agriculture (FAO), Rome, base de données FAOSTAT, dernier accès mai 2018.

1 For statistical purposes, the data for China do not include those for the Hong Kong Special Administrative Region (Hong Kong SAR), Macao Special Administrative Region (Macao SAR) and Taiwan Province of China.

1 Pour la présentation des statistiques, les données pour la Chine ne comprennent pas la région administrative spéciale de Hong Kong (Hong Kong RAS), la région administrative spéciale de Macao (Macao RAS) et la province chinoise de Taïwan.

21 Total imports, exports and balance of trade

Imports CIF, exports FOB and balance: millions of US dollars

Total des importations, des exportations et balance commerciale

Importations CAF, exportations FAB et balance: en millions de dollars É.-U.

Region, country or area [&]	Sys.[t]	1995	2005	2010	2014	2015	2016	2017	Région, pays ou zone [&]
Total, all countries or areas									**Total, tous pays ou zones**
Imports		**5 099 057**	**10 577 013**	**15 261 844**	**18 762 833**	**16 453 455**	**15 960 482**	**17 507 492**	**Importations**
Exports		**5 050 238**	**10 373 445**	**15 100 194**	**18 832 791**	**16 406 967**	**15 860 881**	**17 177 323**	**Exportations**
Balance		**-48 819**	**-203 568**	**-161 649**	**69 958**	**-46 488**	**-99 601**	**-330 169**	**Balance**
Africa									**Afrique**
Imports		114 352	246 228	468 146	614 317	535 592	473 741	480 744	Importations
Exports		103 460	306 656	496 498	557 380	386 097	338 754	355 742	Exportations
Balance		-10 892	60 428	28 352	-56 936	-149 495	-134 987	-125 002	Balance
Northern Africa									**Afrique septentrionale**
Imports		45 062	87 571	181 147	229 144	205 345	182 480	182 306	Importations
Exports		33 043	114 104	165 544	153 120	108 178	99 289	103 249	Exportations
Balance		-12 019	26 533	-15 603	-76 024	-97 167	-83 191	-79 057	Balance
Sub-Saharan Africa									**Afrique subsaharienne**
Imports		69 290	158 657	287 000	385 173	330 248	291 261	298 438	Importations
Exports		70 417	192 552	330 954	404 260	277 919	239 465	252 493	Exportations
Balance		1 127	33 895	43 955	19 087	-52 328	-51 796	-45 945	Balance
Eastern Africa									**Afrique orientale**
Imports		17 980	31 243	62 688	103 477	102 542	82 761	83 747	Importations
Exports		9 499	16 297	31 652	49 358	42 943	37 502	39 658	Exportations
Balance		-8 481	-14 945	-31 036	-54 119	-59 598	-45 259	-44 090	Balance
Middle Africa									**Afrique centrale**
Imports		5 412	18 680	43 623	59 725	45 012	38 230	35 120	Importations
Exports		10 954	48 958	90 717	101 741	63 801	44 496	30 798	Exportations
Balance		5 542	30 278	47 094	42 016	18 789	6 266	-4 322	Balance
Southern Africa									**Afrique australe**
Imports		26 745	63 786	97 572	119 645	97 655	89 836	98 505	Importations
Exports		28 214	56 076	95 227	107 309	82 944	88 295	101 898	Exportations
Balance		1 470	-7 711	-2 345	-12 336	-14 711	-1 541	3 393	Balance
Western Africa									**Afrique occidentale**
Imports		19 153	44 948	83 116	102 326	85 040	80 434	81 066	Importations
Exports		21 750	71 221	113 358	145 852	88 231	69 173	80 140	Exportations
Balance		2 597	26 273	30 241	43 526	3 191	-11 262	-926	Balance
Americas									**Amériques**
Imports		1 178 848	2 557 150	3 228 657	3 988 282	3 733 045	3 554 576	3 815 365	Importations
Exports		997 709	1 835 325	2 550 360	3 179 783	2 838 253	2 731 857	2 956 598	Exportations
Balance		-181 139	-721 825	-678 297	-808 498	-894 792	-822 720	-858 767	Balance
Northern America									**Amérique septentrionale**
Imports		936 343	2 048 668	2 362 939	2 877 573	2 736 892	2 655 399	2 845 929	Importations
Exports		774 525	1 265 374	1 665 222	2 095 899	1 911 586	1 840 742	1 967 911	Exportations
Balance		-161 818	-783 295	-697 718	-781 675	-825 306	-814 657	-878 017	Balance
Latin America & the Caribbean									**Amérique latine et Caraïbes**
Imports		242 505	508 481	865 718	1 110 708	996 153	899 178	969 436	Importations
Exports		223 184	569 951	885 138	1 083 884	926 667	891 115	988 687	Exportations
Balance		-19 321	61 470	19 420	-26 824	-69 486	-8 063	19 250	Balance
Caribbean									**Caraïbes**
Imports		20 945	36 923	51 238	56 358	50 982	49 008	49 571	Importations
Exports		8 346	21 331	24 192	40 215	37 404	37 963	43 533	Exportations
Balance		-12 598	-15 592	-27 045	-16 143	-13 578	-11 045	-6 037	Balance
Central America									**Amérique centrale**
Imports		87 084	259 847	366 171	471 696	464 406	454 798	492 280	Importations
Exports		87 067	233 506	336 529	447 113	426 909	419 845	458 759	Exportations
Balance		-17	-26 340	-29 642	-24 583	-37 497	-34 953	-33 522	Balance
South America									**Amérique du Sud**
Imports		134 476	211 711	448 308	582 655	480 765	395 372	427 585	Importations
Exports		127 771	315 113	524 416	596 556	462 353	433 307	486 394	Exportations
Balance		-6 706	103 402	76 108	13 902	-18 411	37 935	58 809	Balance
Asia									**Asie**
Imports		1 500 432	3 172 210	5 444 317	7 150 655	6 189 526	5 942 566	6 577 637	Importations
Exports		1 557 385	3 569 857	5 893 417	7 694 315	6 845 218	6 538 596	6 963 850	Exportations
Balance		56 953	397 647	449 100	543 660	655 692	596 030	386 213	Balance
Central Asia									**Asie centrale**
Imports		9 375	25 644	40 686	66 212	50 773	46 767	52 271	Importations
Exports		10 782	36 890	74 861	98 648	66 182	55 406	69 031	Exportations
Balance		1 407	11 246	34 175	32 436	15 408	8 639	16 760	Balance

21

Total imports, exports and balance of trade *(continued)*
Imports CIF, exports FOB and balance: millions of US dollars

Total des importations, des exportations et balance commerciale *(suite)*
Importations CAF, exportations FAB et balance: en millions de dollars É.-U.

Region, country or area &	Sys.t	1995	2005	2010	2014	2015	2016	2017	Région, pays ou zone &
Eastern Asia									**Asie orientale**
Imports		804 190	1 744 378	2 967 396	3 916 577	3 317 929	3 163 173	3 600 614	Importations
Exports		894 718	1 937 757	3 219 245	4 137 629	3 942 643	3 761 758	4 069 183	Exportations
Balance		90 528	193 379	251 849	221 053	624 714	598 585	468 569	Balance
South-eastern Asia									**Asie du Sud-Est**
Imports		353 943	584 010	950 481	1 231 251	1 088 638	1 088 037	1 265 884	Importations
Exports		320 454	655 071	1 051 556	1 290 957	1 158 879	1 148 308	1 299 270	Exportations
Balance		-33 489	71 061	101 076	59 706	70 241	60 272	33 386	Balance
Southern Asia									**Asie méridionale**
Imports		74 082	229 179	497 340	639 001	561 542	527 299	514 174	Importations
Exports		65 912	193 182	354 892	467 627	393 497	371 038	317 138	Exportations
Balance		-8 171	-35 997	-142 448	-171 373	-168 046	-156 261	-197 036	Balance
Western Asia									**Asie occidentale**
Imports		155 335	407 407	737 099	1 023 770	942 135	886 360	884 788	Importations
Exports		154 177	557 564	919 156	1 385 890	1 003 998	921 607	891 649	Exportations
Balance		-1 159	150 158	182 058	362 121	61 863	35 247	6 861	Balance
Europe									**Europe**
Imports		2 228 669	4 439 990	5 873 573	6 721 299	5 743 778	5 749 302	6 348 032	Importations
Exports		2 320 042	4 527 059	5 907 021	7 104 971	6 102 296	6 015 274	6 619 661	Exportations
Balance		91 373	87 068	33 447	383 672	358 518	265 972	271 629	Balance
Eastern Europe									**Europe orientale**
Imports		161 835	490 657	867 387	1 054 924	847 830	854 663	1 003 499	Importations
Exports		176 871	594 285	993 297	1 276 700	1 024 049	1 000 018	1 178 501	Exportations
Balance		15 036	103 628	125 910	221 776	176 219	145 355	175 002	Balance
Northern Europe									**Europe septentrionale**
Imports		470 870	937 990	1 122 240	1 283 589	1 133 055	1 141 770	1 204 673	Importations
Exports		494 552	913 599	1 045 978	1 198 220	1 046 684	980 643	1 070 228	Exportations
Balance		23 682	-24 391	-76 262	-85 369	-86 371	-161 128	-134 445	Balance
Southern Europe									**Europe méridionale**
Imports		400 631	861 881	1 039 442	1 075 792	925 618	922 324	1 045 973	Importations
Exports		372 435	660 817	830 354	1 026 036	887 637	899 845	996 859	Exportations
Balance		-28 196	-201 064	-209 088	-49 756	-37 981	-22 479	-49 114	Balance
Western Europe									**Europe occidentale**
Imports		1 195 333	2 149 462	2 844 504	3 306 994	2 837 275	2 830 544	3 093 887	Importations
Exports		1 276 184	2 358 357	3 037 392	3 604 015	3 143 926	3 134 768	3 374 073	Exportations
Balance		80 851	208 895	192 888	297 021	306 651	304 224	280 185	Balance
Oceania									**Océanie**
Imports		76 756	161 435	247 151	288 281	251 513	240 296	285 713	Importations
Exports		71 642	134 548	252 899	296 342	235 103	236 399	281 470	Exportations
Balance		-5 114	-26 888	5 748	8 060	-16 411	-3 897	-4 243	Balance
Australia and New Zealand									**Australie et Nouvelle-Zélande**
Imports		71 338	151 453	231 861	270 042	236 642	225 619	268 570	Importations
Exports		66 374	127 740	243 041	282 080	222 150	223 500	268 213	Exportations
Balance		-4 965	-23 714	11 179	12 038	-14 493	-2 119	-357	Balance
Melanesia									**Mélanésie**
Imports		3 432	5 397	9 665	11 308	7 968	7 505	9 398	Importations
Exports		4 039	5 199	8 112	12 307	10 997	10 856	11 193	Exportations
Balance		607	-197	-1 553	999	3 029	3 351	1 795	Balance
Micronesia									**Micronésie**
Imports		897	2 379	3 292	4 383	4 629	4 949	5 340	Importations
Exports		1 028	1 295	1 508	1 695	1 737	1 785	1 833	Exportations
Balance		131	-1 084	-1 783	-2 688	-2 892	-3 164	-3 507	Balance
Polynesia									**Polynésie**
Imports		1 089	2 206	2 333	2 548	2 275	2 222	2 405	Importations
Exports		201	314	238	259	220	257	231	Exportations
Balance		-887	-1 893	-2 095	-2 289	-2 055	-1 965	-2 174	Balance
Afghanistan									**Afghanistan**
Imports	G	...	...	5 154	7 697	7 723	6 534	* 7 384	Importations
Exports	G	...	...	388	571	571	596	* 700	Exportations
Balance	G	...	...	-4 766	-7 127	-7 151	-5 938	* -6 684	Balance
Albania									**Albanie**
Imports	G	* 713	2 614	4 603	5 230	4 320	4 669	5 826	Importations
Exports	G	* 202	658	1 550	2 431	1 930	1 962	2 262	Exportations
Balance	G	* -511	-1 956	-3 053	-2 799	-2 391	-2 707	-3 565	Balance

Total imports, exports and balance of trade *(continued)*
Imports CIF, exports FOB and balance: millions of US dollars

Total des importations, des exportations et balance commerciale *(suite)*
Importations CAF, exportations FAB et balance: en millions de dollars É.-U.

Region, country or area &	Sys.t	1995	2005	2010	2014	2015	2016	2017	Région, pays ou zone &
Algeria									**Algérie**
Imports	S	10 782	20 357	41 000	58 618	51 803	47 091	46 053	Importations
Exports	S	9 357	46 002	57 051	60 388	34 796	29 992	35 191	Exportations
Balance	S	-1 426	25 645	16 051	1 770	-17 007	-17 099	-10 862	Balance
Andorra									**Andorre**
Imports	S	1 025	* 1 796	1 541	1 556	* 1 295	* 1 355	* 1 480	Importations
Exports	S	48	143	92	95	* 87	* 100	* 120	Exportations
Balance	S	-978	* -1 653	-1 448	-1 461	* -1 209	* -1 255	* -1 360	Balance
Angola [1]									**Angola** [1]
Imports	S	* 1 466	* 8 321	* 18 143	* 28 753	* 16 758	* 7 331	* 3 845	Importations
Exports	S	* 3 592	* 23 835	* 52 612	* 58 672	* 33 048	* 21 161	* 13 311	Exportations
Balance	S	* 2 126	* 15 514	34 469	29 919	16 290	* 13 831	* 9 466	Balance
Anguilla									**Anguilla**
Imports	S	* 53	* 133	* 150	* 175	* 204	* 193	* 194	Importations
Exports	S	* 1	* 7	* 12	* 5	* 11	* 7	* 3	Exportations
Balance	S	* -52	* -126	* -137	* -169	* -193	* -186	* -191	Balance
Antigua and Barbuda									**Antigua-et-Barbuda**
Imports	G	* 344	525	501	552	465	491	630	Importations
Exports	G	* 53	121	35	23	26	61	62	Exportations
Balance	G	* -291	-405	-466	-529	-439	-429	-567	Balance
Argentina									**Argentine**
Imports	S	20 122	28 689	56 792	65 230	59 757	55 610	66 899	Importations
Exports	S	20 963	40 106	68 174	68 407	56 788	57 733	58 384	Exportations
Balance	S	841	11 418	11 382	3 178	-2 969	2 124	-8 515	Balance
Armenia									**Arménie**
Imports	S	* 674	1 692	3 782	4 160	3 257	3 218	4 077	Importations
Exports	S	* 271	937	1 011	1 490	1 483	1 808	2 041	Exportations
Balance	S	* -403	-755	-2 770	-2 669	-1 774	-1 411	-2 035	Balance
Aruba									**Aruba**
Imports	S	* 566	1 030	1 071	1 284	1 165	1 117	* 1 152	Importations
Exports	S	* 15	106	125	116	80	95	* 95	Exportations
Balance	S	* -551	-924	-947	-1 168	-1 085	-1 022	* -1 057	Balance
Australia [1]									**Australie** [1]
Imports	G	* 57 381	125 221	201 703	227 544	200 114	189 406	228 442	Importations
Exports	G	* 52 628	106 011	212 109	240 445	187 792	189 630	230 163	Exportations
Balance	G	* -4 752	-19 210	10 405	12 900	-12 322	224	1 721	Balance
Austria									**Autriche**
Imports	S	* 66 331	119 950	150 593	172 447	147 935	149 987	* 166 551	Importations
Exports	S	* 53 460	117 722	144 882	169 715	145 277	144 701	* 159 785	Exportations
Balance	S	* -12 871	-2 228	-5 711	-2 732	-2 658	-5 287	* -6 766	Balance
Azerbaijan									**Azerbaïdjan**
Imports	G	* 666	4 211	6 597	9 179	9 211	8 516	8 767	Importations
Exports	G	* 637	4 347	21 278	21 752	11 327	9 067	13 798	Exportations
Balance	G	* -30	136	14 682	12 573	2 116	551	5 031	Balance
Bahamas [2]									**Bahamas** [2]
Imports	G	* 1 243	2 567	2 862	3 790	3 161	* 2 903	* 2 660	Importations
Exports	G	* 176	271	620	689	443	* 360	* 280	Exportations
Balance	G	* -1 067	-2 296	-2 242	-3 101	-2 719	* -2 544	* -2 380	Balance
Bahrain									**Bahreïn**
Imports	G	3 679	9 339	16 002	20 074	16 378	14 749	* 12 613	Importations
Exports	G	3 475	10 239	16 059	23 746	16 684	12 892	* 9 666	Exportations
Balance	G	-204	899	58	3 672	307	-1 856	* -2 947	Balance
Bangladesh									**Bangladesh**
Imports	G	5 438	12 631	30 504	* 41 065	48 059	* 50 210	* 47 743	Importations
Exports	G	3 407	9 332	19 231	* 23 070	31 734	* 32 013	* 31 367	Exportations
Balance	G	-2 031	-3 299	-11 273	* -17 995	-16 325	* -18 197	* -16 376	Balance
Barbados									**Barbade**
Imports	G	766	1 672	1 196	1 740	1 618	1 621	1 600	Importations
Exports	G	238	361	314	481	483	517	485	Exportations
Balance	G	-528	-1 311	-883	-1 260	-1 135	-1 104	-1 114	Balance
Belarus									**Bélarus**
Imports	G	* 5 382	16 699	34 884	40 502	30 291	27 610	* 34 235	Importations
Exports	G	* 4 623	15 977	25 283	36 081	26 660	23 537	* 29 207	Exportations
Balance	G	* -759	-722	-9 601	-4 422	-3 631	-4 073	* -5 027	Balance

21

Total imports, exports and balance of trade *(continued)*
Imports CIF, exports FOB and balance: millions of US dollars

Total des importations, des exportations et balance commerciale *(suite)*
Importations CAF, exportations FAB et balance: en millions de dollars É.-U.

Region, country or area [&]	Sys.[t]	1995	2005	2010	2014	2015	2016	2017	Région, pays ou zone [&]
Belgium									**Belgique**
Imports	S	153 388[3]	319 085	391 256	452 773	371 025	372 713	406 412	Importations
Exports	S	168 154[3]	335 692	407 596	472 201	397 739	398 033	429 980	Exportations
Balance	S	14 765[3]	16 606	16 340	19 429	26 714	25 321	23 568	Balance
Belize									**Belize**
Imports	G	259	439	700	962	996	952	913	Importations
Exports	G	162	208	282	358	314	246	278	Exportations
Balance	G	-97	-231	-418	-604	-682	-706	-636	Balance
Benin									**Bénin**
Imports	S	* 745	899	2 134	3 704	2 475	2 630	* 2 690	Importations
Exports	S	* 415	288	534	968	626	410	* 160	Exportations
Balance	S	* -329	-611	-1 600	-2 735	-1 849	-2 220	* -2 530	Balance
Bermuda									**Bermudes**
Imports	G	633	988	970	961	929	971	1 078	Importations
Exports	G	63	* 49	* 15	12	9	8	12	Exportations
Balance	G	-570	* -939	* -955	-949	-920	-963	-1 066	Balance
Bhutan									**Bhoutan**
Imports	G	* 113	387	854	* 934	* 1 062	* 1 003	* 983	Importations
Exports	G	* 103	258	413	* 584	* 549	* 525	* 520	Exportations
Balance	G	* -9	-129	-440	* -351	* -512	* -478	* -463	Balance
Bolivia (Plurin. State of)									**Bolivie (État plurin. de)**
Imports	G	1 396	2 343	5 604	10 492	9 766	8 427	9 302	Importations
Exports	G	1 181	2 797	6 965	12 856	8 726	7 082	7 852	Exportations
Balance	G	-215	454	1 361	2 364	-1 041	-1 345	-1 450	Balance
Bosnia and Herzegovina									**Bosnie-Herzégovine**
Imports	S	* 1 068	7 054	9 223	10 990	8 994	9 142	10 444	Importations
Exports	S	* 152	2 388	4 803	5 891	5 099	5 328	6 367	Exportations
Balance	S	* -917	-4 665	-4 420	-5 100	-3 895	-3 814	-4 078	Balance
Botswana									**Botswana**
Imports	G	…	3 162	5 657	7 830	7 626	6 103	5 283	Importations
Exports	G	…	4 431	4 693	7 915	6 319	7 321	5 898	Exportations
Balance	G	…	1 268	-964	85	-1 307	1 218	615	Balance
Brazil									**Brésil**
Imports	G	53 734	73 600	181 768	229 154	171 446	137 552	150 749	Importations
Exports	G	46 505	118 529	201 915	225 098	191 127	185 235	217 739	Exportations
Balance	G	-7 229	44 928	20 147	-4 056	19 681	47 683	66 990	Balance
British Virgin Islands									**Îles Vierges britanniques**
Imports	G	* 122	* 227	* 313	* 403	* 430	* 457	* 403	Importations
Exports	G	* 11	* ~0	* ~0	* ~0	* ~0	* ~0	* ~0	Exportations
Balance	G	* -110	* -226	* -313	* -403	* -430	* -457	* -403	Balance
Brunei Darussalam									**Brunéi Darussalam**
Imports	S	2 078	* 1 447	2 539	3 599	3 229	2 679	3 085	Importations
Exports	S	2 379	* 6 242	8 908	10 509	6 353	4 875	5 571	Exportations
Balance	S	301	* 4 794	6 369	6 910	3 124	2 197	2 486	Balance
Bulgaria									**Bulgarie**
Imports	S	5 469	18 162	25 360	34 740	29 265	28 875	34 149	Importations
Exports	S	5 220	11 739	20 608	29 387	25 779	26 088	30 182	Exportations
Balance	S	-249	-6 423	-4 752	-5 354	-3 486	-2 787	-3 967	Balance
Burkina Faso									**Burkina Faso**
Imports	G	484	1 161	2 048	3 575	2 980	3 343	* 4 083	Importations
Exports	G	171	332	1 288	2 846	2 177	2 520	* 2 262	Exportations
Balance	G	-313	-828	-760	-729	-802	-823	* -1 821	Balance
Burundi									**Burundi**
Imports	S	270	258	404	673	561	625	725	Importations
Exports	S	179	114	118	142	114	123	142	Exportations
Balance	S	-92	-144	-286	-531	-447	-502	-583	Balance
Cabo Verde									**Cabo Verde**
Imports	G	* 252	438	731	769	606	672	794	Importations
Exports	G	* 9	89	220	357	215	60	50	Exportations
Balance	G	* -243	-349	-511	-412	-391	-612	-744	Balance
Cambodia									**Cambodge**
Imports	S	* 217	2 552	4 903	9 702	10 669	12 371	* 13 155	Importations
Exports	S	* 76	3 019	5 590	6 846	8 542	10 069	* 12 440	Exportations
Balance	S	* -142	467	688	-2 856	-2 126	-2 302	* -716	Balance

21 Total imports, exports and balance of trade *(continued)*
Imports CIF, exports FOB and balance: millions of US dollars

Total des importations, des exportations et balance commerciale *(suite)*
Importations CAF, exportations FAB et balance: en millions de dollars É.-U.

Region, country or area &	Sys.ᵗ	1995	2005	2010	2014	2015	2016	2017	Région, pays ou zone &
Cameroon									**Cameroun**
Imports	S	1 079	2 800	5 133	7 561	6 037	4 899	* 4 224	Importations
Exports	S	1 539	2 849	3 878	5 160	4 053	* 2 984	* 2 433	Exportations
Balance	S	460	49	-1 255	-2 402	-1 984	* -1 915	* -1 791	Balance
Canada [1]									**Canada** [1]
Imports	G	164 371	314 444	392 109	463 089	419 693	402 966	432 721	Importations
Exports	G	191 118	360 552	386 580	475 177	408 804	389 071	420 502	Exportations
Balance	G	26 747	46 108	-5 529	12 088	-10 889	-13 895	-12 219	Balance
Cayman Islands									**Îles Caïmanes**
Imports	G	* 390	* 1 191	* 828	* 977	915	* 941	* 988	Importations
Exports	G	* 4	* 52	* 13	* 26	* 99	* 88	* 79	Exportations
Balance	G	* -386	* -1 138	* -815	* -951	* -817	* -853	* -909	Balance
Central African Republic									**République centrafricaine**
Imports	S	265	185	210	308	457	401	* 333	Importations
Exports	S	120	111	90	21	97	88	* 41	Exportations
Balance	S	-146	-75	-120	-287	-360	-313	* -292	Balance
Chad									**Tchad**
Imports	S	* 214	* 953	* 2 507	* 3 494	* 2 198	* 1 373	* 844	Importations
Exports	S	* 243	* 3 095	* 3 410	* 4 194	* 2 900	* 1 990	* 1 344	Exportations
Balance	S	* 28	* 2 142	* 904	* 700	* 702	* 617	* 499	Balance
Chile									**Chili**
Imports	S	14 903	32 927	59 007	72 850	62 387	58 761	65 062	Importations
Exports	S	15 901	41 973	71 106	75 083	62 033	60 733	69 229	Exportations
Balance	S	998	9 046	12 099	2 234	-354	1 972	4 168	Balance
China [4]									**Chine** [4]
Imports	S	* 131 353	659 953	1 396 002	1 959 235	1 679 564	1 587 921	* 1 844 183	Importations
Exports	S	148 616	761 953	1 577 764	2 342 293	2 273 468	2 097 637	* 2 238 669	Exportations
Balance	S	* 17 263	102 001	181 762	383 058	593 904	509 716	* 394 485	Balance
China, Hong Kong SAR									**Chine, RAS de Hong Kong**
Imports	G	196 072	300 160	441 369	600 613	559 306	547 124	589 824	Importations
Exports	G	173 871	292 119	400 692	524 065	510 553	516 588	550 240	Exportations
Balance	G	-22 201	-8 042	-40 677	-76 548	-48 753	-30 536	-39 584	Balance
China, Macao SAR									**Chine, RAS de Macao**
Imports	G	2 025	4 514	5 629	11 396	10 603	8 924	* 9 449	Importations
Exports	G	2 025	2 474	870	1 240	1 339	1 257	* 1 406	Exportations
Balance	G	-1	-2 040	-4 760	-10 156	-9 264	-7 668	* -8 043	Balance
Colombia									**Colombie**
Imports	G	13 883	21 204	40 683	64 028	54 036	44 831	* 45 878	Importations
Exports	G	10 201	21 190	39 820	54 795	35 691	31 045	* 38 463	Exportations
Balance	G	-3 682	-14	-863	-9 233	-18 345	-13 786	* -7 414	Balance
Comoros									**Comores**
Imports	S	62	85	181	* 43	* 92	* 193	* 167	Importations
Exports	S	11	4	14	* 4	* 9	* 20	* 18	Exportations
Balance	S	-51	-81	-167	* -39	* -83	* -173	* -149	Balance
Congo									**Congo**
Imports	S	556	* 1 342	4 369	3 348	* 4 183	* 9 793	* 12 380	Importations
Exports	S	1 090	* 4 744	6 918	6 550	* 3 536	* 2 540	* 1 387	Exportations
Balance	S	534	* 3 402	2 548	3 202	* -647	* -7 253	* -10 993	Balance
Cook Islands									**Îles Cook**
Imports	G	* 49	81	91	* 121	* 109	* 107	* 130	Importations
Exports	G	* 5	5	5	* 18	* 14	* 13	* 21	Exportations
Balance	G	* -44	-76	-85	* -103	* -95	* -93	* -109	Balance
Costa Rica									**Costa Rica**
Imports	S	3 205	9 173	13 920	17 185	15 504	15 322	* 15 907	Importations
Exports	S	2 702	7 151	9 045	11 243	9 578	9 908	* 10 642	Exportations
Balance	S	-504	-2 023	-4 875	-5 942	-5 926	-5 414	* -5 265	Balance
Côte d'Ivoire									**Côte d'Ivoire**
Imports	S	2 472	5 865	7 849	11 178	9 532	* 7 675	* 9 555	Importations
Exports	S	* 3 736	7 248	10 284	12 985	11 845	* 10 054	* 12 437	Exportations
Balance	S	* 1 264	1 383	2 434	1 807	2 313	* 2 379	* 2 881	Balance
Croatia									**Croatie**
Imports	G	7 509	18 560	20 067	22 907	20 580	21 830	24 513	Importations
Exports	G	4 633	8 773	11 811	13 844	12 844	13 648	15 732	Exportations
Balance	G	-2 877	-9 788	-8 256	-9 063	-7 737	-8 182	-8 780	Balance

21 Total imports, exports and balance of trade *(continued)*

Imports CIF, exports FOB and balance: millions of US dollars

Total des importations, des exportations et balance commerciale *(suite)*

Importations CAF, exportations FAB et balance: en millions de dollars É.-U.

Region, country or area [&]	Sys.[t]	1995	2005	2010	2014	2015	2016	2017	Région, pays ou zone [&]
Cuba									**Cuba**
Imports	S	* 2 874	8 084	* 10 913	* 6 413	* 5 613	* 4 913	* 4 304	Importations
Exports	S	* 1 491	2 319	* 4 945	* 11 703	* 14 515	* 18 003	* 22 329	Exportations
Balance	S	* -1 384	-5 766	* -5 968	* 5 289	* 8 902	* 13 090	* 18 025	Balance
Cyprus									**Chypre**
Imports	G	3 694	6 382	8 645	6 829	5 699	6 604	9 292	Importations
Exports	G	1 231	1 546	1 506	1 924	1 935	1 920	3 368	Exportations
Balance	G	-2 463	-4 836	-7 138	-4 905	-3 764	-4 684	-5 924	Balance
Czechia									**Tchéquie**
Imports	S	25 303	76 527	125 691	153 225	140 716	142 328	162 058	Importations
Exports	S	21 686	78 209	132 141	174 279	157 194	162 087	180 010	Exportations
Balance	S	-3 618	1 681	6 450	21 054	16 478	19 760	17 952	Balance
Dem. People's Rep. Korea									**Rép. pop. dém. de Corée**
Imports	G	* 3 122	* 1 466	* 1 957	* 2 460	* 2 604	* 2 758	* 2 920	Importations
Exports	G	* 1 739	* 787	* 882	* 965	* 987	* 1 010	* 1 033	Exportations
Balance	G	* -1 382	* -679	* -1 075	* -1 495	* -1 617	* -1 748	* -1 887	Balance
Dem. Rep. of the Congo									**Rép. dém. du Congo**
Imports	S	* 869	* 2 268	* 4 500	* 6 494	* 6 196	* 5 907	* 5 655	Importations
Exports	S	* 1 562	* 2 190	* 5 300	* 6 599	* 5 789	* 5 114	* 4 491	Exportations
Balance	S	* 693	* -78	* 800	* 105	* -407	* -793	* -1 165	Balance
Denmark									**Danemark**
Imports	S	43 142	72 716	82 724	99 568	85 327	85 133	92 248	Importations
Exports	S	48 789	82 278	96 217	110 749	94 619	94 355	101 646	Exportations
Balance	S	5 648	9 562	13 492	11 181	9 291	9 222	9 398	Balance
Djibouti									**Djibouti**
Imports	G	* 176	* 277	* 603	* 803	* 890	* 987	* 1 094	Importations
Exports	G	* 13	* 39	* 470	* 129	* 132	* 134	* 137	Exportations
Balance	G	* -163	* -238	* -133	* -674	* -758	* -852	* -956	Balance
Dominica									**Dominique**
Imports	S	117	165	225	* 230	* 214	* 214	* 231	Importations
Exports	S	45	42	34	* 36	* 30	* 23	* 21	Exportations
Balance	S	-72	-124	-190	* -194	* -184	* -191	* -210	Balance
Dominican Republic [1,5]									**République dominicaine** [1,5]
Imports	G	* 3 155	6 804	15 138	17 752	17 348	17 789	19 524	Importations
Exports	G	* 872	6 183	4 767	9 928	8 384	8 745	8 856	Exportations
Balance	G	* -2 283	-621	-10 371	-7 824	-8 964	-9 044	-10 669	Balance
Ecuador									**Équateur**
Imports	G	4 195	9 609	20 591	27 518	21 387	16 189	19 845	Importations
Exports	G	4 361	9 869	17 490	25 724	18 331	16 798	19 122	Exportations
Balance	G	166	261	-3 101	-1 794	-3 057	609	-722	Balance
Egypt [6]									**Égypte** [6]
Imports	G	11 739	19 812	53 003	71 338	74 361	58 053	66 339	Importations
Exports	G	3 444	10 646	26 332	26 812	21 967	22 507	25 943	Exportations
Balance	G	-8 295	-9 166	-26 672	-44 526	-52 394	-35 545	-40 396	Balance
El Salvador									**El Salvador**
Imports	S	2 628	6 809	8 416	10 513	10 415	9 855	10 593	Importations
Exports	S	985	3 436	4 499	5 273	5 485	5 335	5 760	Exportations
Balance	S	-1 642	-3 373	-3 917	-5 240	-4 930	-4 519	-4 833	Balance
Equatorial Guinea									**Guinée équatoriale**
Imports	G	* 50	* 1 309	* 5 679	* 6 492	* 6 010	* 5 457	* 4 887	Importations
Exports	G	* 86	* 7 062	* 9 964	* 11 587	* 9 301	* 7 753	* 6 196	Exportations
Balance	G	* 36	* 5 753	* 4 285	* 5 094	* 3 291	* 2 297	* 1 309	Balance
Eritrea									**Érythrée**
Imports	G	* 432	* 503	* 1 187	* 2 359	* 2 800	* 3 326	* 3 949	Importations
Exports	G	* 73	* 11	* 13	* 15	* 15	* 16	* 16	Exportations
Balance	G	* -359	* -493	* -1 175	* -2 344	* -2 785	* -3 310	* -3 932	Balance
Estonia									**Estonie**
Imports	S	2 546	11 018	13 197	20 185	15 732	* 16 205	17 320	Importations
Exports	S	1 840	8 247	12 811	17 466	13 908	* 14 270	15 353	Exportations
Balance	S	-706	-2 770	-385	-2 719	-1 824	* -1 934	-1 967	Balance
Eswatini									**Eswatini**
Imports	G	...	1 656	* 1 710	* 1 184	* 791	* 541	* 483	Importations
Exports	G	...	1 278	* 1 557	* 1 873	* 1 592	* 1 400	* 1 588	Exportations
Balance	G	...	-378	* -153	* 690	* 801	* 858	* 1 106	Balance

21 Total imports, exports and balance of trade *(continued)*

Imports CIF, exports FOB and balance: millions of US dollars

Total des importations, des exportations et balance commerciale *(suite)*

Importations CAF, exportations FAB et balance: en millions de dollars É.-U.

Region, country or area &	Sys.†	1995	2005	2010	2014	2015	2016	2017	Région, pays ou zone &
Ethiopia									**Éthiopie**
Imports	G	1 141	4 095	8 602	21 914	25 815	19 121	* 16 252	Importations
Exports	G	422	926	2 330	5 667	5 028	1 724	* 1 385	Exportations
Balance	G	-719	-3 169	-6 272	-16 247	-20 788	-17 397	* -14 867	Balance
Falkland Islands (Malvinas)									**Îles Falkland (Malvinas)**
Imports	G	* 27	* 8	* 50	* 26	* 21	* 17	* 13	Importations
Exports	G	* 4	* 11	* 9	* 5	* 4	* 4	* 3	Exportations
Balance	G	* -23	* 2	* -41	* -21	* -17	* -13	* -10	Balance
Faroe Islands									**Îles Féroé**
Imports	G	* 314	747	* 780	* 1 040	* 909	* 978	* 1 066	Importations
Exports	G	* 362	602	* 839	* 1 110	* 1 024	* 1 192	* 1 405	Exportations
Balance	G	* 48	-145	* 59	* 71	* 114	* 214	* 338	Balance
Fiji									**Fidji**
Imports	G	* 891	1 607	1 808	3 250	2 081	2 316	2 420	Importations
Exports	G	* 619	702	841	1 373	895	926	956	Exportations
Balance	G	* -273	-906	-967	-1 877	-1 186	-1 391	-1 464	Balance
Finland									**Finlande**
Imports	G	29 520	58 473	68 767	76 773	60 174	60 502	70 100	Importations
Exports	G	40 409	65 238	70 117	74 339	59 682	57 326	67 281	Exportations
Balance	G	10 889	6 766	1 349	-2 434	-492	-3 176	-2 820	Balance
France									**France**
Imports	S	273 387	475 857[7]	599 172[7]	659 872[7]	563 398[7]	560 555[7]	* 617 386[7]	Importations
Exports	S	277 079	434 354[7]	511 651[7]	566 656[7]	493 941[7]	488 885[7]	* 526 267[7]	Exportations
Balance	S	3 692	-41 503[7]	-87 520[7]	-93 216[7]	-69 457[7]	-71 670[7]	* -91 119[7]	Balance
French Guiana [8]									**Guyane française [8]**
Imports	S	783	...	...	...	...	...	...	Importations
Exports	S	158	...	...	...	...	...	...	Exportations
Balance	S	-625	...	...	...	...	...	...	Balance
French Polynesia									**Polynésie française**
Imports	S	* 848	1 702	1 726	1 762	1 527	* 1 491	* 1 638	Importations
Exports	S	* 173	210	153	170	130	* 173	* 153	Exportations
Balance	S	* -675	-1 491	-1 573	-1 592	-1 397	* -1 319	* -1 485	Balance
Gabon									**Gabon**
Imports	S	* 884	1 451	* 2 969	* 3 104	* 3 032	* 2 931	* 2 805	Importations
Exports	S	* 2 718	5 068	* 8 539	* 8 949	* 5 069	* 2 854	* 1 584	Exportations
Balance	S	* 1 834	3 617	* 5 570	* 5 844	* 2 037	* -77	* -1 220	Balance
Gambia									**Gambie**
Imports	G	215	260	284	387	* 395	384	* 386	Importations
Exports	G	19	7	68	104	* 122	94	* 120	Exportations
Balance	G	-196	-252	-215	-283	* -273	-290	* -265	Balance
Georgia									**Géorgie**
Imports	G	396	2 490	5 236	8 602	7 730	7 236	7 982	Importations
Exports	G	152	865	1 677	2 861	2 205	2 114	2 728	Exportations
Balance	G	-245	-1 624	-3 558	-5 741	-5 525	-5 122	-5 254	Balance
Germany									**Allemagne**
Imports	S	464 145	779 819	1 066 817	1 214 956	1 057 616	1 060 672	1 173 628	Importations
Exports	S	518 224	977 132	1 271 096	1 498 158	1 328 549	1 340 752	1 450 215	Exportations
Balance	S	54 079	197 313	204 280	283 202	270 933	280 080	276 587	Balance
Ghana									**Ghana**
Imports	G	* 1 897	4 878	8 057	* 13 104	* 12 450	11 361	* 10 124	Importations
Exports	G	* 1 755	3 060	5 233	* 13 351	* 12 132	10 656	* 7 982	Exportations
Balance	G	* -142	-1 819	-2 824	* 246	* -318	-705	* -2 141	Balance
Gibraltar									**Gibraltar**
Imports		* 408	* 501	* 627	* 701	* 776	* 861	* 743	Importations
Exports		* 114	* 195	* 259	* 267	* 295	* 327	* 362	Exportations
Balance		* -294	* -306	* -368	* -434	* -480	* -535	* -382	Balance
Greece									**Grèce**
Imports	S	25 805	54 894	66 453	62 181	47 264	47 595	55 301	Importations
Exports	S	* 10 896	17 434	27 586	35 755	28 289	27 811	32 155	Exportations
Balance	S	* -14 909	-37 459	-38 867	-26 425	-18 975	-19 784	-23 146	Balance
Greenland									**Groenland**
Imports	G	421	700	854	768	586	623	* 743	Importations
Exports	G	364	402	391	540	395	553	* 549	Exportations
Balance	G	-57	-297	-463	-228	-191	-71	* -194	Balance

Total imports, exports and balance of trade *(continued)*
Imports CIF, exports FOB and balance: millions of US dollars

Total des importations, des exportations et balance commerciale *(suite)*
Importations CAF, exportations FAB et balance: en millions de dollars É.-U.

Region, country or area &	Sys.†	1995	2005	2010	2014	2015	2016	2017	Région, pays ou zone &
Grenada									**Grenade**
Imports	S	129	334	* 306	* 340	* 372	* 350	* 419	Importations
Exports	S	22	28	* 25	* 37	* 33	* 30	* 23	Exportations
Balance	S	-107	-306	* -281	* -303	* -339	* -321	* -396	Balance
Guadeloupe [8]									**Guadeloupe [8]**
Imports	S	1 901	...	...	...	...	...	...	Importations
Exports	S	162	...	...	...	...	...	...	Exportations
Balance	S	-1 739	...	...	...	...	...	...	Balance
Guatemala									**Guatemala**
Imports	S	3 292	10 500	13 830	18 263	17 637	16 979	* 18 190	Importations
Exports	S	1 936	5 381	8 460	10 891	10 677	10 591	* 11 108	Exportations
Balance	S	-1 357	-5 119	-5 370	-7 373	-6 960	-6 387	* -7 082	Balance
Guinea									**Guinée**
Imports	S	819	1 648	* 1 405	2 509	2 139	* 2 122	* 2 065	Importations
Exports	S	702	796	* 1 471	1 947	1 574	* 1 743	* 1 942	Exportations
Balance	S	-117	-852	* 66	-563	-565	* -378	* -123	Balance
Guinea-Bissau									**Guinée-Bissau**
Imports	G	* 134	112	* 197	* 230	* 221	* 212	* 204	Importations
Exports	G	* 45	23	* 120	* 339	* 548	* 885	* 1 430	Exportations
Balance	G	* -89	-88	* -77	* 109	* 327	* 673	* 1 226	Balance
Guyana									**Guyana**
Imports	S	* 472	778	1 452	1 783	2 186	1 625	1 762	Importations
Exports	S	* 455	539	901	1 174	1 286	1 453	1 790	Exportations
Balance	S	* -17	-239	-551	-609	-900	-172	28	Balance
Haiti									**Haïti**
Imports	G	650	* 1 449	* 3 147	* 3 734	* 3 523	* 3 405	* 3 470	Importations
Exports	G	35	* 470	* 579	* 950	* 1 018	* 982	* 941	Exportations
Balance	G	-615	* -979	* -2 568	* -2 785	* -2 505	* -2 423	* -2 530	Balance
Honduras									**Honduras**
Imports	S	1 728	4 419	6 895	7 984	8 381	7 912	8 612	Importations
Exports	S	656	1 294	3 104	4 533	4 201	4 085	4 970	Exportations
Balance	S	-1 072	-3 125	-3 791	-3 450	-4 179	-3 827	-3 642	Balance
Hungary									**Hongrie**
Imports	S	15 186	65 920	87 432	104 178	90 761	92 044	104 284	Importations
Exports	S	12 452	62 272	94 749	112 536	100 297	103 071	113 382	Exportations
Balance	S	-2 734	-3 648	7 317	8 358	9 536	11 027	9 098	Balance
Iceland									**Islande**
Imports	G	1 751	4 979	3 914	5 372	5 285	5 703	6 945	Importations
Exports	G	1 803	3 091	4 603	5 051	4 722	4 450	4 850	Exportations
Balance	G	51	-1 888	689	-321	-563	-1 254	-2 094	Balance
India [9]									**Inde [9]**
Imports	G	36 592	140 862	350 029	459 369	390 745	356 705	337 414	Importations
Exports	G	31 699	100 353	220 408	317 545	264 381	260 327	216 913	Exportations
Balance	G	-4 893	-40 509	-129 621	-141 825	-126 364	-96 378	-120 501	Balance
Indonesia									**Indonésie**
Imports	S	40 629	57 701	135 663	178 179	142 695	135 653	157 388	Importations
Exports	S	45 418	85 660	157 779	176 036	150 366	144 490	168 810	Exportations
Balance	S	4 789	27 959	22 116	-2 143	7 671	8 837	11 422	Balance
Iran (Islamic Republic of) [10,11]									**Iran (Rép. islamique d') [10,11]**
Imports	S	* 13 882	* 38 869	54 697	* 53 563	* 42 488	* 35 342	* 29 519	Importations
Exports	S	* 18 360	60 012	83 785	* 88 795	* 62 928	* 45 629	* 33 103	Exportations
Balance	S	* 4 478	21 143	29 088	* 35 232	* 20 439	* 10 286	* 3 585	Balance
Iraq									**Iraq**
Imports	S	* 445	* 12 861	31 764	37 064	32 667	45 831	* 40 362	Importations
Exports	S	* 555	19 773	52 483	84 506	49 403	43 774	* 24 266	Exportations
Balance	S	* 110	* 6 912	20 718	47 442	16 736	-2 056	* -16 096	Balance
Ireland									**Irlande**
Imports	G	32 321	70 284	64 601	82 595	77 795	82 029	88 828	Importations
Exports	G	43 789	110 003	120 645	123 071	124 731	132 010	138 072	Exportations
Balance	G	11 468	39 719	56 045	40 476	46 935	49 981	49 244	Balance
Israel [12]									**Israël [12]**
Imports	S	* 28 328	45 032	59 194	72 332	62 068	65 803	69 693	Importations
Exports	S	* 19 046	42 771	58 413	68 965	64 062	60 571	53 791	Exportations
Balance	S	* -9 282	-2 262	-781	-3 367	1 994	-5 232	-15 901	Balance

21 Total imports, exports and balance of trade *(continued)*
Imports CIF, exports FOB and balance: millions of US dollars

Total des importations, des exportations et balance commerciale *(suite)*
Importations CAF, exportations FAB et balance: en millions de dollars É.-U.

Region, country or area[&]	Sys.[t]	1995	2005	2010	2014	2015	2016	2017	Région, pays ou zone[&]
Italy									**Italie**
Imports	S	200 320	384 836	486 984	474 083	410 933	404 578	451 416	Importations
Exports	S	230 441	372 957	446 840	529 529	456 989	461 529	503 054	Exportations
Balance	S	30 122	-11 878	-40 145	55 446	46 055	56 951	51 638	Balance
Jamaica									**Jamaïque**
Imports	G	2 773	4 885	5 225	5 836	4 993	4 767	5 818	Importations
Exports	G	1 424	1 514	1 328	1 452	1 263	1 202	1 310	Exportations
Balance	G	-1 349	-3 370	-3 898	-4 384	-3 730	-3 565	-4 508	Balance
Japan									**Japon**
Imports	G	336 094	515 866	694 059	812 185	625 568	606 924	671 474	Importations
Exports	G	442 937	594 941	769 774	690 217	624 874	644 932	698 097	Exportations
Balance	G	106 843	79 074	75 715	-121 967	-695	38 008	26 623	Balance
Jordan									**Jordanie**
Imports	G	3 696	10 455	15 262	22 740	20 475	19 207	20 407	Importations
Exports	G	1 769	4 284	7 023	8 385	7 833	7 509	7 469	Exportations
Balance	G	-1 928	-6 170	-8 239	-14 355	-12 642	-11 698	-12 938	Balance
Kazakhstan									**Kazakhstan**
Imports	G	3 805	17 333	24 024	41 295	30 567	25 175	29 346	Importations
Exports	G	5 227	27 846	57 244	79 459	45 954	36 775	48 342	Exportations
Balance	G	1 422	10 513	33 220	38 163	15 387	11 601	18 996	Balance
Kenya									**Kenya**
Imports	G	2 818	5 846	12 093	* 18 437	* 16 097	* 14 098	* 16 652	Importations
Exports	G	1 826	3 420	5 169	* 5 690	* 5 908	* 5 695	* 5 805	Exportations
Balance	G	-992	-2 426	-6 924	* -12 748	* -10 189	* -8 403	* -10 847	Balance
Kiribati									**Kiribati**
Imports	G	34	74	73	116	111	117	* 183	Importations
Exports	G	7	4	4	10	10	11	* 11	Exportations
Balance	G	-27	-70	-69	-106	-101	-107	* -172	Balance
Kuwait									**Koweït**
Imports	S	7 790	* 15 801	22 691	31 489	31 907	30 820	33 590	Importations
Exports	S	12 944	* 44 869	62 698	101 132	55 162	46 242	54 807	Exportations
Balance	S	5 155	* 29 068	40 007	69 643	23 254	15 422	21 217	Balance
Kyrgyzstan									**Kirghizistan**
Imports	S	522	1 108	3 223	* 5 674	4 068	3 844	4 474	Importations
Exports	S	412	672	1 488	* 1 638	1 441	1 423	1 784	Exportations
Balance	S	-110	-436	-1 734	* -4 036	-2 627	-2 421	-2 690	Balance
Lao People's Dem. Rep.									**Rép. dém. populaire lao**
Imports	S	* 588	* 874	1 837	4 452	3 778	4 107	* 4 804	Importations
Exports	S	* 311	* 552	1 909	2 572	2 985	3 124	* 2 759	Exportations
Balance	S	* -277	* -322	72	-1 880	-793	-983	* -2 045	Balance
Latvia									**Lettonie**
Imports	S	1 818	8 770	11 143	16 798	13 850	13 593	15 886	Importations
Exports	S	1 305	5 303	8 851	13 603	11 491	11 470	12 895	Exportations
Balance	S	-513	-3 468	-2 292	-3 196	-2 359	-2 123	-2 991	Balance
Lebanon									**Liban**
Imports	G	* 7 295	9 327	17 970	20 487	* 18 069	18 703	* 19 579	Importations
Exports	G	* 826	1 879	4 254	3 312	* 2 151	2 977	* 2 843	Exportations
Balance	G	* -6 469	-7 448	-13 716	-17 175	* -15 919	-15 726	* -16 736	Balance
Lesotho									**Lesotho**
Imports	G	...	* 1 410	1 277	* 2 207	* 1 949	* 1 726	* 1 608	Importations
Exports	G	...	* 650	503	* 924	* 773	* 648	* 571	Exportations
Balance	G	...	* -760	-773	* -1 283	* -1 177	* -1 079	* -1 036	Balance
Liberia									**Libéria**
Imports	S	* 358	* 309	* 710	* 1 045	* 899	* 761	* 464	Importations
Exports	S	* 452	* 130	* 222	* 579	* 627	* 649	* 697	Exportations
Balance	S	* 94	* -179	* -488	* -465	* -272	* -113	* 233	Balance
Libya									**Libye**
Imports	G	* 4 912	* 6 058	17 674	* 18 991	* 12 999	* 8 789	* 5 743	Importations
Exports	G	* 9 363	* 31 272	36 440	* 20 994	* 9 717	* 4 902	* 2 273	Exportations
Balance	G	* 4 451	* 25 215	18 766	* 2 003	* -3 282	* -3 887	* -3 470	Balance
Lithuania									**Lituanie**
Imports	G	3 649	15 704	23 378	35 217	28 176	27 349	32 530	Importations
Exports	G	2 706	12 070	20 814	32 394	25 411	25 023	29 910	Exportations
Balance	G	-943	-3 634	-2 564	-2 823	-2 765	-2 326	-2 620	Balance

21 Total imports, exports and balance of trade *(continued)*

Imports CIF, exports FOB and balance: millions of US dollars

Total des importations, des exportations et balance commerciale *(suite)*

Importations CAF, exportations FAB et balance: en millions de dollars É.-U.

Region, country or area [&]	Sys.[t]	1995	2005	2010	2014	2015	2016	2017	Région, pays ou zone [&]
Luxembourg									**Luxembourg**
Imports	S	...	17 586	20 400	23 850	19 296	19 124	21 071	Importations
Exports	S	...	12 715	13 911	14 791	12 626	12 838	13 959	Exportations
Balance	S	...	-4 871	-6 489	-9 059	-6 671	-6 285	-7 112	Balance
Madagascar									**Madagascar**
Imports	S	550	1 686	2 546	3 355	2 961	2 965	* 2 820	Importations
Exports	S	360	836	1 082	2 243	2 164	2 256	* 2 312	Exportations
Balance	S	-190	-850	-1 464	-1 112	-796	-709	* -508	Balance
Malawi									**Malawi**
Imports	G	500	1 165	2 173	2 774	2 312	* 1 416	* 999	Importations
Exports	G	433	495	1 066	1 342	1 080	* 1 023	* 941	Exportations
Balance	G	-67	-670	-1 107	-1 432	-1 232	* -394	* -57	Balance
Malaysia									**Malaisie**
Imports	G	77 046	114 290	164 586	208 823	176 175	168 375	193 856	Importations
Exports	G	73 778	141 624	198 791	234 135	200 211	189 414	216 428	Exportations
Balance	G	-3 267	27 334	34 204	25 312	24 036	21 039	22 572	Balance
Maldives									**Maldives**
Imports	G	268	745	1 095	1 993	1 897	2 128	* 2 338	Importations
Exports	G	50	154	74	145	144	140	* 175	Exportations
Balance	G	-218	-591	-1 021	-1 848	-1 753	-1 988	* -2 163	Balance
Mali									**Mali**
Imports	S	* 774	1 544	4 704	* 3 154	* 3 169	3 845	* 5 000	Importations
Exports	S	* 443	1 075	1 996	* 2 475	* 2 530	2 848	* 1 902	Exportations
Balance	S	* -331	-468	-2 707	* -679	* -639	-998	* -3 098	Balance
Malta									**Malte**
Imports	G	2 942	3 865	5 732	8 445	6 788	7 182	* 6 827	Importations
Exports	G	1 913	2 431	3 717	4 971	3 915	4 039	* 3 193	Exportations
Balance	G	-1 029	-1 435	-2 015	-3 474	-2 873	-3 143	* -3 634	Balance
Marshall Islands									**Îles Marshall**
Imports	G	* 75	* 68	* 76	* 83	* 84	* 86	* 60	Importations
Exports	G	* 23	* 11	* 17	* 23	* 25	* 28	* 26	Exportations
Balance	G	* -52	* -57	* -60	* -59	* -59	* -59	* -35	Balance
Martinique [8]									**Martinique** [8]
Imports	S	1 970	...	...	...	...	...	...	Importations
Exports	S	242	...	...	...	...	...	...	Exportations
Balance	S	-1 728	...	...	...	...	...	...	Balance
Mauritania									**Mauritanie**
Imports	S	* 326	1 342	1 708	3 642	* 3 677	2 174	3 522	Importations
Exports	S	* 550	556	1 819	2 140	* 1 522	1 623	1 989	Exportations
Balance	S	* 225	-786	111	-1 502	* -2 156	-551	-1 533	Balance
Mauritius									**Maurice**
Imports	G	2 000	3 160	4 402	5 607	4 458	4 655	5 269	Importations
Exports	G	1 538	2 144	1 850	2 663	2 481	2 194	2 103	Exportations
Balance	G	-462	-1 016	-2 553	-2 944	-1 977	-2 461	-3 167	Balance
Mayotte									**Mayotte**
Imports	G	...	309	...	...	...	...	...	Importations
Exports	G	...	6	...	...	...	...	...	Exportations
Balance	G	...	-303	...	...	...	...	...	Balance
Mexico [1,13]									**Mexique** [1,13]
Imports	G	72 453	221 819	301 482	399 977	395 232	387 064	420 369	Importations
Exports	G	79 541	214 207	298 305	396 882	380 638	373 893	409 451	Exportations
Balance	G	7 088	-7 612	-3 177	-3 095	-14 595	-13 172	-10 918	Balance
Micronesia (Fed. States of) [1]									**Micronésie (États féd. de)** [1]
Imports	S	* 100	128	168	* 117	* 68	* 40	* 23	Importations
Exports	S	* 43	13	23	* 15	* 11	* 6	* 3	Exportations
Balance	S	* -56	-115	-145	* -102	* -58	* -34	* -20	Balance
Mongolia									**Mongolie**
Imports	G	* 415	1 183	* 3 172	5 131	3 797	3 340	* 4 295	Importations
Exports	G	* 473	1 064	* 2 883	5 774	4 669	4 916	* 6 112	Exportations
Balance	G	* 58	-118	* -289	643	873	1 577	* 1 817	Balance
Montenegro									**Monténégro**
Imports	S	...	...	2 182	2 367	2 050	2 263	2 611	Importations
Exports	S	...	...	437	441	353	354	421	Exportations
Balance	S	...	...	-1 745	-1 926	-1 697	-1 908	-2 190	Balance

21

Total imports, exports and balance of trade *(continued)*
Imports CIF, exports FOB and balance: millions of US dollars

Total des importations, des exportations et balance commerciale *(suite)*
Importations CAF, exportations FAB et balance: en millions de dollars É.-U.

Region, country or area [&]	Sys.[t]	1995	2005	2010	2014	2015	2016	2017	Région, pays ou zone [&]
Montserrat									**Montserrat**
Imports	S	* 51	30	* 29	42	* 39	* 36	* 29	Importations
Exports	S	* 2	1	1	3	* 3	* 4	* 5	Exportations
Balance	S	* -49	-28	-28	-39	* -36	* -32	* -24	Balance
Morocco									**Maroc**
Imports	S	8 540	20 803	35 379	46 192	37 546	41 696	* 34 293	Importations
Exports	S	4 719	11 185	17 765	23 816	22 037	22 858	* 21 249	Exportations
Balance	S	-3 822	-9 618	-17 614	-22 376	-15 509	-18 838	* -13 044	Balance
Mozambique									**Mozambique**
Imports	S	727	2 408	3 564	8 743	7 908	5 295	* 3 352	Importations
Exports	S	174	1 745	2 243	4 725	3 196	3 352	* 3 296	Exportations
Balance	S	-553	-663	-1 321	-4 018	-4 712	-1 943	* -57	Balance
Myanmar									**Myanmar**
Imports	G	* 1 346	* 1 907	4 164	16 220	16 907	15 696	19 253	Importations
Exports	G	* 860	* 3 776	7 625	11 452	12 197	11 673	13 879	Exportations
Balance	G	* -487	* 1 869	3 461	-4 768	-4 710	-4 023	-5 375	Balance
Namibia									**Namibie**
Imports	G	...	2 525	5 980	8 531	7 697	6 721	* 8 101	Importations
Exports	G	...	2 726	5 848	5 984	4 628	4 816	* 5 573	Exportations
Balance	G	...	201	-131	-2 547	-3 069	-1 905	* -2 529	Balance
Nepal									**Népal**
Imports	G	* 1 330	* 2 282	5 116	7 590	6 612	8 879	10 038	Importations
Exports	G	* 345	* 863	874	901	660	729	741	Exportations
Balance	G	* -985	* -1 419	-4 242	-6 689	-5 952	-8 150	-9 297	Balance
Netherlands									**Pays-Bas**
Imports	S	157 929	310 591	439 987	508 042	424 851	398 336	* 441 338	Importations
Exports	S	177 626	349 813	492 646	571 348	473 834	444 867	* 494 558	Exportations
Balance	S	19 697	39 222	52 659	63 305	48 983	46 531	* 53 220	Balance
Netherlands Antilles [former]									**Antilles néerlandaises [anc.]**
Imports	S	* 1 830	894	* 1 254	...	...	...	...	Importations
Exports	S	* 1 354	91	* 109	...	...	...	...	Exportations
Balance	S	* -476	-803	* -1 145	...	...	...	...	Balance
New Caledonia									**Nouvelle-Calédonie**
Imports	S	* 840	1 774	3 303	3 315	2 529	* 2 257	* 2 515	Importations
Exports	S	* 570	1 114	1 268	1 619	1 239	* 1 267	* 1 460	Exportations
Balance	S	* -270	-660	-2 036	-1 696	-1 291	* -989	* -1 055	Balance
New Zealand									**Nouvelle-Zélande**
Imports	G	13 958	26 232	30 158	42 498	36 528	36 213	40 128	Importations
Exports	G	13 745	21 729	30 932	41 636	34 357	33 870	38 050	Exportations
Balance	G	-212	-4 504	774	-862	-2 171	-2 343	-2 078	Balance
Nicaragua									**Nicaragua**
Imports	G	1 009	2 536	4 191	5 746	5 866	7 476	7 704	Importations
Exports	G	509	866	1 848	4 974	4 667	4 592	4 926	Exportations
Balance	G	-500	-1 670	-2 343	-773	-1 199	-2 884	-2 778	Balance
Niger									**Niger**
Imports	S	345	736	2 273	2 151	2 458	1 861	* 1 617	Importations
Exports	S	273	486	479	1 050	790	927	* 639	Exportations
Balance	S	-71	-250	-1 794	-1 101	-1 669	-933	* -978	Balance
Nigeria									**Nigéria**
Imports	G	* 8 221	* 21 314	44 235	46 532	* 34 912	35 194	31 270	Importations
Exports	G	* 12 342	* 55 145	86 568	102 878	* 50 108	32 883	44 466	Exportations
Balance	G	* 4 121	* 33 831	42 333	56 346	* 15 196	-2 311	13 196	Balance
Northern Mariana Islands									**Îles Mariannes du Nord**
Imports	G	* 628	* 1 952	* 2 867	* 3 902	* 4 215	* 4 553	* 4 916	Importations
Exports	G	* 941	* 1 254	* 1 453	* 1 635	* 1 684	* 1 735	* 1 787	Exportations
Balance	G	* 313	* -699	* -1 414	* -2 266	* -2 531	* -2 818	* -3 129	Balance
Norway									**Norvège**
Imports	G	32 706	55 488	77 330	89 439	77 193	72 810	85 526	Importations
Exports	G	41 740	103 759	130 657	144 611	104 800	89 628	101 976	Exportations
Balance	G	9 034	48 271	53 327	55 172	27 607	16 819	16 450	Balance
Oman									**Oman**
Imports	G	4 249	8 970	19 775	29 303	29 007	23 260	* 18 893	Importations
Exports	G	5 917	18 692	36 600	50 718	31 927	24 455	* 17 652	Exportations
Balance	G	1 669	9 722	16 825	21 415	2 919	1 195	* -1 241	Balance

21 Total imports, exports and balance of trade *(continued)*
Imports CIF, exports FOB and balance: millions of US dollars

Total des importations, des exportations et balance commerciale *(suite)*
Importations CAF, exportations FAB et balance: en millions de dollars É.-U.

Region, country or area &	Sys.t	1995	2005	2010	2014	2015	2016	2017	Région, pays ou zone &
Other non-specified areas									**Autres zones non-spécifiées**
Imports		103 506	181 592	251 315	273 845	228 508	230 930	* 259 906	Importations
Exports		111 343	189 393	273 706	313 563	280 019	280 479	* 317 579	Exportations
Balance		7 838	7 801	22 391	39 718	51 511	49 549	* 57 673	Balance
Pakistan									**Pakistan**
Imports	G	11 704	25 097	37 537	47 545	43 990	46 998	57 440	Importations
Exports	G	8 158	16 050	21 413	24 722	22 089	20 534	21 878	Exportations
Balance	G	-3 546	-9 046	-16 124	-22 823	-21 901	-26 464	-35 562	Balance
Palau									**Palaos**
Imports	S	* 60	* 156	107	165	150	154	158	Importations
Exports	S	* 14	* 14	* 12	11	6	7	6	Exportations
Balance	S	* -47	* -143	* -96	-154	-144	-147	-151	Balance
Panama									**Panama**
Imports	S	2 511	4 152	16 737	11 066	10 375	9 238	* 9 992	Importations
Exports	S	577	963	10 987	12 960	11 348	11 195	* 11 624	Exportations
Balance	S	-1 933	-3 189	-5 751	1 894	973	1 957	* 1 632	Balance
Papua New Guinea									**Papouasie-Nvl-Guinée**
Imports	G	* 1 451	* 1 728	* 3 950	* 3 935	* 2 537	* 2 101	* 3 578	Importations
Exports	G	* 2 653	* 3 276	* 5 742	* 8 793	* 8 423	* 8 176	* 8 240	Exportations
Balance	G	* 1 202	* 1 548	* 1 792	* 4 859	* 5 887	* 6 074	* 4 661	Balance
Paraguay									**Paraguay**
Imports	S	3 136	3 274	10 033	12 169	10 291	9 753	11 873	Importations
Exports	S	919	3 153	6 517	9 636	8 328	8 501	8 680	Exportations
Balance	S	-2 217	-121	-3 517	-2 533	-1 964	-1 251	-3 194	Balance
Peru 1									**Pérou** 1
Imports	S	7 584	12 502	29 966	42 177	38 026	36 148	39 764	Importations
Exports	S	5 440	17 114	35 807	38 646	33 667	36 310	44 238	Exportations
Balance	S	-2 144	4 612	5 842	-3 531	-4 359	162	4 474	Balance
Philippines									**Philippines**
Imports	G	28 487	49 487	58 468	67 719	70 153	85 909	101 889	Importations
Exports	G	17 447	41 255	51 498	61 810	58 648	56 313	68 713	Exportations
Balance	G	-11 040	-8 233	-6 970	-5 909	-11 505	-29 596	-33 177	Balance
Poland									**Pologne**
Imports	S	29 019	101 539	174 128	216 687	189 696	188 518	217 979	Importations
Exports	S	22 862	89 378	157 065	214 477	194 461	196 455	221 308	Exportations
Balance	S	-6 157	-12 161	-17 063	-2 210	4 765	7 937	3 329	Balance
Portugal									**Portugal**
Imports	S	33 565	63 904	77 682	78 396	66 871	67 632	77 834	Importations
Exports	S	23 370	38 672	49 414	63 834	55 259	55 677	62 170	Exportations
Balance	S	-10 195	-25 232	-28 268	-14 562	-11 612	-11 955	-15 664	Balance
Qatar									**Qatar**
Imports	S	3 398	10 061	23 240	30 448	32 610	32 060	* 29 451	Importations
Exports	S	3 557	25 762	74 964	131 592	77 971	57 311	* 67 444	Exportations
Balance	S	159	15 702	51 725	101 144	45 361	25 250	* 37 993	Balance
Republic of Korea									**République de Corée**
Imports	G	135 109	261 236	425 208	525 557	436 487	406 182	478 469	Importations
Exports	G	* 125 056	284 418	466 381	573 075	526 753	495 418	573 627	Exportations
Balance	G	* -10 052	23 183	41 173	47 518	90 266	89 236	95 158	Balance
Republic of Moldova									**République de Moldova**
Imports	G	841	2 292	3 855	5 317	3 987	4 020	4 831	Importations
Exports	G	746	1 091	1 541	2 340	1 967	2 045	2 425	Exportations
Balance	G	-95	-1 201	-2 314	-2 977	-2 020	-1 976	-2 406	Balance
Réunion 8									**Réunion** 8
Imports	S	2 711	...	...	...	...	...	...	Importations
Exports	S	209	...	...	...	...	...	...	Exportations
Balance	S	-2 502	...	...	...	...	...	...	Balance
Romania									**Roumanie**
Imports	S	10 278	40 463	62 007	77 889	69 858	74 605	85 318	Importations
Exports	S	7 910	27 730	49 413	69 878	60 605	63 581	70 627	Exportations
Balance	S	-2 368	-12 733	-12 593	-8 011	-9 253	-11 024	-14 691	Balance
Russian Federation									**Fédération de Russie**
Imports	G	* 46 710	98 707	228 912	286 649	182 782	182 257	228 213	Importations
Exports	G	* 79 869	241 452	397 068	497 834	343 908	* 309 228	* 403 406	Exportations
Balance	G	* 33 159	142 744	168 156	211 185	161 126	* 126 970	* 175 194	Balance

21

Total imports, exports and balance of trade *(continued)*
Imports CIF, exports FOB and balance: millions of US dollars

Total des importations, des exportations et balance commerciale *(suite)*
Importations CAF, exportations FAB et balance: en millions de dollars É.-U.

Region, country or area [&]	Sys.[t]	1995	2005	2010	2014	2015	2016	2017	Région, pays ou zone [&]
Rwanda									**Rwanda**
Imports	G	* 241	374	1 405	1 954	1 858	1 778	* 1 794	Importations
Exports	G	* 8	150	242	653	579	622	* 984	Exportations
Balance	G	* -233	-224	-1 163	-1 301	-1 279	-1 157	* -810	Balance
Saint Helena [14]									**Sainte-Hélène [14]**
Imports	G	* 13	* 12	* 20	* 33	* 41	* 48	* 55	Importations
Exports	G	* 1	* 1	* ~0	* ~0	* ~0	* ~0	* ~0	Exportations
Balance	G	* -12	* -12	* -20	* -33	* -40	* -48	* -55	Balance
Saint Kitts and Nevis									**Saint-Kitts-et-Nevis**
Imports	S	132	210	270	268	297	334	309	Importations
Exports	S	19	34	32	39	32	37	33	Exportations
Balance	S	-113	-176	-238	-229	-265	-297	-276	Balance
Saint Lucia									**Sainte-Lucie**
Imports	S	* 306	486	647	642	583	669	* 731	Importations
Exports	S	* 109	64	215	146	181	120	* 104	Exportations
Balance	S	* -197	-422	-432	-496	-403	-549	* -627	Balance
Saint Pierre and Miquelon									**Saint-Pierre-et-Miquelon**
Imports	S	* 96	* 216	* 747	* 1 900	* 2 259	* 2 629	* 2 991	Importations
Exports	S	* 16	* 31	* 137	* 426	* 533	* 653	* 780	Exportations
Balance	S	* -80	* -185	* -610	* -1 473	* -1 726	* -1 976	* -2 211	Balance
Saint Vincent & Grenadines									**Saint-Vincent-Grenadines**
Imports	S	134	240	379	* 361	334	* 335	* 315	Importations
Exports	S	59	40	42	* 48	46	* 47	* 39	Exportations
Balance	S	-75	-201	-338	* -313	-288	* -288	* -276	Balance
Samoa									**Samoa**
Imports	S	* 95	239	310	388	371	350	356	Importations
Exports	S	* 9	87	70	51	59	56	44	Exportations
Balance	S	* -86	-151	-240	-337	-312	-294	-312	Balance
Sao Tome and Principe									**Sao Tomé-et-Principe**
Imports	S	* 29	50	112	170	142	139	147	Importations
Exports	S	* 5	3	6	10	9	10	11	Exportations
Balance	S	* -24	-46	-106	-159	-133	-129	-136	Balance
Saudi Arabia									**Arabie saoudite**
Imports	S	28 085	57 233	103 622	168 240	163 821	129 796	* 123 934	Importations
Exports	S	49 030	180 278	250 577	341 947	201 492	207 572	* 251 648	Exportations
Balance	S	20 944	123 045	146 955	173 708	37 671	77 776	* 127 714	Balance
Senegal									**Sénégal**
Imports	G	* 1 413	3 498	4 782	6 503	5 595	5 478	6 729	Importations
Exports	G	* 412	1 471	2 088	2 750	2 612	2 640	2 989	Exportations
Balance	G	* -1 001	-2 027	-2 694	-3 753	-2 984	-2 838	-3 740	Balance
Serbia									**Serbie**
Imports	S	...	...	16 735	20 609	18 210	19 231	22 146	Importations
Exports	S	...	...	9 795	14 843	13 379	14 852	16 959	Exportations
Balance	S	...	...	-6 940	-5 765	-4 831	-4 379	-5 187	Balance
Serbia and Monten. [former]									**Serbie-et-Monténégro [anc.]**
Imports	S	* 2 666	* 11 393	...	...	...	...	...	Importations
Exports	S	* 1 531	* 4 430	...	...	...	...	...	Exportations
Balance	S	* -1 135	* -6 963	...	...	...	...	...	Balance
Seychelles									**Seychelles**
Imports	G	255	675	1 180	1 075	975	1 648	* 2 141	Importations
Exports	G	53	340	418	551	474	484	* 497	Exportations
Balance	G	-202	-335	-763	-524	-501	-1 164	* -1 644	Balance
Sierra Leone									**Sierra Leone**
Imports	S	* 131	341	* 776	2 057	1 759	958	* 893	Importations
Exports	S	* 42	154	* 319	279	93	466	* 324	Exportations
Balance	S	* -89	-187	* -457	-1 778	-1 666	-492	* -569	Balance
Singapore									**Singapour**
Imports	G	124 503	200 724	310 791	366 247	296 745	291 908	327 710	Importations
Exports	G	118 263	230 344	351 867	409 769	346 638	338 082	373 255	Exportations
Balance	G	-6 240	29 619	41 076	43 521	49 893	46 174	45 545	Balance
Slovakia									**Slovaquie**
Imports	S	8 162	34 226	64 382	81 354	72 958	75 156	82 994	Importations
Exports	S	8 374	* 32 210	63 999	85 976	75 051	77 565	84 525	Exportations
Balance	S	212	* -2 016	-383	4 622	2 094	2 409	1 532	Balance

21 Total imports, exports and balance of trade *(continued)*
Imports CIF, exports FOB and balance: millions of US dollars

Total des importations, des exportations et balance commerciale *(suite)*
Importations CAF, exportations FAB et balance: en millions de dollars É.-U.

Region, country or area[&]	Sys.[t]	1995	2005	2010	2014	2015	2016	2017	Région, pays ou zone[&]
Slovenia									**Slovénie**
Imports	S	9 492	19 626	26 592	30 049	25 870	26 690	28 192	Importations
Exports	S	8 316	17 896	24 435	30 522	26 587	27 658	28 773	Exportations
Balance	S	-1 176	-1 730	-2 157	473	717	967	581	Balance
Solomon Islands									**Îles Salomon**
Imports	S	* 154	139	328	500	466	454	572	Importations
Exports	S	* 168	70	215	459	400	437	500	Exportations
Balance	S	* 14	-68	-112	-41	-65	-17	-72	Balance
Somalia									**Somalie**
Imports	G	* 38	* 469	* 496	* 519	* 525	* 530	* 537	Importations
Exports	G	* 38	* 379	* 568	* 786	* 853	* 925	* 1 003	Exportations
Balance	G	* -~0	* -90	* 72	* 267	* 328	* 394	* 466	Balance
South Africa[1,15]									**Afrique du Sud**[1,15]
Imports	G	...	55 033	82 949	99 893	79 591	74 744	83 031	Importations
Exports	G	...	46 991	82 626	90 612	69 631	74 111	88 268	Exportations
Balance	G	...	-8 042	-323	-9 281	-9 960	-633	5 237	Balance
South Sudan									**Soudan du sud**
Imports	G	...	...	...	* 537	* 635	* 750	* 886	Importations
Exports	G	...	...	...	* 4 030	* 3 103	* 2 389	* 1 840	Exportations
Balance	G	...	...	...	* 3 493	* 2 469	* 1 639	* 953	Balance
Spain									**Espagne**
Imports	S	113 399	289 611	315 547	350 978	305 266	302 539	350 922	Importations
Exports	S	89 616	192 798	246 265	318 649	278 122	281 777	319 622	Exportations
Balance	S	-23 783	-96 812	-69 282	-32 328	-27 144	-20 762	-31 300	Balance
Sri Lanka									**Sri Lanka**
Imports	G	* 4 756	8 307	12 354	19 244	18 967	19 501	21 316	Importations
Exports	G	* 3 790	6 160	8 304	11 295	10 440	10 546	11 741	Exportations
Balance	G	* -966	-2 147	-4 050	-7 949	-8 528	-8 955	-9 575	Balance
State of Palestine									**État de Palestine**
Imports	S	...	2 668	3 959	5 683	5 225	5 364	* 5 624	Importations
Exports	S	...	335	576	944	958	926	* 1 035	Exportations
Balance	S	...	-2 332	-3 383	-4 739	-4 268	-4 437	* -4 589	Balance
Sudan									**Soudan**
Imports	G	...	...	...	* 9 211	8 413	* 7 365	* 9 163	Importations
Exports	G	...	...	...	* 4 350	5 588	* 5 455	* 4 061	Exportations
Balance	G	...	...	...	* -4 861	-2 826	* -1 910	* -5 102	Balance
Sudan [former]									**Soudan [anc.]**
Imports	G	1 185	7 367	11 875	...	...	...	...	Importations
Exports	G	685	4 506	11 529	...	...	...	...	Exportations
Balance	G	-500	-2 861	-346	...	...	...	...	Balance
Suriname									**Suriname**
Imports	G	583	1 050	1 397	1 827	* 1 826	1 174	1 209	Importations
Exports	G	483	997	2 026	1 918	* 1 468	1 235	1 441	Exportations
Balance	G	-100	-53	628	91	* -359	61	232	Balance
Sweden									**Suède**
Imports	G	61 647	111 351	148 788	162 257	138 361	141 101	153 856	Importations
Exports	G	77 436	130 264	158 411	164 680	140 001	139 456	153 106	Exportations
Balance	G	15 790	18 912	9 622	2 423	1 641	-1 645	-751	Balance
Switzerland									**Suisse**
Imports	S	80 152	126 574	176 281	275 054	253 152	269 157	267 501	Importations
Exports	S	81 641	130 930	195 609	311 146	291 959	304 691	299 309	Exportations
Balance	S	1 489	4 356	19 329	36 092	38 807	35 534	31 807	Balance
Syrian Arab Republic									**République arabe syrienne**
Imports	S	* 4 645	7 898	17 562	* 4 311	* 3 206	* 2 383	* 1 773	Importations
Exports	S	* 3 561	6 450	11 353	* 2 250	* 1 685	* 1 265	* 949	Exportations
Balance	S	* -1 084	-1 448	-6 209	* -2 061	* -1 521	* -1 118	* -824	Balance
Tajikistan									**Tadjikistan**
Imports	G	* 809	* 1 329	* 2 659	* 4 296	* 3 435	* 3 030	* 2 775	Importations
Exports	G	* 748	* 905	* 1 207	* 1 080	* 891	* 899	* 1 198	Exportations
Balance	G	* -61	* -424	* -1 452	* -3 216	* -2 544	* -2 132	* -1 577	Balance
Thailand									**Thaïlande**
Imports	S	70 781	118 164	182 393	227 932	202 019	195 714	* 225 681	Importations
Exports	S	56 439	110 110	195 312	227 573	210 883	213 593	* 233 695	Exportations
Balance	S	-14 341	-8 054	12 918	-359	8 864	17 879	* 8 013	Balance

Total imports, exports and balance of trade *(continued)*
Imports CIF, exports FOB and balance: millions of US dollars

Total des importations, des exportations et balance commerciale *(suite)*
Importations CAF, exportations FAB et balance: en millions de dollars É.-U.

Region, country or area[&]	Sys.[t]	1995	2005	2010	2014	2015	2016	2017	Région, pays ou zone[&]
TFYR of Macedonia									**ex-R.Y. de Macédoine**
Imports	S	1 719	3 228	5 474	7 301	6 400	6 757	7 719	Importations
Exports	S	1 204	2 041	3 351	4 964	4 490	4 785	5 670	Exportations
Balance	S	-515	-1 187	-2 123	-2 337	-1 910	-1 972	-2 049	Balance
Timor-Leste									**Timor-Leste**
Imports	S	* 112	102	* 298	* 538	* 492	* 647	* 724	Importations
Exports	S	* 34	43	* 42	* 39	* 38	* 94	* 197	Exportations
Balance	S	* -78	-58	* -256	* -499	* -454	* -553	* -527	Balance
Togo									**Togo**
Imports	S	556	593	1 205	1 753	1 731	1 716	1 615	Importations
Exports	S	383	360	648	804	710	715	749	Exportations
Balance	S	-174	-233	-557	-949	-1 021	-1 001	-866	Balance
Tokelau									**Tokélaou**
Imports	G	* 1	* 1	* 1	* 1	* 1	* 1	* 1	Importations
Exports	G	* ~0	* ~0	* ~0	* ~0	* ~0	* ~0	* ~0	Exportations
Balance	G	* -~0	* -1	* -1	* -1	* -1	* -1	* -1	Balance
Tonga									**Tonga**
Imports	G	* 77	120	159	218	* 206	* 209	* 212	Importations
Exports	G	* 15	10	8	19	* 15	* 14	* 10	Exportations
Balance	G	* -63	-110	-151	-199	* -191	* -195	* -201	Balance
Trinidad and Tobago									**Trinité-et-Tobago**
Imports	S	* 1 386	5 694	6 480	11 412	9 298	* 8 084	* 6 425	Importations
Exports	S	* 2 007	9 611	10 982	14 526	10 756	* 7 639	* 8 863	Exportations
Balance	S	* 622	3 918	4 502	3 114	1 458	* -446	* 2 439	Balance
Tunisia									**Tunisie**
Imports	G	* 7 903	13 174	22 215	24 793	20 223	19 487	* 20 715	Importations
Exports	G	* 5 475	10 494	16 427	16 760	14 073	13 575	* 14 532	Exportations
Balance	G	* -2 428	-2 681	-5 789	-8 034	-6 149	-5 912	* -6 183	Balance
Turkey									**Turquie**
Imports	S	35 707	116 774	185 544	242 177	207 207	198 618	233 792	Importations
Exports	S	21 599	73 476	113 883	157 610	143 850	142 530	157 055	Exportations
Balance	S	-14 109	-43 298	-71 661	-84 567	-63 356	-56 089	-76 737	Balance
Turkmenistan									**Turkménistan**
Imports	G	* 1 364	* 2 217	* 2 400	* 2 533	* 2 554	* 2 616	* 2 679	Importations
Exports	G	* 677	* 3 009	* 3 335	* 3 600	* 3 670	* 3 741	* 3 813	Exportations
Balance	G	* -687	* 792	* 935	* 1 068	* 1 116	* 1 125	* 1 135	Balance
Turks and Caicos Islands									**Îles Turques-et-Caïques**
Imports	G	* 51	304	* 302	* 406	* 410	* 389	* 370	Importations
Exports	G	* 5	15	* 16	* 6	* 5	* 4	* 4	Exportations
Balance	G	* -46	-289	* -286	* -400	* -405	* -385	* -366	Balance
Tuvalu									**Tuvalu**
Imports	G	* 6	13	* 12	* 12	* 12	* 12	* 12	Importations
Exports	G	* ~0	~0	* ~0	* ~0	* ~0	* ~0	* ~0	Exportations
Balance	G	* -6	-13	* -12	* -12	* -12	* -12	* -12	Balance
Uganda									**Ouganda**
Imports	G	1 038	2 054	4 664	6 074	5 528	4 829	* 4 809	Importations
Exports	G	575	813	1 619	2 262	2 267	2 482	* 2 852	Exportations
Balance	G	-462	-1 241	-3 046	-3 812	-3 261	-2 347	* -1 957	Balance
Ukraine									**Ukraine**
Imports	G	* 15 484	36 122	60 737	54 381	37 516	39 250	49 439	Importations
Exports	G	* 13 128	34 228	51 430	53 913	38 127	36 361	43 428	Exportations
Balance	G	* -2 356	-1 894	-9 307	-468	611	-2 889	-6 011	Balance
United Arab Emirates									**Émirats arabes unis**
Imports	G	* 20 776	80 814	187 001	298 611	287 025	270 882	* 237 797	Importations
Exports	G	* 27 691	115 453	198 362	380 340	333 362	298 651	* 220 453	Exportations
Balance	G	* 6 915	34 639	11 361	81 728	46 338	27 769	* -17 345	Balance
United Kingdom									**Royaume-Uni**
Imports	G	261 456	528 461	627 618	694 344	630 251	636 368	640 365	Importations
Exports	G	234 372	392 744	422 014	511 145	466 296	411 463	443 734	Exportations
Balance	G	-27 084	-135 717	-205 603	-183 199	-163 955	-224 905	-196 631	Balance
United Rep. of Tanzania									**Rép.-Unie de Tanzanie**
Imports	G	1 653	3 247	8 013	12 691	14 706	7 876	* 7 706	Importations
Exports	G	685	1 672	4 051	5 705	5 854	4 742	* 4 500	Exportations
Balance	G	-968	-1 575	-3 962	-6 986	-8 852	-3 134	* -3 206	Balance

21 Total imports, exports and balance of trade *(continued)*

Imports CIF, exports FOB and balance: millions of US dollars

Total des importations, des exportations et balance commerciale *(suite)*

Importations CAF, exportations FAB et balance: en millions de dollars É.-U.

Region, country or area &	Sys.†	1995	2005	2010	2014	2015	2016	2017	Région, pays ou zone &
United States of America [16]									**États-Unis d'Amérique** [16]
Imports	G	770 821	1 732 321	1 968 260	2 410 855	2 313 425	2 248 209	2 408 395	Importations
Exports	G	582 965	904 339	1 278 099	1 619 743	1 501 846	1 450 457	1 546 069	Exportations
Balance	G	-187 857	-827 981	-690 161	-791 113	-811 579	-797 752	-862 326	Balance
Uruguay									**Uruguay**
Imports	G	2 866	3 879	8 622	10 762	9 489	8 137	8 458	Importations
Exports	G	2 106	3 422	6 724	9 166	7 670	6 964	7 889	Exportations
Balance	G	-760	-457	-1 898	-1 597	-1 820	-1 173	-568	Balance
Uzbekistan									**Ouzbékistan**
Imports	G	* 2 874	* 3 657	* 8 381	* 12 415	* 10 150	* 12 101	* 12 998	Importations
Exports	G	* 3 718	* 4 458	* 11 587	* 12 871	* 14 225	* 12 568	* 13 894	Exportations
Balance	G	* 844	* 801	* 3 206	* 456	* 4 076	* 466	* 896	Balance
Vanuatu									**Vanuatu**
Imports	G	* 95	* 149	276	* 308	* 355	* 377	* 313	Importations
Exports	G	* 28	* 38	46	* 63	* 39	* 50	* 38	Exportations
Balance	G	* -67	* -111	-230	* -246	* -316	* -327	* -275	Balance
Venezuela (Boliv. Rep. of)									**Venezuela (Rép. boliv. du)**
Imports	G	10 791	21 848	32 343	* 44 639	* 40 146	* 17 150	* 6 771	Importations
Exports	G	19 093	55 413	66 963	* 74 047	* 37 236	* 20 215	* 11 563	Exportations
Balance	G	8 302	33 565	34 620	* 29 409	* -2 910	* 3 065	* 4 792	Balance
Viet Nam									**Viet Nam**
Imports	G	* 8 155	36 761	84 839	147 839	165 776	174 978	* 218 338	Importations
Exports	G	* 5 449	32 447	72 237	150 217	162 017	176 581	* 203 526	Exportations
Balance	G	* -2 706	-4 314	-12 602	2 378	-3 759	1 602	* -14 813	Balance
Wallis and Futuna Islands									**Îles Wallis-et-Futuna**
Imports	S	* 13	51	* 35	* 46	* 49	* 53	* 57	Importations
Exports	S	* ~0	* 1	* 1	* 1	* 1	* 1	* 1	Exportations
Balance	S	* -13	* -50	* -34	* -45	* -48	* -51	* -55	Balance
Yemen									**Yémen**
Imports	S	* 1 812	5 400	9 255	12 042	6 573	* 3 311	* 7 162	Importations
Exports	S	* 1 917	5 608	6 437	2 417	510	* 24	* 637	Exportations
Balance	S	* 105	208	-2 818	-9 625	-6 063	* -3 286	* -6 525	Balance
Zambia									**Zambie**
Imports	S	708	2 558	5 321	9 539	8 420	* 7 457	* 9 145	Importations
Exports	S	1 055	1 810	7 200	9 688	6 983	* 6 490	* 8 363	Exportations
Balance	S	347	-748	1 879	149	-1 437	* -967	* -782	Balance
Zimbabwe									**Zimbabwe**
Imports	G	2 659	2 072	5 852	6 380	6 002	5 212	* 5 449	Importations
Exports	G	1 846	1 394	3 199	3 064	2 704	2 832	* 3 465	Exportations
Balance	G	-813	-679	-2 653	-3 316	-3 298	-2 379	* -1 985	Balance

Source:

United Nations Statistics Division, New York, Commodity Trade Statistics Database (UN COMTRADE), last accessed June 2018.

Source:

Organisation des Nations Unies, Division de statistique, New York, Comtrade base de données de l'ONU, dernier accès juin 2018.

& Systems of trade: Two systems of recording trade, the General trade system (G) and the Special trade system (S), are in common use. They differ mainly in the way warehoused and re-exported goods are recorded. See the Technical notes for an explanation of the trade systems.

& Systèmes de commerce : Deux systèmes d'enregistrement du commerce sont couramment utilisés, le Commerce général (G) et le Commerce spécial (S). Ils ne diffèrent que par la façon dont sont enregistrées les marchandises entreposées et les marchandises réexportées. Voir les Notes techniques pour une explication des Systèmes de commerce.

1. Imports FOB.
2. Trade statistics exclude certain oil and chemical products.
3. Data refer to Belgium and Luxembourg.
4. For statistical purposes, the data for China do not include those for the Hong Kong Special Administrative Region (Hong Kong SAR), Macao Special Administrative Region (Macao SAR) and Taiwan Province of China.

1. Importations FAB.
2. Les statistiques commerciales font exclusion de certains produits pétroliers et chimiques.
3. Les données se rapportent à Belgique et Luxembourg.
4. Pour la présentation des statistiques, les données pour la Chine ne comprennent pas la région administrative spéciale de Hong Kong (Hong Kong RAS), la région administrative spéciale de Macao (Macao RAS) et la province chinoise de Taïwan.

5 Export and import values exclude trade in the processing zone.
6 Imports exclude petroleum imported without stated value. Exports cover domestic exports.
7 Including French Guiana, Guadeloupe, Martinique and Réunion.
8 After 1995, import and exports included in France.
9 Excluding military goods, fissionable materials, bunkers, ships and aircraft.
10 Data include oil and gas. The value of oil exports and total exports are rough estimates based on information published in various petroleum industry journals.
11 Year ending 20 March of the year stated.
12 Imports and exports net of returned goods. The figures also exclude Judea and Samaria and the Gaza area.
13 Trade data include maquiladoras and exclude goods from customs-bonded warehouses. Total exports include revaluation and exports of silver.
14 Year ending 31 March of the following year.
15 Exports include gold.
16 Including the trade of the U.S. Virgin Islands and Puerto Rico but excluding shipments of merchandise between the United States and its other possessions (Guam and American Samoa). Data include imports and exports of non-monetary gold.

5 Les valeurs à l'exportation et à l'importation excluent le commerce de la zone de transformation.
6 Non compris le pétrole brute dont la valeur des importations ne sont pas stipulée. Les exportations sont les exportations d'intérieur.
7 Y compris Guadeloupe, Guyane française, Martinique et Réunion.
8 Après 1995, importations et exportations incluses en France.
9 À l'exclusion des marchandises militaires, des matières fissibles, des soutes, des bateaux et de l'avion.
10 Les données comprennent le pétrole et le gaz. La valeur des exportations de pétrole et des exportations totales sont des évaluations grossières basées sur l'information publiée à divers journaux d'industrie de pétrole.
11 Année finissant le 20 mars de l'année indiquée.
12 Importations et exportations nettes des marchandises retournées excluant les régions de Judée et Samarie et Gaza.
13 Les statistiques du commerce extérieur comprennent maquiladoras et ne comprennent pas les marchandises provenant des entrepôts en douane. Les exportations comprennent la réévaluation et les données sur les exportations d'argent.
14 Année finissant le 31 Mars de l'année suivante.
15 Les exportations comprennent l'or.
16 Incluant les Iles Vierges américaines et Porto Rico excluant l'expédition de marchandises avec Guam et les Samoa américaines. Incluant le commerce d'or non-monétaire.

22 Major trading partner

Three largest trade partners as a percentage of total international merchandise trade in US dollars, as at 2017

Partenaire commercial principal

Trois principaux partenaires commerciaux en pourcentage du total de commerce international de marchandises en dollars américains, en 2017

Country or area	Major trading partner	Percentage of exports 2005	2010	2017	Major trading partner	Percentage of imports 2005	2010	2017	Pays ou zone
Afghanistan									**Afghanistan**
Partner 1	Pakistan	...	39.0	*47.5	Iran (Islamic Rep.), Iran (Rép. islamique)	...	7.5	*19.4	Partenaire 1
Partner 2	India, Inde	...	16.8	38.6	Pakistan	...	11.6	*18.3	Partenaire 2
Partner 3	Iran (Islamic Rep.), Iran (Rép. islamique)	...	8.2	*3.2	China, Chine	...	13.7	*16.7	Partenaire 3
Albania									**Albanie**
Partner 1	Italy, Italie	72.4	50.8	54.5	Italy, Italie	29.3	28.2	26.0	Partenaire 1
Partner 2	Serbia, Serbie	...	8.3	7.8	Areas nes, Zones nsa [1]	...	...	13.0	Partenaire 2
Partner 3	Spain, Espagne	0.1	3.4	5.6	Turkey, Turquie	7.5	5.7	7.4	Partenaire 3
Algeria									**Algérie**
Partner 1	Italy, Italie	16.4	15.4	16.0	China, Chine	6.5	11.2	18.1	Partenaire 1
Partner 2	France	10.0	6.6	12.6	France	22.0	14.9	9.3	Partenaire 2
Partner 3	Spain, Espagne	11.0	10.4	11.7	Italy, Italie	7.5	10.0	8.2	Partenaire 3
Andorra									**Andorre**
Partner 1	Spain, Espagne	59.2	67.4	*29.6	Spain, Espagne	*51.5	59.9	*67.3	Partenaire 1
Partner 2	Sri Lanka	...	...	15.3	France	*22.3	17.6	*18.8	Partenaire 2
Partner 3	United States, États-Unis	0.1	0.1	*13.0	Germany, Allemagne	*5.3	4.5	*3.0	Partenaire 3
Angola									**Angola**
Partner 1	China, Chine	*29.8	39.8	*43.2	China, Chine	*4.8	10.1	*16.9	Partenaire 1
Partner 2	India, Inde	*~0.0	9.7	8.1	Portugal	*12.9	14.4	*14.6	Partenaire 2
Partner 3	Spain, Espagne	*3.1	1.9	*6.8	Republic of Korea, République de Corée	*19.6	1.1	*8.6	Partenaire 3
Anguilla									**Anguilla**
Partner 1	United States, États-Unis	*26.5	*17.0	*26.5	United States, États-Unis	*61.7	*59.4	*69.2	Partenaire 1
Partner 2	Thailand, Thaïlande	...	...	26.4	Trinidad and Tobago, Trinité-et-Tobago	*6.9	*14.5	*5.1	Partenaire 2
Partner 3	Saint Lucia, Sainte-Lucie	*8.5	...	*8.3	Poland, Pologne	*~0.0	*~0.0	*4.2	Partenaire 3
Antigua and Barbuda									**Antigua-et-Barbuda**
Partner 1	United Kingdom, Royaume-Uni	16.7	19.7	52.5	United States, États-Unis	48.9	34.5	44.3	Partenaire 1
Partner 2	United States, États-Unis	7.7	29.7	16.2	Undisclosed, Non divulgués	...	...	14.5	Partenaire 2
Partner 3	Spain, Espagne	~0.0	0.7	12.8	Japan, Japon	2.8	2.7	4.7	Partenaire 3
Argentina									**Argentine**
Partner 1	Brazil, Brésil	15.8	21.2	15.9	Brazil, Brésil	37.0	*32.5	26.7	Partenaire 1
Partner 2	United States, États-Unis	12.1	5.4	7.7	China, Chine	5.3	*13.5	18.4	Partenaire 2
Partner 3	China, Chine	7.9	8.5	7.4	United States, États-Unis	16.3	*11.8	11.4	Partenaire 3
Armenia									**Arménie**
Partner 1	Russian Federation, Fédération de Russie	12.4	17.5	26.5	Russian Federation, Fédération de Russie	14.8	22.0	28.7	Partenaire 1
Partner 2	Bulgaria, Bulgarie	0.1	15.5	14.0	China, Chine	1.5	10.6	11.7	Partenaire 2
Partner 3	Switzerland, Suisse	3.7	1.7	11.8	Turkey, Turquie	3.1	5.6	5.6	Partenaire 3
Aruba									**Aruba**
Partner 1	Colombia, Colombie	11.9	27.2	*24.2	United States, États-Unis	*55.7	50.0	*55.1	Partenaire 1
Partner 2	United States, États-Unis	*11.3	*6.1	*19.5	Netherlands, Pays-Bas	*12.7	11.3	*12.8	Partenaire 2
Partner 3	Netherlands, Pays-Bas	*33.5	*5.1	*16.6	Areas nes, Zones nsa [1]	0.1	2.0	*12.1	Partenaire 3
Australia									**Australie**
Partner 1	China, Chine	11.6	*25.5	29.6	China, Chine	13.8	*18.7	21.9	Partenaire 1
Partner 2	Areas nes, Zones nsa [1]	0.1	*0.4	*15.0	United States, États-Unis	13.9	*12.4	10.3	Partenaire 2
Partner 3	Japan, Japon	20.5	*18.5	10.4	Japan, Japon	11.0	*8.7	7.2	Partenaire 3
Austria									**Autriche**
Partner 1	Germany, Allemagne	31.7	*30.9	*30.0	Germany, Allemagne	42.2	*38.7	*36.8	Partenaire 1
Partner 2	United States, États-Unis	5.6	*4.4	*6.5	Italy, Italie	6.6	*6.6	*6.1	Partenaire 2
Partner 3	Italy, Italie	8.6	*7.7	*6.2	China, Chine	3.1	*4.7	*5.9	Partenaire 3
Azerbaijan									**Azerbaïdjan**
Partner 1	Italy, Italie	30.3	*33.1	31.9	Russian Federation, Fédération de Russie	17.0	17.4	16.8	Partenaire 1
Partner 2	Turkey, Turquie	6.3	*0.8	*9.9	Turkey, Turquie	7.4	11.7	14.7	Partenaire 2
Partner 3	Israel, Israël	4.5	8.2	4.6	China, Chine	4.1	8.9	11.2	Partenaire 3
Bahamas									**Bahamas**
Partner 1	United States, États-Unis	60.9	76.0	*83.1	United States, États-Unis	*85.9	*90.9	*81.9	Partenaire 1
Partner 2	France	13.1	3.5	4.4	Areas nes, Zones nsa [1]	0.1	0.8	*3.0	Partenaire 2
Partner 3	Finland, Finlande	...	...	*3.2	Dominica, Dominique	...	...	*1.5	Partenaire 3
Bahrain									**Bahreïn**
Partner 1	Saudi Arabia, Arabie saoudite	*6.3	7.2	*18.1	Areas nes, Zones nsa [1]	44.6	36.6	*21.4	Partenaire 1
Partner 2	United Arab Emirates, Émirats arabes unis	*1.6	*2.7	*17.3	China, Chine	4.1	7.4	*9.7	Partenaire 2
Partner 3	United States, États-Unis	*2.7	1.5	*11.0	United States, États-Unis	3.7	4.5	*8.6	Partenaire 3

22

Major trading partner *(continued)*
Three largest trade partners as a percentage of total international merchandise trade in US dollars, as at 2017

Partenaire commercial principal *(suite)*
Trois principaux partenaires commerciaux en pourcentage du total de commerce international de marchandises en dollars américains, en 2017

Country or area	Major trading partner	Percentage of exports 2005	2010	2017	Major trading partner	Percentage of imports 2005	2010	2017	Pays ou zone
Bangladesh									**Bangladesh**
Partner 1	United States, États-Unis	*28.5	*24.3	*19.3	China, Chine	*15.9	17.5	*21.5	Partenaire 1
Partner 2	Germany, Allemagne	*15.7	*13.8	*14.7	India, Inde	*10.9	11.5	*12.2	Partenaire 2
Partner 3	United Kingdom, Royaume-Uni	*10.1	*8.9	*11.0	Singapore, Singapour	*3.5	5.4	*9.2	Partenaire 3
Barbados									**Barbade**
Partner 1	United States, États-Unis	*13.4	24.9	25.8	United States, États-Unis	35.9	43.9	39.5	Partenaire 1
Partner 2	Areas nes, Zones nsa [1]	~0.0	...	19.5	Trinidad and Tobago, Trinité-et-Tobago	21.2	7.2	16.8	Partenaire 2
Partner 3	Trinidad and Tobago, Trinité-et-Tobago	10.6	8.4	7.5	China, Chine	2.9	4.8	5.8	Partenaire 3
Belarus									**Bélarus**
Partner 1	Russian Federation, Fédération de Russie	35.8	39.4	*46.3	Russian Federation, Fédération de Russie	60.4	55.8	*54.2	Partenaire 1
Partner 2	Ukraine	5.7	10.1	12.0	China, Chine	1.7	4.6	*7.7	Partenaire 2
Partner 3	United Kingdom, Royaume-Uni	7.0	3.7	*4.6	Germany, Allemagne	6.7	6.8	*4.8	Partenaire 3
Belgium									**Belgique**
Partner 1	Germany, Allemagne	19.2	18.5	16.6	Netherlands, Pays-Bas	17.6	18.6	17.2	Partenaire 1
Partner 2	France	17.2	16.6	14.9	Germany, Allemagne	17.1	16.1	13.8	Partenaire 2
Partner 3	Netherlands, Pays-Bas	11.7	11.9	12.0	France	11.3	11.0	9.5	Partenaire 3
Belize									**Belize**
Partner 1	United Kingdom, Royaume-Uni	19.9	26.1	27.7	United States, États-Unis	40.3	47.9	35.6	Partenaire 1
Partner 2	United States, États-Unis	53.9	49.1	26.3	China, Chine	2.2	9.7	11.2	Partenaire 2
Partner 3	Jamaica, Jamaïque	4.6	2.6	5.4	Mexico, Mexique	11.6	10.0	11.2	Partenaire 3
Benin									**Bénin**
Partner 1	India, Inde	6.9	4.6	*15.4	India, Inde	1.6	0.9	*14.9	Partenaire 1
Partner 2	Malaysia, Malaisie	2.8	1.5	13.2	Thailand, Thaïlande	6.7	8.6	*12.4	Partenaire 2
Partner 3	Bangladesh	0.4	0.6	*10.2	France	18.4	14.7	*10.1	Partenaire 3
Bermuda									**Bermudes**
Partner 1	United States, États-Unis	*7.0	*69.1	81.2	United States, États-Unis	77.0	71.7	66.5	Partenaire 1
Partner 2	Canada	*20.1	*5.8	*4.9	Canada	4.0	8.0	9.5	Partenaire 2
Partner 3	United Kingdom, Royaume-Uni	*1.1	*8.2	4.4	United Kingdom, Royaume-Uni	3.3	3.7	4.0	Partenaire 3
Bhutan									**Bhoutan**
Partner 1	India, Inde	87.6	82.4	*77.2	India, Inde	75.1	75.1	*80.2	Partenaire 1
Partner 2	Bangladesh	4.9	4.8	12.7	Thailand, Thaïlande	1.6	2.5	*5.7	Partenaire 2
Partner 3	Nepal, Népal	0.4	0.2	*2.6	Republic of Korea, République de Corée	1.5	5.1	*2.5	Partenaire 3
Bolivia (Plurin. State of)									**Bolivie (État plurin. de)**
Partner 1	Brazil, Brésil	36.3	*34.6	18.5	China, Chine	5.8	11.7	21.8	Partenaire 1
Partner 2	Argentina, Argentine	*9.5	*8.0	*15.7	Brazil, Brésil	21.9	*18.0	16.8	Partenaire 2
Partner 3	Republic of Korea, République de Corée	2.2	*5.3	7.8	Argentina, Argentine	16.7	12.7	12.5	Partenaire 3
Bosnia and Herzegovina									**Bosnie-Herzégovine**
Partner 1	Germany, Allemagne	11.3	*15.8	14.4	Germany, Allemagne	14.4	10.5	11.6	Partenaire 1
Partner 2	Croatia, Croatie	20.5	*15.3	*11.6	Italy, Italie	8.9	8.9	11.4	Partenaire 2
Partner 3	Italy, Italie	13.1	*12.2	10.9	Serbia, Serbie	...	10.5	11.2	Partenaire 3
Botswana									**Botswana**
Partner 1	Belgium, Belgique	0.2	3.3	22.8	South Africa, Afrique du Sud	84.1	72.8	64.3	Partenaire 1
Partner 2	India, Inde	0.1	0.9	19.7	Canada	0.5	0.1	8.8	Partenaire 2
Partner 3	United Arab Emirates, Émirats arabes unis	0.1	0.1	16.6	Namibia, Namibie	0.5	1.2	6.7	Partenaire 3
Brazil									**Brésil**
Partner 1	China, Chine	5.7	15.2	21.8	China, Chine	7.3	14.1	18.1	Partenaire 1
Partner 2	United States, États-Unis	19.8	10.0	12.5	United States, États-Unis	17.5	15.0	16.7	Partenaire 2
Partner 3	Argentina, Argentine	8.3	9.2	8.1	Argentina, Argentine	8.5	7.9	6.3	Partenaire 3
British Virgin Islands									**Îles Vierges britanniques**
Partner 1	Ghana	*~0.0	...	*60.0	United States, États-Unis	*8.9	*9.9	*39.5	Partenaire 1
Partner 2	Mexico, Mexique	*1.3	*0.1	*8.4	Areas nes, Zones nsa [1]	...	...	*38.5	Partenaire 2
Partner 3	United States, États-Unis	*24.3	*14.0	*3.1	Switzerland, Suisse	*2.0	*3.9	*5.1	Partenaire 3
Brunei Darussalam									**Brunéi Darussalam**
Partner 1	Japan, Japon	*37.7	43.5	29.3	China, Chine	*6.2	7.8	20.8	Partenaire 1
Partner 2	Republic of Korea, République de Corée	*12.9	16.7	14.2	Singapore, Singapour	*18.3	19.1	18.5	Partenaire 2
Partner 3	Malaysia, Malaisie	*1.4	1.5	11.2	Malaysia, Malaisie	*20.1	23.6	18.2	Partenaire 3
Bulgaria									**Bulgarie**
Partner 1	Germany, Allemagne	9.8	10.6	13.4	Germany, Allemagne	13.6	11.7	12.2	Partenaire 1
Partner 2	Italy, Italie	12.0	*9.7	*8.3	Russian Federation, Fédération de Russie	15.6	16.1	10.2	Partenaire 2
Partner 3	Romania, Roumanie	3.8	*9.2	8.2	Italy, Italie	9.0	7.4	7.3	Partenaire 3

22 Major trading partner *(continued)*

Three largest trade partners as a percentage of total international merchandise trade in US dollars, as at 2017

Partenaire commercial principal *(suite)*

Trois principaux partenaires commerciaux en pourcentage du total de commerce international de marchandises en dollars américains, en 2017

Country or area	Major trading partner	Percentage of exports 2005	2010	2017	Major trading partner	Percentage of imports 2005	2010	2017	Pays ou zone
Burkina Faso									**Burkina Faso**
Partner 1	Switzerland, Suisse	9.4	63.5	* 59.4	China, Chine	2.7	9.7	* 14.5	Partenaire 1
Partner 2	Singapore, Singapour	2.2	4.9	9.1	Côte d'Ivoire	* 17.9	16.0	* 8.6	Partenaire 2
Partner 3	India, Inde	~0.0	0.1	* 5.2	France	* 18.7	10.3	* 8.1	Partenaire 3
Burundi									**Burundi**
Partner 1	United Arab Emirates, Émirats arabes unis	25.3	8.8	27.1	India, Inde	4.1	6.0	14.2	Partenaire 1
Partner 2	Dem. Rep. of Congo, Rép. Dém. du Congo	0.9	6.2	17.0	China, Chine	4.2	12.0	13.8	Partenaire 2
Partner 3	Pakistan	~0.0	...	9.2	Saudi Arabia, Arabie saoudite	0.3	0.6	9.1	Partenaire 3
Cabo Verde									**Cabo Verde**
Partner 1	Spain, Espagne	8.1	* 32.2	70.8	Portugal	40.4	45.5	42.9	Partenaire 1
Partner 2	Portugal	* 22.9	* 24.4	* 24.8	Spain, Espagne	7.0	6.8	12.6	Partenaire 2
Partner 3	United States, États-Unis	6.0	* 0.4	2.3	Italy, Italie	4.3	2.0	6.1	Partenaire 3
Cambodia									**Cambodge**
Partner 1	United States, États-Unis	52.9	34.1	* 21.3	China, Chine	16.6	24.2	* 36.8	Partenaire 1
Partner 2	United Kingdom, Royaume-Uni	4.1	4.2	9.5	Thailand, Thaïlande	* 11.4	14.1	15.4	Partenaire 2
Partner 3	Germany, Allemagne	7.5	2.0	* 9.0	Viet Nam	* 7.1	9.9	11.4	Partenaire 3
Cameroon									**Cameroun**
Partner 1	Netherlands, Pays-Bas	7.5	13.1	* 15.7	China, Chine	4.4	10.6	21.4	Partenaire 1
Partner 2	India, Inde	0.4	3.6	11.5	France	18.0	14.6	12.0	Partenaire 2
Partner 3	China, Chine	2.4	8.5	* 10.9	Nigeria, Nigéria	26.8	18.2	4.6	Partenaire 3
Canada									**Canada**
Partner 1	United States, États-Unis	83.7	74.7	76.0	United States, États-Unis	56.5	50.4	51.4	Partenaire 1
Partner 2	China, Chine	1.7	3.3	4.3	China, Chine	7.8	11.0	12.6	Partenaire 2
Partner 3	United Kingdom, Royaume-Uni	1.9	4.1	3.2	Mexico, Mexique	3.8	5.5	6.3	Partenaire 3
Cayman Islands									**Îles Caïmanes**
Partner 1	Netherlands, Pays-Bas	* ~0.0	* ~0.0	* 33.3	United States, États-Unis	* 50.8	11.7	85.4	Partenaire 1
Partner 2	Malta, Malte	* 0.1	* 4.9	* 30.0	Bahamas	* 0.0	~0.0	2.9	Partenaire 2
Partner 3	Seychelles	...	* 0.0	* 28.5	Denmark, Danemark	* 0.2	~0.0	2.0	Partenaire 3
Central African Republic									**République centrafricaine**
Partner 1	France	* 19.6	16.0	* 48.6	France	* 14.0	24.1	21.1	Partenaire 1
Partner 2	Burundi	...	...	14.2	Japan, Japon	4.0	3.6	11.3	Partenaire 2
Partner 3	China, Chine	0.3	8.0	* 10.2	United States, États-Unis	* 0.5	4.6	9.9	Partenaire 3
Chad									**Tchad**
Partner 1	United States, États-Unis	* 72.7	* 68.0	* 47.4	France	* 23.5	12.2	21.6	Partenaire 1
Partner 2	United Arab Emirates, Émirats arabes unis	* ~0.0	* 0.1	* 12.9	China, Chine	* 3.7	22.5	16.5	Partenaire 2
Partner 3	China, Chine	* 8.8	* 16.0	* 11.7	Cameroon, Cameroun	* 6.5	24.7	12.4	Partenaire 3
Chile									**Chili**
Partner 1	China, Chine	11.7	24.4	27.6	China, Chine	9.6	16.8	23.8	Partenaire 1
Partner 2	United States, États-Unis	16.0	* 9.9	* 14.4	United States, États-Unis	15.5	17.7	18.0	Partenaire 2
Partner 3	Japan, Japon	* 11.9	10.9	9.3	Brazil, Brésil	11.6	8.3	8.6	Partenaire 3
China									**Chine**
Partner 1	United States, États-Unis	21.4	18.0	* 18.4	Republic of Korea, République de Corée	11.6	9.9	10.0	Partenaire 1
Partner 2	China, Hong Kong SAR, Chine, RAS Hong Kong	16.3	13.8	13.7	Japan, Japon	15.2	12.7	9.2	Partenaire 2
Partner 3	Japan, Japon	11.0	7.7	* 6.2	Asia nes, Asie nsa [2]	11.3	8.3	8.7	Partenaire 3
China, Hong Kong SAR									**Chine, RAS de Hong Kong**
Partner 1	China, Chine	44.5	52.4	54.2	China, Chine	45.0	44.7	44.6	Partenaire 1
Partner 2	United States, États-Unis	15.9	10.7	7.7	Asia nes, Asie nsa	7.2	6.6	7.2	Partenaire 2
Partner 3	India, Inde	1.0	2.5	3.8	Singapore, Singapour	5.8	7.0	6.4	Partenaire 3
China, Macao SAR									**Chine, RAS de Macao**
Partner 1	Areas nes, Zones nsa [1]	4.1	69.5	* 61.9	China, Chine	37.4	29.1	* 31.4	Partenaire 1
Partner 2	China, Hong Kong SAR, Chine, RAS Hong Kong	9.8	9.6	29.8	Areas nes, Zones nsa	...	...	* 11.6	Partenaire 2
Partner 3	China, Chine	14.9	5.5	* 5.9	China, Hong Kong SAR, Chine, RAS Hong Kong	8.6	10.4	* 8.5	Partenaire 3
Colombia									**Colombie**
Partner 1	United States, États-Unis	* 41.8	* 43.1	* 32.9	United States, États-Unis	28.5	25.9	26.7	Partenaire 1
Partner 2	Panama	* 1.2	* 2.4	* 6.2	China, Chine	7.6	13.5	19.3	Partenaire 2
Partner 3	Netherlands, Pays-Bas	* 2.1	* 4.1	* 3.9	Mexico, Mexique	8.3	9.5	7.6	Partenaire 3
Comoros									**Comores**
Partner 1	India, Inde	6.1	5.2	* 25.2	United Rep. Tanzania, Rép.-Unie Tanzanie	1.7	1.6	38.4	Partenaire 1
Partner 2	France	74.9	22.0	12.2	China, Chine	1.6	7.7	12.1	Partenaire 2
Partner 3	United Arab Emirates, Émirats arabes unis	1.7	3.6	* 11.8	France	17.9	20.6	11.4	Partenaire 3

22

Major trading partner *(continued)*
Three largest trade partners as a percentage of total international merchandise trade in US dollars, as at 2017

Partenaire commercial principal *(suite)*
Trois principaux partenaires commerciaux en pourcentage du total de commerce international de marchandises en dollars américains, en 2017

Country or area	Major trading partner	Percentage of exports 2005	2010	2017	Major trading partner	Percentage of imports 2005	2010	2017	Pays ou zone
Congo									**Congo**
Partner 1	China, Chine	* 36.1	20.9	* 47.8	China, Chine	* 9.2	3.5	25.9	Partenaire 1
Partner 2	United Arab Emirates, Émirats arabes unis	* 0.4	0.1	10.9	France	* 20.9	12.2	20.3	Partenaire 2
Partner 3	Italy, Italie	* 0.5	0.8	* 9.4	Norway, Norvège	* 0.3	0.4	4.4	Partenaire 3
Cook Islands									**Îles Cook**
Partner 1	Japan, Japon	30.8	49.7	* 40.2	New Zealand, Nouvelle-Zélande	* 73.9	76.4	54.2	Partenaire 1
Partner 2	Thailand, Thaïlande	...	...	11.0	Fiji, Fidji	1.2	9.4	8.7	Partenaire 2
Partner 3	Greece, Grèce	...	...	* 8.4	Italy, Italie	~0.0	~0.0	5.8	Partenaire 3
Costa Rica									**Costa Rica**
Partner 1	United States, États-Unis	42.8	* 37.4	* 41.0	United States, États-Unis	41.1	46.8	37.3	Partenaire 1
Partner 2	Netherlands, Pays-Bas	6.3	7.0	5.8	China, Chine	3.8	7.1	13.6	Partenaire 2
Partner 3	Panama	2.6	* 4.8	* 5.7	Mexico, Mexique	4.7	6.4	7.0	Partenaire 3
Côte d'Ivoire									**Côte d'Ivoire**
Partner 1	Netherlands, Pays-Bas	11.0	14.2	* 12.1	Nigeria, Nigéria	24.5	* 26.3	* 15.2	Partenaire 1
Partner 2	United States, États-Unis	14.1	* 10.3	* 8.1	France	27.7	* 11.9	* 13.8	Partenaire 2
Partner 3	Belgium, Belgique	2.2	* 0.1	* 6.5	China, Chine	3.1	* 7.0	* 11.7	Partenaire 3
Croatia									**Croatie**
Partner 1	Italy, Italie	21.2	18.7	13.6	Germany, Allemagne	14.8	12.5	15.8	Partenaire 1
Partner 2	Germany, Allemagne	10.7	10.3	12.3	Italy, Italie	16.0	15.2	12.9	Partenaire 2
Partner 3	Slovenia, Slovénie	8.1	7.8	10.7	Slovenia, Slovénie	6.8	5.8	10.7	Partenaire 3
Cuba									**Cuba**
Partner 1	Canada	20.3	* 22.7	* 21.6	China, Chine	11.5	18.6	* 26.2	Partenaire 1
Partner 2	China, Chine	4.9	* 27.4	* 16.9	Spain, Espagne	* 8.7	13.6	* 14.0	Partenaire 2
Partner 3	Spain, Espagne	6.9	* 6.1	* 10.1	Mexico, Mexique	* 3.6	* 5.4	5.0	Partenaire 3
Cyprus									**Chypre**
Partner 1	Libya, Libye	* 0.5	0.7	9.0	Greece, Grèce	17.1	18.7	18.6	Partenaire 1
Partner 2	Bunkers, Com. de soute	15.7	0.1	8.2	Italy, Italie	10.1	9.3	7.3	Partenaire 2
Partner 3	Greece, Grèce	* 11.4	* 21.5	7.7	China, Chine	3.8	5.3	7.1	Partenaire 3
Czechia									**Tchéquie**
Partner 1	Germany, Allemagne	33.5	33.4	32.8	Germany, Allemagne	30.0	26.9	25.8	Partenaire 1
Partner 2	Slovakia, Slovaquie	8.6	8.2	7.8	China, Chine	5.1	12.1	12.6	Partenaire 2
Partner 3	Poland, Pologne	5.5	6.0	6.1	Poland, Pologne	5.0	6.1	7.7	Partenaire 3
Dem. People's Rep. Korea									**Rép. pop. dém. de Corée**
Partner 1	China, Chine	* 35.0	* 55.7	* 92.2	China, Chine	* 45.0	* 62.8	* 91.4	Partenaire 1
Partner 2	Pakistan	* 0.9	* 0.9	* 0.9	Russian Federation, Fédération de Russie	* 9.3	* 1.3	* 2.2	Partenaire 2
Partner 3	India, Inde	* 0.6	* 6.8	* 0.8	Thailand, Thaïlande	* 8.6	* 0.8	* 1.5	Partenaire 3
Dem. Rep. of the Congo									**Rép. dém. du Congo**
Partner 1	China, Chine	* 11.6	* 43.3	* 37.4	China, Chine	* 3.1	10.8	19.7	Partenaire 1
Partner 2	Zambia, Zambie	* 1.4	* 21.9	* 15.9	South Africa, Afrique du Sud	* 17.0	19.3	16.4	Partenaire 2
Partner 3	Republic of Korea, République de Corée	* ~0.0	* 1.7	* 9.2	Zambia, Zambie	* 6.0	7.6	11.6	Partenaire 3
Denmark									**Danemark**
Partner 1	Undisclosed, Non divulgués [3]	3.1	1.4	15.0	Germany, Allemagne	21.0	20.7	21.4	Partenaire 1
Partner 2	Germany, Allemagne	* 17.2	* 19.8	* 14.2	Sweden, Suède	14.1	13.3	11.9	Partenaire 2
Partner 3	Sweden, Suède	* 14.8	* 14.2	10.6	Netherlands, Pays-Bas	6.7	7.1	7.7	Partenaire 3
Djibouti									**Djibouti**
Partner 1	United States, États-Unis	* 1.0	* 0.4	* 25.3	China, Chine	* 11.0	* 3.2	* 50.6	Partenaire 1
Partner 2	Saudi Arabia, Arabie saoudite	* 0.1	* 0.8	* 19.9	Indonesia, Indonésie	* 4.2	* 0.2	* 4.5	Partenaire 2
Partner 3	United Arab Emirates, Émirats arabes unis	* 5.3	* 1.0	* 7.3	United Arab Emirates, Émirats arabes unis	* 17.6	* 18.5	* 4.3	Partenaire 3
Dominica									**Dominique**
Partner 1	Bahamas	0.4	0.4	* 40.3	United States, États-Unis	36.6	41.8	* 57.0	Partenaire 1
Partner 2	Indonesia, Indonésie	...	...	14.1	China, Chine	2.2	4.0	* 8.3	Partenaire 2
Partner 3	Saudi Arabia, Arabie saoudite	...	...	* 6.7	Mexico, Mexique	0.5	0.5	* 7.1	Partenaire 3
Dominican Republic									**République dominicaine**
Partner 1	United States, États-Unis	70.3	57.7	53.3	United States, États-Unis	54.8	39.0	44.4	Partenaire 1
Partner 2	Haiti, Haïti	2.7	16.8	9.6	China, Chine	5.4	10.7	13.2	Partenaire 2
Partner 3	Canada	0.6	0.5	8.9	Mexico, Mexique	2.8	6.0	4.6	Partenaire 3
Ecuador									**Équateur**
Partner 1	United States, États-Unis	* 50.1	* 34.7	31.7	United States, États-Unis	19.2	* 27.9	20.0	Partenaire 1
Partner 2	Viet Nam	~0.0	~0.0	7.6	China, Chine	6.5	7.8	18.6	Partenaire 2
Partner 3	Peru, Pérou	8.8	* 7.6	6.7	Colombia, Colombie	14.4	* 9.8	8.1	Partenaire 3

22 Major trading partner *(continued)*

Three largest trade partners as a percentage of total international merchandise trade in US dollars, as at 2017

Partenaire commercial principal *(suite)*

Trois principaux partenaires commerciaux en pourcentage du total de commerce international de marchandises en dollars américains, en 2017

Country or area	Major trading partner	Percentage of exports 2005	2010	2017	Major trading partner	Percentage of imports 2005	2010	2017	Pays ou zone
Egypt									**Égypte**
Partner 1	United Arab Emirates, Émirats arabes unis	2.9	2.3	10.6	China, Chine	5.0	9.2	12.2	Partenaire 1
Partner 2	Italy, Italie	10.1	8.4	8.5	Germany, Allemagne	10.4	7.6	6.8	Partenaire 2
Partner 3	Turkey, Turquie	3.1	3.7	7.2	Italy, Italie	4.2	5.6	6.3	Partenaire 3
El Salvador									**El Salvador**
Partner 1	United States, États-Unis	52.9	48.4	44.9	United States, États-Unis	36.5	37.0	31.8	Partenaire 1
Partner 2	Honduras	14.1	12.9	13.8	China, Chine	3.2	5.7	13.7	Partenaire 2
Partner 3	Guatemala	12.4	14.0	13.8	Guatemala	8.7	9.6	9.9	Partenaire 3
Equatorial Guinea									**Guinée équatoriale**
Partner 1	China, Chine	* 21.7	* 6.2	* 16.5	Spain, Espagne	* 11.2	* 5.8	* 19.6	Partenaire 1
Partner 2	India, Inde	* ~0.0	* 1.3	* 12.7	China, Chine	* 1.9	* 8.9	* 17.6	Partenaire 2
Partner 3	Republic of Korea, République de Corée	...	* 7.9	* 11.4	United States, États-Unis	* 24.8	* 5.3	* 12.4	Partenaire 3
Eritrea									**Érythrée**
Partner 1	China, Chine	* 0.7	* 5.8	* 49.2	Egypt, Égypte	* 2.3	* 10.9	* 26.7	Partenaire 1
Partner 2	Republic of Korea, République de Corée	...	* 0.1	* 20.2	China, Chine	* 2.7	* 7.6	* 19.1	Partenaire 2
Partner 3	United Arab Emirates, Émirats arabes unis	* 0.3	* 13.3	* 20.0	United Arab Emirates, Émirats arabes unis	* 12.2	* 14.2	* 10.1	Partenaire 3
Estonia									**Estonie**
Partner 1	Finland, Finlande	24.6	15.3	15.2	Finland, Finlande	11.7	11.5	10.7	Partenaire 1
Partner 2	Sweden, Suède	12.2	14.0	12.7	Germany, Allemagne	12.8	10.6	10.3	Partenaire 2
Partner 3	Russian Federation, Fédération de Russie	9.8	14.8	10.3	China, Chine	5.7	7.0	8.5	Partenaire 3
Eswatini									**Eswatini**
Partner 1	South Africa, Afrique du Sud	37.5	* 50.1	* 66.2	South Africa, Afrique du Sud	80.9	* 81.2	* 78.7	Partenaire 1
Partner 2	Nigeria, Nigéria	...	* 2.4	* 5.1	Guinea, Guinée	...	...	* 3.8	Partenaire 2
Partner 3	Zimbabwe	~0.0	* 0.7	* 2.2	China, Chine	4.0	* 1.4	* 2.8	Partenaire 3
Ethiopia									**Éthiopie**
Partner 1	United States, États-Unis	4.7	4.4	* 9.8	China, Chine	12.6	24.0	* 31.9	Partenaire 1
Partner 2	Saudi Arabia, Arabie saoudite	6.3	6.3	9.7	United States, États-Unis	9.2	5.6	* 8.8	Partenaire 2
Partner 3	Germany, Allemagne	13.1	11.4	* 8.6	India, Inde	6.0	7.2	* 7.5	Partenaire 3
Falkland Islands (Malvinas)									**Îles Falkland (Malvinas)**
Partner 1	Spain, Espagne	* 78.1	* 79.5	* 72.6	United Kingdom, Royaume-Uni	* 73.1	* 77.7	* 47.9	Partenaire 1
Partner 2	Namibia, Namibie	...	...	12.5	Spain, Espagne	* 0.8	* 1.2	* 28.7	Partenaire 2
Partner 3	United States, États-Unis	* 5.6	* 3.1	* 5.0	Greece, Grèce	...	* 6.7	* 10.6	Partenaire 3
Faroe Islands									**Îles Féroé**
Partner 1	Russian Federation, Fédération de Russie	3.6	* 4.0	* 24.1	Denmark, Danemark	26.7	* 30.4	* 59.9	Partenaire 1
Partner 2	United Kingdom, Royaume-Uni	28.4	* 17.3	* 17.5	Norway, Norvège	17.4	* 18.1	* 11.5	Partenaire 2
Partner 3	Denmark, Danemark	14.6	* 11.0	* 13.5	Germany, Allemagne	6.6	* 6.1	* 6.2	Partenaire 3
Fiji									**Fidji**
Partner 1	United States, États-Unis	15.4	11.4	19.4	Singapore, Singapour	29.9	33.1	19.1	Partenaire 1
Partner 2	Australia, Australie	20.4	21.1	15.4	New Zealand, Nouvelle-Zélande	* 18.2	15.9	17.2	Partenaire 2
Partner 3	New Zealand, Nouvelle-Zélande	5.1	5.8	6.8	Australia, Australie	* 24.6	20.3	16.6	Partenaire 3
Finland									**Finlande**
Partner 1	Germany, Allemagne	* 10.6	* 9.5	14.0	Germany, Allemagne	* 14.9	* 13.2	15.2	Partenaire 1
Partner 2	Sweden, Suède	* 10.7	* 11.4	* 10.2	Russian Federation, Fédération de Russie	* 13.9	* 17.7	13.1	Partenaire 2
Partner 3	Netherlands, Pays-Bas	* 4.7	* 6.6	6.7	Sweden, Suède	* 10.6	* 10.0	10.9	Partenaire 3
France									**France**
Partner 1	Germany, Allemagne	14.5	16.2	* 16.1	Germany, Allemagne	17.2	17.3	* 16.9	Partenaire 1
Partner 2	Spain, Espagne	10.2	7.4	7.5	China, Chine	5.5	8.2	* 9.1	Partenaire 2
Partner 3	United States, États-Unis	7.2	5.7	* 7.4	Italy, Italie	8.6	7.5	* 7.5	Partenaire 3
French Polynesia									**Polynésie française**
Partner 1	Japan, Japon	28.3	20.1	* 26.1	France	35.5	28.1	* 25.6	Partenaire 1
Partner 2	China, Hong Kong SAR, Chine, RAS Hong Kong	28.0	30.0	24.5	China, Chine	6.4	9.4	* 13.2	Partenaire 2
Partner 3	United States, États-Unis	13.8	11.6	* 18.0	United States, États-Unis	* 10.0	10.1	10.4	Partenaire 3
Gabon									**Gabon**
Partner 1	China, Chine	4.0	* 8.0	* 29.9	France	39.3	* 32.9	* 26.4	Partenaire 1
Partner 2	Trinidad and Tobago, Trinité-et-Tobago	...	...	14.4	China, Chine	1.7	* 4.9	* 19.0	Partenaire 2
Partner 3	Australia, Australie	1.3	* ~0.0	* 8.2	Belgium, Belgique	12.2	* 15.7	* 7.6	Partenaire 3
Gambia									**Gambie**
Partner 1	Guinea-Bissau, Guinée-Bissau	0.3	3.1	* 62.9	Côte d'Ivoire	12.6	19.4	* 16.8	Partenaire 1
Partner 2	Viet Nam	...	~0.0	12.0	Brazil, Brésil	4.3	10.0	* 11.6	Partenaire 2
Partner 3	Senegal, Sénégal	7.1	26.3	* 11.1	Spain, Espagne	1.3	3.4	* 11.0	Partenaire 3

22 Major trading partner *(continued)*

Three largest trade partners as a percentage of total international merchandise trade in US dollars, as at 2017

Partenaire commercial principal *(suite)*

Trois principaux partenaires commerciaux en pourcentage du total de commerce international de marchandises en dollars américains, en 2017

Country or area	Major trading partner	Percentage of exports 2005	2010	2017	Major trading partner	Percentage of imports 2005	2010	2017	Pays ou zone
Georgia									**Géorgie**
Partner 1	Russian Federation, Fédération de Russie	17.8	* 2.7	14.5	Turkey, Turquie	11.5	16.9	17.2	Partenaire 1
Partner 2	Azerbaijan, Azerbaïdjan	9.6	* 15.3	* 10.0	Russian Federation, Fédération de Russie	15.4	* 4.6	9.9	Partenaire 2
Partner 3	Turkey, Turquie	14.1	* 12.5	7.9	China, Chine	1.9	6.4	9.2	Partenaire 3
Germany									**Allemagne**
Partner 1	United States, États-Unis	8.8	6.8	8.7	China, Chine	6.5	9.5	9.8	Partenaire 1
Partner 2	France	10.1	* 9.6	* 8.2	Netherlands, Pays-Bas	8.3	7.8	8.1	Partenaire 2
Partner 3	China, Chine	2.7	5.6	6.7	France	8.6	7.7	6.2	Partenaire 3
Ghana									**Ghana**
Partner 1	Switzerland, Suisse	4.5	4.1	* 17.5	China, Chine	8.1	13.2	* 17.3	Partenaire 1
Partner 2	India, Inde	1.4	0.9	14.6	United Kingdom, Royaume-Uni	7.6	4.8	* 9.7	Partenaire 2
Partner 3	United Arab Emirates, Émirats arabes unis	0.3	6.8	* 13.4	United States, États-Unis	7.1	13.7	* 7.8	Partenaire 3
Gibraltar									**Gibraltar**
Partner 1	Mauritania, Mauritanie	...	* ~0.0	* 27.6	Areas nes, Zones nsa [1]	...	* 15.0	* 38.4	Partenaire 1
Partner 2	Germany, Allemagne	* 42.3	* 2.1	* 19.4	United Kingdom, Royaume-Uni	* 16.7	* 14.8	* 12.3	Partenaire 2
Partner 3	Netherlands, Pays-Bas	* 0.1	* 0.1	* 13.8	Spain, Espagne	* 16.9	* 10.8	* 10.9	Partenaire 3
Greece									**Grèce**
Partner 1	Italy, Italie	10.5	* 9.2	10.6	Germany, Allemagne	13.3	10.7	10.2	Partenaire 1
Partner 2	Germany, Allemagne	12.5	* 9.3	* 7.1	Italy, Italie	12.3	9.7	7.6	Partenaire 2
Partner 3	Turkey, Turquie	5.4	* 6.0	6.9	Russian Federation, Fédération de Russie	7.7	9.6	7.0	Partenaire 3
Greenland									**Groenland**
Partner 1	Denmark, Danemark	86.7	88.9	* 81.3	Denmark, Danemark	71.5	* 57.6	* 72.2	Partenaire 1
Partner 2	Portugal	...	4.1	8.3	Sweden, Suède	16.1	* 21.6	* 9.8	Partenaire 2
Partner 3	Areas nes, Zones nsa [1]	~0.0	2.3	* 6.0	China, Chine	~0.0	1.8	* 2.6	Partenaire 3
Grenada									**Grenade**
Partner 1	United States, États-Unis	21.4	* 16.3	* 31.1	United States, États-Unis	37.5	* 31.9	* 36.1	Partenaire 1
Partner 2	Saint Lucia, Sainte-Lucie	9.3	* 11.2	* 9.9	Trinidad and Tobago, Trinité-et-Tobago	20.9	* 25.2	* 15.7	Partenaire 2
Partner 3	Germany, Allemagne	1.6	* 6.0	* 8.1	United Kingdom, Royaume-Uni	5.8	* 4.2	* 4.6	Partenaire 3
Guatemala									**Guatemala**
Partner 1	United States, États-Unis	50.1	38.8	* 34.5	United States, États-Unis	33.9	37.1	* 38.5	Partenaire 1
Partner 2	El Salvador	12.1	11.7	11.4	Mexico, Mexique	8.7	11.2	* 11.4	Partenaire 2
Partner 3	Honduras	7.3	8.3	* 8.6	China, Chine	7.2	7.1	* 10.9	Partenaire 3
Guinea									**Guinée**
Partner 1	China, Chine	0.2	* 1.4	* 86.6	Côte d'Ivoire	14.4	* 1.7	* 22.3	Partenaire 1
Partner 2	Belgium, Belgique	10.6	* 0.5	* 6.8	China, Chine	3.9	* 6.7	* 11.6	Partenaire 2
Partner 3	Singapore, Singapour	* ~0.0	* ~0.0	* 1.7	Spain, Espagne	0.6	* 2.2	* 8.8	Partenaire 3
Guinea-Bissau									**Guinée-Bissau**
Partner 1	India, Inde	86.6	* 76.2	* 61.1	Portugal	37.2	* 24.2	* 26.6	Partenaire 1
Partner 2	Viet Nam	...	* 4.2	* 21.3	Gambia, Gambie	1.6	* 0.9	* 19.6	Partenaire 2
Partner 3	Belarus, Bélarus	...	* ~0.0	* 10.0	Senegal, Sénégal	40.9	* 21.4	* 15.4	Partenaire 3
Guyana									**Guyana**
Partner 1	Canada	16.0	39.6	22.9	Trinidad and Tobago, Trinité-et-Tobago	33.3	22.0	27.5	Partenaire 1
Partner 2	United States, États-Unis	15.5	10.2	15.9	United States, États-Unis	31.1	27.7	26.5	Partenaire 2
Partner 3	Trinidad and Tobago, Trinité-et-Tobago	5.5	3.5	11.4	China, Chine	4.1	5.8	8.9	Partenaire 3
Haiti									**Haïti**
Partner 1	United States, États-Unis	* 83.7	* 81.2	* 82.7	United States, États-Unis	* 49.3	* 35.2	* 34.1	Partenaire 1
Partner 2	Dominican Republic, Rép. dominicaine	* 4.2	* 2.3	* 3.7	Dominican Republic, Rép. dominicaine	* 12.0	* 23.4	* 21.0	Partenaire 2
Partner 3	Canada	* 3.8	* 3.6	* 2.9	China, Chine	* 2.2	* 7.4	* 11.9	Partenaire 3
Honduras									**Honduras**
Partner 1	United States, États-Unis	41.6	* 38.9	40.2	United States, États-Unis	36.8	38.5	34.7	Partenaire 1
Partner 2	Germany, Allemagne	8.3	7.5	7.9	China, Chine	2.3	7.7	15.0	Partenaire 2
Partner 3	Belgium, Belgique	5.2	4.3	7.0	Guatemala	7.8	8.9	8.6	Partenaire 3
Hungary									**Hongrie**
Partner 1	Germany, Allemagne	30.1	27.1	27.4	Germany, Allemagne	27.6	27.0	26.5	Partenaire 1
Partner 2	Romania, Roumanie	3.7	5.3	5.2	Austria, Autriche	6.6	6.0	6.2	Partenaire 2
Partner 3	Italy, Italie	5.5	5.3	5.1	Poland, Pologne	3.8	4.7	5.6	Partenaire 3
Iceland									**Islande**
Partner 1	Netherlands, Pays-Bas	12.5	34.0	25.5	Germany, Allemagne	13.8	7.5	10.6	Partenaire 1
Partner 2	Spain, Espagne	7.4	4.7	13.5	Norway, Norvège	7.0	9.1	9.1	Partenaire 2
Partner 3	United Kingdom, Royaume-Uni	17.8	10.1	9.4	China, Chine	5.1	6.0	6.9	Partenaire 3

22 Major trading partner *(continued)*

Three largest trade partners as a percentage of total international merchandise trade in US dollars, as at 2017

Partenaire commercial principal *(suite)*

Trois principaux partenaires commerciaux en pourcentage du total de commerce international de marchandises en dollars américains, en 2017

Country or area	Major trading partner	Percentage of exports 2005	2010	2017	Major trading partner	Percentage of imports 2005	2010	2017	Pays ou zone
India									**Inde**
Partner 1	United States, États-Unis	16.5	11.2	16.0	China, Chine	* 7.2	11.8	16.6	Partenaire 1
Partner 2	United Arab Emirates, Émirats arabes unis	8.4	12.3	9.6	United States, États-Unis	* 6.0	5.5	5.7	Partenaire 2
Partner 3	China, Hong Kong SAR, Chine, RAS Hong Kong	4.4	4.3	5.0	United Arab Emirates, Émirats arabes unis	* 3.6	8.8	4.9	Partenaire 3
Indonesia									**Indonésie**
Partner 1	China, Chine	7.8	9.9	13.6	China, Chine	10.1	15.1	21.9	Partenaire 1
Partner 2	United States, États-Unis	11.5	9.1	10.5	Singapore, Singapour	16.4	14.9	10.8	Partenaire 2
Partner 3	Japan, Japon	21.1	16.3	10.5	Japan, Japon	12.0	12.5	9.0	Partenaire 3
Iran (Islamic Republic of)									**Iran (Rép. islamique d')**
Partner 1	China, Chine	0.8	5.3	* 27.7	China, Chine	* 6.4	10.4	* 31.8	Partenaire 1
Partner 2	Republic of Korea, République de Corée	0.2	0.5	12.9	United Arab Emirates, Émirats arabes unis	* 18.7	28.6	* 11.8	Partenaire 2
Partner 3	India, Inde	1.1	2.0	* 12.3	Republic of Korea, République de Corée	* 5.5	6.7	* 7.3	Partenaire 3
Iraq									**Iraq**
Partner 1	Areas nes, Zones nsa [1]	...	...	* 99.8	Areas nes, Zones nsa [1]	69.0	* 94.8	* 68.2	Partenaire 1
Partner 2	Singapore, Singapour	...	...	0.2	Turkey, Turquie	* 7.1	* 1.0	* 8.3	Partenaire 2
Partner 3	United Arab Emirates, Émirats arabes unis	0.5	* ~0.0	* ~0.0	China, Chine	* 1.0	* 0.2	* 7.4	Partenaire 3
Ireland									**Irlande**
Partner 1	United States, États-Unis	18.7	* 23.7	27.1	United Kingdom, Royaume-Uni	31.2	* 28.8	22.1	Partenaire 1
Partner 2	United Kingdom, Royaume-Uni	17.1	* 13.9	* 11.8	United States, États-Unis	14.1	* 15.4	20.6	Partenaire 2
Partner 3	Belgium, Belgique	* 15.1	* 14.9	10.9	France	3.4	* 8.2	13.3	Partenaire 3
Israel									**Israël**
Partner 1	United States, États-Unis	* 37.8	* 33.2	27.0	China, Chine	* 4.2	* 8.0	13.1	Partenaire 1
Partner 2	United Kingdom, Royaume-Uni	* 3.9	* 3.9	* 8.4	United States, États-Unis	* 13.6	* 11.2	11.8	Partenaire 2
Partner 3	Areas nes, Zones nsa [1]	1.6	0.4	7.5	Areas nes, Zones nsa [1]	1.7	2.2	9.7	Partenaire 3
Italy									**Italie**
Partner 1	Germany, Allemagne	* 13.1	14.3	12.5	Germany, Allemagne	18.1	16.0	16.3	Partenaire 1
Partner 2	France	* 12.2	11.5	10.3	France	10.2	8.7	8.8	Partenaire 2
Partner 3	United States, États-Unis	* 8.0	6.1	9.1	China, Chine	4.6	7.8	7.1	Partenaire 3
Jamaica									**Jamaïque**
Partner 1	United States, États-Unis	25.6	49.6	45.0	United States, États-Unis	42.8	37.4	43.7	Partenaire 1
Partner 2	Netherlands, Pays-Bas	2.3	5.1	12.0	Japan, Japon	4.4	2.3	6.3	Partenaire 2
Partner 3	Canada	19.4	12.3	9.6	China, Chine	2.9	4.6	6.3	Partenaire 3
Japan									**Japon**
Partner 1	United States, États-Unis	22.9	15.6	19.3	China, Chine	21.0	22.1	24.5	Partenaire 1
Partner 2	China, Chine	13.5	19.4	19.1	United States, États-Unis	12.7	10.0	11.0	Partenaire 2
Partner 3	Republic of Korea, République de Corée	7.8	8.1	7.6	Australia, Australie	4.8	6.5	5.8	Partenaire 3
Jordan									**Jordanie**
Partner 1	United States, États-Unis	* 26.1	* 13.2	21.5	China, Chine	9.2	10.8	13.5	Partenaire 1
Partner 2	Free zones, Zones franches	5.6	7.5	12.5	Saudi Arabia, Arabie saoudite	23.7	* 19.8	13.5	Partenaire 2
Partner 3	Saudi Arabia, Arabie saoudite	* 5.9	* 9.6	11.3	United States, États-Unis	5.6	5.6	9.8	Partenaire 3
Kazakhstan									**Kazakhstan**
Partner 1	Italy, Italie	15.0	16.7	17.9	Russian Federation, Fédération de Russie	38.0	22.8	39.1	Partenaire 1
Partner 2	China, Chine	8.7	17.7	12.0	China, Chine	7.2	16.5	16.0	Partenaire 2
Partner 3	Netherlands, Pays-Bas	3.2	7.3	9.8	Germany, Allemagne	7.5	7.6	5.1	Partenaire 3
Kenya									**Kenya**
Partner 1	United States, États-Unis	6.7	5.5	* 10.5	China, Chine	5.2	12.6	* 35.7	Partenaire 1
Partner 2	Netherlands, Pays-Bas	7.1	6.6	9.3	India, Inde	5.6	10.8	* 8.0	Partenaire 2
Partner 3	Pakistan	5.4	4.4	* 8.3	Japan, Japon	5.2	6.1	* 4.6	Partenaire 3
Kiribati									**Kiribati**
Partner 1	Malaysia, Malaisie	...	...	* 33.2	Australia, Australie	35.6	28.1	* 21.8	Partenaire 1
Partner 2	United States, États-Unis	~0.0	...	21.2	Fiji, Fidji	20.9	26.8	* 21.8	Partenaire 2
Partner 3	Fiji, Fidji	15.5	2.2	* 14.9	China, Chine	2.3	5.4	* 9.6	Partenaire 3
Kuwait									**Koweït**
Partner 1	Areas nes, Zones nsa [1]	* 0.2	...	90.5	China, Chine	* 6.8	12.5	16.4	Partenaire 1
Partner 2	India, Inde	* 1.0	* 11.9	* 1.4	United States, États-Unis	* 10.8	11.4	10.3	Partenaire 2
Partner 3	Saudi Arabia, Arabie saoudite	* 0.7	* 0.8	1.2	United Arab Emirates, Émirats arabes unis	* 4.5	4.5	8.7	Partenaire 3
Kyrgyzstan									**Kirghizistan**
Partner 1	Switzerland, Suisse	9.7	26.1	27.4	China, Chine	9.3	20.7	33.4	Partenaire 1
Partner 2	Kazakhstan	17.3	12.2	16.5	Russian Federation, Fédération de Russie	34.2	33.6	26.4	Partenaire 2
Partner 3	Russian Federation, Fédération de Russie	20.0	17.3	14.7	Kazakhstan	16.3	12.0	13.1	Partenaire 3

22 Major trading partner *(continued)*

Three largest trade partners as a percentage of total international merchandise trade in US dollars, as at 2017

Partenaire commercial principal *(suite)*

Trois principaux partenaires commerciaux en pourcentage du total de commerce international de marchandises en dollars américains, en 2017

Country or area	Major trading partner	Percentage of exports 2005	2010	2017	Major trading partner	Percentage of imports 2005	2010	2017	Pays ou zone
Lao People's Dem. Rep.									**Rép. dém. populaire lao**
Partner 1	China, Chine	* 4.2	11.7	* 36.1	Thailand, Thaïlande	* 68.4	71.8	* 61.9	Partenaire 1
Partner 2	Thailand, Thaïlande	* 37.0	53.5	31.3	China, Chine	* 9.2	9.8	* 18.2	Partenaire 2
Partner 3	Viet Nam	* 15.9	6.5	* 17.2	Viet Nam	* 6.2	6.6	* 10.1	Partenaire 3
Latvia									**Lettonie**
Partner 1	Lithuania, Lituanie	* 10.5	16.2	16.8	Lithuania, Lituanie	13.5	17.1	18.6	Partenaire 1
Partner 2	Estonia, Estonie	* 10.4	13.5	11.6	Germany, Allemagne	13.6	11.5	11.3	Partenaire 2
Partner 3	Russian Federation, Fédération de Russie	8.3	10.6	9.1	Poland, Pologne	6.3	7.9	9.1	Partenaire 3
Lebanon									**Liban**
Partner 1	South Africa, Afrique du Sud	0.2	8.1	* 21.1	China, Chine	* 7.9	9.1	* 11.2	Partenaire 1
Partner 2	Saudi Arabia, Arabie saoudite	7.4	* 5.8	* 9.0	Italy, Italie	* 10.4	7.8	* 7.5	Partenaire 2
Partner 3	United Arab Emirates, Émirats arabes unis	* 8.5	* 9.8	* 8.0	United States, États-Unis	* 5.9	10.7	* 6.3	Partenaire 3
Lesotho									**Lesotho**
Partner 1	United States, États-Unis	* 44.5	21.4	* 29.9	South Africa, Afrique du Sud	* 77.1	78.9	* 86.7	Partenaire 1
Partner 2	South Africa, Afrique du Sud	* 42.3	74.9	29.3	Asia nes, Asie nsa	* 5.6	5.3	* 3.9	Partenaire 2
Partner 3	Belgium, Belgique	* 0.8	...	* 28.1	China, Chine	* 3.8	2.6	* 3.8	Partenaire 3
Liberia									**Libéria**
Partner 1	Areas nes, Zones nsa [1]	20.1	...	* 20.9	Areas nes, Zones nsa [1]	...	...	* 60.1	Partenaire 1
Partner 2	Switzerland, Suisse	* 0.2	* 0.5	* 17.3	China, Chine	* 10.0	* 29.6	* 14.7	Partenaire 2
Partner 3	United Arab Emirates, Émirats arabes unis	* 0.1	* 6.0	* 9.6	India, Inde	* 3.1	* 2.2	* 3.9	Partenaire 3
Libya									**Libye**
Partner 1	Italy, Italie	* 36.7	42.3	* 17.6	China, Chine	* 3.3	9.8	* 13.4	Partenaire 1
Partner 2	Germany, Allemagne	* 16.2	2.6	15.7	Italy, Italie	* 18.3	9.4	* 13.0	Partenaire 2
Partner 3	Spain, Espagne	* 9.8	9.2	* 13.8	Turkey, Turquie	* 1.8	10.6	* 9.3	Partenaire 3
Lithuania									**Lituanie**
Partner 1	Russian Federation, Fédération de Russie	11.4	15.6	14.9	Russian Federation, Fédération de Russie	27.5	32.7	13.0	Partenaire 1
Partner 2	Latvia, Lettonie	10.0	9.5	9.9	Germany, Allemagne	14.8	10.9	12.3	Partenaire 2
Partner 3	Poland, Pologne	5.3	7.7	8.1	Poland, Pologne	8.2	8.8	10.6	Partenaire 3
Luxembourg									**Luxembourg**
Partner 1	Germany, Allemagne	25.4	28.4	26.9	Belgium, Belgique	33.8	* 24.9	24.3	Partenaire 1
Partner 2	France	17.2	16.2	14.8	Germany, Allemagne	25.9	* 25.6	24.1	Partenaire 2
Partner 3	Belgium, Belgique	11.4	12.6	11.6	France	11.8	* 14.9	11.8	Partenaire 3
Madagascar									**Madagascar**
Partner 1	France	* 34.4	* 33.1	* 23.8	China, Chine	* 13.9	12.2	* 21.3	Partenaire 1
Partner 2	United States, États-Unis	22.0	* 4.2	* 13.0	France	* 15.6	14.4	* 6.9	Partenaire 2
Partner 3	Germany, Allemagne	* 6.4	* 7.3	* 8.4	India, Inde	* 5.9	2.4	* 6.5	Partenaire 3
Malawi									**Malawi**
Partner 1	Belgium, Belgique	1.4	12.4	* 10.6	South Africa, Afrique du Sud	32.7	30.1	* 18.1	Partenaire 1
Partner 2	Zimbabwe	2.2	5.4	9.3	China, Chine	2.9	9.1	* 13.1	Partenaire 2
Partner 3	Mozambique	3.5	3.4	* 9.2	United Arab Emirates, Émirats arabes unis	2.3	5.0	* 11.0	Partenaire 3
Malaysia									**Malaisie**
Partner 1	Singapore, Singapour	15.5	13.3	14.3	China, Chine	11.5	12.6	19.6	Partenaire 1
Partner 2	China, Chine	6.5	12.6	13.5	Singapore, Singapour	11.7	11.4	11.1	Partenaire 2
Partner 3	United States, États-Unis	19.6	9.5	9.5	United States, États-Unis	12.9	10.7	8.3	Partenaire 3
Maldives									**Maldives**
Partner 1	Thailand, Thaïlande	15.3	29.9	* 34.4	United Arab Emirates, Émirats arabes unis	15.7	18.8	* 15.7	Partenaire 1
Partner 2	Sri Lanka	12.2	19.6	10.2	Singapore, Singapour	24.1	17.9	* 14.3	Partenaire 2
Partner 3	United States, États-Unis	2.9	0.7	* 8.9	China, Chine	2.1	2.9	* 13.4	Partenaire 3
Mali									**Mali**
Partner 1	South Africa, Afrique du Sud	34.9	57.1	* 47.0	Senegal, Sénégal	11.5	13.6	* 19.4	Partenaire 1
Partner 2	Switzerland, Suisse	30.3	12.1	15.0	China, Chine	4.9	9.9	* 15.6	Partenaire 2
Partner 3	United Arab Emirates, Émirats arabes unis	~0.0	1.0	* 7.6	Côte d'Ivoire	10.2	7.9	* 9.8	Partenaire 3
Malta									**Malte**
Partner 1	United States, États-Unis	* 13.5	7.0	* 20.3	Italy, Italie	30.7	24.6	* 19.2	Partenaire 1
Partner 2	Bunkers, Com. de soute	0.1	0.1	10.7	Cayman Islands, Îles Caïmanes	~0.0	1.0	* 10.2	Partenaire 2
Partner 3	Germany, Allemagne	* 12.1	* 10.5	* 10.7	Canada	0.2	2.2	* 9.0	Partenaire 3
Marshall Islands									**Îles Marshall**
Partner 1	Spain, Espagne	* ~0.0	* ~0.0	* 16.5	Areas nes, Zones nsa [1]	...	...	87.4	Partenaire 1
Partner 2	United States, États-Unis	* 25.9	* 12.9	* 15.2	United States, États-Unis	21.5	7.6	5.8	Partenaire 2
Partner 3	Thailand, Thaïlande	* 35.4	* 33.6	* 13.9	China, Chine	* 11.4	24.3	3.8	Partenaire 3

22 Major trading partner *(continued)*

Three largest trade partners as a percentage of total international merchandise trade in US dollars, as at 2017

Partenaire commercial principal *(suite)*

Trois principaux partenaires commerciaux en pourcentage du total de commerce international de marchandises en dollars américains, en 2017

Country or area	Major trading partner	Percentage of exports 2005	2010	2017	Major trading partner	Percentage of imports 2005	2010	2017	Pays ou zone
Mauritania									**Mauritanie**
Partner 1	China, Chine	1.5	39.4	35.1	Republic of Korea, République de Corée	* ~0.0	0.1	18.1	Partenaire 1
Partner 2	Switzerland, Suisse	...	13.1	15.4	United Arab Emirates, Émirats arabes unis	* 0.9	12.1	8.9	Partenaire 2
Partner 3	Spain, Espagne	10.7	7.2	11.6	Norway, Norvège	* 0.8	~0.0	7.8	Partenaire 3
Mauritius									**Maurice**
Partner 1	France	15.7	16.2	15.8	China, Chine	9.8	13.3	16.4	Partenaire 1
Partner 2	United Kingdom, Royaume-Uni	30.0	23.7	11.9	India, Inde	6.9	22.3	16.4	Partenaire 2
Partner 3	United States, États-Unis	9.2	10.9	11.2	South Africa, Afrique du Sud	8.6	8.4	8.5	Partenaire 3
Mexico									**Mexique**
Partner 1	United States, États-Unis	86.0	80.2	80.0	United States, États-Unis	53.6	48.2	46.4	Partenaire 1
Partner 2	Canada	2.0	3.6	2.8	China, Chine	8.0	15.1	17.6	Partenaire 2
Partner 3	Germany, Allemagne	1.1	1.2	1.7	Japan, Japon	5.9	5.0	4.3	Partenaire 3
Micronesia (Fed. States of)									**Micronésie (États féd. de)**
Partner 1	Thailand, Thaïlande	* 82.0	* 30.6	* 59.5	Republic of Korea, République de Corée	4.0	2.4	* 26.2	Partenaire 1
Partner 2	China, Chine	...	* 3.8	* 11.7	United States, États-Unis	42.9	48.7	* 23.0	Partenaire 2
Partner 3	Philippines	* 5.9	* 1.5	* 11.5	Asia nes, Asie nsa [2]	1.7	0.8	14.1	Partenaire 3
Mongolia									**Mongolie**
Partner 1	China, Chine	48.1	* 81.8	* 79.0	China, Chine	24.9	* 41.5	* 31.1	Partenaire 1
Partner 2	United Kingdom, Royaume-Uni	8.2	* 2.1	* 16.0	Russian Federation, Fédération de Russie	35.3	* 26.8	* 25.8	Partenaire 2
Partner 3	Russian Federation, Fédération de Russie	2.6	* 2.5	* 1.1	Japan, Japon	6.4	* 4.6	* 9.9	Partenaire 3
Montenegro									**Monténégro**
Partner 1	Serbia, Serbie	...	* 28.2	17.8	Serbia, Serbie	...	26.2	21.5	Partenaire 1
Partner 2	Bosnia-Herzegovina, Bosnie-Herzégovine	...	7.3	12.7	China, Chine	...	5.4	9.6	Partenaire 2
Partner 3	Areas nes, Zones nsa [1]	...	0.1	9.4	Germany, Allemagne	...	7.1	8.5	Partenaire 3
Montserrat									**Montserrat**
Partner 1	Mexico, Mexique	...	...	* 73.4	United States, États-Unis	56.6	* 68.5	* 47.6	Partenaire 1
Partner 2	United States, États-Unis	23.6	28.5	7.4	Trinidad and Tobago, Trinité-et-Tobago	14.6	* 6.1	* 10.1	Partenaire 2
Partner 3	France	1.2	25.9	* 6.1	United Kingdom, Royaume-Uni	7.8	* 5.6	* 9.8	Partenaire 3
Morocco									**Maroc**
Partner 1	Spain, Espagne	20.0	* 17.0	* 23.3	Spain, Espagne	11.6	10.6	* 15.7	Partenaire 1
Partner 2	France	30.1	22.5	21.1	France	18.2	15.6	* 13.2	Partenaire 2
Partner 3	Italy, Italie	5.0	4.5	* 4.6	China, Chine	5.1	8.4	* 9.1	Partenaire 3
Mozambique									**Mozambique**
Partner 1	South Africa, Afrique du Sud	* 16.5	* 20.8	* 21.0	South Africa, Afrique du Sud	* 40.6	34.4	* 30.0	Partenaire 1
Partner 2	Netherlands, Pays-Bas	* 59.7	* 52.7	* 20.9	Singapore, Singapour	1.0	0.2	* 8.1	Partenaire 2
Partner 3	India, Inde	* 1.8	* 1.4	* 20.2	China, Chine	* 2.9	3.6	* 7.9	Partenaire 3
Myanmar									**Myanmar**
Partner 1	China, Chine	* 7.2	6.2	38.9	China, Chine	* 29.0	27.1	31.8	Partenaire 1
Partner 2	Thailand, Thaïlande	* 47.1	41.7	19.4	Singapore, Singapour	* 18.5	27.0	15.2	Partenaire 2
Partner 3	Japan, Japon	* 5.4	2.8	6.5	Thailand, Thaïlande	* 21.9	11.4	11.3	Partenaire 3
Namibia									**Namibie**
Partner 1	Switzerland, Suisse	0.3	0.9	* 18.8	South Africa, Afrique du Sud	83.2	* 72.4	* 57.2	Partenaire 1
Partner 2	South Africa, Afrique du Sud	28.2	29.0	16.0	Botswana	0.2	* 0.3	* 6.8	Partenaire 2
Partner 3	Botswana	0.4	0.7	* 14.1	Zambia, Zambie	0.1	1.3	* 4.1	Partenaire 3
Nepal									**Népal**
Partner 1	India, Inde	* 52.4	65.3	56.7	India, Inde	* 53.0	63.6	65.0	Partenaire 1
Partner 2	United States, États-Unis	* 29.1	6.3	11.2	China, Chine	* 8.4	11.0	12.6	Partenaire 2
Partner 3	Turkey, Turquie	* 0.2	1.0	6.4	Areas nes, Zones nsa [1]	* ~0.0	...	2.0	Partenaire 3
Netherlands									**Pays-Bas**
Partner 1	Germany, Allemagne	23.8	22.1	* 22.2	Germany, Allemagne	19.0	20.3	* 18.2	Partenaire 1
Partner 2	Belgium, Belgique	11.7	9.8	10.3	Belgium, Belgique	10.8	8.9	* 10.5	Partenaire 2
Partner 3	United Kingdom, Royaume-Uni	9.2	7.4	* 9.0	China, Chine	7.6	9.3	* 9.0	Partenaire 3
New Caledonia									**Nouvelle-Calédonie**
Partner 1	China, Chine	5.6	3.5	* 35.7	France	32.3	22.3	* 25.7	Partenaire 1
Partner 2	Japan, Japon	18.3	18.8	15.9	China, Chine	4.7	17.6	* 10.2	Partenaire 2
Partner 3	Republic of Korea, République de Corée	13.1	11.6	* 15.1	Singapore, Singapour	15.0	12.9	* 8.2	Partenaire 3
New Zealand									**Nouvelle-Zélande**
Partner 1	China, Chine	5.1	11.1	22.3	China, Chine	10.8	16.0	19.3	Partenaire 1
Partner 2	Australia, Australie	21.0	23.0	16.4	Australia, Australie	20.6	18.2	12.2	Partenaire 2
Partner 3	United States, États-Unis	14.9	8.6	9.9	United States, États-Unis	11.0	10.4	10.7	Partenaire 3

22 Major trading partner *(continued)*

Three largest trade partners as a percentage of total international merchandise trade in US dollars, as at 2017

Partenaire commercial principal *(suite)*

Trois principaux partenaires commerciaux en pourcentage du total de commerce international de marchandises en dollars américains, en 2017

Country or area	Major trading partner	Percentage of exports 2005	2010	2017	Major trading partner	Percentage of imports 2005	2010	2017	Pays ou zone
Nicaragua									**Nicaragua**
Partner 1	United States, États-Unis	35.4	32.8	58.6	United States, États-Unis	20.7	20.7	23.5	Partenaire 1
Partner 2	Mexico, Mexique	5.1	2.8	6.6	China, Chine	5.9	8.7	15.2	Partenaire 2
Partner 3	El Salvador	14.2	10.7	5.6	Mexico, Mexique	8.5	7.7	11.0	Partenaire 3
Niger									**Niger**
Partner 1	France	*22.2	*9.0	*31.3	France	15.8	11.0	*28.3	Partenaire 1
Partner 2	Thailand, Thaïlande	*~0.0	1.2	11.6	China, Chine	5.5	43.8	*16.2	Partenaire 2
Partner 3	Malaysia, Malaisie	...	0.7	*11.1	United States, États-Unis	5.4	6.1	*7.8	Partenaire 3
Nigeria									**Nigéria**
Partner 1	India, Inde	*9.3	10.5	17.9	China, Chine	*13.8	16.6	18.7	Partenaire 1
Partner 2	United States, États-Unis	*45.0	34.4	12.8	Belgium, Belgique	*5.1	3.9	12.9	Partenaire 2
Partner 3	Spain, Espagne	*8.0	3.3	9.9	Netherlands, Pays-Bas	*3.1	0.8	9.2	Partenaire 3
Northern Mariana Islands									**Îles Mariannes du Nord**
Partner 1	Areas nes, Zones nsa [1]	91.1	*91.1	*91.1	Areas nes, Zones nsa [1]	56.5	*66.2	*66.1	Partenaire 1
Partner 2	Republic of Korea, République de Corée	*0.5	*0.6	*3.6	China, Hong Kong SAR, Chine, RAS Hong Kong	*12.3	*11.4	*13.5	Partenaire 2
Partner 3	Singapore, Singapour	*0.1	*0.7	*2.6	Republic of Korea, République de Corée	*10.6	*4.3	3.9	Partenaire 3
Norway									**Norvège**
Partner 1	United Kingdom, Royaume-Uni	25.0	27.4	21.1	Sweden, Suède	14.4	14.0	11.5	Partenaire 1
Partner 2	Germany, Allemagne	12.6	11.0	15.5	Germany, Allemagne	13.4	12.3	11.1	Partenaire 2
Partner 3	Netherlands, Pays-Bas	9.9	11.9	9.9	China, Chine	5.6	8.5	9.8	Partenaire 3
Oman									**Oman**
Partner 1	China, Chine	*27.5	25.6	*43.6	United Arab Emirates, Émirats arabes unis	26.1	28.4	*45.1	Partenaire 1
Partner 2	Areas nes, Zones nsa [1]	9.7	16.8	10.3	Areas nes, Zones nsa [1]	1.6	...	*11.2	Partenaire 2
Partner 3	United Arab Emirates, Émirats arabes unis	*7.3	11.6	*7.5	China, Chine	2.4	4.8	*4.8	Partenaire 3
Other non-specified areas									**Autres zones non-spécifiées**
Partner 1	China, Chine	21.6	28.0	26.3	China, Chine	*11.0	14.3	*19.1	Partenaire 1
Partner 2	China, Hong Kong SAR, Chine, RAS Hong Kong	16.3	13.8	13.7	Japan, Japon	25.3	20.7	*17.6	Partenaire 2
Partner 3	United States, États-Unis	15.1	11.5	12.0	United States, États-Unis	11.6	10.2	*12.5	Partenaire 3
Pakistan									**Pakistan**
Partner 1	United States, États-Unis	24.8	17.2	16.3	China, Chine	*9.4	14.0	26.8	Partenaire 1
Partner 2	United Kingdom, Royaume-Uni	5.7	5.2	7.5	United Arab Emirates, Émirats arabes unis	9.9	14.0	13.1	Partenaire 2
Partner 3	China, Chine	2.7	6.7	6.9	United States, États-Unis	6.1	4.3	4.9	Partenaire 3
Palau									**Palaos**
Partner 1	Areas nes, Zones nsa [1]	...	...	38.9	United States, États-Unis	31.5	34.9	35.8	Partenaire 1
Partner 2	Japan, Japon	*90.8	*82.5	*23.4	Singapore, Singapour	...	17.9	15.3	Partenaire 2
Partner 3	Guam	...	*3.1	14.5	Japan, Japon	14.2	12.3	12.5	Partenaire 3
Panama									**Panama**
Partner 1	United States, États-Unis	*44.8	*19.8	*20.6	China, Chine	*6.4	24.9	*31.3	Partenaire 1
Partner 2	Colombia, Colombie	*1.6	*15.6	*9.5	Singapore, Singapour	*0.1	10.4	*18.9	Partenaire 2
Partner 3	Areas nes, Zones nsa [1]	1.0	0.2	*8.9	United States, États-Unis	*26.8	20.5	*9.5	Partenaire 3
Papua New Guinea									**Papouasie-Nvl-Guinée**
Partner 1	Australia, Australie	*56.7	*42.8	*26.0	Australia, Australie	*58.7	*39.5	*30.7	Partenaire 1
Partner 2	Japan, Japon	*3.9	*7.0	*24.4	China, Chine	*3.2	*7.3	*16.2	Partenaire 2
Partner 3	China, Chine	*4.0	*6.4	*19.1	Singapore, Singapour	*7.2	*11.1	*10.8	Partenaire 3
Paraguay									**Paraguay**
Partner 1	Brazil, Brésil	48.9	33.7	32.0	China, Chine	19.6	34.2	30.9	Partenaire 1
Partner 2	Argentina, Argentine	11.9	8.5	13.1	Brazil, Brésil	27.2	24.1	23.0	Partenaire 2
Partner 3	Chile, Chili	2.0	9.3	7.3	Argentina, Argentine	19.9	15.7	10.3	Partenaire 3
Peru									**Pérou**
Partner 1	China, Chine	10.9	15.2	26.3	China, Chine	8.5	17.2	22.3	Partenaire 1
Partner 2	United States, États-Unis	30.7	17.1	15.7	United States, États-Unis	17.8	19.4	20.3	Partenaire 2
Partner 3	Switzerland, Suisse	4.6	10.7	5.3	Brazil, Brésil	8.2	7.3	6.2	Partenaire 3
Philippines									**Philippines**
Partner 1	Japan, Japon	17.5	15.2	15.8	China, Chine	6.3	8.5	18.1	Partenaire 1
Partner 2	United States, États-Unis	18.0	14.7	14.1	Japan, Japon	17.1	12.5	11.6	Partenaire 2
Partner 3	China, Hong Kong SAR, Chine, RAS Hong Kong	8.1	8.4	13.1	Republic of Korea, République de Corée	4.8	6.9	8.7	Partenaire 3
Poland									**Pologne**
Partner 1	Germany, Allemagne	28.2	26.1	27.2	Germany, Allemagne	24.7	21.7	22.7	Partenaire 1
Partner 2	United Kingdom, Royaume-Uni	5.6	6.3	6.4	China, Chine	5.4	9.5	12.1	Partenaire 2
Partner 3	Czechia, Tchéquie	4.6	5.9	6.4	Russian Federation, Fédération de Russie	8.8	10.5	6.8	Partenaire 3

22

Major trading partner *(continued)*

Three largest trade partners as a percentage of total international merchandise trade in US dollars, as at 2017

Partenaire commercial principal *(suite)*

Trois principaux partenaires commerciaux en pourcentage du total de commerce international de marchandises en dollars américains, en 2017

Country or area	Major trading partner	Percentage of exports 2005	2010	2017	Major trading partner	Percentage of imports 2005	2010	2017	Pays ou zone
Portugal									**Portugal**
Partner 1	Spain, Espagne	27.5	27.0	25.2	Spain, Espagne	30.7	32.0	32.0	Partenaire 1
Partner 2	France	13.4	12.0	12.5	Germany, Allemagne	14.3	13.9	13.7	Partenaire 2
Partner 3	Germany, Allemagne	12.3	13.0	11.3	France	8.7	7.2	7.4	Partenaire 3
Qatar									**Qatar**
Partner 1	Japan, Japon	40.0	28.7	* 19.1	United States, États-Unis	11.6	11.8	* 14.4	Partenaire 1
Partner 2	Republic of Korea, République de Corée	15.8	16.0	15.6	China, Chine	5.2	9.1	* 10.4	Partenaire 2
Partner 3	India, Inde	3.5	8.6	* 12.9	Germany, Allemagne	9.2	7.2	* 9.3	Partenaire 3
Republic of Korea									**République de Corée**
Partner 1	China, Chine	21.8	25.1	24.7	China, Chine	14.8	16.8	20.5	Partenaire 1
Partner 2	United States, États-Unis	14.6	10.7	12.0	Japan, Japon	18.5	15.1	11.5	Partenaire 2
Partner 3	Viet Nam	1.2	2.1	8.3	United States, États-Unis	11.8	9.5	10.6	Partenaire 3
Republic of Moldova									**République de Moldova**
Partner 1	Romania, Roumanie	10.2	16.0	24.8	Romania, Roumanie	11.2	10.0	14.4	Partenaire 1
Partner 2	Russian Federation, Fédération de Russie	31.8	26.2	10.5	Russian Federation, Fédération de Russie	11.7	15.2	11.8	Partenaire 2
Partner 3	Italy, Italie	12.2	9.6	9.7	Ukraine	20.9	13.7	10.6	Partenaire 3
Romania									**Roumanie**
Partner 1	Germany, Allemagne	14.0	18.1	23.0	Germany, Allemagne	14.0	16.7	20.1	Partenaire 1
Partner 2	Italy, Italie	19.4	13.8	11.2	Italy, Italie	* 15.5	11.6	10.0	Partenaire 2
Partner 3	France	7.4	8.3	6.8	Hungary, Hongrie	3.3	8.7	7.5	Partenaire 3
Russian Federation									**Fédération de Russie**
Partner 1	Areas nes, Zones nsa [1]	~0.0	0.5	* 11.0	China, Chine	7.4	17.0	21.2	Partenaire 1
Partner 2	China, Chine	5.4	* 5.0	* 9.7	Germany, Allemagne	13.4	11.6	10.0	Partenaire 2
Partner 3	Netherlands, Pays-Bas	10.2	13.4	8.8	United States, États-Unis	4.6	4.3	5.6	Partenaire 3
Rwanda									**Rwanda**
Partner 1	Dem. Rep. of Congo, Rép. Dém. du Congo	2.6	7.5	* 31.8	China, Chine	3.7	15.0	* 21.2	Partenaire 1
Partner 2	Kenya	22.0	16.3	16.0	Uganda, Ouganda	13.2	12.7	* 11.2	Partenaire 2
Partner 3	United Arab Emirates, Émirats arabes unis	~0.0	0.2	* 14.0	Kenya	13.5	10.1	* 7.8	Partenaire 3
Saint Helena									**Sainte-Hélène**
Partner 1	United States, États-Unis	* 22.3	* 34.2	* 45.6	South Africa, Afrique du Sud	* 13.9	* 14.1	* 42.5	Partenaire 1
Partner 2	Japan, Japon	* 19.8	* 21.5	* 13.8	United Kingdom, Royaume-Uni	* 49.4	* 45.9	* 42.2	Partenaire 2
Partner 3	Czechia, Tchéquie	* 1.2	* ~0.0	* 10.3	Greece, Grèce	* 0.1	...	* 6.3	Partenaire 3
Saint Kitts and Nevis									**Saint-Kitts-et-Nevis**
Partner 1	United States, États-Unis	91.9	* 74.2	68.7	United States, États-Unis	57.9	68.0	67.0	Partenaire 1
Partner 2	Saint Lucia, Sainte-Lucie	0.3	* 3.5	* 6.8	Trinidad and Tobago, Trinité-et-Tobago	14.1	6.5	4.4	Partenaire 2
Partner 3	Trinidad and Tobago, Trinité-et-Tobago	2.0	1.9	6.5	Canada	2.2	2.0	2.7	Partenaire 3
Saint Lucia									**Sainte-Lucie**
Partner 1	United States, États-Unis	14.0	57.8	* 43.2	United States, États-Unis	44.0	42.0	* 46.9	Partenaire 1
Partner 2	Areas nes, Zones nsa [1]	2.1	...	12.4	Trinidad and Tobago, Trinité-et-Tobago	14.2	21.0	* 12.7	Partenaire 2
Partner 3	Trinidad and Tobago, Trinité-et-Tobago	22.5	19.1	* 8.4	Areas nes, Zones nsa [1]	0.2	...	* 5.0	Partenaire 3
Saint Pierre and Miquelon									**Saint-Pierre-et-Miquelon**
Partner 1	Canada	* 0.2	* 21.4	* 39.6	France	* 49.3	* 62.5	* 58.7	Partenaire 1
Partner 2	France	* 9.1	* 14.6	* 15.3	Canada	* 31.7	* 33.1	* 34.2	Partenaire 2
Partner 3	Portugal	* 0.2	* 12.0	* 14.8	Netherlands, Pays-Bas	* 0.9	* 0.8	* 3.0	Partenaire 3
Saint Vincent & Grenadines									**Saint-Vincent-Grenadines**
Partner 1	Barbados, Barbade	12.7	11.3	* 17.8	United States, États-Unis	33.3	33.0	* 38.2	Partenaire 1
Partner 2	Saint Lucia, Sainte-Lucie	10.9	20.6	17.2	Trinidad and Tobago, Trinité-et-Tobago	23.6	27.1	* 17.6	Partenaire 2
Partner 3	Antigua and Barbuda, Antigua-et-Barbuda	6.2	7.4	* 14.5	United Kingdom, Royaume-Uni	9.4	5.7	* 7.2	Partenaire 3
Samoa									**Samoa**
Partner 1	American Samoa, Samoa américaines	13.4	4.5	26.6	New Zealand, Nouvelle-Zélande	33.4	30.7	26.4	Partenaire 1
Partner 2	Australia, Australie	74.8	65.3	21.4	Singapore, Singapour	4.4	5.9	16.6	Partenaire 2
Partner 3	New Zealand, Nouvelle-Zélande	2.0	9.3	19.7	United States, États-Unis	14.0	11.5	11.1	Partenaire 3
Sao Tome and Principe									**Sao Tomé-et-Principe**
Partner 1	Netherlands, Pays-Bas	38.5	15.9	29.6	Portugal	57.0	* 62.4	54.5	Partenaire 1
Partner 2	Spain, Espagne	...	~0.0	16.6	Angola	20.4	15.6	19.8	Partenaire 2
Partner 3	France	1.8	0.3	16.1	China, Chine	0.2	2.2	5.0	Partenaire 3
Saudi Arabia									**Arabie saoudite**
Partner 1	Areas nes, Zones nsa [1]	7.8	6.2	* 79.0	China, Chine	7.5	11.9	* 14.5	Partenaire 1
Partner 2	United Arab Emirates, Émirats arabes unis	1.3	1.5	3.2	United States, États-Unis	15.1	13.4	* 13.4	Partenaire 2
Partner 3	China, Chine	0.7	1.4	* 2.0	Germany, Allemagne	8.3	7.9	* 6.3	Partenaire 3

22

Major trading partner *(continued)*

Three largest trade partners as a percentage of total international merchandise trade in US dollars, as at 2017

Partenaire commercial principal *(suite)*

Trois principaux partenaires commerciaux en pourcentage du total de commerce international de marchandises en dollars américains, en 2017

Country or area	Major trading partner	Percentage of exports 2005	2010	2017	Major trading partner	Percentage of imports 2005	2010	2017	Pays ou zone
Senegal									**Sénégal**
Partner 1	Mali	* 19.2	* 26.1	19.8	France	20.9	19.7	14.7	Partenaire 1
Partner 2	Switzerland, Suisse	0.2	* 7.9	* 10.1	China, Chine	3.6	8.3	9.7	Partenaire 2
Partner 3	Bunkers, Com. de soute	11.4	7.6	5.1	Nigeria, Nigéria	10.4	10.2	7.9	Partenaire 3
Serbia									**Serbie**
Partner 1	Italy, Italie	...	11.4	13.2	Germany, Allemagne	...	10.6	12.7	Partenaire 1
Partner 2	Germany, Allemagne	...	10.3	12.6	Italy, Italie	...	8.6	10.0	Partenaire 2
Partner 3	Bosnia-Herzegovina, Bosnie-Herzégovine	...	11.1	8.0	China, Chine	...	7.2	8.2	Partenaire 3
Seychelles									**Seychelles**
Partner 1	United Arab Emirates, Émirats arabes unis	0.1	37.9	* 26.3	Cayman Islands, Îles Caïmanes	...	0.0	* 30.8	Partenaire 1
Partner 2	France	14.7	19.2	22.8	United Arab Emirates, Émirats arabes unis	3.8	48.0	* 15.3	Partenaire 2
Partner 3	United Kingdom, Royaume-Uni	28.5	18.6	* 15.4	France	6.6	5.0	* 8.9	Partenaire 3
Sierra Leone									**Sierra Leone**
Partner 1	Côte d'Ivoire	~0.0	* 0.2	* 34.7	China, Chine	* 5.5	* 12.2	* 12.6	Partenaire 1
Partner 2	United States, États-Unis	* 3.6	* 8.1	* 31.0	United States, États-Unis	3.5	* 7.5	* 9.8	Partenaire 2
Partner 3	Belgium, Belgique	* 87.5	* 26.6	* 19.3	India, Inde	2.8	* 5.4	* 7.8	Partenaire 3
Singapore									**Singapour**
Partner 1	China, Chine	8.6	10.3	14.5	China, Chine	10.2	10.8	13.8	Partenaire 1
Partner 2	China, Hong Kong SAR, Chine, RAS Hong Kong	9.4	11.7	12.3	Malaysia, Malaisie	13.6	11.7	11.9	Partenaire 2
Partner 3	Malaysia, Malaisie	13.3	11.9	10.6	United States, États-Unis	11.7	11.5	10.6	Partenaire 3
Slovakia									**Slovaquie**
Partner 1	Germany, Allemagne	* 25.6	19.2	20.6	Germany, Allemagne	20.6	16.1	16.7	Partenaire 1
Partner 2	Czechia, Tchéquie	* 14.3	13.7	11.5	Czechia, Tchéquie	12.8	10.3	10.3	Partenaire 2
Partner 3	Poland, Pologne	* 6.2	7.3	7.6	Europe nes, Europe nsa [4]	8.4	12.1	8.6	Partenaire 3
Slovenia									**Slovénie**
Partner 1	Germany, Allemagne	19.9	19.6	20.3	Germany, Allemagne	17.2	16.2	17.1	Partenaire 1
Partner 2	Italy, Italie	12.7	12.1	11.5	Italy, Italie	17.4	15.6	14.4	Partenaire 2
Partner 3	Croatia, Croatie	9.1	6.7	8.0	Austria, Autriche	7.9	7.9	8.1	Partenaire 3
Solomon Islands									**Îles Salomon**
Partner 1	China, Chine	45.8	49.1	65.2	Australia, Australie	42.0	32.4	19.9	Partenaire 1
Partner 2	Italy, Italie	...	3.1	7.7	Singapore, Singapour	6.3	24.1	13.8	Partenaire 2
Partner 3	Switzerland, Suisse	...	...	3.9	New Zealand, Nouvelle-Zélande	6.5	5.9	13.2	Partenaire 3
Somalia									**Somalie**
Partner 1	Saudi Arabia, Arabie saoudite	* 3.4	* 35.7	* 48.6	China, Chine	* 3.0	* 5.7	* 18.9	Partenaire 1
Partner 2	Oman	* 3.4	* 19.0	* 20.5	United Arab Emirates, Émirats arabes unis	* 39.1	* 22.8	* 17.8	Partenaire 2
Partner 3	United Arab Emirates, Émirats arabes unis	* 38.0	* 21.4	* 10.8	India, Inde	* 6.5	* 5.6	* 15.9	Partenaire 3
South Africa									**Afrique du Sud**
Partner 1	China, Chine	2.9	9.9	9.8	China, Chine	9.0	13.8	18.3	Partenaire 1
Partner 2	United States, États-Unis	10.4	8.7	7.5	Germany, Allemagne	14.0	10.9	11.5	Partenaire 2
Partner 3	Germany, Allemagne	7.1	6.7	6.6	United States, États-Unis	7.9	7.2	6.6	Partenaire 3
South Sudan									**Soudan du sud**
Partner 1	China, Chine	...	...	* 95.9	Uganda, Ouganda	...	...	* 69.0	Partenaire 1
Partner 2	India, Inde	...	...	3.8	China, Chine	...	...	* 12.4	Partenaire 2
Partner 3	Uganda, Ouganda	...	...	* 0.1	United States, États-Unis	...	...	* 3.2	Partenaire 3
Spain									**Espagne**
Partner 1	France	19.2	18.2	14.7	Germany, Allemagne	14.7	11.7	12.5	Partenaire 1
Partner 2	Germany, Allemagne	11.3	11.5	10.9	France	14.1	10.7	10.7	Partenaire 2
Partner 3	Italy, Italie	8.4	9.0	7.8	China, Chine	5.0	7.9	8.3	Partenaire 3
Sri Lanka									**Sri Lanka**
Partner 1	United States, États-Unis	32.6	21.3	24.9	India, Inde	17.3	20.6	21.1	Partenaire 1
Partner 2	United Kingdom, Royaume-Uni	12.6	12.3	8.9	China, Chine	7.6	10.0	19.7	Partenaire 2
Partner 3	India, Inde	9.1	5.6	6.7	United Arab Emirates, Émirats arabes unis	2.7	2.7	7.3	Partenaire 3
State of Palestine									**État de Palestine**
Partner 1	Israel, Israël	86.6	84.9	* 83.2	Israel, Israël	70.2	72.6	* 58.2	Partenaire 1
Partner 2	Jordan, Jordanie	5.2	5.4	5.6	Turkey, Turquie	4.5	4.5	* 8.9	Partenaire 2
Partner 3	United Arab Emirates, Émirats arabes unis	0.4	2.0	* 2.5	China, Chine	4.2	4.6	* 7.1	Partenaire 3
Sudan									**Soudan**
Partner 1	China, Chine	...	...	* 56.4	China, Chine	...	...	* 22.8	Partenaire 1
Partner 2	United Arab Emirates, Émirats arabes unis	...	...	14.4	Jordan, Jordanie	...	...	* 8.6	Partenaire 2
Partner 3	Saudi Arabia, Arabie saoudite	...	...	* 14.4	India, Inde	...	...	* 8.5	Partenaire 3

22 Major trading partner *(continued)*

Three largest trade partners as a percentage of total international merchandise trade in US dollars, as at 2017

Partenaire commercial principal *(suite)*

Trois principaux partenaires commerciaux en pourcentage du total de commerce international de marchandises en dollars américains, en 2017

Country or area	Major trading partner	Percentage of exports 2005	2010	2017	Major trading partner	Percentage of imports 2005	2010	2017	Pays ou zone
Suriname									**Suriname**
Partner 1	Switzerland, Suisse	0.3	8.8	32.0	United States, États-Unis	18.9	24.6	31.8	Partenaire 1
Partner 2	China, Hong Kong SAR, Chine, RAS Hong Kong	0.1	~0.0	22.5	Netherlands, Pays-Bas	17.7	17.5	13.8	Partenaire 2
Partner 3	Belgium, Belgique	10.2	10.1	10.8	Trinidad and Tobago, Trinité-et-Tobago	19.1	23.7	9.7	Partenaire 3
Sweden									**Suède**
Partner 1	Germany, Allemagne	10.4	11.4	10.7	Germany, Allemagne	18.1	18.0	18.7	Partenaire 1
Partner 2	Norway, Norvège	8.7	10.0	10.1	Netherlands, Pays-Bas	6.7	6.2	8.9	Partenaire 2
Partner 3	Finland, Finlande	6.1	6.4	6.9	Norway, Norvège	8.2	8.7	8.1	Partenaire 3
Switzerland									**Suisse**
Partner 1	Germany, Allemagne	19.4	19.3	15.2	Germany, Allemagne	31.6	31.9	20.7	Partenaire 1
Partner 2	United States, États-Unis	10.9	10.1	12.3	United States, États-Unis	5.6	5.4	8.0	Partenaire 2
Partner 3	China, Chine	2.1	3.7	8.2	Italy, Italie	10.5	10.2	7.5	Partenaire 3
Syrian Arab Republic									**République arabe syrienne**
Partner 1	Lebanon, Liban	2.9	3.8	* 16.9	Turkey, Turquie	4.3	9.5	* 28.0	Partenaire 1
Partner 2	Egypt, Égypte	2.3	* 3.4	* 13.7	China, Chine	* 8.1	8.8	* 20.1	Partenaire 2
Partner 3	Saudi Arabia, Arabie saoudite	5.7	4.8	* 11.3	Russian Federation, Fédération de Russie	3.8	6.3	* 5.7	Partenaire 3
Tajikistan									**Tadjikistan**
Partner 1	Kazakhstan	* 2.1	* 1.4	* 29.8	China, Chine	* 13.7	* 43.4	* 51.1	Partenaire 1
Partner 2	Turkey, Turquie	* 6.0	* 23.1	* 18.6	Russian Federation, Fédération de Russie	* 22.8	* 21.2	* 19.1	Partenaire 2
Partner 3	Switzerland, Suisse	* 1.1	* ~0.0	* 14.9	Kazakhstan	* 14.3	* 8.2	* 12.7	Partenaire 3
Thailand									**Thaïlande**
Partner 1	United States, États-Unis	15.5	10.4	* 11.4	China, Chine	9.4	13.3	* 21.6	Partenaire 1
Partner 2	China, Chine	8.3	11.0	11.0	Japan, Japon	22.0	20.8	* 15.8	Partenaire 2
Partner 3	Japan, Japon	13.7	10.5	* 9.5	United States, États-Unis	7.4	5.9	* 6.2	Partenaire 3
TFYR of Macedonia									**ex-R.Y. de Macédoine**
Partner 1	Germany, Allemagne	17.8	21.3	47.0	Germany, Allemagne	10.4	11.2	11.8	Partenaire 1
Partner 2	Serbia, Serbie	...	21.2	8.4	United Kingdom, Royaume-Uni	1.4	5.2	10.1	Partenaire 2
Partner 3	Bulgaria, Bulgarie	3.7	8.8	5.9	Greece, Grèce	9.2	8.2	8.0	Partenaire 3
Timor-Leste									**Timor-Leste**
Partner 1	Singapore, Singapour	0.4	...	* 52.2	Indonesia, Indonésie	47.0	* 19.3	* 36.9	Partenaire 1
Partner 2	Thailand, Thaïlande	0.2	* ~0.0	* 30.7	China, Chine	1.7	* 4.7	* 28.4	Partenaire 2
Partner 3	United States, États-Unis	23.9	...	* 4.0	Viet Nam	4.5	* 5.8	* 8.8	Partenaire 3
Togo									**Togo**
Partner 1	Burkina Faso	* 18.8	* 10.5	17.9	China, Chine	13.2	15.1	19.6	Partenaire 1
Partner 2	Benin, Bénin	* 11.6	* 5.3	* 14.3	France	17.6	13.6	10.8	Partenaire 2
Partner 3	Ghana	* 20.3	* 5.9	7.6	Japan, Japon	1.8	3.0	5.1	Partenaire 3
Tokelau									**Tokélaou**
Partner 1	Indonesia, Indonésie	...	* 0.1	* 70.7	Nigeria, Nigéria	...	* ~0.0	* 69.5	Partenaire 1
Partner 2	Bangladesh	* 32.4	* 25.3	* 6.8	Germany, Allemagne	* 6.0	* 18.3	* 9.1	Partenaire 2
Partner 3	France	* 5.4	* 5.8	* 5.0	Samoa	* 0.8	* 0.1	* 6.9	Partenaire 3
Tonga									**Tonga**
Partner 1	United States, États-Unis	23.9	16.2	* 27.4	New Zealand, Nouvelle-Zélande	38.3	31.9	* 31.7	Partenaire 1
Partner 2	Republic of Korea, République de Corée	0.2	0.6	20.6	China, Chine	3.7	5.3	* 20.8	Partenaire 2
Partner 3	New Zealand, Nouvelle-Zélande	13.4	16.5	* 17.6	Netherlands, Pays-Bas	~0.0	0.1	* 11.2	Partenaire 3
Trinidad and Tobago									**Trinité-et-Tobago**
Partner 1	United States, États-Unis	* 58.6	48.1	* 41.7	United States, États-Unis	29.2	28.0	* 32.0	Partenaire 1
Partner 2	Argentina, Argentine	0.2	0.8	6.8	Gabon	2.1	12.9	* 12.5	Partenaire 2
Partner 3	Colombia, Colombie	1.6	2.6	* 4.1	China, Chine	3.0	5.8	* 7.1	Partenaire 3
Tunisia									**Tunisie**
Partner 1	France	* 32.9	* 28.7	* 32.0	France	* 23.5	* 18.9	* 15.4	Partenaire 1
Partner 2	Italy, Italie	* 24.1	19.9	17.4	Italy, Italie	20.9	17.6	* 14.5	Partenaire 2
Partner 3	Germany, Allemagne	* 8.5	8.5	* 10.5	China, Chine	2.9	6.1	* 9.3	Partenaire 3
Turkey									**Turquie**
Partner 1	Germany, Allemagne	* 12.9	* 10.1	9.6	China, Chine	* 5.9	9.3	10.0	Partenaire 1
Partner 2	United Kingdom, Royaume-Uni	8.1	* 6.3	* 6.1	Germany, Allemagne	* 11.7	* 9.5	9.1	Partenaire 2
Partner 3	United Arab Emirates, Émirats arabes unis	* 2.3	2.9	5.8	Russian Federation, Fédération de Russie	11.1	11.6	8.3	Partenaire 3
Turkmenistan									**Turkménistan**
Partner 1	China, Chine	* 0.4	* 39.0	* 78.6	Turkey, Turquie	* 8.6	* 23.5	* 26.6	Partenaire 1
Partner 2	Turkey, Turquie	* 3.3	* 14.4	* 4.9	Germany, Allemagne	* 6.3	* 7.0	* 10.9	Partenaire 2
Partner 3	Afghanistan	...	* 4.4	* 4.9	China, Chine	* 4.3	* 10.8	* 9.3	Partenaire 3

22

Major trading partner *(continued)*

Three largest trade partners as a percentage of total international merchandise trade in US dollars, as at 2017

Partenaire commercial principal *(suite)*

Trois principaux partenaires commerciaux en pourcentage du total de commerce international de marchandises en dollars américains, en 2017

Country or area	Major trading partner	Percentage of exports 2005	2010	2017	Major trading partner	Percentage of imports 2005	2010	2017	Pays ou zone
Turks and Caicos Islands									**Îles Turques-et-Caïques**
Partner 1	Bahamas	...	* ~0.0	* 30.2	United States, États-Unis	98.3	* 98.3	* 89.9	Partenaire 1
Partner 2	Zimbabwe	...	...	25.1	Dominican Republic, Rép. dominicaine	0.1	* 0.2	* 1.4	Partenaire 2
Partner 3	United States, États-Unis	99.7	* 99.1	* 21.9	Japan, Japon	~0.0	* ~0.0	* 1.1	Partenaire 3
Tuvalu									**Tuvalu**
Partner 1	Thailand, Thaïlande	...	* 75.2	* 93.3	Singapore, Singapour	17.5	* 0.4	* 27.7	Partenaire 1
Partner 2	Japan, Japon	...	* 7.8	* 4.2	Japan, Japon	3.7	* 16.3	* 23.3	Partenaire 2
Partner 3	Bosnia-Herzegovina, Bosnie-Herzégovine	...	...	* 0.4	Fiji, Fidji	19.7	* 23.9	* 14.3	Partenaire 3
Uganda									**Ouganda**
Partner 1	Kenya	8.9	11.8	* 16.3	China, Chine	5.3	8.9	* 18.4	Partenaire 1
Partner 2	United Arab Emirates, Émirats arabes unis	10.4	7.5	15.0	India, Inde	6.4	14.7	* 17.3	Partenaire 2
Partner 3	South Sudan, Soudan du Sud	...	...	* 9.7	Kenya	25.3	11.0	* 9.5	Partenaire 3
Ukraine									**Ukraine**
Partner 1	Russian Federation, Fédération de Russie	21.9	* 26.1	9.1	Russian Federation, Fédération de Russie	35.6	36.5	14.6	Partenaire 1
Partner 2	Poland, Pologne	3.0	* 3.5	* 6.3	China, Chine	5.0	7.7	11.4	Partenaire 2
Partner 3	Turkey, Turquie	5.9	5.9	5.8	Germany, Allemagne	9.4	7.6	10.5	Partenaire 3
United Arab Emirates									**Émirats arabes unis**
Partner 1	Areas nes, Zones nsa [1]	29.3	26.5	* 51.4	Areas nes, Zones nsa [1]	0.7	30.2	* 30.2	Partenaire 1
Partner 2	Asia nes, Asie nsa [2]	* 10.7	* 34.4	* 13.9	China, Chine	8.5	* 7.3	* 8.3	Partenaire 2
Partner 3	India, Inde	4.6	* 11.0	* 3.8	United States, États-Unis	6.9	* 6.0	* 7.6	Partenaire 3
United Kingdom									**Royaume-Uni**
Partner 1	United States, États-Unis	14.4	13.9	13.3	Germany, Allemagne	13.0	12.2	13.9	Partenaire 1
Partner 2	Germany, Allemagne	10.6	10.6	10.5	China, Chine	6.8	9.8	9.3	Partenaire 2
Partner 3	France	9.3	7.5	7.4	United States, États-Unis	8.4	9.0	9.2	Partenaire 3
United Rep. of Tanzania									**Rép.-Unie de Tanzanie**
Partner 1	Switzerland, Suisse	8.7	17.5	* 16.2	China, Chine	6.9	10.9	* 20.8	Partenaire 1
Partner 2	India, Inde	4.7	5.6	14.8	India, Inde	5.9	11.2	* 18.1	Partenaire 2
Partner 3	South Africa, Afrique du Sud	17.6	10.7	* 13.3	United Arab Emirates, Émirats arabes unis	6.3	8.4	* 7.5	Partenaire 3
United States of America									**États-Unis d'Amérique**
Partner 1	Canada	23.3	19.5	18.2	China, Chine	15.0	19.5	21.8	Partenaire 1
Partner 2	Mexico, Mexique	13.3	12.8	15.7	Mexico, Mexique	10.0	11.8	13.2	Partenaire 2
Partner 3	China, Chine	4.6	7.2	8.4	Canada	16.8	14.2	12.7	Partenaire 3
Uruguay									**Uruguay**
Partner 1	China, Chine	* 4.5	* 10.4	18.8	China, Chine	6.2	13.0	20.0	Partenaire 1
Partner 2	Brazil, Brésil	* 13.4	* 23.4	* 16.5	Brazil, Brésil	21.3	18.3	19.5	Partenaire 2
Partner 3	Free zones, Zones franches	0.9	4.1	16.4	Argentina, Argentine	20.3	17.0	12.6	Partenaire 3
Uzbekistan									**Ouzbékistan**
Partner 1	Switzerland, Suisse	* 0.1	* 0.5	* 37.9	Russian Federation, Fédération de Russie	* 26.0	* 20.0	* 23.7	Partenaire 1
Partner 2	China, Chine	* 11.5	* 19.3	* 19.2	China, Chine	* 7.0	* 14.2	* 19.4	Partenaire 2
Partner 3	Russian Federation, Fédération de Russie	* 22.0	* 22.5	* 10.6	Kazakhstan	* 7.4	* 13.3	* 11.3	Partenaire 3
Vanuatu									**Vanuatu**
Partner 1	Mauritania, Mauritanie	...	...	* 28.4	China, Chine	* 5.2	9.9	* 18.0	Partenaire 1
Partner 2	Japan, Japon	* 4.1	4.5	27.9	Australia, Australie	* 41.3	30.9	* 14.9	Partenaire 2
Partner 3	Philippines	* 2.0	12.8	* 8.1	New Zealand, Nouvelle-Zélande	* 15.6	13.6	* 8.7	Partenaire 3
Venezuela (Boliv. Rep. of)									**Venezuela (Rép. boliv. du)**
Partner 1	United States, États-Unis	45.2	* 7.6	* 44.5	United States, États-Unis	31.6	30.5	* 33.3	Partenaire 1
Partner 2	China, Chine	0.4	* 5.8	* 22.5	China, Chine	3.7	11.1	* 21.4	Partenaire 2
Partner 3	India, Inde	~0.0	* ~0.0	* 15.0	Mexico, Mexique	6.9	4.5	* 8.6	Partenaire 3
Viet Nam									**Viet Nam**
Partner 1	United States, États-Unis	18.3	19.7	* 21.7	China, Chine	16.0	23.8	* 28.6	Partenaire 1
Partner 2	China, Chine	10.0	10.7	12.4	Republic of Korea, République de Corée	9.8	11.5	* 18.4	Partenaire 2
Partner 3	Japan, Japon	13.4	10.7	* 8.3	Japan, Japon	11.1	10.6	* 8.6	Partenaire 3
Wallis and Futuna Islands									**Îles Wallis-et-Futuna**
Partner 1	Singapore, Singapour	...	...	* 29.7	France	32.0	* 23.1	* 26.4	Partenaire 1
Partner 2	United Kingdom, Royaume-Uni	0.1	* 0.1	* 22.5	New Caledonia, Nouvelle-Calédonie	5.6	* 17.1	* 20.7	Partenaire 2
Partner 3	France	* 6.8	* 1.6	* 8.8	Fiji, Fidji	5.8	* 13.4	* 18.4	Partenaire 3
Yemen									**Yémen**
Partner 1	Saudi Arabia, Arabie saoudite	1.8	3.2	* 32.2	United Arab Emirates, Émirats arabes unis	* 8.2	* 11.7	* 11.5	Partenaire 1
Partner 2	Oman	* 0.1	* 0.2	* 17.0	China, Chine	* 6.4	* 7.9	* 10.8	Partenaire 2
Partner 3	Areas nes, Zones nsa [1]	0.5	0.9	* 10.6	Saudi Arabia, Arabie saoudite	* 6.4	6.1	* 8.6	Partenaire 3

22 Major trading partner *(continued)*

Three largest trade partners as a percentage of total international merchandise trade in US dollars, as at 2017

Partenaire commercial principal *(suite)*

Trois principaux partenaires commerciaux en pourcentage du total de commerce international de marchandises en dollars américains, en 2017

Country or area	Major trading partner	Percentage of exports 2005	2010	2017	Major trading partner	Percentage of imports 2005	2010	2017	Pays ou zone
Zambia4									**Zambie**
Partner 1	Switzerland, Suisse	28.7	51.0	* 44.3	South Africa, Afrique du Sud	47.6	34.4	* 30.9	Partenaire 1
Partner 2	China, Chine	2.1	20.2	14.5	Dem. Rep. of Congo, Rép. Dém. du Congo	0.9	23.8	* 11.2	Partenaire 2
Partner 3	Singapore, Singapour	0.1	~0.0	* 7.8	China, Chine	3.3	5.4	* 8.2	Partenaire 3
Zimbabwe									**Zimbabwe**
Partner 1	South Africa, Afrique du Sud	41.5	54.2	* 79.4	South Africa, Afrique du Sud	15.0	48.0	* 41.3	Partenaire 1
Partner 2	Mozambique	2.8	2.9	9.5	Singapore, Singapour	0.2	0.3	* 21.5	Partenaire 2
Partner 3	United Arab Emirates, Émirats arabes unis	0.7	10.3	* 4.1	China, Chine	2.4	5.5	* 7.0	Partenaire 3

Source:

United Nations Statistics Division, New York, Commodity Trade Statistics Database (UN COMTRADE), last accessed June 2018.

1 Areas not elsewhere specified.
2 Asia not elsewhere specified.
3 Undisclosed (Special categories).
4 Europe not elsewhere specified.

Source:

Organisation des Nations Unies, Division de statistique, New York, Comtrade base de données de l'ONU, dernier accès juin 2018.

1 Zones non spécifiées ailleurs.
2 Asie non spécifiées ailleurs.
3 Pays non divulgués.
4 Europe non spécifiées ailleurs.

Part Three

Energy, environment and infrastructure

Chapter XII	Energy (table 23)
Chapter XIII	Environment (tables 24 - 25)
Chapter XIV	Science and technology (tables 26 – 28)
Chapter XV	Communication (table 29)
Chapter XVI	International tourism and transport (table 30)
Chapter XVII	Development assistance (tables 31 and 32)

Troisième partie

Energie, environnement et infrastructures

Chapitre XII	Énergie (tableau 23)
Chapitre XIII	Environnement (tableaux 24 - 25)
Chapitre XIV	Science et technologie (tableaux 26 - 28)
Chapitre XV	Communication (tableau 29)
Chapitre XVI	Tourisme international et transport (tableau 30)
Chapitre XVII	Aide au développement (tableaux 31 et 32)

23 Production, trade and supply of energy

Petajoules and gigajoules per capita

Production, commerce et fourniture d'énergie

pétajoules et gigajoules par habitant

Region, country or area	1990	1995	2000	2005	2010	2013	2014	2015	Région, pays ou zone
Total, all countries or areas									**Total, tous pays ou zones**
Primary Energy production	**357 639**	**377 236**	**408 238**	**476 469**	**530 321**	**559 530**	**567 004**	**572 353**	**Production d'énergie primaire**
Net imports	**-7 091**	**-8 863**	**-10 813**	**-13 751**	**-13 098**	**-18 406**	**-16 670**	**-18 196**	**Importations nettes**
Changes in stocks	**4 140**	**164**	**-2 930**	**-289**	**12**	**374**	**3 205**	**2 469**	**Variations des stocks**
Total supply	**346 408**	**368 210**	**400 355**	**463 007**	**517 211**	**540 751**	**547 128**	**551 688**	**Approv.total**
Supply per capita	**62**	**64**	**65**	**71**	**75**	**75**	**75**	**75**	**Approv.par habitant**
Africa									**Afrique**
Primary Energy production	27 878	32 055	37 184	44 963	47 676	45 533	45 152	45 242	Production d'énergie primaire
Net imports	-12 213	-13 034	-16 304	-20 474	-19 455	-15 069	-13 414	-13 162	Importations nettes
Changes in stocks	-10	291	31	10	-63	-47	252	-43	Variations des stocks
Total supply	15 674	18 730	20 849	24 480	28 284	30 511	31 487	32 123	Approv.total
Supply per capita	25	26	26	27	27	27	27	27	Approv.par habitant
North America									**Amérique du Nord**
Primary Energy production	89 464	93 298	96 207	97 911	100 215	107 868	114 238	114 073	Production d'énergie primaire
Net imports	* 7 789	* 9 145	* 15 610	* 20 179	* 12 979	* 3 474	* 1 510	* 1 441	Importations nettes
Changes in stocks	1 783	-922	-2 221	-124	-602	-1 541	903	2 067	Variations des stocks
Total supply	95 470	103 366	114 038	118 213	113 796	112 882	114 844	113 447	Approv.total
Supply per capita	223	226	234	230	208	200	202	198	Approv.par habitant
South America									**Amérique du Sud**
Primary Energy production	16 259	20 317	24 080	26 630	29 391	30 966	31 216	31 660	Production d'énergie primaire
Net imports	-3 752	-5 789	-7 316	-8 057	-7 250	-7 213	-6 780	-7 861	Importations nettes
Changes in stocks	86	-6	-13	-323	-64	9	150	-63	Variations des stocks
Total supply	12 420	14 534	16 776	18 897	22 206	23 743	24 284	23 862	Approv.total
Supply per capita	42	45	48	51	56	58	59	57	Approv.par habitant
Asia									**Asie**
Primary Energy production	103 897	129 663	145 546	192 204	236 026	257 286	259 212	263 383	Production d'énergie primaire
Net imports	-11 565	-8 920	-9 710	-9 662	227	3 458	7 087	7 871	Importations nettes
Changes in stocks	1 712	604	-739	-398	1 615	1 779	1 400	130	Variations des stocks
Total supply	90 620	120 140	136 575	182 940	234 638	258 965	264 900	271 125	Approv.total
Supply per capita	29	35	37	46	56	60	61	62	Approv.par habitant
Europe									**Europe**
Primary Energy production	112 829	93 292	94 623	102 546	102 514	102 582	100 943	101 099	Production d'énergie primaire
Net imports	15 404	13 521	12 271	10 782	8 107	5 624	4 654	3 836	Importations nettes
Changes in stocks	366	94	245	582	-1 154	20	452	308	Variations des stocks
Total supply	127 865	106 719	106 649	112 746	111 775	108 186	105 145	104 626	Approv.total
Supply per capita	118	147	147	154	152	147	142	141	Approv.par habitant
Oceania									**Océanie**
Primary Energy production	7 314	8 611	10 598	12 214	14 500	15 296	16 244	16 897	Production d'énergie primaire
Net imports	-2 752	-3 785	-5 363	-6 518	-7 707	-8 679	-9 728	-10 320	Importations nettes
Changes in stocks	203	103	-233	-37	280	155	48	71	Variations des stocks
Total supply	4 358	4 723	5 468	5 731	6 511	6 463	6 469	6 506	Approv.total
Supply per capita	160	163	176	171	179	169	167	165	Approv.par habitant
Afghanistan									**Afghanistan**
Primary Energy production	19	16	18	23	41	59	63	60	Production d'énergie primaire
Net imports	* 28	* 13	* 8	14	96	* 87	* 72	* 85	Importations nettes
Changes in stocks	* 0	* 0	* 0	...	...	...	...	...	Variations des stocks
Total supply	* 46	* 29	25	36	137	145	135	145	Approv.total
Supply per capita	* 4	* 1	1	1	5	5	4	4	Approv.par habitant
Albania									**Albanie**
Primary Energy production	99	43	34	48	69	85	84	87	Production d'énergie primaire
Net imports	15	4	31	43	22	27	33	10	Importations nettes
Changes in stocks	* 23	0	...	0	0	10	13	6	Variations des stocks
Total supply	92	47	65	91	91	102	103	92	Approv.total
Supply per capita	28	15	21	29	31	35	36	32	Approv.par habitant
Algeria									**Algérie**
Primary Energy production	4 380	4 748	6 556	7 534	6 200	5 676	5 900	5 883	Production d'énergie primaire
Net imports	* -3 263	* -3 485	* -5 414	* -5 952	* -4 551	* -3 714	* -3 732	* -3 694	Importations nettes
Changes in stocks	* 41	-8	-27	0	9	3	44	-33	Variations des stocks
Total supply	1 075	1 270	1 170	1 583	1 641	1 959	2 123	2 221	Approv.total
Supply per capita	43	45	38	48	46	51	55	56	Approv.par habitant
Andorra									**Andorre**
Primary Energy production	* 0	* 0	* 0	0	1	1	1	1	Production d'énergie primaire
Net imports	* 6	7	9	10	9	8	8	8	Importations nettes
Total supply	* 7	7	9	10	10	9	9	9	Approv.total
Supply per capita	* 130	111	138	130	114	118	119	124	Approv.par habitant

Region, country or area	1990	1995	2000	2005	2010	2013	2014	2015	Région, pays ou zone
Angola									**Angola**
Primary Energy production	1 198	1 585	1 803	2 934	4 057	4 001	3 902	4 137	Production d'énergie primaire
Net imports	*-960	*-1 224	*-1 475	*-2 565	*-3 547	*-3 421	*-3 280	*-3 534	Importations nettes
Changes in stocks	...	17	21	5	1	0	8	1	Variations des stocks
Total supply	238	343	308	363	509	581	613	602	Approv.total
Supply per capita	23	28	22	22	24	25	25	24	Approv.par habitant
Anguilla									**Anguilla**
Primary Energy production	*0	*0	*0	*0	*0	*0	*0	*0	Production d'énergie primaire
Net imports	*1	*1	*1	*2	*2	*2	*2	*2	Importations nettes
Total supply	*1	*1	*1	*2	*2	*2	*2	*2	Approv.total
Supply per capita	*87	*94	*117	*132	*155	*118	*136	*151	Approv.par habitant
Antigua and Barbuda									**Antigua-et-Barbuda**
Primary Energy production	...	...	...	...	0	...	...	...	Production d'énergie primaire
Net imports	*5	*4	*5	*7	*8	*8	*8	*8	Importations nettes
Total supply	*4	*4	*5	*6	*8	*8	*8	*8	Approv.total
Supply per capita	*68	*60	*65	*75	*86	*84	*84	*85	Approv.par habitant
Argentina									**Argentine**
Primary Energy production	2 064	2 722	3 404	3 609	3 343	2 981	3 065	3 100	Production d'énergie primaire
Net imports	-144	-535	-866	-683	-21	403	460	497	Importations nettes
Changes in stocks	-8	-6	-17	8	16	4	6	-12	Variations des stocks
Total supply	1 928	2 194	2 556	2 919	3 307	3 379	3 519	3 610	Approv.total
Supply per capita	59	63	69	75	80	79	82	83	Approv.par habitant
Armenia									**Arménie**
Primary Energy production	...	10	27	36	52	47	50	46	Production d'énergie primaire
Net imports	...	59	57	69	*70	90	91	84	Importations nettes
Changes in stocks	...	...	...	...	*3	...	...	1	Variations des stocks
Total supply	...	68	84	105	*119	138	141	129	Approv.total
Supply per capita	...	21	27	34	*40	46	47	43	Approv.par habitant
Aruba									**Aruba**
Primary Energy production	0	0	*5	*5	*5	*1	*1	*1	Production d'énergie primaire
Net imports	*7	*10	*21	*26	*23	*12	*12	*12	Importations nettes
Changes in stocks	0	...	...	...	...	...	...	...	Variations des stocks
Total supply	*7	*10	*26	30	*28	*12	*12	*13	Approv.total
Supply per capita	*108	*121	*284	299	*273	*119	*120	*123	Approv.par habitant
Australia [1]									**Australie** [1]
Primary Energy production	6 547	7 784	9 731	11 451	13 620	14 429	15 282	15 938	Production d'énergie primaire
Net imports	-2 694	-3 752	-5 412	-6 717	-7 924	-8 952	-9 981	-10 595	Importations nettes
Changes in stocks	203	104	-221	-28	264	145	49	81	Variations des stocks
Total supply	3 650	3 928	4 540	4 762	5 431	5 333	5 252	5 261	Approv.total
Supply per capita	213	217	237	233	245	229	222	220	Approv.par habitant
Austria									**Autriche**
Primary Energy production	340	367	410	414	503	508	507	500	Production d'énergie primaire
Net imports	712	737	777	1 003	885	854	880	826	Importations nettes
Changes in stocks	14	-14	-10	0	-38	-29	39	-48	Variations des stocks
Total supply	1 038	1 119	1 197	1 416	1 427	1 391	1 348	1 374	Approv.total
Supply per capita	135	141	150	172	170	164	158	161	Approv.par habitant
Azerbaijan									**Azerbaïdjan**
Primary Energy production	...	628	803	1 155	2 759	2 502	2 475	2 472	Production d'énergie primaire
Net imports	...	-91	-319	-547	-2 239	-1 922	-1 899	-1 891	Importations nettes
Changes in stocks	...	0	-2	35	34	11	-9	-22	Variations des stocks
Total supply	...	536	485	573	486	569	585	603	Approv.total
Supply per capita	...	69	60	67	53	60	61	62	Approv.par habitant
Bahamas									**Bahamas**
Primary Energy production	...	...	...	0	0	0	0	0	Production d'énergie primaire
Net imports	*35	*22	*26	*27	*34	*45	*30	*29	Importations nettes
Changes in stocks	*9	*-1	*-1	*0	...	*4	*-4	*-5	Variations des stocks
Total supply	*26	*24	*27	*26	35	41	34	*34	Approv.total
Supply per capita	*100	*86	*91	*83	96	109	89	*87	Approv.par habitant
Bahrain									**Bahreïn**
Primary Energy production	294	341	706	672	849	911	961	957	Production d'énergie primaire
Net imports	*-87	-94	-382	-353	-339	-360	-407	-382	Importations nettes
Changes in stocks	*-6	-10	-6	-28	-3	0	-5	-4	Variations des stocks
Total supply	213	257	331	348	513	551	559	579	Approv.total
Supply per capita	433	459	518	480	407	408	410	420	Approv.par habitant

23 Production, trade and supply of energy *(continued)*

Petajoules and gigajoules per capita

Production, commerce et fourniture d'énergie *(suite)*

pétajoules et gigajoules par habitant

Region, country or area	1990	1995	2000	2005	2010	2013	2014	2015	Région, pays ou zone
Bangladesh									**Bangladesh**
Primary Energy production	682	792	857	1 027	1 304	1 414	1 438	1 509	Production d'énergie primaire
Net imports	93	* 122	139	165	163	212	236	274	Importations nettes
Changes in stocks	-6	-4	-6	3	-21	1	-13	-6	Variations des stocks
Total supply	782	918	1 001	1 189	1 489	1 627	1 687	1 789	Approv.total
Supply per capita	7	8	8	8	10	10	11	11	Approv.par habitant
Barbados									**Barbade**
Primary Energy production	5	5	6	5	4	3	2	3	Production d'énergie primaire
Net imports	9	8	10	12	16	17	14	15	Importations nettes
Changes in stocks	-1	0	-1	0	0	0	0	1	Variations des stocks
Total supply	16	13	16	18	20	19	17	17	Approv.total
Supply per capita	62	49	61	65	72	68	58	58	Approv.par habitant
Belarus									**Bélarus**
Primary Energy production	...	138	147	159	166	167	155	146	Production d'énergie primaire
Net imports	...	912	881	962	980	982	1 012	890	Importations nettes
Changes in stocks	...	6	-1	-4	-8	7	5	-16	Variations des stocks
Total supply	...	1 043	1 029	1 125	1 155	1 142	1 162	1 053	Approv.total
Supply per capita	...	102	102	115	122	120	122	111	Approv.par habitant
Belgium									**Belgique**
Primary Energy production	544	495	570	577	646	624	525	444	Production d'énergie primaire
Net imports	1 457	1 771	1 835	1 877	1 886	1 734	1 707	1 823	Importations nettes
Changes in stocks	-4	29	-21	18	18	21	23	40	Variations des stocks
Total supply	2 005	2 237	2 426	2 436	2 515	2 337	2 209	2 226	Approv.total
Supply per capita	202	222	238	234	230	210	197	197	Approv.par habitant
Belize									**Belize**
Primary Energy production	4	4	5	4	14	10	9	9	Production d'énergie primaire
Net imports	4	6	6	7	-2	3	3	5	Importations nettes
Changes in stocks	...	...	...	...	0	0	0	0	Variations des stocks
Total supply	8	10	11	11	13	13	13	15	Approv.total
Supply per capita	44	44	44	39	40	37	37	41	Approv.par habitant
Benin									**Bénin**
Primary Energy production	74	79	62	70	86	102	108	114	Production d'énergie primaire
Net imports	* 1	* 10	* 20	* 37	* 67	* 66	* 71	* 78	Importations nettes
Changes in stocks	0	0	0	2	0	0	2	1	Variations des stocks
Total supply	74	89	83	105	153	167	177	190	Approv.total
Supply per capita	16	16	13	14	16	16	17	17	Approv.par habitant
Bermuda									**Bermudes**
Primary Energy production	...	...	...	...	* 1	* 1	* 1	* 1	Production d'énergie primaire
Net imports	* 7	* 7	* 7	* 7	* 9	* 7	* 9	* 7	Importations nettes
Changes in stocks	...	...	...	...	...	0	0	0	Variations des stocks
Total supply	* 7	* 8	* 7	* 8	* 9	8	10	8	Approv.total
Supply per capita	* 118	* 123	* 115	* 124	* 138	120	153	133	Approv.par habitant
Bhutan									**Bhoutan**
Primary Energy production	41	43	46	53	73	75	75	77	Production d'énergie primaire
Net imports	-3	* -4	* -2	-5	-14	-11	-10	-14	Importations nettes
Total supply	37	39	44	48	59	63	64	63	Approv.total
Supply per capita	67	76	77	73	81	84	84	82	Approv.par habitant
Bolivia (Plurin. State of)									**Bolivie (État plurin. de)**
Primary Energy production	202	235	282	586	656	910	959	871	Production d'énergie primaire
Net imports	-97	-85	-78	-366	-397	-592	-621	-534	Importations nettes
Changes in stocks	0	1	-2	0	-1	-1	0	1	Variations des stocks
Total supply	105	149	206	220	259	318	338	337	Approv.total
Supply per capita	16	20	25	24	26	31	32	31	Approv.par habitant
Bonaire, St. Eustatius & Saba									**Bonaire, St-Eustache et Saba**
Primary Energy production	...	...	...	...	...	0	0	0	Production d'énergie primaire
Net imports	...	...	...	...	...	* 5	* 5	* 5	Importations nettes
Total supply	...	...	...	...	...	* 5	* 5	* 5	Approv.total
Supply per capita	...	...	...	...	...	* 219	* 214	* 212	Approv.par habitant
Bosnia and Herzegovina									**Bosnie-Herzégovine**
Primary Energy production	...	28	126	152	182	192	252	257	Production d'énergie primaire
Net imports	...	29	52	54	84	79	72	85	Importations nettes
Changes in stocks	...	...	-1	-1	-3	5	-1	11	Variations des stocks
Total supply	...	56	179	206	269	266	325	331	Approv.total
Supply per capita	...	17	48	54	70	70	85	87	Approv.par habitant

23 Production, trade and supply of energy *(continued)*
Petajoules and gigajoules per capita

Production, commerce et fourniture d'énergie *(suite)*
pétajoules et gigajoules par habitant

Region, country or area	1990	1995	2000	2005	2010	2013	2014	2015	Région, pays ou zone
Botswana									**Botswana**
Primary Energy production	24	27	28	29	30	42	47	56	Production d'énergie primaire
Net imports	* 15	* 17	* 29	* 36	* 45	* 50	* 45	* 36	Importations nettes
Changes in stocks	0	...	...	0	0	3	-7	* 11	Variations des stocks
Total supply	39	44	57	65	74	89	98	80	Approv.total
Supply per capita	28	28	32	35	36	41	44	35	Approv.par habitant
Brazil									**Brésil**
Primary Energy production	4 490	5 038	6 308	8 344	10 050	10 360	10 965	11 456	Production d'énergie primaire
Net imports	1 555	1 918	1 713	900	859	1 760	1 638	874	Importations nettes
Changes in stocks	86	-106	1	-8	-8	-30	41	-20	Variations des stocks
Total supply	5 960	7 062	8 020	9 252	10 916	12 149	12 562	12 350	Approv.total
Supply per capita	40	44	46	50	55	59	61	59	Approv.par habitant
British Virgin Islands									**Îles Vierges britanniques**
Primary Energy production	0	0	0	0	0	0	0	0	Production d'énergie primaire
Net imports	* 1	* 1	* 1	* 2	* 2	* 2	* 3	* 3	Importations nettes
Total supply	* 1	* 1	* 1	* 2	* 2	* 2	* 3	* 3	Approv.total
Supply per capita	* 56	* 66	* 72	* 85	* 89	* 85	* 85	* 84	Approv.par habitant
Brunei Darussalam									**Brunéi Darussalam**
Primary Energy production	668	752	813	848	775	710	679	673	Production d'énergie primaire
Net imports	* -594	-683	-744	-772	-648	-582	-528	-560	Importations nettes
Changes in stocks	* -33	-1	-4	-1	-7	0	3	0	Variations des stocks
Total supply	107	71	73	76	136	127	149	114	Approv.total
Supply per capita	424	246	224	210	345	310	357	269	Approv.par habitant
Bulgaria									**Bulgarie**
Primary Energy production	407	428	410	444	442	444	474	505	Production d'énergie primaire
Net imports	730	546	358	384	291	265	257	275	Importations nettes
Changes in stocks	-44	7	-5	2	-9	6	-14	6	Variations des stocks
Total supply	1 181	966	773	826	741	703	744	775	Approv.total
Supply per capita	134	116	97	107	100	97	103	108	Approv.par habitant
Burkina Faso									**Burkina Faso**
Primary Energy production	85	96	69	98	118	123	124	126	Production d'énergie primaire
Net imports	* 9	* 10	* 12	* 16	* 26	* 42	* 40	* 48	Importations nettes
Changes in stocks	* 0	1	-1	* 0	* -2	* 2	* -2	* 4	Variations des stocks
Total supply	93	104	83	114	145	162	165	169	Approv.total
Supply per capita	10	10	7	8	9	9	9	9	Approv.par habitant
Burundi									**Burundi**
Primary Energy production	54	62	51	79	86	56	56	56	Production d'énergie primaire
Net imports	* 4	* 4	* 5	* 3	* 4	* 4	* 4	* 3	Importations nettes
Changes in stocks	0	0	0	0	0	0	0	0	Variations des stocks
Total supply	58	66	55	81	89	60	60	59	Approv.total
Supply per capita	10	11	9	11	9	6	6	5	Approv.par habitant
Cabo Verde									**Cabo Verde**
Primary Energy production	1	1	1	2	1	2	2	* 2	Production d'énergie primaire
Net imports	* 1	* 2	* 4	* 6	* 7	* 7	* 7	* 8	Importations nettes
Changes in stocks	0	...	...	...	...	...	...	...	Variations des stocks
Total supply	* 2	* 3	* 4	8	9	9	9	* 9	Approv.total
Supply per capita	* 7	* 7	* 10	16	19	17	17	* 17	Approv.par habitant
Cambodia									**Cambodge**
Primary Energy production	103	98	114	105	152	171	178	184	Production d'énergie primaire
Net imports	* 18	22	28	39	72	80	88	111	Importations nettes
Total supply	121	119	142	144	223	251	267	295	Approv.total
Supply per capita	13	11	11	11	16	17	17	19	Approv.par habitant
Cameroon									**Cameroun**
Primary Energy production	501	457	532	442	351	373	406	446	Production d'énergie primaire
Net imports	* -326	* -219	* -268	* -152	* -73	* -83	* -81	* -120	Importations nettes
Changes in stocks	* 0	* 2	0	-5	-13	0	...	...	Variations des stocks
Total supply	176	237	264	295	291	290	325	326	Approv.total
Supply per capita	14	17	17	17	14	13	14	14	Approv.par habitant
Canada									**Canada**
Primary Energy production	11 460	14 587	15 531	16 597	16 450	18 308	19 322	19 321	Production d'énergie primaire
Net imports	-2 538	-5 047	-5 377	-5 468	-5 859	-7 300	-7 599	-8 126	Importations nettes
Changes in stocks	170	-145	-351	-106	-303	-154	176	44	Variations des stocks
Total supply	8 752	9 684	10 504	11 235	10 895	11 162	11 546	11 151	Approv.total
Supply per capita	316	331	343	348	319	317	324	310	Approv.par habitant

23 Production, trade and supply of energy *(continued)*
Petajoules and gigajoules per capita

Production, commerce et fourniture d'énergie *(suite)*
pétajoules et gigajoules par habitant

Region, country or area	1990	1995	2000	2005	2010	2013	2014	2015	Région, pays ou zone
Cayman Islands									**Îles Caïmanes**
Net imports	4	* 6	* 7	7	8	8	8	8	Importations nettes
Total supply	4	* 5	* 7	7	8	8	8	8	Approv.total
Supply per capita	138	* 159	* 166	130	144	131	132	132	Approv.par habitant
Central African Republic									**République centrafricaine**
Primary Energy production	28	28	19	19	19	19	19	19	Production d'énergie primaire
Net imports	* 3	* 3	* 4	* 3	* 4	* 5	* 5	* 5	Importations nettes
Changes in stocks	0	* 0	* 0	...	...	...	...	...	Variations des stocks
Total supply	31	31	22	22	23	23	23	23	Approv.total
Supply per capita	11	9	6	5	5	5	5	5	Approv.par habitant
Chad									**Tchad**
Primary Energy production	43	48	55	433	324	275	288	* 225	Production d'énergie primaire
Net imports	* 2	* 2	* 2	* -367	* -252	* -198	* -209	* -145	Importations nettes
Changes in stocks	0	0	...	...	...	...	...	...	Variations des stocks
Total supply	45	50	57	66	73	77	79	* 80	Approv.total
Supply per capita	7	7	7	7	6	6	6	* 6	Approv.par habitant
Chile									**Chili**
Primary Energy production	326	344	358	390	384	626	539	540	Production d'énergie primaire
Net imports	284	437	722	791	888	1 013	927	969	Importations nettes
Changes in stocks	24	10	7	3	-6	26	6	4	Variations des stocks
Total supply	587	772	1 073	1 178	1 278	1 613	1 459	1 504	Approv.total
Supply per capita	45	54	70	72	75	92	82	84	Approv.par habitant
China [2]									**Chine** [2]
Primary Energy production	32 727	39 692	40 783	63 831	88 642	101 417	101 498	100 864	Production d'énergie primaire
Net imports	-1 370	-397	1 426	4 251	14 225	18 890	19 634	18 874	Importations nettes
Changes in stocks	959	132	-251	-752	1 248	1 895	1 444	-187	Variations des stocks
Total supply	30 398	39 163	42 461	68 833	101 618	118 412	119 688	119 926	Approv.total
Supply per capita	27	32	33	53	76	87	87	87	Approv.par habitant
China, Hong Kong SAR									**Chine, RAS de Hong Kong**
Net imports	321	382	571	578	680	592	590	640	Importations nettes
Changes in stocks	5	* -16	1	-2	130	6	-10	58	Variations des stocks
Total supply	316	398	570	579	550	585	599	583	Approv.total
Supply per capita	54	65	84	85	79	82	83	80	Approv.par habitant
China, Macao SAR									**Chine, RAS de Macao**
Primary Energy production	...	...	...	* 2	* 2	* 2	* 2	* 2	Production d'énergie primaire
Net imports	15	18	23	26	* 29	* 29	31	38	Importations nettes
Changes in stocks	0	0	0	0	0	0	0	1	Variations des stocks
Total supply	15	18	24	28	31	30	34	40	Approv.total
Supply per capita	40	45	55	58	57	54	58	68	Approv.par habitant
Colombia									**Colombie**
Primary Energy production	1 882	2 419	3 046	3 335	4 486	5 702	5 397	5 593	Production d'énergie primaire
Net imports	* -891	-1 267	-1 987	-2 139	-3 081	-4 161	-3 751	-4 157	Importations nettes
Changes in stocks	7	48	-43	16	3	18	121	-38	Variations des stocks
Total supply	983	1 104	1 103	1 180	1 402	1 522	1 525	1 475	Approv.total
Supply per capita	30	30	28	27	31	32	32	31	Approv.par habitant
Comoros									**Comores**
Primary Energy production	1	2	2	2	2	3	3	3	Production d'énergie primaire
Net imports	* 1	* 1	* 1	* 2	* 2	* 3	* 2	* 3	Importations nettes
Total supply	2	3	3	* 4	* 5	* 5	5	5	Approv.total
Supply per capita	5	6	6	* 6	* 7	* 7	6	7	Approv.par habitant
Congo									**Congo**
Primary Energy production	361	419	609	563	724	612	648	623	Production d'énergie primaire
Net imports	* -325	* -375	* -569	* -519	* -649	* -516	* -525	* -512	Importations nettes
Changes in stocks	0	0	...	0	6	-12	14	...	Variations des stocks
Total supply	36	44	40	45	70	109	109	111	Approv.total
Supply per capita	15	16	13	13	17	25	24	24	Approv.par habitant
Cook Islands									**Îles Cook**
Primary Energy production	...	...	...	...	...	* 0	* 0	* 0	Production d'énergie primaire
Net imports	* 1	* 1	* 1	1	* 1	* 1	* 1	* 1	Importations nettes
Total supply	* 0	* 1	* 1	1	* 1	* 1	* 1	* 1	Approv.total
Supply per capita	* 28	* 30	* 36	39	* 36	* 42	* 44	* 41	Approv.par habitant
Costa Rica									**Costa Rica**
Primary Energy production	30	46	67	93	104	110	110	110	Production d'énergie primaire
Net imports	40	65	70	85	99	97	103	97	Importations nettes
Changes in stocks	1	0	-1	0	0	-2	1	0	Variations des stocks
Total supply	68	110	137	177	203	210	213	207	Approv.total
Supply per capita	22	32	35	41	45	45	45	43	Approv.par habitant

23 Production, trade and supply of energy *(continued)*
Petajoules and gigajoules per capita

Production, commerce et fourniture d'énergie *(suite)*
pétajoules et gigajoules par habitant

Region, country or area	1990	1995	2000	2005	2010	2013	2014	2015	Région, pays ou zone
Côte d'Ivoire									**Côte d'Ivoire**
Primary Energy production	179	178	242	451	467	540	540	526	Production d'énergie primaire
Net imports	*26	*68	*28	*-27	*-40	*24	*38	*10	Importations nettes
Changes in stocks	*1	*0	*-8	*5	3	-2	-3	-6	Variations des stocks
Total supply	204	245	278	418	425	566	580	543	Approv.total
Supply per capita	16	17	17	23	21	26	26	24	Approv.par habitant
Croatia									**Croatie**
Primary Energy production	...	209	178	199	215	186	182	184	Production d'énergie primaire
Net imports	...	115	166	212	180	164	146	168	Importations nettes
Changes in stocks	...	-2	-4	4	5	-2	-8	2	Variations des stocks
Total supply	...	325	349	407	390	352	335	350	Approv.total
Supply per capita	...	70	77	92	90	82	79	83	Approv.par habitant
Cuba									**Cuba**
Primary Energy production	*213	170	241	205	200	202	212	212	Production d'énergie primaire
Net imports	*404	286	232	*207	*301	*250	*243	*268	Importations nettes
Changes in stocks	-5	4	10	...	...	...	...	...	Variations des stocks
Total supply	623	452	462	412	501	451	454	480	Approv.total
Supply per capita	59	41	42	37	44	40	40	42	Approv.par habitant
Curaçao									**Curaçao**
Primary Energy production	...	...	...	...	...	0	0	0	Production d'énergie primaire
Net imports	...	...	...	...	...	77	85	93	Importations nettes
Total supply	...	...	...	...	...	77	85	93	Approv.total
Supply per capita	...	...	...	...	...	499	545	592	Approv.par habitant
Cyprus									**Chypre**
Primary Energy production	0	0	0	0	4	5	5	5	Production d'énergie primaire
Net imports	57	72	88	94	104	78	76	83	Importations nettes
Changes in stocks	-1	2	0	3	5	1	-2	3	Variations des stocks
Total supply	57	70	88	92	103	82	83	85	Approv.total
Supply per capita	75	82	93	89	94	71	72	73	Approv.par habitant
Czechia									**Tchéquie**
Primary Energy production	...	1 367	1 289	1 387	1 339	1 277	1 245	1 213	Production d'énergie primaire
Net imports	...	367	411	527	476	489	527	555	Importations nettes
Changes in stocks	...	-30	-49	16	-77	-41	13	4	Variations des stocks
Total supply	...	1 764	1 748	1 898	1 891	1 807	1 758	1 764	Approv.total
Supply per capita	...	171	171	186	180	171	167	167	Approv.par habitant
Dem. People's Rep. Korea									**Rép. pop. dém. de Corée**
Primary Energy production	1 211	838	787	923	872	853	871	788	Production d'énergie primaire
Net imports	181	83	41	-28	-77	-395	-367	-457	Importations nettes
Changes in stocks	...	...	2	...	...	...	...	...	Variations des stocks
Total supply	1 391	921	826	896	795	459	505	332	Approv.total
Supply per capita	69	42	36	38	32	18	20	13	Approv.par habitant
Dem. Rep. of the Congo									**Rép. dém. du Congo**
Primary Energy production	490	616	677	866	855	1 149	1 179	1 218	Production d'énergie primaire
Net imports	*-13	*-33	*-43	*-41	*-24	*2	*23	*-8	Importations nettes
Changes in stocks	0	0	-1	0	0	...	...	...	Variations des stocks
Total supply	477	584	635	825	831	1 151	1 202	1 209	Approv.total
Supply per capita	13	13	13	14	13	16	16	16	Approv.par habitant
Denmark [3]									**Danemark** [3]
Primary Energy production	420	649	1 149	1 298	968	690	664	662	Production d'énergie primaire
Net imports	298	217	-383	-498	-204	33	21	28	Importations nettes
Changes in stocks	-7	57	-19	14	-45	10	15	21	Variations des stocks
Total supply	725	811	785	786	810	713	669	668	Approv.total
Supply per capita	141	155	147	145	146	127	118	118	Approv.par habitant
Djibouti									**Djibouti**
Primary Energy production	2	2	3	3	3	3	3	4	Production d'énergie primaire
Net imports	*5	*5	*5	*6	*7	*7	*7	*7	Importations nettes
Changes in stocks	0	...	...	...	*0	...	...	...	Variations des stocks
Total supply	*6	*7	8	*9	11	*11	*11	*10	Approv.total
Supply per capita	*12	*11	11	*11	13	*13	*13	*11	Approv.par habitant
Dominica									**Dominique**
Primary Energy production	0	0	0	0	0	0	0	0	Production d'énergie primaire
Net imports	*1	1	1	*2	*2	*2	*2	*3	Importations nettes
Changes in stocks	...	*0	...	...	0	*0	*0	*0	Variations des stocks
Total supply	*1	1	2	*2	2	*2	*2	*3	Approv.total
Supply per capita	*14	19	24	*31	34	*33	*34	*37	Approv.par habitant

23 Production, trade and supply of energy *(continued)*
Petajoules and gigajoules per capita

Production, commerce et fourniture d'énergie *(suite)*
pétajoules et gigajoules par habitant

Region, country or area	1990	1995	2000	2005	2010	2013	2014	2015	Région, pays ou zone
Dominican Republic									**République dominicaine**
Primary Energy production	22	24	24	28	27	29	28	25	Production d'énergie primaire
Net imports	122	212	259	239	271	277	272	302	Importations nettes
Changes in stocks	1	0	0	2	0	-2	0	0	Variations des stocks
Total supply	143	236	283	266	298	309	301	328	Approv.total
Supply per capita	20	30	33	29	30	30	29	31	Approv.par habitant
Ecuador									**Équateur**
Primary Energy production	683	915	959	1 251	1 077	1 249	1 324	1 297	Production d'énergie primaire
Net imports	-428	* -577	-612	-772	-513	-635	-649	-641	Importations nettes
Changes in stocks	0	...	20	4	2	2	-2	4	Variations des stocks
Total supply	255	339	328	475	562	611	677	651	Approv.total
Supply per capita	25	30	27	35	38	39	43	40	Approv.par habitant
Egypt									**Égypte**
Primary Energy production	2 376	2 684	2 773	3 383	3 692	3 448	3 240	3 051	Production d'énergie primaire
Net imports	* -1 084	* -709	* -449	* -645	* -511	* -10	* 262	* 405	Importations nettes
Changes in stocks	* 21	369	36	-4	-60	0	-1	-1	Variations des stocks
Total supply	1 271	1 605	2 288	2 742	3 242	3 438	3 503	3 457	Approv.total
Supply per capita	22	26	34	37	40	39	39	38	Approv.par habitant
El Salvador									**El Salvador**
Primary Energy production	60	70	89	104	95	86	86	87	Production d'énergie primaire
Net imports	32	67	77	85	81	81	82	92	Importations nettes
Changes in stocks	-1	2	0	0	-2	0	-1	-1	Variations des stocks
Total supply	92	135	166	189	178	167	170	180	Approv.total
Supply per capita	17	24	28	31	29	27	28	29	Approv.par habitant
Equatorial Guinea									**Guinée équatoriale**
Primary Energy production	4	34	285	823	813	800	842	879	Production d'énergie primaire
Net imports	* 1	* -28	* -276	* -770	* -745	* -733	* -770	* -808	Importations nettes
Changes in stocks	...	* 1	...	...	...	...	...	...	Variations des stocks
Total supply	5	5	9	52	68	68	73	* 71	Approv.total
Supply per capita	13	11	18	86	94	85	89	* 84	Approv.par habitant
Eritrea									**Érythrée**
Primary Energy production	...	31	21	21	24	26	27	27	Production d'énergie primaire
Net imports	...	* 13	* 9	* 10	* 7	* 7	* 8	* 8	Importations nettes
Changes in stocks	...	...	0	-2	0	0	0	...	Variations des stocks
Total supply	...	43	30	32	31	33	34	36	Approv.total
Supply per capita	...	14	8	7	7	7	7	7	Approv.par habitant
Estonia									**Estonie**
Primary Energy production	...	139	129	163	205	237	242	233	Production d'énergie primaire
Net imports	...	74	66	57	30	21	16	13	Importations nettes
Changes in stocks	...	-3	-1	0	-2	1	5	15	Variations des stocks
Total supply	...	217	196	220	236	258	254	230	Approv.total
Supply per capita	...	151	143	164	177	195	193	176	Approv.par habitant
Eswatini									**Eswatini**
Primary Energy production	20	19	34	36	33	38	37	38	Production d'énergie primaire
Net imports	...	* 2	* 7	* 3	* 11	* 13	* 10	* 11	Importations nettes
Changes in stocks	...	...	...	* 0	* 0	...	...	...	Variations des stocks
Total supply	20	21	41	40	44	51	47	49	Approv.total
Supply per capita	23	22	39	36	37	41	37	38	Approv.par habitant
Ethiopia									**Éthiopie**
Primary Energy production	...	885	977	1 070	1 212	1 285	1 308	1 334	Production d'énergie primaire
Net imports	...	* 31	* 43	* 60	* 82	* 111	* 128	* 136	Importations nettes
Changes in stocks	...	* -2	-2	-3	1	1	-1	0	Variations des stocks
Total supply	...	918	1 022	1 132	1 293	1 394	1 438	1 471	Approv.total
Supply per capita	...	16	16	15	15	15	15	15	Approv.par habitant
Falkland Islands (Malvinas)									**Îles Falkland (Malvinas)**
Primary Energy production	0	* 0	* 0	* 0	* 0	* 0	* 0	* 0	Production d'énergie primaire
Net imports	0	* 0	* 0	* 1	* 1	* 1	* 1	* 1	Importations nettes
Total supply	1	* 1	* 1	* 1	* 1	* 1	* 1	* 1	Approv.total
Supply per capita	271	* 239	* 178	* 235	* 261	* 258	* 257	* 257	Approv.par habitant
Faroe Islands									**Îles Féroé**
Primary Energy production	0	0	0	0	0	0	1	1	Production d'énergie primaire
Net imports	* 11	* 9	* 10	* 11	* 9	* 9	* 8	* 9	Importations nettes
Total supply	10	* 8	* 10	* 10	* 9	* 10	* 9	* 9	Approv.total
Supply per capita	220	* 191	* 216	* 216	* 184	* 202	* 182	* 188	Approv.par habitant

23 Production, trade and supply of energy *(continued)*
Petajoules and gigajoules per capita

Production, commerce et fourniture d'énergie *(suite)*
pétajoules et gigajoules par habitant

Region, country or area	1990	1995	2000	2005	2010	2013	2014	2015	Région, pays ou zone
Fiji									**Fidji**
Primary Energy production	10	13	11	9	6	8	8	8	Production d'énergie primaire
Net imports	9	* 11	* 11	* 16	* 16	* 18	* 22	* 30	Importations nettes
Changes in stocks	-1	...	...	* 0	...	...	...	...	Variations des stocks
Total supply	21	* 23	22	24	22	* 25	* 30	38	Approv.total
Supply per capita	28	* 30	27	29	25	* 29	* 34	43	Approv.par habitant
Finland									**Finlande**
Primary Energy production	504	549	622	699	727	759	759	734	Production d'énergie primaire
Net imports	712	636	725	761	721	659	681	617	Importations nettes
Changes in stocks	26	-27	2	27	-78	30	25	1	Variations des stocks
Total supply	1 190	1 212	1 346	1 433	1 526	1 387	1 415	1 349	Approv.total
Supply per capita	239	237	260	273	284	254	258	245	Approv.par habitant
France [4]									**France [4]**
Primary Energy production	4 652	5 314	5 427	5 692	5 623	5 638	5 695	5 720	Production d'énergie primaire
Net imports	4 801	4 619	5 258	5 689	5 197	4 918	4 510	4 565	Importations nettes
Changes in stocks	71	10	148	49	-109	-32	55	-24	Variations des stocks
Total supply	9 381	9 924	10 537	11 332	10 929	10 589	10 149	10 310	Approv.total
Supply per capita	165	171	178	186	173	166	158	155	Approv.par habitant
French Guiana									**Guyane française**
Primary Energy production	0	1	2	2	3	3	3	3	Production d'énergie primaire
Net imports	* 9	* 8	6	8	* 9	* 9	* 10	* 9	Importations nettes
Total supply	9	9	8	10	* 12	* 12	* 13	* 12	Approv.total
Supply per capita	79	62	47	49	* 51	* 47	* 49	* 46	Approv.par habitant
French Polynesia									**Polynésie française**
Primary Energy production	0	0	1	1	1	* 1	* 1	* 1	Production d'énergie primaire
Net imports	* 6	* 6	* 8	* 11	* 11	* 10	* 9	* 10	Importations nettes
Total supply	* 7	7	9	12	12	11	11	12	Approv.total
Supply per capita	* 34	32	37	46	46	41	40	41	Approv.par habitant
Gabon									**Gabon**
Primary Energy production	609	822	630	622	590	558	559	556	Production d'énergie primaire
Net imports	* -509	* -765	* -572	* -545	* -527	* -451	* -451	* -451	Importations nettes
Changes in stocks	50	2	-4	5	-29	0	...	...	Variations des stocks
Total supply	50	56	62	72	93	107	109	106	Approv.total
Supply per capita	54	52	50	53	60	65	64	62	Approv.par habitant
Gambia									**Gambie**
Primary Energy production	4	5	6	6	6	7	7	7	Production d'énergie primaire
Net imports	* 3	* 3	* 4	* 5	* 6	* 6	* 7	* 7	Importations nettes
Changes in stocks	0	...	...	...	...	...	...	...	Variations des stocks
Total supply	7	8	9	10	12	13	14	* 14	Approv.total
Supply per capita	7	7	7	7	7	7	7	* 7	Approv.par habitant
Georgia									**Géorgie**
Primary Energy production	...	22	28	53	58	63	61	58	Production d'énergie primaire
Net imports	...	37	65	82	82	104	127	140	Importations nettes
Changes in stocks	...	0	0	0	0	0	0	1	Variations des stocks
Total supply	...	59	93	135	140	167	188	197	Approv.total
Supply per capita	...	12	20	30	33	41	47	49	Approv.par habitant
Germany									**Allemagne**
Primary Energy production	...	6 050	5 645	5 706	5 377	5 032	5 004	5 007	Production d'énergie primaire
Net imports	...	7 849	8 207	8 360	8 088	8 202	7 765	7 859	Importations nettes
Changes in stocks	...	-137	-183	46	-179	-36	-14	-16	Variations des stocks
Total supply	...	14 037	14 034	14 020	13 643	13 270	12 783	12 882	Approv.total
Supply per capita	...	171	170	170	170	165	159	160	Approv.par habitant
Ghana									**Ghana**
Primary Energy production	138	211	192	164	148	350	357	372	Production d'énergie primaire
Net imports	* 49	* 66	* 79	* 87	* 120	* -32	* -33	* -31	Importations nettes
Changes in stocks	0	...	...	...	0	12	3	1	Variations des stocks
Total supply	187	277	271	251	267	306	321	339	Approv.total
Supply per capita	13	16	14	12	11	12	12	12	Approv.par habitant
Gibraltar									**Gibraltar**
Net imports	3	5	6	7	8	8	9	9	Importations nettes
Changes in stocks	0	...	...	...	...	...	...	...	Variations des stocks
Total supply	2	4	5	6	7	8	8	9	Approv.total
Supply per capita	90	162	197	219	238	242	257	272	Approv.par habitant

23 Production, trade and supply of energy *(continued)*

Petajoules and gigajoules per capita

Production, commerce et fourniture d'énergie *(suite)*

pétajoules et gigajoules par habitant

Region, country or area	1990	1995	2000	2005	2010	2013	2014	2015	Région, pays ou zone
Greece									**Grèce**
Primary Energy production	385	391	419	432	396	388	368	355	Production d'énergie primaire
Net imports	506	581	741	831	762	573	613	676	Importations nettes
Changes in stocks	-10	10	12	-18	-11	-28	-2	45	Variations des stocks
Total supply	902	963	1 148	1 280	1 169	989	983	985	Approv.total
Supply per capita	89	90	104	115	105	89	89	90	Approv.par habitant
Greenland									**Groenland**
Primary Energy production	*0	1	1	1	1	1	2	2	Production d'énergie primaire
Net imports	*5	*5	*7	9	10	8	7	8	Importations nettes
Changes in stocks	...	...	...	*1	1	0	0	1	Variations des stocks
Total supply	5	5	7	9	11	9	9	9	Approv.total
Supply per capita	90	94	127	165	186	165	154	158	Approv.par habitant
Grenada									**Grenade**
Primary Energy production	0	0	0	0	0	0	0	0	Production d'énergie primaire
Net imports	*2	*2	*3	3	4	5	4	4	Importations nettes
Changes in stocks	0	0	0	0	0	0	0	0	Variations des stocks
Total supply	2	2	3	3	4	5	4	4	Approv.total
Supply per capita	17	23	29	33	38	44	35	38	Approv.par habitant
Guadeloupe									**Guadeloupe**
Primary Energy production	1	*2	*2	5	*2	5	5	5	Production d'énergie primaire
Net imports	16	19	24	28	*30	29	27	27	Importations nettes
Total supply	18	21	26	33	*32	34	32	33	Approv.total
Supply per capita	47	52	61	75	*71	72	68	71	Approv.par habitant
Guatemala									**Guatemala**
Primary Energy production	143	178	229	255	279	310	327	316	Production d'énergie primaire
Net imports	52	75	75	112	108	132	149	180	Importations nettes
Changes in stocks	0	*1	-4	6	0	3	12	20	Variations des stocks
Total supply	195	252	307	361	387	439	465	476	Approv.total
Supply per capita	22	25	27	28	26	28	29	29	Approv.par habitant
Guernsey									**Guernesey**
Net imports	...	...	...	1	1	0	1	1	Importations nettes
Total supply	...	...	...	1	1	0	1	1	Approv.total
Supply per capita	...	...	...	17	14	6	9	13	Approv.par habitant
Guinea									**Guinée**
Primary Energy production	91	110	107	109	112	113	113	116	Production d'énergie primaire
Net imports	*14	*16	*21	*26	*36	*31	*33	*37	Importations nettes
Changes in stocks	0	...	...	...	...	...	...	...	Variations des stocks
Total supply	105	126	128	135	147	144	146	152	Approv.total
Supply per capita	18	17	15	15	13	12	12	12	Approv.par habitant
Guinea-Bissau									**Guinée-Bissau**
Primary Energy production	17	18	20	22	24	25	25	25	Production d'énergie primaire
Net imports	*3	*4	*3	*4	*5	*5	*4	*4	Importations nettes
Total supply	20	21	23	26	28	29	30	30	Approv.total
Supply per capita	20	19	19	19	17	17	17	16	Approv.par habitant
Guyana									**Guyana**
Primary Energy production	9	8	9	9	8	7	7	7	Production d'énergie primaire
Net imports	*16	*21	22	20	24	27	28	27	Importations nettes
Changes in stocks	...	0	0	0	0	0	0	0	Variations des stocks
Total supply	25	29	32	29	32	34	35	35	Approv.total
Supply per capita	34	39	43	39	43	45	46	45	Approv.par habitant
Haiti									**Haïti**
Primary Energy production	51	58	65	115	131	140	136	139	Production d'énergie primaire
Net imports	11	13	20	28	28	31	38	40	Importations nettes
Changes in stocks	-1	...	...	...	...	-1	0	0	Variations des stocks
Total supply	64	71	84	142	159	171	174	179	Approv.total
Supply per capita	9	9	10	15	16	16	16	17	Approv.par habitant
Honduras									**Honduras**
Primary Energy production	91	92	96	77	93	106	105	113	Production d'énergie primaire
Net imports	32	51	65	89	98	112	110	97	Importations nettes
Changes in stocks	0	1	5	-4	0	0	-9	-29	Variations des stocks
Total supply	122	142	157	170	191	217	224	237	Approv.total
Supply per capita	25	25	25	25	25	28	28	29	Approv.par habitant

23 Production, trade and supply of energy *(continued)*
Petajoules and gigajoules per capita

Production, commerce et fourniture d'énergie *(suite)*
pétajoules et gigajoules par habitant

Region, country or area	1990	1995	2000	2005	2010	2013	2014	2015	Région, pays ou zone
Hungary									**Hongrie**
Primary Energy production	615	583	486	434	496	479	462	471	Production d'énergie primaire
Net imports	594	521	573	729	627	501	593	565	Importations nettes
Changes in stocks	-2	11	10	8	9	-26	55	-21	Variations des stocks
Total supply	1 211	1 093	1 049	1 155	1 113	1 006	1 000	1 058	Approv.total
Supply per capita	117	106	103	115	111	101	101	107	Approv.par habitant
Iceland									**Islande**
Primary Energy production	59	63	109	127	252	283	285	285	Production d'énergie primaire
Net imports	28	27	31	31	26	26	27	29	Importations nettes
Changes in stocks	0	0	2	1	-1	1	0	1	Variations des stocks
Total supply	87	90	139	158	278	309	312	313	Approv.total
Supply per capita	341	338	494	534	875	951	952	950	Approv.par habitant
India									**Inde**
Primary Energy production	9 218	10 985	12 090	18 315	22 598	22 401	23 103	23 538	Production d'énergie primaire
Net imports	1 196	* 2 010	3 890	4 689	6 558	10 690	* 12 120	13 208	Importations nettes
Changes in stocks	45	* -41	-155	194	252	-103	-169	48	Variations des stocks
Total supply	10 370	13 035	16 135	22 809	28 903	33 195	35 391	36 697	Approv.total
Supply per capita	12	14	15	20	23	26	27	28	Approv.par habitant
Indonesia									**Indonésie**
Primary Energy production	6 735[5]	8 320[5]	8 129[5]	11 351	16 854	19 088	18 457	17 926	Production d'énergie primaire
Net imports	-2 753[5]	-3 634[5]	-3 577[5]	-4 243	-8 530	-10 758	-10 263	-8 523	Importations nettes
Changes in stocks	223[5]	100[5]	-417[5]	21	2	62	282	-48	Variations des stocks
Total supply	3 759[5]	4 587[5]	4 970[5]	7 087	8 322	8 267	7 912	9 452	Approv.total
Supply per capita	20[5]	23[5]	23[5]	31	34	33	31	37	Approv.par habitant
Iran (Islamic Republic of)									**Iran (Rép. islamique d')**
Primary Energy production	7 454	9 302	11 121	13 006	14 283	12 540	13 368	13 637	Production d'énergie primaire
Net imports	-4 634	-5 415	-5 787	-5 682	-5 634	-3 369	-3 414	-3 640	Importations nettes
Changes in stocks	0	0	-52	103	69	-30	-32	7	Variations des stocks
Total supply	2 819	3 887	5 386	7 221	8 579	9 201	9 986	9 989	Approv.total
Supply per capita	51	65	82	104	116	119	128	126	Approv.par habitant
Iraq									**Iraq**
Primary Energy production	4 411	1 265	5 482	4 147	5 274	6 514	6 772	7 565	Production d'énergie primaire
Net imports	* -3 656	-193	-4 487	-2 656	-3 835	-4 443	-4 629	-5 719	Importations nettes
Changes in stocks	* 169	0	0	3	1	19	87	-152	Variations des stocks
Total supply	586	1 072	995	1 488	1 437	2 051	2 055	1 997	Approv.total
Supply per capita	34	53	42	54	47	60	58	55	Approv.par habitant
Ireland									**Irlande**
Primary Energy production	145	172	90	69	77	94	84	80	Production d'énergie primaire
Net imports	281	303	482	544	522	486	454	489	Importations nettes
Changes in stocks	10	28	-2	2	-8	34	3	14	Variations des stocks
Total supply	416	446	573	610	608	546	534	555	Approv.total
Supply per capita	118	124	151	147	132	117	114	118	Approv.par habitant
Isle of Man									**Île de Man**
Primary Energy production	...	...	...	* 0	* 0	* 0	* 0	* 0	Production d'énergie primaire
Net imports	...	...	...	0	0	* 0	* 0	* 0	Importations nettes
Total supply	...	...	...	* 0	0	* 0	* 0	* 0	Approv.total
Supply per capita	...	...	...	* 6	2	* 4	* 3	* 3	Approv.par habitant
Israel									**Israël**
Primary Energy production	18	23	27	87	162	241	283	308	Production d'énergie primaire
Net imports	450	625	719	685	804	712	618	650	Importations nettes
Changes in stocks	-12	-1	-17	5	0	21	10	2	Variations des stocks
Total supply	480	649	763	767	966	931	891	955	Approv.total
Supply per capita	107	122	127	116	130	119	112	118	Approv.par habitant
Italy [6]									**Italie [6]**
Primary Energy production	1 072	1 235	1 183	1 269	1 384	1 542	1 539	1 509	Production d'énergie primaire
Net imports	5 375	5 481	6 239	6 509	6 009	4 965	4 628	4 888	Importations nettes
Changes in stocks	80	3	190	-70	69	-23	-1	-5	Variations des stocks
Total supply	6 366	6 714	7 230	7 847	7 324	6 530	6 168	6 402	Approv.total
Supply per capita	112	118	127	134	123	109	103	107	Approv.par habitant
Jamaica									**Jamaïque**
Primary Energy production	13	9	11	15	6	7	8	* 8	Production d'énergie primaire
Net imports	97	118	144	139	95	104	96	101	Importations nettes
Changes in stocks	-2	-3	7	1	-2	-1	1	1	Variations des stocks
Total supply	113	130	148	151	103	113	104	108	Approv.total
Supply per capita	48	53	57	56	38	41	37	39	Approv.par habitant

23 Production, trade and supply of energy *(continued)*
Petajoules and gigajoules per capita

Production, commerce et fourniture d'énergie *(suite)*
pétajoules et gigajoules par habitant

Region, country or area	1990	1995	2000	2005	2010	2013	2014	2015	Région, pays ou zone
Japan									**Japon**
Primary Energy production	3 121	4 088	4 384	4 175	4 118	1 161	1 099	1 269	Production d'énergie primaire
Net imports	15 341	16 662	17 453	17 700	16 739	17 800	17 198	16 665	Importations nettes
Changes in stocks	147	55	166	100	-6	-21	-121	-50	Variations des stocks
Total supply	18 314	20 697	21 671	21 774	20 862	18 981	18 418	17 984	Approv.total
Supply per capita	150	166	172	172	164	149	145	142	Approv.par habitant
Jersey									**Jersey**
Primary Energy production	...	...	...	* 0	* 0	* 1	* 1	* 1	Production d'énergie primaire
Net imports	...	1	1	2	2	2	2	2	Importations nettes
Total supply	...	1	1	3	3	3	3	3	Approv.total
Supply per capita	...	9	17	28	28	27	27	29	Approv.par habitant
Jordan									**Jordanie**
Primary Energy production	6	10	10	10	9	7	7	8	Production d'énergie primaire
Net imports	136	160	190	285	300	311	349	359	Importations nettes
Changes in stocks	4	-2	-5	7	5	-10	5	5	Variations des stocks
Total supply	138	172	205	289	303	328	352	362	Approv.total
Supply per capita	40	39	42	54	46	45	47	48	Approv.par habitant
Kazakhstan									**Kazakhstan**
Primary Energy production	...	2 663	3 367	5 131	6 770	7 198	7 092	7 338	Production d'énergie primaire
Net imports	...	-477	-1 819	-2 771	* -3 318	-3 568	-3 722	-4 120	Importations nettes
Changes in stocks	...	...	-12	8	88	80	16	-41	Variations des stocks
Total supply	...	2 185	1 560	2 352	3 363	3 550	3 354	3 258	Approv.total
Supply per capita	...	137	104	155	206	208	193	185	Approv.par habitant
Kenya									**Kenya**
Primary Energy production	217	239	248	338	* 650	* 719	750	761	Production d'énergie primaire
Net imports	* 71	* 98	* 141	* 109	* 137	* 149	* 159	* 189	Importations nettes
Changes in stocks	0	...	...	4	-5	-1	0	0	Variations des stocks
Total supply	289	337	388	443	* 793	* 868	909	949	Approv.total
Supply per capita	12	12	12	12	* 20	* 20	20	21	Approv.par habitant
Kiribati									**Kiribati**
Primary Energy production	0	0	0	0	0	0	0	0	Production d'énergie primaire
Net imports	* 0	* 0	0	* 1	1	1	1	* 1	Importations nettes
Total supply	* 0	* 0	0	* 1	1	1	1	* 1	Approv.total
Supply per capita	* 5	* 5	6	* 9	8	7	7	* 8	Approv.par habitant
Kuwait [7]									**Koweït** [7]
Primary Energy production	2 799	4 802	4 748	6 080	5 557	7 107	6 943	7 003	Production d'énergie primaire
Net imports	* -2 090	-3 968	-3 941	-4 915	-4 229	-5 710	-5 626	-5 531	Importations nettes
Changes in stocks	* 142	-1	-17	31	-22	-21	-22	14	Variations des stocks
Total supply	566	835	824	1 133	1 350	1 418	1 339	1 458	Approv.total
Supply per capita	271	513	424	500	441	394	357	375	Approv.par habitant
Kyrgyzstan									**Kirghizistan**
Primary Energy production	...	53	60	61	53	74	80	75	Production d'énergie primaire
Net imports	...	51	38	53	63	96	93	103	Importations nettes
Changes in stocks	...	3	-2	0	1	2	2	12	Variations des stocks
Total supply	...	101	101	114	115	167	171	167	Approv.total
Supply per capita	...	22	20	23	21	29	29	28	Approv.par habitant
Lao People's Dem. Rep.									**Rép. dém. populaire lao**
Primary Energy production	54	57	70	73	117	* 141	141	185	Production d'énergie primaire
Net imports	5	7	-1	3	2	* -10	-8	* 2	Importations nettes
Total supply	60	63	70	76	119	* 130	133	187	Approv.total
Supply per capita	14	13	13	13	19	* 20	20	28	Approv.par habitant
Latvia									**Lettonie**
Primary Energy production	...	60	59	78	95	98	108	98	Production d'énergie primaire
Net imports	...	138	94	116	78	100	70	84	Importations nettes
Changes in stocks	...	1	-4	5	-29	2	-17	3	Variations des stocks
Total supply	...	197	157	190	203	196	196	179	Approv.total
Supply per capita	...	79	66	82	97	98	99	91	Approv.par habitant
Lebanon									**Liban**
Primary Energy production	5	8	7	10	9	10	7	8	Production d'énergie primaire
Net imports	* 108	166	198	197	253	279	300	305	Importations nettes
Changes in stocks	...	...	-1	...	...	...	...	...	Variations des stocks
Total supply	* 113	173	207	206	262	289	306	312	Approv.total
Supply per capita	* 38	50	55	51	60	55	55	53	Approv.par habitant

23 Production, trade and supply of energy *(continued)*
Petajoules and gigajoules per capita

Production, commerce et fourniture d'énergie *(suite)*
pétajoules et gigajoules par habitant

Region, country or area	1990	1995	2000	2005	2010	2013	2014	2015	Région, pays ou zone
Lesotho									**Lesotho**
Primary Energy production	19	22	28	25	27	31	31	31	Production d'énergie primaire
Net imports	* 17	* 19	* 20	* 22	* 25	* 27	* 28	* 28	Importations nettes
Total supply	36	41	48	47	52	58	59	59	Approv.total
Supply per capita	22	23	24	23	26	28	28	27	Approv.par habitant
Liberia									**Libéria**
Primary Energy production	32	25	43	53	64	71	73	76	Production d'énergie primaire
Net imports	* 7	* 7	* 6	* 9	* 11	* 12	* 16	* 16	Importations nettes
Total supply	38	31	49	62	75	83	89	92	Approv.total
Supply per capita	18	15	17	19	19	19	20	20	Approv.par habitant
Libya									**Libye**
Primary Energy production	3 020	3 190	3 117	4 062	4 294	2 635	1 505	1 496	Production d'énergie primaire
Net imports	* -2 676	* -2 538	* -2 433	* -3 335	* -3 365	* -2 016	* -688	* -475	Importations nettes
Changes in stocks	-124	...	...	...	69	-185	74	...	Variations des stocks
Total supply	468	653	685	727	860	805	743	1 022	Approv.total
Supply per capita	108	137	131	126	137	129	119	163	Approv.par habitant
Liechtenstein									**Liechtenstein**
Primary Energy production	...	...	...	...	1	1	1	1	Production d'énergie primaire
Net imports	...	...	...	...	2	2	2	2	Importations nettes
Total supply	...	...	...	...	3	3	3	3	Approv.total
Supply per capita	...	...	...	...	81	79	75	76	Approv.par habitant
Lithuania									**Lituanie**
Primary Energy production	...	157	139	170	64	69	74	76	Production d'énergie primaire
Net imports	...	234	175	196	225	210	214	223	Importations nettes
Changes in stocks	...	14	8	4	3	-2	1	4	Variations des stocks
Total supply	...	376	306	362	286	282	287	294	Approv.total
Supply per capita	...	104	87	106	92	95	98	102	Approv.par habitant
Luxembourg									**Luxembourg**
Primary Energy production	1	2	3	4	5	6	6	6	Production d'énergie primaire
Net imports	143	130	140	179	173	163	156	150	Importations nettes
Changes in stocks	0	-1	2	-1	-1	0	0	-1	Variations des stocks
Total supply	143	133	142	185	178	168	161	157	Approv.total
Supply per capita	376	327	325	405	351	308	290	278	Approv.par habitant
Madagascar									**Madagascar**
Primary Energy production	72	89	92	104	124	127	129	132	Production d'énergie primaire
Net imports	* 13	* 18	* 26	* 24	* 25	* 39	* 41	* 46	Importations nettes
Changes in stocks	* 0	0	...	0	-1	0	* 0	* 0	Variations des stocks
Total supply	85	108	118	127	150	166	171	179	Approv.total
Supply per capita	8	8	8	7	7	7	7	7	Approv.par habitant
Malawi									**Malawi**
Primary Energy production	56	55	56	60	64	67	68	68	Production d'énergie primaire
Net imports	* 8	* 11	* 8	* 10	* 13	* 13	* 13	* 11	Importations nettes
Total supply	64	65	65	69	77	80	81	78	Approv.total
Supply per capita	7	7	6	5	5	5	5	5	Approv.par habitant
Malaysia									**Malaisie**
Primary Energy production	1 794	2 791	3 082	3 770	3 450	3 529	3 738	3 748	Production d'énergie primaire
Net imports	-1 019	* -1 018	-1 116	-1 031	* -495	-57	-240	-365	Importations nettes
Changes in stocks	3	* 5	8	21	* -10	54	-37	-41	Variations des stocks
Total supply	773	1 768	1 958	2 717	2 965	3 417	3 535	3 424	Approv.total
Supply per capita	42	85	84	104	105	116	118	113	Approv.par habitant
Maldives									**Maldives**
Primary Energy production	0	0	0	0	0	0	0	0	Production d'énergie primaire
Net imports	* 3	* 4	* 6	* 9	* 13	* 15	* 18	* 19	Importations nettes
Total supply	* 2	4	6	9	13	16	19	19	Approv.total
Supply per capita	* 11	14	24	30	40	45	53	52	Approv.par habitant
Mali									**Mali**
Primary Energy production	37	42	45	49	52	53	55	55	Production d'énergie primaire
Net imports	* 5	* 6	* 11	* 12	* 26	* 34	* 36	* 40	Importations nettes
Total supply	43	49	57	61	78	87	91	95	Approv.total
Supply per capita	5	5	5	5	5	5	5	5	Approv.par habitant
Malta									**Malte**
Primary Energy production	...	...	...	0	0	0	1	1	Production d'énergie primaire
Net imports	28	30	28	37	35	37	31	25	Importations nettes
Changes in stocks	0	1	1	0	-1	4	-2	-2	Variations des stocks
Total supply	28	29	28	37	35	32	33	27	Approv.total
Supply per capita	76	74	70	91	86	78	78	65	Approv.par habitant

23 Production, trade and supply of energy *(continued)*
Petajoules and gigajoules per capita

Production, commerce et fourniture d'énergie *(suite)*
pétajoules et gigajoules par habitant

Region, country or area	1990	1995	2000	2005	2010	2013	2014	2015	Région, pays ou zone
Marshall Islands									**Îles Marshall**
Primary Energy production	...	* 0	* 0	* 0	* 0	* 0	* 0	* 0	Production d'énergie primaire
Net imports	...	* 1	* 1	* 2	* 2	* 2	* 2	* 2	Importations nettes
Total supply	...	* 1	* 2	* 2	* 2	* 2	* 2	* 2	Approv.total
Supply per capita	...	* 28	* 30	* 35	* 41	* 41	* 40	* 42	Approv.par habitant
Martinique									**Martinique**
Primary Energy production	0	0	* 0	* 0	* 1	* 1	* 1	* 1	Production d'énergie primaire
Net imports	* 21	* 21	* 22	* 28	* 26	* 29	* 30	* 31	Importations nettes
Changes in stocks	0	...	...	...	...	...	...	...	Variations des stocks
Total supply	21	* 21	* 22	29	27	* 30	* 31	* 31	Approv.total
Supply per capita	57	* 57	* 58	73	69	* 76	* 79	* 79	Approv.par habitant
Mauritania									**Mauritanie**
Primary Energy production	11	12	13	15	34	32	31	30	Production d'énergie primaire
Net imports	* 13	* 14	* 16	* 21	* 7	* 15	* 23	* 24	Importations nettes
Changes in stocks	0	...	...	0	* -3	...	...	...	Variations des stocks
Total supply	* 23	* 26	29	36	45	48	54	* 54	Approv.total
Supply per capita	* 11	* 11	11	12	12	12	14	* 13	Approv.par habitant
Mauritius									**Maurice**
Primary Energy production	13	15	13	12	11	10	10	12	Production d'énergie primaire
Net imports	* 21	* 28	* 34	* 44	* 49	* 56	* 53	* 57	Importations nettes
Changes in stocks	1	2	-3	-1	-2	2	-2	3	Variations des stocks
Total supply	33	41	49	57	63	64	65	67	Approv.total
Supply per capita	31	36	41	45	50	50	51	52	Approv.par habitant
Mayotte									**Mayotte**
Primary Energy production	* 0	0	0	0	0	0	0	0	Production d'énergie primaire
Net imports	* 1	* 1	* 2	* 3	* 4	* 4	* 5	* 5	Importations nettes
Changes in stocks	...	...	...	...	0	...	...	...	Variations des stocks
Total supply	* 1	* 2	* 2	* 3	4	4	5	5	Approv.total
Supply per capita	* 12	* 13	* 14	* 17	20	20	20	21	Approv.par habitant
Mexico									**Mexique**
Primary Energy production	8 170	8 488	9 613	10 716	9 040	8 843	8 514	8 006	Production d'énergie primaire
Net imports	-2 985	-2 997	-3 167	-3 301	-1 623	-858	-650	-183	Importations nettes
Changes in stocks	7	-7	91	-19	5	9	45	-60	Variations des stocks
Total supply	5 179	5 498	6 356	7 434	7 413	7 976	7 818	7 883	Approv.total
Supply per capita	61	60	64	70	62	64	62	62	Approv.par habitant
Micronesia (Fed. States of)									**Micronésie (États féd. de)**
Primary Energy production	...	* 0	0	0	0	0	0	0	Production d'énergie primaire
Net imports	...	* 2	* 2	2	2	* 2	* 2	* 2	Importations nettes
Total supply	...	* 2	* 2	2	2	* 2	* 2	* 2	Approv.total
Supply per capita	...	* 15	* 17	16	17	* 21	* 22	* 22	Approv.par habitant
Mongolia									**Mongolie**
Primary Energy production	82	72	66	138	655	799	677	654	Production d'énergie primaire
Net imports	33	17	21	-35	-449	-327	-384	-365	Importations nettes
Changes in stocks	...	...	...	-1	41	-24	-50	17	Variations des stocks
Total supply	116	89	87	104	164	498	342	272	Approv.total
Supply per capita	53	39	36	41	61	174	118	92	Approv.par habitant
Montenegro									**Monténégro**
Primary Energy production	...	...	...	25	35	32	29	30	Production d'énergie primaire
Net imports	...	...	...	17	14	9	11	12	Importations nettes
Changes in stocks	...	...	...	...	...	...	0	0	Variations des stocks
Total supply	...	...	...	42	48	41	40	42	Approv.total
Supply per capita	...	...	...	67	77	66	64	68	Approv.par habitant
Montserrat									**Montserrat**
Net imports	* 0	* 1	* 0	* 1	* 1	* 1	* 1	* 1	Importations nettes
Changes in stocks	...	...	...	...	0	* 0	0	0	Variations des stocks
Total supply	* 0	* 0	* 0	* 1	1	1	1	1	Approv.total
Supply per capita	* 41	* 48	* 75	* 93	175	146	133	149	Approv.par habitant
Morocco									**Maroc**
Primary Energy production	83	85	73	72	81	59	56	59	Production d'énergie primaire
Net imports	* 267	* 354	* 401	* 530	* 686	* 752	* 784	* 752	Importations nettes
Changes in stocks	-2	10	-2	0	10	44	64	15	Variations des stocks
Total supply	352	428	477	603	758	767	777	796	Approv.total
Supply per capita	14	16	17	20	23	23	23	23	Approv.par habitant

23 Production, trade and supply of energy *(continued)*
Petajoules and gigajoules per capita

Production, commerce et fourniture d'énergie *(suite)*
pétajoules et gigajoules par habitant

Region, country or area	1990	1995	2000	2005	2010	2013	2014	2015	Région, pays ou zone
Mozambique									**Mozambique**
Primary Energy production	236	248	302	429	517	738	776	810	Production d'énergie primaire
Net imports	* 12	* 16	* -11	* -65	* -94	* -192	* -193	* -230	Importations nettes
Changes in stocks	0	0	0	-1	0	67	35	* 41	Variations des stocks
Total supply	248	264	292	364	424	478	549	538	Approv.total
Supply per capita	18	17	16	18	17	18	20	19	Approv.par habitant
Myanmar									**Myanmar**
Primary Energy production	446	464	648	927	969	974	1 076	1 141	Production d'énergie primaire
Net imports	6	27	-113	-307	-305	-292	-305	-299	Importations nettes
Changes in stocks	2	-7	-3	1	2	1	-31	-4	Variations des stocks
Total supply	449	498	538	619	663	682	802	846	Approv.total
Supply per capita	11	12	12	13	13	13	15	16	Approv.par habitant
Namibia									**Namibie**
Primary Energy production	...	13	16	17	17	19	19	20	Production d'énergie primaire
Net imports	...	* 24	* 26	* 37	* 48	* 40	* 54	* 56	Importations nettes
Changes in stocks	...	...	...	...	0	* 0	...	0	Variations des stocks
Total supply	...	38	42	53	65	59	74	76	Approv.total
Supply per capita	...	23	22	26	30	25	31	31	Approv.par habitant
Nauru									**Nauru**
Primary Energy production	...	...	...	...	* 0	* 0	0	* 0	Production d'énergie primaire
Net imports	* 2	* 2	* 2	* 1	* 1	* 1	* 1	* 1	Importations nettes
Changes in stocks	...	...	...	...	* 0	0	0	0	Variations des stocks
Total supply	* 2	* 1	* 1	* 1	1	* 1	* 1	* 1	Approv.total
Supply per capita	* 188	* 148	* 119	* 84	58	* 61	* 63	* 65	Approv.par habitant
Nepal									**Népal**
Primary Energy production	146	271	310	349	384	409	451	430	Production d'énergie primaire
Net imports	9	29	39	39	62	74	91	75	Importations nettes
Changes in stocks	-1	-1	...	...	...	...	* 0	...	Variations des stocks
Total supply	156	301	349	388	446	483	542	505	Approv.total
Supply per capita	8	14	14	14	17	17	19	18	Approv.par habitant
Netherlands									**Pays-Bas**
Primary Energy production	2 533	2 796	2 416	2 610	2 917	2 894	2 447	1 990	Production d'énergie primaire
Net imports	260	174	769	783	565	327	552	1 265	Importations nettes
Changes in stocks	5	-81	84	43	36	38	-4	219	Variations des stocks
Total supply	2 788	3 051	3 101	3 350	3 446	3 182	3 003	3 034	Approv.total
Supply per capita	187	198	196	205	207	189	178	179	Approv.par habitant
Netherlands Antilles [former]									**Antilles néerlandaises [anc.]**
Primary Energy production	0	0	0	0	0	...	...	...	Production d'énergie primaire
Net imports	* 71	* 94	83	84	68	...	...	...	Importations nettes
Changes in stocks	* -11	...	...	...	...	...	...	...	Variations des stocks
Total supply	82	* 95	83	84	69	...	...	...	Approv.total
Supply per capita	432	* 500	464	452	334	...	...	...	Approv.par habitant
New Caledonia									**Nouvelle-Calédonie**
Primary Energy production	2	1	2	1	1	2	1	2	Production d'énergie primaire
Net imports	* 20	* 26	* 28	* 36	48	53	61	62	Importations nettes
Changes in stocks	...	...	...	...	2	2	-3	1	Variations des stocks
Total supply	21	27	30	37	47	53	65	63	Approv.total
Supply per capita	125	140	141	161	192	205	251	240	Approv.par habitant
New Zealand									**Nouvelle-Zélande**
Primary Energy production	500	544	628	572	770	736	780	775	Production d'énergie primaire
Net imports	58	82	106	167	76	143	144	156	Importations nettes
Changes in stocks	1	-3	-12	-8	12	11	-3	-16	Variations des stocks
Total supply	556	629	747	747	833	868	927	946	Approv.total
Supply per capita	163	171	194	181	191	194	206	209	Approv.par habitant
Nicaragua									**Nicaragua**
Primary Energy production	59	66	56	62	66	89	91	92	Production d'énergie primaire
Net imports	28	37	49	57	56	57	61	72	Importations nettes
Changes in stocks	0	0	-1	0	-3	2	0	0	Variations des stocks
Total supply	86	102	107	119	125	144	152	165	Approv.total
Supply per capita	21	22	21	22	22	24	25	27	Approv.par habitant
Niger									**Niger**
Primary Energy production	54	65	74	* 70	56	101	* 101	99	Production d'énergie primaire
Net imports	* 7	* 9	* 7	* 7	* 13	* -13	* -8	* -5	Importations nettes
Changes in stocks	0	0	0	0	0	0	1	0	Variations des stocks
Total supply	62	73	81	* 77	70	87	* 92	95	Approv.total
Supply per capita	8	8	7	* 6	4	5	* 5	5	Approv.par habitant

Production, trade and supply of energy *(continued)*
Petajoules and gigajoules per capita

Production, commerce et fourniture d'énergie *(suite)*
pétajoules et gigajoules par habitant

Region, country or area	1990	1995	2000	2005	2010	2013	2014	2015	Région, pays ou zone
Nigeria									**Nigéria**
Primary Energy production	6 091	6 856	8 247	9 734	10 595	10 406	10 585	10 603	Production d'énergie primaire
Net imports	* -3 312	* -3 804	* -4 595	* -5 324	* -5 612	* -4 799	* -4 979	* -4 876	Importations nettes
Changes in stocks	-2	-30	53	-9	-35	3	-26	-107	Variations des stocks
Total supply	2 780	3 082	3 599	4 420	5 018	5 605	5 631	5 832	Approv.total
Supply per capita	29	28	29	32	31	32	32	32	Approv.par habitant
Niue									**Nioué**
Primary Energy production	0	0	0	0	0	0	0	0	Production d'énergie primaire
Net imports	* 0	* 0	* 0	0	0	0	0	0	Importations nettes
Total supply	* 0	* 0	* 0	0	0	0	0	0	Approv.total
Supply per capita	* 34	* 34	* 42	42	53	61	62	64	Approv.par habitant
Norway [8]									**Norvège** [8]
Primary Energy production	4 977	7 543	9 340	9 372	8 759	8 134	8 158	8 615	Production d'énergie primaire
Net imports	-4 024	-6 559	-8 250	-8 240	-7 334	-6 770	-7 026	-7 376	Importations nettes
Changes in stocks	77	20	15	15	-1	-2	-20	20	Variations des stocks
Total supply	876	964	1 075	1 117	1 425	1 365	1 153	1 219	Approv.total
Supply per capita	207	221	239	242	291	269	224	234	Approv.par habitant
Oman									**Oman**
Primary Energy production	1 531	1 931	2 359	2 356	2 793	3 150	3 101	3 481	Production d'énergie primaire
Net imports	-1 392	* -1 710	-2 079	-1 912	-2 022	-2 136	-2 090	-2 202	Importations nettes
Changes in stocks	-14	-15	-38	0	-7	-4	-2	-2	Variations des stocks
Total supply	153	236	319	445	778	1 018	1 014	1 280	Approv.total
Supply per capita	82	106	141	183	264	261	239	285	Approv.par habitant
Other non-specified areas									**Autres zones non-spécifiées**
Primary Energy production	456	453	489	518	538	562	566	511	Production d'énergie primaire
Net imports	1 649	2 327	3 060	3 750	4 112	3 947	4 095	4 081	Importations nettes
Changes in stocks	100	117	41	28	-1	-8	60	51	Variations des stocks
Total supply	2 005	2 663	3 509	4 240	4 651	4 517	4 601	4 542	Approv.total
Supply per capita	98	125	158	186	200	194	197	194	Approv.par habitant
Pakistan									**Pakistan**
Primary Energy production	906	1 192	1 403	2 020	2 255	2 379	2 390	2 415	Production d'énergie primaire
Net imports	385	529	680	633	843	790	961	947	Importations nettes
Changes in stocks	...	...	0	10	2	* -5	26	* 3	Variations des stocks
Total supply	1 290	1 722	2 082	2 642	3 095	3 174	3 325	3 360	Approv.total
Supply per capita	12	14	14	17	18	18	18	18	Approv.par habitant
Palau									**Palaos**
Net imports	...	* 2	* 3	* 3	3	* 3	* 3	* 3	Importations nettes
Total supply	...	* 3	* 3	* 3	3	* 3	* 3	* 3	Approv.total
Supply per capita	...	* 158	* 152	* 156	141	* 152	* 155	* 147	Approv.par habitant
Panama									**Panama**
Primary Energy production	24	22	28	32	26	31	31	36	Production d'énergie primaire
Net imports	42	41	75	88	98	130	122	114	Importations nettes
Changes in stocks	4	1	-1	0	-20	-12	-15	-21	Variations des stocks
Total supply	62	62	104	120	144	173	167	171	Approv.total
Supply per capita	26	23	35	37	40	45	43	44	Approv.par habitant
Papua New Guinea									**Papouasie-Nvl-Guinée**
Primary Energy production	251	263	220	174	95	114	166	* 168	Production d'énergie primaire
Net imports	* -162	* -171	* -121	* -48	* 47	32	-3	* -3	Importations nettes
Changes in stocks	0	* 3	* 0	0	2	-2	5	* 5	Variations des stocks
Total supply	88	89	99	126	141	148	157	* 159	Approv.total
Supply per capita	21	19	18	21	21	20	21	* 21	Approv.par habitant
Paraguay									**Paraguay**
Primary Energy production	* 145	194	276	288	327	340	324	329	Production d'énergie primaire
Net imports	* -60	-80	-122	-109	-98	-108	-77	-68	Importations nettes
Changes in stocks	* 0	-4	2	-1	-4	-5	1	0	Variations des stocks
Total supply	* 84	118	153	180	234	237	246	260	Approv.total
Supply per capita	* 20	25	29	31	38	37	38	39	Approv.par habitant
Peru									**Pérou**
Primary Energy production	439	414	391	455	786	953	1 019	961	Production d'énergie primaire
Net imports	-28	60	130	108	-20	-160	-92	-25	Importations nettes
Changes in stocks	-3	23	7	-3	-12	-38	12	-2	Variations des stocks
Total supply	415	450	514	565	779	831	915	937	Approv.total
Supply per capita	19	19	20	20	27	27	30	30	Approv.par habitant

Production, trade and supply of energy *(continued)*
Petajoules and gigajoules per capita

Production, commerce et fourniture d'énergie *(suite)*
pétajoules et gigajoules par habitant

Region, country or area	1990	1995	2000	2005	2010	2013	2014	2015	Région, pays ou zone
Philippines									**Philippines**
Primary Energy production	540	533	695	762	924	933	986	999	Production d'énergie primaire
Net imports	512	759	860	697	718	821	875	1 067	Importations nettes
Changes in stocks	13	28	4	-10	11	-27	-11	14	Variations des stocks
Total supply	1 039	1 264	1 551	1 469	1 631	1 780	1 871	2 050	Approv.total
Supply per capita	17	18	20	17	18	18	19	20	Approv.par habitant
Poland									**Pologne**
Primary Energy production	4 350	4 161	3 318	3 281	2 808	2 969	2 820	2 834	Production d'énergie primaire
Net imports	99	58	438	686	1 351	1 091	1 168	1 196	Importations nettes
Changes in stocks	43	-36	-24	82	-93	-61	21	31	Variations des stocks
Total supply	4 406	4 256	3 780	3 886	4 251	4 122	3 966	3 999	Approv.total
Supply per capita	116	111	99	102	110	107	103	104	Approv.par habitant
Portugal [9]									**Portugal** [9]
Primary Energy production	142	139	161	151	242	240	250	222	Production d'énergie primaire
Net imports	596	714	864	969	717	631	610	692	Importations nettes
Changes in stocks	19	12	0	16	-15	-16	-15	7	Variations des stocks
Total supply	720	840	1 026	1 104	975	887	875	907	Approv.total
Supply per capita	73	83	99	105	92	85	84	88	Approv.par habitant
Puerto Rico									**Porto Rico**
Primary Energy production	* 1	0	1	0	0	1	1	1	Production d'énergie primaire
Net imports	...	...	12	24	27	55	55	58	Importations nettes
Total supply	* 1	0	13	24	27	56	56	60	Approv.total
Supply per capita	* 0	0	3	6	7	15	15	16	Approv.par habitant
Qatar									**Qatar**
Primary Energy production	1 009	1 364	2 449	3 718	7 428	9 271	9 166	9 225	Production d'énergie primaire
Net imports	-832	-811	-1 921	-2 991	-6 261	-7 861	-7 287	-7 221	Importations nettes
Changes in stocks	-22	0	-56	-1	3	15	29	110	Variations des stocks
Total supply	199	553	584	728	1 165	1 395	1 850	1 895	Approv.total
Supply per capita	420	1 102	988	886	660	664	852	848	Approv.par habitant
Republic of Korea									**République de Corée**
Primary Energy production	941	878	1 420	1 776	1 855	1 799	2 024	2 116	Production d'énergie primaire
Net imports	2 840	5 319	6 505	6 810	8 703	9 257	9 192	9 314	Importations nettes
Changes in stocks	-69	115	71	-179	117	49	51	67	Variations des stocks
Total supply	3 851	6 083	7 854	8 764	10 441	11 007	11 165	11 364	Approv.total
Supply per capita	90	136	171	186	213	221	223	226	Approv.par habitant
Republic of Moldova									**République de Moldova**
Primary Energy production	...	4	3	4	8	12	15	15	Production d'énergie primaire
Net imports	...	184	64	85	80	75	70	69	Importations nettes
Changes in stocks	...	2	0	0	-2	1	0	0	Variations des stocks
Total supply	...	186	66	89	91	86	86	84	Approv.total
Supply per capita	...	43	16	24	22	21	21	21	Approv.par habitant
Réunion									**Réunion**
Primary Energy production	8	9	7	7	8	9	9	9	Production d'énergie primaire
Net imports	* 16	* 23	* 36	* 44	* 50	* 48	* 49	* 51	Importations nettes
Changes in stocks	0	0	1	1	0	0	-1	1	Variations des stocks
Total supply	24	31	42	49	58	57	58	59	Approv.total
Supply per capita	39	47	57	61	70	67	68	69	Approv.par habitant
Romania									**Roumanie**
Primary Energy production	1 695	1 335	1 194	1 173	1 155	1 090	1 109	1 116	Production d'énergie primaire
Net imports	936	591	331	446	311	240	214	217	Importations nettes
Changes in stocks	11	2	-8	-7	-7	-11	-4	-7	Variations des stocks
Total supply	2 620	1 925	1 532	1 626	1 474	1 342	1 326	1 340	Approv.total
Supply per capita	113	85	69	75	73	68	67	69	Approv.par habitant
Russian Federation									**Fédération de Russie**
Primary Energy production	...	40 589	41 030	50 506	53 679	55 887	55 400	56 024	Production d'énergie primaire
Net imports	...	-13 397	-14 842	-22 870	-24 601	-25 405	-24 793	-26 109	Importations nettes
Changes in stocks	...	472	195	298	147	225	150	75	Variations des stocks
Total supply	...	26 720	25 994	27 338	28 932	30 258	30 457	29 841	Approv.total
Supply per capita	...	180	177	190	202	211	212	208	Approv.par habitant
Rwanda									**Rwanda**
Primary Energy production	28	48	46	63	76	* 83	* 84	* 85	Production d'énergie primaire
Net imports	* 8	* 7	* 8	* 7	* 8	* 11	* 11	* 13	Importations nettes
Changes in stocks	...	...	...	0	...	...	...	...	Variations des stocks
Total supply	35	54	54	71	84	* 94	* 96	* 97	Approv.total
Supply per capita	5	10	7	8	8	* 9	* 8	* 8	Approv.par habitant

Production, trade and supply of energy *(continued)*
Petajoules and gigajoules per capita

Production, commerce et fourniture d'énergie *(suite)*
pétajoules et gigajoules par habitant

Region, country or area	1990	1995	2000	2005	2010	2013	2014	2015	Région, pays ou zone
Saint Helena									**Sainte-Hélène**
Primary Energy production	* 0	0	0	0	0	0	* 0	0	Production d'énergie primaire
Net imports	0	* 0	0	0	0	0	* 0	* 0	Importations nettes
Total supply	0	* 0	0	0	0	0	* 0	* 0	Approv.total
Supply per capita	17	* 27	36	33	38	40	* 39	* 37	Approv.par habitant
Saint Kitts and Nevis									**Saint-Kitts-et-Nevis**
Primary Energy production	1	1	1	1	0	* 0	* 0	* 0	Production d'énergie primaire
Net imports	* 2	* 2	* 3	* 3	3	* 3	* 3	* 4	Importations nettes
Total supply	* 2	* 2	* 3	* 3	3	* 3	* 3	* 3	Approv.total
Supply per capita	* 53	* 56	* 63	* 67	61	* 59	* 60	* 60	Approv.par habitant
Saint Lucia									**Sainte-Lucie**
Primary Energy production	0	0	0	0	0	0	0	0	Production d'énergie primaire
Net imports	2	* 4	* 5	* 6	* 6	* 6	* 6	* 6	Importations nettes
Total supply	2	5	5	* 5	6	6	6	6	Approv.total
Supply per capita	18	31	31	* 33	33	33	33	33	Approv.par habitant
Saint Pierre and Miquelon									**Saint-Pierre-et-Miquelon**
Primary Energy production	...	...	* 0	0	0	0	0	0	Production d'énergie primaire
Net imports	2	1	* 1	* 1	* 1	* 1	* 1	* 1	Importations nettes
Total supply	1	1	* 1	* 1	* 1	* 1	* 1	* 1	Approv.total
Supply per capita	206	164	* 125	* 149	* 160	* 163	* 175	* 175	Approv.par habitant
Saint Vincent & Grenadines									**Saint-Vincent-Grenadines**
Primary Energy production	0	0	0	0	0	0	0	0	Production d'énergie primaire
Net imports	* 1	* 2	2	* 3	3	3	* 3	* 3	Importations nettes
Total supply	* 1	* 2	2	* 3	3	3	* 3	* 3	Approv.total
Supply per capita	* 12	* 19	21	* 31	31	29	* 30	* 31	Approv.par habitant
Samoa									**Samoa**
Primary Energy production	1	1	1	2	* 2	* 2	* 2	* 1	Production d'énergie primaire
Net imports	* 2	* 2	* 2	* 3	* 3	3	* 3	4	Importations nettes
Changes in stocks	...	...	...	...	0	0	...	...	Variations des stocks
Total supply	* 3	* 3	* 3	* 4	* 5	5	* 5	6	Approv.total
Supply per capita	* 16	* 17	* 19	* 21	* 24	24	* 24	29	Approv.par habitant
Sao Tome and Principe									**Sao Tomé-et-Principe**
Primary Energy production	1	1	1	1	1	1	1	1	Production d'énergie primaire
Net imports	* 1	* 1	* 1	* 1	* 2	* 2	* 2	* 2	Importations nettes
Total supply	* 1	1	* 2	* 2	2	* 3	* 3	* 3	Approv.total
Supply per capita	* 12	12	* 12	* 13	14	* 14	* 14	* 14	Approv.par habitant
Saudi Arabia [7]									**Arabie saoudite** [7]
Primary Energy production	16 769	19 932	20 284	24 162	22 115	25 573	25 904	28 571	Production d'énergie primaire
Net imports	* -13 721	-16 427	-15 797	-18 116	-14 727	-17 702	-17 114	-17 284	Importations nettes
Changes in stocks	* 172	-12	0	0	-319	-114	-87	115	Variations des stocks
Total supply	2 875	3 516	4 487	6 047	7 707	7 985	8 876	11 172	Approv.total
Supply per capita	178	190	224	252	274	264	287	354	Approv.par habitant
Senegal									**Sénégal**
Primary Energy production	40	44	50	52	86	75	77	80	Production d'énergie primaire
Net imports	* 41	* 43	* 46	* 65	* 74	* 79	* 84	* 91	Importations nettes
Changes in stocks	0	0	1	3	-4	-2	-1	-1	Variations des stocks
Total supply	* 81	* 87	96	114	165	155	163	171	Approv.total
Supply per capita	* 11	* 10	10	11	13	11	11	11	Approv.par habitant
Serbia [10]									**Serbie** [10]
Primary Energy production	...	...	...	431	440	474	393	449	Production d'énergie primaire
Net imports	...	...	...	243	212	145	148	164	Importations nettes
Changes in stocks	...	...	...	2	4	0	-7	1	Variations des stocks
Total supply	...	...	...	672	648	618	550	612	Approv.total
Supply per capita	...	...	...	68	72	69	62	69	Approv.par habitant
Serbia and Monten. [former]									**Serbie-et-Monténégro [anc.]**
Primary Energy production	...	497	479	...	...	...	...	...	Production d'énergie primaire
Net imports	...	* 25	77	...	...	...	...	...	Importations nettes
Total supply	...	522	556	...	...	...	...	...	Approv.total
Supply per capita	...	48	52	...	...	...	...	...	Approv.par habitant
Seychelles									**Seychelles**
Primary Energy production	0	0	0	0	0	0	0	0	Production d'énergie primaire
Net imports	* 1	* 4	* 9	* 10	* 6	* 4	* 7	* 6	Importations nettes
Changes in stocks	* 0	0	* 0	...	...	...	...	...	Variations des stocks
Total supply	2	* 3	8	10	6	5	6	6	Approv.total
Supply per capita	31	* 39	102	115	66	48	62	65	Approv.par habitant

23 Production, trade and supply of energy *(continued)*

Petajoules and gigajoules per capita

Production, commerce et fourniture d'énergie *(suite)*

pétajoules et gigajoules par habitant

Region, country or area	1990	1995	2000	2005	2010	2013	2014	2015	Région, pays ou zone
Sierra Leone									**Sierra Leone**
Primary Energy production	43	42	49	50	52	53	53	54	Production d'énergie primaire
Net imports	* 7	* 5	* 6	* 7	* 9	* 15	* 17	* 13	Importations nettes
Changes in stocks	0	...	...	...	...	...	...	...	Variations des stocks
Total supply	50	47	55	56	60	67	69	67	Approv.total
Supply per capita	13	12	13	11	10	11	11	10	Approv.par habitant
Singapore									**Singapour**
Primary Energy production	...	...	...	...	25	27	27	28	Production d'énergie primaire
Net imports	493	641	783	774	1 058	1 080	1 123	1 246	Importations nettes
Changes in stocks	-163	2	27	-31	-25	-10	8	41	Variations des stocks
Total supply	656	640	756	805	1 109	1 117	1 142	1 233	Approv.total
Supply per capita	218	184	193	189	218	207	207	220	Approv.par habitant
Sint Maarten (Dutch part)									**St-Martin (partie néerland.)**
Net imports	...	...	...	...	...	* 11	* 11	* 12	Importations nettes
Total supply	...	...	...	...	...	* 11	* 11	* 12	Approv.total
Supply per capita	...	...	...	...	...	* 306	* 303	* 305	Approv.par habitant
Slovakia									**Slovaquie**
Primary Energy production	...	210	263	265	250	269	264	265	Production d'énergie primaire
Net imports	...	514	485	516	475	424	408	407	Importations nettes
Changes in stocks	...	-22	4	4	-12	-7	15	-4	Variations des stocks
Total supply	...	746	744	778	737	700	658	677	Approv.total
Supply per capita	...	139	138	144	136	129	121	125	Approv.par habitant
Slovenia									**Slovénie**
Primary Energy production	...	124	129	146	157	150	153	142	Production d'énergie primaire
Net imports	...	129	141	160	149	133	123	133	Importations nettes
Changes in stocks	...	-1	2	0	0	-3	-2	-1	Variations des stocks
Total supply	...	254	269	306	306	287	279	275	Approv.total
Supply per capita	...	129	136	153	149	139	135	133	Approv.par habitant
Solomon Islands									**Îles Salomon**
Primary Energy production	* 3	* 3	* 3	* 3	* 3	* 3	* 3	* 3	Production d'énergie primaire
Net imports	* 2	* 2	* 3	* 3	* 3	* 3	* 3	* 3	Importations nettes
Total supply	* 5	* 5	* 5	* 6	* 6	* 6	* 6	* 6	Approv.total
Supply per capita	* 17	* 15	* 13	* 12	* 11	* 11	* 11	* 10	Approv.par habitant
Somalia									**Somalie**
Primary Energy production	58	69	85	103	124	128	129	129	Production d'énergie primaire
Net imports	* 10	* 8	* 5	* 4	* 1	* 8	* 8	* 8	Importations nettes
Changes in stocks	* 0	* 0	...	...	...	...	...	...	Variations des stocks
Total supply	68	77	90	107	126	137	137	137	Approv.total
Supply per capita	10	12	12	13	13	13	13	13	Approv.par habitant
South Africa									**Afrique du Sud**
Primary Energy production	4 767	5 691	6 175	6 648	6 906	6 997	7 110	7 049	Production d'énergie primaire
Net imports	* -587	* -1 009	* -1 171	* -1 183	* -605	* -739	* -621	* -683	Importations nettes
Changes in stocks	0	-68	-41	0	1	18	-12	-1	Variations des stocks
Total supply	4 179	4 750	5 044	5 465	6 299	6 240	6 501	6 367	Approv.total
Supply per capita	114	115	113	114	122	117	120	117	Approv.par habitant
South Sudan									**Soudan du sud**
Primary Energy production	...	...	...	...	...	217	337	321	Production d'énergie primaire
Net imports	...	...	...	...	...	* -190	* -308	* -297	Importations nettes
Total supply	...	...	...	...	...	28	29	23	Approv.total
Supply per capita	...	...	...	...	...	2	2	2	Approv.par habitant
Spain [11]									**Espagne** [11]
Primary Energy production	1 442	1 313	1 314	1 256	1 419	1 420	1 432	1 368	Production d'énergie primaire
Net imports	2 308	2 949	3 812	4 738	3 991	3 295	3 352	3 497	Importations nettes
Changes in stocks	6	69	52	78	73	-125	52	-40	Variations des stocks
Total supply	3 744	4 191	5 074	5 915	5 337	4 841	4 732	4 905	Approv.total
Supply per capita	96	106	126	136	115	104	102	106	Approv.par habitant
Sri Lanka									**Sri Lanka**
Primary Energy production	135	146	156	163	184	184	179	181	Production d'énergie primaire
Net imports	54	80	144	161	170	188	211	217	Importations nettes
Changes in stocks	2	-1	4	1	-7	-8	-18	-36	Variations des stocks
Total supply	187	225	296	324	360	380	408	433	Approv.total
Supply per capita	11	12	16	16	18	19	20	21	Approv.par habitant

23 Production, trade and supply of energy *(continued)*
Petajoules and gigajoules per capita

Production, commerce et fourniture d'énergie *(suite)*
pétajoules et gigajoules par habitant

Region, country or area	1990	1995	2000	2005	2010	2013	2014	2015	Région, pays ou zone
State of Palestine									**État de Palestine**
Primary Energy production	* 4	* 5	* 5	8	9	8	9	9	Production d'énergie primaire
Net imports	* 16	* 18	33	49	45	53	57	63	Importations nettes
Changes in stocks	...	...	...	0	0	0	-2	0	Variations des stocks
Total supply	* 20	* 22	38	58	54	61	69	72	Approv.total
Supply per capita	...	* 8	12	16	13	14	15	16	Approv.par habitant
Sudan									**Soudan**
Primary Energy production	...	...	...	...	...	679	682	658	Production d'énergie primaire
Net imports	...	...	...	...	...	* -63	* -57	* -4	Importations nettes
Changes in stocks	...	...	...	...	...	* -1	0	0	Variations des stocks
Total supply	...	...	...	...	...	617	626	655	Approv.total
Supply per capita	...	...	...	...	...	16	16	16	Approv.par habitant
Sudan [former]									**Soudan [anc.]**
Primary Energy production	379	448	851	1 145	1 473	...	...	...	Production d'énergie primaire
Net imports	* 73	* 59	* -287	* -480	* -762	...	...	...	Importations nettes
Changes in stocks	* 1	1	8	12	...	...	...	...	Variations des stocks
Total supply	451	506	556	654	711	...	...	...	Approv.total
Supply per capita	17	17	16	17	16	...	...	...	Approv.par habitant
Suriname									**Suriname**
Primary Energy production	15	17	33	32	43	41	40	40	Production d'énergie primaire
Net imports	* 15	* 16	* 1	* -4	* -4	* -5	* -4	* -11	Importations nettes
Changes in stocks	0	0	...	...	0	0	0	0	Variations des stocks
Total supply	29	34	36	26	40	36	36	29	Approv.total
Supply per capita	72	78	76	53	77	68	68	54	Approv.par habitant
Sweden									**Suède**
Primary Energy production	1 235	1 312	1 257	1 430	1 364	1 450	1 430	1 408	Production d'énergie primaire
Net imports	726	747	724	739	714	594	581	505	Importations nettes
Changes in stocks	-5	-29	9	32	-33	-6	10	26	Variations des stocks
Total supply	1 967	2 089	1 971	2 137	2 112	2 050	2 001	1 887	Approv.total
Supply per capita	230	237	222	237	225	213	206	193	Approv.par habitant
Switzerland [12]									**Suisse** [12]
Primary Energy production	428	468	500	458	526	540	552	509	Production d'énergie primaire
Net imports	584	521	524	628	564	569	491	499	Importations nettes
Changes in stocks	-5	-14	-18	6	-2	-5	0	-16	Variations des stocks
Total supply	1 017	1 003	1 041	1 080	1 091	1 113	1 043	1 024	Approv.total
Supply per capita	152	142	145	145	139	136	126	123	Approv.par habitant
Syrian Arab Republic									**République arabe syrienne**
Primary Energy production	1 036	1 403	1 417	1 171	1 165	304	237	196	Production d'énergie primaire
Net imports	* -554	-813	-690	-431	-233	226	218	223	Importations nettes
Changes in stocks	6	* 5	...	1	20	0	0	...	Variations des stocks
Total supply	476	585	729	740	911	530	454	419	Approv.total
Supply per capita	39	41	46	40	44	27	24	23	Approv.par habitant
Tajikistan									**Tadjikistan**
Primary Energy production	...	56	53	66	65	73	77	82	Production d'énergie primaire
Net imports	...	40	38	33	29	24	32	32	Importations nettes
Total supply	...	95	91	99	94	97	109	114	Approv.total
Supply per capita	...	17	15	15	12	12	13	13	Approv.par habitant
Thailand									**Thaïlande**
Primary Energy production	1 089	1 322	1 700	2 144	2 952	3 060	3 137	2 929	Production d'énergie primaire
Net imports	699	1 289	1 308	1 869	2 027	2 145	2 235	2 470	Importations nettes
Changes in stocks	4	-25	-67	-54	33	-163	-57	-13	Variations des stocks
Total supply	1 784	2 635	3 075	4 067	4 945	5 367	5 428	5 412	Approv.total
Supply per capita	31	44	49	61	74	80	80	80	Approv.par habitant
TFYR of Macedonia									**ex-R.Y. de Macédoine**
Primary Energy production	...	112	118	108	68	65	61	58	Production d'énergie primaire
Net imports	...	43	48	52	53	55	59	60	Importations nettes
Changes in stocks	...	5	-4	-4	-1	-2	0	0	Variations des stocks
Total supply	...	151	169	163	121	122	120	118	Approv.total
Supply per capita	...	77	84	80	59	59	58	57	Approv.par habitant
Timor-Leste									**Timor-Leste**
Primary Energy production	...	...	...	201	186	168	142	* 147	Production d'énergie primaire
Net imports	...	...	...	* -196	* -182	* -161	* -135	* -139	Importations nettes
Total supply	...	...	...	* 4	* 4	* 7	* 8	* 8	Approv.total
Supply per capita	...	...	...	* 4	* 4	* 6	* 7	* 7	Approv.par habitant

23 Production, trade and supply of energy *(continued)*
Petajoules and gigajoules per capita

Production, commerce et fourniture d'énergie *(suite)*
pétajoules et gigajoules par habitant

Region, country or area	1990	1995	2000	2005	2010	2013	2014	2015	Région, pays ou zone
Togo									**Togo**
Primary Energy production	44	57	74	84	99	108	111	113	Production d'énergie primaire
Net imports	*11	*15	*16	*15	*29	*25	*26	*26	Importations nettes
Changes in stocks	0	0	0	-1	-2	-2	-2	-3	Variations des stocks
Total supply	55	71	89	99	130	134	139	143	Approv.total
Supply per capita	15	17	19	18	20	19	19	20	Approv.par habitant
Tonga									**Tonga**
Primary Energy production	0	0	0	0	0	0	0	0	Production d'énergie primaire
Net imports	1	1	1	*2	*2	*2	*2	*2	Importations nettes
Changes in stocks	...	...	...	...	...	*0	*0	*0	Variations des stocks
Total supply	1	1	1	*2	2	2	2	2	Approv.total
Supply per capita	12	14	15	*16	16	15	15	16	Approv.par habitant
Trinidad and Tobago									**Trinité-et-Tobago**
Primary Energy production	529	511	799	1 464	1 786	1 673	1 663	1 577	Production d'énergie primaire
Net imports	-271	-264	-378	-777	-954	-863	-847	-753	Importations nettes
Changes in stocks	6	-12	7	10	-13	-13	-6	9	Variations des stocks
Total supply	251	258	414	678	845	824	822	816	Approv.total
Supply per capita	206	205	321	516	636	611	607	600	Approv.par habitant
Tunisia									**Tunisie**
Primary Energy production	222	205	253	274	341	298	274	260	Production d'énergie primaire
Net imports	*-27	*6	*47	*71	*79	*135	*162	*198	Importations nettes
Changes in stocks	3	-9	7	-4	-7	2	2	7	Variations des stocks
Total supply	192	220	293	349	427	430	435	452	Approv.total
Supply per capita	23	25	31	35	40	39	39	40	Approv.par habitant
Turkey									**Turquie**
Primary Energy production	1 087	1 112	1 085	1 004	1 352	1 310	1 303	1 314	Production d'énergie primaire
Net imports	1 138	1 532	2 113	2 517	3 039	3 584	3 744	4 111	Importations nettes
Changes in stocks	35	45	-3	-28	-28	23	-4	87	Variations des stocks
Total supply	2 190	2 598	3 201	3 549	4 419	4 872	5 051	5 338	Approv.total
Supply per capita	40	44	50	52	61	64	65	68	Approv.par habitant
Turkmenistan									**Turkménistan**
Primary Energy production	...	1 376	1 928	2 584	1 982	3 208	3 270	3 407	Production d'énergie primaire
Net imports	...	-802	-1 303	-1 779	-1 030	-2 109	-2 148	-2 248	Importations nettes
Total supply	...	574	625	805	951	1 100	1 123	1 160	Approv.total
Supply per capita	...	137	139	170	189	210	212	216	Approv.par habitant
Turks and Caicos Islands									**Îles Turques-et-Caïques**
Primary Energy production	0	0	0	0	0	0	0	0	Production d'énergie primaire
Net imports	*0	*1	*1	*2	*3	*3	*3	*3	Importations nettes
Total supply	*0	*1	*1	*2	*3	*3	*3	*3	Approv.total
Supply per capita	*34	*43	*52	*57	*84	*79	*83	*84	Approv.par habitant
Tuvalu									**Tuvalu**
Primary Energy production	...	...	...	...	...	...	...	0	Production d'énergie primaire
Net imports	*0	*0	*0	*0	0	*0	*0	*0	Importations nettes
Total supply	*0	*0	*0	*0	0	*0	*0	*0	Approv.total
Supply per capita	*8	*9	*10	*13	13	*13	*13	*14	Approv.par habitant
Uganda									**Ouganda**
Primary Energy production	271	300	302	390	477	548	573	595	Production d'énergie primaire
Net imports	*9	*12	*17	*26	*46	*49	*52	*60	Importations nettes
Changes in stocks	0	...	...	...	...	...	...	...	Variations des stocks
Total supply	281	312	319	417	523	596	625	655	Approv.total
Supply per capita	16	15	13	15	16	16	17	17	Approv.par habitant
Ukraine									**Ukraine**
Primary Energy production	...	3 661	3 231	3 328	3 238	3 579	3 206	2 552	Production d'énergie primaire
Net imports	...	3 411	2 343	2 458	1 762	1 320	1 160	1 268	Importations nettes
Changes in stocks	...	0	0	-86	-490	54	-68	66	Variations des stocks
Total supply	...	7 073	5 574	5 872	5 491	4 846	4 434	3 753	Approv.total
Supply per capita	...	138	114	125	120	107	99	84	Approv.par habitant
United Arab Emirates									**Émirats arabes unis**
Primary Energy production	5 177	5 661	6 571	7 293	7 496	8 948	9 052	9 682	Production d'énergie primaire
Net imports	*-4 375	*-4 533	-4 853	-5 450	*-4 860	*-5 866	-5 787	-6 096	Importations nettes
Changes in stocks	12	21	...	...	...	...	...	...	Variations des stocks
Total supply	791	1 108	1 719	1 842	2 635	3 082	3 265	3 587	Approv.total
Supply per capita	437	472	567	453	316	341	359	392	Approv.par habitant

23 Production, trade and supply of energy *(continued)*
Petajoules and gigajoules per capita

Production, commerce et fourniture d'énergie *(suite)*
pétajoules et gigajoules par habitant

Region, country or area	1990	1995	2000	2005	2010	2013	2014	2015	Région, pays ou zone
United Kingdom [13]									**Royaume-Uni** [13]
Primary Energy production	8 595	10 588	11 247	8 483	6 217	4 574	4 504	4 926	Production d'énergie primaire
Net imports	-151	-1 928	-2 169	736	1 959	3 372	3 089	2 460	Importations nettes
Changes in stocks	-84	-265	-138	0	-265	26	132	-112	Variations des stocks
Total supply	8 527	8 925	9 216	9 219	8 442	7 919	7 462	7 498	Approv.total
Supply per capita	149	154	157	153	135	124	116	116	Approv.par habitant
United Rep. of Tanzania									**Rép.-Unie de Tanzanie**
Primary Energy production	315	434	543	665	782	882	928	958	Production d'énergie primaire
Net imports	* 27	* 30	* 30	* 57	* 64	* 113	* 111	* 128	Importations nettes
Changes in stocks	0	...	...	...	...	...	...	...	Variations des stocks
Total supply	341	463	572	722	847	995	1 039	1 087	Approv.total
Supply per capita	13	15	17	19	19	20	20	20	Approv.par habitant
United States of America [14]									**États-Unis d'Amérique** [14]
Primary Energy production	68 588	68 963	69 339	68 124	71 882	77 910	83 581	84 007	Production d'énergie primaire
Net imports	12 528	16 273	23 218	28 307	19 895	10 884	8 999	8 794	Importations nettes
Changes in stocks	1 606	-764	-1 980	-16	-263	-1 374	703	2 110	Variations des stocks
Total supply	79 510	86 000	94 538	96 447	92 040	90 168	91 877	90 691	Approv.total
Supply per capita	314	323	335	325	297	284	288	282	Approv.par habitant
United States Virgin Islands									**Îles Vierges américaines**
Primary Energy production	...	...	...	...	...	* 0	* 0	* 0	Production d'énergie primaire
Total supply	...	...	...	...	...	* 0	* 0	* 0	Approv.total
Supply per capita	...	...	...	...	...	* 0	* 1	* 1	Approv.par habitant
Uruguay									**Uruguay**
Primary Energy production	51	45	46	45	89	95	113	* 126	Production d'énergie primaire
Net imports	44	66	70	75	85	94	85	89	Importations nettes
Changes in stocks	-2	4	-2	-5	1	-7	-1	3	Variations des stocks
Total supply	96	107	119	126	173	197	199	212	Approv.total
Supply per capita	31	33	36	38	51	58	58	62	Approv.par habitant
Uzbekistan									**Ouzbékistan**
Primary Energy production	...	2 045	2 307	2 446	2 309	2 268	2 339	2 344	Production d'énergie primaire
Net imports	...	-170	-177	-395	-499	-469	-510	-561	Importations nettes
Changes in stocks	...	88	...	...	...	...	...	...	Variations des stocks
Total supply	...	1 787	2 130	2 050	1 809	1 799	1 829	1 783	Approv.total
Supply per capita	...	78	86	79	65	62	62	60	Approv.par habitant
Vanuatu									**Vanuatu**
Primary Energy production	0	0	1	1	1	1	1	1	Production d'énergie primaire
Net imports	* 1	* 1	* 1	* 1	* 2	* 2	* 3	* 2	Importations nettes
Changes in stocks	...	...	...	...	* 0	* 0	* 0	0	Variations des stocks
Total supply	1	1	* 2	2	3	3	3	3	Approv.total
Supply per capita	8	7	* 11	8	11	10	12	11	Approv.par habitant
Venezuela (Boliv. Rep. of)									**Venezuela (Rép. boliv. du)**
Primary Energy production	5 953	7 962	8 965	8 283	8 139	7 698	7 460	7 337	Production d'énergie primaire
Net imports	-4 027	-5 772	-6 320	-5 883	* -4 983	-4 858	-4 733	-4 890	Importations nettes
Changes in stocks	-18	24	15	-336	-54	39	-33	-2	Variations des stocks
Total supply	1 944	2 167	2 629	2 737	3 211	2 802	2 760	2 449	Approv.total
Supply per capita	99	98	108	103	111	93	90	79	Approv.par habitant
Viet Nam									**Viet Nam**
Primary Energy production	787	1 136	1 733	2 612	2 747	2 878	2 975	3 043	Production d'énergie primaire
Net imports	-3	-207	-421	-786	-422	-267	-142	27	Importations nettes
Changes in stocks	-7	20	50	70	5	* 86	* 58	* 77	Variations des stocks
Total supply	791	908	1 262	1 756	2 319	2 524	2 775	2 994	Approv.total
Supply per capita	12	12	16	21	26	28	30	32	Approv.par habitant
Wallis and Futuna Islands									**Îles Wallis-et-Futuna**
Net imports	...	...	...	0	0	0	0	0	Importations nettes
Total supply	...	...	...	0	0	0	0	0	Approv.total
Supply per capita	...	...	...	26	27	26	26	26	Approv.par habitant
Yemen									**Yémen**
Primary Energy production	...	713	908	844	804	759	678	172	Production d'énergie primaire
Net imports	...	-571	-712	-529	-477	-416	-374	-28	Importations nettes
Changes in stocks	...	0	0	40	...	...	...	...	Variations des stocks
Total supply	...	142	197	274	326	344	304	145	Approv.total
Supply per capita	...	9	11	13	14	13	12	5	Approv.par habitant

Region, country or area	1990	1995	2000	2005	2010	2013	2014	2015	Région, pays ou zone
Zambia									**Zambie**
Primary Energy production	207	224	248	280	319	362	374	385	Production d'énergie primaire
Net imports	* 14	* 19	* 13	* 25	* 29	* 35	* 34	* 45	Importations nettes
Changes in stocks	...	-1	1	0	0	-1	-6	...	Variations des stocks
Total supply	222	244	260	305	348	398	415	430	Approv.total
Supply per capita	28	27	25	27	25	26	26	27	Approv.par habitant
Zimbabwe									**Zimbabwe**
Primary Energy production	372	362	379	379	368	400	482	449	Production d'énergie primaire
Net imports	* 30	* 64	* 53	* 36	* 24	* 54	* 49	* 47	Importations nettes
Changes in stocks	0	5	-5	1	...	...	67	24	Variations des stocks
Total supply	402	422	438	414	392	454	464	472	Approv.total
Supply per capita	38	36	35	33	28	30	30	30	Approv.par habitant

Source:

United Nations Statistics Division, New York, Energy Statistics Yearbook 2015, last accessed December 2017.

Source:

Organisation des Nations Unies, Division de statistique, New York, Annuaire des statistiques de l'énergie 2015, dernier accès decembre 2017.

1 Excluding overseas territories.
2 For statistical purposes, the data for China do not include those for the Hong Kong Special Administrative Region (Hong Kong SAR), Macao Special Administrative Region (Macao SAR) and Taiwan Province of China.
3 Excluding the Faroe Islands and Greenland.
4 Including Monaco.
5 Data include Timor-Leste.
6 Data include San Marino and the Holy See.
7 The data for crude oil production include 50 per cent of the output of the Neutral Zone.
8 Including Svalbard and Jan Mayen Islands.
9 Data includes the Azores and Madeira.
10 Excluding Kosovo.
11 Data include the Canary Islands.
12 Including Liechtenstein.
13 Shipments of coal and oil to Jersey, Guernsey and the isle of Man from the United Kingdom are not classed as exports. Supplies of coal and oil to these islands are, therefore, included as part of UK supply. Exports of natural gas to the Isle of Man included with the exports to Ireland.
14 Oil and coal trade statistics include overseas territories.

1 Non compris les départements d'outre-mer.
2 Pour la présentation des statistiques, les données pour la Chine ne comprennent pas la région administrative spéciale de Hong Kong (Hong Kong RAS), la région administrative spéciale de Macao (Macao RAS) et la province chinoise de Taïwan.
3 Non compris les Îles Féroé et le Groenland.
4 Y compris Monaco.
5 Les données comprennent Timor-Leste.
6 Les données comprennent Saint-Marin et le Saint-Siège.
7 Les données relatives à la production de pétrole brut comprennent 50 pour cent de la production de la Zone Neutre.
8 Y compris les îles Svalbard-et-Jan Mayen.
9 Les données comprennent Azores et Madère.
10 Non compris Kosovo.
11 Les données comprennent les îles Canaries.
12 Y compris Liechtenstein.
13 Les livraisons de charbon et de pétrole du Royaume-Uni à Jersey, Guernesey et à l'île de Man ne sont pas considérées comme des exportations ; l'Approv.de charbon et pétrole à ces îles fait donc partie de l'Approv.du Royaume-Uni. Les exportations de gaz naturel vers l'île de Man sont inclues dans les exportations vers l'Irlande.
14 Les données sur le pétrole et le charbon incluent les territoires d'outre-mer.

24 Land

Thousand hectares and percent of total land

Terres

Milliers d'hectares et pourcentage de la superficie totale

Region, country or area Région, pays ou zone	Year Année	Area – Superficie ('000 hectares) Total land Superficie totale	Arable land Terres arables	Permanent crops Cultures permanentes	Forest cover Superficie forestière	Area – Superficie (Percent of total)[&] Arable land Terres arables	Permanent crops Cultures Permanentes[&]	Forest cover Superficie forestière	Sites protected for terrestrial biodiversity Sites pour la bio. terre. dans aires protég. (%)[&&]
Total, all countries or areas	**2005**	**13 011 699**	**1 405 843**	**148 372**	**4 032 743**	**10.8**	**1.1**	**31.0**	**40.10**
Total, tous pays ou zones	**2010**	**13 009 625**	**1 388 254**	**159 210**	**4 015 673**	**10.7**	**1.2**	**30.9**	**44.37**
	2015	**13 008 983**	**1 425 919**	**164 831**	**3 999 134**	**11.0**	**1.3**	**30.7**	**46.50**
	2018	**...**	**...**	**...**	**...**	**...**	**...**	**...**	**46.65**
Africa	2005	2 964 823	216 296	30 844	654 679	7.3	1.0	22.1	...
Afrique	2010	2 964 894	226 593	33 026	638 282	7.6	1.1	21.5	...
	2015	2 964 921	235 169	33 892	624 103	7.9	1.1	21.0	...
Northern Africa	2005	838 039	41 430	5 310	36 954	4.9	0.6	4.4	21.13
Afrique septentrionale	2010	838 039	42 525	5 806	36 813	5.1	0.7	4.4	24.84
	2015	838 039	42 935	6 216	28 836	5.1	0.7	3.4	37.72
	2018	...	...	...	...	...	...	...	37.96
Sub-Saharan Africa	2005	2 126 784[1]	174 866[1]	25 534[1]	617 725[1]	8.2[1]	1.2[1]	29.0[1]	34.94
Afrique subsaharienne	2010	2 126 855[1]	184 068[1]	27 221[1]	601 469[1]	8.7[1]	1.3[1]	28.3[1]	40.17
	2015	2 126 882[1]	192 234[1]	27 676[1]	595 267[1]	9.0[1]	1.3[1]	28.0[1]	41.57
	2018	...	...	...	...	...	...	...	41.99
Eastern Africa	2005	605 629	55 768	6 913	203 745	9.2	1.1	33.6	...
Afrique orientale	2010	605 700	62 720	7 604	196 249	10.4	1.3	32.4	...
	2015	605 727	66 395	7 908	197 308	11.0	1.3	32.6	...
Middle Africa	2005	649 682	23 346	2 762	310 491	3.6	0.4	47.8	...
Afrique centrale	2010	649 682	24 364	3 015	306 378	3.8	0.5	47.2	...
	2015	649 682	25 904	3 201	303 251	4.0	0.5	46.7	...
Southern Africa	2005	265 067	14 730	406	29 429	5.6	0.2	11.1	...
Afrique australe	2010	265 067	14 089	460	28 489	5.3	0.2	10.7	...
	2015	265 067	14 146	444	27 635	5.3	0.2	10.4	...
Western Africa	2005	606 406	81 022	15 453	74 060	13.4	2.5	12.2	...
Afrique occidentale	2010	606 406	82 895	16 142	70 353	13.7	2.7	11.6	...
	2015	606 406	85 789	16 123	67 073	14.1	2.7	11.1	...
Americas	2005	3 880 552	367 910	29 413	1 616 564	9.5	0.8	41.7	...
Amériques	2010	3 879 102	364 013	27 990	1 602 412	9.4	0.7	41.3	...
	2015	3 878 860	371 369	27 792	1 592 663	9.6	0.7	41.1	...
Northern America	2005	1 866 616	210 385	9 573	652 337	11.3	0.5	34.9	21.83
Amérique septentrionale	2010	1 865 166	199 327	7 621	656 026	10.7	0.4	35.2	25.50
	2015	1 865 166	195 872	7 300	657 168	10.5	0.4	35.2	26.23
	2018	...	...	...	...	...	...	...	26.23
Latin America & the Caribbean	2005	2 013 936[1]	157 525[1]	19 840[1]	964 227[1]	7.8[1]	1.0[1]	47.9[1]	33.57
Amérique latine et Caraïbes	2010	2 013 936[1]	164 686[1]	20 369[1]	946 386[1]	8.2[1]	1.0[1]	47.0[1]	36.89
	2013	2 013 714[1]	172 124[1]	20 454[1]	939 851[1]	8.5[1]	1.0[1]	46.7[1]	38.32
	2015	2 013 694[1]	175 497[1]	20 492[1]	935 495[1]	8.7[1]	1.0[1]	...	38.96
	2018	...	...	...	...	...	...	...	39.13
Caribbean	2005	22 598	5 699	1 324	6 340	25.2	5.9	28.1	...
Caraïbes	2010	22 598	5 579	1 317	6 744	24.7	5.8	29.8	...
	2015	22 356	5 184	1 355	7 194	23.2	6.1	32.2	...
Central America	2005	245 227	29 276	4 837	89 276	11.9	2.0	36.4	...
Amérique centrale	2010	245 227	28 796	5 127	87 508	11.7	2.1	35.7	...
	2015	245 227	27 994	5 243	86 290	11.4	2.1	35.2	...
South America	2005	1 746 111	122 551	13 679	868 611	7.0	0.8	49.7	...
Amérique du Sud	2010	1 746 111	130 311	13 925	852 133	7.5	0.8	48.8	...
	2015	1 746 111	142 319	13 894	842 011	8.2	0.8	48.2	...
Asia	2005	3 103 540	492 151	70 530	580 868	15.9	2.3	18.7	...
Asie	2010	3 103 331	480 787	81 156	589 405	15.5	2.6	19.0	...
	2015	3 103 224	495 618	86 495	593 362	16.0	2.8	19.1	...
Central Asia	2005	392 679	37 043	705	12 038	9.4	0.2	3.1	12.32
Asie centrale	2010	392 679	37 001	701	11 799	9.4	0.2	3.0	15.70
	2015	392 562	37 746	777	11 705	9.6	0.2	3.0	16.34
	2018	...	...	...	...	...	...	...	16.48
Eastern Asia	2005	1 156 002	121 906	13 296	241 841	10.5	1.2	20.9	48.68
Asie orientale	2010	1 156 045	116 625	15 468	250 504	10.1	1.3	21.7	49.47
	2015	1 156 071	128 177	16 951	257 047	11.1	1.5	22.2	50.99
	2018	...	...	...	...	...	...	...	51.11

24 Land *(continued)*

Thousand hectares and percent of total land

Terres *(suite)*

Milliers d'hectares et pourcentage de la superficie totale

Region, country or area Région, pays ou zone	Year Année	Area – Superficie ('000 hectares) Total land Superficie totale	Arable land Terres arables	Permanent crops Cultures permanentes	Forest cover Superficie forestière	Area – Superficie (Percent of total)& Arable land Terres arables	Permanent crops Cultures Permanentes&	Forest cover Superficie forestière	Sites protected for terrestrial biodiversity Sites pour la bio. terre. dans aires protég. (%)&&
South-eastern Asia Asie du Sud-Est	2005	434 076	65 548	36 521	217 123	15.1	8.4	50.0	31.37
	2010	434 067	68 194	42 500	214 594	15.7	9.8	49.4	33.66
	2015	434 050	70 217	44 975	210 759	16.2	10.4	48.6	35.21
	2018	...	...	...	...	...	...	...	35.25
Southern Asia Asie méridionale	2005	640 034	225 413	14 631	91 519	35.2	2.3	14.3	29.18
	2010	640 034	220 858	16 865	93 406	34.5	2.6	14.6	30.28
	2015	640 034	220 637	17 804	94 087	34.5	2.8	14.7	32.77
	2018	...	...	...	...	...	...	...	32.78
Western Asia Asie occidentale	2005	480 749	42 240	5 377	18 347	8.8	1.1	3.8	11.07
	2010	480 506	38 110	5 623	19 103	7.9	1.2	4.0	13.94
	2015	480 507	38 842	5 989	19 764	8.1	1.2	4.1	15.27
	2018	...	...	...	...	...	...	...	15.38
Europe Europe	2005	2 214 130	279 161	16 166	1 004 147	12.6	0.7	45.4	57.59
	2010	2 213 644	273 241	15 435	1 013 572	12.3	0.7	45.8	63.58
	2015	2 213 324	276 492	15 124	1 015 482	12.5	0.7	45.9	65.54
	2018	...	...	...	...	...	...	...	65.59
Eastern Europe Europe orientale	2005	1 805 641	195 108	4 505	852 968	10.8	0.2	47.2	...
	2010	1 805 269	190 941	4 275	859 827	10.6	0.2	47.6	...
	2015	1 805 260	195 255	4 110	860 425	10.8	0.2	47.7	...
Northern Europe Europe septentrionale	2005	170 310	18 781	139	74 437	11.0	0.1	43.7	...
	2010	170 245	19 208	115	74 570	11.3	0.1	43.8	...
	2015	169 890	19 244	119	74 735	11.3	0.1	44.0	...
Southern Europe Europe méridionale	2005	129 659	31 185	10 069	43 296	24.1	7.8	33.4	...
	2010	129 633	29 255	9 685	45 100	22.6	7.5	34.8	...
	2015	129 657	27 993	9 551	45 639	21.6	7.4	35.2	...
Western Europe Europe occidentale	2005	108 521	34 086	1 453	33 446	31.4	1.3	30.8	...
	2010	108 497	33 837	1 359	34 076	31.2	1.3	31.4	...
	2015	108 518	34 000	1 344	34 684	31.3	1.2	32.0	...
Oceania Océanie	2005	848 655	50 326	1 419	176 485	5.9	0.2	20.8	26.15
	2010	848 655	43 620	1 602	172 002	5.1	0.2	20.3	32.84
	2015	848 655	47 271	1 528	173 524	5.6	0.2	20.4	36.01
	2018	...	...	...	...	...	...	...	36.60
Australia and New Zealand Australie et Nouvelle-Zélande	2005	794 565	49 827	403	137 824	6.3	0.1	17.3	40.00
	2010	794 565	43 067	471	133 362	5.4	0.1	16.8	45.70
	2015	794 565	46 716	397	134 903	5.9	0.1	17.0	50.89
	2018	...	...	...	...	...	...	...	51.39
Melanesia Mélanésie	2005	52 959	453	873	38 103	0.9	1.6	71.9	...
	2010	52 959	511	994	38 058	1.0	1.9	71.9	...
	2015	52 959	511	994	38 040	1.0	1.9	71.8	...
Micronesia Micronésie	2005	317	11	70	185	3.3	22.2	58.4	...
	2010	317	9	69	185	2.8	21.9	58.2	...
	2015	317	9	68	184	2.8	21.4	58.0	...
Polynesia Polynésie	2005	814	36	73	372	4.4	9.0	45.8	...
	2010	814	33	68	397	4.1	8.3	48.8	...
	2015	814	35	69	396	4.2	8.5	48.7	...
Antarctica Antarctique	2005	...	...	...	...	...	...	...	7.13
	2010	...	...	...	...	...	...	...	7.13
	2018	...	...	...	...	...	...	...	10.05
Afghanistan Afghanistan	2005	* 65 286	7 805	105	* 1 350	* 12.0	* 0.2	* 2.1	0.04
	2010	* 65 286	7 793	118	* 1 350	* 11.9	* 0.2	* 2.1	6.14
	2015	* 65 286	7 765	145	* 1 350	* 11.9	* 0.2	* 2.1	6.14
	2018	...	...	...	...	...	...	...	6.14
Albania Albanie	2005	2 740	538	121	* 782	19.6	4.4	* 28.6	43.98
	2010	2 740	626	70	* 776	22.8	2.6	* 28.3	58.81
	2015	* 2 740	615	81	* 772	* 22.4	* 3.0	* 28.2	66.98
	2018	...	...	...	...	...	...	...	66.98
Algeria Algérie	2005	238 174	7 511	852	1 536	3.2	0.4	0.6	38.43
	2010	238 174	7 502	909	1 918	3.1	0.4	0.8	38.43
	2015	238 174	7 462	1 000	1 956	3.1	0.4	0.8	38.81
	2018	...	...	...	...	...	...	...	38.81

24 Land *(continued)*
Thousand hectares and percent of total land

Terres *(suite)*
Milliers d'hectares et pourcentage de la superficie totale

Region, country or area Région, pays ou zone	Year Année	Area – Superficie ('000 hectares) Total land Superficie totale	Arable land Terres arables	Permanent crops Cultures permanentes	Forest cover Superficie forestière	Area – Superficie (Percent of total)& Arable land Terres arables	Permanent crops Cultures Permanentes&	Forest cover Superficie forestière	Sites protected for terrestrial biodiversity Sites pour la bio. terre. dans aires protég. (%)&&
American Samoa Samoa américaines	2005	20	* 3	* 2	* 18	* 16.5	* 8.5	* 89.4	61.50
	2010	20	* 3	* 2	* 18	* 15.0	* 9.5	* 88.6	61.50
	2015	20	* 3	* 2	* 18	* 15.0	* 9.5	* 87.7	61.50
	2018	...	...	...	...	...	...	...	61.50
Andorra Andorre	2005	47	1	...	* 16	1.7	...	* 34.0	17.90
	2010	47	1	...	* 16	1.6	...	* 34.0	17.90
	2015	47	1	...	* 16	1.7	...	* 34.0	26.08
	2018	...	...	...	...	...	...	...	26.08
Angola Angola	2005	124 670	* 3 300	* 290	59 104	* 2.6	* 0.2	47.4	28.37
	2010	124 670	* 4 100	* 290	58 480	* 3.3	* 0.2	46.9	28.37
	2015	124 670	* 4 900	* 290	57 856	* 3.9	* 0.2	46.4	28.37
	2018	...	...	...	...	...	...	...	28.37
Anguilla Anguilla	2005	9	...	...	* 6	...	...	* 61.1	0.15
	2010	9	...	...	* 6	...	...	* 61.1	0.15
	2015	9	...	...	* 6	...	...	* 61.1	0.15
	2018	...	...	...	...	...	...	...	0.15
Antigua and Barbuda Antigua-et-Barbuda	2005	44	* 4	* 1	* 10	* 9.1	* 2.3	* 22.3	18.44
	2010	44	* 4	* 1	* 10	* 9.1	* 2.3	* 22.3	18.44
	2015	44	* 4	* 1	* 10	* 9.1	* 2.3	* 22.3	18.44
	2018	...	...	...	...	...	...	...	18.44
Argentina Argentine	2005	* 273 669	* 32 898	* 1 000	30 186	* 12.0	* 0.4	* 11.0	29.69
	2010	* 273 669	* 37 981	* 1 000	28 596	* 13.9	* 0.4	* 10.4	32.00
	2015	* 273 669	* 39 200	* 1 000	27 112	* 14.3	* 0.4	* 9.9	32.88
	2018	...	...	...	...	...	...	...	33.21
Armenia Arménie	2005	2 847	* 455	50	332	* 16.0	1.8	11.7	24.84
	2010	2 847	449	55	331	15.8	1.9	11.6	30.54
	2015	* 2 847	447	57	332	* 15.7	* 2.0	* 11.7	30.54
	2018	...	...	...	...	...	...	...	30.54
Aruba Aruba	2005	18	* 2	...	* ~0	* 11.1	...	* 2.3	47.85
	2010	18	* 2	...	* ~0	* 11.1	...	* 2.3	47.85
	2015	18	* 2	...	* ~0	* 11.1	...	* 2.3	47.85
	2018	...	...	...	...	...	...	...	47.85
Australia Australie	2005	768 230	* 49 402	* 340	127 641	* 6.4	* ~0.0	16.6	38.69
	2010	768 230	* 42 568	* 400	123 211	* 5.5	* 0.1	16.0	46.22
	2015	* 768 230	* 46 126	* 330	124 751	* 6.0	* ~0.0	* 16.2	53.53
	2018	...	...	...	...	...	...	...	54.27
Austria Autriche	2005	* 8 258	1 381	66	3 851	* 16.7	* 0.8	* 46.6	63.47
	2010	8 257	1 364	65	3 860	16.5	0.8	46.7	66.09
	2015	* 8 252	1 346	65	3 869	* 16.3	* 0.8	* 46.9	66.34
	2018	...	...	...	...	...	...	...	66.35
Azerbaijan Azerbaïdjan	2005	8 266	1 843	222	* 877	22.3	2.7	* 10.6	33.27
	2010	8 266	1 884	227	* 1 008	22.8	2.8	* 12.2	39.42
	2015	* 8 266	1 938	237	* 1 139	* 23.4	* 2.9	* 13.8	39.42
	2018	...	...	...	...	...	...	...	39.42
Bahamas Bahamas	2005	* 1 001	* 7	* 4	* 515	* 0.7	* 0.4	* 51.4	6.96
	2010	* 1 001	* 9	* 4	* 515	* 0.9	* 0.4	* 51.4	7.03
	2015	* 1 001	* 8	* 4	* 515	* 0.8	* 0.4	* 51.4	24.72
	2018	...	...	...	...	...	...	...	24.72
Bahrain Bahreïn	2005	74	* 2	* 3	* ~0	* 2.0	* 4.3	* 0.6	19.61
	2010	76	* 2	* 3	* 1	* 2.1	* 3.9	* 0.7	27.46
	2015	77	* 2	* 3	* 1	* 2.1	* 3.9	* 0.8	27.46
	2018	...	...	...	...	...	...	...	27.46
Bangladesh Bangladesh	2005	13 017	* 7 911	* 800	1 455	* 60.8	* 6.1	11.2	37.92
	2010	* 13 017	* 7 791	* 850	1 442	* 59.9	* 6.5	* 11.1	48.00
	2015	* 13 017	* 7 764	* 830	1 429	* 59.6	* 6.4	* 11.0	48.02
	2018	...	...	...	...	...	...	...	48.02
Barbados Barbade	2005	43	* 13	* 1	6	* 30.2	* 2.3	14.7	2.07
	2010	43	* 12	* 1	6	* 27.9	* 2.3	14.7	2.07
	2015	43	* 11	* 1	6	* 25.6	* 2.3	14.7	2.07
	2018	...	...	...	...	...	...	...	2.07

Land *(continued)*
Thousand hectares and percent of total land

Terres *(suite)*
Milliers d'hectares et pourcentage de la superficie totale

Region, country or area Région, pays ou zone	Year Année	Area – Superficie ('000 hectares) Total land Superficie totale	 Arable land Terres arables	 Permanent crops Cultures permanentes	 Forest cover Superficie forestière	Area – Superficie (Percent of total)& Arable land Terres arables	 Permanent crops Cultures Permanentes&	 Forest cover Superficie forestière	Sites protected for terrestrial biodiversity Sites pour la bio. terre. dans aires protég. (%)&&
Belarus	2005	20 283	5 542	118	8 436	27.3	0.6	41.6	34.99
Bélarus	2010	20 290	5 535	122	8 534	27.3	0.6	42.1	35.40
	2015	* 20 291	* 5 685	113	8 634	* 28.0	* 0.6	* 42.5	49.07
	2018	...	...	...	...	...	...	...	49.07
Belgium	2005	3 028	843	21	674	27.8	0.7	22.3	80.53
Belgique	2010	3 028	834	22	681	27.5	0.7	22.5	80.58
	2015	* 3 028	830	23	683	* 27.4	* 0.7	* 22.6	80.77
	2018	...	...	...	...	...	...	...	80.77
Belize	2005	2 281	* 70	* 32	* 1 417	* 3.1	* 1.4	* 62.1	45.75
Belize	2010	* 2 281	* 75	* 32	* 1 391	* 3.3	* 1.4	* 61.0	45.77
	2015	* 2 281	* 78	* 32	* 1 366	* 3.4	* 1.4	* 59.9	45.96
	2018	...	...	...	...	...	...	...	45.96
Benin	2005	* 11 276	* 2 700	* 270	4 811	* 23.9	* 2.4	* 42.7	77.38
Bénin	2010	* 11 276	* 2 540	* 350	4 561	* 22.5	* 3.1	* 40.4	77.38
	2015	* 11 276	* 2 700	* 500	4 311	* 23.9	* 4.4	* 38.2	77.38
	2018	...	...	...	...	...	...	...	77.38
Bermuda	2005	5	~0	...	* 1	8.0	...	* 20.0	16.21
Bermudes	2010	5	~0	...	* 1	6.0	...	* 20.0	16.21
	2015	* 5	* ~0	...	* 1	* 6.0	...	* 20.0	16.21
	2018	...	...	...	...	...	...	...	16.21
Bhutan	2005	3 812	* 167	* 19	2 656	* 4.4	* 0.5	69.7	38.56
Bhoutan	2010	3 812	101	12	2 705	2.6	0.3	71.0	41.23
	2015	3 812	100	12	2 755	2.6	0.3	72.3	42.92
	2018	...	...	...	...	...	...	...	42.92
Bolivia (Plurin. State of)	2005	108 330	3 806	199	58 734	3.5	0.2	54.2	52.77
Bolivie (État plurin. de)	2010	* 108 330	* 4 297	* 219	56 209	* 4.0	* 0.2	* 51.9	54.64
	2015	* 108 330	* 4 473	* 232	54 764	* 4.1	* 0.2	* 50.6	56.23
	2018	...	...	...	...	...	...	...	56.23
Bonaire, St. Eustatius & Saba	2005	...	...	...	...	...	...	...	39.26
Bonaire, St-Eustache et	2010	...	...	...	...	...	...	...	39.26
Saba	2018	...	...	...	...	...	...	...	39.26
Bosnia and Herzegovina	2005	5 120	1 025	95	* 2 185	20.0	1.9	* 42.7	0.00
Bosnie-Herzégovine	2010	5 120	1 004	105	* 2 185	19.6	2.1	* 42.7	11.98
	2015	5 120	1 029	105	* 2 185	20.1	2.1	* 42.7	11.99
	2018	...	...	...	...	...	...	...	11.99
Botswana	2005	* 56 673	* 240	2	11 943	* 0.4	* ~0.0	* 21.1	47.10
Botswana	2010	* 56 673	259	* 2	11 351	* 0.5	* ~0.0	* 20.0	47.10
	2015	* 56 673	* 399	* 2	10 840	* 0.7	* ~0.0	* 19.1	47.10
	2018	...	...	...	...	...	...	...	47.10
Brazil	2005	* 835 814	* 69 157	* 7 276	506 734	* 8.3	* 0.9	* 60.6	42.31
Brésil	2010	* 835 814	* 70 363	* 7 100	498 458	* 8.4	* 0.8	* 59.6	47.46
	2015	* 835 814	* 80 017	* 6 572	493 538	* 9.6	* 0.8	* 59.0	47.58
	2018	...	...	...	...	...	...	...	47.58
British Indian Ocean Terr.	2005	...	...	...	...	...	...	...	99.91
Terr. brit. de l'océan Indien	2010	...	...	...	...	...	...	...	99.91
	2018	...	...	...	...	...	...	...	99.91
British Virgin Islands	2005	15	* 1	* 1	* 4	* 6.7	* 6.7	* 24.4	9.35
Îles Vierges britanniques	2010	15	* 1	* 1	* 4	* 6.7	* 6.7	* 24.3	9.35
	2015	15	* 1	* 1	* 4	* 6.7	* 6.7	* 24.1	9.35
	2018	...	...	...	...	...	...	...	9.35
Brunei Darussalam	2005	527	* 2	* 5	* 389	* 0.4	* 0.9	* 73.8	62.88
Brunéi Darussalam	2010	* 527	* 4	* 6	* 380	* 0.8	* 1.1	* 72.1	62.88
	2015	* 527	* 5	* 6	* 380	* 0.9	* 1.1	* 72.1	62.88
	2018	...	...	...	...	...	...	...	62.88
Bulgaria	2005	10 864	3 173	188	3 651	29.2	1.7	33.6	41.19
Bulgarie	2010	* 10 856	3 186	164	3 737	* 29.3	* 1.5	* 34.4	95.55
	2015	* 10 856	3 510	134	3 823	* 32.3	* 1.2	* 35.2	95.55
	2018	...	...	...	...	...	...	...	95.55
Burkina Faso	2005	* 27 360	* 4 900	* 70	5 949	* 17.9	* 0.3	* 21.7	66.71
Burkina Faso	2010	* 27 360	* 6 000	* 80	5 649	* 21.9	* 0.3	* 20.6	71.83
	2015	* 27 360	* 6 000	* 100	5 350	* 21.9	* 0.4	* 19.6	71.83
	2018	...	...	...	...	...	...	...	71.83

Land *(continued)*
Thousand hectares and percent of total land

Terres *(suite)*
Milliers d'hectares et pourcentage de la superficie totale

Region, country or area Région, pays ou zone	Year Année	Area – Superficie ('000 hectares) Total land Superficie totale	Arable land Terres arables	Permanent crops Cultures permanentes	Forest cover Superficie forestière	Area – Superficie (Percent of total)& Arable land Terres arables	Permanent crops Cultures Permanentes&	Forest cover Superficie forestière	Sites protected for terrestrial biodiversity Sites pour la bio. terre. dans aires protég. (%)&&
Burundi Burundi	2005	* 2 568	* 956	* 380	181	* 37.2	* 14.8	* 7.0	51.03
	2010	* 2 568	* 950	* 400	253	* 37.0	* 15.6	* 9.9	51.03
	2015	* 2 568	* 1 200	* 350	276	* 46.7	* 13.6	* 10.7	51.19
	2018	...	...	...	...	...	...	...	51.19
Cabo Verde Cabo Verde	2005	403	* 48	* 2	84	* 11.9	* 0.5	20.7	14.95
	2010	403	* 50	* 3	85	* 12.4	* 0.7	21.1	14.95
	2015	403	* 50	* 4	90	* 12.4	* 1.0	22.3	15.14
	2018	...	...	...	...	...	...	...	15.14
Cambodia Cambodge	2005	17 652	* 3 700	156	10 731	* 21.0	0.9	60.8	38.12
	2010	* 17 652	* 3 800	* 155	10 094	* 21.5	* 0.9	* 57.2	39.54
	2015	* 17 652	* 3 800	* 155	9 457	* 21.5	* 0.9	* 53.6	39.54
	2018	...	...	...	...	...	...	...	39.54
Cameroon Cameroun	2005	47 271	5 963	* 1 250	21 016	12.6	* 2.6	44.5	25.41
	2010	* 47 271	* 6 200	* 1 500	19 916	* 13.1	* 3.2	* 42.1	28.45
	2015	* 47 271	* 6 200	* 1 550	18 816	* 13.1	* 3.3	* 39.8	36.31
	2018	...	...	...	...	...	...	...	36.31
Canada Canada	2005	909 351	* 45 266	* 6 873	347 576	* 5.0	* 0.8	38.2	21.18
	2010	909 351	* 43 397	* 5 021	347 302	* 4.8	* 0.6	38.2	25.43
	2015	909 351	* 43 606	* 4 700	347 069	* 4.8	* 0.5	38.2	25.66
	2018	...	...	...	...	...	...	...	25.66
Cayman Islands Îles Caïmanes	2005	24	* ~0	* 1	* 13	* 0.8	* 2.1	* 52.9	31.64
	2010	24	* ~0	* 1	* 13	* 0.8	* 2.1	* 52.9	31.67
	2015	24	* ~0	* 1	* 13	* 0.8	* 2.1	* 52.9	32.51
	2018	...	...	...	...	...	...	...	32.51
Central African Republic République centrafricaine	2005	62 298	* 1 930	* 85	22 326	* 3.1	* 0.1	35.8	74.23
	2010	62 298	* 1 800	* 80	22 248	* 2.9	* 0.1	35.7	74.37
	2015	62 298	* 1 800	* 80	22 170	* 2.9	* 0.1	35.6	74.37
	2018	...	...	...	...	...	...	...	74.37
Chad Tchad	2005	125 920	* 4 500	* 30	6 141	* 3.6	* ~0.0	4.9	70.63
	2010	125 920	* 4 500	* 35	5 508	* 3.6	* ~0.0	4.4	70.63
	2015	* 125 920	* 4 900	* 35	4 875	* 3.9	* ~0.0	* 3.9	70.63
	2018	...	...	...	...	...	...	...	70.63
Channel Islands Îles Anglo-Normandes	*2005	19	4	...	1	20.0	...	4.2	...
	*2010	19	4	...	1	22.6	...	4.2	...
	*2015	19	4	...	1	20.5	...	4.2	...
Chile Chili	2005	74 353	* 1 450	* 435	16 042	* 2.0	* 0.6	21.6	33.42
	2010	74 353	* 1 271	* 457	16 231	* 1.7	* 0.6	21.8	35.19
	2015	* 74 353	* 1 313	* 457	17 735	* 1.8	* 0.6	* 23.9	35.66
	2018	...	...	...	...	...	...	...	35.71
China [2] Chine [2]	2005	* 938 821	* 112 250	* 12 350	193 044	* 12.0	* 1.3	* 20.6	46.58
	2010	* 938 821	* 107 220	* 14 500	200 610	* 11.4	* 1.5	* 21.4	47.10
	2015	* 938 821	* 119 000	16 000	208 321	* 12.7	* 1.7	* 22.2	47.59
	2018	...	...	...	...	...	...	...	47.59
China, Hong Kong SAR Chine, RAS de Hong Kong	2005	105	* 5	* 1	...	* 4.8	* 1.0	...	56.66
	2010	* 105	* 4	* 1	...	* 3.3	* 1.0	...	56.66
	2015	* 105	* 3	* 1	...	* 3.0	* 1.0	...	56.66
	2018	...	...	...	...	...	...	...	56.66
China, Macao SAR Chine, RAS de Macao	2005	3	...	...	...	...	...	...	0.00
	2010	3	...	...	...	...	...	...	0.00
	2015	3	...	...	...	...	...	...	0.00
	2018	...	...	...	...	...	...	...	0.00
Christmas Island Île Christmas	2005	...	...	...	...	...	...	...	60.43
	2010	...	...	...	...	...	...	...	60.43
	2018	...	...	...	...	...	...	...	60.43
Colombia Colombie	2005	110 950	* 2 026	* 1 587	60 201	* 1.8	* 1.4	54.3	24.99
	2010	110 950	* 1 763	* 1 590	58 635	* 1.6	* 1.4	52.8	30.30
	2015	110 950	* 1 689	* 1 906	58 502	* 1.5	* 1.7	52.7	37.97
	2018	...	...	...	...	...	...	...	37.97
Comoros Comores	2005	186	* 65	* 53	* 42	* 34.9	* 28.5	* 22.6	5.00
	2010	186	* 65	* 53	* 39	* 34.9	* 28.5	* 21.0	10.42
	2015	186	* 65	* 53	* 37	* 34.9	* 28.5	* 19.9	10.42
	2018	...	...	...	...	...	...	...	10.42

24 Land *(continued)*
Thousand hectares and percent of total land

Terres *(suite)*
Milliers d'hectares et pourcentage de la superficie totale

Region, country or area Région, pays ou zone	Year Année	Area – Superficie ('000 hectares) Total land Superficie totale	Arable land Terres arables	Permanent crops Cultures permanentes	Forest cover Superficie forestière	Area – Superficie (Percent of total)& Arable land Terres arables	Permanent crops Cultures Permanentes&	Forest cover Superficie forestière	Sites protected for terrestrial biodiversity Sites pour la bio. terre. dans aires protég. (%)&&
Congo	2005	* 34 150	* 490	* 57	22 471	* 1.4	* 0.2	* 65.8	51.53
Congo	2010	* 34 150	* 510	* 66	22 411	* 1.5	* 0.2	* 65.6	61.21
	2015	* 34 150	* 550	* 77	22 334	* 1.6	* 0.2	* 65.4	72.12
	2018	...	...	...	...	...	...	...	72.12
Cook Islands	2005	24	* 1	* 1	15	* 5.2	* 6.2	62.9	7.63
Îles Cook	2010	24	* 1	* 1	15	* 2.9	* 2.7	62.9	7.63
	2015	24	* 1	* 1	15	* 4.2	* 2.1	62.9	7.63
	2018	...	...	...	...	...	...	...	22.45
Costa Rica	2005	* 5 106	* 210	* 280	2 491	* 4.1	* 5.5	* 48.8	44.76
Costa Rica	2010	* 5 106	* 225	* 315	2 605	* 4.4	* 6.2	* 51.0	45.33
	2015	* 5 106	* 232	* 314	2 756	* 4.5	* 6.1	* 54.0	45.33
	2018	...	...	...	...	...	...	...	45.33
Côte d'Ivoire	2005	* 31 800	* 2 800	* 4 200	* 10 405	* 8.8	* 13.2	* 32.7	79.13
Côte d'Ivoire	2010	* 31 800	* 2 900	* 4 500	* 10 403	* 9.1	* 14.2	* 32.7	79.13
	2015	* 31 800	* 2 900	* 4 500	* 10 401	* 9.1	* 14.2	* 32.7	79.13
	2018	...	...	...	...	...	...	...	79.13
Croatia	2005	5 596	873	73	1 903	15.6	1.3	34.0	22.75
Croatie	2010	5 596	904	84	1 920	16.2	1.5	34.3	24.41
	2015	* 5 596	844	76	1 922	* 15.1	* 1.3	* 34.3	72.04
	2018	...	...	...	...	...	...	...	72.04
Cuba	2005	10 644	* 3 672	425	2 697	* 34.5	4.0	25.3	42.08
Cuba	2010	* 10 644	* 3 384	* 420	2 932	* 31.8	* 3.9	* 27.5	68.33
	2015	* 10 402	* 3 014	504	3 200	* 29.0	* 4.8	* 30.8	73.42
	2018	...	...	...	...	...	...	...	73.42
Curaçao	2005	...	...	...	...	...	...	...	6.07
Curaçao	2010	...	...	...	...	...	...	...	6.07
	2018	...	...	...	...	...	...	...	40.41
Cyprus	2005	924	123	43	173	13.3	4.7	18.7	36.08
Chypre	2010	924	83	30	173	8.9	3.2	18.7	54.55
	2015	924	99	26	173	10.7	2.9	18.7	57.81
	2018	...	...	...	...	...	...	...	57.81
Czechia	2005	7 726	3 209	77	2 647	41.5	1.0	34.3	87.83
Tchéquie	2010	7 724	3 171	77	2 657	41.1	1.0	34.4	92.30
	2015	7 722	3 136	76	2 667	40.6	1.0	34.5	92.30
	2018	...	...	...	...	...	...	...	92.30
Dem. People's Rep. Korea	2005	* 12 041	* 2 350	* 200	* 6 299	* 19.5	* 1.7	* 52.3	10.16
Rép. pop. dém. de Corée	2010	* 12 041	* 2 400	* 230	* 5 666	* 19.9	* 1.9	* 47.1	10.16
	2015	* 12 041	* 2 350	* 230	* 5 031	* 19.5	* 1.9	* 41.8	10.16
	2018	...	...	...	...	...	...	...	10.16
Dem. Rep. of the Congo	2005	* 226 705	* 6 700	* 750	155 692	* 3.0	* 0.3	* 68.7	36.63
Rép. dém. du Congo	2010	* 226 705	* 6 800	* 765	154 135	* 3.0	* 0.3	* 68.0	38.50
	2015	* 226 705	* 7 100	* 900	152 578	* 3.1	* 0.4	* 67.3	38.50
	2018	...	...	...	...	...	...	...	40.10
Denmark	2005	4 243	2 332	* 7	558	55.0	0.2	13.1	89.16
Danemark	2010	4 243	2 421	5	587	57.1	0.1	13.8	89.63
	2015	* 4 199	2 351	5	612	* 56.0	* 0.1	* 14.6	89.65
	2018	...	...	...	...	...	...	...	89.65
Djibouti	2005	* 2 318	* 1	...	* 6	* ~0.0	...	* 0.2	0.00
Djibouti	2010	* 2 318	2	...	* 6	* 0.1	...	* 0.2	0.00
	2015	* 2 318	* 2	...	* 6	* 0.1	...	* 0.2	0.95
	2018	...	...	...	...	...	...	...	0.95
Dominica	2005	75	* 5	* 15	* 46	* 6.7	* 20.0	* 61.3	44.26
Dominique	2010	75	* 6	* 17	* 45	* 8.0	* 22.7	* 59.5	44.26
	2015	75	* 6	* 17	* 43	* 8.0	* 22.7	* 57.8	44.26
	2018	...	...	...	...	...	...	...	44.26
Dominican Republic	2005	4 831	* 820	* 400	1 652	* 17.0	* 8.3	34.2	72.89
République dominicaine	2010	4 831	* 800	* 400	1 817	* 16.6	* 8.3	37.6	72.89
	2015	* 4 831	* 800	* 355	1 983	* 16.6	* 7.3	* 41.0	76.23
	2018	...	...	...	...	...	...	...	76.23

24 Land (continued)

Thousand hectares and percent of total land

Terres (suite)

Milliers d'hectares et pourcentage de la superficie totale

Region, country or area Région, pays ou zone	Year Année	Area – Superficie ('000 hectares) Total land Superficie totale	Arable land Terres arables	Permanent crops Cultures permanentes	Forest cover Superficie forestière	Area – Superficie (Percent of total)& Arable land Terres arables	Permanent crops Cultures Permanentes&	Forest cover Superficie forestière	Sites protected for terrestrial biodiversity Sites pour la bio. terre. dans aires protég. (%)&&
Ecuador Équateur	2005	24 836	1 296	1 214	13 335	5.2	4.9	53.7	25.53
	2010	24 836	1 186	1 391	12 942	4.8	5.6	52.1	27.89
	2015	* 24 836	1 067	1 483	12 548	* 4.3	* 6.0	* 50.5	29.00
	2018	...	...	...	...	...	...	...	29.00
Egypt Égypte	2005	99 545	* 2 563	960	67	* 2.6	1.0	0.1	37.86
	2010	* 99 545	* 2 873	798	70	* 2.9	* 0.8	* 0.1	39.64
	2015	* 99 545	2 896	924	73	* 2.9	* 0.9	* 0.1	39.64
	2018	...	...	...	...	...	...	...	39.64
El Salvador El Salvador	2005	* 2 072	* 702	227	309	* 33.9	* 11.0	* 14.9	9.88
	2010	* 2 072	* 673	* 225	287	* 32.5	* 10.9	* 13.9	22.39
	2015	* 2 072	* 750	* 215	265	* 36.2	* 10.4	* 12.8	26.58
	2018	...	...	...	...	...	...	...	26.58
Equatorial Guinea Guinée équatoriale	2005	2 805	* 130	* 90	1 685	* 4.6	* 3.2	60.1	100.00
	2010	2 805	* 120	* 70	1 626	* 4.3	* 2.5	58.0	100.00
	2015	2 805	* 120	* 60	1 568	* 4.3	* 2.1	55.9	100.00
	2018	...	...	...	...	...	...	...	100.00
Eritrea Érythrée	2005	* 10 100	* 620	* 2	* 1 554	* 6.1	* ~0.0	* 15.4	13.34
	2010	* 10 100	* 690	* 2	* 1 532	* 6.8	* ~0.0	* 15.2	13.34
	2015	* 10 100	* 690	* 2	* 1 510	* 6.8	* ~0.0	* 15.0	13.34
	2018	...	...	...	...	...	...	...	13.34
Estonia Estonie	2005	4 239	592	11	2 252	14.0	0.3	53.1	94.67
	2010	4 239	645	7	2 234	15.2	0.2	52.7	94.76
	2015	* 4 239	670	6	2 232	* 15.8	* 0.1	* 52.7	94.91
	2018	...	...	...	...	...	...	...	94.92
Eswatini Eswatini	2005	* 1 720	* 178	* 14	541	* 10.3	* 0.8	* 31.5	29.98
	2010	* 1 720	* 175	* 15	563	* 10.2	* 0.9	* 32.7	29.98
	2015	* 1 720	* 175	* 15	586	* 10.2	* 0.9	* 34.1	30.27
	2018	...	...	...	...	...	...	...	30.27
Ethiopia Éthiopie	2005	* 100 000	12 823	768	13 000	* 12.8	* 0.8	* 13.0	18.59
	2010	* 100 000	14 565	1 118	12 296	* 14.6	* 1.1	* 12.3	19.77
	2015	* 100 000	* 15 119	* 1 140	12 499	* 15.1	* 1.1	* 12.5	19.77
	2018	...	...	...	...	...	...	...	19.77
Falkland Islands (Malvinas) Îles Falkland (Malvinas)	2005	1 217	...	...	* 0	...	...	* 0.0	10.90
	2010	1 217	...	...	* 0	...	...	* 0.0	10.90
	2015	1 217	...	...	* 0	...	...	* 0.0	10.90
	2018	...	...	...	...	...	...	...	10.90
Faroe Islands Îles Féroé	2005	140	* 3	...	* ~0	* 2.1	...	* 0.1	0.00
	2010	140	* 3	...	* ~0	* 2.1	...	* 0.1	0.00
	2015	140	* 3	...	* ~0	* 2.1	...	* 0.1	6.67
	2018	...	...	...	...	...	...	...	6.67
Fiji Fidji	2005	* 1 827	* 170	* 83	997	* 9.3	* 4.5	* 54.6	3.30
	2010	* 1 827	* 165	* 85	993	* 9.0	* 4.7	* 54.3	4.89
	2015	* 1 827	* 165	* 85	1 017	* 9.0	* 4.7	* 55.7	4.89
	2018	...	...	...	...	...	...	...	4.89
Finland Finlande	2005	30 459	2 237	4	22 143	7.3	~0.0	72.7	72.04
	2010	30 390	2 255	4	22 218	7.4	~0.0	73.1	72.24
	2015	30 391	2 242	3	22 218	7.4	~0.0	73.1	72.64
	2018	...	...	...	...	...	...	...	72.65
France France	2005	* 54 756	18 378	1 111	15 861	* 33.6	* 2.0	* 29.0	68.81
	2010	* 54 756	18 301	1 011	16 424	* 33.4	* 1.8	* 30.0	80.13
	2015	* 54 756	18 479	986	16 989	* 33.7	* 1.8	* 31.0	81.17
	2018	...	...	...	...	...	...	...	81.17
French Guiana Guyane française	2005	* 8 220	12	4	8 168	* 0.1	* ~0.0	* 99.4	58.57
	2010	* 8 220	12	4	8 138	* 0.1	* ~0.0	* 99.0	67.03
	2015	* 8 220	14	5	8 130	* 0.2	* 0.1	* 98.9	67.39
	2018	...	...	...	...	...	...	...	67.39
French Polynesia Polynésie française	2005	* 366	* 3	* 22	* 130	* 0.8	* 6.0	* 35.5	3.99
	2010	* 366	* 3	* 22	* 155	* 0.7	* 6.0	* 42.3	5.36
	2015	* 366	* 3	* 23	* 155	* 0.7	* 6.3	* 42.3	5.36
	2018	...	...	...	...	...	...	...	5.36

24 Land *(continued)*
Thousand hectares and percent of total land

Terres *(suite)*
Milliers d'hectares et pourcentage de la superficie totale

Region, country or area Région, pays ou zone	Year Année	Area – Superficie ('000 hectares) Total land Superficie totale	Arable land Terres arables	Permanent crops Cultures permanentes	Forest cover Superficie forestière	Area – Superficie (Percent of total)& Arable land Terres arables	Permanent crops Cultures Permanentes&	Forest cover Superficie forestière	Sites protected for terrestrial biodiversity Sites pour la bio. terre. dans aires protég. (%)&&
French Southern Territories Terres australes françaises	2005	...	...	...	...	...	...	...	0.00
	2010	...	...	...	...	...	...	...	71.86
	2018	...	...	...	...	...	...	...	83.96
Gabon Gabon	2005	25 767	* 325	* 170	22 000	* 1.3	* 0.7	85.4	61.17
	2010	25 767	* 325	* 170	22 000	* 1.3	* 0.7	85.4	61.17
	2015	25 767	* 325	* 170	23 000	* 1.3	* 0.7	89.3	61.17
	2018	...	...	...	...	...	...	...	61.67
Gambia Gambie	2005	1 012	* 325	* 5	471	* 32.1	* 0.5	46.5	34.59
	2010	1 012	450	* 5	480	44.5	* 0.5	47.4	34.59
	2015	* 1 012	* 440	* 5	488	* 43.5	* 0.5	* 48.2	34.59
	2018	...	...	...	...	...	...	...	34.59
Georgia Géorgie	2005	6 949	* 470	* 110	2 773	* 6.8	* 1.6	39.9	19.16
	2010	* 6 949	* 415	* 125	2 822	* 6.0	* 1.8	* 40.6	21.27
	2015	* 6 949	* 448	* 160	2 822	* 6.4	* 2.3	* 40.6	28.38
	2018	...	...	...	...	...	...	...	28.38
Germany Allemagne	2005	34 876	11 904	198	11 384	34.1	0.6	32.6	70.71
	2010	34 857	11 846	199	11 409	34.0	0.6	32.7	78.06
	2015	* 34 886	11 849	205	11 419	* 34.0	* 0.6	* 32.7	78.56
	2018	...	...	...	...	...	...	...	78.56
Ghana Ghana	2005	* 22 754	* 4 000	* 2 800	9 053	* 17.6	* 12.3	* 39.8	84.96
	2010	22 754	* 4 620	* 2 700	9 195	* 20.3	* 11.9	40.4	84.96
	2015	* 22 754	* 4 700	* 2 700	9 337	* 20.7	* 11.9	* 41.0	84.96
	2018	...	...	...	...	...	...	...	84.96
Gibraltar Gibraltar	2005	1	...	...	* 0	...	...	* 0.0	34.98
	2010	1	...	...	* 0	...	...	* 0.0	34.98
	2015	1	...	...	* 0	...	...	* 0.0	34.98
	2018	...	...	...	...	...	...	...	34.98
Greece Grèce	2005	* 12 890	2 639	1 136	* 3 752	* 20.5	* 8.8	* 29.1	66.10
	2010	* 12 890	2 567	1 137	* 3 903	* 19.9	* 8.8	* 30.3	73.17
	2015	* 12 890	* 2 224	* 1 109	* 4 054	* 17.3	* 8.6	* 31.5	73.17
	2018	...	...	...	...	...	...	...	73.17
Greenland Groenland	2005	41 045	1	...	* ~0	~0.0	...	* ~0.0	26.11
	2010	41 045	1	...	* ~0	~0.0	...	* ~0.0	26.37
	2015	41 045	1	...	* ~0	~0.0	...	* ~0.0	30.26
	2018	...	...	...	...	...	...	...	30.26
Grenada Grenade	2005	34	* 2	* 4	* 17	* 5.9	* 11.8	* 50.0	30.16
	2010	34	* 3	* 4	* 17	* 8.8	* 11.8	* 50.0	30.16
	2015	34	* 3	* 4	* 17	* 8.8	* 11.8	* 50.0	42.66
	2018	...	...	...	...	...	...	...	42.66
Guadeloupe Guadeloupe	2005	169	19	4	* 74	11.2	2.4	* 43.8	53.38
	2010	* 169	21	3	* 73	* 12.4	* 2.0	* 43.1	80.65
	2015	* 169	23	3	* 73	* 13.5	* 1.8	* 43.0	80.75
	2018	...	...	...	...	...	...	...	80.75
Guam Guam	2005	54	* 2	* 10	* 25	* 3.7	* 18.5	* 46.3	40.17
	2010	54	* 1	* 9	* 25	* 1.9	* 16.7	* 46.3	40.17
	2015	54	* 1	* 9	* 25	* 1.9	* 16.7	* 46.3	40.17
	2018	...	...	...	...	...	...	...	40.17
Guatemala Guatemala	2005	10 716	1 400	841	3 938	13.1	7.8	36.7	27.65
	2010	* 10 716	* 1 196	* 970	3 722	* 11.2	* 9.1	* 34.7	30.75
	2015	* 10 716	934	1 061	3 540	* 8.7	* 9.9	* 33.0	30.75
	2018	...	...	...	...	...	...	...	30.75
Guinea Guinée	2005	* 24 572	* 2 741	* 680	6 724	* 11.2	* 2.8	* 27.4	76.38
	2010	* 24 572	* 2 900	* 700	6 544	* 11.8	* 2.8	* 26.6	76.38
	2015	* 24 572	* 3 100	* 700	6 364	* 12.6	* 2.8	* 25.9	76.38
	2018	...	...	...	...	...	...	...	76.38
Guinea-Bissau Guinée-Bissau	2005	* 2 812	* 280	* 250	* 2 072	* 10.0	* 8.9	* 73.7	52.18
	2010	* 2 812	* 300	* 250	* 2 022	* 10.7	* 8.9	* 71.9	52.18
	2015	* 2 812	* 300	* 250	* 1 972	* 10.7	* 8.9	* 70.1	52.60
	2018	...	...	...	...	...	...	...	52.60
Guyana Guyana	2005	* 19 685	* 420	* 28	16 602	* 2.1	* 0.1	* 84.3	...
	2010	* 19 685	* 420	* 28	16 576	* 2.1	* 0.1	* 84.2	...
	2015	* 19 685	* 420	* 30	16 526	* 2.1	* 0.2	* 84.0	...

24 Land *(continued)*
Thousand hectares and percent of total land

Terres *(suite)*
Milliers d'hectares et pourcentage de la superficie totale

Region, country or area Région, pays ou zone	Year Année	Area – Superficie ('000 hectares) Total land Superficie totale	Arable land Terres arables	Permanent crops Cultures permanentes	Forest cover Superficie forestière	Area – Superficie (Percent of total)& Arable land Terres arables	Permanent crops Cultures Permanentes&	Forest cover Superficie forestière	Sites protected for terrestrial biodiversity Sites pour la bio. terre. dans aires protég. (%)&&
Haiti Haïti	2005	* 2 756	* 900	* 280	105	* 32.7	* 10.2	* 3.8	10.45
	2010	* 2 756	* 1 100	* 280	101	* 39.9	* 10.2	* 3.7	10.45
	2015	* 2 756	* 1 070	* 280	97	* 38.8	* 10.2	* 3.5	10.45
	2018	...	...	...	...	...	...	...	10.45
Heard Is. and McDonald Is. Île Heard-et-Îles MacDonald	2005	...	...	...	...	...	...	...	100.00
	2010	...	...	...	...	...	...	...	100.00
	2018	...	...	...	...	...	...	...	100.00
Honduras Honduras	2005	* 11 189	* 1 050	* 400	5 792	* 9.4	* 3.6	* 51.8	57.47
	2010	* 11 189	* 1 020	* 450	5 192	* 9.1	* 4.0	* 46.4	57.58
	2015	* 11 189	* 1 020	* 455	4 592	* 9.1	* 4.1	* 41.0	65.03
	2018	...	...	...	...	...	...	...	65.03
Hungary Hongrie	2005	8 961	4 601	205	1 983	51.3	2.3	22.1	81.02
	2010	9 053	4 392	188	2 046	48.5	2.1	22.6	82.86
	2015	* 9 053	4 412	173	2 069	* 48.7	* 1.9	* 22.9	82.90
	2018	...	...	...	...	...	...	...	82.90
Iceland Islande	2005	10 025	129	...	37	1.3	...	0.4	15.00
	2010	10 025	123	...	43	1.2	...	0.4	15.65
	2015	* 10 025	121	...	49	* 1.2	...	* 0.5	18.02
	2018	...	...	...	...	...	...	...	18.02
India Inde	2005	297 319	* 159 444	* 10 230	67 709	* 53.6	* 3.4	22.8	22.57
	2010	* 297 319	* 157 009	* 12 225	69 790	* 52.8	* 4.1	* 23.5	22.57
	2015	* 297 319	* 156 463	* 13 000	70 682	* 52.6	* 4.4	* 23.8	26.09
	2018	...	...	...	...	...	...	...	26.10
Indonesia Indonésie	2005	181 157	* 22 946	* 17 900	97 857	* 12.7	* 9.9	54.0	21.25
	2010	* 181 157	* 23 600	* 21 000	94 432	* 13.0	* 11.6	* 52.1	22.81
	2015	* 181 157	* 23 500	* 22 500	91 010	* 13.0	* 12.4	* 50.2	23.48
	2018	...	...	...	...	...	...	...	23.48
Iran (Islamic Republic of) Iran (Rép. islamique d')	2005	162 876	16 533	1 574	10 692	10.2	1.0	6.6	47.90
	2010	162 876	15 390	1 672	10 692	9.4	1.0	6.6	48.62
	2015	* 162 876	* 14 687	* 1 789	10 692	* 9.0	* 1.1	* 6.6	48.62
	2018	...	...	...	...	...	...	...	48.62
Iraq Iraq	2005	* 43 737	* 5 200	* 190	* 825	* 11.9	* 0.4	* 1.9	0.00
	2010	* 43 432	* 4 000	* 220	* 825	* 9.2	* 0.5	* 1.9	1.34
	2015	* 43 432	* 5 034	* 235	* 825	* 11.6	* 0.5	* 1.9	4.93
	2018	...	...	...	...	...	...	...	5.10
Ireland Irlande	2005	6 889	1 184	3	695	17.2	~0.0	10.1	86.72
	2010	6 889	1 011	2	726	14.7	~0.0	10.5	89.30
	2015	* 6 889	* 1 029	1	754	* 14.9	* ~0.0	* 10.9	89.93
	2018	...	...	...	...	...	...	...	89.93
Isle of Man Île de Man	2005	57	18	...	* 3	31.2	...	* 6.1	...
	2010	57	25	...	* 3	44.5	...	* 6.1	...
	2015	57	23	...	* 3	40.7	...	* 6.1	...
Israel Israël	2005	2 164	* 311	70	155	* 14.4	3.2	7.2	13.84
	2010	2 164	* 294	77	154	* 13.6	3.6	7.1	15.60
	2015	2 164	* 297	97	165	* 13.7	4.5	7.6	15.66
	2018	...	...	...	...	...	...	...	15.66
Italy Italie	2005	29 414	7 780	2 554	8 759	26.5	8.7	29.8	75.14
	2010	* 29 414	7 042	2 588	9 028	* 23.9	* 8.8	* 30.7	77.95
	2015	* 29 414	6 601	2 447	9 297	* 22.4	* 8.3	* 31.6	77.96
	2018	...	...	...	...	...	...	...	77.96
Jamaica Jamaïque	2005	* 1 083	* 128	* 110	339	* 11.8	* 10.2	* 31.3	22.01
	2010	* 1 083	* 120	* 95	337	* 11.1	* 8.8	* 31.1	22.01
	2015	* 1 083	* 120	* 95	335	* 11.1	* 8.8	* 31.0	22.03
	2018	...	...	...	...	...	...	...	22.03
Japan Japon	2005	* 36 450	4 360	332	24 935	* 12.0	* 0.9	* 68.4	64.47
	2010	* 36 455	4 282	311	24 966	* 11.7	* 0.9	* 68.5	64.65
	2015	* 36 456	* 4 201	* 295	24 958	* 11.5	* 0.8	* 68.5	68.47
	2018	...	...	...	...	...	...	...	68.47
Jordan Jordanie	2005	8 824	185	86	* 98	2.1	1.0	* 1.1	...
	2010	8 878	178	83	* 98	2.0	0.9	* 1.1	...
	2015	* 8 878	* 228	86	* 98	* 2.6	* 1.0	* 1.1	...

24 Land *(continued)*

Thousand hectares and percent of total land

Terres *(suite)*

Milliers d'hectares et pourcentage de la superficie totale

Region, country or area Région, pays ou zone	Year Année	Area – Superficie ('000 hectares) Total land Superficie totale	Arable land Terres arables	Permanent crops Cultures permanentes	Forest cover Superficie forestière	Area – Superficie (Percent of total)& Arable land Terres arables	Permanent crops Cultures Permanentes&	Forest cover Superficie forestière	Sites protected for terrestrial biodiversity Sites pour la bio. terre. dans aires protég. (%)&&
Kazakhstan	2005	* 269 970	* 28 562	116	* 3 337	* 10.6	* ~0.0	* 1.2	9.64
Kazakhstan	2010	* 269 970	28 684	116	* 3 309	* 10.6	* ~0.0	* 1.2	14.75
	2015	* 269 970	* 29 395	* 132	* 3 309	* 10.9	* ~0.0	* 1.2	15.99
	2018	...	...	...	...	...	...	...	16.29
Kenya	2005	* 56 914	* 5 264	438	4 047	* 9.2	* 0.8	* 7.1	35.52
Kenya	2010	* 56 914	* 5 500	* 520	4 230	* 9.7	* 0.9	* 7.4	36.80
	2015	* 56 914	* 5 800	* 530	4 413	* 10.2	* 0.9	* 7.8	37.50
	2018	...	...	...	...	...	...	...	37.50
Kiribati	2005	81	* 2	* 32	* 12	* 2.5	* 3 200.0	* 15.0	12.54
Kiribati	2010	* 81	* 2	* 32	* 12	* 2.5	* 3 200.0	* 15.0	52.54
	2015	* 81	* 2	* 32	* 12	* 2.5	* 3 200.0	* 15.0	52.54
	2018	...	...	...	...	...	...	...	52.54
Kuwait	2005	1 782	* 11	* 3	* 6	* 0.6	* 0.2	* 0.3	46.27
Koweït	2010	1 782	* 10	* 6	* 6	* 0.6	* 0.3	* 0.4	46.27
	2015	1 782	* 8	6	* 6	* 0.4	0.3	* 0.4	59.03
	2018	...	...	...	...	...	...	...	59.03
Kyrgyzstan	2005	* 19 180	1 284	72	869	* 6.7	* 0.4	* 4.5	22.36
Kirghizistan	2010	* 19 180	1 276	74	677	* 6.7	* 0.4	* 3.5	22.36
	2015	* 19 180	* 1 281	* 75	637	* 6.7	* 0.4	* 3.3	22.62
	2018	...	...	...	...	...	...	...	22.62
Lao People's Dem. Rep.	2005	23 080	* 1 150	* 85	16 870	* 5.0	* 0.4	73.1	44.04
Rép. dém. populaire lao	2010	* 23 080	* 1 400	* 130	17 816	* 6.1	* 0.6	* 77.2	45.48
	2015	* 23 080	* 1 525	* 169	18 761	* 6.6	* 0.7	* 81.3	45.48
	2018	...	...	...	...	...	...	...	45.48
Latvia	2005	6 220	1 092	13	3 297	17.6	0.2	53.0	97.22
Lettonie	2010	6 224	1 173	7	3 354	18.8	0.1	53.9	97.26
	2015	* 6 218	1 230	7	3 356	* 19.8	* 0.1	* 54.0	97.26
	2018	...	...	...	...	...	...	...	97.26
Lebanon	2005	* 1 023	* 142	141	137	* 13.9	* 13.8	* 13.3	11.57
Liban	2010	* 1 023	114	126	137	* 11.1	* 12.3	* 13.4	11.57
	2015	* 1 023	* 132	* 126	137	* 12.9	* 12.3	* 13.4	13.08
	2018	...	...	...	...	...	...	...	13.08
Lesotho	2005	3 036	323	* 4	43	10.6	* 0.1	1.4	15.27
Lesotho	2010	3 036	322	* 4	44	10.6	* 0.1	1.4	15.27
	2015	3 036	* 272	* 5	49	* 9.0	* 0.2	1.6	15.27
	2018	...	...	...	...	...	...	...	15.27
Liberia	2005	9 632	* 400	* 215	4 479	* 4.2	* 2.2	46.5	16.36
Libéria	2010	9 632	* 480	* 180	4 329	* 5.0	* 1.9	44.9	16.36
	2015	9 632	* 500	* 200	4 179	* 5.2	* 2.1	43.4	16.36
	2018	...	...	...	...	...	...	...	16.36
Libya	2005	175 954	* 1 750	* 335	* 217	* 1.0	* 0.2	* 0.1	4.60
Libye	2010	175 954	* 1 716	* 335	* 217	* 1.0	* 0.2	* 0.1	4.60
	2015	* 175 954	* 1 720	* 330	* 217	* 1.0	* 0.2	* 0.1	4.60
	2018	...	...	...	...	...	...	...	4.60
Liechtenstein	2005	16	* 4	...	* 7	* 24.4	...	* 43.1	75.82
Liechtenstein	2010	16	* 3	...	* 7	* 20.6	...	* 43.1	75.82
	2015	16	* 2	...	* 7	* 13.5	...	* 43.1	75.82
	2018	...	...	...	...	...	...	...	75.82
Lithuania	2005	6 268	1 907	40	2 121	30.4	0.6	33.8	89.59
Lituanie	2010	6 268	2 127	31	2 170	33.9	0.5	34.6	91.56
	2015	6 265	* 2 173	* 34	2 180	* 34.7	* 0.5	34.8	91.56
	2018	...	...	...	...	...	...	...	91.56
Luxembourg	2005	259	60	2	* 87	23.2	0.8	* 33.5	62.77
Luxembourg	2010	259	62	2	* 87	23.9	0.6	* 33.5	62.77
	2015	259	63	2	* 87	24.2	0.6	* 33.5	78.61
	2018	...	...	...	...	...	...	...	78.68
Madagascar	2005	* 58 154	* 3 000	* 600	12 838	* 5.2	* 1.0	* 22.1	19.68
Madagascar	2010	* 58 154	* 3 500	* 600	12 553	* 6.0	* 1.0	* 21.6	21.74
	2015	* 58 180	* 3 500	* 620	12 473	* 6.0	* 1.1	* 21.4	22.11
	2018	...	...	...	...	...	...	...	24.25

24 Land *(continued)*
Thousand hectares and percent of total land

Terres *(suite)*
Milliers d'hectares et pourcentage de la superficie totale

Region, country or area Région, pays ou zone	Year Année	Area – Superficie ('000 hectares) Total land Superficie totale	Arable land Terres arables	Permanent crops Cultures permanentes	Forest cover Superficie forestière	Area – Superficie (Percent of total)& Arable land Terres arables	Permanent crops Cultures Permanentes&	Forest cover Superficie forestière	Sites protected for terrestrial biodiversity Sites pour la bio. terre. dans aires protég. (%)&&
Malawi Malawi	2005	9 428	* 3 200	* 130	3 402	* 33.9	* 1.4	36.1	81.64
	2010	9 428	* 3 700	* 135	3 237	* 39.2	* 1.4	34.3	81.64
	2015	* 9 428	* 3 800	* 140	3 147	* 40.3	* 1.5	* 33.4	81.64
	2018	...	...	...	...	...	...	...	81.64
Malaysia Malaisie	2005	* 32 855	* 958	* 5 900	20 890	* 2.9	* 18.0	* 63.6	39.08
	2010	* 32 855	* 931	* 6 250	22 124	* 2.8	* 19.0	* 67.3	39.50
	2015	* 32 855	* 954	* 6 600	22 195	* 2.9	* 20.1	* 67.6	39.50
	2018	...	...	...	...	...	...	...	39.50
Maldives Maldives	2005	30	* 3	* 5	* 1	* 10.0	* 16.7	* 3.3	0.00
	2010	30	* 4	* 3	* 1	* 13.0	* 10.0	* 3.3	0.00
	2015	* 30	* 4	* 3	* 1	* 13.0	* 10.0	* 3.3	0.00
	2018	...	...	...	...	...	...	...	0.00
Mali Mali	2005	122 019	* 5 603	* 150	5 505	* 4.6	* 0.1	4.5	33.77
	2010	* 122 019	* 6 261	* 150	5 110	* 5.1	* 0.1	* 4.2	33.77
	2015	* 122 019	* 6 411	* 150	4 715	* 5.3	* 0.1	* 3.9	33.77
	2018	...	...	...	...	...	...	...	33.77
Malta Malte	2005	32	8	1	* ~0	25.6	3.4	* 1.1	99.40
	2010	32	9	1	* ~0	28.4	3.9	* 1.1	99.40
	2015	32	9	1	* ~0	28.0	3.9	* 1.1	99.40
	2018	...	...	...	...	...	...	...	99.40
Marshall Islands Îles Marshall	2005	18	2	8	* 13	11.1	44.4	* 70.2	16.80
	2010	18	* 2	* 8	* 13	* 11.1	* 44.4	* 70.2	23.42
	2015	18	* 2	* 7	* 13	* 11.1	* 36.1	* 70.2	25.38
	2018	...	...	...	...	...	...	...	25.38
Martinique Martinique	2005	* 106	10	8	49	* 9.4	* 7.5	* 45.8	75.08
	2010	* 106	10	7	49	* 9.6	* 7.0	* 45.8	99.12
	2015	* 106	11	6	49	* 10.5	* 6.0	* 45.8	99.12
	2018	...	...	...	...	...	...	...	99.12
Mauritania Mauritanie	2005	103 070	* 400	* 11	267	* 0.4	* ~0.0	0.3	14.62
	2010	103 070	* 450	* 11	242	* 0.4	* ~0.0	0.2	14.62
	2015	103 070	* 450	* 11	225	* 0.4	* ~0.0	0.2	14.62
	2018	...	...	...	...	...	...	...	14.62
Mauritius Maurice	2005	203	* 85	* 4	38	* 41.9	* 2.0	18.8	9.49
	2010	203	* 80	* 4	38	* 39.4	* 2.0	18.9	9.57
	2015	* 203	* 74	* 4	39	* 36.5	* 2.0	* 19.0	10.39
	2018	...	...	...	...	...	...	...	10.39
Mayotte Mayotte	2005	37	* 8	* 10	* 8	* 20.6	* 26.7	* 20.7	15.63
	2010	37	* 9	3	* 7	* 23.3	9.1	* 18.2	54.09
	2015	37	* 9	* 3	* 6	* 23.8	* 8.7	* 15.6	54.09
	2018	...	...	...	...	...	...	...	54.09
Mexico Mexique	2005	194 395	* 23 296	2 607	67 083	* 12.0	1.3	34.5	24.15
	2010	194 395	* 23 507	2 651	66 498	* 12.1	1.4	34.2	29.05
	2015	* 194 395	* 22 913	2 695	66 040	* 11.8	* 1.4	* 34.0	31.03
	2018	...	...	...	...	...	...	...	33.39
Micronesia (Fed. States of) Micronésie (États féd. de)	2005	70	* 3	* 17	* 64	* 3.6	* 24.3	* 91.4	1.29
	2010	70	* 2	* 17	* 64	* 2.9	* 24.3	* 91.6	1.29
	2015	70	* 2	* 17	* 64	* 2.9	* 24.3	* 91.8	1.29
	2018	...	...	...	...	...	...	...	1.29
Mongolia Mongolie	2005	* 155 356	* 695	* 2	11 308	* 0.4	* ~0.0	* 7.3	36.45
	2010	* 155 356	* 614	* 3	13 039	* 0.4	* ~0.0	* 8.4	39.09
	2015	* 155 356	* 567	* 5	12 553	* 0.4	* ~0.0	* 8.1	41.98
	2018	...	...	...	...	...	...	...	43.67
Montenegro Monténégro	2005	...	...	...	...	...	...	...	11.86
	2010	* 1 345	172	16	827	* 12.8	* 1.2	* 61.5	11.86
	2015	* 1 345	9	5	827	* 0.6	* 0.4	* 61.5	11.86
	2018	...	...	...	...	...	...	...	11.86
Montserrat Montserrat	2005	10	* 2	...	* 3	* 20.0	...	* 25.0	0.00
	2010	10	* 2	...	* 3	* 20.0	...	* 25.0	0.00
	2015	10	* 2	...	* 3	* 20.0	...	* 25.0	30.63
	2018	...	...	...	...	...	...	...	30.63

24 Land *(continued)*

Thousand hectares and percent of total land

Terres *(suite)*

Milliers d'hectares et pourcentage de la superficie totale

Region, country or area Région, pays ou zone	Year Année	Area – Superficie ('000 hectares) Total land Superficie totale	Arable land Terres arables	Permanent crops Cultures permanentes	Forest cover Superficie forestière	Area – Superficie (Percent of total)& Arable land Terres arables	Permanent crops Cultures Permanentes&	Forest cover Superficie forestière	Sites protected for terrestrial biodiversity Sites pour la bio. terre. dans aires protég. (%)&&
Morocco Maroc	2005	* 44 630	* 8 122	* 867	5 401	* 18.2	* 1.9	* 12.1	13.32
	2010	* 44 630	7 729	1 259	5 672	* 17.3	* 2.8	* 12.7	14.72
	2015	* 44 630	* 8 130	* 1 462	5 632	* 18.2	* 3.3	* 12.6	43.00
	2018	...	...	...	...	...	...	...	43.00
Mozambique Mozambique	2005	78 638	* 5 000	* 250	40 079	* 6.4	* 0.3	51.0	19.02
	2010	78 638	* 5 650	* 300	38 972	* 7.2	* 0.4	49.6	19.02
	2015	78 638	* 5 650	* 300	37 940	* 7.2	* 0.4	48.2	31.31
	2018	...	...	...	...	...	...	...	31.31
Myanmar Myanmar	2005	65 336	10 059	896	33 321	15.4	1.4	51.0	22.46
	2010	65 326	10 811	1 406	31 773	16.5	2.2	48.6	22.46
	2015	* 65 308	* 10 879	* 1 550	29 041	* 16.7	* 2.4	* 44.5	22.46
	2018	...	...	...	...	...	...	...	22.91
Namibia Namibie	2005	* 82 329	* 814	* 6	7 661	* 1.0	* ~0.0	* 9.3	44.58
	2010	* 82 329	* 800	* 9	7 290	* 1.0	* ~0.0	* 8.9	82.37
	2015	* 82 329	* 800	* 9	6 919	* 1.0	* ~0.0	* 8.4	85.38
	2018	...	...	...	...	...	...	...	85.38
Nauru Nauru	2005	2	...	* ~0	* 0	...	* 20.0	* 0.0	0.00
	2010	2	...	* ~0	* 0	...	* 20.0	* 0.0	0.00
	2015	2	...	* ~0	* 0	...	* 20.0	* 0.0	0.00
	2018	...	...	...	...	...	...	...	0.00
Nepal Népal	2005	14 335	* 2 280	* 133	3 636	* 15.9	* 0.9	25.4	50.32
	2010	14 335	* 2 180	* 152	3 636	* 15.2	* 1.1	25.4	54.63
	2015	14 335	* 2 114	* 212	3 636	* 14.7	* 1.5	25.4	54.63
	2018	...	...	...	...	...	...	...	54.64
Netherlands Pays-Bas	2005	3 376	1 111	32	365	32.9	0.9	10.8	91.32
	2010	3 373	1 023	36	373	30.3	1.1	11.1	91.37
	2015	* 3 369	1 033	38	376	* 30.7	* 1.1	* 11.2	91.37
	2018	...	...	...	...	...	...	...	91.37
Netherlands Antilles [former] Antilles néerlandaises [anc.]	2005	80	* 8	...	* 1	* 10.0	...	* 1.5	...
	2010	80	* 8	...	* 1	* 10.0	...	* 1.5	...
	2015	80	* 8	...	* 1	* 10.0	...	* 1.5	...
New Caledonia Nouvelle-Calédonie	2005	* 1 828	* 7	* 4	* 839	* 0.4	* 0.2	* 45.9	15.50
	2010	1 828	* 7	* 4	* 839	* 0.4	* 0.2	* 45.9	66.12
	2015	* 1 828	* 6	* 4	* 839	* 0.3	* 0.2	* 45.9	66.39
	2018	...	...	...	...	...	...	...	66.39
New Zealand Nouvelle-Zélande	2005	26 331	425	63	10 183	1.6	0.2	38.7	42.48
	2010	26 331	499	71	10 151	1.9	0.3	38.6	44.00
	2015	* 26 331	* 590	* 67	10 152	* 2.2	* 0.3	* 38.6	44.27
	2018	...	...	...	...	...	...	...	44.27
Nicaragua Nicaragua	2005	12 034	* 2 000	* 290	3 464	* 16.6	* 2.4	28.8	73.68
	2010	12 034	* 1 531	* 295	3 114	* 12.7	* 2.5	25.9	73.68
	2015	12 034	* 1 504	* 286	3 114	* 12.5	* 2.4	25.9	73.68
	2018	...	...	...	...	...	...	...	73.68
Niger Niger	2005	* 126 670	* 14 123	* 60	1 266	* 11.1	* ~0.0	* 1.0	40.66
	2010	* 126 670	* 15 100	* 100	1 204	* 11.9	* 0.1	* 1.0	40.66
	2015	* 126 670	* 16 800	* 100	1 142	* 13.3	* 0.1	* 0.9	42.75
	2018	...	...	...	...	...	...	...	42.75
Nigeria Nigéria	2005	* 91 077	* 36 000	* 6 400	11 089	* 39.5	* 7.0	* 12.2	69.18
	2010	* 91 077	* 33 000	* 6 700	9 041	* 36.2	* 7.4	* 9.9	79.62
	2015	* 91 077	* 34 000	* 6 500	6 993	* 37.3	* 7.1	* 7.7	79.62
	2018	...	...	...	...	...	...	...	79.62
Niue Nioué	2005	26	* 1	* 3	* 19	* 3.8	* 10.8	* 73.5	95.28
	2010	26	* 1	* 3	* 19	* 3.8	* 11.5	* 71.5	95.28
	2015	26	* 1	* 3	* 18	* 3.8	* 11.5	* 69.6	95.28
	2018	...	...	...	...	...	...	...	95.28
Norfolk Island Île Norfolk	2005	4	...	...	* ~0	...	...	* 11.5	44.38
	2010	4	...	...	* ~0	...	...	* 11.5	44.38
	2015	4	...	...	* ~0	...	...	* 11.5	59.00
	2018	...	...	...	...	...	...	...	59.00

24 Land *(continued)*
Thousand hectares and percent of total land

Terres *(suite)*
Milliers d'hectares et pourcentage de la superficie totale

Region, country or area Région, pays ou zone	Year Année	Area – Superficie ('000 hectares) Total land Superficie totale	Arable land Terres arables	Permanent crops Cultures permanentes	Forest cover Superficie forestière	Area – Superficie (Percent of total)& Arable land Terres arables	Permanent crops Cultures Permanentes&	Forest cover Superficie forestière	Sites protected for terrestrial biodiversity Sites pour la bio. terre. dans aires protég. (%)&&
Northern Mariana Islands Îles Mariannes du Nord	2005	46	*1	*1	*31	*2.2	*2.2	*67.7	3.84
	2010	46	*1	*1	*30	*2.2	*2.2	*65.9	40.59
	2015	46	*1	*1	*30	*2.2	*2.2	*64.1	40.59
	2018	...	...	...	...	...	...	...	40.59
Norway Norvège	2005	36 525	862	5	12 092	2.4	~0.0	33.1	51.98
	2010	36 525	826	5	12 102	2.3	~0.0	33.1	53.85
	2015	*36 525	*806	*5	12 112	*2.2	*~0.0	*33.2	54.85
	2018	...	...	...	...	...	...	...	55.91
Oman Oman	2005	30 950	28	37	2	0.1	0.1	~0.0	7.82
	2010	30 950	34	38	2	0.1	0.1	~0.0	7.82
	2015	*30 950	*38	*31	2	*0.1	*0.1	*~0.0	11.46
	2018	...	...	...	...	...	...	...	11.46
Other non-specified areas Autres zones non-spécifiées	*2005	3 541	603	230	...	17.0	6.5	...	...
	*2010	3 541	598	215	...	16.9	6.1	...	...
	*2015	3 541	592	205	...	16.7	5.8	...	...
Pakistan Pakistan	2005	77 088	30 170	795	*1 902	39.1	1.0	*2.5	36.64
	2010	*77 088	29 390	852	*1 687	*38.1	*1.1	*2.2	36.64
	2015	*77 088	*30 440	*812	*1 472	*39.5	*1.1	*1.9	36.64
	2018	...	...	...	...	...	...	...	36.64
Palau Palaos	2005	*46	*1	*2	40	*2.2	*4.3	*87.6	17.90
	2010	*46	*1	*2	40	*2.2	*4.3	*87.6	17.90
	2015	*46	*1	*2	40	*2.2	*4.3	*87.6	36.55
	2018	...	...	...	...	...	...	...	36.55
Panama Panama	2005	7 434	*548	*160	4 782	*7.4	*2.2	64.3	37.84
	2010	*7 434	569	189	4 699	*7.7	*2.5	*63.2	38.84
	2015	*7 434	*563	*185	4 617	*7.6	*2.5	*62.1	38.84
	2018	...	...	...	...	...	...	...	38.84
Papua New Guinea Papouasie-Nvl-Guinée	2005	*45 286	*240	*600	33 586	*0.5	*1.3	*74.2	7.32
	2010	*45 286	*300	*700	33 573	*0.7	*1.5	*74.1	7.32
	2015	*45 286	*300	*700	33 559	*0.7	*1.5	*74.1	7.32
	2018	...	...	...	...	...	...	...	7.32
Paraguay Paraguay	2005	*39 730	*3 460	*100	18 475	*8.7	*0.3	*46.5	23.31
	2010	*39 730	*4 145	*85	16 950	*10.4	*0.2	*42.7	23.31
	2015	*39 730	*4 800	*85	15 323	*12.1	*0.2	*38.6	23.31
	2018	...	...	...	...	...	...	...	23.31
Peru Pérou	2005	*128 000	*3 930	*1 090	75 528	*3.1	*0.9	*59.0	...
	2010	*128 000	*4 085	*1 307	74 811	*3.2	*1.0	*58.4	...
	2015	*128 000	*4 152	*1 379	73 973	*3.2	*1.1	*57.8	...
Philippines Philippines	2005	29 817	*5 005	*4 850	7 074	*16.8	*16.3	23.7	38.72
	2010	29 817	*5 300	*5 300	6 840	*17.8	*17.8	22.9	41.40
	2015	29 817	*5 590	*5 350	8 040	*18.7	*17.9	27.0	41.68
	2018	...	...	...	...	...	...	...	41.68
Pitcairn Pitcairn	2005	5	...	...	*4	...	...	*74.5	0.00
	2010	5	...	...	*4	...	...	*74.5	0.00
	2015	5	...	...	*4	...	...	*74.5	0.00
	2018	...	...	...	...	...	...	...	27.68
Poland Pologne	2005	30 633	12 141	378	9 200	39.6	1.2	30.0	73.43
	2010	30 628	10 829	390	9 329	35.4	1.3	30.5	87.87
	2015	30 619	10 887	391	9 435	35.6	1.3	30.8	88.10
	2018	...	...	...	...	...	...	...	88.10
Portugal Portugal	2005	*9 147	*1 278	*774	3 296	*14.0	*8.5	*36.0	60.46
	2010	*9 159	1 148	714	3 239	*12.5	*7.8	*35.4	70.97
	2015	*9 161	1 132	751	3 182	*12.4	*8.2	*34.7	73.90
	2018	...	...	...	...	...	...	...	73.90
Puerto Rico Porto Rico	2005	887	*66	*37	463	*7.5	*4.2	52.2	33.98
	2010	*887	*57	*50	479	*6.4	*5.6	*54.0	33.98
	2015	*887	*61	*50	496	*6.9	*5.6	*55.9	33.98
	2018	...	...	...	...	...	...	...	33.98
Qatar Qatar	2005	1 161	*12	*3	*0	*1.0	*0.2	*0.0	49.97
	2010	1 161	*13	3	*0	*1.1	0.2	*0.0	49.97
	2015	*1 161	*13	*3	*0	*1.1	*0.2	*0.0	49.97
	2018	...	...	...	...	...	...	...	49.97

Land *(continued)*
Thousand hectares and percent of total land

Terres *(suite)*
Milliers d'hectares et pourcentage de la superficie totale

		Area – Superficie ('000 hectares)				Area – Superficie (Percent of total)&			Sites protected for terrestrial biodiversity
Region, country or area Région, pays ou zone	Year Année	Total land Superficie totale	Arable land Terres arables	Permanent crops Cultures permanentes	Forest cover Superficie forestière	Arable land Terres arables	Permanent crops Cultures Permanentes&	Forest cover Superficie forestière	Sites pour la bio. terre. dans aires protég. (%)&&
Republic of Korea République de Corée	2005	9 685	1 643	181	6 255	17.0	1.9	64.6	27.31
	2010	* 9 723	* 1 507	208	6 222	* 15.5	* 2.1	* 64.0	36.40
	2015	* 9 748	* 1 465	215	6 184	* 15.0	* 2.2	* 63.4	36.61
	2018	...	...	...	...	...	...	...	36.61
Republic of Moldova République de Moldova	2005	3 289	1 833	302	* 363	55.7	9.2	* 11.0	23.61
	2010	3 285	1 813	299	* 386	55.2	9.1	* 11.8	23.61
	2015	* 3 287	1 823	289	* 409	* 55.5	* 8.8	* 12.4	23.61
	2018	...	...	...	...	...	...	...	23.61
Réunion Réunion	2005	* 250	35	3	85	* 14.0	* 1.2	* 34.0	0.58
	2010	* 250	35	3	88	* 14.1	* 1.2	* 35.2	45.82
	2015	* 251	34	3	88	* 13.6	* 1.2	* 35.1	45.82
	2018	...	...	...	...	...	...	...	45.82
Romania Roumanie	2005	22 998	8 985	510	6 391	39.1	2.2	27.8	14.84
	2010	23 005	9 146	463	6 515	39.8	2.0	28.3	64.98
	2015	* 23 008	8 757	423	6 861	* 38.1	* 1.8	* 29.8	77.23
	2018	...	...	...	...	...	...	...	77.29
Russian Federation Fédération de Russie	2005	1 638 139	121 781	1 800	808 790	7.4	0.1	49.4	26.81
	2010	* 1 637 687	* 119 000	* 1 650	815 136	* 7.3	* 0.1	* 49.8	26.84
	2015	* 1 637 687	* 123 122	* 1 600	814 931	* 7.5	* 0.1	* 49.8	26.84
	2018	...	...	...	...	...	...	...	26.88
Rwanda Rwanda	2005	* 2 467	* 1 083	* 250	385	* 43.9	* 10.1	* 15.6	45.67
	2010	* 2 467	* 1 124	* 250	446	* 45.6	* 10.1	* 18.1	45.67
	2015	* 2 467	* 1 152	* 250	480	* 46.7	* 10.1	* 19.5	45.67
	2018	...	...	...	...	...	...	...	45.67
Saint Barthélemy Saint-Barthélemy	2005	...	...	...	...	...	...	...	23.26
	2010	...	...	...	...	...	...	...	62.29
	2018	...	...	...	...	...	...	...	62.29
Saint Helena Sainte-Hélène	2005	39	* 4	...	* 2	* 10.3	...	* 5.1	0.58[3]
	2010	* 39	* 4	...	* 2	* 10.3	...	* 5.1	16.67[3]
	2015	* 39	* 4	...	* 2	* 10.3	...	* 5.1	54.85[3]
	2018[3]	...	...	...	...	...	...	...	54.85
Saint Kitts and Nevis Saint-Kitts-et-Nevis	2005	26	4	~0	11	15.3	0.1	42.3	29.20
	2010	26	5	~0	11	17.3	0.4	42.3	29.20
	2015	* 26	* 5	* ~0	11	* 19.2	* 0.4	* 42.3	29.20
	2018	...	...	...	...	...	...	...	29.20
Saint Lucia Sainte-Lucie	2005	* 61	* 2	* 8	21	* 3.6	* 12.6	* 34.3	40.32
	2010	* 61	* 3	* 7	21	* 4.9	* 11.5	* 33.8	46.05
	2015	* 61	* 3	* 7	20	* 4.9	* 11.5	* 33.3	46.05
	2018	...	...	...	...	...	...	...	46.05
Saint Martin (French part) St-Martin (partie française)	2005	...	...	...	...	...	...	...	29.21
	2010	...	...	...	...	...	...	...	59.34
	2018	...	...	...	...	...	...	...	59.39
Saint Pierre and Miquelon Saint-Pierre-et-Miquelon	2005	* 23	* 3	...	3	* 13.0	...	* 13.0	...
	2010	* 23	* 3	...	3	* 13.0	...	* 12.6	...
	2015	* 23	* 2	...	3	* 8.7	...	* 12.2	...
Saint Vincent & Grenadines Saint-Vincent-Grenadines	2005	39	* 5	* 3	* 26	* 12.8	* 7.7	* 66.7	42.66
	2010	39	* 5	* 3	* 27	* 12.8	* 7.7	* 69.2	42.66
	2015	39	* 5	* 3	* 27	* 12.8	* 7.7	* 69.2	42.66
	2018	...	...	...	...	...	...	...	42.66
Samoa Samoa	2005	* 283	* 11	* 27	* 171	* 3.9	* 9.5	* 60.4	31.17
	2010	* 283	* 8	* 22	* 171	* 2.8	* 7.8	* 60.4	31.17
	2015	* 283	* 8	* 22	* 171	* 2.8	* 7.8	* 60.4	31.17
	2018	...	...	...	...	...	...	...	36.53
San Marino Saint-Marin	2005	6	* 1	...	* 0	* 16.7	...	* 0.0	...
	2010	6	* 1	...	* 0	* 16.7	...	* 0.0	...
	2015	6	* 1	...	* 0	* 16.7	...	* 0.0	...
Sao Tome and Principe Sao Tomé-et-Principe	2005	* 96	* 8	* 40	56	* 8.3	* 41.7	* 58.3	0.00
	2010	* 96	* 9	* 39	54	* 8.9	* 40.6	* 55.8	58.01
	2015	* 96	* 9	* 39	54	* 9.1	* 40.6	* 55.8	58.01
	2018	...	...	...	...	...	...	...	58.01

24 Land *(continued)*
Thousand hectares and percent of total land

Terres *(suite)*
Milliers d'hectares et pourcentage de la superficie totale

Region, country or area Région, pays ou zone	Year Année	Area – Superficie ('000 hectares) Total land Superficie totale	Arable land Terres arables	Permanent crops Cultures permanentes	Forest cover Superficie forestière	Area – Superficie (Percent of total)& Arable land Terres arables	Permanent crops Cultures Permanentes&	Forest cover Superficie forestière	Sites protected for terrestrial biodiversity Sites pour la bio. terre. dans aires protég. (%)&&
Saudi Arabia	2005	214 969	* 3 500	217	* 977	* 1.6	0.1	* 0.5	20.98
Arabie saoudite	2010	214 969	* 3 180	226	* 977	* 1.5	0.1	* 0.5	20.98
	2015	* 214 969	* 3 502	* 145	* 977	* 1.6	* 0.1	* 0.5	20.98
	2018	...	...	...	...	...	...	...	20.98
Senegal	2005	* 19 253	* 3 126	* 50	8 673	* 16.2	* 0.3	* 45.0	41.12
Sénégal	2010	* 19 253	* 3 800	* 58	8 473	* 19.7	* 0.3	* 44.0	41.12
	2015	* 19 253	* 3 200	* 68	8 273	* 16.6	* 0.4	* 43.0	41.16
	2018	...	...	...	...	...	...	...	41.16
Serbia	2005	...	...	...	...	...	...	...	24.09
Serbie	2010	* 8 746	2 654	190	2 713	* 30.3	* 2.2	* 31.0	26.35
	2015	* 8 746	2 591	188	2 720	* 29.6	* 2.1	* 31.1	30.17
	2018	...	...	...	...	...	...	...	30.23
Serbia and Monten. [former] Serbie-et-Monténégro [anc.]	2005	* 10 200	* 3 505	* 317	3 102	* 34.4	* 3.1	* 30.4	...
Seychelles	2005	46	* 1	* 3	41	* 2.2	* 6.5	88.4	19.46
Seychelles	2010	* 46	* 1	* 2	41	* 2.0	* 3.3	* 88.4	19.71
	2015	* 46	* ~0	* 1	41	* 0.3	* 3.0	* 88.4	19.71
	2018	...	...	...	...	...	...	...	19.71
Sierra Leone	2005	* 7 218	* 1 472	* 140	2 824	* 20.4	* 1.9	* 39.1	55.39
Sierra Leone	2010	* 7 218	* 1 580	* 150	2 726	* 21.9	* 2.1	* 37.8	68.98
	2015	* 7 218	* 1 584	* 165	3 044	* 21.9	* 2.3	* 42.2	80.32
	2018	...	...	...	...	...	...	...	80.32
Singapore	2005	* 69	* 1	* ~0	16	* 1.0	* 0.1	* 23.7	21.14
Singapour	2010	* 70	* 1	* ~0	16	* 0.9	* 0.1	* 23.3	21.14
	2015	* 71	* 1	* ~0	16	* 0.8	* 0.1	* 23.1	21.14
	2018	...	...	...	...	...	...	...	21.14
Sint Maarten (Dutch part)	2005	...	...	...	...	...	...	...	6.37
St-Martin (partie néerland.)	2010	...	...	...	...	...	...	...	6.37
	2018	...	...	...	...	...	...	...	6.37
Slovakia	2005	4 810	1 391	26	1 932	28.9	0.5	40.2	73.09
Slovaquie	2010	4 809	1 392	25	1 939	28.9	0.5	40.3	76.30
	2015	4 808	* 1 383	19	1 940	* 28.8	0.4	40.3	83.62
	2018	...	...	...	...	...	...	...	83.62
Slovenia	2005	2 014	176	28	1 243	8.7	1.4	61.7	86.07
Slovénie	2010	2 014	185	52	1 247	9.2	2.6	61.9	86.08
	2015	2 014	184	53	1 248	9.1	2.7	62.0	88.65
	2018	...	...	...	...	...	...	...	88.65
Solomon Islands	2005	* 2 799	* 16	* 65	* 2 241	* 0.6	* 2.3	* 80.1	7.11
Îles Salomon	2010	* 2 799	* 19	* 80	* 2 213	* 0.7	* 2.9	* 79.1	9.53
	2015	* 2 799	* 20	* 80	* 2 185	* 0.7	* 2.9	* 78.1	9.53
	2018	...	...	...	...	...	...	...	9.53
Somalia	2005	* 62 734	* 1 350	* 27	7 131	* 2.2	* ~0.0	* 11.4	0.00
Somalie	2010	* 62 734	* 1 100	* 28	6 747	* 1.8	* ~0.0	* 10.8	0.00
	2015	* 62 734	* 1 100	* 25	6 363	* 1.8	* ~0.0	* 10.1	0.00
	2018	...	...	...	...	...	...	...	0.00
South Africa	2005	121 309	* 13 175	* 380	9 241	* 10.9	* 0.3	7.6	33.47
Afrique du Sud	2010	121 309	12 533	430	9 241	10.3	0.4	7.6	35.08
	2015	* 121 309	* 12 500	* 413	9 241	* 10.3	* 0.3	* 7.6	37.71
	2018	...	...	...	...	...	...	...	37.71
South Georgia & Sandwich Is.	2005	...	...	...	...	...	...	...	0.00
Géorgie du S.-Îles	2010	...	...	...	...	...	...	...	0.00
Sandwich	2018	...	...	...	...	...	...	...	100.00
South Sudan	2005	...	...	...	...	...	...	...	30.26
Soudan du sud	2010	...	...	...	...	...	...	...	33.64
	2015	...	...	...	7 157	...	...	...	33.64
	2018	...	...	...	...	...	...	...	33.64
Spain	2005	49 909	12 913	4 931	17 282	25.9	9.9	34.6	53.01
Espagne	2010	50 001	12 528	4 693	18 247	25.1	9.4	36.5	54.56
	2015	50 023	12 338	4 696	18 418	24.7	9.4	36.8	56.26
	2018	...	...	...	...	...	...	...	56.26

24 Land *(continued)*
Thousand hectares and percent of total land

Terres *(suite)*
Milliers d'hectares et pourcentage de la superficie totale

Region, country or area Région, pays ou zone	Year Année	Area – Superficie ('000 hectares) Total land Superficie totale	Arable land Terres arables	Permanent crops Cultures permanentes	Forest cover Superficie forestière	Area – Superficie (Percent of total)& Arable land Terres arables	Permanent crops Cultures Permanentes&	Forest cover Superficie forestière	Sites protected for terrestrial biodiversity Sites pour la bio. terre. dans aires protég. (%)&&
Sri Lanka Sri Lanka	2005	6 271	* 1 100	* 970	2 118	* 17.5	* 15.5	33.8	41.74
	2010	6 271	* 1 200	* 980	2 103	* 19.1	* 15.6	33.5	47.49
	2015	6 271	* 1 300	* 1 000	2 070	* 20.7	* 15.9	33.0	49.85
	2018	...	...	...	...	...	...	...	49.85
State of Palestine État de Palestine	2005	602	* 99	115	* 9	* 16.4	19.1	* 1.5	2.47
	2010	602	44	54	* 9	7.3	9.0	* 1.5	2.47
	2015	602	* 64	84	* 9	* 10.6	14.0	* 1.5	2.47
	2018	...	...	...	...	...	...	...	2.47
Sudan Soudan	2005	...	...	...	...	...	...	...	9.09
	2010	...	...	...	...	...	...	...	18.62
	2015	...	* 19 823	* 168	19 210	...	...	...	18.62
	2018	...	...	...	...	...	...	...	25.00
Sudan [former] Soudan [anc.]	2005	237 600	18 750	* 130	28 111	7.9	* 0.1	11.8	...
	2010	237 600	19 878	142	27 239	8.4	0.1	11.5	...
Suriname Suriname	2005	* 15 600	49	* 6	15 371	* 0.3	* ~0.0	* 98.5	51.19
	2010	* 15 600	55	6	15 351	* 0.4	* ~0.0	* 98.4	51.19
	2015	* 15 600	* 65	* 6	15 332	* 0.4	* ~0.0	* 98.3	51.19
	2018	...	...	...	...	...	...	...	51.19
Svalbard and Jan Mayen Is. Îles Svalbard-et-Jan Mayen	2005	...	...	...	...	...	...	...	63.12
	2010	...	...	...	...	...	...	...	67.67
	2018	...	...	...	...	...	...	...	67.69
Sweden Suède	2005	41 034	* 2 694	* 9	28 218	* 6.6	* ~0.0	68.8	56.65
	2010	41 034	* 2 625	* 9	28 073	* 6.4	* ~0.0	68.4	57.79
	2015	40 731	* 2 581	* 9	28 073	* 6.3	* ~0.0	68.9	58.18
	2018	...	...	...	...	...	...	...	58.81
Switzerland Suisse	2005	3 952	406	23	1 217	10.3	0.6	30.8	28.51
	2010	3 952	405	24	1 235	10.2	0.6	31.3	35.22
	2015	* 3 952	398	* 26	1 254	* 10.1	* 0.6	* 31.7	35.23
	2018	...	...	...	...	...	...	...	35.23
Syrian Arab Republic République arabe syrienne	2005	18 357	4 675	887	* 461	25.5	4.8	* 2.5	1.12
	2010	18 363	4 687	1 009	* 491	25.5	5.5	* 2.7	1.12
	2015	* 18 363	* 4 662	* 1 071	* 491	* 25.4	* 5.8	* 2.7	1.12
	2018	...	...	...	...	...	...	...	1.12
Tajikistan Tadjikistan	2005	13 996	* 757	117	410	* 5.4	0.8	2.9	20.46
	2010	* 13 996	* 751	* 130	410	* 5.4	* 0.9	* 2.9	20.46
	2015	* 13 879	* 730	* 140	412	* 5.3	* 1.0	* 3.0	20.99
	2018	...	...	...	...	...	...	...	20.99
Thailand Thaïlande	2005	* 51 089	* 15 200	* 3 610	16 100	* 29.8	* 7.1	* 31.5	67.95
	2010	* 51 089	* 15 760	* 4 500	16 249	* 30.8	* 8.8	* 31.8	71.01
	2015	* 51 089	* 16 810	* 4 500	16 399	* 32.9	* 8.8	* 32.1	71.74
	2018	...	...	...	...	...	...	...	71.74
TFYR of Macedonia ex-R.Y. de Macédoine	2005	2 543	448	39	* 975	17.6	1.5	* 38.3	20.78
	2010	2 522	414	35	* 998	16.4	1.4	* 39.6	21.06
	2015	2 522	415	39	* 998	16.5	1.5	* 39.6	21.06
	2018	...	...	...	...	...	...	...	21.06
Timor-Leste Timor-Leste	2005	1 487	* 170	* 65	* 798	* 11.4	* 4.4	* 53.7	14.91
	2010	* 1 487	* 150	* 72	* 742	* 10.1	* 4.8	* 49.9	38.73
	2015	* 1 487	* 155	* 75	* 686	* 10.4	* 5.0	* 46.1	38.73
	2018	...	...	...	...	...	...	...	38.73
Togo Togo	2005	* 5 439	* 2 100	* 150	386	* 38.6	* 2.8	* 7.1	75.00
	2010	* 5 439	* 2 460	* 205	287	* 45.2	* 3.8	* 5.3	96.98
	2015	* 5 439	* 2 650	* 170	188	* 48.7	* 3.1	* 3.5	96.98
	2018	...	...	...	...	...	...	...	96.98
Tokelau Tokélaou	2005	1	...	* 1	* 0	...	* 60.0	* 0.0	2.59
	2010	1	...	* 1	* 0	...	* 60.0	* 0.0	2.59
	2015	1	...	* 1	* 0	...	* 60.0	* 0.0	2.59
	2018	...	...	...	...	...	...	...	2.59
Tonga Tonga	2005	* 72	* 15	* 11	9	* 20.8	* 15.3	* 12.5	9.31
	2010	72	* 17	* 11	9	* 23.6	* 15.3	12.5	9.31
	2015	72	* 18	* 11	9	* 25.0	* 15.3	12.5	9.31
	2018	...	...	...	...	...	...	...	9.31

24 Land *(continued)*
Thousand hectares and percent of total land

Terres *(suite)*
Milliers d'hectares et pourcentage de la superficie totale

Region, country or area Région, pays ou zone	Year Année	Area – Superficie ('000 hectares) Total land Superficie totale	Arable land Terres arables	Permanent crops Cultures permanentes	Forest cover Superficie forestière	Area – Superficie (Percent of total)& Arable land Terres arables	Permanent crops Cultures Permanentes&	Forest cover Superficie forestière	Sites protected for terrestrial biodiversity Sites pour la bio. terre. dans aires protég. (%)&&
Trinidad and Tobago Trinité-et-Tobago	2005	513	* 25	* 22	230	* 4.9	* 4.3	44.8	40.67
	2010	513	* 25	* 22	226	* 4.9	* 4.3	44.1	40.67
	2015	513	* 25	* 22	234	* 4.9	* 4.3	45.7	40.67
	2018	...	...	...	...	...	...	...	40.67
Tunisia Tunisie	2005	15 536	2 730	2 166	915	17.6	13.9	5.9	15.97
	2010	15 536	2 823	2 363	990	18.2	15.2	6.4	27.21
	2015	* 15 536	* 2 900	* 2 332	1 041	* 18.7	* 15.0	* 6.7	40.85
	2018	...	...	...	...	...	...	...	40.85
Turkey Turquie	2005	76 963	23 830	2 776	10 662	31.0	3.6	13.9	2.11
	2010	76 963	21 384	3 011	11 203	27.8	3.9	14.6	2.24
	2015	76 963	20 645	3 284	11 715	26.8	4.3	15.2	2.29
	2018	...	...	...	...	...	...	...	2.29
Turkmenistan Turkménistan	2005	* 46 993	* 2 040	* 60	* 4 127	* 4.3	* 0.1	* 8.8	14.41
	2010	* 46 993	* 1 940	* 60	* 4 127	* 4.1	* 0.1	* 8.8	14.60
	2015	* 46 993	* 1 940	* 60	* 4 127	* 4.1	* 0.1	* 8.8	14.60
	2018	...	...	...	...	...	...	...	14.60
Turks and Caicos Islands Îles Turques-et-Caïques	2005	95	* 1	...	* 34	* 1.1	...	* 36.2	27.96
	2010	95	* 1	...	* 34	* 1.1	...	* 36.2	27.96
	2015	95	* 1	...	* 34	* 1.1	...	* 36.2	27.96
	2018	...	...	...	...	...	...	...	27.96
Tuvalu Tuvalu	2005	3	...	* 2	* 1	...	* 56.7	* 33.3	...
	2010	3	...	* 2	* 1	...	* 60.0	* 33.3	...
	2015	3	...	* 2	* 1	...	* 60.0	* 33.3	...
Uganda Ouganda	2005	19 981	* 5 950	* 2 200	3 429	* 29.8	* 11.0	17.2	61.02
	2010	20 052	* 6 750	* 2 200	2 753	* 33.7	* 11.0	13.7	72.05
	2015	20 052	* 6 900	* 2 200	2 077	* 34.4	* 11.0	10.4	72.05
	2018	...	...	...	...	...	...	...	72.05
Ukraine Ukraine	2005	57 938	32 452	901	9 575	56.0	1.6	16.5	23.26
	2010	57 932	32 477	897	9 548	56.1	1.5	16.5	23.26
	2015	* 57 929	32 541	* 893	9 657	* 56.2	* 1.5	* 16.7	23.66
	2018	...	...	...	...	...	...	...	23.66
United Arab Emirates Émirats arabes unis	2005	8 360	* 68	189	* 312	* 0.8	2.3	* 3.7	0.00
	2010	* 8 360	51	42	* 317	* 0.6	* 0.5	* 3.8	13.23
	2015	* 8 360	* 38	* 40	* 323	* 0.4	* 0.5	* 3.9	26.79
	2018	...	...	...	...	...	...	...	30.78
United Kingdom Royaume-Uni	2005	24 193	5 729	47	3 021	23.7	0.2	12.5	81.71
	2010	24 193	5 970	46	3 059	24.7	0.2	12.6	83.84
	2015	* 24 193	6 011	49	3 144	* 24.8	* 0.2	* 13.0	84.11
	2018	...	...	...	...	...	...	...	84.36
United Rep. of Tanzania Rép.-Unie de Tanzanie	2005	88 580	* 9 700	* 1 660	49 920	* 11.0	* 1.9	56.4	52.55
	2010	* 88 580	* 11 600	* 1 850	47 920	* 13.1	* 2.1	* 54.1	57.03
	2015	* 88 580	* 13 500	* 2 150	46 060	* 15.2	* 2.4	* 52.0	57.03
	2018	...	...	...	...	...	...	...	57.03
U.S. Minor Outlying islands Îles min. éloignées des É-U	2005	...	...	...	...	...	...	...	75.00
	2010	...	...	...	...	...	...	...	100.00
	2018	...	...	...	...	...	...	...	100.00
United States of America États-Unis d'Amérique	2005	916 192	* 165 115	* 2 700	304 757	* 18.0	* 0.3	33.3	...
	2010	914 742	* 155 926	* 2 600	308 720	* 17.0	* 0.3	33.7	...
	2015	* 914 742	* 152 263	* 2 600	310 095	* 16.6	* 0.3	* 33.9	...
United States Virgin Islands Îles Vierges américaines	2005	35	* 2	* 1	19	* 5.7	* 2.9	53.5	33.13
	2010	35	* 1	* 1	18	* 2.9	* 2.9	51.9	34.01
	2015	35	* 1	* 1	18	* 2.9	* 2.9	50.3	39.38
	2018	...	...	...	...	...	...	...	39.38
Uruguay Uruguay	2005	17 502	* 1 392	* 40	1 522	* 8.0	* 0.2	8.7	10.38
	2010	17 502	* 2 033	38	1 731	* 11.6	0.2	9.9	20.72
	2015	17 502	* 2 411	* 39	1 845	* 13.8	* 0.2	10.5	20.80
	2018	...	...	...	...	...	...	...	20.80
Uzbekistan Ouzbékistan	2005	42 540	* 4 400	* 340	3 295	* 10.3	* 0.8	7.7	11.71
	2010	* 42 540	* 4 350	* 320	3 276	* 10.2	* 0.8	* 7.7	15.88
	2015	* 42 540	* 4 400	* 370	3 220	* 10.3	* 0.9	* 7.6	15.88
	2018	...	...	...	...	...	...	...	15.88

24 Land *(continued)*

Thousand hectares and percent of total land

Terres *(suite)*

Milliers d'hectares et pourcentage de la superficie totale

		Area – Superficie ('000 hectares)				Area – Superficie (Percent of total)&			
Region, country or area Région, pays ou zone	Year Année	Total land Superficie totale	Arable land Terres arables	Permanent crops Cultures permanentes	Forest cover Superficie forestière	Arable land Terres arables	Permanent crops Cultures Permanentes&	Forest cover Superficie forestière	Sites protected for terrestrial biodiversity Sites pour la bio. terre. dans aires protég. (%)&&
Vanuatu Vanuatu	2005	* 1 219	* 20	* 121	* 440	* 1.6	* 9.9	* 36.1	6.39
	2010	* 1 219	* 20	* 125	* 440	* 1.6	* 10.3	* 36.1	6.39
	2015	* 1 219	* 20	* 125	* 440	* 1.6	* 10.3	* 36.1	6.39
	2018	...	...	...	...	...	...	...	6.39
Venezuela (Boliv. Rep. of) Venezuela (Rép. boliv. du)	2005	* 88 205	* 2 655	* 700	47 713	* 3.0	* 0.8	* 54.1	67.37
	2010	* 88 205	* 2 700	* 700	47 505	* 3.1	* 0.8	* 53.9	67.37
	2015	* 88 205	* 2 700	* 700	46 683	* 3.1	* 0.8	* 52.9	67.37
	2018	...	...	...	...	...	...	...	67.37
Viet Nam Viet Nam	2005	* 31 007	6 358	3 054	13 077	* 20.5	* 9.8	* 42.2	27.16
	2010	* 31 007	6 437	3 681	14 128	* 20.8	* 11.9	* 45.6	29.97
	2015	* 31 007	6 998	* 4 070	14 773	* 22.6	* 13.1	* 47.6	40.88
	2018	...	...	...	...	...	...	...	40.88
Wallis and Futuna Islands Îles Wallis-et-Futuna	2005	14	* 1	* 5	6	* 7.1	* 35.7	41.5	0.00
	2010	14	* 1	* 5	6	* 7.1	* 35.7	41.6	0.00
	2015	14	* 1	* 5	6	* 7.1	* 35.7	41.6	0.00
	2018	...	...	...	...	...	...	...	0.00
Western Sahara Sahara occidental	*2005	26 600	4	...	707	~0.0	...	2.7	...
	*2010	26 600	4	...	707	~0.0	...	2.7	...
	*2015	26 600	4	...	707	~0.0	...	2.7	...
Yemen Yémen	2005	52 797	* 1 287	236	* 549	* 2.4	0.4	* 1.0	20.04
	2010	* 52 797	* 1 291	288	* 549	* 2.4	* 0.5	* 1.0	31.08
	2015	* 52 797	* 1 248	* 298	* 549	* 2.4	* 0.6	* 1.0	31.08
	2018	...	...	...	...	...	...	...	31.08
Zambia Zambie	2005	* 74 339	* 2 727	* 35	50 301	* 3.7	* ~0.0	* 67.7	46.29
	2010	* 74 339	* 3 400	* 36	49 468	* 4.6	* ~0.0	* 66.5	48.33
	2015	* 74 339	* 3 800	* 36	48 635	* 5.1	* ~0.0	* 65.4	48.33
	2018	...	...	...	...	...	...	...	48.33
Zimbabwe Zimbabwe	2005	* 38 685	* 3 900	* 100	17 259	* 10.1	* 0.3	* 44.6	80.73
	2010	* 38 685	* 4 000	* 100	15 624	* 10.3	* 0.3	* 40.4	80.73
	2015	* 38 685	* 4 000	* 100	14 062	* 10.3	* 0.3	* 36.4	85.88
	2018	...	...	...	...	...	...	...	85.88

Source:

Food and Agriculture Organization of the United Nations (FAO), Rome, FAOSTAT data last accessed May 2018.
United Nations Environment Programme (UNEP) World Conservation Monitoring Centre (WCWC) and World Conservation Union (IUCN) and BirdLife International, Cambridge, Sustainable Development Goals database, May 2018.

Source:

Organisation des Nations Unies pour l'alimentation et l'agriculture (FAO), Rome, base de données FAOSTAT, dernier accès mai 2018.
Le Programme des Nations Unies pour l'environnement (PNUE) Le Centre mondial de surveillance de la conservation (CMSC) et l'Union mondiale pour la nature (IUCN) et BirdLife International, Cambridge, base de données sur les Objectifs de développement durable (ODD), May 2018.

& Figures calculated by the United Nations Statistics Division. && Based on spatial overlap between polygons for Key Biodiversity Areas from the World Database of key Biodiveristy Areas and polygons for protected areas from the World Database on Protected Areas.

& Chiffres calculés par la Division de statistique des Nations Unies. && basées sur un chevauchement spatial entre les zones clés pour la biodiversité de la base de données mondiale pour les zones clés pour la biodiversité et les polygones pour les zones protégées de la base de données mondiale sur les zones protégées.

1 Calculated by the UN Statistics Division.
2 For statistical purposes, the data for China do not include those for the Hong Kong Special Administrative Region (Hong Kong SAR), Macao Special Administrative Region (Macao SAR) and Taiwan Province of China.
3 Including Ascension and Tristan da Cunha.

1 Calculés par la Division de statistique des Nations Unies.
2 Pour la présentation des statistiques, les données pour la Chine ne comprennent pas la région administrative spéciale de Hong Kong (Hong Kong RAS), la région administrative spéciale de Macao (Macao RAS) et la province chinoise de Taïwan.
3 Y compris Ascension et Tristan da Cunha.

25 Threatened species

Number of species by taxonomic group

Espèces menacées

Nombre d'espèces menacées par groupe taxonomique

Country or area &	2004	2010	2014	2015	2016	2017	2018	Pays ou zone &
Afghanistan								**Afghanistan**
Vertebrates	31	31	32	31	35	35	34	Vertébrés
Invertebrates	1	1	2	2	2	2	2	Invertébrés
Plants	1	2	3	5	5	5	5	Plantes
Total	33	34	37	38	42	42	41	Total
Albania								**Albanie**
Vertebrates	33	53	53	54	63	62	62	Vertébrés
Invertebrates	4	47	56	58	62	68	71	Invertébrés
Plants	0	0	0	0	0	0	4	Plantes
Total	37	100	109	112	125	130	137	Total
Algeria								**Algérie**
Vertebrates	36	69	71	71	78	79	80	Vertébrés
Invertebrates	12	21	25	26	29	38	40	Invertébrés
Plants	2	15	17	17	18	18	23	Plantes
Total	50	105	113	114	125	135	143	Total
American Samoa								**Samoa américaines**
Vertebrates	18	21	25	25	27	27	27	Vertébrés
Invertebrates	5	57	64	64	64	64	64	Invertébrés
Plants	1	1	1	1	1	1	1	Plantes
Total	24	79	90	90	92	92	92	Total
Andorra								**Andorre**
Vertebrates	1	4	4	4	5	5	6	Vertébrés
Invertebrates	4	4	7	7	7	8	8	Invertébrés
Plants	0	0	0	0	0	0	0	Plantes
Total	5	8	11	11	12	13	14	Total
Angola								**Angola**
Vertebrates	44	77	87	87	99	103	108	Vertébrés
Invertebrates	6	7	9	9	9	9	11	Invertébrés
Plants	26	33	34	34	34	34	35	Plantes
Total	76	117	130	130	142	146	154	Total
Anguilla								**Anguilla**
Vertebrates	15	20	29	37	38	38	40	Vertébrés
Invertebrates	0	10	10	10	10	10	10	Invertébrés
Plants	3	3	3	4	4	4	4	Plantes
Total	18	33	42	51	52	52	54	Total
Antarctica								**Antarctique**
Vertebrates	8	6	6	6	6	6	6	Vertébrés
Invertebrates	0	0	0	0	0	0	0	Invertébrés
Plants	0	0	0	0	0	0	0	Plantes
Total	8	6	6	6	6	6	6	Total
Antigua and Barbuda								**Antigua-et-Barbuda**
Vertebrates	18	23	30	38	38	40	41	Vertébrés
Invertebrates	0	11	11	11	11	11	11	Invertébrés
Plants	4	4	4	4	4	4	4	Plantes
Total	22	38	45	53	53	55	56	Total
Argentina								**Argentine**
Vertebrates	134	157	160	160	172	172	186	Vertébrés
Invertebrates	10	12	13	13	14	14	14	Invertébrés
Plants	42	44	70	70	70	70	70	Plantes
Total	186	213	243	243	256	256	270	Total
Armenia								**Arménie**
Vertebrates	27	29	31	31	34	34	33	Vertébrés
Invertebrates	7	6	9	9	9	9	9	Invertébrés
Plants	1	1	71	71	71	71	73	Plantes
Total	35	36	111	111	114	114	115	Total
Aruba								**Aruba**
Vertebrates	17	20	19	25	28	28	28	Vertébrés
Invertebrates	1	1	2	2	2	2	2	Invertébrés
Plants	0	1	2	2	2	2	2	Plantes
Total	18	22	23	29	32	32	32	Total
Australia [1]								**Australie** [1]
Vertebrates	282	297	304	304	319	323	358	Vertébrés
Invertebrates	283	489	511	514	514	531	534	Invertébrés
Plants	56	67	91	91	# 93	94	106	Plantes
Total	621	853	906	909	926	948	998	Total

Country or area &	2004	2010	2014	2015	2016	2017	2018	Pays ou zone &
Austria								**Autriche**
Vertebrates	20	23	24	24	27	26	28	Vertébrés
Invertebrates	44	55	70	69	69	71	74	Invertébrés
Plants	3	4	13	13	# 21	21	25	Plantes
Total	67	82	107	106	117	118	127	Total
Azerbaijan								**Azerbaïdjan**
Vertebrates	32	41	43	43	47	48	47	Vertébrés
Invertebrates	6	4	7	7	7	7	7	Invertébrés
Plants	0	0	42	42	42	42	43	Plantes
Total	38	45	92	92	96	97	97	Total
Bahamas								**Bahamas**
Vertebrates	36	44	52	61	65	66	71	Vertébrés
Invertebrates	1	11	12	12	12	12	12	Invertébrés
Plants	5	7	8	8	8	8	7	Plantes
Total	42	62	72	81	85	86	90	Total
Bahrain								**Bahreïn**
Vertebrates	18	19	20	19	23	23	27	Vertébrés
Invertebrates	0	13	13	13	13	13	13	Invertébrés
Plants	0	0	0	0	0	0	0	Plantes
Total	18	32	33	32	36	36	40	Total
Bangladesh								**Bangladesh**
Vertebrates	73	104	108	109	120	123	125	Vertébrés
Invertebrates	0	2	7	7	7	7	7	Invertébrés
Plants	12	16	17	21	21	21	22	Plantes
Total	85	122	132	137	148	151	154	Total
Barbados								**Barbade**
Vertebrates	18	24	31	37	39	42	43	Vertébrés
Invertebrates	0	10	11	11	11	11	11	Invertébrés
Plants	2	2	3	3	3	3	3	Plantes
Total	20	36	45	51	53	56	57	Total
Belarus								**Bélarus**
Vertebrates	10	10	12	11	14	15	15	Vertébrés
Invertebrates	8	6	9	9	9	9	10	Invertébrés
Plants	0	0	1	1	1	1	1	Plantes
Total	18	16	22	21	24	25	26	Total
Belgium								**Belgique**
Vertebrates	25	15	17	16	23	22	23	Vertébrés
Invertebrates	11	11	14	14	14	14	15	Invertébrés
Plants	0	1	0	0	# 1	1	1	Plantes
Total	36	27	31	30	38	37	39	Total
Belize								**Belize**
Vertebrates	36	48	60	70	70	69	69	Vertébrés
Invertebrates	1	12	12	12	12	12	12	Invertébrés
Plants	30	32	33	35	36	36	43	Plantes
Total	67	92	105	117	118	117	124	Total
Benin								**Bénin**
Vertebrates	17	47	55	55	66	68	70	Vertébrés
Invertebrates	0	1	3	3	3	3	3	Invertébrés
Plants	14	14	16	16	17	17	19	Plantes
Total	31	62	74	74	86	88	92	Total
Bermuda								**Bermudes**
Vertebrates	18	18	25	28	35	36	36	Vertébrés
Invertebrates	25	28	28	28	28	28	28	Invertébrés
Plants	4	4	7	8	8	8	8	Plantes
Total	47	50	60	64	71	72	72	Total
Bhutan								**Bhoutan**
Vertebrates	40	50	52	52	54	52	51	Vertébrés
Invertebrates	1	1	1	1	1	1	1	Invertébrés
Plants	7	8	12	18	18	18	43	Plantes
Total	48	59	65	71	73	71	95	Total
Bolivia (Plurin. State of)								**Bolivie (État plurin. de)**
Vertebrates	79	90	114	114	124	124	129	Vertébrés
Invertebrates	1	1	3	3	3	3	3	Invertébrés
Plants	70	72	99	99	104	104	104	Plantes
Total	150	163	216	216	231	231	236	Total

25 Threatened species *(continued)*
Number of species by taxonomic group

Espèces menacées *(suite)*
Nombre d'espèces menacées par groupe taxonomique

Country or area &	2004	2010	2014	2015	2016	2017	2018	Pays ou zone &
Bonaire, St. Eustatius & Saba								**Bonaire, St-Eustache et Saba**
Vertebrates	...	...	32	41	42	42	42	Vertébrés
Invertebrates	...	...	11	11	11	11	11	Invertébrés
Plants	...	...	3	3	3	3	3	Plantes
Total	...	...	46	55	56	56	56	Total
Bosnia and Herzegovina								**Bosnie-Herzégovine**
Vertebrates	29	44	46	48	51	51	50	Vertébrés
Invertebrates	10	22	36	36	36	39	42	Invertébrés
Plants	1	1	1	1	1	1	3	Plantes
Total	40	67	83	85	88	91	95	Total
Botswana								**Botswana**
Vertebrates	15	18	22	22	24	26	28	Vertébrés
Invertebrates	0	0	0	0	0	0	0	Invertébrés
Plants	0	0	2	2	2	2	2	Plantes
Total	15	18	24	24	26	28	30	Total
Bouvet Island								**Île Bouvet**
Vertebrates	1	2	3	3	3	3	3	Vertébrés
Invertebrates	0	0	0	0	0	0	0	Invertébrés
Plants	0	0	0	0	0	0	0	Plantes
Total	1	2	3	3	3	3	3	Total
Brazil								**Brésil**
Vertebrates	282[2]	341[2]	395	396	397	403	407	Vertébrés
Invertebrates	34	45	54	54	55	55	55	Invertébrés
Plants	381	387	516	516	521	532	538	Plantes
Total	697	773	965	966	973	990	1 000	Total
British Indian Ocean Terr.								**Terr. brit. de l'océan Indien**
Vertebrates	6	10	11	11	14	15	15	Vertébrés
Invertebrates	0	65	69	69	69	69	69	Invertébrés
Plants	1	1	1	1	1	1	1	Plantes
Total	7	76	81	81	84	85	85	Total
British Virgin Islands								**Îles Vierges britanniques**
Vertebrates	20	23	33	41	41	47	48	Vertébrés
Invertebrates	0	10	10	10	10	10	10	Invertébrés
Plants	10	10	10	10	10	10	20	Plantes
Total	30	43	53	61	61	67	78	Total
Brunei Darussalam								**Brunéi Darussalam**
Vertebrates	49	70	75	77	80	81	82	Vertébrés
Invertebrates	0	1	8	8	8	8	9	Invertébrés
Plants	99	99	104	104	104	104	116	Plantes
Total	148	170	187	189	192	193	207	Total
Bulgaria								**Bulgarie**
Vertebrates	35	39	43	42	49	50	49	Vertébrés
Invertebrates	9	27	37	37	38	48	57	Invertébrés
Plants	0	0	6	6	6	6	9	Plantes
Total	44	66	86	85	93	104	115	Total
Burkina Faso								**Burkina Faso**
Vertebrates	9	20	25	25	27	27	26	Vertébrés
Invertebrates	0	1	1	1	1	1	1	Invertébrés
Plants	2	3	3	3	3	3	3	Plantes
Total	11	24	29	29	31	31	30	Total
Burundi								**Burundi**
Vertebrates	22	43	46	45	44	46	46	Vertébrés
Invertebrates	4	7	7	7	7	7	7	Invertébrés
Plants	2	2	7	8	8	8	89	Plantes
Total	28	52	60	60	59	61	142	Total
Cabo Verde								**Cabo Verde**
Vertebrates	21	28	35	35	49	49	51	Vertébrés
Invertebrates	0	0	13	13	13	13	13	Invertébrés
Plants	2	3	3	3	3	3	51	Plantes
Total	23	31	51	51	65	65	115	Total
Cambodia								**Cambodge**
Vertebrates	72	107	128	130	137	141	145	Vertébrés
Invertebrates	0	67	77	77	79	79	79	Invertébrés
Plants	31	30	32	36	36	35	37	Plantes
Total	103	204	237	243	252	255	261	Total

Country or area &	2004	2010	2014	2015	2016	2017	2018	Pays ou zone &
Cameroon								**Cameroun**
Vertebrates	146	222	236	237	255	258	263	Vertébrés
Invertebrates	4	24	27	27	27	27	25	Invertébrés
Plants	334	378	425	433	490	490	544	Plantes
Total	484	624	688	697	772	775	832	Total
Canada								**Canada**
Vertebrates	62	63	69	68	79	81	86	Vertébrés
Invertebrates	11	12	18	22	25	27	37	Invertébrés
Plants	1	2	6	7	# 14	14	25	Plantes
Total	74	77	93	97	118	122	148	Total
Cayman Islands								**Îles Caïmanes**
Vertebrates	16	21	28	38	38	41	41	Vertébrés
Invertebrates	1	11	11	11	11	11	11	Invertébrés
Plants	2	2	22	22	22	22	22	Plantes
Total	19	34	61	71	71	74	74	Total
Central African Republic								**République centrafricaine**
Vertebrates	15	19	31	32	33	36	38	Vertébrés
Invertebrates	0	0	0	0	0	0	0	Invertébrés
Plants	15	17	22	22	24	24	25	Plantes
Total	30	36	53	54	57	60	63	Total
Chad								**Tchad**
Vertebrates	18	24	29	29	31	33	36	Vertébrés
Invertebrates	1	4	4	4	4	4	4	Invertébrés
Plants	2	2	5	5	6	6	6	Plantes
Total	21	30	38	38	41	43	46	Total
Chile								**Chili**
Vertebrates	83	95	98	98	111	112	132	Vertébrés
Invertebrates	0	9	12	12	13	13	13	Invertébrés
Plants	40	41	72	72	72	72	72	Plantes
Total	123	145	182	182	196	197	217	Total
China [3]								**Chine** [3]
Vertebrates	326	374	416	420	428	430	431	Vertébrés
Invertebrates	4	32	76	76	76	76	76	Invertébrés
Plants	443	453	503	544	# 575	574	588	Plantes
Total	773	859	995	1 040	1 079	1 080	1 095	Total
China, Hong Kong SAR								**Chine, RAS de Hong Kong**
Vertebrates	32	37	45	45	46	47	49	Vertébrés
Invertebrates	1	6	8	8	8	8	8	Invertébrés
Plants	6	6	6	7	9	9	8	Plantes
Total	39	49	59	60	63	64	65	Total
China, Macao SAR								**Chine, RAS de Macao**
Vertebrates	5	9	10	10	10	10	10	Vertébrés
Invertebrates	0	0	1	1	1	1	1	Invertébrés
Plants	0	0	0	0	0	0	0	Plantes
Total	5	9	11	11	11	11	11	Total
Christmas Island								**Île Christmas**
Vertebrates	12	16	18	18	20	20	18	Vertébrés
Invertebrates	0	16	18	18	18	18	19	Invertébrés
Plants	1	1	1	1	1	1	1	Plantes
Total	13	33	37	37	39	39	38	Total
Cocos (Keeling) Islands								**Îles des Cocos (Keeling)**
Vertebrates	5	11	12	11	12	13	13	Vertébrés
Invertebrates	0	17	20	20	20	20	20	Invertébrés
Plants	0	0	0	0	0	0	0	Plantes
Total	5	28	32	31	32	33	33	Total
Colombia								**Colombie**
Vertebrates	371	424	463	473	518	525	537	Vertébrés
Invertebrates	0	30	33	33	52	52	53	Invertébrés
Plants	222	227	245	245	257	258	261	Plantes
Total	593	681	741	751	827	835	851	Total
Comoros								**Comores**
Vertebrates	18	21	26	26	29	33	34	Vertébrés
Invertebrates	4	63	73	73	73	74	76	Invertébrés
Plants	5	5	7	7	7	7	9	Plantes
Total	27	89	106	106	109	114	119	Total

25 Threatened species *(continued)*
Number of species by taxonomic group

Espèces menacées *(suite)*
Nombre d'espèces menacées par groupe taxonomique

Country or area &	2004	2010	2014	2015	2016	2017	2018	Pays ou zone &
Congo								**Congo**
Vertebrates	29	61	70	71	81	82	86	Vertébrés
Invertebrates	1	5	7	7	7	7	7	Invertébrés
Plants	35	37	41	41	45	45	47	Plantes
Total	65	103	118	119	133	134	140	Total
Cook Islands								**Îles Cook**
Vertebrates	22	27	30	30	31	32	32	Vertébrés
Invertebrates	0	25	32	32	32	32	32	Invertébrés
Plants	1	1	11	11	11	11	11	Plantes
Total	23	53	73	73	74	75	75	Total
Costa Rica								**Costa Rica**
Vertebrates	112	142	156	162	166	169	171	Vertébrés
Invertebrates	9	27	30	30	31	31	31	Invertébrés
Plants	110	116	131	131	140	140	144	Plantes
Total	231	285	317	323	337	340	346	Total
Côte d'Ivoire								**Côte d'Ivoire**
Vertebrates	61	100	113	113	127	130	133	Vertébrés
Invertebrates	1	4	6	6	6	6	7	Invertébrés
Plants	105	106	107	107	112	113	117	Plantes
Total	167	210	226	226	245	249	257	Total
Croatia								**Croatie**
Vertebrates	46	77	84	84	93	94	93	Vertébrés
Invertebrates	11	21	66	67	68	73	79	Invertébrés
Plants	0	3	8	8	# 9	9	9	Plantes
Total	57	101	158	159	170	176	181	Total
Cuba								**Cuba**
Vertebrates	106	123	133	138	138	137	146	Vertébrés
Invertebrates	3	15	23	23	23	23	23	Invertébrés
Plants	163	166	176	176	179	179	179	Plantes
Total	272	304	332	337	340	339	348	Total
Curaçao								**Curaçao**
Vertebrates	...	...	29	36	36	38	38	Vertébrés
Invertebrates	...	...	11	11	11	11	11	Invertébrés
Plants	...	...	2	2	2	2	2	Plantes
Total	...	...	42	49	49	51	51	Total
Cyprus								**Chypre**
Vertebrates	24	31	33	34	41	42	42	Vertébrés
Invertebrates	0	4	7	8	12	12	15	Invertébrés
Plants	1	8	18	18	18	18	21	Plantes
Total	25	43	58	60	71	72	78	Total
Czechia								**Tchéquie**
Vertebrates	22	10	11	11	14	14	14	Vertébrés
Invertebrates	19	19	25	24	24	24	29	Invertébrés
Plants	4	4	10	10	# 15	15	31	Plantes
Total	45	33	46	45	53	53	74	Total
Dem. People's Rep. Korea								**Rép. pop. dém. de Corée**
Vertebrates	40	44	52	53	57	58	60	Vertébrés
Invertebrates	1	2	3	3	3	3	3	Invertébrés
Plants	3	6	8	8	17	17	17	Plantes
Total	44	52	63	64	77	78	80	Total
Dem. Rep. of the Congo								**Rép. dém. du Congo**
Vertebrates	84	162	172	171	183	182	187	Vertébrés
Invertebrates	22	51	53	53	53	53	55	Invertébrés
Plants	65	83	107	109	113	114	148	Plantes
Total	171	296	332	333	349	349	390	Total
Denmark								**Danemark**
Vertebrates	21	18	20	20	27	28	29	Vertébrés
Invertebrates	11	12	15	15	15	15	16	Invertébrés
Plants	3	3	1	1	# 4	4	4	Plantes
Total	35	33	36	36	46	47	49	Total
Djibouti								**Djibouti**
Vertebrates	19	29	34	34	38	38	43	Vertébrés
Invertebrates	0	50	57	57	57	57	57	Invertébrés
Plants	2	2	3	3	3	3	3	Plantes
Total	21	81	94	94	98	98	103	Total

25 Threatened species *(continued)*
Number of species by taxonomic group

Espèces menacées *(suite)*
Nombre d'espèces menacées par groupe taxonomique

Country or area &	2004	2010	2014	2015	2016	2017	2018	Pays ou zone &
Dominica								**Dominique**
Vertebrates	22	27	33	40	42	44	44	Vertébrés
Invertebrates	0	11	11	11	11	11	11	Invertébrés
Plants	11	10	11	11	11	11	11	Plantes
Total	33	48	55	62	64	66	66	Total
Dominican Republic								**République dominicaine**
Vertebrates	72	80	90	95	95	126	130	Vertébrés
Invertebrates	2	16	16	16	16	16	16	Invertébrés
Plants	30	30	41	42	42	42	45	Plantes
Total	104	126	147	153	153	184	191	Total
Ecuador								**Équateur**
Vertebrates	288	356	394	395	417	426	434	Vertébrés
Invertebrates	48	62	65	65	70	70	70	Invertébrés
Plants	1 815	1 837	1 840	1 848	# 1 866	1 862	1 864	Plantes
Total	2 151	2 255	2 299	2 308	2 353	2 358	2 368	Total
Egypt								**Égypte**
Vertebrates	43	73	82	83	96	97	99	Vertébrés
Invertebrates	1	46	54	55	56	56	56	Invertébrés
Plants	2	2	3	3	3	3	8	Plantes
Total	46	121	139	141	155	156	163	Total
El Salvador								**El Salvador**
Vertebrates	23	39	47	47	47	47	47	Vertébrés
Invertebrates	1	6	7	7	10	10	10	Invertébrés
Plants	25	27	29	29	29	29	30	Plantes
Total	49	72	83	83	86	86	87	Total
Equatorial Guinea								**Guinée équatoriale**
Vertebrates	38	60	69	71	85	85	86	Vertébrés
Invertebrates	2	2	5	5	5	5	4	Invertébrés
Plants	61	68	77	79	88	87	95	Plantes
Total	101	130	151	155	178	177	185	Total
Eritrea								**Érythrée**
Vertebrates	31	44	51	51	58	59	67	Vertébrés
Invertebrates	0	50	58	58	58	58	58	Invertébrés
Plants	3	3	4	4	4	5	5	Plantes
Total	34	97	113	113	120	122	130	Total
Estonia								**Estonie**
Vertebrates	8	8	11	11	14	15	15	Vertébrés
Invertebrates	4	3	6	6	6	6	7	Invertébrés
Plants	0	0	0	0	# 2	2	2	Plantes
Total	12	11	17	17	22	23	24	Total
Eswatini								**Eswatini**
Vertebrates	12	18	23	23	25	23	26	Vertébrés
Invertebrates	0	0	0	0	0	0	0	Invertébrés
Plants	11	11	11	11	11	11	12	Plantes
Total	23	29	34	34	36	34	38	Total
Ethiopia								**Éthiopie**
Vertebrates	65	79	89	89	92	90	95	Vertébrés
Invertebrates	6	15	15	15	15	15	15	Invertébrés
Plants	22	26	40	41	41	43	47	Plantes
Total	93	120	144	145	148	148	157	Total
Falkland Islands (Malvinas)								**Îles Falkland (Malvinas)**
Vertebrates	21	18	18	18	18	18	17	Vertébrés
Invertebrates	0	0	0	0	0	0	0	Invertébrés
Plants	5	5	5	5	5	5	5	Plantes
Total	26	23	23	23	23	23	22	Total
Faroe Islands								**Îles Féroé**
Vertebrates	11	13	13	14	20	20	22	Vertébrés
Invertebrates	0	0	0	0	0	0	0	Invertébrés
Plants	0	0	0	0	# 1	1	1	Plantes
Total	11	13	13	14	21	21	23	Total
Fiji								**Fidji**
Vertebrates	33	37	48	48	52	55	55	Vertébrés
Invertebrates	2	90	165	165	165	165	165	Invertébrés
Plants	66	65	65	65	65	71	78	Plantes
Total	101	192	278	278	282	291	298	Total

25 Threatened species *(continued)*
Number of species by taxonomic group

Espèces menacées *(suite)*
Nombre d'espèces menacées par groupe taxonomique

Country or area &	2004	2010	2014	2015	2016	2017	2018	Pays ou zone &
Finland								**Finlande**
Vertebrates	14	10	13	13	17	18	19	Vertébrés
Invertebrates	10	7	10	10	10	10	10	Invertébrés
Plants	1	1	2	2	# 8	8	8	Plantes
Total	25	18	25	25	35	36	37	Total
France								**France**
Vertebrates	53	62	70	70	80	82	84	Vertébrés
Invertebrates	65	91	132	133	137	153	160	Invertébrés
Plants	2	15	32	33	# 43	43	55	Plantes
Total	120	168	234	236	260	278	299	Total
French Guiana								**Guyane française**
Vertebrates	33	40	50	51	55	55	56	Vertébrés
Invertebrates	0	0	0	0	0	0	0	Invertébrés
Plants	16	16	16	16	18	18	18	Plantes
Total	49	56	66	67	73	73	74	Total
French Polynesia								**Polynésie française**
Vertebrates	46	54	63	63	63	66	66	Vertébrés
Invertebrates	29	59	65	65	65	62	62	Invertébrés
Plants	47	47	47	47	47	47	48	Plantes
Total	122	160	175	175	175	175	176	Total
French Southern Territories								**Terres australes françaises**
Vertebrates	17	21	22	22	24	25	25	Vertébrés
Invertebrates	0	0	0	0	0	0	0	Invertébrés
Plants	0	0	0	0	0	0	0	Plantes
Total	17	21	22	22	24	25	25	Total
Gabon								**Gabon**
Vertebrates	31	84	92	93	105	105	107	Vertébrés
Invertebrates	1	0	3	3	3	3	4	Invertébrés
Plants	107	120	132	135	162	162	172	Plantes
Total	139	204	227	231	270	270	283	Total
Gambia								**Gambie**
Vertebrates	17	39	48	48	60	60	63	Vertébrés
Invertebrates	0	0	2	2	2	2	2	Invertébrés
Plants	4	4	5	5	5	5	5	Plantes
Total	21	43	55	55	67	67	70	Total
Georgia								**Géorgie**
Vertebrates	33	37	39	38	42	43	42	Vertébrés
Invertebrates	10	9	15	15	15	15	15	Invertébrés
Plants	0	0	61	61	# 62	62	63	Plantes
Total	43	46	115	114	119	120	120	Total
Germany								**Allemagne**
Vertebrates	35	33	35	33	39	40	40	Vertébrés
Invertebrates	31	34	58	57	57	57	61	Invertébrés
Plants	12	12	17	17	# 24	19	43	Plantes
Total	78	79	110	107	120	116	144	Total
Ghana								**Ghana**
Vertebrates	43	83	99	99	112	114	118	Vertébrés
Invertebrates	0	1	5	5	5	5	5	Invertébrés
Plants	117	118	119	119	119	119	118	Plantes
Total	160	202	223	223	236	238	241	Total
Gibraltar								**Gibraltar**
Vertebrates	16	20	20	21	28	26	28	Vertébrés
Invertebrates	2	2	4	5	5	5	5	Invertébrés
Plants	0	0	0	0	0	0	1	Plantes
Total	18	22	24	26	33	31	34	Total
Greece								**Grèce**
Vertebrates	62	107	111	111	120	121	123	Vertébrés
Invertebrates	11	36	117	122	181	192	308	Invertébrés
Plants	2	13	58	58	# 60	61	71	Plantes
Total	75	156	286	291	361	374	502	Total
Greenland								**Groenland**
Vertebrates	11	13	16	16	21	22	24	Vertébrés
Invertebrates	0	0	0	0	0	0	0	Invertébrés
Plants	1	1	1	1	1	1	1	Plantes
Total	12	14	17	17	22	23	25	Total

Threatened species *(continued)*
Number of species by taxonomic group

Espèces menacées *(suite)*
Nombre d'espèces menacées par groupe taxonomique

Country or area &	2004	2010	2014	2015	2016	2017	2018	Pays ou zone &
Grenada								**Grenade**
Vertebrates	20	24	32	38	40	41	42	Vertébrés
Invertebrates	0	10	10	10	10	10	10	Invertébrés
Plants	3	3	3	3	3	3	3	Plantes
Total	23	37	45	51	53	54	55	Total
Guadeloupe [4]								**Guadeloupe** [4]
Vertebrates	25	30	37	45	45	48	50	Vertébrés
Invertebrates	1	16	16	16	16	16	16	Invertébrés
Plants	7	8	9	9	9	9	9	Plantes
Total	33	54	62	70	70	73	75	Total
Guam								**Guam**
Vertebrates	16	24	31	31	34	35	35	Vertébrés
Invertebrates	5	6	60	60	60	60	60	Invertébrés
Plants	3	4	4	4	4	4	4	Plantes
Total	24	34	95	95	98	99	99	Total
Guatemala								**Guatemala**
Vertebrates	115	140	168	176	176	176	175	Vertébrés
Invertebrates	8	8	9	9	13	13	13	Invertébrés
Plants	85	82	94	97	102	101	113	Plantes
Total	208	230	271	282	291	290	301	Total
Guernsey								**Guernesey**
Vertebrates	...	2	2	2	5	5	5	Vertébrés
Invertebrates	...	0	0	0	0	0	0	Invertébrés
Plants	...	0	0	0	0	0	0	Plantes
Total	...	2	2	2	5	5	5	Total
Guinea								**Guinée**
Vertebrates	42	107	122	122	132	134	138	Vertébrés
Invertebrates	3	5	7	7	7	7	8	Invertébrés
Plants	22	22	34	34	44	44	69	Plantes
Total	67	134	163	163	183	185	215	Total
Guinea-Bissau								**Guinée-Bissau**
Vertebrates	17	48	59	59	69	70	73	Vertébrés
Invertebrates	1	0	2	2	2	2	2	Invertébrés
Plants	4	4	5	5	5	5	5	Plantes
Total	22	52	66	66	76	77	80	Total
Guyana								**Guyana**
Vertebrates	41	46	62	63	65	67	73	Vertébrés
Invertebrates	1	1	1	1	1	1	1	Invertébrés
Plants	23	22	23	23	26	26	26	Plantes
Total	65	69	86	87	92	94	100	Total
Haiti								**Haïti**
Vertebrates	86	94	106	113	113	149	153	Vertébrés
Invertebrates	2	14	14	14	14	14	14	Invertébrés
Plants	28	29	39	42	42	42	80	Plantes
Total	116	137	159	169	169	205	247	Total
Heard Is. and McDonald Is.								**Île Heard-et-Îles MacDonald**
Vertebrates	12	12	12	12	12	12	12	Vertébrés
Invertebrates	0	0	0	0	0	0	0	Invertébrés
Plants	0	0	0	0	0	0	0	Plantes
Total	12	12	12	12	12	12	12	Total
Holy See								**Saint-Siège**
Vertebrates	...	1	1	1	1	1	1	Vertébrés
Invertebrates	...	0	0	0	0	0	0	Invertébrés
Plants	...	0	0	0	0	0	0	Plantes
Total	...	1	1	1	1	1	1	Total
Honduras								**Honduras**
Vertebrates	93	110	147	156	156	157	157	Vertébrés
Invertebrates	2	17	18	18	21	21	21	Invertébrés
Plants	111	113	119	120	123	123	131	Plantes
Total	206	240	284	294	300	301	309	Total
Hungary								**Hongrie**
Vertebrates	25	20	22	22	25	26	26	Vertébrés
Invertebrates	25	26	36	35	35	29	34	Invertébrés
Plants	1	1	10	10	# 12	11	45	Plantes
Total	51	47	68	67	72	66	105	Total

25 Threatened species *(continued)*
Number of species by taxonomic group

Espèces menacées *(suite)*
Nombre d'espèces menacées par groupe taxonomique

Country or area &	2004	2010	2014	2015	2016	2017	2018	Pays ou zone &
Iceland								**Islande**
Vertebrates	15	17	19	21	26	27	29	Vertébrés
Invertebrates	0	0	0	0	0	0	0	Invertébrés
Plants	0	0	0	0	0	0	0	Plantes
Total	15	17	19	21	26	27	29	Total
India								**Inde**
Vertebrates	283	390	521	520	528	530	540	Vertébrés
Invertebrates	23	113	135	135	135	135	135	Invertébrés
Plants	246	255	332	384	388	387	392	Plantes
Total	552	758	988	1 039	1 051	1 052	1 067	Total
Indonesia								**Indonésie**
Vertebrates	419	503	529	530	540	564	572	Vertébrés
Invertebrates	31	246	288	290	290	290	287	Invertébrés
Plants	383	393	408	426	427	427	436	Plantes
Total	833	1 142	1 225	1 246	1 257	1 281	1 295	Total
Iran (Islamic Republic of)								**Iran (Rép. islamique d')**
Vertebrates	65	82	94	94	105	106	111	Vertébrés
Invertebrates	3	19	24	24	24	24	24	Invertébrés
Plants	1	1	3	3	3	4	5	Plantes
Total	69	102	121	121	132	134	140	Total
Iraq								**Iraq**
Vertebrates	33	45	51	51	54	53	54	Vertébrés
Invertebrates	2	15	17	17	17	17	17	Invertébrés
Plants	0	0	1	1	1	2	2	Plantes
Total	35	60	69	69	72	72	73	Total
Ireland								**Irlande**
Vertebrates	18	24	31	32	40	41	42	Vertébrés
Invertebrates	3	2	6	6	6	6	6	Invertébrés
Plants	1	1	1	1	# 3	3	5	Plantes
Total	22	27	38	39	49	50	53	Total
Isle of Man								**Île de Man**
Vertebrates	...	2	3	3	3	3	3	Vertébrés
Invertebrates	...	0	0	0	0	0	0	Invertébrés
Plants	...	0	0	0	0	0	0	Plantes
Total	...	2	3	3	3	3	3	Total
Israel								**Israël**
Vertebrates	47	73	78	78	89	90	91	Vertébrés
Invertebrates	10	58	73	74	74	74	74	Invertébrés
Plants	0	0	0	0	9	10	23	Plantes
Total	57	131	151	152	172	174	188	Total
Italy								**Italie**
Vertebrates	53	70	76	76	85	87	89	Vertébrés
Invertebrates	58	77	134	136	141	194	222	Invertébrés
Plants	3	27	66	67	# 79	78	109	Plantes
Total	114	174	276	279	305	359	420	Total
Jamaica								**Jamaïque**
Vertebrates	54	58	63	69	71	82	87	Vertébrés
Invertebrates	5	15	15	15	15	15	15	Invertébrés
Plants	208	209	214	214	214	214	214	Plantes
Total	267	282	292	298	300	311	316	Total
Japan								**Japon**
Vertebrates	148	158	171	171	180	184	198	Vertébrés
Invertebrates	45	157	170	170	171	171	174	Invertébrés
Plants	12	15	21	23	# 46	49	50	Plantes
Total	205	330	362	364	397	404	422	Total
Jersey								**Jersey**
Vertebrates	...	2	2	2	5	5	5	Vertébrés
Invertebrates	...	0	1	1	1	1	1	Invertébrés
Plants	...	0	0	0	0	0	0	Plantes
Total	...	2	3	3	6	6	6	Total
Jordan								**Jordanie**
Vertebrates	27	41	41	40	47	47	48	Vertébrés
Invertebrates	3	48	61	61	61	61	61	Invertébrés
Plants	0	1	1	1	5	5	8	Plantes
Total	30	90	103	102	113	113	117	Total

25 Threatened species *(continued)*
Number of species by taxonomic group

Espèces menacées *(suite)*
Nombre d'espèces menacées par groupe taxonomique

Country or area &	2004	2010	2014	2015	2016	2017	2018	Pays ou zone &
Kazakhstan								**Kazakhstan**
Vertebrates	48	53	55	55	57	59	59	Vertébrés
Invertebrates	4	4	7	7	7	7	7	Invertébrés
Plants	1	16	15	16	16	16	14	Plantes
Total	53	73	77	78	80	82	80	Total
Kenya								**Kenya**
Vertebrates	99	137	157	157	162	162	169	Vertébrés
Invertebrates	27	72	84	84	84	86	87	Invertébrés
Plants	103	129	187	222	222	232	234	Plantes
Total	229	338	428	463	468	480	490	Total
Kiribati								**Kiribati**
Vertebrates	10	17	19	19	21	23	23	Vertébrés
Invertebrates	1	73	81	81	81	81	81	Invertébrés
Plants	0	0	0	0	0	0	0	Plantes
Total	11	90	100	100	102	104	104	Total
Kuwait								**Koweït**
Vertebrates	20	28	29	29	36	36	39	Vertébrés
Invertebrates	0	13	13	13	13	13	13	Invertébrés
Plants	0	0	0	0	0	0	0	Plantes
Total	20	41	42	42	49	49	52	Total
Kyrgyzstan								**Kirghizistan**
Vertebrates	12	23	23	23	26	26	26	Vertébrés
Invertebrates	3	3	4	4	4	4	4	Invertébrés
Plants	1	14	14	14	14	14	13	Plantes
Total	16	40	41	41	44	44	43	Total
Lao People's Dem. Rep.								**Rép. dém. populaire lao**
Vertebrates	72	107	147	148	153	147	149	Vertébrés
Invertebrates	0	3	21	21	21	21	21	Invertébrés
Plants	19	22	32	41	41	41	54	Plantes
Total	91	132	200	210	215	209	224	Total
Latvia								**Lettonie**
Vertebrates	15	9	13	13	16	17	18	Vertébrés
Invertebrates	8	9	12	12	12	12	12	Invertébrés
Plants	0	0	0	0	# 1	1	1	Plantes
Total	23	18	25	25	29	30	31	Total
Lebanon								**Liban**
Vertebrates	25	44	47	48	58	58	57	Vertébrés
Invertebrates	1	5	15	16	16	17	18	Invertébrés
Plants	0	1	2	5	10	12	24	Plantes
Total	26	50	64	69	84	87	99	Total
Lesotho								**Lesotho**
Vertebrates	11	10	10	10	11	11	13	Vertébrés
Invertebrates	1	2	3	3	3	3	3	Invertébrés
Plants	1	4	4	4	4	4	4	Plantes
Total	13	16	17	17	18	18	20	Total
Liberia								**Libéria**
Vertebrates	45	91	98	98	108	109	112	Vertébrés
Invertebrates	3	9	11	11	11	11	10	Invertébrés
Plants	46	47	49	49	52	52	53	Plantes
Total	94	147	158	158	171	172	175	Total
Libya								**Libye**
Vertebrates	24	42	45	49	55	56	56	Vertébrés
Invertebrates	0	0	1	2	4	4	4	Invertébrés
Plants	1	2	3	3	3	3	5	Plantes
Total	25	44	49	54	62	63	65	Total
Liechtenstein								**Liechtenstein**
Vertebrates	3	0	0	0	2	2	2	Vertébrés
Invertebrates	5	2	4	4	4	4	6	Invertébrés
Plants	0	0	0	0	0	0	0	Plantes
Total	8	2	4	4	6	6	8	Total
Lithuania								**Lituanie**
Vertebrates	12	12	15	14	17	17	18	Vertébrés
Invertebrates	5	5	7	7	7	7	8	Invertébrés
Plants	0	0	1	1	# 2	2	2	Plantes
Total	17	17	23	22	26	26	28	Total

25

Threatened species *(continued)*
Number of species by taxonomic group

Espèces menacées *(suite)*
Nombre d'espèces menacées par groupe taxonomique

Country or area &	2004	2010	2014	2015	2016	2017	2018	Pays ou zone &
Luxembourg								**Luxembourg**
Vertebrates	6	1	2	2	4	4	4	Vertébrés
Invertebrates	4	4	7	7	7	7	7	Invertébrés
Plants	0	0	0	0	0	0	0	Plantes
Total	10	5	9	9	11	11	11	Total
Madagascar								**Madagascar**
Vertebrates	222	283	445	446	527	543	551	Vertébrés
Invertebrates	32	100	110	110	110	172	194	Invertébrés
Plants	276	280	374	409	607	609	871	Plantes
Total	530	663	929	965	1 244	1 324	1 616	Total
Malawi								**Malawi**
Vertebrates	25	127	132	130	135	136	136	Vertébrés
Invertebrates	11	17	16	16	16	16	14	Invertébrés
Plants	14	14	23	25	24	24	26	Plantes
Total	50	158	171	171	175	176	176	Total
Malaysia								**Malaisie**
Vertebrates	190	246	268	269	282	288	280	Vertébrés
Invertebrates	19	242	262	262	262	264	265	Invertébrés
Plants	683	692	706	721	721	720	712	Plantes
Total	892	1 180	1 236	1 252	1 265	1 272	1 257	Total
Maldives								**Maldives**
Vertebrates	12	20	23	23	29	29	29	Vertébrés
Invertebrates	0	39	46	46	46	46	46	Invertébrés
Plants	0	0	0	0	0	0	0	Plantes
Total	12	59	69	69	75	75	75	Total
Mali								**Mali**
Vertebrates	19	23	31	31	34	34	35	Vertébrés
Invertebrates	0	0	0	0	0	0	0	Invertébrés
Plants	6	6	8	8	8	8	11	Plantes
Total	25	29	39	39	42	42	46	Total
Malta								**Malte**
Vertebrates	22	20	23	23	30	30	30	Vertébrés
Invertebrates	3	3	4	4	5	5	5	Invertébrés
Plants	0	3	4	4	4	4	4	Plantes
Total	25	26	31	31	39	39	39	Total
Marshall Islands								**Îles Marshall**
Vertebrates	12	17	22	22	25	28	28	Vertébrés
Invertebrates	1	67	73	73	73	73	73	Invertébrés
Plants	0	0	0	0	0	0	0	Plantes
Total	13	84	95	95	98	101	101	Total
Martinique								**Martinique**
Vertebrates	20	22	28	34	33	37	37	Vertébrés
Invertebrates	1	1	2	2	2	2	2	Invertébrés
Plants	8	8	9	9	9	9	9	Plantes
Total	29	31	39	45	44	48	48	Total
Mauritania								**Mauritanie**
Vertebrates	25	57	66	66	80	83	85	Vertébrés
Invertebrates	1	1	3	3	3	3	3	Invertébrés
Plants	0	0	0	0	0	0	0	Plantes
Total	26	58	69	69	83	86	88	Total
Mauritius								**Maurice**
Vertebrates	28	36	41	41	45	47	48	Vertébrés
Invertebrates	32	98	118	118	118	120	120	Invertébrés
Plants	87	88	91	90	90	90	91	Plantes
Total	147	222	250	249	253	257	259	Total
Mayotte								**Mayotte**
Vertebrates	6	9	15	15	18	18	19	Vertébrés
Invertebrates	1	60	69	69	69	70	70	Invertébrés
Plants	0	0	0	0	0	0	3	Plantes
Total	7	69	84	84	87	88	92	Total
Mexico								**Mexique**
Vertebrates	446	609	628	639	648	655	657	Vertébrés
Invertebrates	41	79	92	93	102	106	106	Invertébrés
Plants	261	255	371	377	402	401	450	Plantes
Total	748	943	1 091	1 109	1 152	1 162	1 213	Total

25 Threatened species *(continued)*
Number of species by taxonomic group

Espèces menacées *(suite)*
Nombre d'espèces menacées par groupe taxonomique

Country or area &	2004	2010	2014	2015	2016	2017	2018	Pays ou zone &
Micronesia (Fed. States of)								**Micronésie (États féd. de)**
Vertebrates	22	35	43	44	48	49	50	Vertébrés
Invertebrates	4	108	115	115	115	114	114	Invertébrés
Plants	4	5	5	4	4	4	4	Plantes
Total	30	148	163	163	167	167	168	Total
Monaco								**Monaco**
Vertebrates	9	11	13	13	17	18	18	Vertébrés
Invertebrates	0	0	2	3	3	3	3	Invertébrés
Plants	0	0	0	0	0	0	1	Plantes
Total	9	11	15	16	20	21	22	Total
Mongolia								**Mongolie**
Vertebrates	36	33	33	33	37	38	37	Vertébrés
Invertebrates	3	3	3	3	3	3	3	Invertébrés
Plants	0	0	0	0	0	0	0	Plantes
Total	39	36	36	36	40	41	40	Total
Montenegro								**Monténégro**
Vertebrates	...	44	47	49	57	57	56	Vertébrés
Invertebrates	...	28	34	34	35	39	42	Invertébrés
Plants	...	0	2	2	2	2	3	Plantes
Total	...	72	83	85	94	98	101	Total
Montserrat								**Montserrat**
Vertebrates	18	21	29	37	36	38	39	Vertébrés
Invertebrates	0	11	11	11	11	11	11	Invertébrés
Plants	3	3	5	6	6	6	6	Plantes
Total	21	35	45	54	53	55	56	Total
Morocco								**Maroc**
Vertebrates	40	86	89	90	101	103	105	Vertébrés
Invertebrates	8	40	46	52	60	66	69	Invertébrés
Plants	2	31	34	34	# 38	38	49	Plantes
Total	50	157	169	176	199	207	223	Total
Mozambique								**Mozambique**
Vertebrates	64	98	117	117	127	129	132	Vertébrés
Invertebrates	5	59	67	67	67	67	67	Invertébrés
Plants	46	52	77	84	84	113	122	Plantes
Total	115	209	261	268	278	309	321	Total
Myanmar								**Myanmar**
Vertebrates	107	143	161	163	178	183	187	Vertébrés
Invertebrates	2	64	77	77	77	77	77	Invertébrés
Plants	38	42	47	61	61	61	61	Plantes
Total	147	249	285	301	316	321	325	Total
Namibia								**Namibie**
Vertebrates	44	66	74	73	81	84	85	Vertébrés
Invertebrates	1	0	4	4	4	4	4	Invertébrés
Plants	24	26	27	28	28	27	27	Plantes
Total	69	92	105	105	113	115	116	Total
Nauru								**Nauru**
Vertebrates	5	12	12	12	14	14	14	Vertébrés
Invertebrates	0	62	68	68	68	68	68	Invertébrés
Plants	0	0	0	0	0	0	0	Plantes
Total	5	74	80	80	82	82	82	Total
Nepal								**Népal**
Vertebrates	69	83	85	85	87	84	84	Vertébrés
Invertebrates	1	3	3	3	3	3	3	Invertébrés
Plants	7	7	12	17	17	17	17	Plantes
Total	77	93	100	105	107	104	104	Total
Netherlands								**Pays-Bas**
Vertebrates	27	18	20	19	26	27	28	Vertébrés
Invertebrates	7	6	10	10	10	10	11	Invertébrés
Plants	0	0	0	0	# 3	3	4	Plantes
Total	34	24	30	29	39	40	43	Total
Netherlands Antilles [former]								**Antilles néerlandaises [anc.]**
Vertebrates	26	24	...	...	...	...	...	Vertébrés
Invertebrates	0	11	...	...	...	...	...	Invertébrés
Plants	2	3	...	...	...	...	...	Plantes
Total	28	38	...	...	...	...	...	Total

25

Threatened species *(continued)*
Number of species by taxonomic group

Espèces menacées *(suite)*
Nombre d'espèces menacées par groupe taxonomique

Country or area &	2004	2010	2014	2015	2016	2017	2018	Pays ou zone &
New Caledonia								**Nouvelle-Calédonie**
Vertebrates	34	61	109	109	114	116	117	Vertébrés
Invertebrates	11	97	125	125	125	125	125	Invertébrés
Plants	217	257	259	259	286	285	350	Plantes
Total	262	415	493	493	525	526	592	Total
New Zealand								**Nouvelle-Zélande**
Vertebrates	114	117	130	130	128	130	131	Vertébrés
Invertebrates	14	15	46	46	46	46	61	Invertébrés
Plants	21	21	21	21	# 23	23	24	Plantes
Total	149	153	197	197	197	199	216	Total
Nicaragua								**Nicaragua**
Vertebrates	49	61	73	79	78	78	79	Vertébrés
Invertebrates	2	17	18	18	20	20	20	Invertébrés
Plants	39	43	43	44	46	46	50	Plantes
Total	90	121	134	141	144	144	149	Total
Niger								**Niger**
Vertebrates	12	22	27	27	29	30	32	Vertébrés
Invertebrates	1	2	1	1	1	1	1	Invertébrés
Plants	2	2	3	3	3	3	3	Plantes
Total	15	26	31	31	33	34	36	Total
Nigeria								**Nigéria**
Vertebrates	61	113	127	127	145	148	148	Vertébrés
Invertebrates	1	12	17	17	17	17	13	Invertébrés
Plants	170	172	188	189	197	196	203	Plantes
Total	232	297	332	333	359	361	364	Total
Niue								**Nioué**
Vertebrates	12	20	20	20	22	22	22	Vertébrés
Invertebrates	0	23	30	30	30	30	30	Invertébrés
Plants	0	0	0	0	0	0	0	Plantes
Total	12	43	50	50	52	52	52	Total
Norfolk Island								**Île Norfolk**
Vertebrates	21	19	17	17	18	19	19	Vertébrés
Invertebrates	12	21	23	23	23	23	23	Invertébrés
Plants	1	1	1	1	1	2	2	Plantes
Total	34	41	41	41	42	44	44	Total
Northern Mariana Islands								**Îles Mariannes du Nord**
Vertebrates	22	29	37	37	39	40	40	Vertébrés
Invertebrates	2	51	57	57	57	57	...	Invertébrés
Plants	4	5	5	5	5	5	5	Plantes
Total	28	85	99	99	101	102	102	Total
Norway								**Norvège**
Vertebrates	22	27	30	30	38	40	42	Vertébrés
Invertebrates	9	7	10	10	10	10	10	Invertébrés
Plants	2	2	3	4	# 14	14	21	Plantes
Total	33	36	43	44	62	64	73	Total
Oman								**Oman**
Vertebrates	48	47	54	53	62	62	68	Vertébrés
Invertebrates	1	26	31	31	31	31	31	Invertébrés
Plants	6	6	6	6	6	6	6	Plantes
Total	55	79	91	90	99	99	105	Total
Other non-specified areas								**Autres zones non-spécifiées**
Vertebrates	79	104	115	114	123	123	129	Vertébrés
Invertebrates	0	122	128	128	128	128	128	Invertébrés
Plants	78	78	82	83	# 85	86	85	Plantes
Total	157	304	325	325	336	337	342	Total
Pakistan								**Pakistan**
Vertebrates	70	92	100	99	110	110	115	Vertébrés
Invertebrates	0	15	18	18	18	18	18	Invertébrés
Plants	2	2	5	12	12	12	12	Plantes
Total	72	109	123	129	140	140	145	Total
Palau								**Palaos**
Vertebrates	13	22	27	27	31	32	34	Vertébrés
Invertebrates	5	102	146	146	146	146	146	Invertébrés
Plants	3	4	4	4	4	4	4	Plantes
Total	21	128	177	177	181	182	184	Total

25 Threatened species *(continued)*

Number of species by taxonomic group

Espèces menacées *(suite)*

Nombre d'espèces menacées par groupe taxonomique

Country or area &	2004	2010	2014	2015	2016	2017	2018	Pays ou zone &
Panama								**Panama**
Vertebrates	113	125	138	148	151	153	154	Vertébrés
Invertebrates	2	20	22	22	22	22	22	Invertébrés
Plants	195	202	203	203	208	208	211	Plantes
Total	310	347	363	373	381	383	387	Total
Papua New Guinea								**Papouasie-Nvl-Guinée**
Vertebrates	141	139	145	146	155	160	161	Vertébrés
Invertebrates	12	171	181	181	181	181	180	Invertébrés
Plants	142	143	145	151	152	152	158	Plantes
Total	295	453	471	478	488	493	499	Total
Paraguay								**Paraguay**
Vertebrates	40	38	39	39	40	40	43	Vertébrés
Invertebrates	0	0	0	0	0	0	0	Invertébrés
Plants	10	10	19	19	19	19	19	Plantes
Total	50	48	58	58	59	59	62	Total
Peru								**Pérou**
Vertebrates	232	274	316	317	351	351	377	Vertébrés
Invertebrates	2	3	8	8	8	8	8	Invertébrés
Plants	274	274	318	318	334	326	328	Plantes
Total	508	551	642	643	693	685	713	Total
Philippines								**Philippines**
Vertebrates	225	262	291	291	302	306	302	Vertébrés
Invertebrates	19	213	237	237	237	238	238	Invertébrés
Plants	212	222	233	239	239	239	245	Plantes
Total	456	697	761	767	778	783	785	Total
Pitcairn								**Pitcairn**
Vertebrates	15	20	20	20	21	21	21	Vertébrés
Invertebrates	5	15	16	16	16	16	16	Invertébrés
Plants	7	7	7	7	7	7	7	Plantes
Total	27	42	43	43	44	44	44	Total
Poland								**Pologne**
Vertebrates	27	17	20	19	23	23	24	Vertébrés
Invertebrates	15	16	23	22	22	22	28	Invertébrés
Plants	4	4	10	10	# 13	13	14	Plantes
Total	46	37	53	51	58	58	66	Total
Portugal								**Portugal**
Vertebrates	51	71	79	81	92	94	98	Vertébrés
Invertebrates	82	79	94	94	97	103	197	Invertébrés
Plants	15	21	81	81	# 83	84	104	Plantes
Total	148	171	254	256	272	281	399	Total
Puerto Rico								**Porto Rico**
Vertebrates	44	49	62	70	69	69	72	Vertébrés
Invertebrates	1	1	0	0	0	0	0	Invertébrés
Plants	52	53	57	57	57	57	63	Plantes
Total	97	103	119	127	126	126	135	Total
Qatar								**Qatar**
Vertebrates	12	19	22	22	26	26	32	Vertébrés
Invertebrates	0	13	13	13	13	13	13	Invertébrés
Plants	0	0	0	0	0	0	0	Plantes
Total	12	32	35	35	39	39	45	Total
Republic of Korea								**République de Corée**
Vertebrates	54	58	64	65	72	74	78	Vertébrés
Invertebrates	1	3	4	4	5	5	8	Invertébrés
Plants	0	3	7	7	# 32	32	32	Plantes
Total	55	64	75	76	109	111	118	Total
Republic of Moldova								**République de Moldova**
Vertebrates	22	24	22	22	26	27	26	Vertébrés
Invertebrates	5	3	5	5	5	6	6	Invertébrés
Plants	0	0	2	2	2	2	2	Plantes
Total	27	27	29	29	33	35	34	Total
Réunion								**Réunion**
Vertebrates	18	16	22	22	24	24	24	Vertébrés
Invertebrates	16	73	87	87	87	89	89	Invertébrés
Plants	14	15	17	17	17	17	18	Plantes
Total	48	104	126	126	128	130	131	Total

25 Threatened species *(continued)*
Number of species by taxonomic group

Espèces menacées *(suite)*
Nombre d'espèces menacées par groupe taxonomique

Country or area &	2004	2010	2014	2015	2016	2017	2018	Pays ou zone &
Romania								**Roumanie**
Vertebrates	40	39	43	42	49	50	50	Vertébrés
Invertebrates	22	24	39	38	38	49	68	Invertébrés
Plants	1	1	5	5	5	5	7	Plantes
Total	63	64	87	85	92	104	125	Total
Russian Federation								**Fédération de Russie**
Vertebrates	114	93	126	126	134	136	139	Vertébrés
Invertebrates	30	25	37	36	36	39	39	Invertébrés
Plants	7	8	54	55	# 60	60	60	Plantes
Total	151	126	217	217	230	235	238	Total
Rwanda								**Rwanda**
Vertebrates	30	49	53	51	51	50	52	Vertébrés
Invertebrates	4	2	2	2	2	4	4	Invertébrés
Plants	3	4	6	8	8	8	41	Plantes
Total	37	55	61	61	61	62	97	Total
Saint Barthélemy								**Saint-Barthélemy**
Vertebrates	...	4	7	16	18	18	19	Vertébrés
Invertebrates	...	11	11	11	11	11	11	Invertébrés
Plants	...	2	2	2	2	2	2	Plantes
Total	...	17	20	29	31	31	32	Total
Saint Helena [5]								**Sainte-Hélène** [5]
Vertebrates	32	31	37	37	39	41	41	Vertébrés
Invertebrates	2	2	13	13	15	15	33	Invertébrés
Plants	26	27	30	30	44	44	44	Plantes
Total	60	60	80	80	98	100	118	Total
Saint Kitts and Nevis								**Saint-Kitts-et-Nevis**
Vertebrates	17	24	32	39	39	40	40	Vertébrés
Invertebrates	0	10	10	10	10	10	10	Invertébrés
Plants	2	2	2	2	2	2	2	Plantes
Total	19	36	44	51	51	52	52	Total
Saint Lucia								**Sainte-Lucie**
Vertebrates	23	29	35	41	43	45	45	Vertébrés
Invertebrates	0	11	11	11	11	11	11	Invertébrés
Plants	6	6	6	6	6	6	6	Plantes
Total	29	46	52	58	60	62	62	Total
Saint Martin (French part)								**St-Martin (partie française)**
Vertebrates	...	4	30	38	37	39	40	Vertébrés
Invertebrates	...	11	10	10	10	10	10	Invertébrés
Plants	...	2	3	3	3	3	3	Plantes
Total	...	17	43	51	50	52	53	Total
Saint Pierre and Miquelon								**Saint-Pierre-et-Miquelon**
Vertebrates	2	4	7	7	11	12	14	Vertébrés
Invertebrates	0	0	0	0	0	0	0	Invertébrés
Plants	0	0	0	0	0	0	0	Plantes
Total	2	4	7	7	11	12	14	Total
Saint Vincent & Grenadines								**Saint-Vincent-Grenadines**
Vertebrates	20	24	33	39	41	43	44	Vertébrés
Invertebrates	0	10	10	10	10	10	10	Invertébrés
Plants	4	4	5	5	5	5	5	Plantes
Total	24	38	48	54	56	58	59	Total
Samoa								**Samoa**
Vertebrates	15	23	26	26	29	29	29	Vertébrés
Invertebrates	1	53	62	62	62	62	62	Invertébrés
Plants	2	2	2	2	2	2	2	Plantes
Total	18	78	90	90	93	93	93	Total
San Marino								**Saint-Marin**
Vertebrates	...	0	0	0	0	0	0	Vertébrés
Invertebrates	...	0	1	1	1	1	1	Invertébrés
Plants	...	0	0	0	0	0	0	Plantes
Total	...	0	1	1	1	1	1	Total
Sao Tome and Principe								**Sao Tomé-et-Principe**
Vertebrates	24	33	38	38	51	52	51	Vertébrés
Invertebrates	2	2	5	5	5	5	4	Invertébrés
Plants	35	35	38	38	38	37	49	Plantes
Total	61	70	81	81	94	94	104	Total

25 Threatened species *(continued)*
Number of species by taxonomic group

Espèces menacées *(suite)*
Nombre d'espèces menacées par groupe taxonomique

Country or area &	2004	2010	2014	2015	2016	2017	2018	Pays ou zone &
Saudi Arabia								**Arabie saoudite**
Vertebrates	37	47	54	57	66	68	69	Vertébrés
Invertebrates	1	53	59	59	59	59	59	Invertébrés
Plants	3	3	3	3	3	4	4	Plantes
Total	41	103	116	119	128	131	132	Total
Senegal								**Sénégal**
Vertebrates	40	72	83	82	95	98	101	Vertébrés
Invertebrates	0	1	13	13	13	13	13	Invertébrés
Plants	7	9	11	11	12	12	13	Plantes
Total	47	82	107	106	120	123	127	Total
Serbia								**Serbie**
Vertebrates	...	29	29	29	35	35	35	Vertébrés
Invertebrates	...	16	23	22	24	30	35	Invertébrés
Plants	...	1	5	5	# 6	6	7	Plantes
Total	...	46	57	56	65	71	77	Total
Serbia and Monten. [former]								**Serbie-et-Monténégro [anc.]**
Vertebrates	42	...	...	...	...	...	...	Vertébrés
Invertebrates	19	...	...	...	...	...	...	Invertébrés
Plants	1	...	...	...	...	...	...	Plantes
Total	62	...	...	...	...	...	...	Total
Seychelles								**Seychelles**
Vertebrates	35	45	54	54	55	57	58	Vertébrés
Invertebrates	4	100	319	319	319	320	320	Invertébrés
Plants	45	45	62	62	62	62	61	Plantes
Total	84	190	435	435	436	439	439	Total
Sierra Leone								**Sierra Leone**
Vertebrates	35	77	90	92	103	103	105	Vertébrés
Invertebrates	4	6	8	8	8	8	8	Invertébrés
Plants	47	48	58	58	65	66	71	Plantes
Total	86	131	156	158	176	177	184	Total
Singapore								**Singapour**
Vertebrates	30	58	56	56	63	63	67	Vertébrés
Invertebrates	1	162	173	173	173	173	173	Invertébrés
Plants	54	57	58	58	58	57	60	Plantes
Total	85	277	287	287	294	293	300	Total
Sint Maarten (Dutch part)								**St-Martin (partie néerland.)**
Vertebrates	...	...	29	37	37	39	40	Vertébrés
Invertebrates	...	...	10	10	10	10	10	Invertébrés
Plants	...	...	2	2	2	2	3	Plantes
Total	...	...	41	49	49	51	53	Total
Slovakia								**Slovaquie**
Vertebrates	27	15	16	16	19	20	21	Vertébrés
Invertebrates	19	17	23	22	22	24	32	Invertébrés
Plants	2	2	7	7	# 10	10	28	Plantes
Total	48	34	46	45	51	54	81	Total
Slovenia								**Slovénie**
Vertebrates	32	36	41	42	50	51	53	Vertébrés
Invertebrates	42	59	75	76	77	81	83	Invertébrés
Plants	0	0	7	7	# 11	11	11	Plantes
Total	74	95	123	125	138	143	147	Total
Solomon Islands								**Îles Salomon**
Vertebrates	52	63	70	70	75	77	75	Vertébrés
Invertebrates	6	141	151	151	151	151	151	Invertébrés
Plants	16	16	17	17	17	17	16	Plantes
Total	74	220	238	238	243	245	242	Total
Somalia								**Somalie**
Vertebrates	46	56	62	60	66	67	71	Vertébrés
Invertebrates	1	51	62	62	62	62	62	Invertébrés
Plants	17	21	42	43	43	46	46	Plantes
Total	64	128	166	165	171	175	179	Total
South Africa								**Afrique du Sud**
Vertebrates	155	185	210	209	219	233	248	Vertébrés
Invertebrates	127	159	202	202	202	202	208	Invertébrés
Plants	75	97	116	116	116	146	151	Plantes
Total	357	441	528	527	537	581	607	Total

25 Threatened species *(continued)*
Number of species by taxonomic group

Espèces menacées *(suite)*
Nombre d'espèces menacées par groupe taxonomique

Country or area &	2004	2010	2014	2015	2016	2017	2018	Pays ou zone &
South Georgia & Sandwich Is.								**Géorgie du S.-Îles Sandwich**
Vertebrates	12	10	9	9	9	9	9	Vertébrés
Invertebrates	0	0	0	0	0	0	0	Invertébrés
Plants	0	0	0	0	0	0	0	Plantes
Total	12	10	9	9	9	9	9	Total
South Sudan								**Soudan du sud**
Vertebrates	...	...	27	26	30	34	36	Vertébrés
Invertebrates	...	...	0	0	0	0	1	Invertébrés
Plants	...	...	15	16	15	15	16	Plantes
Total	...	...	42	42	45	49	53	Total
Spain								**Espagne**
Vertebrates	76	118	122	123	135	138	142	Vertébrés
Invertebrates	63	67	216	215	236	258	288	Invertébrés
Plants	14	55	214	213	# 221	221	251	Plantes
Total	153	240	552	551	592	617	681	Total
Sri Lanka								**Sri Lanka**
Vertebrates	112	149	159	159	167	167	172	Vertébrés
Invertebrates	2	120	130	130	130	130	130	Invertébrés
Plants	280	283	287	291	291	290	294	Plantes
Total	394	552	576	580	588	587	596	Total
State of Palestine								**État de Palestine**
Vertebrates	4	16	18	20	23	24	26	Vertébrés
Invertebrates	0	2	4	4	4	4	4	Invertébrés
Plants	0	0	0	0	3	3	6	Plantes
Total	4	18	22	24	30	31	36	Total
Sudan								**Soudan**
Vertebrates	36	49	56	57	63	67	73	Vertébrés
Invertebrates	2	45	50	50	50	50	50	Invertébrés
Plants	17	18	16	16	16	16	17	Plantes
Total	55	112	122	123	129	133	140	Total
Suriname								**Suriname**
Vertebrates	32	38	48	49	55	55	57	Vertébrés
Invertebrates	0	1	1	1	1	1	1	Invertébrés
Plants	27	26	26	26	27	27	27	Plantes
Total	59	65	75	76	83	83	85	Total
Svalbard and Jan Mayen Is.								**Îles Svalbard-et-Jan Mayen**
Vertebrates	9	3	5	5	7	7	9	Vertébrés
Invertebrates	0	0	0	0	0	0	0	Invertébrés
Plants	0	0	0	0	0	0	0	Plantes
Total	9	3	5	5	7	7	9	Total
Sweden								**Suède**
Vertebrates	20	15	17	16	24	25	27	Vertébrés
Invertebrates	13	11	15	15	15	15	16	Invertébrés
Plants	3	3	4	5	# 14	14	15	Plantes
Total	36	29	36	36	53	54	58	Total
Switzerland								**Suisse**
Vertebrates	17	14	15	15	18	20	22	Vertébrés
Invertebrates	30	28	43	43	43	44	47	Invertébrés
Plants	2	3	4	4	# 10	10	10	Plantes
Total	49	45	62	62	71	74	79	Total
Syrian Arab Republic								**République arabe syrienne**
Vertebrates	26	68	84	84	94	94	91	Vertébrés
Invertebrates	3	7	19	20	20	20	22	Invertébrés
Plants	0	3	4	4	13	18	26	Plantes
Total	29	78	107	108	127	132	139	Total
Tajikistan								**Tadjikistan**
Vertebrates	20	24	27	26	29	30	32	Vertébrés
Invertebrates	2	2	3	3	3	3	3	Invertébrés
Plants	2	14	12	12	12	12	12	Plantes
Total	24	40	42	41	44	45	47	Total
Thailand								**Thaïlande**
Vertebrates	136	201	233	234	245	248	255	Vertébrés
Invertebrates	1	185	211	211	211	211	211	Invertébrés
Plants	84	91	133	150	150	152	155	Plantes
Total	221	477	577	595	606	611	621	Total

25 Threatened species *(continued)*
Number of species by taxonomic group

Espèces menacées *(suite)*
Nombre d'espèces menacées par groupe taxonomique

Country or area &	2004	2010	2014	2015	2016	2017	2018	Pays ou zone &
TFYR of Macedonia								**ex-R.Y. de Macédoine**
Vertebrates	24	31	31	31	34	35	34	Vertébrés
Invertebrates	5	59	69	69	70	75	86	Invertébrés
Plants	0	0	0	0	0	0	5	Plantes
Total	29	90	100	100	104	110	125	Total
Timor-Leste								**Timor-Leste**
Vertebrates	11	18	19	19	20	22	24	Vertébrés
Invertebrates	0	0	1	1	1	1	1	Invertébrés
Plants	0	0	1	1	1	1	1	Plantes
Total	11	18	21	21	22	24	26	Total
Togo								**Togo**
Vertebrates	22	43	50	51	63	65	70	Vertébrés
Invertebrates	0	1	3	3	3	3	3	Invertébrés
Plants	10	10	12	12	12	12	12	Plantes
Total	32	54	65	66	78	80	85	Total
Tokelau								**Tokélaou**
Vertebrates	6	10	11	11	14	14	14	Vertébrés
Invertebrates	0	31	35	35	35	35	35	Invertébrés
Plants	0	0	0	0	0	0	0	Plantes
Total	6	41	46	46	49	49	49	Total
Tonga								**Tonga**
Vertebrates	11	19	23	23	26	28	28	Vertébrés
Invertebrates	2	35	47	47	47	47	47	Invertébrés
Plants	3	4	4	4	4	4	5	Plantes
Total	16	58	74	74	77	79	80	Total
Trinidad and Tobago								**Trinité-et-Tobago**
Vertebrates	32	37	45	53	56	57	58	Vertébrés
Invertebrates	0	10	10	10	10	10	10	Invertébrés
Plants	1	1	2	2	2	2	50	Plantes
Total	33	48	57	65	68	69	118	Total
Tunisia								**Tunisie**
Vertebrates	31	57	61	61	70	70	71	Vertébrés
Invertebrates	5	11	14	15	17	19	20	Invertébrés
Plants	0	7	7	7	7	7	10	Plantes
Total	36	75	82	83	94	96	101	Total
Turkey								**Turquie**
Vertebrates	76	130	191	191	199	199	201	Vertébrés
Invertebrates	13	15	70	76	78	82	85	Invertébrés
Plants	3	5	103	103	# 105	107	114	Plantes
Total	92	150	364	370	382	388	400	Total
Turkmenistan								**Turkménistan**
Vertebrates	35	37	38	38	42	43	46	Vertébrés
Invertebrates	5	5	7	7	7	7	7	Invertébrés
Plants	0	3	4	4	4	4	4	Plantes
Total	40	45	49	49	53	54	57	Total
Turks and Caicos Islands								**Îles Turques-et-Caïques**
Vertebrates	18	22	29	37	37	41	42	Vertébrés
Invertebrates	0	10	10	10	10	10	10	Invertébrés
Plants	2	2	9	9	9	9	9	Plantes
Total	20	34	48	56	56	60	61	Total
Tuvalu								**Tuvalu**
Vertebrates	7	14	15	15	17	18	18	Vertébrés
Invertebrates	1	71	78	78	78	78	78	Invertébrés
Plants	0	0	0	0	0	0	0	Plantes
Total	8	85	93	93	95	96	96	Total
Uganda								**Ouganda**
Vertebrates	77	110	121	117	116	119	124	Vertébrés
Invertebrates	19	15	19	19	19	24	30	Invertébrés
Plants	38	41	49	52	52	53	64	Plantes
Total	134	166	189	188	187	196	218	Total
Ukraine								**Ukraine**
Vertebrates	40	45	48	47	52	53	53	Vertébrés
Invertebrates	14	15	24	23	23	31	38	Invertébrés
Plants	1	1	16	17	# 19	18	23	Plantes
Total	55	61	88	87	94	102	114	Total

25 Threatened species *(continued)*
Number of species by taxonomic group

Espèces menacées *(suite)*
Nombre d'espèces menacées par groupe taxonomique

Country or area &	2004	2010	2014	2015	2016	2017	2018	Pays ou zone &
United Arab Emirates								**Émirats arabes unis**
Vertebrates	23	32	34	33	41	41	45	Vertébrés
Invertebrates	0	16	15	15	15	15	15	Invertébrés
Plants	0	0	0	0	0	0	0	Plantes
Total	23	48	49	48	56	56	60	Total
United Kingdom								**Royaume-Uni**
Vertebrates	32	48	53	53	61	62	64	Vertébrés
Invertebrates	10	11	17	18	18	18	19	Invertébrés
Plants	13	14	15	16	# 22	22	48	Plantes
Total	55	73	85	87	101	102	131	Total
United Rep. of Tanzania								**Rép.-Unie de Tanzanie**
Vertebrates	144	313	346	346	355	355	360	Vertébrés
Invertebrates	33	80	129	129	129	125	129	Invertébrés
Plants	239	298	504	602	602	602	632	Plantes
Total	416	691	979	1 077	1 086	1 082	1 121	Total
U.S. Minor Outlying islands								**Îles min. éloignées des É-U**
Vertebrates	15	23	24	24	25	26	26	Vertébrés
Invertebrates	0	44	47	47	47	47	47	Invertébrés
Plants	0	0	0	0	0	0	0	Plantes
Total	15	67	71	71	72	73	73	Total
United States of America								**États-Unis d'Amérique**
Vertebrates	342	376	438	444	454	456	462	Vertébrés
Invertebrates	561	531	570	575	578	580	580	Invertébrés
Plants	240	245	279	280	# 447	477	498	Plantes
Total	1 143	1 152	1 287	1 299	# 1 479	1 513	1 540	Total
United States Virgin Islands								**Îles Vierges américaines**
Vertebrates	22	21	32	41	42	46	46	Vertébrés
Invertebrates	0	0	0	0	0	0	0	Invertébrés
Plants	9	12	12	12	12	12	17	Plantes
Total	31	33	44	53	54	58	63	Total
Uruguay								**Uruguay**
Vertebrates	48	78	79	79	82	82	85	Vertébrés
Invertebrates	1	1	2	2	2	2	2	Invertébrés
Plants	1	1	22	22	22	22	22	Plantes
Total	50	80	103	103	106	106	109	Total
Uzbekistan								**Ouzbékistan**
Vertebrates	29	34	35	34	39	39	43	Vertébrés
Invertebrates	1	1	3	3	3	3	3	Invertébrés
Plants	1	15	17	17	17	17	16	Plantes
Total	31	50	55	54	59	59	62	Total
Vanuatu								**Vanuatu**
Vertebrates	19	32	35	35	37	36	38	Vertébrés
Invertebrates	0	79	92	92	92	91	91	Invertébrés
Plants	10	10	10	10	10	10	10	Plantes
Total	29	121	137	137	139	137	139	Total
Venezuela (Boliv. Rep. of)								**Venezuela (Rép. boliv. du)**
Vertebrates	151	179	202	209	212	220	228	Vertébrés
Invertebrates	1	21	26	26	26	26	26	Invertébrés
Plants	67	70	77	77	82	82	81	Plantes
Total	219	270	305	312	320	328	335	Total
Viet Nam								**Viet Nam**
Vertebrates	144	186	235	239	260	260	278	Vertébrés
Invertebrates	0	92	126	127	152	152	152	Invertébrés
Plants	145	146	177	199	204	204	231	Plantes
Total	289	424	538	565	616	616	661	Total
Wallis and Futuna Islands								**Îles Wallis-et-Futuna**
Vertebrates	12	16	22	22	24	24	24	Vertébrés
Invertebrates	0	57	65	65	65	64	64	Invertébrés
Plants	1	1	1	1	1	1	1	Plantes
Total	13	74	88	88	90	89	89	Total
Western Sahara								**Sahara occidental**
Vertebrates	18	38	37	36	44	46	48	Vertébrés
Invertebrates	1	1	3	3	3	3	3	Invertébrés
Plants	0	0	0	0	0	0	0	Plantes
Total	19	39	40	39	47	49	51	Total

25 Threatened species *(continued)*
Number of species by taxonomic group

Espèces menacées *(suite)*
Nombre d'espèces menacées par groupe taxonomique

Country or area &	2004	2010	2014	2015	2016	2017	2018	Pays ou zone &
Yemen								**Yémen**
Vertebrates	34	48	55	57	67	68	72	Vertébrés
Invertebrates	2	62	68	68	68	68	68	Invertébrés
Plants	159	159	162	162	162	162	163	Plantes
Total	195	269	285	287	297	298	303	Total
Zambia								**Zambie**
Vertebrates	24	44	51	49	51	53	54	Vertébrés
Invertebrates	7	14	14	14	14	14	15	Invertébrés
Plants	8	9	14	20	20	21	22	Plantes
Total	39	67	79	83	85	88	91	Total
Zimbabwe								**Zimbabwe**
Vertebrates	24	34	38	38	39	41	42	Vertébrés
Invertebrates	2	5	5	5	5	5	7	Invertébrés
Plants	17	16	17	17	17	43	46	Plantes
Total	43	55	60	60	61	89	95	Total
Areas n.e.s								**Zones n.s.a**
Vertebrates	1	1	1	1	3	3	5	Vertébrés
Invertebrates	0	0	1	1	1	1	1	Invertébrés
Plants	0	0	0	0	0	0	0	Plantes
Total	1	1	2	2	4	4	6	Total

Source:

World Conservation Union (IUCN), Gland and Cambridge, IUCN Red List of Threatened Species publication, last accessed July 2018.

Source:

Union internationale pour la conservation de la nature et de ses ressources (UICN), Gland et Cambridge, Liste rouge des espèces menacées publiée par l'UICN, dernier accès juillet 2018.

& Vertebrates consists of mammals, birds, reptiles, amphibians and fish. Invertebrates consists of molluscs and other invertebrates. Plants consists of plants, and since 2016, fungi and protists. Reptiles, fishes, molluscs, other invertebrates, plants, fungi & protists: please note that for these groups, there are still many species that have not yet been assessed for the IUCN Red List and therefore their status is not known (i.e. these groups have not yet been completely assessed). Therefore the figures presented below for these groups should be interpreted as the number of species known to be threatened within those species that have been assessed to date, and not as the overall total number of threatened species for each group.

& Les vertébrés se composent de mammifères, oiseaux, reptiles, amphibiens et poissons; les invertébrés se composent de mollusques et autres invertébrés. A partir de 2016, les plantes incluent aussi les champignons et les protistes. Veuillez noter que beaucoup d'espèces tels que les reptiles, les poissons, les mollusques et autres invertébrés, les plantes, les champignons et les protistes n'ont pas été encore évaluées dans le cadre de la Liste rouge de l'UICN , donc leur statut est inconnu pour le moment (c.-à-d. ces groupes ne sont que partiellement évalués). En conséquent, les données présentées ci-dessous pour chaque groupe doivent être interprétées comme le nombre d'espèces connues et menacées parmi les espèces évaluées à ce jour, et non comme le nombre total d'espèces menacées dans chaque groupe.

1. Excluding overseas territories.
2. The figures for Amphibians displayed here are those that were agreed at the GAA Brazil workshop in April 2003; the "consistent Red List Categories" were not yet accepted by the Brazilian experts.
3. For statistical purposes, the data for China do not include those for the Hong Kong Special Administrative Region (Hong Kong SAR), Macao Special Administrative Region (Macao SAR) and Taiwan Province of China.
4. Excluding the north islands, Saint Barthélemy and Saint Martin (French part).
5. Including Ascension and Tristan da Cunha.

1. Non compris les départements d'outre-mer.
2. Les chiffres concernant les amphibiens sont ceux qui ont été convenus lors de l'atelier de l'Évaluation mondiale des amphibiens du Brésil en avril 2003 ; les "catégories conformes à la Liste rouge" n'ont pas encore été acceptées par les experts brésiliens.
3. Pour la présentation des statistiques, les données pour la Chine ne comprennent pas la région administrative spéciale de Hong Kong (Hong Kong RAS), la région administrative spéciale de Macao (Macao RAS) et la province chinoise de Taïwan.
4. Les îles du Nord, Saint-Barthélemy et Saint-Martin (partie française) sont exclues.
5. Y compris Ascension et Tristan da Cunha.

26 Population employed in research and development (R&D)

Full-time equivalent (FTE)

Population employé dans la recherche et le développement (R-D)

Equivalent temps plein (ETP)

Country or area Pays ou zone	Year Année	Total R & D personnel Total du personnel de R - D	Researchers Chercheurs		Technicians and equivalent staff Techniciens et personnel assimilé		Other supporting staff Autre personnel de soutien	
			Total M & F Total H & F	Females Femmes	Total M & F Total H & F	Females Femmes	Total M & F Total H & F	Females Femmes
Albania[1] Albanie[1]	2008	779	467	207	120	...	192	...
Algeria[1] Algérie[1]	2005	7 331	5 593	2 043	1 134	...	604	...
American Samoa[1] Samoa américaines[1]	2005	6	6	...	...	...	...	...
Angola Angola	2011	2 038	1 150	320	858	242	30	6
Argentina	2005	45 361	31 868	15 416	7 788	...	5 705	...
Argentine	2010	65 299	46 199	23 041[2]	10 143	...	8 957	...
	2014	76 904	51 665	26 280[2]	13 703	...	11 536	...
Armenia[3]	2005[1]	6 892[4]	5 056	2 329	345	...	1 491[4]	...
Arménie[3]	2010[1]	6 558[4]	4 981	2 261	479	...	672	...
	2015[2,5]	5 044[4]	3 856	2 023	308	186	503	270
Australia	2004	116 194	81 192	...	...	...	...	...
Australie	2008	137 489	92 649	...	24 243	...	20 597	...
	*2010	...	100 414	...	...	...	...	...
Austria	2004	42 891	25 955	4 740	12 067	2 901	4 869	2 471
Autriche	*2005	47 625	28 470	...	...	...	...	...
	2009	56 438	34 664	7 765	16 709	3 903	5 065	2 398
	*2010	59 923	36 581	...	...	...	...	...
	2013	66 186	40 426	9 286	20 310	4 263	5 451	2 343
	*2015	69 318	42 339	...	...	...	...	...
Azerbaijan[3]	2005	18 164[4]	11 603	6 056	1 825	...	3 086	...
Azerbaïdjan[3]	2010	17 924[4]	11 037	6 101	1 819	1 087	3 531	1 866
	2015	23 093[4]	16 137	8 849	1 881	1 005	2 571	1 378
Bahrain Bahreïn	2014	562	493	205	23	12	41	16
Belarus[3]	2005	30 222[4]	18 267	7 897	2 112	...	5 763	...
Bélarus[3]	2010	31 712[4]	19 879	8 392	2 248	...	9 585[4]	...
	2015	26 153[4]	16 953	6 863	1 736	...	7 464[4]	...
Belgium	2005	53 517	33 146	9 769	15 047	4 585	5 324	2 702
Belgique	2010	60 075	40 832	12 962	14 401	5 079	4 841	2 517
	2011	62 895	42 686	13 545	15 176	5 232	5 033	2 575
	* #2015	77 864	55 087	...	...	...	...	...
Benin[1,3] Bénin[1,3]	2007	...	1 000	...	...	...	...	...
Bermuda[3]	2010	80	41	17	10	...	29	13
Bermudes[3]	2015	60	34	11	4	...	22	12
Bolivia (Plurin. State of)	2002	1 090	1 040	...	...	...	50	...
Bolivie (État plurin. de)	2010	2 497	1 646	...	258	...	593	...
Bosnia and Herzegovina	2005[1]	731	253	...	198	...	280	...
Bosnie-Herzégovine	2007[1]	1 554	745	...	270	...	536	...
	2015	2 173	1 253	547	227	115	210	118
Botswana[3]	2005[1]	2 140	1 732	533	408	...	...	...
Botswana[3]	2013	1 716	760	225	328	110	628	282
Brazil	2005	196 283	109 410	...	86 873	...	...	...
Brésil	2010	266 709	138 653	...	128 056	...	...	...
Brunei Darussalam[1]	2003	140	98	...	...	...	...	...
Brunéi Darussalam[1]	#2004	...	102	...	...	...	...	...
Bulgaria	2005	15 853	10 053	4 673	3 778	2 256	2 022	1 349
Bulgarie	2010	16 574	10 979	5 506	3 704	2 189	1 891	1 172
	2011	16 986	11 902	5 940	3 263	1 970	1 821	1 139
	2014	19 335	13 201	6 571	...	...	...	...
	2015	22 421	14 224	...	...	...	...	...
Burkina Faso[3]	2005	942[1,6]	301[1,6]	37	225[1,6]	...	416[1,6]	...
Burkina Faso[3]	#2010	2 548	1 144	264	608	149	796	256
Burundi[3]	2010	744[1]	374[1]	56	117[1]	...	253[1]	...
Burundi[3]	2011	746[1]	379[1]	55	125[1]	...	242[1]	...

26 Population employed in research and development (R&D) *(continued)*
Full-time equivalent (FTE)

Population employé dans la recherche et le développement (R-D) *(suite)*
Equivalent temps plein (ETP)

Country or area Pays ou zone	Year Année	Total R & D personnel Total du personnel de R - D	Researchers / Chercheurs Total M & F Total H & F	Researchers / Chercheurs Females Femmes	Technicians and equivalent staff / Techniciens et personnel assimilé Total M & F Total H & F	Technicians and equivalent staff / Techniciens et personnel assimilé Females Femmes	Other supporting staff / Autre personnel de soutien Total M & F Total H & F	Other supporting staff / Autre personnel de soutien Females Femmes
Cabo Verde [1]	2002	151	60	...	15	...	76	...
Cabo Verde [1]	2011[7]	# 37	# 25	9	# 4	2	# 8	5
Cambodia	2002[1]	494	223	50	170	...	102	...
Cambodge	2015	# 1 895	# 471	# 126	# 945	330	# 478	216
Cameroon [3]								
Cameroun [3]	2008	5 600	4 562	994	338	...	700	...
Canada	2005	218 590	136 700	...	52 825	...	29 072	...
Canada	2010	233 060	158 660	...	51 930	...	22 470	...
	2013	226 620	159 190	...	46 540	...	20 890	...
Central African Republic [3]	2005[1]	...	11	...	...	...	...	...
	2007[7]	...	41[1]	17	...	...	...	...
République centrafricaine [3]	#2009[1]	...	134	...	...	...	...	...
Chile	2010[8]	11 491	5 440	1 671	3 909	1 590	2 142	941
Chili	*2015	15 261	8 175	2 692	5 117	2 220	1 970	877
China [9]	2005[10]	1 364 799	1 118 698	...	...	...	...	...
Chine [9]	2010	2 553 829	1 210 841	...	...	...	...	...
	2015	3 758 848	1 619 028	...	...	...	...	...
China, Hong Kong SAR	2005	22 053	18 024	...	2 346	...	1 683	...
Chine, RAS de Hong	2010	24 060	20 582	...	2 159	...	1 319	...
Kong	2014	27 378	23 831	...	1 985	...	1 563	...
	2015	...	23 675	...	...	...	...	...
China, Macao SAR [1]	#2005	413	298	77	110	...	5	...
Chine, RAS de Macao	2010	676	350	116	313	158	13	9
[1]	2015	1 464	769	245	667	301	29	23
Colombia	2005	...	5 264	1 808	...	...	...	...
Colombie	2010	...	8 369	3 067	...	...	...	...
	2014	...	5 491	2 032	...	...	...	...
Congo								
Congo	2000	217[1]	102[1]	13	111[1]	22	4[1]	...
Costa Rica [3]	2005	...	1 444	569	...	...	...	...
Costa Rica [3]	2010	6 156[2]	3 569[2]	1 475[2]	1 326[2]	388	1 261[2]	476
	2014[2]	6 370	4 072	1 803	1 342	416	956	292
Côte d'Ivoire [1]								
Côte d'Ivoire [1]	2005	...	1 269	210	...	...	...	...
Croatia	2005	9 270	5 727	2 710	2 633	1 196	910	584
Croatie	2010	10 859	7 104	3 485	2 601	1 280	1 154	768
	2014	10 027	6 117	3 119	2 879	1 310	1 031	675
	2015	10 645	6 367	...	3 157	...	1 121	...
Cuba [3]	2005	33 988	5 526	2 703	...	...	28 462[11]	...
Cuba [3]	2010	16 641	4 872	2 381	...	...	11 769	...
	2014	14 418	4 355	2 098	...	...	10 063	...
	2015	23 552	3 853	...	...	...	19 699	...
Cyprus	2005	1 157	682	239	273	98	201	105
Chypre	2010	1 302	905	337	216	89	181	101
	2014	1 269	888	343	224	99	158	89
	*2015	1 245	860	...	...	...	...	...
Czechia	#2005	43 370	24 169	6 349	13 773	5 153	5 429	2 633
Tchéquie	2010	52 290	29 228	7 429	15 971	5 141	7 092	3 369
	2014	64 444	36 040	8 701	19 846	6 065	8 558	4 154
	*2015	66 433	38 081	...	19 350	...	9 002	...
Dem. Rep. of the Congo [3,4]	2005	33 478	10 411	...	1 510	...	21 557	...
Rép. dém. du Congo [3,4]	2009	34 820	12 470	...	1 843	...	20 507	...
Denmark	2005	43 499	28 179	8 113	10 781	5 364	4 538	2 534
Danemark	2010	56 623	37 435	* 11 654	12 557	* 4 959	6 631	* 3 433
	2011	57 585	39 181	12 376	11 856	4 694	6 548	3 112
	2013	57 744	39 868	13 544	...	...	...	...
	*2015	59 532	42 425	...	...	...	...	...

26 Population employed in research and development (R&D) *(continued)*
Full-time equivalent (FTE)

Population employé dans la recherche et le développement (R-D) *(suite)*
Equivalent temps plein (ETP)

Country or area Pays ou zone	Year Année	Total R & D personnel Total du personnel de R - D	Researchers Chercheurs Total M & F Total H & F	 Females Femmes	Technicians and equivalent staff Techniciens et personnel assimilé Total M & F Total H & F	 Females Femmes	Other supporting staff Autre personnel de soutien Total M & F Total H & F	 Females Femmes
Ecuador	2003	...	645	...	...	...	...	...
Équateur	2010	4 769	2 110	854	1 029	300	1 630	783
	2014	8 948	6 373	2 630	1 435	714	1 140	649
Egypt	2010	86 455[1]	40 752[1,5]	16 972	20 758[1,6]	...	24 945[1,6]	...
Égypte	2015	112 752	62 208	26 477	31 795[5]	...	18 748[5]	...
El Salvador [3]	2005	...	260	81	...	...	...	...
El Salvador [3]	2010	...	516	190	...	...	...	...
	2015	...	828	315	...	...	...	...
Estonia	2005	4 362	3 331	1 317	567	274	464	305
Estonie	2010	5 277	4 077	1 688	907	404	293	211
	2014	5 796	4 323	1 865	896	438	577	423
	*2015	5 464	4 186	...	890	...	388	...
Ethiopia	2005	5 112	1 608	111	779	...	2 725	...
Éthiopie	2007	6 051	1 615	125	978	...	3 458	...
	#2010	8 282	3 701	...	1 441	...	3 140	...
	2013	11 501	4 267	556	3 157	757	4 078	1 316
Faroe Islands Îles Féroé	2003	131	86	21	41	...	4	...
Finland	2005	57 471	39 582	...	...	...	...	...
Finlande	2010	55 897	41 425	...	...	...	...	...
	2015	50 367	37 516	...	...	...	...	...
France	2005	349 681	202 507	...	105 171	...	42 003	...
France	2010	# 397 756	# 243 533	46 001[8]	# 118 364	...	# 35 860	...
	2014	417 129	267 308	# 70 939[8]	114 190	...	35 631	...
Gabon [1,3]	2004[6]	188	80	25	68	...	40	...
Gabon [1,3]	2009	# 839	# 531	# 118	# 142	55	# 166	66
Gambia [3]	2005[1]	84	46	4	28	...	10	...
Gambie [3]	2008	# 855	# 155	31	# 200	...	# 500	...
	2009	926	179	...	198	...	549	...
	2011	# 1 055	# 60[1]	12	# 737	...	# 233	...
Georgia [3]	2005	13 415	8 112	4 275	1 810	...	3 493	...
Géorgie [3]	2015[1,2,5]	12 486	9 069	4 591	1 589	990	1 825	963
Germany	2005	475 278	272 148	47 666	94 578	29 657	108 553	44 729
Allemagne	2009	534 975	317 307	65 258	111 660	34 277	106 008	44 018
	2010	548 723	* 327 996	...	* 113 211	...	* 107 515	...
	2013	588 615	354 463	80 353	138 770	38 432	95 382	44 089
	2014	605 252	351 923	...	153 387	...	99 943	...
	*2015	613 740	357 538	...	...	...	...	...
Ghana Ghana	2010	# 3 005	# 941	163	# 731	186	# 1 333	288
Greece	2005	33 603	19 593	6 213	8 450	3 070	5 559	3 007
Grèce	*2007	35 531	21 014	...	...	...	...	...
	#2011	36 913	24 674	9 602	6 336	2 973	5 903	2 897
	2013	42 188	29 228	11 361	...	...	...	...
	*2015	50 512	35 069	...	...	...	...	...
Greenland Groenland	2004	48	40	11	8[12]	...	...	...
Guam Guam	2005	51	48	...	...	...	...	...
Guatemala [1]	2005	851	388	...	139	...	324	...
Guatemala [1]	2010	876	363	145	273	...	240	...
	2012	920	411	172	276	...	233	...
Guinea [1,3]	2000	3 711	2 117	122	768	...	826	...
Guinée [1,3]	2013	# 752	# 214	# 21	# 33	3	# 75	22
Honduras [3] Honduras [3]	2003	2 280	539	143	...	...	1 741	731
Hungary	2005	23 239	15 878	...	4 591	...	2 770	...
Hongrie	2010	31 480	21 342	6 447	5 967	3 230	4 171	2 346
	2014	37 329	26 213	6 908	6 833	3 524	4 283	2 266
	2015	36 847	25 316	...	7 112	...	4 419	...

26 Population employed in research and development (R&D) *(continued)*
Full-time equivalent (FTE)

Population employé dans la recherche et le développement (R-D) *(suite)*
Equivalent temps plein (ETP)

Country or area Pays ou zone	Year Année	Total R & D personnel Total du personnel de R - D	Researchers Chercheurs Total M & F Total H & F	Researchers Chercheurs Females Femmes	Technicians and equivalent staff Techniciens et personnel assimilé Total M & F Total H & F	Technicians and equivalent staff Techniciens et personnel assimilé Females Femmes	Other supporting staff Autre personnel de soutien Total M & F Total H & F	Other supporting staff Autre personnel de soutien Females Femmes
Iceland	2005	3 226	2 155	784	669	299	402	181
Islande	2009	3 397	2 505	1 000	626	279	266	96
	#2011	3 244	2 258	812	604	192	381	246
	2015	2 941	# 1 944	...	# 694	...	# 303	...
India	2000	318 443	115 936	11 304[8]	90 045[13]	10 363	112 462[13]	19 531
Inde	2005	391 149	154 827	19 707[8]	105 808[13]	...	130 514[13]	...
	2010	441 126	192 819	27 532	124 188[13]	...	124 119[13]	...
	2015	528 219	282 994	39 389	125 184	15 644	120 041	22 673
Indonesia [3]	2005	# 55 118[1]	# 35 564[1]	10 874	# 9 253[1]	...	# 10 301[1]	...
Indonésie [3]	#2009[1]	...	41 143	...	...	...	...	...
Iran (Islamic Republic of)	2010[5,14]	...	54 813	14 775	...	...	...	...
Iran (Rép. islamique d')	2012	80 886	52 656	15 484	14 189	3 978	14 041	4 705
Iraq	2010[2,5]	16 857[4]	12 849[4]	4 380	1 927[4]	...	1 988[4]	...
Iraq	2015	3 657	2 341	955	889	390	427	169
Ireland	2005	16 690	11 587	3 241	3 043	797	2 060	881
Irlande	*2010	19 722	14 176	4 672	3 052	813	2 494	1 044
	2013	* 24 129	* 16 844	4 933	* 4 490	876	* 2 795	1 086
	*2015	29 444	21 451	...	4 955	...	3 039	...
Israel [15]	2011	70 401	55 184	11 700	9 818	2 320	5 399	2 006
Israël [15]	*2012	77 143	63 521	...	7 676	...	5 946	...
Italy	2005	175 248	82 489	26 797	...	...	...	...
Italie	2010	225 632	103 424	35 792	...	...	...	...
	2014	249 467	118 183	42 700	...	...	...	...
	*2015	248 140	120 677	...	...	...	...	...
Japan	2005	896 855	680 631	...	71 726	...	144 498	...
Japon	2010	877 928	656 032	...	74 857	...	147 039	...
	2015	875 005	662 071	...	66 802	...	146 131	...
Jordan [3]	2003	42 153	15 891	3 385	19 322	2 073	6 940	2 101
Jordanie [3]	2008	...	11 310[1]	# 2 548	...	...	...	...
	#2015[1]	11 908[16]	9 092	1 790	2 816	626	...	...
Kazakhstan	2010	8 325	6 022	...	454	...	1 179	...
Kazakhstan	#2013	17 586	12 552	...	3 012	...	2 022	...
	2015	...	18 454	...	...	...	...	...
Kenya Kenya	2010	# 42 566	# 9 305	1 861	# 26 384	12 024	# 6 877	2 735
Kuwait [1,6]	2005	800	384	...	96	...	320	...
Koweït [1,6]	2010	829	407	152	87	23	335	145
	2012	825	439	159	66	17	320	155
Kyrgyzstan [3]	2005	3 419[4]	2 187	977	226	...	498	...
Kirghizistan [3]	2010	3 129[4]	1 974	876	261	...	428	...
	2015[5]	4 557[4]	3 441	1 742	314	161	403	272
Lao People's Dem. Rep. [1] Rép. dém. populaire lao [1]	2002	268	87	...	...	...	...	...
Latvia	2005	5 483	3 282	1 636	1 062	554	1 139	594
Lettonie	2010	5 563	3 896	1 823	915	401	752	439
	2011	5 432	3 947	2 045	819	387	666	440
	2013	5 396	3 625	1 829	...	...	...	...
	*2015	5 570	3 613	...	...	...	...	...
Lesotho	2004	51[1]	20[1]	10[8]	21[1]	...	10[1]	...
Lesotho	2009[1]	105	46	16[8]	47	...	11	...
	2015[2,5]	72	50	20	14	7	8	2
Libya [3]	2004[1]	772	215	...	164	...	...	...
Libye [3]	2009	1 131[1]	460[1]	101	229[1]	...	268[1]	...
Lithuania	2005	11 002	7 637	3 706	1 436	939	1 929	1 280
Lituanie	2010	12 315	8 599	4 367	1 691	887	2 025	1 281
	2011	11 173	8 390	4 099	1 426	812	1 357	888
	2014	11 791	9 075	4 221	...	...	...	...
	*2015	10 523	8 124	...	...	...	...	...

26 Population employed in research and development (R&D) *(continued)*
Full-time equivalent (FTE)

Population employé dans la recherche et le développement (R-D) *(suite)*
Equivalent temps plein (ETP)

Country or area Pays ou zone	Year Année	Total R & D personnel Total du personnel de R - D	Researchers Chercheurs Total M & F Total H & F	Researchers Chercheurs Females Femmes	Technicians and equivalent staff Techniciens et personnel assimilé Total M & F Total H & F	Technicians and equivalent staff Techniciens et personnel assimilé Females Femmes	Other supporting staff Autre personnel de soutien Total M & F Total H & F	Other supporting staff Autre personnel de soutien Females Femmes
Luxembourg	2005	4 392	2 227	392	1 558	258	607	250
Luxembourg	2009	4 711	2 396	534	1 423	384	891	437
	2010	4 972	2 613	…	1 708	…	651	…
	2013	4 975	2 503	683	1 596	284	875	267
	*2015	5 593	2 869	…	1 783	…	942	…
Madagascar [3]	2005	2 414[1]	1 607[1]	563	195[1]	…	612[1]	…
Madagascar [3]	2010	# 3 020[1]	# 2 334[1]	821	# 326[1]	…	# 360[1]	…
	2014[1]	# 5 782	# 1 828	# 587	# 575	246	# 2 369	929
Malawi								
Malawi	2010	1 721[2]	732[2]	136	873[2]	155	116[2]	15
Malaysia	2004	17 887	12 670	4 701	1 598	…	3 619	…
Malaisie	2010	50 484	41 253	19 029	3 676	…	5 555	…
	2015	82 360	69 864	33 931	4 007	1 245	8 490	4 155
Mali								
Mali	2010	856	443	62	342	44	71	34
Malta	2005	825	479	121	222	20	124	65
Malte	2010	1 125	595	153	349	36	181	88
	2014	1 444	786	231	410	50	248	115
	*2015	1 391	817	…	311	…	263	…
Mauritius [2]								
Maurice [2]	2012	627	228	94	68	34	331	57
Mexico	2005	83 685	43 922	…	25 796	…	13 967	…
Mexique	2010	70 997	38 497	…	20 760	…	11 740	…
	2013	59 073	29 921	…	16 345	…	12 807	…
Monaco [1]								
Monaco [1]	2005	18	10	5	5	…	3	…
Mongolia [3]	2000	2 113[1]	1 631[1]	…	294[1]	150	188[1]	…
Mongolie [3]	2005	2 283[1]	1 731[1]	819	81[1]	…	471[1]	…
	2010	2 517[1]	1 739[1]	865[1]	129[1]	48	649[1]	399
	2015[1]	2 515	1 867	915	97	33	551	329
Montenegro								
Monténégro	2015	673	523	239	81	39	68[1]	47
Morocco	2010	28 041[1]	23 280[1]	7 744	1 697[1,6]	…	1 747[1,6]	…
Maroc	2012	31 099[1]	# 28 265	9 018[2,5]	1 414[1,6]	217[6]	1 420[1,6]	341[6]
	2014	37 859[1]	35 025	…	1 414[1,6]	217[6]	1 420[1,6]	341[6]
Mozambique	2010	# 2 164[2]	# 912[2]	294	# 1 093[2]	…	# 159[2]	…
Mozambique	2015	2 320	1 162	336	723	217	435	144
Myanmar [1]								
Myanmar [1]	2002	7 418	837	…	6 499	…	82	…
Namibia [3]	2010	949	748	327	118	…	83[1]	41
Namibie [3]	2014[1]	1 132	749	290	255	95	128	79
Nauru [1,3]								
Nauru [1,3]	2003	77	19	3	18	…	36	…
Nepal [3]	2002	* 13 500	* 3 000	* 450	* 6 000	…	4 500[1]	…
Népal [3]	2010	# 41 911[1,17]	# 5 123[1]	399	# 12 053[1]	…	# 21 167[1]	…
Netherlands	2005	93 599	47 854	…	23 265	…	22 480	…
Pays-Bas	2010	100 544	53 703	…	22 128	…	24 714	…
	#2011	117 436	61 335	15 629	34 107	7 340	21 993	8 723
	2014	124 066	76 229	19 525	…	…	…	…
	*2015	128 327	76 977	…	…	…	…	…
New Zealand	2005	18 929	12 986	…	3 200	…	2 800	…
Nouvelle-Zélande	2009	23 200	16 100	…	4 100	…	2 900	…
	2013	24 900	17 900	…	4 520	…	2 580	…
Nicaragua [3]	2002	456	256	96[8]	…	…	200[1]	…
Nicaragua [3]	2004	371	326	…	45	15	…	…
	2012	…	874	…	…	…	…	…
Niger [1]								
Niger [1]	2005	595	101	…	137	…	357	…
Nigeria [1,3]	2005	66 574	28 533	4 839	10 854	…	27 187	…
Nigéria [1,3]	#2007	32 802[2]	17 624[2]	4 106	4 647[2]	1 026	10 531[2]	3 759

26 Population employed in research and development (R&D) *(continued)*

Full-time equivalent (FTE)

Population employé dans la recherche et le développement (R-D) *(suite)*

Equivalent temps plein (ETP)

Country or area Pays ou zone	Year Année	Total R & D personnel Total du personnel de R - D	Researchers Chercheurs Total M & F Total H & F	Researchers Chercheurs Females Femmes	Technicians and equivalent staff Techniciens et personnel assimilé Total M & F Total H & F	Technicians and equivalent staff Techniciens et personnel assimilé Females Femmes	Other supporting staff Autre personnel de soutien Total M & F Total H & F	Other supporting staff Autre personnel de soutien Females Femmes
Norway	2005	29 966	21 200	...	...	...	...	...
Norvège	2010	36 121	26 451	...	...	...	...	...
	*2015	42 695	30 826	...	...	...	...	...
Oman Oman	2015	1 567	907	246	224	75	436	101
Pakistan	2005	53 159[2,5]	12 689[2,5]	2 053	6 471[2,5]	...	33 999[2,5]	...
Pakistan	2009	74 695[2,5]	27 602[2,5]	6 534	10 993[2,5]	...	36 100[2,5]	...
	2015[2,5]	101 519	55 611	19 097	13 450	1 259	32 458	2 504
Panama	2002	1 331[18]	297	...	...	...	1 034	...
Panama	2005	1 302[18]	344	...	...	...	...	...
	2008	1 449	463	...	377	...	609	...
	2009	531[18]	394	...	...	...	# 137	...
	2013	1 178	150	74	595	298	433	166
Paraguay	2005	# 614	419	...	...	...	# 195	...
Paraguay	2008	667	466	...	...	...	201	...
	2011	# 496	# 317	...	79	...	# 100	...
	2015[2]	...	1 222	575	...	...	...	...
Peru [3]	2004	8 434	4 965	...	1 757	...	1 712	...
Pérou [3]	#2010	...	434	...	...	...	...	...
	2014	...	3 737	...	...	...	...	...
Philippines	2005	9 407[4]	6 896	3 500	897	...	1 440	...
Philippines	2009	10 366	7 505	3 882	1 116	381	1 743	708
	2013	26 577	18 481	8 872	2 765	1 041	5 140	2 086
Poland	2005	76 761	62 162	24 521	8 947	...	5 652	...
Pologne	2010	81 843	64 511	24 745	10 939	...	6 393	...
	2014	104 359	78 622	27 765	16 703	...	9 034	...
	2015	109 249	82 594	...	16 872	...	9 783	...
Portugal	2005	25 728	21 126	9 530	2 918	1 177	1 683	954
Portugal	2010	47 616	41 523	18 175	4 004	1 481	2 088	894
	2014	46 878	38 155	16 691	7 389	3 069	1 334	642
	*2015	48 478	39 580	...	...	...	...	...
Puerto Rico [3]	2009	5 776	2 986	...	2 790	...	...	...
Porto Rico [3]	2013	4 793	1 976	...	2 516	...	301[13]	...
Qatar Qatar	2012	1 952	1 203	243	394	135	354	147
Republic of Korea	2005[19]	215 345	179 812	...	26 272	...	9 261	...
République de Corée	2010	335 228	264 118	...	47 557	...	23 554	...
	2015	442 027	356 447	...	61 604	...	23 975	...
Republic of Moldova	2005	4 672[8]	2 583[8]	1 120	334[8]	...	1 755[8]	...
République de	2010	4 316	2 709	1 258	287	202	1 320	773
Moldova	2015	4 169	2 694	1 341	240	163	1 235	653
Romania	2005	33 222	22 958	10 617	4 998	2 859	5 266	2 414
Roumanie	2010	26 171	19 780	8 797	3 139	1 695	3 252	1 424
	2014	31 391	18 109	8 142	4 510	2 119	8 772	3 898
	2015	31 331	17 459	...	5 328	...	8 544	...
Russian Federation	2005	919 716	464 577	...	74 253	...	380 886	...
Fédération de Russie	2010	839 992	442 071	...	68 042	...	329 879	...
	2015	833 654	449 180	...	70 121	...	314 353	...
Rwanda [3,7] Rwanda [3,7]	2009	1 001[1]	564[1]	123	8[1]	...	429[1]	...
Saint Helena Sainte-Hélène	2000	33[1]	2[1]	...	8[1]	4	23[1]	...
Saint Vincent & Grenadines [3] Saint-Vincent-Grenadines [3]	2002	131	21	...	110	...	...	...
Saudi Arabia [3]	2002[1,7]	4 182	1 513	263	1 674	...	995	...
Arabie saoudite [3]	2009	2 655[1,6]	1 271[1,6]	18	658[1,6]	...	726[1,6]	...
	2013[4]	# 751 927	# 35 324	# 8 198	# 100 053	39 420	# 616 550	276 272
Senegal Sénégal	2010	5 642	4 679	1 162	441	101	523	161

26 Population employed in research and development (R&D) *(continued)*

Full-time equivalent (FTE)

Population employé dans la recherche et le développement (R-D) *(suite)*

Equivalent temps plein (ETP)

Country or area Pays ou zone	Year Année	Total R & D personnel Total du personnel de R - D	Researchers Chercheurs Total M & F Total H & F	Researchers Chercheurs Females Femmes	Technicians and equivalent staff Techniciens et personnel assimilé Total M & F Total H & F	Technicians and equivalent staff Techniciens et personnel assimilé Females Femmes	Other supporting staff Autre personnel de soutien Total M & F Total H & F	Other supporting staff Autre personnel de soutien Females Femmes
Serbia	2010[20]	17 274	10 985	5 370	2 428	1 475	3 861	1 954
Serbie	2015	21 573[20]	14 657[20]	7 201	2 974[20]	1 507	3 942[20]	1 981
Seychelles [1]								
Seychelles [1]	2005	180	13	4	53	...	114	...
Singapore	2005	28 586	23 789	...	2 375	...	2 422	...
Singapour	2010	37 013	32 031	...	2 342	...	2 641	...
	2014	42 543	36 666	...	2 490	...	3 387	...
Slovakia	2005	14 404	10 921	4 484	2 245	1 218	1 238	670
Slovaquie	2010	18 188	15 183	6 376	2 087	1 046	918	589
	2014	17 594	14 742	6 090	1 990	833	862	508
	2015	17 591	14 406	...	2 116	...	1 070	...
Slovenia	2005	8 994	5 253	1 777	2 820	1 067	921	501
Slovénie	2010	12 940	7 703	2 668	3 928	1 386	1 309	642
	2014	14 866	8 574	2 973	4 946	1 594	1 345	598
	*2015	14 225	7 900	...	4 970	...	1 354	...
South Africa	2005	28 798	17 303	6 272	5 248	1 749	6 247	2 928
Afrique du Sud	2010	29 486	18 720	7 649	5 410	2 016	5 357	2 546
	2013	37 956	23 346	10 165	6 905	2 565	7 705	3 757
Spain	2005	174 773	109 720	41 371	39 904	13 259	25 149	11 390
Espagne	2010	222 022	134 653	51 831	60 697	24 052	26 672	12 988
	2014	200 233	122 235	47 136	54 405	21 335	23 592	11 460
	2015	200 866	122 437	...	...	...	...	...
Sri Lanka	#2004	5 475	2 679	861	1 474	...	1 322	...
Sri Lanka	2010	5 714	2 140	842	1 851	...	1 723	...
	2013	* 4 601	2 276	851	* 1 258	303	1 067	347
State of Palestine							1,1	
État de Palestine							4,2	
	2007	566[1,14,20]	280[1,14,20]	94	91[1,14,20]	...	195[0]	...
	2010[2]	2 074	1 312	...	291	...	471[21]	...
	2013[2]	5 161	2 492	...	772	...	# 1 483	...
Sudan [former] [3]								
Soudan [anc.] [3]	*2005	23 726	11 208	4 483	5 569	...	6 949	...
Sweden [8]	#2005	77 557	55 001	15 960[22]	...	...	...	...
Suède [8]	2009	77 363	47 308	14 080	19 686	4 849	10 369	3 817
	*2010	77 418	49 312	...	...	...	...	...
	2011	78 445	48 702	14 721	19 194	4 860	10 551	3 941
	2013	80 957	# 64 194	# 17 989	...	...	...	...
	*2015	84 523	68 670	...	...	...	...	...
Switzerland	2004	52 250	25 400	...	17 130	...	9 720	...
Suisse	2008	62 066	25 142	...	21 763	...	15 161	...
	2012	75 476	35 950	...	22 179	...	17 347	...
Tajikistan [3]	2004	2 487[4]	1 548	407	247	...	692[4]	...
Tadjikistan [3]	2005	3 220[4]	1 993	...	324	...	903[4]	...
	2006	3 110[4]	1 895	735	202	...	1 013[4]	...
	2010[2,5]	2 827[4]	1 802	...	329	...	427	...
	2015[2,5]	3 704[4]	2 467	886	410	212	448	212
Thailand	2005	36 967	20 506	10 241	10 520	...	5 941	...
Thaïlande	2009	# 60 344	22 000	11 064	# 15 036	...	# 23 308	...
	2015	89 617	59 416	16 577[2]	16 539	3 950[2]	5 701	2 662[2]
TFYR of Macedonia	2005	1 434	1 113	576	168	94	153	81
ex-R.Y. de Macédoine	2010	1 434	1 102	620	170	104	162	106
	2015	2 024	1 785	905	155	83	84	48
Togo	#2005[7]	312	186	...	126	...	...	...
Togo	2010	# 444[2]	# 220[2]	21	# 54[2]	10	# 169[2]	14
	2014[2]	539	272	24	64	20	204	42
Trinidad and Tobago [3]	2005	954	548	183	406	180	...	...
Trinité-et-Tobago [3]	2010	1 351	951	462	400	152	...	...
	2014	2 115	1 228	671	415	163	472	227
Tunisia	2010	15 589	14 727	7 654	499[6]	197[6]	363[6]	228[6]
Tunisie	2015	21 294	20 113	11 844	710[6]	289[6]	471[6]	283[6]

26 Population employed in research and development (R&D) *(continued)*
Full-time equivalent (FTE)

Population employé dans la recherche et le développement (R-D) *(suite)*
Equivalent temps plein (ETP)

Country or area Pays ou zone	Year Année	Total R & D personnel Total du personnel de R - D	Researchers Chercheurs		Technicians and equivalent staff Techniciens et personnel assimilé		Other supporting staff Autre personnel de soutien	
			Total M & F Total H & F	Females Femmes	Total M & F Total H & F	Females Femmes	Total M & F Total H & F	Females Femmes
Turkey Turquie	2005	49 251[8]	39 139	13 381	4 753[8]	988[8]	5 360[8]	978[8]
	2010	81 792[8]	64 341	21 056	10 352[8]	1 741[8]	7 099[8]	1 551[8]
	2014	115 444[8]	89 657	29 240	16 084[8]	2 977[8]	9 703[8]	2 609[8]
Uganda [3] Ouganda [3]	2005	1 686	776	291	472	...	438	...
	2010	4 270	# 2 823	687	# 922	254	# 525	155
Ukraine Ukraine	2007	132 926[8]	67 493[8]	29 620	15 045[8]	...	25 160[8]	...
	2010[8]	116 321	60 812	...	13 053	...	21 593	...
	2015[8]	81 854[20]	43 016[20]	...	7 983[20]	...	15 754	...
United Arab Emirates Émirats arabes unis	2011	11 400	...	...	...	...	...	...
	2015	...	18 345	...	...	...	...	...
United Kingdom Royaume-Uni	*2005	# 324 917[8]	# 248 599	...	41 494	...	# 34 824[8]	...
	*2010	350 766[8]	256 585	...	59 290	...	# 34 891[8]	...
	*2015	416 538[8]	289 330	...	87 110[8]	...	40 098	...
United Rep. of Tanzania Rép.-Unie de Tanzanie	2010	2 929[1,2]	1 600[1,2]	393	472[1,2]	112	857[1,2]	310
	2013[1,2]	1 967	929	228	301	62	737	277
United States of America États-Unis d'Amérique	*2005	...	1 101 105	...	...	...	...	...
	*2010	...	1 198 777	...	...	...	...	...
	*2014	...	1 351 903	...	...	...	...	...
United States Virgin Islands [1,3] Îles Vierges américaines [1,3]	2000	33	11	2	6	...	16	...
	2005	37	6	...	12	...	11	...
	2007	42	6	...	13	...	14	...
Uruguay [3] Uruguay [3]	2002	4 323	3 839	1 813	...	...	484	114
	2006	3 436	3 182	1 349	172	84	# 82	# 69
	2010	...	2 889	1 473	...	...	...	...
	2015	...	2 288	1 117	...	...	...	...
Uzbekistan [3] Ouzbékistan [3]	2010	36 358[4]	30 343	12 487	1 900	...	1 978	...
	2015	36 830[4]	31 680	13 018	1 835	883	1 910	836
Venezuela (Boliv. Rep. of) [1] Venezuela (Rép. boliv. du) [1]	2005	...	3 248	...	...	...	...	...
	2009	...	5 209	2 782	...	...	...	...
	2010	...	5 803	...	...	...	...	...
	2013	...	10 834	...	...	...	...	...
Viet Nam [3] Viet Nam [3]	2002	...	41 117	17 585	...	...	...	...
	2013	164 744	128 998	56 846	12 799	5 033	15 149	8 412
Zambia [3] Zambie [3]	2005	3 285[1]	792[1]	116[8]	1 240[1]	...	1 253[1]	...
	#2008	2 219	612	188	835	270	772	360
Zimbabwe Zimbabwe	2012	1 741[2]	1 305[2]	332	141[2]	41	295[2]	100

Source:

United Nations Educational, Scientific and Cultural Organization (UNESCO), Montreal, the UNESCO Institute for Statistics (UIS) statistics database, last accessed November 2017.

Source:

Organisation des Nations Unies pour l'éducation, la science et la culture (UNESCO), Montréal, base de données statistiques de l'Institut de statistique (ISU) de l'UNESCO, dernier accès novembre 2017.

1 Partial data.
2 Excluding business enterprise.
3 Head count instead of Full-time equivalent.
4 Overestimated or based on overestimated data.
5 Excluding private non-profit.
6 Government only.
7 Higher Education only.
8 Underestimated or based on underestimated data.
9 For statistical purposes, the data for China do not include those for the Hong Kong Special Administrative Region (Hong Kong SAR), Macao Special Administrative Region (Macao SAR) and Taiwan Province of China.

1 Données partielles.
2 Ne comprend pas les entreprises commerciales.
3 Personnes physiques au lieu d'Equivalents temps plein.
4 Surestimé ou fondé sur des données surestimées.
5 Non compris les organisations privées à but non lucratif.
6 Etat seulement.
7 Enseignement supérieur seulement.
8 Sous-estimé ou basé sur des données sous-estimées.
9 Pour la présentation des statistiques, les données pour la Chine ne comprennent pas la région administrative spéciale de Hong Kong (Hong Kong RAS), la région administrative spéciale de Macao (Macao RAS) et la province chinoise de Taïwan.

Population employed in research and development (R&D) *(continued)*
Full-time equivalent (FTE)

Population employé dans la recherche et le développement (R-D) *(suite)*
Equivalent temps plein (ETP)

10 Do not correspond exactly to Frascati Manual recommendations.
11 Including technicians and equivalent staff.
12 Including other supporting staff.
13 Excluding Higher Education.
14 Excluding government.
15 Excluding Defence (all or mostly).
16 Excluding data for other supporting staff.
17 Including other classes.
18 Excluding technicians and equivalent staff.
19 Excluding social sciences and humanities.
20 Excluding data from some regions, provinces or states.
21 Included in others/Not specified.
22 University graduates instead of researchers.

10 Ne corresponds pas exactement aux recommendations du Manuel de Frascati.
11 Y compris les techniciens y le personnel assimilé.
12 Y compris autre personnel de soutien.
13 Non compris l'enseignement supérieur.
14 Non compris l'état.
15 À l'exclusion de la défense (en totalité ou en grande partie).
16 Non compris les données pour le personnel de soutien.
17 Comprend d'autres catégories.
18 Non compris les techniciens y le personnel assimilé.
19 Non compris les sciences sociales et les sciences humaines.
20 Non compris les données de certaines régions, provinces ou états.
21 Inclus dans autres/Non spécifié.
22 Diplômes universitaires au lieu de chercheurs.

27 Gross domestic expenditure on research and development (R&D)

As a percentage of GDP and by source of funds

Dépenses intérieures brutes de recherche et développement (R-D)

En pourcentage du PIB et répartition par source de financement

Country or area Pays ou zone	Year Année	Expenditure on R&D as a % of GDP Dépenses en R&D en % du PIB	Source of funds (%) / Source de financement (%) Business enterprises Entreprises	Govern-ment Etat	Higher education Enseigne-ment supérieur	Private non-profit Institut. Privées sans but lucratif	Funds from abroad Fonds de l'étranger	Not specified/ Non précisé
Total, all countries or areas	**2005**	**1.5**	...	...	...	...	...	...
Total, tous pays ou zones	**2010**	**1.6**	...	...	...	...	...	...
	2014	**1.7**	...	...	...	...	...	...
Northern Africa	2005	0.3	...	...	...	...	...	...
Afrique septentrionale	2010	0.4	...	...	...	...	...	...
	2014	0.5	...	...	...	...	...	...
Sub-Saharan Africa	2005	0.4	...	...	...	...	...	...
Afrique subsaharienne	2010	0.4	...	...	...	...	...	...
	2014	0.4	...	...	...	...	...	...
Northern America	2005	2.5	...	...	...	...	...	...
Amérique septentrionale	2010	2.7	...	...	...	...	...	...
	2014	2.6	...	...	...	...	...	...
Latin America & the Caribbean	2005	0.6	...	...	...	...	...	...
Amérique latine et Caraïbes	2010	0.6	...	...	...	...	...	...
	2014	0.7	...	...	...	...	...	...
Central Asia	2005	0.2	...	...	...	...	...	...
Asie centrale	2010	0.2	...	...	...	...	...	...
	2014	0.2	...	...	...	...	...	...
Eastern Asia	2005	2.1	...	...	...	...	...	...
Asie orientale	2010	2.2	...	...	...	...	...	...
	2014	2.5	...	...	...	...	...	...
South-eastern Asia	2005	0.6	...	...	...	...	...	...
Asie du Sud-Est	2010	0.8	...	...	...	...	...	...
	2014	0.8	...	...	...	...	...	...
Southern Asia	2005	0.7	...	...	...	...	...	...
Asie méridionale	2010	0.7	...	...	...	...	...	...
	2014	0.7	...	...	...	...	...	...
Western Asia	2005	0.5	...	...	...	...	...	...
Asie occidentale	2010	0.5	...	...	...	...	...	...
	2014	0.6	...	...	...	...	...	...
Europe	2005	1.6	...	...	...	...	...	...
Europe	2010	1.7	...	...	...	...	...	...
	2014	1.8	...	...	...	...	...	...
Oceania	2005	1.9	...	...	...	...	...	...
Océanie	2010	2.2	...	...	...	...	...	...
	2014	2.0	...	...	...	...	...	...
Australia and New Zealand	2005	1.9	...	...	...	...	...	...
Australie et Nouvelle-Zélande	2010	2.2	...	...	...	...	...	...
	2014	2.1	...	...	...	...	...	...
Albania [1] Albanie [1]	2008	0.2	3.3	80.8	8.6	...	7.4	...
Algeria [1] Algérie [1]	2005	0.1	...	...	...	...	...	...
Argentina	2005	0.4	31.0	59.6	5.7	3.0	0.7	~0.0
Argentine	2008	0.5	26.5	67.6	4.4	1.0	0.6	~0.0
	2010	0.6	...	...	...	...	...	...
	2014	0.6	...	...	...	...	...	...
Armenia	2005[1]	0.3	...	77.5	...	...	4.7	17.8
Arménie	2010[1]	0.2	...	84.5	...	...	11.7	3.8
	2015[2,3]	0.3	...	73.8	...	...	2.3	23.9
Australia	2004	1.9	54.6	40.3	0.4	1.9	2.9	...
Australie	2008	2.4	61.9	34.6	0.1	1.8	1.6	...
	*2010	2.4	...	...	...	...	...	...
	*2013	2.2	...	...	...	...	...	...

27 Gross domestic expenditure on research and development (R&D) *(continued)*
As a percentage of GDP and by source of funds

Dépenses intérieures brutes de recherche et développement (R-D) *(suite)*
En pourcentage du PIB et répartition par source de financement

Country or area Pays ou zone	Year Année	Expenditure on R&D as a % of GDP Dépenses en R&D en % du PIB	Source of funds (%) / Source de financement (%) Business enterprises Entreprises	Govern-ment Etat	Higher education Enseigne-ment supérieur	Private non-profit Institut. Privées sans but lucratif	Funds from abroad Fonds de l'étranger	Not specified/ Non précisé
Austria	2004	2.2	47.2	32.6	0.4	0.5	19.4	...
Autriche	*2005	2.4	45.6	35.9	...	0.4	18.0	...
	2009	2.6	47.1	34.9	0.7	0.6	16.8	...
	*2010	2.7	45.1	38.3[4]	...	0.5	16.1	...
	2013	3.0	48.7	33.6	0.6	0.5	16.6	...
	*2015	3.1	47.0	36.6[4]	...	0.5	15.9	...
Azerbaijan	2005	0.2[5]	18.7	77.5	~0.0	1.3	2.4	...
Azerbaïdjan	2010	0.2	# 9.6	# 88.2	0.3	1.9	~0.0	...
	2014	0.2	30.5	67.6	0.8	0.9	0.2	...
	2015	0.2	32.2	65.8	0.4	1.7	...	...
Bahrain								
Bahreïn	2014	0.1	21.8	41.5	21.2	2.0	12.4	1.1
Belarus	2002	0.6	24.4	63.4	2.2	~0.0	10.1	...
Bélarus	2005	0.7	21.2	71.9	0.7	...	6.3	...
	2008	0.7	36.5	57.6	0.3	0.1	5.5	...
	2010	0.7	27.1	58.7	...	0.6	13.6	...
	2011	0.7	45.8	45.5	...	~0.0	8.7	...
	2015	0.5	41.3	46.0	...	...	12.7	...
Belgium	2005	1.8	59.7	24.7	2.6	0.6	12.4	...
Belgique	2010	2.1	57.6	25.4	3.1	0.6	13.3	...
	2013	2.4	61.3	24.1	1.0	0.4	13.2	...
	*2015	2.5	...	...	...	...	...	...
Bermuda [6]	2010[7]	0.2	...	...	...	...	...	...
Bermudes [6]	2015	0.2	...	...	...	...	...	...
Bolivia (Plurin. State of)	2002	0.3	16.0	20.0	31.0	19.0	14.0	...
Bolivie (État plurin. de)	#2009	0.2	5.2	51.2	26.5	2.1	1.9	13.2
Bosnia and Herzegovina	2005[1]	~0.0	...	...	...	...	...	...
Bosnie-Herzégovine	2009[1]	~0.0	...	...	...	...	...	...
	2013	0.3	1.8	25.3	...	~0.0	53.9	18.9
	2015	0.2	31.4	37.6	14.1	~0.0	16.9	...
Botswana	2005	0.5	...	...	...	...	...	...
Botswana	#2012	0.3	5.8	73.9	12.6	0.7	6.8	0.2
	2013	0.5	17.7	59.7	0.9	...	21.7	...
Brazil	2005	1.0	50.4	47.7	1.9	...	...	...
Brésil	2010	1.2	47.0	51.1	1.8	...	...	~0.0
	2011	1.1	45.2	52.9	1.9	...	...	~0.0
	2014	1.2	36.4	61.4	2.2	...	...	...
Brunei Darussalam	2003	~0.0[1]	6.7	86.8	...	...	6.6	...
Brunéi Darussalam	#2004	~0.0[1]	1.6	91.0	7.4	...	...	...
Bulgaria	2005	0.4	27.8	63.9	0.4	0.3	7.6	...
Bulgarie	2010	0.6	16.7	43.2	0.5	0.1	39.6	...
	2014	0.8	22.3	26.4	~0.0	0.4	50.9	...
	*2015	1.0	...	...	...	...	...	...
Burkina Faso	2005	0.2[1]	...	100.0	...	...	...	...
Burkina Faso	2009	0.2	11.9	9.1	12.2	1.3	59.6	5.9
Burundi [1]	2008	0.2	...	59.9	0.2	...	39.9	...
Burundi [1]	2010	0.1	...	...	...	...	...	...
	2011	0.1	...	...	...	...	...	...
Cabo Verde [1,8]								
Cabo Verde [1,8]	2011	0.1	...	100.0	...	...	...	...
Cambodia	2002[1]	~0.0	...	17.9	...	43.0	28.4	10.6
Cambodge	#2015	0.1	19.4	23.5	0.1	22.1	34.9	...
Canada	2005	2.0	49.3	* 31.8	* 7.3	2.8	8.8	...
Canada	2010	1.8	47.0	* 35.2	* 7.8	3.5	6.5	...
	*2014	1.6	45.4	34.6	10.3	3.7	6.0	...
Chile	2010	0.3	25.4	40.4	12.7	1.7	19.8	...
Chili	*2015	0.4	32.8	42.6	11.1	0.6	12.9	...

27 Gross domestic expenditure on research and development (R&D) *(continued)*

As a percentage of GDP and by source of funds

Dépenses intérieures brutes de recherche et développement (R-D) *(suite)*

En pourcentage du PIB et répartition par source de financement

Country or area / Pays ou zone	Year / Année	Expenditure on R&D as a % of GDP / Dépenses en R&D en % du PIB	Source of funds (%) / Source de financement (%): Business enterprises / Entreprises	Govern-ment / Etat	Higher education / Enseigne-ment supérieur	Private non-profit Institut. / Privées sans but lucratif	Funds from abroad / Fonds de l'étranger	Not specified / Non précisé
China[9] / Chine[9]	2005	1.3	67.0	26.3	…	…	0.9	…
	2010	1.7	71.7	24.0	…	…	1.3	…
	2015	2.1	74.7	21.3	…	…	0.7	…
China, Hong Kong SAR / Chine, RAS de Hong Kong	2005	0.8	53.0[10]	44.1	0.4	…	2.5	…
	2010	0.7	47.6[10]	47.3	0.1	…	4.9	…
	2014	0.7	46.4[10]	46.5	~0.0	…	7.0	…
	2015	0.8	…	…	…	…	…	…
China, Macao SAR / Chine, RAS de Macao	2005	0.1[1]	* 0.2	* 88.0	* 10.0	* 0.4	…	* 1.4
	2007	# 0.1[1]	0.1	89.3	5.8	2.8	0.6	1.6
	2008	0.1[1]	0.2	91.7	6.4	1.4	…	0.3
	2010[1]	0.1	…	…	…	…	…	…
	2015[1]	0.1	…	87.2	6.2	0.5	…	6.1
Colombia / Colombie	2005	0.2	25.4	36.9	29.4	3.8	4.5	…
	2010	0.2	28.8	38.7	23.2	6.0	3.3	…
	2015	0.2	33.6	43.3	17.4	3.3	2.4	…
Costa Rica / Costa Rica	2004	0.4	…	…	…	…	…	…
	2010	0.5	20.7	62.6	…	0.4	11.8	4.6
	2014	0.6	1.5	56.2	…	0.5	1.4	40.4
Croatia / Croatie	2005	0.9	34.3	58.1	4.9	~0.0	2.6	…
	2010	0.7	38.8	49.2	2.0	0.2	9.9	…
	2015	0.9	46.6	36.4	2.0	0.5	14.5	…
Cuba / Cuba	2005	0.5	35.0	60.0	…	…	5.0	…
	2010	0.6	15.0	75.0	…	…	10.0	…
	2015	0.4	40.0	55.0	…	…	5.0	…
Cyprus / Chypre	2005	0.4	16.8	67.0	4.2	1.2	10.9	…
	2010	0.4	12.7	68.3	3.5	0.5	15.0	…
	2014	0.5	13.7	56.5	5.6	0.6	23.7	…
	*2015	0.5	…	…	…	…	…	…
Czechia / Tchéquie	2005	1.2	48.2	45.2	1.2	~0.0	5.4	…
	2010	1.3	40.8	44.4	0.9	~0.0	13.9	…
	*2015	1.9	34.5	32.2	0.7	0.1	32.5	…
Dem. Rep. of the Congo / Rép. dém. du Congo	2005	# 0.1[11,12]	…	100.0	…	…	…	…
	2009	0.1[11,12]	…	100.0	…	…	…	…
Denmark / Danemark	2005	2.4	59.5	27.6	…	2.8	10.1	…
	2010	2.9	* 61.1	* 28.2[4]	…	* 3.5	* 7.2	…
	*2015	3.0	59.4	29.4[4]	…	4.7	6.5	…
Ecuador / Équateur	2003	0.1	…	…	…	…	…	…
	2010	0.4	1.0[3]	40.2[3]	9.6[3]	0.5[3]	5.3[3]	43.4[13]
	2014	0.4	0.1[3]	42.4[3]	12.6[3]	0.1[3]	2.5[3]	42.3[13]
Egypt / Égypte	2005[1,11]	0.2	…	…	…	…	…	…
	2010[2,3]	0.4	…	…	…	…	…	…
	2014	0.6	8.1	91.7[14]	…	0.1	0.1	…
	2015	0.7	6.2	93.7[14]	…	0.1	…	…
El Salvador / El Salvador	2010	0.1	0.6	70.1	20.8	~0.0	8.3	0.1
	2013	0.1	0.7	42.7	37.0	2.8	16.4	0.3
	2014	0.1	0.7	33.0	48.6	0.9	16.9	…
	2015	0.1	…	…	…	…	…	…
Estonia / Estonie	2005	0.9	38.5	43.5	0.8	0.2	17.1	…
	2010	1.6	43.6	44.1	0.6	0.2	11.4	…
	*2015	1.5	41.0	46.4	0.2	0.2	12.2	…
Ethiopia / Éthiopie	2005	0.2[1]	…	69.2	…	0.1	30.8	…
	2010	# 0.2	10.8	56.0	1.1	~0.0	30.0	2.2
	2013	0.6	0.7	79.1	1.8	0.2	2.1	16.0
Faroe Islands / Îles Féroé	2003	0.9	20.4	…	…	0.3	18.7	60.6[6,14,15]
Finland / Finlande	2005	3.3	66.9	25.7	0.2	1.0	# 6.3	…
	2010	3.7	66.1	25.7	0.2	1.1	6.9	…
	2015	2.9	54.8	28.9	0.3	1.5	14.5	…

27

Gross domestic expenditure on research and development (R&D) *(continued)*
As a percentage of GDP and by source of funds

Dépenses intérieures brutes de recherche et développement (R-D) *(suite)*
En pourcentage du PIB et répartition par source de financement

			Source of funds (%) / Source de financement (%)					
Country or area Pays ou zone	Year Année	Expenditure on R&D as a % of GDP Dépenses en R&D en % du PIB	Business enterprises Entreprises	Govern-ment Etat	Higher education Enseigne-ment supérieur	Private non-profit Institut. Privées sans but lucratif	Funds from abroad Fonds de l'étranger	Not specified/ Non précisé
France France	2005	2.0	51.9	38.6	1.0	0.9	7.5	...
	#2010	2.2	53.5	37.1	1.0	0.8	7.5	...
	2014	2.2	55.7	34.6	1.0	1.0	7.8	...
	*2015	2.2	...	...	...	...	...	...
Gabon Gabon	2009	0.6	29.3	58.1	9.5	...	3.1	~0.0
Gambia Gambie	2009[1]	~0.0	...	...	...	...	...	...
	2011[6]	0.1	...	38.5	...	45.6	15.9	...
Georgia Géorgie	2005	0.2	...	...	...	...	...	...
	2014	# 0.2[1,2,3]	...	42.1[8,16]	41.8[8,16]	2.1[8,16]	14.3[8,16]	0.3[8,16]
	2015[1,2,3]	0.3	...	...	...	...	...	...
Germany Allemagne	2005	2.4	67.6	28.4	...	0.3	3.7	...
	2010	2.7	65.5	30.4	...	0.2	3.9	...
	2014	2.9	65.8	28.8	...	0.3	5.0	...
	*2015	2.9	...	...	...	...	...	...
Ghana Ghana	2010	# 0.4	# 0.1	# 68.3	0.3	0.1	31.2	...
Greece Grèce	2005	0.6	31.1	46.8	1.7	1.5	19.0	...
	*2010	0.6	36.5	48.3	2.3	1.0	11.9	...
	*2015	1.0	31.8	52.7	2.5	0.2	12.8	...
Greenland Groenland	2004	0.7	...	...	...	...	...	...
Guam Guam	2001	...	...	100.0	...	...	...	...
Guatemala[1] Guatemala[1]	2005	~0.0	...	42.1	57.9	...	...	...
	2010	~0.0	...	18.3	30.9	...	50.8	...
	2012	~0.0	...	23.5	27.5	...	49.0	...
Honduras Honduras	2004	~0.0	...	...	...	...	...	...
Hungary Hongrie	2005	0.9	39.4[16]	49.4[16]	...	0.3[16]	10.7[16]	...
	2010	1.1	47.4	39.3	...	0.9	12.4	...
	2015	1.4	49.7	34.6	...	0.7	15.0	...
Iceland Islande	2005	2.7	48.0	40.5	...	0.3	11.2	...
	2009	2.7	47.8	40.2	...	0.6	11.4	...
	2015	2.2	33.3	32.0	4.2	4.2	26.4	...
India Inde	2005	0.8	...	...	...	...	...	...
	*2010	0.8	...	...	...	...	...	...
	2015	0.6	...	...	...	...	...	...
Indonesia Indonésie	2001	~0.0[1]	14.7[1,10]	84.5	0.2	...	...	0.7
	#2009[1]	0.1	...	...	...	...	...	...
	*2013	0.1	...	...	...	...	...	...
Iran (Islamic Republic of) Iran (Rép. islamique d')	2005	0.6	12.2	76.2	11.6	...	...	...
	2008	0.7	30.9	61.6	7.4	...	...	...
	2010[2,17]	0.3	...	...	...	...	...	...
	2012	0.3	...	...	...	...	...	...
Iraq Iraq	2010	~0.0[18]	...	100.0[14]	...	...	...	...
	2015	~0.0	1.1	96.4	2.1	0.3	0.1	...
Ireland Irlande	2005	1.2	57.4	32.0	1.7	0.2	8.6	...
	*2010	1.6	52.2	29.4	0.9	0.5	17.0	...
	*2014	1.5	52.8	27.3	0.7	0.6	18.6	...
Israel[19] Israël[19]	2005	4.0	56.2	14.5	2.8	1.8	24.7	...
	2010	3.9	36.2	14.2	1.2	1.1	47.3	...
	2013	4.1	37.0	12.5	0.2	1.0	49.2	...
	2015	4.3	...	...	...	...	...	...
Italy Italie	2005	1.0	39.7	50.7	0.1	1.6	8.0	...
	2010	1.2	44.7	41.6	0.9	3.1	9.8	...
	*2014	1.4	46.2	40.8	1.0	2.6	9.3	...
	*2015	1.3	...	...	...	...	...	...

Gross domestic expenditure on research and development (R&D) *(continued)*

As a percentage of GDP and by source of funds

Dépenses intérieures brutes de recherche et développement (R-D) *(suite)*

En pourcentage du PIB et répartition par source de financement

Country or area Pays ou zone	Year Année	Expenditure on R&D as a % of GDP Dépenses en R&D en % du PIB	Source of funds (%) / Source de financement (%) Business enterprises Entreprises	Govern-ment Etat	Higher education Enseigne-ment supérieur	Private non-profit Institut. Privées sans but lucratif	Funds from abroad Fonds de l'étranger	Not specified/ Non précisé
Jamaica Jamaïque	2002	0.1	...	...	...	...	...	...
Japan Japon	2005	3.2	76.1	* 16.8	* 6.1	0.7	0.3	...
	2010	3.1	75.9	* 17.2	* 5.7	0.8	0.4	...
	2015	3.3	78.0	* 15.4	* 5.4	0.7	0.5	...
Jordan Jordanie	2002	0.3	...	...	...	...	...	...
	2008	0.4	...	...	...	...	...	...
Kazakhstan Kazakhstan	2005	0.3	39.1	44.5	13.4	1.3	1.5	...
	2010	0.2	36.6	36.7	17.2	8.9	0.6	...
	2011	0.2	51.6	24.9	16.3	6.9	0.3	...
	2013	0.2	28.9	63.7	...	...	0.8	6.6
	2015	0.2	...	...	...	...	...	...
Kenya Kenya	#2010	0.8	4.3	26.0	19.0	3.5	47.1	...
Kuwait Koweït	2003[11]	0.1[1]	# 4.4	# 94.7	~0.0	...	0.9	...
	2004[11]	0.1[1]	6.0	93.2	...	...	0.8	...
	2005[11]	0.1[1]	7.3	92.3	...	0.4	...	...
	2009[11]	0.1[1]	2.3	96.5	...	...	1.2	...
	2010[11]	0.1[1]	5.2	94.8	...	~0.0	...	...
	2013[2,3]	# 0.3	1.4	92.9	0.2	5.5	...	...
Kyrgyzstan Kirghizistan	2003	0.2	53.7	45.1	0.1	...	1.1	...
	2005	0.2	36.4	63.6	...	...	~0.0	...
	2010	0.2	...	...	...	...	...	...
	2015[2]	0.1	8.7	89.2	0.2	...	1.0	0.8
Lao People's Dem. Rep. [1] Rép. dém. populaire lao [1]	2002	~0.0	36.0	8.0	2.0	...	54.0	...
Latvia Lettonie	2005	0.5	34.3	46.0	1.2	...	18.5	...
	2010	0.6	38.8	26.4	1.4	...	33.4	...
	*2015	0.6	20.1	32.7	2.2	...	45.0	...
Lesotho Lesotho	2004[1]	0.1	...	...	...	...	...	...
	2009[1]	~0.0	3.4	15.0	2.8	...	...	78.9
	2011[1]	~0.0[8]	...	...	44.7[15]	...	3.4	51.9
	2015[2,3]	0.1	0.8	91.1	...	0.3	7.8	...
Lithuania Lituanie	2005	0.7	20.8	62.7	5.7	0.2	10.5	...
	2010	0.8	32.4	46.0	1.5	0.2	19.9	...
	*2015	1.0	28.0	35.6	1.5	0.3	34.6	...
Luxembourg Luxembourg	2005	1.6	79.7	16.6	~0.0	0.1	3.6	...
	2010	1.5	43.5	35.1	0.6	0.1	20.6	...
	2013	1.3	16.5	48.4	1.7	1.0	32.3	...
	*2015	1.3	...	...	...	...	...	...
Madagascar Madagascar	2005	0.2[1]	...	89.8[14]	...	...	10.2	...
	2009	0.1[1]	...	89.4[14]	...	...	10.6	...
	2010	0.1[1]	...	# 100.0[14]	...	...	...	...
	2011	0.1[1]	...	100.0[15]	...	...	...	...
	#2014[1,11]	~0.0	...	...	...	...	...	...
Malaysia Malaisie	2004	0.6	71.2	21.5	6.9	...	0.4	...
	2010	1.0	59.6	36.4	3.5	...	0.4	0.1
	2015	1.3	11.4[20]	# 35.7	7.0	...	1.7	44.3[4]
Mali Mali	2007[1]	0.2[17]	10.1	40.9	...	...	49.0	...
	2010	0.6[3]	...	# 91.2	...	...	8.8	...
Malta Malte	2005	0.5	# 46.8	# 25.9	0.4	0.1	26.9	...
	2010	0.6	51.8	34.6	1.3	0.1	12.2	...
	*2015	0.8	44.1	33.3	1.2	0.1	21.3	...
Mauritius Maurice	2005[6,18]	0.4	...	100.0	...	...	...	...
	2012[3]	# 0.2	0.3	72.4	20.7	0.1	6.4	...
Mexico Mexique	2005	0.4	41.5	49.2	7.3	0.9	1.1	...
	2010	0.5	32.9	62.3	2.8	1.6	0.5	...
	*2015	0.6	20.6	71.2	3.5	4.4	0.4	...

27

Gross domestic expenditure on research and development (R&D) *(continued)*
As a percentage of GDP and by source of funds

Dépenses intérieures brutes de recherche et développement (R-D) *(suite)*
En pourcentage du PIB et répartition par source de financement

Country or area Pays ou zone	Year Année	Expenditure on R&D as a % of GDP Dépenses en R&D en % du PIB	Source of funds (%) / Source de financement (%) Business enterprises Entreprises	Govern-ment Etat	Higher education Enseigne-ment supérieur	Private non-profit Institut. Privées sans but lucratif	Funds from abroad Fonds de l'étranger	Not specified/ Non précisé
Monaco [1] Monaco [1]	2005	~0.0	...	98.8	...	...	...	1.2
Mongolia Mongolie	2005	0.2[1]	10.4	77.8	0.8	...	4.4	6.5
	2010[1]	0.2	7.2	61.1	1.5	...	4.2	25.9
	2014[1]	0.2	7.5	75.8	3.2	...	2.8	10.7
	2015[1]	0.2	7.3	80.1	9.7	...	...	2.9
Montenegro Monténégro	2005	0.9	...	...	...	...	...	...
	2007	1.1	...	...	...	...	...	...
	2015	0.4	29.9	57.8	6.4	~0.0	5.9	...
Morocco Maroc	2003	0.6	12.3	40.3	47.4	...	...	...
	2010	0.7	29.9	23.1	45.3	...	1.7	...
Mozambique Mozambique	2002[6,12]	0.4	...	34.7	...	...	65.3	...
	2010	# 0.4[3]	...	18.8[14]	...	3.0	78.1	...
	2015	0.3	0.5[1]	43.5	13.3	...	39.9	2.8
Myanmar [1] Myanmar [1]	2002	0.2	...	...	...	...	...	...
Namibia Namibie	2010	0.1[1,17]	19.8	78.6	...	...	1.5	...
	2014[1]	0.3	11.1	63.2	6.0	3.9	15.8	...
Nepal [1,18] Népal [1,18]	2010	0.3	...	...	...	...	...	...
Netherlands Pays-Bas	2005	1.8	46.3	38.8	0.3	2.6	12.0	...
	2009	1.7	45.1	40.9	0.3	2.8	10.8	...
	2010	1.7	...	...	...	...	...	...
	*2015	2.0	48.7	33.4	0.2	2.6	15.1	...
New Zealand Nouvelle-Zélande	2005	1.1	41.1	43.2	8.9	1.7	5.2	...
	2009	1.3	39.0	44.7	8.3	2.8	5.2	...
	2013	1.2	39.8	39.8	10.1	3.1	7.2	...
Nicaragua Nicaragua	2002	~0.0	...	...	...	...	...	...
	2015[8]	0.1	...	...	...	...	...	...
Nigeria Nigéria	2007	0.2[3]	0.2	96.4	0.1	1.7	1.0	0.6
Norway Norvège	2005	1.5	46.8	43.6	0.7	0.9	8.1	...
	2009	1.7	43.6	46.8	0.4	1.0	8.2	...
	2010	1.7	...	...	...	...	...	...
	2013	1.7	43.1	45.8	0.5	1.0	9.5	...
	*2015	1.9	...	...	...	...	...	...
Oman Oman	2013	0.2	24.5	48.6	24.4	0.1	~0.0	2.3
	2015	0.2	21.4	55.7	22.8	0.2	...	...
Pakistan Pakistan	2005	0.4[2,3]	...	87.0	11.9	...	0.3	0.8
	2009	0.4[2,3]	...	84.0	12.1	1.7	0.9	1.3
	2015[2,3]	0.2	...	67.0	25.5	0.3	2.7	4.6
Panama Panama	2003	0.3	0.6	25.5	1.8	1.0	71.0	0.1
	2005	0.2	0.4	38.5	1.4	0.7	58.9	...
	2010	0.1	3.4	53.9	6.0	14.0	22.7	~0.0
	2011	0.2	18.9	46.7	5.0	8.7	20.7	~0.0
	2013	0.1	10.8	80.9	8.0	...	0.3	...
Paraguay Paraguay	2005	0.1	# 0.3	# 74.9	# 8.6	# 2.0	# 14.2	...
	2008	0.1	0.3	76.2	9.2	2.1	12.3	...
	2015[3]	0.1	0.3	73.1	2.1	4.2	10.3	10.1
Peru Pérou	2004	0.2	...	...	...	...	...	...
	2015	0.1	...	...	...	...	...	...
Philippines Philippines	2005	0.1	62.6	25.6	6.0	0.7	4.8	0.3
	2009	0.1	57.5	26.7	7.8	0.4	4.2	3.4
	2013	0.1	36.9	51.6	9.0	0.2	1.8	0.5
Poland Pologne	2005	0.6	33.4	57.7	2.9	0.3	5.7	...
	2010	0.7	24.4	60.9	2.5	0.3	11.8	...
	2015	1.0	39.0	41.8	2.2	0.2	16.7	...

27 Gross domestic expenditure on research and development (R&D) *(continued)*

As a percentage of GDP and by source of funds

Dépenses intérieures brutes de recherche et développement (R-D) *(suite)*

En pourcentage du PIB et répartition par source de financement

Country or area Pays ou zone	Year Année	Expenditure on R&D as a % of GDP Dépenses en R&D en % du PIB	Source of funds (%) / Source de financement (%) Business enterprises Entreprises	Govern-ment Etat	Higher education Enseigne-ment supérieur	Private non-profit Institut. Privées sans but lucratif	Funds from abroad Fonds de l'étranger	Not specified/ Non précisé
Portugal Portugal	2005	0.8	36.3	55.2	1.0	2.8	4.7	...
	2010	1.5	43.9	45.1	3.2	4.6	3.2	...
	2014	1.3	41.8	47.1	4.2	1.3	5.6	...
	*2015	1.3	...	...	...	...	...	...
Puerto Rico Porto Rico	2009	0.5	...	...	...	...	...	...
	2013	0.4	65.4	24.9	8.9	0.5	...	0.3
	2015	0.4	...	...	...	...	...	...
Qatar Qatar	2012	0.5	24.2	31.2	36.6	5.6	2.4	0.1
Republic of Korea République de Corée	2005[21]	2.6	75.0	23.0	0.9	0.4	0.7	...
	2010	3.5	71.8	26.7	0.9	0.4	0.2	...
	2015	4.2	74.5	23.7	0.6	0.4	0.8	...
Republic of Moldova République de Moldova	2005	0.4	...	...	...	...	3.8	96.2[4]
	2010	0.4	...	...	...	...	7.4	92.6[4]
	2015	0.4	...	...	...	...	11.6	88.4[4]
Romania Roumanie	2005	0.4	37.2	53.5	4.0	~0.0	5.3	...
	2010	0.5	32.3	54.4	2.2	~0.0	11.1	...
	2015	0.5	37.3	41.7	1.7	0.1	19.2	...
Russian Federation Fédération de Russie	2005	1.1	30.0	61.9	0.4	~0.0	7.6	...
	2010	1.1	25.5	70.3	0.5	0.1	3.5	...
	2015	1.1	26.5	69.5	1.2	0.2	2.6	...
Saint Vincent & Grenadines Saint-Vincent-Grenadines	2002	0.1	...	...	...	...	...	...
Saint Arabia [18] Arabie saoudite [18]	2005[1]	~0.0	...	...	...	...	...	...
	#2010[6]	0.9	...	...	...	...	...	...
	2013[6]	0.8	...	...	...	...	...	...
Senegal Sénégal	2010	0.5	4.1	47.6	~0.0	3.2	40.5	4.5
Serbia Serbie	2005[22,23]	0.4	...	...	...	...	...	...
	2010	0.7[22]	8.6	59.4	28.4	~0.0	3.6	...
	2015	0.9[22]	12.8	50.6	24.0	~0.0	12.6	...
Seychelles Seychelles	2005	0.3	...	...	...	...	...	...
Singapore Singapour	2005	2.2	58.8	36.4	0.5	...	4.4	...
	2010	2.0	53.1	40.2	1.8	...	4.9	...
	2014	2.2	54.1	37.1	2.0	...	6.8	...
Slovakia Slovaquie	2005	0.5	36.6	57.0[20]	0.3	~0.0	6.0	...
	2010	0.6	35.1	49.6[20]	0.4	0.3	14.7	...
	2015	1.2	25.1	31.9[20]	3.3	0.3	39.4	...
Slovenia Slovénie	2005	1.4	54.8	37.2	0.7	~0.0	7.3	...
	2010	2.1	58.4	35.3	0.3	0.1	6.0	...
	*2015	2.2	69.2	19.9	0.3	~0.0	10.6	...
South Africa Afrique du Sud	2005	0.9	43.9	38.2	3.0	1.4	13.6	...
	2010	0.7	40.1	44.5	0.1	3.2	12.1	...
	2013	0.7	41.4	42.9	0.7	2.1	12.9	...
Spain Espagne	2005	1.1	46.3	43.0	4.1	0.9	5.7	...
	2010	1.4	43.0	46.6	3.9	0.7	5.7	...
	2014	1.2	46.4	41.4	4.1	0.7	7.4	...
	2015	1.2	...	...	...	...	...	...
Sri Lanka Sri Lanka	#2000[1]	0.1	7.7	51.7	18.5	~0.0	4.5	17.5
	#2004	0.2	0.6[10]	67.5[14]	...	...	22.6	9.3
	2010	0.1	# 40.9	55.9	0.2	~0.0	2.7	0.3
	2013	0.1	40.7	53.9	...	...	5.0	0.4
State of Palestine [3] État de Palestine [3]	2010	0.4	0.9	21.3	2.3	4.9	52.4	18.2
	2013	0.5	3.8	29.4	4.6	17.1	24.2	21.1
Sudan [6] Soudan [6]	2005	0.3	...	...	...	...	...	...

27 Gross domestic expenditure on research and development (R&D) *(continued)*
As a percentage of GDP and by source of funds

Dépenses intérieures brutes de recherche et développement (R-D) *(suite)*
En pourcentage du PIB et répartition par source de financement

Country or area Pays ou zone	Year Année	Expenditure on R&D as a % of GDP Dépenses en R&D en % du PIB	Source of funds (%) / Source de financement (%) Business enterprises Entreprises	Govern-ment Etat	Higher education Enseigne-ment supérieur	Private non-profit Institut. Privées sans but lucratif	Funds from abroad Fonds de l'étranger	Not specified/ Non précisé
Sweden	#2005	3.4	63.9	24.4	0.7	2.9	8.1	...
Suède	2009	3.4	59.5	27.0	0.6	2.6	10.3	...
	*2010	3.2	...	...	...	...	...	...
	2013[20]	3.3	61.0	28.3	1.0	3.1	6.7	...
	*2015	3.3	...	...	...	...	...	...
Switzerland	2004	2.7	69.7	22.7	1.5	0.8	5.2	...
Suisse	2008	2.7	68.2	22.8	2.3	0.7	6.0	...
	2012	3.0	60.8	25.4	1.2	0.6	12.1	...
Tajikistan	2001	0.1	0.6	97.3	...	...	0.2	1.9
Tadjikistan	2005	0.1	2.2[16]	91.5[16]	0.3[16]	...	...	5.5[16]
	2006	0.1	0.2[16]	76.3[16]	0.2[16]	...	0.6[16]	19.9[16]
	2010	0.1[2,3]	1.9[16]	76.2[16]	0.4[16]	...	...	19.7[16]
	2011	0.1[2,3]	1.6[16]	82.1[16]	0.1[16]	...	...	15.1[16]
	2013	0.1[2,3]	...	92.5	0.2	...	0.2	7.1
	2015[2,3]	0.1	...	100.0	...	...	...	...
Thailand	2005	0.2	48.7	31.5	14.9	0.7	1.8	2.4
Thaïlande	2009	0.2	41.4	37.9	17.8	0.3	1.0	1.6
	2015	0.6	66.2	20.5	5.5	0.1	1.5	6.0
TFYR of Macedonia	2002	0.2	* 7.8	* 76.3	* 7.3	* ~0.0	* 8.6	...
ex-R.Y. de Macédoine	2005	0.2	...	...	...	...	...	...
	2010	0.2	...	...	...	...	...	...
	2015	0.4	16.8	52.9	25.0	0.1	5.2	...
Togo	2010	0.3[3]	...	88.3	...	...	11.7	...
Togo	2012	0.2[3]	...	84.9	...	3.1	12.1	...
	2014[3]	0.3[2]	...	94.5	...	...	5.5	...
Trinidad and Tobago	2005	0.1	...	...	...	...	...	...
Trinité-et-Tobago	2010	~0.0	...	...	...	...	...	...
	2014	0.1	...	...	...	...	...	...
Tunisia	2005	0.7	14.4	79.2	...	...	6.4	...
Tunisie	2010	0.7	17.1	78.1	...	...	4.8	...
	2015	* 0.6	18.9	77.1	...	...	3.9	...
Turkey	2005	0.6	43.3[4]	50.1[4]	...	5.8[4]	0.8	...
Turquie	2010	0.8	45.1	30.8	19.6	3.7	0.8	...
	2014	1.0	50.9	26.3	18.4	3.4	1.1	...
Uganda	2002	0.4	1.3	33.8	1.3	...	63.6	...
Ouganda	2005	0.2	1.7	41.5	...	...	56.9	...
	2010	0.5	13.7	21.9	1.0	6.0	57.3	...
Ukraine	2005	1.0	# 32.3	# 40.1	# 0.1	# 0.4	# 24.4	# 2.8
Ukraine	2010	0.8	26.2	46.7	0.2	0.1	25.7	1.1
	2015	0.6[22]	40.3	39.4	0.2	~0.0	18.2	2.0
United Arab Emirates	2014	0.7	74.3[24]	25.7[11]	...	...	...	...
Émirats arabes unis	2015	0.9	...	...	...	...	...	...
United Kingdom	2005	1.6	42.1	32.7	1.2	4.7	19.3	...
Royaume-Uni	*2010	1.7	44.0	32.3	1.2	4.8	17.6	...
	*2015	1.7	48.4	28.0	1.2	4.8	17.6	...
United Rep. of Tanzania	2010	0.4[1,3]	0.1	57.5	0.3	0.1	42.0	...
Rép.-Unie de Tanzanie	2013[3]	0.5	...	...	...	...	...	...
United States of America	2005[7]	2.5	63.3	30.8	2.8	3.1	...	...
États-Unis d'Amérique	2010	2.7[7]	56.9[7]	32.6[7]	3.0[7]	3.8[7]	3.7	...
	2015	* 2.8[7]	64.2[7]	* 24.0[7]	* 3.4[7]	* 3.7[7]	* 4.7	...
United States Virgin Islands [1]	2002	...	...	70.8	28.0	1.2	...	...
Îles Vierges américaines [1]	2005	...	...	100.0	...	...	...	...
	2007	...	...	100.0	...	...	...	...
Uruguay	2000	0.2	39.3	20.3	35.7	...	4.8	~0.0
Uruguay	2002	0.2	46.7	17.1	31.4	0.1	4.7	...
	2010	0.3	47.1	22.9	26.6	0.9	1.7	0.8
	2011	0.3	8.5	30.8	45.2	0.1	6.5	8.9
	2014	0.3	4.6	28.6	59.2	0.3	7.4	...

Gross domestic expenditure on research and development (R&D) *(continued)*

As a percentage of GDP and by source of funds

Dépenses intérieures brutes de recherche et développement (R-D) *(suite)*

En pourcentage du PIB et répartition par source de financement

			Source of funds (%) / Source de financement (%)					
Country or area Pays ou zone	Year Année	Expenditure on R&D as a % of GDP Dépenses en R&D en % du PIB	Business enterprises Entreprises	Government Etat	Higher education Enseignement supérieur	Private non-profit Institut. Privées sans but lucratif	Funds from abroad Fonds de l'étranger	Not specified/ Non précisé
Uzbekistan	2005	0.2	...	...	...	...	...	...
Ouzbékistan	2010	0.2	...	...	...	...	...	...
	2015	0.2	38.9	57.0[14]	...	...	1.2	2.9
Viet Nam	2002	0.2	18.1	74.1	0.7[10]	...	6.3	0.8
Viet Nam	2013	0.4	40.0	55.9	0.8	...	1.5	1.8
Zambia	2005[1]	~0.0	...	...	...	...	...	...
Zambie	#2008	0.3	3.2	94.8	...	0.3	1.6	...

Source:

United Nations Educational, Scientific and Cultural Organization (UNESCO), Montreal, the UNESCO Institute for Statistics (UIS) statistics database, last accessed November 2017.

1 Partial data.
2 Excluding private non-profit.
3 Excluding business enterprise.
4 Including other classes.
5 Data have been converted from the former national currency using the appropriate conversion rate.
6 Overestimated or based on overestimated data.
7 Excluding most or all capital expenditures.
8 Higher Education only.
9 For statistical purposes, the data for China do not include those for the Hong Kong Special Administrative Region (Hong Kong SAR), Macao Special Administrative Region (Macao SAR) and Taiwan Province of China.
10 Including private non-profit.
11 Government only.
12 S&T budget instead of R&D expenditure.
13 Including business enterprise.
14 Including higher education.
15 Including Government.
16 The sum of the breakdown does not add to the total.
17 Excluding government.
18 R&D budget instead of R&D expenditure or based on R&D budget.
19 Excluding Defence (all or mostly).
20 Underestimated or based on underestimated data.
21 Excluding social sciences and humanities.
22 Excluding data from some regions, provinces or states.
23 Do not correspond exactly to Frascati Manual recommendations.
24 Business enterprise only.

Source:

Organisation des Nations Unies pour l'éducation, la science et la culture (UNESCO), Montréal, base de données statistiques de l'Institut de statistique (ISU) de l'UNESCO, dernier accès novembre 2017.

1 Données partielles.
2 Non compris les organisations privées à but non lucratif.
3 Ne comprend pas les entreprises commerciales.
4 Comprend d'autres catégories.
5 Les données ont été converties à partir de l'ancienne monnaie nationale et du taux de conversion approprié.
6 Surestimé ou fondé sur des données surestimées.
7 Exclut toutes ou presque toutes des dépenses en capital.
8 Enseignement supérieur seulement.
9 Pour la présentation des statistiques, les données pour la Chine ne comprennent pas la région administrative spéciale de Hong Kong (Hong Kong RAS), la région administrative spéciale de Macao (Macao RAS) et la province chinoise de Taïwan.
10 Y compris les fonds privés à but non lucratif.
11 Etat seulement.
12 Budget pour la science et technologie au lieu des dépenses de recherche et développement.
13 Y compris les fonds d'entreprises.
14 Y compris l'enseignement supérieur.
15 Y compris l'état.
16 La somme de toutes les valeurs diffère du total.
17 Non compris l'état.
18 Basé sur le budget de la recherche-développement au lieu des dépenses.
19 À l'exclusion de la défense (en totalité ou en grande partie).
20 Sous-estimé ou basé sur des données sous-estimées.
21 Non compris les sciences sociales et les sciences humaines.
22 Non compris les données de certaines régions, provinces ou états.
23 Ne corresponds pas exactement aux recommandations du Manuel de Frascati.
24 Les entreprises commerciales seulement.

28 Patents

Resident filings (per million population), grants and patents in force

Brevets

Demandes émanant de résidents (par million d'habitants), délivrances et brevets en vigueur

Region, country or area	1985	1995	2005	2010	2014	2015	2016	Région, pays ou zone
Total, all countries or areas								**Total, tous pays ou zones**
Grants of patents	**397 580**	**430 700**	**634 000**	**915 500**	**1 179 900**	**1 241 000**	**1 351 600**	**Brevets délivrés**
Africa								**Afrique**
Grants of patents	...	...	4 800	9 600	13 900	8 500	7 800	Brevets délivrés
Northern America								**Amérique septentrionale**
Grants of patents	...	...	159 300	238 700	324 400	320 600	329 500	Brevets délivrés
Latin America & the Caribbean								**Amérique latine et Caraïbes**
Grants of patents	...	...	15 000	17 900	18 700	18 500	19 600	Brevets délivrés
Asia								**Asie**
Grants of patents	...	...	288 700	469 600	636 900	700 500	771 000	Brevets délivrés
Europe								**Europe**
Grants of patents	...	...	151 000	160 800	161 800	165 400	195 900	Brevets délivrés
Oceania								**Océanie**
Grants of patents	...	...	15 200	18 900	24 200	27 500	27 800	Brevets délivrés
Albania								**Albanie**
Resident filings (per mil. pop.)	...	...	...	...	4	5	8	Dem. de rés. (par mil. d'hab.)
Grants of patents	...	...	395	349	5	10	5	Brevets délivrés
Patents in force	...	...	...	349	...	...	...	Brevets en vigueur
Algeria								**Algérie**
Resident filings (per mil. pop.)	...	1	2	2	2	2	3	Dem. de rés. (par mil. d'hab.)
Grants of patents	...	118	443	1 076	281	353	383	Brevets délivrés
Patents in force	...	...	498	...	4 340	5 145	5 618	Brevets en vigueur
Argentina								**Argentine**
Resident filings (per mil. pop.)	...	19	27	13	12	13	20	Dem. de rés. (par mil. d'hab.)
Grants of patents	...	1 003	1 798	1 366	1 360	1 559	1 879	Brevets délivrés
Armenia								**Arménie**
Resident filings (per mil. pop.)	...	58	69	49	42	39	44	Dem. de rés. (par mil. d'hab.)
Grants of patents	...	52	126	124	108	81	93	Brevets délivrés
Patents in force	...	...	110	278	279	248	226	Brevets en vigueur
Australia								**Australie**
Resident filings (per mil. pop.)	...	99	125	109	85	96	109	Dem. de rés. (par mil. d'hab.)
Grants of patents	6 764	9 406	10 979	14 557	19 304	23 098	23 744	Brevets délivrés
Patents in force	...	...	96 403	96 293	128 407	117 906	132 994	Brevets en vigueur
Austria								**Autriche**
Resident filings (per mil. pop.)	300	217	404	497	475	486	471	Dem. de rés. (par mil. d'hab.)
Grants of patents	2 571	1 777	938	1 130	962	1 356	1 135	Brevets délivrés
Patents in force	...	...	95 618	102 113	118 494	121 367	142 875	Brevets en vigueur
Azerbaijan								**Azerbaïdjan**
Resident filings (per mil. pop.)	...	29	33	30	21	23	19	Dem. de rés. (par mil. d'hab.)
Grants of patents	...	9	195	126	97	88	131	Brevets délivrés
Patents in force	...	...	...	...	87	82	345	Brevets en vigueur
Bahamas								**Bahamas**
Resident filings (per mil. pop.)	13	...	...	...	3	5	8	Dem. de rés. (par mil. d'hab.)
Grants of patents	66	...	...	...	238	192	47	Brevets délivrés
Patents in force	...	...	...	...	1 117	1 132	1 077	Brevets en vigueur
Bahrain								**Bahreïn**
Resident filings (per mil. pop.)	...	...	...	...	5	7	6	Dem. de rés. (par mil. d'hab.)
Grants of patents	31	...	...	...	...	...	...	Brevets délivrés
Patents in force	...	...	...	...	117	...	...	Brevets en vigueur
Bangladesh								**Bangladesh**
Resident filings (per mil. pop.)	...	1	...	...	...	...	...	Dem. de rés. (par mil. d'hab.)
Grants of patents	118	80	182	92	121	101	106	Brevets délivrés
Patents in force	...	...	...	...	1 077	...	...	Brevets en vigueur
Barbados								**Barbade**
Resident filings (per mil. pop.)	...	...	...	...	4	...	...	Dem. de rés. (par mil. d'hab.)
Grants of patents	...	...	7	...	3	10	26	Brevets délivrés
Patents in force	...	...	49	57	...	...	...	Brevets en vigueur
Belarus								**Bélarus**
Resident filings (per mil. pop.)	...	61	121	197	82	75	60	Dem. de rés. (par mil. d'hab.)
Grants of patents	...	633	955	1 222	1 938	902	949	Brevets délivrés
Patents in force	...	...	...	4 444	5 176	2 676	2 503	Brevets en vigueur

Region, country or area	1985	1995	2005	2010	2014	2015	2016	Région, pays ou zone
Belgium								**Belgique**
Resident filings (per mil. pop.)	78	72	208	244	251	265	286	Dem. de rés. (par mil. d'hab.)
Grants of patents	1 976	1 216	708	532	373	567	1 620	Brevets délivrés
Patents in force	...	...	...	89 999	90 012	90 648	97 639	Brevets en vigueur
Belize								**Belize**
Grants of patents	...	...	...	...	28	8	4	Brevets délivrés
Patents in force	...	...	...	...	120	128	132	Brevets en vigueur
Bolivia (Plurin. State of)								**Bolivie (État plurin. de)**
Resident filings (per mil. pop.)	1	2	...	...	1	...	1	Dem. de rés. (par mil. d'hab.)
Grants of patents	62	47	...	...	97	75	86	Brevets délivrés
Patents in force	...	...	...	...	601	...	...	Brevets en vigueur
Bosnia and Herzegovina								**Bosnie-Herzégovine**
Resident filings (per mil. pop.)	...	...	17	15	11	...	17	Dem. de rés. (par mil. d'hab.)
Grants of patents	...	...	46	173	5	...	12	Brevets délivrés
Patents in force	...	...	120	716	503	...	375	Brevets en vigueur
Botswana								**Botswana**
Resident filings (per mil. pop.)	...	...	...	...	2	...	...	Dem. de rés. (par mil. d'hab.)
Grants of patents	...	...	...	...	...	...	1	Brevets délivrés
Patents in force	...	...	...	...	883	...	...	Brevets en vigueur
Brazil								**Brésil**
Resident filings (per mil. pop.)	14	17	22	21	23	23	25	Dem. de rés. (par mil. d'hab.)
Grants of patents	3 934	2 659	2 439	3 251	2 749	3 411	4 195	Brevets délivrés
Patents in force	...	...	32 571	40 022	24 976	23 952	24 153	Brevets en vigueur
Brunei Darussalam								**Brunéi Darussalam**
Resident filings (per mil. pop.)	...	...	...	...	63	...	...	Dem. de rés. (par mil. d'hab.)
Grants of patents	...	42	26	40	71	...	...	Brevets délivrés
Bulgaria								**Bulgarie**
Resident filings (per mil. pop.)	...	44	36	34	35	44	35	Dem. de rés. (par mil. d'hab.)
Grants of patents	130	375	313	251	72	37	42	Brevets délivrés
Patents in force	...	...	2 203	6 812	10 203	10 721	11 511	Brevets en vigueur
Burundi								**Burundi**
Grants of patents	...	1	...	...	...	...	...	Brevets délivrés
Cambodia								**Cambodge**
Grants of patents	...	...	...	...	...	1	...	Brevets délivrés
Canada								**Canada**
Resident filings (per mil. pop.)	81	83	160	134	118	119	112	Dem. de rés. (par mil. d'hab.)
Grants of patents	18 697	9 139	15 516	19 120	23 749	22 201	26 424	Brevets délivrés
Patents in force	...	...	125 110	133 355	161 442	166 771	175 236	Brevets en vigueur
Chile								**Chili**
Resident filings (per mil. pop.)	10	12	22	19	26	25	22	Dem. de rés. (par mil. d'hab.)
Grants of patents	448	133	311	1 020	1 168	1 058	2 077	Brevets délivrés
Patents in force	...	...	...	8 121	9 987	11 163	12 512	Brevets en vigueur
China [1]								**Chine [1]**
Resident filings (per mil. pop.)	4	8	72	219	587	706	874	Dem. de rés. (par mil. d'hab.)
Grants of patents	44	3 393	53 305	135 110	233 228	359 316	404 208	Brevets délivrés
Patents in force	...	...	182 396	564 760	1 196 497	1 472 374	1 772 203	Brevets en vigueur
China, Hong Kong SAR								**Chine, RAS de Hong Kong**
Resident filings (per mil. pop.)	3	4	23	19	27	33	32	Dem. de rés. (par mil. d'hab.)
Grants of patents	1 030	1 960	6 518	5 353	5 932	5 963	5 698	Brevets délivrés
Patents in force	...	...	...	33 225	40 865	42 306	43 359	Brevets en vigueur
China, Macao SAR								**Chine, RAS de Macao**
Resident filings (per mil. pop.)	...	...	6	7	3	5	...	Dem. de rés. (par mil. d'hab.)
Grants of patents	...	2	5	156	16	36	57	Brevets délivrés
Patents in force	...	...	12	377	451	470	467	Brevets en vigueur
Colombia								**Colombie**
Resident filings (per mil. pop.)	2	4	2	3	5	7	11	Dem. de rés. (par mil. d'hab.)
Grants of patents	169	365	256	639	1 212	1 003	917	Brevets délivrés
Patents in force	...	...	...	...	6 710	7 858	6 623	Brevets en vigueur
Congo								**Congo**
Grants of patents	...	15	...	...	...	...	...	Brevets délivrés
Costa Rica								**Costa Rica**
Resident filings (per mil. pop.)	...	...	...	2	3	4	2	Dem. de rés. (par mil. d'hab.)
Grants of patents	...	...	...	45	114	130	67	Brevets délivrés
Patents in force	...	...	...	239	518	635	678	Brevets en vigueur

Patents *(continued)*
Resident filings (per million population), grants and patents in force

Brevets *(suite)*
Demandes émanant de résidents (par million d'habitants), délivrances et brevets en vigueur

Region, country or area	1985	1995	2005	2010	2014	2015	2016	Région, pays ou zone
Croatia								**Croatie**
Resident filings (per mil. pop.)	...	57	82	62	43	42	45	Dem. de rés. (par mil. d'hab.)
Grants of patents	...	25	140	82	90	45	35	Brevets délivrés
Patents in force	...	...	1 094	2 134	4 838	5 621	6 606	Brevets en vigueur
Cuba								**Cuba**
Resident filings (per mil. pop.)	...	10	9	...	2	...	3	Dem. de rés. (par mil. d'hab.)
Grants of patents	18	77	64	...	94	...	93	Brevets délivrés
Patents in force	...	...	653	...	927	...	857	Brevets en vigueur
Cyprus								**Chypre**
Resident filings (per mil. pop.)	...	...	54	35	44	37	43	Dem. de rés. (par mil. d'hab.)
Grants of patents	43	...	68	19	...	...	...	Brevets délivrés
Patents in force	...	...	3 521	333	149	114	79	Brevets en vigueur
Czechia								**Tchéquie**
Resident filings (per mil. pop.)	...	61	65	99	102	104	93	Dem. de rés. (par mil. d'hab.)
Grants of patents	...	1 299	1 551	911	688	749	781	Brevets délivrés
Patents in force	...	...	10 165	23 415	32 590	34 837	37 889	Brevets en vigueur
Dem. People's Rep. Korea								**Rép. pop. dém. de Corée**
Resident filings (per mil. pop.)	...	...	245	326	...	...	...	Dem. de rés. (par mil. d'hab.)
Grants of patents	...	...	3 583	6 290	...	...	...	Brevets délivrés
Denmark								**Danemark**
Resident filings (per mil. pop.)	167	236	523	625	595	596	597	Dem. de rés. (par mil. d'hab.)
Grants of patents	1 054	1 120	389	155	292	430	409	Brevets délivrés
Patents in force	...	...	56 978	47 732	51 345	52 321	55 715	Brevets en vigueur
Dominican Republic								**République dominicaine**
Resident filings (per mil. pop.)	...	...	...	...	1	2	2	Dem. de rés. (par mil. d'hab.)
Grants of patents	...	...	...	...	62	24	21	Brevets délivrés
Patents in force	...	...	...	...	294	311	265	Brevets en vigueur
Ecuador								**Équateur**
Resident filings (per mil. pop.)	...	1	1	...	2	1	3	Dem. de rés. (par mil. d'hab.)
Grants of patents	...	90	38	28	20	14	10	Brevets délivrés
Patents in force	...	...	38	199	...	...	...	Brevets en vigueur
Egypt								**Égypte**
Resident filings (per mil. pop.)	3	6	6	7	8	8	10	Dem. de rés. (par mil. d'hab.)
Grants of patents	298	346	147	321	415	472	450	Brevets délivrés
Patents in force	...	...	...	3 316	4 012	3 703	3 189	Brevets en vigueur
El Salvador								**El Salvador**
Resident filings (per mil. pop.)	3	1	...	...	...	1	1	Dem. de rés. (par mil. d'hab.)
Grants of patents	70	61	...	...	77	35	40	Brevets délivrés
Patents in force	...	...	...	...	1 642	...	...	Brevets en vigueur
Estonia								**Estonie**
Resident filings (per mil. pop.)	...	11	19	83	61	47	55	Dem. de rés. (par mil. d'hab.)
Grants of patents	...	...	163	120	38	24	27	Brevets délivrés
Patents in force	...	...	1 395	5 317	7 904	8 356	8 924	Brevets en vigueur
Eswatini								**Eswatini**
Grants of patents	30	...	...	...	2	2	...	Brevets délivrés
Ethiopia								**Éthiopie**
Grants of patents	...	...	9	...	...	...	...	Brevets délivrés
Fiji								**Fidji**
Grants of patents	15	...	...	...	...	...	...	Brevets délivrés
Finland								**Finlande**
Resident filings (per mil. pop.)	352	403	637	628	662	601	560	Dem. de rés. (par mil. d'hab.)
Grants of patents	2 160	2 347	1 757	923	787	931	815	Brevets délivrés
Patents in force	...	...	39 450	46 622	47 344	48 242	48 588	Brevets en vigueur
France								**France**
Resident filings (per mil. pop.)	212	209	354	373	379	377	369	Dem. de rés. (par mil. d'hab.)
Grants of patents	24 195	17 918	11 473	9 899	11 889	12 699	12 374	Brevets délivrés
Patents in force	...	...	343 568	435 915	510 490	520 069	535 554	Brevets en vigueur
Gambia								**Gambie**
Grants of patents	...	...	2	...	...	...	...	Brevets délivrés
Georgia								**Géorgie**
Resident filings (per mil. pop.)	...	61	54	47	30	27	26	Dem. de rés. (par mil. d'hab.)
Grants of patents	...	133	320	258	209	206	177	Brevets délivrés
Patents in force	...	...	1 040	1 044	1 486	1 650	1 394	Brevets en vigueur

Patents *(continued)*
Resident filings (per million population), grants and patents in force

Brevets *(suite)*
Demandes émanant de résidents (par million d'habitants), délivrances et brevets en vigueur

Region, country or area	1985	1995	2005	2010	2014	2015	2016	Région, pays ou zone
Germany								**Allemagne**
Resident filings (per mil. pop.)	415	467	875	910	912	884	890	Dem. de rés. (par mil. d'hab.)
Grants of patents	19 500	16 000	17 063	13 678	15 030	14 795	15 652	Brevets délivrés
Patents in force	...	...	434 663	514 046	576 273	602 013	617 307	Brevets en vigueur
Ghana								**Ghana**
Grants of patents	...	...	...	...	...	...	25	Brevets délivrés
Patents in force	...	...	...	...	...	...	25	Brevets en vigueur
Greece								**Grèce**
Resident filings (per mil. pop.)	113	25	48	73	68	59	63	Dem. de rés. (par mil. d'hab.)
Grants of patents	3 294	350	320	479	316	262	271	Brevets délivrés
Patents in force	...	...	...	32 120	27 230	26 506	26 479	Brevets en vigueur
Grenada								**Grenade**
Grants of patents	...	...	...	...	...	9	14	Brevets délivrés
Guatemala								**Guatemala**
Resident filings (per mil. pop.)	9	3	1	...	1	...	...	Dem. de rés. (par mil. d'hab.)
Grants of patents	166	22	104	104	105	51	52	Brevets délivrés
Patents in force	...	...	...	590	840	867	883	Brevets en vigueur
Guyana								**Guyana**
Resident filings (per mil. pop.)	1	...	...	...	1	...	...	Dem. de rés. (par mil. d'hab.)
Grants of patents	22	...	...	...	1	...	57	Brevets délivrés
Patents in force	...	...	...	...	17	12	29	Brevets en vigueur
Haiti								**Haïti**
Resident filings (per mil. pop.)	1	...	...	...	...	...	...	Dem. de rés. (par mil. d'hab.)
Grants of patents	9	3	11	10	...	...	...	Brevets délivrés
Honduras								**Honduras**
Resident filings (per mil. pop.)	3	1	...	...	...	...	1	Dem. de rés. (par mil. d'hab.)
Grants of patents	19	...	85	81	94	69	53	Brevets délivrés
Patents in force	...	...	...	...	...	...	82	Brevets en vigueur
Hungary								**Hongrie**
Resident filings (per mil. pop.)	273	106	78	75	67	68	74	Dem. de rés. (par mil. d'hab.)
Grants of patents	2 095	1 910	1 126	65	376	365	271	Brevets délivrés
Patents in force	...	...	9 125	13 853	20 426	21 851	23 782	Brevets en vigueur
Iceland								**Islande**
Resident filings (per mil. pop.)	87	71	253	343	281	257	218	Dem. de rés. (par mil. d'hab.)
Grants of patents	21	11	101	139	54	17	22	Brevets délivrés
Patents in force	...	...	349	1 892	4 089	4 920	5 941	Brevets en vigueur
India								**Inde**
Resident filings (per mil. pop.)	1	2	4	7	9	10	10	Dem. de rés. (par mil. d'hab.)
Grants of patents	1 814	1 613	4 320	7 138	6 153	6 022	8 248	Brevets délivrés
Patents in force	...	...	16 419	47 224	49 272	47 113	49 575	Brevets en vigueur
Indonesia								**Indonésie**
Resident filings (per mil. pop.)	...	...	1	2	3	4	...	Dem. de rés. (par mil. d'hab.)
Grants of patents	...	...	...	...	...	1 911	3 674	Brevets délivrés
Iran (Islamic Republic of)								**Iran (Rép. islamique d')**
Resident filings (per mil. pop.)	4	5	58	149	175	...	186	Dem. de rés. (par mil. d'hab.)
Grants of patents	339	166	2 890	5 372	3 060	2 936	3 268	Brevets délivrés
Iraq								**Iraq**
Resident filings (per mil. pop.)	19	4	...	...	...	9	...	Dem. de rés. (par mil. d'hab.)
Grants of patents	103	32	...	...	...	312	...	Brevets délivrés
Ireland								**Irlande**
Resident filings (per mil. pop.)	205	233	264	274	191	179	184	Dem. de rés. (par mil. d'hab.)
Grants of patents	1 042	3 525	349	243	148	126	164	Brevets délivrés
Patents in force	...	...	...	79 040	111 109	118 273	147 125	Brevets en vigueur
Israel								**Israël**
Resident filings (per mil. pop.)	187	228	241	190	137	153	152	Dem. de rés. (par mil. d'hab.)
Grants of patents	1 636	2 029	2 269	2 293	3 984	4 492	4 938	Brevets délivrés
Patents in force	...	...	...	26 494	26 645	28 666	30 922	Brevets en vigueur
Italy								**Italie**
Resident filings (per mil. pop.)	35	...	...	219	201	...	215	Dem. de rés. (par mil. d'hab.)
Grants of patents	...	9 164	5 534	16 106	7 795	7 153	6 429	Brevets délivrés
Patents in force	...	...	...	65 417	63 071	...	...	Brevets en vigueur
Jamaica								**Jamaïque**
Resident filings (per mil. pop.)	...	3	4	5	12	2	7	Dem. de rés. (par mil. d'hab.)
Grants of patents	...	4	...	...	28	74	5	Brevets délivrés
Patents in force	...	...	527	...	324	375	328	Brevets en vigueur

Patents *(continued)*
Resident filings (per million population), grants and patents in force

Brevets *(suite)*
Demandes émanant de résidents (par million d'habitants), délivrances et brevets en vigueur

Region, country or area	1985	1995	2005	2010	2014	2015	2016	Région, pays ou zone
Japan								**Japon**
Resident filings (per mil. pop.)	2 272	2 661	2 880	2 265	2 090	2 036	2 049	Dem. de rés. (par mil. d'hab.)
Grants of patents	50 100	109 100	122 944	222 693	227 142	189 358	203 087	Brevets délivrés
Patents in force	...	...	1 123 055	1 423 432	1 920 490	1 946 568	1 980 985	Brevets en vigueur
Jordan								**Jordanie**
Resident filings (per mil. pop.)	...	...	9	6	5	4	2	Dem. de rés. (par mil. d'hab.)
Grants of patents	...	...	55	64	115	83	121	Brevets délivrés
Patents in force	...	...	...	312	377	427	463	Brevets en vigueur
Kazakhstan								**Kazakhstan**
Resident filings (per mil. pop.)	...	65	101	105	105	75	59	Dem. de rés. (par mil. d'hab.)
Grants of patents	...	1 281	...	1 868	1 504	1 504	1 011	Brevets délivrés
Patents in force	...	...	...	581	5 184	3 934	3 218	Brevets en vigueur
Kenya								**Kenya**
Resident filings (per mil. pop.)	...	...	1	2	3	3	3	Dem. de rés. (par mil. d'hab.)
Grants of patents	98	...	48	54	53	24	26	Brevets délivrés
Kiribati								**Kiribati**
Grants of patents	1	...	...	...	...	...	...	Brevets délivrés
Kyrgyzstan								**Kirghizistan**
Resident filings (per mil. pop.)	...	26	...	26	23	22	15	Dem. de rés. (par mil. d'hab.)
Grants of patents	...	133	...	109	100	111	120	Brevets délivrés
Patents in force	...	...	...	112	375	347	274	Brevets en vigueur
Latvia								**Lettonie**
Resident filings (per mil. pop.)	...	85	53	101	56	83	55	Dem. de rés. (par mil. d'hab.)
Grants of patents	...	629	122	184	141	147	68	Brevets délivrés
Patents in force	...	...	4 012	5 680	6 763	6 938	7 419	Brevets en vigueur
Lebanon								**Liban**
Resident filings (per mil. pop.)	...	...	...	...	14	19	...	Dem. de rés. (par mil. d'hab.)
Grants of patents	...	...	...	...	316	279	...	Brevets délivrés
Lesotho								**Lesotho**
Resident filings (per mil. pop.)	...	5	...	...	...	...	...	Dem. de rés. (par mil. d'hab.)
Grants of patents	...	7	...	...	...	...	...	Brevets délivrés
Libya								**Libye**
Resident filings (per mil. pop.)	...	1	...	...	...	...	...	Dem. de rés. (par mil. d'hab.)
Liechtenstein								**Liechtenstein**
Resident filings (per mil. pop.)	...	...	4 355	8 056	7 493	9 920	10 000	Dem. de rés. (par mil. d'hab.)
Lithuania								**Lituanie**
Resident filings (per mil. pop.)	...	29	21	38	50	48	42	Dem. de rés. (par mil. d'hab.)
Grants of patents	...	494	116	84	120	133	103	Brevets délivrés
Patents in force	...	...	768	642	520	530	522	Brevets en vigueur
Luxembourg								**Luxembourg**
Resident filings (per mil. pop.)	221	86	441	990	1 053	952	1 067	Dem. de rés. (par mil. d'hab.)
Grants of patents	418	...	29	87	152	153	184	Brevets délivrés
Patents in force	...	...	...	21 346	19 360	19 040	19 960	Brevets en vigueur
Madagascar								**Madagascar**
Resident filings (per mil. pop.)	...	2	...	...	...	...	...	Dem. de rés. (par mil. d'hab.)
Grants of patents	...	25	32	55	24	23	19	Brevets délivrés
Patents in force	...	...	249	387	390	414	386	Brevets en vigueur
Malawi								**Malawi**
Grants of patents	43	23	...	1	...	1	7	Brevets délivrés
Malaysia								**Malaisie**
Resident filings (per mil. pop.)	1	7	20	44	45	41	36	Dem. de rés. (par mil. d'hab.)
Grants of patents	1 150	1 753	2 508	2 160	2 705	2 877	3 324	Brevets délivrés
Patents in force	...	...	...	20 908	21 568	23 538	25 117	Brevets en vigueur
Malta								**Malte**
Resident filings (per mil. pop.)	...	29	...	104	150	215	...	Dem. de rés. (par mil. d'hab.)
Grants of patents	20	19	...	4	4	10	6	Brevets délivrés
Patents in force	...	...	...	832	490	428	423	Brevets en vigueur
Mauritius								**Maurice**
Resident filings (per mil. pop.)	4	3	...	...	2	1	2	Dem. de rés. (par mil. d'hab.)
Grants of patents	4	3	...	8	9	4	2	Brevets délivrés
Mexico								**Mexique**
Resident filings (per mil. pop.)	8	5	5	8	10	11	10	Dem. de rés. (par mil. d'hab.)
Grants of patents	977	3 538	8 098	9 399	9 819	9 338	8 652	Brevets délivrés
Patents in force	...	...	48 374	82 017	106 340	106 648	109 238	Brevets en vigueur

28 Patents *(continued)*
Resident filings (per million population), grants and patents in force

Brevets *(suite)*
Demandes émanant de résidents (par million d'habitants), délivrances et brevets en vigueur

Region, country or area	1985	1995	2005	2010	2014	2015	2016	Région, pays ou zone
Monaco								**Monaco**
Resident filings (per mil. pop.)	521	423	503	539	735	862	1 117	Dem. de rés. (par mil. d'hab.)
Grants of patents	66	36	9	5	5	8	9	Brevets délivrés
Patents in force	...	...	37 483	53 859	53 893	63 777	85 132	Brevets en vigueur
Mongolia								**Mongolie**
Resident filings (per mil. pop.)	...	57	40	41	48	37	37	Dem. de rés. (par mil. d'hab.)
Grants of patents	5	117	197	96	216	234	157	Brevets délivrés
Patents in force	...	...	13 663	2 645	...	4 338	4 324	Brevets en vigueur
Montenegro								**Monténégro**
Resident filings (per mil. pop.)	...	...	...	37	21	37	16	Dem. de rés. (par mil. d'hab.)
Grants of patents	...	...	...	264	14	10	8	Brevets délivrés
Patents in force	...	...	...	264	1 933	2 372	...	Brevets en vigueur
Morocco								**Maroc**
Resident filings (per mil. pop.)	2	3	5	5	10	6	7	Dem. de rés. (par mil. d'hab.)
Grants of patents	313	354	556	808	...	...	352	Brevets délivrés
Patents in force	...	...	9 872	...	...	...	...	Brevets en vigueur
Mozambique								**Mozambique**
Resident filings (per mil. pop.)	...	...	...	1	1	1	1	Dem. de rés. (par mil. d'hab.)
Grants of patents	...	...	14	...	60	54	35	Brevets délivrés
Nepal								**Népal**
Grants of patents	1	1	3	...	...	2	...	Brevets délivrés
Patents in force	...	...	...	...	72	...	...	Brevets en vigueur
Netherlands								**Pays-Bas**
Resident filings (per mil. pop.)	134	137	614	511	543	549	536	Dem. de rés. (par mil. d'hab.)
Grants of patents	2 145	673	2 373	1 947	1 722	1 377	1 914	Brevets délivrés
Patents in force	...	...	135 215	135 127	156 261	160 214	164 264	Brevets en vigueur
New Zealand								**Nouvelle-Zélande**
Resident filings (per mil. pop.)	310	350	458	364	363	258	229	Dem. de rés. (par mil. d'hab.)
Grants of patents	1 732	2 641	4 189	4 347	4 677	4 259	3 910	Brevets délivrés
Patents in force	...	...	34 182	34 800	28 854	40 802	38 906	Brevets en vigueur
Nicaragua								**Nicaragua**
Resident filings (per mil. pop.)	1	...	...	...	...	...	...	Dem. de rés. (par mil. d'hab.)
Grants of patents	25	1	...	...	62	...	...	Brevets délivrés
Patents in force	...	...	...	...	387	...	...	Brevets en vigueur
Norway								**Norvège**
Resident filings (per mil. pop.)	222	259	247	334	318	321	335	Dem. de rés. (par mil. d'hab.)
Grants of patents	2 165	2 014	542	1 631	1 413	1 446	2 525	Brevets délivrés
Patents in force	...	...	...	16 534	21 882	23 087	27 930	Brevets en vigueur
Pakistan								**Pakistan**
Resident filings (per mil. pop.)	...	...	1	1	1	1	1	Dem. de rés. (par mil. d'hab.)
Grants of patents	...	474	393	238	185	131	214	Brevets délivrés
Patents in force	...	...	...	...	185	...	1 848	Brevets en vigueur
Panama								**Panama**
Resident filings (per mil. pop.)	6	6	...	...	3	4	17	Dem. de rés. (par mil. d'hab.)
Grants of patents	72	80	228	378	166	78	13	Brevets délivrés
Patents in force	...	...	...	378	1 725	1 684	1 734	Brevets en vigueur
Papua New Guinea								**Papouasie-Nvl-Guinée**
Grants of patents	...	...	...	...	...	70	...	Brevets délivrés
Patents in force	...	...	...	...	...	71	...	Brevets en vigueur
Paraguay								**Paraguay**
Resident filings (per mil. pop.)	2	...	4	3	...	...	...	Dem. de rés. (par mil. d'hab.)
Grants of patents	8	...	...	...	...	...	...	Brevets délivrés
Peru								**Pérou**
Resident filings (per mil. pop.)	2	...	1	1	3	2	2	Dem. de rés. (par mil. d'hab.)
Grants of patents	148	...	388	365	332	362	403	Brevets délivrés
Patents in force	...	...	2 252	2 435	2 651	2 643	2 779	Brevets en vigueur
Philippines								**Philippines**
Resident filings (per mil. pop.)	2	2	2	2	3	4	3	Dem. de rés. (par mil. d'hab.)
Grants of patents	1 281	589	1 642	1 153	2 159	2 200	4 006	Brevets délivrés
Patents in force	...	...	...	52 527	...	...	...	Brevets en vigueur
Poland								**Pologne**
Resident filings (per mil. pop.)	138	67	56	90	116	138	123	Dem. de rés. (par mil. d'hab.)
Grants of patents	4 467	2 608	2 522	3 004	2 852	2 572	3 548	Brevets délivrés
Patents in force	...	...	14 578	30 021	53 183	57 951	65 006	Brevets en vigueur

28 Patents *(continued)*

Resident filings (per million population), grants and patents in force

Brevets *(suite)*

Demandes émanant de résidents (par million d'habitants), délivrances et brevets en vigueur

Region, country or area	1985	1995	2005	2010	2014	2015	2016	Région, pays ou zone
Portugal								**Portugal**
Resident filings (per mil. pop.)	8	8	19	55	80	103	85	Dem. de rés. (par mil. d'hab.)
Grants of patents	960	960	231	140	97	76	38	Brevets délivrés
Patents in force	…	…	35 871	39 076	35 561	35 080	35 649	Brevets en vigueur
Qatar								**Qatar**
Resident filings (per mil. pop.)	…	…	…	…	4	…	9	Dem. de rés. (par mil. d'hab.)
Republic of Korea								**République de Corée**
Resident filings (per mil. pop.)	66	1 313	2 536	2 660	3 233	3 279	3 189	Dem. de rés. (par mil. d'hab.)
Grants of patents	2 268	12 512	73 512	68 843	129 786	101 873	108 875	Brevets délivrés
Patents in force	…	…	420 906	640 412	885 959	912 442	950 526	Brevets en vigueur
Republic of Moldova								**République de Moldova**
Resident filings (per mil. pop.)	…	73	105	42	19	18	26	Dem. de rés. (par mil. d'hab.)
Grants of patents	…	227	269	132	54	61	70	Brevets délivrés
Patents in force	…	…	1 108	1 018	384	348	343	Brevets en vigueur
Romania								**Roumanie**
Resident filings (per mil. pop.)	185	80	43	69	49	51	53	Dem. de rés. (par mil. d'hab.)
Grants of patents	2 786	1 860	759	447	356	305	355	Brevets délivrés
Patents in force	…	…	8 627	2 915	17 268	17 089	18 906	Brevets en vigueur
Russian Federation								**Fédération de Russie**
Resident filings (per mil. pop.)	…	118	166	203	169	205	188	Dem. de rés. (par mil. d'hab.)
Grants of patents	…	25 633	23 390	30 322	33 950	34 706	33 536	Brevets délivrés
Patents in force	…	…	123 089	181 904	208 320	218 974	230 870	Brevets en vigueur
Rwanda								**Rwanda**
Grants of patents	1	…	3	…	…	…	…	Brevets délivrés
Patents in force	…	…	…	…	135	108	…	Brevets en vigueur
Samoa								**Samoa**
Resident filings (per mil. pop.)	…	…	…	…	5	5	…	Dem. de rés. (par mil. d'hab.)
Grants of patents	4	2	…	…	…	64	…	Brevets délivrés
Patents in force	…	…	…	…	96	64	…	Brevets en vigueur
San Marino								**Saint-Marin**
Resident filings (per mil. pop.)	…	…	…	…	306	303	392	Dem. de rés. (par mil. d'hab.)
Grants of patents	…	…	…	…	201	290	462	Brevets délivrés
Saudi Arabia								**Arabie saoudite**
Resident filings (per mil. pop.)	…	1	6	12	31	29	41	Dem. de rés. (par mil. d'hab.)
Grants of patents	…	3	225	194	561	763	595	Brevets délivrés
Patents in force	…	…	…	…	2 338	2 664	3 104	Brevets en vigueur
Serbia								**Serbie**
Resident filings (per mil. pop.)	…	…	50	40	30	26	27	Dem. de rés. (par mil. d'hab.)
Grants of patents	…	…	265	427	105	86	68	Brevets délivrés
Patents in force	…	…	…	1 477	2 964	3 329	3 790	Brevets en vigueur
Serbia and Monten. [former]								**Serbie-et-Monténégro [anc.]**
Grants of patents	1 053	510	…	…	…	…	…	Brevets délivrés
Seychelles								**Seychelles**
Grants of patents	2	1	…	…	…	…	…	Brevets délivrés
Sierra Leone								**Sierra Leone**
Grants of patents	…	5	…	…	…	…	…	Brevets délivrés
Singapore								**Singapour**
Resident filings (per mil. pop.)	1	41	133	176	238	265	286	Dem. de rés. (par mil. d'hab.)
Grants of patents	416	1 750	7 530	4 442	5 538	7 054	7 341	Brevets délivrés
Patents in force	…	…	43 024	43 591	47 422	46 906	48 603	Brevets en vigueur
Slovakia								**Slovaquie**
Resident filings (per mil. pop.)	…	50	32	48	44	51	48	Dem. de rés. (par mil. d'hab.)
Grants of patents	…	381	560	376	94	82	122	Brevets délivrés
Patents in force	…	…	4 033	10 565	15 014	15 366	16 363	Brevets en vigueur
Slovenia								**Slovénie**
Resident filings (per mil. pop.)	…	158	215	282	…	…	…	Dem. de rés. (par mil. d'hab.)
Grants of patents	…	380	285	250	…	…	…	Brevets délivrés
Patents in force	…	…	5 201	1 485	…	…	…	Brevets en vigueur
Solomon Islands								**Îles Salomon**
Grants of patents	4	…	…	…	…	…	…	Brevets délivrés
Somalia								**Somalie**
Grants of patents	7	…	…	…	…	…	…	Brevets délivrés
South Africa								**Afrique du Sud**
Resident filings (per mil. pop.)	123	21	21	16	15	16	50	Dem. de rés. (par mil. d'hab.)
Grants of patents	6 768	5 113	1 831	5 331	5 065	4 499	4 255	Brevets délivrés
Patents in force	…	…	…	…	55 031	58 624	89 049	Brevets en vigueur

28 Patents *(continued)*

Resident filings (per million population), grants and patents in force

Brevets *(suite)*

Demandes émanant de résidents (par million d'habitants), délivrances et brevets en vigueur

Region, country or area	1985	1995	2005	2010	2014	2015	2016	Région, pays ou zone
Spain								**Espagne**
Resident filings (per mil. pop.)	56	52	92	107	95	93	93	Dem. de rés. (par mil. d'hab.)
Grants of patents	9 115	686	2 769	2 773	3 235	2 561	2 308	Brevets délivrés
Patents in force	...	...	39 297	175 687	137 836	115 591	115 070	Brevets en vigueur
Sri Lanka								**Sri Lanka**
Resident filings (per mil. pop.)	2	4	8	11	...	10	13	Dem. de rés. (par mil. d'hab.)
Grants of patents	112	159	180	504	...	262	123	Brevets délivrés
Patents in force	...	...	...	...	...	...	710	Brevets en vigueur
Sudan								**Soudan**
Resident filings (per mil. pop.)	...	...	...	7	...	7	7	Dem. de rés. (par mil. d'hab.)
Grants of patents	...	...	174	125	190	196	164	Brevets délivrés
Patents in force	...	...	...	...	...	196	164	Brevets en vigueur
Sweden								**Suède**
Resident filings (per mil. pop.)	460	446	555	614	604	599	564	Dem. de rés. (par mil. d'hab.)
Grants of patents	5 681	1 541	1 911	1 380	588	889	866	Brevets délivrés
Patents in force	...	...	102 741	96 796	93 348	92 607	93 545	Brevets en vigueur
Switzerland								**Suisse**
Resident filings (per mil. pop.)	493	410	897	1 069	1 018	1 035	1 043	Dem. de rés. (par mil. d'hab.)
Grants of patents	6 421	1 303	...	741	677	687	617	Brevets délivrés
Patents in force	...	...	99 531	123 033	144 859	162 761	193 883	Brevets en vigueur
Syrian Arab Republic								**République arabe syrienne**
Resident filings (per mil. pop.)	...	9	6	...	...	11	...	Dem. de rés. (par mil. d'hab.)
Grants of patents	...	71	72	...	...	14	32	Brevets délivrés
Tajikistan								**Tadjikistan**
Resident filings (per mil. pop.)	...	6	4	1	...	...	...	Dem. de rés. (par mil. d'hab.)
Grants of patents	...	47	...	3	...	...	...	Brevets délivrés
Patents in force	...	...	...	248	...	237	...	Brevets en vigueur
Thailand								**Thaïlande**
Resident filings (per mil. pop.)	1	2	14	18	15	15	16	Dem. de rés. (par mil. d'hab.)
Grants of patents	45	470	553	772	1 286	1 364	1 838	Brevets délivrés
Patents in force	...	...	...	10 201	11 623	11 681	12 193	Brevets en vigueur
TFYR of Macedonia								**ex-R.Y. de Macédoine**
Resident filings (per mil. pop.)	...	50	26	13	...	...	...	Dem. de rés. (par mil. d'hab.)
Grants of patents	...	163	373	406	...	...	...	Brevets délivrés
Trinidad and Tobago								**Trinité-et-Tobago**
Resident filings (per mil. pop.)	...	19	1	...	3	2	2	Dem. de rés. (par mil. d'hab.)
Grants of patents	...	87	...	...	39	33	60	Brevets délivrés
Tunisia								**Tunisie**
Resident filings (per mil. pop.)	2	3	6	11	13	16	21	Dem. de rés. (par mil. d'hab.)
Grants of patents	...	141	338	620	552	589	583	Brevets délivrés
Turkey								**Turquie**
Resident filings (per mil. pop.)	3	3	15	48	67	74	85	Dem. de rés. (par mil. d'hab.)
Grants of patents	385	763	823	...	1 276	1 723	1 764	Brevets délivrés
Patents in force	...	...	...	24 969	53 908	54 673	63 575	Brevets en vigueur
Uganda								**Ouganda**
Grants of patents	26	...	...	...	1	...	...	Brevets délivrés
Patents in force	...	...	...	...	26	...	19	Brevets en vigueur
Ukraine								**Ukraine**
Resident filings (per mil. pop.)	...	93	75	56	54	50	50	Dem. de rés. (par mil. d'hab.)
Grants of patents	...	1 350	3 719	3 874	3 319	3 014	2 813	Brevets délivrés
Patents in force	...	...	37 336	24 622	26 183	25 737	24 760	Brevets en vigueur
United Arab Emirates								**Émirats arabes unis**
Resident filings (per mil. pop.)	...	...	...	...	5	4	...	Dem. de rés. (par mil. d'hab.)
Grants of patents	...	...	...	...	110	177	222	Brevets délivrés
Patents in force	...	...	...	...	561	653	673	Brevets en vigueur
United Kingdom								**Royaume-Uni**
Resident filings (per mil. pop.)	348	321	372	333	308	306	290	Dem. de rés. (par mil. d'hab.)
Grants of patents	20 880	9 473	10 159	5 594	4 986	5 464	5 602	Brevets délivrés
Patents in force	...	...	377 259	412 519	498 904	458 422	507 973	Brevets en vigueur
United Rep. of Tanzania								**Rép.-Unie de Tanzanie**
Grants of patents	30	...	3	1	4	1	...	Brevets délivrés
United States of America								**États-Unis d'Amérique**
Resident filings (per mil. pop.)	268	466	703	782	895	899	914	Dem. de rés. (par mil. d'hab.)
Grants of patents	71 661	101 419	143 806	219 614	300 678	298 407	303 049	Brevets délivrés
Patents in force	...	...	1 683 968	2 017 318	2 527 750	2 644 697	2 763 055	Brevets en vigueur

28 Patents *(continued)*

Resident filings (per million population), grants and patents in force

Brevets *(suite)*

Demandes émanant de résidents (par million d'habitants), délivrances et brevets en vigueur

Region, country or area	1985	1995	2005	2010	2014	2015	2016	Région, pays ou zone
Uruguay								**Uruguay**
Resident filings (per mil. pop.)	21	11	7	7	11	8	...	Dem. de rés. (par mil. d'hab.)
Grants of patents	196	36	...	29	31	19	...	Brevets délivrés
Patents in force	...	...	...	877	646	606	...	Brevets en vigueur
Uzbekistan								**Ouzbékistan**
Resident filings (per mil. pop.)	...	46	10	13	11	9	11	Dem. de rés. (par mil. d'hab.)
Grants of patents	...	1 233	407	192	179	153	166	Brevets délivrés
Patents in force	...	...	1 263	1 253	1 141	1 081	977	Brevets en vigueur
Venezuela (Boliv. Rep. of)								**Venezuela (Rép. boliv. du)**
Resident filings (per mil. pop.)	13	...	...	...	...	...	...	Dem. de rés. (par mil. d'hab.)
Grants of patents	351	...	...	...	...	...	...	Brevets délivrés
Viet Nam								**Viet Nam**
Resident filings (per mil. pop.)	...	...	2	4	5	6	6	Dem. de rés. (par mil. d'hab.)
Grants of patents	...	56	668	822	1 397	1 388	1 423	Brevets délivrés
Patents in force	...	...	...	9 103	14 593	16 149	14 398	Brevets en vigueur
Yemen								**Yémen**
Resident filings (per mil. pop.)	...	...	1	1	1	...	1	Dem. de rés. (par mil. d'hab.)
Grants of patents	...	...	...	...	20	15	...	Brevets délivrés
Zambia								**Zambie**
Resident filings (per mil. pop.)	...	...	...	...	1	...	...	Dem. de rés. (par mil. d'hab.)
Grants of patents	74	43	14	12	23	...	...	Brevets délivrés
Patents in force	...	...	2 695	3 858	4 161	...	...	Brevets en vigueur
Zimbabwe								**Zimbabwe**
Resident filings (per mil. pop.)	4	5	...	...	...	1	...	Dem. de rés. (par mil. d'hab.)
Grants of patents	212	105	...	...	...	...	...	Brevets délivrés
OAPI [2]								**OAPI [2]**
Grants of patents	...	23	374	...	550	526	360	Brevets délivrés
Patents in force	...	...	...	...	2 112	2 184	2 220	Brevets en vigueur
ARIPO [3]								**ARIPO [3]**
Grants of patents	1	64	164	111	254	443	468	Brevets délivrés
Patents in force	...	...	...	...	2 550	2 964	3 421	Brevets en vigueur
EAPO [4]								**EAPO [4]**
Grants of patents	...	...	1 201	1 802	1 600	1 757	3 081	Brevets délivrés
EPO [5]								**OEB [5]**
Grants of patents	15 117	41 609	53 258	58 108	64 608	68 431	95 956	Brevets délivrés
GCC [6]								**CCG [6]**
Grants of patents	...	...	105	362	503	662	673	Brevets délivrés
Patents in force	...	...	...	...	3 609	3 242	4 308	Brevets en vigueur

Source:

World Intellectual Property Organization (WIPO), Geneva, WIPO statistics database, last accessed February 2018.

Source:

Organisation mondiale de la propriété intellectuelle (OMPI), Genève, la base de données statistiques de l'OMPI, dernier accès février 2018.

1 For statistical purposes, the data for China do not include those for the Hong Kong Special Administrative Region (Hong Kong SAR), Macao Special Administrative Region (Macao SAR) and Taiwan Province of China.

2 Members of the African Intellectual Property Organization (OAPI), which includes Benin, Burkina Faso, Cameroon, Central African Republic, Chad, Congo, Côte d'Ivoire, Equatorial Guinea, Gabon, Guinea, Guinea-Bissau, Mali, Mauritania, Niger, Senegal and Togo.

3 Members of the African Regional Intellectual Property Organization (ARIPO), which includes Botswana, Eswatini, Gambia, Ghana, Kenya, Lesotho, Liberia, Malawi, Mozambique, Namibia, Rwanda, Sao Tome and Principe, Sierra Leone, Somalia, Sudan, Tanzania, Uganda, Zambia and Zimbabwe.

4 Members of the Eurasian Patent Organization (EAPO), which includes Armenia, Azerbaijan, Belarus, Kazakhstan, Kyrgyzstan, the Republic of Moldova, the Russian Federation, Tajikistan and Turkmenistan.

1 Pour la présentation des statistiques, les données pour la Chine ne comprennent pas la région administrative spéciale de Hong Kong (Hong Kong RAS), la région administrative spéciale de Macao (Macao RAS) et la province chinoise de Taïwan.

2 Les membres de l'Organisation africaine de la propriété intellectuelle (OAPI) incluent: Bénin, Burkina Faso, Cameroun, Congo, Côte d'Ivoire, Gabon, Guinée, Guinée-Bissau, Guinée équatoriale, Mali, Mauritanie, Niger, République centrafricaine, Sénégal, Tchad et Togo.

3 Les membres de l'Organisation régionale africaine de la propriété intellectuelle (ARIPO) incluent: Botswana, Eswatini, Gambie, Ghana, Kenya, Lesotho, Libéria, Malawi, Mozambique, Namibie, Ouganda, Rwanda, Sao Tomé-et-Principe, Sierra Leone, Somalie, Soudan, Tanzanie, Zambie et Zimbabwe.

4 Les membres de l'Organisation eurasienne de la propriété intellectuelle (EAPO) incluent: Arménie, Azerbaïdjan, Bélarus, Fédération de Russie, Kazakhstan, Kirghizistan, Moldavie, Tadjikistan et Turkménistan.

5 Members of the European Patent Organisation (EPO), which includes Albania, Austria, Belgium, Bulgaria, Croatia, Cyprus, Czechia, Denmark, Estonia, Finland, France, Germany, Greece, Hungary, Iceland, Ireland, Italy, Latvia, Liechtenstein, Lithuania, Luxembourg, Malta, Monaco, Netherlands, Norway, Poland, Portugal, Romania, San Marino, Serbia, Slovenia, Slovakia, Spain, Sweden, Switzerland, the Former Yugoslav Republic of Macedonia, Turkey and the United Kingdom.

6 Members of the Gulf Cooperation Council (GCC) Patent Office, which includes Bahrain, Kuwait, Oman, Qatar, Saudi Arabia and the United Arab Emirates.

5 Les membres de l'Organisation européenne des brevets (OEB) incluent: Albanie, Allemagne, Autriche, Belgique, Bulgarie, Croatie, Danemark, Espagne, Estonie, Finlande, France, Grèce, Hongrie, Irlande, Islande, Italie, L'ex-République yougoslave de Macédoine, Lettonie, Liechtenstein, Lituanie, Luxembourg, Malte, Monaco, Norvège, Pays-Bas, Pologne, Portugal, République tchèque, Roumanie, Royaume-Uni, Saint-Marin, Serbie, Slovaquie, Slovénie, Suède, Suisse, Tchéquie et Turquie.

6 Les États suivants sont membres de l'Organisation de la propriété intellectuelle pour la Conseil de coopération du Golfe (CCG) incluent: Bahreïn, Arabie saoudite, Émirats arabes unis, Koweït, Oman et Qatar.

29 Internet usage

Percentage of individuals per country

Utilisation d'Internet

Pourcentage de personnes par pays

Country or area	2000	2005	2010	2013	2014	2015	2016	Pays ou zone
Total, all countries or areas	**6.7**	**15.6**	**28.7**	**36.6**	**39.7**	**43.0**	**45.7**	**Total, tous pays ou zones**
Northern Africa	0.6	9.6	24.6	31.6	35.3	38.9	41.7	Afrique septentrionale
Sub-Saharan Africa	0.5	2.1	6.6	11.9	14.3	17.5	19.6	Afrique subsaharienne
Eastern Africa	0.2	1.3	5.4	...	...	15.3	...	Afrique orientale
Middle Africa	0.1	0.7	2.0	...	...	8.3	...	Afrique centrale
Southern Africa	4.9	7.0	22.0	...	...	48.3	...	Afrique australe
Western Africa	0.1	2.5	14.3	...	...	31.1	...	Afrique occidentale
Northern America	43.9	68.3	72.5	72.9	74.4	76.0	77.6	Amérique septentrionale
Latin America & the Carib.	3.9	16.6	34.7	46.3	48.8	54.3	56.8	Amérique latine et Caraïbes
Caribbean	2.9	12.6	23.8	...	...	41.5	...	Caraïbes
Asia	3.2	9.1	22.7	31.5	35.2	38.8	42.0	Asie
Central Asia	0.5	3.3	18.4	...	...	43.5	...	Asie centrale
Eastern Asia	5.9	16.1	39.5	...	...	54.4	...	Asie orientale
South-eastern Asia	2.4	8.7	18.8	...	...	34.2	...	Asie du Sud-Est
Southern Asia	0.5	2.8	7.6	...	...	24.6	...	Asie méridionale
Western Asia	3.6	11.1	32.5	...	...	50.3	...	Asie occidentale
Europe	15.2	40.2	61.4	71.5	73.8	75.6	77.5	Europe
Oceania	35.1	47.2	57.6	63.8	64.8	66.0	68.6	Océanie
Australia and New Zealand	46.9	63.0	76.7	83.3	84.2	85.2	88.3	Australie et Nouvelle-Zélande
Afghanistan	...	1.2	* 4.0	* 5.9	* 7.0	* 8.3	* 10.6	Afghanistan
Albania	0.1	6.0	45.0	* 57.2	* 60.1	* 63.3	* 66.4	Albanie
Algeria	0.5	5.8	12.5	* 22.5	* 29.5	* 38.2	* 42.9	Algérie
Andorra	10.5	37.6	81.0	* 94.0	* 95.9	* 96.9	* 97.9	Andorre
Angola	0.1	1.1	* 2.8	* 8.9	10.2[1,2]	* 12.4	* 13.0	Angola
Anguilla	22.4	* 29.0	* 49.6	* 64.8	* 70.4	* 76.0	* 81.6	Anguilla
Antigua and Barbuda	6.5	* 27.0	* 47.0	* 63.4	* 67.8	* 70.0	* 73.0	Antigua-et-Barbuda
Argentina	7.0	17.7	* 45.0	* 59.9	* 64.7	68.0	* 70.2	Argentine
Armenia	1.3	5.3	* 25.0	41.9	54.6	59.1	* 62.0	Arménie
Aruba	15.4	* 25.4	* 62.0	* 78.9	* 83.8	* 88.7	* 93.5	Aruba
Australia	46.8	63.0[3]	* 76.0	83.5[3]	* 84.0	84.6[3]	* 88.2	Australie
Austria	33.7[4]	58.0[5]	75.2[5]	80.6[5]	81.0[5]	83.9[5]	84.3	Autriche
Azerbaijan	0.1	8.0	46.0[6]	73.0[6]	75.0[6]	77.0[6]	78.2	Azerbaïdjan
Bahamas	* 8.0	* 25.0	* 43.0	* 72.0	* 76.9	* 78.0	* 80.0	Bahamas
Bahrain	6.2	21.3	55.0	90.0[3]	90.5[3]	93.5[3]	98.0	Bahreïn
Bangladesh	* 0.1	* 0.2	* 3.7	6.6	* 13.9	* 14.4	* 18.2	Bangladesh
Barbados	4.0	* 52.5	* 65.1	* 71.8	* 75.2	* 76.1	* 79.5	Barbade
Belarus	1.9	...	31.8[7]	# 54.2[8]	59.0[8]	# 67.3[9]	71.1	Bélarus
Belgium	29.4	* 55.8	75.0	82.2[5]	85.0[5,10]	85.1[5,10]	86.5[5,10]	Belgique
Belize	6.0	* 17.0	28.2[1]	* 33.6	* 38.7	* 41.6	* 44.6	Belize
Benin	0.2	1.3	3.1	* 4.9	* 6.0	* 11.3	* 12.0	Bénin
Bermuda	42.9	65.4	* 84.2	* 95.3	* 96.8	* 98.3	* 98.0	Bermudes
Bhutan	0.4	3.8	* 13.6	* 22.4	* 30.3	* 39.8	* 41.8	Bhoutan
Bolivia (Plurin. State of)	* 1.4	5.2	* 22.4	37.0[1,10]	34.6[1,10]	* 35.6	* 39.7	Bolivie (État plurin. de)
Bosnia and Herzegovina	1.1	21.3	* 42.8	* 57.8	* 60.8	* 65.1	* 69.3	Bosnie-Herzégovine
Botswana	2.9	* 3.3	6.0	* 30.0	36.7	* 37.3	* 39.4	Botswana
Brazil	2.9	21.0[10,11]	40.7[10,11]	51.0[11]	54.6[11]	58.3	* 59.7	Brésil
British Virgin Islands	...	...	37.0	...	...	...	...	Îles Vierges britanniques
Brunei Darussalam	9.0	36.5	* 53.0	* 64.5	* 68.8	* 71.2	75.0	Brunéi Darussalam
Bulgaria	5.4	20.0[5]	46.2[5]	53.1[5]	55.5[5]	56.7[5]	59.8	Bulgarie
Burkina Faso	0.1	0.5	* 2.4	* 9.1	* 9.4	* 11.4	* 14.0	Burkina Faso
Burundi	0.1	0.5	* 1.0	1.3[1]	* 1.4	* 4.9	* 5.2	Burundi
Cabo Verde	1.8	6.1	* 30.0	* 37.5	* 40.3	* 48.0	* 48.2	Cabo Verde
Cambodia	~0.0	0.3	1.3	* 6.8	* 14.0	* 19.0	25.6	Cambodge
Cameroon	0.3	1.4	* 4.3	* 10.0	16.2[3]	* 20.7	* 25.0	Cameroun
Canada	51.3	71.7[7]	# 80.3[7]	* 85.8	* 87.1	* 88.5	* 89.8	Canada
Cayman Islands	...	38.0	* 66.0	* 71.4	* 74.1	* 77.0	* 79.0	Îles Caïmanes
Central African Republic	0.1	* 0.3	* 2.0	* 3.4	* 3.6	* 3.8	* 4.0	République centrafricaine
Chad	~0.0	0.4	* 1.7	* 2.5	* 2.9	* 3.5	* 5.0	Tchad
Chile	16.6[1]	* 31.2[1]	* 45.0[1]	58.0[1]	* 61.1	* 64.3	* 66.0	Chili
China [12]	1.8	8.5	34.3	* 45.8[8,13,14]	* 47.9[8,13,14]	* 50.3[8,13,14]	53.2	Chine [12]
China, Hong Kong SAR	27.8[2,11]	56.9[11]	72.0[11]	74.2[11]	79.9[11]	84.9[11]	* 87.3	Chine, RAS de Hong Kong

29 Internet usage *(continued)*
Percentage of individuals per country

Utilisation d'Internet *(suite)*
Pourcentage de personnes par pays

Country or area	2000	2005	2010	2013	2014	2015	2016	Pays ou zone
China, Macao SAR	* 13.6	* 34.9	55.2[15]	65.8[15]	69.8[15]	77.6[15]	81.6	Chine, RAS de Macao
Colombia	2.2	11.0	36.5[1]	51.7[1]	52.6[1]	55.9[1]	58.1	Colombie
Comoros	0.3	* 2.0	* 5.1	* 6.5	* 7.0	* 7.5	* 7.9	Comores
Congo	~0.0	* 1.5	* 5.0	* 6.6	* 7.1	* 7.6	* 8.1	Congo
Cook Islands	* 15.7	* 26.2	35.7	* 45.0	* 48.0	* 51.0	* 54.0	Îles Cook
Costa Rica	5.8	22.1[1]	36.5[1,10]	# 46.0[10]	* 53.0	59.8[1,10]	66.0	Costa Rica
Côte d'Ivoire	0.2	1.0	* 2.7	* 12.0	* 19.3	* 21.9	* 26.5	Côte d'Ivoire
Croatia	6.6	33.1[5]	56.6[5]	66.7[5]	68.6[5]	69.8[5]	72.7	Croatie
Cuba	0.5[16]	9.7[17]	15.9[17]	27.9[8,17]	29.1[8]	37.3[8]	* 38.8	Cuba
Cyprus	15.3	32.8[5]	53.0[5]	65.5[5]	69.3[5]	71.7[5]	75.9	Chypre
Czechia	9.8	35.3[5]	68.8[5]	74.1[5]	74.2[7]	75.7[7]	76.5[7]	Tchéquie
Dem. People's Rep. Korea	0.0[18]	0.0[18]	* 0.0	...	...	...	...	Rép. pop. dém. de Corée
Dem. Rep. of the Congo	* ~0.0	* 0.2	* 0.7	* 2.2	* 3.0	* 3.8	* 6.2	Rép. dém. du Congo
Denmark	39.2[19]	82.7[5]	88.7[5]	94.6[5]	96.0[5]	96.3[5]	97.0	Danemark
Djibouti	0.2	1.0	* 6.5	* 9.5	* 10.7	* 11.9	* 13.1	Djibouti
Dominica	8.8	* 38.5	47.5	* 51.0	57.5	* 65.0	* 67.0	Dominique
Dominican Republic	3.7	11.5	* 31.4	45.9[20]	* 49.6	54.2[20]	* 61.3	République dominicaine
Ecuador	1.5	* 6.0	29.0[1]	40.3[1]	45.6[1]	48.9[1]	54.1	Équateur
Egypt	* 0.6	12.8	21.6[8]	29.4[8]	33.9[8]	37.8[8]	* 39.2	Égypte
El Salvador	1.2	* 4.2[11]	15.9[11]	23.1[2,11]	24.8[11]	26.8	* 29.0	El Salvador
Equatorial Guinea	0.1	1.1	6.0	* 16.4	* 18.9	* 21.3	* 23.8	Guinée équatoriale
Eritrea	0.1	...	* 0.6	* 0.9	* 1.0	* 1.1	* 1.2	Érythrée
Estonia	28.6	61.5[5]	74.1[5,10]	80.0[5]	84.2[5]	88.4[5]	87.2	Estonie
Eswatini	0.9	* 3.7	11.0	* 24.7	* 26.2	* 25.6	* 28.6	Eswatini
Ethiopia	~0.0	0.2	* 0.8	* 4.6	* 7.7	* 11.6	15.4	Éthiopie
Falkland Islands (Malvinas)	58.6	* 84.0	95.8	* 96.9	* 97.6	* 98.3	* 99.0	Îles Falkland (Malvinas)
Faroe Islands	32.9	* 67.9	75.2	* 90.0	* 93.3	* 94.2	* 95.1	Îles Féroé
Fiji	1.5	8.5	* 20.0	* 35.2	* 37.4	* 42.5	* 46.5	Fidji
Finland	37.2[3,21]	74.5[5]	86.9[5]	91.5[5]	# 86.5[22]	86.4[22]	87.7[22]	Finlande
France	14.3[2,3]	42.9[23,24]	77.3[5,25]	81.9[5,25]	83.8[5,25]	84.7[5,25]	85.6[25]	France
French Polynesia	6.4	21.5	49.0	* 56.8	* 60.7	* 64.6	* 68.4	Polynésie française
Gabon	1.2	4.9	* 13.0	* 30.5	* 38.1	* 45.8	* 48.1	Gabon
Gambia	0.9	* 3.8	9.2	* 14.0	* 15.6	* 16.5	* 18.5	Gambie
Georgia	0.5	* 6.1	26.9	43.3[2,8]	* # 44.0[8,10]	# 47.6[8,10]	* 50.0	Géorgie
Germany	30.2	68.7[5]	82.0[5]	84.2[5]	86.2[5]	87.6[5]	89.6	Allemagne
Ghana	0.2	1.8	# 7.8[20]	* 15.0	* 25.5	* 31.4	* 34.7	Ghana
Gibraltar	19.1	* 39.1	65.0	...	...	...	* 94.4	Gibraltar
Greece	9.1	24.0[5]	44.4[5]	59.9[5]	63.2[5]	66.8[5]	69.1	Grèce
Greenland	31.7	57.7	63.0	* 65.8	* 66.7	* 67.6	* 68.5	Groenland
Grenada	4.1	* 20.5	* 27.0	* 35.0	51.6	* 53.8	* 55.9	Grenade
Guam	16.1	38.6	* 54.0	* 65.4	* 69.3	* 73.1	* 77.0	Guam
Guatemala	0.7	5.7	* 10.5	* 19.7	* 23.4	* 28.8	* 34.5	Guatemala
Guernsey	31.9	73.6	...	...	...	...	...	Guernesey
Guinea	0.1	0.5	* 1.0	* 4.5	* 6.4	* 8.2	* 9.8	Guinée
Guinea-Bissau	0.2	1.9	* 2.5	* 3.1	* 3.3	* 3.5	* 3.8	Guinée-Bissau
Guyana	6.6	...	29.9	* 31.0	* 32.0	* 34.0	* 35.7	Guyana
Haiti	0.2	* 6.4	* 8.4	* 10.6	* 11.4	* 12.2	* 12.2	Haïti
Honduras	1.2	* 6.5[1]	11.1	17.8	* 19.1	* 27.6	* 30.0	Honduras
Hungary	7.0	39.0[5]	65.0[5]	72.6[5]	75.7[5]	72.8[5]	79.3	Hongrie
Iceland	44.5	87.0[5]	93.4[5,10]	96.5[5]	98.2[5]	* 98.2	* 98.2	Islande
India	0.5	* 2.4	* 7.5	* 15.1	* 21.0	* 26.0	* 29.5	Inde
Indonesia	0.9	3.6	10.9[26]	14.9[1]	17.1[1]	22.0[1]	25.4	Indonésie
Iran (Islamic Republic of)	0.9	* 8.1	15.9[8]	30.0[8]	* 39.4	* 45.3	53.2	Iran (Rép. islamique d')
Iraq	...	* 0.9	2.5	* 9.2	13.2	* 17.2	* 21.2	Iraq
Ireland	17.9[3]	41.6[5]	69.9[5]	78.2[5]	79.7[5,10]	80.1[5,10]	82.2[5,10]	Irlande
Israel	20.9	25.2	67.5[27]	70.3[10,27]	75.0[27]	77.4[27]	* 79.8	Israël
Italy	23.1	35.0[5]	53.7[5]	58.5[5]	# 55.6[8]	58.1[8]	61.3[8]	Italie
Jamaica	3.1	* 12.8	27.7[4]	37.1[4]	40.4[4]	* 42.2	* 45.0	Jamaïque
Japan	30.0[28]	66.9[8]	78.2[8]	88.2[8]	89.1[8]	91.1	* 92.0	Japon
Jersey	9.2	31.3	...	...	...	...	...	Jersey
Jordan	2.6	12.9	27.2[1]	41.4[1]	46.2[1]	* 60.1	* 62.3	Jordanie
Kazakhstan	0.7	3.0	31.6[5,29]	* 63.0	* 66.0	72.9[30]	76.8	Kazakhstan
Kenya	0.3	3.1	7.2	* 13.0	* 16.5	* 21.0	* 26.0	Kenya

Country or area	2000	2005	2010	2013	2014	2015	2016	Pays ou zone
Kiribati	* 1.8	* 4.0	9.1	* 11.5	* 12.3	* 13.0	* 13.7	Kiribati
Kuwait	6.7	25.9	* 61.4	* 75.5	* 78.7	* 77.5	* 78.4	Koweït
Kyrgyzstan	1.0	10.5	* 16.3	* 23.0	* 28.3	* 30.2	* 34.5	Kirghizistan
Lao People's Dem. Rep.	0.1	0.9	7.0	* 12.5	* 14.3	* 18.2	* 21.9	Rép. dém. populaire lao
Latvia	6.3	46.0[5]	68.4[5]	75.2[5]	75.8[5]	79.2[5]	79.9	Lettonie
Lebanon	8.0	10.1[8]	* 43.7[3]	* 70.5	* 73.0	* 74.0	* 76.1	Liban
Lesotho	0.2	* 2.6	* 3.9	* 15.0	* 22.0	* 25.0	27.4	Lesotho
Liberia	~0.0	...	2.3	* 3.2	* 5.4	* 5.9	* 7.3	Libéria
Libya	0.2	* 3.9	* 14.0	* 16.5	* 17.8	* 19.0	* 20.3	Libye
Liechtenstein	36.5	63.4	* 80.0	* 93.8	* 95.2	* 96.6	* 98.1	Liechtenstein
Lithuania	6.4	36.2[2,5]	62.1[2,5]	68.5[5]	72.1[5]	71.4[5]	74.4	Lituanie
Luxembourg	22.9	70.0[5]	90.6[5]	93.8[5]	94.7[5]	97.3[5]	97.5	Luxembourg
Madagascar	0.2	* 0.6	* 1.7	* 3.0	* 3.7	* 4.2	* 4.7	Madagascar
Malawi	0.1	0.4	2.3	* 5.1	* 5.8	* 9.3	* 9.6	Malawi
Malaysia	21.4	48.6	56.3[26]	57.1[3]	63.7[3]	71.1[3]	78.8	Malaisie
Maldives	* 2.2[31]	* 6.9[31]	26.5[3]	* 44.1	* 49.3	* 54.5	* 59.1	Maldives
Mali	0.1	0.5	* 2.0	* 3.5	* 7.0	* 10.3	11.1	Mali
Malta	13.1	41.2[5]	63.0[5]	68.9[5]	73.2[5]	76.2[5]	77.3	Malte
Marshall Islands	1.5	3.9	* 7.0	* 14.0	* 16.8	* 19.3	* 29.8	Îles Marshall
Mauritania	0.2	0.7	* 4.0	* 6.2	* 10.7	* 15.2	* 18.0	Mauritanie
Mauritius	7.3	* 15.2	28.3[1]	40.1[1]	44.8[1]	50.1[1]	* 53.2	Maurice
Mayotte	1.2	...	...	...	...	...	...	Mayotte
Mexico	5.1	* 17.2	* 31.1[32]	43.5[8]	44.4[8]	# 57.4[8]	59.5	Mexique
Micronesia (Fed. States of)	3.7	11.9	* 20.0	* 27.8	* 29.7	* 31.5	33.4	Micronésie (États féd. de)
Monaco	42.2	55.5	75.0	* 90.7	* 92.4	* 93.4	* 95.2	Monaco
Mongolia	1.3	...	10.2	17.7	19.9	21.4	22.3	Mongolie
Montenegro	...	* 27.1	* 37.5	60.3[5]	* 61.0	68.1[5]	69.9	Monténégro
Montserrat	...	...	35.0	...	...	...	...	Montserrat
Morocco	0.7	15.1[23,33]	* 52.0[30,34]	56.0[2,35]	56.8[10,35]	57.1[1,10]	58.3	Maroc
Mozambique	0.1	* 0.9	4.2	* 7.3	* 9.2	* 16.9	* 17.5	Mozambique
Myanmar	...	0.1	0.3	* 8.0	* 11.5	* 21.7	* 25.1	Myanmar
Namibia	1.6	* 4.0	11.6	* 13.9	* 14.8	* 25.7	* 31.0	Namibie
Nepal	0.2	0.8	7.9[32]	* 13.3	* 15.4	* 17.6	* 19.7	Népal
Netherlands	44.0	81.0[2,5]	90.7[2,5]	94.0[5]	# 91.7[20]	91.7[20]	90.4[20]	Pays-Bas
New Caledonia	13.9	32.4	* 42.0	* 66.0	* 70.0	* 74.0	...	Nouvelle-Calédonie
New Zealand	* 47.4	* 62.7	* 80.5	* 82.8	* 85.5	* 88.2	* 88.5	Nouvelle-Zélande
Nicaragua	1.0	2.6	* 10.0	* 15.5	* 17.6	* 19.7	* 24.6	Nicaragua
Niger	~0.0	* 0.2	* 0.8	* 1.7	* 2.0	* 2.5	* 4.3	Niger
Nigeria	0.1	* 3.5	* 11.5	* 19.1	* 21.0	* 24.5	* 25.7	Nigéria
Niue	26.5	51.7	* 77.0	...	...	...	...	Nioué
Norway	* 52.0	82.0[5]	93.4[5]	95.1[5]	96.3[5]	96.8[5]	97.3	Norvège
Oman	* 3.5	6.7	35.8[1]	66.5[1,36]	* 70.2	* 66.1	69.8	Oman
Other non-specified areas	28.1	58.0	71.5	76.3[20]	78.0[20]	78.0[20]	79.7	Autres zones non-spécifiées
Pakistan	...	6.3	* 8.0	* 10.9	* 12.0	* 14.0	15.5	Pakistan
Panama	6.6	11.5	* 40.1	44.0[11]	44.9[11]	51.2[11]	* 54.0	Panama
Papua New Guinea	0.8	1.7	1.3[11]	* 5.1	* 6.5	* 7.9	* 9.6	Papouasie-Nvl-Guinée
Paraguay	0.7	7.9[10,11]	19.8[10,11]	36.9[10,11]	43.0[10,11]	48.4[11]	* 51.3	Paraguay
Peru	* 3.1	* 17.1	34.8[8]	39.2[8]	40.2[8]	40.9[8]	45.5	Pérou
Philippines	2.0	* 5.4	25.0	48.1[37]	* 49.6	* 53.7	* 55.5	Philippines
Poland	7.3	38.8[5]	62.3[5]	62.8[5]	66.6[5,10]	68.0[5,10]	73.3[5,10]	Pologne
Portugal	* 16.4	35.0[5]	53.3[5]	62.1[5]	64.6[5]	68.6[5]	70.4	Portugal
Puerto Rico	10.5	* 23.4	45.3[20]	69.0[38]	76.1[38]	* 79.5	* 80.3	Porto Rico
Qatar	4.9	24.7	69.0	* 85.3	* 91.5	92.9[3]	* 94.3	Qatar
Republic of Korea	44.7[15,23]	73.5[15]	83.7[15]	84.8[15]	87.6[5]	89.6[5]	92.7	République de Corée
Republic of Moldova	1.3	14.6	* 32.3	* 45.0	* 46.6	63.3	71.0	République de Moldova
Réunion	13.8	28.1	...	...	...	...	...	Réunion
Romania	3.6	* 21.5[5]	39.9[5]	49.8[5]	54.1[5]	55.8[5]	59.5	Roumanie
Russian Federation	2.0	15.2	43.0[5]	68.0[39]	70.5[2,39]	73.4[2,39]	76.4[2,39]	Fédération de Russie
Rwanda	0.1	* 0.6	* 8.0	* 9.0	* 10.6	* 18.0	* 20.0	Rwanda
Saint Helena	5.9	15.9	24.9	...	...	...	...	Sainte-Hélène
Ascension	34.9	...	35.0	...	...	...	...	Ascension
Saint Kitts and Nevis	5.9	* 34.0	63.0	* 64.6	68.0	* 75.7	* 76.8	Saint-Kitts-et-Nevis
Saint Lucia	5.1	21.6	43.3	* 46.2	* 50.0	* 42.5	* 46.7	Sainte-Lucie

Internet usage *(continued)*
Percentage of individuals per country

Utilisation d'Internet *(suite)*
Pourcentage de personnes par pays

Country or area	2000	2005	2010	2013	2014	2015	2016	Pays ou zone
Saint Vincent & Grenadines	* 3.2	* 9.2	* 33.7	* 43.5	47.4	* 51.8	* 55.6	Saint-Vincent-Grenadines
Samoa	0.6	3.4	* 7.0	* 15.3	* 21.2	* 25.4	* 29.4	Samoa
San Marino	48.8	50.3	...	...	...	...	...	Saint-Marin
Sao Tome and Principe	4.6	* 13.8	18.8	* 23.0	* 24.4	* 25.8	* 28.0	Sao Tomé-et-Principe
Saudi Arabia	2.2	12.7	41.0	* 60.5	64.7[33]	69.6[33]	73.8	Arabie saoudite
Senegal	0.4	4.8	* 8.0	* 13.1	* 17.7	* 21.7	* 25.7	Sénégal
Serbia	...	* 26.3[5]	40.9	53.5[5]	62.1[5]	65.3[5]	67.1	Serbie
Seychelles	* 7.4	25.4	* 41.0	* 50.4	* 51.3	* 54.3	* 56.5	Seychelles
Sierra Leone	0.1	0.2	* 0.6	* 4.0	* 6.1	* 6.3	* 11.8	Sierra Leone
Singapore	36.0	61.0[3]	* 71.0[6]	80.9[6]	79.0	79.0	* 81.0	Singapour
Slovakia	9.4	55.2[5]	75.7[5,10]	77.9[5]	80.0[5,10]	77.6[5,10]	80.5[5,10]	Slovaquie
Slovenia	15.1	46.8[10]	70.0[5]	72.7[5]	71.6[5]	73.1[5]	75.5	Slovénie
Solomon Islands	0.5	0.8	* 5.0	* 8.0	* 9.0	* 10.0	* 11.0	Îles Salomon
Somalia	~0.0	* 1.1	...	* 1.5	* 1.6	* 1.8	* 1.9	Somalie
South Africa	5.3	7.5	* 24.0	* 46.5	* 49.0	* 51.9	* 54.0	Afrique du Sud
South Sudan	...	...	* 7.0	* 14.1	* 15.9	* 17.9	...	Soudan du sud
Spain	13.6[4,40]	47.9[2,5]	65.8[11]	71.6[5]	76.2[5]	78.7[5]	80.6	Espagne
Sri Lanka	0.6	* 1.8	12.0	* 21.9	25.8	* 30.0	* 32.1	Sri Lanka
State of Palestine	1.1	* 16.0[11]	* 37.4	* 46.6	53.7[11]	* 57.4	* 61.2	État de Palestine
Sudan	~0.0	1.3	* 16.7	* 22.7	* 24.6	* 26.6	* 28.0	Soudan
Suriname	2.5	6.4	31.6	* 37.4	* 40.1	* 42.8	* 45.4	Suriname
Sweden	45.7	84.8[5]	90.0[41]	94.8[5]	92.5[5]	90.6[5]	91.5	Suède
Switzerland	47.1[4,13]	70.1[4,13]	83.9[4,13]	86.3[4,13]	87.4[4,13]	87.5[4,13]	89.4	Suisse
Syrian Arab Republic	0.2	* 5.6	20.7	* 26.2	* 28.1	* 30.0	* 31.9	République arabe syrienne
Tajikistan	~0.0	0.3	* 11.6	* 16.0	* 17.5	* 19.0	* 20.5	Tadjikistan
Thailand	3.7	15.0	22.4	28.9[8]	# 34.9[8]	39.3[8]	47.5	Thaïlande
TFYR of Macedonia	2.5	* 26.5[5]	51.9[42]	65.2[5,10]	68.1[5,10]	70.4[5]	72.2	ex-R.Y. de Macédoine
Timor-Leste	...	0.1	* 3.0	* 11.0	* 17.5	* 23.0	* 25.2	Timor-Leste
Togo	* 0.8	* 1.8	* 3.0	* 4.5	* 5.7	* 7.1	* 11.3	Togo
Tonga	2.4	* 4.9	* 16.0	* 32.8	* 36.0	* 38.7	* 40.0	Tonga
Trinidad and Tobago	7.7	* 29.0	* 48.5	* 63.8	* 65.1	* 69.2	* 73.3	Trinité-et-Tobago
Tunisia	2.8	9.7	36.8	* 43.8	* 46.2	* 48.5	* 50.9	Tunisie
Turkey	3.8[5]	15.5[2,5]	39.8[2,5]	46.3[2,5]	51.0[2,5]	53.7[5]	58.3	Turquie
Turkmenistan	0.1	* 1.0	* 3.0	* 9.6	* 12.2	* 15.0	* 18.0	Turkménistan
Tuvalu	5.2	...	* 25.0	* 37.0	* 39.2	* 42.7	* 46.0	Tuvalu
Uganda	0.2	1.7	12.5	* 15.5	* 16.9	* 17.8	* 21.9	Ouganda
Ukraine	0.7	* 3.7[23,43]	23.3	41.0	46.2	48.9	* 52.5	Ukraine
United Arab Emirates	23.6	* 40.0	68.0	* 88.0	90.4[10,42]	* 90.5	90.6[10,42]	Émirats arabes unis
United Kingdom	26.8[7,10]	70.0[5]	85.0[5]	89.8[5]	91.6[5]	92.0[5]	94.8	Royaume-Uni
United Rep. of Tanzania	0.1	* 1.1	* 2.9	* 4.4	* 7.0	* 10.0	* 13.0	Rép.-Unie de Tanzanie
United States of America	* 43.1	* 68.0	71.7[15]	71.4[15]	* 73.0	74.6[15]	* 76.2	États-Unis d'Amérique
United States Virgin Islands	13.8	* 27.3	* 31.2	* 45.3	* 50.1	* 54.8	* 59.6	Îles Vierges américaines
Uruguay	10.5	20.1	46.4[8]	57.7[8]	61.5[8]	64.6[8]	66.4	Uruguay
Uzbekistan	0.5	3.3	* 15.9	* 26.8	* 35.5	* 42.8	* 46.8	Ouzbékistan
Vanuatu	2.1	5.1	8.0	* 11.3	* 18.8	* 22.4	* 24.0	Vanuatu
Venezuela (Boliv. Rep. of)	3.4	12.6	* 37.4	* 54.9	* 57.0	* 61.9	* 60.0	Venezuela (Rép. boliv. du)
Viet Nam	0.3	12.7	30.7	* 38.5	* 41.0	* 43.5	* 46.5	Viet Nam
Wallis and Futuna Islands	4.8	6.7	8.2	...	...	...	...	Îles Wallis-et-Futuna
Yemen	0.1	* 1.0	12.4	* 20.0	* 22.6	* 24.1	* 24.6	Yémen
Zambia	0.2	* 2.9	10.0	* 15.4	* 19.0	* 21.0	* 25.5	Zambie
Zimbabwe	* 0.4	* 2.4	* 6.4	* 15.5	16.4[15]	* 22.7	* 23.1	Zimbabwe

Source:

International Telecommunication Union (ITU), Geneva, the ITU database, last accessed February 2018.

Source:

Union internationale des télécommunications (UIT), Genève, la base de données de l'UIT, dernier accès février 2018.

1 Population aged 5 years and over.
2 Users in the last 12 months.
3 Population aged 15 years and over.

1 Population âgée de 5 ans et plus.
2 Utilisateurs au cours des 12 derniers mois.
3 Population âgée de 15 ans et plus.

Internet usage *(continued)*
Percentage of individuals per country

Utilisation d'Internet *(suite)*
Pourcentage de personnes par pays

4 Population aged 14 years and over.
5 Population aged 16 to 74 years.
6 Population aged 7 years and over.
7 Population aged 16 years and over.
8 Population aged 6 years and over.
9 Population aged 6 to 72 years.
10 Users in the last 3 months.
11 Population aged 10 years and over.
12 For statistical purposes, the data for China do not include those for the Hong Kong Special Administrative Region (Hong Kong SAR), Macao Special Administrative Region (Macao SAR) and Taiwan Province of China.
13 Users in the last 6 months.
14 Data refer to permanent residents.
15 Population aged 3 years and over.
16 Refers only to users with access to the international network.
17 Including users of the international network and also those having access only to the Cuban network.
18 Commercially not available. Local Intranet available in country.
19 E-mail users.
20 Population aged 12 years and over.
21 Has used at least one other Internet application besides e-mail in last 3 months.
22 Population aged 16 to 89 years.
23 Users in the last month.
24 Population aged 11 years and over.
25 Including Guadeloupe, Martinique, Réunion and French Guiana.
26 Refers to the total population.
27 Population aged 20 years and over.
28 PC-based only.
29 According to sample surveys.
30 Population aged 6 to 74 years.
31 Excluding mobile internet users.
32 December.
33 Population aged 12 to 65 years.
34 Living in electrified areas.
35 Population aged 5 to 75 years.
36 Excluding population living in workers' camps.
37 Population aged 10 to 64 years
38 Population aged 18 years and over.
39 Population aged 15 to 72 years.
40 November.
41 Population aged 16 to 75 years.
42 Population aged 15 to 74 years.
43 Population aged 15 to 59 years.

4 Population âgée de 14 ans et plus.
5 Population âgée de 16 à 74 ans.
6 Population âgée de 7 ans et plus.
7 Population âgée de 16 ans et plus.
8 Population âgée de 6 ans et plus.
9 Population âgée de 6 à 72 ans.
10 Utilisateurs au cours des 3 derniers mois.
11 Population âgée de 10 ans et plus.
12 Pour la présentation des statistiques, les données pour la Chine ne comprennent pas la région administrative spéciale de Hong Kong (Hong Kong RAS), la région administrative spéciale de Macao (Macao RAS) et la province chinoise de Taïwan.
13 Utilisateurs au cours des 6 derniers mois.
14 Les données concernent les résidents permanents.
15 Population âgée de 3 ans et plus.
16 Uniquement utilisateurs ayant accès au réseau international.
17 Y compris les utilisateurs du réseau international et ceux qui n'ont accès qu'au réseau cubain.
18 Non disponible commercialement, seul l'intranet local est accessible dans le pays.
19 Utilisateurs du courrier électronique
20 Population âgée de 12 ans et plus.
21 Ayant au moins utilisé une application Internet autre que le courrier électronique au cours des trois derniers mois. Population âgée de plus de 15 ans.
22 Population âgée de 16 à 89 ans.
23 Utilisateurs au cours du mois passé.
24 Population âgée de 11 ans et plus.
25 Y compris Guadeloupe, Martinique, Réunion et Guyane française.
26 Fait référence à la population totale.
27 Population âgée de 20 ans et plus.
28 Sur ordinateur PC seulement.
29 Selon un échantillon d'enquêtes.
30 Population âgée de 6 à 74 ans.
31 Les utilisateurs d'Internet mobile non-inclus.
32 Décembre.
33 Population âgée de 12 à 65 ans.
34 Vivant dans des zones électrifiées.
35 Population âgée de 5 à 75 ans.
36 Non compris la population vivant dans les camps de travailleurs.
37 Population âgée de 10 à 64 ans.
38 Population âgée de 18 ans et plus.
39 Population âgée de 15 à 72 ans.
40 Novembre.
41 Population âgée de 16 à 75 ans.
42 Population âgée de 15 à 74 ans.
43 Population âgée de 15 à 59 ans.

30 Tourist/visitor arrivals and tourism expenditure

Thousands arrivals and millions of US dollars

Arrivées de touristes/visiteurs et dépenses touristiques

Milliers d'arrivées et millions de dollars É.-U.

Country or area of destination	Series& Série&	1995	2005	2010	2014	2015	2016	Pays ou zone de destination
Afghanistan								**Afghanistan**
Tourism expenditure		...	...	169	92	88	51	Dépenses touristiques
Albania								**Albanie**
Tourist/visitor arrivals [1]	TF	...	...	2 191	3 341	3 784	4 070	Arrivées de touristes/visiteurs [1]
Tourism expenditure		70	880	1 780	1 849	1 614	1 821	Dépenses touristiques
Algeria								**Algérie**
Tourist/visitor arrivals [2]	VF	520	1 443	2 070	2 301	1 710	2 039	Arrivées de touristes/visiteurs [2]
Tourism expenditure		...	477	324	348	357	243	Dépenses touristiques
American Samoa								**Samoa américaines**
Tourist/visitor arrivals	TF	34	25	23	22	20	20	Arrivées de touristes/visiteurs
Andorra								**Andorre**
Tourist/visitor arrivals	TF	...	2 418	# 1 808	# 2 363	# 2 663	# 2 831	Arrivées de touristes/visiteurs
Angola								**Angola**
Tourist/visitor arrivals	TF	9	210	425	595	592	397	Arrivées de touristes/visiteurs
Tourism expenditure		27	103	726	1 597	1 171	628	Dépenses touristiques
Anguilla								**Anguilla**
Tourist/visitor arrivals [1]	TF	39	62	62	71	73	79	Arrivées de touristes/visiteurs [1]
Tourism expenditure [3]		50	86	99	136	134	138	Dépenses touristiques [3]
Antigua and Barbuda								**Antigua-et-Barbuda**
Tourist/visitor arrivals [1]	TF	220	245	230	249[4]	250[4]	265[4]	Arrivées de touristes/visiteurs [1]
Tourism expenditure [3]		247	309	298	708	714	693	Dépenses touristiques [3]
Argentina								**Argentine**
Tourist/visitor arrivals	TF	2 289	3 823	5 325	# 5 931	# 5 736	# 5 559	Arrivées de touristes/visiteurs
Tourism expenditure		2 550	3 209	5 605	5 645	5 441	5 186	Dépenses touristiques
Armenia								**Arménie**
Tourist/visitor arrivals	TF	12	319	684	1 204	1 192	1 260	Arrivées de touristes/visiteurs
Tourism expenditure		14	243	694	994	956	988	Dépenses touristiques
Aruba								**Aruba**
Tourist/visitor arrivals [4]	TF	619	733	824	1 072	1 225	1 102	Arrivées de touristes/visiteurs [4]
Tourism expenditure		554	...	1 254	1 625	1 659	1 638	Dépenses touristiques
Australia								**Australie**
Tourist/visitor arrivals [5]	VF	3 726	5 499	5 790	6 884	7 444	8 263	Arrivées de touristes/visiteurs [5]
Tourism expenditure		11 915	19 719	31 064	33 619	30 872	34 475	Dépenses touristiques
Austria								**Autriche**
Tourist/visitor arrivals [6]	TCE	17 173	19 952	22 004	25 291	26 728	28 121	Arrivées de touristes/visiteurs [6]
Tourism expenditure [3]		13 435	16 243	18 758	20 907	18 288	19 241	Dépenses touristiques [3]
Azerbaijan								**Azerbaïdjan**
Tourist/visitor arrivals	TF	...	693	1 280	2 160	1 922	2 044	Arrivées de touristes/visiteurs
Tourism expenditure		87	100	792	2 713	2 535	2 855	Dépenses touristiques
Bahamas								**Bahamas**
Tourist/visitor arrivals	TF	1 598	1 608	1 370	1 427	1 484	1 482	Arrivées de touristes/visiteurs
Tourism expenditure		1 356	2 081	2 159	2 336	2 554	2 627	Dépenses touristiques
Bahrain								**Bahreïn**
Tourist/visitor arrivals [1]	VF	2 311	6 313	11 952	10 452	# 9 670	# 10 158	Arrivées de touristes/visiteurs [1]
Tourism expenditure		593	1 603	2 163	1 915	...	...	Dépenses touristiques
Bangladesh								**Bangladesh**
Tourist/visitor arrivals	TF	156	208	303	125	...	...	Arrivées de touristes/visiteurs
Tourism expenditure		...	82	104	154	148	175	Dépenses touristiques
Barbados								**Barbade**
Tourist/visitor arrivals	TF	442	548	532	521	592	632	Arrivées de touristes/visiteurs
Tourism expenditure		630	1 081	1 074	...	...	...	Dépenses touristiques
Belarus								**Bélarus**
Tourist/visitor arrivals	TF	161[7,8]	91[7,8]	119[7,8]	# 5 375[7]	4 386[7]	9 424[9]	Arrivées de touristes/visiteurs
Tourism expenditure		28	346	665	1 230	1 013	1 019	Dépenses touristiques
Belgium								**Belgique**
Tourist/visitor arrivals	TCE	5 560	6 747	7 186	7 887	# 8 355	# 7 481	Arrivées de touristes/visiteurs
Tourism expenditure		...	10 881	...	15 244	13 084	12 772	Dépenses touristiques
Belize								**Belize**
Tourist/visitor arrivals	TF	131	237	242	321	341	386	Arrivées de touristes/visiteurs
Tourism expenditure [3]		78	214	264	380	372	391	Dépenses touristiques [3]
Benin								**Bénin**
Tourist/visitor arrivals	TF	138	176	199	242	255	267	Arrivées de touristes/visiteurs
Tourism expenditure		...	108	149	153	148	...	Dépenses touristiques

30 Tourist/visitor arrivals and tourism expenditure *(continued)*

Thousands arrivals and millions of US dollars

Arrivées de touristes/visiteurs et dépenses touristiques *(suite)*

Milliers d'arrivées et millions de dollars É.-U.

Country or area of destination	Series& Série&	1995	2005	2010	2014	2015	2016	Pays ou zone de destination
Bermuda								**Bermudes**
Tourist/visitor arrivals [1,4]	TF	387	270	232	224	220	244	Arrivées de touristes/visiteurs [1,4]
Tourism expenditure		...	...	...	407	386	445	Dépenses touristiques
Bhutan								**Bhoutan**
Tourist/visitor arrivals	TF	5	14	# 41[10]	133	155	210	Arrivées de touristes/visiteurs
Tourism expenditure		5	19	64	120	120	137	Dépenses touristiques
Bolivia (Plurin. State of)								**Bolivie (État plurin. de)**
Tourist/visitor arrivals	TF	284	524	679	871	882	959	Arrivées de touristes/visiteurs
Tourism expenditure		92	345	339	746	810	801	Dépenses touristiques
Bonaire								**Bonaire**
Tourist/visitor arrivals	TF	59	63	71	...	...	...	Arrivées de touristes/visiteurs
Tourism expenditure [3]		37	87	...	...	...	...	Dépenses touristiques [3]
Sint Eustatius [11]								**Saint-Eustache [11]**
Tourist/visitor arrivals	TF	9	10	11	...	...	...	Arrivées de touristes/visiteurs
Saba								**Saba**
Tourist/visitor arrivals	TF	10	12	12	...	...	...	Arrivées de touristes/visiteurs
Bosnia and Herzegovina								**Bosnie-Herzégovine**
Tourist/visitor arrivals	TCE	...	217	365	536	678	777	Arrivées de touristes/visiteurs
Tourism expenditure		...	557	662	755	702	770	Dépenses touristiques
Botswana								**Botswana**
Tourist/visitor arrivals	TF	521	1 474	1 973	1 966	1 528	...	Arrivées de touristes/visiteurs
Tourism expenditure		176	563	781	978	1 037	1 075	Dépenses touristiques
Brazil								**Brésil**
Tourist/visitor arrivals [2]	TF	1 991	5 358	5 161	6 430	6 306	6 578	Arrivées de touristes/visiteurs [2]
Tourism expenditure		1 085	4 168	5 522	7 405	6 254	6 613	Dépenses touristiques
British Virgin Islands								**Îles Vierges britanniques**
Tourist/visitor arrivals	TF	219	337	330	386	393	408	Arrivées de touristes/visiteurs
Tourism expenditure		211	412	389	459	484	...	Dépenses touristiques
Brunei Darussalam								**Brunéi Darussalam**
Tourist/visitor arrivals [4]	TF	...	126	214	201	218	219	Arrivées de touristes/visiteurs [4]
Tourism expenditure [3]		...	191	...	79	147	144	Dépenses touristiques [3]
Bulgaria								**Bulgarie**
Tourist/visitor arrivals	TF	3 466	4 837	6 047	7 311	7 099	8 252	Arrivées de touristes/visiteurs
Tourism expenditure		662	3 063	3 807	4 518	3 583	4 164	Dépenses touristiques
Burkina Faso								**Burkina Faso**
Tourist/visitor arrivals	THS	124	245	274	191	163	152	Arrivées de touristes/visiteurs
Tourism expenditure		...	46	105	183	...	...	Dépenses touristiques
Burundi								**Burundi**
Tourist/visitor arrivals [2]	TF	34	148	# 142	# 235	# 131	# 187	Arrivées de touristes/visiteurs [2]
Tourism expenditure		1	2	2	4	2	2	Dépenses touristiques
Cabo Verde								**Cabo Verde**
Tourist/visitor arrivals	TF	28[4]	198	336	494	520	598	Arrivées de touristes/visiteurs
Tourism expenditure		29	177	387	453	380	402	Dépenses touristiques
Cambodia								**Cambodge**
Tourist/visitor arrivals	TF	220[4]	1 422	2 508	4 503	4 775	5 012	Arrivées de touristes/visiteurs
Tourism expenditure		71	929	1 671	3 220	3 418	3 523	Dépenses touristiques
Cameroon								**Cameroun**
Tourist/visitor arrivals	VF	...	...	573	822	...	...	Arrivées de touristes/visiteurs
Tourism expenditure		75	229	171	630	476	...	Dépenses touristiques
Canada								**Canada**
Tourist/visitor arrivals	TF	16 932	18 771	16 219	16 537	17 971	19 824	Arrivées de touristes/visiteurs
Tourism expenditure		9 176	15 887	18 438	20 802	19 273	...	Dépenses touristiques
Cayman Islands								**Îles Caïmanes**
Tourist/visitor arrivals [4]	TF	361	168	288	383	385	385	Arrivées de touristes/visiteurs [4]
Tourism expenditure		394	356	465	541	651	...	Dépenses touristiques
Central African Republic								**République centrafricaine**
Tourist/visitor arrivals [12]	TF	26	12	54	96	121	...	Arrivées de touristes/visiteurs [12]
Tourism expenditure		4	7	14	...	...	...	Dépenses touristiques
Chad								**Tchad**
Tourist/visitor arrivals	TF	...	...	71	122	120	...	Arrivées de touristes/visiteurs
Tourism expenditure		43	...	...	...	...	...	Dépenses touristiques
Chile								**Chili**
Tourist/visitor arrivals	TF	1 540	2 027	2 801[2]	3 674[2]	4 478[2]	5 641[2]	Arrivées de touristes/visiteurs
Tourism expenditure		1 186	1 608	2 362	3 202	3 412	3 697	Dépenses touristiques

30 Tourist/visitor arrivals and tourism expenditure *(continued)*
Thousands arrivals and millions of US dollars

Arrivées de touristes/visiteurs et dépenses touristiques *(suite)*
Milliers d'arrivées et millions de dollars É.-U.

Country or area of destination	Series& Série&	1995	2005	2010	2014	2015	2016	Pays ou zone de destination
China[13]								**Chine**[13]
Tourist/visitor arrivals	TF	20 034	46 809	55 664	55 622	56 886	59 270	Arrivées de touristes/visiteurs
Tourism expenditure[3]		8 730	29 296	45 814	44 044	44 969	44 432	Dépenses touristiques[3]
China, Hong Kong SAR								**Chine, RAS de Hong Kong**
Tourist/visitor arrivals	TF	...	14 773	20 085	27 770	26 686	26 553	Arrivées de touristes/visiteurs
Tourism expenditure		...	13 588	27 208	46 079	42 229	37 976	Dépenses touristiques
China, Macao SAR								**Chine, RAS de Macao**
Tourist/visitor arrivals	TF	* 4 202	* 9 014	* 11 926	* 14 566	* 14 308	* 15 704	Arrivées de touristes/visiteurs
Tourism expenditure		3 233	7 181	22 688	43 303	31 488	30 568	Dépenses touristiques
Colombia								**Colombie**
Tourist/visitor arrivals	TF	1 399	# 933	1 405	2 552	2 978	3 317	Arrivées de touristes/visiteurs
Tourism expenditure		887	1 891	3 441	4 887	5 235	5 835	Dépenses touristiques
Comoros								**Comores**
Tourist/visitor arrivals[4]	TF	23	26	15	23	24	27	Arrivées de touristes/visiteurs[4]
Tourism expenditure		22	24	35	...	...	...	Dépenses touristiques
Congo								**Congo**
Tourist/visitor arrivals[2]	TF	...	35	194	226	220	211	Arrivées de touristes/visiteurs[2]
Tourism expenditure[3]		14	40	27	55	...	...	Dépenses touristiques[3]
Cook Islands								**Îles Cook**
Tourist/visitor arrivals	TF	48	88	104	121	125	146	Arrivées de touristes/visiteurs
Tourism expenditure		28	91	111	175	154	179	Dépenses touristiques
Costa Rica								**Costa Rica**
Tourist/visitor arrivals	TF	785	1 679	2 100	2 527	2 660	2 925	Arrivées de touristes/visiteurs
Tourism expenditure		763	1 810	2 179	3 137	3 408	3 956	Dépenses touristiques
Côte d'Ivoire								**Côte d'Ivoire**
Tourist/visitor arrivals[14]	VF	...	...	252	471	1 441	1 583	Arrivées de touristes/visiteurs[14]
Tourism expenditure		103	93	213	195	214	...	Dépenses touristiques
Croatia								**Croatie**
Tourist/visitor arrivals	TCE	1 485	* 7 743	9 111[15]	11 623[15]	12 683[15]	13 809[15]	Arrivées de touristes/visiteurs
Tourism expenditure		...	7 625	8 299	10 079	9 018	9 820	Dépenses touristiques
Cuba								**Cuba**
Tourist/visitor arrivals[4]	TF	742	2 261	2 507	2 970	3 491	3 968	Arrivées de touristes/visiteurs[4]
Tourism expenditure		1 100	2 591	2 396	2 546	2 819	3 069	Dépenses touristiques
Curaçao								**Curaçao**
Tourist/visitor arrivals[4]	TF	224	222	342	452	468	441	Arrivées de touristes/visiteurs[4]
Tourism expenditure		175	244	438	820	712	644	Dépenses touristiques
Cyprus								**Chypre**
Tourist/visitor arrivals	TF	2 100	2 470	2 173	2 441	2 659	3 187	Arrivées de touristes/visiteurs
Tourism expenditure		2 019	2 618	2 424	2 920	2 489	2 756	Dépenses touristiques
Czechia								**Tchéquie**
Tourist/visitor arrivals	TF	...	9 404	8 629	10 649	11 619	12 090	Arrivées de touristes/visiteurs
Tourism expenditure		...	5 772	8 068	7 614	6 766	7 041	Dépenses touristiques
Dem. Rep. of the Congo								**Rép. dém. du Congo**
Tourist/visitor arrivals	TF	35	61	81[4]	...	...	...	Arrivées de touristes/visiteurs
Tourism expenditure[3]		...	3	11	45	~0	4	Dépenses touristiques[3]
Denmark								**Danemark**
Tourist/visitor arrivals	TCE	...	# 9 587	9 425	# 10 267	10 424	10 781	Arrivées de touristes/visiteurs
Tourism expenditure[3]		3 691	5 293	5 704	7 617	6 685	7 046	Dépenses touristiques[3]
Djibouti								**Djibouti**
Tourist/visitor arrivals	THS	21	30	51	...	...	...	Arrivées de touristes/visiteurs
Tourism expenditure[3]		5	7	18	25	31	34	Dépenses touristiques[3]
Dominica								**Dominique**
Tourist/visitor arrivals	TF	60	79	77	82	75	78	Arrivées de touristes/visiteurs
Tourism expenditure[3]		42	57	94	216	215	235	Dépenses touristiques[3]
Dominican Republic								**République dominicaine**
Tourist/visitor arrivals[4]	TF	1 776	3 691	4 125	5 141	5 600	5 959	Arrivées de touristes/visiteurs[4]
Tourism expenditure[3]		1 571	3 518	4 163	5 630	6 116	6 723	Dépenses touristiques[3]
Ecuador								**Équateur**
Tourist/visitor arrivals[1]	VF	440	860	1 047	1 557	1 544	1 418	Arrivées de touristes/visiteurs[1]
Tourism expenditure		315	488	786	1 487	1 557	1 449	Dépenses touristiques
Egypt								**Égypte**
Tourist/visitor arrivals	TF	2 871	8 244	14 051	9 628	9 139	5 258	Arrivées de touristes/visiteurs
Tourism expenditure		2 954	7 206	13 633	7 979	6 897	3 305	Dépenses touristiques

30 Tourist/visitor arrivals and tourism expenditure *(continued)*
Thousands arrivals and millions of US dollars

Arrivées de touristes/visiteurs et dépenses touristiques *(suite)*
Milliers d'arrivées et millions de dollars É.-U.

Country or area of destination	Series& Série&	1995	2005	2010	2014	2015	2016	Pays ou zone de destination
El Salvador								**El Salvador**
Tourist/visitor arrivals	TF	235	1 127	1 150	1 345	1 402	1 434	Arrivées de touristes/visiteurs
Tourism expenditure		152	656	646	1 285	1 203	1 161	Dépenses touristiques
Equatorial Guinea								**Guinée équatoriale**
Tourism expenditure		1	...	...	...	...	...	Dépenses touristiques
Eritrea								**Érythrée**
Tourist/visitor arrivals [2]	VF	315	83	84	119	114	142	Arrivées de touristes/visiteurs [2]
Tourism expenditure		58	66	...	...	...	48	Dépenses touristiques
Estonia								**Estonie**
Tourist/visitor arrivals	TF	530	1 917[16,17]	2 372[16,18]	2 918[16,18]	2 989[16,18]	3 147[16,18]	Arrivées de touristes/visiteurs
Tourism expenditure		452	1 229	...	2 231	1 843	1 896	Dépenses touristiques
Eswatini								**Eswatini**
Tourist/visitor arrivals	TF	300[19]	837	868	939	873	947	Arrivées de touristes/visiteurs
Tourism expenditure		54	77	51	16	14	13	Dépenses touristiques
Ethiopia								**Éthiopie**
Tourist/visitor arrivals	TF	103[20]	227	468	770	864	871	Arrivées de touristes/visiteurs
Tourism expenditure		177	533	1 434	2 107	2 279	2 138	Dépenses touristiques
Fiji								**Fidji**
Tourist/visitor arrivals [1]	TF	318	545	632	693	755	792	Arrivées de touristes/visiteurs [1]
Tourism expenditure		369	722	825	1 034	1 037	...	Dépenses touristiques
Finland								**Finlande**
Tourist/visitor arrivals	TCE	1 779	# 2 080	2 319	2 731	2 622	2 789	Arrivées de touristes/visiteurs
Tourism expenditure [3]		1 640	2 180	3 040	3 679	2 560	2 717	Dépenses touristiques [3]
France								**France**
Tourist/visitor arrivals	TF	60 033[21]	74 988[22]	76 647[22]	83 701[22]	84 452[22]	* 82 570[22]	Arrivées de touristes/visiteurs
Tourism expenditure		31 295	52 139	56 187	67 382	52 959	50 883	Dépenses touristiques
French Guiana								**Guyane française**
Tourist/visitor arrivals [23]	TF	...	95	189	185	199	...	Arrivées de touristes/visiteurs [23]
Tourism expenditure		...	44	...	...	...	...	Dépenses touristiques
French Polynesia								**Polynésie française**
Tourist/visitor arrivals [1,4]	TF	172	208	154	181	184	192	Arrivées de touristes/visiteurs [1,4]
Tourism expenditure [3]		...	530	405	510	466	...	Dépenses touristiques [3]
Gabon								**Gabon**
Tourist/visitor arrivals [24]	TF	125	269	...	...	...	...	Arrivées de touristes/visiteurs [24]
Tourism expenditure		94	13	...	...	...	...	Dépenses touristiques
Gambia								**Gambie**
Tourist/visitor arrivals [2,25]	TF	45	108	91	156	135	161	Arrivées de touristes/visiteurs [2,25]
Tourism expenditure		...	59	80	110	121	120	Dépenses touristiques
Georgia								**Géorgie**
Tourist/visitor arrivals	TF	...	...	1 067	2 229	2 282	2 721	Arrivées de touristes/visiteurs
Tourism expenditure		...	287	737	1 972	2 117	2 370	Dépenses touristiques
Germany								**Allemagne**
Tourist/visitor arrivals	TCE	14 847	21 500	26 875	32 999	34 970	35 555	Arrivées de touristes/visiteurs
Tourism expenditure		24 052	40 531	49 126	58 701	50 645	52 129	Dépenses touristiques
Ghana								**Ghana**
Tourist/visitor arrivals [2]	TF	286	429	931	825	897	...	Arrivées de touristes/visiteurs [2]
Tourism expenditure		30	867	706	1 027	911	952	Dépenses touristiques
Greece								**Grèce**
Tourist/visitor arrivals	TF	10 130	14 765	15 007	22 033	23 599	24 799	Arrivées de touristes/visiteurs
Tourism expenditure		4 182	13 453	13 858	19 481	17 260	16 533	Dépenses touristiques
Grenada								**Grenade**
Tourist/visitor arrivals	TF	108	99	110	150	155	156	Arrivées de touristes/visiteurs
Tourism expenditure [3]		76	71	112	466	493	510	Dépenses touristiques [3]
Guadeloupe								**Guadeloupe**
Tourist/visitor arrivals [4,26]	TF	640[27]	372	392	486	512	581	Arrivées de touristes/visiteurs [4,26]
Tourism expenditure		458	306	510	...	614	...	Dépenses touristiques
Guam								**Guam**
Tourist/visitor arrivals	TF	1 362	1 228	1 197	1 343	1 409	1 535	Arrivées de touristes/visiteurs
Guatemala								**Guatemala**
Tourist/visitor arrivals	TF	...	...	1 119	1 371	1 473	1 585	Arrivées de touristes/visiteurs
Tourism expenditure [3]		213	791	1 378	1 564	1 580	1 550	Dépenses touristiques [3]
Guinea								**Guinée**
Tourist/visitor arrivals [28]	TF	...	45	12	33	35	...	Arrivées de touristes/visiteurs [28]
Tourism expenditure		1	...	2	17	27	17	Dépenses touristiques

Tourist/visitor arrivals and tourism expenditure *(continued)*
Thousands arrivals and millions of US dollars

Arrivées de touristes/visiteurs et dépenses touristiques *(suite)*
Milliers d'arrivées et millions de dollars É.-U.

Country or area of destination	Series& Série&	1995	2005	2010	2014	2015	2016	Pays ou zone de destination
Guinea-Bissau								**Guinée-Bissau**
Tourist/visitor arrivals [4]	TF	...	5	22	36	44	...	Arrivées de touristes/visiteurs [4]
Tourism expenditure [3]		...	2	13	21	17	...	Dépenses touristiques [3]
Guyana								**Guyana**
Tourist/visitor arrivals	TF	106	117[29]	152[29]	206[29]	207[29]	235[29]	Arrivées de touristes/visiteurs
Tourism expenditure [3]		33	35	80	79	65	...	Dépenses touristiques [3]
Haiti								**Haïti**
Tourist/visitor arrivals [4]	TF	145	112	255[2]	465[2]	516[2]	...	Arrivées de touristes/visiteurs [4]
Tourism expenditure [3]		90	80	383	578	609	511	Dépenses touristiques [3]
Honduras								**Honduras**
Tourist/visitor arrivals	TF	271	673	863	868	880	...	Arrivées de touristes/visiteurs
Tourism expenditure		85	465	627	642	652	692	Dépenses touristiques
Hungary								**Hongrie**
Tourist/visitor arrivals	TF	...	9 979	9 510	12 140	14 316	15 255	Arrivées de touristes/visiteurs
Tourism expenditure		2 938	4 761	6 595	7 483	6 929	7 481	Dépenses touristiques
Iceland								**Islande**
Tourist/visitor arrivals	TF	190	374	489	998	1 289	1 792	Arrivées de touristes/visiteurs
Tourism expenditure [3]		186	413	562	1 375	1 618	2 411	Dépenses touristiques [3]
India								**Inde**
Tourist/visitor arrivals	TF	2 124[1]	3 919[1]	5 776[1]	13 107[2]	13 284[2]	14 569[2]	Arrivées de touristes/visiteurs
Tourism expenditure		...	7 659	...	20 756	21 472	23 111	Dépenses touristiques
Indonesia								**Indonésie**
Tourist/visitor arrivals	VF	4 324	5 002	7 003	9 435	10 407	11 519	Arrivées de touristes/visiteurs
Tourism expenditure		...	5 094	7 618	11 567	12 054	12 599	Dépenses touristiques
Iran (Islamic Republic of)								**Iran (Rép. islamique d')**
Tourist/visitor arrivals	VF	568	...	2 938	4 967	5 237	4 942	Arrivées de touristes/visiteurs
Tourism expenditure		205	1 025	2 631	4 197	4 086	...	Dépenses touristiques
Iraq								**Iraq**
Tourist/visitor arrivals	VF	61	...	1 518	...	...	...	Arrivées de touristes/visiteurs
Tourism expenditure		...	186	1 736	2 504	4 076	2 479	Dépenses touristiques
Ireland								**Irlande**
Tourist/visitor arrivals [30]	TF	4 818	7 333	# 7 134	8 813	9 528	10 100	Arrivées de touristes/visiteurs [30]
Tourism expenditure		2 698	6 780	8 187	11 093	10 802	11 427	Dépenses touristiques
Israel								**Israël**
Tourist/visitor arrivals [1]	TF	2 215	1 903	2 803	2 927	2 799	2 900	Arrivées de touristes/visiteurs [1]
Tourism expenditure		3 491	2 750	5 511	6 495	6 500	6 426	Dépenses touristiques
Italy								**Italie**
Tourist/visitor arrivals [31]	TF	31 052	36 513	43 626	48 576	50 732	52 372	Arrivées de touristes/visiteurs [31]
Tourism expenditure [3]		28 731	35 319	38 438	45 547	39 420	40 373	Dépenses touristiques [3]
Jamaica								**Jamaïque**
Tourist/visitor arrivals [2]	TF	1 147	1 479	1 922	2 080	2 123	2 182	Arrivées de touristes/visiteurs [2]
Tourism expenditure [3]		1 069	1 545	2 001	2 255	2 401	2 539	Dépenses touristiques [3]
Japan								**Japon**
Tourist/visitor arrivals [1]	VF	3 345	6 728	8 611	13 413	19 737	24 040	Arrivées de touristes/visiteurs [1]
Tourism expenditure		4 894	15 554	15 356	20 790	27 285	33 427	Dépenses touristiques
Jordan								**Jordanie**
Tourist/visitor arrivals [2]	TF	1 075	2 987	# 4 207	# 3 990	# 3 761	# 3 858	Arrivées de touristes/visiteurs [2]
Tourism expenditure		973	1 759	4 390	5 518	4 968	4 943	Dépenses touristiques
Kazakhstan								**Kazakhstan**
Tourist/visitor arrivals	TF	...	3 143	2 991	4 560	...	...	Arrivées de touristes/visiteurs
Tourism expenditure		155	801	1 236	1 701	1 734	1 716	Dépenses touristiques
Kenya								**Kenya**
Tourist/visitor arrivals [1]	TF	918	1 399	1 470	1 261	1 114	1 268	Arrivées de touristes/visiteurs [1]
Tourism expenditure		785	969	1 620	1 745	1 596	1 620	Dépenses touristiques
Kiribati								**Kiribati**
Tourist/visitor arrivals [32]	TF	4	4	5	5	4	6	Arrivées de touristes/visiteurs [32]
Tourism expenditure [3]		...	...	4	3	2	3	Dépenses touristiques [3]
Kuwait								**Koweït**
Tourist/visitor arrivals	VF	1 443	3 474	5 208	6 528	6 941	7 055	Arrivées de touristes/visiteurs
Tourism expenditure		307	413	574	615	931	831	Dépenses touristiques
Kyrgyzstan								**Kirghizistan**
Tourist/visitor arrivals	VF	...	...	855	2 849	3 051	2 930	Arrivées de touristes/visiteurs
Tourism expenditure		...	94	212	468	482	477	Dépenses touristiques

Tourist/visitor arrivals and tourism expenditure *(continued)*
Thousands arrivals and millions of US dollars

Arrivées de touristes/visiteurs et dépenses touristiques *(suite)*
Milliers d'arrivées et millions de dollars É.-U.

Country or area of destination	Series& Série&	1995	2005	2010	2014	2015	2016	Pays ou zone de destination
Lao People's Dem. Rep.								**Rép. dém. populaire lao**
Tourist/visitor arrivals	TF	60	672	1 670	3 164	3 543	3 315	Arrivées de touristes/visiteurs
Tourism expenditure		52	143	385	642	725	713	Dépenses touristiques
Latvia								**Lettonie**
Tourist/visitor arrivals [33]	TF	539	1 116	1 373	1 843	2 024	1 793	Arrivées de touristes/visiteurs [33]
Tourism expenditure		37	446	...	1 298	1 279	1 282	Dépenses touristiques
Lebanon								**Liban**
Tourist/visitor arrivals [34]	TF	450	1 140	2 168	1 355	1 518	1 688	Arrivées de touristes/visiteurs [34]
Tourism expenditure		710	5 969	8 026	6 835	7 087	7 153	Dépenses touristiques
Lesotho								**Lesotho**
Tourist/visitor arrivals	VF	209	304	426	# 1 079	1 082	1 196	Arrivées de touristes/visiteurs
Tourism expenditure [3]		27	27	23	16	34	48	Dépenses touristiques [3]
Liberia [3]								**Libéria [3]**
Tourism expenditure		...	67	12	55	46	...	Dépenses touristiques
Libya								**Libye**
Tourist/visitor arrivals	THS	...	81	...	...	...	...	Arrivées de touristes/visiteurs
Tourism expenditure		4	301	170	...	...	...	Dépenses touristiques
Liechtenstein								**Liechtenstein**
Tourist/visitor arrivals	TCE	...	...	64	61[35]	57[35]	69[35]	Arrivées de touristes/visiteurs
Lithuania								**Lituanie**
Tourist/visitor arrivals	TF	650	2 000	1 507	2 063	2 071	2 296	Arrivées de touristes/visiteurs
Tourism expenditure [3]		77	920	958	1 383	1 153	1 210	Dépenses touristiques [3]
Luxembourg								**Luxembourg**
Tourist/visitor arrivals	TCE	768	913	805	1 038	1 090	1 054	Arrivées de touristes/visiteurs
Tourism expenditure		...	3 770	4 519	6 042	4 753	4 583	Dépenses touristiques
Madagascar								**Madagascar**
Tourist/visitor arrivals [36]	TF	75	277	196	222	244	293	Arrivées de touristes/visiteurs [36]
Tourism expenditure		106	275	425	739	696	913	Dépenses touristiques
Malawi								**Malawi**
Tourist/visitor arrivals [37]	TF	192	438	746	819	805	849	Arrivées de touristes/visiteurs [37]
Tourism expenditure		22	48	45	36	39	43	Dépenses touristiques
Malaysia								**Malaisie**
Tourist/visitor arrivals [38]	TF	7 469	16 431	24 577	27 437	25 721	26 757	Arrivées de touristes/visiteurs [38]
Tourism expenditure [3]		3 969	8 846	18 152	22 600	17 666	18 084	Dépenses touristiques [3]
Maldives								**Maldives**
Tourist/visitor arrivals [4]	TF	315	395	792	1 205	1 234	1 286	Arrivées de touristes/visiteurs [4]
Tourism expenditure		...	...	...	2 811	2 691	2 864	Dépenses touristiques
Mali								**Mali**
Tourist/visitor arrivals	TF	...	...	169	168	159	173	Arrivées de touristes/visiteurs
Tourism expenditure		26	149	208	214	...	...	Dépenses touristiques
Malta								**Malte**
Tourist/visitor arrivals	TF	1 116	1 171[39]	1 339[39]	1 690[39]	1 783[39]	1 966[39]	Arrivées de touristes/visiteurs
Tourism expenditure [3]		656	755	1 066	1 521	1 381	1 451	Dépenses touristiques [3]
Marshall Islands								**Îles Marshall**
Tourist/visitor arrivals	TF	6[4]	9[40]	5[4]	5[4]	6[4]	10	Arrivées de touristes/visiteurs
Tourism expenditure		3	4	4	5	...	...	Dépenses touristiques
Martinique								**Martinique**
Tourist/visitor arrivals	TF	457	484	478	490	487	519	Arrivées de touristes/visiteurs
Tourism expenditure		384	280	472	483	340	365	Dépenses touristiques
Mauritania								**Mauritanie**
Tourism expenditure		...	...	...	42	31	33	Dépenses touristiques
Mauritius								**Maurice**
Tourist/visitor arrivals	TF	422	761	935	1 038	1 151	1 275	Arrivées de touristes/visiteurs
Tourism expenditure		616	1 189	1 585	1 719	1 679	1 824	Dépenses touristiques
Mexico								**Mexique**
Tourist/visitor arrivals [2]	TF	20 241	21 915	23 290	29 346	32 093	35 079	Arrivées de touristes/visiteurs [2]
Tourism expenditure		6 847	12 801	12 628	16 606	18 729	20 619	Dépenses touristiques
Micronesia (Fed. States of)								**Micronésie (États féd. de)**
Tourist/visitor arrivals [41]	TF	...	19	45	35	31	30	Arrivées de touristes/visiteurs [41]
Tourism expenditure [3]		...	...	24	29	25	...	Dépenses touristiques [3]
Monaco								**Monaco**
Tourist/visitor arrivals	THS	233	286	279	329	331	336	Arrivées de touristes/visiteurs
Mongolia								**Mongolie**
Tourist/visitor arrivals [42]	TF	108	338	456	393	386	404	Arrivées de touristes/visiteurs [42]
Tourism expenditure		33	203	288	257	279	379	Dépenses touristiques

30 Tourist/visitor arrivals and tourism expenditure *(continued)*
Thousands arrivals and millions of US dollars

Arrivées de touristes/visiteurs et dépenses touristiques *(suite)*
Milliers d'arrivées et millions de dollars É.-U.

Country or area of destination	Series& Série&	1995	2005	2010	2014	2015	2016	Pays ou zone de destination
Montenegro								**Monténégro**
Tourist/visitor arrivals	TCE	...	272	1 088	1 350	1 560	1 662	Arrivées de touristes/visiteurs
Tourism expenditure		...	...	765	959	947	978	Dépenses touristiques
Montserrat								**Montserrat**
Tourist/visitor arrivals	TF	18	10	6	9	9	9	Arrivées de touristes/visiteurs
Tourism expenditure [3]		17	9	6	9	9	9	Dépenses touristiques [3]
Morocco								**Maroc**
Tourist/visitor arrivals [2]	TF	2 602	5 843	9 288	10 283	10 177	10 332	Arrivées de touristes/visiteurs [2]
Tourism expenditure		1 469	5 426	8 176	9 070	7 765	7 921	Dépenses touristiques
Mozambique								**Mozambique**
Tourist/visitor arrivals	TF	...	578[43]	1 718[44]	1 661[44]	1 552[44]	1 639[44]	Arrivées de touristes/visiteurs
Tourism expenditure		...	138	135	225	202	114	Dépenses touristiques
Myanmar								**Myanmar**
Tourist/visitor arrivals	TF	194	660	792	3 081	4 681	# 2 907	Arrivées de touristes/visiteurs
Tourism expenditure		169	83	91	1 687	2 266	2 269	Dépenses touristiques
Namibia								**Namibie**
Tourist/visitor arrivals	TF	272	778	984	1 320	1 388	1 469	Arrivées de touristes/visiteurs
Tourism expenditure		...	363	473	552	546	378	Dépenses touristiques
Nepal								**Népal**
Tourist/visitor arrivals [45]	TF	363	375	603	790	539	753	Arrivées de touristes/visiteurs [45]
Tourism expenditure		232	160	378	511	509	498	Dépenses touristiques
Netherlands								**Pays-Bas**
Tourist/visitor arrivals	TCE	6 574	10 012	10 883	13 925	15 007	15 828	Arrivées de touristes/visiteurs
Tourism expenditure		10 611	...	...	19 726	17 592	18 317	Dépenses touristiques
New Caledonia								**Nouvelle-Calédonie**
Tourist/visitor arrivals [2]	TF	86	101	99	107	114	116	Arrivées de touristes/visiteurs [2]
Tourism expenditure [3]		108	149	129	187	158	...	Dépenses touristiques [3]
New Zealand								**Nouvelle-Zélande**
Tourist/visitor arrivals	TF	...	2 353	2 435	2 772	3 039	3 370	Arrivées de touristes/visiteurs
Tourism expenditure [3]		2 318	6 486	6 523	8 402	9 140	9 418	Dépenses touristiques [3]
Nicaragua								**Nicaragua**
Tourist/visitor arrivals	TF	281	712[2]	1 011[2]	1 330[2]	1 386[2]	1 504[2]	Arrivées de touristes/visiteurs
Tourism expenditure [3]		50	206	313	445	529	642	Dépenses touristiques [3]
Niger								**Niger**
Tourist/visitor arrivals	TF	35	58	74	135	135	152	Arrivées de touristes/visiteurs
Tourism expenditure		...	44	106	100	80	...	Dépenses touristiques
Nigeria								**Nigéria**
Tourist/visitor arrivals	TF	656	1 010	1 555	...	1 255	1 889	Arrivées de touristes/visiteurs
Tourism expenditure		47	139	736	601	470	1 085	Dépenses touristiques
Niue								**Nioué**
Tourist/visitor arrivals [46]	TF	2	3	6	7	* 8	...	Arrivées de touristes/visiteurs [46]
Tourism expenditure		2	1	2	...	...	...	Dépenses touristiques
Northern Mariana Islands								**Îles Mariannes du Nord**
Tourist/visitor arrivals	VF	676	507	379	460	479	531	Arrivées de touristes/visiteurs
Tourism expenditure		655	...	...	...	...	...	Dépenses touristiques
Norway								**Norvège**
Tourist/visitor arrivals	TF	2 880[47]	3 824	4 767	4 855	5 361	5 960	Arrivées de touristes/visiteurs
Tourism expenditure		2 730	4 243	5 299	7 503	6 370	6 196	Dépenses touristiques
Oman								**Oman**
Tourist/visitor arrivals	TF	...	891	1 441	1 611	1 909	2 292	Arrivées de touristes/visiteurs
Tourism expenditure		...	627	1 072	1 972	2 247	2 497	Dépenses touristiques
Other non-specified areas								**Autres zones non-spécifiées**
Tourist/visitor arrivals [2]	VF	2 332	3 378	5 567	9 910	10 440	10 690	Arrivées de touristes/visiteurs [2]
Tourism expenditure		3 985	5 740	10 387	17 419	16 987	15 833	Dépenses touristiques
Pakistan								**Pakistan**
Tourist/visitor arrivals	TF	378	798	907	...	...	...	Arrivées de touristes/visiteurs
Tourism expenditure		582	828	998	971	915	879	Dépenses touristiques
Palau								**Palaos**
Tourist/visitor arrivals [48]	TF	53	81	85	140	162	138	Arrivées de touristes/visiteurs [48]
Tourism expenditure [49]		...	63	76	131	156	...	Dépenses touristiques [49]
Panama								**Panama**
Tourist/visitor arrivals	TF	345	702	1 324	1 745	2 110	2 007	Arrivées de touristes/visiteurs
Tourism expenditure		372	1 108	2 621	5 749	5 754	6 455	Dépenses touristiques

30 Tourist/visitor arrivals and tourism expenditure *(continued)*
Thousands arrivals and millions of US dollars

Arrivées de touristes/visiteurs et dépenses touristiques *(suite)*
Milliers d'arrivées et millions de dollars É.-U.

Country or area of destination	Series& Série&	1995	2005	2010	2014	2015	2016	Pays ou zone de destination
Papua New Guinea								**Papouasie-Nvl-Guinée**
Tourist/visitor arrivals	TF	42	69	140	182	184	...	Arrivées de touristes/visiteurs
Tourism expenditure		...	9	2	3	...	2	Dépenses touristiques
Paraguay								**Paraguay**
Tourist/visitor arrivals [5]	TF	438	341	465	649	1 215	1 308	Arrivées de touristes/visiteurs [5]
Tourism expenditure		162	96	243	314	348	356	Dépenses touristiques
Peru								**Pérou**
Tourist/visitor arrivals [2]	TF	479	1 571[50]	2 299[50]	3 215[50]	3 456[50]	* 3 744[50]	Arrivées de touristes/visiteurs [2]
Tourism expenditure		521	1 438	2 475	3 907	4 140	4 303	Dépenses touristiques
Philippines								**Philippines**
Tourist/visitor arrivals [2]	TF	1 760	2 623	3 520	4 833	5 361	5 967	Arrivées de touristes/visiteurs [2]
Tourism expenditure		1 141	2 863	3 441	6 059	6 415	6 333	Dépenses touristiques
Poland								**Pologne**
Tourist/visitor arrivals	TF	19 215[16]	15 200[16]	12 470[16]	16 000	16 728	17 471	Arrivées de touristes/visiteurs
Tourism expenditure		6 927	7 161	10 037	12 924	11 355	12 052	Dépenses touristiques
Portugal								**Portugal**
Tourist/visitor arrivals [51]	TCE	* 4 572	* 5 769	* 6 756	* 9 092	* 9 957	* 11 223	Arrivées de touristes/visiteurs [51]
Tourism expenditure		5 646	9 042	12 985	17 718	15 823	17 185	Dépenses touristiques
Puerto Rico								**Porto Rico**
Tourist/visitor arrivals [36]	TF	3 131	3 686	3 186	3 246	3 542	3 736	Arrivées de touristes/visiteurs [36]
Tourism expenditure [52]		1 828	3 239	3 211	3 439	3 825	3 985	Dépenses touristiques [52]
Qatar								**Qatar**
Tourist/visitor arrivals	TF	...	...	1 700	2 839	2 941	2 938	Arrivées de touristes/visiteurs
Tourism expenditure		...	...	...	10 576	12 131	12 593	Dépenses touristiques
Republic of Korea								**République de Corée**
Tourist/visitor arrivals	VF	3 753	6 023	8 798	14 202	13 232	17 242	Arrivées de touristes/visiteurs
Tourism expenditure		6 670	8 290	14 367	22 704	19 055	21 053	Dépenses touristiques
Republic of Moldova								**République de Moldova**
Tourist/visitor arrivals [53]	TCE	...	67	64	94	94	121	Arrivées de touristes/visiteurs [53]
Tourism expenditure		71	138	222	328	291	331	Dépenses touristiques
Réunion								**Réunion**
Tourist/visitor arrivals [4]	TF	304	409	420	406	426	458	Arrivées de touristes/visiteurs [4]
Tourism expenditure		216	384	392	387	339	360	Dépenses touristiques
Romania								**Roumanie**
Tourist/visitor arrivals	VF	5 445	5 839	7 498	8 442	9 331	10 223	Arrivées de touristes/visiteurs
Tourism expenditure		689	1 324	1 631	2 225	2 097	2 166	Dépenses touristiques
Russian Federation								**Fédération de Russie**
Tourist/visitor arrivals	VF	10 290	22 201	22 281	32 421	33 729	24 571	Arrivées de touristes/visiteurs
Tourism expenditure		...	7 805	13 239	19 451	13 204	12 823	Dépenses touristiques
Rwanda								**Rwanda**
Tourist/visitor arrivals	TF	...	...	504	926	987	932	Arrivées de touristes/visiteurs
Tourism expenditure		4	67	224	376	457	470	Dépenses touristiques
Saint Kitts and Nevis								**Saint-Kitts-et-Nevis**
Tourist/visitor arrivals [36]	TF	79	141	98	113	122	...	Arrivées de touristes/visiteurs [36]
Tourism expenditure [3]		63	121	90	310	308	331	Dépenses touristiques [3]
Saint Lucia								**Sainte-Lucie**
Tourist/visitor arrivals [1]	TF	231	318	306	338	345	348	Arrivées de touristes/visiteurs [1]
Tourism expenditure [3]		230	382	309	778	810	770	Dépenses touristiques [3]
Saint Vincent & Grenadines								**Saint-Vincent-Grenadines**
Tourist/visitor arrivals [36]	TF	60	96	72	71	75	79	Arrivées de touristes/visiteurs [36]
Tourism expenditure [3]		53	104	86	175	202	208	Dépenses touristiques [3]
Samoa								**Samoa**
Tourist/visitor arrivals	TF	68	102	122	120	128	134	Arrivées de touristes/visiteurs
Tourism expenditure		36	74	124	147	126	...	Dépenses touristiques
San Marino [54]								**Saint-Marin [54]**
Tourist/visitor arrivals	THS	28	50	120	75	54	60	Arrivées de touristes/visiteurs
Sao Tome and Principe								**Sao Tomé-et-Principe**
Tourist/visitor arrivals	TF	6	16	8	...	26	29	Arrivées de touristes/visiteurs
Tourism expenditure		...	...	...	56	63	69	Dépenses touristiques
Saudi Arabia								**Arabie saoudite**
Tourist/visitor arrivals	TF	3 325	8 037	10 850	18 260	17 994	18 049	Arrivées de touristes/visiteurs
Tourism expenditure		...	...	7 536	9 263	11 183	12 139	Dépenses touristiques
Senegal								**Sénégal**
Tourist/visitor arrivals	TF	...	769	* 900	* 963	* 1 007	...	Arrivées de touristes/visiteurs
Tourism expenditure		168	334	464	481	...	...	Dépenses touristiques

30 Tourist/visitor arrivals and tourism expenditure *(continued)*
Thousands arrivals and millions of US dollars

Arrivées de touristes/visiteurs et dépenses touristiques *(suite)*
Milliers d'arrivées et millions de dollars É.-U.

Country or area of destination	Series& Série&	1995	2005	2010	2014	2015	2016	Pays ou zone de destination
Serbia								**Serbie**
Tourist/visitor arrivals	TCE	...	453	683	1 029	1 132	1 281	Arrivées de touristes/visiteurs
Tourism expenditure		...	308	950	1 352	1 322	1 460	Dépenses touristiques
Seychelles								**Seychelles**
Tourist/visitor arrivals	TF	121	129	175	233	276	303	Arrivées de touristes/visiteurs
Tourism expenditure		224	269	352	480	483	505	Dépenses touristiques
Sierra Leone								**Sierra Leone**
Tourist/visitor arrivals [4]	TF	14	40	39	44	24	55	Arrivées de touristes/visiteurs [4]
Tourism expenditure [3]		57	64	26	35	37	...	Dépenses touristiques [3]
Singapore								**Singapour**
Tourist/visitor arrivals	TF	6 070	7 079	9 161	11 864	12 051	12 914	Arrivées de touristes/visiteurs
Tourism expenditure [3]		7 611	6 209	14 178	19 134	16 563	18 386	Dépenses touristiques [3]
Sint Maarten (Dutch part)								**St-Martin (partie néerland.)**
Tourist/visitor arrivals [55]	TF	460	468	443	500	505	528	Arrivées de touristes/visiteurs [55]
Tourism expenditure		...	...	681	922	913	871	Dépenses touristiques
Slovakia								**Slovaquie**
Tourist/visitor arrivals [56]	TCE	903	1 515	1 327	1 475	1 721	2 027	Arrivées de touristes/visiteurs [56]
Tourism expenditure		630	1 282	2 335	2 642	2 480	2 800	Dépenses touristiques
Slovenia								**Slovénie**
Tourist/visitor arrivals	TCE	732	1 555	1 869	2 411	2 707	3 032	Arrivées de touristes/visiteurs
Tourism expenditure		1 128	1 894	2 721	2 944	2 521	2 627	Dépenses touristiques
Solomon Islands								**Îles Salomon**
Tourist/visitor arrivals	TF	12	9[57]	21	20	22	23	Arrivées de touristes/visiteurs
Tourism expenditure		17	6	51	65	60	71	Dépenses touristiques
South Africa								**Afrique du Sud**
Tourist/visitor arrivals	TF	4 488[58]	7 369[58]	# 8 074	# 9 549[59]	8 904[59]	10 044[59]	Arrivées de touristes/visiteurs
Tourism expenditure		2 654	8 629	10 309	10 484	9 140	8 807	Dépenses touristiques
South Sudan								**Soudan du sud**
Tourism expenditure		...	...	...	...	22	24	Dépenses touristiques
Spain								**Espagne**
Tourist/visitor arrivals	TF	32 971	55 914	52 677	64 939	68 175[60]	# 75 315	Arrivées de touristes/visiteurs
Tourism expenditure [3]		25 368	49 565	54 305	65 099	56 532	60 605	Dépenses touristiques [3]
Sri Lanka								**Sri Lanka**
Tourist/visitor arrivals [1]	TF	403	549	654	1 527	1 798	2 051	Arrivées de touristes/visiteurs [1]
Tourism expenditure		367	729	1 044	3 278	3 978	4 591	Dépenses touristiques
State of Palestine								**État de Palestine**
Tourist/visitor arrivals	THS	...	88	522	556	432	400	Arrivées de touristes/visiteurs
Tourism expenditure [3,61]		255	52	409	412	312	284	Dépenses touristiques [3,61]
Sudan								**Soudan**
Tourist/visitor arrivals	TF	29	246[2]	495[2]	684[2]	741[2]	...	Arrivées de touristes/visiteurs
Tourism expenditure [3]		8	114	82	967	949	1 009	Dépenses touristiques [3]
Suriname								**Suriname**
Tourist/visitor arrivals	TF	43[62]	161	205	252	228	256	Arrivées de touristes/visiteurs
Tourism expenditure		52	96	69	103	99	74	Dépenses touristiques
Sweden								**Suède**
Tourist/visitor arrivals	TF	...	...	...	19 945	...	...	Arrivées de touristes/visiteurs
Tourism expenditure [3]		3 471	6 554	8 336	11 846	11 307	12 633	Dépenses touristiques [3]
Switzerland								**Suisse**
Tourist/visitor arrivals	THS	6 946	7 229	8 628	9 158	9 305	9 205	Arrivées de touristes/visiteurs
Tourism expenditure		11 354	11 952	17 614	21 444	19 639	19 220	Dépenses touristiques
Syrian Arab Republic								**République arabe syrienne**
Tourist/visitor arrivals	TCE	815	3 571[2]	8 546[2,63]	...	...	...	Arrivées de touristes/visiteurs
Tourism expenditure		...	2 035	6 308	...	...	...	Dépenses touristiques
Tajikistan								**Tadjikistan**
Tourist/visitor arrivals	VF	...	...	160	213	414	...	Arrivées de touristes/visiteurs
Tourism expenditure		...	9	142	220	146	150	Dépenses touristiques
Thailand								**Thaïlande**
Tourist/visitor arrivals	TF	6 952[2]	11 567[2]	15 936	24 810	29 923	32 530	Arrivées de touristes/visiteurs
Tourism expenditure		9 257	12 103	23 796	42 047	48 527	52 465	Dépenses touristiques
TFYR of Macedonia								**ex-R.Y. de Macédoine**
Tourist/visitor arrivals	TCE	147	197	262	425	486	510	Arrivées de touristes/visiteurs
Tourism expenditure		...	116	199	298	268	283	Dépenses touristiques
Timor-Leste								**Timor-Leste**
Tourist/visitor arrivals [64]	TF	...	...	40	60	62	66	Arrivées de touristes/visiteurs [64]
Tourism expenditure [3]		...	...	24	35	51	58	Dépenses touristiques [3]

30 Tourist/visitor arrivals and tourism expenditure *(continued)*

Thousands arrivals and millions of US dollars

Arrivées de touristes/visiteurs et dépenses touristiques *(suite)*

Milliers d'arrivées et millions de dollars É.-U.

Country or area of destination	Series& Série&	1995	2005	2010	2014	2015	2016	Pays ou zone de destination
Togo								**Togo**
Tourist/visitor arrivals	THS	53	81	202	282	273	338	Arrivées de touristes/visiteurs
Tourism expenditure		...	27	105	233	212	...	Dépenses touristiques
Tonga								**Tonga**
Tourist/visitor arrivals [4]	TF	29	42	47	50	54	59	Arrivées de touristes/visiteurs [4]
Tourism expenditure		...	15	28	...	...	...	Dépenses touristiques
Trinidad and Tobago								**Trinité-et-Tobago**
Tourist/visitor arrivals [4]	TF	260	463	388	412	440	410	Arrivées de touristes/visiteurs [4]
Tourism expenditure		232	593	630	875	809	708	Dépenses touristiques
Tunisia								**Tunisie**
Tourist/visitor arrivals	TF	4 120[1]	6 378[1]	7 828	7 163	5 359	5 724	Arrivées de touristes/visiteurs
Tourism expenditure		1 838	2 800	3 477	3 042	1 869	1 706	Dépenses touristiques
Turkey								**Turquie**
Tourist/visitor arrivals	TF	7 083	20 273	31 364[65]	39 811[65]	39 478[65]	30 289[65]	Arrivées de touristes/visiteurs
Tourism expenditure		...	20 760	26 318	38 766	35 451	26 695	Dépenses touristiques
Turkmenistan								**Turkménistan**
Tourist/visitor arrivals	TF	218	12	...	...	...	...	Arrivées de touristes/visiteurs
Turks and Caicos Islands								**Îles Turques-et-Caïques**
Tourist/visitor arrivals	TF	79	176	281	357	386	454	Arrivées de touristes/visiteurs
Tourism expenditure		53	...	...	...	...	...	Dépenses touristiques
Tuvalu								**Tuvalu**
Tourist/visitor arrivals	TF	1	1	2	1	2	3	Arrivées de touristes/visiteurs
Tourism expenditure [3]		...	1	2	...	...	...	Dépenses touristiques [3]
Uganda								**Ouganda**
Tourist/visitor arrivals	TF	160	468	946	1 266	1 303	1 323	Arrivées de touristes/visiteurs
Tourism expenditure		...	382	802	810	1 180	...	Dépenses touristiques
Ukraine								**Ukraine**
Tourist/visitor arrivals	TF	3 716	17 631	21 203	12 712	12 428	13 333	Arrivées de touristes/visiteurs
Tourism expenditure		...	3 542	4 696	2 264	1 662	1 723	Dépenses touristiques
United Arab Emirates								**Émirats arabes unis**
Tourist/visitor arrivals [66]	THS	2 315	7 126	...	...	...	...	Arrivées de touristes/visiteurs [66]
Tourism expenditure		632	3 218	8 577	15 221	17 481	19 496	Dépenses touristiques
United Kingdom								**Royaume-Uni**
Tourist/visitor arrivals	TF	21 719	28 039	28 295	32 613	34 436	35 814	Arrivées de touristes/visiteurs
Tourism expenditure		27 577	41 736	41 468	62 604	60 807	55 558	Dépenses touristiques
United Rep. of Tanzania								**Rép.-Unie de Tanzanie**
Tourist/visitor arrivals	TF	285	590	754	1 113	1 104	1 233	Arrivées de touristes/visiteurs
Tourism expenditure		...	835	1 279	2 047	1 924	2 157	Dépenses touristiques
United States of America								**États-Unis d'Amérique**
Tourist/visitor arrivals	TF	43 318	49 206	60 010	# 75 022	# 77 465	# 75 608	Arrivées de touristes/visiteurs
Tourism expenditure		93 743	122 077	167 996	235 990	247 394	244 708	Dépenses touristiques
United States Virgin Islands								**Îles Vierges américaines**
Tourist/visitor arrivals	TF	454	594	572	615	642	...	Arrivées de touristes/visiteurs
Tourism expenditure		822	1 432	1 223	1 319	1 324	...	Dépenses touristiques
Uruguay								**Uruguay**
Tourist/visitor arrivals	TF	2 022	1 808	2 353	2 682	2 773	3 037	Arrivées de touristes/visiteurs
Tourism expenditure		725	699	1 669	1 869	1 880	2 156	Dépenses touristiques
Uzbekistan								**Ouzbékistan**
Tourist/visitor arrivals	TF	92	242	975	...	...	...	Arrivées de touristes/visiteurs
Tourism expenditure [3]		...	28	121	...	...	...	Dépenses touristiques [3]
Vanuatu								**Vanuatu**
Tourist/visitor arrivals	TF	44	62	97	109	90	95	Arrivées de touristes/visiteurs
Tourism expenditure		...	104	242	284	254	...	Dépenses touristiques
Venezuela (Boliv. Rep. of)								**Venezuela (Rép. boliv. du)**
Tourist/visitor arrivals	TF	700	706	526	857	789	601	Arrivées de touristes/visiteurs
Tourism expenditure		995	722	885	900	654	546	Dépenses touristiques
Viet Nam								**Viet Nam**
Tourist/visitor arrivals	VF	1 351	3 477	5 050	7 874	7 944	10 013	Arrivées de touristes/visiteurs
Tourism expenditure		...	2 300	4 450	7 410	7 350	8 250	Dépenses touristiques
Yemen								**Yémen**
Tourist/visitor arrivals	TF	61	336	1 025[2]	1 018[2]	367[2]	...	Arrivées de touristes/visiteurs
Tourism expenditure		...	...	1 291	1 199	116	...	Dépenses touristiques
Zambia								**Zambie**
Tourist/visitor arrivals	TF	163	669	815	947	932	956	Arrivées de touristes/visiteurs
Tourism expenditure [3]		...	447	492	642	660	683	Dépenses touristiques [3]

30 Tourist/visitor arrivals and tourism expenditure *(continued)*
Thousands arrivals and millions of US dollars

Arrivées de touristes/visiteurs et dépenses touristiques *(suite)*
Milliers d'arrivées et millions de dollars É.-U.

Country or area of destination	Series& Série&	1995	2005	2010	2014	2015	2016	Pays ou zone de destination
Zimbabwe								**Zimbabwe**
Tourist/visitor arrivals	VF	1 416	1 559	2 239	1 880	2 057	2 168	Arrivées de touristes/visiteurs
Tourism expenditure		145	99	135	186	191	194	Dépenses touristiques

Source:

World Tourism Organization (UNWTO), Madrid, the UNWTO Statistics Database, last accessed January 2018.

The majority of the expenditure data have been provided to the WTO by the International Monetary Fund (IMF). & Series (by order of priority, see Annex II): TF: Arrivals of non-resident tourists at national borders. VF: Arrivals of non-resident visitors at national borders. TCE: Arrivals of non-resident tourists in all types of accommodation establishments. THS: Arrivals of non-resident tourists in hotels and similar establishments.

1 Excluding nationals residing abroad.
2 Including nationals residing abroad.
3 Excluding passenger transport.
4 Arrivals by air.
5 Excluding nationals residing abroad and crew members.
6 Only paid accommodation; excluding stays at friends and relatives and second homes.
7 Excludes the Belarusian-Russian border segment.
8 Package tour only.
9 Includes estimation of the Belarusian-Russian border segment.
10 Including regional high end tourists.
11 Excluding Netherlands Antillean residents.
12 Arrivals by air at Bangui only.
13 For statistical purposes, the data for China do not include those for the Hong Kong Special Administrative Region (Hong Kong SAR), Macao Special Administrative Region (Macao SAR) and Taiwan Province of China.
14 Arrivals to Félix Houphouët Boigny Airport only.
15 Excluding arrivals in ports of nautical tourism.
16 Border statistics are not collected any more, surveys used instead.
17 Calculated on the basis of accommodation statistics and "Foreign Visitor Survey" carried out by the Statistical Office of Estonia.
18 Based on mobile positioning data.
19 Arrivals in hotels only.
20 Arrivals to Bole airport only.
21 Estimated based on surveys at national borders.
22 Arrivals of non-resident visitors.
23 Survey at Cayenne-Rochambeau airport on departure.
24 Arrivals of non-resident tourists at Libreville airport.
25 Charter tourists only.
26 Excluding the north islands, Saint Barthélemy and Saint Martin (French part).
27 Non-resident tourists staying in all types of accommodation establishments.
28 Arrivals by air at Conakry airport.
29 Arrivals to Timehri airport only.
30 Including tourists from Northern Ireland.
31 Excluding seasonal and border workers.
32 Air arrivals. Tarawa and Christmas Island.

Source:

Organisation mondiale du tourisme (OMT), Madrid, base de données statistiques de l'OMT, dernier accés janvier 2018.

La majorité des données sur les dépenses touristiques sont celles que le Fonds monétaire international (FMI) a fournies à l'Organisation mondiale du tourisme (OMT). & Série (par ordre de priorite, voir annexe II): TF: Arrivées de touristes non résidents aux frontières nationales. VF: Arrivées de visiteurs non résidents aux frontières nationales. TCE: Arrivées de touristes non résidents dans tous les types d'établissements d'hébergement touristique. THS: Arrivées de touristes non résidents dans les hôtels et établissements assimilés.

1 À l'exclusion des nationaux résidant à l'étranger.
2 Y compris les nationaux du pays résidant à l'étranger.
3 Non compris le transport de passagers.
4 Arrivées par voie aérienne.
5 À l'exclusion des nationaux du pays résidant à l'étranger et des membres des équipages.
6 Seulement logement payé; sont exclus les séjours chez des amis et membres de la famille et des résidences secondaires.
7 Exclut le segment de la frontière biélorusse-russe.
8 Tourisme organisé.
9 Comprend l'estimation du segment frontalier biélorusse-russe.
10 Y compris les touristes régionaux haut de gamme.
11 A l'exclusion des résidents des Antilles Néerlandaises.
12 Arrivées par voie aérienne à Bangui uniquement.
13 Pour la présentation des statistiques, les données pour la Chine ne comprennent pas la région administrative spéciale de Hong Kong (Hong Kong RAS), la région administrative spéciale de Macao (Macao RAS) et la province chinoise de Taïwan.
14 Arrivées à l'aéroport Félix Houphouët Boigny seulement.
15 À l'exclusion des arrivées dans des ports à tourisme nautique.
16 Statistiques frontaliers ne sont plus collectés, les enquêtes utilisées à la place.
17 Calculé sur la base des statistiques d'hébergement et de la « Foreign Visitor Survey » menée par la « Statistical Office of Estonia ». À partir de 2004, les statistiques de frontière ne sont plus collectées.
18 Basé sur les données de positionnement mobile.
19 Arrivées dans les hôtels uniquement.
20 Arrivées à l'aéroport de Bole uniquement.
21 Estimations à partir d'enquêtes aux frontières.
22 Arrivées de touristes non résidents.
23 Enquête au départ de l'aéroport de Cayenne-Rochambeau.
24 Arrivées de touristes non résidents à l'aéroport de Libreville.
25 Arrivées en vols à la demande seulement.
26 Les îles du Nord, Saint-Barthélemy et Saint-Martin (partie française) sont exclues.
27 Arrivées de touristes non résidents dans tous les types d'établissements d'hébergement touristique.
28 Arrivées par voie aérienne à l'aéroport de Conakry.
29 Arrivées à l'aéroport de Timehri seulement.
30 Y compris touristes à Irlande du Nord.
31 À l'exclusion des travailleurs saisonniers et frontaliers.
32 Arrivées par voie aérienne. Tarawa et île Christmas.

33 Non-resident departures. Survey of persons crossing the state border.
34 Excluding the Lebanon, Syria and Palestine nationalities.
35 Excluding long term tourists on campgrounds and in holiday flats.
36 Arrivals of non-resident tourists by air.
37 Departures.
38 Including Singapore residents crossing the frontier by road through Johore Causeway.
39 Departures by air and by sea.
40 Air and sea arrivals.
41 Arrivals in the States of Kosrae, Chuuk, Pohnpei and Yap; excluding FSM citizens.
42 Excluding diplomats and foreign residents in Mongolia.
43 The data correspond only to 12 border posts.
44 The data of all the border posts of the country are used.
45 Including arrivals from India.
46 Including Niueans residing usually in New Zealand.
47 Non-resident tourists staying in registered hotels.
48 Air arrivals (Palau International Airport).
49 Data refer to fiscal years ending 30 September.
50 Including tourists with identity document other than a passport.
51 Includes establishments with 10 or more bed places: hotels, apartment hotels, "pousadas", tourist apartments and tourist villages, as well as other accommodation establishments: boarding houses, motels and inns. Includes camping sites and recreation centres. Does not include tourism in rural areas neither local accommodation.
52 Data refer to fiscal years beginning 1 July.
53 Excluding the left side of the river Nistru and the municipality of Bender.
54 Including Italian tourists.
55 Arrivals by air. Including arrivals to Saint Martin (French part).
56 Non-resident tourists staying in commercial accommodation only (representing approximately 25% of all tourists).
57 Without first quarter.
58 Excluding arrivals for work and contract workers.
59 Excluding transit.
60 Data calculated by extrapolating the data of Turespaña until September to calculate the data for October, November and December. Since October 2015 this operation is carried out by the National Statistics Institute - INE.
61 West Bank and Gaza.
62 Arrivals at Zanderij Airport.
63 Including Iraqi nationals.
64 Arrivals by air at Dili Airport.
65 Turkish citizens resident abroad are included.
66 Arrivals in hotels only. Including domestic tourism and nationals of the country residing abroad.

33 Départs de non-résidents. Enquête menée auprès de personnes franchissant la frontière de l'État.
34 À l'exclusion des nationalités libanaise, syrienne et palestinienne.
35 À l'exclusion des touristes à long terme en camping ou dans des appartements de vacances.
36 Arrivées de touristes non résidents par voie aérienne.
37 Départs.
38 Y compris les résidents de Singapour traversant la frontière par voie terrestre à travers le Johore Causeway.
39 Départs par voies aérienne et maritime.
40 Arrivées par voie aérienne et maritime.
41 Arrivées dans les États de Kosrae, Chuuk, Pohnpei et Yap; non compris les citoyens FSM.
42 Sont exclus les diplomates et les étrangers qui résident en Mongolie.
43 les données ne couvrent que 12 postes frontière.
44 Les données de l'ensemble des postes frontières du pays sont utilisées.
45 Y compris les arrivées à Inde.
46 Y compris les nationaux de Nioué résidant habituellement en Nouvelle-Zélande.
47 Non résidents touristes dans les hôtels enregistrés.
48 Arrivées par voie aérienne (Aéroport international de Palaos).
49 Les données se réfèrent aux exercices budgétaires finissant le 30 septembre.
50 Nouvelle série estimée comprenant les touristes avec une pièce d'identité autre qu'un passeport.
51 Comprend les établissements avec 10 ou plus de places lits: hôtels, aparthôtels, "pousadas", appartements et villages pour touristes ainsi que d'autres établissements d'hébergement: pensions, motels et auberges. Comprend les terrains de camping et les centres de loisirs. N'inclut pas le tourisme dans les zones rurales ou l'hébergement local.
52 Les données se réfèrent aux exercices budgétaires commençant le 1er juillet.
53 La rive gauche de la rivière Nistru et la municipalité de Bender sont exclues.
54 Y compris les touristes italiens.
55 Arrivées par voie aérienne. Y compris les arrivées à Saint-Martin (partie française).
56 Les touristes non-résidents séjournant dans un logement commercial seulement (représentant environ 25% de tous les touristes).
57 Sans premier trimestre.
58 À l'exclusion des arrivées par travail et les travailleurs contractuels.
59 À l'exclusion des personnes en transit.
60 Données calculées en extrapolant les données de Turespaña jusqu'à septembre pour calculer les données d'octobre, novembre et décembre. À partir de 2015, cette opération est menée par l'Institut national de la statistique – INE.
61 Cisjordanie et Gaza.
62 Arrivées à l'aéroport de Zanderij.
63 Y compris les ressortissants iraquiens.
64 Arrivées par voie aérienne à l'aéroport de Dili.
65 Citoyens turcs résidant à l'étranger sont inclus.
66 Arrivées dans les hôtels uniquement. Y compris le tourisme interne et les nationaux résidant à l'étranger.

31 Net disbursements of official development assistance to recipients

Total, bilateral and multilateral aid (millions of US dollars); and as a percentage of Gross National Income (GNI)

Décaissements nets d'aide publique au développement aux bénéficiaires

Total, bilatérale et multilatérale d'aide (millions de dollars É.-U.); et en pourcentage du Revenu National Brut (RNB)

Region, country or area&	1975	1985	1995	2005	2010	2014	2015	2016	Région, pays ou zone&
Total, all countries or areas [1]									**Total, tous pays ou zones [1]**
Bilateral	**15 189**	**26 348**	**48 268**	**82 923**	**94 441**	**119 778**	**117 372**	**116 519**	**Bilatérale**
Multilateral	**3 597**	**5 920**	**11 004**	**25 620**	**37 133**	**41 952**	**35 368**	**40 493**	**Multilatérale**
Total	**18 785**	**32 268**	**59 272**	**108 542**	**131 574**	**161 730**	**152 740**	**157 011**	**Total**
% of GNI	**1.7**	**1.3**	**1.1**	**1.2**	**0.7**	**0.6**	**0.6**	**0.6**	**% du RNB**
Africa [1]									**Afrique [1]**
Bilateral	5 671	10 076	16 828	24 081	30 087	34 927	34 907	31 159	Bilatérale
Multilateral	1 105	2 247	5 015	11 740	17 732	19 156	16 137	18 794	Multilatérale
Total	6 775	12 323	21 843	35 821	47 820	54 083	51 044	49 954	Total
% of GNI	4.3	4.0	4.6	3.7	2.6	2.3	2.3	2.4	% du RNB
Northern Africa [1,2]									**Afrique septentrionale [1,2]**
Bilateral	3 062	2 849	2 703	1 705	1 844	5 552	3 712	3 585	Bilatérale
Multilateral	179	142	277	980	823	1 774	1 294	1 783	Multilatérale
Total	3 241	2 991	2 981	2 685	2 667	7 326	5 006	5 368	Total
% of GNI	8.2	2.7	1.9	0.8	0.5	1.1	0.8	0.9	% du RNB
Sub-Saharan Africa [1,3]									**Afrique subsaharienne [1,3]**
Bilateral	2 557	7 017	13 771	21 889	27 172	27 649	28 445	25 928	Bilatérale
Multilateral	926	1 968	4 594	10 532	16 425	16 614	14 268	15 880	Multilatérale
Total	3 483	8 985	18 365	32 420	43 597	44 262	42 714	41 808	Total
% of GNI	3.0	4.5	5.8	5.1	3.4	2.6	2.8	2.9	% du RNB
Americas [1]									**Amériques [1]**
Bilateral	777	3 015	5 484	4 559	8 143	7 856	8 179	8 941	Bilatérale
Multilateral	597	398	935	2 106	2 854	2 140	2 027	2 342	Multilatérale
Total	1 375	3 413	6 418	6 665	10 997	9 995	10 206	11 283	Total
% of GNI	0.4	0.5	0.4	0.3	0.2	0.2	0.2	0.3	% du RNB
North America [1]									**Amérique du Nord [1]**
Bilateral	254	1 989	2 988	2 285	4 974	3 195	3 652	5 675	Bilatérale
Multilateral	280	203	513	1 011	1 886	1 249	916	1 210	Multilatérale
Total	534	2 193	3 501	3 296	6 860	4 445	4 567	6 885	Total
% of GNI	0.4	0.9	0.8	0.3	0.5	0.3	0.3	0.5	% du RNB
South America [1]									**Amérique du Sud [1]**
Bilateral	435	903	2 268	2 038	1 942	3 542	3 393	2 790	Bilatérale
Multilateral	317	150	344	792	858	699	928	1 003	Multilatérale
Total	752	1 052	2 612	2 829	2 800	4 241	4 321	3 793	Total
% of GNI	0.3	0.2	0.2	0.2	0.1	0.1	0.1	0.1	% du RNB
Asia [1]									**Asie [1]**
Bilateral	6 393	9 033	14 201	39 027	26 898	41 953	35 682	32 778	Bilatérale
Multilateral	1 813	2 747	4 415	7 579	9 896	11 847	9 737	10 735	Multilatérale
Total	8 206	11 780	18 616	46 606	36 794	53 800	45 419	43 513	Total
% of GNI	1.5	0.9	0.6	1.0	0.3	0.3	0.3	0.3	% du RNB
Eastern and South-Eastern Asia [1,4]									**Asie orientale et du Sud-Est [1,4]**
Bilateral	1 495	2 448	7 387	6 613	5 019	3 479	3 496	2 571	Bilatérale
Multilateral	371	498	1 411	1 779	2 515	2 742	1 901	1 915	Multilatérale
Total	1 866	2 946	8 798	8 391	7 534	6 221	5 397	4 486	Total
% of GNI	0.7	0.5	0.4	0.3	0.1	0.1	~0.0	~0.0	% du RNB
South-central Asia [1,5]									**Asie centrale et du Sud [1,5]**
Bilateral	2 457	2 678	4 049	7 262	13 215	12 600	13 525	11 072	Bilatérale
Multilateral	1 308	1 998	2 409	4 395	5 499	7 184	6 155	6 915	Multilatérale
Total	3 765	4 676	6 458	11 658	18 713	19 783	19 680	17 987	Total
% of GNI	2.8	1.6	1.3	1.0	0.8	0.7	0.6	0.6	% du RNB
Western Asia [1,6]									**Asie occidentale [1,6]**
Bilateral	2 407	3 856	2 449	24 324	7 766	23 282	17 587	18 429	Bilatérale
Multilateral	134	181	504	1 182	1 709	1 738	1 530	1 715	Multilatérale
Total	2 541	4 037	2 954	25 506	9 475	25 020	19 117	20 144	Total
% of GNI	1.9	0.9	0.7	3.6	1.2	3.2	6.1	6.8	% du RNB
Europe [1,7]									**Europe [1,7]**
Bilateral	96	383	1 753	2 446	3 123	3 661	2 783	3 420	Bilatérale
Multilateral	58	28	534	1 605	2 787	4 880	4 002	4 802	Multilatérale
Total	154	410	2 288	4 051	5 910	8 541	6 784	8 222	Total
% of GNI	0.3	0.6	1.0	0.6	0.5	0.7	0.6	0.8	% du RNB

31

Net disbursements of official development assistance to recipients *(continued)*
Total, bilateral and multilateral aid (millions of US dollars); and as a percentage of Gross National Income (GNI)

Décaissements nets d'aide publique au développement aux bénéficiaires *(suite)*
Total, bilatérale et multilatérale d'aide (millions de dollars É.-U.); et en pourcentage du Revenu National Brut (RNB)

Region, country or area&	1975	1985	1995	2005	2010	2014	2015	2016	Région, pays ou zone&
Oceania [1]									**Océanie** [1]
Bilateral	589	859	1 807	803	1 619	1 609	1 624	1 229	Bilatérale
Multilateral	24	38	62	341	269	281	295	454	Multilatérale
Total	613	897	1 868	1 144	1 888	1 890	1 919	1 683	Total
% of GNI	17.1	14.5	12.3	11.6	12.3	7.5	24.2	20.8	% du RNB
Areas not specified									**Zones non spécifiées**
Bilateral	...	2 982	8 196	12 007	24 571	29 773	34 197	38 992	Bilatérale
Multilateral	...	462	42	2 248	3 595	3 647	3 171	3 365	Multilatérale
Total	1 662	3 445	8 238	14 254	28 166	33 420	37 368	42 357	Total
Afghanistan									**Afghanistan**
Bilateral	41	7	129	2 296	5 757	4 378	3 871	3 500	Bilatérale
Multilateral	29	9	84	542	713	565	366	564	Multilatérale
Total	69	16	213	2 838	6 470	4 943	4 237	4 064	Total
% of GNI	2.9	...	...	45.2	40.4	24.4	21.3	20.6	% du RNB
Albania									**Albanie**
Bilateral	...	...	118	192	253	167	232	86	Bilatérale
Multilateral	...	...	63	123	112	114	102	82	Multilatérale
Total	...	...	181	315	365	281	334	169	Total
% of GNI	...	...	7.3	3.8	3.1	2.2	3.0	1.4	% du RNB
Algeria									**Algérie**
Bilateral	213	161	272	252	131	103	36	103	Bilatérale
Multilateral	23	11	24	96	71	58	51	54	Multilatérale
Total	235	172	296	347	201	161	87	157	Total
% of GNI	1.5	0.3	0.8	0.4	0.1	0.1	0.1	0.1	% du RNB
Angola									**Angola**
Bilateral	4	72	304	217	146	100	276	63	Bilatérale
Multilateral	1	19	113	198	89	135	104	144	Multilatérale
Total	5	90	416	415	235	235	380	207	Total
% of GNI	...	1.4	11.3	1.7	0.3	0.2	0.4	0.2	% du RNB
Anguilla									**Anguilla**
Bilateral	2	2	3	4	-1	...	...	...	Bilatérale
Multilateral	~0	1	1	~0	9	...	...	...	Multilatérale
Total	2	3	3	4	8	...	...	...	Total
Antigua and Barbuda									**Antigua-et-Barbuda**
Bilateral	2	2	2	7	6	1	1	-2	Bilatérale
Multilateral	1	1	~0	1	14	2	1	2	Multilatérale
Total	2	3	2	8	20	3	1	~0	Total
% of GNI	...	1.2	0.4	0.8	1.8	0.2	0.1	0.0	% du RNB
Argentina									**Argentine**
Bilateral	3	30	126	62	99	12	-45	-200	Bilatérale
Multilateral	23	9	17	32	30	37	26	203	Multilatérale
Total	26	39	143	94	129	49	-19	3	Total
% of GNI	0.1	0.1	0.1	0.1	~0.0	~0.0	0.0	0.0	% du RNB
Armenia									**Arménie**
Bilateral	...	...	111	105	232	130	174	144	Bilatérale
Multilateral	...	...	107	67	111	137	173	183	Multilatérale
Total	...	...	218	173	343	267	347	327	Total
% of GNI	...	...	14.9	3.4	3.5	2.2	3.2	3.0	% du RNB
Aruba									**Aruba**
Bilateral	...	...	23	...	...	...	...	...	Bilatérale
Multilateral	...	...	3	...	...	...	...	...	Multilatérale
Total	...	12	26	...	...	...	...	...	Total
Azerbaijan									**Azerbaïdjan**
Bilateral	...	...	67	119	82	133	23	34	Bilatérale
Multilateral	...	...	53	91	80	83	47	44	Multilatérale
Total	...	...	120	211	162	217	70	78	Total
% of GNI	...	...	3.9	1.8	0.3	0.3	0.1	0.2	% du RNB
Bahamas									**Bahamas**
Bilateral	~0	~0	3	...	...	...	...	...	Bilatérale
Multilateral	1	1	2	...	...	...	...	...	Multilatérale
Total	1	1	4	...	...	...	...	...	Total
% of GNI	0.1	~0.0	0.1	...	...	...	...	...	% du RNB

31

Net disbursements of official development assistance to recipients *(continued)*
Total, bilateral and multilateral aid (millions of US dollars); and as a percentage of Gross National Income (GNI)

Décaissements nets d'aide publique au développement aux bénéficiaires *(suite)*
Total, bilatérale et multilatérale d'aide (millions de dollars É.-U.); et en pourcentage du Revenu National Brut (RNB)

Region, country or area&	1975	1985	1995	2005	2010	2014	2015	2016	Région, pays ou zone&
Bahrain									**Bahreïn**
Bilateral	25	73	100	...	...	...	...	...	Bilatérale
Multilateral	1	1	~0	...	...	...	...	...	Multilatérale
Total	26	74	100	...	...	...	...	...	Total
% of GNI	...	2.2	1.7	...	...	...	...	...	% du RNB
Bangladesh									**Bangladesh**
Bilateral	777	619	907	590	582	1 346	1 606	1 371	Bilatérale
Multilateral	295	508	375	731	822	1 077	964	1 133	Multilatérale
Total	1 072	1 127	1 282	1 320	1 405	2 423	2 570	2 503	Total
% of GNI	5.5	5.0	3.3	1.8	1.1	1.3	1.2	1.1	% du RNB
Barbados									**Barbade**
Bilateral	3	6	-2	-5	-1	...	...	...	Bilatérale
Multilateral	3	1	1	3	18	...	...	...	Multilatérale
Total	5	7	-1	-2	16	...	...	...	Total
% of GNI	...	0.5	-0.1	-0.1	0.4	...	...	...	% du RNB
Belarus									**Bélarus**
Bilateral	...	...	...	40	94	78	71	-66	Bilatérale
Multilateral	...	...	...	18	42	43	34	43	Multilatérale
Total	...	...	...	58	136	121	105	-22	Total
% of GNI	...	...	...	0.2	0.2	0.2	0.2	-0.1	% du RNB
Belize									**Belize**
Bilateral	8	21	12	6	9	12	11	6	Bilatérale
Multilateral	1	1	7	6	16	25	17	29	Multilatérale
Total	9	22	19	12	25	38	28	35	Total
% of GNI	8.2	11.0	3.2	1.2	2.0	2.4	1.7	2.1	% du RNB
Benin									**Bénin**
Bilateral	36	62	229	175	388	311	250	244	Bilatérale
Multilateral	18	32	52	174	301	289	180	249	Multilatérale
Total	54	94	281	349	689	599	430	493	Total
% of GNI	8.0	9.2	13.2	7.3	10.0	6.2	5.2	5.7	% du RNB
Bermuda									**Bermudes**
Bilateral	...	1	-2	...	...	...	...	...	Bilatérale
Multilateral	...	~0	0	...	...	...	...	...	Multilatérale
Total	~0	1	-2	...	...	...	...	...	Total
% of GNI	~0.0	0.1	-0.1	...	...	...	...	...	% du RNB
Bhutan									**Bhoutan**
Bilateral	~0	9	64	52	87	67	59	32	Bilatérale
Multilateral	2	14	10	38	44	63	38	20	Multilatérale
Total	2	23	73	90	131	131	97	52	Total
% of GNI	...	17.0	27.5	11.2	8.8	7.2	5.2	2.5	% du RNB
Bolivia (Plurin. State of)									**Bolivie (État plurin. de)**
Bilateral	27	166	559	486	569	562	589	524	Bilatérale
Multilateral	29	30	153	157	148	113	203	173	Multilatérale
Total	56	196	712	643	718	675	791	696	Total
% of GNI	2.2	4.0	11.0	7.0	3.8	2.2	2.5	2.1	% du RNB
Bosnia and Herzegovina									**Bosnie-Herzégovine**
Bilateral	...	...	900	309	290	278	119	196	Bilatérale
Multilateral	...	...	66	231	222	352	236	249	Multilatérale
Total	...	...	966	540	511	630	355	445	Total
% of GNI	...	...	59.4	4.6	2.9	3.4	2.2	2.7	% du RNB
Botswana									**Botswana**
Bilateral	39	71	71	8	95	51	41	65	Bilatérale
Multilateral	12	24	19	40	60	49	24	25	Multilatérale
Total	51	96	90	48	155	99	66	91	Total
% of GNI	14.4	9.4	1.9	0.5	1.3	0.6	0.5	0.6	% du RNB
Brazil									**Brésil**
Bilateral	101	91	245	88	361	832	719	572	Bilatérale
Multilateral	66	31	34	104	88	82	284	103	Multilatérale
Total	166	122	279	193	449	914	1 003	675	Total
% of GNI	0.1	0.1	~0.0	~0.0	~0.0	~0.0	0.1	~0.0	% du RNB
British Virgin Islands									**Îles Vierges britanniques**
Bilateral	2	2	~0	...	...	...	...	...	Bilatérale
Multilateral	~0	~0	1	...	...	...	...	...	Multilatérale
Total	2	2	1	...	...	...	...	...	Total

31

Net disbursements of official development assistance to recipients *(continued)*
Total, bilateral and multilateral aid (millions of US dollars); and as a percentage of Gross National Income (GNI)

Décaissements nets d'aide publique au développement aux bénéficiaires *(suite)*
Total, bilatérale et multilatérale d'aide (millions de dollars É.-U.); et en pourcentage du Revenu National Brut (RNB)

Region, country or area&	1975	1985	1995	2005	2010	2014	2015	2016	Région, pays ou zone&
Brunei Darussalam									**Brunéi Darussalam**
Bilateral	~0	1	4	...	...	...	...	...	Bilatérale
Multilateral	0	~0	~0	...	...	...	...	...	Multilatérale
Total	~0	1	4	...	...	...	...	...	Total
% of GNI	...	...	0.1	...	...	...	...	...	% du RNB
Burkina Faso									**Burkina Faso**
Bilateral	62	134	350	382	554	676	526	485	Bilatérale
Multilateral	27	54	140	316	491	448	471	538	Multilatérale
Total	89	188	490	698	1 045	1 123	997	1 023	Total
% of GNI	9.5	12.2	20.7	12.8	11.4	9.4	9.2	8.7	% du RNB
Burundi									**Burundi**
Bilateral	33	91	147	163	279	263	185	560	Bilatérale
Multilateral	15	46	140	202	349	252	181	183	Multilatérale
Total	47	137	287	366	628	515	367	742	Total
% of GNI	11.5	12.1	29.0	33.2	31.2	16.7	11.9	24.8	% du RNB
Cabo Verde									**Cabo Verde**
Bilateral	4	42	91	112	248	183	111	75	Bilatérale
Multilateral	5	22	25	51	79	48	42	38	Multilatérale
Total	9	64	116	163	327	231	153	113	Total
% of GNI	...	48.0	23.9	17.4	20.6	13.1	10.1	7.4	% du RNB
Cambodia									**Cambodge**
Bilateral	78	9	434	374	524	559	522	552	Bilatérale
Multilateral	4	5	117	165	210	243	157	177	Multilatérale
Total	82	14	551	539	734	803	679	728	Total
% of GNI	...	...	16.3	9.0	6.8	5.1	4.0	3.9	% du RNB
Cameroon									**Cameroun**
Bilateral	72	134	380	279	303	515	433	489	Bilatérale
Multilateral	37	18	64	138	237	342	230	267	Multilatérale
Total	110	152	444	417	540	856	663	756	Total
% of GNI	4.5	1.9	5.4	2.6	2.3	2.7	2.4	3.2	% du RNB
Cayman Islands									**Îles Caïmanes**
Bilateral	1	-~0	-1	...	...	...	...	...	Bilatérale
Multilateral	1	~0	~0	...	...	...	...	...	Multilatérale
Total	2	~0	-1	...	...	...	...	...	Total
Central African Republic									**République centrafricaine**
Bilateral	39	73	126	37	78	290	295	261	Bilatérale
Multilateral	16	31	42	52	183	321	192	239	Multilatérale
Total	55	104	168	89	261	611	487	500	Total
% of GNI	14.5	12.1	15.3	6.6	13.1	35.7	30.6	28.4	% du RNB
Chad									**Tchad**
Bilateral	33	118	165	166	275	168	1	276	Bilatérale
Multilateral	34	61	70	221	215	224	606	348	Multilatérale
Total	67	179	235	386	490	392	607	624	Total
% of GNI	7.7	17.4	16.3	6.9	4.8	2.9	5.8	6.6	% du RNB
Chile									**Chili**
Bilateral	96	37	147	88	145	199	36	163	Bilatérale
Multilateral	31	3	9	83	44	47	18	16	Multilatérale
Total	127	40	157	170	189	246	54	178	Total
% of GNI	1.7	0.3	0.2	0.2	0.1	0.1	~0.0	0.1	% du RNB
China [8]									**Chine** [8]
Bilateral	...	697	2 560	1 471	344	-1 242	-584	-981	Bilatérale
Multilateral	...	242	921	329	327	295	252	190	Multilatérale
Total	...	939	3 481	1 799	672	-947	-332	-791	Total
% of GNI	...	0.3	0.5	0.1	~0.0	-~0.0	0.0	-~0.0	% du RNB
China, Hong Kong SAR									**Chine, RAS de Hong Kong**
Bilateral	-1	18	14	...	...	...	...	...	Bilatérale
Multilateral	~0	2	4	...	...	...	...	...	Multilatérale
Total	-1	20	18	...	...	...	...	...	Total
% of GNI	-~0.0	0.1	~0.0	...	...	...	...	...	% du RNB
China, Macao SAR									**Chine, RAS de Macao**
Bilateral	~0	~0	-4	...	...	...	...	...	Bilatérale
Multilateral	0	~0	0	...	...	...	...	...	Multilatérale
Total	~0	~0	-4	...	...	...	...	...	Total
% of GNI	...	~0.0	-0.1	...	...	...	...	...	% du RNB

31 Net disbursements of official development assistance to recipients *(continued)*
Total, bilateral and multilateral aid (millions of US dollars); and as a percentage of Gross National Income (GNI)

Décaissements nets d'aide publique au développement aux bénéficiaires *(suite)*
Total, bilatérale et multilatérale d'aide (millions de dollars É.-U.); et en pourcentage du Revenu National Brut (RNB)

Region, country or area&	1975	1985	1995	2005	2010	2014	2015	2016	Région, pays ou zone&
Colombia									**Colombie**
Bilateral	51	45	158	542	576	1 113	1 275	1 003	Bilatérale
Multilateral	32	17	12	83	98	111	81	103	Multilatérale
Total	83	61	170	625	674	1 224	1 356	1 107	Total
% of GNI	0.7	0.2	0.2	0.4	0.2	0.3	0.5	0.4	% du RNB
Comoros									**Comores**
Bilateral	19	32	27	5	23	26	30	21	Bilatérale
Multilateral	2	15	15	18	47	49	36	33	Multilatérale
Total	22	47	42	23	70	75	66	54	Total
% of GNI	35.9	41.7	17.9	6.1	13.2	11.6	11.5	8.7	% du RNB
Congo									**Congo**
Bilateral	43	55	117	1 350	1 048	47	38	35	Bilatérale
Multilateral	13	14	10	76	267	59	51	53	Multilatérale
Total	56	69	127	1 426	1 315	106	89	88	Total
% of GNI	7.6	3.4	10.3	35.4	14.6	0.9	1.1	1.2	% du RNB
Cook Islands									**Îles Cook**
Bilateral	5	9	12	7	13	25	22	-9	Bilatérale
Multilateral	~0	1	1	1	1	4	4	27	Multilatérale
Total	6	10	13	8	14	28	26	17	Total
Costa Rica									**Costa Rica**
Bilateral	16	265	19	13	79	21	87	74	Bilatérale
Multilateral	14	14	13	13	16	33	25	27	Multilatérale
Total	30	279	32	26	95	55	111	101	Total
% of GNI	1.6	6.2	0.3	0.1	0.3	0.1	0.2	0.2	% du RNB
Côte d'Ivoire									**Côte d'Ivoire**
Bilateral	82	110	949	16	478	417	302	246	Bilatérale
Multilateral	18	7	264	75	368	508	351	413	Multilatérale
Total	100	117	1 212	91	845	925	653	658	Total
% of GNI	2.7	1.9	12.1	0.6	3.5	2.7	2.1	1.9	% du RNB
Croatia									**Croatie**
Bilateral	...	...	48	58	11	...	...	...	Bilatérale
Multilateral	...	...	5	65	121	...	...	...	Multilatérale
Total	...	...	53	123	132	...	...	...	Total
% of GNI	...	...	0.2	0.3	0.2	...	...	...	% du RNB
Cuba									**Cuba**
Bilateral	11	31	46	67	82	229	527	2 650	Bilatérale
Multilateral	9	11	17	23	51	33	25	28	Multilatérale
Total	20	42	64	90	132	262	553	2 678	Total
% of GNI	0.2	0.2	0.2	0.2	0.2	...	...	...	% du RNB
Cyprus									**Chypre**
Bilateral	18	31	15	...	...	...	...	...	Bilatérale
Multilateral	13	6	7	...	...	...	...	...	Multilatérale
Total	31	37	21	...	...	...	...	...	Total
% of GNI	6.3	1.5	0.2	...	...	...	...	...	% du RNB
Dem. People's Rep. Korea									**Rép. pop. dém. de Corée**
Bilateral	...	...	3	33	28	109	104	86	Bilatérale
Multilateral	...	...	11	54	50	45	27	34	Multilatérale
Total	...	6	13	87	79	154	131	120	Total
Dem. Rep. of the Congo									**Rép. dém. du Congo**
Bilateral	219	223	136	1 094	1 042	1 315	1 663	1 063	Bilatérale
Multilateral	39	83	59	788	2 442	1 085	936	1 044	Multilatérale
Total	258	305	195	1 882	3 484	2 400	2 599	2 107	Total
% of GNI	2.5	4.5	4.0	16.4	17.8	7.8	7.8	6.6	% du RNB
Djibouti									**Djibouti**
Bilateral	34	71	94	46	105	114	136	141	Bilatérale
Multilateral	~0	11	12	29	27	52	33	44	Multilatérale
Total	34	81	106	74	132	166	170	185	Total
% of GNI	...	...	20.5	9.6	...	...	...	...	% du RNB
Dominica									**Dominique**
Bilateral	6	13	18	13	3	10	4	-2	Bilatérale
Multilateral	2	4	7	8	30	6	8	11	Multilatérale
Total	8	17	25	21	32	16	12	9	Total
% of GNI	...	17.8	11.9	6.2	6.7	3.2	2.3	1.7	% du RNB

31 Net disbursements of official development assistance to recipients *(continued)*

Total, bilateral and multilateral aid (millions of US dollars); and as a percentage of Gross National Income (GNI)

Décaissements nets d'aide publique au développement aux bénéficiaires *(suite)*

Total, bilatérale et multilatérale d'aide (millions de dollars É.-U.); et en pourcentage du Revenu National Brut (RNB)

Region, country or area&	1975	1985	1995	2005	2010	2014	2015	2016	Région, pays ou zone&
Dominican Republic									**République dominicaine**
Bilateral	13	195	107	9	60	92	241	125	Bilatérale
Multilateral	17	12	13	67	116	74	39	51	Multilatérale
Total	30	207	120	76	177	166	280	177	Total
% of GNI	0.8	4.4	0.8	0.2	0.3	0.3	0.4	0.3	% du RNB
Ecuador									**Équateur**
Bilateral	21	116	197	159	102	122	172	126	Bilatérale
Multilateral	49	19	27	74	49	43	146	118	Multilatérale
Total	69	135	224	232	151	165	318	244	Total
% of GNI	0.9	0.8	1.0	0.6	0.2	0.2	0.3	0.3	% du RNB
Egypt									**Égypte**
Bilateral	2 413	1 692	1 873	730	412	3 224	2 316	1 728	Bilatérale
Multilateral	100	82	155	316	187	314	184	403	Multilatérale
Total	2 513	1 774	2 028	1 046	599	3 538	2 499	2 130	Total
% of GNI	22.5	5.7	3.4	1.2	0.3	1.2	0.8	0.6	% du RNB
El Salvador									**El Salvador**
Bilateral	4	327	277	127	203	72	66	72	Bilatérale
Multilateral	34	18	19	72	78	26	24	57	Multilatérale
Total	37	345	296	199	282	98	90	129	Total
% of GNI	2.0	9.4	3.2	1.2	1.4	0.4	0.4	0.5	% du RNB
Equatorial Guinea									**Guinée équatoriale**
Bilateral	1	9	23	18	75	-3	3	3	Bilatérale
Multilateral	1	8	10	20	10	4	5	4	Multilatérale
Total	2	17	33	38	85	1	7	7	Total
% of GNI	2.1	29.5	28.3	0.9	0.9	0.0	0.1	0.1	% du RNB
Eritrea									**Érythrée**
Bilateral	...	...	119	229	49	2	54	16	Bilatérale
Multilateral	...	...	29	121	114	83	40	51	Multilatérale
Total	2	...	148	350	162	84	94	67	Total
% of GNI	...	...	25.3	32.1	7.7	...	...	...	% du RNB
Eswatini									**Eswatini**
Bilateral	5	18	49	-1	21	42	42	77	Bilatérale
Multilateral	10	6	9	47	70	44	51	70	Multilatérale
Total	14	24	58	47	91	86	93	147	Total
% of GNI	...	...	3.2	1.4	2.2	2.0	2.4	4.1	% du RNB
Ethiopia									**Éthiopie**
Bilateral	73	541	653	1 205	2 223	2 193	2 238	2 492	Bilatérale
Multilateral	59	177	224	724	1 232	1 391	996	1 582	Multilatérale
Total	132	718	877	1 929	3 455	3 584	3 234	4 074	Total
% of GNI	...	7.6	11.5	15.6	11.6	6.5	5.0	5.7	% du RNB
Fiji									**Fidji**
Bilateral	18	28	41	32	56	75	73	95	Bilatérale
Multilateral	2	3	4	34	19	19	30	23	Multilatérale
Total	19	32	44	66	76	94	102	117	Total
% of GNI	2.9	2.8	2.3	2.2	2.5	2.2	2.5	2.7	% du RNB
French Polynesia									**Polynésie française**
Bilateral	71	171	448	...	...	...	...	...	Bilatérale
Multilateral	~0	1	3	...	...	...	...	...	Multilatérale
Total	72	172	451	...	...	...	...	...	Total
% of GNI	10.4	11.4	11.3	...	...	...	...	...	% du RNB
Gabon									**Gabon**
Bilateral	58	55	140	1	82	92	81	22	Bilatérale
Multilateral	3	6	4	50	24	19	17	19	Multilatérale
Total	60	61	144	50	106	111	99	42	Total
% of GNI	3.0	2.0	3.4	0.6	0.9	0.7	0.8	0.3	% du RNB
Gambia									**Gambie**
Bilateral	4	33	25	7	52	29	69	7	Bilatérale
Multilateral	4	15	20	53	70	71	39	85	Multilatérale
Total	8	48	45	61	121	100	108	92	Total
% of GNI	7.0	19.1	5.9	10.3	12.8	12.2	11.8	9.8	% du RNB
Georgia									**Géorgie**
Bilateral	...	...	104	183	357	308	255	210	Bilatérale
Multilateral	...	...	106	110	270	255	194	252	Multilatérale
Total	...	...	209	293	627	564	449	463	Total
% of GNI	...	...	8.1	4.5	5.6	3.5	3.3	3.4	% du RNB

31

Net disbursements of official development assistance to recipients *(continued)*
Total, bilateral and multilateral aid (millions of US dollars); and as a percentage of Gross National Income (GNI)

Décaissements nets d'aide publique au développement aux bénéficiaires *(suite)*
Total, bilatérale et multilatérale d'aide (millions de dollars É.-U.); et en pourcentage du Revenu National Brut (RNB)

Region, country or area&	1975	1985	1995	2005	2010	2014	2015	2016	Région, pays ou zone&
Ghana									**Ghana**
Bilateral	99	105	362	660	1 132	641	1 023	714	Bilatérale
Multilateral	25	89	288	493	565	482	746	603	Multilatérale
Total	124	194	650	1 153	1 697	1 123	1 769	1 316	Total
% of GNI	4.5	4.4	10.3	10.9	5.4	3.0	4.9	3.2	% du RNB
Gibraltar									**Gibraltar**
Bilateral	...	...	~0	...	...	...	...	...	Bilatérale
Multilateral	...	...	0	...	...	...	...	...	Multilatérale
Total	3	29	~0	...	...	...	...	...	Total
Grenada									**Grenade**
Bilateral	2	32	8	33	10	14	7	-4	Bilatérale
Multilateral	1	2	3	20	24	26	17	13	Multilatérale
Total	3	34	11	53	34	40	24	9	Total
% of GNI	...	21.2	3.3	7.9	4.6	4.5	2.5	0.9	% du RNB
Guatemala									**Guatemala**
Bilateral	25	71	181	189	322	188	331	199	Bilatérale
Multilateral	15	12	27	65	67	92	80	67	Multilatérale
Total	40	83	208	254	389	280	411	265	Total
% of GNI	1.1	0.9	1.4	1.0	1.0	0.5	0.7	0.4	% du RNB
Guinea									**Guinée**
Bilateral	20	74	305	89	47	238	246	243	Bilatérale
Multilateral	4	39	111	104	174	325	292	319	Multilatérale
Total	24	113	416	193	221	563	538	561	Total
% of GNI	...	...	11.5	7.3	5.1	9.2	8.6	9.7	% du RNB
Guinea-Bissau									**Guinée-Bissau**
Bilateral	17	34	95	8	-32	16	29	132	Bilatérale
Multilateral	4	22	23	59	161	94	66	67	Multilatérale
Total	21	56	118	67	129	110	95	199	Total
% of GNI	18.7	35.3	49.8	11.6	15.3	10.0	9.0	17.8	% du RNB
Guyana									**Guyana**
Bilateral	7	21	59	80	106	125	12	15	Bilatérale
Multilateral	3	6	27	70	62	36	20	55	Multilatérale
Total	10	27	86	150	167	161	32	70	Total
% of GNI	2.1	7.0	15.2	19.3	7.4	5.2	1.0	2.0	% du RNB
Haiti									**Haïti**
Bilateral	18	120	603	260	2 373	811	837	831	Bilatérale
Multilateral	38	29	120	165	700	272	209	244	Multilatérale
Total	56	149	722	426	3 073	1 082	1 046	1 075	Total
% of GNI	...	...	...	10.0	46.3	12.3	11.9	13.3	% du RNB
Honduras									**Honduras**
Bilateral	24	245	301	509	436	457	412	307	Bilatérale
Multilateral	26	25	101	183	198	149	128	105	Multilatérale
Total	51	270	402	692	634	606	541	412	Total
% of GNI	4.6	7.8	11.0	7.5	4.2	3.3	2.8	2.1	% du RNB
India									**Inde**
Bilateral	879	844	876	669	1 639	1 118	1 801	935	Bilatérale
Multilateral	726	743	862	1 207	1 192	1 874	1 373	1 743	Multilatérale
Total	1 605	1 587	1 738	1 876	2 831	2 992	3 174	2 679	Total
% of GNI	1.7	0.7	0.5	0.2	0.2	0.2	0.2	0.1	% du RNB
Indonesia									**Indonésie**
Bilateral	455	514	1 252	2 255	967	-569	-167	-288	Bilatérale
Multilateral	232	83	50	281	423	187	133	178	Multilatérale
Total	687	597	1 303	2 537	1 390	-382	-33	-111	Total
% of GNI	2.4	0.7	0.7	0.9	0.2	-~0.0	0.0	-~0.0	% du RNB
Iran (Islamic Republic of)									**Iran (Rép. islamique d')**
Bilateral	-12	2	162	61	72	48	91	79	Bilatérale
Multilateral	13	9	25	40	40	33	19	37	Multilatérale
Total	2	11	187	101	112	81	111	116	Total
% of GNI	0.0	~0.0	0.2	0.1	~0.0	~0.0	...	...	% du RNB
Iraq									**Iraq**
Bilateral	101	19	273	21 999	2 040	1 232	1 347	2 104	Bilatérale
Multilateral	9	1	60	58	138	137	136	182	Multilatérale
Total	110	20	333	22 057	2 178	1 369	1 483	2 287	Total
% of GNI	...	~0.0	...	43.5	1.6	0.6	0.8	1.3	% du RNB

31

Net disbursements of official development assistance to recipients *(continued)*

Total, bilateral and multilateral aid (millions of US dollars); and as a percentage of Gross National Income (GNI)

Décaissements nets d'aide publique au développement aux bénéficiaires *(suite)*

Total, bilatérale et multilatérale d'aide (millions de dollars É.-U.); et en pourcentage du Revenu National Brut (RNB)

Region, country or area&	1975	1985	1995	2005	2010	2014	2015	2016	Région, pays ou zone&
Israel									**Israël**
Bilateral	466	1 978	334	...	...	...	...	...	Bilatérale
Multilateral	2	~0	2	...	...	...	...	...	Multilatérale
Total	467	1 978	336	...	...	...	...	...	Total
% of GNI	3.7	8.5	0.4	...	...	...	...	...	% du RNB
Jamaica									**Jamaïque**
Bilateral	16	161	82	-9	-10	27	15	-17	Bilatérale
Multilateral	9	7	27	48	150	69	44	44	Multilatérale
Total	24	169	109	40	139	96	59	27	Total
% of GNI	0.8	9.2	2.0	0.4	1.1	0.7	0.4	0.2	% du RNB
Jordan									**Jordanie**
Bilateral	471	598	462	593	692	2 450	1 911	2 426	Bilatérale
Multilateral	21	9	78	117	263	247	241	313	Multilatérale
Total	492	607	540	710	955	2 697	2 152	2 739	Total
% of GNI	35.0	12.4	8.4	5.5	3.6	7.6	5.8	7.1	% du RNB
Kazakhstan									**Kazakhstan**
Bilateral	...	...	54	194	140	51	6	27	Bilatérale
Multilateral	...	...	11	31	72	42	77	33	Multilatérale
Total	...	...	65	225	212	93	83	60	Total
% of GNI	...	...	0.3	0.4	0.2	0.1	0.1	0.1	% du RNB
Kenya									**Kenya**
Bilateral	99	366	506	475	1 163	1 549	1 655	1 379	Bilatérale
Multilateral	26	61	227	281	468	1 112	809	809	Multilatérale
Total	125	427	733	757	1 631	2 661	2 464	2 189	Total
% of GNI	3.9	7.2	8.4	4.0	4.1	4.4	3.9	3.1	% du RNB
Kiribati									**Kiribati**
Bilateral	6	11	14	20	21	61	50	49	Bilatérale
Multilateral	~0	1	2	8	2	20	15	12	Multilatérale
Total	6	12	15	28	23	81	65	61	Total
% of GNI	...	38.8	16.9	17.5	10.5	23.5	19.2	23.2	% du RNB
Kosovo									**Kosovo**
Bilateral	...	...	...	...	215	360	251	236	Bilatérale
Multilateral	...	...	...	0	312	219	186	134	Multilatérale
Total	...	...	...	...	528	579	438	370	Total
% of GNI	...	...	...	...	8.9	7.7	6.7	5.5	% du RNB
Kuwait									**Koweït**
Bilateral	-2	3	4	...	...	...	...	...	Bilatérale
Multilateral	2	1	~0	...	...	...	...	...	Multilatérale
Total	~0	4	4	...	...	...	...	...	Total
% of GNI	0.0	~0.0	~0.0	...	...	...	...	...	% du RNB
Kyrgyzstan									**Kirghizistan**
Bilateral	...	...	191	176	257	457	598	311	Bilatérale
Multilateral	...	...	94	91	127	170	172	205	Multilatérale
Total	...	...	285	267	384	627	770	515	Total
% of GNI	...	...	17.5	11.3	8.6	8.8	12.0	8.2	% du RNB
Lao People's Dem. Rep.									**Rép. dém. populaire lao**
Bilateral	26	19	253	161	285	349	394	283	Bilatérale
Multilateral	13	21	55	137	128	126	77	117	Multilatérale
Total	38	40	308	297	413	474	471	399	Total
% of GNI	...	1.7	17.5	11.1	6.2	3.7	3.4	2.6	% du RNB
Lebanon									**Liban**
Bilateral	7	65	147	142	319	584	788	970	Bilatérale
Multilateral	7	17	44	89	126	237	187	169	Multilatérale
Total	14	82	191	231	445	821	975	1 139	Total
% of GNI	...	...	1.6	1.1	1.2	1.8	2.1	2.4	% du RNB
Lesotho									**Lesotho**
Bilateral	12	65	81	26	92	52	40	51	Bilatérale
Multilateral	16	28	31	42	164	55	43	62	Multilatérale
Total	28	92	113	68	256	107	83	113	Total
% of GNI	11.4	18.4	8.4	3.1	8.5	3.8	3.2	4.6	% du RNB
Liberia									**Libéria**
Bilateral	8	72	51	118	959	451	764	566	Bilatérale
Multilateral	12	19	72	104	457	299	330	249	Multilatérale
Total	20	90	123	222	1 416	750	1 094	815	Total
% of GNI	3.3	11.2	...	56.4	127.2	44.6	62.4	44.8	% du RNB

31

Net disbursements of official development assistance to recipients *(continued)*
Total, bilateral and multilateral aid (millions of US dollars); and as a percentage of Gross National Income (GNI)

Décaissements nets d'aide publique au développement aux bénéficiaires *(suite)*
Total, bilatérale et multilatérale d'aide (millions de dollars É.-U.); et en pourcentage du Revenu National Brut (RNB)

Region, country or area&	1975	1985	1995	2005	2010	2014	2015	2016	Région, pays ou zone&
Libya									**Libye**
Bilateral	-6	3	4	17	1	173	132	149	Bilatérale
Multilateral	8	2	2	6	7	38	26	30	Multilatérale
Total	2	5	6	24	8	210	157	179	Total
% of GNI	...	...	...	0.1	~0.0	...	...	...	% du RNB
Madagascar									**Madagascar**
Bilateral	43	118	192	517	264	263	400	246	Bilatérale
Multilateral	39	67	107	399	214	326	277	376	Multilatérale
Total	82	185	299	916	477	588	677	622	Total
% of GNI	3.6	6.7	10.0	18.5	5.5	5.7	7.2	6.5	% du RNB
Malawi									**Malawi**
Bilateral	43	72	286	301	560	533	694	774	Bilatérale
Multilateral	20	41	149	272	456	398	355	469	Multilatérale
Total	63	112	435	574	1 017	931	1 049	1 243	Total
% of GNI	10.1	10.4	32.2	15.9	14.8	15.8	16.9	23.4	% du RNB
Malaysia									**Malaisie**
Bilateral	88	219	104	17	-33	6	-14	-64	Bilatérale
Multilateral	11	10	5	12	27	14	13	13	Multilatérale
Total	99	229	108	29	-6	20	-1	-52	Total
% of GNI	1.1	0.8	0.1	~0.0	0.0	~0.0	0.0	-~0.0	% du RNB
Maldives									**Maldives**
Bilateral	2	6	51	50	72	4	17	14	Bilatérale
Multilateral	1	3	7	27	40	19	10	13	Multilatérale
Total	3	9	58	77	112	23	27	27	Total
% of GNI	...	7.7	15.3	7.0	5.6	0.8	0.9	0.8	% du RNB
Mali									**Mali**
Bilateral	67	308	401	395	770	774	790	729	Bilatérale
Multilateral	76	70	139	330	322	462	414	480	Multilatérale
Total	144	379	540	725	1 091	1 236	1 204	1 209	Total
% of GNI	17.6	27.7	20.3	12.0	10.6	9.1	9.8	8.9	% du RNB
Malta									**Malte**
Bilateral	33	18	7	...	...	...	...	...	Bilatérale
Multilateral	1	~0	2	...	...	...	...	...	Multilatérale
Total	34	18	9	...	...	...	...	...	Total
% of GNI	6.4	1.5	0.3	...	...	...	...	...	% du RNB
Marshall Islands									**Îles Marshall**
Bilateral	...	...	36	55	26	55	56	12	Bilatérale
Multilateral	...	...	2	2	7	1	1	1	Multilatérale
Total	...	...	39	57	33	56	57	13	Total
% of GNI	...	...	25.4	31.7	16.4	24.5	24.0	5.3	% du RNB
Mauritania									**Mauritanie**
Bilateral	68	179	163	91	277	176	240	174	Bilatérale
Multilateral	15	28	67	97	97	85	78	117	Multilatérale
Total	83	208	230	189	374	261	318	291	Total
% of GNI	18.7	32.9	17.2	8.4	8.7	5.0	6.8	6.4	% du RNB
Mauritius									**Maurice**
Bilateral	15	24	16	13	41	19	30	-31	Bilatérale
Multilateral	13	3	8	22	84	26	48	73	Multilatérale
Total	28	27	24	34	125	45	78	42	Total
% of GNI	...	2.6	0.6	0.6	1.2	0.4	0.7	0.4	% du RNB
Mayotte									**Mayotte**
Bilateral	...	20	107	201	603	...	...	...	Bilatérale
Multilateral	...	~0	1	~0	1	...	...	...	Multilatérale
Total	...	21	108	201	604	...	...	...	Total
Mexico									**Mexique**
Bilateral	-6	121	367	173	406	657	270	643	Bilatérale
Multilateral	62	23	24	29	56	158	51	166	Multilatérale
Total	56	144	391	202	462	815	321	809	Total
% of GNI	0.1	0.1	0.1	~0.0	~0.0	0.1	~0.0	0.1	% du RNB
Micronesia (Fed. States of)									**Micronésie (États féd. de)**
Bilateral	...	...	74	104	62	114	77	42	Bilatérale
Multilateral	...	...	3	3	1	3	4	9	Multilatérale
Total	...	...	77	106	63	117	81	51	Total
% of GNI	...	...	33.0	41.1	20.8	34.1	21.9	13.1	% du RNB

31

Net disbursements of official development assistance to recipients *(continued)*
Total, bilateral and multilateral aid (millions of US dollars); and as a percentage of Gross National Income (GNI)

Décaissements nets d'aide publique au développement aux bénéficiaires *(suite)*
Total, bilatérale et multilatérale d'aide (millions de dollars É.-U.); et en pourcentage du Revenu National Brut (RNB)

Region, country or area&	1975	1985	1995	2005	2010	2014	2015	2016	Région, pays ou zone&
Mongolia									**Mongolie**
Bilateral	...	...	184	160	222	240	191	241	Bilatérale
Multilateral	...	...	25	61	81	77	45	84	Multilatérale
Total	...	5	209	221	303	317	236	325	Total
% of GNI	...	0.2	14.7	8.9	4.6	2.8	2.2	3.2	% du RNB
Montenegro									**Monténégro**
Bilateral	...	...	...	4	54	20	27	25	Bilatérale
Multilateral	...	...	...	0	26	80	73	60	Multilatérale
Total	...	...	...	4	80	100	100	86	Total
% of GNI	...	...	...	0.2	2.0	2.2	2.4	2.0	% du RNB
Montserrat									**Montserrat**
Bilateral	4	2	9	27	16	36	...	39	Bilatérale
Multilateral	~0	~0	1	1	10	5	...	~0	Multilatérale
Total	4	2	9	28	26	40	52	39	Total
Morocco									**Maroc**
Bilateral	260	836	447	395	708	1 332	836	1 189	Bilatérale
Multilateral	10	30	54	338	278	908	645	803	Multilatérale
Total	270	866	501	733	986	2 240	1 481	1 992	Total
% of GNI	3.0	6.0	1.3	1.2	1.1	2.1	1.5	2.0	% du RNB
Mozambique									**Mozambique**
Bilateral	14	242	799	806	1 432	1 484	1 306	940	Bilatérale
Multilateral	6	54	264	483	512	622	509	592	Multilatérale
Total	20	296	1 063	1 290	1 943	2 106	1 815	1 531	Total
% of GNI	...	6.8	44.1	17.5	19.8	12.6	12.5	14.2	% du RNB
Myanmar									**Myanmar**
Bilateral	17	237	109	34	212	1 109	927	1 125	Bilatérale
Multilateral	40	107	42	111	143	275	242	410	Multilatérale
Total	58	344	150	145	355	1 384	1 169	1 536	Total
% of GNI	...	...	...	1.2	0.7	2.2	2.0	...	% du RNB
Namibia									**Namibie**
Bilateral	...	...	170	56	207	159	106	74	Bilatérale
Multilateral	...	...	20	58	55	67	37	97	Multilatérale
Total	...	5	190	113	261	226	142	170	Total
% of GNI	...	0.4	4.6	1.6	2.4	1.8	1.2	1.7	% du RNB
Nauru									**Nauru**
Bilateral	...	...	3	9	27	20	30	21	Bilatérale
Multilateral	...	...	~0	~0	1	2	1	2	Multilatérale
Total	~0	~0	3	9	28	23	31	23	Total
% of GNI	...	...	...	...	48.7	16.1	25.2	17.7	% du RNB
Nepal									**Népal**
Bilateral	14	105	303	284	444	503	819	645	Bilatérale
Multilateral	29	126	126	139	370	381	406	419	Multilatérale
Total	44	231	430	423	814	884	1 225	1 064	Total
% of GNI	2.8	8.8	9.8	5.2	5.1	4.4	5.7	4.9	% du RNB
Netherlands Antilles [former]									**Antilles néerlandaises [anc.]**
Bilateral	28	64	97	...	...	...	...	...	Bilatérale
Multilateral	5	1	2	...	...	...	...	...	Multilatérale
Total	33	65	98	...	...	...	...	...	Total
New Caledonia									**Nouvelle-Calédonie**
Bilateral	65	145	448	...	...	...	...	...	Bilatérale
Multilateral	~0	~0	3	...	...	...	...	...	Multilatérale
Total	65	145	451	...	...	...	...	...	Total
% of GNI	7.9	17.0	12.4	...	...	...	...	...	% du RNB
Nicaragua									**Nicaragua**
Bilateral	17	91	585	594	539	314	341	305	Bilatérale
Multilateral	25	17	65	171	121	118	117	126	Multilatérale
Total	41	108	649	765	660	432	458	431	Total
% of GNI	2.8	4.3	17.2	12.4	7.8	3.7	3.7	3.3	% du RNB
Niger									**Niger**
Bilateral	106	226	211	270	402	399	489	490	Bilatérale
Multilateral	31	72	61	254	339	519	379	462	Multilatérale
Total	137	298	272	523	741	918	868	951	Total
% of GNI	13.2	21.3	14.9	15.4	13.1	11.3	12.3	12.8	% du RNB

31 Net disbursements of official development assistance to recipients *(continued)*

Total, bilateral and multilateral aid (millions of US dollars); and as a percentage of Gross National Income (GNI)

Décaissements nets d'aide publique au développement aux bénéficiaires *(suite)*

Total, bilatérale et multilatérale d'aide (millions de dollars É.-U.); et en pourcentage du Revenu National Brut (RNB)

Region, country or area&	1975	1985	1995	2005	2010	2014	2015	2016	Région, pays ou zone&
Nigeria									**Nigéria**
Bilateral	65	19	88	5 954	1 072	1 238	1 492	1 364	Bilatérale
Multilateral	16	13	122	448	980	1 240	939	1 137	Multilatérale
Total	81	32	211	6 402	2 052	2 479	2 432	2 501	Total
% of GNI	0.3	0.1	0.8	6.5	0.6	0.5	0.5	0.6	% du RNB
Niue									**Nioué**
Bilateral	...	...	8	19	14	13	19	13	Bilatérale
Multilateral	...	...	~0	2	1	1	~0	1	Multilatérale
Total	2	4	8	21	15	14	20	14	Total
Northern Mariana Islands									**Îles Mariannes du Nord**
Bilateral	81	158	~0	...	...	...	...	...	Bilatérale
Multilateral	~0	1	-1	...	...	...	...	...	Multilatérale
Total	81	159	-1	...	...	...	...	...	Total
Oman									**Oman**
Bilateral	138	75	74	15	-24	...	...	...	Bilatérale
Multilateral	2	2	1	4	2	...	...	...	Multilatérale
Total	140	78	75	19	-22	...	...	...	Total
% of GNI	7.8	0.8	0.6	0.1	-~0.0	...	...	...	% du RNB
Other non-specified areas									**Autres zones non-spécifiées**
Bilateral	18	-10	0	...	...	...	...	...	Bilatérale
Multilateral	...	...	0	...	...	...	...	...	Multilatérale
Total	18	-10	~0	...	...	...	...	...	Total
Pakistan									**Pakistan**
Bilateral	628	405	474	886	2 181	2 006	2 302	1 791	Bilatérale
Multilateral	119	363	349	731	840	1 610	1 446	1 162	Multilatérale
Total	747	767	823	1 617	3 021	3 616	3 748	2 953	Total
% of GNI	6.5	2.3	1.4	1.5	1.6	1.4	1.3	1.0	% du RNB
Palau									**Palaos**
Bilateral	...	...	142	23	28	23	13	15	Bilatérale
Multilateral	...	...	0	~0	1	1	1	3	Multilatérale
Total	...	...	142	24	29	23	14	18	Total
% of GNI	...	...	145.2	12.9	16.3	9.8	5.1	6.3	% du RNB
Panama									**Panama**
Bilateral	18	61	32	-3	114	-212	-2	2	Bilatérale
Multilateral	15	8	8	23	14	18	12	20	Multilatérale
Total	33	69	40	20	127	-193	10	23	Total
% of GNI	1.5	1.1	0.4	0.1	0.5	-0.4	~0.0	0.1	% du RNB
Papua New Guinea									**Papouasie-Nvl-Guinée**
Bilateral	294	241	343	212	418	472	484	424	Bilatérale
Multilateral	11	16	28	54	94	110	107	107	Multilatérale
Total	305	257	371	267	512	582	591	532	Total
% of GNI	23.8	11.0	8.5	5.9	5.6	3.5	...	...	% du RNB
Paraguay									**Paraguay**
Bilateral	11	42	130	39	70	35	30	43	Bilatérale
Multilateral	26	8	10	13	51	27	30	46	Multilatérale
Total	37	50	139	51	121	62	60	89	Total
% of GNI	...	...	1.7	0.7	0.7	0.2	0.2	0.3	% du RNB
Peru									**Pérou**
Bilateral	52	291	341	366	-365	271	295	251	Bilatérale
Multilateral	24	21	31	89	69	57	39	69	Multilatérale
Total	77	312	372	456	-296	328	335	320	Total
% of GNI	0.5	2.0	0.7	0.6	-0.2	0.2	0.2	0.2	% du RNB
Philippines									**Philippines**
Bilateral	150	422	853	490	390	528	409	177	Bilatérale
Multilateral	27	37	60	77	151	149	106	106	Multilatérale
Total	177	459	912	568	541	677	515	283	Total
% of GNI	1.2	1.6	1.2	0.4	0.2	0.2	0.2	0.1	% du RNB
Qatar									**Qatar**
Bilateral	-1	1	4	...	...	...	...	...	Bilatérale
Multilateral	1	1	-~0	...	...	...	...	...	Multilatérale
Total	1	2	4	...	...	...	...	...	Total
% of GNI	~0.0	~0.0	0.1	...	...	...	...	...	% du RNB

31 Net disbursements of official development assistance to recipients *(continued)*

Total, bilateral and multilateral aid (millions of US dollars); and as a percentage of Gross National Income (GNI)

Décaissements nets d'aide publique au développement aux bénéficiaires *(suite)*

Total, bilatérale et multilatérale d'aide (millions de dollars É.-U.); et en pourcentage du Revenu National Brut (RNB)

Region, country or area&	1975	1985	1995	2005	2010	2014	2015	2016	Région, pays ou zone&
Republic of Korea									**République de Corée**
Bilateral	208	-13	54	...	...	...	...	...	Bilatérale
Multilateral	40	4	3	...	...	...	...	...	Multilatérale
Total	248	-9	57	...	...	...	...	...	Total
% of GNI	1.2	-~0.0	~0.0	...	...	...	...	...	% du RNB
Republic of Moldova									**République de Moldova**
Bilateral	...	...	...	94	213	326	204	146	Bilatérale
Multilateral	...	...	...	75	260	192	108	182	Multilatérale
Total	...	...	...	170	473	518	313	328	Total
% of GNI	...	...	...	5.1	7.5	5.9	4.5	4.6	% du RNB
Rwanda									**Rwanda**
Bilateral	54	123	403	271	602	518	713	634	Bilatérale
Multilateral	36	54	291	302	431	517	373	515	Multilatérale
Total	90	177	695	573	1 033	1 035	1 085	1 148	Total
% of GNI	15.9	10.4	53.5	22.4	18.0	13.2	13.5	14.1	% du RNB
Saint Helena									**Sainte-Hélène**
Bilateral	...	...	12	22	...	126	82	102	Bilatérale
Multilateral	...	...	~0	~0	...	5	~0	4	Multilatérale
Total	3	12	13	23	54	131	82	106	Total
Saint Kitts and Nevis									**Saint-Kitts-et-Nevis**
Bilateral	1	3	2	1	-2	...	...	...	Bilatérale
Multilateral	~0	1	2	2	13	...	...	...	Multilatérale
Total	2	4	4	3	11	...	...	...	Total
% of GNI	...	4.2	1.4	0.5	1.7	...	...	...	% du RNB
Saint Lucia									**Sainte-Lucie**
Bilateral	8	4	31	4	~0	8	1	-7	Bilatérale
Multilateral	1	3	17	6	41	11	13	22	Multilatérale
Total	9	7	48	11	41	19	14	15	Total
% of GNI	...	2.9	8.0	1.2	3.4	1.4	1.0	1.1	% du RNB
Saint Vincent & Grenadines									**Saint-Vincent-Grenadines**
Bilateral	6	3	32	4	-~0	2	3	-5	Bilatérale
Multilateral	~0	3	15	4	17	8	11	14	Multilatérale
Total	6	5	48	8	17	10	14	9	Total
% of GNI	18.1	3.8	15.6	1.5	2.5	1.4	1.8	1.2	% du RNB
Samoa									**Samoa**
Bilateral	4	14	38	24	98	64	63	-14	Bilatérale
Multilateral	9	6	5	20	50	30	31	102	Multilatérale
Total	13	19	43	44	148	94	94	89	Total
% of GNI	...	...	...	10.0	23.7	12.1	11.9	11.6	% du RNB
Sao Tome and Principe									**Sao Tomé-et-Principe**
Bilateral	~0	6	72	10	36	18	33	24	Bilatérale
Multilateral	1	6	12	23	14	23	16	24	Multilatérale
Total	1	12	84	33	50	41	49	47	Total
% of GNI	...	...	...	26.6	25.4	11.7	15.4	13.4	% du RNB
Saudi Arabia									**Arabie saoudite**
Bilateral	-6	16	17	23	...	...	...	...	Bilatérale
Multilateral	9	12	~0	2	...	...	...	...	Multilatérale
Total	3	27	17	25	...	...	...	...	Total
% of GNI	~0.0	~0.0	~0.0	~0.0	...	...	...	...	% du RNB
Senegal									**Sénégal**
Bilateral	103	249	489	429	654	822	628	433	Bilatérale
Multilateral	36	42	163	272	283	287	251	303	Multilatérale
Total	139	290	652	701	936	1 109	879	736	Total
% of GNI	6.5	10.3	13.8	8.2	7.3	7.4	6.6	5.2	% du RNB
Serbia									**Serbie**
Bilateral	...	...	92	838	300	9	-75	219	Bilatérale
Multilateral	...	...	3	231	361	358	387	414	Multilatérale
Total	...	...	95	1 068	661	367	312	633	Total
% of GNI	...	...	...	4.1	1.7	0.9	0.9	1.8	% du RNB
Seychelles									**Seychelles**
Bilateral	7	19	12	12	43	-~0	1	-7	Bilatérale
Multilateral	~0	3	2	6	11	12	6	13	Multilatérale
Total	7	22	13	17	54	12	7	6	Total
% of GNI	15.6	13.5	2.7	1.9	5.9	0.9	0.5	0.4	% du RNB

31 Net disbursements of official development assistance to recipients *(continued)*

Total, bilateral and multilateral aid (millions of US dollars); and as a percentage of Gross National Income (GNI)

Décaissements nets d'aide publique au développement aux bénéficiaires *(suite)*

Total, bilatérale et multilatérale d'aide (millions de dollars É.-U.); et en pourcentage du Revenu National Brut (RNB)

Region, country or area[&]	1975	1985	1995	2005	2010	2014	2015	2016	Région, pays ou zone[&]
Sierra Leone									**Sierra Leone**
Bilateral	7	43	136	131	221	587	708	471	Bilatérale
Multilateral	10	20	76	209	237	327	239	223	Multilatérale
Total	17	64	212	340	458	914	946	693	Total
% of GNI	2.5	7.7	26.0	21.4	17.3	18.7	22.6	21.1	% du RNB
Singapore									**Singapour**
Bilateral	8	21	16	...	...	...	...	...	Bilatérale
Multilateral	5	2	1	...	...	...	...	...	Multilatérale
Total	12	23	17	...	...	...	...	...	Total
% of GNI	0.2	0.1	~0.0	...	...	...	...	...	% du RNB
Slovenia									**Slovénie**
Bilateral	...	...	40	...	...	...	...	...	Bilatérale
Multilateral	...	...	12	...	...	...	...	...	Multilatérale
Total	...	...	53	...	...	...	...	...	Total
% of GNI	...	...	0.2	...	...	...	...	...	% du RNB
Solomon Islands									**Îles Salomon**
Bilateral	22	16	42	167	301	181	170	152	Bilatérale
Multilateral	1	5	6	32	40	19	21	23	Multilatérale
Total	22	21	48	198	340	201	190	176	Total
% of GNI	45.5	13.5	14.9	47.7	68.5	18.2	17.0	15.2	% du RNB
Somalia									**Somalie**
Bilateral	110	249	134	117	309	905	1 028	955	Bilatérale
Multilateral	55	102	54	123	197	204	225	215	Multilatérale
Total	165	351	188	240	506	1 109	1 253	1 169	Total
% of GNI	...	...	...	...	...	21.3	23.0	20.4	% du RNB
South Africa									**Afrique du Sud**
Bilateral	...	...	358	423	800	690	901	930	Bilatérale
Multilateral	...	...	28	259	236	387	519	251	Multilatérale
Total	...	...	386	681	1 036	1 077	1 420	1 181	Total
% of GNI	...	...	0.3	0.3	0.3	0.3	0.5	0.4	% du RNB
South Sudan									**Soudan du sud**
Bilateral	...	...	...	...	...	1 676	1 407	1 300	Bilatérale
Multilateral	...	...	...	...	...	288	267	290	Multilatérale
Total	...	...	...	...	...	1 964	1 675	1 590	Total
% of GNI	...	...	...	...	...	16.6	21.1	...	% du RNB
Sri Lanka									**Sri Lanka**
Bilateral	81	343	412	902	284	232	173	29	Bilatérale
Multilateral	67	125	142	263	296	259	254	337	Multilatérale
Total	148	468	555	1 165	580	492	427	366	Total
% of GNI	4.4	7.9	4.3	4.8	1.0	0.6	0.5	0.5	% du RNB
State of Palestine									**État de Palestine**
Bilateral	...	...	374	640	1 818	1 978	1 395	1 970	Bilatérale
Multilateral	...	...	140	376	695	510	477	432	Multilatérale
Total	...	...	514	1 016	2 513	2 488	1 871	2 402	Total
% of GNI	...	...	13.8	19.6	26.4	17.5	13.0	16.0	% du RNB
Sudan									**Soudan**
Bilateral	227	972	183	1 450	1 557	671	751	591	Bilatérale
Multilateral	67	153	54	376	469	204	148	219	Multilatérale
Total	294	1 125	237	1 826	2 026	875	900	810	Total
% of GNI	5.3	9.4	1.8	7.4	3.4	1.2	1.0	0.9	% du RNB
Suriname									**Suriname**
Bilateral	50	9	74	31	79	11	11	10	Bilatérale
Multilateral	3	2	3	13	25	2	5	6	Multilatérale
Total	53	11	77	44	104	13	16	17	Total
% of GNI	11.6	1.2	11.1	2.6	2.4	0.3	0.3	0.5	% du RNB
Syrian Arab Republic									**République arabe syrienne**
Bilateral	803	591	306	-3	-31	3 992	4 668	8 578	Bilatérale
Multilateral	25	19	50	74	162	182	222	289	Multilatérale
Total	827	610	356	71	131	4 174	4 890	8 868	Total
% of GNI	11.7	3.6	3.1	0.3	...	...	...	...	% du RNB
Tajikistan									**Tadjikistan**
Bilateral	...	...	49	143	255	227	280	188	Bilatérale
Multilateral	...	...	16	110	178	129	147	146	Multilatérale
Total	...	...	65	252	433	356	426	334	Total
% of GNI	...	...	5.5	11.3	6.2	3.1	4.5	4.1	% du RNB

31 Net disbursements of official development assistance to recipients *(continued)*

Total, bilateral and multilateral aid (millions of US dollars); and as a percentage of Gross National Income (GNI)

Décaissements nets d'aide publique au développement aux bénéficiaires *(suite)*

Total, bilatérale et multilatérale d'aide (millions de dollars É.-U.); et en pourcentage du Revenu National Brut (RNB)

Region, country or area[&]	1975	1985	1995	2005	2010	2014	2015	2016	Région, pays ou zone[&]
Thailand									**Thaïlande**
Bilateral	67	403	814	-239	-132	259	-2	170	Bilatérale
Multilateral	18	55	25	72	111	96	61	58	Multilatérale
Total	85	457	839	-167	-20	355	59	228	Total
% of GNI	0.6	1.2	0.5	-0.1	-~0.0	0.1	~0.0	0.1	% du RNB
TFYR of Macedonia									**ex-R.Y. de Macédoine**
Bilateral	...	...	34	154	127	62	55	54	Bilatérale
Multilateral	...	...	45	74	67	150	159	115	Multilatérale
Total	...	...	79	227	194	212	214	168	Total
% of GNI	...	...	1.8	3.7	2.1	1.9	2.2	1.6	% du RNB
Timor-Leste									**Timor-Leste**
Bilateral	...	...	~0	149	252	198	174	178	Bilatérale
Multilateral	...	...	0	35	40	51	39	46	Multilatérale
Total	~0	...	~0	185	291	250	212	224	Total
% of GNI	...	...	...	22.2	8.9	7.1	7.8	...	% du RNB
Togo									**Togo**
Bilateral	31	74	156	42	205	81	110	64	Bilatérale
Multilateral	11	37	35	41	198	130	90	101	Multilatérale
Total	42	111	191	83	403	211	200	165	Total
% of GNI	6.8	15.3	15.1	4.0	14.6	5.2	5.4	4.1	% du RNB
Tokelau									**Tokélaou**
Bilateral	...	2	3	16	14	19	...	14	Bilatérale
Multilateral	...	~0	~0	~0	~0	~0	...	~0	Multilatérale
Total	~0	2	4	16	15	19	9	14	Total
Tonga									**Tonga**
Bilateral	3	11	37	23	59	61	52	63	Bilatérale
Multilateral	1	2	2	9	11	19	16	20	Multilatérale
Total	3	13	39	32	70	80	68	83	Total
% of GNI	...	21.2	18.9	12.1	18.5	17.9	15.7	20.9	% du RNB
Trinidad and Tobago									**Trinité-et-Tobago**
Bilateral	3	3	14	-11	2	...	...	...	Bilatérale
Multilateral	3	4	11	9	2	...	...	...	Multilatérale
Total	5	7	25	-2	4	...	...	...	Total
% of GNI	0.2	0.1	0.5	-~0.0	~0.0	...	...	...	% du RNB
Tunisia									**Tunisie**
Bilateral	176	144	49	240	426	511	144	216	Bilatérale
Multilateral	38	17	27	128	124	412	331	412	Multilatérale
Total	214	160	75	368	550	923	475	627	Total
% of GNI	5.1	2.0	0.4	1.2	1.3	2.0	1.1	1.6	% du RNB
Turkey									**Turquie**
Bilateral	19	168	297	-57	715	997	139	1 028	Bilatérale
Multilateral	40	12	16	457	334	2 450	2 006	2 585	Multilatérale
Total	58	180	314	399	1 050	3 447	2 145	3 613	Total
% of GNI	0.1	0.3	0.2	0.1	0.1	0.4	0.3	0.4	% du RNB
Turkmenistan									**Turkménistan**
Bilateral	...	...	27	20	29	20	13	19	Bilatérale
Multilateral	...	...	4	10	15	15	11	14	Multilatérale
Total	...	...	31	29	44	34	24	33	Total
% of GNI	...	...	1.2	0.4	0.2	0.1	0.1	0.1	% du RNB
Turks and Caicos Islands									**Îles Turques-et-Caïques**
Bilateral	3	5	5	3	...	...	...	...	Bilatérale
Multilateral	~0	1	1	2	...	...	...	...	Multilatérale
Total	3	6	6	5	...	...	...	...	Total
Tuvalu									**Tuvalu**
Bilateral	...	3	7	6	14	26	42	-30	Bilatérale
Multilateral	...	~0	1	4	~0	9	8	54	Multilatérale
Total	~0	3	8	9	14	34	50	24	Total
% of GNI	...	...	...	24.7	27.5	68.6	88.7	44.4	% du RNB
Uganda									**Ouganda**
Bilateral	37	84	571	699	1 112	1 091	1 127	1 137	Bilatérale
Multilateral	15	96	263	497	578	543	502	620	Multilatérale
Total	52	179	834	1 195	1 690	1 634	1 628	1 757	Total
% of GNI	2.2	5.2	14.6	13.7	8.5	6.0	5.9	7.0	% du RNB

31

Net disbursements of official development assistance to recipients *(continued)*
Total, bilateral and multilateral aid (millions of US dollars); and as a percentage of Gross National Income (GNI)

Décaissements nets d'aide publique au développement aux bénéficiaires *(suite)*
Total, bilatérale et multilatérale d'aide (millions de dollars É.-U.); et en pourcentage du Revenu National Brut (RNB)

Region, country or area&	1975	1985	1995	2005	2010	2014	2015	2016	Région, pays ou zone&
Ukraine									**Ukraine**
Bilateral	...	...	...	248	442	950	1 198	1 062	Bilatérale
Multilateral	...	...	...	156	214	454	251	461	Multilatérale
Total	...	...	...	404	657	1 404	1 449	1 523	Total
% of GNI	...	...	...	0.5	0.5	1.1	1.6	1.7	% du RNB
United Arab Emirates									**Émirats arabes unis**
Bilateral	3	3	6	...	...	...	...	...	Bilatérale
Multilateral	1	1	-~0	...	...	...	...	...	Multilatérale
Total	4	4	5	...	...	...	...	...	Total
United Rep. of Tanzania									**Rép.-Unie de Tanzanie**
Bilateral	237	400	613	823	1 923	1 572	1 716	1 507	Bilatérale
Multilateral	57	77	258	670	1 037	1 078	866	810	Multilatérale
Total	293	477	871	1 492	2 960	2 651	2 582	2 318	Total
% of GNI	...	...	17.0	9.0	9.5	5.6	5.8	5.0	% du RNB
Uruguay									**Uruguay**
Bilateral	-1	3	60	1	31	78	12	4	Bilatérale
Multilateral	13	2	6	17	17	14	12	14	Multilatérale
Total	12	5	66	18	48	92	23	18	Total
% of GNI	0.4	0.1	0.4	0.1	0.1	0.2	0.1	~0.0	% du RNB
Uzbekistan									**Ouzbékistan**
Bilateral	...	...	76	128	153	156	287	288	Bilatérale
Multilateral	...	...	8	41	81	169	161	169	Multilatérale
Total	...	...	84	169	234	325	448	457	Total
% of GNI	...	...	0.6	1.2	0.6	0.5	0.7	0.7	% du RNB
Vanuatu									**Vanuatu**
Bilateral	12	20	43	29	104	98	169	81	Bilatérale
Multilateral	~0	2	2	11	3	3	18	48	Multilatérale
Total	12	22	46	40	108	100	187	129	Total
% of GNI	...	17.7	21.0	10.8	16.0	12.3	...	...	% du RNB
Venezuela (Boliv. Rep. of)									**Venezuela (Rép. boliv. du)**
Bilateral	-~0	9	35	13	33	28	22	30	Bilatérale
Multilateral	19	2	8	36	20	16	15	14	Multilatérale
Total	18	11	43	49	53	43	37	43	Total
% of GNI	0.1	~0.0	0.1	~0.0	~0.0	...	...	...	% du RNB
Viet Nam									**Viet Nam**
Bilateral	367	115	724	1 386	2 010	2 828	2 240	2 028	Bilatérale
Multilateral	22	38	111	525	938	1 387	918	867	Multilatérale
Total	390	153	835	1 911	2 948	4 216	3 157	2 895	Total
% of GNI	...	...	4.1	3.4	2.6	2.4	1.7	1.5	% du RNB
Wallis and Futuna Islands									**Îles Wallis-et-Futuna**
Bilateral	2	~0	1	72	123	99	106	85	Bilatérale
Multilateral	~0	~0	~0	~0	5	~0	~0	~0	Multilatérale
Total	2	~0	1	72	127	100	106	85	Total
Yemen									**Yémen**
Bilateral	211	342	109	127	418	851	1 385	1 715	Bilatérale
Multilateral	40	89	63	169	249	313	146	211	Multilatérale
Total	251	431	172	296	667	1 163	1 531	1 926	Total
% of GNI	...	...	4.2	2.0	2.3	2.9	4.2	7.1	% du RNB
Zambia									**Zambie**
Bilateral	68	244	1 765	692	654	733	564	629	Bilatérale
Multilateral	18	75	266	478	266	264	234	334	Multilatérale
Total	86	319	2 031	1 169	919	998	797	963	Total
% of GNI	3.5	15.9	57.0	15.2	4.9	3.8	3.8	5.1	% du RNB
Zimbabwe									**Zimbabwe**
Bilateral	4	218	438	162	478	499	507	398	Bilatérale
Multilateral	~0	18	53	211	234	262	281	257	Multilatérale
Total	4	235	492	373	713	761	788	655	Total
% of GNI	0.1	4.3	7.2	6.8	7.5	5.1	5.1	4.2	% du RNB

Source:

Organisation for Economic Co-operation and Development (OECD), Paris, the OECD Development Assistance Committee (DAC) database, last accessed May 2018.

Source:

Organisation de coopération et de développement économiques (OCDE), Paris, base de données du Comité d'aide au développement (CAD) de l'OCDE, dernier accès May 2018.

31 Net disbursements of official development assistance to recipients *(continued)*

Total, bilateral and multilateral aid (millions of US dollars); and as a percentage of Gross National Income (GNI)

Décaissements nets d'aide publique au développement aux bénéficiaires *(suite)*

Total, bilatérale et multilatérale d'aide (millions de dollars É.-U.); et en pourcentage du Revenu National Brut (RNB)

Official Development Assistance (ODA) is defined as those flows to developing countries and multilateral institutions provided by official agencies, including state and local governments, or by their executive agencies, each transaction of which meets the following tests: i) it is administered with the promotion of the economic development and welfare of developing countries as its main objective; and ii) it is concessional in character and conveys a grant element of at least 25 per cent.

1 Including regional aid disbursements in addition to the disbursements made to individual countries and areas.
2 Excluding Sudan.
3 Including Sudan.
4 Excludes Myanmar.
5 Includes Armenia, Azerbaijan, Georgia and Myanmar. Excludes Iran (Islamic Rep. of).
6 Excluding Armenia, Azerbaijan, Cyprus, Georgia and Turkey. Includes Iran (Islamic Rep. of).
7 Including Turkey and Cyprus.
8 For statistical purposes, the data for China do not include those for the Hong Kong Special Administrative Region (Hong Kong SAR), Macao Special Administrative Region (Macao SAR) and Taiwan Province of China.

On entend par Aide publique au développement (APD), l'ensemble des flux financiers à destination des pays en développement et des institutions multilatérales par des organismes publics (y compris les autorités étatiques et locales) ou par leurs organes exécutifs satisfaisant les critères suivants: i) elle est administrée dans le but premier de promouvoir le développement économique et social des pays en développement ; ii) elle est accordée à des conditions de faveur et comporte une élément de subvention d'au moins 25 pour cent.

1 Y compris les versements d'aides régionales en plus des versements effectués aux aux différents pays et régions.
2 Exclut le Soudan.
3 Y compris le Soudan.
4 Non compris Myanmar.
5 Y compris l'Arménie, l'Azerbaïdjan, la Géorgie et le Myanmar. Non compris la Rép. Islamique d 'Iran.
6 Non compris l'Arménie, l'Azerbaïdjan, Chypre, la Géorgie et la Turquie. Y compris la Rép. Islamique d 'Iran.
7 Y compris la Turquie et Chypre.
8 Pour la présentation des statistiques, les données pour la Chine ne comprennent pas la région administrative spéciale de Hong Kong (Hong Kong RAS), la région administrative spéciale de Macao (Macao RAS) et la province chinoise de Taïwan.

32 Net disbursements of official development assistance from donors

Millions of US dollars and as a percentage of gross national income (GNI)

Décaissements nets d'aide publique au développement par des donateurs

Millions de dollares É.-U. et en pourcentage du revenu national brut (RNB)

Country or area	1975	1985	1995	2005	2010	2014	2015	2016	2017	Pays ou zone
Total										**Total**
$ millions	20 183	33 855	65 424	120 771	147 644	178 552	162 782	176 575	* 177 595	$millions
DAC total										**CAD total**
$ millions	13 315	28 858	58 896	108 397	128 484	137 539	131 563	144 965	* 146 600	$millions
% of GNI	0.34	0.33	0.26	0.32	0.31	0.30	0.30	0.32	* 0.31	% du RNB
Australia [1]										**Australie** [1]
$ millions	552	749	1 194	1 680	3 826	4 382	3 494	3 278	* 2 957	$millions
% of GNI	0.65	0.48	0.34	0.25	0.32	0.31	0.29	0.27	* 0.23	% du RNB
Austria [1]										**Autriche** [1]
$ millions	79	248	620	1 573	1 208	1 235	1 324	1 635	* 1 230	$millions
% of GNI	0.21	0.38	0.27	0.52	0.32	0.28	0.35	0.42	* 0.30	% du RNB
Azerbaijan										**Azerbaïdjan**
$ millions	...	...	...	...	...	16	13	13	...	$millions
% of GNI	...	...	...	...	...	0.02	0.02	0.04	...	% du RNB
Belgium [1]										**Belgique** [1]
$ millions	378	440	1 034	1 963	3 004	2 446	1 904	2 300	* 2 204	$millions
% of GNI	0.60	0.55	0.38	0.53	0.64	0.46	0.42	0.50	* 0.45	% du RNB
Bulgaria										**Bulgarie**
$ millions	...	...	...	...	40	49	41	68	* 62	$millions
% of GNI	...	...	...	...	0.09	0.09	0.09	0.13	* 0.11	% du RNB
Canada [1]										**Canada** [1]
$ millions	880	1 631	2 067	3 756	5 214	4 240	4 277	3 930	* 4 277	$millions
% of GNI	0.54	0.49	0.38	0.34	0.34	0.24	0.28	0.26	* 0.26	% du RNB
Croatia										**Croatie**
$ millions	...	...	...	...	...	72	51	41	* 50	$millions
% of GNI	...	...	...	...	...	0.13	0.09	0.07	* 0.09	% du RNB
Cyprus [2]										**Chypre** [2]
$ millions	...	...	...	15	51	19	18	...	...	$millions
% of GNI	...	...	...	0.09	0.23	0.09	0.09	...	...	% du RNB
Czechia [1]										**Tchéquie** [1]
$ millions	...	...	...	135	228	212	199	260	* 272	$millions
% of GNI	...	...	...	0.11	0.13	0.11	0.12	0.14	* 0.13	% du RNB
Denmark [1]										**Danemark** [1]
$ millions	205	440	1 623	2 109	2 871	3 003	2 566	2 369	* 2 401	$millions
% of GNI	0.55	0.80	0.96	0.81	0.91	0.86	0.85	0.75	* 0.72	% du RNB
Estonia										**Estonie**
$ millions	...	...	...	10	19	38	34	43	* 42	$millions
% of GNI	...	...	...	0.08	0.10	0.15	0.15	0.19	* 0.17	% du RNB
Finland [1]										**Finlande** [1]
$ millions	48	211	388	902	1 333	1 635	1 288	1 060	* 1 054	$millions
% of GNI	0.17	0.40	0.31	0.46	0.55	0.59	0.55	0.44	* 0.41	% du RNB
France [1]										**France** [1]
$ millions	1 493	3 134	8 443	10 026	12 915	10 620	9 039	9 622	* 11 363	$millions
% of GNI	0.44	0.61	0.55	0.47	0.50	0.37	0.37	0.38	* 0.43	% du RNB
Germany [1]										**Allemagne** [1]
$ millions	1 689	2 942	7 524	10 082	12 985	16 566	17 940	24 736	* 24 681	$millions
% of GNI	0.40	0.47	0.31	0.36	0.39	0.42	0.52	0.70	* 0.66	% du RNB
Greece [1]										**Grèce** [1]
$ millions	...	...	...	384	508	247	239	369	* 317	$millions
% of GNI	...	...	...	0.17	0.17	0.11	0.12	0.19	* 0.16	% du RNB
Hungary [1]										**Hongrie** [1]
$ millions	29	84	...	100	114	144	156	199	* 149	$millions
% of GNI	...	...	...	0.11	0.09	0.11	0.13	0.17	* 0.11	% du RNB
Iceland [1]										**Islande** [1]
$ millions	...	...	...	27	29	37	40	59	* 69	$millions
% of GNI	...	...	...	0.18	0.26	0.22	0.24	0.28	* 0.29	% du RNB
Ireland [1]										**Irlande** [1]
$ millions	8	39	153	719	895	816	718	803	* 808	$millions
% of GNI	0.09	0.24	0.29	0.42	0.52	0.38	0.32	0.32	* 0.30	% du RNB
Israel										**Israël**
$ millions	...	...	...	95	145	200	233	351	* 342	$millions
% of GNI	...	...	...	0.07	0.07	0.07	0.08	0.11	* 0.10	% du RNB

32

Net disbursements of official development assistance from donors *(continued)*
Millions of US dollars and as a percentage of gross national income (GNI)

Décaissements nets d'aide publique au développement par des donateurs *(suite)*
Millions de dollares É.-U. et en pourcentage du revenu national brut (RNB)

Country or area	1975	1985	1995	2005	2010	2014	2015	2016	2017	Pays ou zone
Italy [1]										**Italie** [1]
$ millions	182	1 098	1 623	5 091	2 996	4 009	4 003	5 087	* 5 734	$millions
% of GNI	0.10	0.26	0.15	0.29	0.15	0.19	0.22	0.27	* 0.29	% du RNB
Japan [1]										**Japon** [1]
$ millions	1 148	3 797	14 489	13 126	11 058	9 483	9 203	10 417	* 11 475	$millions
% of GNI	0.23	0.29	0.27	0.28	0.20	0.20	0.20	0.20	* 0.23	% du RNB
Kazakhstan										**Kazakhstan**
$ millions	...	...	...	...	...	33	43	24	...	$millions
% of GNI	...	...	...	...	...	0.02	0.02	0.02	...	% du RNB
Kuwait										**Koweït**
$ millions	859[3]	647[3]	384[3]	218[3]	232[3]	277[3]	304[3]	# 1 080[4]	...	$millions
Latvia										**Lettonie**
$ millions	...	...	...	11	16	25	23	30	* 32	$millions
% of GNI	...	...	...	0.07	0.06	0.08	0.09	0.11	* 0.11	% du RNB
Liechtenstein										**Liechtenstein**
$ millions	...	...	...	...	27	27	24	25	...	$millions
% of GNI	...	...	...	...	0.62	0.50	...	...	...	% du RNB
Lithuania										**Lituanie**
$ millions	...	...	...	16	37	46	48	57	* 59	$millions
% of GNI	...	...	...	0.06	0.10	0.10	0.12	0.14	* 0.13	% du RNB
Luxembourg [1]										**Luxembourg** [1]
$ millions	...	8	65	256	403	423	363	391	* 424	$millions
% of GNI	...	0.17	0.36	0.79	1.05	1.06	0.95	1.00	* 1.00	% du RNB
Malta										**Malte**
$ millions	...	...	...	...	14	20	17	21	* 26	$millions
% of GNI	...	...	...	...	0.18	0.20	0.17	0.20	* 0.22	% du RNB
Netherlands [1]										**Pays-Bas** [1]
$ millions	608	1 136	3 226	5 115	6 357	5 573	5 726	4 966	* 4 955	$millions
% of GNI	0.74	0.91	0.81	0.82	0.81	0.64	0.75	0.65	* 0.60	% du RNB
New Zealand [1]										**Nouvelle-Zélande** [1]
$ millions	66	54	123	274	342	506	442	447	* 436	$millions
% of GNI	0.52	0.25	0.23	0.27	0.26	0.27	0.27	0.25	* 0.23	% du RNB
Norway [1]										**Norvège** [1]
$ millions	184	574	1 244	2 794	4 372	5 086	4 278	4 380	* 4 123	$millions
% of GNI	0.65	1.01	0.86	0.94	1.05	1.00	1.05	1.12	* 0.99	% du RNB
Other non-specified areas										**Autres zones non-spécifiées**
$ millions	...	...	92	483	381	274	255	328	...	$millions
% of GNI	...	...	...	0.14	0.10	0.05	0.05	0.06	...	% du RNB
Poland [1]										**Pologne** [1]
$ millions	32	19	...	205	378	452	441	663	* 674	$millions
% of GNI	...	...	...	0.07	0.08	0.09	0.10	0.15	* 0.13	% du RNB
Portugal [1]										**Portugal** [1]
$ millions	...	10	258	377	649	430	308	343	* 378	$millions
% of GNI	...	0.05	0.25	0.21	0.29	0.19	0.16	0.17	* 0.18	% du RNB
Republic of Korea [1]										**République de Corée** [1]
$ millions	...	...	116	752	1 174	1 857	1 915	2 246	* 2 205	$millions
% of GNI	...	...	0.02	0.10	0.12	0.13	0.14	0.16	* 0.14	% du RNB
Romania										**Roumanie**
$ millions	...	...	...	...	114	214	158	269	...	$millions
% of GNI	...	...	...	...	0.07	0.11	0.09	0.15	...	% du RNB
Russian Federation										**Fédération de Russie**
$ millions	...	...	...	...	472	876[5]	1 161[5]	1 258[5]	* 1 194[5]	$millions
% of GNI	...	...	...	...	0.03	0.05[5]	0.09[5]	0.10[5]	* 0.08[5]	% du RNB
Saudi Arabia [6]										**Arabie saoudite** [6]
$ millions	2 569	2 443	305	1 026	3 480	13 634	6 758	...	...	$millions
Slovakia [1]										**Slovaquie** [1]
$ millions	...	...	...	57	74	83	85	106	* 113	$millions
% of GNI	...	...	...	...	0.09	0.09	0.10	0.12	* 0.12	% du RNB
Slovenia [1]										**Slovénie** [1]
$ millions	...	...	...	35	59	62	63	81	* 76	$millions
% of GNI	...	...	...	0.11	0.13	0.12	0.15	0.19	* 0.16	% du RNB
Spain [1]										**Espagne** [1]
$ millions	...	169	1 348	3 018	5 949	1 877	1 397	4 278	* 2 415	$millions
% of GNI	...	0.10	0.24	0.27	0.43	0.13	0.12	0.35	* 0.19	% du RNB

32

Net disbursements of official development assistance from donors *(continued)*
Millions of US dollars and as a percentage of gross national income (GNI)

Décaissements nets d'aide publique au développement par des donateurs *(suite)*
Millions de dollares É.-U. et en pourcentage du revenu national brut (RNB)

Country or area	1975	1985	1995	2005	2010	2014	2015	2016	2017	Pays ou zone
Sweden [1]										**Suède** [1]
$ millions	566	840	1 704	3 362	4 533	6 233	7 089	4 894	* 5 512	$millions
% of GNI	0.78	0.86	0.77	0.94	0.97	1.09	1.40	0.94	* 1.01	% du RNB
Switzerland [1]										**Suisse** [1]
$ millions	104	303	1 084	1 772	2 300	3 522	3 529	3 582	* 3 097	$millions
% of GNI	0.18	0.31	0.33	0.42	0.39	0.50	0.51	0.53	* 0.46	% du RNB
Thailand										**Thaïlande**
$ millions	...	...	...	...	4	69	62	168	...	$millions
% of GNI	...	...	...	...	~0.00	0.02	0.02	0.05	...	% du RNB
Timor-Leste										**Timor-Leste**
$ millions	...	...	...	...	...	3	4	...	...	$millions
Turkey										**Turquie**
$ millions	...	...	107	601	967	3 591	3 919	6 488	* 8 143	$millions
% of GNI	...	...	0.06	0.17	0.13	0.45	0.50	0.76	* 0.95	% du RNB
United Arab Emirates [7]										**Émirats arabes unis** [7]
$ millions	1 998	366	...	510	414	5 080	4 381	4 241	* 4 595	$millions
% of GNI	...	...	...	...	0.14	1.26	1.18	1.21	* 1.31	% du RNB
United Kingdom [1]										**Royaume-Uni** [1]
$ millions	904	1 530	3 202	10 772	13 053	19 263	18 553	18 053	* 17 940	$millions
% of GNI	0.38	0.33	0.29	0.47	0.57	0.70	0.70	0.70	* 0.70	% du RNB
United States of America [1]										**États-Unis d'Amérique** [1]
$ millions	4 161	9 403	7 367	27 935	29 656	33 096	30 986	34 412	* 35 261	$millions
% of GNI	0.27	0.24	0.10	0.23	0.20	0.19	0.17	0.19	* 0.18	% du RNB
Areas not specified										**Zones non spécifiées**
$ millions	721	32	...	...	...	...	...	...	...	$millions
European Union (EU) [1,8]										**Union européenne (UE)** [1,8]
$ millions	722	1 510	5 398	9 390	12 747	16 451	13 670	17 106	* 16 450	$millions

Source:

Organisation for Economic Co-operation and Development (OECD), Paris, the OECD Development Assistance Committee (DAC) database, last accessed May 2018.

Source:

Organisation de coopération et de développement économiques (OCDE), Paris, base de données du Comité d'aide au développement (CAD) de l'OCDE, dernier accès May 2018.

1 Development Assistance Committee member (OECD).
2 Data refer to government controlled areas.
3 Includes Kuwait Fund grants only.
4 Includes Kuwait Fund grants, State of Kuwait grants administered by Kuwait Fund as well as State of Kuwait grants.
5 Some of the debt relief reported may correspond to the credits. Statistics currently published on ODA by Russia and the estimates from the previous Chairman's reports should not be used at the same time.
6 Saudi Arabia's reporting to the OECD on its development co-operation programme consists of aggregate figures on humanitarian and development assistance by region, multilateral aid and loan disbursements and repayments by the Saudi Fund for Development.
7 Data reported at activity level, represent flows from all government agencies.
8 Refers to European Union institutions.

1 Le Comité d'aide au développement (l'OCDE).
2 Les données se rapportent aux zones contrôlées par le Gouvernement.
3 Inclut les subventions du Fonds koweïtien seulement.
4 Inclut les subventions du Fonds koweïtien, les subventions de l'État du Koweït administrées par le Kuwait Fund ainsi que les subventions de l'État du Koweït.
5 Une partie de l'allégement de la dette rapporté peut correspondre aux crédits. Les statistiques actuellement publiées sur l'APD par la Russie et les estimations des précédents rapports du Président ne devraient pas être utilisées en même temps.
6 La déclaration de l'Arabie saoudite auprès de l'OCDE relatif au programme de coopération au développement est constituée de données globales sur l'aide humanitaire, l'aide au développement par région, l'aide multilatérale, et les déboursements et les remboursements de prêts par les Fonds saoudien pour le développement.
7 Les données rapportées au niveau d'activité, ces données représentent les flux de tous les organismes gouvernementaux.
8 Se réfèrent aux institutions de l'Union Européenne.

Annex I - Country and area nomenclature, regional and other groupings

The *Statistical Yearbook* lists countries or areas based on the United Nations Standard Country Codes (Series M, No. 49), prepared by the Statistics Division of the United Nations Secretariat and first issued in 1970[1]. The list of countries or areas; the composition of geographical regions and economic, trade and other groupings used within this yearbook (as at 31 July 2018) are presented in this Annex. The names of countries or areas refer to their short form used in day-to-day operations of the United Nations and not necessarily to their official name as used in formal documents[2]. As an aid to statistical data processing, a unique standard three-digit numerical code is assigned to each country or area and to each geographical region and grouping of countries or areas. For reference, these codes, where applicable, are presented to the left of each country or area listed in this Annex. These codes range from 000 to 899, inclusive.

A. Changes in country or area names (since 31 July 2008)

The geographical extent of a country or area, or the composition of a geographical region, may change over time and users should take such changes into account in interpreting the tables in this Yearbook. A change in the name of a country or area while its geographical coverage remains the same is not usually accompanied by a change in its numerical code. Changes in numerical codes and names in the general period covered by the statistics (since 31 July 2008) in the *Yearbook*, are shown below;

Numerical code	Country or area (added or changed)	Date of change	Numerical code	Country or area (Name changes with no change in code)	Date of change
728	South Sudan	2011	748	Eswatini, *previously Swaziland*	2018
729	Sudan	2011	203	Czechia, *previously Czech Republic*	2016
531	Curaçao	2010	132	Cabo Verde, *previously Cape Verde*	2013
534	Sint Maarten (Dutch part)	2010	275	State of Palestine, *previously Occupied Palestinian Territory*	2013
535	Bonaire, Sint Eustatius and Saba	2010			
			434	Libya, *previously Libyan Arab Jamahiriya*	2011
			068	Bolivia (Plurinational State of), *previously Bolivia*	2009
			498	Republic of Moldova, *previously Moldova*	2008

B. Regional groupings

The scheme of regional groupings given on the next page is based mainly on 6 continents; these continental regions, except Antarctica, are further subdivided into 22 sub-regions and 2 intermediary regions (Sub-Saharan Africa and Latin America and the Caribbean) that are drawn as to obtain greater homogeneity in sizes of population, demographic circumstances and accuracy of demographic statistics. This nomenclature is widely used in international statistics and is followed to the greatest extent possible in the present *Yearbook* in order to promote consistency and facilitate comparability and analysis. However, it is by no means universal in international statistical compilation, even at the level of continental regions, and variations in international statistical sources and methods dictate many unavoidable differences in particular fields in the present *Yearbook*. General differences are indicated in the footnotes to the classification presented below. More detailed differences are given in the footnotes and technical notes to individual tables.

Neither is there international standardization in the use of the terms "developed" and "developing" countries, areas or regions. These terms are used in the present publication to refer to regional groupings generally considered as "developed": these are Northern America (numerical code 021), Europe (150), Cyprus (196), Israel (376), Japan (392) and Australia and New Zealand (053). These designations are intended for statistical convenience and do not necessarily express a judgement about the stage reached by a particular country or area in the development process. Differences from this usage are indicated in the notes to individual tables.

[1] Four revisions of this document were published in 1975, 1982, 1996 and 1999. Further revisions are now published on the United Nations Statistics Division website under the M49 section.

[2] A listing in the 6 official languages of the United Nations is contained in Terminology Bulletin No. 347/Rev.1 or the UNTERM website, prepared by the Department of General Assembly Affairs and Conference Services of the United Nations Secretariat.

001 World

002 Africa

202 Sub-Saharan Africa

014 Eastern Africa

086	British Indian Ocean Territory
108	Burundi
174	Comoros
262	Djibouti
232	Eritrea
231	Ethiopia
260	French Southern Territories
404	Kenya
450	Madagascar
454	Malawi
480	Mauritius
175	Mayotte
508	Mozambique
638	Réunion
646	Rwanda
690	Seychelles
706	Somalia
728	South Sudan note 736
800	Uganda
834	United Republic of Tanzania note /a
894	Zambia
716	Zimbabwe

017 Middle Africa

024	Angola
120	Cameroon
140	Central African Republic
148	Chad
178	Congo
180	Democratic Republic of the Congo
226	Equatorial Guinea
266	Gabon
678	Sao Tome and Principe

018 Southern Africa

072	Botswana
748	Eswatini
426	Lesotho
516	Namibia
710	South Africa

011 Western Africa

204	Benin
854	Burkina Faso
132	Cabo Verde
384	Côte d'Ivoire
270	Gambia
288	Ghana
324	Guinea
624	Guinea-Bissau
430	Liberia
466	Mali
478	Mauritania
562	Niger
566	Nigeria
654	Saint Helena note /b
686	Senegal
694	Sierra Leone
768	Togo

015 Northern Africa

012	Algeria
818	Egypt
434	Libya
504	Morocco
729	Sudan note 736
788	Tunisia
732	Western Sahara

Note **Tables may list**

736 *Sudan [former]*

/a Includes

--- *Zanzibar*

/b Includes

--- *Ascension*

--- *Tristan da Cunha*

019 Americas

419 Latin America and the Caribbean

029 Caribbean

660	Anguilla
028	Antigua and Barbuda
533	Aruba
044	Bahamas
052	Barbados
535	Bonaire, Sint Eustatius and Saba note 530
092	British Virgin Islands
136	Cayman Islands
192	Cuba
531	Curaçao note 530
212	Dominica
214	Dominican Republic
308	Grenada
312	Guadeloupe
332	Haiti
388	Jamaica
474	Martinique
500	Montserrat
630	Puerto Rico
652	Saint Barthélemy
659	Saint Kitts and Nevis
662	Saint Lucia
663	Saint Martin (French part)
670	Saint Vincent and the Grenadines
534	Sint Maarten (Dutch part) note 530
780	Trinidad and Tobago
796	Turks and Caicos Islands
850	United States Virgin Islands

013 Central America

084	Belize
188	Costa Rica
222	El Salvador
320	Guatemala
340	Honduras
484	Mexico
558	Nicaragua
591	Panama

005 South America

032	Argentina
068	Bolivia (Plurinational State of)
074	Bouvet Island
076	Brazil
152	Chile
170	Colombia
218	Ecuador
238	Falkland Islands (Malvinas)
254	French Guiana
328	Guyana
600	Paraguay
604	Peru
740	Suriname
239	South Georgia and the South Sandwich Islands
858	Uruguay
862	Venezuela (Bolivarian Republic of)

021 Northern America note 003

060	Bermuda
124	Canada
304	Greenland
666	Saint Pierre and Miquelon
840	United States of America

Note

003 *The continent of* **North America** *comprises Northern America, Caribbean and Central America.*

Tables may list

530 *Netherlands Antilles [former]*

010 Antarctica

001 World

142 Asia

143 Central Asia
398 Kazakhstan
417 Kyrgyzstan
762 Tajikistan
795 Turkmenistan
860 Uzbekistan

030 Eastern Asia
156 China
344 China, Hong Kong Special Administrative Region
446 China, Macao Special Administrative Region
408 Democratic People's Republic of Korea
392 Japan
496 Mongolia
410 Republic of Korea

035 South-eastern Asia
096 Brunei Darussalam
116 Cambodia
360 Indonesia
418 Lao People's Democratic Republic
458 Malaysia
104 Myanmar
608 Philippines
702 Singapore
764 Thailand
626 Timor-Leste
704 Viet Nam

034 Southern Asia
004 Afghanistan
050 Bangladesh
064 Bhutan
356 India
364 Iran (Islamic Republic of)
462 Maldives
524 Nepal
586 Pakistan
144 Sri Lanka

145 Western Asia
051 Armenia
031 Azerbaijan
048 Bahrain
196 Cyprus
268 Georgia
368 Iraq
376 Israel
400 Jordan
414 Kuwait
422 Lebanon
512 Oman
634 Qatar
682 Saudi Arabia
275 State of Palestine
760 Syrian Arab Republic
792 Turkey
784 United Arab Emirates
887 Yemen

150 Europe

151 Eastern Europe
112 Belarus
100 Bulgaria
203 Czechia
348 Hungary
616 Poland
498 Republic of Moldova
642 Romania
643 Russian Federation
703 Slovakia
804 Ukraine

154 Northern Europe
248 Åland Islands
208 Denmark
233 Estonia
234 Faroe Islands
246 Finland
831 Guernsey note 830
352 Iceland
372 Ireland
833 Isle of Man
832 Jersey note 830
428 Latvia
440 Lithuania
578 Norway
744 Svalbard and Jan Mayen Islands
752 Sweden
826 United Kingdom of Great Britain and Northern Ireland

039 Southern Europe
008 Albania
020 Andorra
070 Bosnia and Herzegovina
191 Croatia
292 Gibraltar
300 Greece
336 Holy See
380 Italy
470 Malta
499 Montenegro note 891
620 Portugal
674 San Marino
688 Serbia note 891 & /c
705 Slovenia
724 Spain
807 The former Yugoslav Republic of Macedonia

155 Western Europe
040 Austria
056 Belgium
250 France
276 Germany
438 Liechtenstein
442 Luxembourg
492 Monaco
528 Netherlands
756 Switzerland

Note **Tables may list**
830 *Channel Islands*
891 *Serbia and Montenegro [former]*
/c *Kosovo*

009 Oceania

053 Australia and New Zealand
036 Australia
162 Christmas Island
166 Cocos (Keeling) Islands
334 Heard Island and McDonald Islands
554 New Zealand
574 Norfolk Island

054 Melanesia
242 Fiji
540 New Caledonia
598 Papua New Guinea
090 Solomon Islands
548 Vanuatu

057 Micronesia
316 Guam
296 Kiribati
584 Marshall Islands
583 Micronesia (Federated States of)
520 Nauru
580 Northern Mariana Islands
585 Palau
581 United States minor outlying islands

061 Polynesia
016 American Samoa
184 Cook Islands
258 French Polynesia
570 Niue
612 Pitcairn
882 Samoa
772 Tokelau
776 Tonga
798 Tuvalu
876 Wallis and Futuna Islands

Other groupings

Following is a list of other groupings and their compositions presented in the *Yearbook*. These groupings are organized mainly around economic and trade interests in regional associations.

063 Andean Common Market (ANCOM)

068	Bolivia (Plurinational State of)	170	Colombia	218	Ecuador	604	Peru

066 Asia-Pacific Economic Cooperation (APEC)

036	Australia	344	China, Hong Kong Special Administrative Region	554	New Zealand	702	Singapore
096	Brunei Darussalam	360	Indonesia	598	Papua New Guinea	158	Taiwan Province of China
124	Canada	392	Japan	604	Peru	764	Thailand
152	Chile	458	Malaysia	608	Philippines	840	United States of America
156	China	484	Mexico	410	Republic of Korea	704	Viet Nam
				643	Russian Federation		

073 Association of Southeast Asian Nations (ASEAN)

096	Brunei Darussalam	360	Indonesia	458	Malaysia	608	Philippines	764	Thailand
116	Cambodia	418	Lao PDR	104	Myanmar	702	Singapore	704	Viet Nam

130 Caribbean Community and Common Market (CARICOM)

028	Antigua and Barbuda	084	Belize	332	Haiti	662	Saint Lucia
044	Bahamas (member of the Community only)	212	Dominica	388	Jamaica	670	Saint Vincent and the Grenadines
		308	Grenada	500	Montserrat	740	Suriname
052	Barbados	328	Guyana	659	Saint Kitts and Nevis	780	Trinidad and Tobago

395 Central American Common Market (CACM)

188	Costa Rica	222	El Salvador	320	Guatemala	340	Honduras	558	Nicaragua

171 Common Market for Eastern and Southern Africa (COMESA)

108	Burundi	262	Djibouti	231	Ethiopia	454	Malawi	729	Sudan
174	Comoros	818	Egypt	404	Kenya	480	Mauritius	800	Uganda
180	Democratic Republic of the Congo	232	Eritrea	434	Libya	646	Rwanda	894	Zambia
		748	Eswatini	450	Madagascar	690	Seychelles	716	Zimbabwe

172 Commonwealth of Independent States (CIS)[3]

051	Armenia	398	Kazakhstan	643	Russian Federation	804	Ukraine
031	Azerbaijan	417	Kyrgyzstan	762	Tajikistan	860	Uzbekistan
112	Belarus	498	Republic of Moldova	795	Turkmenistan		

692 Economic and Monetary Community of Central Africa (EMCCA)

120	Cameroon	140	Central African Republic	148	Chad	178	Congo	226	Equatorial Guinea	266	Gabon

892 Economic Community of West African States (ECOWAS)

204	Benin	384	Côte d'Ivoire	324	Guinea	466	Mali	686	Senegal
854	Burkina Faso	270	Gambia	624	Guinea-Bissau	562	Niger	694	Sierra Leone
132	Cabo Verde	288	Ghana	430	Liberia	566	Nigeria	768	Togo

098 Euro Area

040	Austria	246	Finland	372	Ireland	528	Netherlands	724	Spain
056	Belgium	250	France	380	Italy	620	Portugal		
196	Cyprus	276	Germany	442	Luxembourg	703	Slovakia		
233	Estonia	300	Greece	470	Malta	705	Slovenia		

197 European Free Trade Association (EFTA)

352	Iceland	438	Liechtenstein	578	Norway	756	Switzerland

097 European Union (EU)

040	Austria	208	Denmark	348	Hungary	470	Malta	705	Slovenia
056	Belgium	233	Estonia	372	Ireland	528	Netherlands	724	Spain
100	Bulgaria	246	Finland	380	Italy	616	Poland	752	Sweden

[3] Georgia (numerical code 268) can be listed as part of this group; for example, in International Merchandise Trade statistics.

097 European Union (EU) *(Continued)*

191	Croatia	250	France	428	Latvia	620	Portugal	826	United Kingdom
196	Cyprus	276	Germany	440	Lithuania	642	Romania		
203	Czech Republic	300	Greece	442	Luxembourg	703	Slovakia		

095 Latin American Integration Association (LAIA)

032	Argentina	170	Colombia	591	Panama	862	Venezuela (Bolivarian Republic of)
068	Bolivia (Plurinational State of)	192	Cuba	600	Paraguay		
076	Brazil	218	Ecuador	604	Peru		
152	Chile	484	Mexico	858	Uruguay		

199 Least developed countries (LDCs)

004	Afghanistan	262	Djibouti	450	Madagascar	706	Somalia
024	Angola	226	Equatorial Guinea	454	Malawi	728	South Sudan
050	Bangladesh	232	Eritrea	466	Mali	729	Sudan
204	Benin	231	Ethiopia	478	Mauritania	626	Timor-Leste
064	Bhutan	270	Gambia	508	Mozambique	768	Togo
854	Burkina Faso	324	Guinea	104	Myanmar	798	Tuvalu
108	Burundi	624	Guinea-Bissau	524	Nepal	800	Uganda
116	Cambodia	332	Haiti	562	Niger	834	United Republic of Tanzania
140	Central African Republic	296	Kiribati	646	Rwanda		
148	Chad	418	Lao People's Democratic Republic	678	Sao Tome and Principe	548	Vanuatu
174	Comoros			686	Senegal	887	Yemen
180	Democratic Republic of the Congo	426	Lesotho	694	Sierra Leone	894	Zambia
		430	Liberia	090	Solomon Islands		

071 North American Free Trade Agreement (NAFTA)

124	Canada	484	Mexico	840	United States of America

198 Organisation for Economic Co-operation and Development (OECD)

036	Australia	250	France	442	Luxembourg	705	Slovenia
040	Austria	276	Germany	484	Mexico	724	Spain
056	Belgium	300	Greece	528	Netherlands	752	Sweden
124	Canada	348	Hungary	554	New Zealand	756	Switzerland
152	Chile	352	Iceland	578	Norway	792	Turkey
203	Czech Republic	372	Ireland	616	Poland	826	United Kingdom of Great Britain and Northern Ireland
208	Denmark	376	Israel	620	Portugal		
233	Estonia	380	Italy	410	Republic of Korea		
246	Finland	392	Japan	703	Slovakia	840	United States of America

399 Organization of the Petroleum Exporting Countries (OPEC)

012	Algeria	364	Iran (Islamic Republic of)	566	Nigeria	862	Venezuela (Bolivarian Republic of)
024	Angola	368	Iraq	634	Qatar		
218	Ecuador	414	Kuwait	682	Saudi Arabia		
360	Indonesia	434	Libya	784	United Arab Emirates		

711 Southern African Customs Union (SACU)

072	Botswana	748	Eswatini	426	Lesotho	516	Namibia	710	South Africa

069 Southern Common Market (MERCOSUR)

032	Argentina	076	Brazil	858	Uruguay
068	Bolivia (Plurinational State of)	600	Paraguay	862	Venezuela (Bolivarian Republic of)

Annexe I - Nomenclature des pays ou zones, groupements régionaux et autres groupements

L'Annuaire statistique répertorie de pays ou de zones sur la base de l'opuscule United Nations Standard Country Codes (Série M, nº 49) rédigée par la Division de statistique du Secrétariat de l'Organisation des Nations Unies et publiée en 1970[1]. La liste des pays ou zones; la composition des régions géographiques et économiques, commerciales et d'autres groupements utilisés dans cet annuaire (au 31 juillet 2018) sont présentées dans la présente annexe. On a eu recours à la forme brève des noms des pays et des zones usitées au cours des activités courantes des Nations Unies, et pas nécessairement aux désignations officielles utilisées dans les documents officiels[2]. Afin de faciliter le traitement des données statistiques, un code numérique unique et standard à trois chiffres est attribué à chaque pays ou zone et à chaque région géographique et groupement de pays ou de zones. Pour référence, ces codes, le cas échéant, sont présentés à la gauche de chaque pays ou zone visées dans cette annexe. Ces codes s'échelonnent entre 000 et 899.

A. Changements dans le nom des pays ou zones (depuis 31 juillet 2008)

L'étendue géographique d'un pays ou d'une zone ou la composition d'une région géographique peuvent varier au fil du temps et les utilisateurs devront tenir compte de telles modifications lorsqu'ils ont recours aux codes indiques dans la présente publication et qu'ils établissent des rapports entre les données portant sur différentes périodes. La modification du nom d'un pays ou d'une zone alors que son espace géographique demeure le même n'est pas habituellement accompagnée d'un changement de son code numérique. Changements dans les codes numériques et noms dans la période générale couverts par les statistiques (depuis le 31 juillet 2008) dans l'Annuaire, sont présentés ci-dessous;

Code numérique	Pays ou region (nouveaux codes et codes modifies)	Date de la modification	Code numérique	Pays ou region (Changements de nom sans modification du code)	Date de la modification
728	Soudan du Sud	2011	748	Eswatini, *ex-Swaziland*	2018
729	Soudan	2011	203	Tchéquie, *ex-République tchèque*	2016
531	Curaçao	2010	132	Cabo Verde, *ex-Cap-Vert*	2013
534	Saint-Martin (partie néerlandaise)	2010	434	État de Palestine, *ex-Territoire palestinien occupé*	2013
535	Bonaire, Saint-Eustache et Saba	2010	275	Libye, *ex-Jamahiriya arabe libyenne*	2011
			068	Bolivie (État plurinational de), *ex-Bolivie*	2009
			498	République de Moldova, *ex-Moldova*	2008

B. Groupements régionaux

Le système des groupements régionaux à la page suivante est principalement basé sur les 6 continents; ces régions continentales, à l'exception de l'Antarctique, sont subdivisées en 22 sous-régions et 2 régions intermédiaires (Afrique subsaharienne et l'Amérique latine et Caraïbes) afin d'obtenir une homogénéité accrue les effectifs de population, les situations démographiques et la précision des statistiques démographiques. Cette nomenclature est couramment utilisée aux fins des statistiques internationales et a été appliquée autant qu'il a été possible dans le présent *Annuaire* en vue de renforcer la cohérence et de faciliter la comparaison et l'analyse. Son utilisation pour l'établissement des statistiques internationales n'est cependant rien moins qu'universelle, même au niveau des régions continentales, et les variations que présentent les sources et méthodes statistiques internationales entraînent inévitablement de nombreuses différences dans certains domaines de cet *Annuaire*. Les différences d'ordre général sont indiquées dans les notes figurant au bas de la classification présentée ci-dessous. Les différences plus spécifiques sont mentionnées dans les notes techniques et notes de bas de page accompagnant les divers tableaux.

L'application des expressions "développés" et "en développement" aux pays, zones ou régions n'est pas non plus normalisée à l'échelle internationale. Ces expressions sont utilisées dans la présente publication en référence aux groupements régionaux généralement considérés comme "développés", à savoir l'Amérique septentrionale (code numérique 021), l'Europe (150), Chypre (196), Israël (376), le Japon (392) et l'Australie et la Nouvelle-Zélande (053). Ces appellations sont employées pour des raisons de commodité statistique et n'expriment pas nécessairement un jugement sur le stade de développement atteint par tel ou tel pays ou zone. Les cas différant de cet usage sont signalés dans les notes accompagnant les tableaux concernés.

[1] Quatre révisions de ce document ont été publiés en 1975, 1982, 1996 et 1999. D'autres révisions sont maintenant publiés sur le site internet de la Division de statistique des Nations Unies.

[2] Le Bulletin terminologique No 347/Rev.1 ou UNTERM website, intitulé "Noms de pays" établi par le Département des affaires de l'Assemblée générale et des services de conférence du Secrétariat de l'Organisation des Nations Unies, répertorie les noms des États Membres dans les six langues de l'Organisation.

001 Monde

002 Afrique

202 Afrique subsaharienne

014 Afrique orientale

108 Burundi
174 Comores
262 Djibouti
232 Érythrée
231 Éthiopie
404 Kenya
450 Madagascar
454 Malawi
480 Maurice
175 Mayotte
508 Mozambique
800 Ouganda
834 République-Unie de Tanzanie note /a
638 Réunion
646 Rwanda
690 Seychelles
706 Somalie
728 Soudan du Sud note 736
260 Terres australes françaises
086 Territoire britannique de l'océan Indien
894 Zambie
716 Zimbabwe

017 Afrique centrale

024 Angola
120 Cameroun
178 Congo
266 Gabon
226 Guinée équatoriale
140 République centrafricaine
180 République démocratique du Congo
678 Sao Tomé-et-Principe
148 Tchad

018 Afrique australe

710 Afrique du Sud
072 Botswana
748 Eswatini
426 Lesotho
516 Namibie

011 Afrique occidentale

204 Bénin
854 Burkina Faso
132 Cabo Verde
384 Côte d'Ivoire
270 Gambie
288 Ghana
324 Guinée
624 Guinée-Bissau
430 Libéria
466 Mali
478 Mauritanie
562 Niger
566 Nigéria
654 Sainte-Hélène note /b
686 Sénégal
694 Sierra Leone
768 Togo

015 Afrique septentrionale

012 Algérie
818 Égypte
434 Libye
504 Maroc
732 Sahara occidental
729 Soudan note 736
788 Tunisie

Note **Certains tableaux peuvent**

736 *Soudan [anc.]*

/a Incluent
--- *Zanzibar*

/b Incluent
--- *Ascension*
--- *Tristan da Cunha*

019 Amériques

419 Amérique latine et Caraïbes

029 Caraïbes

660 Anguilla
028 Antigua-et-Barbuda
533 Aruba
044 Bahamas
052 Barbade
535 Bonaire, Saint-Eustache et Saba note 530
192 Cuba
531 Curaçao note 530
212 Dominique
308 Grenade
312 Guadeloupe
332 Haïti
136 Îles Caïmanes
796 Îles Turques-et-Caïques
850 Îles Vierges américaines
092 Îles Vierges britanniques
388 Jamaïque
474 Martinique
500 Montserrat
630 Porto Rico
214 République dominicaine
652 Saint-Barthélemy
659 Saint-Kitts-et-Nevis
662 Sainte-Lucie
663 Saint-Martin (partie française)
534 Saint-Martin (partie néerlandaise) note 530
670 Saint-Vincent-et-les Grenadines
780 Trinité-et-Tobago

013 Amérique centrale

084 Belize
188 Costa Rica
222 El Salvador
320 Guatemala
340 Honduras
484 Mexique
558 Nicaragua
591 Panama

005 Amérique du Sud

032 Argentine
068 Bolivie (État plurinational de)
076 Brésil
152 Chili
170 Colombie
218 Équateur
239 Géorgie du Sud-et-les Îles Sandwich du Sud
328 Guyana
254 Guyane française
074 Île Bouvet
238 Îles Falkland (Malvinas)
600 Paraguay
604 Pérou
740 Suriname
858 Uruguay
862 Venezuela (République bolivarienne du)

021 Amérique septentrionale note 003

060 Bermudes
124 Canada
840 États-Unis d'Amérique
304 Groenland
666 Saint-Pierre-et-Miquelon

Note

003 *Le continent de* ***l'Amérique du Nord*** *comprend l'Amérique septentrionale, les Caraïbes et l'Amérique centrale*

Certains tableaux peuvent

530 *Antilles néerlandaises [anc.]*

010 Antarctique

001 Monde

142 Asie

143 Asie centrale

398 Kazakhstan
417 Kirghizistan
860 Ouzbékistan
762 Tadjikistan
795 Turkménistan

030 Asie orientale

156 Chine
344 Chine, région administrative spéciale de Hong Kong
446 Chine, région administrative spéciale de Macao
392 Japon
496 Mongolie
410 République de Corée
408 République populaire démocratique de Corée

035 Asie du Sud-Est

096 Brunéi Darussalam
116 Cambodge
360 Indonésie
458 Malaisie
104 Myanmar
608 Philippines
418 République démocratique populaire lao
702 Singapour
764 Thaïlande
626 Timor-Leste
704 Viet Nam

034 Asie méridionale

004 Afghanistan
050 Bangladesh
064 Bhoutan
356 Inde
364 Iran (République islamique d')
462 Maldives
524 Népal
586 Pakistan
144 Sri Lanka

145 Asie occidentale

682 Arabie saoudite
051 Arménie
031 Azerbaïdjan
048 Bahreïn
196 Chypre
784 Émirats arabes unis
275 État de Palestine
268 Géorgie
368 Iraq
376 Israël
400 Jordanie
414 Koweït
422 Liban
512 Oman
634 Qatar
760 République arabe syrienne
792 Turquie
887 Yémen

150 Europe

151 Europe orientale

112 Bélarus
100 Bulgarie
643 Fédération de Russie
348 Hongrie
616 Pologne
498 République de Moldova
642 Roumanie
703 Slovaquie
203 Tchéquie
804 Ukraine

154 Europe septentrionale

208 Danemark
233 Estonie
246 Finlande
831 Guernesey note 830
833 Île de Man
248 Îles d'Åland
234 Îles Féroé
744 Îles Svalbard-et-Jan Mayen
372 Irlande
352 Islande
832 Jersey note 830
428 Lettonie
440 Lituanie
578 Norvège
826 Royaume-Uni de Grande-Bretagne et d'Irlande du Nord
752 Suède

039 Europe méridionale

008 Albanie
020 Andorre
070 Bosnie-Herzégovine
191 Croatie
724 Espagne
807 Ex-République yougoslave de Macédoine
292 Gibraltar
300 Grèce
380 Italie
470 Malte
499 Monténégro note 891
620 Portugal
674 Saint-Marin
336 Saint-Siège
688 Serbie note 891 & /c
705 Slovénie

155 Europe occidentale

276 Allemagne
040 Autriche
056 Belgique
250 France
438 Liechtenstein
442 Luxembourg
492 Monaco
528 Pays-Bas
756 Suisse

Note **Certains tableaux peuvent énumérer**

830 *Îles Anglo-Normandes*
891 *Serbie-et-Monténégro [anc.]*
/c *Kosovo*

009 Océanie

053 Australie et Nouvelle-Zélande

036 Australie
162 Île Christmas
334 Île Heard-et-Îles MacDonald
574 Île Norfolk
166 Îles des Cocos (Keeling)
554 Nouvelle-Zélande

054 Mélanésie

242 Fidji
090 Îles Salomon
540 Nouvelle-Calédonie
598 Papouasie-Nouvelle-Guinée
548 Vanuatu

057 Micronésie

316 Guam
580 Îles Mariannes du Nord
584 Îles Marshall
581 Îles mineures éloignées des États-Unis
296 Kiribati
583 Micronésie (États fédérés de)
520 Nauru
585 Palaos

061 Polynésie

184 Îles Cook
876 Îles Wallis-et-Futuna
570 Nioué
612 Pitcairn
258 Polynésie française
882 Samoa
016 Samoa américaines
772 Tokélaou[corrigée]
776 Tonga
798 Tuvalu

C. Autres groupements

On trouvera ci-après une liste des autres groupements et de leur composition, présentée dans l'*Annuaire*. Ces groupements correspondent essentiellement à des intérêts économiques et commerciaux d'après les associations régionales.

071 Accord de libre-échange nord-américain (ALENA)

124 Canada; 840 États-Unis d'Amérique; 484 Mexique

073 Association des nations de l'Asie du Sud-Est (ANASE)

096 Brunéi Darussalam; 116 Cambodge; 360 Indonésie; 458 Malaisie; 104 Myanmar; 608 Philippines; 418 République démocratique populaire lao; 702 Singapour; 764 Thaïlande; 704 Viet Nam

197 Association européenne de libre-échange (AELE)

352 Islande; 438 Liechtenstein; 578 Norvège; 756 Suisse

095 Association latino-américaine d'intégration (ALAI)

032 Argentine; 068 Bolivie (État plurinational de); 076 Brésil; 152 Chili; 170 Colombie; 192 Cuba; 218 Équateur; 484 Mexique; 591 Panama; 600 Paraguay; 604 Pérou; 858 Uruguay; 862 Venezuela (République bolivarienne du)

130 Communauté des Caraïbes et Marché commun des Caraïbes (CARICOM)

028 Antigua-et-Barbuda; 044 Bahamas (membre de la communauté seulement); 052 Barbade; 084 Belize; 212 Dominique; 308 Grenade; 328 Guyana; 332 Haïti; 388 Jamaïque; 500 Montserrat; 659 Saint-Kitts-et-Nevis; 662 Sainte-Lucie; 670 Saint-Vincent-et-les Grenadines; 740 Suriname; 780 Trinité-et-Tobago

172 Communauté d'Etats indépendants (CEI)[3]

051 Arménie; 031 Azerbaïdjan; 112 Bélarus; 643 Fédération de Russie; 268 Géorgie; 398 Kazakhstan; 417 Kirghizistan; 860 Ouzbékistan; 498 République de Moldova; 762 Tadjikistan; 795 Turkménistan; 804 Ukraine

892 Communauté économique des Etats de l'Afrique de l'Ouest (CEDEAO)

204 Bénin; 854 Burkina Faso; 132 Cabo Verde; 384 Côte d'Ivoire; 270 Gambie; 288 Ghana; 324 Guinée; 624 Guinée-Bissau; 430 Libéria; 466 Mali; 562 Niger; 566 Nigéria; 686 Sénégal; 694 Sierra Leone; 768 Togo

692 Communauté économique et monétaire des Etats de l'Afrique Centrale (CEMAC)

120 Cameroun; 178 Congo; 266 Gabon; 226 Guinée équatoriale; 140 République centrafricaine; 148 Tchad

066 Coopération économique Asie-Pacifique (CEAP)

036 Australie; 096 Brunéi Darussalam; 124 Canada; 152 Chili; 156 Chine; 344 Chine, région administrative spéciale de Hong Kong; 840 États-Unis d'Amérique; 643 Fédération de Russie; 360 Indonésie; 392 Japon; 458 Malaisie; 484 Mexique; 554 Nouvelle-Zélande; 598 Papouasie-Nouvelle-Guinée; 604 Pérou; 608 Philippines; 158 Province chinoise de Taïwan; 410 République de Corée; 702 Singapour; 764 Thaïlande; 704 Viet Nam

063 Marché commun andin (ANCOM)

068 Bolivie (État plurinational de); 170 Colombie; 218 Équateur; 604 Pérou

395 Marché commun centraméricain (MCCA)

188 Costa Rica; 222 El Salvador; 320 Guatemala; 340 Honduras; 558 Nicaragua

171 Marché commun de l'Afrique de l'Est et de l'Afrique australe (COMESA)

108 Burundi; 174 Comores; 262 Djibouti; 818 Égypte; 232 Érythrée; 748 Eswatini; 231 Éthiopie; 404 Kenya; 434 Libye; 450 Madagascar; 454 Malawi; 480 Maurice; 800 Ouganda; 180 République démocratique du Congo; 646 Rwanda; 690 Seychelles; 729 Soudan; 894 Zambie; 716 Zimbabwe

[3] La Géorgie (code numérique 268) peut figurer dans ce groupe; par exemple, dans le cadre des statistiques du commerce international de marchandises.

069 Marché commun du Sud (MERCOSUR)

032	Argentine	076	Brésil	858	Uruguay
068	Bolivie (État plurinational de)	600	Paraguay	862	Venezuela (République bolivarienne du)

198 Organisation de coopération et de développement économiques (OCDE)

276	Allemagne	840	États-Unis d'Amérique	392	Japon	203	République tchèque
036	Australie	246	Finlande	442	Luxembourg	826	Royaume-Uni de Grande-Bretagne et d'Irlande du Nord
040	Autriche	250	France	484	Mexique		
056	Belgique	300	Grèce	578	Norvège		
124	Canada	348	Hongrie	554	Nouvelle-Zélande	703	Slovaquie
152	Chili	372	Irlande	528	Pays-Bas	705	Slovénie
208	Danemark	376	Israël	616	Pologne	752	Suède
724	Espagne	352	Islande	620	Portugal	756	Suisse
233	Estonie	380	Italie	410	République de Corée	792	Turquie

399 Organisation des pays exportateurs de pétrole (OPEP)

012	Algérie	218	Équateur	434	Libye	862	Venezuela (République bolivarienne du)
024	Angola	360	Indonésie	414	Koweït		
682	Arabie saoudite	364	Iran (République islamique d')	566	Nigéria		
784	Émirats arabes unis	368	Iraq	634	Qatar		

199 Pays les moins avancés (PMA)

004	Afghanistan	270	Gambie	478	Mauritanie	686	Sénégal
024	Angola	324	Guinée	508	Mozambique	694	Sierra Leone
050	Bangladesh	226	Guinée équatoriale	104	Myanmar	706	Somalie
204	Bénin	624	Guinée-Bissau	524	Népal	728	Soudan du Sud
064	Bhoutan	332	Haïti	562	Niger	729	Soudan
854	Burkina Faso	090	Îles Salomon	800	Ouganda	148	Tchad
108	Burundi	296	Kiribati	140	République centrafricaine	626	Timor-Leste
116	Cambodge	426	Lesotho	180	République démocratique du Congo	768	Togo
174	Comores	430	Libéria	418	République démocratique populaire lao	798	Tuvalu
262	Djibouti	450	Madagascar	834	République-Unie de Tanzanie	548	Vanuatu
232	Érythrée	454	Malawi	646	Rwanda	887	Yémen
231	Éthiopie	466	Mali	678	Sao Tomé-et-Principe	894	Zambie

711 Union douanière d'Afrique australe

710	Afrique du Sud	072	Botswana	748	Eswatini	426	Lesotho	516	Namibie

097 Union européenne (UE)

276	Allemagne	208	Danemark	348	Hongrie	470	Malte	826	Royaume-Uni de Grande-Bretagne et d'Irlande du Nord
040	Autriche	724	Espagne	372	Irlande	528	Pays-Bas		
056	Belgique	233	Estonie	380	Italie	616	Pologne		
100	Bulgarie	246	Finlande	428	Lettonie	620	Portugal	703	Slovaquie
191	Croatie	250	France	440	Lituanie	203	République tchèque	705	Slovénie
196	Chypre	300	Grèce	442	Luxembourg	642	Roumanie	752	Suède

098 Zone euro

276	Allemagne	724	Espagne	300	Grèce	470	Malte	705	Slovénie
040	Autriche	233	Estonie	372	Irlande	528	Pays-Bas		
056	Belgique	246	Finlande	380	Italie	620	Portugal		
196	Chypre	250	France	442	Luxembourg	703	Slovaquie		

Annex II: Technical notes

Chapter I: World summary

Table 1: World statistics – selected series

These world aggregates are obtained from other tables in this *Yearbook*, where available, and are compiled from statistical publications and databases of the United Nations and the specialized agencies and other institutions. The technical notes of the relevant table in this *Yearbook* should be consulted for detailed information on definition, source, compilation and coverage.

Chapter II: Population and migration

Table 2: Population, surface area and density

The total, male and female population, sex ratio, population age distribution and population density are taken from the estimates and projections prepared by the United Nations Population Division, published in *World Population Prospects: The 2017 Revision.* Surface area are obtained from the *Demographic Yearbook*, through this source only official national data are reported.

Total, male and female population refers to the de facto population in a country, area or region as of 1 July of the year indicated, unless otherwise stated in a footnote. Figures are presented in millions. The total population of a country may comprise either all usual residents of the country (de jure population) or all persons present in the country (de facto population) at the time of the census; for purposes of international comparisons, the de facto definition is used, unless otherwise stated in a footnote.

Population aged 0-14 years / 60 years and over refers to the percentage of the population aged 0-14 years and aged 60 years and older, respectively as of 1 July of the year indicated, unless otherwise stated in a footnote.

Population density refers to the population, as of 1 July of the year indicated, per square kilometre of surface area, unless otherwise stated in a footnote.

Sex ratio is calculated as the ratio of the population of men to that of 100 women as of 1 July of the year indicated, unless otherwise stated in a footnote.

Surface area refers to land area plus inland water, unless otherwise stated in a footnote.

Table 3: Population in the capital city, urban and rural areas

The statistics on population in the capital city and urban areas and their rates of growth for each country or area are estimates and projections published by the Population Division of the Department of Economic and Social Affairs of the United Nations Secretariat in the *World Urbanization Prospects: The 2018 Revision*. Because of national differences in the specific characteristics that distinguish urban from rural areas, there are no internationally agreed definitions of urban and rural. In most countries, the distinction is mainly based on size of locality. For the latest available census definition of urban areas in a particular country or area, reference should be made to the *Demographic Yearbook.* Annual rates of change in urban and rural population are computed as average annual percentage changes using mid-year population estimates.

Table 4: International migrants and refugees

International migrant stock are taken from the estimates and projections prepared by the United Nations Population Division, published in *International migrant stock: The 2017 Revision.* "Refugees and others of concern to UNHCR" are obtained from the United Nations High Commissioner for Refugees, published in the Population Statistics database.

International migrant stock represents the number of persons born in a country other than that in which they live. When information on country of birth was not recorded, data on the number of persons having foreign citizenship was used instead. In the absence of any empirical data, estimates were imputed. Figures for international migrant stock as a percentage of the population are the outcome of dividing the estimated international migrant stock by the estimated total population and multiplying the result by 100.

Refugees include individuals recognised under the 1951 Convention relating to the Status of Refugees; its 1967 Protocol; the 1969 OAU Convention Governing the Specific Aspects of Refugee Problems in Africa; those recognised in accordance with the UNHCR Statute; individuals granted complementary forms of protection; or those enjoying temporary protection. Since 2007, the refugee population also includes people in a refugee-like situation.

Asylum-seekers are individuals who have sought international protection and whose claims for refugee status have not yet been determined, irrespective of when they may have been lodged.

"Other" represents the following 5 categories:

- Internally displaced persons (IDPs) are people or groups of individuals who have been forced to leave their homes or places of habitual residence, in particular as a result of, or in order to avoid the effects of armed conflict, situations of generalised violence, violations of human rights, or natural or man-made disasters, and who have not crossed an international border. For the purposes of UNHCR's statistics, this population only includes conflict-generated IDPs to whom the Office extends protection and/or assistance. Since 2007, the IDP population also includes people in an IDP-like situation. For global IDP estimates, see www.internal-displacement.org.
- Returned refugees are former refugees who have returned to their country of origin spontaneously or in an organised fashion but are yet to be fully integrated. Such return would normally only take place in conditions of safety and dignity.
- Returned IDPs refer to those IDPs who were beneficiaries of UNHCR's protection and assistance activities and who returned to their areas of origin or habitual residence during the year.
- Stateless persons are defined under international law as persons who are not considered as nationals by any State under the operation of its law. In other words, they do not possess the nationality of any State. UNHCR statistics refer to persons who fall under the agency's statelessness mandate because they are stateless according to this international definition, but data from some countries may also include persons with undetermined nationality.
- Others of concern refers to individuals who do not necessarily fall directly into any of the groups above, but to whom UNHCR extends its protection and/or assistance services, based on humanitarian or other special grounds.

Chapter III: Gender

Table 5: Proportion of seats held by women in national parliament

The table shows the percentage of seats held by women members in single or lower chambers of national parliaments as at January/ February each year (see table footnotes for specific details). National parliaments can be bicameral or unicameral. This table covers the single chamber in unicameral parliaments and the lower chamber in bicameral parliaments. It does not cover the upper chamber of bi-cameral parliaments. Seats are usually won by members in general parliamentary elections. Seats may also be filled by nomination, appointment, indirect election, rotation of members and by-election. The proportion of seats held by women in national parliament is derived by dividing the total number of seats occupied by women by the total number of seats in parliament. There is no weighting or normalising of statistics. The source for this table is the Inter-Parliamentary Union (IPU), see www.ipu.org for further information.

Table 6: Ratio of girls to boys in primary, secondary and tertiary education

The ratio of girls to boys (gender parity index) in primary, secondary and tertiary education is the ratio of the number of female students enrolled at primary, secondary and tertiary levels of education to the number of male students in each level. To standardise the effects of the population structure of the appropriate age groups, the Gender Parity Index (GPI) of the Gross Enrolment Ratio (GER) for each level of education is used. The source for this table is the UNESCO Institute for Statistics (UIS), see www.uis.unesco.org for further information.

Chapter IV: Education

Data in Tables 7 and 8 are presented using the 2011 revision of UNESCO's International Standard Classification of Education (ISCED). Data are presented in the tables based on the three main levels of educations defined as follows;

"Primary education" (ISCED level 1) programmes are typically designed to provide students with fundamental skills in reading, writing and mathematics (i.e. literacy and numeracy) and establish a solid foundation for learning and understanding core areas of knowledge, personal and social development, in preparation for lower secondary education. It focuses on learning at a basic level of complexity with little, if any, specialisation.

"Secondary education" (ISCED level 2 and 3) is divided into two different stages, i.e. lower secondary and upper secondary. Lower secondary education programmes are typically designed to build on the learning outcomes from primary. Usually, they aim to lay the foundation for lifelong learning and human development upon which education systems may then expand further educational opportunities. Upper secondary education programmes are typically designed to complete secondary education in preparation for tertiary education or provide skills relevant to employment, or both. Programmes at this level offer students more varied, specialised and in-depth instruction than programmes at lower secondary. They are more differentiated, with an increased range of options and streams available. Teachers are often highly qualified in the subjects or fields of specialisation they teach, particularly in the higher grades.

Tertiary education (ISCED levels 5-8) builds on secondary education, providing learning activities in specialised fields of education. It aims at learning at a high level of complexity and specialisation. Tertiary education includes what is commonly understood as academic education but also includes advanced vocational or professional education. It comprises ISCED levels 5, 6, 7 and 8, which are labelled as short-cycle tertiary education, Bachelor's or equivalent level, Master's or equivalent level, and doctoral or equivalent level, respectively. The content of programmes at the tertiary level is more complex and advanced than in lower ISCED levels.

For more information about the International Standard Classification of Education (ISCED) 2011 please refer to: http://www.uis.unesco.org/Education/Documents/isced-2011-en.pdf

Table 7: Education at the primary, secondary and tertiary levels

The table shows the number of students enrolled as well as the gross enrolment ratio which is the number of students enrolled, regardless of age, expressed as a percentage of the eligible official school-age population corresponding to the same level of education in a given school year. Enrolment is measured at the beginning of the school or academic year. The gross enrolment ratio at each level will include all pupils whatever their ages, whereas the population is limited to the range of official school ages. Therefore, for countries with almost universal education among the school-age population, the gross enrolment ratio can exceed 100 if the actual age distribution of pupils extends beyond the official school ages.

Table 8: Teaching staff at the primary, secondary and tertiary levels

The table shows the total number of teachers at a given level of education, as well as the proportion of female teachers expressed as a percentage of the total (male and female) at the same level in a given school year. The data sources include school census or surveys and teachers' records. Teachers (or teaching staff) are defined as persons employed full-time or part-time in an official capacity to guide and direct the learning experience of pupils and students, irrespective of their qualifications or the delivery mechanism, i.e. face-to-face and/or at a distance. This definition excludes educational personnel who have no active teaching duties (e.g. headmasters, headmistresses or principals who do not teach) or who work occasionally or in a voluntary capacity in educational institutions.

Table 9: Public expenditure on education

Public expenditure on education consists of current and capital expenditures on education by local, regional and national governments, including municipalities. Household contributions are excluded. Current expenditure on education includes expenditure for goods and services consumed within the current year and which would need to be renewed if needed the following year. It includes expenditure on: staff salaries and benefits; contracted or purchased services; other resources including books and teaching materials; welfare services; and other current expenditure such as subsidies to students and households, furniture and equipment, minor repairs, fuel, telecommunications, travel, insurance and rents. Capital expenditure on education includes expenditure for assets that last longer than one year. It includes expenditure for construction, renovation and major repairs of buildings and the purchase of heavy equipment or vehicles.

Chapter V: Health

Table 10: Health personnel

The table shows four main categories of health personnel (out of 9 categories available in the source); Physicians which includes generalist medical practitioners and specialist medical practitioners; Nursing and midwifery personnel which includes nursing professionals, midwifery professionals, nursing associate professionals and midwifery associate professionals. Traditional midwives are not included here; Dentistry personnel includes dentists, dental assistants, dental technicians and related occupations; and Pharmaceutical personnel which includes pharmacists, pharmaceutical assistants, pharmaceutical technicians and related occupations.

The data are obtained from the World Health Organisation's (WHO) Global Health Workforce Statistics database which are compiled from several sources such as national population censuses, labour force and employment surveys, national statistical products and routine administrative information systems. As a result, considerable variability remains across countries in the coverage, quality and reference year of the original data. In general, the denominator data for health workforce density (i.e. national population estimates) were obtained from the United Nations Population Division's *World Population Prospects* publication. In some cases, the official report provided only workforce density indicators, from which estimates of the stock were then calculated.

The classification of health workers used is based on criteria for vocational education and training, regulation of health professions, and activities and tasks of jobs, i.e. a framework for categorizing key workforce variables according to shared characteristics. The WHO framework largely draws on the latest revisions to the internationally standardized classification systems of the International Labour Organization (International Standard Classification of Occupations), United Nations Educational, Scientific and Cultural Organization (International Standard Classification of Education), and the United Nations Statistics Division (International Standard Industrial Classification of All Economic Activities). Depending on the nature of each country's situation and the means of measurement, data are available for up to 9 categories of health workers in the aggregated set, and up to 18 categories in the disaggregated set. The latter essentially reflects attempts to better distinguish some subgroups of the workforce according to assumed differences in skill level and skill specialization.

Table 11: Expenditure on health

The series "Current expenditure" refers to all health care goods and services used or consumed during a year excluding capital spending, or rather "gross capital formation", which is the purchase of new assets used repeatedly over several years. These estimates are in line with the 2011 System of Health Accounts (SHA). Current expenditure is expressed as a proportion of Gross Domestic Product (GDP). The series Domestic General government expenditures are composed of public and private domestic sources. The Domestic public sources include domestic revenue as internal transfers and grants, transfers, subsidies to voluntary health insurance beneficiaries, Non-profit institutions serving households (NPISH) or enterprise financing schemes as well as compulsory prepayment and social health insurance contributions. All these transfers and subsidies represent public sources for health and indicate the overall governments' contribution to funding healthcare relative to other sources of funding from domestic private and external sources. Domestic General government expenditure is expressed as a proportion of general government expenditures.

Chapter VI: Crime

Table 12: Intentional homicides and other crimes

"Intentional homicides" and "other crimes" are taken from the United Nations Office on Drugs and Crime, published in their statistics database.

"Intentional Homicide" means unlawful death purposefully inflicted on a person by another person. Data on intentional homicide should also include serious assault leading to death and death as a result of a terrorist attack. It should exclude attempted homicide, manslaughter, death due to legal intervention, justifiable homicide in self-defence and death due to armed conflict.

"Assault" means physical attack against the body of another person resulting in serious bodily injury, excluding indecent/sexual assault, threats and slapping/punching. 'Assault' leading to death should also be excluded.

"Kidnapping" means unlawfully detaining a person or persons against their will (including through the use of force, threat, fraud or enticement) for the purpose of demanding for their liberation an illicit gain or any other economic gain or other material benefit, or in order to oblige someone to do or not to do something. "Kidnapping" excludes disputes over child custody.

"Theft" means depriving a person or organisation of property without force with the intent to keep it . "Theft" excludes Burglary, housebreaking, Robbery, and Theft of a Motor Vehicle, which are recorded separately.

Total "Sexual violence" means rape and sexual assault, including Sexual Offences against Children.

Chapter VII: National accounts

The National Accounts Main Aggregates Database (available at http://unstats.un.org/unsd/snaama) presents national accounts data for more than 200 countries and areas of the world. It is the basis for the publication of National Account Statistics: Analysis of Main Aggregates (AMA), a publication prepared by the Statistics Division of the Department for Economic and Social Affairs of the United Nations Secretariat with the generous co-operation of national statistical offices. The database is updated in December of each year with newly available national accounts data for all countries and areas.

The National Accounts Main Aggregates Database is based on the data obtained from the United Nations National Accounts Questionnaire (NAQ) introduced in October 1999, which in turn is based on the System of National Accounts 1993 (1993 SNA). The data are supplemented with estimates prepared by the Statistics Division. The updated SNA, called the System of National Accounts 2008 (2008 SNA) was finalised in September 2009. As of 2017, 83 countries and territories (European Union Member States Albania, Argentina, Armenia, Australia, Belarus, Brazil, British Virgin Islands, Brunei Darussalam, Canada, Chile, China (mainland), China, Hong Kong SAR, China, Macao SAR, Costa Rica, Dominican Republic, Ecuador, Eswatini, Fiji, Iceland, India, Indonesia, Israel, Japan, Kenya, Lao People's Democratic Republic, Lebanon, Liechtenstein, Malaysia, Mauritius, Mexico, Mongolia, Montenegro, Morocco, New Zealand, Nigeria, Norway, Pakistan, Peru, Philippines, Republic of Korea, Saudi Arabia, Serbia, Singapore, Sint Maarten, South Africa, Sri Lanka, Switzerland, TFYR of Macedonia, Thailand, Timor-Leste, Turkey, Uganda, Ukraine, the United States of America and Zambia) have started submitting data according to the 2008 SNA.

Every effort has been made to present the estimates of the various countries or areas in a form designed to facilitate international comparability. To this end, important differences in concept, scope, coverage and classification have been described in the footnotes for individual countries. Such differences should be taken into account to avoid misleading comparisons. Data contained in the tables relate to the calendar year for which they are shown, except in several cases. These special cases are posted on the National Accounts Main Aggregates Database website (http://unstats.un.org/unsd/snaama/notes.asp). The figures shown are the most recent estimates and revisions available at the time of compilation. In general, figures for the most recent year are to be regarded as provisional. The sums of the components in the tables may not necessarily add up to totals shown because of rounding.

Table 13: Gross domestic product and gross domestic product per capita

This table shows gross domestic product (GDP) and GDP per capita in US dollars at current prices, GDP at constant 2005 prices and the corresponding real rates of growth. The tables are intended to facilitate international comparisons of levels of income generated in production. Official data and estimates of total and per capita GDP at current prices have been converted to US dollars, while total GDP at constant prices are converted to 2005 prices before conversion to US dollars using the 2005 exchange rates. The conversion methodology to US dollars is described in the document on the methodology for the National Accounts Main Aggregates Database (http://unstats.un.org/unsd/snaama/methodology.pdf). For inter-country comparisons over time, it would be more appropriate to use the growth rate in the table based on constant price data, which are more indicative of inter-country and intra-grouping comparisons of trends in total GDP. The growth rate shown in the table is computed as geometric mean of annual growth rates expressed as percentages for the years.

Table 14: Gross value added by kind of economic activity

This table presents the shares of the components of gross value added at current prices by kind of economic activity.

Sector	Comprises of (in terms of ISIC 3):
Agriculture	Agriculture, hunting, forestry and fishing (ISIC A-B)
Industry	Mining and quarrying, Manufacturing, Electricity, gas and water supply (ISIC C-E) Construction (ISIC F)
Services	Wholesale and retail trade; repair of motor vehicles, motorcycles and personal and household goods, Hotels and restaurants (ISIC G-H) Transport, storage and communications (ISIC I) Other activities which includes financial intermediation, real estate, renting and business activities, public administration and defense; compulsory social security, education, health and social work, other community, social and personal service activities, private households with employed persons (ISIC J-P).

Chapter VIII: Finance

Detailed information and current figures relating to table 15? are contained in International Financial Statistics, published by the International Monetary Fund (see also http://elibrary-data.imf.org) and in the United Nations Monthly Bulletin of Statistics.

Table 15: Balance of payments summary

A balance of payments can be broadly described as the record of an economy's international economic transactions. It shows (a) transactions in goods, services and income between an economy and the rest of the world, (b) changes of ownership and other changes in that economy's monetary gold, special drawing rights (SDRs) and claims on and liabilities to the rest of the world, and (c) unrequited transfers and counterpart entries needed to balance in the accounting sense any entries for the foregoing transactions and changes which are not mutually offsetting. The balance of payments data are presented on the basis of the methodology and presentation of the sixth edition of the Balance of Payments Manual (BPM6), published by the International Monetary Fund in November 2013. The BPM6 incorporates several major changes to take account of developments in international trade and finance over the years, and to better harmonize the Fund's balance of payments methodology with the methodology of the 2008 System of National Accounts (SNA). The detailed definitions concerning the content of the basic categories of the balance of payments are given in the Balance of Payments Manual (sixth edition)

Brief explanatory notes are given below to clarify the scope of the major items.

Current account is a record of all transactions in the balance of payments covering the exports and imports of goods and services, payments of income, and current transfers between residents of a country and non-residents.

Capital account, n.i.e. refers mainly to capital transfers linked to the acquisition of a fixed asset other than transactions relating to debt forgiveness plus the disposal of nonproduced, nonfinancial assets, and to capital transfers linked to the disposal of fixed assets by the donor or to the financing of capital formation by the recipient, plus the acquisition of nonproduced, nonfinancial assets.

Financial account, n.i.e. is the net sum of the balance of direct investment, portfolio investment, and other investment transactions.

Reserves and related items is the sum of transactions in reserve assets, LCFARs, exceptional financing, and use of Fund credit and loans.

Table 16: Exchange rates

Foreign exchange rates are shown in units of national currency per US dollar. The exchange rates are classified into three broad categories, reflecting both the role of the authorities in the determination of the exchange and/or the multiplicity of exchange rates in a country. The market rate is used to describe exchange rates determined largely by market forces; the official rate is an exchange rate deter-mined by the authorities, sometimes in a flexible manner. For countries maintaining multiple exchange arrangements, the rates are labelled principal rate, secondary rate, and tertiary rate. Unless otherwise stated, the table refers to end of period and period averages of market exchange rates or official exchange rates.

Chapter IX: Labour market

A comparable and comprehensive collection of data on labour force and related topics are available from the International Labour Organisation's (ILO) *Key Indicators of the Labour Market (KILM)* publication, which is updated every 2 years. More timely information is contained in the ILO's ILOSTAT data repository (see www.ilo.org/ilostat) which publishes data as it is received from the countries either on an annual, quarterly or monthly basis but does not include all the consistency checks nor include all the sources used by KILM. For various reasons, national definitions of employment and unemployment often differ from the recommended international standard definitions and thereby limit international comparability. Inter-country comparisons are also complicated by a variety of types of data collection systems used to obtain information on employed and unemployed persons. The ILOSTAT website provides a comprehensive description of the methodology underlying the labour series.

Table 17: Labour force and unemployment

Labour force participation rate is calculated by expressing the number of persons in the labour force as a percentage of the working-age population. The labour force is the sum of the number of persons employed and the number of unemployed (see ILO's current International Recommendations on Labour Statistics). The working-age population is the population above a certain age, prescribed for the measurement of economic characteristics. The data refer to the age group of 15 years and over and are based on ILO's modelled estimates, unless otherwise stated in a footnote.

Unemployment" is defined to include persons above a certain age who, during a specified period of time were:

(a) "Without work", i.e. were not in paid employment or self-employment;

(b) "Currently available for work", i.e. were available for paid employment or self-employment during the reference period; and

(c) "Seeking work", i.e. had taken specific steps in a specified period to find paid employment or self-employment

Persons not considered to be unemployed include:

(a) Persons intending to establish their own business or farm, but who had not yet arranged to do so and who were not seeking work for pay or profit;

(b) Former unpaid family workers not at work and not seeking work for pay or profit.

The series generally represent the total number of persons wholly unemployed or temporarily laid-off. Percentage figures, where given, are calculated by comparing the number of unemployed to the total members of that group of the labour force on which the unemployment data are based.

Table 18: Employment by economic activity

The employment table presents the percentage distribution of employed persons by economic activity, according to International Standard Industry Classification (ISIC) version 4.

Chapter X: Price and production indices

Table 19: Consumer price indices

A consumer price index is usually estimated as a series of summary measures of the period-to-period proportional change in the prices of a fixed set of consumer goods and services of constant quantity and characteristics, acquired, used or paid for by the reference population. Each summary measure is constructed as a weighted average of a large number of elementary aggregate indices. Each of the elementary aggregate indices is estimated using a sample of prices for a defined set of goods and services obtained in, or by residents of, a specific region from a given set of outlets or other sources of consumption goods and services. The table presents the general consumer price index for all groups of consumption items combined, and the food index including non-alcoholic beverages only. Where alcoholic beverages and/or tobacco are included, this is indicated in footnotes.

Table 20: Agricultural production

"Agriculture" relates to the production of all crops and livestock products. The "Food Index" includes those commodities which are considered edible and contain nutrients. The index numbers of agricultural output and food production are calculated by the Laspeyres formula with the base year period 2004-2006. The latter is provided in order to diminish the impact of annual fluctuations in agricultural output during base years on the indices for the period. Production quantities of each commodity are weighted by 2004-2006 average national producer prices and summed for each year. The index numbers are based on production data for a calendar year. These may differ in some instances from those actually produced and published by the individual countries themselves due to variations in concepts, coverage, weights and methods of calculation. Efforts have been made to estimate these methodological differences to achieve a better international comparability of data. Detailed data on agricultural production are published by FAO in its *Statistical Yearbook*.

Chapter XI: International merchandise trade

The *International Trade Statistics Yearbook* (ITSY) provides an overview of the latest trends of trade in goods and services of most countries and areas in the world, a publication prepared by the Statistics Division of the Department for Economic and Social Affairs of the United Nations Secretariat. The yearbook, see http://comtrade.un.org/pb/, is released in two volumes; Volume I is compiled earlier in the year to present an advanced overview of international merchandise trade from the previous year, Volume II, generally released six months later, contains detailed tables showing international trade for individual commodities and 11 world trade tables covering trade values and indices. Volume II also contains updated versions of world trade tables. The table in this yearbook are also updated monthly in the United Nations Monthly Bulletin of Statistics and on the trade statistics website, see http://unstats.un.org/unsd/trade/data/tables.asp#annual.

The statistics in this Yearbook have been compiled by national statistical authorities largely consistent with the United Nations recommended International Merchandise Trade Statistics, Concepts and Definitions 2010 (IMTS 2010). Depending on what parts of the economic territory are included in the statistical territory, the trade data-compilation system adopted by a country (its trade system) may be referred to as general or special.

General trade system	The statistical territory coincides with the economic territory. Consequently, it is recommended that the statistical territory of a country applying the general trade system comprises all applicable territorial elements. In this case, imports include goods entering the free circulation area, premises for inward processing, industrial free zones, premises for customs warehousing or commercial free zones and exports include goods leaving those territorial elements
Special trade system	(strict definition) The statistical territory comprises only a particular part of the economic territory, so that certain flows of goods which are in the scope of IMTS 2010 are not included in either import or export statistics of the compiling country. The strict definition of the special trade system is in use when the statistical territory comprises only the free circulation area, that is, the part within which goods "may be disposed of without customs restriction". Consequently, in such a case, imports include only goods entering the free circulation area of a compiling country and exports include only goods leaving the free circulation area of a compiling country
	(relaxed definition) (a) goods that enter a country for, or leave it after, inward processing, as well as (b) goods that enter or leave an industrial free zone, are also recorded and included in international merchandise trade statistics

Generally, all countries report their detailed merchandise trade data according to the Harmonized Commodity Description and Coding System (HS) and the data correspond and are then presented by Standard International Trade Classifications (SITC, Rev.3). Data refer to calendar years; however, for those countries which report according to some other reference year, the data are presented in the year which covers the majority of the reference year used by the country.

FOB-type values include the transaction value of the goods and the value of services performed to deliver goods to the border of the exporting country. CIF-type values include the transaction value of the goods, the value of services performed to deliver goods to the border of the exporting country and the value of the services performed to deliver the goods from the border of the exporting country to the border of the importing country. Therefore, data for the statistical value of imported goods are presented as a CIF-type value and the statistical value of exported goods as an FOB-type value.

Conversion of values from national currencies into United States dollars is done by means of currency conversion factors based on official exchange rates. Values in currencies subject to fluctuation are converted into United States dollars using weighted average exchange rates specially calculated for this purpose. The weighted average exchange rate for a given currency for a given year is the component monthly factors, furnished by the International Monetary Fund in its International Financial Statistics publication, weighted by the value of the relevant trade in each month; a monthly factor is the exchange rate (or the simple average rate) in effect during that month. These factors are applied to total imports and exports and to the trade in individual commodities with individual countries.

Table 21: Total imports, exports and balance of trade

Figures on the total imports and exports of countries (or areas) presented in this table are mainly taken from International Financial Statistics published monthly by the International Monetary Fund (IMF) but also from other sources such as national publications and websites and the United Nations *Monthly Bulletin of Statistics* Questionnaire, see the *International Trade Statistics Yearbook* for further details. Estimates for missing data are made in order to arrive to regional totals but are otherwise not shown. The estimation process is automated using quarterly year-on-year growth rates for the extrapolation of missing quarterly data (unless quarterly data can be estimated using available monthly data within the quarter). The conversion factors applied to data in this table are published quarterly in the United Nations *Monthly Bulletin of Statistics* and are also available on the United Nations trade statistics website: http://unstats.un.org/unsd/trade/data/tables.asp#annual.

Table 22: Major trading partners

Figures on major trading partners show the three largest trade partners (countries of last known destination and origin or consignment) in international merchandise trade transactions. In some cases a special partner is shown (i.e. Areas nes, bunkers, etc.) instead of a country and refers to one of the following special categories. Areas not elsewhere specified (i.e. Areas nes) is used (a) for low value trade, (b) if the partner designation was unknown to the country or if an error was made in the partner assignment and (c) for reasons of confidentiality. If a specific geographical location can be identified within Areas nes, then they are recorded accordingly (i.e. Asia nes). Bunkers are ship stores and aircraft supplies, which consists mostly of fuels and food. Free zones belong to the geographical and economic territory of a country but not to its customs territory. For the purpose of trade statistics the transactions between the customs territory and the free zones are recorded, if the reporting country uses the Special Trade System. Free zones can be commercial free zones (duty free shops) or industrial free zones. Data are expressed as percentages of total exports and of total imports of the country, area or special partner.

Data in this table consists of data as reported by UN Comtrade (at three-digit level of SITC Rev. 3 and detailed trading partners breakdown) and estimated data for missing reporters. The data are estimated either through the extrapolation of the data of the two adjacent years, or, if this is not possible, through the use of the data reported by the trading partners (so called mirror data). Mirror statistics is also used in case the partner distribution or confidential data make it necessary to adjust the reported data. In addition, modifications to the received data are made in cases where the provided data are obviously incomplete, in particular in the case of unreported petroleum oils exports in merchandise data.

Chapter XII: Energy

The Energy Statistics Yearbook (available at http://unstats.un.org/unsd/energy/yearbook) is a comprehensive collection of international energy statistics for over 220 countries and areas. The yearbook is prepared by the Statistics Division of the Department for Economic and Social Affairs of the United Nations Secretariat. The yearbook is produced every year with newly available data on energy production, trade, stock changes, bunkers and consumption for all countries and areas, and a historical series back to 1950 are available. The data are compiled primarily from the annual energy questionnaire distributed by the United Nations Statistics Division and supplemented by official national statistical publications, as well as publications from international and regional organizations. Where official data are not available or are inconsistent, estimates are made by the Statistics Division based on governmental, professional or commercial materials.

The period to which the data refer is the calendar year, with the exception of the data of the following countries which refer to the fiscal year: Afghanistan and Iran (Islamic Rep. of) – beginning 21 March of the year stated; Australia, Bangladesh, Bhutan, Egypt (for the latter two, electricity only), Nepal - ending June of the year stated; Pakistan - starting July of the year stated; India, Myanmar and New Zealand – beginning April of the year stated. Data on a per capita basis use population data from the United Nations Population Division as a denominator.

Table 23: Production, trade and consumption of energy

Data are presented in petajoules (gigajoules per capita), to which the individual energy commodities are converted in the interests of international uniformity and comparability. To convert from original units to joules, the data in original units (metric tons, metric tons of oil equivalent, kilowatt hours, cubic metres) are multiplied by conversion factors. For a list of the relevant conversion factors and a detailed description of methods, see the Energy Statistics Yearbook.

Included in the production of commercial primary energy for solids are hard coal, lignite, peat and oil shale; liquids are comprised of crude petroleum, natural gas liquids, other hydrocarbons, additives and oxygenates, and liquid biofuels; gas comprises natural gas and primary steam/heat; and electricity is comprised of primary electricity generation from hydro, nuclear, geothermal, wind, tide, wave and solar sources.

Net imports (imports less exports and bunkers) and changes in stocks, refer to all primary and secondary forms of energy (including feedstocks). Within net imports; bunkers refer to bunkers of aviation gasoline, jet fuel and of hard coal, gas-diesel oil and residual fuel oil. International trade of energy commodities is based on the "general trade" system, that is, all goods entering and leaving the national boundary of a country are recorded as imports and exports.

Included in the consumption of energy are primary forms of solid fuels, net imports and changes in stocks of secondary fuels; liquids which is energy use of oil products includes feedstocks and refinery gas, and direct use of crude petroleum; gases include the consumption of natural gas and primary heat, net imports and changes in stocks of manufactured gases;

and electricity which is primary electricity production and net imports of electricity. Consumption for some of the petroleum products is negative due to the exclusion of inter-product transfers from the calculations. Negative consumption of electricity is due to negligible primary electricity production as compared to net exports. More generally, negative consumption can represent a residual or statistical difference between production and exports when a particular product is mainly exported.

Chapter XIII: Environment

Table 24: Land

The data on land are compiled by the Food and Agriculture Organization of the United Nations (FAO). FAO's definitions of the land categories are as follows:

Land area	Total area excluding area under inland water bodies. The definition of inland water bodies generally includes major rivers and lakes
Arable land	Land under temporary crops (multiple cropped areas are counted only once); temporary meadows for mowing or pasture; land under market and kitchen gardens; and land temporarily fallow (less than five years). Abandoned land resulting from shifting cultivation is not included in this category. Data for "arable land" are not meant to indicate the amount of land that is potentially cultivable.
Permanent crops	Land cultivated with crops that occupy the land for long periods and need not be replanted after each harvest, such as cocoa, coffee and rubber. This category includes land under flowering shrubs, fruit trees, nut trees and vines, but excludes land under trees grown for wood or timber
Forest	In the Global Forest Resources Assessment 2010 the following definition is used for forest: Land spanning more than 0.5 hectares with trees higher than 5 metres and a canopy cover of more than 10 percent, or trees able to reach these thresholds in situ. It does not include land that is predominantly under agricultural or urban land use.
Sites protected for terrestrial biodiversity	Land which contributes significantly to the global persistence of biodiversity measured as a proportion of which is wholly covered by a designated protected area. Data are based on spatial overlap between polygons for Key Biodiversity Areas from the World Database of key Biodiversity Areas and polygons for protected areas from the World Database on Protected Areas. Figures for each region are calculated as the proportion of each Key Biodiversity Area covered by protected areas, averaged (i.e. calculated as the mean) across all Key Biodiversity Areas within the region.

Table 25: Threatened species

Data on the number of threatened species in each group of animals and plants are compiled by the World Conservation Union (IUCN)/ Species Survival Commission (SSC) and published in the IUCN Red List of Threatened Species. The list provides a catalogue of those species that are considered globally threatened. The number of threatened species for any particular country will change between years for a number of reasons, including:

- New information being available to refine the assessment (e.g., confirmation that the species occurs or does not occur in a particular country, confirmation that the species is or is not threatened, etc.)
- Taxonomic changes (e.g., what was previously recognised as one species is now split into several separate species, or has now been merged with another species).
- Corrections (e.g., the previous assessment may have missed a particular country out of its country occurrence list or included a specific country by mistake).
- Genuine status changes (e.g., a species may have genuinely deteriorated or improved in status and therefore has moved into or out of the threatened categories).

The categories used in the Red List are as follows; extinct, extinct in the wild, critically endangered; endangered, vulnerable, near threatened and data deficient.

Chapter XIV: Science and technology

Table 26: Human resources in research and development (R&D)

The data presented on human resources in research and development (R&D) are compiled by the UNESCO Institute for Statistics. Data for certain countries are provided to UNESCO by OECD, Eurostat and the Latin-American Network on Science and Technology Indicators (RICYT). The definitions and classifications applied by UNESCO in the table are based on those set out in the Frascati Manual (OECD, 2002). The three categories of personnel shown are defined as follows:

Researchers	Professionals engaged in the conception or creation of new knowledge, products, processes, methods and systems and also in the management of the projects concerned. Postgraduate students at the PhD level (ISCED level 8) engaged in R&D are considered as researchers.
Technicians and equivalent staff	Persons whose main tasks require technical knowledge and experience in one or more fields of engineering, physical and life sciences (technicians) or social sciences and humanities (equivalent staff). They participate in R&D by performing scientific and technical tasks involving the application of concepts and operational methods, normally under the supervision of researchers.
Other supporting staff	Skilled and unskilled craftsmen, secretarial and clerical staff participating in R&D projects or directly associated with (or providing services to researchers involved in) such projects.

Headcount data reflect the total number of persons employed in R&D, independently from their dedication. Full-time equivalent (FTE) may be thought of as one person-year. Thus, a person who normally spends 30% of his/her time on R&D and the rest on other activities (such as teaching, university administration and student counselling) should be considered as 0.3 FTE. Similarly, if a full-time R&D worker is employed at an R&D unit for only six months, this results in an FTE of 0.5.

Table 27: Gross domestic expenditure on research and development (R&D)

The data presented on gross domestic expenditure on research and development are compiled by the UNESCO Institute for Statistics. Data for certain countries are provided to UNESCO by OECD, EUROSTAT and the Network on Science and Technology Indicators (RICYT). Gross domestic expenditure on R&D (GERD) is total intramural expenditure on R&D performed on the national territory during a given period. It includes R&D performed within a country and funded from abroad but excludes payments made abroad for R&D. The sources of funds for GERD are classified according to the following five categories:

Business enterprise funds	Funds allocated to R&D by all firms, organizations and institutions whose primary activity is the market production of goods and services (other than the higher education sector) for sale to the general public at an economically significant price, and those private non-profit institutes mainly serving these firms, organizations and institutions.
Government funds	Funds allocated to R&D by all departments, offices and other bodies which furnish, but normally do not sell to the community, those common services, other than higher education, which cannot otherwise be conveniently and economically provided, as well as those that administer the state and the economic and social policy of the community. Public enterprises, mainly engaged in market production and sale of goods and services, funds are included in the business enterprise funds sector. Government funds also include private non-profit institutes controlled and mainly financed by government, not administered by the higher education sector.
Higher education funds	Funds allocated to R&D by institutions of higher education comprising all universities, colleges of technology, other institutions providing tertiary education (i.e. ISCED 5, 6, 7 or 8), whatever their source or finance or legal status. They also include all research institutes, experimental stations and clinics operating under the direct control of or administered by or associated with higher education institutions.
Private non-profit funds	Funds allocated to R&D by non-market, private non-profit institutions serving households (i.e. the general public), as well as by private individuals and households.
Funds from abroad	Funds allocated to R&D by all institutions and individuals located outside the political borders of a country; and all international organizations (except business enterprises), including facilities and operations within the country's borders.

The absolute figures for R&D expenditure should not be compared country by country. Such comparisons would require the conversion of national currencies into a common currency by means of special R&D exchange rates. Official exchange rates do not always reflect the real costs of R&D activities and comparisons that are based on such rates can result in misleading conclusions, although they can be used to indicate a gross order of magnitude.

Table 28: Patents

A patent is granted by a national patent office or by a regional office that does the work for a number of countries, such as the European Patent Office and the African Regional Intellectual Property Organisation. Under such regional systems, an applicant requests protection for the invention in one or more countries, and each country decides as to whether to offer patent protection within its borders. The World Intellectual Property Organisation (WIPO) administered Patent Cooperation Treaty (PCT) provides for the filling of a single international patent application which has the same effect as national applications filed in the designated countries. Data include resident intensity, patents granted and patents in force. Patent intensity is presented as the resident patent fillings per million population, where as resident Intellectual Property (IP) filling refers to an application filed by an applicant at its national IP office. IP grant (registration) data are based on the same concept. In force refers to a patent or other form of IP protection that is currently valid. Country of origin is used to categorise IP data by resident (domestic) and non-resident (foreign). The residence of the first-named applicant (or inventor) recorded in the IP document (e.g. patent or trademark application) is used to classify IP data by country of origin. The data are compiled and published by the WIPO.

Chapter XV: Communication

Table 29: Internet usage

The table shows percentage of individuals using the internet and replaces the statistics shown in previous yearbooks such as the "Number (thousands) of fixed (wired) internet subscriptions" and "fixed (wired) internet subscriptions per 100 inhabitants". Besides capturing the use of the Internet, this indicator is able to measure changes in Internet access and use. In countries where many people access the Internet at work, at school, at cybercafés or other public locations, increases in public access serve to increase the number of users despite limited numbers of Internet subscriptions and of households with Internet access. Developing countries especially tend to have many Internet users per Internet subscriptions, reflecting that home access is not the primary location of access.

Chapter XVI: International tourism and transport

The data on international tourism have been supplied by the World Tourism Organization (UNWTO) from detailed tourism information published in either the *Yearbook of Tourism Statistics* or *Compendium of Tourism Statistics,* see www.unwto.org/statistics for further information. For statistical purposes, the term "international visitor" describes "any person who travels to a country other than that in which he/she has his/her usual residence but outside his/her usual environment for a period not exceeding 12 months and whose main purpose of visit is other than the exercise of an activity remunerated from within the country visited". There are four series presented in the UNWTO *yearbook* and *compendium*, but only one series is selected to be presented in this yearbook, generally based on the following priority order to best describe an "international visitor";

Order	Series code	Series name
1	TF	*Arrivals of non-resident tourists at national borders* are visitors who stay at least one night in a collective or private accommodation in the country visited (excludes same-day visitors)
2	VF	*Arrivals of non-resident visitors at national borders* are visitors as defined in series "TF" as well as same-day visitors who do not spend the night in a collective or private accommodation in the country visited
3	TCE	*Arrivals of non-resident tourists in all types of accommodation establishments*
4	THS	*Arrivals of non-resident tourists in hotels and similar establishments*

The figures do not include immigrants, residents in a frontier zone, persons domiciled in one country or area and working in an adjoining country or area, members of the armed forces and diplomats and consular representatives when they travel from their country of origin to the country in which they are stationed and vice-versa. The figures also exclude persons in transit who do not formally enter the country through passport control, such as air transit passengers who remain for a short period in a designated area of the air terminal or ship passengers who are not permitted to disembark. This category includes passengers transferred directly between airports or other terminals. Other passengers in transit through a country are classified as visitors.

Table 30: Tourist/visitor arrivals and tourism expenditure

Data on arrivals of non-resident (or international) visitors may be obtained from different sources. In some cases data are obtained from border statistics derived from administrative records (police, immigration, traffic counts and other types of controls), border surveys and registrations at accommodation establishments. Totals correspond to the total number of arrivals from the regions indicated in the table. When a person visits the same country several times a year, an equal number of arrivals is recorded. Likewise, if a person visits several countries during the course of a single trip, his/her arrival in each country is recorded separately. Consequently, arrivals cannot be assumed to be equal to the number of persons travelling.

Expenditure associated with tourism activity of visitors has been traditionally identified with the travel item of the Balance of Payments (BOP): in the case of inbound tourism, those expenditures in the country of reference associated with non-resident visitors are registered as "credits" in the BOP and refer to "travel receipts". The new conceptual framework approved by the United Nations Statistical Commission in relation to the measurement of tourism macroeconomic activity (the so-called Tourism Satellite Account) considers that "tourism industries and products" includes transport of passengers. Consequently, a better estimate of tourism-related expenditures by resident and non-resident visitors in an international scenario would be, in terms of the BOP, the value of the travel item plus that of the passenger transport item. Nevertheless, users should be aware that BOP estimates include, in addition to expenditures associated with visitors, those related to other types of individuals. The data published should allow international comparability and therefore correspond to those published by the International Monetary Fund and provided by the Central Banks, any exceptions are listed within the *Compendium of Tourism Statistics* and the *Yearbook of Tourism Statistics,* see www.unwto.org/statistics for further information.

Chapter XVII: Development assistance

Table 31: Net disbursements of official development assistance to recipients

The table presents estimates of flows of financial resources to individual recipients either directly (bilaterally) or through multilateral institutions (multilaterally). The multilateral institutions include the World Bank Group, regional banks, financial institutions of the European Union and a number of United Nations institutions, programmes and trust funds. The source of data is the Development Assistance Committee (DAC) of OECD to which member countries reported data on their flow of resources to developing countries and territories, countries and territories in transition, and multilateral institutions. Additional information on definitions, methods and sources can be found in OECD's *Geographical Distribution of Financial Flows to Developing Countries* publication, also see http://stats.oecd.org/ for further information.

Table 32: Net disbursements of official development assistance from donors

The table presents the development assistance expenditures of donor countries. This table includes donors' contributions to multilateral agencies; therefore, the overall totals differ from those in table 32, which include disbursements by multilateral agencies.

***

Annexe II: Notes techniques

Chapitre I: Aperçu mondial

Tableau 1: Statistiques mondiales – séries principales

Ces séries d'agrégats mondiaux sont obtenues à partir d'autres tableaux figurant dans le présent *Annuaire*, lorsque c'est possible, et sont établies à partir de publications et de bases de données statistiques des Nations Unies et des organismes spécialisés ainsi que d'autres institutions. Pour davantage d'information sur les définitions, les sources, les méthodes de compilation et la couverture des données, il convient de se référer aux notes techniques du tableau correspondant dans le présent *Annuaire*.

Chapitre II: Population et migration

Tableau 2: Population, superficie et densité

Les données concernant la population totale, masculine et féminine, le rapport des sexes, la répartition de la population par âge et la densité de la population proviennent des estimations et des projections préparées par la Division de la population de l'Organisation des Nations Unies, qui sont publiées dans *Perspectives de la population mondiale : Révision de 2017*. Les données concernant la superficie sont extraites de l'*Annuaire démographique*, qui ne contient que les données nationales officielles.

La population totale, masculine et féminine correspond à la population de fait dans un pays, un territoire ou une région à compter du 1er juillet de l'année indiquée, sauf indication contraire dans une note en bas de page. Les chiffres sont présentés en millions. La population totale d'un pays peut consister de tous les résidents habituels (population de droit) ou toutes les personnes présentes dans le pays (population de fait) au moment du recensement ; pour permettre les comparaisons internationales, la population de fait est utilisée, sauf indication contraire dans une note en bas de page.

La population âgée de 0 à 14 ans/ 60 ans et plus correspond au pourcentage de la population âgée de 0 à 14 ans et 60 ans et plus, respectivement à compter du 1er juillet de l'année indiquée, sauf indication contraire dans une note en bas de page.

La densité de la population correspond à la population, à compter du 1er juillet de l'année indiquée, par kilomètre carré de superficie, sauf indication contraire dans une note en bas de page.

Le rapport des sexes est calculé en tant que le rapport de la population des hommes à celui de 100 femmes à compter du 1er juillet de l'année indiquée, sauf indication contraire dans une note en bas de page.

La superficie correspond aux territoires plus eaux intérieures, sauf indication contraire dans une note en bas de page.

Tableau 3: : Population et taux de croissance dans les zones urbaines et capitales

Les statistiques sur la population dans la capitale, la population urbaine, la population rurale et les taux d'accroissement de chaque pays ou zone sont des estimations et projections publiées par la Division de la population du Département des affaires économiques et sociales du Secrétariat des Nations Unies dans Perspectives d'urbanisation, révision 2018. Il n'existe pas de définition reconnue à l'échelle internationale des zones urbaines et rurales parce que les caractéristiques retenues pour distinguer ces deux types de zone diffèrent d'un pays à un autre. Dans la plupart des pays, cette distinction est essentiellement une fonction de la taille des agglomérations. Pour la définition la plus récente des zones urbaines utilisée dans une région ou un pays donné, se reporter à l'Annuaire démographique. Les taux annuels de variation des populations urbaines et rurales se calculent sur la base de la variation annuelle moyenne en pourcentage déterminée à partir des estimations de la population au milieu de l'année.

Tableau 4: Migrants internationaux et réfugiés

Le stock international de migrants provient d'estimations et de projections préparées par la Division de la population de l'Organisation des Nations Unies, publiées dans *International migrant stock: The 2017 Revision*. Les données sur les «réfugiés et autres personnes relevant de la compétence du HCR» ont été obtenues auprès du Haut-Commissaire des Nations Unies pour les réfugiés, et sont publiées dans la base de données de statistiques démographiques.

Le stock international de migrants représente le nombre de personnes nées dans un autre pays que celui dans lequel elles vivent. Lorsque les informations concernant le pays d'origine font défaut, on a utilisé les données sur le nombre de personnes de nationalité étrangère. Et à défaut de données empiriques, on a eu recours à des estimations. Les données font référence au milieu de l'année 2015. Le stock international de migrants en pourcentage de la population est obtenu en divisant le stock international de migrants estimé par la population totale estimée et en multipliant le résultat par 100.

Les réfugiés sont les personnes reconnues comme telles au sens de la Convention de 1951 relative au statut des réfugiés, de son protocole de 1967 ou de la Convention de l'OUA de 1969 régissant les aspects propres aux problèmes des réfugiés en

Afrique; celles reconnues comme réfugiés conformément au Statut du HCR; les personnes qui bénéficient d'une forme de protection complémentaire ou jouissent d'une protection temporaire. Depuis 2007, la population des réfugiés inclut également les personnes dont la situation est assimilable à celle des réfugiés.

Les demandeurs d'asile sont des personnes qui ont déposé une demande de protection internationale et qui n'ont pas encore obtenu le statut de réfugié, quelle que soit la date à laquelle la demande a été présentée.

Les « autres personnes relevant de la compétence du HCR » se composent des cinq catégories suivantes :

Les personnes déplacées sont des personnes ou groupes de personnes qui ont été forcés ou contraints de fuir ou de quitter leurs foyers ou leur lieu de résidence habituel, notamment en raison d'un conflit armé, de situations de violence généralisée, de violations des droits de l'homme ou de catastrophes naturelles ou provoquées par l'homme, ou pour en éviter les effets, et qui n'ont pas franchi les frontières internationalement reconnues d'un État. Aux fins des statistiques du HCR, cette population ne comprend que les personnes déplacées en raison d'un conflit qui bénéficient de la protection et/ou de l'assistance du HCR. Depuis 2007, la population de personnes déplacées inclut également les personnes dont la situation est assimilable à celle des personnes déplacées. On trouvera des estimations de la population mondiale des personnes déplacées sur le site www.internal-displacement.org.

Les réfugiés de retour sont d'anciens réfugiés rentrés dans leur pays d'origine, soit spontanément, soit de façon organisée, mais qui ne sont pas encore pleinement intégrés. Ces retours ne se font normalement que lorsque leur sécurité et leur dignité peuvent être garanties.

Les déplacés de retour sont des personnes déplacée qui bénéficiaient des activités de protection et d'assistance du HCR et qui sont revenues à leur lieu d'origine ou de résidence habituel au cours de l'année.

Les apatrides sont définis par le droit international comme des personnes qu'aucun État ne considère comme ses ressortissants par application de sa législation. En d'autres termes, les apatrides ne possèdent la nationalité d'aucun État. Les statistiques du HCR incluent les personnes qui relèvent de sa compétence en vertu de cette définition, mais les données de certains pays peuvent aussi inclure des personnes de nationalité indéterminée.

Les autres personnes relevant de la compétence du HCR sont des personnes qui ne relèvent pas directement d'une des catégories ci-dessus, mais auxquelles le HCR assure protection et/ou assistance pour des raisons humanitaires ou d'autre motifs particuliers.

Chapitre III: La situation des femmes

Tableau 5: Proportion de sièges occupés par des femmes au parlement national

Ce tableau indique le pourcentage des sièges des chambres uniques ou basses des parlements nationaux occupés par des femmes, en janvier ou février de chaque année (voir les notes du tableau pour plus de détails). Les parlements nationaux peuvent être bicaméraux ou unicaméraux. Ce tableau porte sur la chambre unique des parlements unicaméraux et sur la chambre basse des parlements bicaméraux. Il ne porte pas sur la chambre haute des parlements bicaméraux. Les sièges sont habituellement attribués aux membres à l'issue d'élections parlementaires générales. Certains sièges peuvent aussi être pourvus à l'issue de nominations, de désignations, d'élections indirectes, de roulement des membres et d'élections partielles. La proportion d'élues est obtenue en divisant le nombre total de sièges occupés par des femmes par le nombre total de sièges que compte le parlement. Les statistiques ne sont ni pondérées ni normalisées. La source de ce tableau est l'Union interparlementaire, voir www.ipu.org pour plus d'informations

Tableau 6: Rapport filles/garçons dans l'enseignement primaire, secondaire et supérieur

Ce tableau indique la proportion de filles par rapport aux garçons (indice de parité des sexes) dans l'enseignement primaire, secondaire et supérieur, à savoir le rapport entre le nombre de filles inscrites dans l'enseignement primaire, secondaire et supérieur et le nombre de garçons à chaque niveau. Pour normaliser les effets de la pyramide des âges, l'indice de parité des sexes du taux brut de scolarisation pour chaque niveau d'enseignement est utilisé. La source de ce tableau est l'Institut de statistique de l'UNESCO, voir www.uis.unesco.org pour plus d'informations.

Chapitre IV: Éducation

Les données des tableaux 7 et 8 sont présentées conformément à la Classification internationale type de l'éducation de l'UNESCO (CITE, révision de 2011). Les données sont présentées dans les tableaux sur la base des trois principaux niveaux d'éducation, présentés comme suit :

L'enseignement primaire (CITE niveau 1) désigne les programmes éducatifs habituellement conçus pour apporter aux élèves les compétences fondamentales en lecture, écriture et en mathématiques (c'est-à-dire en calcul) afin d'établir une base solide pour la compréhension et l'apprentissage des principaux domaines de la connaissance et favoriser le développement personnel et social dans le but de les préparer à l'entrée dans le premier cycle de l'enseignement secondaire. Il privilégie l'enseignement à un niveau de complexité élémentaire avec peu ou pas de spécialisation.

L'enseignement secondaire (niveaux 2 et 3 de la CITE) est divisé en deux parties : le premier et le second cycles du secondaire. Les programmes du premier cycle de l'enseignement secondaire sont généralement conçus de manière à renforcer les acquis scolaires du primaire. L'objectif consiste habituellement à établir la base d'un apprentissage et d'un développement humain valables pour toute la vie et que les systèmes éducatifs pourront ensuite enrichir par de nouvelles possibilités d'éducation. Les programmes du deuxième cycle de l'enseignement secondaire visent en général à achever l'enseignement secondaire et à préparer à l'entrée dans l'enseignement supérieur et/ou à enseigner des compétences utiles à l'exercice d'un emploi. Les programmes de ce niveau offrent aux élèves un enseignement plus varié, spécialisé et approfondi que les programmes du premier cycle. Ils sont davantage différenciés et proposent un éventail plus large d'options et de filières. Les enseignants sont souvent hautement qualifiés dans les matières ou domaines spécialisés qu'ils enseignent, en particulier dans les classes supérieures.

L'enseignement supérieur (niveaux 5 à 8 de la CITE) se fonde sur les acquis de l'enseignement secondaire et offre des activités d'apprentissage dans des domaines d'éducation spécialisés. Il vise à transmettre des connaissances très spécialisées et d'un niveau de complexité élevé. L'enseignement supérieur inclut ce que l'on qualifie habituellement d'enseignement académique mais il comprend aussi l'enseignement technique ou professionnel avancé. Il comprend les niveaux 5, 6, 7 et 8 de la CITE, appelés respectivement enseignement supérieur de cycle court, enseignement du niveau de la licence ou équivalent, niveau master ou équivalent, et niveau doctorat ou équivalent. Le contenu des programmes de l'enseignement supérieur est plus complexe et plus avancé que celui des niveaux inférieurs de la CITE.

On trouvera davantage d'informations sur la Classification internationale type de l'éducation (CITE) 2011 sur le site : http://www.uis.unesco.org/Education/Documents/isced-2011-fr.pdf.

Tableau 7: Enseignement primaire, secondaire et supérieur

Le tableau montre le nombre d'élèves scolarisés ainsi que le taux de scolarisation brut qui est le nombre d'étudiants inscrits, quel que soit leur âge, exprimé en pourcentage de la population d'âge scolaire officiellement admissible correspondant au même niveau d'enseignement pour une année scolaire donnée. Les inscriptions sont mesurées au début de l'année scolaire ou universitaire. Le taux de scolarisation brut pour chaque niveau comprend tous les élèves, quel que soit leur âge, tandis que la population générale considérée ne comprend que ceux dont l'âge correspond à l'âge scolaire officiel. De ce fait, pour les pays dont la population d'âge scolaire est quasi totalement scolarisée, le taux de scolarisation brut peut dépasser 100 si la répartition des âges effectifs des élèves s'étend au-delà des âges scolaires officiels.

Tableau 8: Personnel enseignant au niveau primaire, secondaire et supérieur

Le tableau montre le nombre total d'enseignants à chaque niveau ainsi que la proportion des enseignantes exprimée en pourcentage du nombre total d'enseignants (hommes et femmes) au même niveau au cours d'une année scolaire donnée. Les données proviennent de recensements ou d'enquêtes dans les écoles et des dossiers des enseignants.

Les enseignants (ou personnel enseignant) sont définis comme des personnes qui, dans l'exercice de leur métier, guident et dirigent le parcours didactique des élèves et étudiants, indépendamment de leurs qualifications et du mécanisme de transmission des connaissances (autrement dit soit face-à-face et/ou à distance). L'enseignement consiste à planifier, organiser, et mener des activités de groupe ou les connaissances, aptitudes et compétences des élèves sont développés comme précisé dans le programme d'éducation. Cette définition exclut le personnel enseignant qui n'a pas de fonctions pédagogiques à la période de référence (par exemple les directeurs ou chefs d'établissements scolaires qui n'enseignent pas) et les personnes qui travaillent ponctuellement ou bénévolement dans des établissements d'enseignement.

Le personnel enseignant universitaire est le personnel employé dont la mission principale est l'enseignement et /ou la recherche. Cela comprend le personnel qui détient un grade universitaire avec des titres tels que professeur, professeur agrégé, professeur adjoint, maitre de conférences ou l'équivalent. Le personnel, comme par exemple doyen, directeur, vice-doyen, doyen adjoint, président ou chef de département, est également inclus si leur activité principale est l'enseignement ou la recherche.

Tableau 9: Dépenses publiques afférentes à l'éducation

Les dépenses publiques afférentes à l'éducation consistent en dépenses courantes et dépenses en capital engagées par l'administration aux niveaux local, régional et national, y compris les municipalités. Les contributions des ménages sont exclues. Les dépenses d'éducation courantes comprennent les dépenses en biens et en services consommés dans l'année en cours et qui devront être renouvelées au besoin l'année suivante. Elles comprennent les dépenses au titre des salaires et avantages du personnel; des services achetés ou obtenus par contrat; d'autres ressources, notamment de manuels et autres matériels d'enseignement; des services sociaux; et d'autres dépenses courantes telles que les subventions aux étudiants et aux ménages, l'ameublement et le matériel, les petites réparations, le combustible, les télécommunications, les voyages, l'assurance et les loyers. Les dépenses en capital pour l'éducation consistent en achats de biens dont la durée dépasse une année. Elles comprennent les dépenses de construction, de rénovation et de grosses réparations de bâtiments ainsi que l'achat de matériel lourd et de véhicules.

Chapitre V: Santé

Tableau 10: Le personnel de santé

Le tableau présente quatre grandes catégories de personnel de santé (sur les 9 catégories disponibles à la source) : la catégorie des médecins, qui comprend les médecins généralistes et les spécialistes; celle des infirmiers et sages-femmes comprend les infirmiers et sages-femmes qualifiés, les infirmiers auxiliaires professionnels et les sages-femmes auxiliaires professionnelles. Les accoucheuses traditionnelles ne sont pas incluses; le personnel de dentisterie comprend les dentistes, les assistants dentaires, les techniciens dentaires et les professions associées; et le personnel du secteur pharmaceutique comprend les pharmaciens, les pharmaciens assistants, les préparateurs en pharmacie et les professions associées.

Les données sont extraites des statistiques mondiales des personnels de santé de la base de données de l'Organisation mondiale de la Santé (OMS), qui sont établies à partir de plusieurs sources comme les recensements de population nationaux, les enquêtes sur la population active et l'emploi, les productions statistiques nationales et les données régulières des administrations. Il existe de ce fait d'un pays à l'autre une variabilité considérable dans la couverture, la qualité et l'année de référence des données. Généralement, les données du dénominateur pour le calcul de la densité du personnel de santé (c'est-à-dire les estimations de la population nationale) sont extraites des *Perspectives de la population*

mondiale publiées par la Division de la population de l'Organisation des Nations Unies. Parfois le rapport officiel ne fournit que les indicateurs de la densité du personnel de santé, à partir desquels le stock est ensuite estimé.

La classification des personnels du secteur de la santé utilisée repose sur les critères de l'enseignement et formation techniques et professionnels, la réglementation des professions de santé et les activités et tâches des postes, c'est-à-dire sur un cadre de catégorisation des principales variables des personnels selon des caractéristiques communes. Le cadre de l'OMS repose en grande partie sur les révisions les plus récentes des systèmes de classification internationaux normalisés de l'Organisation internationale du Travail (Classification internationale type des professions), de l'Organisation des Nations Unies pour l'éducation, la science et la culture (Classification internationale type de l'éducation) et de la Division de statistique de l'ONU (Classification internationale type, par industrie, de toutes les branches d'activité économique). En fonction de la situation propre à chaque pays et des moyens de mesure, les données disponibles dans l'ensemble agrégé décrivent jusqu'à 9 catégories de personnels de santé, et jusqu'à 18 catégories dans l'ensemble désagrégé. Ce dernier reflète essentiellement une tentative de mieux distinguer certains sous-groupes des personnels du secteur de la santé en fonction de différences supposées dans les niveaux de compétence et de spécialisation.

Tableau 11: Dépenses de santé

La série « Dépenses courantes » fait référence aux biens et aux services de santé utilisés ou consommés au cours d'une année, à l'exclusion des dépenses en capital, ou plutôt de la « formation brute de capital », qui correspond à l'achat de nouveaux actifs sur plusieurs années. Ces estimations sont conformes au Système de comptes de la santé (SCS) de 2011. La dépense courante est exprimée en proportion du produit intérieur brut (PIB). Les séries des dépenses des administrations publiques générales sont composées de sources nationales publiques et privées. Les séries des dépenses des administrations publiques générales sont composées de sources nationales publiques et privées. Les sources publiques nationales comprennent les recettes intérieures sous forme de transferts et de subventions internes, les transferts, les subventions aux bénéficiaires de l'assurance maladie volontaire, les institutions sans but lucratif au service des ménages ou les régimes de financement des entreprises ainsi que les cotisations obligatoires. Tous ces transferts et subventions représentent des sources publiques de santé et indiquent la contribution globale des gouvernements au financement des soins de santé par rapport à d'autres sources de financement provenant de sources privées et extérieures nationales. Les dépenses des administrations publiques nationales sont exprimées en proportion des dépenses des administrations publiques. (voir http://apps.who.int/nha/database/DocumentationCentre/Index/fr).

Chapitre VI: Criminalité

Tableau 12: Homicides intentionnels et autres crimes

Les données des «homicides intentionnels» et des «autres crimes» proviennent des données recueillies dans la base de données statistiques de l'Office des Nations Unies contre la drogue et le crime.

L'homicide intentionnel est défini comme la mort illégale d'une personne causée par une autre ayant l'intention de tuer ou de blesser gravement. Les données de l'homicide intentionnel doivent aussi inclure les violences suivies de mort et la mort résultant d'une attaque terroriste. Elles excluent la tentative d'homicide intentionnel, l'homicide involontaire, la mort causée par une intervention légale, l'homicide justifiable en état de légitime défense et la mort causée par un conflit armé.

L'agression est une atteinte à l'intégrité physique d'une autre personne entraînant des dommages corporels graves, à l'exclusion des actes préjudiciables à caractère sexuel, des menaces et des gifles/coups de poing. Les agressions graves ayant entraîné la mort sont également exclues.

L'enlèvement désigne la détention et soustraction illégales d'une ou de plusieurs personnes contre leur volonté (y compris par le recours à la force, aux menaces, à la fraude ou à l'incitation) aux fins d'exiger pour leur libération un gain illicite ou un autre avantage économique ou matériel, ou pour contraindre une personne à suivre ou à ne pas suivre une ligne de conduite. L'enlèvement exclut les différends relatifs à la garde d'un enfant.

Le vol est l'appropriation ou l'obtention illégale d'un bien dans l'intention d'en priver une personne ou une organisation de manière permanente sans son consentement et sans recours à la force. Le vol exclut le cambriolage, l'entrée avec effraction, le vol qualifié et le vol de véhicule motorisé, qui sont comptabilisés séparément.

La violence sexuelle désigne le viol et l'agression sexuelle, y compris les agressions sexuelles contre les enfants.

Chapitre VII: Comptes nationaux

La base de données des principaux agrégats des comptes nationaux (consultable sur le site http://unstats.un.org/unsd/snaama) présente les données des comptes nationaux de plus de 200 pays et régions du monde. Elle constitue la base de l'analyse des principaux agrégats des statistiques de la comptabilité nationale (*National Account Statistics: Analysis of Main Aggregates*), une publication préparée par la Division de statistique du Département des affaires économiques et sociales du Secrétariat des Nations Unies avec le généreux concours des offices nationaux de la statistique. La base de données est mise à jour chaque année au mois de décembre avec les données nouvellement disponibles des comptes nationaux de tous les pays et régions.

La base de données des principaux agrégats des comptes nationaux repose sur les données extraites du Questionnaire sur la comptabilité nationale des Nations Unies (NAQ) introduit en octobre 1999, qui lui-même repose sur le Système de comptes nationaux 1993 (SCN 1993). Les données sont complétées par des estimations préparées par la Division de statistique. Le SCN actualisé, appelé Système de comptes nationaux 2008 (SCN 2008) a été finalisé en septembre 2009. En 2017, 83 pays et territoires (États membres de l'Union européenne, Albanie, Arabie saoudite, Argentine, Arménie, Australie, Bélarus, Brésil, Brunéi Darussalam, Canada, Chili, Chine, Chine, RAS de Hong Kong, Chine, RAS de Macao, Costa Rica, République dominicaine, Équateur, Eswatini, Fidji, Îles Vierges britanniques, Inde, Indonésie, Islande, Israël, Japon, Kenya, Rép. dém. populaire lao, Liban, Liechtenstein, ex-R.Y. de Macédoine, Malaisie, Maroc, Maurice, Mexique, Mongolie, Monténégro, Nouvelle-Zélande, Nigéria, Norvège, Pakistan, Pérou, Philippines, République de Corée, Serbie, Singapour, St-Martin, Afrique du Sud, Sri Lanka, Suisse, Thaïlande, Timor-Leste, Turquie, Ouganda, Ukraine, États-Unis d'Amérique et Zambie) ont commencé de soumettre des données conformément au SCN 2008.

Tout est mis en œuvre pour présenter les estimations des divers pays ou régions sous une forme conçue pour faciliter la comparabilité internationale. À cette fin, les différences importantes entre les concepts, la portée, la couverture et la classification sont décrites dans les notes de chaque pays. Ces différences doivent être prises en compte afin d'éviter les comparaisons fallacieuses. Les données contenues dans les tableaux se rapportent à l'année civile pour laquelle elles sont présentées, sauf exceptions. Ces exceptions sont affichées sur le site Web de la base de données des principaux agrégats des comptes nationaux (http://unstats.un.org/unsd/snaama/notes.asp). Les chiffres présentés sont les estimations et révisions les plus récentes disponibles au moment de leur établissement. En général, les chiffres de l'année la plus récente doivent être considérés comme provisoires. Les sommes des composantes des tableaux ne correspondent pas nécessairement aux totaux indiqués en raison des arrondis.

Tableau 13: Produit intérieur brut et produit intérieur brut par habitant

Ce tableau présente le produit intérieur brut (PIB) et le PIB par habitant en dollars des États-Unis aux prix courants, le PIB à prix constants de 2005 et les taux de croissance réels correspondants. Les tableaux sont destinés à faciliter les comparaisons internationales des niveaux de revenu générés par la production. Les données et les estimations officielles du PIB total et du PIB par habitant aux prix courants sont converties en dollars des États-Unis, tandis que celles du PIB total à prix constants sont converties aux prix de 2005 avant conversion en dollars aux taux de change en vigueur en 2005. La méthode de conversion en dollars des États-Unis est décrite dans le document sur la méthodologie de la base de données des principaux agrégats des comptes nationaux (http://unstats.un.org/unsd/snaama/methodology.pdf). Pour les comparaisons entre pays sur la durée, il est plus approprié d'utiliser les taux de croissance à prix constants du tableau, qui représentent mieux les tendances du PIB total dans les comparaisons entre pays et entre groupes de pays. Le taux de croissance indiqué dans le tableau est calculé comme la moyenne géométrique des taux de croissance annuelle exprimés en pourcentages pour les années.

Tableau 14: Valeur ajoutée brute par type d'activité économique

Ce tableau présente les parts des composantes de la valeur ajoutée brute aux prix courants par type d'activité économique.

Secteur	Composé de (selon la nomenclature CITI 3)
Agriculture	Agriculture, chasse, sylviculture et pêches (CITI A-B)
Industrie	Activités extractives, activités de fabrication, production et distribution d'électricité, de gaz et d'eau (CITI C-E) Construction (CITI F)
Services	Commerce de gros et de détail; réparation de véhicules automobiles, de motocycles et de biens personnels et domestiques, hôtels et restaurants (CITI G-H) Transports, entreposage et communications (CITI I) Autres activités, y compris intermédiation financière, immobilier, location et activités de services aux entreprises, administration publique et défense, sécurité sociale obligatoire, éducation, santé et action sociale, autres activités de services collectifs, sociaux et personnels, ménages privés employant du personnel domestique (CITI J-P).

Chapitre VIII: Finances

Des informations détaillées et les chiffres courants concernant le tableau 15 figurent dans *Statistiques financières internationales*, une publication du Fonds monétaire international (voir aussi http://elibrary-data.imf.org) et dans le *Bulletin mensuel de statistique des Nations Unies*.

Tableau 15: Résumé de la balance des paiements

La balance des paiements peut être décrite d'une façon générale comme l'enregistrement des transactions économiques internationales d'une économie. Elle présente : a) les transactions en biens, services et revenus entre une économie et le reste du monde, b) les changements de propriété et les autres changements des avoirs de cette économie en or monétaire, droits de tirage spéciaux (DTS) et en créances et engagements envers le reste du monde, et c) les transferts sans contrepartie et les écritures de contrepartie nécessaires pour équilibrer au sens comptable les écritures au titre des transactions et changements susmentionnés qui ne s'annulent pas mutuellement. Les données de la balance des paiements sont présentées sur la base de la méthodologie et de la présentation de la sixième édition du *Manuel de la balance des paiements* (MBP6), publiée par le Fonds monétaire international en novembre 2013. Le MBP6 incorpore plusieurs modifications majeures pour tenir compte des évolutions du commerce international et de la finance internationale au fil des années, et de mieux harmoniser la méthodologie de la balance des paiements du Fonds avec celle du Système de comptes nationaux 2008 (SCN 2008). Les définitions détaillées concernant le contenu des catégories fondamentales de la balance des paiements sont données dans le *Manuel de la balance des paiements* (sixième édition).

De brèves notes explicatives sont données ci-dessous pour clarifier la portée des principaux éléments.

Le compte des transactions courantes enregistre toutes les transactions de la balance des paiements couvrant les exportations et les importations de biens et de services, les revenus et les transferts courants entre les résidents d'un pays et des non-résidents.

Le compte de capital, n.i.a. porte principalement sur les transferts de capital liés à l'acquisition d'un actif fixe autres que les transactions relatives à l'annulation de la dette, plus la cession d'actifs non financiers non produits, et les transferts de capital liés à la cession d'actifs fixes par le donateur ou au financement de la formation de capital par le récipiendaire, plus l'acquisition d'actifs non financiers non produits.

Le compte d'opérations financières, n.i.a. représente le solde net de l'investissement direct, de l'investissement de portefeuille et des autres transactions d'investissement.

Les réserves sont la somme des transactions sur actifs de réserve, les engagements constituant des avoirs de réserve pour les autorités étrangères, le financement exceptionnel et l'utilisation des crédits du FMI.

Tableau 16: Cours des changes

Les taux des changes sont exprimés par le nombre d'unités de monnaie nationale pour un dollar des Etats-Unis. Les taux de change sont classés en trois catégories, qui dénotent le rôle des autorités dans l'établissement des taux de change et/ou la multiplicité des taux de change dans un pays. Par taux du marché, on entend les taux de change déterminés essentiellement par les forces du marché; le taux officiel est un taux de change établi par les autorités, parfois selon des dispositions souples. Pour les pays qui continuent à mettre en œuvre des régimes de taux de change multiples, les taux sont désignés par les appellations suivantes: "taux principal", "taux secondaire" et "taux tertiaire". Sauf indication contraire, le tableau indique des taux de fin de période et les moyennes sur la période, des taux de change du marché ou des taux de change officiels.

Chapitre IX: Marché du travail

Une collection complète de données comparables sur la population active et les sujets connexes est disponible sous la forme des *Indicateurs clé du marché du travail* (KILM) publiés par l'Organisation internationale du Travail (OIT), et mis à jour tous les deux ans. Des données plus contemporaines sont accessibles sur ILOSTAT (www.ilo.org/ilostat), le dépôt de données de l'OIT, qui publie des données annuellement, trimestriellement ou mensuellement à mesure de leur communication par les pays mais sans procéder à toutes les vérifications de leur cohérence ni inclure toutes les sources utilisées par les KILM. Pour diverses raisons, les définitions nationales de l'emploi et du chômage diffèrent souvent des définitions internationales normalisées recommandées, ce qui limite la comparabilité internationale. Les comparaisons entre pays se trouvent en outre compliquées par la diversité des systèmes de collecte de données utilisés pour recueillir des informations sur les personnes employées et les chômeurs. Le site Web d'ILOSTAT offre une description complète de la méthodologie employée pour établir les séries sur la main-d'œuvre.

Tableau 17: Population active et chômage

Le taux de participation à la population active est calculé en exprimant le nombre de personnes de la population active sous forme de pourcentage de la population en âge de travailler. La population active est la somme du nombre de personnes employées et du nombre de personnes sans emploi (voir les Recommandations internationales en vigueur sur les statistiques du travail de l'OIT). La population en âge de travailler est la population d'âge supérieur à un certain seuil, prescrit pour la mesure des caractéristiques économiques. Les données concernent le groupe des personnes de 15 ans et plus et reposent sur les estimations modélisées de l'OIT, sauf indication contraire en note de bas de page.

La définition du chômage inclut les personnes en âge de travailler qui, au cours d'une certaine période, étaient :

a) « Sans emploi », c'est-à-dire sans emploi rémunéré ou indépendant;

b) « Disponibles », c'est-à-dire libres de contracter un emploi rémunéré ou de pratiquer un emploi indépendant au cours de la période de référence; et

c) « À la recherche d'un emploi », c'est-à-dire qui ont pris des mesures déterminées pour trouver un emploi rémunéré ou indépendant au cours de la période spécifiée

Ne sont pas considérées comme sans emploi :

a) Les personnes qui ont l'intention d'établir leur propre activité ou exploitation agricole, mais n'ont pas encore pris les dispositions nécessaires à cet effet et ne recherchent pas un emploi en vue d'une rémunération ou d'un profit;

b) Les anciens travailleurs familiaux non rémunérés qui n'ont pas d'emploi et ne sont pas à la recherche d'un emploi pour rémunération ou profit.

Les séries représentent généralement le nombre total des personnes au chômage complet ou temporairement mises à pied. Les données exprimées en pourcentages, lorsqu'elles figurent dans le tableau, sont calculées en comparant le nombre des chômeurs au total des membres du groupe de la population active sur lequel les données du chômage sont basées.

Tableau 18: Emploi par activité économique

Le tableau de l'emploi présente, exprimée en pourcentages, la répartition des personnes employées par activité économique, conformément à la Classification internationale type, par industrie, de toutes les branches d'activité économique (CITI) version 4.

Chapitre X: Indices des prix et de la production

Tableau 19 : Indices des prix à la consommation

Un indice des prix à la consommation est généralement estimé sous forme d'une série de mesures synthétiques des variations relatives, d'une période à l'autre, des prix d'un ensemble fixe de biens et de services de consommation d'une quantité et de caractéristiques constantes, acquis, utilisés ou payés par la population de référence. Chaque mesure synthétique est construite comme la moyenne pondérée d'un grand nombre d'indices d'agrégats élémentaires. L'indice de chaque agrégat élémentaire est estimé au moyen d'un échantillon de prix pour un ensemble défini de biens et de services obtenus dans une région donnée ou par ses résidents auprès d'un ensemble donné de points de vente ou d'autres sources de biens et de services de consommation. Le tableau présente les indices généraux des prix à la consommation pour tous les groupes d'articles de consommation combinés, et un indice des prix des produits alimentaires ne comprenant que les boissons non alcoolisées. Lorsque les prix des boissons alcoolisées et/ou du tabac sont inclus, cela est indiqué en note.

Tableau 20: Indices de la production agricole

L'agriculture désigne la production de tous les produits de culture et d'élevage. L'indice des produits alimentaires comprend les produits qui sont considérés comme comestibles et qui contiennent des éléments nutritifs. Les indices de la production agricole et de la production alimentaire sont calculés par la formule de Laspeyres avec comme période de base les années 2004-2006. Le choix d'une période de base de plusieurs années permet de réduire l'incidence des fluctuations annuelles de la production agricole sur les indices de cette période. Les quantités de chaque denrée produites sont pondérées par la moyenne nationale des prix à la production pour la période 2004-2006 et sommées pour chaque année. Les indices reposent sur les données de la production d'une année civile. Ceux-ci peuvent différer dans certains cas de ceux effectivement produits et publiés par les pays eux-mêmes en raison de différences dans les concepts, la couverture, les coefficients de pondération et les méthodes de calcul. On s'efforce d'estimer ces différences méthodologiques pour obtenir une meilleure comparabilité internationale des données. Des données détaillées sur la production agricole sont publiées par la FAO dans son *Annuaire statistique*.

Chapitre XI: Commerce international des marchandises

Préparé par la Division de statistique du Département des affaires économiques et sociales du Secrétariat des Nations Unies, l'*Annuaire statistique du commerce international* (ITSY) offre un aperçu des tendances récentes du commerce de biens et de services de la plupart des pays et régions du monde. L'*Annuaire*, voir http://comtrade.un.org/pb/, est publié en deux volumes; le Volume I est établi plus tôt dans l'année pour présenter un aperçu préliminaire du commerce international de marchandises de l'année précédente; le Volume II, publié généralement six mois plus tard, contient des tableaux détaillés qui présentent le commerce international par produit et 11 tableaux du commerce mondial couvrant les valeurs commerciales et les indices. Le Volume II contient également des versions actualisées des tableaux du commerce mondial. Les tableaux de cet *Annuaire* sont également mis à jour mensuellement dans le Bulletin mensuel de statistique des Nations Unies et sur le site des statistiques du commerce, voir http://unstats.un.org/unsd/trade/data/tables.asp#annual.

Les statistiques présentées dans cet *Annuaire* sont établies par les autorités statistiques nationales de façon largement conforme aux concepts et définitions des statistiques du commerce international de marchandises recommandés par les Nations Unies en 2010 (IMTS 2010). En fonction des parties du territoire économique incluses dans le territoire statistique, le système d'établissement des données du commerce adopté par un pays (son système de commerce) sera appelé général ou spécial.

Système de commerce général	Le territoire statistique coïncide avec le territoire économique. Il est donc recommandé que le territoire statistique d'un pays qui applique le système de commerce général englobe tous les éléments territoriaux applicables. Dans ce cas, les importations comprennent les biens qui entrent dans la zone de libre circulation, les installations de perfectionnement actif, les zones franches industrielles, les entrepôts sous douane ou les zones franches commerciales, et les exportations comprennent les biens qui quittent ces éléments territoriaux.
Système de commerce	(définition stricte) Le territoire statistique ne comprend qu'une partie spécifique du territoire économique, de sorte que certains flux de marchandises auxquels les recommandations IMTS 2010 sont applicables ne sont inclus ni dans les statistiques d'importation ni dans les statistiques

spécial	d'exportation du pays déclarant. La définition stricte du système de commerce spécial est utilisée lorsque le territoire statistique ne comprend que la zone de libre circulation, c'est-à-dire la partie dans laquelle les marchandises « peuvent être écoulées sans restriction douanière ». Par conséquent, dans ce cas, les importations ne comprennent que les marchandises qui entrent dans la zone de libre circulation du pays déclarant et les exportations ne comprennent que les marchandises qui quittent la zone de libre circulation du pays déclarant .
	(définition assouplie) a) les marchandises qui entrent dans un pays aux fins du perfectionnement actif ou en ressortent après, ainsi que b) les marchandises qui entrent dans une zone franche industrielle ou en sortent, sont aussi enregistrées et incluses dans les statistiques du commerce international de marchandises.

Tous les pays communiquent en général leurs données détaillées du commerce de marchandises conformément au Système harmonisé de désignation et de codification des marchandises (SH) et les données correspondent à la Classification type pour le commerce international (CTCI, rév. 3), dans laquelle elles sont ensuite présentées. Les données se réfèrent à des années civiles; cependant, pour les pays qui communiquent leurs données selon une autre année de référence, les données sont présentées dans l'année qui couvre la plus grande partie de l'année de référence utilisée par le pays.

Les valeurs FOB comprennent la valeur transactionnelle des marchandises et la valeur des services fournis pour livrer les marchandises à la frontière du pays exportateur. Les valeurs CIF comprennent la valeur transactionnelle des marchandises, la valeur des services fournis pour livrer les marchandises à la frontière du pays exportateur et la valeur des services fournis pour livrer les marchandises depuis la frontière du pays exportateur jusqu'à la frontière du pays importateur. De ce fait, les données de la valeur statistique des marchandises importées sont présentées dans le format CIF et celles de la valeur statistique des marchandises exportées dans le format FOB.

La conversion des valeurs libellées en monnaies nationales en dollars des États-Unis s'effectue au moyen de facteurs de conversion de devises fondés sur les taux de change officiels. Les valeurs libellées en monnaies sujettes à des fluctuations sont converties en dollars des États-Unis au moyen de taux de change moyens pondérés calculés spécialement à cette fin. Le taux de change moyen pondéré d'une monnaie donnée pour une année donnée est donné par les facteurs composants mensuels, fournis par le Fonds monétaire international dans sa publication *Statistiques financières internationales*, pondérés par la valeur du commerce concerné pour chaque mois; les facteurs mensuels sont les taux de change (ou les taux moyens simples) en vigueur au cours de ce mois. Ces facteurs sont appliqués aux importations et aux exportations totales et au commerce de chaque produit avec chaque pays.

Tableau 21: Total des importations, des exportations et balance commerciale

Les données des importations totales et des exportations totales des pays (ou régions) présentées dans ce tableau proviennent principalement des *Statistiques financières internationales* publiées mensuellement par le Fonds monétaire international (FMI) mais aussi d'autres sources comme les publications et les sites web nationaux et le Questionnaire du *Bulletin mensuel de statistique* des Nations Unies, voir l'*Annuaire statistique du commerce international* pour plus de détails. Les données manquantes sont estimées afin de parvenir à des totaux régionaux mais ne sont pas présentées. La procédure d'estimation est automatisée au moyen des taux de croissance en glissement annuel trimestriels pour l'extrapolation des données trimestrielles manquantes (sauf si les données trimestrielles peuvent être estimées au moyen des données mensuelles disponibles au cours du trimestre). Les facteurs de conversion appliqués aux données de ce tableau sont publiés trimestriellement dans le *Bulletin mensuel de statistique* des Nations Unies et sont aussi disponibles sur le site Web des statistiques du commerce de l'ONU : http://unstats.un.org/unsd/trade/data/tables.asp#annual.

Table 22: Principaux partenaires commerciaux

Les chiffres sur les principaux partenaires commerciaux montrent les trois plus grands partenaires commerciaux (les pays de dernière destination et d'origine ou de provenance) dans les transactions du commerce international de marchandises. Dans certains cas un partenaire privilégié est présenté (zones nca, abris fortifiés, etc.). Les zones ni compris ailleurs (zones nca) sont utilisées (a) pour le commerce de faible valeur, (b)si le partenaire choisi est inconnu ou si une erreur a été commise en choisissant le partenaire et (c) pour des raisons de confidentialité. Si un emplacement géographique précis peut être identifie dans zones nca, elles sont alors enregistrées en conséquence (par exemple, Asie nca). Les abris fortifiés sont des magasins de navires et d'aéronefs, qui consistent pour la plupart de combustibles et de denrées alimentaires. Les zones franches appartiennent au territoire économique et géographique d'un pays et non à leurs territoires douaniers. Aux fins des statistiques sur le commerce les opérations entre les territoires douaniers et les zones franches sont enregistrées, si le pays déclarant utilise le Système de Commerce Spécial. Les zones franches peuvent être des zones franches commerciales (boutiques hors taxes) ou des zones franches industrielles. Les données sont exprimées en pourcentage des exportations totales et des importations totales d'un pays, zone ou partenaire privilégié.

Les données dans ce tableau sont des données telles que rapportées par l'UN Comtrade (au niveau à trois chiffres de la CTCI Rév. 3 et une ventilation détaillée des partenaires commerciaux) et des données estimées pour les rapporteurs manquants. Les données sont estimées soit par extrapolation des données des deux années adjacentes, soit, si cela n'est pas possible, par l'utilisation des données déclarées par les partenaires commerciaux (données dites miroir). Les statistiques de miroir sont également utilisées dans le cas où la distribution du partenaire ou des données confidentielles rendent nécessaire l'ajustement des données rapportées. En outre, des modifications sont apportées aux données reçues dans les cas où les données fournies sont manifestement incomplètes, en particulier dans le cas d'exportations d'huiles de pétrole non déclarées dans les données sur les marchandises.

Chapitre XII: Énergie

L'*Annuaire statistique de l'énergie* (consultable sur le site http://unstats.un.org/unsd/energy/yearbook) est une collection complète de statistiques internationales de l'énergie qui couvre plus de 220 pays et régions. L'*Annuaire* est préparé par la Division de statistique du Département des affaires économiques et sociales du Secrétariat des Nations Unies. L'*Annuaire* est produit chaque année avec les nouvelles données disponibles sur la production d'énergie, le commerce, les variations de stocks, les réserves et la consommation de tous les pays et régions, et une série historique remontant à 1950 est disponible. Les données sont établies essentiellement à partir du questionnaire annuel sur l'énergie diffusé par la Division de statistique des Nations Unies et complétées par des publications statistiques officielles nationales, ainsi que des publications des organisations internationales et régionales. Lorsque les données officielles ne sont pas disponibles ou ne sont pas cohérentes, la Division de statistique établit des estimations en s'appuyant sur des éléments d'origine gouvernementale, professionnelle ou commerciale.

Les données se réfèrent à l'année civile, sauf celles des pays suivants qui se rapportent à l'exercice budgétaire : Afghanistan et Iran (République islamique d') – commençant le 21 mars de l'année indiquée; Australie, Bangladesh, Bhoutan, Égypte (électricité seulement pour ces deux derniers pays), Népal – finissant en juin de l'année indiquée; Pakistan – commençant en juillet de l'année indiquée; Inde, Myanmar et Nouvelle-Zélande – commençant en avril de l'année indiquée. Les données exprimées par habitant utilisent comme dénominateur les données démographiques de la Division de la population de l'Organisation des Nations Unies.

Tableau 23: Production, commerce et consommation d'énergie

Les données sont présentées en pétajoules (ou en gigajoules par habitant), unités auxquelles chaque produit énergétique est converti afin d'assurer l'uniformité et la comparabilité internationales des données. Pour convertir en joules les unités originelles, celles-ci (tonnes métriques, tonnes métriques d'équivalent pétrole, kilowattheures, mètres cubes) sont multipliées par des facteurs de conversion. Voir l'*Annuaire statistique de l'énergie* pour une liste des facteurs de conversion et une description détaillée des méthodes utilisées.

Les combustibles solides inclus dans la production commerciale d'énergie primaire sont l'anthracite, la lignite, la tourbe et le schiste bitumineux; les liquides comprennent le pétrole brut, les condensats de gaz naturel, les autres hydrocarbures, additifs et oxygénats, et les biocarburants liquides; les gaz comprennent le gaz naturel et la vapeur/chaleur primaire; et l'électricité comprend la production primaire d'électricité d'origine hydraulique, nucléaire, géothermique, éolienne, marémotrice, houlomotrice et solaire.

Les importations nettes (importations moins exportations et bunkers) et les variations des stocks font référence à toutes les formes d'énergie primaire et secondaire (y compris les produits intermédiaires). Dans les importations nettes, les bunkers font référence aux bunkers d'essence aviation, de carburéacteur et d'anthracite, de gazole/carburant diesel et de fiouls résiduels. Le commerce international de produits énergétiques repose sur le système du « commerce général », c'est-à-dire que toutes les marchandises entrant sur le territoire national d'un pays ou en sortant sont enregistrées comme importations ou exportations.

La consommation d'énergie comprend les formes primaires des combustibles solides, les importations nettes et les variations des stocks des combustibles secondaires; les liquides comprennent les produits pétroliers utilisés à des fins de production d'énergie y compris les produits intermédiaires, le gaz de raffinerie et le pétrole brut utilisé directement; les gaz comprennent la consommation de gaz naturel et de chaleur primaire, les importations nettes et les variations des stocks de gaz manufacturés; et l'électricité comprend la production primaire d'électricité et les importations nettes d'électricité. La consommation de certains produits pétroliers est négative en raison de l'exclusion des calculs des transferts entre produits. La consommation négative d'électricité est due à une production d'électricité primaire négligeable par rapport aux exportations nettes. Plus généralement, une consommation négative peut représenter une différence résiduelle ou statistique entre la production et les exportations lorsqu'un produit donné est principalement exporté.

Chapitre XIII: Environnement

Tableau 24: Terres

Les données relatives aux terres sont compilées par l'Organisation des Nations Unies pour l'alimentation et l'agriculture (FAO). Les définitions de la FAO en ce qui concerne les terres sont les suivantes:

Superficie totale des terres	Superficie totale, à l'exception des eaux intérieures. Les eaux intérieures désignent généralement les principaux fleuves et lacs.
Terres arables	Terres affectées aux cultures temporaires (les terres sur lesquelles est pratiquée la double culture ne sont comptabilisées qu'une fois); prairies temporaires à faucher ou à pâturer, jardins maraîchers ou potagers et terres en jachère temporaire (moins de cinq ans). Cette définition ne comprend pas les terres abandonnées du fait de la culture itinérante. Les données relatives aux terres arables ne peuvent être utilisées pour calculer la superficie des terres aptes à l'agriculture.
Cultures permanentes	Superficie des terres avec des cultures qui occupent la terre pour de longues périodes et qui ne nécessitent pas d'être replantées après chaque récolte, comme le cacao, le café et le caoutchouc. Cette catégorie comprend les terres plantées d'arbustes à fleurs, d'arbres fruitiers, d'arbres à noix et de vignes, mais ne comprend pas les terres plantées d'arbres destinés à la coupe.
Superficie forestière	Dans l'Évaluation des ressources forestières mondiales 2010, la FAO a défini les forêts comme suit : Terres occupant une superficie de plus de 0,5 hectares avec des arbres atteignant une hauteur supérieure à cinq mètres et un couvert arboré de plus de dix pour cent, ou avec des arbres capables d'atteindre ces seuils en situ. Sont exclues les terres à vocation agricole ou urbaine prédominante.
Sites importants pour la biodiversité terrestre dans les aires protégées	Les terres contribuant énormément à la persistance globale de la biodiversité mesurées en proportion entièrement couverte par des zones protégées désignées. Les données sont fondées sur un chevauchement entre les polygones pour les zones clés de la biodiversité provenant de la base des données mondiales sur les zones clés pour la biodiversité et les polygones pour les zones protégées provenant de la base des données mondiales sur les zones protégées. Les chiffres pour chaque région sont calculés comme la proportion de chaque zone clé pour la biodiversité couverte par des zones protégées, moyennés (c'est-à-dire, calculés comme la moyenne) à travers toutes les zones clés de la biodiversité dans la région.

Tableau 25: Espèces menacées

Les données relatives au nombre d'espèces menacées dans chaque groupe d'animaux et de plantes sont établies par l'Union internationale pour la conservation de la nature et de ses ressources (UICN)/ Commission de sauvegarde des espèces (CSE) et publiées dans la liste rouge des espèces menacées de l'UICN. Cette liste fournit le catalogue des espèces considérées comme menacées au niveau mondial. Le nombre d'espèces menacées dans un pays donné change au cours des années pour diverses raisons, entre autres :

- La disponibilité d'informations nouvelles permet de raffiner l'évaluation (de confirmer par exemple que l'espèce est ou n'est pas présente dans un pays donné, que l'espèce est ou n'est pas menacée, etc.);
- L'évolution de la taxonomie (par exemple ce qu'on reconnaissait auparavant comme une certaine espèce est à présent réparti entre plusieurs espèces distinctes, ou fusionné avec une autre espèce);
- Les corrections (par exemple l'évaluation précédente peut avoir omis d'inscrire un pays donné dans la liste appropriée ou avoir inclus un pays donné par erreur);
- Changement de statut réel (par exemple la situation d'une espèce peut s'être réellement détériorée ou améliorée et l'espèce avoir par conséquent été incorporée aux catégories menacées ou en avoir été retirée).

Les catégories utilisées dans la Liste rouge sont les suivantes : espèce éteinte, éteinte à l'état sauvage, gravement menacée d'extinction; menacée d'extinction, vulnérable, quasi menacée et données insuffisantes.

Chapitre XIV: Science et technologie

La recherche et le développement expérimental (R-D) englobe tous les travaux de création entrepris de façon systématique en vue d'accroître la somme des connaissances, y compris la connaissance de l'homme, de la culture et de la société, ainsi que l'utilisation de cette somme de connaissances pour de nouvelles applications. Pour tout renseignement complémentaire, voir le site Web de l'Institut de statistique de l'UNESCO www.uis.unesco.org.

Tableau 26: Personnel employé dans la recherche et le développement (R–D)

Les données présentées sur le personnel employé dans la recherche et le développement (R-D) sont compilées par l'Institut de statistique de l'UNESCO. Les données de certains pays ont été fournies à l'UNESCO par l'OCDE, EUROSTAT et "la Red de Indicadores de Ciencia y Technología (RICYT)". Les définitions et classifications appliquées par l'UNESCO sont basées sur le Manuel de Frascati (OCDE, 2002).

Les trois catégories du personnel présentées sont définies comme suivant:

Les chercheurs	Les chercheurs sont des spécialistes travaillant à la conception ou à la création de connaissances, de produits, de procédés, de méthodes et de systèmes nouveaux et à la gestion des projets concernés. Les étudiants diplômés au niveau du doctorat (CITE niveau 8) ayant des activités de R-D sont considérés comme des chercheurs.
Techniciens et personnel assimilé	Personnes dont les tâches principales requièrent des connaissances et une expérience technique dans un ou plusieurs domaines de l'ingénierie, des sciences physiques et de la vie ou des sciences sociales et humaines. Ils participent à la R-D en exécutant des tâches scientifiques et techniques faisant intervenir l'application de principes et de méthodes opérationnelles, généralement sous le contrôle de chercheurs.
Autre personnel de soutien	les travailleurs, qualifiés ou non, et le personnel de secrétariat et de bureau participant à l'exécution des projets de R-D ou qui sont directement associés à l'exécution de tels projets.

Personnes physiques est le nombre total de personnes qui sont principalement ou partiellement affectées à la R-D. Ce dénombrement inclut les employés à 'temps plein' et les employés à 'temps partiel'. Équivalent temps plein (ETP) peut être considéré comme une année-personne. Ainsi, une personne qui consacre 30% de son temps en R&D et le reste à d'autres activités (enseignement, administration universitaire ou direction d'étudiants) compte pour 0.3 ETP en R&D. De façon analogue, si un employé travaille à temps plein dans un centre de R&D pendant six mois seulement, il compte pour 0.5 ETP.

Tableau 27: Dépenses intérieures brutes de recherche et développement (R–D)

Les données présentées sur les dépenses intérieures brutes de recherche et développement sont compilées par l'Institut de statistique de l'UNESCO. Les données de certains pays ont été fournies à l'UNESCO par l'OCDE, EUROSTAT et "la Red de Indicadores de Ciencia y Technología (RICYT)". La dépense intérieure brute de R-D (DIRD) est la dépense totale intra-muros afférente aux travaux de R-D exécutés sur le territoire national pendant une période donnée. Elle comprend la R-D exécutée sur le territoire national et financée par l'étranger mais ne tient pas compte des paiements effectués à l'étranger pour des travaux de R-D. Les sources de financement pour la DIRD sont classées selon les cinq catégories suivantes:

Les fonds des entreprises	Les fonds alloués à la R-D par toutes les firmes, organismes et institutions dont l'activité première est la production marchande de biens ou de services (autres que dans le secteur d'enseignement supérieur) en vue de leur vente au public, à un prix qui correspond à la réalité économique, et les institutions privées sans but lucratif principalement au service de ces entreprises, organismes et institutions.
Les fonds de l'Etat	Les fonds fournis à la R-D par le gouvernement central (fédéral), d'état ou par les autorités locales. Ceci inclut tous les ministères, bureaux et autres organismes qui fournissent, sans normalement les vendre, des services collectifs autres que d'enseignement supérieur, qu'il n'est pas possible d'assurer de façon pratique et économique par d'autres moyens et qui, de surcroît, administrent les affaires publiques et appliquent la politique économique et sociale de la collectivité. Les fonds des entreprises publiques sont compris dans ceux du secteur des entreprises. Les fonds de l'Etat incluent également les institutions privées sans but lucratif contrôlées et principalement financées par l'Etat.
Les fonds de l'enseignement supérieur	Les fonds fournis à la R-D par les établissements d'enseignement supérieur tels que toutes les universités, grandes écoles, instituts de technologie et autres établissements postsecondaires, ainsi que tous les instituts de recherche, les stations d'essais et les cliniques qui travaillent sous le contrôle direct des établissements d'enseignement supérieur ou qui sont administrés par ces derniers ou leur sont associés
Les fonds d'institutions privées sans but lucratif	Les fonds destinés à la R-D par les institutions privées sans but lucratif non marchandes au service du public, ainsi que par les simples particuliers ou les ménages.
Les fonds étrangers	Les fonds destinés à la R-D par les institutions et les individus se trouvant en dehors des frontières politiques d'un pays, à l'exception des véhicules, navires, avions et satellites utilisés par des

	institutions nationales, ainsi que des terrains d'essai acquis par ces institutions, et par toutes les organisations internationales (à l'exception des entreprises), y compris leurs installations et leurs activités à l'intérieur des frontières d'un pays

Il faut éviter de comparer les chiffres absolus concernant les dépenses de R-D d'un pays à l'autre. On ne pourrait procéder à des comparaisons détaillées qu'en convertissant en une même monnaie les sommes libellées en monnaie nationale au moyen de taux de change spécialement applicables aux activités de R-D. Les taux de change officiels ne reflètent pas toujours le coût réel des activités de R-D, et les comparaisons établies sur la base de ces taux peuvent conduire à des conclusions trompeuses; toutefois, elles peuvent être utilisées pour donner une idée de l'ordre de grandeur.

Tableau 28: Brevets

Les brevets sont accordés par un office national des brevets ou un office régional qui accomplit cette tâche pour de nombreux pays, comme l'Office européen des brevets et l'African Regional Intellectual Property Organisation. Dans le cadre de ces systèmes régionaux, le requérant demande que son invention soit protégée dans un ou plusieurs pays, et il appartient à chaque pays d'accorder ou non la protection d'un brevet sur son territoire. Le Traité de coopération en matière de brevets (PCT), administré par l'Organisation mondiale de la propriété intellectuelle (OMPI) prévoit le dépôt d'une demande de brevet international unique dotée de la même validité que des demandes nationales déposées dans les pays désignés. Les données comprennent l'intensité de l'activité des résidents, les brevets délivrés et les brevets en vigueur. L'intensité du dépôt de brevets est présentée comme le nombre de demandes de brevet déposées par des résidents par million d'habitants, tandis que le dépôt d'une demande de propriété intellectuelle (PI) par des résidents fait référence à une demande déposée par un requérant auprès de son office national de la propriété intellectuelle. Les statistiques des droits de propriété intellectuelle (enregistrement) reposent sur le même concept. L'expression « en vigueur » désigne un brevet ou une autre forme de protection de la PI en cours de validité. Le pays d'origine sert à catégoriser les données de PI en PI résidente (intérieure) et non résidente (étrangère). La résidence du premier demandeur cité (ou inventeur) enregistré dans le document de PI (par exemple une demande de brevet ou de dépôt de marque) sert à classer les données de PI par pays d'origine. Les données sont établies et publiées par l'OMPI.

Chapter XV: Communication

Table 29: Utilisation d'Internet

Le tableau indique le pourcentage de personnes qui utilisent Internet et remplace les statistiques présentées dans les annuaires précédents comme le « Nombre (en milliers) d'abonnements à l'Internet fixe (filaire) » et le « Nombre d'abonnements à l'Internet fixe (filaire) pour 100 habitants ». Cet indicateur, outre qu'il saisit l'usage d'Internet, permet de mesurer les évolutions de l'accès à Internet et de son utilisation. Dans les pays où de nombreuses personnes accèdent à Internet au travail, à l'école, dans les cybercafés ou d'autres lieux publics, la multiplication des accès publics accroît le nombre d'utilisateurs malgré le nombre limité des abonnements et des foyers qui ont accès à Internet. Les pays en développement en particulier comptent souvent de nombreux utilisateurs par abonnement à Internet, ce qui traduit le fait que le foyer n'est pas le lieu principal d'accès.

Chapitre XVI: Tourisme et transport internationaux

Les données sur le tourisme international sont fournies par l'Organisation mondiale du tourisme (OMT) qui publie des renseignements détaillés sur le tourisme dans l'*Annuaire des statistiques du tourisme* ou le *Compendium des statistiques du tourisme*, voir www.unwto.org/statistics pour des informations plus complètes. Aux fins de l'établissement des statistiques, l'expression «visiteur international» décrit «toute personne qui se rend dans un pays autre que celui dans lequel il ou elle a son lieu de résidence habituelle, mais différent de son environnement habituel, pour une période de 12 mois au maximum, dans un but principal autre que celui d'y exercer une activité rémunérée». L'*Annuaire* et le *Compendium* de l'OMT comportent quatre séries distinctes, mais une seule est retenue pour inclusion dans le présent *Annuaire*, en fonction en général de l'ordre de priorité suivant afin de décrire au mieux le «visiteur international»;

Ordre	Code de la série	Nom de la série
1	TF	*Arrivées de touristes non résidents aux frontières nationales* désigne les visiteurs qui passent au moins une nuit dans un logement collectif ou privé dans le pays visité (exclut les visiteurs d'un jour)
2	VF	*Arrivées de visiteurs non résidents aux frontières nationales* désigne les visiteurs définis dans la série « TF » ainsi que les visiteurs d'un jour qui ne passent pas la nuit dans un logement collectif

		ou privé dans le pays visité
3	TCE	*Arrivées de touristes non résidents dans tous les types d'établissements d'hébergement*
4	THS	*Arrivées de touristes non résidents dans les hôtels et établissements similaires*

Ces chiffres ne comprennent pas les immigrants, les résidents frontaliers, les personnes domiciliées dans un pays ou une région et qui travaillent dans un pays ou une région limitrophe, les membres des forces armées et les diplomates et les représentants consulaires lorsqu'ils se rendent de leur pays d'origine au pays où ils sont en poste et vice-versa. Ne sont pas inclus non plus les voyageurs en transit qui n'entrent pas formellement dans le pays en faisant viser leur passeport, comme les passagers d'un vol en escale qui demeurent pendant un court laps de temps dans une zone distincte d'une aérogare ou les passagers d'un navire qui ne sont pas autorisés à débarquer. Cette catégorie inclut les passagers transférés directement d'une aérogare à une autre ou à un autre terminal. Les autres passagers en transit dans un pays sont classés comme visiteurs.

Tableau 30: Arrivées de touristes/visiteurs et dépenses touristiques

Les données relatives aux arrivées de visiteurs non résidents (ou internationaux) peuvent être obtenues de différentes sources. Dans certains cas, elles proviennent des statistiques frontalières tirées des registres administratifs (contrôles de police, de l'immigration, comptages du trafic routier et autres types de contrôle), des enquêtes statistiques aux frontières et des enregistrements d'établissements d'hébergement. Les totaux correspondent au nombre total d'arrivées depuis les régions indiquées dans le tableau. Lorsqu'une personne visite le même pays plusieurs fois dans l'année, un même nombre d'arrivées est enregistré. De même, si une personne visite plusieurs pays au cours d'un même voyage, son arrivée dans chaque pays est enregistrée séparément. On ne peut donc pas supposer que le nombre des arrivées soit égal au nombre de personnes qui voyagent.

Les dépenses associées à l'activité touristique des visiteurs sont traditionnellement identifiées au poste «Voyages» de la balance des paiements (BDP): dans le cas du tourisme dans le pays récepteur, les dépenses dans le pays de référence associées aux visiteurs non résidents sont enregistrées comme « crédits » dans la BDP et il s'agit de « recettes au titre des voyages». Le nouveau cadre conceptuel approuvé par la Commission de statistique des Nations Unies concernant la mesure de l'activité touristique à l'échelle macroéconomique (le compte satellite du tourisme) considère que la notion « industries et produits touristiques » inclut le transport de passagers. Par conséquent, une meilleure estimation des dépenses liées au tourisme par des visiteurs résidents et non résidents dans un scénario international serait, du point de vue de la BDP, la somme des valeurs du poste « Voyages » et du poste «Transport de passagers». Néanmoins, les utilisateurs doivent être conscients de ce que les estimations de la BDP comprennent, outre les dépenses associées aux visiteurs, celles liées à d'autres types d'individus. Les données publiées doivent permettre la comparabilité internationale et donc correspondre à celles publiées par le Fonds monétaire international et fournies par les banques centrales, les exceptions sont listées dans le *Compendium des statistiques du tourisme* et l'*Annuaire des statistiques du tourisme*, voir www.unwto.org/statistics pour des informations plus complètes.

Chapitre XVII: Aide au développement

Tableau 31: Décaissements nets d'aide publique au développement aux bénéficiaires

Le tableau présente des estimations des flux de ressources financières à destination des pays bénéficiaires soit directement (aide bilatérale) soit par l'intermédiaire d'institutions multilatérales (aide multilatérale). Les institutions multilatérales comprennent le Groupe de la Banque mondiale, des banques régionales, les institutions financières de l'Union européenne et un certain nombre d'institutions, de programmes et de fonds d'affectation spéciale des Nations Unies. Les données ont été obtenues auprès du Comité d'aide au développement (CAD) de l'OCDE, auquel les pays membres communiquent des données sur les flux de ressources qu'ils mettent à la disposition de pays et territoires en développement, de pays et territoires en transition, et des institutions multilatérales. On trouvera davantage d'informations sur les définitions, les méthodes et les sources dans la publication de l'OCDE intitulée *Répartition géographique des ressources financières allouées aux pays en développement*, ainsi que sur le site http://stats.oecd.org/.

Tableau 32: Décaissements nets d'aide publique au développement par des donateurs

Le tableau présente les dépenses d'aide au développement des pays donateurs. Ce tableau inclut les contributions des donateurs aux institutions multilatérales; les totaux diffèrent donc de ceux du tableau 32, qui incluent les décaissements des institutions multilatérales.

* * *

Annex III

Conversion coefficients and factors

The metric system of weights and measures is employed in the *Statistical Yearbook*. In this system, the relationship between units of volume and capacity is: 1 litre = 1 cubic decimetre (dm^3) exactly (as decided by the 12th International Conference of Weights and Measures, New Delhi, November 1964).

Section A shows the equivalents of the basic metric, British imperial and United States units of measurements. According to an agreement between the national standards institutions of English-speaking nations, the British and United States units of length, area and volume are now identical, and based on the yard = 0.9144 metre exactly. The weight measures in both systems are based on the pound = 0.45359237 kilogram exactly (Weights and Measures Act 1963 (London), and *Federal Register announcement of 1 July 1959: Refinement of Values for the Yard and Pound* (Washington D.C.)).

Section B shows various derived or conventional conversion coefficients and equivalents.

Section C shows other conversion coefficients or factors which have been utilized in the compilation of certain tables in the *Statistical Yearbook*. Some of these are only of an approximate character and have been employed solely to obtain a reasonable measure of international comparability in the tables.

For a comprehensive survey of international and national systems of weights and measures and of units' weights for a large number of commodities in different countries, see *World Weights and Measures*.

Annexe III

Coefficients et facteurs de conversion

L'*Annuaire statistique* utilise le système métrique pour les poids et mesures. La relation entre unités métriques de volume et de capacité est: 1 litre = 1 décimètre cube (dm^3) exactement (comme fut décidé à la Conférence internationale des poids et mesures, New Delhi, novembre 1964).

La section A fournit les principaux équivalents des systèmes de mesure métrique, britannique et américain. Suivant un accord entre les institutions de normalisation nationales des pays de langue anglaise, les mesures britanniques et américaines de longueur, superficie et volume sont désormais identiques, et sont basées sur le yard = 0.9144 mètre exactement. Les mesures de poids se rapportent, dans les deux systèmes, à la livre (pound) = 0.45359237 kilogramme exactement (*Weights and Measures Act 1963* (Londres), et *Federal Register Announcement of 1 July 1959: Refinement of Values for the Yard and Pound* (Washington, D.C.)).

La section B fournit divers coefficients et facteurs de conversion conventionnels ou dérivés.

La section C fournit d'autres coefficients ou facteurs de conversion utilisés dans l'élaboration de certains tableaux de l'*Annuaire statistique*. Certains coefficients ou facteurs de conversion ne sont que des approximations et ont été utilisés uniquement pour obtenir un degré raisonnable de comparabilité sur le plan international.

Pour une étude d'ensemble des systèmes internationaux et nationaux de poids et mesures, et d'unités de poids pour un grand nombre de produits dans différents pays, voir *World Weights and Measures*.

A. Equivalents of metric, British imperial and United States units of measure

A. Equivalents des unités métriques, britanniques et des Etats-Unis

Metric units Unités métriques	British imperial and US equivalents Equivalents en mesures britanniques et des Etats-Unis		British imperial and US units Unités britanniques et des Etats-Unis	Metric equivalents Equivalents en mesures métriques
Length — Longueur				
1 centimetre – centimètre (cm)	0.3937008	inch	1 inch	2.540 cm
1 metre – mètre (m)	3.280840	feet	1 foot	30.480 cm
	1.093613	yard	1 yard	0.9144 m
1 kilometre – kilomètre (km)	0.6213712	mile	1 mile	1609.344 m
	0.5399568	international nautical mile	1 international nautical mile	1852.000 m
Area — Superficie				
1 square centimetre – (cm^2)	0.1550003	square inch	1 square inch	6.45160 cm^2
1 square metre – (m^2)	10.763910	square feet	1 square foot	9.290304 dm^2
	1.195990	square yards	1 square yard	0.83612736 m^2
1 hectare – (ha)	2.471054	acres	1 acre	0.4046856 ha
1 square kilometre – (km^2)	0.3861022	square mile	1 square mile	2.589988 km^2
Volume				
1 cubic centimetre – (cm^3)	0.06102374	cubic inch	1 cubic inch	16.38706 cm^3
1 cubic metre – (m^3)	35.31467	cubic feet	1 cubic foot	28.316847 dm^3
	1.307951	cubic yards	1 cubic yard	0.76455486 m^3
Capacity — Capacité				
1 litre (l)	0.8798766	British imperial quart	1 British imperial quart	1.136523 l
	1.056688	U.S. liquid quart	1 U.S. liquid quart	0.9463529 l
	0.908083	U.S. dry quart	1 U.S. dry quart	1.1012208 l
1 hectolitre (hl)	21.99692	British imperial gallons	1 British imperial gallon	4.546092 l
	26.417200	U.S. gallons	1 U.S. gallon	3.785412 l
	2.749614	British imperial bushels	1 imperial bushel	36.368735 l
	2.837760	U.S. bushels	1 U.S. bushel	35.239067 l

Metric units Unités métriques	British imperial and US equivalents Equivalents en mesures britanniques et des Etats-Unis		British imperial and US units Unités britanniques et des Etats-Unis	Metric equivalents Equivalents en mesures métriques	
Weight or mass — Poids					
1 kilogram (kg)	35.27396	av. ounces	1 av. ounce	28.349523	g
	32.15075	troy ounces	1 troy ounce	31.10348	g
	2.204623	av. pounds	1 av. pound	453.59237	g
			1 cental (100 lb.)	45.359237	kg
			1 hundredweight (112 lb.)	50.802345	kg
1 ton – tonne (t)	1.1023113	short tons	1 short ton (2 000 lb.)	0.9071847	t
	0.9842065	long tons	1 long ton (2 240 lb.)	1.0160469	t

B. Various conventional or derived coefficients

Air transport

1 passenger-mile = 1.609344 passenger kilometre
1 short ton-mile = 1.459972 tonne-kilometre
1 long ton-mile = 1.635169 tonne kilometre

Electric energy

1 Kilowatt (kW) = 1.34102 British horsepower (hp)
1.35962 cheval vapeur (cv)

C. Other coefficients or conversion factors employed in *Statistical Yearbook* tables

Roundwood

Equivalent in solid volume without bark.

Sugar

1 metric ton raw sugar = 0.9 metric ton refined sugar
For the United States and its possessions:
1 metric ton refined sugar = 1.07 metric tons raw sugar

Energy

1 metric ton peat = .325 metric ton of coal oil equivalent
1 ton oil equivalent = .4186 GJ or 11.63 MWh

B. Divers coefficients conventionnels ou dérivés

Transport aérien

1 voyageur (passager) – kilomètre = 0.621371 passenger-mile
1 tonne-kilomètre = 0.684945 short ton-mile
0.611558 long ton-mile

Energie électrique

1 British horsepower (hp) = 0.7457 kW
1 cheval vapeur (cv) = 0.735499 kW

C. Autres coefficients ou facteurs de conversion utilisés dans les tableaux de l'*Annuaire statistique*

Bois rond

Equivalences en volume solide sans écorce.

Sucre

1 tonne métrique de sucre brut = 0.9 tonne métrique de sucre raffiné
Pour les États-Unis et leurs possessions:
1 tonne métrique de sucre raffiné = 1.07 tonne métrique de sucre brut

Energie

1 tonne métrique d'équivalent charbon = 3.08 tonnes métrique de tourbe
1 GJ = 2.39 tonne d'équivalent pétrol or 1 MWh = .086 tonne métrique d'équivalent pétrol

Annex IV - Tables added, omitted and discontinued

A. Tables added

The present issue of the *Statistical Yearbook* includes the following tables which were not presented in the previous issue:

Table 3	Population and rates of growth in urban areas and capital cities
Table 19	Consumer price indices
Table 29	Internet usage

B. Tables omitted

The following tables which were presented in previous issues are not presented in the present issue. They will be updated in future issues of the *Yearbook* when new data become available:

- Population growth and indicators of fertility and mortality
- CO2 emissions estimates
- Water supply and sanitation coverage
- Civil aviation: scheduled airline traffic
- Index of industrial production

C. Tables discontinued

- Mobile telephone subscriptions

Annexe IV - Tableaux ajoutés, supprimés et discontinués

A. Tableaux ajoutés

Dans ce numéro de l'Annuaire statistique, les tableaux suivants n'ont pas été présentés dans le numéro antérieur, et ont été ajoutés:

Tableau 3	Population et taux de croissance dans les zones urbaines et capitales
Tableau 19	Indices des prix à la consommation
Tableau 29	Utilisation d'internet

B. Tableaux supprimés

Les tableaux suivants qui ont été repris dans les éditions antérieures n'ont pas été repris dans la présente édition. Ils seront actualisés dans les futures livraisons de l'Annuaire à mesure que des données nouvelles deviendront disponibles:

- Croissance démographique et indicateurs de fécondité et moralité
- Estimation des émissions de CO2
- Services d'alimentation en eau potable et d'assainissement
- Aviation civile : trafic aérien régulier
- Indices de la production industrielle

C. Tableaux discontinués

Les tableaux suivants ont été discontinués

- Abonnements aux services de téléphone cellulaire mobile

Annexe IV. [illegible]

Dans ce document [illegible]

[illegible] zones arides et sèches [illegible]

[illegible]

Les [illegible]

[illegible]